Preface

The goal of this book is to show you how to develop professional Windows applications using MFC and tools like the AppWizard and ClassWizard. The book is designed to move you rapidly and confidently to the point where you can create your own rich, full-featured applications with C++ and MFC.

The most important feature of this book is its constant attention to advanced features. As your skills develop, the book probes deeply into the concepts and capabilities that will let you build applications that are unique and useful. Features like these:

- Subclassed controls with customized appearance and behavior
- Splash screens
- Expanding dialog boxes
- Bitmaps stretched over the backgrounds of dialogs and client areas
- Windows 95 controls
- Property sheets
- Floating palettes and tool bars
- Popup menus
- Customized system menus
- MDI applications with multiple document types
- Multi-threaded applications
- OLE-capable servers, clients, and controls
- Client/server databases

These features make the difference between a normal application and a stunning application, and all of these different topics are explained in this book with straightforward examples and clear English descriptions.

Version Free

This book is designed to be "version free." The goal is to create a book that can be updated on the web each time Visual C++ changes versions so that we can save you the cost of buying a new book every six months. To accomplish this goal, we have isolated all version-specific features in Appendix B. When a new version appears on the market, we will update this appendix on the web immediately, and you can access our updates, changes and supplements free of charge. See http://www.iftech.com/mfc for details.

Audience

As described in the chapter "Getting Your Bearings," this book is designed with several different entry points to help different kinds of programmers get started quickly. If you have no prior experience with GUI application development, Visual C++ or MFC, you can start at Chapter 1 and learn the basics, covering the concepts and theory behind MFC from the ground up. By the time you finish Part 1 you will feel comfortable with MFC and will be ready to start learning some of its more intricate details.

If you are already familiar with GUI development but want to learn more about the development tools like the AppWizard and ClassWizard, you can start at Part 2 or 3. Part 3 shows you how to accelerate your development cycle with the different tools built into Visual C++. Once you have mastered these tools, you are ready to begin adding professional features so move on to Parts 4 and 5.

If you are migrating from another operating system to Windows NT or Windows 95, this book will help you to quickly map your existing knowledge into the NT framework. See Chapter 0 for a list of the 110 most common Visual C++ programming questions, as well as the sections that contain the answers. If you are a C programmer with no C++ experience, use Appendix A to come up to speed on C++ and then start with Chapter 1.

Organization

This book is organized in five different parts, each one discussing a particular type of subject matter.

Part 1 provides introductory material on GUI development, event-driven programming, and the MFC hierarchy. If you have never seen MFC before, start here and it will teach you the fundamentals. Part 1 shows you how to create and understand the simplest MFC application, how to create new controls, how to customize the behavior and appearance of those controls, and how to respond to events with message maps. By the end of Part 1 you are well-grounded in the concepts and principles that make any MFC program work properly.

Part 2 contains more advanced MFC details. In this part of the book you learn about most of the different MFC classes: canned dialogs, list and edit controls, the MFC application class, and the Windows drawing model. You also learn about the debugging features built into MFC, along with a variety of utility classes that make MFC programming easier.

Part 3 focuses on the AppWizard and ClassWizard tools in Visual C++. These tools are designed to help you create MFC applications quickly and easily. This part of the book starts with an introduction to the tools and shows how they work. It then explores four in-depth example applications: A drawing editor, a text editor, a form-based application and an address list application. These programs all show you how to set up a framework and then add in menu options, dialogs, tool and status bars, printing features, and so on.

Part 4 is a collection of advanced features that you will want to add to your own applications as your skills develop. For example, Part 4 shows you how to create splash screens, expanding dialogs, popup menus, and so on. Browse though the different chapters in this part to get more in-depth material on MFC or to find application features that are important to you.

Part 5 talks about advanced MFC classes. In particular, it shows you how to add database and OLE support to your applications. It also demonstrates how to use Win32 threads to improve your application's performance.

The CD-ROM and the On-line Index

The CD-ROM included with this book contains the source code for all of the examples in the book, as well as the source code and data for an on-line indexing program. There is also an EXAMPLES directory that contains all of the code from each section of the book in a text file. If you want to follow along with the book and work through the examples on your own, these text files will save you the trouble of retyping the code in each step.

The index on the CD-ROM is broken down by sections and includes every word found in the manuscript. To use the index, follow the directions in the README file on the CD-ROM to compile the program. When you run the index, you will see a display that contains an edit area, three buttons (Help, Search and Quit), and a list area. Any words that you type in the edit area are used to search for appropriate sections. For example, if you want to find out how to create a Splash Screen, you would type "Splash Screens" in the edit area. Press the "Search" button to begin the search. The index program will list all sections that contain all three of those words. Enter as many words as you like to hone the search. Word matching is exact and case-insensitive. If a word does not appear in the book the program will tell you.

There are many cases where an exact match does not work well. For example, there may be a section that contains "thread" and "create" but not "creating" and "threads", so if you enter the line "creating threads" on the edit line you get no matches. You can use the "*" wild card character at the end of a word to solve this problem. For example, by entering "creat*" the system will OR together all words with the root "creat" ("create", "creates", "creation", etc.). You may want to get in the habit of using the wild card character at the end of all words: "creat* thread*", for example. This often yields more accurate results.

If an obvious word seems to be missing from the index, try to find it in the book to make sure you are spelling it correctly. For example, "toolbar" is sometimes spelled as one or two words in the book, and you need to spell it the same way in your search.

Contacting the Authors: Questions, Comments, and Version Changes

One thing about Microsoft is that it never stands still for very long. Its compilers change versions and the libraries are upgraded constantly. One of the goals in creating this book is to make its code compatible with existing and future releases of Microsoft compiler products. Another goal is to give you "investment-grade" knowledge—

knowledge that does not loose its value over time, and that is transferable between as many different platforms as possible.

As things change however, you need a way to get updates and corrections. You may also have questions, comments or suggestions for improving this book. If so, we would like to hear from you. See Appendix C for information on asking questions via email. You can also visit our World Wide Web server at http://www.iftech.com/mfc.

Acknowledgments

We would like to sincerely thank several people for their help and support in creating this book. Mike Meehan, our publisher, has shown tremendous flexibility and good humor as this book has moved through versions and grown larger each time. There really is an infinite amount of material to cover, and he has not ever stopped us from trying to conquer it all, despite the logistical problems. Leigh Ann Brain, the book's designer and layout pro, has similarly shown tremendous patience and fortitude in the face of a gigantic book. We thank you both for making this book possible.

Dave Morey of Ziff-Davis has been extremely helpful in answering questions and providing support. He also assisted in the production of the CD.

Tina Kasparian and Leigh Ann Brain have shown extreme patience, putting up with our long phone calls at all hours and our constant babbling about controls and frameworks. We couldn't have done it without you both.

GETTING YOUR BEARINGS

You are probably opening this book because you are new to Windows Programming or because you are new to MFC (Microsoft Foundation Classes) or the Visual C++ programming environment. For example, you might be an experienced UNIX or Macintosh programmer. Or perhaps you have a lot of talent with C programming and command-driven user interfaces on PCs and want to move over to Windows. You may be experienced with Windows programming in C, but have never before used MFC and C++ to develop Windows applications. Regardless of your origin, you will find that as you try to make your transition you are hampered by two problems. The purpose of this book is to quickly solve those problems so that you can begin creating your own professional applications with Visual C++ as quickly as possible.

The first problem is mental: you have to get past the wall that surrounds Visual C++. That wall arises because of the obvious complexity of the Windows and C++ programming environments. When you load Visual C++ from its CD, you notice that there are tens of thousands of pages of documentation, hundreds of sample programs, and untold megabytes of help files. No one has the time to sort through *all* of this material, but you know that hidden in those megabytes are hundreds of important concepts that you need to master.

The second problem is more pedestrian: you have to pick a place to start. But where should you begin? How do you write a simple Windows application? How do you learn how to write an advanced one?

This book is designed to help you move into the Visual C++ environment rapidly and confidently. The purpose of this chapter is to help you get your bearings in this new environment. It will introduce you to Visual C++ and then give you a starting point and a direction so that you can become an accomplished Windows programmer very quickly using the most modern tools and techniques available.

What is Visual C++?

The Visual C++ environment is huge and can be extremely intimidating initially. Visual C++ combines a complete suite of powerful tools into a single application development environment, and the first time you face all of these tools it can be very difficult to discern what they all do or how to use them. When you look at the book reader application that comes with the Visual C++ CD-ROM, you face another hurdle: You find thousands and thousands of pages in many different books. The thought of wading through all of these manuals can be daunting.

So let's start at the beginning and look at Visual C++ in an organized way. First of all, what is it? Here is a brief summary:

- Visual C++ is a C++ compiler
- Visual C++ is a debugging environment
- Visual C++ is an application framework generator
- Visual C++ is a project manager
- Visual C++ is an easy way to design and implement menus, dialogs, and other "resources"
- Visual C++ is a programmer accelerator—several tools inside Visual C++ are designed to make you more efficient by making your life as a programmer easier or by reducing the code you must write

In other words, Visual C++ is a complete and extremely powerful application development environment. In order to take full advantage of this environment, you have to become comfortable with all the tools, and you have to know how they can work together to accelerate your software development cycle.

In its most basic form, Visual C++ is simply a C++ compiler. You can use it to create simple text programs in C or C++. If you would like to try this out, go to Appendix B.1 and work through the example there. You will find that it is *extremely* easy to write, compile, and debug simple text programs using Visual C++.

Most people who purchase Visual C++ do not want to create text programs, however. They want to create advanced Windows applications that make effective use of the Windows 95 and Windows NT user interface. To do this, you must know C++, and you must understand the MFC hierarchy. MFC is designed make you as productive as possible by encapsulating common Windows code in classes that are already written, tested, and debugged. Once you invest the time to learn MFC, you are greatly rewarded in increased speed, flexibility and robustness.

Part 1 of this book gives you a thorough introduction to MFC. It shows you the basic principles used in every MFC program you write. Part 2 gives a complete overview of all the controls and features that MFC offers. Part 2 contains hundreds of examples that make it easy to understand the different MFC classes.

Once you feel comfortable with MFC, you are ready to begin creating professional Windows applications. Part 3 introduces the AppWizard, the ClassWizard, and the resource editing tools of Visual C++. The AppWizard is your starting point when creating any full-blown Windows application: It helps you by generating a complete file framework that organizes the entire application around a consistent core of MFC classes. The ClassWizard, in combination with the resource editing features that the Visual C++ environment provides, then makes it easy to add to and complete your application by helping you design, create, and install menus, dialog boxes, and other application resources. The ClassWizard also helps you add the code that lets your application respond to user input properly. Using these three tools—the AppWizard, the ClassWizard, and the resource editors—together with the MFC class hierarchy, it is extremely easy to complete professional applications very quickly. Part 3 contains four different example applications to help demonstrate the process.

Part 4 continues by demonstrating advanced features. It shows you how to use a variety of techniques to create such things as expanding dialogs, property sheets, dialog bars, splash screens, self-drawn controls and bitmapped backgrounds. These techniques add significant utility to your applications when used appropriately. Finally, Part 5 concludes the book by discussing advanced MFC classes for database connectivity, OLE features, and so on.

Available Documentation

The Visual C++ CD-ROM contains over 100 megabytes of on-line documentation covering various aspects of Windows, MFC, and the tools available in Visual C++. It contains many more megabytes of sample code. The MFC class hierarchy contains hundreds of different classes holding thousands of member functions. The Win32 API contains thousands of functions as well. All of this material is documented in on-line help files. Obviously, there is no lack of documentation with this product.

This book, therefore, makes no attempt to replace the documentation. Its goal is to help you wind your way through the Visual C++ forest and find what you need. Using the base you gain from reading this book, you will be able to approach Visual C++ and begin using it in productive ways very quickly.

There are currently seven different types of documentation provided by Microsoft for Visual C++ and MFC:

1. On-line Books – A series of manuals on the CD-ROM that act as the documentation for the system. The collection of books is visible in the InforView pane (see Appendix B.6.2). Look at the titles of all the different books and articles available. You will find that there are many .

2. Tech Notes – One of the sections in the on-line book collection is a set of MFC technical notes. These notes provide a set of useful explanations and discussions on MFC and migration issues.

3. MFC Encyclopedia – Another section in books on-line is the MFC encyclopedia, an extremely useful collection of notes and programming hints for the MFC class hierarchy.

4. Sample Code – The Visual C++ directory contains a sample directory that contains source code demonstrating a wide variety of techniques. Some of the samples are written in C, while other samples use MFC and C++.

5. Developer CD – Microsoft's Developer's Network CD provides quite a bit of additional sample code, along with books and files containing a variety of valuable information. You receive this CD when you become a member of the Microsoft Developer's Network.

6. Compuserve – Microsoft supports most of its products and environments on Compuserve. The MSMFC forum is particularly useful for MFC programmers, as is the Visual C++ section of the MSLANG forum.

7. Internet News Groups—The following news groups are of interest to MFC programmers: comp.os.ms-windows.programmer.tools.mfc and comp.os.ms-windows.programmer.win32.

Using all of these different forms of documentation, you can find anything you need to know. The key is understanding where and how to look for what you need. This book will help accelerate that process tremendously.

Road Map

The tools in Visual C++ require a great deal of prior knowledge if you want to use them effectively. For example, when you open the Visual C++ package and load the CD, you may have the impression that you can use the AppWizard to generate any program you like. Unfortunately, the code that the AppWizard generates is virtually worthless unless you know a good bit about MFC already. That is why this book is structured the way it is. The progression presented in this book is exactly the progression you will need to follow if you do not already know MFC. However, different people come into Visual C++ with varying levels of experience and different goals. Here is a road map to guide you through the material so that you can find the best starting point for your particular situation:

- If you do not know C++, you will need to learn it. Proceed to the accelerated introduction to C++ in Appendix A of this book.
- If you want to simply try out Visual C++ and compile some simple programs, proceed to Appendix B. It will show you how the compiler works and how to compile and debug simple applications.
- If you know C++ but have never done any Windows programming of any kind, proceed to Part 1. It will teach you the fundamentals of event-driven programming and then quickly introduce you to MFC programming.
- If you have experience with Windows programming in C but have never done Windows programming using C++ and MFC, proceed to Part 1. It will quickly introduce you to the MFC class hierarchy and MFC programming.
- If you have used MFC before (for example, if you are familiar with MFC version 1.0) but are unfamiliar with the new application development tools like the AppWizard and the ClassWizard, skim Part 2 and then proceed to Part 3 for a complete introduction to the tools.
- If you are familiar with Visual C++ and MFC but want to learn about a variety of techniques that can make your applications look more professional,

4

turn to Part 4. It will show you how to create things like splash screens, expanding dialogs, property sheets, and self-drawn controls.

- If you are a corporate programmer who needs to attach to a client/server database, pay particular attention to Chapter 33 in Part 5.

Common Questions

The goal of this section is to show you how to find answers to the most common questions about Visual C++ and MFC. You may wish to scan this list now and periodically in the future to quickly find answers to your questions.

Part 1

1. What is MFC? Why does it exist? See Chapter 1
2. How do I compile and run a simple MFC program? See Appendix B.3 and Chapter 1.
3. How do I create a simple "Hello World!" program in MFC? What does the code actually mean? See Chapter 2.
4. I have found the AppWizard, but when I run it I find it generates 15 files that make absolutely no sense to me. What do I do? See the discussion at the beginning of Part 3 of this book.
5. How do I create a simple MFC control? See Chapter 3.
6. How do I customize MFC controls and change their styles? See Chapter 3.
7. How do I create a push button and respond to its events in MFC? See Chapter 4.
8. What is a message map? See Chapter 4.
9. How do I create a scroll bar and respond to its events? See Chapter 4.
10. How do I create an edit control and respond to its events? See Chapter 5 and Chapter 8.
11. How do I create simple applications? See Chapter 5.
12. How do I make a simple application appropriately handle tab keys, accelerators, etc.? See Chapter 5.

Part 2

13. What is a resource? What is a resource file? What are the advantages of resources? See Chapter 6.
14. How do I create and use icon, dialog, menu, string table, and accelerator resources? See Chapter 6.
15. How do I create a message dialog? A File Open dialog? A Font dialog? A Color dialog? A Print dialog? A Find/Replace dialog? See Chapter 7.
16. What is the difference between modal and modeless dialogs? See Chapter 7.
17. How do I use an edit control in single and multi-line modes? See Chapter 8.
18. How do I create a simple text editor? See Chapter 8.

19. How do I create and use lists, drop down lists, and combo boxes in my applications? See Chapter 9 and Chapter 20.

20. How do I make multi-column and tabbed lists? See Chapter 9.

21. How do I load and display system and custom icons? See Chapters 6 and 10.

22. How do I change the application cursor? See Chapter 10 and 11.5.3.

23. How do I display a watch cursor? See Chapter 10.

24. How do I perform background processing while the application is idle? See Chapter 10.

25. What is a document template? See Chapter 10 and Chapter 16.

26. How do I create an MRU file list? See Chapter 10.

27. How do I use INI files with my applications? See Chapter 10.

28. How do I draw lines, rectangles, circles, etc. in my application's window? See Chapter 11.

29. How do I add graphics to an application? See Chapter 11.

30. How do I respond to mouse clicks in a drawing? See Chapter 11.

31. How do I create rubber-banded lines, rectangles, etc. in a drawing?

32. How do I create a drawing space larger than the current window? See Chapters 11 and 15.

33. How do I create animated drawings? See Chapter 11.

34. How do I work with text and binary files in MFC? See Chapter 12.

35. How do I work with strings in MFC? See Chapter 12.

36. How do I work with time values in MFC? See Chapter 12.

37. Is there an easy way to create arrays, lists and hash tables in MFC? See Chapter 12.

38. What debugging facilities are built into MFC? How do I make use of the MFC exception handling mechanisms? See Chapter 13.

39. How do I use TRACE and ASSERT statements? See Chapter 13.

40. How do I prevent and detect memory leaks in my applications? See Chapter 13.

Part 3

41. Are there any simple applications in this book showing me how to use the AppWizard and ClassWizard? See the drawing example, the editor example, the form example and the address list example in Part 3 of this book.

42. What is the AppWizard? What is the ClassWizard? How do I use them to speed up application development? See Chapter 14.

43. How do I create a simple framework with the AppWizard? See Chapter 14.

44. What do all of the files generated by the AppWizard do? See Chapter 14.

45. What is the document/view paradigm? See Chapters 14, 15 and 18.

46. What do the STDAFX files do? See Chapter 14.

47. Can you give me a simple example of the AppWizard and ClassWizard in action? See Chapter 14.

48. How do I create a simple drawing program with the AppWizard and the document/view paradigm? See Chapter 15.

49. What is the difference between an SDI and an MDI application? See Chapter 15.

50. How do I understand what is going on inside the AppWizard framework? See Section 15.3 and Chapter 21.

51. How do I add new menus and menu options to an application? See Chapter 15.

52. How do I add scrolling to a drawing application? How do I use splitter windows? See Chapter 15.

53. How do I add a new dialog to an AppWizard framework? How do I use DDX and DDV? See Chapters 15 and 18.

54. How do I add a dialog class with the ClassWizard? See Chapters 15 and 18.

55. How do I add printing to an application? What do the MFC printing functions do? How do I handle multi-page printing? See Chapters 15 and 18.

56. How do I create a text editor with the AppWizard? See Chapter 16.

57. How do I handle multiple document types in a single MDI application? See Chapter 16.

58. What is a document template? See Chapter 16.

59. How do I use form views? How do I put controls on the face of an application? See Chapter 17.

60. Can you give me an example that combines all of these different concepts in a single application? See Chapter 18.

61. How do I create a resizable tabbed list in a form view? See Chapter 18.

62. How do I enable and disable menu options? See Chapters 18 and 6.

63. How do I customize the tool bar and status bar? See Chapter 18.

64. How do I work with the clipboard in an application? See Chapter 18.

65. How do I print text information from an application? See Chapter 18.

66. How do I add context sensitive help to my applications? See Chapter 19.

67. What is the help compiler and how do I use it? See Chapter 19.

68. How do I use the Windows 95 controls in my applications? See Chapter 20.

69. How do I create Property sheets (tabbed dialogs) in my applications? See Chapter 20.

Part 4

70. How do DDX and DDV really work behind the scenes? See Chapter 22.

71. How do I integrate all of the different types of controls and use DDX to access them? See Chapter 22.

72. Is there a way to create new DDX functions for different data types? See Chapter 22.

73. How does MFC really work? What is happening inside of MFC? How does a C++ program using MFC compare to a C program? See Chapter 23.

74. How does MFC handle window handles? See Chapter 23.

75. Where is the window procedure in an MFC program? See Chapter 23.

76. How does subclassing work with Windows controls? See Chapter 23.

77. How can I take an existing control, like the CEdit control, and enhance its behavior without completely rewriting it? How do I integrate a new control like this into a dialog? See Chapter 24.

78. How do I create list boxes and combo boxes that contain icons, bitmaps or other graphical elements? See Chapter 26.

79. How do I handle owner-drawn controls in MFC? See Chapter 26.

80. How do I enumerate fonts and other resources under Windows? See Chapter 26.

81. How can I add a splash screen to my applications? See Chapter 27.

82. How do I add expanding dialogs to my applications? See Chapter 28.

83. How do I stretch a bitmap over an area? See Chapter 29.

84. How can I draw onto a CStatic control? See Chapter 29.

85. How do I add a bitmap or a drawing to the background of a dialog or a window? See Chapter 29.

86. How do I create my own floating palettes and tool bars? See Chapter 30.

87. How do I accept files dragged from the File Manager? See Chapter 32.

88. How do I make an application float so that it is "always on top." See Chapter 32.

89. How do I start an application in a minimized or maximized state? See Chapter 32.

90. How do I create a modelss dialog box? See Chapter 32.

91. How do I create a mini-frame window? See Chapter 32.

92. How do I create a popup menu activated by the right mouse button? See Chapter 32.

93. How do I customize the system menu? See Chapter 32.

Part 5

94. How to I access SQL databases from an MFC program? Chapter 33.

95. What is a relational database? What is SQL? See Chapter 33.

96. What is ODBC? How do I create ODBC data sources? See Chapter 33.

97. What is the CRecordset class? How do I access databases with it? See Chapter 33.

This book is continuously updated. See http://www.iftech.com/mfc

98. How do I retrieve records from a database? How do I add and delete records? See Chapter 33.

99. What is OLE? How can I use it in my applications? See Chapter 34.

100. What features does OLE support? See Chapter 34.

101. What is the registry? What is a class ID? See Chapter 34.

102. How do I create OLE servers and containers with MFC? See Chapter 34.

103. How do I create an OLE automation server? How do I access an automation server from a Visual Basic or Visual C++? See Chapter 34.

104. What is an OCX? How do I create an OLE control? See Chapter 34.

105. What is a thread? How can I use threads to improve applications? See Chapter 35.

106. What is the difference between worker and user-interface threads? See Chapter 35.

107. How do thread priorities work? What are they? See Chapter 35.

108. What is C++? How do I move from C to C++? See Appendix A.

109. How do I use the Visual C++ compiler, debugger and browser? See Appendix B.

110. What is OpenGL and how do I use it to create realistic graphical images? See Appendix D.

Part 1

In Part 1 of this book, you will learn about the fundamental concepts and vocabulary that drive Visual C++ and the Microsoft Foundation Class (MFC) hierarchy. Part 1 introduces you to simple MFC controls, customization, message maps for event handling, and other central ideas that make MFC programs work properly. You will also learn how to compile MFC programs in Visual C++. By the end of Part 1 you will understand how to create simple MFC programs of your own. Parts 2, 3, 4, and 5 show you how to increase your knowledge so you can create complete, professional applications with Visual C++.

INTRODUCTION

Visual C++ is much more than a compiler. It is a complete application development environment that, when used as intended, lets you fully exploit the object-oriented nature of C++ to create professional Windows applications. To take advantage of these features, you need to understand the C++ programming language. If you have never used C++, please turn to Appendix A for an introduction. You must then understand the Microsoft Foundation Class (MFC) hierarchy. This class hierarchy encapsulates the user interface portion of the Windows API, supplies other useful classes, and makes it significantly easier to create Windows applications in an object-oriented way.

This chapter introduces the fundamental concepts and vocabulary behind MFC and event-driven programming. In this chapter you will enter, compile, and run a simple MFC program using Visual C++. If you already feel comfortable with the concepts, read section 1.1 and then move straight to Section 1.4, which will show you how to start using Visual C++ immediately. Chapter 2 provides a detailed explanation of the code used in Chapter 1. Chapter 3 discusses MFC controls and their customization. Chapter 4 covers message maps, which let you handle events in MFC. Finally, Chapter 5 completes this section with several simple example applications that integrate the different concepts you have learned.

1.1 What is the Microsoft Foundation Class Library?

Let's say you want to create a Windows application. You might, for example, need to create a specialized text or drawing editor, or a program that finds files on a large network, or an application that lets a user visualize the interrelationships in a big data set. Where do you begin?

A good starting place is the design of the user interface. First, decide what the user should be able to do with the program, and then pick a set of user interface objects accordingly. The Windows user interface has a number of standard controls, such as buttons, menus, scroll bars, and lists, that are already familiar to Windows users. With this in mind, you can choose a set of controls and decide how they should be arranged on screen. You might start with a rough sketch of the interface if the program is small, or go through a complete user interface specification and design cycle if the program is large.

The next step is to implement the code. When creating a program for any Windows platform, the programmer has two choices: C or C++. With C, the programmer codes at the level of the Windows Application Program Interface (API). This interface consists of a collection of hundreds of C functions described in the Window's API Reference books. The more modern version of the API, first introduced in Windows NT, is typically referred to as the "Win32 API," to distinguish it from the original 16-bit API of earlier Windows products like Windows 3.1.

Microsoft also provides a C++ library that sits on top of the Windows API and makes the programmer's job easier. Called the MFC library, this library's primary advantage is efficiency. It greatly reduces the amount of code that must be written to create a Windows program. It also provides all the advantages normally found in C++ programming, such as inheritance and encapsulation. MFC is portable across versions of Windows and the Mac, so that, for example, code created under Windows 3.1 can move to Windows NT or Windows 95 very easily. MFC is therefore the preferred method for developing Windows applications and will be used throughout this book.

When you use MFC, you write code that creates the necessary user interface controls and customizes their appearance. You also write code that responds when the user manipulates these controls. For example, if the user clicks a button, you want to have code in place that responds appropriately. It is this sort of event-handling code that will form the bulk of any application. Once the application responds correctly to all of the available controls, it is finished.

You can see from this discussion that the creation of a Windows program is a straightforward process when using MFC. The goal of this book is to fill in the details and to show the techniques you can use to create professional applications as quickly as possible. The Visual C++ application development environment is specifically tuned to MFC, so by learning MFC and Visual C++ together you can significantly increase your power as an application developer.

1.2 Windows Vocabulary

The vocabulary used to talk about user interface features and software development in Windows is basic but unique. Here we review a few definitions to make discussion easier for those who are new to the environment.

Each application on the screen has a main application window. This is the window you see when the program executes, and it normally contains the main pull-down menu, user controls, and so on. A simple main window is shown in Figure 1.1 Under Windows 95 things look a little different but do the same things.

This main window contains several standard elements. The bar at the top of the window is called the *title bar*. From left to right it contains the *system menu* (or control menu) box, the *title* (or caption) containing the word "Clock," and the *minimize* and

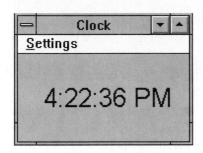

Figure 1.1
A typical Windows application

maximize buttons used to iconify and expand the window, respectively. Around the window a thick frame allows the user to resize the window.

Below the title bar is a *menu bar*, here containing the single menu named "Settings." The "S" of "Settings" is underlined to indicate its use as a *menu mnemonic*. If you hit **Alt-S** on the keyboard, it is the same as clicking the settings menu with the mouse.

The area below the menu bar is left for the application itself, and it is called the *client area*. In Figure 1.1 the client area holds the current time. Typically, the client area is filled with controls or child windows. Windows applications can use any of a number of standard user controls:

- Static text labels
- Push buttons
- List boxes
- Combo boxes (a more advanced form of list)
- Radio boxes
- Check boxes
- Editable text areas (single and multi-line)
- Scroll bars

Windows supports several types of application windows. A typical application will live inside a *frame window*. A frame window is a full-featured main window that the user can resize, minimize to an icon, maximize to fill the screen, and so on. Windows also supports two types of dialog boxes: *modal* and *modeless*. A modal dialog box, once on the screen, blocks input to the rest of the application until it is answered. A modeless dialog box can appear at the same time as the application and seems to "float above" it to keep from being overlaid.

Windows also provides an organizing scheme called the *Multiple Document Interface*, or MDI, an example of which is shown in Figure 1.2. The MDI system allows the user to view multiple documents at the same time within a single instance of an application. For example, a text editor might allow the user to open multiple files simultaneously. When implemented with MDI, the application presents a large application window that can hold multiple sub-windows, each containing a document. The single main menu is held by the main application window and it applies to the topmost window held within the MDI frame. Individual windows can be iconified or expanded as desired within the MDI frame, or the entire MDI frame can be minimized into a single icon on the desktop. The MDI interface gives the impression of a second desktop out on the desktop, and it goes a long way toward organizing and removing window clutter.

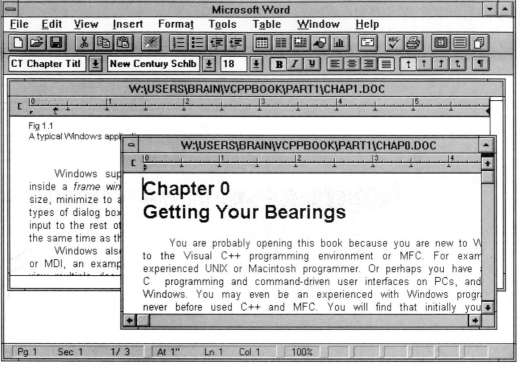

Figure 1.2
A typical MDI application

Each application that you create will use its own unique set of controls, its own menu structure, and its own dialog boxes. A great deal of the effort that goes into creating any good application interface lies in the choice and organization of these interface objects. Visual C++, along with its resource editors and ClassWizard, makes the creation and customization of these interface objects extremely easy.

1.3 Event-driven Software and Vocabulary

All window-based GUIs contain the same basic elements and all operate in the same way. On screen the user sees a group of windows, each of which contains controls, icons, objects, and so on that are manipulated with the mouse or the keyboard. The interface objects seen by the user are the same from system to system: push buttons, scroll bars, icons, dialog boxes, pull-down menus, etc. These interface objects all work the same way, although some have minor differences in their "look and feel." For example, scroll bars look slightly different as you move from Windows to the Mac, but they all do the same thing.

This book is continuously updated. See http://www.iftech.com/mfc

From a programmer's standpoint, the systems are all similar in concept, although they differ radically in their specifics. To create a GUI program, the programmer first puts all the needed user interface controls into a window. For example, if the programmer is trying to create a simple program such as a Fahrenheit to Celsius converter, then the programmer selects user interface objects appropriate to the task and displays them on screen. In this example, the programmer might let the user enter a temperature in an editable text area, display the converted temperature in another un-editable text area, and let the user exit the program by clicking on a push button labeled "Quit." This structure is shown in Figure 1.3.

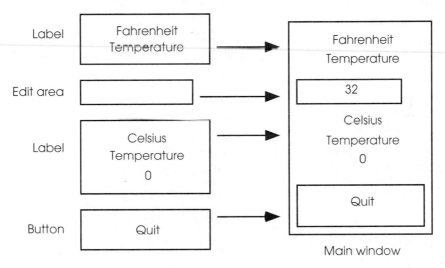

Figure 1.3
Elements of a typical application showing the selection of user interface controls in a Fahrenheit to Celsius conversion program

As the user manipulates the application's controls, the program must respond appropriately. For example, if the user clicks the Quit button, the button must update the screen appropriately, highlighting itself as necessary. Then the program must respond by quitting. Normally the button manages its appearance itself, and the program in some way receives a message from the button that says, "The Quit button was pressed. Do something about it." The program responds by exiting.

Windows follows this same general pattern. In a typical application you will create a main window and place inside it different user interface controls. These controls are often referred to as *child windows*—each control is like a smaller and more specialized sub-window inside the main application window. As the application programmer, you manipulate the controls by sending them messages via function calls, and they respond to user actions by sending messages back to your code.

If you have never done any "event-driven" programming, then all of this may seem foreign to you. However, the event-driven style of programming is easy to understand when compared to a normal command-driven user interface.

In a command-driven user interface, the system interacts with the user in three steps. First, the system prompts the user for a command. The prompt could be something explanatory such as:

```
Please enter the next command>
```

Or it could be something more obtuse:

```
%
```

The user is expected to know all the commands in the system and to type whichever one is needed. Second, the user types a command at the prompt and the system reads it. Third, the system parses the command and any modifiers following the command. The parsing step allows the system to call appropriate code to "execute" the command. Once command execution is complete, the program issues a new command prompt and the cycle repeats. Users of DOS or UNIX are familiar with this process.

An event-driven user interface works somewhat differently. The exact details depend on the system and the level at which you are interfacing with it, but the basic concepts are similar. In an event-driven interface, the application paints several (or many) user interface objects such as buttons, text areas, and menus onto the screen. Now the application waits–typically in a piece of code called an *event loop*–for the user to do something. The user can do anything to any of the objects on screen using either the mouse or the keyboard. The user might click one of the buttons, for example. The mouse click is called an *event*. Event-driven systems define events for user actions such as mouse clicks and keystrokes, as well as for system activities such as screen updating.

At the lowest level of abstraction, you have to respond to each event in a fair amount of detail. This is the case when you are writing normal C code directly to the API. In such a scenario, you receive the mouse-click event in some sort of structure. Code in your event loop looks at different fields in the structure, determines which user interface object was affected, perhaps highlights the object in some way to give the user visual feedback, and then performs the appropriate action for that object and event. When there are many objects on the screen, the application becomes very large. It can take a quite a bit of code simply to figure out which object was clicked and what to do about it.

Fortunately, you can work at a much higher level of abstraction. In MFC, almost all these low-level implementation details are handled for you. If you want to place a user interface object on the screen, you create it with two lines of code. If the user clicks on a button, the button does everything needed to update its appearance on the screen and then calls a pre-arranged function in your program. This function contains the code that implements the appropriate action for the button. MFC handles all the details for you: You create the button and tell it about a specific handler function, and it calls your function when the user presses it.

The labor involved in creating MFC applications is almost completely devoted to the creation of the handler functions. Visual C++ contains tools, described in Part 3 of this book, that make this process easy and intuitive.

1.4 An Example

One of the best ways to begin understanding the structure and style of a typical MFC program is to enter, compile, and run a small example. Listing 1.1 contains a simple "Hello World" program. Figure 1.4 shows a screen dump of the program during execution. If this is the first time you've seen this sort of program, it probably will not make a lot of sense initially. Don't worry about that. We will examine the code in detail in the next chapter. For now, the goal is to use the Visual C++ environment to create, compile, and execute this simple program.

Listing 1.1

hello.cpp – A simple "Hello World" program in MFC.

```
//hello.cpp

#include <afxwin.h>

// Declare the application class
class CHelloApp : public CWinApp
{
public:
    virtual BOOL InitInstance();
};

// Create an instance of the application class
CHelloApp HelloApp;

// Declare the main window class
class CHelloWindow : public CFrameWnd
{
    CStatic* cs;
public:
    CHelloWindow();
};

// The InitInstance function is called each
// time the application first executes.
BOOL CHelloApp::InitInstance()
{
    m_pMainWnd = new CHelloWindow();
    m_pMainWnd->ShowWindow(m_nCmdShow);
    m_pMainWnd->UpdateWindow();
    return TRUE;
}

// The constructor for the window class
CHelloWindow::CHelloWindow()
{
    // Create the window itself
    Create(NULL,
        "Hello World!",
        WS_OVERLAPPEDWINDOW,
```

```
        CRect(0,0,200,200));
// Create a static label
cs = new CStatic();
cs->Create("hello world",
    WS_CHILD|WS_VISIBLE|SS_CENTER,
    CRect(50,80,150,150),
    this);
}
```

Figure 1.4
Screen dump of the "Hello World" program
during execution

This small program does three things. First, it creates an "application object." Every MFC program you write will have a single application object that handles the initialization details of MFC and Windows. Next, the application creates a single window on the screen to act as the main application window. Finally, inside that window the application creates a single static text label containing the words "Hello World." We will look at this program in detail in the next chapter to gain a complete understanding of its structure.

The steps necessary to enter and compile this program are straightforward. If you have not yet installed Visual C++ on your machine, do so now. You will have the option of creating standard and custom installations. For the purposes of this book a standard installation is suitable and after answering two or three simple questions the rest of the installation is quick and painless. *Then turn to Appendix B.3.*

1.5 Conclusion

In this chapter you have successfully compiled and executed your first program. You will use these same steps for each of the programs you create in Parts 1 and 2 of this book. You will find that you can either create a separate directory for each project or you can create a single project file and directory, and then add and remove different source files. For more information on the compiler, debugger, browser, and so on, please see Appendix B.

In the next chapter, we will examine the program in Listing 1.1 in detail so you gain a more complete understanding of its structure.

UNDERSTANDING AN MFC PROGRAM

2

In this chapter we will examine a simple MFC program piece by piece to gain an understanding of its structure and conceptual framework. We will start by looking at MFC itself and then examine how you use MFC to create applications.

2.1 An Introduction to MFC

MFC is a large and extensive C++ class hierarchy that makes Windows application development significantly easier. MFC encapsulates much of the Windows API, letting you take advantage of all the features of C++ when writing Windows code. As each new version of Windows comes out, MFC gets modified so that old code compiles and works under the new system. MFC also grows over time, adding new capabilities to the hierarchy and making it easier to create complete applications.

The advantage of using MFC and C++–as opposed to directly accessing the Windows API from a C program–is that MFC already contains and encapsulates all the normal "boilerplate" code that all Windows programs written in C must contain. Programs written in MFC are therefore much smaller than equivalent C programs. In addition, aspects of Windows programming that are quite complicated when dealt with in C become almost trivial in MFC. For example, creating an MDI framework in MFC is trivial, but is rather complex in C. On the other hand, MFC is a fairly thin covering over the C functions, so there is little or no performance penalty imposed by its use. It is also easy to customize things using the standard C calls when necessary because MFC does not modify or hide the basic structure of a Windows program.

The best part about using MFC is that it does all the hard work for you. The hierarchy contains thousands and thousands of lines of correct, optimized, and robust Windows code. Many of the member functions that you call invoke code that would have taken you weeks to write yourself. In this way MFC tremendously accelerates your project-development cycle.

MFC is fairly large. For example, Version 4.0 of the hierarchy contains over 200 different classes. Fortunately, you don't need to use all of them in a typical program. In fact, it is possible to create some fairly spectacular software using only ten or so of the different classes available in MFC. The hierarchy is broken down into six different class categories:

- Application Architecture
- Visual Objects
- General Purpose
- Collections
- OLE 2
- Database

We will concentrate on visual objects initially. Part 2 contains an overview, with examples, of a majority of the classes in the hierarchy. Figure 2.1 shows the critical portion of the class hierarchy that deals with application support and windows support.

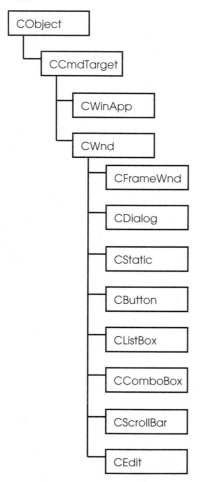

Figure 2.1
The portion of the Microsoft Foundation Class Library that deals with applications and windows.

There are several things to notice in Figure 2.1. First, most classes in MFC derive from a base class called **CObject**. This class contains data members and member functions that are common to most MFC classes. The second thing to notice is the simplicity of the diagram. The **CWinApp** class is used whenever you create an application and it is used only once in any program. The **CWnd** class collects all the common features found in windows, dialog boxes, and controls. The **CFrameWnd** class inherits from **CWnd** and implements a normal framed application window. **CDialog** handles the two normal flavors of dialogs: modeless and modal, respectively. Finally, Windows supports six native control types: static text, editable text, push buttons, scroll bars, lists, and combo boxes (an extended form of list). Once you understand this fairly small number of pieces, you are well on your way to a complete understanding of MFC. The other classes in the MFC hierarchy implement other features such as memory management, document control, database support, and so on.

To create a program in MFC, you either use its classes directly or, more commonly, you derive new classes from the existing classes. In the derived classes you create new member functions that allow instances of the class to behave properly in your application. You can see this derivation process in the simple program we used in Chapter 1, which is described in greater detail in Section 2.3. Both **CHelloApp** and **CHelloWindow** in Listing 1.1 are derived from existing MFC classes.

2.2 Designing a Program

Before discussing the code itself, it is worthwhile to briefly discuss the program design process under MFC. As an example, imagine that you want to create a program that displays the message "Hello World" to the user. This is obviously a very simple application but it still requires some thought.

A "Hello World" application first needs to create a window on the screen that holds the words "Hello World." It then needs to get the actual "Hello World" words into that window. Three objects are required to accomplish this task:

1. An application object that initializes the application and hooks it to Windows. The application object handles all low-level event processing.
2. A window object that acts as the main application window.
3. A static text object that will hold the static text label "Hello World."

Every program that you create in MFC will contain the first two objects. The third object is unique to this particular application. Each application will define its own set of user interface objects that display the application's output as well as gather input from the user.

Once you have completed the user interface design and decided on the controls necessary to implement the interface, you write the code to create the controls on the screen. You also write the code that handles the messages generated by these controls as they are manipulated by the user. In the case of a "Hello World" application, only one user interface control is necessary. It holds the words "Hello World." More realistic applications may have hundreds of controls arranged in the main window and dialog boxes.

2.3 Understanding the Code for "Hello World"

Listing 2.1 shows the code for the simple "Hello World" program that you entered, compiled, and executed in Chapter 1. Line numbers have been added to allow discussion of the code in the sections that follow. By walking through this program line by line, you can gain a good understanding of the way MFC is used to create simple applications. Part 3 of this book discusses how to create more complicated applications using the AppWizard to generate an MFC application framework for you.

If you have not done so already, please compile and execute Listing 2.1 by following the instructions given in Appendix B.3.

Listing 2.1
hello.cpp - A simple "Hello World" program

```
1   //hello.cpp

2   #include <afxwin.h>

3   // Declare the application class
4   class CHelloApp : public CWinApp
5   {
6   public:
7       virtual BOOL InitInstance();
8   };

9   // Create an instance of the application class
10  CHelloApp HelloApp;

11  // Declare the main window class
12  class CHelloWindow : public CFrameWnd
13  {
14      CStatic* cs;
15  public:
16      CHelloWindow();
17  };

18  // The InitInstance function is called each
19  // time the application first executes.
20  BOOL CHelloApp::InitInstance()
21  {
22      m_pMainWnd = new CHelloWindow();
23      m_pMainWnd->ShowWindow(m_nCmdShow);
24      m_pMainWnd->UpdateWindow();
25      return TRUE;
26  }

27  // The constructor for the window class
28  CHelloWindow::CHelloWindow()
29  {
30      // Create the window itself
31      Create(NULL,
32          "Hello World!",
33          WS_OVERLAPPEDWINDOW,
34          CRect(0,0,200,200));
35      // Create a static label
36      cs = new CStatic();
```

```
37      cs->Create("hello world",
38          WS_CHILD|WS_VISIBLE|SS_CENTER,
39          CRect(50,80,150,150),
40          this);
41  }
```

Some of the variable names in Listing 2.1 may seem a bit odd because Microsoft code uses something called "Hungarian notation" to prefix its variable names. This notational system encodes information about the variable's type in the variable's name. For example, a variable named **bFlag** starts with "b" to indicate that it is a Boolean variable. The name **szString** uses "sz" to indicate that it is a null (zero) terminated string. In Listing 2.1, the name **m_pMainWnd** uses "m_" to indicate that the variable is a class member and "p" to indicate that it is a pointer. By looking at several variable names and their types, you will quickly learn what each character means. Here is a table of common letters and their translations:

b	BOOL
c	char
h	handle
i	int
l	long
m_	member
p	pointer
sz	null terminated string
w	UINT

You will find that each programmer tends to have slightly different preferences, so the notation may vary slightly from program to program. You will also find that you either like or dislike this system. If you dislike it, don't use it. There is no requirement that your variable names comply with this system.

Take a moment and look though this program. Get a feeling for the "lay of the land." The program consists of six small parts, each of which does something important.

1. The program first includes `afxwin.h` (line 2). This header file contains all the types, classes, functions, and variables used in MFC. It also includes other header files for such things as the Windows API libraries.
2. Lines 3 through 8 derive a new application class named **CHelloApp** from the standard **CWinApp** application class declared in MFC. The new class is created so the **InitInstance** member function in the **CWinApp** class can be overridden.

InitInstance is a virtual function that is called as the application begins execution.

3. In Line 10, the code declares an instance of the application object as a global variable. This instance is important because it causes the program to execute. When the application is loaded into memory and begins running, the creation of that global variable causes the default constructor for the **CWinApp** class to execute. This constructor automatically calls the **InitInstance** function in lines 18 though 26.

4. In lines 11 through 17, the **CHelloWindow** class is derived from the **CFrameWnd** class declared in MFC. **CHelloWindow** acts as the application's window on the screen. A new class is created so that a new constructor and data member can be implemented.

5. Lines 18 through 26 implement the **InitInstance** function. This function creates an instance of the **CHelloWindow** class, thereby causing the constructor for the class in Lines 27 through 41 to execute. It also gets the new window onto the screen.

6. Lines 27 through 41 implement the window's constructor. The constructor actually creates the window and then creates a static control inside it.

An interesting thing to notice in this program is that there is no **main** or **Win-Main** function, and no apparent event loop. Yet we know from executing it in Chapter 1 that it processed events. The window could be minimized and maximized, moved around, and so on. All this activity is hidden in the main application class **CWinApp** and we therefore don't have to worry about it.Event handling is totally automatic and invisible in MFC.

The following sections describe the different pieces of this program in more detail. It is unlikely that all of this information will make complete sense to you right now. It's best to read through it to get your first exposure to the concepts. In Chapter 3, where a number of specific examples are discussed, the different pieces will come together and begin to clarify themselves.

2.3.1 The Application Object

Every program that you create in MFC will contain a single application object that you derive from the **CWinApp** class. This object must be declared globally (line 10) and can exist only once in any given program.

An object derived from the **CWinApp** class handles initialization of the application, as well as the main event loop for the program. The **CWinApp** class has several data members and a number of member functions. We will look at all these different functions and variables in detail in later chapters (see in particular Chapter 10). For now, almost all are unimportant. If you would like to browse through some of these functions, however, search for **CWinApp** in the MFC documentation. In the program above, we have overridden only one virtual function in **CWinApp**, that being the **Init-Instance** function.

The purpose of the application object is to initialize and control your application. Because Windows allows multiple instances of the same application to run simultaneously, MFC breaks the initialization process into two parts and uses two functions– **InitApplication** and **InitInstance**–to handle it. Here we have used only the **InitInstance** function because of the simplicity of the application. **InitInstance** is called each time a new instance of the application is invoked. The code in Lines 3 through 8 creates a class called **CHelloApp** derived from **CWinApp**. It contains a new **InitInstance** function that overrides the existing function in **CWinApp** (which does nothing):

```
3    // Declare the application class
4    class CHelloApp : public CWinApp
5    {
6    public:
7        virtual BOOL InitInstance();
8    };
```

Inside the overridden **InitInstance** function at lines 18 through 26, the program creates and displays the window using **CWinApp**'s data member named **m_pMainWnd**:

```
18   // The InitInstance function is called each
19   // time the application first executes.
20   BOOL CHelloApp::InitInstance()
21   {
22       m_pMainWnd = new CHelloWindow();
23       m_pMainWnd->ShowWindow(m_nCmdShow);
24       m_pMainWnd->UpdateWindow();
25       return TRUE;
26   }
```

The **InitInstance** function returns a TRUE value to indicate that initialization was completed successfully. Had the function returned a FALSE value, the application would terminate immediately. We will see more details of the window initialization process in the next section.

When the application object is created at line 10, its data members (inherited from **CWinApp**) are automatically initialized. For example, **m_pszAppName**, **m_lpCommandLine**, and **m_nCmdShow** all contain appropriate values. See the MFC documentation for more information. We'll see a use for one of these variables in a moment.

2.3.2 The Window Object

MFC defines two types of windows: 1) frame windows, which are fully functional windows that can be resized, minimized, and so on, and 2) dialog windows, which are not resizable. A frame window (or a MDI frame window) is typically used for the main application window of a program.

In the code shown in Listing 2.1, a new class named **CHelloWindow** is derived from the **CFrameWnd** class in lines 8 through 14:

```
11   // Declare the main window class
12   class CHelloWindow : public CFrameWnd
13   {
14       CStatic* cs;
```

```
15  public:
16      CHelloWindow();
17  };
```

The derivation contains a new constructor, along with a data member that will point to the single user interface control used in the program. Each application that you create will have a unique set of controls residing in the main application window. Therefore, the derived class will have an overridden constructor that creates all the controls required in the main window. Typically this class will also have an overridden destructor to delete them when the window closes, but the destructor is not used here (See Section 2.4 for details). In Chapter 4, we will see that the derived window class will also declare a message handler to handle messages that these controls produce in response to user events.

Typically, any application you create will have a single main application window. The **CWinApp** application class therefore contains a data member named **m_pMainWnd** that can point to this main window. To create the main window for this application, the **InitInstance** function (lines 18 through 26) creates an instance of **CHelloWindow** and uses **m_pMainWnd** to point to the new window. Our **CHelloWindow** object is created at line 22:

```
18  // The InitInstance function is called each
19  // time the application first executes.
20  BOOL CHelloApp::InitInstance()
21  {
22      m_pMainWnd = new CHelloWindow();
23      m_pMainWnd->ShowWindow(m_nCmdShow);
24      m_pMainWnd->UpdateWindow();
25      return TRUE;
26  }
```

Simply creating a frame window is not enough, however. Two other steps are required to make sure that the new window appears on screen correctly. First, the code must call the window's **ShowWindow** function to make the window appear on screen (line 18). Second, the program must call the **UpdateWindow** function to make sure that each control, and any drawing done in the interior of the window, is painted correctly onto the screen (line 19).

You may wonder where the **ShowWindow** and **UpdateWindow** functions are defined. For example, if you wanted to look them up to learn more about them, you might look in the MFC documentation at the **CFrameWnd** class description. **CFrameWnd** does not contain either of these member functions, however. It turns out that **CFrameWnd** inherits its behavior—as do all controls and windows in MFC—from the **CWnd** class (see figure 2.1). If you refer to **CWnd** in the MFC documentation, you will find that it is a huge class containing more than 200 different functions. Obviously, you are not going to master this particular class in a couple of minutes, but among the many useful functions are **ShowWindow** and **UpdateWindow**. We will be referring to the **CWnd** class throughout this book, and you will gain a thorough familiarity with it.

While we are on the subject, take a minute now to look up the **CWnd::Show-Window** function in the MFC documentation. Notice that **ShowWindow** accepts a

28

single parameter, and that the parameter can be set to one of ten different values. We have set it to a data member held by **CHelloApp** in our program, **m_nCmdShow** (line 23). The **m_nCmdShow** variable is initialized based on conditions set by the user at application start-up. For example, the user may have started the application from the Program Manager and told the Program Manager to start the application in the minimized state by setting the check box in the application's properties dialog. The **m_nCmdShow** variable will be set to SW_SHOWMINIMIZED, and the application will start in an iconic state. The **m_nCmdShow** variable is a way for the outside world to communicate with the new application at start-up. If you would like to experiment, you can try replacing **m_nCmdShow** in the call to **ShowWindow** with the different constant values defined for **ShowWindow**. Recompile the program and see what they do.

Line 22 instantiates the window. It allocates memory for it by calling the **new** function. At this point in the program's execution the constructor for the **CHelloWindow** is called. The constructor is called whenever an instance of the class is allocated. Inside the window's constructor, the window must create itself. It does this by calling the **Create** member function for the **CFrameWnd** class at line 31:

```
27  // The constructor for the window class
28  CHelloWindow::CHelloWindow()
29  {
30      // Create the window itself
31      Create(NULL,
32          "Hello World!",
33          WS_OVERLAPPEDWINDOW,
34          CRect(0,0,200,200));
```

Four parameters are passed to the create function. By looking in the MFC documentation you can see the different types. The initial NULL parameter indicates that a default class name be used (more on this in Chapter 10). The second parameter is the title of the window that will appear in the title bar. The third parameter is the style attribute for the window. This example indicates that a normal, overlappable window should be created. Style attributes are covered in detail in Chapter 3. The fourth parameter specifies that the window should be placed onto the screen with its upper left corner at point 0,0 and that the initial size of the window should be 200 x 200 pixels. If the value **rectDefault** is used as the fourth parameter instead, Windows will place and size the window automatically for you.

Because this is an extremely simple program, it creates a single static text control inside the window. In later chapters, we will see far more involved derivations from the **CFrameWnd** class. In this particular example, the program uses a single static text label as its only control, and it is created at lines 25 through 40. This step is described in more detail in the next section.

2.3.3 The Static Text Control

The program derives the **CHelloWindow** class from the **CFrameWnd** class (lines 11 through 17). In doing so it declares a private data member of type **CStatic***, as well as a constructor.

As seen in the previous section, the **CHelloWindow** constructor does two things. First it creates the application's window by calling the **Create** function (line 31), and then it allocates and creates the control that belongs inside the window. In this case a single static label is used as the only control. Object creation is always a two-step process in MFC. First, the memory for the instance of the class is allocated, thereby calling the constructor to initialize any variables. Next, an explicit **Create** function is called to actually create the object on screen (see Section XXX for an explanation). The code allocates and creates a single static text object using this two-step process at lines 36 through 40:

```
27  // The constructor for the window class
28  CHelloWindow::CHelloWindow()
29  {
30      // Create the window itself
31      Create(NULL,
32          "Hello World!",
33          WS_OVERLAPPEDWINDOW,
34          CRect(0,0,200,200));
35      // Create a static label
36      cs = new CStatic();
37      cs->Create("hello world",
38          WS_CHILD|WS_VISIBLE|SS_CENTER,
39          CRect(50,80,150,150),
40          this);
41  }
```

The constructor for the **CStatic** item is called when the memory for it is allocated, and then an explicit **Create** function is called to create the **CStatic** control's window. The parameters used in the **Create** function here are similar to those used for window creation at line 31. The first parameter specifies the text to be displayed by the control. The second parameter specifies the style attributes. The style attributes are discussed in detail in the next chapter, but here we request that the control be a child window (and therefore displayed within another window), that it should be visible, and that the text within the control should be centered. The third parameter determines the size and position of the static control, as shown in Figure 2.2. The fourth indicates the parent window for which this control is the child. Having created the static control, it will appear in the application's window and display the specified text.

2.4 Completing the Program

The code demonstrated so far in Listings 1.1 and 2.1 is not quite complete. It will run correctly, but if you were to turn on the trace option and run it under the debugger (see Appendix B.2) you would get complaints that the application does not free up its allocated memory properly. To fix that problem, you need to create a destructor for the **CHelloWindow** class and delete the memory allocated for the **CStatic** label. This correction is shown in Listing 2.2.

Listing 2.2
hello.cpp – The simple "Hello World" program with a proper destructor

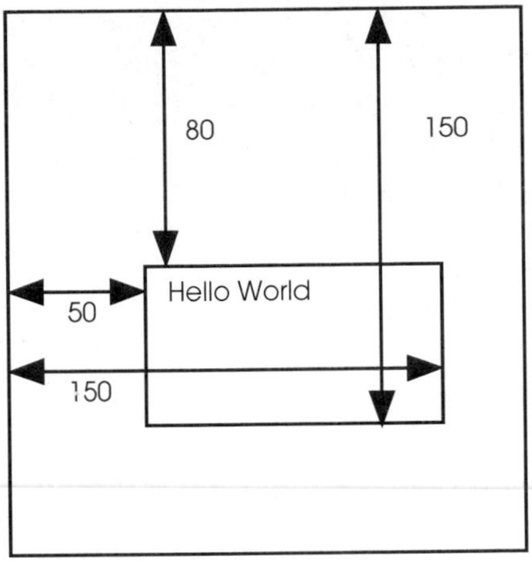
80
150
Hello World
50
150

Figure 2.2
Placement of the CStatic label

```
//hello.cpp

#include <afxwin.h>

// Declare the application class
class CHelloApp : public CWinApp
{
public:
    virtual BOOL InitInstance();
};

// Create an instance of the application class
CHelloApp HelloApp;

// Declare the main window class
class CHelloWindow : public CFrameWnd
{
    CStatic* cs;
public:
    CHelloWindow();
    ~CHelloWindow();
};

// The InitInstance function is called each
// time the application first executes.
BOOL CHelloApp::InitInstance()
{
    m_pMainWnd = new CHelloWindow();
    m_pMainWnd->ShowWindow(m_nCmdShow);
    m_pMainWnd->UpdateWindow();
    return TRUE;
}

// The constructor for the window class
CHelloWindow::CHelloWindow()
{
    // Create the window itself
    Create(NULL,
```

```
            "Hello World!",
            WS_OVERLAPPEDWINDOW,
            CRect(0,0,200,200));
    // Create a static label
    cs = new CStatic();
    cs->Create("hello world",
            WS_CHILD|WS_VISIBLE|SS_CENTER,
            CRect(50,80,150,150),
            this);
}


// The destructor for the window class
CHelloWindow::~CHelloWindow()
{
    delete cs;
}
```

2.5 MFC Application Structure

In this chapter you have seen the simplest possible MFC program. However, the structure of this program applies to all MFC applications, whether the code fits in 100 lines or 100,000. There are six pieces that every MFC application will always have:

1. A class derived from **CWinApp** that acts as the application class for the program. This class will always override the **InitInstance** function.
2. An instance of that application class declared as a global variable. The constructor for the **CWinApp** class automatically calls **InitInstance**.
3. A class derived from **CFrameWnd** (or **CMDIFrameWnd** or **CMiniFrameWnd**) that acts as the application's main window on the screen.
4. Code implementing the **InitInstance** function that creates the window.
5. Code for the window class's constructor.
6. Code for the window class's destructor.

You will find all these pieces in the "hello world" application created above. You will also find them in the code generated by the AppWizard, although the AppWizard will add quite a few other pieces as well. Your goal is to understand these pieces so well that when you see them generated by the AppWizard you understand why they are there and how to modify them.

2.6 Conclusion

In looking at this code for the first time, it will be unfamiliar and therefore potentially annoying. Don't worry about it. The only part in the entire program that matters from an application programmer's perspective is the **CStatic** creation code at lines 36 through 40. The rest you will type in once and then ignore. In the next chapter you will come to a full understanding of what lines 36 through 40 do and see a number of options that you have in customizing a **CStatic** control.

CUSTOMIZING CONTROLS

3

Controls are the user interface objects that create interfaces for Windows applications. Most Windows applications and dialog boxes that you see are nothing but a collection of controls arranged in a way that appropriately implements the functionality of the program. To build effective applications, you must completely understand how to use the controls available in Windows. There are only six basic controls–**CStatic**, **CButton**, **CEdit**, **CList**, **CComboBox**, and **CScrollBar**–along with an additional collection of Windows 95 controls discussed in Chapter 20. You need to understand what each control can do, how you can tune its appearance and behavior, and how to make the controls respond appropriately to user events. By combining this knowledge with an understanding of menus and dialogs (discussed in Chapters 6 and 7 of this book), you gain the ability to create any Windows application that you can imagine.

The simplest of the controls, **CStatic**, displays static text. The **CStatic** class has no data members and only four member functions: the constructor, the **Create** function, and two functions for getting and setting icons on static controls. It does not respond to user events. Because of its simplicity, it is a good place to start learning about Windows controls.

In this chapter we will look at the **CStatic** class to understand how controls can be modified and customized. In the following chapter, we examine the **CButton** and **CScrollBar** classes to gain an understanding of event handling. Chapter 5 then integrates the concepts you have learned in Part 1 by creating two very simple applications. Part 2 contains descriptions of all other controls, as well as a variety of other useful MFC classes. Once you understand all the controls and classes, you are ready to build complete applications as discussed in Part 3.

3.1 The Basics

A **CStatic** object displays static text messages to the user. These messages can serve purely informational purposes (for example, text in a message dialog that describes an error), or they can serve as small labels that identify other controls. Figure

3.1 shows the standard **File Open** dialog box. In this dialog you find six text labels. Five of the labels identify the lists, text area, and check box and do not ever change. The sixth displays the current directory and changes each time the current directory changes.

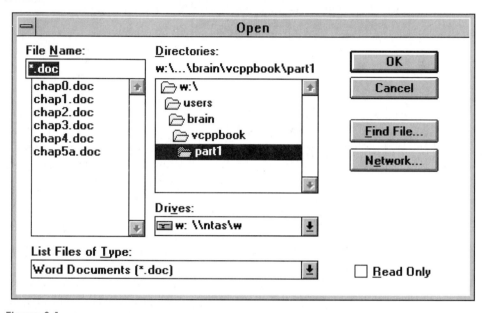

Figure 3.1
A file open dialog that uses six text labels

CStatic objects have several other display formats, each of which is demonstrated in Figure 3.2. By changing the style of a label it can display itself as a solid rectangle, as a border, or as an icon. The rectangular solid and frame forms of the **CStatic** class allow you to visually group related interface elements and to add separators between controls.

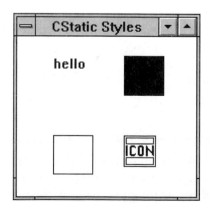

Figure 3.2
The four different display formats for a **CStatic** object. Clockwise from top left: static text, black rectangle, icon, black frame

A **CStatic** control is always a child window to some parent window. Typically, the parent window is the main window for an application or a dialog box. You create the static control, as discussed in Chapter 2, with two lines of code and a variable declaration:

```
// declaration
CStatic *cs;
...

// allocation
cs = new CStatic();
// creation
cs->Create("hello world",
    WS_CHILD|WS_VISIBLE|SS_CENTER,
    CRect(50,80, 150, 150),
    this);
```

This two-line creation style is typical of all controls created programmatically using MFC. The call to **new** allocates memory for an instance of the **CStatic** class and, in the process, calls the constructor for the class. The constructor performs any initialization needed by the class. The **Create** function creates the control at the Windows level and puts it on the screen. See Chapter 23 for details.

Note that there is another way to create static controls—you can use a dialog template, as described in Chapter 6, Part 3, and Part 4. This technique makes positioning easier, but you must then create code that gets a pointer to the static control if you want to manipulate it. Once you have that pointer, you use the same techniques discussed in this chapter to manipulate the control. You simply avoid the creation step, because the dialog template performs the creation automatically.

The **Create** function accepts up to five parameters, as described in the MFC documentation.

CStatic::CreateCreates a CStatic object

```
BOOL CStatic::Create(LPCSTR lpText,
    DWORD dwStyle,
    const RECT& rect,
    CWnd* pParentWnd,
    UINT nID = 0xffff);
```

lpText	Text displayed by the control
dwStyle	Control's window style
rect	Position and size of the control within its parent window
pParentWnd	Parent window (NULL is invalid. It must have a parent.)
nID	Resource ID for the control (optional)

This function returns TRUE if successful, FALSE otherwise.

Most of these values are self-explanatory. The **lpText** parameter specifies the text displayed by the label. The **rect** parameter controls the position, size, and shape of the text when it is displayed in its parent window. The **pParentWnd** parameter indicates the parent of the **CStatic** control. The control will appear in the parent window, and the position of the control will be relative to the upper left corner of the client area of the parent. The **nID** parameter is an integer value used as a control ID by certain functions in the API. We'll see examples of this parameter in the next chapter.

The **dwStyle** parameter is the most important parameter. It controls the appearance and behavior of the control. The following sections describe this parameter in detail.

3.2 CStatic Styles

All controls have a variety of display *styles*. Styles are determined at creation using the **dwStyle** parameter passed to the **Create** function. The style parameter is a bit mask that you build by or-ing together different mask constants. The constants available to a **CStatic** control can be found in the MFC documentation (Find the page for the **CStatic::Create** function and click on the **Static Styles** item that you find on that page) and are also briefly described below:

Valid styles for the CStatic class
Styles inherited from CWnd:

WS_CHILD	Mandatory for CStatic.
WS_VISIBLE	The control should be visible to the user.
WS_DISABLED	The control should reject user events.
WS_BORDER	The control's text is framed by a border.

Styles native to CStatic:

SS_BLACKFRAME	The control displays itself as a rectangular border. Color is the same as window frames.
SS_BLACKRECT	The control displays itself as a filled rectangle. Color is the same as window frames.
SS_CENTER	The text is center justified.
SS_GRAYFRAME	The control displays itself as a rectangular border. Color is the same as the desktop.
SS_GRAYRECT	The control displays itself as a filled rectangle. Color is the same as the desktop.
SS_ICON	The control displays itself as an icon. The text string is used as the name of the icon in a resource file. The rect parameter controls only positioning.
SS_LEFT	The text displayed is left justified. Extra text is word-wrapped.
SS_LEFTNOWORDWRAP	The text is left justified, but extra text is clipped.
SS_NOPREFIX	"&" characters in the text string indicate accelerator prefixes unless this attribute is used.
SS_RIGHT	The text displayed is right justified. Extra text is word-wrapped.
SS_SIMPLE	A single line of text is displayed left justified. Any CTLCOLOR messages must be ignored by the parent.
SS_USERITEM	User-defined item.

| SS_WHITEFRAME | The control displays itself as a rectangular border. Color is the same as window backgrounds. |
| SS_WHITERECT | The control displays itself as a filled rectangular. Color is the same as window backgrounds. |

These constants come from two different sources. The "SS" (Static Style) constants apply only to **CStatic** controls. The "WS" (Window Style) constants apply to all windows and are therefore defined in the **CWnd** object from which **CStatic** inherits its behavior. There are many other "WS" style constants defined in **CWnd**. They can be found by looking up the **CWnd::Create** function in the MFC documentation. The four above are the only ones that apply to a **CStatic** object.

A **CStatic** object will always have at least two style constants or-ed together: WS_CHILD and WS_VISIBLE. The control is not created unless it is the child of another window, and it will be invisible unless WS_VISIBLE is specified. WS_DISABLED controls the label's response to events. Because a label has no sensitivity to events such as keystrokes or mouse clicks anyway, specifically disabling it is redundant.

All the other style attributes are optional and control the appearance of the label. By modifying the style attributes passed to the **CStatic::Create** function, you control how the static object appears on screen. You can learn quite a bit about the different styles by using style attributes to modify the text appearance of the **CStatic** object, as discussed in the next section.

3.3 CStatic Text Appearance

The code shown in Listing 3.1 is useful for understanding the behavior of the **CStatic** object. It is similar to the listing discussed in Chapter 2, but it modifies the creation of the **CStatic** object slightly. If you compile and execute Listing 3.1, you will see output similar to the screen dump shown in Figure 3.3. Please turn to Appendix B.3 for instructions on entering and compiling this code.

Listing 3.1
static1.cpp - A simple CStatic test program

```
//static1.cpp

#include <afxwin.h>
#pragma hdrstop

// Declare the application class
class CTestApp : public CWinApp
{
public:
    virtual BOOL InitInstance();
};

// Create an instance of the application class
CTestApp TestApp;
```

```
// Declare the main window class
class CTestWindow : public CFrameWnd
{
    CStatic* cs;
public:
    CTestWindow();
};

// The InitInstance function is called
// once when the application first executes
BOOL CTestApp::InitInstance()
{
    m_pMainWnd = new CTestWindow();
    m_pMainWnd->ShowWindow(m_nCmdShow);
    m_pMainWnd->UpdateWindow();
    return TRUE;
}

// The constructor for the window class
CTestWindow::CTestWindow()
{
    CRect r;

    // Create the window itself
    Create(NULL,
        "CStatic Tests",
        WS_OVERLAPPEDWINDOW,
        CRect(0,0,200,200));

    // Get the size of the client rectangle
    GetClientRect(&r);
    r.InflateRect(-20,-20);

    // Create a static label
    cs = new CStatic();
    cs->Create("hello world",
        WS_CHILD|WS_VISIBLE|WS_BORDER|SS_CENTER,
        r,
        this);
}
```

The code of interest in Listing 3.1 is in the window constructor, which is repeated below with line numbers:

```
    CTestWindow::CTestWindow()
    {
        CRect r;

        // Create the window itself
1       Create(NULL,
            "CStatic Tests",
            WS_OVERLAPPEDWINDOW,
            CRect(0,0,200,200));

        // Get the size of the client rectangle
```

This book is continuously updated. See http://www.iftech.com/mfc

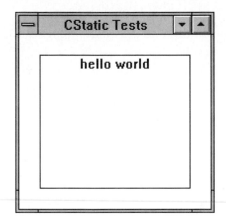

Figure 3.3
Screen dump for the simple CStatic test program shown in Listing 3.1

```
2        GetClientRect(&r);
3        r.InflateRect(-20,-20);

         // Create a static label
4        cs = new CStatic();
5        cs->Create("hello world",
         WS_CHILD|WS_VISIBLE|WS_BORDER|SS_CENTER,
         r,
         this);
    }
```

The function first calls the **CTestWindow::Create** function for the window at line 1. This is the **Create** function for the **CFrameWnd** object, because **CTestWindow** inherits its behavior from **CFrameWnd**. The code in line 1 specifies that the window should have a size of 200 by 200 pixels and that the upper left corner of the window should be initially placed at location 0,0 on the screen. The constant **rectDefault** can replace the **CRect** parameter if desired.

At line 2, the code calls **CTestWindow::GetClientRect**, passing it the parameter **&r**. The **GetClientRect** function is inherited from the **CWnd** class (see the sidebar for search strategies to use when trying to look up functions in the Microsoft documentation). The variable **r** is of type **CRect** and is declared as a local variable at the beginning of the function.

Two questions arise here in trying to understand this code: 1) What does the **GetClientRect** function do? and 2) What does a **CRect** variable do? Let's start with question 1. When you look up the **CWnd::GetClientRect** function you find it returns a value of type **CRect** that contains the size of the client rectangle of the particular window. It stores the value at the address passed in as a parameter, in this case **&r**. That address should point to a location of type **CRect**. The **CRect** type is a class defined in MFC. It is a convenience class used to manage rectangles. If you look up the class in the MFC documentation, you will find that it defines more than 30 member functions and operators to manipulate rectangles.

In our case, we want to center the words "Hello World" in the window. Therefore, we use **GetClientRect** to get the rectangle coordinates for the client area. In line 3 we then call **CRect::InflateRect**, which symmetrically increases or decreases the size of a rectangle. Here we have decreased the rectangle by 20 pixels on all sides. Had we not, the border surrounding the label would have blended into the window frame and we would not be able to see it.

The actual **CStatic** label is created in lines 4 and 5. The style attributes specify that the words displayed by the label should be centered and surrounded by a border. The size and position of the border is determined by the **CRect** parameter **r**. The resulting screen dump shown in Figure 3.3 is as expected.

By modifying the different style attributes you can gain an understanding of the different capabilities of the **CStatic** object. For example, Listing 3.2 contains a replacement for the **CTestWindow** constructor function in Listing 3.1. Figure 3.4 shows a screen dump for this code.

Listing 3.2
A demonstration of CStatic's word-wrapping abilities.

```
CTestWindow::CTestWindow()
{
    CRect r;

    // Create the window itself
    Create(NULL,
        "CStatic Tests",
        WS_OVERLAPPEDWINDOW,
        CRect(0,0,200,200));

    // Get the size of the client rectangle
    GetClientRect(&r);
    r.InflateRect(-20,-20);

    // Create a static label
    cs = new CStatic();
    cs->Create("Now is the time for all good men to \
come to the aid of their country",
        WS_CHILD|WS_VISIBLE|WS_BORDER|SS_CENTER,
        r,
        this);
}
```

The code of Listing 3.2 is identical to that of Listing 3.1 except the text string is much longer. As you can see in Figure 3.4, the **CStatic** object has wrapped the text within the specified bounding rectangle and centered each line individually.

If the bounding rectangle is too small to contain all the lines of text, then the text is clipped as needed to make it fit the available space. This feature of the **CStatic** Object is shown in Listing 3.3 and Figure 3.5. In Listing 3.3, the bounding rectangle has been reduced to the point where it forces truncation (compare **InflateRect** parameters).

Looking up functions in the Microsoft documentation

Say you want to find out about the **GetClientRect** function. How do you look it up? This is not a trivial matter in a system as big as Windows. **GetClientRect** could be defined somewhere in MFC, in the normal Windows API, in the standard C run-time library, or in some standard C++ library like `iostream.h`. It can be literally anywhere among the thousands of pages of documentation and, when you are new to the documentation, finding it can be difficult. Once you are familiar with the system, you will know where all the common functions come from. Right now, just finding the right page is a problem. You need an organized approach to find anything.

The best place to start your search for the **GetClientRect** function is with the current object. We are in a function called **CTestWindow::CTestWindow**, which is the constructor for the **CTestWindow** class. The first place to look, therefore, is at the class declaration for **CTestWindow** to see if **GetClientRect** has been defined there. We look at the top of Listing 3.1, at the definition of **CTestWindow**, and we find only a constructor defined. **GetClientRect** must be elsewhere.

The next place to look is the class from which **CTestWindow** inherits its behavior. Again, this can be found in the class declaration for **CTestWindow**. Looking there we find that this class inherits behavior from **CFrameWnd**. Looking up **CFrameWnd** in the MFC documentation, we again find nothing for **GetClientRect**.

The next step is to continue following the inheritance chain to its end. **CFrameWnd** inherits its behavior from **CWnd**–you can see that by looking at the first line in the MFC documentation for the **CFrameWnd** class where it says:

```
class CFrameWnd : public CWnd
```

You can also see it by looking at a diagram for the MFC class hierarchy, as partially shown in Figure 2.1. It is in the **CWnd** class that we find **GetClientRect**.

But say it wasn't there and you had to keep looking. You would follow the inheritance chain to **CObject**, which is always the end of the chain in MFC. Then you would look in the Windows API. For example, if we had been looking up the function **MessageBeep** we would have found it in the API. If it wasn't in the API we would then try the C run-time library. This documents all the normal C and C++ run-time functions like **printf**, **time**, and so on. The function **strftime**, for example, is found here, as are all the standard C functions such as **sin**. If not there, we would look at the top of the code file for the inclusion of unusual header files, then we would track the function down in one of those. The system makes this relatively painless by showing all of the different possibilities in a list. Your job is to select one item from the list. It gets easier as you become more familiar with MFC.

Figure 3.4
Screen dump for code in Listing 3 showing CStatic word wrapping

Compiling multiple executables

This chapter contains several different example programs. There are two different ways for you to compile and run them. The first way is to place each different program into its own directory and then create a new project for each one. Using this technique, you can compile each program separately and work with each executable simultaneously or independently. The disadvantage of this approach is the amount of disk space it consumes.

In the second approach, you create a single directory that contains all of the source files from this chapter. You then create a single project file in that directory. To compile each program, you can edit the project and change its source file (see Appendix B.1.4). Simply add a different source file into the project, remove the old file, and rebuild. This arrangement minimizes disk consumption, and is generally preferred for short example programs like the ones in this chapter. For big multi-file applications it makes sense to create a separate directory and project for each application that you create. Starting in Version 4.0 a project can contain multiple EXEs.

Listing 3.3
A long string and a small bounding rectangle force CStatic to truncate text.

```
CTestWindow::CTestWindow()
{
    CRect r;

    // Create the window itself
    Create(NULL,
        "CStatic Tests",
        WS_OVERLAPPEDWINDOW,
        CRect(0,0,200,200));
```

This book is continuously updated. See http://www.iftech.com/mfc

```
    // Get the size of the client rectangle
    GetClientRect(&r);
    r.InflateRect(-50,-50);

    // Create a static label
    cs = new CStatic();
    cs->Create("Now is the time for all good men to come to \
        the aid of their country",
        WS_CHILD|WS_VISIBLE|WS_BORDER|SS_CENTER,
        r,
        this);
}
```

Figure 3.5
CStatic's truncation feature as exercised by Listing 3.3

In all the code we have seen so far, the style SS_CENTER has been used to center the text. The **CStatic** object also allows for left or right justification. Figure 3.6 shows an example of left justification, created by replacing the SS_CENTER attribute with an SS_LEFT attribute. Right justification aligns the words to the right margin rather than the left and is specified with the SS_RIGHT attribute.

One other text attribute is available. It turns off the word wrap feature and is used often for simple labels that identify other controls (see Figure 3.1 for an example). The SS_LEFTNOWORDWRAP style forces left justification and causes no wrapping to take place. The effect of this style is shown in Figure 3.7. Despite the height available in the bounding rectangle, the object has not made use of it.

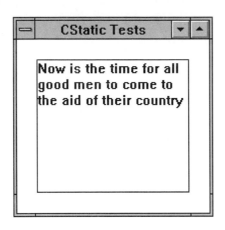

Figure 3.6
An example of left justification

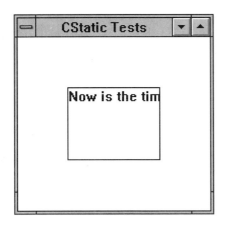

Figure 3.7
The effect of the SS_LEFTNOWORDWRAP style

3.4 Rectangular Display Modes for CStatic

The **CStatic** object also supports two different rectangular display modes: solid filled rectangles and frames. You normally use these two styles to visually group other controls within a window. For example, you might place a black rectangular frame in a window to collect together several related editable areas. You can choose from six different styles when creating these rectangles: SS_BLACKFRAME, SS_BLACKRECT, SS_GRAYFRAME, SS_GRAYRECT, SS_WHITEFRAME, and SS_WHITERECT. The RECT form is a filled rectangle, while the FRAME form is a border. The color names are a little misleading—for example, SS_WHITERECT displays a rectangle of the same color as the window background. Although this color defaults to white, the user can change it with the Control Panel and the rectangle may not be actually white on some machines.

When a rectangle or frame attribute is specified, the **CStatic**'s text string is ignored. Typically, an empty string is passed. The process of creating a rectangle is shown in Listing 3.4 and Figure 3.8.

Listing 3.4
The creation of a black rectangle.

```
CTestWindow::CTestWindow()
{
    CRect r;

    // Create the window itself
    Create(NULL,
        "CStatic Tests",
        WS_OVERLAPPEDWINDOW,
        CRect(0,0,200,200));

    // Get the size of the client rectangle
    GetClientRect(&r);
    r.InflateRect(-50,-50);

    // Create a static label
    cs = new CStatic();
    cs->Create("",
        WS_CHILD|WS_VISIBLE|SS_BLACKRECT,
        r,
        this);
}
```

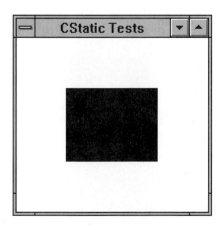

Figure 3.8
A black rectangle frame produced by Listing 3.4

A frame window can hold many controls. Figure 3.9 shows a gray rectangle overlaid by a static text label. Listing 3.5 produced this figure. The only difference here are two CStatic objects–**cs1** and **cs2**–which are declared in the **CTestWindow** class and then deleted in its destructor. Note that the order of creation determines the stacking order. Also note that if **cs2** has a large enough rectangle, it can completely obscure the gray rectangle underneath it and make it invisible.

Listing 3.5

Code that creates a gray rectangle overlaid by text.

```
CTestWindow::CTestWindow()
{
    CRect r;

    // Create the window itself
    Create(NULL,
        "CStatic Tests",
        WS_OVERLAPPEDWINDOW,
        CRect(0,0,200,200));

    // Get the size of the client rectangle
    GetClientRect(&r);
    r.InflateRect(-50,-50);

    // Create the grey rectangle
    cs1 = new CStatic();
    cs1->Create("",
        WS_CHILD|WS_VISIBLE|SS_GRAYRECT,
        r,
        this);

    // Create the text that sits on top of it
    r.InflateRect(-10,-10);
    cs2 = new CStatic();
    cs2->Create("Now is the time",
        WS_CHILD|WS_VISIBLE|SS_LEFTNOWORDWRAP,
        r,
        this);
}
```

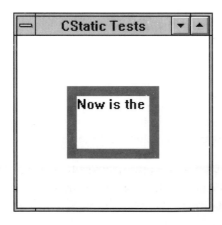

Figure 3.9
Screen dump for Listing 3.5

This book is continuously updated. See http://www.iftech.com/mfc

3.5 Fonts

You can change the font of a **CStatic** object by creating a **CFont** object. Doing so demonstrates how one MFC class can interact with another in certain cases to modify behavior of a control. The **CFont** class in MFC holds a single instance of a particular Windows font. For example, one instance of the **CFont** class might hold a Times font at 18 points while another might hold a Courier font at 10 points. You can modify the font used by a static label by calling the **SetFont** function that **CStatic** inherits from **CWnd**. Listing 3.6 shows the code required to implement fonts, and Figure 3.10 shows a screen dump of this code.

Listing 3.6
Code for modifying the font of a CStatic object.

```
CTestWindow::CTestWindow()
{
    CRect r;

    // Create the window itself
    Create(NULL,
        "CStatic Tests",
        WS_OVERLAPPEDWINDOW,
        CRect(0,0,200,200));

    // Get the size of the client rectangle
    GetClientRect(&r);
    r.InflateRect(-20,-20);

    // Create a static label
    cs = new CStatic();
    cs->Create("Hello World",
        WS_CHILD|WS_VISIBLE|WS_BORDER|SS_CENTER,
        r,
        this);

    // Create a new 36 point Arial font
    font = new CFont;
    font->CreateFont(36,0,0,0,700,0,0,0,
                ANSI_CHARSET,OUT_DEFAULT_PRECIS,
                CLIP_DEFAULT_PRECIS,
                DEFAULT_QUALITY,
                DEFAULT_PITCH|FF_DONTCARE,
                "arial");

    // Cause the label to use the new font
    cs->SetFont(font);
}
```

The code in Listing 3.9 starts by creating the window and the **CStatic** object as usual. The code then creates an object of type **CFont**. The font variable should be declared as a data member in the **CTestWindow** class with the line "CFont *font". The

Figure 3.10
A modified font produced by Listing 3.6

CFont::Create function has 15 parameters, but only three matter in most cases (see Chapter 11 for details). For example, the 36 specifies the size of the font in points, the 700 specifies the density of the font (400 is "normal," 700 is "bold," and values can range from 1 to 1000. The constants FW_NORMAL and FW_BOLD have the same meanings. See the FW constants in the documentation), and the word "arial" names the font to use. Windows always ships with five True Type fonts (Arial, Courier New, Symbol, Times New Roman, and Wingdings), and by sticking to one of these you can be fairly certain that the font will exist on just about any machine. If you specify a font name that is unknown to the system, then the **CFont** class will choose the default font seen in all the other examples used in this chapter.

For more information on the **CFont** class see the MFC documentation and Chapter 11. There is also a good overview on fonts. Search for "Fonts and Text Overview."

The **SetFont** function comes from the **CWnd** class. It sets the font of a window, in this case the **CStatic** child window. One question you may have at this point is, "How do I know which functions available in **CWnd** apply to the **CStatic** class?" You learn this by experience. Take half an hour and read through all the functions in **CWnd**. You will learn quite a bit and you will find many functions that allow you to customize controls. We will see other **Set** functions found in the **CWnd** class in the next chapter.

3.6 Conclusion

In this chapter we looked at the many different capabilities of the **CStatic** object. One we ignored is the SS_ICON style. It is discussed in Chapter 6 because it requires an understanding of resource files. We also left out some of the **Set** functions inherited from the **CWnd** class so they can be discussed in Chapter 4 where they are more appropriate. Chapter 11 contains more information on fonts. Chapter 5 contains two programs that use multiple static labels.

Handling Events

Any user interface object that an application places in a window has two controllable features: 1) its appearance, and 2) its behavior when responding to events. In the last chapter you gained an understanding of the **CStatic** control and saw how you can use style attributes to customize the appearance of user interface objects. These concepts apply to all the different control classes available in MFC.

In this chapter we will examine the **CButton** control to gain an understanding of message maps and simple event handling. We'll then look at the **CScrollBar** control to see a somewhat more involved example and also look at how an application can handle system messages.

4.1 Understanding Message Maps

As discussed in Chapter 2, MFC programs do not contain a main function or event loop. All the event handling happens "behind the scenes" in C++ code that is part of the **CWinApp** class. Because it is hidden, we need a way to tell the invisible event loop to notify us about events of interest to the application. This is done with a mechanism called a *message map*. The message map identifies interesting events and then indicates functions to call in response to those events.

For example, say you want to write a program that will quit whenever the user presses a button labeled "Quit." In the program you place code to specify the button's creation: you indicate where the button goes, what it says, etc. Next, you create a message map for the parent of the button–whenever a user clicks the button, it tries to send a message to its parent. By installing a message map for the parent window, you create a mechanism to intercept and use the button's messages. The message map will request that MFC call a specific function whenever a specific button event occurs. In this case, a click on the Quit button is the event of interest. You then put the code for quitting the application in the indicated function.

MFC does the rest. When the program executes and the user clicks the Quit button, the button will highlight itself as expected. MFC then automatically calls the right function and the program terminates. With just a few lines of code your program becomes sensitive to user events.

4.2 The CButton Class

The **CStatic** control discussed in Chapter 3 is unique in that it cannot respond to user events. No amount of clicking, typing, or dragging will do anything to a **CStatic** control because it ignores the user completely. However, the **CStatic** class is an anomaly. All the other controls available in Windows respond to user events in two ways. First, they update their appearance automatically when the user manipulates them (e.g., when the user clicks on a button it highlights itself to give the user visual feedback). Second, each different control tries to send messages to your code so the program can respond to the user as needed. For example, a button sends a *button clicked* whenever it gets clicked. If you write code to receive the messages, then your code can respond to user events.

To gain an understanding of this process, we will start with the **CButton** control. Listing 4.1 demonstrates the creation of a button, and Figure 4.1 shows a screen dump for this piece of code.

Listing 4.1
Creating a CButton object.

```
// button1.cpp

#include <afxwin.h>

#define IDC_BUTTON 100

// Declare the application class
class CButtonApp : public CWinApp
{
public:
    virtual BOOL InitInstance();
};

// Create an instance of the application class
CButtonApp ButtonApp;

// Declare the main window class
class CButtonWindow : public CFrameWnd
{
    CButton *button;
public:
    CButtonWindow();
};

// The InitInstance function is called once
// when the application first executes
BOOL CButtonApp::InitInstance()
{
    m_pMainWnd = new CButtonWindow();
```

```
        m_pMainWnd->ShowWindow(m_nCmdShow);
        m_pMainWnd->UpdateWindow();
        return TRUE;
}
// The constructor for the window class
CButtonWindow::CButtonWindow()
{
        CRect r;

        // Create the window itself
        Create(NULL,
            "CButton Tests",
            WS_OVERLAPPEDWINDOW,
            CRect(0,0,200,200));

        // Get the size of the client rectangle
        GetClientRect(&r);
        r.InflateRect(-20,-20);

        // Create a button
        button = new CButton();
        button->Create("Push me",
            WS_CHILD|WS_VISIBLE|BS_PUSHBUTTON,
            r,
            this,
            IDC_BUTTON);
}
```

Figure 4.1
Appearance of a CButton object as created by Listing 4.1

The code in listing 4.1 is nearly identical to the code discussed in previous chapters. The **Create** function for the **CButton** class, as seen in the MFC documentation, accepts five parameters. The first four are exactly the same as those found in the **CStatic** class. The fifth parameter indicates the resource ID for the button. The resource ID is a unique integer value used to identify the button in the message map. A constant value IDC_BUTTON has been defined at the top of the program for this value. The "IDC_" is arbitrary, but here indicates that the constant is an ID value for a control.

It is given a value of 100 because values less than 100 are reserved for system-defined IDs. You can use any value above 99.

The style attributes available for the **CButton** class are different from those for the **CStatic** class, as discussed in Chapter 3. Eleven different "BS" ("Button Style") constants are defined. See the **CButton::Create** function in the MFC documentation for a complete list. Here we have used the BS_PUSHBUTTON style for the button, indicating that we want this button to display itself as a normal push button. We have also used two familiar "WS" attributes: WS_CHILD and WS_VISIBLE. We will examine some of the other styles in later sections.

When you run the code, you will notice that the button responds to user events. That is, it highlights as you would expect. It does nothing else because we haven't told it what to do. We need to wire in a message map to make the button do something interesting.

4.3 Creating a Message Map

The code in Listing 4.2 contains a message map as well as a new function that handles the button click so the program beeps when the user clicks on the button. The portions of the code that differ from Listing 4.1 are shown in boldface.

Listing 4.2
A program that creates a button and beeps when the button is pressed.

```
// button2.cpp

#include <afxwin.h>

#define IDC_BUTTON 100

// Declare the application class
class CButtonApp : public CWinApp
{
public:
    virtual BOOL InitInstance();
};

// Create an instance of the application class
CButtonApp ButtonApp;

// Declare the main window class
class CButtonWindow : public CFrameWnd
{
    CButton *button;
public:
    CButtonWindow();
    afx_msg void HandleButton();

    DECLARE_MESSAGE_MAP()
};

// The message handler function
```

```
void CButtonWindow::HandleButton()
{
    MessageBeep(0xFFFFFFFF);
}

// The message map
BEGIN_MESSAGE_MAP(CButtonWindow, CFrameWnd)
    ON_BN_CLICKED(IDC_BUTTON, HandleButton)
END_MESSAGE_MAP()

// The InitInstance function is called once
// when the application first executes
BOOL CButtonApp::InitInstance()
{
    m_pMainWnd = new CButtonWindow();
    m_pMainWnd->ShowWindow(m_nCmdShow);
    m_pMainWnd->UpdateWindow();
    return TRUE;
}

// The constructor for the window class
CButtonWindow::CButtonWindow()
{
    CRect r;

    // Create the window itself
    Create(NULL,
        "CButton Tests",
        WS_OVERLAPPEDWINDOW,
        CRect(0,0,200,200));

    // Get the size of the client rectangle
    GetClientRect(&r);
    r.InflateRect(-20,-20);

    // Create a button
    button = new CButton();
    button->Create("Push me",
        WS_CHILD|WS_VISIBLE|BS_PUSHBUTTON,
        r,
        this,
        IDC_BUTTON);
}
```

Three modifications have been made to Listing 4.1 to create Listing 4.2:

1. The class declaration for **CButtonWindow** now contains a new member function as well as a macro that indicates a message map is defined for the class. The **HandleButton** function, which is identified as a message handler by the use of the **afx_msg** tag, is a normal C++ function. There are some special constraints on this function that we will discuss shortly (e.g., it must be **void** and it cannot accept any parameters). The DECLARE_MESSAGE_MAP macro makes the creation of a message map possible. *Both the function and the macro must be public.*

2. The **HandleButton** function is created in the same way as any member function. In this function, we called the **MessageBeep** function available from the Windows API. You could also call **Beep** or any other function.

3. Special MFC macros create a message map. In the code, you can see that the BEGIN_MESSAGE_MAP macro accepts two parameters. The first is the name of the specific class to which the message map applies. The second is the base class from which the specific class is derived. It is followed by an ON_BN_CLICKED macro that accepts two parameters: The ID of the control and the function to call whenever that ID sends a command message. Finally, the message map ends with the END_MESSAGE_MAP macro. *Note the placement of parentheses and the lack of semicolons on the macros.*

When a user clicks the button, it sends a command message containing its ID to its parent, which is the window containing the button. That is default behavior for a button, and that is why this code works. The button sends the message to its parent because it is a child window. The parent window intercepts this message and uses the message map to determine the function to call. MFC handles the routing, and whenever the specified message is seen, the indicated function gets called. The program beeps whenever the user clicks the button.

The ON_BN_CLICKED message is one of two messages a **CButton** object can send. It is equivalent to the ON_COMMAND message in the **CWnd** class and is simply a convenient synonym for it. ON_BN_DOUBLECLICKED is the other possible message for a **CButton** (Note that ON_BN_DOUBLE CLICKED will not work unless you modify the parent window's class to contain the CS_DBLCLKS style. See Chapter 11 for details on registering new window styles.). You can find information about these messages by looking up the **CButton** class description in the documentation.

4.4 Sizing Messages

In Listing 4.2 the code for the application's window, which is derived from the **CFrameWnd** class, recognized the button-click message generated by the button and responded to it because of its message map. The ON_BN_CLICKED macro added into the message map (search for the **CButton** overview as well as the ON_COMMAND macro in the MFC documentation) specifies the ID of the button and the function that the window should call when it receives a command message from that button. Because the button automatically sends to its parent its ID in a command message whenever the user clicks it, this arrangement allows the code to handle button events properly.

Windows is also capable of sending messages itself. There are about 100 different messages available, all inherited from the **CWnd** class. By browsing through the member functions for the **CWnd** class in the MFC documentation you can see what all these messages are. Look for any member function beginning with the word "On". Many of them are quite interesting.

You may have noticed that all the code demonstrated so far does not handle re-sizing very well. When the window resizes, the frame of the window adjusts accordingly but the contents stay where they were placed originally. It is possible to make resized windows respond more attractively by recognizing re-sizing events. One of the messages that is sent by Windows is a sizing message. The message is generated whenever the window changes shape. We can use this message to control the size of child windows inside the frame, as shown in Listing 4.3.

Listing 4.3
Handling window re-sizing with the ON_WM_SIZE message.

```
// button3.cpp

#include <afxwin.h>

#define IDC_BUTTON 100

// Declare the application class
class CButtonApp : public CWinApp
{
public:
    virtual BOOL InitInstance();
};

// Create an instance of the application class
CButtonApp ButtonApp;

// Declare the main window class
class CButtonWindow : public CFrameWnd
{
    CButton *button;
public:
    CButtonWindow();
    afx_msg void HandleButton();
    afx_msg void OnSize(UINT, int, int);

    DECLARE_MESSAGE_MAP()
};

// A message handler function
void CButtonWindow::HandleButton()
{
    MessageBeep(0xFFFFFFFF);
}

// A message handler function
void CButtonWindow::OnSize(UINT nType, int cx,
    int cy)
{
    CRect r;

    GetClientRect(&r);
    r.InflateRect(-20,-20);
```

```
        button->MoveWindow(r);
    }

    // The message map
    BEGIN_MESSAGE_MAP(CButtonWindow, CFrameWnd)
        ON_BN_CLICKED(IDC_BUTTON, HandleButton)
        ON_WM_SIZE()
    END_MESSAGE_MAP()

    // The InitInstance function is called once
    // when the application first executes
    BOOL CButtonApp::InitInstance()
    {
        m_pMainWnd = new CButtonWindow();
        m_pMainWnd->ShowWindow(m_nCmdShow);
        m_pMainWnd->UpdateWindow();
        return TRUE;
    }
    // The constructor for the window class
    CButtonWindow::CButtonWindow()
    {
        CRect r;

        // Create the window itself
        Create(NULL,
            "CButton Tests",
            WS_OVERLAPPEDWINDOW,
            CRect(0,0,200,200));

        // Get the size of the client rectangle
        GetClientRect(&r);
        r.InflateRect(-20,-20);

        // Create a button
        button = new CButton();
        button->Create("Push me",
            WS_CHILD|WS_VISIBLE|BS_PUSHBUTTON,
            r,
            this,
            IDC_BUTTON);
    }
```

To understand this code, start by looking in the message map for the window. There you will find the entry ON_WM_SIZE. This entry indicates that the message map is sensitive to sizing messages coming from the **CButtonWindow** object. Sizing messages are generated on this window whenever the user resizes it.

Notice also that the ON_WM_SIZE entry in the message map has no parameters. As you can see in the MFC documentation under the **CWnd** class, it is understood that the ON_WM_SIZE entry in the message map will always call a function named **OnSize**, and that function must accept the three parameters shown. The **OnSize** function must be a member function of the class owning the message map, and the function must be declared in the class as an **afx_msg** function (as shown in the definition of the **CButtonWindow** class).

If you look in the MFC documentation, there are almost 100 functions named "On..." in the **CWnd** class. **CWnd::OnSize** is one of them. All these functions have a corresponding tag in the message map with the form ON_WM_. For example, ON_WM_SIZE corresponds to **OnSize**. None of the ON_WM_ entries in the message map accept parameters.

The **OnSize** function always corresponds to the ON_WM_SIZE entry in the message map. You must name the handler function **OnSize**, and it must accept the three parameters shown in the listing. You can find the specific parameter requirements of any **On...** function by looking up that function in the MFC documentation. You can look the function up directly by typing **OnSize** into the search window or you can find it as a member function to the **CWnd** class.

Inside the **OnSize** function itself, three lines of code modify the size of the button held in the window:

```
void CButtonWindow::OnSize(UINT nType, int cx,
    int cy)
{
    CRect r;

    GetClientRect(&r);
    r.InflateRect(-20,-20);
    button->MoveWindow(r);
}
```

The call to **GetClientRect** retrieves the new size of the window's client rectangle. This rectangle is then deflated and the **MoveWindow** function is called on the button. **MoveWindow** is inherited from **CWnd** and resizes and moves the child window for the button in one step.

When you execute the program in Listing 4.3 and resize the application's window, you will find the button resizes itself correctly. In the code, the resize event generates a call through the message map to the **OnSize** function, which calls the **MoveWindow** function to resize the button appropriately.

4.5 Window Messages

By looking in the MFC documentation, you can see the wide variety of **CWnd** messages that the main window handles. Some are similar to the sizing message seen in the previous section. For example, ON_WM_MOVE messages are sent when a user moves a window and ON_WM_PAINT messages are sent when any part of the window has to be repainted. In all our programs so far, repainting has happened automatically because controls are responsible for their own appearance. In Chapter 11, however, we will see that the application is responsible for repainting any drawings it places directly in the window. In this context the ON_WM_PAINT message is important.

There are also some event messages sent to the window that are more esoteric. For example, you can use the ON_WM_TIMER message in conjunction with the **SetTimer** function to cause the window to receive messages at pre-set intervals. The code in Listing 4.4 demonstrates the process. When you run this code, the program will beep once each second. The beeping can be replaced by a number of useful processes. For example, in Chapter 11 we will see one example of this capability–the timer is used to update the face of a simple digital clock.

Listing 4.4
The SetTimer function and ON_WM_TIMER message cause the application to beep once each second.

```
// button4.cpp

#include <afxwin.h>

#define IDC_BUTTON 100
#define IDT_TIMER1 200

// Declare the application class
class CButtonApp : public CWinApp
{
public:
    virtual BOOL InitInstance();
};

// Create an instance of the application class
CButtonApp ButtonApp;

// Declare the main window class
class CButtonWindow : public CFrameWnd
{
    CButton *button;
public:
    CButtonWindow();
    afx_msg void HandleButton();
    afx_msg void OnSize(UINT, int, int);
    afx_msg void OnTimer(UINT);

    DECLARE_MESSAGE_MAP()
};

// A message handler function
void CButtonWindow::HandleButton()
{
    MessageBeep(0xFFFFFFFF);
}

// A message handler function
void CButtonWindow::OnSize(UINT nType, int cx,
    int cy)
{
    CRect r;

    GetClientRect(&r);
    r.InflateRect(-20,-20);
    button->MoveWindow(r);
}
```

This book is continuously updated. See http://www.iftech.com/mfc

```
// A message handler function
void CButtonWindow::OnTimer(UINT id)
{
    MessageBeep(0xFFFFFFFF);
}

// The message map
BEGIN_MESSAGE_MAP(CButtonWindow, CFrameWnd)
    ON_BN_CLICKED(IDC_BUTTON, HandleButton)
    ON_WM_SIZE()
    ON_WM_TIMER()
END_MESSAGE_MAP()

// The InitInstance function is called once
// when the application first executes
BOOL CButtonApp::InitInstance()
{
    m_pMainWnd = new CButtonWindow();
    m_pMainWnd->ShowWindow(m_nCmdShow);
    m_pMainWnd->UpdateWindow();
    return TRUE;
}

// The constructor for the window class
CButtonWindow::CButtonWindow()
{
    CRect r;

    // Create the window itself
    Create(NULL,
        "CButton Tests",
        WS_OVERLAPPEDWINDOW,
        CRect(0,0,200,200));

    // Set up the timer
    SetTimer(IDT_TIMER1, 1000, NULL); // 1000 ms.

    // Get the size of the client rectangle
    GetClientRect(&r);
    r.InflateRect(-20,-20);

    // Create a button
    button = new CButton();
    button->Create("Push me",
        WS_CHILD|WS_VISIBLE|BS_PUSHBUTTON,
        r,
        this,
        IDC_BUTTON);
}
```

Inside the program in Listing 4.4 we created a button, as shown previously, and left its re-sizing code in place. In the constructor for the window we also added a call to the **SetTimer** function. This function accepts three parameters: an ID for the timer (so that multiple timers can be active simultaneously, the ID is sent to the function called each time a timer goes off), the time in milliseconds that is to be the timer's increment, and a function. Here, we passed NULL for the function so that the window's message map will route the function automatically. In the message map we have wired in the ON_WM_TIMER message, and it will automatically call the **OnTimer** function passing it the ID of the timer that went off.

When the program runs, it beeps once each 1,000 milliseconds. Each time the timer's increment elapses, the window sends a message to itself. The message map routes the message to the **OnTimer** function, which beeps. You can place a wide variety of useful code into this function.

4.6 Scroll Bar Controls

Windows has two different ways to handle scroll bars. Some controls, such as the edit control (Chapters 5 and 8) and the list control (Chapter 9), can be created with scroll bars already attached. When this is the case, the master control handles the scroll bars automatically. For example, if an edit control has its scroll bars active, then when the scroll bars are used, the edit control scrolls as expected without any additional code.

Scroll bars can also work on a stand-alone basis. When used this way they are seen as independent controls in their own right. You can learn more about scroll bars by referring to the **CScrollBar** section of the MFC documentation. Scroll bar controls are created the same way we created static labels and buttons. They have four member functions that allow you to get and set both the range and position of a scroll bar.

The code shown in listing 4.5 demonstrates the creation of a horizontal scroll bar and its message map. Figure 4.2 shows a screen dump for this listing.

Listing 4.5
The creation of a horizontal scroll bar and its message map.

```
// sb1.cpp
#include <afxwin.h>

#define IDC_SCROLLBAR 100
const int MAX_RANGE=100;
const int MIN_RANGE=0;

// Declare the application class
class CScrollBarApp : public CWinApp
{
public:
    virtual BOOL InitInstance();
};

// Create an instance of the application class
CScrollBarApp ScrollBarApp;

// Declare the main window class
```

```
class CScrollBarWindow : public CFrameWnd
{
    CScrollBar *sb;
public:
    CScrollBarWindow();
    afx_msg void OnHScroll(UINT nSBCode, UINT nPos,
        CScrollBar* pScrollBar);

    DECLARE_MESSAGE_MAP()
};

// The message handler function
void CScrollBarWindow::OnHScroll(UINT nSBCode,
    UINT nPos, CScrollBar* pScrollBar)
{
    MessageBeep(0xFFFFFFFF);
}


// The message map
BEGIN_MESSAGE_MAP(CScrollBarWindow, CFrameWnd)
    ON_WM_HSCROLL()
END_MESSAGE_MAP()

// The InitInstance function is called once
// when the application first executes
BOOL CScrollBarApp::InitInstance()
{
    m_pMainWnd = new CScrollBarWindow();
    m_pMainWnd->ShowWindow(m_nCmdShow);
    m_pMainWnd->UpdateWindow();
    return TRUE;
}


// The constructor for the window class
CScrollBarWindow::CScrollBarWindow()
{
    CRect r;

    // Create the window itself
    Create(NULL,
        "CScrollBar Tests",
        WS_OVERLAPPEDWINDOW,
        CRect(0,0,200,200));

    // Get the size of the client rectangle
    GetClientRect(&r);
    // Create a scroll bar
    sb = new CScrollBar();
    sb->Create(WS_CHILD|WS_VISIBLE|SBS_HORZ,
        CRect(10,10,r.Width()-10,30),
        this,
        IDC_SCROLLBAR);
    sb->SetScrollRange(MIN_RANGE,MAX_RANGE,TRUE);
}
```

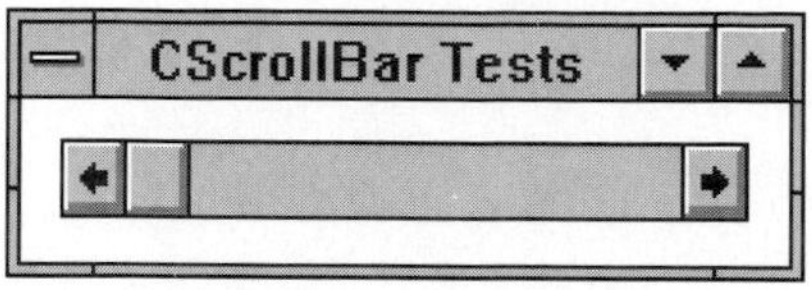

Figure 4.2
A simple horizontal scroll bar as produced
by Listing 4.5

Windows distinguishes between horizontal and vertical scroll bars and also supports an object called a *size box* in the **CScrollBar** class. A size box is a small square. It is formed at the intersection of a horizontal and vertical scroll bar and can be dragged by the mouse to automatically resize a window. Looking at the code in Listing 4.5, you can see that the **Create** function creates a horizontal scroll bar using the SBS_HORIZ style. Immediately following creation, the range of the scroll bar is set for 0 to 100 using the two constants MIN_RANGE and MAX_RANGE (defined at the top of the listing) in the **SetRange** function.

The event-handling function **OnHScroll** comes from the **CWnd** class. We have used this function because the code creates a horizontal scroll bar. For a vertical scroll bar you should use **OnVScroll**. In the code here the message map wires in the scrolling function and causes the scroll bar to beep whenever the user manipulates it. When you run the code you can click on the arrows, drag the thumb, and so on. Each event will generate a beep, but the thumb will not actually move because we have not wired in the code for movement yet.

Each time the scroll bar is used and **OnHScroll** is called, your code needs a way to determine the user's action. Inside the **OnHScroll** function you can examine the first parameter passed to the message handler, as shown in Listing 4.6. If you use this code with Listing 4.5, the scroll bar's thumb will move appropriately with each user manipulation.

Listing 4.6
A scroll bar message handler that handles all possible user actions.

```
// The message handling function
void CScrollBarWindow::OnHScroll(UINT nSBCode,
    UINT nPos, CScrollBar* pScrollBar)
{
    int pos;

    pos = sb->GetScrollPos();
    switch ( nSBCode )
    {
        case SB_LINEUP:
            pos -= 1;
            break;

        case SB_LINEDOWN:
            pos += 1;
            break;
```

```
        case SB_PAGEUP:
            pos -= 10;
            break;

        case SB_PAGEDOWN:
            pos += 10;
            break;

        case SB_TOP:
            pos = MIN_RANGE;
            break;

        case SB_BOTTOM:
            pos = MAX_RANGE;
            break;

        case SB_THUMBPOSITION:
            pos = nPos;
            break;

        default:
            return;
    }

    if ( pos < MIN_RANGE )
        pos = MIN_RANGE;
    else if ( pos > MAX_RANGE )
        pos = MAX_RANGE;
    sb->SetScrollPos( pos, TRUE );
}
```

The different constant values such as SB_LINEUP and SB_LINEDOWN are described in the **OnHScroll** function documentation in the documentation. The code in Listing 4.6 starts by retrieving the current scroll bar position using **GetScroll-Pos**. It then decides what the user did to the scroll bar using a switch statement. The constant value names imply a vertical orientation but are used in horizontal scroll bars as well: SB_LINEUP and SB_LINEDOWN apply when the user clicks the left and right arrows. SB_PAGEUP and SB_PAGEDOWN apply when the user clicks in the shaft of the scroll bar itself. SB_TOP and SB_BOTTOM apply when the user moves the thumb to the top or bottom of the bar. SB_THUMBPOSITION applies when the user drags the thumb to a specific position. The code adjusts the position accordingly, then makes sure that it's still in range before setting the scroll bar to its new position. Once the scroll bar is set, the thumb moves on the screen to inform the user visually.

A vertical scroll bar is handled the same way as a horizontal scroll bar except that you use the SBS_VERT style and the **OnVScroll** function. You can also use several alignment styles to align both the scroll bars and the grow box in a given client rectangle.

4.7 Understanding Message Maps

The message map structure is unique to MFC. It is important that you understand why it exists and how it actually works so you can exploit this structure in your own code.

Any C++ purist who looks at a message map has an immediate question: Why didn't Microsoft use virtual functions instead? Virtual functions are the standard C++ way to handle what message maps are doing in MFC, so the use of rather bizarre macros like DECLARE_MESSAGE_MAP and BEGIN_MESSAGE_MAP seems like the work of eccentrics.

MFC uses message maps to get around a fundamental problem with virtual functions. Look at the **CWnd** class in the MFC documentation. It contains more than 100 event-handling member functions (they start with "On"), all of which would have to be virtual if message maps were not used. Now look at all the classes that derive from the **CWnd** class. For example, search for "Hierarchy Charts" in the MFC documentation and look at the object hierarchy. Thirty or so classes in MFC use **CWnd** as their base class. This set includes all the visual controls such as buttons, static labels, and lists. Now imagine that MFC used virtual functions and you created an application that contained 20 controls. The virtual function tables for all those functions would create quite a bit of overhead. Because the vast majority of those tables are never used, they are unneeded.

Message maps duplicate the action of a virtual function table, but do so on an on-demand basis. When you create an entry in a message map, you are saying to the system, "when you see the specified message, please call the specified function." Only those functions that actually get overridden appear in the message map, saving memory and CPU overhead.

When you declare a message map with DECLARE_MESSAGE_MAP and BEGIN_MESSAGE_MAP, the system routes all messages through to your message map. If your map handles a given message, then your function gets called and the message stops there. However, if your message map does not contain an entry for a message, then the system sends that message to the class specified in the second parameter of BEGIN_MESSAGE_MAP. That class may or may not handle it and the process repeats. Eventually, if no message map handles a given message, the message arrives at a default handler that eats it.

You can see that message maps do approximately the same thing as virtual functions, but on a function-by-function basis. The construction of a message map lets you specify just one or two overrides for a class without any additional overhead. See Chapter 23 for details.

4.8 Conclusion

All the message handling concepts described in this chapter apply to every one of the controls available in Windows. We will see examples of these concepts throughout Part 2.

Chapter 5 uses the scroll bar and button controls described in this chapter to create two simple applications. Chapter 11 uses the timer capability described in Section 4.5 to create a simple digital clock.

Simple Applications

In the last four chapters we discussed the basic structure of any MFC application. You have learned about the static label, button, and scroll bar controls. The purpose of this chapter is to consolidate that knowledge by creating two small applications: a Fahrenheit to Celsius converter and an interest calculator.

5.1 Designing an Application

There are many different ways to fill an application's window using MFC. The following list identifies the five most common:

1. Text editing programs fill their main window with a re-sizable text editor of some sort. Examples include the Notepad, Write, and Microsoft Word.
2. Drawing and paint editors fill their main window with some kind of re-sizable graphics manipulator. Examples include Paintbrush and Microsoft Draw. Drawing editors are discussed in Chapter 11.
3. List windows use a scrollable list of items to allow selection. Examples include the output of the Search function in the File Manager and the output of other search engines, as well as applications like the User Manager in Windows NT. Lists are discussed in Chapter 9.
4. Many applications use some sort of custom interface that is painted on the screen "by hand" to implement a unique interaction method. Examples include spreadsheets and the Control Panel. Usually the drawing is done using techniques described in Chapter 11.
5. Control windows fill the main application window with standard controls. Examples include the PIF editor and the Calculator. The calculator, for example, fills the main window with buttons, and a text area displays the current value. Almost all normal dialog boxes are built using this technique.

Part 3 discusses the creation of these different types of applications using the *AppWizard*. The AppWizard automatically generates an MFC code framework for the application. A second tool called the *ClassWizard*, in conjunction with the *resource editors* available in Visual C++, makes it easy to add user interface elements such as menus and dialogs to the framework. See Chapter 6 for details.

In this chapter we will discuss the creation of two Category 5 applications. Here we will create them "by hand," so that you can contrast this approach with the automatic approach presented in Part 3. Those who are impatient may wish to move directly to Part 2 or 3 now.

The two example programs presented in this chapter are simple applications that use standard controls to implement the user interface. A surprising number of applications fit this mold, including most Input-Process-Output or "IPO" programs. These programs accept input from the user and then calculate and display a result. For simple applications of this type, it is occasionally easier to write the code yourself, as discussed in this chapter, rather than bring the full power of the AppWizard to bear on the problem. You can also better understand and appreciate what the AppWizard is doing if you know what is going on behind the scenes.

Imagine that you want to create a simple IPO application in MFC. For example, you might want to create a Fahrenheit to Celsius converter or a simple calculator of some sort. Where do you start? Probably the best place to begin, as described in Chapter 1, is the user interface. Decide what the program should be able to do and then choose a set of user interface objects that accomplish those goals. You have to decide which controls are best suited for accepting input from the user and which are most useful for displaying program output. You can sketch the layout of these objects to decide on their placement.

You now possess enough knowledge to create your own applications. You know how to create a main application window and you are familiar with three important controls available in MFC: the static label, the button, and the scroll bar. Let's start by creating the Fahrenheit to Celsius conversion program.

What controls does the user need to operate this program? The user definitely needs a way to input the Fahrenheit temperature. In most GUIs there are only two built-in controls to gather numeric input: an edit area in which the user types a value or some type of sliding control which the user manipulates with the mouse. We have not discussed edit areas yet, so for now we are constrained to the scroll bar.

We also need a way to output the result of the conversion, as well as a formal way to quit the application. We can use a **CStatic** control to display the temperature in Celsius and Fahrenheit. A **CButton** control labeled "Quit" can be used to handle quitting. A rough sketch of the proposed application using these different controls is shown in Figure 5.1.

You will use this same basic technique to design any Windows application. Even a large application with hundreds of dialog boxes is really nothing but a collection of user interface controls or custom interactive drawings (see Chapter 11) arranged on screen. The interface is designed so the user can comfortably manipulate all the data held by the application.

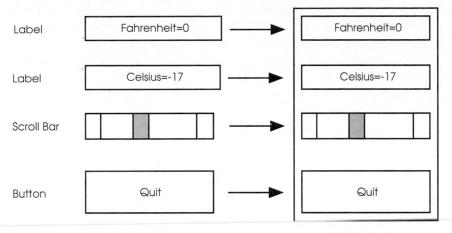

Label	Fahrenheit=0	→	Fahrenheit=0
Label	Celsius=-17	→	Celsius=-17
Scroll Bar		→	
Button	Quit	→	Quit

Main window

Figure 5.1
Proposed layout for the controls for the Fahrenheit to Celsius converter

5.2 Implementing the Fahrenheit to Celsius Converter

Using the code examples from the previous chapters, we can easily piece together most of the Fahrenheit to Celsius converter. The results are shown in Listing 5.1. A screen dump of this program during execution is shown in Figure 5.2.

Listing 5.1
Code to implement a Fahrenheit to Celsius converter.

```
// f2c.cpp

#include <afxwin.h>
#include <strstrea.h>

const int IDC_SB1=100;
const int IDC_CS1=101;
const int IDC_CS2=102;
const int IDC_BUTTON=103;

const int MIN_RANGE=0;
const int MAX_RANGE=100;

// Define an application object
class CApp : public CWinApp
{
public:
    virtual BOOL InitInstance();
};

// Create an instance of the application object
CApp App;
```

```
// Define the window object
class CWindow : public CFrameWnd
{
    CScrollBar* sb1;
    CStatic* cs1;
    CStatic* cs2;
    CButton* button;
public:
    CWindow();
    afx_msg void OnHScroll(UINT nSBCode,
        UINT nPos, CScrollBar* pScrollBar);
    afx_msg void handleButton();
    DECLARE_MESSAGE_MAP()
};

// The message map
BEGIN_MESSAGE_MAP( CWindow, CFrameWnd )
    ON_WM_HSCROLL()
    ON_BN_CLICKED(IDC_BUTTON, handleButton)
END_MESSAGE_MAP()

// Window constructor
CWindow::CWindow()
{
    // Create the window
    Create(NULL, "c2f", WS_OVERLAPPEDWINDOW,
        CRect(0,0,208,208));

    // Create the fahrenheit label
    cs1 = new CStatic();
    cs1->Create("Farhenheit = 32",
        WS_CHILD|WS_VISIBLE|WS_BORDER,
        CRect(0,0,200,50),
        this, IDC_CS1);

    // Create celsius label
    cs2 = new CStatic();
    cs2->Create("Celsius = 0",
        WS_CHILD|WS_VISIBLE|WS_BORDER,
        CRect(0,51,200,100),
        this, IDC_CS2);

    // Create the scroll bar
    sb1 = new CScrollBar();
    sb1->Create(WS_CHILD|WS_VISIBLE|SBS_HORZ,
        CRect(0,101,200,130),
        this, IDC_SB1);
    sb1->SetScrollRange(MIN_RANGE,MAX_RANGE,TRUE);
    sb1->SetScrollPos(32);

    // Create quit button
    button = new CButton();
    button -> Create("Quit",
        WS_CHILD|WS_VISIBLE|WS_BORDER,
        CRect(0,131,200,180),
        this, IDC_BUTTON);
```

```
    }

    // Handle the horizontal scroll bar
    void CWindow::OnHScroll( UINT nSBCode,
        UINT nPos, CScrollBar* pScrollBar )
    {
        int pos;

        pos = pScrollBar->GetScrollPos();
        switch ( nSBCode )
        {
            case SB_LINEUP:
                pos -= 1;
                break;
            case SB_LINEDOWN:
                pos += 1;
                break;
            case SB_PAGEUP:
                pos -= 10;
                break;
            case SB_PAGEDOWN:
                pos +- 10;
                break;
            case SB_TOP:
                pos = MIN_RANGE;
                break;
            case SB_BOTTOM:
                pos = MAX_RANGE;
                break;
            case SB_THUMBPOSITION:
                pos = nPos;
                break;
            default:
                return;
        }
        if ( pos < MIN_RANGE )
            pos = MIN_RANGE;
        else if ( pos > MAX_RANGE )
            pos = MAX_RANGE;
        sb1->SetScrollPos( pos, TRUE );

        // set the labels to the new values
        char s[100];
        ostrstream ostr(s,100);
        ostr << "Fahrenheit= " << pos << ends;
        SetDlgItemText(IDC_CS1,s);
        ostr.seekp(ios::beg);
        ostr << "Celsius= " << (pos-32)*5/9 << ends;
        SetDlgItemText(IDC_CS2,s);
    }

    void CWindow::handleButton()
    // Quits the application
    {
        DestroyWindow();
    }
```

```
// Init the application and the main window
BOOL CApp::InitInstance()
{
    m_pMainWnd = new CWindow();
    m_pMainWnd->ShowWindow(m_nCmdShow);
    m_pMainWnd->UpdateWindow();
    return TRUE;
}
```

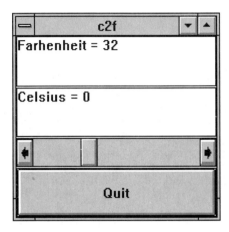

Figure 5.2
Screen dump of the Fahrenheit to Celsius converter shown in Listing 5.1

Looking at this program you see a number of familiar pieces. The **CApp** class is derived from **CWinApp** and overrides the **InitInstance** function. The **CWindow** class is derived from **CFrameWnd**. It declares pointers to the four user interface controls, declares the message map, and defines two functions that handle messages sent by the scroll bar and the button.

The constructor for **CWindow** creates two static labels, a scroll bar, and a button. It sets the range for the scroll bar and its initial position. The techniques used here are the same as those used in Chapters 3 and 4 to create labels, buttons, and scroll bars.

The two functions, **CWindow::OnHScroll** and **CWindow::HandleButton**, handle messages returned by the scroll bar and the button, respectively. The **OnHScroll** function uses the same process seen in Chapter 4. It determines which action the user has performed on the scroll bar and then updates the scroll bar's position accordingly. This function also updates the two static labels so they display the appropriate Fahrenheit and Celsius temperatures, using the following lines:

```
char s[100];
ostrstream ostr(s,100);
ostr << "Fahrenheit= " << pos << ends;
SetDlgItemText(IDC_CS1,s);
ostr.seekp(ios::beg);
ostr << "Celsius= " << (pos-32)*5/9 << ends;
SetDlgItemText(IDC_CS2,s);
```

This code uses the C++ string stream library to format strings into memory. An alternative implementation in C would use **sprintf** instead.

Changing Controls

At this point in your MFC career, you may have noticed a trend. There are at least three different ways to change the appearance of any control:

1. You can modify some aspects of the control at creation using its style constants (WS_BORDER, SS_CENTER, etc.)
2. You can modify some aspects of the control during execution using special functions in the **CWnd** class like **CWnd::SetFont**.
3. You can modify the control's data using **SetDlgItemText** and **SetDlgItemInt** and the control's ID.

There are other ways as well. The **SetWindowLong** function in the API lets you change a control's attributes. Many controls also have functions that you can call to modify the control in specific ways: Examples include **CStatic::SetIcon** and **CListBox::AddString**.

How do you discover all of these different techniques? One way is through experience, such as the experience you are gaining through this book. You can also gain experience by reading other people's code. Look in the SAMPLES directory that came with Visual C++ for many megabytes of sample code. You should look through the MFC documentation and read about the functions in the **CWnd** class and the control classes.

You might also consider searching the documentation for the word "Set". There are perhaps 100 functions that start with that word and many of them are quite interesting.

The function **SetDlgItemText** is inherited from **CWnd**. The name of this function assumes that controls are found only in dialog boxes, but our program uses controls in a normal window. The **SetDlgItemText** function, and its nearly identical partner **SetDlgItemInt**, set the string of **CStatic**, **CButton**, and **CEdit** controls. The text version accepts a normal C string (or an MFC **CString** object–see Chapter 12) and places it in the control specified by the ID parameter. The integer version accepts an integer instead. The first parameter is the resource ID of the control to set, while the second is the new value. Note that the control's ID is determined in the **Create** function for the control. In this program, all four controls are given a unique ID at creation by using constants defined at the top of the program.

The **handleButton** function is the button handler. It simply calls the **Destroy-Window** function to quit.

The main window for this application allows re-sizing and maximization. Because the controls in the window do not readjust their size or position in response to the extra screen space, the program looks unattractive after resizing. One way to solve this problem is to disable resizing altogether. This is the approach taken, for example, by the Calculator accessory shipped with Windows. If you run the calculator you will notice it has a thin border that disables re-sizing. You can take advantage of this effect by changing the style attributes for the window from WS_OVERLAPPEDWINDOW to the following:

WS_OVERLAPPED | WS_MINIMIZE | WS_SYSMENU

The WS_OVERLAPPEDWINDOW style automatically includes a thick resizing frame and a maximize button. By switching to the WS_OVERLAPPED style you can choose the specific border decorations that you want to include. By leaving out the thick frame and the maximize button, the application cannot resize itself. See the **CWnd::Create** function in the MFC documentation for more information.

One last feature you may wish to add to this application is an appropriate icon. Addition of an icon requires the use of resource files, discussed in Chapter 6.

5.3 The CEdit Control

Scroll bars work well when input is restricted to integer values that fall within a small range. However, if the user needed to select values between zero and 1,000,000, then a scroll bar doesn't work well because its gradations are too coarse. When scroll bars are inappropriate (e.g., when reading floating point values, large integers, or text), single- line edit areas work well. The **CEdit** class implements this control. The **CEdit** class can also be used in much more advanced ways to create complete text editors. These applications are discussed in detail in Chapter 8. Here we'll focus on using **CEdit** to implement a simple single-line text input control.

The code in Listing 5.2 demonstrates the creation of a simple **CEdit** object.

Listing 5.2
Code demonstrating the use of a CEdit control.

```
// edit.cpp

#include <afxwin.h>

const int ED=100;
const int CS=101;

// Define an application object
class CApp : public CWinApp
{
public:
    virtual BOOL InitInstance();
};

CApp App;

// Define the window object
class CWindow : public CFrameWnd
{
    CEdit* ed;
    CStatic* cs;
```

```
public:
    CWindow();
    afx_msg void HandleChange();
    DECLARE_MESSAGE_MAP()
};


// Message map
BEGIN_MESSAGE_MAP( CWindow, CFrameWnd )
    ON_EN_CHANGE(ED, HandleChange)
END_MESSAGE_MAP()

// Window constructor
CWindow::CWindow()
{
    // Create the window
    Create(NULL, "Interest",
        WS_OVERLAPPEDWINDOW,
        CRect(CPoint(10,10),CSize(150,100)));

    // Create the edit control
    ed = new CEdit();
    ed->Create(WS_CHILD|WS_VISIBLE|WS_BORDER,
        CRect(CPoint(5,5),CSize(100,24)),
        this, ED);
    ed->LimitText(10);

    // Create a static label
    cs = new CStatic();
    cs->Create("xxx",
        WS_CHILD|WS_VISIBLE|WS_BORDER,
        CRect(CPoint(5,30),CSize(100,24)),
        this, CS);
    ed->SetFocus();
}

void CWindow::HandleChange()
// Handles any change to the edit control
{
    UINT amount=GetDlgItemInt(ED);
    SetDlgItemInt(CS,amount);
}

// Init the application and the main window
BOOL CApp::InitInstance()
{
    m_pMainWnd = new CWindow();
    m_pMainWnd->ShowWindow(m_nCmdShow);
    m_pMainWnd->UpdateWindow();
    return TRUE;
}
```

In Listing 5.2, the constructor for the main window creates both a single-line edit control and a static label. Notice that this code uses a new technique for specifying the location and size of the bounding rectangles of the controls. Instead of specifying the top left and bottom right coordinates, it specifies the top left corner along with the width and height of the bounding rectangle. The two techniques are interchangeable. The **LimitText** function sets the maximum length of the text entry to 10 characters. The call to **SetFocus** at the bottom of the window constructor ensures that the edit control will have user focus when the window initially appears.

The message map wires in the ON_EN_CHANGE map entry so that the EN_CHANGE (EN = Edit Notification) message generated by the edit control is intercepted. This message is sent by an edit control each time its value changes (look at the description of the **CEdit** class in the MFC documentation for a discussion). An alternative would place a button in the window that the user presses to accept the value typed into the edit control. This alternative creates an interface that has a "Press return at the end of the line" feel to it.

The code in Listing 5.2 demonstrates how to extract integer values from an edit control. Each time the user modifies the edit control, the **HandleChange** function is called via the message map. The **HandleChange** function calls **GetDlgItemInt** to extract the current value from the edit control and then calls **SetDlgItemInt** to set the value into the static label. When you execute the program, notice that the value displayed in the label changes with each character typed. Also notice that invalid input is rejected. For example, if you enter "123aaa" in the edit control, only "123" will appear in the label.

Retrieval of text rather than integer input from an edit control is just as easy. Modify the code in **HandleChange** so that it calls **GetDlgItemText** and **SetDlgItemText**. Retrieval of values such as real numbers requires slightly more work. The following replacement for the **HandleChange** function demonstrates the process. This code interprets the contents of the edit area as the radius of a circle and calculates the circle's area:

```
void CWindow::HandleChange()
// Handles any change to the edit control
{
    float f;
    char s[100], t[100];

    GetDlgItemText(ED,s,100);

    // convert s to a float
    istrstream istr(s,100);
    istr >> f;

    // calculate the area of a circle
    f = (float) 3.14159 * f * f;

    // convert the area back to a string for display
    ostrstream ostr(t,100);
    ostr << "area = " << setprecision(10);
    ostr << f << ends;
    SetDlgItemText(CS,t);
}
```

The code uses the **strstream** library and therefore must include <strstrea.h> and <iomanip.h> at the top of the program. See Appendix A for details. In this version of **HandleChange**, the code uses **GetDlgItemText** to retrieve the current value of the edit control. This value is then converted to a floating point value. The insertion operator used to convert the string to a floating point value is smart enough to ignore data that is irrelevant, so characters other than digits or a period are ignored. The code then calculates the area of the circle and converts that value back to a string that can be displayed in the static label using **SetDlgItemText**.

There are several style attributes that you can apply to the edit control to customize its behavior. For example, it can be forced to display all input as upper- or lower-case characters or it can obscure input for applications such as password acceptance. See the description of the **CEdit** control in the MFC documentation for details on these styles, as well as Chapter 8. Experiment with the different options in the code shown above.

5.4 An Interest Calculator

As a final example of the **CEdit** control we will use it to create an interest calculator. Here is an English description of the calculator application:

The program should display three editable areas labeled "Amount," "Interest Rate," and "Time." The user can input account information in these three areas. The program should use the three values to calculate the future value of the account and display the result.

Probably the best way to accept the values is with edit controls. The purpose of each edit control can be identified for the user using static text labels, and the account balance can also be displayed in a label. A quit button at the bottom will allow the user to quit. The code in Listing 5.3 implements this program. Figure 5.3 shows a screen dump of the program during execution.

Listing 5.3
Implementation of the interest calculator.

```
// interest.cpp

#include <afxwin.h>
#include <math.h>
#include <strstrea.h>
#include <iomanip.h>

const int IDC_ED1=100;
const int IDC_ED2=101;
const int IDC_ED3=102;
const int IDC_RESULT=103;
const int IDC_BUTTON=104;

// Define an application object
class CApp : public CWinApp
{
```

```
public:
    virtual BOOL InitInstance();
};

// Create an instance of the application
CApp App;

// Define the window object
class CWindow : public CFrameWnd
{
    CEdit* ed1;
    CEdit* ed2;
    CEdit* ed3;
    CStatic* cs1;
    CStatic* cs2;
    CStatic* cs3;
    CStatic* result;
    CButton* button;
public:
    CWindow();
    afx_msg void HandleChange();
    afx_msg void HandleButton();
    DECLARE_MESSAGE_MAP()
    virtual BOOL PreTranslateMessage(MSG* msg);
};

// This function interprets tab keys properly
BOOL CWindow::PreTranslateMessage(MSG *msg)
{
    return ::IsDialogMessage(m_hWnd,msg);
}

// Message map
BEGIN_MESSAGE_MAP( CWindow, CFrameWnd )
    ON_EN_CHANGE(IDC_ED1, HandleChange)
    ON_EN_CHANGE(IDC_ED2, HandleChange)
    ON_EN_CHANGE(IDC_ED3, HandleChange)
    ON_BN_CLICKED(IDC_BUTTON, HandleButton)
END_MESSAGE_MAP()

// Window constructor
CWindow::CWindow()
{
    // Create the window
    Create(NULL, "Interest",
        WS_OVERLAPPED | WS_MINIMIZEBOX | WS_SYSMENU,
        CRect(CPoint(10,10),CSize(144,226)));

    // Create the labels
    cs1 = new CStatic();
    cs1->Create("Amount",
        WS_CHILD|WS_VISIBLE,
        CRect(CPoint(8,10),CSize(66,16)),
        this);
    cs2 = new CStatic();
    cs2->Create("Rate(%)",
```

```
            WS_CHILD|WS_VISIBLE,
            CRect(CPoint(8,46),CSize(66,16)),
            this);
        cs3 = new CStatic();
        cs3->Create("Time(yrs)",
            WS_CHILD|WS_VISIBLE,
            CRect(CPoint(8,80),CSize(66,16)),
            this);

        // Create the edit controls
        ed1 = new CEdit();
        ed1->Create(
            WS_CHILD|WS_VISIBLE|WS_BORDER|WS_TABSTOP,
            CRect(CPoint(76,10),CSize(64,24)),
            this, IDC_ED1);
        ed2 = new CEdit();
        ed2->Create(
            WS_CHILD|WS_VISIBLE|WS_BORDER|WS_TABSTOP,
            CRect(CPoint(76,46),CSize(64,24)),
            this, IDC_ED2);
        ed3 = new CEdit();
        ed3->Create(
            WS_CHILD|WS_VISIBLE|WS_BORDER|WS_TABSTOP,
            CRect(CPoint(76,80),CSize(64,24)),
            this, IDC_ED3);

        // Create the result label
        result = new CStatic();
        result->Create("Result=0",
            WS_CHILD|WS_VISIBLE,
            CRect(CPoint(10,120),CSize(200,24)),
            this, IDC_RESULT);

        // Create quit button
        button = new CButton();
        button -> Create("&Quit",
            WS_CHILD|WS_VISIBLE|WS_TABSTOP,
            CRect(CPoint(2,162),CSize(138,38)),
            this, IDC_BUTTON);
        ed1->SetFocus();
}

// Handle the quit button
void CWindow::HandleButton()
// Quits the application
{
    DestroyWindow ();
}

// Handle changes to any edit area
void CWindow::HandleChange()
// Handles modifications to any edit control
{
    UINT amount=GetDlgItemInt(ED1);
    UINT rate=GetDlgItemInt(ED2);
    UINT time=GetDlgItemInt(ED3);
```

```
    double result=amount*
        exp((double)rate/100.0*time);
    char s[100];
    ostrstream ostr(s,100);
    ostr << "Result = ";
//  ostr << setprecision(2);
//  ostr << setiosflags( ios::fixed );
// The above line currently causes a crash
// on large values.
    ostr << setprecision(10);
    ostr << result << ends;
    SetDlgItemText(IDC_RESULT,s);
}

// Init the application and the main window
BOOL CApp::InitInstance()
{
    m_pMainWnd = new CWindow();
    m_pMainWnd->ShowWindow(m_nCmdShow);
    m_pMainWnd->UpdateWindow();
    return TRUE;
}
```

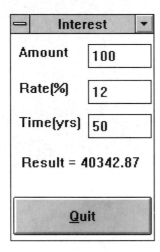

Figure 5.3
Screen dump for the interest calculator

The code for this program is straightforward. The window constructor creates the eight controls and the **HandleButton** function quits the application. The message map routes EN_CHANGE messages from all three edit controls to the same **HandleChange** function. This function extracts the contents of the three controls and calculates the account balance. The result is displayed in the result label. The code currently uses integer input values. However, it would be a straightforward modification to use code from the previous section and allow real number input.

The interest calculator application includes a unique feature that improves its user interface. The window class overrides a virtual function named **PreTranslate-**

Message inherited from **CWnd**. This virtual function allows the application to intercept messages intended for any window or control that you create (because they all inherit from **CWnd**) before they are processed by MFC. In the code above, the application passes the messages to the **IsDialogMessage** function. This function extracts keystrokes such as the tab key and interprets them in the same way that a dialog box would. By setting the WS_TABSTOP attribute for the three edit controls and the button, the user can tab between these four items using the keyboard as well as the mouse. This technique is the basis for *forms* as automatically implemented by the AppWizard and first discussed in Part 3.

Also notice that the label on the button, "&Quit," contains an "&." The placement of this ampersand indicates that the "Q," which is the character immediately following the ampersand, be used as a mnemonic. You will find the application responds to the ALT-Q keystroke by quitting the application because of this mnemonic and the pre-translation of messages.

5.5 Conclusion

In this chapter you have combined your initial knowledge of MFC gained in previous chapters with some simple user interface design rules to create your first useful applications. Part 2 discusses other MFC user interface features so we can build larger, more complicated applications. Part 3 shows how to combine these features with application design and development tools in Visual C++ to significantly speed your application development cycle.

Part 2

VISUAL C++ AND MFC DETAILS

Part 1 of this book introduced you to the fundamentals of MFC programming. In Part 3 you will learn about application development tools like the AppWizard and Class-Wizard that make the creation and implementation of Windows applications so easy in Visual C++. The purpose of Part 2 is to help you become familiar with the details of MFC and Visual C++. You will need to understand these details in order to get the most out of Part 3.

The AppWizard is a code-generation tool. It makes it extremely easy to create a new application by generating the initial MFC code framework for you. Note, however, that the code generated by the AppWizard requires quite a bit of MFC knowledge before you can use it appropriately. For example, the AppWizard generates code that makes extensive use of the MFC debugging features. Until you understand these features completely (see Chapter 13), it is difficult to appropriately modify source code generated by the AppWizard to take advantage of the debugging capabilities. Part 2 familiarizes you with these details.

You, therefore, have two choices at this point in the book. You can work through Part 2 and prepare yourself fully for Part 3. Or you can jump to Part 3 and read about topics in Part 2 as the need arises. If you are the "jump-in-immediately" type, you may wish to visit Chapter 6 first to pick up information on resource files and the resource editors, and then proceed directly to Part 3 to start creating applications immediately. For those who prefer to know what they are doing before they jump in, work through Part 2 and then proceed to Part 3 fully prepared.

Part 2 starts by introducing you to the concept of *resource files* and *resource editors*. You may have noticed in Chapter 5 that you had to write quite a bit of code to create the controls that make up even a very simple application. You can imagine that in a large application the amount of code could quickly become ridiculous. Resources solve this problem. Resources are also extremely important in Part 3, so the introduction that you receive in Chapter 6 makes it much easier to understand some of the mechanics of the AppWizard and ClassWizard.

Chapter 7 discusses the canned dialogs available in MFC. For example, any time you need to ask the user for a file name you can use the **CFileDialog** class to present the standard File Open dialog. The canned dialogs make most standard tasks such as file opening, color selection, and message production much easier. Part 2 then completes your introduction to the Windows controls with two chapters that introduce you to the **CEdit**, **CListBox,** and **CComboBox** controls. The **CStatic**, **CButton,** and **CScrollBar** controls were covered in Part 1: If you look at the visual object hierarchy chart, you will find that these six controls make up the total set of controls available in Windows.

Chapter 10 then gives you an in-depth overview of the features and capabilities of the **CWinApp** class. This class is central in MFC, and extremely important to the AppWizard, so a good understanding of its features is important. Chapter 11 provides a tremendous amount of detail about the Windows drawing model. While it is possible to create many different types of programs with the available controls, Windows is, at its heart, a graphical environment. Therefore, many programs that you want to create will be graphical in nature, presenting the user with drawings and diagrams instead of lists and text. This chapter explains the important concepts that help you to use the drawing features of Windows effectively.

Chapter 12 discusses utility and collection classes in MFC. Part of the joy of using MFC is the fact that it contains classes that make your life as a programmer easier. This chapter discusses many of these classes and shows examples of how to use them effectively. Finally, Chapter 13 immerses you in the MFC debugging features. The designers of MFC took the long-term run-time stability of the hierarchy very seriously and incorporated a number of debugging and diagnostic features into MFC. This chapter will show you how to use those features to reduce your debugging time.

Resources, Dialogs, and Menus

One of the most powerful features of Visual C++ and the MFC class hierarchy is the ability to create, and easily integrate into your applications, something called *resources*. Resources help you solve one of the more bothersome problems seen in Chapter 5. In that chapter you created two small, simple applications, and you ended up having to write a tremendous amount of code to create and position the controls. For example, if you look back at the window constructor for the interest calculator example in Listing 5.3, you find that it takes 50 lines of code just to set up the eight controls displayed in the application's main window. You can easily imagine that any "real" application will have hundreds of controls, and it would take quite a bit of time to create these controls if you had to do it "by hand" like this.

What if you need to create a dialog that lets the user enter name and address information for a company database? You would like to use a tool that lets you lay out the dialog controls and position them visually. In Visual C++ you can do just that, using a tool called a *dialog editor* to set up the dialog. Then you use a class called **CDialog** in MFC to make the process of communicating with the dialog resource easy and straightforward.

Visual C++ contains several customized resource editors for the general task of editing *resource files*. These files and editors handle not only dialogs, but also such things as menus, accelerator tables, icons, and bitmaps. This chapter will introduce you to the concept of resource files and help you understand how to create and modify them with the tools available in Visual C++. In Part 3 you will see how to easily use these tools to rapidly develop your own complex applications.

6.1 Resources and Resource Files

Resources are program objects such as icons, menus, and dialog boxes that are defined outside your program's C++ code in special text and binary files. These files, called *resource files* or *resource scripts*, describe the different resources by using a programming language understood by the *resource compiler*. The resource compiler is invoked through your normal Visual C++ project file, and its output is linked to the program's executable just like any other binary object file. The application loads the resources and uses them to implement different elements of the user interface.

In the not-so-distant past, you created resource scripts "by hand." That is, you typed resource-creation code into resource scripts just like you type C++ code into text files now. Then you ran the resource code through the resource compiler and linked the output to your executable. In Visual C++ this process is completely automated, using graphical editors that make the process extremely quick and straightforward.

Resources make application development easier. There are several important advantages to using resources in your applications:

1. Resource files can be modified without touching your code, and this allows you to make changes much more quickly. For example, you can reposition a control in a dialog box very easily in a resource file without ever touching or recompiling the C++ program that uses it.

2. Resource files concentrate text strings in one place, allowing you to easily handle different human languages. For example, a program will place all its menus and dialog box labels in its resource script. Dialog boxes and menus generally contain all the language-specific text strings used in an application, so if you want to change the language, you simply change the resource file. You can maintain several different resource files, one for each language your application supports (English, French, German, Spanish, etc.), and link them in as needed.

3. You can build resources very quickly with the resource editors. These tools let you visually manipulate things like dialogs and menus, and this increases your productivity tremendously. The dialog editor, for example, allows you to create and position the controls for a dialog using a point-and-click user interface. It is, therefore, very easy to re-size and move the different dialog controls.

A resource-definition file, commonly called a *script* or *rc* file, is a text file with the extension .RC. With the resource editors, you never have to actually look at or touch the script file. You simply include it into the project and Visual C++ invokes the resource compiler on it automatically. The application can access the resources by using a unique name or constant value assigned to each resource in the script file. A header file, generally named RESOURCE.H, accompanies the script file and contains all the constant names and values.

Here are five facts about resource files that will make them easier to understand in the following sections:

1. A resource file, or RC file, contains one or more of the following resource categories:
   - Accelerator
   - Bitmap
   - Cursor
   - Dialog

- Icon
- Menu
- Toolbar
- String Table
- Version

In the case of the first seven resource categories, each category can contain zero or more resources of its type. For example, a program might have 15 different dialogs, three menus, five icons, two bit maps and three accelerator tables. In the case of string tables and version information, on the other hand, the program contains just one resource of that type.

2. To add a new resource to a resource file see Appendix B.5.1. Each type of resource has its own special editor in Visual C++. The appropriate editor will appear when you create the new resource, allowing you to modify the resource.

3. All resources have *properties*. You can select a specific resource and then select the **Properties** option in the **Edit** menu (or double-click on the resource) to view the properties for the resource. One property is the constant ID or name of the resource. Other common properties include things like width and height. Generally, you can easily modify any resource using its property dialog.

4. Resources can be identified by an integer constant or by a name. An integer constant is the default identification chosen by the resource editors for any new resource, but many functions in MFC prefer to work with resource names. Constant values must be included into the application, so the resource editors manipulate a header file called RESOURCE.H that contains the constant values. A typical constant identifier is IDI_ICON1. The "ID" portion identifies it as a resource ID, the "I" identities it as an icon, and the "ICON1" is a unique name for the specific icon. In RESOURCE.H, this constant name might be associated with the value 105. To replace a constant value with a name, choose the **Properties** option in the **Edit** menu and type the name, *in quotes*, into the **ID** field.

5. Resource scripts get compiled and linked to your application through the project file. All you have to do is include the header file for the resource file in your application and add the RC file to your project. The header file contains constant values defined in the script file and needed by your code to retrieve different resources. The RC file describes the resources for the resource compiler. The project file knows how to invoke the resource compiler on the RC file and then link the resources into your application. Figure 6.1 illustrates the process.

The goal of this chapter is to show you how resource files integrate into Visual C++ programs and to demonstrate the editors to you. You will then learn in Part 3 how to use these editors within the AppWizard framework and the ClassWizard to accelerate the application development process.

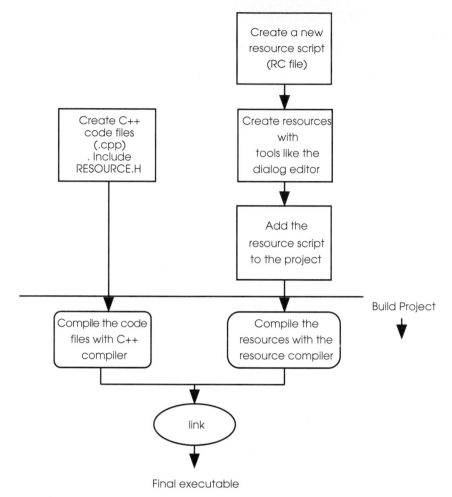

Figure 6.1
Compiling and linking resource files

6.2 The Icon Resource

It may take several passes to get used to the idea of resource files, so let's start with the simplest possible example. In Chapter 3 we experimented extensively with the **CStatic** control. One option we omitted was the ability of a static control to display *icons*. Icons in applications are almost always handled through resource files. In this section and the next we will walk through the creation of a resource file and icon resource and show how to display the icon resource from a normal MFC program like the ones you developed in Part 1.

The code shown in Listing 6.1 creates a **CStatic** control that can display an icon. The screen dump in Figure 6.2 demonstrates the output of the program.

Listing 6.1
Code that creates a CStatic label displaying an icon.

```cpp
// icon.cpp

#include <afxwin.h>

// Declare the application class
class CApp : public CWinApp
{
public:
    virtual BOOL InitInstance();
};

// Create an instance of the application class
CApp App;

//Declare the window class
class CWindow : public CFrameWnd
{
    CStatic* cs;
public:
    CWindow();
    ~CWindow();
};

// The InitInstance function is called once
// when the application first executes
BOOL CApp::InitInstance()
{
    m_pMainWnd = new CWindow();
    m_pMainWnd->ShowWindow(m_nCmdShow);
    m_pMainWnd->UpdateWindow();
    return TRUE;
}

// The constructor for the window class
CWindow::CWindow()
{
    CRect r;

    // Create the window
    Create(NULL,
        "Icon Test",
        WS_OVERLAPPEDWINDOW,
        CRect(0,0,200,200));

    // Create a label that holds an icon
    cs = new CStatic();
    cs->Create("icon",
        WS_CHILD|WS_VISIBLE|SS_ICON,
        CRect(20,20,0,0),
        this);
}
```

```
// The destructor for the window
CWindow::~CWindow()
{
    delete cs;
}
```

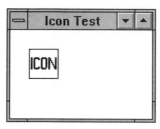

Figure 6.2
An icon displayed by a CStatic label

In the code in Listing 6.1, the line that creates the **CStatic** control is important. The SS_ICON style attribute tells the control that it should display an icon, and in this context the name "icon" passed as the first parameter names the icon that should be displayed.

If you try to compile and run the application in Listing 6.2 using the techniques discussed in Appendix B.3 of the book, you will find that it does not work. To display the icon, the application needs to be able to load the bit-level description for the icon from a resource file using the name "icon". The creation of this resource is described in the next section.

6.3 Creating a Resource File

You use the resource editors in Visual C++ to create and edit any type of resource. The collection of editors include a dialog editor, a menu editor, an accelerator table editor, an icon editor, a cursor editor, a bitmap editor, a string resource editor, the toolbar editor, and a version editor. To use any of these editors you must first create a new resource script. Let's walk through the whole process of creating a new project, adding in the C++ code, creating a resource script, and then adding an icon resource. This will allow you to see how resource scripts and C++ files work together to create complete applications.

6.3.1 Step 1– Create a New Project

We will use the same technique discussed in Appendix B.3 to create a new project. Call the project ICON and the code file for Listing 6.1 ICON.CPP.

6.3.2 Step 2 – Create a New Resource Script

To create a new resource script for this application see Appendix B.5.2.

6.3.3 Step 3 – Add the RC File to the Project

Now add the RC file to the project in exactly the same way you added the CPP file to it.

6.3.4 Step 4 – Create the Icon Resource

To create the icon resource used by Listing 6.1, create a new icon resource as described in Appendix B.5.3.

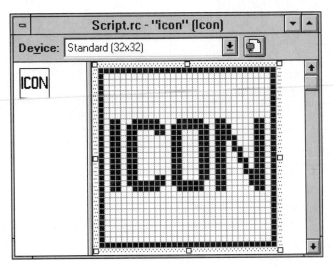

Figure 6.3
Editing the icon resource

Create an icon like the one shown in Figure 6.3, or make up your own, using the various drawing and painting tools in the palette. If the pal ette is not visible see Appendix B.5.4. The resource editor will give the icon an arbitrary constant value named IDI_ICON1.

When you have finished your icon, choose the **Save** option in the **File** menu. If you now look in the resource view, you will see that it shows a new resource.

6.3.5 Step 5 – Change the Icon ID

When the icon editor created the new icon, it gave it a *constant value* and named that constant IDI_ICON1. It placed this constant name and value in a file it created called RESOURCE.H. We need to change this. In our case, because of the way the code appears in Listing 6.1, the icon needs to have the *name* "icon" rather than a *constant value*. To do this, open IDI_ICON1 by double-clicking it in the resource view. Choose the **Properties** item in the **Edit** menu. You will see an Icon Properties dialog. In the ID field, type the word "icon" (*be sure to include the quotes*) in place of IDI_ICON1. Close the properties dialog. The new name should appear in the title bar of the icon's window, and also in the resource view.

6.3.6 Step 6 – Compile and Run

You should now be able to compile and run the application. Provided you have followed all the steps correctly, Visual C++ will compile the resource file, compile the CPP file, link the two together, and produce an executable. When you run the application you should find that it looks like the application in Figure 6.2.

6.3.7 Review

Here is a review of the steps taken to display an icon in a **CStatic** control:

1. Create a new MFC project. See Appendix B.3 for details.
2. Create a CPP file that includes the **CStatic** control and give the control the SS_ICON style. (See the **style** part of the **CStatic::Create** function in the MFC documentation for more information on the SS_ICON style.)
3. Add the CPP file to the project.
4. Create a new resource script. See Appendix B.5 for details.
5. Add the new resource script to the project.
6. Create a new icon resource.
7. In the properties dialog for the new icon give the icon the name "icon". Note that this is a quoted string: *Include the quotes in the ID field of the properties dialog.*
8. Build and run the application.

After you do it several times and get comfortable with the process and tools, you will find that using resource scripts and resource editors to create resources is extremely easy.

An interesting side effect of knowing how to create icon resources is that you can now give the application an icon when it is minimized on the desktop. Create a new icon and, in the ID field of the Properties dialog for the icon, use the name AFX_IDI_STD_FRAME. This constant name is recognized automatically by MFC as the identifier for the application's icon. When you run the application, it will have its own icon on the desktop. The AppWizard leverages automatic features like this constantly to make it easy to create full-fledged applications. Be sure to create both 16x16 and 32x32 bit icons as described in Appendix B.5.3.

You may also want to use the **LoadIcon** and **SetIcon** functions to change the icon. See Chapter 10 for an example.

For complete information on the icon editor, press the F1 key while the icon editor window is visible in Visual C++.

6.4 Menus

Menus are another resource that you commonly create with a resource editor. Visual C++ provides a menu editor that is extremely easy to use.

The code in Listing 6.2 creates a simple application that displays a menu. To try out this code, create a new project using the same steps you followed in Section 6.3.1, and add the code shown in Listing 6.2 to the project. If you compile and run the application now it will execute, but you will see no menu because we have not yet created the menu resource named "MainMenu" with the resource editor. As with the icon resource in Section 6.3, Visual C++ simply does not load the resource if it cannot find it.

Listing 6.2
Creating a menu with a menu resource.

```
// menu.cpp
#include <afxwin.h>

// Define the application object class
class CApp : public CWinApp
{
public:
    virtual BOOL InitInstance();
};

// Define the edit window class
class CWindow : public CFrameWnd
{
    CMenu *menu;
public:
    CWindow();
    DECLARE_MESSAGE_MAP()
};

// Create and instance of the application object
CApp App;

// The message map
BEGIN_MESSAGE_MAP(CWindow, CFrameWnd)
END_MESSAGE_MAP()

// CWindow constructor
CWindow::CWindow()
{
    Create( NULL, "Menu Samp", WS_OVERLAPPEDWINDOW, rectDefault);
    menu = new CMenu();
    menu->LoadMenu("MainMenu");
    SetMenu(menu);
    DrawMenuBar();
}

// Initialize the CApp m_pMainWnd data member
BOOL CApp::InitInstance()
{
    m_pMainWnd = new CWindow();
    m_pMainWnd -> ShowWindow( m_nCmdShow );
    m_pMainWnd -> UpdateWindow();
    return( TRUE );
}
```

In Listing 6.2, the window's constructor loads the menu resource. It loads a menu by the name of "MainMenu."

To create the menu resource, create a new resource script for this project following the steps in Appendix B.5.2, and then add the new script to the project. Create a new **Menu** resource as described in Appendix B.5.5. You will see a window like the one shown in Figure 6.4.

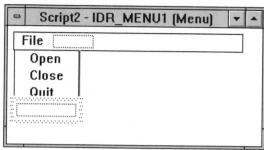

Figure 6.4
The menu editor showing a simple menu

Looking at Figure 6.4, you can see several different objects. First, there is a menu named **File**. The **File** menu contains the options **Open**, **Close,** and **Quit**. Below the **Quit** option and to the right of the **File** menu there are blank boxes. These indicate areas where you can add new options or menus. You can drag these blank boxes, or the menus and options themselves, to different positions. If you click on one of the blank boxes and begin typing you can create a new menu or menu option. If you double-click on any existing menu option (or single-click and choose the **Properties** option in the **Edit** menu), its Properties dialog will appear.

Create the menu structure shown in Figure 6.4 on your own. Simply click on a blank box in the menu bar or a menu and type, for example, the word "File". The Properties dialog will appear automatically and the word "File" will fall into the **Caption** field. At the end of the word press return and the Properties dialog will disappear. You will find that it takes just a minute or two to create the menu. Then double-click on the new **Open** option to see its properties again.

In the Properties dialog for the **Open** option in the **File** menu that you just created you should note several important fields:

1. The ID field contains the name of the constant for the menu option. You will use this constant inside message maps to detect when the user selects that option, as we will see in a moment. The resource editor has given this constant an obvious name (ID_FILE_OPEN), but you can change it to anything you like. In fact, you should change it. If you leave it as it is, the compiler will generate a number of warnings when you compile the code because the constants chosen for the menu option IDs are already used by MFC and the AppWizard. To eliminate the warnings, you should rename each menu option ID using an IDM_ preface in place of ID_. Double-click on each menu option and then change its name in the ID field to IDM_FILE_OPEN, IDM_FILE_CLOSE, and IDM_FILE_QUIT, respectively (yes, you can change it to **Exit** if you like).

2. The Caption field contains the text that appears in the menu. This is the text you typed when you created the option. You can change it at any time, although the ID field will not reflect the new name unless you manually change it as well.

3. The Prompt field contains a message that goes in the status bar of applications equipped with a status bar. We will see how to use the status bar in Chapter 18.

4. The dialog contains several different check boxes to control the menu item's behavior.

 Try some of these out on your different menus. Each one is explained below:
 - Separator – If selected, the menu option will appear as a horizontal line.
 - Checked – If selected, the menu option will initially have a check mark next to it.
 - Popup – If selected, the option becomes a popup menu. The File menu is a popup. You create multi-level menus by placing a popup inside another pop-up.
 - Grayed – If selected, the menu item is grayed out and inactive.
 - Inactive – If selected, the menu option is initially inactive but not grayed to indicate that. Use Grayed instead.

After creating the menu, you need to rename it "MainMenu" so the application can find it. By default the menu resource editor has assigned the new menu resource the ID of IDR_MENU1. To change it, go back to the resource file's main window. Single-click on IDR_MENU1 as shown and then select the **Properties** option in the **Edit** menu. In the ID field of the Properties dialog, type "MainMenu", *making sure that you include the quotes and use the correct capitalization*. Close the dialog and save the resource file by selecting the **Save** option in the **File** menu. Make sure you are saving it to the proper directory. Name the file SCRIPT.RC.

To include the menu in your application, take the same steps as for the icon in the previous section. *Include the file RESOURCE.H at the top of Listing 6.2.* You have to do this because RESOURCE.H contains the constant values for IDM_FILE_OPEN, IDM_FILE_CLOSE, and IDM_FILE_QUIT. *Add the resource file to your project.* You have to do this or the resource file will not be compiled and linked to the application. Build the modified project.

When you run the application you should see the menu bar and it should work as expected. None of the items will be enabled initially, but we will see in a moment how to remedy that. If you do not see the menu bar, assume that there is a problem with the naming of the menu or with the resource file itself and fix the problem.

Here is a review of the steps taken to display a menu in an MFC application:

1. Create a new MFC project.
2. Create a CPP file that loads a menu resource in the window's constructor.
3. Add the CPP file to the project.
4. Create a new resource script.
5. Add the new resource script to the project.

6. Create a new menu resource.

7. In the properties dialog for the new menu, give the menu the ID "MainMenu". Note that this is a quoted string: *Include the quotes in the ID field of the properties dialog.*

8. Build and run the application.

For more information on the menu editor, press the F1 button with the menu editor window visible.

6.5 Responding to Menus

You respond to menu options chosen by the user through the message map. No menu item is enabled unless it has an entry in a message map (you can change this behavior by modifying the **m_bAutoMenuEnable** member in the **CFrameWnd** class). If a message map entry exists for a menu option, the menu option sends a message containing its ID to the window each time the user selects it. If you place an ON_COMMAND entry for a menu item in the message map and give that entry a function to call, the menu will respond to the user by calling the function. The mechanism is identical to the mechanism used to recognize clicks in push buttons, as described in Chapter 4.

For example, the code in Listing 6.3 demonstrates how to respond to the **Quit** option in the **File** menu.

Listing 6.3
Responding to the quit option

```
// menu2.cpp

#include <afxwin.h>
#include "resource.h"

// Define the application object class
class CApp : public CWinApp
{
public:
    virtual BOOL InitInstance();
};

// Define the edit window class
class CWindow : public CFrameWnd
{
    CMenu *menu;
public:
    CWindow();
    afx_msg void HandleQuit();
    DECLARE_MESSAGE_MAP()
};

// Create and instance of the application object
CApp App;
```

```
// The message map
BEGIN_MESSAGE_MAP(CWindow, CFrameWnd)
    ON_COMMAND(IDM_FILE_QUIT, HandleQuit)
END_MESSAGE_MAP()

void CWindow::HandleQuit()
{
    DestroyWindow();
}

// CWindow constructor
CWindow::CWindow()
{
    Create( NULL, "Menu Sample", WS_OVERLAPPEDWINDOW,
        rectDefault);
    menu = new CMenu();
    menu->LoadMenu("MainMenu");
    SetMenu(menu);
    DrawMenuBar();
}

// Initialize the CApp m_pMainWnd data member
BOOL CApp::InitInstance()
{
    m_pMainWnd = new CWindow();
    m_pMainWnd -> ShowWindow( m_nCmdShow );
    m_pMainWnd -> UpdateWindow();
    return( TRUE );
}
```

Listing 6.3 has three modifications that distinguishes it from Listing 6.2:

1. The **CWindow** class contains a new member function named **HandleQuit**.
2. The message map contains an ON_COMMAND entry that recognizes IDM_FILE_QUIT and calls **HandleQuit** in response to it.
3. The **HandleQuit** function calls **DestroyWindow** to close the application.

See Chapter 4 for more information on message maps.

When you build Listing 6.3 and run the application, you will find that the **Quit** option is enabled and when selected it terminates the application properly.

You will follow this same three-step pattern in the message map to respond to any menu option. In Part 3 you will learn about a tool called the *ClassWizard* that automates the process of adding message handlers to your applications and makes menus even easier to create.

The following sections demonstrate several menu features that are important when you create complete applications.

6.5.1 Checked and Enabled Menu Items

The code below demonstrates how to handle checked menu options. When you select a checked option it toggles back and forth between checked and unchecked. To create this effect in the sample program, first use the menu resource editor to add a new menu option named **Word Wrap** to the **File** menu. Then modify the class definition for **CWindow** and its message map, and add a new function as shown in the code fragment below:

```
// Define the edit window class
class CWindow : public CFrameWnd
{
    CMenu *menu;
    BOOL wordwrap; // init in the constructor
public:
    CWindow();
    afx_msg void HandleQuit();
    afx_msg void OnWordWrap();
    DECLARE_MESSAGE_MAP()
};


// The message map
BEGIN_MESSAGE_MAP(CWindow, CFrameWnd)
    ON_COMMAND(IDM_FILE_QUIT, HandleQuit)
    ON_COMMAND(IDM_FILE_WORDWRAP, OnWordWrap)
END_MESSAGE_MAP()

void CWindow::OnWordWrap()
{
    if (wordwrap)
        menu->CheckMenuItem(IDM_FILE_WORDWRAP,
            MF_BYCOMMAND|MF_UNCHECKED);
    else
        menu->CheckMenuItem(IDM_FILE_WORDWRAP,
            MF_BYCOMMAND|MF_CHECKED);
    wordwrap = !wordwrap;
}
```

When you build and run the modified program, you will find that the **Word Wrap** option toggles between a checked and unchecked state. If you wish for it to be initially checked, then select the **Checked** option in the menu item's property dialog.

To disable and enable menu options dynamically in a program, use the **Enable-MenuItem** function in a manner identical to the way the **CheckMenuItem** is demonstrated above. For example:

```
menu->EnableMenuItem(IDM_FILE_CLOSE,
        MF_BYCOMMAND|MF_DISABLE);
```

You will find an example of this feature in Chapter 8. However, you will find in Part 3 that MFC contains a **CCmdUI** class that automates the menu enabling process and makes it even easier. You can use it for handling check marks as well.

6.5.2 Creating Mnemonics

When you create a caption for a menu or a menu option, you have the option of placing an "&" (ampersand) character in front of any one of the characters in the caption. For example, you might type "&File" instead of "File" for the caption of the **File** menu. The ampersand preceeding a character marks that character as the menu's or option's *mnemonic character*. Try adding ampersands to the captions of each item in the menu you created above. Double-click on each item in the menu editor and add the ampersand in the caption of the property dialog that appears. The only constraint is that you cannot mark the same character as a mnemonic character more than once in the same menu or menu bar.

Recompile and run the program and you will find that your menu has mnemonic characters just like any other Windows application.

6.5.3 Creating Accelerators

Most applications allow you to use accelerators as "hot keys" for different menu options. Some accelerators are standard, like Alt-F4 for exiting an application. Others are completely arbitrary and determined by the application's designer. Accelerators are provided to make it easier to access frequently used menu options.

To activate the accelerator keys, your code must load an *accelerator table* from the resource file, usually in the window's constructor immediately following menu loading. Use the **LoadAccelTable** function to load the table and create an Accelerators resource to hold the table.

An accelerator table consists of a set of accelerator specifications, each one displayed on a separate line in the table. Each line defines one accelerator key and maps it to a command ID. The line format is described below. You can double-click on the first blank line in a new table to modify it and add an accelerator to the application. The Accelerators Properties dialog will let you enter four things:

1. *ID* – Indicates the integer constant of the message that is generated when the accelerator is used. Typically this ID corresponds to the ID of one of the available menu options, such as IDM_FILE_OPEN. However, this is not always the case--you might create an accelerator with the ID of ID_INSERT_TOGGLE and associate it with the Insert key on the keyboard.
2. *Key* – Indicates the keystroke for this accelerator. The keystroke can be either an ASCII character or a virtual key like a function key. Typically ASCII characters, when used, are modified by a key like the Control or Alt key. If you click the **Next Key Typed** button to set the keystroke, the accelerator resource editor will automatically choose whether to use an ASCII keystroke or a VirtKey for you and you do not have to worry about the distinction.
3. *Type* – ASCII or VIRTKEY. See *Key*.
4. *Modifiers* – One or more of ALT, SHIFT, and CONTROL can be used to select special key combinations.

For example, you might associate the Ctrl-O keystroke with the **Open** option in the **File** menu by choosing IDM_FILE_OPEN for the accelerator ID. Then click the **Next Key Typed** button and hit the Ctrl-O key combination. You will see the accelerator's entry as a single line in the accelerator table.

If you create an accelerator in the accelerator table and correctly load the accelerator table resource with the **LoadAccelTable** function in the same place that you load the menu, the accelerator will work as you expect. However, the user will not know that the accelerator exists. To show the user the accelerator key as a part of the menu option, modify the caption for the menu option. For example, if you define a Ctrl-Q accelerator for the **Quit** option, and also define "Q" to be the mnemonic character, the proper caption for the **Quit** option is:

```
&Quit\tCrtl-Q
```

You can change it to **Exit** and use Alt-F4. Try it.

For more information on accelerator tables, see Chapters 8 and 18

6.5.4 Creating Hierarchical Menus

To create a hierarchical menu (a menu within a menu), simply select any menu option in the menu resource editor and mark its type as **Popup** in its properties dialog. Then the menu editor will let you add options to it hierarchically and handle all the details for you. No further modifications are required. Items in a hierarchical menu are treated in exactly the same way as normal menu options by the message map.

6.6 Dialog Resources

Visual C++ contains a powerful dialog editor that makes the creation of custom dialog templates extremely easy. Used in combination with MFC's **CDialog** class, you can easily add dialogs to your programs. This section shows a very simple example of how to create a dialog template and dialog class by hand. See also Chapters 15, 18, and 23 for more information on creating dialogs with the dialog editor and **CDialog**-derived classes with the ClassWizard. By using the ClassWizard and its DDX/DDV features, you can create dialogs extremely quickly in Visual C++.

The code in Listing 6.4 shows half of an application that will display a dialog box to the user and extract the string that the user enters. Following the steps in Appendix B.3, create a new project and copy this code to a new code file in that directory. *Add the CPP file to the project. Make sure the project is an MFC project, as described in Appendix B.3.*

Listing 6.4
A program that displays a simple dialog.

```
// dialog.cpp

#include <afxwin.h>
#include "resource.h"
// Define the application object class
class CApp : public CWinApp
{
public:
    virtual BOOL InitInstance();
};

// Define the window class
class CWindow : public CFrameWnd
{
    CMenu *menu;
```

```cpp
public:
    CWindow();
    afx_msg void OnPrompt();
    afx_msg void OnExit();
    DECLARE_MESSAGE_MAP()
};

// Define the Prompt Dialog Class
class CPromptDialog: public CDialog
{
private:
    CStringinputString;
public:
    CPromptDialog( CString initString = NULL,
        CWnd* pParentWnd = NULL )
        : CDialog( IDD_DIALOG1, pParentWnd )
        { inputString = initString; }

    virtual void OnOK();
    virtual BOOL OnInitDialog();
    CString& GetInputString()
        { return inputString; }
};

void CPromptDialog::OnOK()
{
    GetDlgItemText( IDC_EDIT1,
        inputString.GetBuffer(100), 100 );
    inputString.ReleaseBuffer();
    EndDialog( IDOK );
}

// On InitDialog is called just before the dialog
// appears on the screen.
BOOL CPromptDialog::OnInitDialog()
{
    SetDlgItemText( IDC_EDIT1, inputString );
    return TRUE;
}

void CWindow::OnPrompt()
{
    CPromptDialog promptDialog( "initial string",
        this );
    if( promptDialog.DoModal() == IDOK )
    {
        MessageBox( promptDialog.GetInputString(),
            "String Entered", MB_ICONINFORMATION );
    }
}

// On Exit handles the void
void CWindow::OnExit()
{
    DestroyWindow();
}
```

```
      // Creating the app object runs the program.
      CApp app;

      // CWindow constructor
      CWindow::CWindow()
      {
          Create( NULL, "Simple Custom Dialog",
              WS_OVERLAPPEDWINDOW,
              rectDefault, NULL,
              MAKEINTRESOURCE(IDR_MENU1));
      }

      // Initialize the CApp m_pMainWnd data member
      BOOL CApp::InitInstance()
      {
          m_pMainWnd = new CWindow();
          m_pMainWnd -> ShowWindow( m_nCmdShow );
          m_pMainWnd -> UpdateWindow();
          return( TRUE );
      }

      BEGIN_MESSAGE_MAP(CWindow, CFrameWnd)
          ON_COMMAND( IDM_FILE_PROMPT, OnPrompt )
          ON_COMMAND( IDM_FILE_EXIT, OnExit )
      END_MESSAGE_MAP()
```

The other half of the application will be the resource file. The resource file will contain a small menu, along with the template for the dialog box. To create the resource file take the following steps.

6.6.1 Step 1 – Create a New Resource Script

Create a new resource script as described in Appendix B.5.2. Give it the name SCRIPT.RC. *Add* SCRIPT.RC *to the project as described in Appendix B.5.2.*

6.6.2 Step 2 – Create a New Menu

Create a new menu resource (see Appendix B.5.5) consisting simply of a **File** menu and the options **Prompt** and **Exit**. The **Prompt** option will cause the dialog to appear, while the **Exit** option will cause the application to terminate. See Figure 6.5 for a picture of this menu. Change the ID of the two menu options to IDM_FILE_PROMPT and IDM_FILE_EXIT. The resource editor will automatically name the menu IDR_MENU1.

6.6.3 Step 3 – Create a New Dialog

Create a dialog resource like the one shown in Figure 6.6. To do this, create a new dialog resource as described in Appendix B.5.6. A dialog palette will appear, and it lets you choose the different controls that you want to add to the dialog. (If the palette does not appear, see Appendix B.5.4.)

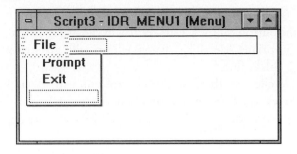

Figure 6.5
A simple menu

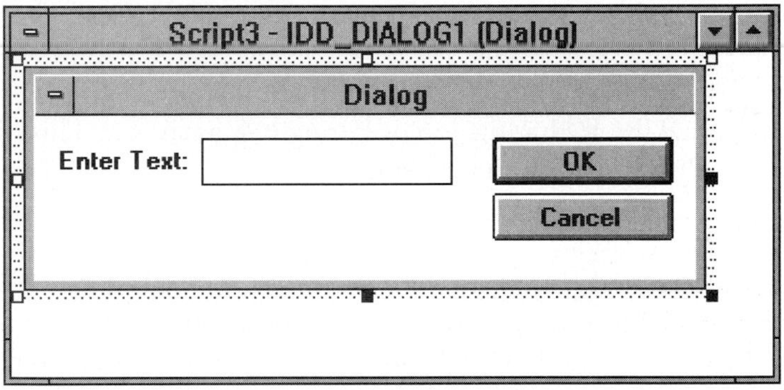

Figure 6.6
A simple dialog box

6.6.4 Step 4 – Add a Static Control to the Dialog

When you create the new dialog, it will automatically have **OK** and **Cancel** buttons. Double click on each one to see their properties. To add the **CStatic** control that says "Enter Text:", click the button for the **CStatic** control in the dialog palette. Drag out a rectangle in your dialog and then enter the string "Enter Text:". The dialog editor will choose the ID IDC_STATIC for this control, and that is fine. However, if you wanted to create code to modify this control, you would change the ID to something unique and then use that ID in functions like **SetDlgItemText** (see Chapter 5).

Once you have created the **CStatic** control, double-click on it to view its properties (or select the **Properties** option in the **Edit** menu after single-clicking on the static control). You will see a property dialog. If you return to Chapter 3 and look at the styles that the **CStatic** control supports, you will find that many (but not all) of the standard **CStatic** styles are supported here using check boxes. The remaining static styles, such as SS_ICON and SS_BLACKFRAME, are supported by the "picture" control.

6.6.5 Step 5 – Add an Edit Control to the Dialog

Now click the button for the **CEdit** control in the dialog palette. Drag out a rectangle of the appropriate size. The dialog editor will give this control the ID IDC_EDIT1, and this is fine.

If you double-click on the new edit control you can see its Properties dialog. This dialog has several different tabs. If you look up the styles for the **CEdit** control in the MFC documentation, you will find that all its styles are supported by check boxes.

Arrange and re-size the different elements of the dialog until they feel comfortable to you. You can use the different alignment tools in the toolbar of the dialog editor if you like. Press the F1 key while the dialog editor is the topmost window for more information. You can also test the dialog by choosing the **Test** option.

6.6.6 Step 6 – Include RESOURCE.H

Include RESOURCE.H at the top of Listing 6.4, as shown. This file contains IDs for the dialog, its controls, and the menu.

6.6.7 Step 7 – Compile and Run

Build the project and execute it. The dialog will appear when the user selects the **Prompt** option in the **File** menu. The dialog will appear with the string "initial string" displayed in the **CEdit** control. This demonstrates that it is possible to pre-load the edit control with a value. You can delete this string and type your own. Once you press the OK button in the dialog, the dialog will close and a message box containing the string you entered will appear.

6.6.8 Step 8 – Understand the Code

The code in Listing 6.4 that makes this all possible is a fairly simple extension of the menu code in Listing 6.3. It uses the same mechanism to display a menu bar and respond to its options. When the user selects the **Prompt** option in the **File** menu, the message map calls the **OnPrompt** function, shown here:

```
void CWindow::OnPrompt()
{
    CPromptDialog promptDialog( "initial string",
        this );
    if( promptDialog.DoModal() == IDOK )
    {
        MessageBox( promptDialog.GetInputString(),
            "String Entered", MB_ICONINFORMATION );
    }
}
```

This function creates an instance of the **CPromptDialog** class called **prompt-Dialog**. It passes the initial string for the **CEdit** control, along with the **this** pointer, to the constructor for the class. It then calls **promptDialog**'s **DoModal** function. If **DoModal** returns IDOK, the function extracts the string from the dialog using the dialog's **GetInputString** function and displays it in a message box.

The **CPromptDialog** class is derived from **CDialog,** as shown in Listing 6.4 and duplicated below:

```
// Define the Prompt Dialog Class
class CPromptDialog: public CDialog
{
private:
    CStringinputString;
public:
    CPromptDialog( CString initString = NULL,
        CWnd* pParentWnd = NULL )
        : CDialog( IDD_DIALOG1, pParentWnd )
        { inputString = initString; }

    virtual void OnOK();
    virtual BOOL OnInitDialog();
    CString& GetInputString()
        { return inputString; }
};

void CPromptDialog::OnOK()
{
    GetDlgItemText( IDC_EDIT1,
        inputString.GetBuffer(100), 100 );
    inputString.ReleaseBuffer();
    EndDialog( IDOK );
}

// On InitDialog is called just before the dialog
// appears on the screen.
BOOL CPromptDialog::OnInitDialog()
{
    SetDlgItemText( IDC_EDIT1, inputString );
    return TRUE;
}
```

If you look up the **CDialog** class in the MFC documentation, you will find that it is designed to facilitate the easy creation of dialogs from dialog resources. The **CPromptDialog** class contains a constructor, new implementations for the **OnOK** and **OnInitDialog** functions, and a new function called **GetInputString** that provides a controlled way to retrieve the input string from the dialog. This latter function follows the model established by the canned dialogs in Chapter 7 for retrieving data from a dialog. It simply returns the value of the member variable named **inputString**.

The constructor calls the constructor for the **CDialog** class, passing it the dialog resource's ID and a parent pointer. It also initializes the **inputString** member. The **CDialog** constructor calls **OnInitDialog** as part of the dialog creation process. The dialog at this point already exists, so **OnInitDialog** can initialize any fields in the dialog. Here it initializes the **CEdit** control. See the page describing **OnInitDialog** in the MFC documentation for more information. In any dialog you create you will use this function to initialize fields in the dialog.

When the user presses the OK button on the dialog, the **OnOK** function gets called automatically before the dialog's destruction. The overridden version shown here extracts the string entered by the user from the **CEdit** control and then destroys the dialog with **EndDialog**, passing back the ID of the button. The value passed to **EndDialog** will be returned by **DoModal** (seen in the **OnPrompt** function).

What you can see in this code is the fact that it is extremely easy to create a dialog using the dialog editor and the **CDialog** class. Simply create a dialog with the dialog resource editor and place into it any controls that it needs. Then create a new class that inherits from the **CDialog** class. In the construct, or specify the dialog resource. In the **OnInitDialog** function, initialize any fields in the dialog. In the **OnOK** function, extract data from any controls that the user could potentially modify. Then create a function to extract that data from the dialog class or simply access it directly through the member variables.

We will see in Part 3 and Part 4 that Visual C++ combines the dialog editor with the ClassWizard and features called Dialog Data Exchange (DDX) and Dialog Data Validation (DDV) to make the creation of any type of modal dialog nearly instantaneous. You will literally have to write no code to create new dialog in your applications when you use the ClassWizard. See Chapters 15, 18, and 22 for examples.

For more information on the dialog editor, press the F1 key while a dialog editor window is visible on the screen.

6.7 String Resources

The string table is an interesting resource type. There is only one string table per resource file. It contains strings and is extremely important to the creation of applications that support different human languages.

Imagine, for example, that you work for a company that produces an application sold internationally. The company wishes to produce versions that run in English, French, German, and Spanish. In the preceeding sections you have seen that resource files go a long way toward making this process easier. For example, the resource file contains all menus and custom dialogs for an application. Therefore, to produce a version of the application for a different language, you can simply create a new resource file and translate the menus and dialogs to the new language. Note that you do not have to touch a single line of source code. You simply substitute the new resource file into the project, re-compile, and the application suddenly speaks in a different tongue.

One problem that can limit the usefulness of this approach, however, is such things as error messages, window titles, information strings, and so on. These elements are often embedded directly in the code. In a large program, say one containing 200,000 lines of source code, this problem can become extremely frustrating. There might be hundreds of message box calls like the one below:

```
MessageBox("The value you have specified is invalid",
    "Problem Report", MB_OK);
```

Searching through 200,000 lines of source code for these sorts of things, and maintaining several different versions of the source code to accommodate the different languages you support, can involve a massive amount of effort.

String tables solve this problem. Instead of using embedded literal strings, you store *all* the application's strings in the string table in the application's resource file. Then you load each string from the string table when you need it. The advantage of this technique is that *all* language-specific strings exist in a single, easily replaceable resource file. The disadvantage is the extra code that you have to write to load those strings each time you need to use them. Fortunately, MFC makes the loading process easy and painless, so the amount of extra code you have to write is minimal.

The code in Listing 6.5 demonstrates how to load strings from a resource file to support a message box and a message label. The following sections outline the steps you must take to create a project and string table suitable for executing this code.

Listing 6.5
Code that uses a string table instead of embedded strings

```
// strings.cpp

#include <afxwin.h>
#include "resource.h"

// Declare the application class
class CApp : public CWinApp
{
public:
    virtual BOOL InitInstance();
};

// Create an instance of the application class
CApp App;

//Declare the window class
class CWindow : public CFrameWnd
{
    CStatic* cs;
public:
    CWindow();
    ~CWindow();
};

// The InitInstance function is called once
// when the application first executes
BOOL CApp::InitInstance()
{
    m_pMainWnd = new CWindow();
    m_pMainWnd->ShowWindow(m_nCmdShow);
    m_pMainWnd->UpdateWindow();
    return TRUE;
}

// The constructor for the window class
CWindow::CWindow()
{
    CRect r;
```

```
    // Create the window
    Create(NULL,
        "Icon Test",
        WS_OVERLAPPEDWINDOW,
        CRect(0,0,200,200));

    // Create a label that holds an icon
    cs = new CStatic();
    CString s;
    AfxFormatString1(s, IDS_HELLOWORLD, "");
    cs->Create(s,
        WS_CHILD|WS_VISIBLE|SS_CENTER,
        CRect(20,20,100, 50),
        this);

    AfxFormatString1(s, IDS_ERROR, "framis");
    MessageBox(s);
}

// The destructor for the window
CWindow::~CWindow()
{
    delete cs;
}
```

Note the use of the **AfxFormatString1** function in the window's constructor. This function and its companion **AfxFormatString2** give you an easy way to extract strings from the resource file using their IDs. To compile and run the code in Listing 6.5, take the following steps.

6.7.1 Step 1 – Create the Project

Create a new project file as described in Appendix B.3.

6.7.2 Step 2 – Create the String Table

Create a new resource script and a string table resource in it as described in Appendix B.5.2 and B.5.7. To add a new string to the table, double-click on the first line. Give the new string the ID of IDS_HELLOWORLD and the caption "Hello World." Close the Property dialog. Double-click on the second blank line in the string table and give this string the ID of IDS_ERROR. Give it the caption, "An error has occurred in the %1 module."

6.7.3 Step 3 – Compile and Run

Save the resource script file to SCRIPT.RC. *Then add SCRIPT.RC to the project as described in Appendix B.5.2.* Compile and execute the program and the message box should contain the error string from the string table. The window should display "Hello World" from the string table as well.

Note that **AfxStringFormat1** has the ability to substitute one string into a string resource in place of the "%1" placeholder. In the case of the **CStatic** label the facility was not used. In the message box's error string it was. In fact, the word you substitute might come from the string table as well. Note that the **AfxFormatString2** does the same thing, but allows the string resource to contain two substitution strings.

You may wish to create a function that handles the call to **AfxStringFormat1** and then returns the string. That way you can call the function directly in the call to **MessageBox**. Note also that **AfxMessageBox** is already overridden so it can accept a string table ID directly. See the MFC documentation for details.

6.8 Conclusion

The concepts demonstrated in this chapter should show you what the resource editors in Visual C++ do and should also make you comfortable with the idea of resource files and resources. We will use these concepts extensively in Part 3.

Canned Dialogs

Dialog boxes are a friendly and easy way to send messages to, and request information from, the user. Using dialog boxes, you can display a nicely formatted message to the user with just one line of code. When you want specific information from the user, you display the appropriate dialog and then extract what you need from it after the user presses the OK button.

MFC has a number of "canned" dialogs to handle common user interface tasks. For example, there is a File Open dialog, a Font dialog, and a Color dialog. By using the canned dialogs you ensure instant user acceptance and ease of use because your program looks like every other. Also, as the operating system changes the canned dialogs are updated. They therefore always look as modern as possible. The dialog images in this chapter were produced in NT 3.51, but may look different in Windows 95 or later versions of NT for this very reason.

For some situations, however, you will want to create custom dialogs. For example, if you are implementing an address list program you might create a custom dialog to get the address information. Custom dialogs are very easy to create using the dialog editor discussed in the previous chapter. See also Parts 3 and 4, which discuss the creation of dialogs within AppWizard frameworks.

In this chapter, we will examine the available canned dialogs. Chapter 8 presents an example of an editor application that demonstrates many of these dialogs in an actual program.

7.1 The Message Box Dialog

The simplest canned dialog box available in Windows is the message box. You use it to display messages such as errors and questions. It allows the user to respond by pressing one or more buttons. The message box is a *modal* dialog. While it is on screen the application cannot accept events itself. You must respond to the dialog before you can continue with the application.

The code in Listing 7.1 demonstrates the creation of a message box handler. Figure 7.1 is a screen dump of the message box.

Listing 7.1
Code that creates and handles a message box.

```cpp
// msgbox.cpp

#include <afxwin.h>

#define IDC_BUTTON 100

// Declare the application class
class CApp : public CWinApp
{
public:
    virtual BOOL InitInstance();
};

// Create an instance of the application class
CApp App;

// Declare the window class
class CWindow : public CFrameWnd
{
    CButton *button;
public:
    CWindow();
    ~CWindow();
    afx_msg void HandleButton();
    DECLARE_MESSAGE_MAP()
};

// Handler for the "Push me" button
void CWindow::HandleButton()
{
    int result;
    result=MessageBox("Is This\nmessage OK?",
        "Message Box",
        MB_ICONQUESTION | MB_YESNO);
    if (result==IDYES)
        Beep(1000,100);
    else
        Beep(200,100);
}

// The message map
BEGIN_MESSAGE_MAP(CWindow, CFrameWnd)
    ON_COMMAND(IDC_BUTTON, HandleButton)
END_MESSAGE_MAP()

// The InitInstance is called once
// when the application begins execution
BOOL CApp::InitInstance()
{
    m_pMainWnd = new CWindow();
    m_pMainWnd->ShowWindow(m_nCmdShow);
```

```
    m_pMainWnd->UpdateWindow();
    return TRUE;
}

// The window constructor
CWindow::CWindow()
{
    CRect r;

    // Create the window
    Create(NULL,
        "Dialog Tests",
        WS_OVERLAPPEDWINDOW,
        CRect(0,0,200,200));

    // Get the client rectangle
    GetClientRect(&r);
    r.InflateRect(-20,-20);

    // Create a button to activate the dialog
    button = new CButton();
    button->Create("Push me",
        WS_CHILD|WS_VISIBLE|BS_PUSHBUTTON,
        r,
        this,
        IDC_BUTTON);
}

// The window's destructor
CWindow::~CWindow()
{
    delete button;
}
```

Figure 7.1
A message box dialog

The code in Listing 7.1 creates a window that displays a push button labeled "Push Me." When you click that button it invokes the **HandleButton** function through the message map:

```
void CWindow::HandleButton()
{
    int result;

    result=MessageBox("Is this\nmessage OK?",
```

```
            "Message Box",
            MB_ICONQUESTION | MB_YESNO);
    if (result==IDYES)
        Beep(1000,100);
    else
        Beep(200,100);
}
```

This function creates a message box dialog and then responds to the value it returns.

The **MessageBox** function, which is a member function of the **CWnd** class, creates the message box (see the documentation for details). The first parameter specifies the message that it should display. The message can contain newline characters as demonstrated in the code, and the message box will parse them as expected. The second parameter is the title for the dialog box's window. The third parameter is used to customize the message box's behavior. The following constants are valid:

MB_ABORTRETRYIGNORE	Abort, Retry, and Ignore buttons displayed.
MB_APPLMODAL	The default – modal to application
MB_DEFBUTTON1	Makes the first button the default button
MB_DEFBUTTON2	Makes the second button the default button
MB_DEFBUTTON3	Makes the third button the default button
MB_ICONEXCLAMATION	Includes an exclamation icon ("!")
MB_ICONINFORMATION	Includes an information icon ("i")
MB_ICONQUESTION	Includes a question icon ("?")
MB_ICONSTOP	Includes a stop sign icon.
MB_OK	Displays an OK button
MB_OKCANCEL	Displays OK and Cancel buttons
MB_RETRYCANCEL	Displays Retry and Cancel buttons
MB_SYSTEMMODAL	Use with caution. Makes dialog system modal
MB_YESNO	Displays Yes and No buttons
MB_YESNOCANCEL	Displays Yes, No, and Cancel buttons

In the example in Listing 7.1, the MB_YESNO and MB_ICONQUESTION constants are combined so that the message box displays a question mark icon and **Yes** and **No** buttons.

The message box returns an integer that specifies the user's action. The following constants are defined for the result:

IDABORT	Abort button
IDCANCEL	Cancel button
IDIGNORE	Ignore button
IDNO	No button
IDOK	OK button
IDRETRY	Retry button
IDYES	Yes button

In cases where the MB_OK style is used, you can ignore the result and simply proceed once the user has responded to the message by clicking on the OK button.

When the message box displays a question, you can use **if** statements or a **switch** statement to respond to the user appropriately.

Because the **MessageBox** function is a member of the **CWnd** class, you can use it only within functions that are members of a class derived from **CWnd**. When this is not the case, use the function **AfxMessageBox** to create the message box.

7.2 The File Open/Save Dialog

You will use the File Open/Save dialog whenever you need to ask the user for a file name in one of your applications. The dialog automatically handles the traversal of directories, the filtering of files in the current directory, and connections to network drives. Figures 7.2a and 7.2b show screen dumps of the File Open/Save dialog in action. Listing 7.2 shows you how to create and read the data from the File Open/Save dialog and how to extract the data from it when it returns.

Listing 7.2
The File Open/Save dialog.

```cpp
// filedlg.cpp

#include <afxwin.h>
#include <afxdlgs.h>
#include <strstrea.h>

#define IDC_BUTTON 100

// Define filters for use with the File Dialog
const char fileDialogFilter[] =
    "C++ Files (*.cpp)|*.cpp|Header Files\
(*.h)|*.h|Resource Files (*.rc)|*.rc||";
const char fileDialogExt[] = "cpp";

// Declare the application class
class CApp : public CWinApp
{
public:
    virtual BOOL InitInstance();
};

// Create an instance of the application class
CApp App;

// Declare the window class
class CWindow : public CFrameWnd
{
    CButton *button;
public:
    CWindow();
    ~CWindow();
    afx_msg void HandleButton();
    DECLARE_MESSAGE_MAP()
};
```

```
// Handler for the "Push me" button
// creates a file dialog
void CWindow::HandleButton()
{
    char s[200];
    ostrstream ostr( s, 200 );

    CFileDialog fileDialog( TRUE,
        fileDialogExt, NULL,
        OFN_FILEMUSTEXIST, fileDialogFilter );

    if( fileDialog.DoModal() == IDOK )
    {
        ostr         << "Pathname: "
                     << fileDialog.GetPathName()
                     << endl
                     << "Filename: "
                     << fileDialog.GetFileName()
                     << endl
                     << "Extension: "
                     << fileDialog.GetFileExt()
                     << endl
                     << "File Title: "
                     << fileDialog.GetFileTitle()
                     << endl
                     << ends;

        MessageBox( s,
            "Dialog Information",
            MB_ICONINFORMATION );
    }
}

// The message map
BEGIN_MESSAGE_MAP(CWindow, CFrameWnd)
    ON_COMMAND(IDC_BUTTON, HandleButton)
END_MESSAGE_MAP()

// The InitInstance is called once
// when the application begins execution
BOOL CApp::InitInstance()
{
    m_pMainWnd = new CWindow();
    m_pMainWnd->ShowWindow(m_nCmdShow);
    m_pMainWnd->UpdateWindow();
    return TRUE;
}

// The window constructor
CWindow::CWindow()
{
    CRect r;

    // Create the window
    Create(NULL,
```

This book is continuously updated. See http://www.iftech.com/mfc

```
        "Dialog Tests",
        WS_OVERLAPPEDWINDOW,
        CRect(0,0,200,200));

    // Get the client rectangle
    GetClientRect(&r);
    r.InflateRect(-20,-20);

    // Create a button to activate the dialog
    button = new CButton();
    button->Create("Push me",
        WS_CHILD|WS_VISIBLE|BS_PUSHBUTTON,
        r,
        this,
        IDC_BUTTON);
}

// The window's destructor
CWindow::~CWindow()
{
    delete button;
}
```

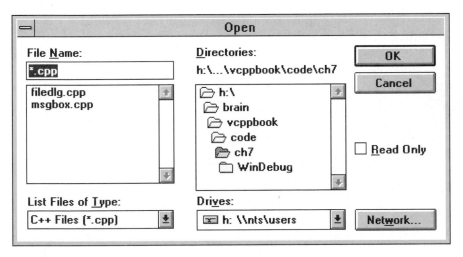

Figure 7.2a
The File Open/Save dialog

Note that you must include AFXDLGS.H when using this canned dialog and those that follow.

The general flow seen in Listing 7.2 is the same as that seen for the message box dialog in the previous section. When the user clicks the button in the application's main window, the code first calls a function that creates the dialog, passing it initial parameters to control its appearance and behavior. The code then displays the dialog by calling the **DoModal** function. This function exits once the user presses the OK or

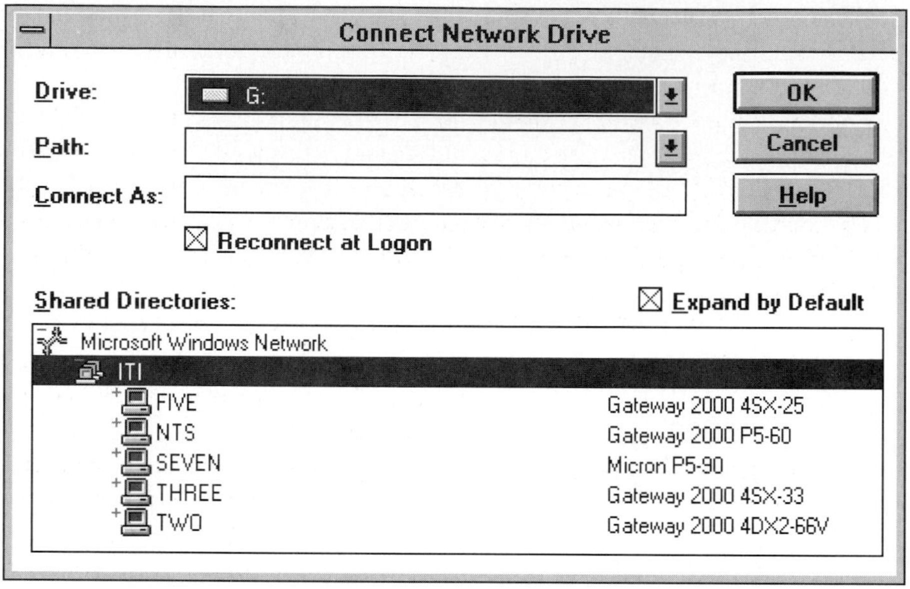

Figure 7.2b
The Network dialog available in the File Open/Save dialog

Cancel button. It returns an integer you can examine to determine which button was pressed. If the user chose a file and pressed OK, you can use several helper functions to examine the result of the user's interaction with the dialog.

The constructor for the **CFileDialog** class accepts six parameters when it is invoked (see the documentation for details). They are demonstrated in listing 7.2 and described below:

```
CFileDialog(BOOL bOpenFileDialog,
        LPCSTR lpszDefExt = NULL,
        LPCSTR lpszFileName = NULL,
        DWORD dwFlags =
            OFN_HIDEREADONLY |
            OFN_OVERWRITEPROMPT,
        LPCSTR lpszFilter = NULL,
        CWnd* pParentWnd = NULL);
```

bOpenFileDialog	TRUE for file open dialog, FALSE for file save dialog
lpszDefExt	Default extension for filenames entered without one
lpszFileName	Initial file name
dwFlags	Style flags
lpszFilter	Filters for "List of files by type" list
pParentWnd	Parent window

The first parameter is a Boolean that specifies whether the dialog is used for opening a file or saving a file. In Save mode, the dialog implements Save As behavior. The user can traverse the directory tree or enter a new file name. In Open mode, the list of files is filled and can be traversed to select a file.

The second parameter is the default file extension. If the user types a file name without an extension, this extension will be added automatically to the file name before the dialog returns it.

The third parameter is the initial file filter or name string. This string will be displayed in the file name box and will control the names visible in the name list below this box. If it is NULL, the first string in the filter list (the fifth parameter) is used.

The fourth parameter is a set of style flags that control the behavior of the dialog. The following flags are defined (see the OPENFILENAME structure description in the API documentation for more information):

OFN_ALLOWMULTISELECT	Allows multiple files to be selected
OFN_CREATEPROMPT	Prompts the user if file name typed does not exist; allows the dialog to be used for creating new file names
OFN_EXTENSIONDIFFERENT	The dialog will recognize when the user selects a file that does not have the default extension
OFN_FILEMUSTEXIST	The user must choose an existing file name
OFN_HIDEREADONLY	Hides the read-only check box
OFN_NOCHANGEDIR	Sets the current directory back to the one in effect when the dialog was invoked
OFN_NONETWORKBUTTON	Hides the Network button
OFN_NOREADONLYRETURN	Rejects read-only files
OFN_NOTESTFILECREATE	The dialog does not attempt to create a test file to check for errors
OFN_NOVALIDATE	Allows dialog to return invalid characters in the file name
OFN_OVERWRITEPROMPT	Displays an overwrite confirmation in save mode
OFN_PATHMUSTEXIST	Rejects non-existing path names
OFN_READONLY	The read-only check box is initially on
OFN_SHOWHELP	The dialog should display a help button

The fifth parameter is a filter string. In the code in Listing 7.2, both this string and the extension string are declared as constants, but they can also come in as **CString**s from a string resource. This filter string specifies the file types that should be shown in the **file type** list. The dialog uses the "|" character to parse the string into separate pieces and uses the "||" characters at the end of the string to mark the end of the chain.

The last parameter is the parent of the dialog.

Once the dialog has been created, you paint it on screen with a call to the **DoModal** function. When this function returns you receive an integer that is set to either IDOK or IDCANCEL. If it is IDCANCEL, the user dismissed the dialog with the **Cancel** button and you can ignore it. If it is IDOK, you will want to extract the file name chosen by the user. Use the five helper functions as shown in the code and listed below:

GetPathName	Full path name of the file
GetFileName	File name only, minus the extension
GetFileExt	Extension, minus the period
GetFileTitle	Title of the file for use as the title text for a window
GetReadOnlyPref	True if the user requested read-only access

If the appropriate style flags are set when you create the dialog, the dialog will automatically handle things such as potential file overwriting for you. There are also three virtual functions declared for the dialog that you can override if you want more control:

```
virtual UINT OnShareViolation(LPCSTR lpszPathName);
virtual BOOL OnFileNameOK();
virtual void OnLBSelChangedNotify(UINT nIDBox,
    UINT iCurSel, UINT nCode);
```

The **OnShareViolation** function is called on share violations and passes the full path name of the selected file to you. If you override the function, you can display a dialog informing the user of the problem or take more aggressive action. The **OnFileNameOK** function is called when the OK button is pressed but before the dialog is dismissed. If you override this function, it allows you to inspect the chosen name. Return TRUE if the name is OK or FALSE if the dialog needs to remain on screen. The **OnLBSelChangeNotify** function is a standard list box function. It gets called whenever the user changes the selection in one of the lists (for more information on lists see Chapter 9). If you override it, you can perform custom actions after each selection change.

As you can see, this dialog gives a tremendous amount of control during the simple act of file name selection. If you want to do nothing more than get a file name, however, it will do that too. Simply use the default style flags and call the **GetPathName** function when **DoModal** returns. Used in this way, the dialog requires only three lines of code to implement a File Open dialog.

This dialog encapsulates the behavior of the **GetOpenFileName** and **GetSaveFileName** functions in the 32-bit API. See the descriptions of those functions if you want to play with some of the more esoteric features of this dialog.

7.3 The Font Dialog

The font dialog allows the user to select a new font. The dialog inspects the fonts available on the system and displays them along with sizing and other information. It also allows the user to view font samples on the fly. Listing 7.3 contains a function demonstrating the creation of the dialog, and Figure 7.3 shows you how the dialog looks.

Listing 7.3
Invoking the font dialog and retrieving results. Substitute this function as a replacement for HandleButton in Listing 7.2.

```
void CWindow::HandleButton()
{
    // Create a font dialog using defaults.
```

```
        CFontDialog fontDialog;

        if( fontDialog.DoModal() == IDOK )
            MessageBox( fontDialog.GetFaceName(),
                "Dialog Information",
                MB_ICONINFORMATION );
    }
```

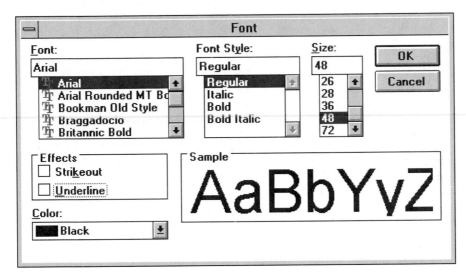

Figure 7.3
The font dialog

The font dialog is created using its constructor, which accepts four parameters (as described in the documentation):

```
CFontDialog(LPLOGFONT lplfInitial = NULL,
        DWORD dwFlags = CF_EFFECTS | CF_SCREENFONTS,
        CDC* pdcPrinter = NULL,
        CWnd* pParentWnd = NULL);
```

lplfInitial   The initial font chosen.
dwFlags   Style flags.
hdcPrinter   The CDC for a printer, if the dialog is being used to set a printer font (see Chapter 11 for more information).
pParentWnd   The parent window.

As shown in Listing 7.3, it is possible to pass no parameters to the constructor. The dialog will behave correctly because of the default parameters. Non-default parameters are needed only when you wish to do something special. The first parameter allows you to specify an initial font in the dialog; you pass in a structure that determines the font. You may recall from Chapter 3 that it takes 15 parameters to specify a particular font (see Chapter 11 for more information on this structure).

The second parameter contains style flags. The following flags can be used (see the CHOOSEFONT structure in the API documentation for more information):

CF_ANSIONLY	Only ANSI fonts are available
CF_APPLY	Displays an Apply button
CF_BOTH	Lists both printer and screen fonts
CF_EFFECTS	Effects selections should be available (strikeout, underline, etc.)
CF_FIXEDPITCHONLY	Only fixed-pitch fonts are available.
CF_FORCEFONTEXIST	Prompts the user if the chosen font does not exist.
CF_INITTOLOGFONTSTRUCT	Use the LOGFONT parameter passed into the constructor
CF_LIMITSIZE	Allow only sizes in the range specified
CF_NOOEMFONTS	Do not allow OEM fonts
CF_NOFACESEL	Do not allow font selections
CF_NOSIMULATIONS	Do not allow simulated fonts
CF_NOSTYLESEL	Do not allow style selections
CF_NOSIZESEL	Do not allow size selections
CF_NOVECTORFONTS	Do not allow vector fonts
CF_PRINTERFONTS	Only fonts supported by the specified printer are allowed
CF_SCALABLEONLY	Only scalable fonts are allowed
CF_SCREENFONTS	Only screen fonts are allowed
CF_SHOWHELP	Displays a help button
CF_TTONLY	Displays only True Type fonts
CF_USESTYLE	Use the supplied style information
CF_WYSIWYG	Only fonts available on both the screen and printer are allowed

The third parameter allows you to pass in a printer device context so that the dialog can determine which fonts the printer allows (see Chapter 11 for more information on Printer DCs). The fourth parameter is the parent.

When the dialog returns from the call to **DoModal**, you can see which font the user has selected by calling any or all of the following functions:

```
CString GetFaceName() const;
CString GetStyleName() const;
int GetSize() const;
COLORREF GetColor() const;
int GetWeight() const;
BOOL IsStrikeOut() const;
BOOL IsUnderline() const;
BOOL IsBold() const;
BOOL IsItalic() const;
```

Each of these functions returns the feature specified. The four Boolean functions return TRUE if their respective check box was selected. It is also possible to copy an entire LOGFONT structure from the m_lf public data member.

Two virtual functions are also available:

```
virtual void OnOK();
virtual void OnCancel();
```

You can create a derived class and override these functions to take special actions when the dialog's buttons are pressed.

The **CFontDialog** class encapsulates the **ChooseFont** function in the 32-bit API. See the description of this function if you wish to customize the behavior of this dialog.

7.4 The Color Dialog

The color dialog gives the user a standardized way to choose colors. You might use this dialog to choose pen colors in a drawing editor (see Chapter 11),or to choose such things as background and foreground colors in an application. This dialog is fairly simple compared to the prior two. Listing 7.4 demonstrates the code needed to use the dialog and Figure 7.4 shows it in action.

Listing 7.4
Code that creates a color editor.

```
void CWindow::HandleButton()
{
    char s[15];
    CColorDialog colorDialog;

    if( colorDialog.DoModal() == IDOK )
    {
        sprintf( s, "0x%x", colorDialog.GetColor() );
        MessageBox( s, "Dialog Information",
            MB_ICONINFORMATION );
    }
}
```

The constructor for the color dialog is shown below (and is described in the documentation):

```
CColorDialog(COLORREF clrInit = 0,
    DWORD dwFlags = 0,
    CWnd* pParentWnd = NULL);
```

clrInit   Initial color selection
dwFlags   Style flags
pParentWnd   Parent window

If a color should be initially selected in the dialog, the first parameter allows you to specify it. The style flags in the second parameter let you specify the behavior of the dialog as listed below:

CC_FULLOPEN	The dialog is initially displayed with the custom color palette visible
CC_PREVENTFULLOPEN	Prevent the user from using the custom color selection area
CC_RGBINIT	Causes the dialog to use the clrInit parameter
CC_SHOWHELP	Displays a help button

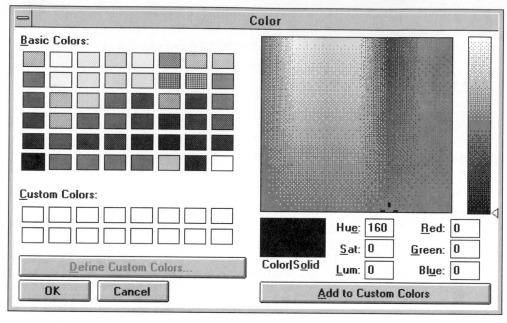

Figure 7.4
The color dialog

The third parameter is the parent window.

When the dialog returns from the **DoModal** function, you use the **GetColor** member function as shown to retrieve the color chosen by the user. **GetColor** returns a value of type COLORREF, which is a 32-bit integer value that contains the Red, Green, Blue (RGB) triplet for the color chosen. The COLORREF type is accepted by all functions that work with colors:

```
COLORREF GetColor() const;
```

Three virtual functions are available in classes that you derive from **CColorDialog**, as follows:

```
virtual void OnOK();
virtual void OnCancel();
virtual BOOL OnColorOK();
```

The **OnColorOK** function allows you to validate the color chosen by the user and display a message if there is a problem.

This dialog encapsulates the behavior of the **ChooseColor** function in the 32-bit API. See that function for more information on customization of this dialog.

7.5 The Print Dialog

The print dialog allows the user to choose a print range for the current document, but also contains a setup button that lets the user choose from available printers (along with options for the specific printer being used). Figures 7.5a, 7.5b, and 7.5c demonstrate the three different panes of this dialog. Listing 7.5 shows how to use the dialog in your code.

Listing 7.5
Code that creates a print dialog.

```
void CWindow::HandleButton()
{
    char s[30];
    CPrintDialog printDialog( FALSE,
        PD_PAGENUMS | PD_NOSELECTION );

    if( printDialog.DoModal() == IDOK )
    {
        sprintf( s, "Number of Copies: %d",
            printDialog.GetCopies() );
        MessageBox( s, "Dialog Information",
            MB_ICONINFORMATION );
    }
}
```

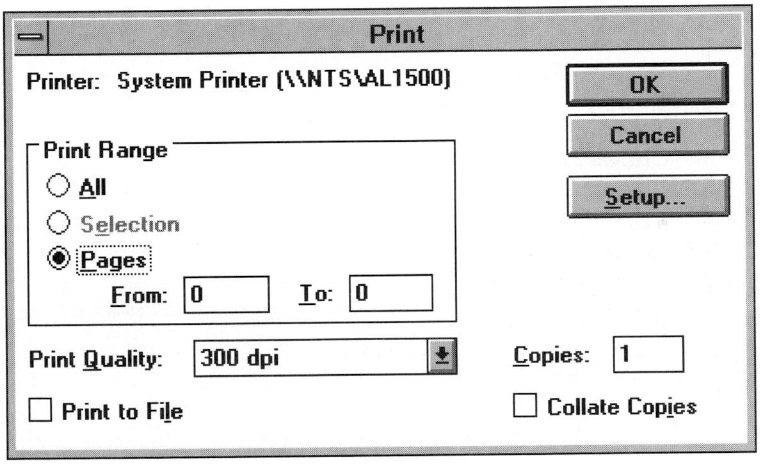

Figure 7.5a
The first pane of the print dialog

The constructor for the print dialog is shown below (and can also be found in the documentation):

```
CPrintDialog(BOOL bPrintSetupOnly,
    DWORD dwFlags = PD_ALLPAGES |
        PD_USEDEVMODECOPIES | PD_NOPAGENUMS|
        PD_HIDEPRINTTOFILE | PD_NOSELECTION,
    CWnd* pParentWnd = NULL);
```

The first parameter should be set to TRUE if you want the dialog to bypass the first pane shown in Figure 7.5a and go directly to the Setup pane. The second param-

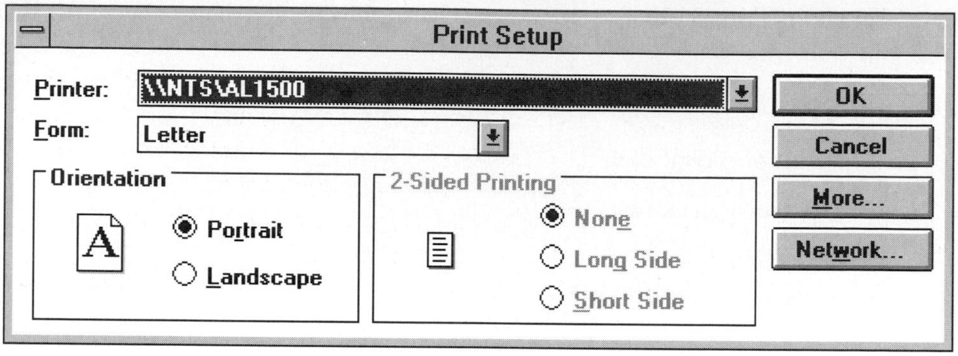

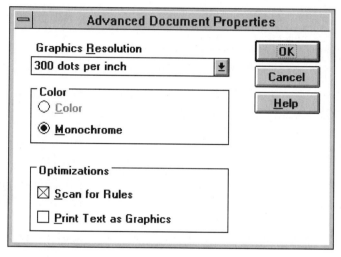

Figure 7.5b
The printer setup dialog

Figure 7.5c
Part two of the printer setup dialog

eter contains style flags as described below (see the PRINTDLG structure in the API documentation for more information):

PD_ALLPAGES	Sets the "all pages" radio button
PD_COLLATE	Checks the collate check box initially
PD_DISABLEPRINTTOFILE	Disables the "Print to file" check box
PD_NOPAGENUMS	Disables the page range portion of the dialog
PD_NOSELECTION	Disables the selection button
PD_NOWARNING	Eliminates "No default printer" warning dialog
PD_PAGENUMS	Causes the page range button to be initially on
PD_PRINTSETUP	Displays the setup pane initially to allow printer setup only

PD_PRINTTOFILE	Causes print-to-file check box to be set initially
PD_RETURNDC	Returns the device context for the selected printer
PD_RETURNDEFAULT	The dialog does not appear and default printer information is copied so that it is available
PD_RETURNIC	Returns an information context
PD_SELECTION	Causes the selection button to be set initially
PD_SHOWHELP	Shows the help button
PD_USEDEVMODECOPIES	Enables multiple copies field if the printer supports it

The third parameter is the parent window.

Once the **DoModal** function returns, the information gathered is available through the member functions listed below:

```
int GetCopies() const;
BOOL GetDefaults() const;
CString GetDeviceName() const;
LPDEVMODE GetDevMode() const;
CString GetDriverName() const;
int GetFromPage() const;
CString GetPortName() const;
HDC GetPrinterDC() const;
int GetToPage() const;
BOOL PrintCollate() const;
BOOL PrintSelection() const;
BOOL PrintAll() const;
BOOL PrintRange() const;
```

Most of these functions are self-explanatory. The functions to get the driver name, device name, port name, and printer DC are discussed along with printing in Chapter 11.

If you derive a class from **CPrintDialog** you can override the following functions:

```
virtual void OnOK();
virtual void OnCancel();
```

This class encapsulates the **PrinterDlg** function in the 32-bit API. For more information on customizing the printer dialog, see the description for **PrinterDlg** in the 32-bit API.

7.6 The Find/Replace Dialog

The Find/Replace dialog makes it easy for you to add Find/Replace capabilities to programs such as text editors. This dialog is unique because it is *modeless*. The dialog and the application can both accept events, with the dialog appearing to "float" above the application at all times. Listing 7.6 demonstrates the code required to use this dialog in a program and Figure 7.6 shows you what the dialog looks like to the user.

Listing 7.6
The Find/Replace dialog.

```
// finddlg.cpp

#include <afxwin.h>
#include <afxdlgs.h>
#include <strstrea.h>

#define IDC_BUTTON 100

// Declare the application class
class CApp : public CWinApp
{
public:
    virtual BOOL InitInstance();
};

// Create an instance of the application class
CApp App;

// Declare the window class
class CWindow : public CFrameWnd
{
    static UINT findMessage;
    CButton *button;
public:
    CWindow();
    ~CWindow();
    afx_msg void HandleButton();
    DECLARE_MESSAGE_MAP()
    afx_msg LONG FindHelper( UINT wParam,
        LONG lParam );
};

// Init find/replace static variables globally.
// findMessage is a Windows message constant
// used in the message map
UINT CWindow::findMessage = ::RegisterWindowMessage(
    FINDMSGSTRING );

void CWindow::HandleButton()
{
    CFindReplaceDialog *findReplaceDialog;

    button->EnableWindow(FALSE);
    findReplaceDialog = new CFindReplaceDialog;
    findReplaceDialog->Create( FALSE, "default" );
}

LONG CWindow::FindHelper( UINT wParam, LONG lParam )
{
    CFindReplaceDialog *findDialog =
        CFindReplaceDialog::GetNotifier(lParam);

    if( findDialog->IsTerminating() )
    {
        button->EnableWindow(TRUE);
    }
```

```
        else if( findDialog->FindNext() )
        {
            // Place search engine code here
            MessageBox( findDialog->GetFindString(),
                "Find String",
                MB_ICONINFORMATION );
        }
        else if( findDialog->ReplaceCurrent() )
        {
            // Place replace code here
            MessageBox( findDialog->GetReplaceString(),
                "Replace String",
                MB_ICONINFORMATION );
        }
        else if( findDialog->ReplaceAll() )
        {
            // Place global find/replace code here
            MessageBox( findDialog->GetReplaceString(),
                "Replace All",
                MB_ICONINFORMATION );
        }
        return 0;
}

// The message map
BEGIN_MESSAGE_MAP(CWindow, CFrameWnd)
    ON_COMMAND(IDC_BUTTON, HandleButton)
    ON_REGISTERED_MESSAGE( findMessage, FindHelper )
END_MESSAGE_MAP()

// The InitInstance is called once
// when the application begins execution
BOOL CApp::InitInstance()
{
    m_pMainWnd = new CWindow();
    m_pMainWnd->ShowWindow(m_nCmdShow);
    m_pMainWnd->UpdateWindow();
    return TRUE;
}

// The window constructor
CWindow::CWindow()
{
    CRect r;

    // Create the window
    Create(NULL,
        "Dialog Tests",
        WS_OVERLAPPEDWINDOW,
        CRect(0,0,200,200));

    // Get the client rectangle
    GetClientRect(&r);
    r.InflateRect(-20,-20);

    // Create a button to activate the dialog
```

```
    button = new CButton();
    button->Create("Push me",
        WS_CHILD|WS_VISIBLE|BS_PUSHBUTTON,
        r,
        this,
        IDC_BUTTON);
}

// The window's destructor
CWindow::~CWindow()
{
    delete button;
}
```

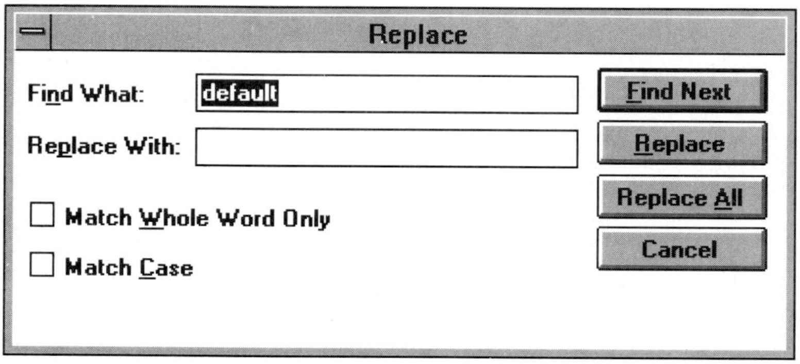

Figure 7.6
The Find/Replace dialog

You can see four separate pieces in Listing 7.6: The **HandleButton** function that creates the dialog, a global declaration for the static member **findMessage**, a "helper" function named **FindHelper**, and a message map that contains the unusual ON_REGISTERED_MESSAGE entry. The message map entry calls the find helper function.

The **HandleButton** function creates and displays the dialog. However, it does not use the **DoModal** function we've seen in the previous examples. Creation here is a two-step process because the find dialog is *modeless*. Once the dialog is created, it will remain on the screen in harmony with the application until it is destroyed. Note that, because the dialog is modeless, the initiating push button must be disabled using the **EnableWindow** function once the user presses it. If it were not disabled, it would be possible to create two or more find dialogs on the screen simultaneously.

The **Create** function for the find dialog looks like this:

```
BOOL Create(BOOL bFindDialogOnly,
        LPCSTR lpszFindWhat,
        LPCSTR lpszReplaceWith  = NULL,
        DWORD dwFlags = FR_DOWN,
        CWnd* pParentWnd = NULL);
```

bFindDialogOnly   Set to TRUE for a find-only dialog

lpszFindWhat	The initial search string
lpszReplaceWith	The initial replacement string
dwFlags	Style flags
pParentWnd	The parent window

The first parameter controls whether the dialog acts as a Find dialog or a Find/Replace dialog. The second and third parameters act as initial values for the Find and Replace text strings. The fourth parameter contains style flags, as described below (see the FINDREPLACE structure in the API documentation for more information):

FR_DOWN	The down check box is initially checked
FR_FINDNEXT	Instructs the dialog to perform a find next
FR_HIDEUPDOWN	Hides the direction check box
FR_HIDEMATCHCASE	Hides the match case check box
FR_HIDEWHOLEWORD	Hides the whole word check box
FR_MATCHCASE	Initially checks the match case check box
FR_NOMATCHCASE	The match case button is disabled
FR_NOUPDOWN	The up/down button is disabled
FR_NOWHOLEWORD	The whole word button is disabled
FR_REPLACE	Instructs the dialog to perform a replace
FR_REPLACEALL	Instructs the dialog to perform a replace all
FR_SHOWHELP	Shows the help button
FR_WHOLEWORD	The whole word button is initially checked

The fifth parameter is the parent.

There is also a helper function. This function is called each time the user clicks any of the buttons in the dialog.

If the user clicks the Cancel button, the dialog will terminate automatically. In response to the Cancel button, the code in Listing 7.6 simply enables the "Push Me" button so the dialog can be created again. If it is not terminating, you need to respond appropriately. What you would normally do is place your search engine at the designated place and search through the text. In order to decide how to search, and what to search for, you can use the following functions:

```
BOOL FindNext();
static CFindReplaceDialog* PASCAL GetNotifier( LPARAM lParam );
CString GetFindString();
CString GetReplaceString();
BOOL IsTerminating() const;
BOOL MatchCase();
BOOL MatchWholeWord();
BOOL ReplaceAll();
BOOL ReplaceCurrent();
BOOL SearchDown();
```

Each of the functions returns the indicated value. You decide whether the user clicked the Find Next, Replace, or Replace All buttons by calling the appropriate function and then extracting the strings from the dialog as shown in the code.

When you run the code shown in Listing 7.6, you will find that the dialog appears along with the application window and both can accept events. For example, you can move and minimize the application window even though the dialog is visible (this is not the case for the modal dialogs seen above). When you press one of the buttons on the Find dialog, a message box will appear. The message box is modal, so the application will stall until you respond to it. The Find dialog will remain on the screen until the user cancels it.

You might be looking at this code and asking yourself, "Why is this code for a modeless dialog so much more complicated than a modal dialog?" The program contains the helper function, the static global variable handling message registration, a message map entry, and all the normal creation code. Briefly, here is what's happening:

The dialog and the application window need to accept events as equal partners. However, the dialog needs a way to communicate back to the application when one of its buttons is pressed. To do this, it sends a message that can be detected by the application. This is not a standard Windows message: It is a custom message created for the Find dialog. The application registers to receive that custom message using the static member **findMessage** and it places a message handler for the message in its message map. The **FindHelper** function is the function that responds to the messages received from the Find dialog.

Once this mechanism is in place, the Find dialog and the application can share the user's attention. When the user clicks a Find dialog button, the dialog sends a message to the application and the application handles the user's request. Thus the application and the dialog can share the screen.

The **CFindDialog** function encapsulates the behavior of the **FindText** and **ReplaceText** functions in the 32-bit API. Read the descriptions of these functions if you wish to customize the behavior of this dialog.

7.7 Conclusion

The dialogs demonstrated in this chapter are used extensively inside the AppWizard framework that you will learn about in Part 3. We will also use several of them in the next chapter to implement a simple text editor.

EDIT CONTROLS AND EDITORS

This chapter demonstrates how to use the **CEdit** control in both its single-line and multi-line modes. We first used the **CEdit** control in its single line mode in Chapter 5. Here, we will exercise its capabilities much more thoroughly so you are aware of its many features. By the end of this chapter you will see how to use the edit control, resource files from Chapter 6, and canned dialogs from Chapter 7 to create a simple but complete text editor. In Part 3 you will see how to create the same editor using **CEdit-View** class and the AppWizard.

8.1 Using the CEdit Control in Single-Line Mode

We used the **CEdit** control for the first time in Chapter 5, where we exercised its single-line mode to retrieve both integer and real values from the user. In its single-line mode, there are several styles and functions you can use to customize the behavior of the edit control: ES_AUTOHSCROLL and **LimitText** are common, for example. You can also set a string into the control using **SetDlgItemText** or **SetDlgItemInt** and retrieve the text with the two corresponding **Get** functions as seen in Chapter 5. The **Set** and **Get** functions are inherited from the **CWnd** class.

Listing 8.1 demonstrates how to use the **CEdit** control in single-line mode to get a name from the user. Here it is done "by hand" as demonstrated in Chapter 5, but as you saw in Chapter 6 it is also easy to create these same controls with the dialog editor (in this case, the **GetDlgItem** function is useful for converting the control's ID in the dialog into an actual **CEdit** pointer so you can call **CEdit** member functions). In Listing 8.1, the maximum length of the name that the user can enter is limited to 20 characters with the **LimitText** member function of the **CEdit** control.

Listing 8.1
Demonstration of a **CEdit** control

```
// limit.cpp
#include <afxwin.h>
```

```
const int EDIT=100;

// Declare the application class
class CApp : public CWinApp
{
public:
    virtual BOOL InitInstance();
};

// Create an instance of the application class
CApp App;

// Declare the main window class
class CWindow : public CFrameWnd
{
    CStatic* cs;
    CEdit *edit;
public:
    CWindow();
};

// The InitInstance function is called each
// time the application first executes.
BOOL CApp::InitInstance()
{
    m_pMainWnd = new CWindow();
    m_pMainWnd->ShowWindow(m_nCmdShow);
    m_pMainWnd->UpdateWindow();
    return TRUE;
}

// The constructor for the window class
CWindow::CWindow()
{
    // Create the window itself
    Create(NULL,
        "CEdit Demo",
        WS_OVERLAPPEDWINDOW,
        CRect(0,0,200,60));
    // Create a static label
    cs = new CStatic();
    cs->Create("Last Name:",
        WS_CHILD|WS_VISIBLE|SS_LEFT,
        CRect(0,4,80,40),
        this);
    edit = new CEdit();
    edit->Create(
        WS_CHILD|WS_VISIBLE|WS_BORDER|
        ES_AUTOHSCROLL,
        CRect(90,2,190,27),
        this, EDIT);
    edit->LimitText(20);
}
```

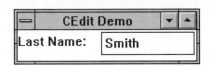

Figure 8.1
Screen Dump from Listing 8.1

Listing 8.1 uses both a **CStatic** and a **CEdit** control to create a window like the one shown in Figure 8.1. Note that when the program creates the **CEdit** control in the window's constructor, the code specifies the ES_AUTOHSCROLL style. This style allows the control to scroll horizontally. Without this style, the control limits the string length to the maximum size of the edit area on the screen. With ES_AUTOHSCROLL specified, the control scrolls as the cursor approaches the last visible character, giving the control the perception of nearly infinite length. You can then constrain the length, if you so choose, with the **LimitText** function, you might want to do this when the data the user enters has to fit inside a specific field in a database.

The **CEdit** control has a number of specialized styles that control its behavior. In code like that shown in Listing 8.1, you set these styles in the control's **Create** function. When working with the control in the dialog editor demonstrated in Chapter 6, you set the styles in the Property dialog for the control. Those styles that are applicable when working in single-line edit mode appear in the following list:

ES_AUTOHSCROLL	Allows the control to accept characters beyond the visible length of the control
ES_CENTER	Causes the control to center the entered text
ES_LEFT	Causes the control to left-justify the entered text
ES_LOWERCASE	Causes the control to convert all entered text to lower case
ES_NOHIDESEL	Causes the control to continue showing selected text even if it does not have focus
ES_OEMCONVERT	Causes the control to convert characters between ANSI and OEM character sets
ES_PASSWORD	Causes the control to display any entered character as a "*"
ES_RIGHT	Causes the control to right justify the entered text
ES_UPPERCASE	Causes the control to convert all entered text to upper case
ES_READONLY	Allows the user to view and scroll text in the edit control, but not to modify it

You should experiment with these styles by modifying the **CEdit** control's **Create** function in Listing 8.1.

The **CEdit** control also has a number of member functions that let you tune the behavior of the control. Several of the more interesting and useful are listed below for a **CEdit** control used in single-line mode. See the MFC documentation for a complete list:

GetModify	Returns TRUE if the user has modified control's text
SetReadOnly	Lets you flip the read-only state of the control

GetSel	Returns the starting and ending index of the selected text
LimitText	Sets the maximum number of characters the control will accept
LineLength	Returns the number of characters in the control
ReplaceSel	Deletes the selected text and inserts the specified text
SetPasswordChar	Lets the programmer set a specific password character (see the ES_PASSWORD style)
SetSel	Lets the programmer select a specific range of characters
Undo	Undoes the last operation on the control
Clear	Deletes the selected text
Copy	Copies any selected text to the clipboard
Cut	Deletes the selected text and copies it to the clipboard
Paste	Inserts the contents of the clipboard into the control (if it is text)

8.2   Using the CEdit Control in Multi-Line Mode

There are two behaviors for the **CEdit** control: single-line and multi-line. You can see the latter when you switch the control to multi-line mode by using the ES_MULTILINE style in the **Create** function. By doing so, you are essentially creating a complete single-font text editor. Listing 8.2 creates a multi-line edit control you can use for experimentation.

Listing 8.2
Creating a multi-line edit control

```
// multi.cpp

#include <afxwin.h>

const int EDIT=100;

// Declare the application class
class CApp : public CWinApp
{
public:
    virtual BOOL InitInstance();
};

// Create an instance of the application class
CApp App;

// Declare the main window class
class CWindow : public CFrameWnd
{
    CEdit *edit;
public:
    CWindow();
};
```

136

```
// The InitInstance function is called each
// time the application first executes.
BOOL CApp::InitInstance()
{
    m_pMainWnd = new CWindow();
    m_pMainWnd->ShowWindow(m_nCmdShow);
    m_pMainWnd->UpdateWindow();
    return TRUE;
}

// The constructor for the window class
CWindow::CWindow()
{
    // Create the window itself
    Create(NULL,
        "CEdit Demo",
        WS_OVERLAPPEDWINDOW,
        CRect(0,0,260,260));
    // Create a multi-line edit control
    edit = new CEdit();
    edit->Create(
        WS_CHILD|WS_VISIBLE|WS_BORDER|
        ES_MULTILINE|ES_AUTOVSCROLL,
        CRect(0, 0, 200, 200),
        this, EDIT);
}
```

In Listing 8.2 the ES_MULTILINE style causes the control to switch to multi-line edit mode. The lack of the ES_AUTOHSCROLL style causes the control to word wrap. If the ES_AUTOHSCROLL style is specified, then the control scrolls horizontally instead of word wrapping.

By browsing through the MFC documentation for **CEdit** you will find a number of useful functions that are activated in multi-line mode:

GetLineCount	Gets the number of lines
GetHandle	Gets a handle to a block of memory containing the current document
SetHandle	Sets the current document in the edit control to the handle passed
FmtLines	Handles soft line-breaks
LineIndex	Returns the starting character number of the given line
SetRect	Resets the formatting rectangle and reformats
SetRectNP	Resets the formatting rectangle without reformatting
SetTabStops	Sets custom tab stops
CanUndo	Indicates if undo is currently possible
GetModify	Indicates that the contents have been modified
SetModify	Sets modification flag
GetRect	Returns the current formatting rectangle

GetSel	Returns the beginning and ending character of the current selection
GetLine	Gets the specified line of text
EmptyUndoBuffer	Clears the undo flag
LimitText	Sets the maximum size of document
LineFromChar	Determines the line number of the specified character index
LineLength	Returns the number of characters in the specified line
LineScroll	Scrolls the number of lines specified up or down
ReplaceSel	Replaces the selected text with the specified string
SetSel	Sets the selected text.
Undo	Undoes the last operation
Clear	Deletes the selected text
Copy	Copies the selected text to the clipboard
Cut	Cuts the selected text to the clipboard
Paste	Pastes the clipboard's contents at the selection point
SetReadOnly	Browse only
GetFirstVisibleLine	Returns the line number of the top line in the control

The **CEdit** control uses a fairly simple data structure to hold the text. Essentially, the entire document is stored in one long character string as shown in Figure 8.2. Lines in a multi-line edit control are separated by '\n' characters embedded in the string. The **CEdit** control keeps track of the starting point of each line and can therefore translate between character indexes and line numbers very easily. When you use the **GetHandle** function, the control returns a handle that points to the text string it is holding (a handle is a pointer to a pointer). You can then work through the string as you would with any other array of characters. The code fragment below demonstrates the process:

```
PSTR stringPointer;
HANDLE stringHandle;
UINT len;

stringHandle = edit.GetHandle();
len = edit.GetWindowTextLength();
stringPointer = (PSTR)::LocalLock(stringHandle);
// Use stringPointer like any
// other string pointer. Unlock the
// handle when you are done.
::LocalUnlock(stringHandle);
```

The locking and unlocking functions come from the 32-bit API and are used to hold a memory block pointed to by a handle at a fixed memory location. The memory manager can, at its discretion, move blocks of memory pointed to by a handle to create larger contiguous blocks on the heap. While a handle is locked, the memory block remains at a fixed position and you can therefore safely reference it through a direct pointer.

The other way to reference data in an edit control is line by line. The **GetLine** function retrieves a copy of the specified line from the edit control.

138

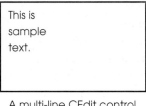

A multi-line CEdit control

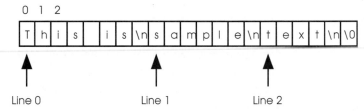

Line 0   Line 1   Line 2

Figure 8.2
The edit control maintains the current document in a normal text string

8.3 Designing a Simple Text Editor

In this section we will develop a complete text editor application. Not only will this section demonstrate most of the features of the **CEdit** control when used in its multi-line mode, but it will also allow you to see how all the different pieces described in the previous chapters fit together to create a complete application. Although we will use a text editor as the example in this section, many of the concepts described here apply to any type of application that you may want to create. For example, the editor uses a complete menu system, modal and modeless dialogs, the clipboard, the file system, and the command line–features that you will use in every application you build. We have chosen an editor as the sample application because it is something that everyone can relate to and understand immediately.

It is also interesting to develop a complete editor application so you can contrast the code you develop here with code you create in Part 3. As it turns out, you will see in Part 3 that you can create an editor nearly equivalent to the one demonstrated in this section without writing a single line of code. All of the functionality described in detail here actually already exists in the **CEditView** class, and you can access that code transparently using the AppWizard. If you are the sort of person who likes to know what is going on "behind the scenes," use this section to enhance your knowledge. If you are not, then look at Part 3.

In this section we want to create a text editor similar to the Notepad application shipped with Windows. Using Notepad as a starting point it is easy to come up with a list of requirements. The editor should be able to:

- Open existing files
- Create new files

- Save the current file to its original name or a new name
- Handle all the normal clipboard functions
- Find a string

From this list of features comes the design for the menu structure. The menu items required to implement the desired features are listed below:

File
    New
    Open
    Save
    Save as
    Exit
Edit
    Undo
    Cut
    Copy
    Paste
    Delete
Search
    Find
    Find Next
Help
    About

To handle all these menu options we will need to use several dialogs. The Open, Save, and Save As options in the file menu can all use the canned Open/Save dialog. Find and Find Next can use the standard modeless find dialog. The About dialog will use a custom dialog built with the dialog editor.

8.4 Creating the Editor Application

This editor application consists of a menu bar and a **CEdit** control that fills the rest of the application window. The first steps to take in creating the text editor application are to set up the **CEdit** control in a window, make sure it is re-sizing and accepting input correctly, and create the menus. The code in Listing 8.3 accomplishes this. It combines Listing 8.2 with the menu-loading concepts from Chapter 6.

To create the menus for this application, use the menu editor described in Chapter 6. Create the **File**, **Edit**, **Search,** and **Help** menus shown in the previous section using the same techniques you learned in Section 6.4. Add appropriate mnemonics and also create several accelerators as described in Section 6.5 and shown in Figure 8.3. Name the resource script SCRIPT.RC. When you are done, *use a text editor* to open SCRIPT.RC as a normal text file and look at its contents. Listing 8.4 contains a resource script that describes the menu bar and its accelerators. If you like you can tune your menu bar, using the resource editor, until it matches the description shown in Listing 8.4.

Listing 8.3
Code that creates the CEdit control and the menu bar.

```
// ed1.cpp - a simple editor with
// non-functional menus and a resizing edit area

#include <afxwin.h>
#include <afxdlgs.h>

#define IDC_EDIT          500

// Define the application object class
class CEditApp : public CWinApp
{
public:
    virtual BOOL InitInstance();
};

// Define the edit window class
class CEditWindow : public CFrameWnd
{
private:
    CEdit m_edit;
public:
    CEditWindow();
protected:
    afx_msg void OnSize( UINT nType, int cx,
        int cy );
    DECLARE_MESSAGE_MAP()
};

// Main application object.
CEditApp editApp;

// constructor for the CEditWindow
CEditWindow::CEditWindow()
{
    CRect rect;

    LoadAccelTable("MainAccelTable");
    Create( NULL, "Ed1", WS_OVERLAPPEDWINDOW,
        rectDefault, NULL, "MainMenu" );

    // Initialize the CEditWindow's CEdit object
    GetClientRect(&rect);
    m_edit.Create(WS_BORDER | WS_HSCROLL |
        WS_VISIBLE | WS_VSCROLL |
        ES_AUTOHSCROLL | ES_AUTOVSCROLL |
        ES_MULTILINE | ES_NOHIDESEL,
        rect, this, IDC_EDIT);
}

// OnSize - handles the resizing of the edit window
void CEditWindow::OnSize( UINT nFlags, int cx,
```

```
        int cy )
{
    CRect rc;
    GetClientRect(&rc);
    m_edit.MoveWindow(rc);
}

// InitInstance - Initialize the CEditApp
// m_pMainWnd data member
BOOL CEditApp::InitInstance()
{
    m_pMainWnd = new CEditWindow();
    m_pMainWnd -> ShowWindow( m_nCmdShow );
    m_pMainWnd -> UpdateWindow();
    return( TRUE );
}

BEGIN_MESSAGE_MAP( CEditWindow, CFrameWnd )
    ON_WM_SIZE()
END_MESSAGE_MAP()
```

Listing 8.4
Portions of the SCRIPT.RC file for the editor.

```
MainMenu MENU DISCARDABLE
BEGIN
    POPUP "&File"
    BEGIN
        MENUITEM "&New",                    IDM_FILE_NEW
        MENUITEM "&Open...\tCtrl+O",         IDM_FILE_OPEN
        MENUITEM "&Save\tCtrl+S",            IDM_FILE_SAVE
        MENUITEM "Save &As...",              IDM_FILE_SAVEAS
        MENUITEM SEPARATOR
        MENUITEM "E&xit",                    IDM_FILE_EXIT
    END
    POPUP "&Edit"
    BEGIN
        MENUITEM "&Undo\tCtrl+Z",            IDM_EDIT_UNDO
        MENUITEM SEPARATOR
        MENUITEM "Cu&t\tCtrl+X",             IDM_EDIT_CUT
        MENUITEM "&Copy\tCtrl+C",            IDM_EDIT_COPY
        MENUITEM "&Paste\tCtrl+V",           IDM_EDIT_PASTE
        MENUITEM "&Delete\tDel",             IDM_EDIT_DELETE
    END
    POPUP "&Search"
    BEGIN
        MENUITEM "&Find...\tCtrl+F",         IDM_SEARCH_FIND
        MENUITEM "Find &Next\tCtrl+N",       IDM_SEARCH_FINDNEXT
    END
    POPUP "&Help"
    BEGIN
        MENUITEM "&About Ed...\tF1",         IDM_HELP_ABOUTED
    END
```

```
END

MainAccelTable ACCELERATORS DISCARDABLE
BEGIN
    "C",          IDM_EDIT_COPY,          VIRTKEY, CONTROL, NOINVERT
    "F",          IDM_SEARCH_FIND,        VIRTKEY, CONTROL, NOINVERT
    "N",          IDM_SEARCH_FINDNEXT,    VIRTKEY, CONTROL, NOINVERT
    "O",          IDM_FILE_OPEN,          VIRTKEY, CONTROL, NOINVERT
    "S",          IDM_FILE_SAVE,          VIRTKEY, CONTROL, NOINVERT
    "V",          IDM_EDIT_PASTE,         VIRTKEY, CONTROL, NOINVERT
    VK_BACK,      IDM_EDIT_UNDO,          VIRTKEY, ALT, NOINVERT
    VK_DELETE,    IDM_EDIT_DELETE,        VIRTKEY, NOINVERT
    VK_DELETE,    IDM_EDIT_CUT,           VIRTKEY, SHIFT, NOINVERT
    VK_F1,        IDM_HELP_ABOUTED,       VIRTKEY, NOINVERT
    VK_INSERT,    IDM_EDIT_COPY,          VIRTKEY, CONTROL, NOINVERT
    VK_INSERT,    IDM_EDIT_PASTE,         VIRTKEY, SHIFT, NOINVERT
    "X",          IDM_EDIT_CUT,           VIRTKEY, CONTROL, NOINVERT
    "Z",          IDM_EDIT_UNDO,          VIRTKEY, CONTROL, NOINVERT
END
```

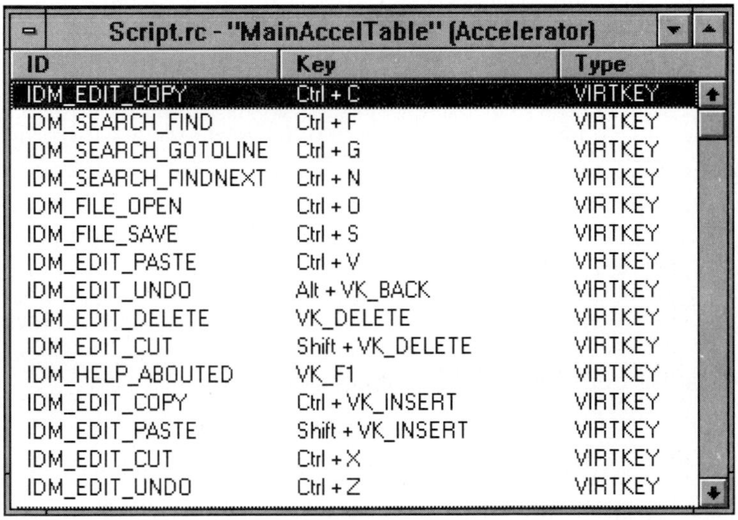
Script.rc - "MainAccelTable" (Accelerator)

ID	Key	Type
IDM_EDIT_COPY	Ctrl + C	VIRTKEY
IDM_SEARCH_FIND	Ctrl + F	VIRTKEY
IDM_SEARCH_GOTOLINE	Ctrl + G	VIRTKEY
IDM_SEARCH_FINDNEXT	Ctrl + N	VIRTKEY
IDM_FILE_OPEN	Ctrl + O	VIRTKEY
IDM_FILE_SAVE	Ctrl + S	VIRTKEY
IDM_EDIT_PASTE	Ctrl + V	VIRTKEY
IDM_EDIT_UNDO	Alt + VK_BACK	VIRTKEY
IDM_EDIT_DELETE	VK_DELETE	VIRTKEY
IDM_EDIT_CUT	Shift + VK_DELETE	VIRTKEY
IDM_HELP_ABOUTED	VK_F1	VIRTKEY
IDM_EDIT_COPY	Ctrl + VK_INSERT	VIRTKEY
IDM_EDIT_PASTE	Shift + VK_INSERT	VIRTKEY
IDM_EDIT_CUT	Ctrl + X	VIRTKEY
IDM_EDIT_UNDO	Ctrl + Z	VIRTKEY

Figure 8.3
The accelerator table for the editor

When you run the program in Listing 8.3, you will see an application like the one shown in Figure 8.4. You will find that the editor itself accepts input, scrolls, deletes text, and so on. The window re-sizes and iconifies properly. The editor's menu system works but none of the options do anything. You have written a surprisingly small amount of code to create this much functionality.

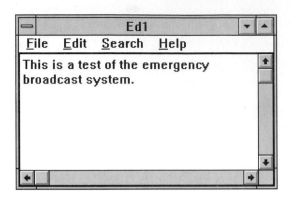

Figure 8.4
The editor in use

8.5 Stubbing in the Menu Handlers

When you are creating your own applications it is beneficial to be able to show a working prototype to potential users very early in the product's life cycle. In the preceeding section we saw that you can implement the complete menu structure very quickly using the menu resource editor. The next step is to create the message map for the menu items and wire in all the different dialog boxes and stubs for the different menu items. Once you have completed this step, users can try out the program—if a menu item should generate a canned dialog then the dialog appears. Otherwise the user sees a simple message box. As you implement the different features you remove the message box stubs and work in the actual code. The program in Listing 8.5 contains the stubbed version of the editor.

Listing 8.5
The stubbed editor containing code that presents all of the dialogs.

```
// ed2.cpp - a simple editor with dialogs
// and stubbed menus and a resizing edit area

#include <afxwin.h>
#include <afxdlgs.h>
#include "resource.h" // resource constants

#define IDC_EDIT              500

// Define filters for use with the File Dialog
const char fileDialogFilter[] =
    "C++ Files (*.cpp)|*.cpp|Header Files (*.h)|*.h|\
Resource Files (*.rc)|*.rc||";
const char fileDialogExt[] = "cpp";

// Define the application object class
class CEditApp : public CWinApp
{
public:
```

```
        virtual BOOL InitInstance();
};

// Define the edit window class
class CEditWindow : public CFrameWnd
{
private:
    static UINT findMessage;
    static UINT gotoLineMessage;
    CEdit m_edit;
public:
    CEditWindow();
    void SaveChanges();
protected:
    afx_msg void OnNew();
    afx_msg void OnOpen();
    afx_msg void OnSave();
    afx_msg void OnSaveAs();
    afx_msg void OnExit();
    afx_msg void OnUndo();
    afx_msg void OnCut();
    afx_msg void OnCopy();
    afx_msg void OnPaste();
    afx_msg void OnDelete();
    afx_msg void OnFind();
    afx_msg void OnFindNext();
    afx_msg LONG FindHelper( UINT wParam,
        LONG lParam );
    afx_msg void OnAbout();
    afx_msg void OnSize( UINT nType, int cx,
        int cy );

    DECLARE_MESSAGE_MAP()
};

// Main application object.
CEditApp editApp;

//-------- Main Message Map -----------//

BEGIN_MESSAGE_MAP( CEditWindow, CFrameWnd )
    ON_COMMAND( IDM_FILE_NEW, OnNew )
    ON_COMMAND( IDM_FILE_OPEN, OnOpen )
    ON_COMMAND( IDM_FILE_SAVE, OnSave )
    ON_COMMAND( IDM_FILE_SAVEAS, OnSaveAs )
    ON_COMMAND( IDM_FILE_EXIT, OnExit )
    ON_COMMAND( IDM_EDIT_UNDO, OnUndo )
    ON_COMMAND( IDM_EDIT_CUT, OnCut )
    ON_COMMAND( IDM_EDIT_COPY, OnCopy )
    ON_COMMAND( IDM_EDIT_PASTE, OnPaste )
    ON_COMMAND( IDM_EDIT_DELETE, OnDelete )
    ON_COMMAND( IDM_SEARCH_FIND, OnFind )
    ON_REGISTERED_MESSAGE( findMessage, FindHelper )
    ON_COMMAND( IDM_SEARCH_FINDNEXT, OnFindNext )
    ON_COMMAND( IDM_HELP_ABOUTED, OnAbout )
    ON_WM_SIZE()
```

```
END_MESSAGE_MAP()

// Initialize message variables
UINT CEditWindow::findMessage =
    ::RegisterWindowMessage( FINDMSGSTRING );
CFindReplaceDialog *findReplaceDialog = NULL;

// constructor for the CEditWindow
CEditWindow::CEditWindow()
{
    CRect rect;

    LoadAccelTable("MainAccelTable");
    Create( NULL, "Ed2", WS_OVERLAPPEDWINDOW,
        rectDefault, NULL, "MainMenu" );

    // Initialize the CEditWindow's CEdit object
    GetClientRect(&rect);
    m_edit.Create(WS_BORDER | WS_HSCROLL |
        WS_VISIBLE | WS_VSCROLL |
        ES_AUTOHSCROLL | ES_AUTOVSCROLL |
        ES_MULTILINE | ES_NOHIDESEL,
        rect, this, IDC_EDIT);
}

// OnSize - handles the resizing of the edit window
void CEditWindow::OnSize( UINT nFlags, int cx,
    int cy )
{
    CRect rc;

    GetClientRect(&rc);
    m_edit.MoveWindow(rc);
}

// InitInstance - Initialize the CEditApp
// m_pMainWnd data member
BOOL CEditApp::InitInstance()
{
    m_pMainWnd = new CEditWindow();
    m_pMainWnd -> ShowWindow( m_nCmdShow );
    m_pMainWnd -> UpdateWindow();
    return( TRUE );
}

// SaveChanges - allows user to save
// or discard changes
void CEditWindow::SaveChanges()
{
    int response;

    response = MessageBox(
        "Save changes before closing?", "Ed",
        MB_ICONQUESTION | MB_YESNOCANCEL );

    if( response == IDYES )
```

```
                MessageBox( "Saving Changes...", "Ed",
                    MB_ICONINFORMATION );
            else if( response == IDNO )
                MessageBox( "Discarding...", "Ed",
                    MB_ICONINFORMATION );
        }

        //-------- File Menu Options -----------//

        void CEditWindow::OnNew()
        {
            SaveChanges();
        }

        void CEditWindow::OnOpen()
        {
            CFileDialog fileDialog( TRUE,
                fileDialogExt, NULL,
                OFN_FILEMUSTEXIST, fileDialogFilter );

            if( fileDialog.DoModal() == IDOK )
                MessageBox( fileDialog.GetPathName(),
                    "Dialog Information",
                    MB_ICONINFORMATION );
        }

        void CEditWindow::OnSave()
        {
            MessageBox( "File Save Selected",
                "Message", MB_ICONINFORMATION );
        }

        void CEditWindow::OnSaveAs()
        {
            CFileDialog fileDialog( FALSE,
                fileDialogExt, NULL,
                OFN_HIDEREADONLY | OFN_OVERWRITEPROMPT,
                fileDialogFilter );

            if( fileDialog.DoModal() == IDOK )
                MessageBox( fileDialog.GetPathName(),
                    "Dialog Information",
                    MB_ICONINFORMATION );
        }

        void CEditWindow::OnExit()
        {
            DestroyWindow();
        }

        //-------- Edit Menu Options -----------//

        void CEditWindow::OnUndo()
        {
            MessageBox( "Edit Undo Selected",
                "Message", MB_ICONINFORMATION );
```

```
}

void CEditWindow::OnCut()
{
    MessageBox( "Edit Cut Selected",
        "Message", MB_ICONINFORMATION );
}

void CEditWindow::OnCopy()
{
    MessageBox( "Edit Copy Selected",
        "Message", MB_ICONINFORMATION );
}

void CEditWindow::OnPaste()
{
    MessageBox( "Edit Paste Selected",
        "Message", MB_ICONINFORMATION );
}

void CEditWindow::OnDelete()
{
    MessageBox( "Edit Delete Selected",
        "Message", MB_ICONINFORMATION );
}

//-------- Search Menu Options -----------//

void CEditWindow::OnFind()
{
    findReplaceDialog = new CFindReplaceDialog;
    findReplaceDialog->Create( FALSE, "default" );
    GetMenu()->EnableMenuItem( IDM_SEARCH_FIND,
        MF_BYCOMMAND | MF_GRAYED );
}

LONG CEditWindow::FindHelper( UINT wParam,
    LONG lParam )
{
    if( findReplaceDialog->IsTerminating() )
    {
        findReplaceDialog = NULL;
        GetMenu()->EnableMenuItem( IDM_SEARCH_FIND,
            MF_BYCOMMAND | MF_ENABLED );
    }
    else if( findReplaceDialog->FindNext() )
        MessageBox(
            findReplaceDialog->GetFindString(),
            "Find String",
            MB_ICONINFORMATION );
    else if( findReplaceDialog->ReplaceCurrent() )
        MessageBox(
            findReplaceDialog->GetReplaceString(),
            "Replace String",
            MB_ICONINFORMATION );
    else if( findReplaceDialog->ReplaceAll() )
```

```
            MessageBox(
                findReplaceDialog->GetReplaceString(),
                "Replace All",
                MB_ICONINFORMATION );

        return 0;
    }

    void CEditWindow::OnFindNext()
    {
        MessageBox( "Search FindNext Selected",
            "Message", MB_ICONINFORMATION );
    }

    //-------- Help Menu Options -----------//

    void CEditWindow::OnAbout()
    {
        CModalDialog aboutDialog( "AboutDialog", this );
        aboutDialog.DoModal();
    }
```

In order to compile Listing 8.5, you will need to create an About dialog. Use the dialog editor as described in Chapter 6. A sample About dialog in shown in Figure 8.5.

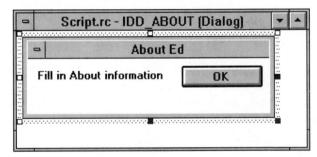

Figure 8.5
The About dialog

In Listing 8.5 every menu option is stubbed appropriately. The following list describes the stubbed behavior of each menu option.

- New – This option currently calls **SaveChanges**, which presents a Yes/No/ Cancel dialog asking the user if the changes made should be saved. Message Boxes stub out the Yes and No responses generated by the user. In the final version this function will be tweaked to check that changes have actually been made to the editor.
- Open – This option calls the File Open dialog and then presents the chosen file name to the user in a message box.
- Save – This option is stubbed with a message box.

- Save As – This option presents a File Save As dialog and then shows the user the file name in a message box.
- Exit – This option terminates the application immediately. In the final version it will need to check for changes using the same code that the New option does.
- Undo – This option is stubbed with a message box.
- Cut – This option is stubbed with a message box.
- Copy – This option is stubbed with a message box.
- Paste – This option is stubbed with a message box.
- Clear – This option is stubbed with a message box.
- Find – This option presents a modeless Find dialog. The application registers the helper function's message appropriately (see Section 7.6) so the dialog can actually be used modelessly. All of its buttons are stubbed with message boxes.
- Find Next – This option is stubbed with a message box.
- About - This option loads a custom dialog named "AboutDialog" from a resource file named about.dlg created by the dialog editor. See Chapter 6 for instructions on using the dialog editor.

With all these stubs in place a user can see the scope of the eventual application and can also try out the look and feel of many of the options such as Open, Save As, and Find. The small amount of code required to develop an early working prototype is one of the many advantages of working with MFC and C++.

8.6 Implementing the Editor

Making the program actually behave like an editor is now simply a matter of replacing the stubs with the actual code. In the following sections we will walk through the different pieces of code used to implement the options. If you add each of the functions described below to the stubbed program shown in the previous section, you will have a working text editor.

8.6.1 New

The **New** option can be called in one of two situations: 1) The editor is displaying a blank screen or a file in which the user has made no changes, or 2) the file on the screen contains changes that should be saved before clearing the edit control. The menu handler for the **New** option reflects the decision that must be made:

```
void CEditWindow::OnNew()
{
    if( SaveChanges() )
        NewFile();
}
```

The **SaveChanges** function checks to see if changes have been made and, if so, queries the user about what to do with the modifications. The user should be able to save the changes, discard them, or return to the editor. When **SaveChanges** finishes querying the user, it returns a Boolean that is TRUE if the system should proceed with clearing the control, and FALSE if not.

```
// Ask user to save or discard changes
BOOL CEditWindow::SaveChanges()
{
    int response;
    BOOL returnCode = FALSE;

    if( m_edit.GetModify() )
    {
        // display MessageBox--filePathName indicates
        // which file we're asking about
        response = MessageBox(
            "Save changes before closing?",
            filePathName,
            MB_ICONQUESTION | MB_YESNOCANCEL );

        switch( response )
        {
            case IDYES:
                if( newFile )
                    returnCode = SaveFileAs();
                else
                    returnCode = SaveFile();
                break;

            case IDNO:
                returnCode = TRUE;
                break;

            case IDCANCEL:
                returnCode = FALSE;
                break;
        }
    }
    else
        returnCode = TRUE;// no changes made to file.

    m_edit.SetFocus();
    return( returnCode );
}
```

The **SaveChanges** function uses a message box in Yes/No/Cancel mode to query the user. If the user wants to save changes, the normal code for the **Save** and **Save As** options can be used to perform the save. The **newFile** variable is a member of **CEditWindow** and it keeps track of whether the current file was previously loaded with **Open** or created fresh with **New**.

The **NewFile** function is responsible for clearing the edit control so it is blank and ready to accept new data.

```
// perform initialization for a new file
void CEditWindow::NewFile()
{
    HANDLE editHandle;
    LPSTR  editBuffer;
    static untitledNum = 0;
    char noName[20];
```

```
// make a simple name for new window
sprintf( noName, "Untitled.%03d",
    ++untitledNum );
SetWindowText( noName );
filePathName = noName;

editHandle = m_edit.GetHandle();
if( LocalReAlloc(editHandle, 1, LHND) == NULL )
{
    MessageBox( "Couldn't allocate memory!",
        "Memory Error", MB_ICONEXCLAMATION );
    return;
}

editBuffer = (LPSTR) LocalLock( editHandle );
editBuffer[0] = 0;
LocalUnlock( editHandle );

m_edit.SetHandle( editHandle );
m_edit.SetModify( FALSE );
m_edit.SetFocus();
newFile = TRUE;
}
```

It creates a dummy file name and places it in the title bar. It then retrieves the handle from the edit control. This handle points to the current string, so the **NewFile** function clears the string by reallocating it to a length of 1 and handing it back to the edit control. The control will make the buffer longer as the user enters new text.

The code at the bottom of the function resets the edit control. **SetModify** sets the edit control's internal flag used by **GetModify**. **SetFocus** sets the focus back to the edit control. The **newFile** variable remembers whether the current file was started with the **New** or **Open** option.

8.6.2 Open

The **Open** option in the **File** menu uses the **SaveChanges** function discussed in Section 8.6.1 to let the user save any changes made to the current file. It then presents a File Open dialog. If the user presses the OK button, it saves the extension of the current file for the next presentation of the dialog and opens the file.

```
void CEditWindow::OnOpen()
{
    if( SaveChanges() )
    {
        CFileDialog fileDialog( TRUE,
            fileDialogExt, lastExtension,
            OFN_FILEMUSTEXIST | OFN_HIDEREADONLY,
            fileDialogFilter );
        if( fileDialog.DoModal() == IDOK )
        {
            // save the extension for use later.
            lastExtension = "*." +
                fileDialog.GetFileExt();
            OpenFile( fileDialog.GetPathName() );
        }
```

```
    }
    m_edit.SetFocus();
}
```

The **OpenFile** function is responsible for actually opening the file. It uses the MFC **CFile** class to handle the file I/O (see the MFC documentation for more information).

```
void CEditWindow::OpenFile( CString pathName )
{
    UINT length;
    HANDLE editHandle;
    LPSTR editBuffer;
    CFile file;

    // try to open the file
    if( !file.Open(pathName, CFile::modeRead) )
    {
        CString msg( "Could not open " +
            pathName + "." );
        MessageBox( msg,
            "File Open Error",
            MB_ICONEXCLAMATION );
        return;
    }

    filePathName = pathName;
    SetWindowText( pathName );

    // get memory to put the file in
    length = (UINT) file.GetLength();
    editHandle = m_edit.GetHandle();
    if( LocalReAlloc(editHandle,
        length + 1, LHND) == NULL )
    {
        file.Close();
        MessageBox( "Couldn't allocate memory!",
            "Memory Error", MB_ICONEXCLAMATION );
        return;
    }

    // read file into the editBuffer
    file.Read( (editBuffer =
        (LPSTR) LocalLock(editHandle)), length );

    // terminate and unlock the edit buffer
    editBuffer[length] = 0;
    LocalUnlock( editHandle );

    // do some initialization
    m_edit.SetHandle( editHandle );
    m_edit.SetModify( FALSE );
    m_edit.SetFocus();
    newFile = FALSE;
    file.Close();
}
```

The **OpenFile** function begins by trying to open the file. If it cannot, it displays an error and returns. If it is successful, it saves the file name and changes the window title. It then tries to allocate enough memory to hold the file. If successful, it reads the file into memory and hands the address of the block back to the edit control.

8.6.3 Save

The **Save** option uses the **newFile** flag to decide whether the file was initially created with **New** or **Open.**

```
void CEditWindow::OnSave()
{
    if( newFile )
        SaveFileAs();
    else
        SaveFile();
}
```

If the file was opened, the **SaveFile** function simply writes the file back to disk using the original file name saved from the open operation. The steps are a reversal of the file-reading steps shown in Section 8.6.2.

```
// save the current file
BOOL CEditWindow::SaveFile()
{
    HANDLE editHandle;
    LPSTR editBuffer;
    UINT length;
    CFile file;

    // try to open the file
    if( !file.Open(filePathName,
        CFile::modeCreate | CFile::modeWrite) )
    {
        CString msg( "Can't open " +
            filePathName +
            "\nCheck the filename." );
        MessageBox( msg,
            "File Save Error",
            MB_ICONEXCLAMATION );
        return FALSE;
    }

    length = m_edit.GetWindowTextLength();

    // get and lock handle to edit text
    editHandle = m_edit.GetHandle();
    editBuffer = (LPSTR) LocalLock( editHandle );

    // write edit text to file, close and unlock
    file.Write( editBuffer, length );
    file.Close();
    LocalUnlock( editHandle );

    // reset our flags
    m_edit.SetModify( FALSE );
```

```
        m_edit.SetFocus();
        newFile = FALSE;
        return TRUE;
    }
```

The **SaveFileAs** function presents a normal File Save As dialog to the user so that the user can enter a new file name.

```
// Manage the SaveAs Dialog
BOOL CEditWindow::SaveFileAs()
{
    BOOL returnCode = FALSE;

    CFileDialog fileDialog( FALSE,
        fileDialogExt, filePathName,
        OFN_HIDEREADONLY | OFN_OVERWRITEPROMPT,
        fileDialogFilter );

    if( fileDialog.DoModal() == IDOK )
    {
        // save old name and get new one
        CString oldPathName( filePathName );
        filePathName = fileDialog.GetPathName();

        // restore old name if save failed--
        // probably due to an invalid filename
        if( !(returnCode = SaveFile() ) )
            filePathName = oldPathName;

        SetWindowText( filePathName );
    }
    else
        returnCode = FALSE;

    m_edit.SetFocus();
    return( returnCode );
}
```

If the user presses the OK button, the new file name is saved and the **SaveFile** function is called to actually save the file. The title of the window is changed to the new file name.

8.6.4 Save As

The **Save As** option works almost exactly the same way as the **Save** option does. The only difference is that it does not have to make a decision between new and opened files—it calls the **SaveFileAs** function seen in Section 8.6.3 automatically.

```
void CEditWindow::OnSaveAs()
{
    SaveFileAs();
}
```

8.6.5 Exit

The **Exit** option calls the **SaveChanges** function from Section 8.6.1 to check whether changes should be saved. If everything is ready to go, it exits the application.

```
void CEditWindow::OnExit()
{
    if( SaveChanges() )
        DestroyWindow();
}
```

8.6.6 Undo, Cut, Copy, Paste, Clear

One of the nicest things about the **CEdit** control is that it handles clipboard operations for you automatically. All the Edit menu options require just one line of code. See the MFC documentation for details on these function calls.

```
void CEditWindow::OnUndo()
{
    m_edit.Undo();
}

void CEditWindow::OnCut()
{
    m_edit.Cut();
}

void CEditWindow::OnCopy()
{
    m_edit.Copy();
}

void CEditWindow::OnPaste()
{
    m_edit.Paste();
}

void CEditWindow::OnDelete()
{
    m_edit.ReplaceSel( "" );
}
```

8.6.7 Find

Preparation for the modeless Find dialog starts with two global variables:

```
UINT CEditWindow::findMessage =
    ::RegisterWindowMessage( FINDMSGSTRING );
CFindReplaceDialog* findReplaceDialog = NULL;
```

The **findMessage** variable holds the message used by the dialog to trigger the message map. The menu manager function (see Section 8.6.11) uses the **findReplace-Dialog** pointer to determine if the menu option should be enabled, thereby preventing multiple instances of the dialog box. When the user selects the **Find** option, the code creates a new modeless find dialog. (See Section 7.6 for details.)

```
void CEditWindow::OnFind()
{
    findReplaceDialog = new CFindReplaceDialog;
    findReplaceDialog->Create( TRUE,
        findString, "", FR_HIDEWHOLEWORD |
        FR_HIDEMATCHCASE | FR_HIDEUPDOWN );
}
```

Once the dialog is on the screen the user can press the **Find Next** or **Cancel** buttons. The result is passed through the message map to the find helper function shown below.

```
// Helper for the find dialog
LONG CEditWindow::FindHelper( UINT wParam,
    LONG lParam )
{
    findString.Empty();
    findString = findReplaceDialog->GetFindString();

    if( findReplaceDialog->IsTerminating() )
        findReplaceDialog = NULL;
    else if( findReplaceDialog->FindNext() )
        Search( findString );
    return 0;
}
```

The function starts by retrieving the string entered by the user. It then decides which button the user pressed. If a search is required, the search engine in the **Search** function is used.

```
// Scan through text looking for findString
void CEditWindow::Search( CString findString )
{
    int cursorPos, startChar, foundChar;
    int lineIndex, charIndex, lineLength;
    CString line, rightLine;

    // ignore case sensitivity
    findString.MakeLower();
    // start from current cursor position
    lineIndex = m_edit.LineFromChar();
    m_edit.GetSel( startChar, charIndex );

    do
    {
        // get the length of current line
        lineLength = m_edit.LineLength( charIndex );

        // determine char index of that line
        cursorPos = charIndex -
            m_edit.LineIndex( lineIndex );

        // put line into a CString.
        // Last param is important.
        m_edit.GetLine( lineIndex,
            line.GetBuffer( lineLength ),
            lineLength );
        line.ReleaseBuffer( lineLength );

        // get chars from cursorPos to end of line
        rightLine = line.Right( lineLength -
            cursorPos );
        rightLine.MakeLower();

        // look for findString
```

```
        foundChar = rightLine.Find( findString );

        // if not found, goto next line
        if( foundChar == -1 )
            charIndex = m_edit.LineIndex( ++lineIndex );
    } while( ( foundChar == -1 ) &&
        ( lineIndex < m_edit.GetLineCount() ) );

    // if found, select the text
    if( foundChar != -1 )
    {
        startChar = charIndex + foundChar;
        m_edit.SetSel( startChar,
            startChar + findString.GetLength() );

        // make the edit window scroll to new line.
        m_edit.LineScroll( m_edit.LineFromChar(
            startChar ) - m_edit.GetFirstVisibleLine() );
        m_edit.SetFocus();
    }

    else
    {
        // Wrap MessageBox in EnableWindow calls so
        // that multiple message boxes
        // can't happen
        if( findReplaceDialog )
            findReplaceDialog->EnableWindow( FALSE );
        MessageBox( "String not found.",
            "Find String",
            MB_ICONINFORMATION );
        if( findReplaceDialog )
            findReplaceDialog->EnableWindow( TRUE );
    }
}
```

There are two ways to search through the text in an edit control. The quicker of the two is to get the handle to the edit control's block of memory and scan the block character by character. Here we have used the line-by-line method instead to demonstrate several of the line-handling functions in the edit control.

The function starts at the current cursor position and retrieves the data in the edit control line by line. The current line is stored in an MFC **CString**, so functions built in to this class can be used to look for a substring on the line. The code spends a fair amount of time jumping between character indexing and line indexing.

If the text is found, it is selected. Otherwise the search finally reaches the end of the data and a message box informs the user.

8.6.8 Find Next

The **Find Next** option uses the search engine presented in the last section and repeats the previous search.

```
void CEditWindow::OnFindNext()
{
    Search( findString );
```

```
    }
```

8.6.9 About

The **About** option loads the About box from a resource file and displays it on the screen.

```
void CEditWindow::OnAbout()
{
    CModalDialog aboutDialog( "AboutDialog", this );
    aboutDialog.DoModal();
}
```

8.6.10 Menu Management

One of the most complicated parts of this program is menu management—the enabling and disabling of the different menu options. You will find in Part 3 that this particular problem is very nicely solved using MFC's **CCmdUI** class.

The **CWnd::OnInitMenu** function is called any time the user selects any menu option before to the actual animation of the menu bar, so this is an appropriate central location to control enabling and disabling:

```
void CEditWindow::OnInitMenu( CMenu *menu )
{
    DWORD selected;
    UINT format, menuState;

    // update the File Save menu item.
    if( m_edit.GetModify() )
        menuState = MF_ENABLED;
    else
        menuState = MF_GRAYED;
    GetMenu()->EnableMenuItem( IDM_FILE_SAVE,
        MF_BYCOMMAND | menuState );

    // update the Edit Undo menu item.
    if( m_edit.CanUndo() )
        menuState = MF_ENABLED;
    else
        menuState = MF_GRAYED;
    GetMenu()->EnableMenuItem( IDM_EDIT_UNDO,
        MF_BYCOMMAND | menuState );

    // update the Edit Cut, Copy, & Delete menu items
    selected = m_edit.GetSel();
    if( HIWORD(selected) != LOWORD(selected) )
        menuState = MF_ENABLED;
    else
        menuState = MF_GRAYED;
    GetMenu()->EnableMenuItem( IDM_EDIT_CUT,
        MF_BYCOMMAND | menuState );
    GetMenu()->EnableMenuItem( IDM_EDIT_COPY,
        MF_BYCOMMAND | menuState );
    GetMenu()->EnableMenuItem( IDM_EDIT_DELETE,
        MF_BYCOMMAND | menuState );
```

```
// Update the Edit Paste menu item by
// looking at what's in the clipboard.
menuState = MF_GRAYED;
if( OpenClipboard() )
{
    format = EnumClipboardFormats( 0 );
    while( format != 0 )
    {
        if( format == CF_TEXT )
        {
            menuState = MF_ENABLED;
            break;
        }
        format = EnumClipboardFormats( format );
    }
    CloseClipboard();
}
GetMenu()->EnableMenuItem( IDM_EDIT_PASTE,
    MF_BYCOMMAND | menuState );

// update the Search Find menu item
if( findReplaceDialog )
    menuState = MF_GRAYED;
else
    menuState = MF_ENABLED;
GetMenu()->EnableMenuItem( IDM_SEARCH_FIND,
    MF_BYCOMMAND | menuState );

// update the Search Find Next menu item
if( findString.GetLength() )
    menuState = MF_ENABLED;
else
    menuState = MF_GRAYED;
GetMenu()->EnableMenuItem( IDM_SEARCH_FINDNEXT,
    MF_BYCOMMAND | menuState );
}
```

The **Open, New, Save As**, **Exit,** and **About** options are always enabled. For all other menus the **OnInitMenu** function checks the appropriate conditions option by option and enables and disables each one. The following conditions are used to determine if an option should be enabled:

- Save – Enabled if the edit control contains modifications
- Undo – Enabled if the edit control reports that there is something to undo
- Cut, Copy, Delete – Enabled if something is selected
- Paste – Enabled if the clipboard contains data in the CD_TEXT format (text data), if the user copies Paintbrush data onto the clipboard, Paste will disable itself
- Search – Enabled if the Find dialog is not already on the screen
- Find Next – Enabled if there are data in the find string to search for

You will also need to add the following line to the bottom of the window's constructor:

```
m_bAutoMenuEnable = FALSE;
```

This line disables default behavior in MFC that causes the **EnableMenuItem** function to misbehave in code not generated by the AppWizard.

8.6.11 Exiting

There are three ways for the user to exit the editor: 1) Choose the **Exit** option in the File menu, 2) choose the **Close** option in the system menu, and 3) log off or shut down Windows. Option 1 is discussed in Section 8.6.5. The **CWnd::OnClose** function handles option 2:

```
void CEditWindow::OnClose()
{
    if( SaveChanges() )
        DestroyWindow();
}
```

This looks just like the Exit function. When the user shuts down Windows or logs out, the **CWnd::OnQueryEndSession** function is called. This gives the user a chance to save changes before the system closes the application:

```
// See if it's Ok to exit Windows
BOOL CEditWindow::OnQueryEndSession()
{
    return SaveChanges();
}
```

Again, this function uses the **SaveChanges** function seen in Section 8.6.1.

8.7 Conclusion

One of the things about this chapter is that it makes everything look easy. It probably took you an hour to read it, and everything seemed fairly straightforward. What you are not seeing is the time spent tweaking things to make them work just right, as well as the time that was wasted on bugs. By showing you a complete application we hope you can save some time by being able to look up these details and bug fixes in an existing piece of code.

There are a number of extensions you can add to this editor if you are so inclined. For example, you might try the following exercises:

- Add case-sensitive searching, backward searching, and whole-word searching.
- Add replace and replace all capabilities.
- Add a font dialog and change the font.
- Add printing—see Chapter 11.

However, you may want to wait until Chapter 16 to make the changes. As mentioned earlier, the AppWizard can make the creation of a simple editor like this one much easier by using the **CEditView** class.

LISTS

Quite a bit of the information we deal with every day is organized in lists. There are lists everywhere in any graphical user interface–lists of files, lists of categories, lists of colors and fonts, lists of options, and so on. Windows is no exception. In this chapter we will discuss the creation of lists using the two controls built into Windows for this purpose: list boxes and combo boxes. A list box is used to display a list of items. A combo box combines a list box with either a **CEdit** control or a **CStatic** control and is frequently used to emulate a radio box in a more space-efficient format.

9.1 Creating a List Box

The **CListBox** control is a fairly intricate user interface object. When you use it in an application, you have a great deal of control over its appearance and behavior. It has 13 different LBS styles in addition to the available WS styles, and it generates six different messages in response to user events. It also has 33 member functions that you can call to insert items into the list, to extract selected items from the list, and to control specific behaviors such as horizontal scrolling. All its functions and data members are described in the MFC documentation.

Though complicated in its implementation, the basic idea behind a list box control is simple. First, you create the list box itself so it appears on screen. Then you fill it with items. When the user selects an item, your code receives a message and it should respond appropriately.

List boxes are typically used in one of two ways. The more common use is in a dialog box. In this case you fill the list when the dialog is initialized, and the list retains a fixed size while the dialog is visible. A second way to use list boxes is as the contents of an entire window. In this case the list box re-sizes with the window.

The code in Listing 9.1 demonstrates the creation of a list box in an application window. Figure 9.1 shows a screen dump for this code when it is running. The code does not provide for any list selection handling—this topic is discussed on its own in Section 9.3.

Listing 9.1
Displaying a list box in a window.

```cpp
// list1.cpp

#include <afxwin.h>
#include <strstrea.h>

const int LIST=100;

// Define an application object
class CApp : public CWinApp
{
public:
    virtual BOOL InitInstance();
};

// Create an instance of the application class
CApp App;

// Define a window object
class CWindow : public CFrameWnd
{
    CListBox* list;
public:
    CWindow();
    afx_msg void OnSize( UINT nFlags,
        int cx, int cy );
    DECLARE_MESSAGE_MAP()
};

// The window's constructor
CWindow::CWindow()
{
    CRect rect;

    // Create the window
    Create(NULL, "List Demo", WS_OVERLAPPEDWINDOW,
        CRect(0,0,250,100));
    GetClientRect(&rect);

    // Create the list box
    list = new CListBox();
    list->Create(
        WS_CHILD|WS_VISIBLE|WS_BORDER|
        WS_VSCROLL|WS_HSCROLL|LBS_NOINTEGRALHEIGHT,
        rect,
        this, LIST);

    // Fill the list box with 100 items
    char s[100];
    ostrstream ostr(s,100);
    int i;
    for (i=0; i<100; i++)
```

```
    {
        ostr.seekp(ios::beg);
        ostr << "This is item number " << i << ends;
        list->AddString(s);
    }
}

// The message map
// see section 9.3 for selection handling
BEGIN_MESSAGE_MAP( CWindow, CFrameWnd )
    ON_WM_SIZE()
END_MESSAGE_MAP()

// Handles window resizing events
void CWindow::OnSize( UINT nFlags, int cx, int cy )
{
    CRect r;

    GetClientRect(&r);
    list->MoveWindow(r);
}

// The InitInstance function executes
// once when the application begins
BOOL CApp::InitInstance()
{
    m_pMainWnd = new CWindow();
    m_pMainWnd->ShowWindow(m_nCmdShow);
    m_pMainWnd->UpdateWindow();
    return TRUE;
}
```

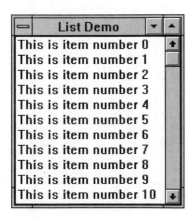

Figure 9.1
A list box in a window

The code in Listing 9.1 creates a **CListBox** in the window's constructor. It uses six different style attributes. The list box, like the **CEdit** control, can automatically handle horizontal and vertical scroll bars if the scroll bar styles are specified at creation. The code also sets the LBS_NOINTEGRALHEIGHT style. With this style set, the list box displays partial lines as the window is re-sized. If this style is not used, the list box will size itself so that only complete lines of the list are visible.

Following creation, the code fills the list box using the list box's **AddString** member function. This function can add strings in one of two ways. If the list is sorted, the string is added at its sorted position. Sorting is specified by choosing the LBS_SORT or the LBS_STANDARD styles when creating the list. If the list is not sorted, then **AddString** adds the new string to the bottom of the list. A second way to add strings to the list is to use the **InsertString** function. This function places the new string at the specified location in the list.

When you run Listing 9.1, note that you can re-size the window and the list box will re-size itself to fit properly. The **OnSize** function, which gets called each time the user change's the window's size, implements this behavior. The **GetClientRect** function gets the new size of the window so the list's borders follow the window's client area exactly.

One thing you might notice when you run the code in Listing 9.1 is that even though a horizontal scroll bar is specified, it does not appear to work correctly. If you shrink the width of the window, as shown in Figure 9.2, the horizontal scroll bar does not appear. You can fix this problem by using the **SetHorizontalExtent** function, which specifies the maximum scrolling range for the horizontal scroll bar. If you add the following line to the code just after list creation, the horizontal scroll bar will appear as in Figure 9.3:

```
list->SetHorizontalExtent(150);
```

Both the horizontal and vertical scroll bars will disappear automatically when the window is made large enough to accommodate the maximum extent in either direction.

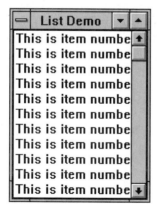

Figure 9.2
A thin list box with the default horizontal extent

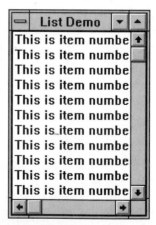

Figure 9.3
A thin list box with a properly set horizontal extent

9.2 Alternate Display Formats

A list box (but not a combo box) can display its data in two alternate formats: multi-column and tabbed. The multi-column mode is useful when the list contains a large number of short items. It allows the list to display many choices in a small area. The tabbed mode lets the list properly display items that contain embedded tab characters. This is especially useful when using a proportional font for the list. You change the font in a list in the same way you change the font for a static label (as shown in Chapter 3).

The code in Listing 9.2 is a replacement for the **CWindow::CWindow** function in Listing 9.1 and demonstrates the creation of a multi-column list. Figure 9.4 shows a screen dump for this code.

Listing 9.2
Creation of a multi-column list.

```
// list2.cpp

// The window's constructor
CWindow::CWindow()
{
    CRect rect;

    // Create the window itself
    Create(NULL, "List Demo", WS_OVERLAPPEDWINDOW,
        CRect(0,0,250,100));
    GetClientRect(&rect);

    // Create the list
    list = new CListBox();
    list->Create(
        WS_CHILD|WS_VISIBLE|WS_BORDER|
        WS_VSCROLL|WS_HSCROLL|LBS_NOINTEGRALHEIGHT|
        LBS_MULTICOLUMN,
        rect,
        this, LIST);
    list->SetColumnWidth(60);

    // Fill the list
    char s[100];
    ostrstream ostr(s,100);
    int i;
    for (i=0; i<100; i++)
    {
        ostr.seekp(ios::beg);
        ostr << "item" << i << ends;
        list->AddString(s);
    }
}
```

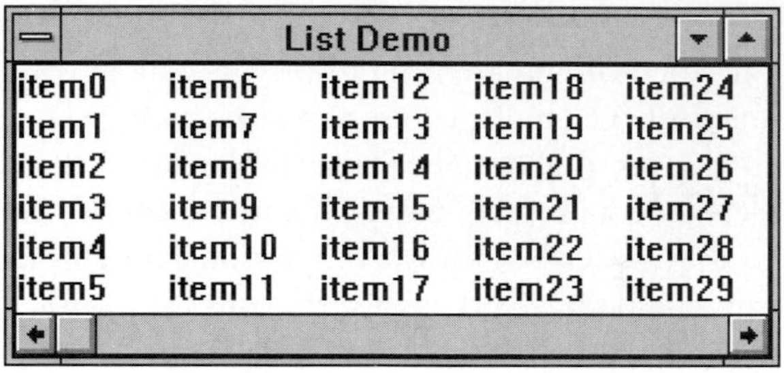

Figure 9.4
Typical multi-column list display

The code in Listing 9.2 differs from Listing 9.1 in two ways. The LBS_MULTICOLUMN style is specified and the column width is set to 60 pixels with a call to the **SetColumnWidth** function. The default width is 32. When in multi-column mode, the horizontal scroll bar is used instead of the vertical scroll bar to page through the available items.

The LBS_USETABSTOPS style causes the list box to interpret tab characters embedded in the data inserted in the list. This display mode is useful when the list displays several different pieces of information on a single line. For example, an address list program (see Chapter 18) might display the name, address, and phone number for each address record on a single line of the list. The tab characters are embedded in the line when the line is created before insertion, and the list box interprets the tab characters to form columns. The tab stops in the list are set by creating an array of integers representing the positions of the stops, and then passing the array to the **CListBox::SetTabStops** function. The code in Listing 9.3 demonstrates the process (replace the window constructor in Listing 9.1 with this code), and Figure 9.5 shows a screen dump for the code.

Listing 9.3
Code demonstrating the display of a tabbed list in a list box.

```
// list3.cpp

// The window's constructor
CWindow::CWindow()
{
    CRect rect;

    // Create the window
    Create(NULL, "Button Demo", WS_OVERLAPPEDWINDOW,
        CRect(0,0,250,100));
    GetClientRect(&rect);

    // Create the list box
    list = new CListBox();
    list->Create(
        WS_CHILD|WS_VISIBLE|WS_BORDER|
```

```
        WS_VSCROLL|WS_HSCROLL|LBS_NOINTEGRALHEIGHT|
        LBS_USETABSTOPS,
        rect,
        this, LIST);

    // Set two tab stops at 30 and 100 dialog units
    int ta[2] = {30, 100};
    list->SetTabStops(2, ta);

    // Fill the list with tabbed lines
    char s[100];
    ostrstream ostr(s,100);
    int i;
    for (i=0; i<100; i++)
    {
        ostr.seekp(ios::beg);
        ostr << "name" << i << '\t';
        ostr << "address" << i << '\t';
        ostr << "phone" << i << ends;
        list->AddString(s);
    }
}
```

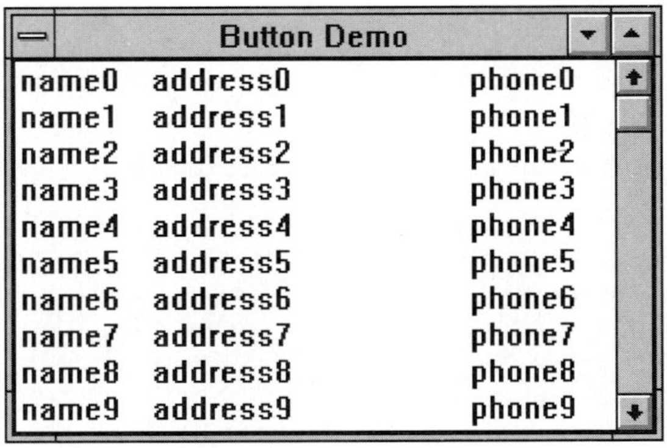

Figure 9.5
Screen dump showing a tabbed list

The code in Listing 9.3 specifies the LBS_USETABSTOPS when the list is created. It initializes an array of integers with the desired tab stop positions, and the array and its size are passed to **SetTabStops**. Tab stops are specified in dialog units rather than pixels (see the **CListBox::SetTabStops** function in the MFC documentation for a description). When the items for the list are created, normal tab characters are embedded within the data. As shown in Figure 9.5, the tabs are interpreted and aligned with the specified stops when the list is displayed.

9.3 Getting User Selections

Once the list box is on the screen, the user can interact with it. The user clicks on items to highlight them, or double-clicks on an item to select it and act upon it in whatever way the application specifies. The list box also supports an extended selection mode which allows the user to shift-click or ctrl-click on multiple items in the list. The application can then retrieve all items selected and act on them simultaneously.

The code in Listing 9.4 demonstrates the creation of a list and the steps that you must take to retrieve user events from the list. Figure 9.6 shows a screen dump of this code during execution.

Listing 9.4
Demonstration of a list box in single select mode.

```
// list4.cpp

#include <afxwin.h>
#include <strstrea.h>

// Define the application class
class CApp : public CWinApp
{
public:
    virtual BOOL InitInstance();
};

// Create an instance of the application class
CApp App;

// Define the window class
class CWindow : public CFrameWnd
{
    CListBox* list;
    CStatic* label;
public:
    CWindow();
    afx_msg void OnSize( UINT nFlags,
        int cx, int cy );
    afx_msg void HandleSelchange();
    afx_msg void HandleDblclk();
    DECLARE_MESSAGE_MAP()
};

const int LIST=100;
const int LABEL=101;

// The window's constructor
CWindow::CWindow()
{
    CRect rect;

    // Create the window
```

```
Create(NULL, "List Demo", WS_OVERLAPPEDWINDOW,
    CRect(0,0,250,100));

// Create the list box. Size it
// so that it leaves 24 pixels
// at the bottom of the window
GetClientRect(&rect);
rect.bottom -= 24;
list = new CListBox();
list->Create(
    WS_CHILD|WS_VISIBLE|WS_BORDER|
    WS_VSCROLL|WS_HSCROLL|LBS_NOINTEGRALHEIGHT|
    LBS_NOTIFY,
    rect, this, LIST);

// Create a label to display the
// selection in the bottom 24 pixels
GetClientRect(&rect);
rect.top = rect.bottom - 24;
label = new CStatic();
label->Create("xxx",
    WS_CHILD|WS_BORDER|WS_VISIBLE,
    rect,
    this,LABEL);

// Fill the list
char s[100];
ostrstream ostr(s,100);
int i;
for (i=0; i<100; i++)
{
    ostr.seekp(ios::beg);
    ostr << "This is item number " << i << ends;
    list->AddString(s);
}
}

// The message map
BEGIN_MESSAGE_MAP( CWindow, CFrameWnd )
    ON_WM_SIZE()
    ON_LBN_SELCHANGE(LIST, HandleSelchange)
    ON_LBN_DBLCLK(LIST, HandleDblclk)
END_MESSAGE_MAP()

// Handle resize events
void CWindow::OnSize( UINT nFlags, int cx, int cy )
{
    CRect rect;

    // Readjust the list
    GetClientRect(&rect);
    rect.bottom -= 24;
    list->MoveWindow(rect);

    // Readjust the label
    GetClientRect(&rect);
```

```
        rect.top = rect.bottom - 24;
        label->MoveWindow(rect);
}


// Handle selections
void CWindow::HandleSelchange()
{
    int i = list->GetCurSel();
    char s[100];
    list->GetText(i,s);
    SetDlgItemText(LABEL, s);
}


// Handle double clicked items
void CWindow::HandleDblclk()
{
    int i = list->GetCurSel();
    char s[100];
    list->GetText(i,s);
    SetDlgItemText(LABEL, s);
    Beep(200,200);
}


// Init the application
BOOL CApp::InitInstance()
{
    m_pMainWnd = new CWindow();
    m_pMainWnd->ShowWindow(m_nCmdShow);
    m_pMainWnd->UpdateWindow();
    return TRUE;
}
```

Figure 9.6
Screen dump of a list box in single select mode

In Listing 9.4, the **CWindow** constructor creates and fills a list box and also creates a static label that will display the selected item. *Note the use of the LBS_NOTIFY style*, which specifies that the list box should generate messages when the user clicks or double-clicks on an item. If you accidentally omit this style, the list box will generate no event messages in response to user actions.

The message map in Listing 9.4 has been augmented to include ON_LBN_SELCHANGE and ON_LBN_DBLCLK. A selection-change message is generated each time the user highlights a new item by clicking on it or using the arrow keys. A double-click message is generated when the user double-clicks on an item. The **HandleSelchange** function is duplicated below:

```
void CWindow::HandleSelchange()
{
    int i = list->GetCurSel();
    char s[100];
    list->GetText(i,s);
    SetDlgItemText(LABEL, s);
}
```

This code gets the item number of the currently selected item by calling the list's **GetCurSel** member function. The index returned is a value between zero and the size of the list minus one (list size can be retrieved with the **GetCount** function). The index is then passed to **GetText**, which retrieves the text for the string at that location. The string is placed into the static label at the bottom of the window to indicate that the function is working correctly. The double-click handler works the same way, but also produces a beep to indicate that a double-click was recognized. You will replace the beep with an action that is appropriate for your application.

List boxes that accept multiple selections are similar in principle but involve slightly more work. When the list box is created, *you should specify the LBS_EXTENDEDSEL style to convert the list over to multiple selection mode*. The code in Listing 9.5 is a replacement for the **HandleSelchange** function in Listing 9.4, and it demonstrates the procedure used to retrieve multiple items. Figure 9.7 shows a screen dump of this code during execution.

Listing 9.5
Retrieving multiple selected items from a list box.

```
// list5.cpp

// Handle selections
void CWindow::HandleSelchange()
{
    int i, *a;
    i = list->GetSelCount();
    a = new int[i];
    list->GetSelItems(i,a);
    char s[100];
    int x;
    ostrstream ostr(s,100);
    for (x=0; x<i; x++)
        ostr << a[x] << " ";
    ostr << ends;
    SetDlgItemText(LABEL, s);
    delete a;
}
```

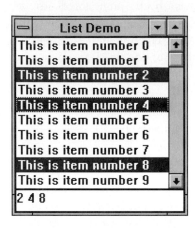

Figure 9.7
Screen dump of a list box in multiple selection mode

The code in Listing 9.5 starts by retrieving a count of the number of items currently selected using the **GetSelCount** function. It uses this count to allocate an integer array capable of holding that many items. The program passes the array and the count to the **GetSelItems** function, which fills the array with the indexes of all selected items in the list. These indexes could then be used with the list's **GetText** function to retrieve the items one by one. Here the integers are instead used to create a string displaying the contents of the array in the static label, demonstrating that the list is working as expected.

9.4 Manipulating Items in a List

When you use list boxes as the contents of an application window (see Chapter 18 for an example), it is common to manipulate the contents of the list over time. For example, a program that finds files by searching their contents for a string will update the list slowly over time. Or the list might display mail that is accumulating in a mailbox or data coming in through a communications port or network socket.

In situations like these, it is helpful to select items in a list box from within your code. For example, if you add a new item to the list on the fly, selecting it brings it to the user's attention. For this purpose, the **SetCurSel** function is used in a list box that is in single-select mode, while the **SetSel** and **SetItemRange** functions perform this task in a list box in extended-selection mode. In an extended-selection List Box, it is also possible to select and retrieve the currently focused item using **SetCaretIndex** and **GetCaretIndex**. Once an item is selected, however, there is no guarantee that it is visible to the user. You can use the **SetTopIndex** function to scroll a specific item onto the top of the list so the user is sure to see it.

The list box provides several functions you can use to manipulate the items in the list. We have seen one: **AddString** adds items to the list, either at their sorted position or at the end of the list, depending on whether LBS_SORT is set.

Other functions used to manipulate the contents of the list are shown below:

InsertString	Inserts a string at the specified location
Dir	Adds file names from the current directory to the list; parameters control the files selected for addition
DeleteString	Deletes the specified string
ResetContent	Deletes all strings from the list
FindString	Finds a string in the list and returns its index
SelectString	Finds a string in the list and selects it

You can use these functions to customize the behavior of a list box in your application. In the following section, you will also recognize the internal use of many of these functions to implement the combo box.

9.5 Combo Boxes

A combo box combines a list box with either an edit control or a static label. When combined with an edit control, characters typed by the user are used to scroll through the data in the list until the first match is found. Typically, this feature is used with a sorted list. When combined with a static label, the user can select items from the list for display in the label. Different styles in the combo box allow the list to be shown at all times or to be hidden most of the time and dropped down when requested by the user. The list box used within a combo box is not quite as capable as the one found in the **CListBox** control. For example, the list box cannot handle tabs or multiple columns, although most of the other capabilities are available in the combo box.

Combo boxes are a convenience–it is almost as easy to create a list and edit control yourself and wire them together. In fact, you are forced to do just that if you want to display tabbed information in the list. However, the combo box is very useful as a small-area replacement for a radio box. For example, a radio box containing 20 items would take up a great deal of space on the screen, but a combo box with a static label can display the same information in a much smaller area–generally the space needed for just one item. When it's time to change the selection, the combo box drops down its list temporarily and then hides it again.

If you look though the styles, messages, and functions available in the combo box, you will find that a combo box is nothing but a straight combination of an edit area (or a static control) and a list box. Almost all the features available have been described in the list box and edit control descriptions here and in Chapter 5. The code shown in Listing 9.6 demonstrates the creation and filling of a combo box control.

Listing 9.6
Creating a combo box.

```
// combo.cpp

#include <afxwin.h>
#include <strstrea.h>
```

```
// Define an application object
class CApp : public CWinApp
{
public:
    virtual BOOL InitInstance();
};

CApp App;

// Define the window class
class CWindow : public CFrameWnd
{
    CComboBox* combo;
public:
    CWindow();
    afx_msg void OnSize( UINT nFlags,
        int cx, int cy );
    DECLARE_MESSAGE_MAP()
};

const int COMBO=100;

// The window's constructor
CWindow::CWindow()
{
    CRect rect;

    Create(NULL, "List Demo", WS_OVERLAPPEDWINDOW,
        CRect(0,0,250,100));
    GetClientRect(&rect);
    combo = new CComboBox();
    combo->Create(
        WS_CHILD|WS_VISIBLE|WS_BORDER|
        CBS_AUTOHSCROLL|CBS_SIMPLE,
        rect,
        this, COMBO);
    char s[100];
    ostrstream ostr(s,100);
    int i;
    for (i=0; i<100; i++)
    {
        ostr.seekp(ios::beg);
        ostr << "Item " << i << ends;
        combo->AddString(s);
    }
}

// The message map
BEGIN_MESSAGE_MAP( CWindow, CFrameWnd )
    ON_WM_SIZE()
END_MESSAGE_MAP()

// Handle resizing
void CWindow::OnSize( UINT nFlags, int cx, int cy )
{
    CRect r;
```

```
    GetClientRect(&r);
    combo->MoveWindow(r);
}

// Init the application
BOOL CApp::InitInstance()
{
    m_pMainWnd = new CWindow();
    m_pMainWnd->ShowWindow(m_nCmdShow);
    m_pMainWnd->UpdateWindow();
    return TRUE;
}
```

There are three modes that can be used when creating a combo box. The first mode is demonstrated in Listing 9.6, where the CBS_SIMPLE style has been specified. This style combines an edit control with a list box that is always visible. The CBS_DROPDOWN style is similar, but the list is hidden and controlled by the user with an arrow button displayed next to the edit area or by the programmer using the **ShowDropDown** function. The CBS_DROPDOWNLIST style is similar to the CBS_DROPDOWN style in its behavior, but the edit control is replaced with a static label. The user changes the label by selecting items from the list when it's visible.

The same functions used with the list box to handle selections are used with the combo box. In particular, the **GetCurSel** function should be used to retrieve the user's current selection in the combo box.

9.6 Conclusion

Lists are extremely important in Windows. See Part 4 for ways to use sub-classing to further customize the appearance of lists in your applications.

THE CWINAPP CLASS

Every application that you create with MFC will contain one instance of the **CWinApp** class. This class is central to the MFC class hierarchy. It embodies the main event loop and dispatches events to other classes in MFC.

Because of its central position in MFC, the **CWinApp** class contains a number of member functions that you can use to customize your application's behavior. The class contains member variables and functions that hold information that is often useful within your application. This chapter discuss a number of the more common capabilities that you can use in the **CWinApp** class.

In Part 3 of the book, when using code generated by the AppWizard, many default features in the **CWinApp** class become extremely important to the default behavior of the application. In particular, the **AddDocTemplate** function in the **CWinApp** class bonds document and view classes created by the AppWizard to the application. To understand everything that an AppWizard framework supports, it is important to have a working knowledge of what the **CWinApp** class is able to do, and why.

10.1 Member Variables

Getting started with the **CWinApp** class is often difficult because it contains a great deal of esoteric and often hidden behavior. Let's therefore start with something simple: the member variables of the class. In MFC, there are a number of member variables in the class, as listed below:

m_pszAppName	The name of the application
m_hInstance	The current instance handle
m_hPrevInstance	The previous instance handle
m_lpCmdLine	A copy of the command line used for invocation
m_nCmdShow	Specifies how window should be shown initially
m_bHelpMode	TRUE if application is in Help context mode (See Chapter 19)

m_pActiveWnd	If the application is an OLE server and is currently in-place active, points to the main window of the container
m_pszExeName	The name of the EXE file
m_pszHelpFilePath	Path to the application's Help file
m_pszProfileName	Name of the application's INI file
m_pszRegistryKey	The registry key of the application (set by **SetRegistryKey**).

In addition to these variables, the following functions are also frequently useful:

AfxGetApp	Returns a pointer to the application's CWinApp object.
AfxGetInstanceHandle	Returns the application's instance handle
AfxGetResourceHandle	Returns a the application's resource handle
AfxGetAppName	Returns the application's name

In particular, the **AfxGetApp** function makes it easy to get a pointer to your application's instance of the **CWinApp** class at any point in the application's code. Once you have this pointer, you can easily access any of the member variables of **CWinApp**. The code in Listing 10.1 demonstrates how to access several of these variables in a message box. Figure 10.1 shows a typical run of Listing 10.1.

Listing 10.1
Dumping the application's variables

```
//vars.cpp

#include <afxwin.h>
#include <strstrea.h>

// Declare the application class
class CApp : public CWinApp
{
public:
    virtual BOOL InitInstance();
};

// Create an instance of the application class
CApp app;

// Declare the main window class
class CWindow : public CFrameWnd
{
public:
    CWindow();
};

// The InitInstance function is called each
// time the application first executes.
BOOL CApp::InitInstance()
{
    m_pMainWnd = new CWindow();
```

```
        m_pMainWnd->ShowWindow(m_nCmdShow);
        m_pMainWnd->UpdateWindow();
        return TRUE;
}


// The constructor for the window class
CWindow::CWindow()
{
    // Create the window
    Create(NULL,
        "CWinApp tests",
        WS_OVERLAPPEDWINDOW,
        CRect(0,0,200,200));

    char s[2000];
    ostrstream ostr( s, 2000 );
    // Access member variables
    ostr << "Application name: "
        << app.m_pszAppName
        << endl
        << "Command line: "
        << app.m_lpCmdLine
        << endl
        << "EXE name: "
        << app.m_pszExeName
        << endl
        << "Help file path: "
        << app.m_pszHelpFilePath
        << endl;
    if (AfxIsValidString(app.m_pszProfileName))
        ostr << "INI file name: "
            << app.m_pszProfileName
            << endl;
    else
        ostr << "No INI file" << endl;
    if (AfxIsValidString(app.m_pszRegistryKey))
        ostr << "Registry key: "
            << app.m_pszRegistryKey
            << endl
            << ends;
    else
        ostr << "No Registry key" << endl << ends;
    MessageBox(s);
}
```

10.2 Icons and Cursors

The **CWinApp** class makes it easy to load both icons and cursors, whether they come from standard system-defined lists or custom resource files. For example, the **LoadStandardIcon** function can load any of the following system-defined icons:

IDI_APPLICATION   Default application icon
IDI_HAND   Stop Sign
IDI_QUESTION   Question mark

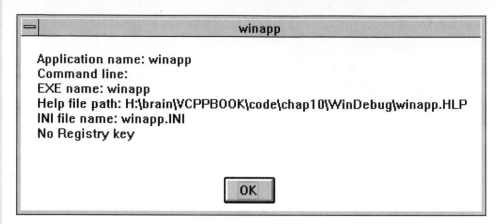

Figure 10.1
Typical output of Listing 10.1

IDI_EXCLAMATION   Exclamation point
IDI_ASTERISK   Asterisk
    Using **CWinApp**'s **LoadIcon** function, you can also load custom icons you
have designed from a resource file. The **LoadIcon** function accepts the ID of the icon
you have created. See Chapter 6 for information on icon resources.
    Listing 10.2 demonstrates how to load and display standard icons in a **CStatic**
control.

Listing 10.2
Code that alternates the CStatic control through two icons at one second intervals.

```
// icon2.cpp

#include <afxwin.h>

// Declare the application class
class CApp : public CWinApp
{
public:
    virtual BOOL InitInstance();
};

// Create an instance of the application class
CApp App;

//Declare the window class
class CWindow : public CFrameWnd
{
    CStatic* cs;
    BOOL flip;
    HICON exclamation, hand;

public:
    CWindow();
```

This book is continuously updated. See http://www.iftech.com/mfc

```
        ~CWindow();
        afx_msg void OnTimer(UINT);
        DECLARE_MESSAGE_MAP()
    };

    // Message handler for timer messages.
    // This function alternates the icon.
    void CWindow::OnTimer(UINT id)
    {
        Beep(200,200);
        flip = !flip;
        if (flip)
            cs->SetIcon(exclamation);
        else
            cs->SetIcon(hand);
    }

    // The message map
    BEGIN_MESSAGE_MAP(CWindow, CFrameWnd)
        ON_WM_TIMER()
    END_MESSAGE_MAP()

    // The InitInstance function is called once
    // when the application first executes
    BOOL CApp::InitInstance()
    {
        m_pMainWnd = new CWindow();
        m_pMainWnd->ShowWindow(m_nCmdShow);
        m_pMainWnd->UpdateWindow();
        return TRUE;
    }

    const int TIMER=100;

    CWindow::CWindow(): flip(FALSE)
    {
        // Create the window
        Create(NULL,
            "Icon Tests",
            WS_OVERLAPPEDWINDOW,
            CRect(0,0,200,200));

        // Initilize the timer event
        SetTimer(TIMER,1000,NULL);

        // Create the label
        cs = new CStatic();
        cs->Create("folder",
            WS_CHILD|WS_VISIBLE|SS_ICON,
            CRect(20,20,0,0),
            this);

        // load the exclamation point icon
        exclamation = App.LoadStandardIcon
            (IDI_EXCLAMATION);
```

```
    // Load the folder icon
    hand = App.LoadStandardIcon
        (IDI_HAND);;
}


    // The window destructor
    CWindow::~CWindow()
    {
        delete cs;
    }
```

In listing 10.2, the variables **exclamation** and **hand** are handles that point to loaded icon resources. Both are loaded from standard system resources using the **Load-StandardIcon** function available from the **CWinApp** class. Inside of the **OnTimer** function (this is the same timer mechanism demonstrated in Chapter 4), the program alternately sets the static label's icon to one of the two icons using the **SetIcon** function.

Using the technique shown in listing 10.2, you could very easily create a set of five or ten sequenced icons that implement a simple animation. When a program is busy executing a long calculation or database search, you can display the animation to show progress.

Cursors are just as easy to load, using either **LoadCursor** to load a custom cursor from a resource file or **LoadStandardCursor** to load a standard cursor. The following cursors are defined system-wide:

IDC_ARROW	Normal arrow
IDC_IBEAM	Text-insertion I-Beam
IDC_WAIT	Hourglass
IDC_CROSS	Cross-hair
IDC_UPARROW	Arrow pointing up
IDC_SIZE	Window resizing
IDC_ICON	File Dragging
IDC_SIZENWSE	Diagonal two-headed arrow
IDC_SIZENESW	Diagonal two-headed arrow
IDC_SIZEWE	Horizontal two-headed arrow
IDC_SIZENS	Vertical two-headed arrow

In general, changing the cursor is not trivial. See Section 11.5.3 for a complete discussion of the problem. However, if you want to display an hourglass cursor the framework provides two functions in the **CCmdTarget** class to handle that task. They are called **BeginWaitCursor** and **EndWaitCursor**. These functions work fine *provided that you call both within a single message-handling function*. If you try to call **BeginWaitCursor** in one message-handler function and then call **EndWaitCursor** in another, it will not work. Again, see Section 11.5.3 for a discussion.

If you want to change the cursor that **BeginWaitCursor** displays, you can do that by overriding **CWinApp::DoWaitCursor**. See the MFC documentation and source code for further information on this function.

10.3 Handling Idle Time

An application is defined as idle, at least as far as MFC is concerned, if there are no user or system events to process in the event queue. As a programmer you will frequently want to perform certain background tasks during this idle time. Prior to MFC 3.0, idle-time processing using the **CWinApp::OnIdle** function was the only facility available to handle background processing. With later versions of MFC, however, you can also create background threads as described in Chapter 35. Therefore, you often have a choice when deciding how to implement a background task.

The **OnIdle** function in the **CWinApp** class is fairly rudimentary. It is called when the event queue is empty. You have the option to override this function and perform processing whenever the function is called. However, you have to keep in mind two limitations:

1. The base functionality of the **CWinApp** class, as well as several different classes in MFC, depends on the **OnIdle** function to handle certain background tasks. Therefore, you must call down to **CWinApp::OnIdle** before you try to perform your own processing.

2. Any processing you do in **OnIdle** must have a very short duration, for example less than 0.10 seconds. If you perform long processing operations in the **OnIdle** function then your interface will stall because the application does not process events until **OnIdle** returns.

When you override **OnIdle**, you will receive an integer parameter called **lCount**. The **lCount** value starts at zero and increments each time **OnIdle** is called. This incrementing continues until the next user or system message arrives in the message queue when MFC stops calling **OnIdle** and processes the message. Then the next time MFC calls **OnIdle** the **lCount** value resets to zero and begins incrementing again. Because of this behavior, and your desire to limit your processing to very short time intervals, you can use **lCount** to segment the activities performed by your **OnIdle** function. For example, when **lCount** is 2 you might perform one type of activity, when it is 3 another, and so on. If you look at the MFC source code, you will find that the base implementation uses the **lCount** values of 0 and 1 to perform its processing.

You must also return a Boolean value from your overridden version of **OnIdle**. If you return TRUE, then MFC will call your overidden version again immediately after checking for new messages in the message queue. If you return FALSE, then MFC will not call **OnIdle** again until another message arrives in the message queue. The **lCount** parameter will be zero on the next call.

The MFC documentation recommends that you call the **CWinApp::OnIdle** function in your overridden implementation of **OnIdle** until it returns FALSE. That indicates that the framework is done with its background tasks. Then you can perform your **OnIdle** processing without interfering with its activities or overburdening the system.

In general, it is better to perform background processing in a separate thread rather than in **OnIdle**. The operating system will provide much smoother time slicing and the background processing will have no impact on the user interface. See Chapter 35 for more information. In certain cases however, such as with icon animation, it is often easier to handle the background processing in **OnIdle**, and in those cases you should take advantage of it.

10.4 Application Functionality

Quite a bit of the functionality built into the **CWinApp** class is there to facilitate the *Document/View paradigm* supported by MFC. The **CWinApp** class's functionality also makes the AppWizard's job much easier by performing a number of standard tasks automatically. See Part 3 for an in-depth discussion of both the document/view paradigm and the AppWizard.

Chapter 16 discusses the use of the AppWizard and the **CEditView** class to create text editor applications. The **CEditView** class is simply a combination of the **CView** and **CEdit** classes that lets the **CEdit** class work within the document/view paradigm. The **CEditView** class also contains a message map that automatically recognizes certain standard menu IDs and implements them for you. For example, if you create a menu bar that contains an item with the ID of ID_EDIT_CUT, and if you use that menu bar in an application that contains an instance of the **CEditView** class, then the instance will automatically detect that ID and respond to it properly. See Chapter 16 and the MFC documentation on **CEditView** for more information.

To get a good understanding of the sort of standard behavior that the **CWinApp** class contains, we will create an extremely simple program that uses **CWinApp**, **CEditView**, several standard resources and the document/view paradigm. The entire set of implications that this combination possesses will seem very large initially, but if you read this section, work through Part 3 of the book, and then return to this section, you will find that you have a very good understanding of the default behavior of the MFC framework invoked by the AppWizard.

Listing 10.3 creates probably the simplest possible program making use of *document templates*. See Chapter 14 for a discussion of document templates. See Chapter 12 and the MFC documentation for a discussion of the DYNCREATE macros. Use the instructions in the following sections to compile and run this code.

Listing 10.3
The simplest possible program using a document template.

```
//docview.cpp
#include <afxwin.h>
#include <afxext.h>
#include "resource.h"

// Declare the application class
class CApp : public CWinApp
{
public:
    virtual BOOL InitInstance();
    DECLARE_MESSAGE_MAP()
```

```
};

// Create an instance of the application class
CApp app;

// Declare the main window class
class CWindow : public CFrameWnd
{
    DECLARE_DYNCREATE(CWindow)
};
IMPLEMENT_DYNCREATE(CWindow, CFrameWnd)

class CDoc : public CDocument
{
    DECLARE_DYNCREATE(CDoc)
public:
    virtual void Serialize(CArchive& ar)
    {
        ((CEditView*)m_viewList.GetHead())->SerializeRaw(ar);
    }
};
IMPLEMENT_DYNCREATE(CDoc, CDocument)

class CEdView : public CEditView
{
    DECLARE_DYNCREATE(CEdView)
};
IMPLEMENT_DYNCREATE(CEdView, CEditView)

// The InitInstance function is called each
// time the application first executes.
BOOL CApp::InitInstance()
{
    CSingleDocTemplate* pDocTemplate;
    pDocTemplate = new CSingleDocTemplate(
        IDR_STANDARD,
        RUNTIME_CLASS(CDoc),
        RUNTIME_CLASS(CWindow),
        RUNTIME_CLASS(CEdView));
    AddDocTemplate(pDocTemplate);

    // command line parsing
    if (m_lpCmdLine[0] == '\0')
        OnFileNew();
    else
        OpenDocumentFile(m_lpCmdLine);

    return TRUE;
}

BEGIN_MESSAGE_MAP(CApp, CWinApp)
    ON_COMMAND(ID_FILE_NEW, CWinApp::OnFileNew)
    ON_COMMAND(ID_FILE_OPEN, CWinApp::OnFileOpen)
END_MESSAGE_MAP()
```

10.4.1 Create the Project

Create a new MFC project as described in Appendix B.3. Call the project "docview."

10.4.2 Create the C++ File

Create a new text file for the C++ code in Listing 10.3. Save the code to a file named DOCVIEW.CPP.

10.4.3 Add the C++ File to the Project

Add the DOCVIEW.CPP file to the project as described in Appendix B.3.

10.4.4 Create a New Resource Script

To create a new resource script for this application see Appendix B.5.2. Call the file SCRIPT.RC.

10.4.5 Add the RC File to the Project

Add the SCRIPT.RC file to the project as shown in Appendix B.5.2.

10.4.6 Add a String Table

Following the directions in Chapter 6, add a string table to the resource script. Create a string in the table with the ID of IDR_STANDARD. Give the string the following caption:

```
edit\n\nEdit\nEdit Files (*.tex)\n.TEX\nEdit.Document\nEdit Document
```
See the section on **CDocTemplate::GetDocString** in the MFC documentation for more information on this string and its components.

10.4.7 Add a Menu

Following the directions in Chapter 6, add a menu to the resource script. The menu should have the ID of IDR_STANDARD (double click on the right side of the new menu bar in the menu resource editor to change the ID). Create a **File** menu and give it the options **New**, **Open** and **Exit**. *The IDs for these three options should be ID_FILE_NEW, ID_FILE_OPEN and ID_APP_EXIT respectively.*

10.4.8 Add an Icon

Following the directions in Chapter 6, add an icon to the resource script. *The ID for the icon should also be IDR_STANDARD.*

10.4.9 Compile and Run

Compile and run the program. You will find that the New and Open options work properly, and that the program exits as it should, asking you if you want to save changed information. For more information on creating an editor like this with the AppWizard and extending its capabilities, see Chapter 16.

10.4.10 Understanding What Just Happened

Why does the code in listing 10.3 work? Why did an application that, at least on the surface, contains no code implement a fairly complete text editor application? The key to understanding the application in Listing 10.3 is the call to **AddDocTemplate**, along with the default behavior it invokes and the peripheral functions in **CWinApp** that leverage the template.

The call to **AddDocTemplate** creates a new *document template* in **CWinApp**'s list of templates. The template specifies four things:

- A set of resources for this template, specified by the resource ID of IDR_STANDARD in this case
- A document class
- A window class
- A view class

The code in Listing 10.3 also uses two different **CWinApp** functions after it creates the template: **OnFileNew**, **OpenDocumentFile**. In the message map it calls **OnFileNew** and **OnFileOpen**.

A document template is a structure held internally in a document template list in the **CWinApp** class. The template bonds together a document class, a view class and a set of resources. As described in detail in Part 3, the view handles the presentation of data to the user, while the document handles data manipulation. The resource ID specifies a collection of resources needed by the document and view, generally including a menu, its accelerator table, a document string and an icon. It is possible (see Chapter 16) for a single MDI application to contain multiple document templates, and this allows the application to display a variety of document types in its MDI shell. For example, Visual C++ can display text files, resources, browser information and so on in its MDI shell. You can easily create applications with this sort of behavior because of the document template facility.

Once the code in Listing 10.3 creates a document template and calls the **AddDocTemplate** function, the instance of the **CWinApp** class is able to do several things. First, it can load the resources having an ID of IDR_STANDARD and use them. Therefore, it can apply a menu bar to the window, give the window an icon, and use the document string in the string table to determine file extensions, title bar information and so on. It can also create instances of the document and view classes. It can then bring the window on to the screen. All of this happens completely automatically.

The code in Listing 10.3 then decides whether the user wants to open an initial file or not. If not, the **OnFileNew** option simply clears the document and view. If there is a file to open, then the **OpenDocumentFile** function opens the file and calls the **Serialize** function (see Chapter 12) in the document template's document class. The **Serialize** function in Listing 10.3 tells the instance of **CEditView** to load the data directly from the text file and display it.

The user can then type into the edit view, or choose a menu option. If the user chooses the **Open** option in the **File** menu, the message map in Listing 10.3 picks it up and calls **CWinApp**'s **OnFileOpen** function. This function creates a File Open dialog (see Chapter 7). Once the user chooses a file, the function calls **OnDocumentOpen**, which was described in the previous paragraph. If the user chooses the **Exit** option, the **CWinApp** class contains an embedded message map that detects ID_APP_EXIT, checks to see if the current file needs saving, saves it if requested to do so by the user, and then exits. Look in the MFC source code for this message map and the function it calls to see the default behavior (use the **Find in Files** option in the **Search** menu of Visual C++ to search the files in the MFC source directory for the ID_APP_EXIT string).

You can see that the document template added with **AddDocTemplate** simply supplies the application's instance of **CWinApp** with some classes. The code in the **CWinApp** class then implements a number of standard behaviors and uses those classes in known ways. For example, when you call **OnFileOpen**, the **CWinApp** class already contains the code that implements the open dialog. The code then calls the **Serialize** function in the document class. That is known behavior. If you fit your code into that known behavior—a process described in Part 3—then you can leverage the existing implementation already contained in MFC to significantly reduce the amount of code that you have to write.

The following functions in the **CWinApp** class are all relevant when creating applications:

DoMessageBox	Standard message box for application
OnContextHelp	Handles context sensitive help (see Chapter 19)
OnFileNew	Handles new file menu option (call from message map)
OnFileOpen	Handles open file menu option (call from message map)
OnFilePrintSetup	Creates print setup dialog (call from message map)
OnHelp	Handles context sensitive help (see Chapter 19)
OnHelpIndex	Activates help window (see Chapter 19)
OnHelpUsing	Activates help on help (see Chapter 19)
OpenDocumentFile	Opens a document file by calling its **Serialize** function
SaveAllModified	Displays a save dialog
WinHelp	Implements **WinHelp** function
AddToRecentFileList	Adds files to MRU file list. Called automatically by **OnFileOpen**

The AppWizard makes use of all of these functions. See the MFC documentation and Part 3 of this book for further information.

10.5 Initialization Features

The **CWinApp** class provides several important functions that you call in the **InitInstance** function to activate different built-in features.

The simplest of these functions is **Enable3dControls**. If you call this function in the first line of the **InitInstance** function in Listing 10.3, then the dialogs produced will have 3D controls. This is especially useful when running under Windows NT. A related function is **SetDialogBkColor**, which changes the background color and the text color on controls in dialogs. It would be better to avoid this function and let the user choose these colors globally in the Control Panel.

It is also possible to integrate your applications with the File Manager and its Associate capability. You can do this by adding the following two lines of code following the addition of the document template in **InitInstance**:

```
RegisterShellFileTypes();
EnableShellOpen();
```

The first line causes the application to use its document string in the string table and register its file extension and name with the File Manager. The user can then associate files with your application using the **Associate** option in the File Manager's **File** menu. The call to **EnableShellOpen** allows the File Manager to launch the application with file names that the user has chosen in the File Manager.

The **CWinApp** class contains automatic handling of INI files (or direct registry entries) through the following six functions:

LoadStdProfileSettings	Loads the INI file and MRU strings
SetRegistryKey	Forces the application to use the registry for INI information
GetProfileInt	Retrieves an integer value from the INI file
WriteProfileInt	Sets an integer value in the INI file
GetProfileString	Retrieves a string value from the INI file
WriteProfileString	Sets an integer value in the INI file

The easiest way to experiment with these functions is to first place a call to **LoadStdProfileSettings** near the top of the **InitInstance** function in Listing 10.3. Pass to the function the value four, as shown here:

```
LoadStdProfileSettings(4);
```

The parameter specifies that the INI file maintain a four item MRU (Most Recently Used) file list. Recompile and run Listing 10.3 after making this change. Use the **Open** menu option to open a file, and then close the application. If you look in the root directory for the NT system files on your machine, you will find that there is a new file named DOCVIEW.INI which contains the path to the file you opened. To enable the display of the MRU file list in the **File** menu of the application, all that you have to do is add a menu option that has the ID of ID_FILE_MRU_FILE1. Give the menu item any caption that you like, although "No Files" might be appropriate. If there are files in the MRU list, then the that Caption will be ignored. Try adding this menu item to the menu associated with Listing 10.3, and compile and rerun. You will find that the MRU list in the **File** menu is now fully functional. By changing the parameter passed to **LoadStdProfileSettings**, you can include up to 16 files in the MRU list in the menu.

Note that the **OnFileOpen** function in the **CWinApp** class automatically adds file names to the MRU list, but you can also add files to it with the **AddToRecent-FileList** function.

An INI file is normally divided into named sections, and each section contains named entries. The entries have values associated with them of type integer or string. You can create any sections and entries that you like in an INI file to store whatever sort of configuration information is important to your application. Use the **WriteProfileInt** and **WriteProfileString** functions to create or change entries, and use the **GetProfileInt** and **GetProfileString** entries to retrieve values you have previously stored. Note that at least one other part of MFC besides the MRU portion places values automatically in the INI file, that being the print preview portion of the hierarchy. It stores the number of preview pages in the INI file.

On systems that support the registry, you should store your INI entries in the registry rather than in an INI file. This is facilitated by the **SetRegistryKey** function. For a complete description of the registry and other important application features under Windows NT and Win32, see the book *"Win32 System Services: The Heart of Windows NT"* by Marshall Brain, ISBN 0-13-097825-6.

10.6 Miscellaneous Features

Other functions available in the **CWinApp** class that are sometimes useful are listed below:

GetPrinterDeviceDefaults	Returns a printer dialog structure from which you can extract the printer's DC. See Chapters 11, 15 and 18 for more information on printing.
InitApplication	Use to perform one-time application initialization
InitInstance	Use to perform per-instance application initialization
ExitInstance	Use to perform any clean-up or closings to reverse the actions of the **InitInstance** function as application terminates
PreTranslateMessage	Use to catch messages before they are translated and dispatched by the message loop (see Chapter 5 for an example)
ProcessMessageFilter	Use to trap specified messages and process them outside of the normal MFC message loop
ProcessWndProcException	Use to handle unhandled exceptions (see Chapter 13)

See the MFC documentation for details.

10.7 Conclusion

The **CWinApp** class is central to the operation of any MFC application. In this chapter you have learned about the basics of its many capabilities. You may find that tracing through many of the **CWinApp** member functions in the MFC source will help to give you a much more complete understanding of what this class can do.

DRADING

Although Windows provides a "graphical user interface," few applications actually make use of drawn graphics. There are two reasons for this. First, while the API encapsulates text editing and list manipulation in easy-to-use objects, there is no single object that encapsulates a drawing editor or a "click-able picture." Second, a tremendous number of functions are available in the graphics library, and getting to know them all can be a daunting task that many people have chosen to ignore.

Drawing turns out to be fairly straightforward, however. Once you understand the basics, it is easy to learn all the different capabilities in the graphics library because everything is related. For example, if you know how to draw a line, it is easy to draw a rectangle, an ellipse, and a polygon because the concepts are the same. Drawing is also an extremely important skill to master for an often overlooked reason: Any printing that you plan to do from Windows must be done by drawing onto a printing device. Learning how to draw is a prelude to learning how to print, a topic covered in detail in Part 3.

The goal of this chapter is to introduce the GDI library so you can add drawn graphics to your applications. We will discuss three major topics in this chapter:

1. Simple drawing concepts using lines, rectangles, circles, and so on.
2. Mouse interaction with drawn graphics.
3. Advanced drawing concepts including mapping and printing.

Once you complete this chapter you will see how easy it is to add graphics to every program you create.

11.1 Introduction to the GDI Library

The GDI library in the Win32 API offers a huge assortment of functions. It acts as a common and independent interface between applications and all the drawing devices that may be attached to a Windows workstation. For example, whether you are drawing to a 640 x 480 VGA screen, a 1280 x 1024 CAD monitor, or a 300 x 300 dpi laser printer, all the drawing commands work exactly the same way. The GDI library abstracts all these devices into a common application interface.

The GDI library can be broken up into groups of related functions. The list below summarizes the library's capabilities so you can get an idea of its breadth and completeness:

- General drawing: lines, rectangles, ellipses, arcs, text
- Drawing tools: pens, brushes, fonts, colors
- Mapping transformations to handle device-independent coordinate systems
- Miscellaneous features: clipping, regions
- Bitmaps: stored rectangular groups of pixels
- Metafiles: stored collections of drawn shapes

The list above is arranged in order of increasing specialization. For example, the first two groups of functions are the most general and will be used in every drawing you create. The groups at the bottom are more specialized and are needed less often.

11.2 GDI Basics

If you've never worked with computer graphics, there are several general concepts and vocabulary words that you need to know before you start. Several Windows-specific concepts also require discussion.

Figure 11.1 shows a typical screen displaying several windows and points out some of the vocabulary used to describe different elements on this screen. The most obvious thing in Figure 11.1 is that both the screen and its windows have their own coordinate systems, but they are almost totally unrelated. Each window manages its own coordinate system. The upper left corner of every window is that window's origin. The positive X direction extends to the right of the origin, while the positive Y direction extends downward unless you modify the mapping mode as described in Section 11.6.1.

Almost everything you do through the GDI library is done in window coordinates. When you draw, you do so relative to the coordinate system of the current window. There are only a few special situations where the screen's coordinate system is used.

All devices that break up their output into individual dots are called *raster devices*. Almost all devices today are raster devices–screens, dot matrix printers, laser printers, and so on. The alternative is a *stroked device* that draws with smooth, continuous strokes. The only stroked device commonly seen anymore is a plotter. The common unit of measure across all raster devices is the *pixel*. A pixel is an individual picture element, or dot, on the screen or printer. A screen is measured in pixels–for example, a typical VGA screen measures 640 x 480 pixels, and a window on the screen has a width and height expressed in pixels as well.

Pixels are not always a good way to think about drawing, however, because they are device-dependent. For example, a normal monitor might spread 640 pixels across ten inches of screen (64 pixels per inch), while most laser printers display 300 or 600 pixels per inch. A large figure drawn in pixel coordinates on screen would therefore

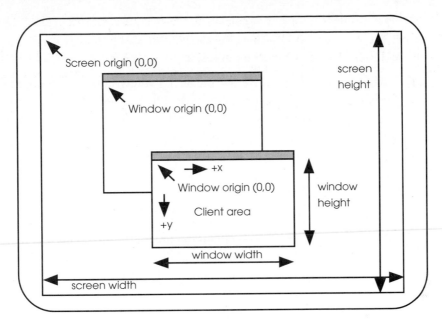

Figure 11.1
Elements of a Windows screen

appear about one-fifth that size when rendered on a 300 dpi laser printer. Windows allows you to change to device-independent coordinate systems, such as 1/100 of a inch or 1/20 of a point. Windows then does the translation from that coordinate system to a specific device for you. These *mappings*, as they're called, are discussed in Section 11.6.1.

Each window contains a drawing area called the *client area*. This area is distinguished from the non-client area: the parts of the window refreshed automatically by Windows itself. Generally the non-client area consists of the title bar, the re-sizing bars, and any scroll bars handled by the window. Anything you draw is *clipped* at the edge of the client area. If you draw a line 600 pixels long into a window that is 200 x 200 pixels, the portion that should be visible in the window is displayed and the rest gets clipped off automatically.

All drawing systems require you to understand a concept called *exposure* and *exposure events*. When a part of a window is exposed, it is the responsibility of the application to redraw it. For example, if your application's window has been covered by another window and that other window closes, part or all of your window is exposed. Your application will receive an event telling it to handle the exposure. The application receives exposure events when it first appears on the screen, when the user re-sizes the window, when the user maximizes the window, or when any part of the window becomes visible to the user because of another window's movement or disappearance. The system calls the **CWnd::OnPaint** function automatically through the message map on each exposure event, as discussed in Section 11.4.1.

11.3 Device Contexts

Before you draw on any Windows device, you must obtain what is called a *Device Context* (DC). The DC serves two purposes:

1. It accesses the proper device driver for the device you wish to draw onto. This is the "Device" portion of DC. For example, the DC that you obtain for a printer has different capabilities than one you obtain for the screen. If a system has multiple printers attached, each one may have a different device driver controlling it. The DC maps the device-independent GDI library calls to a specific device. Once you obtain a DC for a device, you have access to a great deal of information about the device using the **CDC::GetDeviceCaps** function. In fact, you can get far more information about a device through this function than you will normally ever use. Two pieces of information, HORZRES and VERTRES, are very useful. They contain the horizontal and vertical resolution of the device in pixels (also translatable to other units). These values tell you how big a sheet of paper the current printer settings support or the maximum size of a window on the current screen.

2. A DC keeps track of the current drawing context. This is the "Context" portion of DC. When you draw a line, for example, the system needs to know the line's starting and ending points, as well as how thick to make the line and what color it should be. In order to draw text, the system needs to know the font, size, and style, as well as the actual string and where to draw it. The DC stores attributes, such as line color and width or text font.

One way to design a drawing system is to have the programmer pass all the attributes for each shape on every call to the library. This tends to be wasteful in most cases because it turns out there is a lot of identical information from call to call. Generally, a drawing containing 100 lines will use the same color, line width, and mapping mode for each line. The DC remembers (caches, in a way) all the current settings. When you need to change something, like the color of the pen, you change it in the DC and then it applies to all subsequent shapes that you draw with that DC.

The DC contains a number of abstractions and each has default settings when you create a new DC. The abstractions and their defaults are listed below:

- Pen: Any line (including the lines that frame a rectangle or circle) is drawn using the current *pen*, which controls the line style, width, and color. The defaults are black, one pixel wide solid lines.
- Brush: Any filling, as in the filling of the interior of a rectangle or circle, is done using the current *brush*. The brush controls the color and pattern used for the fill. The default is solid white fill.
- Font: Any text is drawn using the current *font*. The font specifies the current type face, size, style, etc., of the characters used. The default is the system font.

198

- Mapping mode: The mapping mode controls the units used for drawing, for example inches, points, or millimeters. The default mode is device-dependent pixel coordinates.

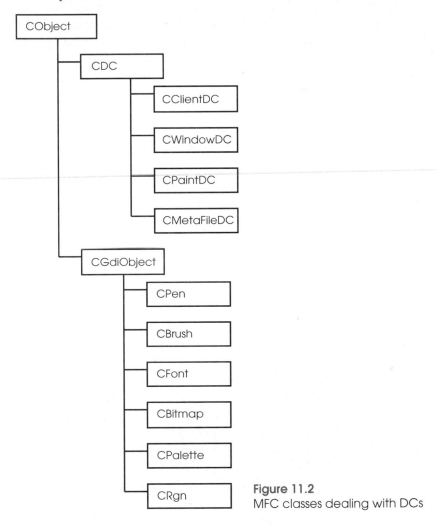

Figure 11.2
MFC classes dealing with DCs

The device context also keeps track of a number of loose pieces of information including:

- Current pen position: The default is (0,0).
- Current background color: The default is white.
- Current text color: The default is black.
- Current drawing mode: The default is R2_COPYPEN.
- Current filling mode for polygons: The default is ALTERNATE.
- Current clipping region: The default is the current client area or sheet of paper.

When you want to draw, you request a certain type of DC, depending on your situation and goals at the moment. For example, if you wish to draw into the current window, you get a Client DC for the window so you can draw in the client area. If you want to draw into a window in response to an ON_WM_PAINT message from an exposure event, you obtain a Paint DC for the window. If you want to print, you get a DC for the desired printer (see Section11.6.3). Or you can create a DC that allows you to draw into a memory bitmap and then copy it to the screen to create animation. Each of these different techniques will be discussed in the following sections.

One thing you need to know about DCs is that they are limited, especially in older versions of Windows. There is no guarantee you will get one when you request it, and you should release them as soon as you have finished using them. The Win32 API alleviates many of the problems associated with DCs, and MFC handles many of the details for you in this regard.

MFC contains the classes shown in Figure 11.2 for working with DCs and drawing. We will see examples of these classes in the following sections.

11.4 Simple Drawing

In this section we examine the techniques used to draw shapes in a window. You will learn how to draw lines, rectangles, circles, arcs, polygons, text, and pixels.

11.4.1 The Basics

Let's say you want to create an extremely simple drawing in Windows. For example, imagine that you would like to open a window and draw a diagonal line across it. There are several basic steps you must follow to create the line, as shown in Listing 11.1.

Listing 11.1
A drawing program that creates a diagonal line across a window

```
// line1.cpp

#include <afxwin.h>

// Define an application class
class CApp : public CWinApp
{
public:
    virtual BOOL InitInstance();
};

CApp App;

// define the window class
class CWindow : public CFrameWnd
{
public:
    CWindow();
    afx_msg void OnPaint();
    DECLARE_MESSAGE_MAP()
};
```

```
// The window's constructor
CWindow::CWindow()
{
    Create(NULL, "Drawing Tests",
        WS_OVERLAPPEDWINDOW,
        CRect(0,0,200,200));
}


// The message map
BEGIN_MESSAGE_MAP( CWindow, CFrameWnd )
    ON_WM_PAINT()
END_MESSAGE_MAP()

// handle exposure events
void CWindow::OnPaint()
{
    CRect rect;
    GetClientRect( rect );
    CPaintDC dc(this);
    dc.MoveTo(0,0);
    dc.LineTo(rect.Width(),rect.Height());
}

// Init the application
BOOL CApp::InitInstance()
{
    m_pMainWnd = new CWindow();
    m_pMainWnd->ShowWindow(m_nCmdShow);
    m_pMainWnd->UpdateWindow();
    return TRUE;
}
```

Listing 11.1 contains the normal instance of **CWinApp** and **CFrameWnd**. The unique code that handles drawing is in the **OnPaint** function:

```
// The message map
BEGIN_MESSAGE_MAP( CWindow, CFrameWnd )
    ON_WM_PAINT()
END_MESSAGE_MAP()

// handle exposure events
void CWindow::OnPaint()
{
    CRect rect;
    GetClientRect( rect );
    CPaintDC dc(this);
    dc.MoveTo(0,0);
    dc.LineTo(rect.Width(),rect.Height());
}
```

The system generates WM_PAINT messages whenever a part of the window becomes exposed. The event is generated when the window first appears on screen, when it is re-sized larger, when it restores itself from an icon, or when another window covering it disappears. The message map calls the **OnPaint** function in response to these events because of its ON_WM_PAINT entry. The **OnPaint** function shown here starts by getting the client rectangle: it needs to know where the bottom right corner of the window is in order to draw a diagonal line. It then creates a Paint DC for the current window by creating an instance of the **CPaintDC** class and passing it the current window (**this**). Whenever you respond to a WM_PAINT event in the **OnPaint** function, you should use a Paint DC because it contains information about the exposed regions of the drawing surface.

Once the function obtains the DC, it can draw. To draw a line, you move to the line's starting point and then draw to its ending point using the **MoveTo** and **LineTo** functions, respectively. **MoveTo** moves the pen to a point without drawing anything, while **LineTo** draws when it moves. Both functions accept the x and y coordinates of the position to which they are moving. These two functions are member functions of the general **CDC** class, from which the **CPaintDC** class derives its behavior. You should look up both classes in the MFC documentation. You will find that the **CDC** class encapsulates everything to do with drawing. It has 100 or so functions representing all the different drawing capabilities offered by MFC. The four specialized DC classes (**CPaintDC, CClientDC, CMetaFileDC,** and **CWindowDC**) inherit their behavior from the **CDC** class.

When you run the program in Listing 11.1, notice that it refreshes itself in all appropriate cases. For example, if you re-size the window, it clears automatically and the **OnPaint** function redraws the diagonal to the new dimensions. If you minimize the window and then restore it, **OnPaint** gets called and redraws the line. Because the diagonal line is drawn in **OnPaint**, it is always visible.

What if this code didn't use the **OnPaint** function? Let's say we eliminate the message map and **OnPaint** function entirely and create the window with the following function:

```
// The window's constructor
CWindow::CWindow()
{
    Create(NULL, "Drawing Tests",
        WS_OVERLAPPEDWINDOW,
        CRect(0,0,200,200));
    CRect rect;
    GetClientRect( rect );
    CClientDC dc(this);
    dc.MoveTo(0,0);
    dc.LineTo(rect.Width(),rect.Height());
}
```

In this new constructor for the window, we create a Client DC and draw the diagonal line right after the window is created. If you try out this code, you'll find it does nothing: The window opens but it is empty. The problem is that although the window has technically been created, the constructor has not completed when it draws the line. As a result, the window is not on the screen yet. The line gets drawn onto a non-existent window. When the window finally does appear, it is blank. Because there is no **OnPaint** function to handle exposure, the window remains blank when it is re-sized or exposed. The use of the **OnPaint** function and the Paint DC in Listing 11.1 solves this problem by waiting until the window actually appears on screen and then responding to the first exposure event.

You use Client DCs, as opposed to Paint DCs, when there is a window already sitting on the screen that needs something drawn in it. You use Client DCs to respond to the application's needs rather than to an exposure event. We will see an example of this technique when integrating mouse functionality into drawing programs.

The **dc** variable declared in the **OnPaint** function in Listing 11.1 is a sensitive resource. Inside the MFC hierarchy, this DC is reserved by a call to **BeginPaint** function in the 32-bit API and it must be released later with a call to **EndPaint**. The **BeginPaint** call occurs in the **CPaintDC** constructor and the **EndPaint** call occurs in the **CPaintDC** destructor. Therefore, if you create the DC as a member of the window class, or as a global variable, it will cause many problems because the **EndPaint** half of the pair will never get called. Always declare a DC variable as a local variable inside of **OnPaint** or in another short-lived function.

11.4.2 Lines and Pens

When we drew the diagonal line in the last section, we used the Paint DC without modifying it in any way. It contained all the standard default settings for line width, color, font, and so on. The default line settings create lines that are one pixel wide and black. You can modify the defaults for drawing a line by creating a new pen with appropriate characteristics. The code in listing 11.2 demonstrates how to draw lines using a different pen. Figure 11.3 shows the output of this code.

Listing 11.2
A set of lines drawn using an alternate pen.

```
// line2.cpp

#include <afxwin.h>

// Define the application class
class CApp : public CWinApp
{
public:
    virtual BOOL InitInstance();
};

CApp App;

// define the window class
class CWindow : public CFrameWnd
{
public:
    CWindow();
    void OnPaint();
    DECLARE_MESSAGE_MAP()
};

// The window's constructor
```

```
CWindow::CWindow()
{
    Create(NULL, "Drawing Tests",
        WS_OVERLAPPEDWINDOW,
        CRect(0,0,250,100));
}

// The message map
BEGIN_MESSAGE_MAP( CWindow, CFrameWnd )
    ON_WM_PAINT()
END_MESSAGE_MAP()

// Handle exposure events
void CWindow::OnPaint()
{
    CRect rect;
    int x;

    GetClientRect( rect );
    CPaintDC dc(this);

    // Modify the pen
    CPen pen(PS_SOLID, 2, RGB(0,0,255)), *oldPen;
    oldPen = dc.SelectObject(&pen);

    // draw a set of lines
    for (x=0; x<rect.Width(); x+=10)
    {
        dc.MoveTo(0,0);
        dc.LineTo(x,rect.Height());
    }

    // Return old pen
    dc.SelectObject(oldPen);
}

// Init the application
BOOL CApp::InitInstance()
{
    m_pMainWnd = new CWindow();
    m_pMainWnd->ShowWindow(m_nCmdShow);
    m_pMainWnd->UpdateWindow();
    return TRUE;
}
```

In the code shown in Listing 11.2, the **OnPaint** function creates a Paint DC and then creates a new pen as an instance of the **CPen** class. The constructor for the **CPen** class accepts parameters that determine the new pen's drawing characteristics, as shown below (see also **CPen::CPen** in the MFC documentation):

```
CPen::CPen( int nPenStyle, int nWidth,
    DWORD crColor );
```

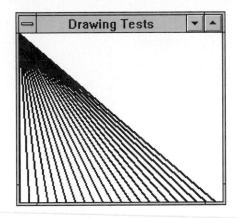

Figure 11.3
A set of lines drawn using an alternate pen. The lines are blue and two pixels wide on a color monitor

nPenStyle	Possible values: PS_SOLID, PS_DASH, PS_DOT, PS_DASHDOT, PS_DASHDOTDOT, PS_NULL, PS_INSIDEFRAME.
nWidth	The width of the pen. Only valid for PEN_SOLID. The value 0 means "one pixel wide regardless of the mapping mode."
crColor	RGB pen color.

The parameters passed in the example code indicate that a two pixel wide solid blue pen should be used. The RGB function accepts intensities for the three RGB colors in the range of 0 to 255 and then displays the closest match possible. The pen is then hooked to the DC with the **SelectObject** function. All subsequent drawing with this DC will use this pen until it changes again.

11.4.3 Rectangles and Brushes

If you replace the **OnPaint** function shown in Listing 11.2 with the version shown in Listing 11.3, you create a filled rectangle as shown in Figure 11.4.

Listing 11.3
Code that creates a filled rectangle. Replace the **OnPaint** function in Listing 11.2 with this function.

```
// rect.cpp

// Handle exposures
void CWindow::OnPaint()
{
    CRect rect;

    GetClientRect( rect );
    CPaintDC dc(this);

    // Create a new pen
    CPen pen(PS_SOLID, 2, RGB(0,0,255)), *oldPen;
    oldPen = dc.SelectObject(&pen);
```

```
// Create a new brush
CBrush brush(HS_CROSS,RGB(255,0,0)), *oldBrush;
oldBrush = dc.SelectObject(&brush);

// Draw a rectangle with the new pen and brush
rect.InflateRect(-20, -20);
dc.Rectangle(rect);

// Return old pen and brush
dc.SelectObject(oldPen)
dc.SelectObject(oldBrush);
}
```

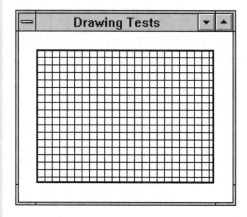

Figure 11.4
A filled rectangle

This new **OnPaint** function starts by creating a Paint DC, attaching a new pen to it, and then creating and attaching a new brush. A brush is used to fill shapes such as rectangles and ellipses, as shown below:

```
CBrush::CBrush(DWORD crColor)
CBrush::CBrush(int nIndex, DWORD crColor)
CBrush(CBitmap *pBitmap)
```

crColor   RGB pen color.
nIndex   possible values: HS_BDIAGONAL, HS_CROSS,
                 HS_DIAGCROSS, HS_FDIAGONAL,
                 HS_HORIZONTAL, HS_VERTICAL.
pBitmap   A pointer to a bitmap.

The first form of the constructor creates a solid brush with the color specified. The second form creates a hatched brush. This is the form used in Listing 11.3. The third form of the constructor uses a bitmap loaded from a resource file to create the brush's pattern (see Chapter 6 for information on resources). Only the upper left 8 x 8 pixels of the bitmap are actually used.

Once you have created the pen and brush and attached them to the DC, you can draw. Listing 11.3 calls the **Rectangle** function to draw the rectangle. This function draws the border of the rectangle with the current pen and fills the interior of the rectangle with the current brush.

If you look at the **CDC** class in the MFC documentation, you will find a number of other functions that deal with rectangles. For example, **FillRect** accepts a **CRect** parameter and a **CBrush** parameter and fills the rectangle using the specified brush. This is a shortcut around attaching the brush to the DC. The **FrameRect** function takes the same two parameters and paints just the border of the rectangle with the specified brush. This function is usually called after a call to **FillRect** to clean up the right and bottom edges of the rectangle. The **InvertRect** function inverts the rectangle's contents. The **RoundRect** function creates a rectangle with rounded corners. You pass **RoundRect** a **CRect** parameter that specifies the size of the rectangle and a **CPoint** parameter that specifies the width and height of an ellipse used to round off the corners. Finally, **DrawFocusRect** draws the specified rectangle in the same way default rectangles are drawn around buttons. This function uses a special drawing mode. If you draw the same focus rectangle a second time, it is removed. This allows you to turn the focus rectangle on and off without disturbing the image underneath.

11.4.4 Circles, Ellipses, Arcs, and Chords

You create ellipses and circles just like rectangles. The rectangle passed as a parameter bounds the ellipse that is drawn. You can replace the call that creates the rectangle in Listing 11.3 with the following code to demonstrate an ellipse. You will see the window shown in Figure 11.5.

```
// ellipse.cpp

dc.Ellipse(rect);
```

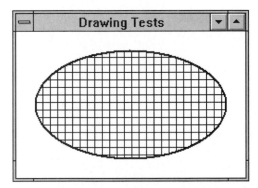

Figure 11.5
An ellipse

The **CDC** class also contains functions for drawing arcs, pie wedges, and chords, as demonstrated in Listing 11.4. If you replace the **OnPaint** function in Listing 11.2 with Listing 11.4, you will see a window similar to the one shown in Figure 11.6.

Listing 11.4
Code that draws an arc, a pie wedge, and a chord. Replace the **OnPaint** function in Listing 11.2 with this function.

```
// arc.cpp

#include <math.h>

// converts angle a to a point on rect r
CPoint Angle(CRect r, double a)
{
    const double pi=3.1415926535;
    //convert from degrees to radians
    a = a * pi / 180.0;
    // find the center of the ellipse
    CPoint c = r.TopLeft();
    c.Offset(r.Width()/2, r.Height()/2);
    // find the point
    c.Offset((int)(cos(a)*r.Width()/2),
        (int)(-sin(a)*r.Height())/2);
    return c;
}

// Handle exposure
void CWindow::OnPaint()
{
    CRect rect;

    GetClientRect( rect );
    CPaintDC dc(this);

    // Modify the pen and brush
    CPen pen(PS_SOLID, 2, RGB(0,0,255)), *oldpen;
    CBrush brush(RGB(255,0,0)), *oldBrush;
    oldpen = dc.SelectObject(&pen);
    oldBrush = dc.SelectObject(&brush);
    rect.InflateRect(-20, -20);

    // Drawn an arc, pie-wedge, and chord
    dc.Arc(rect, Angle(rect, 0.0),
        Angle(rect, 90.0));
    dc.Pie(rect, Angle(rect, 90.0),
        Angle(rect, 180.0));
    dc.Chord(rect, Angle(rect, 180.0),
        Angle(rect, 270.0));

    dc.SelectObject(oldPen);
    dc.SelectObject(oldBrush);
}
```

The **Arc** function is typical of all three and is summarized below:

```
BOOL CDC::Arc(CRect lpRect, CPoint ptStart,
    CPoint ptEnd)
```

lpRect	The rectangle describing the ellipse
ptStart	The starting point of the arc
ptEnd	The ending point of the arc

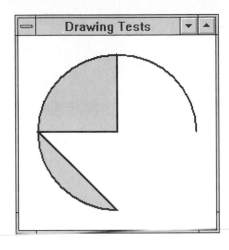

Figure 11.6
A window displaying an arc, a pie wedge,
and a chord

There is also a second form of the **Arc** function that accepts eight integer values instead of the three classes (see the MFC documentation for details).

All three functions require the starting and ending point of the arc being drawn. What you would like to pass is a pair of angles–say 10 degrees and 90 degrees–and draw the arc between those angles. Unfortunately, Windows specifies that the starting and ending points be passed as points on the ellipse. The function **Angle** that appears in Listing 11.4 helps to solve this problem. It accepts the rectangle specifying the complete ellipse, as well as an angle, and calculates the corresponding point on the curve. To use **Angle** in a program, you must include <math.h>.

The **Pie** and **Chord** functions accept the same parameters and draw a filled wedge and a filled chord as shown in the figure.

11.4.5 Polygons

Windows supports the creation of closed, filled polygons that are specified using arrays of points. The code in Listing 11.5 demonstrates the creation of the polygon shown in Figure 11.7. Substitute this code for the **OnPaint** function in Listing 11.2.

Listing 11.5
The creation of a polygon. Replace the **OnPaint** function in Listing 11.2 with this function.

```
//polygon1.cpp

// Handle exposures
void CWindow::OnPaint()
{
    CPaintDC dc(this);

    // Change the pen and brush
    CPen pen(PS_SOLID, 2, RGB(0,0,255)), *oldPen;
    CBrush brush(RGB(255,0,0)), *oldBrush;
    oldPen = dc.SelectObject(&pen);
```

```
oldBrush = dc.SelectObject(&brush);

// Create an array of points for the polygon
CPoint a[10];
a[0] = CPoint(20,50);
a[1] = CPoint(100,20);
a[2] = CPoint(200,150);
a[3] = CPoint(80,200);
dc.Polygon(a, 4);

// Return old pen and brush
dc.SelectObject(oldPen);
dc.SelectObject(oldBrush);
}
```

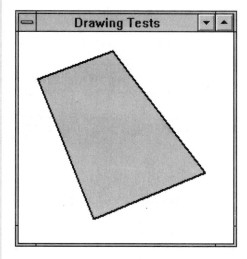

Figure 11.7
A polygon

The code in Listing 11.5 creates an array of **CPoint** structures and fills it with four points. The **Polygon** function draws from point to point in the order specified and then closes the figure if the first and last points are not equal.

If the lines that make up the polygon happen to cross, then the function uses the value set by the **SetPolyFillMode** function to determine how it should fill the polygon. For example, the code shown in Listing 11.6 produced Figure 11.8 using the ALTERNATE filling mode. If you modify the code to use the WINDING mode, you get the polygon shown in Figure 11.9. The default mode is ALTERNATE.

Listing 11.6
A polygon with crossing lines.

```
// polygon2.cpp

// Handle exposure
void CWindow::OnPaint()
{
```

```
CPaintDC dc(this);

// Change the pen and the brush
CPen pen(PS_SOLID, 2, RGB(0,0,255)), *oldPen;
CBrush brush(RGB(255,0,0)), *oldBrush;
oldPen = dc.SelectObject(&pen);
oldBrush = dc.SelectObject(&brush);

// Create the polygon
CPoint a[10];
a[0] = CPoint(20,50);
a[1] = CPoint(100,20);
a[2] = CPoint(100,150);
a[3] = CPoint(10,10);
a[4] = CPoint(200,75);
dc.SetPolyFillMode(ALTERNATE);
dc.Polygon(a, 5);

// Return old pen and brush
dc.SelectObject(oldPen);
dc.SelectObject(oldBrush);
}
```

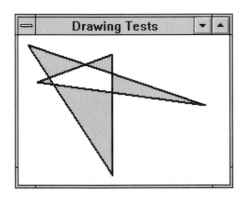

Figure 11.8
The ALTERNATE filling mode

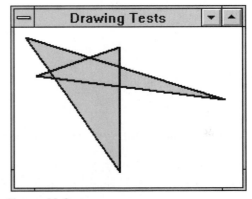

Figure 11.9
The WINDING filling mode

Windows also has a function named **Polyline** that accepts the same parameters as **Polygon**. The **Polyline** function draws line segments from point to point as specified in the array parameter. It does not close the last line back to the starting point as **Polygon** does.

Windows also supports a **PolyPolygon** function that draws groups of polygons simultaneously. It accepts an array of points, followed by an array of integers and an integer. The array of integers contains the number of points in each of the polygons specified in the array of points. For example, if a point array contains 4 points for the first polygon, 6 for the second and 3 for the third, the array of points would contain 13 points. The array of integers would contain 3 integers (4, 6 and 3) to specify the number of points in each polygon. The last integer parameter would contain 3 to specify the number of integers in the integer array.

11.4.6 Text and Fonts

One thing that Windows does well is fonts. The TrueType font model allows the system to create fonts of any size and orientation. These fonts look the same on any device. You use fonts in your drawings the same way you use a pen or a brush–you create the font and then select it for the current DC. Once selected, the new font is applied to all subsequent text output.

The code in Listing 11.7 demonstrates two different ways to create text in a window and also shows how to modify the font as well as several other text attributes. You can replace the **OnPaint** function in Listing 11.2 with this code. The output appears in Figure 11.10.

Listing 11.7
Demonstrations of several text output functions. Replace the **OnPaint** function in Listing 11.2 with this function.

```
// text.cpp

char *s="This is a sample string that contains about 50 characters";

// Handle exposures
void CWindow::OnPaint()
{
    CPaintDC dc(this);

    // demonstrate DrawText
    dc.DrawText(s, -1, CRect(10,10,100,100),
        DT_CENTER | DT_EXPANDTABS | DT_WORDBREAK);
    CRect r(10,10,100,0);
    dc.DrawText(s, -1, r,
        DT_CALCRECT | DT_EXPANDTABS | DT_WORDBREAK);

    // demonstrate ExtTextOut
    dc.SetTextAlign(TA_LEFT | TA_TOP);
    dc.ExtTextOut(10,110,0,
        NULL,s,strlen(s),NULL);

    // demonstrate fonts and colors
    CFont *font = new CFont;
    CFont *oldFont;
    font->CreateFont (36,0,0,0,700,0,0,0,
        ANSI_CHARSET,OUT_DEFAULT_PRECIS,
        CLIP_DEFAULT_PRECIS,
        DEFAULT_QUALITY,
        DEFAULT_PITCH|FF_DONTCARE,
            "Arial");
    oldFont = dc.SelectObject(font);
    dc.SetTextColor(RGB(0,0,255));
    dc.ExtTextOut(10,150,0,
```

```
        NULL,s,strlen(s),NULL);

    // demonstrate text extents
    CSize size = dc.GetTextExtent(s, strlen(s));

    // return old font
    dc.SelectObject(oldFont);
    delete font;
}
```

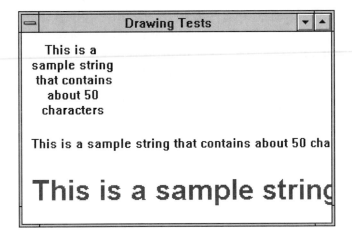

Figure 11.10
Different text output capabilities. The large text is drawn in blue when rendered on
a color monitor

The first function demonstrated is **DrawText**, used in two separate modes. In
the first mode it formats text into a rectangle for display. In the second, it calculates
the height of the minimal bounding rectangle for the same text:

```
dc.DrawText(s, -1, CRect(10,10,100,100),
    DT_CENTER | DT_EXPANDTABS | DT_WORDBREAK);
CRect r(10,10,100,0);
dc.DrawText(s, -1, r,
    DT_CALCRECT | DT_CENTER |
    DT_EXPANDTABS | DT_WORDBREAK);
```

The **DrawText** function accepts four parameters as shown below:

```
int CDC::DrawText(const char FAR* lpString,
    int nCount, LPRECT lpRect, UINT nFormat)
```

lpString   The string to draw

lpCount   The number of characters in the string, or -1 if null termi-
                nated

lpRect   The bounding rectangle

nFormat   Possible values: DT_BOTTOM, DT_CALCRECT,
                DT_CENTER, DT_EXPANDTABS,

DT_EXTERNALLEADING, DT_LEFT, DT_NOCLIP,
DT_NOPREFIX, DT_RIGHT, DT_SINGLELINE,
DT_TABSTOP, DT_TOP, DT_VCENTER,
DT_WORDBREAK

You may notice a great deal of similarity between this function and the text formatting capabilities of the **CStatic** class discussed in Chapter 3. In the first call to **DrawText** we pass in the string **s**, -1 (because it is null terminated), the bounding rectangle of the formatted text, and three formatting constants. The three constants specify that the text should be horizontally centered, that tabs should be expanded, and that the function should break the text at word boundaries. If the word wrap constant is not specified, the entire string will remain as a single line and that line will be centered in the rectangle, clipping off most of it. See the MFC documentation for more information. In Figure 11.10, the uppermost piece of text is the output of this function.

The second call to **DrawText** is similar but includes the DT_CALCRECT constant. This constant causes **DrawText** to calculate either the length of the text if it is a single line or the height of the text if it is multi-line (because of word wrapping or embedded carriage returns). The width or height of **r** is modified by the function when it returns. If you run the above code and output the value of **r.Height( )** in a message box, you will see it is set to a value near 80.

The second part of Listing 11.7 demonstrates the use of the **ExtTextOut** function:

```
dc.SetTextAlign(TA_LEFT | TA_TOP);
dc.ExtTextOut(10,110,0,
    NULL,s,strlen(s),NULL);
```

The **ExtTextOut** function has many of the same capabilities as **DrawText**. In general it should be used for single-line output, and we will use it in this mode in Chapter 18 to demonstrate how to print out pages of text from a program:

```
BOOL CDC::ExtTextOut(int x, inty, UINT nOptions,
    LPRECT lpRect, const char FAR* lpString,
    UINT nCount, LPINT lpDxWidths)
```

x, y	Starting position
nOptions	Possible values: ETO_CLIPPED, ETO_OPAQUE
lpRect	Dimensions of the rectangle
lpString	The string
lpCount	Length of the string
lpDxWidth	Separating distances on a per-character basis

In the example code we left the rectangle and separating distances NULL, so the string is drawn as a single line at the location specified.

The behavior of **ExtTextOut** can be modified with the **SetTextAlign** function as shown here:

```
UINT CDC::SetTextAlign(UINT nFlags)
```

nFlags	Possible values: One of TA_CENTER, TA_LEFT, and TA_RIGHT, plus one of TA_BASELINE, TA_BOTTOM,

and TA_TOP, plus one of TA_UPDATECP and TA_NOUPDATECP.

The constants specify how the code will align the text. For example, TA_LEFT and TA_TOP indicate that the point passed in should be used as the top left corner of the bounding rectangle for this text. TA_UPDATECP indicates that the current position in the DC should be updated after the call.

The next piece of code in the example demonstrates the use of different fonts and colors:

```
CFont *font = new CFont;
font->CreateFont (36,0,0,0,700,0,0,0,
          ANSI_CHARSET,OUT_DEFAULT_PRECIS,
          CLIP_DEFAULT_PRECIS,
          DEFAULT_QUALITY,
          DEFAULT_PITCH|FF_DONTCARE,
          "Arial");
dc.SelectObject(font);
delete font;
dc.SetTextColor(RGB(0,0,255));
dc.ExtTextOut(10,150,0,
    NULL,s,strlen(s),NULL);
```

The first two lines of code in this block were first presented in Chapter 3 to change the font of a **CStatic** label. Here, we create a font and select it into the DC using the same technique we've seen for selecting brushes and pens. The code sets the text color to blue and draws the text with the new font and color.

The **CFont** class allows a huge range of flexibility when creating a font, and you should try experimenting with this class to gain familiarity with it. The parameters are described briefly below:

```
BOOL CreateFont(int nHeight, int nWidth,
    int nEscapement, int nOrientation,
    int nWeight, BYTE bItalic,
    BYTE bUnderline, BYTE cStrikeOut, BYTE nCharSet,
    BYTE nOutPrecision, BYTE nClipPrecision,
    BYTE nQuality, BYTE nPitchAndFamily,
    LPCSTR lpFacename);
```

nHeight, nWidth	Desired height and width of the new font
nEscapement	Rotation angle in 10ths of a degree
nOrientation	Baseline rotation angle in 10ths of a degree
nWeight	Between 0 and 1000. 400=normal, 700=bold
bItalic, bUnderline	Set true if this style is desired
cStrikeOut	The strikeout font to use or 0
nCharSet	Possible values: ANSI_CHARSET, OEM_CHARSET, SYMBOL_CHARSET
nOutPrecision	Desired output precision. Possible values: OUT_CHARACTER_PRECIS, OUT_DEFAULT_PRECIS, OUT_STRING_PRECIS, OUT_STROKE_PRECIS

nClipPrecision	Clipping precision. Possible values: CLIP_CHARACTER_PRECIS, CLIP_DEFAULT_PRECIS, OUT_STROKE_PRECIS
nQuality	Output quality. Possible values: DEFAULT_QUALITY, DRAFT_QUALITY, PROOF_QUALITY
nPitchAndFamily	If the exact typeface specified in lpFacename is not available, this parameter guides the choice of font. Possible values: One of DEFAULT_PITCH, FIXED_PITCH, AND VARIABLE_PITCH or-ed with one of FF_DECORATIVE, FF_DONTCARE, FF_MODERN, FF_ROMAN, FF_SCRIPT, FF_SWISS
lpFacename	The name of a typeface. Windows ships with five True Type fonts: "Arial," "Courier New," "Symbol," "Times New Roman," and "Wingdings," so these are safe bets.

The last line of code in Listing 11.9 calculates the size of a string:

```
CSize size = dc.GetTextExtent(s, strlen(s));
```

The **GetTextExtent** function takes the string passed and the DC's current font and calculates the size of a rectangle necessary to hold that text as a single line.

We can use these different text functions to create a very nice digital clock. What we would like to have is a clock that updates its font size to match the size of the window each time the user re-sizes the application. To do this, we use an **OnSize** function that spins through font sizes trying to find the best fit each time the user re-sizes the window. Then, the **OnPaint** function paints the clock's face at that size. The implementation is shown in Listing 11.8. Figure 11.11 shows sample output for the clock.

Listing 11.8
A clock program demonstrating scaled fonts and text drawing.

```
// clock.cpp

#include <afxwin.h>
#include <time.h>

const int IDT_TIMER = 200;
const int refreshRate = 1000; // milliseconds

// Define the application class
class CApp : public CWinApp
{
public:
    virtual BOOL InitInstance();
};

CApp App;

// Define the window class
class CWindow : public CFrameWnd
{
```

```cpp
    CFont *font;
    CRect client;
public:
    CWindow();
    ~CWindow();
    afx_msg void OnSize(UINT, int, int);
    afx_msg void OnPaint();
    afx_msg void OnTimer(UINT);
    void DrawFace(CDC& dc);
    DECLARE_MESSAGE_MAP()
};

// The message map
BEGIN_MESSAGE_MAP(CWindow, CFrameWnd)
    ON_WM_SIZE()
    ON_WM_TIMER()
    ON_WM_PAINT()
END_MESSAGE_MAP()

// create a font of size x points high
void MakeFont(CFont *font, int x)
{
    font->DeleteObject();
    font->CreateFont (x,0,0,0,700,0,0,0,
        ANSI_CHARSET,OUT_DEFAULT_PRECIS,
        CLIP_DEFAULT_PRECIS,
        DEFAULT_QUALITY,
        DEFAULT_PITCH|FF_DONTCARE,
        "Arial");
}

// Handle resize events
void CWindow::OnSize(UINT nType, int cx, int cy)
{
    CRect r;
    int x=2;
    CClientDC dc(this);
    CFont *oldFont;

    // Get the client rectangle for the window
    GetClientRect(&client);
    do
    {
        x += 10;
        // Try creating a font at size x
        MakeFont(font, x);
        oldFont = dc.SelectObject(font);
        r = client;
        // Calc the size of the string with that font
        dc.DrawText("12:00:00", -1, r,
            DT_CALCRECT | DT_SINGLELINE |
            DT_CENTER | DT_VCENTER);
        dc.SelectObject(oldFont);
    } while (client == (r | client));
    // halt when the string overflows the rect
    MakeFont(font, x-10);
```

This book is continuously updated. See http://www.iftech.com/mfc

```
    }

    // Redraw the clock face
    void CWindow::DrawFace(CDC& dc)
    {
        char s[100];
        CFont *oldFont;

        oldFont = dc.SelectObject(font);
        _strtime(s);
        GetClientRect(&client);
        dc.DrawText(s, -1, client,
            DT_SINGLELINE | DT_CENTER | DT_VCENTER);
        dc.SelectObject(oldFont);
    }

    // Handle timer events
    void CWindow::OnTimer(UINT id)
    {
        CClientDC dc(this);
        DrawFace(dc);
    }

    // Handle exposure events
    void CWindow::OnPaint()
    {
        CPaintDC dc(this);
        DrawFace(dc);
    }

    // init the application
    BOOL CApp::InitInstance()
    {
        m_pMainWnd = new CWindow();
        m_pMainWnd->ShowWindow(m_nCmdShow);
        m_pMainWnd->UpdateWindow();
        return TRUE;
    }

    // The window's constructor
    CWindow::CWindow()
    {
        Create(NULL,
            "Clock",
            WS_OVERLAPPEDWINDOW,
            CRect(0,0,200,200));
        SetTimer(IDT_TIMER, refreshRate, NULL);
        font = new CFont;
    }

    CWindow::~CWindow()
    {
        delete font;
    }
```

This book is continuously updated. See http://www.iftech.com/mfc

Figure 11.11
The clock program

The code in Listing 11.8 uses a timer to generate an event that refreshes the face of the clock periodically. The face is updated every second, as determined by the **refreshRate** constant. The program also uses an **OnSize** function and the ON_WM_SIZE message map entry to recognize re-size events so it can adjust the size of the font to match the available window area. The font fills as much of the window as possible without overflowing horizontally or vertically.

There are several different ways to handle the font re-sizing problem, but the approach chosen here iterates through different font sizes until it finds the largest font. This font is then stored in a data member named **font** so that any exposure event or timer event can use the correct font to display the time without recalculating it. The **OnSize** function contains the logic to find the correct font size:

```
void CWindow::OnSize(UINT nType, int cx, int cy)
{
    CRect r;
    int x=2;
    CClientDC dc(this);
    GetClientRect(&client);
    do
    {
        x += 10;
        MakeFont(font, x);
        dc.SelectObject(font);
        r = client;
        dc.DrawText("12:00:00", -1, r,
            DT_CALCRECT | DT_SINGLELINE |
            DT_CENTER | DT_VCENTER);
    } while (client == (r | client));
    MakeFont(font, x-10);
}
```

This function starts by creating an instance of the **CClientDC** class. In the past, we always used the **CPaintDC** class and drew only in the **OnPaint** function following an exposure event. In Listing 11.8, however, we need to be able to draw into an existing window whenever the timer goes off or when a re-size event arrives. The appropriate DC for these situations is a Client DC, which allows drawing in the client area of the window at any time.

After obtaining the Client DC, the **OnSize** function obtains the window's client rectangle and enters a loop. The font size increases by ten (make it smaller or larger if you like) each time through the loop. The newly generated font is attached to the DC, and then **DrawText** (in its DT_CALCRECT mode) determines the bounding rectangle of the string "12:00:00" using that font. If you want to watch this happen, add an identical call to **DrawText**, excluding the DT_CALCRECT option, at the bottom of the loop. You will see the code try each of the font sizes until the last one gets too big.

The loop needs to decide when the string's bounding rectangle is bigger than the client rectangle. You could accomplish this by comparing the widths and heights of the two rectangles. Instead, the code shown here uses overloaded operators of the **CRect** class (see Chapter 12) to take the union of the font rectangle and the client rectangle. The union returns a rectangle big enough to hold both. If the font fits within the client rectangle, then the union will produce the client rectangle. Otherwise, it will produce something bigger. As soon as it produces something bigger, the loop quits and the code stores the properly sized font.

Notice that the **OnSize** function does not actually draw the string in the window. All it does is choose the correct font and store it. It can do this because an exposure event immediately follows any re-sizing event, so the **OnPaint** function automatically handles the redraw right after the **OnSize** function returns.

This is not necessarily the most efficient way to determine the optimal font size, but it works and is extremely accurate. It is a good way to demonstrate the use of Client DCs and scalable fonts.

11.4.7 Pixels

The CDC class contains several functions that allow you to manipulate pixels in the window directly. For example, the **SetPixel** function sets an individual pixel to a specific color. We will use this function extensively in Section 11.5.4 to create a simple drawing editor. The **BitBlt** function lets you copy groups of pixels from one location to another. You can use this function to create smooth animation as discussed in Section 11.6.3.

The **ExtFloodFill** function also manipulates individual bits based on the current state of the drawing surface. In previous sections you saw how to create filled rectangles, ellipses, and polygons. The **ExtFloodFill** function allows you to fill any arbitrary area. The code in Listing 11.9 demonstrates the use of this function, and Figure 11.12 shows typical output. Replace the **OnPaint** function in Listing 11.2 with the code in Listing 11.9.

Listing 11.9
The flood fill function. Replace the **OnPaint** function in Listing 11.2 with this function.

```
// flood.cpp

// Handle exposure
void CWindow::OnPaint()
{
    CPaintDC dc(this);
    int x;
    for (x=0; x<20; x++)
    {
        dc.MoveTo(rand()%200, rand()%200);
        dc.LineTo(rand()%200, rand()%200);
```

```
    }
    CBrush brush(RGB(0,0,255)), *oldBrush;
    oldBrush = dc.SelectObject(&brush);
    dc.ExtFloodFill(100,100,RGB(0,0,0),
        FLOODFILLBORDER);
    dc.SelectObject(oldBrush);
}
```

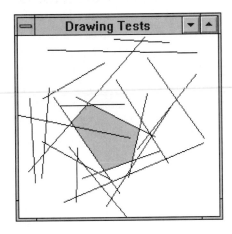

Figure 11.12
The flood fill function at work

Listing 11.9 simply draws 20 random lines and then flood fills starting at the arbitrary point 100,100. A flood fill either paints pixel-by-pixel in all directions until it hits a certain border color, or it paints in all directions as long as the pixels it finds are a certain color, changing them as it goes. In this particular example, **ExtFloodFill** is set up to flood fill in all directions until it hits a border with the color RGB(0,0,0), which is black. It fills with the current brush. If there is even one non-black pixel anywhere in the black border, the flooding will leak out and cover the entire frame if possible.

The other flooding mode is FLOODFILLSURFACE. In this mode, the function fills any pixel contiguous to the starting point and having the same color as the third parameter. In the case shown in Figure 11.12, if you set the starting point onto one of the lines and use FLOODFILLSURFACE with the color black, you can change the color of all the lines simultaneously because they all touch.

The problem with flood filling is that it is extremely slow in comparison to something like a rectangular fill. The computer has to examine every single pixel individually and this takes a great deal of time.

11.4.8 Other Useful Functions

There are many other simple, interesting functions built into the **CDC** class. You can learn a great deal about them by browsing through the MFC documentation. Several of these functions are discussed in this section because of their general utility.

In all the example code shown so far, the background color has been white. If you need a different background color, change it using the **SetBkColor** function. This function accepts an RGB triplet for the new color. Similarly, you can handle erasing by obtaining the current background color with **GetBkColor** and using it in a filled rectangle or other shape. Painting an area with the background color is the same as erasing it.

In Chapter 10, you saw how to load an icon and display it in a **CStatic** label. If you want to paint an icon into the drawing area, you can load it the same way and then use the **DrawIcon** function.

If you want to change the spacing between characters, the **SetTextCharacterExtra** function allows you to place extra pixels between characters as they are drawn.

The **SetBrushOrigin** function lets you change the starting offset of the brush pattern. When using a patterned brush, an 8 x 8 bit array of pixels is repeated across the filled area. This array is aligned with the origin of the window by default, but you can move it as necessary.

The functions in the **CDC** class have several consistent features. Almost all the **Set** functions we have used in this chapter have a corresponding **Get** function that can be used to determine the current state of the variable. You can save this information before changing a value so you can later return it to its original state.

11.5 Using the Mouse with Your Drawings

In the last section, you learned how to draw and fill all the different shapes available in the GDI library. Using these functions you can create a wide variety of graphs, charts, figures, and maps.

There are many cases, however, where static figures are not enough. These are the cases where you want the user to interact with your figures. For example, you might want to display a bar chart and then let the user change the height of different bars. Or you might want to paint a picture of a network configuration and let the user click on different nodes to get more information. In a dental application you might want to display a tooth chart and let the user click on a specific tooth to enter details about a surgical procedure. In a game, the program may need to track mouse motion as the user tries to negotiate a maze.

In all these cases you need the ability to obtain mouse information and then relate it to the drawing. In the following sections, we will look at the techniques used to relate mouse information to your drawings.

11.5.1 Using Normal Controls with Drawings

One very easy way to add user interaction to a drawing is to overlay it with standard controls. For example, if you place buttons on top of a drawing, the buttons will float on top of the drawn elements and act just like the buttons discussed in Chapter 4. The code shown in Listing 11.10 demonstrates the use of buttons with a drawing, and Figure 11.13 shows the output of the program.

Listing 11.10
A simple drawing combined with normal buttons.

```cpp
// btndraw.cpp

#include <afxwin.h>

// Define an application object
class CApp : public CWinApp
{
public:
    virtual BOOL InitInstance();
};

CApp App;

// Define the window class
class CWindow : public CFrameWnd
{
    CButton *b1, *b2, *b3;
public:
    CWindow();
    virtual ~CWindow();
    afx_msg void OnPaint();
    DECLARE_MESSAGE_MAP()
};

// The window constructor
CWindow::CWindow()
{
    Create(NULL, "Drawing Tests",
        WS_OVERLAPPEDWINDOW,
        CRect(0,0,250,100));
    // Create three buttons
    b1 = new CButton;
    b1->Create("One", WS_CHILD | WS_VISIBLE,
        CRect(30,30,70,70), this, 100);
    b2 = new CButton;
    b2->Create("Two", WS_CHILD | WS_VISIBLE,
        CRect(130,30,170,70), this, 101);
    b3 = new CButton;
    b3->Create("Three", WS_CHILD | WS_VISIBLE,
        CRect(70,120,130,160), this, 102);
}

// The message map
BEGIN_MESSAGE_MAP( CWindow, CFrameWnd )
    ON_WM_PAINT()
END_MESSAGE_MAP()

// Handle exposure events
void CWindow::OnPaint()
{
    CRect rect;
```

```
        GetClientRect( rect );
        CPaintDC dc(this);
        // draw lines between the three buttons
        dc.MoveTo(50,50);
        dc.LineTo(150,50);
        dc.LineTo(100,140);
        dc.LineTo(50,50);
}

// The window's destructor
CWindow::~CWindow()
{
        delete b1;
        delete b2;
        delete b3;
}

// Init the application
BOOL CApp::InitInstance()
{
        m_pMainWnd = new CWindow();
        m_pMainWnd->ShowWindow(m_nCmdShow);
        m_pMainWnd->UpdateWindow();
        return TRUE;
}
```

You can see in Listing 11.10 that the code is very similar to the examples in Chapter 4. The window's constructor creates the three buttons, the OnPaint function lays down the drawn elements—in this case three lines—on any exposure event, and the buttons refresh themselves automatically on any exposure.

The advantage of this approach is its simplicity: The buttons handle the clicks and route the events to you through the message map as usual. The disadvantage is that by using buttons, you lose control of the drawing. For example, the buttons cannot be scaled, and they may not fit in with the aesthetics of the figure you have created.

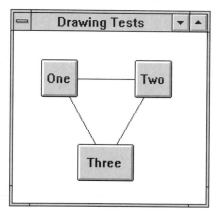

Figure 11.13
A simple drawing combined with normal buttons

11.5.2 Getting Mouse Clicks and Double-Clicks

The **CWnd** class contains 11 functions that you can use to retrieve mouse event information through a normal message map. These functions are listed in the following list.

OnLButtonDblClk	Called when the user double-clicks the left mouse button
OnLButtonDown	Called when the user clicks the left button down
OnLButtonUp	Called when the user releases the left button.
OnMButtonDblClk	Called when the user double-clicks the middle mouse button
OnMButtonDown	Called when the user clicks the middle button down.
OnLButtonUp	Called when the user releases the middle button
OnMouseActivate	Called when the cursor is in an inactive window and the user clicks a mouse button.
OnMouseMove	Called whenever the mouse moves
OnRButtonDblClk	Called when the user double-clicks the right mouse button
OnRButtonDown	Called when the user presses the right button down
OnRButtonUp	Called when the user releases the right button.

The most common use of the mouse is to detect single- and double-clicks within different elements of a drawing. For example, you might display a picture of a network using small rectangles (or icons loaded from a resource file and drawn with **DrawIcon**) to represent the nodes in the network. When the user clicks on a node, the application can pop up a dialog box containing information about the node. The code in Listing 11.11 demonstrates how to achieve this functionality by recognizing single and double-clicks within a rectangle.

Listing 11.11
Detecting mouse clicks within a specific rectangle.

```
// getclcks.cpp

#include <afxwin.h>

// Define the application class
class CApp : public CWinApp
{
public:
    virtual BOOL InitInstance();
};

CApp App;

// define the window class
class CWindow : public CFrameWnd
{
```

```
    BOOL clicked;
    BOOL dblClicked;
    CRect rect;
public:
    CWindow();
    virtual ~CWindow();
    afx_msg void OnPaint();
    afx_msg void OnLButtonUp(UINT, CPoint);
    afx_msg void OnLButtonDblClk(UINT, CPoint);
    DECLARE_MESSAGE_MAP()
};

// The window's constructor
CWindow::CWindow(): rect(10,10,100,100)
{
    clicked=FALSE;
    dblClicked=FALSE;
    Create(NULL, "Drawing Tests",
        WS_OVERLAPPEDWINDOW,
        CRect(0,0,250,100));
}

// The message map
BEGIN_MESSAGE_MAP( CWindow, CFrameWnd )
    ON_WM_PAINT()
    ON_WM_LBUTTONUP()
    ON_WM_LBUTTONDBLCLK()
END_MESSAGE_MAP()

// Handle single clicks
void CWindow::OnLButtonUp(UINT flag, CPoint pos)
{
    if (rect.PtInRect(pos))
    {
        clicked=!clicked;
        Invalidate(TRUE);
    }
}

// Handle double clicks
void CWindow::OnLButtonDblClk(UINT flag,
    CPoint pos)
{
    if (rect.PtInRect(pos))
    {
        dblClicked=!dblClicked;
        Invalidate(TRUE);
    }
}

// Handle exposure
void CWindow::OnPaint()
{
    CPaintDC dc(this);
    if (clicked)
    {
```

```
        CPen pen(PS_SOLID, 2, RGB(0,0,255)), *oldPen;
        oldPen = dc.SelectObject(&pen);
    }
    if (dblClicked)
    {
        CBrush brush(RGB(255,0,0)), *oldBrush;
        oldBrush = dc.SelectObject(&brush);
    }
    dc.Rectangle(rect);
    if (clicked)
        dc.SelectObject(oldPen);
    if (dblClicked)
        dc.SelectObject(oldBrush);
}

// The window's destructor
CWindow::~CWindow()
{
}

// Init the application
BOOL CApp::InitInstance()
{
    m_pMainWnd = new CWindow();
    m_pMainWnd->ShowWindow(m_nCmdShow);
    m_pMainWnd->UpdateWindow();
    return TRUE;
}
```

When you execute this code it displays a rectangle with a black border and a white interior. If you click outside the rectangle nothing happens. If you single-click within the rectangle, its border turns blue. If you double-click inside it, a brush paints the rectangle's interior red. Clicking or double-clicking once more will toggle two Boolean variables so that the border and interior alternately clear and re-highlight themselves.

The **OnPaint** function here is elementary. It simply paints the rectangle, examining the **clicked** and **dblClicked** members to decide whether to highlight the border and interior. The **clicked** and **dblClicked** members are set by the **OnLButtonUp** and **OnLButtonDblClk** functions. The latter is shown here:

```
void CWindow::OnLButtonDblClk(UINT flag,
    CPoint pos)
{
    if (rect.PtInRect(pos))
    {
        dblClicked=!dblClicked;
        Invalidate(TRUE);
    }
}
```

This function receives a flag that indicates if the Shift or Control keys were down at the time of the click (see **CWnd::OnLButtonDblClk** in the MFC documentation), as well as the position of the mouse. The mouse position is used with the **CRect** member function **PtInRect** to decide if the click occurred within the rectangle. If it did occur there, the click is accepted and it toggles the **dblClicked** member. In a more advanced program, the code would then act on the click as appropriate. For example, if you want to pop up a dialog in response to the click then this would be the place to do it.

In this particular piece of code, any click or double-click should redraw the rectangle. The code here simply invalidates the current window using **CWnd::Invalidate**. This causes Windows to generate an exposure event that is routed to the existing **On-Paint** function, and the rectangle is redrawn automatically.

If you have many rectangles on screen and wish to detect clicks within all of them, you will need to create a data structure that holds each rectangle's coordinates. The code can then iterate through the list, checking **PtInRect** for each rectangle. See Chapter 12 for information on storing objects in lists.

When you allow the user to click on something, it is often useful to give the user visual feedback with some sort of highlighting. Normal Windows buttons highlight when the user clicks the mouse button down, and then un-highlight when the user releases the mouse button. In addition, normal buttons employ a safety feature: If the user moves the mouse outside of the button before releasing, the button is not activated. To create this visual effect in a rectangle, you can detect the **OnLButtonDown** event to determine that the mouse button is down. Redraw the rectangle chosen in its highlighted form. If the rectangle contains an icon, you can paint a second highlighted version of the icon. If the rectangle is empty or contains text, you can invert it with **InvertRect**. Then, inside the **OnLButtonUp** handler, un-highlight the rectangle or icon by painting it again. Only if the cursor is still inside the specified rectangle on release should you perform the action.

11.5.3 Simple Drawing Using the Mouse

To handle more complicated user interactions or to create any kind of drawing program, you have to be able to track the motion of the mouse and respond to it. The code in Listing 11.12 demonstrates an extremely simple drawing program that tracks mouse motion using the **OnMouseMove** function. Figure 11.14 shows typical output from this program.

Listing 11.12
Code for a very simple drawing program that draws pixels.

```
// draw1.cpp

#include <afxwin.h>

// Define the application class
class CApp : public CWinApp
{
public:
    virtual BOOL InitInstance();
};
```

```
CApp App;

// define the window class
class CWindow : public CFrameWnd
{
public:
    CWindow();
    afx_msg void OnMouseMove(UINT,CPoint);
    DECLARE_MESSAGE_MAP()
};

// The window's constructor
CWindow::CWindow()
{
    Create(NULL, "Drawing Tests",
        WS_OVERLAPPEDWINDOW,
        CRect(0,0,250,100));
}

// The messahe map
BEGIN_MESSAGE_MAP( CWindow, CFrameWnd )
    ON_WM_MOUSEMOVE()
END_MESSAGE_MAP()

// Handle mouse movement
void CWindow::OnMouseMove(UINT flag,
    CPoint mousePos)
{
    // If the left button is down set the pixel
    if (flag == MK_LBUTTON)
    {
        CClientDC dc(this);
        dc.SetPixel(mousePos,RGB(0,0,255));
    }
}

// Init the application
BOOL CApp::InitInstance()
{
    m_pMainWnd = new CWindow();
    m_pMainWnd->ShowWindow(m_nCmdShow);
    m_pMainWnd->UpdateWindow();
    return TRUE;
}
```

The code in Listing 11.12 sets up its application and window objects in the standard way. It then wires the ON_WM_MOUSEMOVE entry into the message map so the **OnMouseMove** function is called each time the mouse moves within the window:

```
void CWindow::OnMouseMove(UINT flag,
    CPoint mousePos)
{
    // If the left button is down set the pixel
```

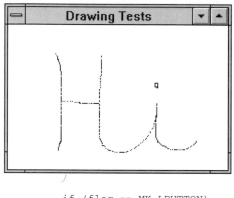

Figure 11.14
Sample output from the simple drawing program

```
if (flag == MK_LBUTTON)
{
    CClientDC dc(this);
    dc.SetPixel(mousePos,RGB(0,0,255));
}
}
```

This function checks to see if the left button is down using the flags parameter (see the **CWnd::OnMouseMove** function in the MFC documentation). If the left button is not down, the function does nothing. If it is down, the function creates a Client DC so it can draw in the client area and paints the pixel at the current mouse position using **SetPixel** (paint rectangles instead of pixels to create a more dramatic drawing). This is another case where the use of a Client DC is appropriate. The given pixel is drawn in response to a user event rather than an exposure event.

It is easy to add improvements to this simple program. Most drawing programs change the cursor when the user is drawing, and we can modify this code so it changes the cursor to a cross hairs cursor. Cursors are pre-defined resources that you must load before they are used, so the first step is to declare a data member in the window class and use it to hold the loaded cursor. For example, you might add the following data member to the **CWindow** class to hold the cross hairs cursor:

```
HCURSOR cross;
```

Then, inside the constructor for the window, you can call the **LoadCursor** function (see Chapter 10) to load in the new cursor shape:

```
cross = AfxGetApp()->LoadStandardCursor(IDC_CROSS);
```

To change the cursor shape in your code, you call the **CWnd::SetCursor** function. For example, you might change the cursor shape right before you set the pixel inside of **OnMouseMove**. That sounds simple enough, but it doesn't work. If you try it in the above code, for example, every time you set the cursor to cross hairs, Windows changes it right back to an arrow–the user sees a very annoying flicker on the screen.

This struggle occurs because your window, as currently constructed, has a "default cursor." Every time the cursor moves in the client area, the window modifies the cursor to that default automatically. Therefore, when you try to change it to something else, the default cursor immediately overrides it. The only way to prevent this behavior is to eliminate the default cursor and manage it yourself. A new version of the program is shown in Listing 11.13.

Listing 11.13
Code that correctly manages a cursor.

```
// draw2.cpp

#include <afxwin.h>

// Define the application class
class CApp : public CWinApp
{
public:
    virtual BOOL InitInstance();
};

CApp App;

// Define the window class
class CWindow : public CFrameWnd
{
    HCURSOR cross;
    HCURSOR arrow;
public:
    CWindow();
    afx_msg void OnMouseMove(UINT,CPoint);
    DECLARE_MESSAGE_MAP()
};

// The window constructor
CWindow::CWindow()
{
    // Load two cursors
    cross = AfxGetApp()->LoadStandardCursor(IDC_CROSS);
    arrow = AfxGetApp()->LoadStandardCursor(IDC_ARROW);

    // Register a custom window class
    const char* wndClass = AfxRegisterWndClass(
            CS_HREDRAW | CS_VREDRAW, NULL,
            (HBRUSH)(COLOR_WINDOW+1), NULL);

    // Create the window with the new class
    Create(wndClass, "Drawing Tests",
        WS_OVERLAPPEDWINDOW,
        CRect(0,0,250,100));
}

// The message map
BEGIN_MESSAGE_MAP( CWindow, CFrameWnd )
    ON_WM_MOUSEMOVE()
END_MESSAGE_MAP()

// Handle mouse movement
```

```
void CWindow::OnMouseMove(UINT flag,
    CPoint mousePos)
{
    // Draw a pixel if the left button is down
    if (flag == MK_LBUTTON)
    {
        CClientDC dc(this);
        ::SetCursor(cross);
        dc.SetPixel(mousePos,RGB(0,0,255));
    }
    else
        ::SetCursor(arrow);
}

// Init the application
BOOL CApp::InitInstance()
{
    m_pMainWnd = new CWindow();
    m_pMainWnd->ShowWindow(m_nCmdShow);
    m_pMainWnd->UpdateWindow();
    return TRUE;
}
```

In Listing 11.13, the **CWindow** class has two new data members to hold the arrow and cross hairs cursors. They are initialized in the constructor. The constructor also registers a new window class using a call to **AfxRegisterWndClass**:

```
const char* wndClass =
        AfxRegisterWndClass(
            CS_HREDRAW | CS_VREDRAW, NULL,
            (HBRUSH)(COLOR_WINDOW+1), NULL);
```

A window class simply gives Windows several pieces of information that it needs to know about the application window. In all previous examples we have used a default window class, but the only way to remove the default cursor is to declare a new class that specifies NULL for the cursor. The new class name is then passed to the **Create** function for the window.

The **AfxRegisterWndClass** function takes several parameters as defined below (see the **RegisterClass** function and the WNDCLASS structure in the Windows API documentation, as well as **AfxRegisterWndClass** in the MFC documentation, for more information):

```
const char* AfxRegisterWndClass( UINT nClassStyle,
    HCURSOR hCursor = 0, HBRUSH hbrBackground = 0,
    HICON hIcon = 0 );
```

nClassStyle	The class style. Possible values (from the WND-CLASS description in the 32-bit API):
CS_BYTEALIGNCLIENT	Improves drawing performance
CS_BYTEALIGNWINDOW	Improves moving and sizing performance.
CS_CLASSDC	One DC is shared by all windows in the class.
CS_DBLCLKS	Double clicks are accepted

CS_GLOBALCLASS	Registers the class globally for all other applications
CS_HREDRAW	Entire window is redrawn on horizontal re-sizing
CS_NOCLOSE	Disables the close option in the system menu
CS_OWNDC	Each window in a class gets its own DC
CS_PARENTDC	Parent window's DC is passed to children
CS_SAVEBITS	Windows repaints exposed areas automatically from a backing store instead of calling On-Paint
CS_VREDRAW	Entire window is redrawn on vertical re-sizing
hCursor	Handle to the default cursor
hbrBackground	Handle to the background color. The following predefined colors are added and cast to HBRUSH as shown below:

COLOR_ACTIVEBORDER
COLOR_ACTIVECAPTION
COLOR_APPWORKSPACE
COLOR_BACKGROUND
COLOR_BTNFACE
COLOR_BTNSHADOW
COLOR_BTNTEXT
COLOR_CAPTIONTEXT
COLOR_GRAYTEXT
COLOR_HIGHLIGHT
COLOR_HIGHLIGHTTEXT
COLOR_INACTIVEBORDER
COLOR_INACTIVECAPTION
COLOR_MENU
COLOR_MENUTEXT
COLOR_SCROLLBAR
COLOR_WINDOW
COLOR_WINDOWFRAME
COLOR_WINDOWTEXT

| hIcon | A handle to the icon, loaded from a resource file. |

In the call to **AfxRegisterWndClass**, the class style is set so the window gets redrawn on any vertical or horizontal re-sizing, the cursor is set to NULL, the background color is set to the normal window color, and the application icon is set to NULL. (Load an icon as shown in Chapter 10 and use its pointer if you like.)

Note that when working with code generated by the AppWizard, you must use a slightly modified technique to register a new window class for the application. In that case, override **CFrameWnd:: PreCreateWindow** and register the new window class there.

Having done all this to eliminate the default cursor, you now have complete control over the cursor's appearance. In Listing 11.13, management occurs in the **On-MouseMove** function by setting the cursor every time the mouse moves. The cursor is guaranteed to have the correct shape at all times. It is also possible to use the **CWnd::OnSetCursor** function to help manage the cursor.

If you use the program in Listing 11.13 for any period of time, you will notice a rather severe problem. Every time the window gets an exposure event, it clears out the client area. The drawing lacks persistence because there is no **OnPaint** function in the code. To solve the problem, you need to create a data structure that remembers all points as they are drawn and then repaints those points on any exposure. The final version of the program is shown in Listing 11.14.

Listing 11.14
A drawing program that uses a data structure to store the drawn points.

```cpp
// draw3.cpp

#include <afxwin.h>
#include <afxcoll.h>

// Define the application class
class CApp : public CWinApp
{
public:
    virtual BOOL InitInstance();
};

CApp App;

const int MAX = 5000;

// The database class
class PointArray
{
    CPoint *points[MAX];
    int count;
public:
    PointArray(): count(0) {}
    ~PointArray()
    {
        for (int i=0; i<count; i++)
            delete(points[i]);
    }
    void Add(CPoint *p)
    {
        if (count<MAX)
            points[count++]=p;
    }
    CPoint *GetAt(int x) {return points[x];}
    int GetSize() {return count;}
};
```

```
// Define the window class
class CWindow : public CFrameWnd
{
    HCURSOR cross;
    HCURSOR arrow;
    PointArray array;
public:
    CWindow();
    afx_msg void OnPaint();
    afx_msg void OnMouseMove(UINT,CPoint);
    DECLARE_MESSAGE_MAP()
};

// The window's constructor
CWindow::CWindow()
{
    // Load two cursors
    cross = AfxGetApp()->LoadStandardCursor(IDC_CROSS);
    arrow = AfxGetApp()->LoadStandardCursor(IDC_ARROW);

    // define a new window class
    const char* pszWndClass =
        AfxRegisterWndClass(
            CS_HREDRAW | CS_VREDRAW, NULL,
            (HBRUSH)(COLOR_WINDOW+1),
            NULL);

    // Create a window with the new class
    Create(pszWndClass, "Drawing Tests",
            WS_OVERLAPPEDWINDOW,
            CRect(0,0,250,100));
}

// The message map
BEGIN_MESSAGE_MAP( CWindow, CFrameWnd )
    ON_WM_PAINT()
    ON_WM_MOUSEMOVE()
END_MESSAGE_MAP()

// Handle mouse movement
void CWindow::OnMouseMove(UINT flag,
    CPoint mousePos)
{
    if (flag == MK_LBUTTON)
    {
        CClientDC dc(this);
        ::SetCursor(cross);
        dc.SetPixel(mousePos,RGB(0,0,255));
        // Add each point to the array
        array.Add(new CPoint(mousePos));
    }
    else
        ::SetCursor(arrow);
}

// Handle exposure
```

```
void CWindow::OnPaint()
{
    int x;
    CPaintDC dc(this);
    // Redraw all points in the array
    for (x=0; x<array.GetSize(); x++)
        dc.SetPixel(* array.GetAt(x),
            RGB(0,0,255));
}

// Init the application
BOOL CApp::InitInstance()
{
    m_pMainWnd = new CWindow();
    m_pMainWnd->ShowWindow(m_nCmdShow);
    m_pMainWnd->UpdateWindow();
    return TRUE;
}
```

The code in Listing 11.14 uses an instance of the class called **PointArray** to hold all the points as they are drawn. The array is declared as a member of the window class, and the functions **Add** and **GetAt** add and retrieve points from the array. MFC also provides its own data structure classes as discussed in Chapter 12, and that chapter shows how to convert this program over to MFC's **CObArray** class.

Each time the user draws a new point, the code adds it to the array in **OnMouse-Move**. Whenever an exposure event triggers **OnPaint**, it can redraw all the points using this array. When you run the new program you will find that re-sizing events and minimization are now handled appropriately, and the window retains its contents throughout execution. It would be a simple matter to write the array to disk on termination and reload at the start of execution to provide persistence across runs as well. See Chapter 12.

You may wish to take the code shown in this section and experiment with it. For example, it would be easy to paint ten randomly clustered pixels instead of one pixel each time the mouse moves and in that way simulate the "spray can" tool found in most paint programs. You could also connect points using a polyline to create a smoother drawing. By adding a menu and some load and save options, you would be well on your way to creating a simple paint program. See Chapter 15 for more information on turning this simple drawing example into a complete application.

11.5.4 Rubber Banding

A technique called *rubber banding* gives the user visual feedback while creating a shape. It is used in all modern drawing programs to create lines, boxes, circles, and so on. The user anchors the starting point with a mouse click and then drags off to the ending point. The shape stretches between the two points dynamically. The technique is useful in many different types of programs. For example, if you want the user to be able to stretch the bars on a bar graph, or to connect nodes in a drawing on a network, rubber banding creates a very appealing user interface.

Listing 11.15 contains code that implements the rubber banding of lines. It could be easily modified to rubber band rectangles and ellipses as well.

Listing 11.15
Code that demonstrates rubber banding.

```cpp
// rubber.cpp

#include <afxwin.h>

// Define the application class
class CApp : public CWinApp
{
public:
    virtual BOOL InitInstance();
};

CApp App;

// Define the window class
class CWindow : public CFrameWnd
{
    HCURSOR cross;
    HCURSOR arrow;
    CPoint start, old;
    BOOL started;
public:
    CWindow();
    afx_msg void OnMouseMove(UINT,CPoint);
    afx_msg void OnLButtonDown(UINT, CPoint);
    afx_msg void OnLButtonUp(UINT, CPoint);
    DECLARE_MESSAGE_MAP()
};

// The window constructor
CWindow::CWindow()
{
    // Load two cursors
    cross = AfxGetApp()->LoadStandardCursor(IDC_CROSS);
    arrow = AfxGetApp()->LoadStandardCursor(IDC_ARROW);
    started=FALSE;

    // Create a custom window class
    const char* pszWndClass = AfxRegisterWndClass(
        CS_HREDRAW | CS_VREDRAW, NULL,
        (HBRUSH)(COLOR_WINDOW+1), NULL);

    // Create the window
    Create(pszWndClass, "Drawing Tests",
        WS_OVERLAPPEDWINDOW,
        CRect(0,0,250,100));
}

// The message map
BEGIN_MESSAGE_MAP( CWindow, CFrameWnd )
```

```
        ON_WM_MOUSEMOVE()
        ON_WM_LBUTTONDOWN()
        ON_WM_LBUTTONUP()
    END_MESSAGE_MAP()

    // Start a new line when the user clicks
    // the mouse button down
    void CWindow::OnLButtonDown(UINT flag,
        CPoint mousePos)
    {
        started = TRUE;
        ::SetCursor(cross);
        // save the starting position of the line
        start = old = mousePos;
        CClientDC dc(this);
        dc.SetROP2(R2_NOT);
        dc.MoveTo(start);
        dc.LineTo(old);
    }


    // Complete the line when the user releases
    // the mouse button
    void CWindow::OnLButtonUp(UINT flag,
        CPoint mousePos)
    {
        if (started)
        {
            started = FALSE;
            ::SetCursor(arrow);
            CClientDC dc(this);
            dc.MoveTo(start);
            dc.LineTo(old);
        }
    }


    // Handle dragging
    void CWindow::OnMouseMove(UINT flag,
        CPoint mousePos)
    {
        // If the mouse button is down and there
        // is a line in progress, rubber band
        if ((flag == MK_LBUTTON) && started)
        {
            ::SetCursor(cross);
            CClientDC dc(this);
            dc.SetROP2(R2_NOT);
            // Undraw the old line
            dc.MoveTo(start);
            dc.LineTo(old);
            // Draw the new line
            dc.MoveTo(start);
            dc.LineTo(mousePos);
            old=mousePos;
        }
        else
            ::SetCursor(arrow);
```

This book is continuously updated. See http://www.iftech.com/mfc

```
}

// Init the application
BOOL CApp::InitInstance()
{
    m_pMainWnd = new CWindow();
    m_pMainWnd->ShowWindow(m_nCmdShow);
    m_pMainWnd->UpdateWindow();
    return TRUE;
}
```

Let's start by examining the basic principles used in this code and then look at the specific implementation. When a user draws a line, what they expect to see is a single line that follows the cursor away from the starting point. In order to implement this behavior, the application needs to draw a new line from the starting point to the cursor each time the mouse moves. The application also has to erase the previous line, as shown in Figure 11.15. If done quickly enough, all this erasing and redrawing is perceived by the user as rubber banding.

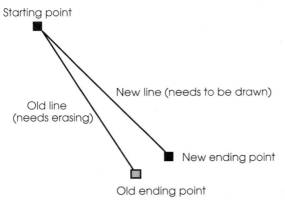

Figure 11.15
Each time the mouse moves, the rubber-banded line must be erased and redrawn

The application cannot simply erase the old line each time the cursor moves. For example, if the application paints over the old line with the background color, as the line is rubber banded across existing parts of the drawing it destroys those parts of the drawing. Instead, the application should invert the existing drawing surface underneath the line when it is first drawn. Then, to erase it, the application can re-invert the line, restoring the drawing to its original state. The rubber-banded line leaves existing figures undisturbed as it passes over them. On the final draw of the line, when the user releases the mouse button after the drag, the application should draw the line one last time in the normal drawing mode.

The code in Listing 11.16 that implements this activity borrows a number of concepts from the previous section. It uses the same cursor-changing technology, for example. The rubber banding process starts when the user first clicks the mouse button down to establish the starting point. This action is detected and handled by **OnLButtonDown**:

```
void CWindow::OnLButtonDown(UINT flag,
    CPoint mousePos)
{
    started = TRUE;
    ::SetCursor(cross);
    start = old = mousePos;
    CClientDC dc(this);
    dc.SetROP2(R2_NOT);
    dc.MoveTo(start);
    dc.LineTo(old);
}
```

The **OnLButtonDown** function changes the cursor and then sets the data members **start** and **old** to the current mouse position. It also changes the drawing mode to R2_NOT. In all previous drawing examples we have used the default mode R2_COPYPEN, which paints the current pen color directly onto the drawing surface without regard for the existing pixels. There are many other drawing modes, however, and each has a special use. The following table is taken from the MFC documentation for the **CDC::SetROP2** function.

R2_BLACK	Pixel is always black
R2_WHITE	Pixel is always white
R2_NOP	Pixel remains unchanged
R2_NOT	Pixel is the inverse of the display color
R2_COPYPEN	Pixel is the pen color
R2_NOTCOPYPEN	Pixel is the inverse of the pen color
R2_MERGEPENNOT	Pixel is a combination of the pen color and the inverse of the display color
R2_MASKPENNOT	Pixel is a combination of the colors common to both the pen and the inverse of the display
R2_MERGENOTPEN	Pixel is a combination of the display color and the inverse of the pen color
R2_MASKNOTPEN	Pixel is a combination of the colors common to both the display and the inverse of the pen
R2_MERGEPEN	Pixel is a combination of the pen color and the display color
R2_NOTMERGEPEN	Pixel is the inverse of the R2_MERGEPEN color
R2_MASKPEN	Pixel is a combination of the colors common to both the pen and the display
R2_NOTMASKPEN	Pixel is the inverse of the R2_MASKPEN color.
R2_XORPEN	Pixel is a combination of the colors in the pen and in the display, but not in both
R2_NOTXORPEN	Pixel is the inverse of the R2_XORPEN color

In the case of this rubber-banding program, we want to use the R2_NOT mode to invert the drawing surface. The **OnLButtonDown** function "primes the pump." It inverts the initial line, even though it's just a single pixel, so subsequent revisions of the line in **OnMouseMove** will work properly.

The **OnMouseMove** function handles the drag phase of the rubber-banding operation:

```
void CWindow::OnMouseMove(UINT flag,
    CPoint mousePos)
{
    if ((flag == MK_LBUTTON) && started)
    {
        ::SetCursor(cross);
        CClientDC dc(this);
        dc.SetROP2(R2_NOT);
        dc.MoveTo(start);
        dc.LineTo(old);
        dc.MoveTo(start);
        dc.LineTo(mousePos);
        old=mousePos;
    }
    else
        ::SetCursor(arrow);
}
```

This function simply un-draws the old line by drawing between **start** and **old** in R2_NOT mode and then drawing in the new line. It stores the new point into **old** so it can un-draw that line the next time through.

The **OnLButtonUp** function cleans up when the user finally releases the button:

```
void CWindow::OnLButtonUp(UINT flag,
    CPoint mousePos)
{
    if (started)
    {
        started = FALSE;
        SetCursor(arrow);
        CClientDC dc(this);
        dc.MoveTo(start);
        dc.LineTo(old);
    }
}
```

This function draws the line one last time in the default R2_COPYPEN mode so the line appears solid on screen.

You might have noticed a Boolean variable named **started** floating through this code. It is there to keep track of whether a line was properly started with a mouse down event. You can see it getting set to TRUE in **OnLButtonDown**, and then both **OnMouseMove** and **OnLButtonUp** check it before they do anything. **OnLButtonUp** sets it back to FALSE upon the successful completion of the line.

The **started** Boolean handles a problem that can arise during icon reconstruction. Try to restore any desktop icon in Windows and watch exactly what happens. You will notice that the icon is replaced by its window on the *down stroke* of the second click. This creates a problem. Imagine the following: The rubber-banding code shown in Listing 11.15 is running, the window for it fills the entire screen, and it is currently minimized. Now you double -click on the icon. The window reappears on the down click of the mouse, so the mouse button is down when the window opens and the window immediately begins to receive mouse motion events. On the final release of the mouse button, the program gets a mouse up event. If the **started** variable were not there to prevent it, the program would try to draw something in response to those events even though they have nothing to do with an actual line.

One thing you might notice while using the rubber banding code is that movement of the mouse outside the application's window causes the window to stop processing events. Because the cursor is not inside the window, mouse events go elsewhere. If you want the application to handle events outside the window during a drag, you should use the **CWnd::SetCapture** function inside the **OnLButtonDown** function to begin capturing all mouse events. Then call **CWnd::ReleaseCapture** function in **OnLButtonUp** to stop capturing events. See the MFC documentation for more information.

11.5.5 Virtual Drawing Spaces

In all the previous examples we have assumed that the entire drawing can fit on one screen. Most production drawing programs, however, allow you to draw onto a drawing surface that is larger than the physical screen. For example, if you are trying to draw a detailed map of New York City for a geographical or navigational information system, the map is not going to fit on one screen. You need the ability to scroll through the map using scroll bars and to scale the map in various ways.

A virtual drawing space allows you to implement this sort of functionality. In a virtual drawing space, the window on the screen displays one small part of a much larger virtual drawing, as shown in Figure 11.16. As the user clicks on the scroll bars, the portion of the virtual drawing that is visible in the window changes.

The data for the virtual drawing is typically stored in a data structure or database that may contain a wide variety of other information beside the drawing data. For example, the database for a geographical information system would contain data describing how to draw each building on the map, but might also contain text data describing each building. The drawing data is stored using its own coordinate system, and then this system is mapped to screen coordinates as the user makes drawing requests with the scroll bars.

Listing 11.16 implements a simple virtual drawing space to show you the principles involved. This program allows the user to draw in and scroll through a drawing space that is HEIGHT pixels high–5,000 in this particular piece of code. It would be a straightforward extrapolation to add horizontal scrolling as well.

Listing 11.16
Implementation of a simple virtual drawing surface

```
// vds.cpp

#include <afxwin.h>

// Define the application class
```

vds origin at 0,0

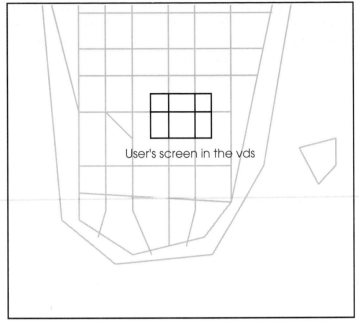

User's screen in the vds

vds maximum extent at 10000, 10000

Figure 11.16
A Virtual Drawing Surface can be much large than the user's screen

```
class CApp : public CWinApp
{
public:
    virtual BOOL InitInstance();
};

CApp App;

// Structure for the vds database
typedef struct LineRec
{
    CPoint lt;
    CPoint rb;
} LineRec;

// Max lines in the database
const int MAX = 1000;
// Max height of the vds
const int HEIGHT = 5000;

// The vds database class
class LineArray
{
    LineRec lines[MAX];
    int count;
```

```
public:
    LineArray(): count(0) {}
    void Add(LineRec l)
    {
        if (count<MAX)
            lines[count++]=l;
    }
    void Add(CPoint p1, CPoint p2)
    {
        if (count<MAX)
        {
            lines[count].lt=p1;
            lines[count].rb=p2;
            count++;
        }
    }
    LineRec Get(int x) {return lines[x];}
    int Size() {return count;}
};

// Define the window class
class CWindow : public CFrameWnd
{
    HCURSOR cross;
    HCURSOR arrow;
    CPoint start, old;
    BOOL started;
    LineArray lines;
    int originY;
public:
    CWindow();
    afx_msg void OnPaint();
    afx_msg void OnMouseMove(UINT,CPoint);
    afx_msg void OnLButtonDown(UINT, CPoint);
    afx_msg void OnLButtonUp(UINT, CPoint);
    afx_msg void OnVScroll(UINT, UINT, CScrollBar*);
    DECLARE_MESSAGE_MAP()
};

// The window constructor
CWindow::CWindow()
{
    originY=0;
    cross = AfxGetApp()->LoadStandardCursor(IDC_CROSS);
    arrow = AfxGetApp()->LoadStandardCursor(IDC_ARROW);
    started=FALSE;
    const char* pszWndClass = AfxRegisterWndClass(
        CS_HREDRAW | CS_VREDRAW, NULL,
        (HBRUSH)(COLOR_WINDOW+1),
        ::LoadIcon(AfxGetInstanceHandle(),
            "xxx"));
    Create(pszWndClass, "Drawing Tests",
        WS_OVERLAPPEDWINDOW | WS_VSCROLL,
        CRect(0,0,250,100));
    SetScrollRange(SB_VERT, 0, HEIGHT);
}
```

```
// The message map
BEGIN_MESSAGE_MAP( CWindow, CFrameWnd )
    ON_WM_PAINT()
    ON_WM_VSCROLL()
    ON_WM_MOUSEMOVE()
    ON_WM_LBUTTONDOWN()
    ON_WM_LBUTTONUP()
END_MESSAGE_MAP()

// Handle vertical scrolling
void CWindow::OnVScroll( UINT code, UINT nPos,
    CScrollBar* sb )
{
    int pos=0;
    CRect rect;

    GetClientRect(&rect);
    pos = GetScrollPos(SB_VERT);
    switch ( code )
    {
    case SB_LINEUP:
        pos -= 1;
        break;
    case SB_LINEDOWN:
        pos += 1;
        break;
    case SB_PAGEUP:
        pos -= 50;
        break;
    case SB_PAGEDOWN:
        pos += 50;
        break;
    case SB_TOP:
        pos = 0;
        break;
    case SB_BOTTOM:
        pos = HEIGHT;
        break;
    case SB_THUMBPOSITION:
        pos = nPos;
        break;
    default:
        return;
    }
    if ( pos < 0 )
        pos = 0;
    if ( pos > HEIGHT-rect.Height() )
        pos = HEIGHT-rect.Height();
    SetScrollPos( SB_VERT, pos );
    originY=pos;
    Invalidate(TRUE);
}

// Start drawing a line
void CWindow::OnLButtonDown(UINT flag,
```

```
        CPoint mousePos)
{
    started = TRUE;
    ::SetCursor(cross);
    start = old = mousePos;
    CClientDC dc(this);
    dc.SetROP2(R2_NOT);
    dc.MoveTo(start);
    dc.LineTo(old);
}


// Complete drawing a line
void CWindow::OnLButtonUp(UINT flag,
    CPoint mousePos)
{
    if (started)
    {
        started = FALSE;
        ::SetCursor(arrow);
        CClientDC dc(this);
        dc.MoveTo(start);
        dc.LineTo(old);
        start.Offset(0,originY);
        old.Offset(0,originY);
        // Store the line in the database
        lines.Add(start, old);
    }
}


// Handle rubber banding of the line
void CWindow::OnMouseMove(UINT flag,
    CPoint mousePos)
{
    if ((flag == MK_LBUTTON) && started)
    {
        ::SetCursor(cross);
        CClientDC dc(this);
        dc.SetROP2(R2_NOT);
        dc.MoveTo(start);
        dc.LineTo(old);
        dc.MoveTo(start);
        dc.LineTo(mousePos);
        old=mousePos;
    }
    else
        ::SetCursor(arrow);
}


// Handle exposures
void CWindow::OnPaint()
{
    CPaintDC dc(this);
    LineRec l;
    int x;
    for (x=0; x<lines.Size(); x++)
```

```
    {
        l=lines.Get(x);
        l.lt.Offset(0,-originY);
        l.rb.Offset(0,-originY);
        dc.MoveTo(l.lt);
        dc.LineTo(l.rb);
    }
}

// Init the application
BOOL CApp::InitInstance()
{
    m_pMainWnd = new CWindow();
    m_pMainWnd->ShowWindow(m_nCmdShow);
    m_pMainWnd->UpdateWindow();
    return TRUE;
}
```

The key to understanding this program is the fact that the virtual drawing space uses its own coordinate system. All lines drawn by the user are stored in the **LineArray** data structure using this private coordinate system. In this example code, the private coordinate system starts at 0,0 and extends to a height of 5,000 pixels, but there is nothing to prevent you from starting the private system at any origin and letting it extend almost infinitely. Figure 11.17 shows the relationship between the private coordinate system and the window's coordinate system.

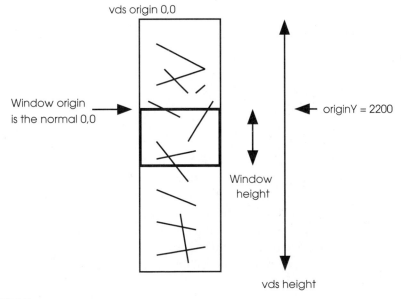

Figure 11.17
The coordinate systems used in a virtual drawing area

The window's coordinate system has its origin at 0,0. Therefore, to adjust the virtual drawing's coordinate system, an **originY** variable keeps track of the window's offset into the virtual drawing space. When the user draws a line on the screen, the line's coordinates are offset by **originY** before the line is stored in the data structure. In Listing 11.16 the offset is added right before the line is stored in the array in **On-LButtonUp**. This step translates the line from screen coordinates to virtual coordinates. Before the line is drawn on the screen again this offset value is subtracted away. In this program the addition and subtraction of the offset values occurs in the **OnLButtonUp**, **OnVScroll**, and **OnPaint** functions, but it would be just as easy to embed it in the **LineArray** class and thereby encapsulate the virtual drawing coordinate system in the data structure.

Most of the code in Listing 11.16 is similar to the rubber-banding program demonstrated in the previous section. To understand the coordinate system, get out a piece of paper and walk through the following example. Say that the user starts this program and, without touching the scroll bar, draws a line on the screen from the point 10,10 to the point 200,200. This line is stored into the **LineArray** data structure. Because the scroll bar has not been manipulated yet, **originY** is zero and the line is stored without any offset. Now say that the user moves the scroll bar 1,000 pixels down in the window. The **OnVScroll** function handles the scrolling and sets **originY** to 1,000. It invalidates the client area, triggering **OnPaint**:

```
void CWindow::OnPaint()
{
    CPaintDC dc(this);
    LineRec l;
    int x;
    for (x=0; x<lines.Size(); x++)
    {
        l=lines.Get(x);
        l.lt.Offset(0,-originY);
        l.rb.Offset(0,-originY);
        dc.MoveTo(l.lt);
        dc.LineTo(l.rb);
    }
}
```

This function traverses the data structure and redraws every line in it. Before it draws each line, however, it applies the **originY** offset to translate the line back to screen coordinates. When the offset of 1,000 is applied to our line, its coordinates are changed from 10,10 and 200,200 to 10,-990 and 200,-800. This line is well outside the window so it is clipped off. On the other hand, a line stored in the data structure with a y coordinate of perhaps 1,010 will still be visible once the offset is subtracted.

In this example program the entire data structure is redrawn on any scrolling request. With a very large data structure--for example, a two gigabyte GIS database representing a city--this simple approach is impractical. Normally you design the database so you can constrain the range of drawing information returned from the database to the area of the current screen. If you are designing a database from scratch and planning to display it in some sort of virtual drawing space, you should consider adding this capability to the design to speed up scrolling.

Chapter 15 demonstrates a drawing program generated by the AppWizard that implements virtual drawing areas using the **CScrollView** class. This class handles the origin manipulations automatically, and you will want to examine it for additional ideas.

11.6 Advanced Drawing Concepts

There are several different capabilities available in the GDI library that allow you to handle special drawing situations. This chapter discusses a few of the more important topics.

11.6.1 Mapping Modes

Let's say you want to create a chart-drawing application. You plan to display the generated charts on the screen, but you also plan to print them on the wide variety of printers that can be attached to a Windows workstation.

If you draw the charts using normal pixel coordinates, as we've done in all previous examples, you will have a problem. When you display one of your charts on the screen, it will look fine. But when you print it on a 150 DPI dot matrix printer, it will be small compared to the screen image. If you print it on a 300 DPI laser printer, it will be smaller still. If you print it on a 600 DPI laser printer, it will be tiny. You will also have problems centering things at the different resolutions.

Windows provides a capability called *mapping* that allows you to solve this problem very easily. By changing over to a different coordinate system–for example, 1/100ths of an inch rather than pixels–Windows will handle the translations from that coordinate system down to a specific device in a device-independent manner. When you print a six-inch-wide bar chart, it will appear six inches wide no matter what type of printer you use. It will also appear 6 inches wide on the user's screen.

Switching to a Metric or English mapping mode is easy. There are five modes to choose from and you call the **CDC::SetMapMode** function to switch to one of them. Once you switch to a new mode, integer coordinate values (logical units) passed to or received from CDC functions are understood in the new coordinate system. For example, in the MM_TEXT mode, a point at 100,100 is 100 pixels to the right and 100 pixels down. In the MM_LOENGLISH mode however, where logical units are understood to indicate 1/100th of an inch, the point 100,100 is one inch to the right and one inch up from the origin. There are also two mapping modes that allow you to create arbitrary mapping systems. The different modes are described below:

MM_TEXT	The default mode. Device-dependent mapping directly from logical units to pixels. Origin is upper left corner, positive X extends to the right, and positive Y extends downward.
MM_LOENGLISH	Logical units indicate 1/100th of an inch. Origin is upper left corner, positive X extends to the right, and positive Y is up.

MM_HIENGLISH	The same as MM_LOENGLISH but logical units map to 1/1000th of an inch.
MM_LOMETRIC	Logical units indicate 1/10th of a millimeter. Origin is upper left corner, positive X extends to the right, and positive Y is up.
MM_HIMETRIC	The same as MM_LOMETRIC but logical units map to 1/100th of a millimeter.
MM_TWIPS	Logical units indicate 1/20 of a point (1/1,440 of an inch). Origin is upper left corner, positive X extends to the right, and positive Y is up.
MM_ANISOTROPIC	Logical units are scaled to an arbitrary coordinate system that you define and that depends on the size of the ultimate output device. You indicate the origin and scaling factors with functionscalls.
MM_ISOTROPIC	Same as MM_ANISOTROPIC, but the two axes are scaled the same way, so one logical unit on the X axis is the same as one logical unit on the Y axis.

Listing 11.17 demonstrates the use of the MM_LOENGLISH mapping mode.

Listing 11.17
The use of the MM_LOENGLISH mapping mode.

```
// mapping.cpp

#include <afxwin.h>

// Define the application class
class CApp : public CWinApp
{
public:
    virtual BOOL InitInstance();
};

CApp App;

// Define the window class
class CWindow : public CFrameWnd
{
public:
    CWindow();
    afx_msg void OnPaint();
    DECLARE_MESSAGE_MAP()
};

// The window's constructor
CWindow::CWindow()
{
    Create(NULL, "Drawing Tests",
        WS_OVERLAPPEDWINDOW,
        CRect(0,0,250,250));
```

```
    }

    // The message map
    BEGIN_MESSAGE_MAP( CWindow, CFrameWnd )
        ON_WM_PAINT()
    END_MESSAGE_MAP()

    // Handle exposure events
    void CWindow::OnPaint()
    {
        CPaintDC dc(this);
        // Adjust the map mode for this DC
        dc.SetMapMode(MM_LOENGLISH);
        CPen pen(PS_SOLID, 2, RGB(0,0,255)), *oldPen;
        CBrush brush(HS_CROSS,RGB(255,0,0)), *oldBrush;
        oldPen = dc.SelectObject(&pen);
        oldBrush = dc.SelectObject(&brush);
        CRect rect(100, -100, 200, -200);
        dc.Rectangle(rect);
        dc.SelectObject(oldPen);
        dc.SelectObject(oldBrush);
    }

    // Init the application
    BOOL CApp::InitInstance()
    {
        m_pMainWnd = new CWindow();
        m_pMainWnd->ShowWindow(m_nCmdShow);
        m_pMainWnd->UpdateWindow();
        return TRUE;
    }
```

The only real difference between listings 11.17 and 11.3 is the use of the **Set-MapMode** function to set the MM_LOENGLISH mapping mode in the **OnPaint** function. Once the new mapping mode is activated, any CDC function that accepts or returns coordinates will do so in the new coordinate system. Therefore, the call to **CDC::Rectangle** shown here produces a rectangle that starts one inch over and one inch down and is one inch wide and high.

The MM_LOENGLISH mapping mode modifies the origin, as shown in Figure 11.18.

As you can see in Figure 11.18, the use of a normal Cartesian coordinate system means that all Y coordinates must be negative if they are to appear in the window. This explains why the Y coordinates in Listing 11.17 are both negative.

As mentioned earlier, the switch to a new mapping mode with **CDC::SetMap-Mode** causes all **CDC** functions to accept and return coordinates in the chosen coordinate system. After the switch to MM_LOENGLISH, for example, all coordinates are understood to be in 1/100ths of an inch. The functions in the **CWnd** class are not affected by the new mode, however. Functions such as **CWnd::GetClientRect** and **OnMouseMove** still return pixel coordinates. You can change these pixel coordinates to the mapping mode coordinate system and back again with the

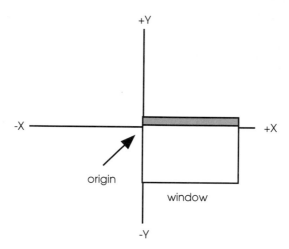

Figure 11.18
A measured coordinate system such as MM_LOENGLISH uses a normal Cartesian coordinate system

CDC::DPtoLP and **CDC::LPtoDP** functions (see the MFC documentation for details and Chapter 15 for an example).

Windows also provides two mapping modes that let you create your own coordinate systems. You tell Windows the maximum extent of the drawing surface and the way you want to map the drawing surface into the current device, and Windows does the rest. Listing 11.18 demonstrates the creation of a 1,000 x 1,000 anisotropic drawing area. The X and Y axis can have different units in an anisotropic mode, while they will be the same units in an isotropic mode.

Listing 11.18
An anisotropic drawing system.

```
// aniso.cpp

#include <afxwin.h>

// Define the application class
class CApp : public CWinApp
{
public:
    virtual BOOL InitInstance();
};

CApp App;

// Define the window class
class CWindow : public CFrameWnd
{
public:
    CWindow();
    void OnPaint();
```

```
        DECLARE_MESSAGE_MAP()
};

// The window's constructor
CWindow::CWindow()
{
    Create(NULL, "Drawing Tests",
        WS_OVERLAPPEDWINDOW,
        CRect(0,0,250,100));
}

// The message map
BEGIN_MESSAGE_MAP( CWindow, CFrameWnd )
    ON_WM_PAINT()
END_MESSAGE_MAP()

// Handle exposures
void CWindow::OnPaint()
{
    CRect rect;
    int x;

    GetClientRect( rect );
    CPaintDC dc(this);
    // Create the anisotropic coord system
    dc.SetMapMode(MM_ANISOTROPIC);
    dc.SetWindowExt(1000, 1000);
    dc.SetViewportExt(rect.Width(), -rect.Height());
    dc.SetViewportOrg(0, rect.Height());

    // Draw a set of lines in the new system
    CPen pen(PS_SOLID, 1, RGB(0,0,255)), *oldpen;
    oldpen = dc.SelectObject(&pen);
    for (x=0; x<1000; x+=10)
    {
        dc.MoveTo(0,0);
        dc.LineTo(x,1000);
    }
    dc.TextOut(500,500,CString("Hello"));
}

// Init the application
BOOL CApp::InitInstance()
{
    m_pMainWnd = new CWindow();
    m_pMainWnd->ShowWindow(m_nCmdShow);
    m_pMainWnd->UpdateWindow();
    return TRUE;
}
```

The particular configuration shown in Listing 11.18 sets up the window so that, as far as the code is concerned, it is always 1,000 x 1,000 logical units wide and high, regardless of how big it is in terms of pixels on the screen. The origin is in the lower right corner, and positive X and Y coordinates extend to the right and up, respectively.

Using a mapping system like this, you know that you can draw in the area between 0,0 and 1000, 1000. No matter how the window shape changes, the figure will be translated from its original 1,000 x 1,000 size into the space available in the window. Note that even the font scales as you re-size the window. This arrangement is especially useful for drawing figures, charts, and graphs. It is generally much easier to draw to a fixed coordinate system and let the machine do the scaling than to have to adjust to changing window sizes, page sizes and so on.

11.6.2 Animation

Computer animation can be implemented in several different ways. For example, the rubber-banding program seen in Section 11.5.3 contains a simple form or animation—the rubber banded line is erased and drawn so quickly that it appears to be a smoothly animated object. For small figures moving on a static background, this erase–redraw technique is appropriate. For example, a digital aquarium could move fish over a static background using the erase–redraw technique. Games using small moving objects often work this way as well.

There are many situations where the erase–redraw technique cannot be used. For example, in a flight simulator the program must redraw the entire screen on every frame because the pilot's perspective changes at each time increment. In this situation you cannot erase the old screen and begin painting the new perspective line-by-line or polygon-by-polygon. The screen shot for a flight simulator demonstrated in Figure 11.19 helps to understand the problem.

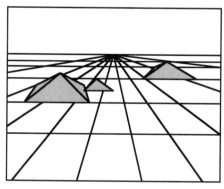

Figure 11.19
A frame from a simple flight simulator program

This simple frame consists of 15 lines and six polygons. An advanced flight simulator will paint hundreds or thousands of polygons for each frame. If they are drawn directly onto the screen they cause flicker. The user's eyes see each frame developing but never see any completed frames.

The easiest way to solve this problem is to draw each frame into an off-screen area and then copy the completed frames to the screen. The user sees a complete frame while the new frame is drawn. This technique creates very convincing animation, even if the frame rate is only three or four frames per second.

Windows allows you to create what is called a Memory DC when an off-screen drawing area is needed. Once created and initialized, a Memory DC is just like a Client DC. You draw into it using the same CDC commands seen throughout the rest of the chapter. Once the frame is finished, you copy it to the on-screen Client DC using the **CDC::BitBlt** function. The word "bitblt" is an abbreviation for "bit block transfer." This function copies bits (words, really) between memory and the display adapter quickly enough to be used at fairly high frame rates without flicker. It can also copy bits from one Memory DC to another.

The code in Listing 11.19 demonstrates how to create a Memory DC, how to draw into it, and how to copy it to the user's window on the screen.

Listing 11.19
Using the **BitBlt** function with an off-screen memory area.

```cpp
// memdc.cpp

#include <afxwin.h>

// Define the application class
class CApp : public CWinApp
{
public:
    virtual BOOL InitInstance();
};

CApp App;

// Define the window class
class CWindow : public CFrameWnd
{
    CDC memDC;
    CBitmap *oldMemDCBitmap, *newMemDCBitmap;
public:
    CWindow();
    ~CWindow();
    afx_msg void OnPaint();
    DECLARE_MESSAGE_MAP()
};

// The constructor for the window
CWindow::CWindow()
{
    Create(NULL, "Drawing Tests",
        WS_OVERLAPPEDWINDOW,
        CRect(0,0,450,450));

    // Create the memory DC
    CClientDC dc(this);
    memDC.CreateCompatibleDC(&dc);
    newMemDCBitmap = new CBitmap;
    CRect rect;
    GetClientRect( &rect );
    newMemDCBitmap->CreateCompatibleBitmap(&dc,
        rect.Width(), rect.Height());
    oldMemDCBitmap =
```

```
        memDC.SelectObject(newMemDCBitmap);
    // Clear the memory DC
    memDC.PatBlt(0,0,450,450,
        WHITENESS);
}


CWindow::~CWindow()
{
    memDC.SelectObject(oldMemDCBitmap);
    delete newMemDCBitmap;
}


// The message map
BEGIN_MESSAGE_MAP( CWindow, CFrameWnd )
    ON_WM_PAINT()
END_MESSAGE_MAP()


// Handle exposure events
void CWindow::OnPaint()
{
    CRect rect(0,0,400,400);
    int x;

    CPaintDC dc(this);
    // Paint into the memory DC
    for (x=0; x<60; x++)
    {
        rect.InflateRect(-3,-3);
        memDC.Rectangle(rect);
    }
    // Transfer the memory DC to the screen
    dc.BitBlt(0,0,400,400,
        &memDC,0,0,SRCCOPY);
}


// Init the application
BOOL CApp::InitInstance()
{
    m_pMainWnd = new CWindow();
    m_pMainWnd->ShowWindow(m_nCmdShow);
    m_pMainWnd->UpdateWindow();
    return TRUE;
}
```

The window's constructor creates the Memory DC. The first line gets the Client DC for the window. This DC is needed because the Memory DC has to be compatible with the window's DC. The memory DC itself is created in the next line with the **CreateCompatibleDC** function. This function creates a DC with the same characteristics—aspect ratio, pixels per inch, colors per pixel, etc.—as the window on the screen.

Next the code creates the area of memory that will hold the "pixels" for this off-screen area by creating a bitmap and attaching it to the Memory DC. The **Create-**

CompatibleBitmap function does this, taking in a DC to match the new bitmap to those characteristics, as well as a width and height for the new bitmap. One thing to keep in mind when creating a bitmap in memory is that bitmaps are resource intensive. For example, a 1,000 x 1,000 pixel bitmap compatible with an eight-bit-per-pixel color display requires almost a megabyte of memory. You generally cannot create 200 of them at once.

The bitmap is associated with the Memory DC using the **SelectObject** function. The bitmap is then cleared to white with the **PatBlt** function, which copies white pixels into the bitmap at the full memory transfer rate. Another way to clear the bitmap is to draw a filled rectangle to the Memory DC. Once the Memory DC's bitmap is clear, you can draw into it just like any other DC.

The **OnPaint** function demonstrates how to draw into the Memory DC and then copy it to the screen. The **for** loop draws nested rectangles to the Memory DC and then bitblts the final frame to the screen. A typical animation program would probably use a timer to control the frame rate. Inside the **OnTimer** function the program would draw a new frame in the Memory DC and then copy it to the Client DC for the window.

An animated application typically uses a fixed-size window for output. If you allow the user to re-size the window, you need to do one of two things: Either you can create the original bitmap attached to the Memory DC big enough to handle the largest window size possible, or you can create a new bitmap each time the window is resized. The following code fragment shows how to properly swap the new bitmap into the Memory DC to avoid memory leaks:

```
CBitmap *temp;
CClientDC dc(this);
CRect rect;

GetClientRect( &rect );
newMemDCBitmap->CreateCompatibleBitmap(&dc,
    rect.Width(), rect.Height());
temp = memDC.SelectObject(newMemDCBitmap);
delete temp;
```

Given the amount of memory that bitmaps can consume, you cannot afford to leak any away.

11.6.3 Simple Printing

As far as your code is concerned, a printer is very similar to the client area of a window. To print something, you simply create a Print DC instead of a Client DC. Once you have created and properly initialized a Print DC, you can draw to it using all the standard CDC functions that we've used throughout the chapter. The code in Listing 11.20 demonstrates the printing process.

Listing 11.20
Simple printing

```
// print.cpp
```

```
#include <afxwin.h>
#include <afxdlgs.h>
#include <strstrea.h>

#define IDM_BUTTON 100

// Declare the application class
class CApp : public CWinApp
{
public:
    virtual BOOL InitInstance();
};

// Create an instance of the application class
CApp App;

// Declare the window class
class CWindow : public CFrameWnd
{
    CButton *button;
public:
    CWindow();
    ~CWindow();
    afx_msg void HandleButton();
    BOOL HandlePrint();
    DECLARE_MESSAGE_MAP()
};

// Get a print DC and draw on it.
BOOL CWindow::HandlePrint()
{
    BOOL error = FALSE;
    CDC* dc = NULL;
    int pageWidth, pageHeight;

    // Let the user select the printer
    CPrintDialog printDialog(FALSE);
    if (printDialog.DoModal() == IDCANCEL)
        return FALSE;

    // Create a print DC
    dc = new CDC;
    if (printDialog.GetPrinterDC() != NULL)
        dc->Attach(printDialog.GetPrinterDC());
    else
        return TRUE;

    // Get the page size for the printer
    pageWidth = dc->GetDeviceCaps(HORZRES);
    pageHeight = dc->GetDeviceCaps(VERTRES);

    // Set mapping modeand convert size of
    // page to logical coordinates
    dc->SetMapMode(MM_LOENGLISH);
    CSize s(pageWidth, pageHeight);
```

```
        dc->DPtoLP(&s);
        pageWidth = s.cx;
        pageHeight = s.cy;

        // Start the doc and print
        if (dc->StartDoc("") >= 0 &&
            dc->StartPage() >= 0)
        {
            // Do the drawing
            // Place your drawing code here.
            dc->Rectangle(0,0,pageWidth,-pageHeight);
            dc->MoveTo(0,0);
            dc->LineTo(pageWidth, -pageHeight);

            CFont *font = new CFont;
            CFont *oldFont;
            font->CreateFont (36,0,0,0,700,0,0,0,
                ANSI_CHARSET,OUT_DEFAULT_PRECIS,
                CLIP_DEFAULT_PRECIS,
                DEFAULT_QUALITY,
                DEFAULT_PITCH|FF_DONTCARE,
                "Arial");
            oldFont = dc->SelectObject(font);
            dc->ExtTextOut(300,-50,0,NULL,"Hello",
                strlen("Hello"),NULL);

            if (dc->EndPage() >= 0)
                dc->EndDoc();
            else
                error = TRUE;
            dc->SelectObject(oldFont);
            delete font;
        }
        else
            error = TRUE;

        if (error)
            dc->AbortDoc();

        delete dc;
        return !error;
}

// Handler for the "Push me" button
void CWindow::HandleButton()
{
    if (HandlePrint())
        MessageBox("Printed successfully",
            "Print status");
    else
        MessageBox(
            " User Canceled or Problems Printing",
            "Print Status");
}

// The message map
```

```
BEGIN_MESSAGE_MAP(CWindow, CFrameWnd)
    ON_COMMAND(IDM_BUTTON, HandleButton)
END_MESSAGE_MAP()

// The InitInstance is called once
// when the application begins execution
BOOL CApp::InitInstance()
{
    m_pMainWnd = new CWindow();
    m_pMainWnd->ShowWindow(m_nCmdShow);
    m_pMainWnd->UpdateWindow();
    return TRUE;
}

// The window constructor
CWindow::CWindow()
{
    CRect r;

    // Create the window
    Create(NULL,
        "Printing Tests",
        WS_OVERLAPPEDWINDOW,
        CRect(0,0,200,200));

    // Get the client rectangle
    GetClientRect(&r);
    r.InflateRect(-20,-20);

    // Create a button to activate the dialog
    button = new CButton();
    button->Create("Push me",
        WS_CHILD|WS_VISIBLE|BS_PUSHBUTTON,
        r,
        this,
        IDM_BUTTON);
}

// The window's destructor
CWindow::~CWindow()
{
    delete button;
}
```

When you execute Listing 11.20 it will present a window containing a button. When you click the button, a Print dialog will appear (see Chapter 7 for details). You can select a printer or use the default. When you click the OK button in the Print dialog, the program will generate one page of output consisting of a rectangle, a diagonal line, and the word "Hello" in a 36-point Arial font.

Inside the code in Listing 11.20, the **HandleButton** function is called when the user presses the button. This function calls **HandlePrint,** which performs the actual printing. **HandlePrint** starts by creating the Print dialog. This step is important—the

Print dialog does the work of acquiring the Printer DC for the printer chosen by the user. To obtain a Printer DC that you can use in your code, you create an instance of the **CDC** class, get the Printer DC from the Print dialog, and attach the latter to the former. Once the attachment is complete any drawing operation performed on **dc** will use the printer as its output device. The code then queries the page size of the printer through the DC using the **GetDeviceCaps** function (look up this function in the MFC documentation—there is quite a bit of data available for the printer), sets the mapping mode, and translates the page size to the logical coordinate system established by the mapping mode.

Printers support the idea of a *document* broken up into individual *pages*. Before you can draw onto the printer you must start a document and then start a page. Anything you draw will appear on the current page. When you are done with a page, you call **EndPage** and **StartPage** again to produce multiple pages within the same document. The code in Listing 13.1 produces a single page of output, but if you would like to experiment you can add the following lines just below the creation of the diagonal line:

```
dc->EndPage();
dc->StartPage();
```

Now the rectangle and line will appear on one page and the text will appear on another.

Once it is done drawing, the program ends the page and the document and the **HandlePrint** function terminates. It returns an error status to its caller so a message box can inform the user of the outcome.

Printing and print preview are greatly simplified by creating your applications with the AppWizard. See Chapters 15 and 18 for examples of printing within an App-Wizard framework.

11.7 Conclusion

This chapter covers a lot of ground, but, in a way, only scratches the surface. The GDI library is so large that it is impossible to cover all its possible uses. What you have gained from this chapter, however, is an introduction that provides a solid foundation. You should be able to use the MFC and API documentation to gather the other bits of knowledge you need to complete your own particular projects.

You will see many of the concepts presented in this chapter later in this book. For example, Chapter 12 shows how to adapt the drawing program to use the built-in MFC data structures. Chapter 15 shows how to create drawing programs within an AppWizard–generated framework.

Utility Classes

One of MFC's goals is to make your life as a programmer more enjoyable by providing you with commonly needed functionality in easy-to-use classes. In this spirit, MFC contains a set of "utility" classes that encapsulate frequently needed concepts. For example, there are MFC classes for both files and strings that help to simplify and organize your use of these two concepts. There are also a number of data structure classes that make it extremely easy to store information in common formats. MFC provides classes for arrays, lists, and mappings. Using these tools, you can easily create any common data structure.

MFC provides the following general utility classes:

CFile	Binary file class
CMemFile	In-Memory file class
CStdioFile	Text file class
CArchive	Binary Stream class
CString	String class
CTime	Time class
CTimeSpan	Relative time class
CPoint	Point class
CRect	Rectangle class
CSize	Size class

MFC also provides the following data structure classes:

CDWordArray	Array of DWORD
CObArray	Array of (CObject *)
CPtrArray	Array of (void *)
CStringArray	Array of CString
CWordArray	Array of WORD
CUIntArray	Array of UINT
CObList	Linked list of CObject
CPtrList	Linked list of (void *)
CStringList	Linked list of CString
CMapPtrToWord	Maps (void *) to WORD
CMapPtrToPtr	Maps (void *) to (void *)

CMapStringToOb	Maps CString to (CObject *)
CMapStringToPtr	Maps CString to (void *)
CMapStringToString	Maps CString to CString
CMapWordToOb	Maps WORD to (CObject *)
CMapWordToPtr	Maps WORDs to (void *)

MFC has its own exception-handling mechanism. The following classes, along with the **try** and **catch** operators, support it:

CException	Base class
CArchiveException	Archive exceptions
DBException	Database exception
CFileException	File exception
CMemoryException	Memory exceptions
CNotSupportedException	Unsupported capability exception
CResourceException	Resource exception
COleException	OLE exception
CUserException	User exceptions

Finally, MFC supports several different debugging classes and macros that can be extremely useful during the debugging phase of an application development cycle:

CDumpContext	Dumping class
CMemoryState	Memory utilization class
CRuntimeClass	Run time class

The next chapter discusses the exception and debugging classes. This chapter deals with the general utility classes and the data structures.

12.1 Utility Classes

MFC encapsulates frequently used concepts such strings, files, and time into classes that make these concepts much easier to use. The following sections describe each of the available classes.

12.1.1 CFile, CMemFile, and CStdioFile classes

You use the **CFile** class to work with binary files. The **CStdioFile** class inherits from the **CFile** class and extends it to provide easy access to text files. The **CMemFile** class also inherits from **CFile** and provides for the creation of binary files in memory rather than on disk. Files in memory are sometimes a useful abstraction that can simplify or speed up some types of data transfers.

Because both **CStdioFile** and **CMemFile** inherit from it, **CFile** is a good place to start learning about files in MFC. You will typically use a **CFile** object to access binary data on disk. For example, if you want to read through a file byte-by-byte, perhaps to create some sort of a hex-dump program, you would use an instance of the **CFile** class to do that. If you want to rapidly copy a file, filtering for certain byte patterns as you go, you would use **CFile**. You will also use **CFile** when you want to read and write files containing fixed-size structures.

When you look in the MFC documentation, you will find that the **CFile** class has more than 20 member functions. These functions map into the following categories:

- Construction (creating, opening, closing)
- Reading and writing
- Seeking
- Locking
- Information
- Operations

Listing 12.1 demonstrates how to open a file using the **CFile** class and how to write, seek, and read from that file.

Listing 12.1
Using the **CFile** class

```
// file1.cpp

#include <afxwin.h>
#include <afxdlgs.h>

const int IDC_BUTTON = 100;
// Define filters for use with the File Dialog
const char fileDialogFilter[] =
    "Data files (*.dat)|*.dat|All files (*.*)|*.*||";
const char fileDialogExt[] = "dat";

// Define the application class
class CApp : public CWinApp
{
public:
    virtual BOOL InitInstance();
};

CApp App;

// Define the window class
class CWindow : public CFrameWnd
{
    CButton *button;
public:
    CWindow();
    afx_msg void HandleButton();
    DECLARE_MESSAGE_MAP()
};

typedef struct _address
{
    char name[20], city[20], state[3];
} address;

// The message handler function
void CWindow::HandleButton()
```

```
    {
        CFileDialog fileDialog( TRUE,
            fileDialogExt, NULL,
            0, fileDialogFilter );
        if( fileDialog.DoModal() == IDOK )
        {
            CFile f;
            CFileException exception;
            BOOL status;

            // Open the file for writing
            status = f.Open(fileDialog.GetPathName(),
                CFile::modeCreate | CFile::modeWrite |
                CFile::shareExclusive,
                &exception);
            // Return on error
            if (!status)
            {
                char s[100];
                sprintf(s, "Error opening file for writing. Code:%d",
                    exception.m_cause);
                MessageBox(s, "Error", MB_OK);
                return;
            }
            else
            {
                address a;

                // Write three records to the file
                try
                {
                    strcpy(a.name, "John Smith");
                    strcpy(a.city, "Zebulon");
                    strcpy(a.state, "NC");
                    f.Write(&a, sizeof(address));
                    strcpy(a.name, "Bob Jones");
                    strcpy(a.city, "Raleigh");
                    strcpy(a.state, "NC");
                    f.Write(&a, sizeof(address));
                    strcpy(a.name, "Bill Clancy");
                    strcpy(a.city, "Wake Forest");
                    strcpy(a.state, "NC");
                    f.Write(&a, sizeof(address));
                }
                // Announce any problems
                catch (CFileException exception)
                {
                    MessageBox("Error writing file",
                        "Error", MB_OK);

                }
                f.Close();
            }
            // Reopen file for reading
            status = f.Open(fileDialog.GetPathName(),
                CFile::modeRead, &exception);
```

```
            if (!status)
            {
                char s[100];
                sprintf(s, "Error opening file for reading. Code:%d",
                    exception.m_cause);
                MessageBox(s, "Error", MB_OK);
                return;
            }
            else
            {
                address a;

                // Read and display one record
                try
                {
                    // print file length
                    char s[100];
                    sprintf(s, "File size = %d", f.GetLength());
                    MessageBox(s, "Length", MB_OK);
                    // Seek and read
                    f.Seek(sizeof(address)*2, CFile::begin);
                    f.Read(&a, sizeof(address));
                    MessageBox(a.name, "Data", MB_OK);
                }
                catch (CFileException exception)
                {
                    MessageBox("Error writing file",
                        "Error", MB_OK);

                }
                f.Close();
            }
        }
}


// The window's constructor
CWindow::CWindow()
{
    // Create a window with the new class
    Create(NULL, "Drawing Tests",
            WS_OVERLAPPEDWINDOW,
            CRect(0,0,250,100));

    // Get the size of the client rectangle
    CRect r;
    GetClientRect(&r);
    r.InflateRect(-20,-20);

    // Create a button
    button = new CButton();
    button->Create("Push me",
        WS_CHILD|WS_VISIBLE|BS_PUSHBUTTON,
        r,
        this,
        IDC_BUTTON);
}
```

```
// The message map
BEGIN_MESSAGE_MAP( CWindow, CFrameWnd )
    ON_COMMAND(IDC_BUTTON, HandleButton)
END_MESSAGE_MAP()

// Init the application
BOOL CApp::InitInstance()
{
    m_pMainWnd = new CWindow();
    m_pMainWnd->ShowWindow(m_nCmdShow);
    m_pMainWnd->UpdateWindow();
    return TRUE;
}
```

The **HandleButton** function in Listing 12.1 contains demonstration code for the **CFile** class. The code starts by declaring and then opening an instance of the **CFile** class. It uses a **CFileDialog** dialog (see Chapter 7) to get a file name from the user:

```
CFileDialog fileDialog( TRUE,
    fileDialogExt, NULL,
    0, fileDialogFilter );
if( fileDialog.DoModal() == IDOK )
{
    CFile f;
    CFileException exception;
    BOOL status;

    // Open the file for writing
    status = f.Open(fileDialog.GetPathName(),
        CFile::modeCreate | CFile::modeWrite |
        CFile::shareExclusive,
        &exception);
    // Return on error
    if (!status)
    {
        char s[100];
        sprintf(s, "Error opening file for writing. Code:%d",
            exception.m_cause);
        MessageBox(s, "Error", MB_OK);
        return;
    }
    else
    {
        . . .
```

When the user clicks the button, a file dialog appears and the user can select a file name. The program then declares instances of the **CFile** and **CFileException** (see Chapter 13) classes and attempts to open that file name. If the file opens, then the status value returned by the **Open** function will be TRUE. Otherwise it is FALSE, and in that case the program produces an error message in a message box. The exception contains an error code that identifies the source of the problem (see the **m_cause** entry in the MFC documentation for a complete list of possibilities). See Chapter 13 for a complete discussion on exceptions and exception handling.

With the file open, Listing 12.1 writes three records to the file using **CFile**'s **Write** function. This function accepts a pointer to a block of memory and the number of bytes to transfer. The block of memory is written at the current file position.

After writing the three records, the program closes the file, reopens it for reading, and display's the file's length using the **GetLength** function. It then uses the **Seek** and **Read** functions to get the third record in the file and display its name:

```
// Print file length
char s[100];
sprintf(s, "File size = %d", f.GetLength());
MessageBox(s, "Length", MB_OK);
// Seek and read
f.Seek(sizeof(address)*2, CFile..begin);
f.Read(&a, sizeof(address));
MessageBox(a.name, "Data", MB_OK);
```

You can see that the process here mimics the seek-read process you are familiar with from the standard I/O library in C. The fact that this functionality is encapsulated in a class, however, makes it easier to use and also provides easy error-trapping mechanisms.

The **GetStatus** and **SetStatus** functions in **CFile** make it easy to get and set a file's status information. Both functions use the **CFileStatus** structure whose members are shown below:

CTime m_ctime	Creation time
CTime m_mtime	Last write time
CTime m_atime	Last read time
LONG m_size	File size
BYTE m_attribute	Attribute byte
char m_szFullName[_MAX_PATH]	The absolute path and file name

On FAT file systems, only the last write time is valid, but on NTFS and HPFS disks all three times contain valid information. The attribute byte contains bits that reflect the current status bits for the file, as shown below:

Normal	0x00
Read Only	0x01
Hidden	0x02
System	0x04
Volume	0x08
Directory	0x10
Archive	0x20

The **CFile** class also provides for file locking using the **LockRange** and **Unlock-Range** member functions. You can lock any block of bytes by indicating the starting location and the length of the block. Typically you would lock one or more structures in a file of structures. When you lock a range of bytes it gives your program exclusive access to them. If you attempt to lock bytes anywhere within an already locked range, MFC throws an exception (see Chapter 13). Because locking prevents access by other processes, you should unlock a range of bytes as quickly as possible to prevent contention among competing processes sharing the same file.

Other useful functions in the **CFile** class include:

Duplicate	Creates a duplicate of the **CFile** instance (not the file)
Flush	Flushes any pending writes to disk
ReadHuge, WriteHuge	Reads and writes blocks over 64K
GetPosition	Returns the current file position in bytes
SetLength	Sets the length of the file (useful for truncating)
Rename	Renames the file
Remove	Deletes the file

As you can see, the **CFile** class simply encapsulates everything associated with binary files in a way that makes binary files much more accessible. Rather than using functions scattered across several APIs, you use the single class.

The **CStdioFile** class inherits its behavior from the **CFile** class and makes it easier to work with text files. The **CStdioFile** class provides two new functions to read and write text information: **ReadString** and **WriteString**. Because of the inherited behavior, you can get status information and also rename and delete text files using the appropriate functions in the **CFile** class.

The **ReadString** member function duplicates the action of the **fgets** function. A typical invocation appears in the example shown in Listing 12.2.

Listing 12.2
A replacement **HandleButton** function for Listing 12.1 that demonstrates the use of the **CStdioFile** class

```
//file2.cpp

// The message handler function
void CWindow::HandleButton()
{
    CFileDialog fileDialog( TRUE,
        fileDialogExt, NULL,
        0, fileDialogFilter );
    if( fileDialog.DoModal() == IDOK )
    {
        CStdioFile f;
        CFileException exception;
        BOOL status;

        // Reopen file for reading
        status = f.Open(fileDialog.GetPathName(),
            CFile::modeRead, &exception);
        if (!status)
        {
            char s[100];
            sprintf(s, "Error opening file for reading. Code:%d",
                exception.m_cause);
            MessageBox(s, "Error", MB_OK);
            return;
```

```
        }
        else
        {
            char s[1000];
            int mbStatus;

            // Read and display lines of text
            do
            {
                try
                {
                    f.ReadString(s, 1000);
                    s[strlen(s)] = '\0'; // Kill CR character
                    mbStatus = MessageBox(s, "Data", MB_OKCANCEL);
                }
                catch (CFileException exception)
                {
                    MessageBox("Error reading file",
                        "Error", MB_OK);
                    mbStatus = IDCANCEL;
                }
            }
            while (mbStatus == IDOK);
            f.Close();
        }
    }
}
```

To execute Listing 12.2, replace the **HandleButton** function in Listing 12.1

Listing 12.2 starts by opening an instance of the **CStdioFile** class in a manner identical to that of Listing 12.1. It then enters a loop that reads each line from the file and displays it in a message box dialog:

```
f.ReadString(s, 1000);
s[strlen(s)] = '\0'; // Kill CR character
mbStatus = MessageBox(s, "Data", MB_OKCANCEL);
```

Like **fgets**, the **ReadString** function reads a '\n' character into the string if it is able to read a complete line from the file. Also like **fgets**, the **ReadString** function returns a zero on end-of-file. In Listing 12.2, the code does not use the end-of-file indicator but instead lets the application throw an exception at the end of the file. The user can also exit the loop by pressing the **Cancel** button on the message box.

The **WriteString** function similarly duplicates the action of the **fputs** function. It writes a string to the file up to a '\0' character. If the string contains '\n' characters, these are written appropriately. See Listing 12.9 for an example.

The **CMemFile** class is identical to the **CFile** class except that the **Duplicate**, **LockRange**, and **UnlockRange** functions are not supported and, therefore, return not-supported exceptions (see Chapter 13). When you read or write from the file, the data is stored in memory rather than on disk and the operation is faster. You may find that memory files are a fast and convenient way to create temporary files that do not consume available disk space and do not need to be deleted when no longer needed.

12.1.2 The CString Class

The **CString** class encapsulates all the functionality of the normal C string library in a single, easy-to-use class that contains more than 30 member functions. The **CString** class has a number of important advantages over a normal C string:

- The **CString** class contains extra capabilities not found in the string library, such as **left**, **right**, and **mid**.
- The **CString** class automatically grows string arrays longer when necessary.
- The **CString** class overrides operators like =, ==, +, and += so string operations are much cleaner.
- You can use instances of the **CString** class in any function or operation that requires a normal C string.

Because of these important advantages, you will get into the habit of using **CString**s whenever you need a string. The code in Listing 12.3 demonstrates some typical uses of the **CString** class.

Listing 12.3
Typical simple uses of the **Cstring** class

```
// declare an instance. The string will be null.
CString s;
// initialize the string
s = "hello";
// concatenate a character and a string to it
s += ' ';
s += "world";
// get the length of the string
int i = s.GetLength();
// find a substring in the string
int j = s.Find("world");
```

In this simple example, the programmer has declared the string **s**, assigned to it, concatenated two other strings to it, and then used the **Find** function to find a substring in **s**. As you can see, the **Cstring** class contains equivalents for **strcpy**, **strcat**, and **strstr** that do the same things but are significantly easier to use.

The **CString** class contains five different types of constructors, as demonstrated below:

```
CString s1;
CString s2("Hello");
CString s3('A', 100);
CString s4("Hello World", 5);
CString s5 = "Hello";
```

The first example creates **s1** as an empty string. The second example creates **s2** containing the characters "Hello". The third example creates **s3** containing a string of

100 As. The fourth example creates **s4** containing the first 5 characters of the string "Hello World". The fifth example creates the string **s5** using the copy constructor.

Note that you do not have to specify a length when creating an instance of **CString**. The class dynamically allocates a block of memory from the heap to satisfy its space requirements. If you concatenate other strings to an existing **CString**, the class automatically reallocates space to satisfy the requirements of the concatenated string. The **CString** class has no maximum string size and always uses exactly as much memory as it needs. Note, however, that if you save an instance of **CString** to a file, what you will get in the file is simply a useless pointer rather than a string. The string itself is stored in a buffer on the heap. That is why Listing 12.1 used normal character arrays for the members of the structure saved to the file.

The **CString** class contains a number of overloaded operators that make the class easy to use: =, +, +=, ==, !=, <, <=, >, >=, and []. The class also contains <</>> for use with the **CArchive** class. The [] operator in particular is extremely nice because it lets you think of a **CSting** as a completely normal array of characters. The **GetAt** and **SetAt** member functions give you additional indexed access paths into the string.

The **GetLength** function performs the same task as the **strlen** function, returning the number of characters in the string. However, it is much quicker than **strlen** is on large strings because the **CString** class contains a data member that knows the length of the string. Therefore, **GetLength** simply returns that data member rather than counting each character in the string. The **IsEmpty** function returns TRUE if the string contains zero characters. The **Empty** function sets the length of the string to zero.

The **CString** class offers a number of utility functions listed below:

Compare	Identical to **strcmp**
CompareNoCase	Case-insensitive compare
Collate	Language-dependent compare like **strcoll**
Find	Finds a target string in a source string, starting at the beginning
FindOneOf	Given a set of characters, finds the first instance of one of them in a set
MakeUpper	Converts string to uppercase
MakeLower	Converts string to lowercase
MakeReverse	Reverses string
Mid	Returns a substring from the middle of an existing string
Left	Returns the leftmost N characters from a string
ReverseFind	Finds a target string in a source string, starting at the end string
Right	Returns the rightmost N characters from a string
SpanIncluding	Given a set of characters, returns the characters in a string from that set
SpanExcluding	Given a set of characters, returns the characters in a string not from that set

As you can see, the class provides much more extensive coverage of common string functions than the normal C string library, and the provided functions are easier to use and often more efficient. In addition, if you want to add extra functionality you can easily inherit the **CString** class and add new functions.

The **GetBuffer** function is unique and important. It allows you to use **CString** objects in places where you specifically need to manipulate the contents of the string memory directly. This capability is generally useful in situations where immediate access to the contents of the string makes operations on the string faster, but is specifically useful when you want to use a **CString** object with a function that returns a string.

For example, say that you want to use a **CString** object named **s** with the **GetDlgItemText** function that you saw in Chapters 4 and 5. As you recall, the **GetDlgItemText** function accepts a parameter in which it returns the contents of a control's text. You cannot simply pass the variable **s** to the function, because **s** is not a pointer to a character. The **GetBuffer** function returns a pointer to a character so you can use it as shown here:

```
GetDlgItemText(IDC_STRING, s.GetBuffer(len), len);
s.ReleaseBuffer();
```

The call to **GetBuffer** returns a normal pointer to character expected by **GetDlgItemText**, and because that pointer is not a **const** pointer you can manipulate the string directly. What **GetBuffer** is returning is the pointer to the memory block that the **CString** class is maintaining on the heap. When you call the **ReleaseBuffer** function, the **CString** class checks the size of the manipulated buffer and updates its internal length.

See also the **GetBufferSetLength** function and the MFC documentation for further information.

12.1.3 The CTime and CTimeSpan Classes

The **CTime** class encapsulates the time functions and structures found in the normal C time library. The class makes many of these functions much easier to use. Additionally, the class provides functions that convert to and from the various standard formats in the C time library, allowing you to easily interface to older C functions and libraries that require these structures. If you have used the time library, these conversion functions will be obvious, but if you have not you may find it useful to read about the time library functions in the documentation.

A typical use of the **CTime** class is shown below:

```
// gettime.cpp

// The message handler function
void CWindow::HandleButton()
{
    CTime t;
    t = CTime::GetCurrentTime();
    CString s = t.Format("Current time and date: %c");
    MessageBox(s, "Time", MB_OK);
}
```

This code demonstrates an extremely common way to use the **CTime** class. You can try it out by using this **HandleButton** function in Listing 12.1. The code creates an instance of the **CTime** class named **t**. It then fills **t** with the current time using the static member function **GetCurrentTime**. Then it uses the **Format** function to create a string representation of **t** and displays it in a message box. You might substitute this code into the clock code in Chapter 11.

The **CTime** constructor has four forms:

```
CTime t1;
CTime t2(t);
CTime t3(dosdate, dostime);
CTime t4(1999, 1, 1, 3, 30, 0);
```

The first example sets **t1** to the time 0. You should plan to fill **t1** in with a valid value shortly afterward, because 0 is an invalid value. This default constructor is provided so that you can create arrays of **CTime**. The second value creates **t2** and initializes it to the value of **t**. Accepted types for **t** are **CTime** and **time_t**. Both FILE-TIME and SYSTEMTIME structures are also accepted. In the third form, values returned by **_dos_getftime** initialize **t3**. In the fourth example, six integer constants set the time to 3:30 on January 1, 1990.

The **CTime** class overloads the following operators: =, +, -, +=, -=, ==, !=, <=,< , >=, > and <</>> (for the **CArchive** class). The addition and subtraction operators use the **CTimeSpan** class described below.

The **CTime** class offers three conversion functions:

GetTime	Returns a **time_t** value
GetGmTime	Returns a pointer to a **tm** structure in GMT (UTC) format
GetLocalTm	Returns a pointer to a **tm** structure in local time format

The **CTime** class also offers a pair of functions that convert the time held in an instance of the class to a string: **Format** and **FormatGmt**. These functions duplicate the **strftime** function in the C time library for local and GMT (UTC) format. You provide either of these functions with a format string similar to a **printf** format string and they return the specified string representation of the time. The following formatting constants are understood:

%a	Name of day (abbreviated)
%A	Name of day
%b	Name of month (abbreviated)
%B	Name of month
%c	Normal representation of date and time
%d	Decimal day of month
%H	Hour (military)
%I	Hour (civilian)
%j	Numeric day of the year (1-366)
%m	Month (numeric)
%M	Minute
%p	AM/PM
%S	Second

%U	Numeric week of the year (0-51), Sunday=first day of week
%W	Numeric week of the year (0-51), Monday=first day of week
%w	Numeric day of the week (Sun=0)
%x	Normal representation of date
%X	Normal representation of time
%y	Year from start of century (0-99)
%Y	Year
%z, %Z	Time zone
%%	Percent character

In the example at the beginning of this section, the "%c" constant was used for simplicity, but you can produce strings as intricate as you like using the above constants.

Finally, the **CTime** function provides six functions that extract integer values from the time held by an instance of the **CTime** class:

GetYear	1970-2038
GetMonth	1-12
GetDay	1-31
GetHour	0-23
GetMinute	0-59
GetSecond	0-59
GetDayOfWeek	Sunday=1, Monday=2, ...

The **CTimeSpan** class supplements the **CTime** class to provide a convenient way to store differences between two times. A typical use appears below:

```
CTime t1(1999,  1, 1, 0, 0, 0);
CTime t2;
t2 = CTime::GetCurrentTime();
CTimeSpan ts = t1 - t2;
CString sd = ts.Format("Difference = %D %H %M %S");
MessageBox(sd, "Time", MB_OK);
```

This example calculates and displays the time difference between the current time and the first second of the year 1999.

The **CTimeSpan** class has three different constructors:

```
CTimeSpan t1;
CTimeSpan t2(t);
CTimeSpan t3(0, 5, 20, 30);
```

The first example creates **t1** and initializes it to zero. The second example creates **t2** and initializes it to either a **time_t** value or a previously created **CTimeSpan** value. The third example creates **t3** and initializes it to 0 days, 5 hours, 20 minutes, and 30 seconds.

A typical way to initialize an instance of the **CTimeSpan** class is shown in the sample code above:

```
CTimeSpan ts = t1 - t2;
```

Here, two instances of the **CTime** class are subtracted and placed in an instance of the **CTimeSpan** class.

The **CTimeSpan** class overloads the following operators: =, +=, -=, +, -, ==, !=, <, <=, >, >=, and <</>> (for the **CArchive** class). These operators make it easy to add, subtract, and compare time differences.

Seven different functions let you easily extract integer representations of the time difference held in an instance of the **CTimeSpan** class:

GetDays	Number of elapsed days
GetHours	Number of hours (-23 through 23).
GetTotalHours	Number of elapsed hours
GetMinutes	Number of minutes (-59 through 59)
GetTotalMinutes	Number of elapsed minutes
GetSeconds	Number of seconds (-59 through 59)
GetTotalSeconds	Number of elapsed seconds

The **format** function makes it easy to print strings showing the value held by instances of the class. The following formatting constants are understood:

%D	Days
%H	Hours
%M	Minutes
%S	Seconds
%%	Percent character

12.1.4 The CRect, CPoint, and CSize Classes

The Windows API, when used in C, supports three common structures named RECT, POINT, and SIZE. These three structures are used in hundreds of different C functions in the API. MFC, therefore, frequently has need for structures of these types. The **CRect**, **CPoint,** and **CSize** classes provide simple and useful encapsulations that preserve the three structures but add a number of functions that make it easier for you to manipulate the structures.

Each of the three classes has a single-member variable of the type RECT, POINT, and SIZE, respectively. This means that you can pass, for example, an instance of **CRect** to any function expecting a RECT parameter.

The following lists briefly describe the functions and operators available in the three classes. Most of the functions have obvious actions. See the MFC documentation for further information.

CRect

```
typedef struct
{
    int left;
    int top;
    int right;
    int bottom;
} RECT;
```

CRect	Constructor
Width	Returns the width of the rectangle
Height	Returns the height of the rectangle
Size	Returns the size

TopLeft	Returns the top-left point
BottomRight	Returns the bottom-right point
IsRectEmpty	Returns TRUE if width or height is zero
IsRectNull	Returns TRUE if all four values are zero
PtInRect	Returns TRUE if the point is inside the rectangle
SetRect	Sets the rectangle
SetRectEmpty	NULLs the rectangle
CopyRect, =	Assignment
EqualRect, ==, !=	Equality and inequality
InflateRect	Modifies the width and height
OffsetRect, +, -	Moves the rectangle's coordinates
SubtractRect, -, -=	Subtraction
IntersectRect, &=, &	Returns the rectangle of intersection
UnionRectSets, |=, |	Returns a rectangle surrounding the two rectangles
LPCRECT	Converts a CRect to an LPCRECT
LPRECT	Converts a CRect to an LPRECT

CPoint

```
typedef struct
{
    int x;
    int y;
} POINT;
```

CPoint	Constructor
Offset	Modifies X and Y
==	Equality
!=	Inequality
+=, +	Addition
-=, -	Subtraction

CSize

```
typedef struct
{
    int cx;
    int cy;
} SIZE;
```

CSize	Constructor
==	Equality
!=	Inequality
+=, +	Addition
-=, -	Subtraction

12.2 Simple Array Classes

One of the most common and frequently used data structures is the normal C array. Arrays are popular because they have several important advantages. First and foremost, they are extremely easy to use. They are also efficient: You can get to any element in an array in a constant amount of time, and this makes them useful for searching and sorting.

C arrays have several problems, however. One of the more bothersome is the fact that they have a fixed size. In C arrays also have unprotected boundaries, and this can lead to a number of difficult-to-track bugs.

MFC provides classes for six different types of arrays. All these arrays share the same basic functionality. There are several important features that distinguish MFC arrays from normal C arrays:

- MFC arrays can grow and shrink. The class allocates or reallocates memory as needed
- MFC arrays perform boundary checks during the debugging phase
- MFC arrays add important and useful capabilities such as insertion into and deletion from the middle of an array

MFC arrays come in two different flavors, one using templates and the other not. The code in Listing 12.4 demonstrates how to create and use an array of unsigned integers using a non-template array class called **CUIntArray**.

Listing 12.4
A simple array of unsigned integers

```cpp
// array.cpp

#include <afxwin.h>
#include <afxcoll.h>

#define IDC_BUTTON 100

// Declare the application class
class CButtonApp : public CWinApp
{
public:
    virtual BOOL InitInstance();
};

// Create an instance of the application class
CButtonApp ButtonApp;

// Declare the main window class
class CButtonWindow : public CFrameWnd
{
    CButton *button;
    CUIntArray array;
    int x;
public:
    CButtonWindow();
    afx_msg void HandleButton();

    DECLARE_MESSAGE_MAP()
};

// The message handler function
```

```
void CButtonWindow::HandleButton()
{
    SetDlgItemInt(100, array.GetAt(x), FALSE);
    x++;
}


// The message map
BEGIN_MESSAGE_MAP(CButtonWindow, CFrameWnd)
    ON_COMMAND(IDC_BUTTON, HandleButton)
END_MESSAGE_MAP()

// The InitInstance function is called once
// when the application first executes
BOOL CButtonApp::InitInstance()
{
    m_pMainWnd = new CButtonWindow();
    m_pMainWnd->ShowWindow(m_nCmdShow);
    m_pMainWnd->UpdateWindow();
    return TRUE;
}


// The constructor for the window class
CButtonWindow::CButtonWindow()
{
    CRect r;

    // Create the window itself
    Create(NULL,
        "CButton Tests",
        WS_OVERLAPPEDWINDOW,
        CRect(0,0,200,200));

    // Get the size of the client rectangle
    GetClientRect(&r);
    r.InflateRect(-20,-20);

    // Create a button
    button = new CButton();
    button->Create("Push me",
        WS_CHILD|WS_VISIBLE|BS_PUSHBUTTON,
        r,
        this,
        IDB_BUTTON);

    int i;
    for (i=0; i<100; i+=2)
        array.Add(i);
}
```

Listing 12.4 creates the array at the bottom of the window's constructor and fills it with 50 integers:

```
int i;
for (i=0; i<100; i+=2)
    array.Add(i);
```

The variable **array** is a data member of the window's class. The code adds elements to the array using the **Add** member function. When the window appears on the screen, it contains a button. Each time you click the button it displays an element of the array. This action demonstrates retrieval.

The **CUintArray** class is one of five simple arrays that MFC supports. The others are **CByteArray**, **CDWordArray**, **CWordArray**, and **CPtrArray**. MFC also supports an array of **CString**s called **CStringArray**, as well as an array of objects derived from **CObject**. Each of these arrays has the same member functions.

The **Add** function seen previously adds an element to the end of the array. If all the memory currently allocated for the array is full, the array increases its size to accommodate the new entry by allocating a new block on the heap and copying the array to that new block. The only limit on array size is set by available virtual memory space.

By default, the array grows by one element each time you add a new entry to the array. That is, each time you call the **Add** function, MFC allocates a new block of memory from the heap that is one element bigger than the current array, and then copies the current contents of the array to the new block. Obviously, this is painfully slow. You can modify the growth behavior, and the initial size of the array, using the **SetSize** function. This function accepts the initial size of the array and the growth size as parameters. *You should use this function only once.* For example, say that you know you will be adding thousands of elements to a UINT array. You might use the following call:

```
CUintArray array;
array.SetSize(0, 10000);
```

This call tells the array to start with 0 elements and to grow the array by 10,000 elements each time it runs out of space. You may want to experiment with the growth size in different applications to find the best trade-off between performance and wasted space.

If you know that the array will need exactly 15,000 elements, you can set that size with the **SetSize** function. For example:

```
CUintArray array;
array.SetSize(15000, 100);
```

This call indicates an initial size of 15,000 elements and a growth size of 100 elements. After doing this, use the **SetAt** or **SetAtGrow** functions to modify existing elements of the array. Both functions accept an index, which is zero-based just like a C array, as well as the value to place at that location. The **SetAt** function will only add new values to existing elements of the array, while **SetAtGrow** will grow the array if necessary to accommodate the new entry.

Note that when you use the **SetSize** function the last element of the array as perceived by the **Add** function is set to the size indicated. In the above example where **SetSize** sets the initial size to 15,000, the next add operation would occur at index 15,000. Use **SetAt** to change values at indexes between 0 and 14,999.

The **GetAt** function returns an element of the array. It will assert an error if you are in debug mode (see Chapter 13) and attempt to reference an element outside the bounds of the array. Note that the [] operator is equivalent to **SetAt** and **GetAt**.

The following functions give you further control over the array:

GetSize	Returns the number of elements in the array
GetUpperBound	Returns GetSize-1
FreeExtra	Deletes any extra memory allocated but not used
RemoveAll	Deletes all elements from the array
InsertAt	Inserts values at the index indicated, bubbling all elements below down to make room
RemoveAt	Removes values at the index indicated, bubbling all elements below up to close the gap
operator []	Sets or gets the element at the specified index.

As you can see, the MFC array implementation is extremely easy to use, but is also quite flexible and robust. You should use it in place of any normal C array.

The template-based form of the array class is called **CArray**. It has the same functions as the pre-defined array classes described above. The template version has the advantage that you can create an array of any type rather than being restricted to specific types. It has the disadvantage that, in most cases, you need to override helper functions in **CArray**. See the MFC documentation (particularly the topic "Collections" in books on-line) for more information on **CArray** and other template classes.

12.3 The CObject class and CObject Arrays

You may have noticed that all the array types listed in the previous section, with the exception of the **CString** and **CObArray** arrays, hold ordinal types: UINT, BYTE, DWORD, WORD, and pointers all fall into this category. If you want to create an array of some other type, MFC also provides the template-based **CArray**. Additionally, it is possible for you to derive new classes from the MFC base class **CObject** and store those objects in an array named **CObArray**. This special array type lets you create your own arrays that can automatically *serialize* themselves to disk, giving you an extremely easy way to read and write data to files.

If you look at the full MFC class hierarchy, you will find that the **CObject** class is extremely important. It is the base class for the vast majority of other classes in the hierarchy. You can see this by searching for "Hierarchy Charts" in the MFC documentation and examining the different hierarchy charts available. Ninety percent of the classes in MFC have **CObject** as their base.

CObject's position in the hierarchy gives it a great deal of control over the behavior of MFC classes. It contains several important characteristics that are broadly shared by all MFC objects:

- Support for runtime class information
- Support for diagnostic information (see Section 12.3)
- Support for serialization
- Support for dynamic creation

By creating your own classes from **CObject**, you can take advantage of these same benefits.

MFC provides six macros that turn on **CObject**'s advanced capabilities:

DECLARE_DYNAMIC
IMPLEMENT_DYNAMIC
DECLARE_DYNCREATE
IMPLEMENT_DYNCREATE
DECLARE_SERIAL
IMPLEMENT_SERIAL

The DYNAMIC macros support runtime class information. Runtime class information allows you (or other parts of the MFC class hierarchy) to query an object derived from **CObject** for its class type. For example, if you call the **IsKindOf** function on an instance of a **CObject**-derived class, the instance will verify if it is derived from a particular class.

The DYNCREATE macros support dynamic creation. Dynamic creation allows the class hierarchy to create instances dynamically at runtime, for example when it is reading serialized object information from disk.

The SERIAL macros support serialization and additionally include the DYNAMIC and DYNCREATE capabilities automatically. By using the SERIAL macros you enable all of capabilities of the **CObject** class.

As an example of how you might use the **CObArray** and **CObject** classes in your own applications, let's revisit DRAW3.CPP from Chapter 11. In that program we created a simple array class that stored the points draw by the user. The array allows the program to properly refresh its client area during **OnPaint** events.

Let's say that we want to extend DRAW3.CPP so it also has the added feature of *persistence*. That is, whenever the user quits the drawing program we want it to save the current picture to disk automatically and then reload that image again the next time the user restarts the application. This is extremely easy to do using the **CObArray** class.

To take advantage of the **CObArray** class, you must derive your data class from **CObject**. Listing 12.5 demonstrates how to do this.

Listing 12.5
The **CObPoint** class

```
class CObPoint : public CObject
{
DECLARE_SERIAL( CObPoint )
protected:
    LONG x, y;
public:
    CObPoint() {x=0; y=0;}
    CObPoint(const CObPoint &p) {x=p.x; y=p.y;}
    CObPoint operator=(const CObPoint& p)
        {x=p.x; y=p.y; return *this;}
    CObPoint(int ix, int iy) {x=ix; y=iy;}
    CObPoint(CPoint &p) {x=p.x; y=p.y;}
    virtual void Serialize(CArchive &archive)
    {
        CObject::Serialize(archive);
```

```
        if (archive.IsStoring())
            archive << x << y;
        else
            archive >> x >> y;
    }
    // The (int) casts in the line below are
    // needed only in Windows 3.1. Remove in
    // WIN32 environments
    CPoint GetPoint() const {return CPoint(x,y);}
};

IMPLEMENT_SERIAL(CObPoint, CObject, 0)
```

The class declared in Listing 12.5 is a complete implementation of a new class derived from **CObject**. It contains the proper default constructor, copy constructor and assignment operator. Technically, the copy constructor and assignment operator are not necessary here because this class does not have members that are pointers. They are included to demonstrate their potential need. See Appendix A for more information. The class contains two converting constructors and a new function **GetPoint** that extracts information from the class. The class also overrides the **Serialize** member function of **CObject** to properly serialize instances of this class. Because it overrides **Serialize**, the class contains the DECLARE_SERIAL macro, and you must also use the IMPLEMENT_SERIAL macro after the compiler finishes compiling the implementation for the class, as shown.

The **Serialize** function gives MFC a way to automatically provide persistence. Each new class that you create from **CObject** should override **Serialize** so it can save itself to an *archive*. An archive is an efficient binary stream (as opposed to a text stream) stored in a file. In **CObPoint::Serialize** you see the class first call the base class's **Serialize** function and then examine the **IsStoring** function to decide on the current data direction. It saves to or loads from the archive depending on the direction using the << or >> operators. All classes in MFC, as well as all standard types (int, char, etc.), have overloaded << and >> operators compatible with the **CArchive** class.

Why go to all this trouble? For example, if you need to create an array of address records, why not create it using your own array rather than inherit an address class from **CObject** and then place the objects in a **CObArray**? Here are three good reasons to base your address class off **CObject**:

1. You automatically gain important debugging features built into the **CObject** class. See Chapter 13.
2. You make integration into the **CDocument** class much easier. This class is extremely important in Part 3.
3. You get access to serialization, which is an efficient and easy way to store data on disk.

To create your own classes based from **CObject**, simply follow the example that appears in Listing 12.5. Create your members and then add functions like those shown to provide access and serialization for the class. See Chapter 13 for information on how to add debugging support to **CObject**-derived classes.

Listing 12.6 shows how to integrate the **CObPoint** class seen in Listing 12.5 into the drawing program from Chapter 11.

Listing 12.6
Using the **CObPoint** class in a drawing program to provide automatic persistence.

```
// drawob.cpp

#include <afxwin.h>
#include <afxcoll.h>

// Define the application class
class CApp : public CWinApp
{
public:
    virtual BOOL InitInstance();
};

CApp App;

class CObPoint : public CObject
{
DECLARE_SERIAL( CObPoint )
protected:
    LONG x, y;
public:
    CObPoint() {x=0; y=0;}
    CObPoint(const CObPoint &p) {x=p.x; y=p.y;}
    CObPoint operator=(const CObPoint& p)
        {x=p.x; y=p.y; return *this;}
    CObPoint(int ix, int iy) {x=ix; y=iy;}
    CObPoint(CPoint &p) {x=p.x; y=p.y;}
    virtual void Serialize(CArchive &archive)
    {
        CObject::Serialize(archive);
        if (archive.IsStoring())
            archive << x << y;
        else
            archive >> x >> y;
    }
    // The (int) casts in the line below are
    // needed only in Windows 3.1. Remove in
    // WIN32 environments
    CPoint GetPoint() const {return CPoint((int)x, (int)y);}
};

IMPLEMENT_SERIAL(CObPoint, CObject, 0)

// Define the window class
class CWindow : public CFrameWnd
{
    CObArray *array;
public:
```

```
    CWindow();
    ~CWindow();
    afx_msg void OnPaint();
    afx_msg void OnMouseMove(UINT,CPoint);
    afx_msg void OnDestroy();
    DECLARE_MESSAGE_MAP()
};

// The window's constructor
CWindow::CWindow()
{
    // Create the window
    Create(NULL, "Drawing Tests",
        WS_OVERLAPPEDWINDOW,
        CRect(0,0,250,250));

    // Read persistent data
    CFile file;
    if (file.Open("data", CFile::modeRead))
    {
        CArchive archive(&file, CArchive::load);
        archive >> array;
        archive.Close();
        file.Close();
    }
    else
        array = new CObArray();
}

// Window's destructor
CWindow::~CWindow()
{
    // delete all elements in the array
    int i;
    for (i=0; i<array->GetSize(); i++)
        delete array->GetAt(i);
    array->RemoveAll();
    delete array;
}

// The message map
BEGIN_MESSAGE_MAP( CWindow, CFrameWnd )
    ON_WM_PAINT()
    ON_WM_MOUSEMOVE()
    ON_WM_DESTROY()
END_MESSAGE_MAP()

// Handle mouse movement
void CWindow::OnMouseMove(UINT flag,
    CPoint mousePos)
{
    if (flag == MK_LBUTTON)
    {
        CClientDC dc(this);
        dc.SetPixel(mousePos,RGB(0,0,255));
        // Add each point to the array
```

```
        array->Add(new CObPoint(mousePos));
    }
}

// Handle exposure
void CWindow::OnPaint()
{
    int x;
    CPaintDC dc(this);
    // Redraw all points in the array
    for (x=0; x<array->GetSize(); x++)
        dc.SetPixel((((CObPoint *)(array->GetAt(x)))->GetPoint(),
            RGB(0,0,255));
}

// Handle destruction by saving object array
void CWindow::OnDestroy()
{
    // Save persistent data
    CFile file;
    if (file.Open("data", CFile::modeCreate | CFile::modeWrite))
    {
        CArchive archive(&file, CArchive::store);
        archive << array;
        archive.Close();
        file.Close();
    }
}

// Init the application
BOOL CApp::InitInstance()
{
    m_pMainWnd = new CWindow();
    m_pMainWnd->ShowWindow(m_nCmdShow);
    m_pMainWnd->UpdateWindow();
    return TRUE;
}
```

Run Listing 12.6, draw something, and then close the application. The **OnDestroy** function will save the data from your drawing to a file arbitrarily named "data." When you rerun the application, the constructor for **CWindow** will read the data back in automatically and you can continue working on the drawing.

This program uses a **CObArray** array to hold the data. The array is a member of the **CWindow** class and is initialized in the constructor for the window. Each time the user does any drawing, the **OnMouseMove** function allocates a new instance of **CObPoint** and uses the **Add** function to add the instance to the array:

```
        array->Add(new CObPoint(mousePos));
```

See the previous section for more information on the **Add** function. Whenever the program receives an exposure event, the **OnPaint** function uses a **for** loop, the **GetSize** function, the **GetAt** function, and the **GetPoint** function of **CObPoint** to retrieve and redraw the points in the drawing:

```
for (x=0; x<array->GetSize(); x++)
    dc.SetPixel(((CObPoint *)(array->GetAt(x)))->GetPoint(),
        RGB(0,0,255));
```

As the window destroys itself on a close, the **OnDestroy** function serializes the array to disk:

```
// Handle destruction by saving object array
void CWindow::OnDestroy()
{
    // Save persistent data
    CFile file;
    if (file.Open("data", CFile::modeCreate | CFile::modeWrite))
    {
        CArchive archive(&file, CArchive::store);
        archive << array;
        archive.Close();
        file.Close();
    }
}
```

The destructor can then free all elements in the array and delete the array itself:

```
// Window's destructor
CWindow::~CWindow()
{
    // delete all elements in the array
    int i;
    for (i=0; i<array->GetSize(); i++)
        delete array->GetAt(i);
    array->RemoveAll();
    delete array;
}
```

The **OnDestroy** function opens a file for writing (see Section 12.1 for more information on **CFile**), attaches that file to an instance of the **CArchive** class, and then dumps the array to the archive. The << operator automatically calls **CObArray**'s **Serialize** member function, which in turn automatically calls the **Serialize** member function for each element it holds. Note that the archive is created here in the "store" direction, and the file is writable.

Loading the file in the window's constructor simply reverses the process:

```
CFile file;
if (file.Open("data", CFile::modeRead))
{
    CArchive archive(&file, CArchive::load);
    archive >> array;
    archive.Close();
    file.Close();
}
```

Here the code opens a readable file and gives the archive a "load" direction. One line of code then brings all the data from the file into the array. Note that nowhere in this code do you have to allocate memory for the array. There is no call to **new** for the **array** member variable, although there is a call to **delete** in the destructor. When the program opens the file and reads in the archive, the archive automatically and dynamically allocates the array and all the points within the array. It can do this because the array and the points are both based off the **CObject** class, which has dynamic creation abilities. You are responsible for deleting the dynamically created objects in the destructor.

Pay special attention to the invocation of the IMPLEMENT_SERIAL macro:

```
IMPLEMENT_SERIAL(CObPoint, CObject, 0)
```

The **CObPoint** class declares itself as serializable at the top of the class with the DECLARE_SERIAL macro. The IMPLEMENT_SERIAL macro, which should only be invoked *once* in an application for any given class, tells MFC two things:

1. The name of **CObPoint**'s base class, **CObject**
2. A "version number," or *schema* that lets MFC handle different versions of the data properly.

The version number is an interesting feature and shows how far MFC goes to make your life easier. For example, this implementation sets the version number to zero. If you were to change the data members of the class in a later program, you could change the version number in IMPLEMENT_SERIAL to one. Then if the user tries to load an old data file, MFC can throw an archive exception (See Chapter 13) to indicate the problem.

Because you can call IMPLEMENT_SERIAL only once for a given class in an application, you typically implement your own **CObject**-derived classes using separate header and implementation files. Listings 12.7 and 12.8 demonstrate the process for the **CObPoint** class. Any program needing to use the **CObPoint** class can simply include the header file and link in the object file for `cobpoint.cpp`.

Listing 12.7
The file cobpoint.h

```
// cobpoint.h

#ifndef _INC_COBPOINT
#define _INC_COBPOINT

class CObPoint : public CObject
{
DECLARE_SERIAL( CObPoint )
protected:
    LONG x, y;
public:
    CObPoint();
    CObPoint(const CObPoint &p);
    CObPoint operator=(const CObPoint& p);
    CObPoint(int ix, int iy);
    CObPoint(CPoint &p);
    virtual void Serialize(CArchive &archive);
    CPoint GetPoint() const;
};
```

```
                        #endif  // _INC_COBPOINT
```

Listing 12.8
The file cobpoint.cpp

```
// cobpoint.cpp

#include <afxwin.h>
#include "cobpoint.h"

CObPoint::CObPoint()
{
    x=y=0;
}

CObPoint::CObPoint(const CObPoint &p)
{
    x=p.x;
    y=p.y;
}

CObPoint CObPoint::operator=(const CObPoint& p)
{
    x=p.x;
    y=p.y;
    return *this;
}

CObPoint::CObPoint(int ix, int iy)
{
    x=ix;
    y=iy;
}

CObPoint::CObPoint(CPoint &p)
{
    x=p.x;
    y=p.y;
}

void CObPoint::Serialize(CArchive &archive)
{
    CObject::Serialize(archive);
    if (archive.IsStoring())
        archive << x << y;
    else
        archive >> x >> y;
}

// The (int) casts in the function below are
// needed only in Windows 3.1. Remove in
// WIN32 environments
CPoint CObPoint::GetPoint() const
```

```
{
    return CPoint((int)x, (int)y);
}

IMPLEMENT_SERIAL(CObPoint, CObject, 0)
```

Note that Listing 12.8 contains the single call to IMPLEMENT_SERIAL needed by the **CObPoint** class.

Note also that the destructor for the **CObArray** class does not dispose of the objects it contains. As seen in the window's destructor in Listing 12.8, you must individually delete each element in the array and then delete the array itself. If you want the array to dispose of its objects automatically, you should derive a new class from **CObArray** and create your own destructor in the new class that deletes each object held by the array. Note that you must use DECLARE_SERIAL and IMPLEMENT_SERIAL for this new array class if it needs to be able to serialize itself.

12.4 List Classes

MFC's list classes give you another way to store collections of objects. MFC supports three different kinds of lists:

- **CStringList** — a linked list of **CString**
- **CObList** — a linked list of **CObject**
- **CPtrList** — a linked list of (void *) pointers

MFC also supports a template-based list class called **CList**. See the MFC documentation for further information.

The MFC lists are implemented as doubly linked lists consisting of individually allocated blocks of memory. There is no limit to the size of a list except for the amount of free virtual memory space in the machine. Because it is a linked list, insertions are fast at the head or the tail or at a known position in the middle of the list. Searching is slow because it has to be sequential.

All MFC lists have the same member functions, listed below:

Constructor	The list constructor
AddHead	Adds elements or other lists to the head of the list
AddTail	Adds elements or other lists to the tail of the list
Find	Returns the POSITION of a pointer value
FindIndex	Returns the POSITION of an index
GetAt	Returns a pointer or reference to a POSITION
GetCount	Returns a count of the elements in the list
GetHead	Returns a pointer or reference to the front element of the list
GetHeadPosition	Returns the POSITION of the front element of the list
GetNext	Returns a pointer or reference to the next element of the list
GetPrev	Returns a pointer or reference to the next element of the list
GetTail	Returns a pointer or reference to the last element of the list
GetTailPosition	Returns the POSITION of the last element of the list

InsertAfter	Given a POSITION, inserts an element behind it
InsertBefore	Give a POSITION, inserts an element in front of it
IsEmpty	Returns TRUE if the list is empty
RemoveAll	Empties the list
RemoveAt	Given a POSITION, deletes the element at that position
RemoveHead	Deletes the list's first element
RemoveTail	Deletes the list's last element
SetAt	Given a POSITION, replaces the object at that position

Many of these functions rely on values of type POSITION. You can best understand this type and how to use it by looking at an example, as shown in Listing 12.9.

Listing 12.9
Adding elements to a sorted list of **CString**.

```
//List.cpp

const char *words[] = {"cat", "dog", "aardvark"
    "boy", "frog", "goat", "horse", "eel",
    "fish", "ant", "llama"};
const int numWords = sizeof(words)/sizeof(char *);
CStringList *list;

void CWindow::SortedAdd(const CString &word)
{
    POSITION p;

    // handle the empty-list case
    if (list->IsEmpty())
        list->AddTail(word);
    // otherwise, find the proper position
    // and add the word
    else
    {
        BOOL done=FALSE;

        p = list->GetHeadPosition();
        while (p != NULL && !done)
        {
            if (word > list->GetAt(p))
                list->GetNext(p);
            else
            {
                list->InsertBefore(p, word);
                done = TRUE;
            }
        }
        if (!done)
            list->AddTail(word);
    }
}

void CWindow::WriteToFile(char *filename)
```

```
    {
        CStdioFile f;
        CFileException e;
        BOOL status;

        status = f.Open(filename,
            CFile::modeCreate | CFile::modeWrite | CFile::typeText, &e);
        if (!status)
        {
            char s[100];
            sprintf(s,"Cause = %d", e.m_cause);
            MessageBox(s, "File error", MB_OK);
        }
        else
        {
            POSITION p;

            p = list->GetHeadPosition();
            while (p != NULL)
                f.WriteString(list->GetNext(p) + "\n");
            f.Close();
        }
    }

// The message handler function
void CWindow::HandleButton()
{
    list = new CStringList;
    int x;

    // unsorted insertions
    for (x=0; x<numWords; x++)
        list->AddTail(words[x]);
    // dump the list to a file
    WriteToFile("string1.dat");

    // sorted insertions
    list->RemoveAll();
    for (x=0; x<numWords; x++)
    {
        // SortedAdd is not in CStringList.
        // It is defined in this listing.
        SortedAdd(words[x]);
    }
    // dump the list to a file
    WriteToFile("string2.dat");

    delete list;
}
```

Listing 12.9 creates a list of **CString**s and adds words to the list one at a time. You can replace the **HandleButton** function in Listing 12.1 to run this code.

Listing 12.9 adds words to the list twice. The first time it adds all words to the end of the list. The second time it maintains the list in sorted order. In both cases it writes the list to a text file after filling it so you can examine the list.

Adding words to the beginning or end of the list is easy. Listing 12.9 repeatedly adds elements to the end of the list using the following **for** loop:

```
for (x=0; x<numWords; x++)
    list->AddTail(words[x]);
```

The **AddTail** function adds each word to the end of the list. Once the **for** loop finishes, the program calls the **WriteToFile** function to create a text file containing the contents of the list. The **WriteToFile** function uses a loop to traverse the list, writing out each element as it goes (Note that serialization [see Section 12.3] would be much easier from a coding standpoint, but serialized files contain binary data rather than text and are not human-readable):

```
POSITION p;


p = list->GetHeadPosition();
while (p != NULL)
    f.WriteString(list->GetNext(p) + "\n");
f.Close();
```

Before entering the loop, the program calls **GetHeadPosition**. This function returns a value of type POSITION. A POSITION is a temporary pointer into the linked list. You can use the **GetAt** or the **GetNext** function to gain access to the object at the POSITION pointer.

The **GetAt** function returns to you either a reference or a pointer to the element held at the position. If the list is constant, **GetAt** returns a pointer to the element held at that position in the list. You can use **GetAt** only on the RHS of an assignment. If the list is not constant, you can use **GetAt** on either the LHS or RHS and you can use it to modify elements in the list. **GetNext** has the same behavior, but additionally moves the POSITION pointer to the next element in the list in addition to returning a pointer or reference to the current element. **GetPrev** does the same thing as **GetNext**, but moves the POSITION pointer to the previous element.

The sorted insertion function adds a word to the list at its proper sorted position. It has to handle three different cases to do this. If the list is empty, the **GetAt** function asserts on the error (see Chapter13), so the code must handle the first insertion separately. When the list is non-empty, the code traverses to find the correct insertion point. Once found, it inserts the value. If the value belongs at the very end of the list, the code handles that situation separately as well to avoid runtime errors:

```
// handle the empty-list case
if (list->IsEmpty())
    list->AddTail(word);
// otherwise, find the proper position
// and add the word
else
{
    BOOL done=FALSE;

    p = list->GetHeadPosition();
```

```
    while (p != NULL && !done)
    {
        if (word > list->GetAt(p))
            list->GetNext(p);
        else
        {
            list->InsertBefore(p, word);
            done = TRUE;
        }
    }
    if (!done)
        list->AddTail(word);
}
```

If you want to modify an element of the list, you can use the **GetAt**, **GetNext**, or **GetPrevious** functions to do it. The code below walks through a list of **CString** and modifies every value in it:

```
POSITION p;
char c = 'a';

p = list->GetHeadPosition();
while (p != NULL)
    list->GetNext(p) = CString(c++, 10);
WriteToFile("string3.dat");
```

The line inside the **while** loop is a little unusual. Because the **GetNext** function returns a reference here, the assignment copies the new **CString** over the existing **CString** in the list. Each element in the list is replaced with a ten-character string such as "aaaaaaaaaa", "bbbbbbbbbb", etc.

You use **CPtrList** and **CObList** in a manner identical to that demonstrated above for **CString**. Keep in mind, however, that neither **CPtrList** nor **CObList** clean up their elements during destruction. If you need for that to happen, derive a new class and create your own destructor there.

12.5 Mapping Classes

The MFC mapping classes let you easily translate values from one type to another. For example, you might have a set of strings associated with a set of **CObject**s. Perhaps the **CObject**s are data records and the strings represent their part numbers. You can easily form a mapping that contains all the associations and then look up objects by their part numbers very quickly. The mapping classes use a hashing algorithm to look things up quickly.

Figure 12.1 shows the different translations possible with the MFC-supplied mappings, and it is easy to derive other mappings of your own to create any mapping you desire.

A list of the mapping class names is shown below:

CMapPtrToWord	Maps (void *) to WORD
CMapPtrToPtr	Maps (void *) to (void *)
CMapStringToOb	Maps CString to (CObject *)
CMapStringToPtr	Maps CString to (void *)

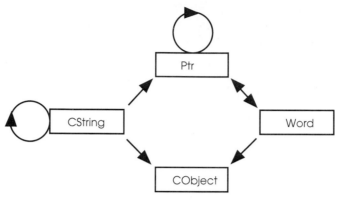

Figure 12.1
The different mappings available in MFC

CMapStringToString	Maps CString to CString
CMapWordToOb	Maps WORD to (CObject *)
CMapWordToPtr	Maps WORDs to (void *)

There is also a template-based mapping class called **CMap**. See the MFC documentation for further information.

To use a mapping class, you must first load it with your associations. For example, you might want to perform one-to-one word translations from nouns in one language to nouns in another, perhaps English to French. You would use the **CMapStringToString** class and load it with associated word pairs. Using the **SetAt** function, you load the specific association for the English word "paper" with the french word "papier." You then associate the English word "window" with the French word "fenetre", and so on. To retrieve an association from the mapping, you would use the **Lookup** function and pass it an English word. It returns the correct French word or NULL if the English word does not exist in the mapping.

The code in Listing 12.10 shows another use for a mapping class. Here the mapping associates file exception error codes from the **CFileException** class (see Chapter 13) with English error strings. You would use this mapping to allow an error dialog to produce an English error message on file exceptions. The program uses the **CMapWordToPtr** class to implement the mapping.

Listing 12.10
A mapping class that translates numeric values from an exception's m_cause field to associated strings.

```
// mapping.cpp

char *errors[] =
{
"No error occurred",
"An unspecified error occurred",
"The file could not be located",
"All or part of the path is invalid",
```

```
    "The permitted number of open files was exceeded",
    "The file could not be accessed",
    "There was an attempt to use an invalid file handle",
    "The current working directory cannot be removed",
    "There are no more directory entries",
    "There was an error trying to set the file pointer",
    "There was a hardware error",
    "SHARE.EXE was not loaded, or a shared region was locked",
    "There was an attempt to lock a region that was already locked",
    "The disk is full",
    "The end of file was reached",
    };
    int numErrors = sizeof(errors)/sizeof(char *);

    class ErrorTranslate : public CMapWordToPtr
    {
    public:
        ErrorTranslate()
        {
            int i;
            for (i=0; i<numErrors; i++)
                SetAt(i, errors[i]);
        }
        char *GetEnglish(int errorNum)
        {
            void *p;
            Lookup(errorNum, p);
            return (char *) p;
        }
    };

    // The message handler function
    void CWindow::HandleButton()
    {
        CFile f;
        CFileException e;
        BOOL status;
        ErrorTranslate err;

        status = f.Open("asdasdasdasd", CFile::modeRead, &e);
        if (!status)
            MessageBox(err.GetEnglish(e.m_cause), "Error", MB_OK);
        else
            f.Close();
    }
```

In Listing 12.10, the **HandleButton** function (which you can use to replace the **HandleButton** function in Listing 12.1) forces a file exception by trying to open a non-existent file. Upon detecting the error, **HandleButton** calls the **GetEnglish** function in the **ErrorTranslate** class. This class is declared locally here but could also appear globally. The constructor for the **ErrorTranslate** class loads associations into the mapping with the **SetAt** function. The **GetEnglish** function then uses the **Look-**

up function to look up a string by error number. See Chapter 13 for more information on **m_cause** and file exceptions.

Mapping classes have several other useful functions:

GetCount	Returns the number of associations in the map
GetNextAssoc	When iterating through the mapping, gets the next association
GetStartPosition	When iterating through the mapping, gets the first association
IsEmpty	Returns TRUE if the mapping contains no associations
Lookup	Looks up an association
operator []	Substitute for **SetAt**
RemoveAll	Deletes all associations in a mapping
RemoveKey	Given a value, removes its association from the mapping
SetAt	Adds an association to the map, replacing a duplicate if necessary

You will find that these functions, combined with the several elementary functions demonstrated in Listing 12.10, give you complete access to the mappings you create.

12.6 Conclusion

It would be possible to write an entire book that exhaustively discusses the different utility and collection classes in MFC. These classes make up about one-half of the hierarchy. Rather than do that, we have chosen to give you a good introduction to the different classes available and leave it at that. The on-line documentation provided in the MFC documentation will help you fill in the details as you need them.

The next chapter discusses the debugging facilities built into MFC.

DEBUGGING AND ROBUSTNESS

13

The MFC class hierarchy provides a number of different tools that help you debug your applications during development. The goal of these tools is to help you release a product that is bug-free and robust. This chapter will show you how to use all these tools and techniques while developing new applications. This chapter also discusses MFC's built-in exception handling mechanism. This mechanism allows you to detect exceptional situations such as out-of-memory errors and file errors at runtime.

Many of the features discussed in this chapter exist because of inherent capabilities built into MFC's base class, **CObject**. You may wish to review the **CObject** class in the MFC documentation and in Section 12.3 before proceeding.

13.1 Setting Up

Many of the features described in this chapter are active only when working with the *debugging version*, as opposed to the *release version*, of MFC. You control the version by specifying the *target* as described in Appendix B.2. The advantage of using the release version is that the final executable for your application is smaller and it compiles and links somewhat more quickly. The advantage of the debugging version is that you can access all the normal debugging facilities, and the MFC library does more thorough tests internally to help catch errors.

When you turn on the debugging mode, three things happen:

1. The "-D_DEBUG" option is added to the compile command, causing debugging statements **ifdef**ed in the header files and code to be included into the application.
2. Debugging information is added into the executable so the debugger can watch variables, single step through code, and so on.
3. The linker links against the debugging version of the MFC DLL rather than the release version.

Note that the conditional compilation variable used in MFC programs to indicate debugging is named "_DEBUG". You will see that value frequently used in many of the example programs in this chapter to switch code in and out of the application.

When you build the debug release of an application, you can use the debugging features in Visual C++. For example, you will probably want to use the **Go** option rather than the **Execute** option in the **Project** menu to run your programs. Using the **Go** option causes the program to run more slowly, but gives you far more control at runtime. In particular, it gives you the ability to halt the program at any time, single step through code, look at variables, and examine the call stack. See Appendix B.2 for details on the different features available in the debug menu.

The following sections show you how to make the most of the debugging facilities built-in to MFC and Visual C++. Keep in mind that while these features help you in the debug target, they are completely stripped out in the release target, and therefore have no impact on the performance of your final product.

13.2 Assertions

One of the easiest to use, and most obvious, debugging features in MFC is called an *assertion*. You use assertions during the debugging phase to verify that your program does not violate any inherent assumptions in the source code that you or other programmers have written. The debugging versions of the MFC libraries use assertions in the same way, making sure that you do not violate any of MFC's assumptions about parameters, working environment, class derivation, and so on.

An *assertion* in a line of source code looks like this:

```
ASSERT (<boolean expression>);
```

The <boolean expression> portion should yield a Boolean value. In debug versions, the program halts and displays an Assertion Failed dialog for any ASSERT statement whose Boolean expression evaluates to FALSE. In release versions of the code, all ASSERT statements are removed by the pre-processor. Note that, because the pre-processor strips out the ASSERT statements in release versions of the code, the boolean expression needs to have no side effects. For example, you should not increment a variable inside an ASSERT statement, because the increment will be lost in the release version of the code.

It is easy to see an example of MFC's assertion mechanism in action: Simply violate an assumption made by MFC. For example, the code in Listing 13.1 violates one of the assumptions that the **CUIntArray::SetSize** function makes.

Listing 13.1
Violating an assumption of the **CUIntArray::SetSize** function

```
// list.cpp

#include <afxwin.h>
#include <afxcoll.h>

// Define the application class
```

```
class CApp : public CWinApp
{
public:
    virtual BOOL InitInstance();
};


CApp App;

// Define the window class
class CWindow : public CFrameWnd
{
    CUIntArray *array;
public:
    CWindow();
};

// The window's constructor
CWindow::CWindow()
{
    // Create a window with the new class
    Create(NULL, "Drawing Tests",
                WS_OVERLAPPEDWINDOW,
                CRect(0,0,250,100));

    array = new CUIntArray;
    array->SetSize(-100);      // This line is a problem
}

// Init the application
BOOL CApp::InitInstance()
{
    m_pMainWnd = new CWindow();
    m_pMainWnd->ShowWindow(m_nCmdShow);
    m_pMainWnd->UpdateWindow();
    return TRUE;
}
```

In Listing 13.1, the constructor for the window allocates an instance of the class **CUIntArray** and then sets the array's initial size to a negative number. If you create a new project, compile Listing 13.1 as a release version program (select release target in the **Target** combo box at the top of the project window), and then run it. It will either die with an unexpected heap error or simply fail to execute. Either error behavior is useless because you have no idea what caused the error.

On the other hand, if you rebuild the project with the debugging information turned on (select the debug target in the **Target** combo box at the top of the project window) and then rerun the application, you will instead see an assertion dialog. This dialog is the standard Assertion Failed dialog and does four things for you:

1. It tells you that you have violated an assumption somewhere.
2. It tells you the exact source file and line where the assumption was tested.
3. It pauses program execution so you can track down the problem.

4. It gives you three options for your next move.

Whenever you violate an assumption, you will have two immediate questions: 1) What was the assumption, and 2) where in my code did I violate it? You can answer both questions using the debugger. Take the following steps to try it out:

1. Create a new project for Listing 13.1. Build a debug version of the project.
2. Run the program under the debugger using the Go option. The program will stop with an assertion error dialog.
3. Click the **Retry** option in the dialog.
4. Select the **Call Stack** option in the **View** menu to look at the current function call stack for the application at the point where you halted execution.

By looking at the Call Stack dialog, you can see a record of which functions were active at the moment execution halted. If you double-click on the top line in the call stack window, you will immediately see the line in the code that violated an assertion. If you double-click on the line for **CUIntArray::SetSize** in the call stack window, you will see the line in the MFC source where the assertion was checked. Being able to look at the ASSERT statement in the MFC source code is useful because there often will be comments around the ASSERT statement that tell you what is being checked and why. At the very least you can look at the Boolean expression. Knowing this information, you can usually fix the problem.

You should use assertions in your own code to test any assumptions that you make. For example, you should test assumptions about incoming parameters, loop extents, and variable values. All these tests will be automatically and totally removed from your code when you create a release version of the program, so they will have no effect on the execution speed of your final application.

Note that these tests are different from standard error checking. For example, you do not want to make an assertion about a file handle right after you open a file. There is a strong likelihood that a file will fail to open in *any* version of the program, debug or release. That is a fact of life with files. Therefore, you want all versions of your application to appropriately test file handles and then respond. You should use an assertion inside a function that assumes it receives an open and valid file handle as an input parameter. The code calling the function should not call the function unless the file is open and valid, so if it does it is violating an assumption inside the function. You want to know about that violated assumption during testing, but it should never occur once the program is fully debugged.

One place where you can use assertions extensively is inside classes that you derive from **CObject** (see Section 12.3). You can use assertions in every member function to guarantee that parameters, and the instance itself, are valid. You can also override **CObject**'s **AssertValid** function to perform further tests. The **AssertValid** function is called by other classes that want to test the *internal state* of a **CObject**-derived class instance. The ASSERT_VALID macro calls the **AssertValid** function. Listing 13.2 shows the **CObPoint** class first seen in Chapter 12, modified appropriately to check all assumptions. For the sake of this example, imagine that negative values for the point's coordinates are considered erroneous.

Listing 13.2
A fully ASSERTed class derived from **CObject**. In this class negative values for **x** and **y** are assumed invalid for the sake of the example.

```
class CObPoint : public CObject
{
DECLARE_SERIAL( CObPoint )
protected:
    LONG x, y;
public:
    CObPoint() {x=0; y=0;}
    CObPoint(const CObPoint &p)
    {
        ASSERT_VALID(&p);
        x=p.x;
        y=p.y;
    }
    CObPoint operator=(const CObPoint& p)
    {
        ASSERT_VALID(&p);
        x=p.x;
        y=p.y;
        return *this;
    }
    CObPoint(int ix, int iy)
    {
        ASSERT (ix >= 0);
        ASSERT (iy >= 0);
        x=ix;
        y=iy;
    }
    CObPoint(CPoint &p)
    {
        ASSERT (p.x >= 0);
        ASSERT (p.y >= 0);
        x=p.x;
        y=p.y;
    }
    virtual void Serialize(CArchive &archive)
    {
        ASSERT_VALID(this);
        CObject::Serialize(archive);
        if (archive.IsStoring())
            archive << x << y;
        else
            archive >> x >> y;
    }
    // The (int) casts in the line below are
    // needed only in Windows 3.1. Remove in
    // WIN32 environments
    CPoint GetPoint() const
    {
```

```
        ASSERT_VALID(this);
        return CPoint((int)x, (int)y);
    }
#ifdef _DEBUG
    virtual void AssertValid() const
    {
        // check base class first
        CObject::AssertValid();

        // check data members...
        ASSERT(x >= 0);
        ASSERT(y >= 0);
    }
#endif //_DEBUG
};

IMPLEMENT_SERIAL(CObPoint, CObject, 0)
```

In Listing 13.2 there are three different things happening:

1. The code uses ASSERT statements to test integer coordinate values to make sure they are positive. As mentioned previously, this stipulation is made simply for the sake of example here.
2. The class declares an **AssertValid** function to override the **CObject::AssertValid** virtual function.
3. The class uses the ASSERT_VALID macro on itself in non-constructor classes.

The **AssertValid** function of the **CObject** class is designed to allow classes to check themselves for basic validity. When you derive a class from **CObject** you should override the **AssertValid** function, call the base class's **AssertValid** function, and then check the validity of all data members with ASSERT or ASSERT_VALID statements. If the class is a list or array class, you should look through all the elements in the container and test each for validity as well. Note that the **AssertValid** function has been placed inside an **ifdef** block so its code is excluded when the compiler forms the release version of the code.

You use the ASSERT_VALID macro to test the validity of any class derived from **CObject**. This macro simply calls the **AssertValid** function on an instance of the class. The advantage of using the macro is that the compiler does not generate any code for the ASSERT_VALID statement in the release version of an application.

The class in Listing 13.2 tests itself using ASSERT_VALID in all non-constructor member functions. It does this because there is no guarantee that the class is valid at any given point in time. By testing the instance with ASSERT_VALID, you are simply verifying that the instance is healthy and catching problems early if it is not. In your own code, you should always add ASSERT_VALID statements to check any variable you use that is an instance of a **CObject**-derived class.

One other macro related to the ASSERT macro is the VERIFY macro. Whereas the compiler removes the ASSERT macro and its statement from the release version of an application, the compiler leaves the statement behind when you use the VERIFY macro. For example, if you make a function call in an ASSERT statement, the call will not exist in the release version of the application. You will find that the debug and release versions of the application behave differently. By placing the function call in a VERIFY statement, you guarantee that the release and debug versions work identically. In general it is best to write your code so it contains no VERIFY macros. Anything requiring a function call or generating a side effect should stand as an independent line of code, and then you should ASSERT the result.

13.3 Tracing

MFC contains a trace facility that, in a debug version of an application, allows you to print messages during runtime to an output window. For example, in front of a piece of code that saves a file to disk, you might place the following trace statement:

```
TRACE("Saving file to disk\n");
```

To see the output of the TRACE statement, you must do two things:

1. You must run an executable in Visual C++'s `bin` directory named `tracer.exe` and use it to turn on tracing.
2. You must run the program using the **Go** option rather than using the **Execute** option.

As an example of how to use the TRACE macro, use Listing 13.3 and take the following steps.

1. Type in the code for Listing 13.3 or copy it from the diskette supplied with the book. Create a new project or add the file to an existing project.
2. Make sure you are building a debug release.
3. Run `tracer.exe` and turn on the first check box to enable basic tracing. The `tracer.exe` file is provided in the BIN directory of Visual C++.
4. Build the project.
5. Run the application using the **Go** option in the **Debug** menu of the **Build** menu.

Listing 13.3 contains a call to the TRACE macro in the window's constructor. Because you are running through the debugger, the trace output will appear directly in the output window of Visual C++. If you do not see any output, select the **Output** option in the **View** menu. If you still see no output, repeat the above steps paying particular attention to steps 2 and 3.

Listing 13.3
Testing the TRACE macro.

```
// trace.cpp

#include <afxwin.h>
#include <afxcoll.h>

// Define the application class
```

```
class CApp : public CWinApp
{
public:
    virtual BOOL InitInstance();
};

CApp App;

// Define the window class
class CWindow : public CFrameWnd
{
    CUIntArray *array;
public:
    CWindow();
};

// The window's constructor
CWindow::CWindow()
{
    // Create a window with the new class
    Create(NULL, "Drawing Tests",
                WS_OVERLAPPEDWINDOW,
                CRect(0,0,250,100));

    array = new CUIntArray;
    TRACE("Array created\n");
}

// Init the application
BOOL CApp::InitInstance()
{
    m_pMainWnd = new CWindow();
    m_pMainWnd->ShowWindow(m_nCmdShow);
    m_pMainWnd->UpdateWindow();
    return TRUE;
}
```

When you run Listing 13.3 and then terminate the application, you will see something like this in the output window of Visual C++:

```
Array created
Detected memory leaks!
Dumping objects ->
{6}
a CUIntArray at $2E0A50
with 0 elements
Object dump complete.
```

The first line is the output of the TRACE statement that you find in the window's constructor. The rest of the output is coming from inside the MFC library. It turns out that MFC is laced with error checks and TRACE statements, and these come out in the debug output once you enable tracing. Here the MFC library has detected unfreed memory, has warned you of that fact, and has dumped (see Section

13.4) the offending object. You can solve this particular problem by making the following change to the **CWindow** class in Listing 13.3 to add a destructor to it:

```
// Define the window class
class CWindow : public CFrameWnd
{
    CUIntArray *array;
public:
    CWindow();
    ~CWindow() { delete array; }
};
```

With the destructor in place, you should see only one line of TRACE output when you run Listing 13.3 again. Note that, because the MFC library automatically generates TRACE output when it detects internal errors, it is a good idea to turn TRACE output on with `tracer.exe` and then run under the debugger at all times while developing an application.

TRACE statements work just like **printf** statements. They accept variable argument lists and the same "%" placeholders that the **printf** function uses. Search on **printf** in the documentation for more information. For example, if **str** is a string and **cnt** is an integer, the following TRACE statement is valid:

```
TRACE("str = %s, cnt = %d\n", str, cnt);
```

Everything you know about the **printf** statement works in the TRACE statement.

When you run `tracer.exe` you will note that it has several different tracing options. Each is described briefly below:

- Multi-App debugging — Prefixes TRACE output with the application name so you can tell which application it comes from.
- Main Message Pump — When **CWinApp** receives a message, it displays it as TRACE output
- Main Message Dispatch — When **CWnd::WindowProc** receives a message, it displays it as a TRACE statement. This causes internal application messages, as well as Windows messages, to be displayed.
- WM_COMMAND Dispatch — Reports information about commands routed through message maps.
- OLE Tracing — Reports OLE messages.
- Database Tracing — Reports database messages.

There are two ways to learn about these different options: Try them out or explore the source code of MFC for specifics. Search on the variable name **afxTraceFlags** as you explore the source.

13.4 Dumping

Every class that MFC derives from **CObject** contains a **Dump** function that allows you to dump the current state of the object to the output window. This information can be useful in certain debugging situations. The code below shows how you could modify the constructor in Listing 13.3 to dump the contents of the **CWindow** object and a **CUIntArray**.

```
    // The window's constructor
    CWindow::CWindow()
    {
        // Create a window with the new class
        Create(NULL, "Drawing Tests",
                    WS_OVERLAPPEDWINDOW,
                    CRect(0,0,250,100));

        array = new CUIntArray;
        array->Add(5);
        array->Add(10);
        array->Add(15);
        TRACE("Array created\n");

#ifdef _DEBUG
        array->Dump(afxDump);
        this->Dump(afxDump);
#endif
    }
```

This code creates an array, adds three elements to it, prints a TRACE statement, and then dumps the state of the array and the window. It uses the variable **afxDump** as the dump site. This is the standard site for all TRACE and **Dump** calls. The output that you will see in the output window when you run this code under the debugger appears below.

```
    Array created

    a CUIntArray at $2E0A50 with 3 elements

    a CFrameWnd at $2E07EC
    m_hWnd = 0xA301C6 (permanent window)
    caption = "Drawing Tests"
    class name = "AfxFrameOrView"
    rect = (L 0, T 0, R 250, B 100)
    parent CWnd* = $0
    style = $4CF0000
    m_hAccelTable = 0x0
    m_nWindow = -1
    m_nIDHelp = 0x0
    m_nIDTracking = 0x0
    m_nIDLastMessage = 0x0
    no active view
```

The array's **Dump** function identifies its class and its size. The window's **Dump** function identifies its class and a variety of useful information about the window. If you do not see any output, see the previous section for instructions on enabling TRACE statements.

When you are creating your own **CObject**-derived classes, you should create a **Dump** function specific to the new class as you create the object. The **Dump** function should dump the contents of the base class as well as the contents of all member variables. For example, you might add the following **Dump** function to the bottom of Listing 13.2.

```
#ifdef _DEBUG
    virtual void Dump( CDumpContext& dumpSite ) const
```

```
    {
        CObject::Dump(dumpSite);

        dumpSite << "x = " << x << "y = " << y;
    }
#endif //_DEBUG
```

When you call this new **Dump** function during debugging, it will print its class and then dump the contents of its **x** and **y** members.

In the previous dump example, the array object dumped itself by declaring the number of elements it contained. However, all the MFC collection classes support the concept of *dump depth*. By changing the depth you tell the collections that you want them to recursively dump their contents as well. By default the depth is set to zero. You change it to a non-zero value using the **SetDepth** function, as shown here:

```
afxDump.SetDepth(1);
```

You can set depth back and forth between zero and one as often as you wish, and the **afxDump** variable will remember the setting you choose until you change it again (because the **afxDump** variable is global to MFC). If you add this call to **SetDepth** to the previous dumping example, you will see output that looks like this for the array:

```
a CUIntArray with 3 elements
[0] = 0x5
[1] = 0xA
[2] = 0xF
```

You can see that this array of UINT dumps its values in hex. A **CObArray** will ask each of the objects it contains to dump themselves.

13.5 Memory State

Another extremely useful feature provided by MFC is the **CMemoryState** class. You can use this class to detect memory leaks in any section of your program. This class not only detects leaks, but can also tell you exactly where they are occurring. The capabilities built into the **CMemoryState** class let you solve memory allocation problems that were once virtually impossible to track.

An instance of the **CMemoryState** class has the ability to hold a snapshot of the current state of the heap at any given point during a program's execution. You use the **CheckPoint** function to take the snapshot. Once you have two different snapshots you can compare them. That is how you discover potential leaks. The **CMemoryState** class has four member functions:

- **CheckPoint** — Stores an image of the current state of the heap in an instance of the class.
- **Difference** — Finds differences between the heap images held in two instances of the class and returns TRUE if there are any.
- **DumpAllObjectsSince** — Performs a standard dump (see the previous section) on all objects allocated on the heap since a snapshot was taken with **CheckPoint**. If **CheckPoint** has not been called and the instance is therefore uninitialized, this function dumps everything currently on the heap.

• **DumpStatistics** — Performs a concise dump of memory statistics, telling you how much memory is allocated in the current snapshot.

The program in Listing 13.4 demonstrates a very simple use of the **CMemoryState** class to detect a memory error.

Listing 13.4
Detecting a memory leak

```
// memstate.cpp

#include <afxwin.h>
#include <afxcoll.h>

// Define the application class
class CApp : public CWinApp
{
public:
    virtual BOOL InitInstance();
};

CApp App;

// Define the window class
class CWindow : public CFrameWnd
{
    CUIntArray *array;
public:
    CWindow();
};

// The window's constructor
CWindow::CWindow()
{
    // Create a window with the new class
    Create(NULL, "Drawing Tests",
            WS_OVERLAPPEDWINDOW,
            CRect(0,0,250,100));

#ifdef _DEBUG
    // Take first snapshot
    CMemoryState startState;
    startState.Checkpoint();
#endif

    array = new CUIntArray;
    array->Add(5);
    array->Add(10);
    array->Add(15);
    TRACE("Array created\n");
    delete array;

#ifdef _DEBUG
    // Take second snapshot
    CMemoryState finishState;
```

```
        finishState.Checkpoint();
        // Look at the difference
        CMemoryState diff;
        if (diff.Difference(startState, finishState))
        {
            TRACE("Memory leak detected.\n");
            diff.DumpStatistics();
            startState.DumpAllObjectsSince();
        }
        else
            TRACE("No memory leaks detected.\n");
    #endif
    }

    // Init the application
    BOOL CApp::InitInstance()
    {
        m_pMainWnd = new CWindow();
        m_pMainWnd->ShowWindow(m_nCmdShow);
        m_pMainWnd->UpdateWindow();
        return TRUE;
    }
```

When you run Listing 13.4 under the debugger, it will produce a single message indicating that the system detected no leaks. However, if you remove the **delete** statement, the difference check will detect a leak and the system will dump all undeleted allocations made since the first snapshot. A typical dump in this situation appears below:

```
Memory leak detected.
0 bytes in 0 Free Blocks.
20 bytes in 1 Object Blocks.
20 bytes in 1 Non-Object Blocks.
Largest number used: 44 bytes.
Total allocations: 44 bytes.
Dumping objects ->
{6} array_u.cpp(111) : non-object block at $002E0AB8, 20 bytes long
{4} a CUIntArray object at $002E0A50, 20 bytes long
Object dump complete.
```

The first part of this dump contains the overall statistics for the leak. It summarizes the allocations that occurred between the two snapshots. *Object Blocks* are blocks directly allocated for **CObject**-derived objects. *Non-Object Blocks* are blocks allocated from the heap by **new** statements but not associated with **CObject**-derived classes. For example, as discussed in Chapter 12, a **CUintArray** allocates a block of memory big enough to hold the elements it contains. Blocks are allocated directly from the heap as non-object blocks.

The object dump gives more information about the individual blocks on the heap. The number in braces is simply a counter. When an MFC program starts, every allocation increments the counter. The creation of the array object was the fourth allocation. The block holding the array's elements was the sixth. If you sequentially add elements to the array, you will probably find that the array is reallocating its memory block in four-integer increments (although this is version dependent).

You can get even more information in the dump by replacing all calls to **new** with the macro DEBUG_NEW. If you make this change in Listing 13.4, you will see the following dump information:

```
Dumping objects ->
{6} array_u.cpp(111) : non-object block at $002E0AB8, 20 bytes long
{4} H:\brain\VCPPBOOK\code\ch13\memstate.cpp(37) :
a CUIntArray object at $002E0A50, 20 bytes long
```

Allocation number four now contains information indicating the file and line number of the statement that allocated it. DEBUG_NEW does not introduce any inefficiency to your code: Any use of DEBUG_NEW is replaced by a normal call to **new** in the release version of an application. You can easily use normal **new** statements in your code if you choose and then #define a replacement for **new** as shown here:

```
#define new DEBUG_NEW
```

Your code will then look normal while still taking advantage of the DEBUG_NEW capability. Be sure to place this particular #define statement below any IMPLEMENT_ macros.

An additional heap check that you can perform whenever you like is contained in the **afxCheckMemory** function. This function scans the entire heap for corrupt blocks. Generally a block gets corrupted when a piece of code overwrites the boundary of the block. For example, if the block is being treated as an array of characters and the code writes too many characters into the block, this will often corrupt the heap. The **afxCheckMemory** function returns a Boolean TRUE if it discovers any invalid blocks.

Whenever you run in debug mode, MFC and the debugger work together to check memory rather carefully. You can tune these checks by adjusting a global variable in MFC named **afxMemDF.** This variable accepts zero or more of the following enumerations or-ed together:

- **allocMemDF**   (the default) Enables debugging in the memory allocator
- **delayFreeMemDF**   Cause blocks of memory freed in your program to remain allocated so the program undergoes increased memory stress
- **checkAlwaysMemDF**   Causes the memory system to automatically call **afxCheckMemory** before any allocation or deallocation operation

The default value for **afxMemDF** is **allocMemDF**. You can turn this default value off by setting **afxMemDF** to zero. Alternatively, you can turn any or all three of the values on by oring them together and assigning them to **afxMemDF**. Note that the **checkAlwaysMemDF** option can significantly slow execution under the debugger.

13.6 Exceptions

The MFC class hierarchy and C++ itself support the concept of an *exception* as its primary mechanism for handling system errors and exceptional situations. For example, if the system runs out of memory during an allocation, your program will receive a memory exception. If the loading or storing of an archive file during serialization fails, your program will receive an archive exception. These exceptions are *thrown* by certain functions in MFC, and by various C++ operations. If your program contains the proper code to *catch* the exception, you can handle the situation and continue execution. If you do not handle the exception yourself, the **CWinApp** class handles it for you.

Exceptions serve the same sort of purpose that error codes returned by functions do. An exception warns you that something went wrong during a function call and gives you the opportunity to do something about it. The use of exceptions tends to reduce the amount of code you have to write. Instead of having to create code to check every return value from every function in a block of code, you can surround the block code in a *try block*. Any exception that occurs inside the block gets handled, or *caught*, by a *catch block* that immediately follows the try block and acts as the exception handler.

MFC supports exceptions of the following types:

CArchiveException	Thrown for errors in archive file loading or saving
CDBException	Thrown for database errors
CFileException	Thrown for file errors
CMemoryException	Thrown for any allocation error that occurs during a call to **new**
CNotSupportedException	Thrown if the specified operation is not supported
COleException	Thrown if an error occurs during an OLE operation
COleDispatchException	Thrown for OLE automation errors
CResourceException	Thrown if a resource cannot be found or created
CUserException	Thrown following notification of a user error

Memory, Not Supported, and Resource exceptions are *unqualified*. Archive, File, and OLE errors are *qualified*. When an exception is qualified it means you can examine an additional variable to determine the exact reason for the exception. For example, a file exception might be generated by a missing file, a lack of disk space, a drive error, etc., and the **m_cause** member variable contains this specific information. This will make a bit more sense after you see several examples.

The code in Listing 13.5 creates an exception and lets you see MFC's default behavior when an exception occurs. The exception is created by attempting to allocate one billion bytes of memory from the heap when the user clicks a push button.

Listing 13.5
A program that creates an exception

```
// except1.cpp

#include <afxwin.h>

const int IDC_BUTTON = 100;

// Define the application class
class CApp : public CWinApp
{
public:
    virtual BOOL InitInstance();
};

CApp App;

// Define the window class
class CWindow : public CFrameWnd
{
    CButton *button;
public:
    CWindow();
    afx_msg void HandleButton();
    DECLARE_MESSAGE_MAP()
};

// The message handler function
void CWindow::HandleButton()
{
    char *p;

    SetDlgItemText(IDC_BUTTON,
        "Allocating one billion bytes");
    p = new(char[1000000000]);
    SetDlgItemText(IDC_BUTTON,
        "Push me");
}

// The window's constructor
CWindow::CWindow()
{
    // Create a window with the new class
    Create(NULL, "Exception Tests",
                WS_OVERLAPPEDWINDOW,
                CRect(0,0,250,100));

    // Get the size of the client rectangle
    CRect r;
    GetClientRect(&r);
    r.InflateRect(-20,-20);

    // Create a button
    button = new CButton();
    button->Create("Push me",
        WS_CHILD|WS_VISIBLE|BS_PUSHBUTTON,
        r, this, IDC_BUTTON);
}
```

```
// The message map
BEGIN_MESSAGE_MAP( CWindow, CFrameWnd )
    ON_COMMAND(IDC_BUTTON, HandleButton)
END_MESSAGE_MAP()

// Init the application
BOOL CApp::InitInstance()
{
    m_pMainWnd = new CWindow();
    m_pMainWnd->ShowWindow(m_nCmdShow);
    m_pMainWnd->UpdateWindow();
    return TRUE;
}
```

Listing 13.5 presents the user with a button. When the user clicks the button, the **HandleButton** function attempts to allocate a block of one billion bytes. On most machines this request will fail. You will see a system-generated message dialog indicating that the program has failed.

If you want to trap the memory error yourself, you need to add exception handling code at the point where the allocations occur. By changing the code in the **HandleButton** function to that shown below, you can trap the exception yourself:

```
// The message handler function
void CWindow::HandleButton()
{
    char *p;

    SetDlgItemText(IDC_BUTTON,
        "Allocating one billion bytes");
    try
    {
        p = new(char[1000000000]);
    }
    catch(CMemoryException* exception)
    {
        MessageBox("Out of memory", "Memory error", MB_OK);
    }
    SetDlgItemText(IDC_BUTTON,
        "Push me");
}
```

By wrapping the call to **new** in a *try block*, you make the application sensitive to the memory exception. The keyword **try** in C++ marks a try block. If an exception occurs anywhere in the block, the system will attempt to find an exception handler, identified by the **catch** keyword, that can catch the exception. The **catch** keyword accepts a parameter that identifies the type of exception that the handler catches (and optionally declares an instance of that type).

In this piece of code, the handler handles memory exceptions. The catch block will automatically create and fill the **exception** instance with information about the exception. At the end of the catch block this instance is automatically destroyed.

When an error occurs, the code in the associated **catch** section executes. In the code shown here a message box appears, and then the program continues execution normally.

Many functions in MFC throw specific exceptions instead of returning error values. The **Rename** function in the **CFile** class is an example of this type of function. If you read about **Rename** in the MFC documentation, you will see in the description that it throws a file exception when a renaming error occurs. The code in Listing 13.6 demonstrates how to use this feature to detect a renaming error (replace the **Handle-Button** function in Listing 13.5 with this code):

Listing 13.6
Catching file exceptions

```
// except2.cpp

// The message handler function
void CWindow::HandleButton()
{
    try
    {
        // call static CFile function to rename
        CFile::Rename( "invalid.xyz",
            "newname.xyz" );
    }
    catch( CFileException *exception )
    {
        if (exception->m_cause==
            CFileException::fileNotFound)
            MessageBox(
                "The file does not exist",
                "Rename Error", MB_OK );
        else
            MessageBox(
                "Disk problem",
                "Rename Error", MB_OK );
    }
}
```

Note the use here of the variable **exception** and the **m_cause** member variable of **CFileException**. If you look up this variable in the MFC documentation, you will find that it is a data member of the **CFileException** class. This data member can hold any of a dozen or so different values that give you specific information about the file error. Here this member allows us to detect whether the renaming failed because the original file did not exist, or because of some other problem. See Section 12.4 for other file exception examples.

13.6.1 Catching Multiple Exceptions

A large block of code could potentially have more than one type of exception that it might generate. For example, the block might generate file exceptions and memory exceptions. There are three different ways to handle this situation. The first technique appears in Listing 13.7, using multiple catch macros:

Listing 13.7
Catching multiple exceptions, version 1

```
// except3.cpp

// The message handler function
void CWindow::HandleButton()
{
    try
    {
        // memory error
        char *p=new(char[1000000000]);
        // file error
        CFile::Rename( "invalid.xyz",
            "newname.xyz" );
    }
    catch( CFileException *exception )
    {
        if (exception->m_cause==
            CFileException::fileNotFound)
            MessageBox(
                "The file does not exist",
                "Rename Error", MB_OK );
        else
            MessageBox(
                "Disk problem",
                "Rename Error", MB_OK );
    }
    catch(CMemoryException *)
    {
        MessageBox("Out of memory", "Memory error", MB_OK);
    }
}
```

When you run this code, the memory allocation will generate an error. If you comment out the allocation statement, the file exception will generate an error. The **catch** blocks work together to handle both cases.

The second technique involves the use of a generic exception in the **catch** block, which you then qualify with **if** statements inside the **catch** block. This technique is shown in Listing 13.8.

Listing 13.8
Catching multiple exceptions, version 2

```
// except4.cpp

// The message handler function
void CWindow::HandleButton()
{
    try
    {
        // memory error
        char *p=new(char[1000000000]);
        // file error
        CFile::Rename( "invalid.xyz",
            "newname.xyz" );
    }
    catch( CException *exception )
    {
        if (exception->
            IsKindOf(RUNTIME_CLASS(CFileException)))
        {
            if (((CFileException *)exception)->m_cause ==
                CFileException::fileNotFound)
                MessageBox(
                    "The file does not exist",
                    "Rename Error", MB_OK );
            else
                MessageBox(
                    "Disk problem",
                    "Rename Error", MB_OK );
        }
        else if (exception->
            IsKindOf(RUNTIME_CLASS(CMemoryException)))
        {
            MessageBox("Out of memory", "Memory error", MB_OK);
        }
    }
}
```

The **catch** block accepts any type of exception. The **IsKindOf** function lets you detect the specific type of exception that occurred.

The third technique uses nesting of try blocks, as shown in Listing 13.9.

Listing 13.9
Catching multiple exceptions, version 3

```
// except5.cpp

// The message handler function
void CWindow::HandleButton()
{
    try
    {
        // memory error
        char *p=new(char[100000000]);
        try
```

```
    {
        // file error
        CFile::Rename( "invalid.xyz",
            "newname.xyz" );
    }
    catch( CFileException *exception )
    {
        if (exception->m_cause==
            CFileException::fileNotFound)
            MessageBox(
                "The file does not exist",
                "Rename Error", MB_OK );
        else
            MessageBox(
                "Disk problem",
                "Rename Error", MB_OK );
    }
}
catch(CMemoryException *)
{
    MessageBox("Out of memory", "Memory error", MB_OK);
}
}
```

In the code shown here, memory exceptions are caught by the outer **try** block. File exceptions are captured for the specific line that causes the error. If a memory exception were to occur in the inner **try** block, then it would be handled by the outer **catch** block. Because the inner block does not handle memory errors, the exception bounces out to the outer block and gets handled there. You can nest **try** blocks as deep as you like. If none of your **catch** blocks handles a given exception, then it gets routed out to the global exception handler in the **CWinApp** class.

The ellipses ("...") used in a catch statement implies "catch all remaining exceptions regardless of type." The code in Listing 13.10 demonstrates the process.

Listing 13.10
Catching other errors

```
try
{
    int i=0;
    int j=5/i;
}
catch(CMemoryException *)
{
    MessageBox("Out of memory", "Memory error", MB_OK);
}
catch(...)
{
    MessageBox("Unknown error", "error", MB_OK);
}
```

This code will correctly catch the divide-by-zero error. The **GetExceptionCode** function in Win32 can be useful for decoding the type of error.

13.6.2 Throwing Exceptions

It is possible to create your own exceptions using the **throw** keyword or special **Afx** functions built into MFC. You might do this if, for example, you created your own memory allocator using **malloc** or some other mechanism. Or you might use the **throw** keyword if you inherited from the **CFile** class and wanted to add new error codes as shown in Listing 13.11.

Listing 13.11
Throwing exceptions

```
// except6.cpp

void TestCondition()
{
    AfxThrowFileException(
        CFileException::generic );
    MessageBox(NULL, "This line will not execute",
        "Skipped over", MB_OK );
}

// The message handler function
void CWindow::HandleButton()
{
    // Call a function that generates an exceptions
    try
    {
        TestCondition();
    }
    catch( CFileException *exception )
    {
        MessageBox( "Caught a File Exception",
            "Exception", MB_OK );
    }
}
```

If you want to create your own exception classes, you should inherit from the **CException** class and, in your code that needs to generate exceptions, use the **throw** keyword to generate the exceptions.

The following exception-throwing functions are provided by MFC:

AfxThrowArchiveException
AfxThrowDBException
AfxThrowFileException
AfxThrowMemoryException
AfxThrowNotSupportedException
AfxThrowOleException

AfxThrowOleDispatchException
AfxThrowResourceException
AfxThrowUserException

For additional information about exceptions, see the MFC documentation and books on line. This is an incredibly rich topic and the documentation has a number of interesting examples.

13.7 Other Debugging Features

MFC contains a number of other debugging facilities that are invoked with **Afx** functions. The list below briefly describes each of these functions:

AfxAbort	Aborts the program after a fatal error
AfxCheckMemroy	Checks the heap and free pool for corruption
AfxDoForAllClasses	Iterates through all **CObject**-derived classes
AfxDoForAllObject	Iterates through all **CObject**-derived objects on heap
AfxEnableMemoryTracking	Enables and disables memory tracking
AfxIsMemoryBlock	Confirms that a pointer points to a valid block on the heap
AfxIsValidAddress	Confirms that an address resides in the program's memory space
AfxIsValidString	Confirms that an address points to a valid string
AfxSetAllocHook	Lets you perform tests before memory allocations
AfxTraceEnabled	Enables and disables trace output
AfxTraceFlags	Lets you customize trace features

See the MFC documentation for complete descriptions of these functions.

13.8 Conclusion

By combining all the different techniques seen in this chapter, you can create applications that are much more robust and much easier to test than normal programs. You will find that as you gain experience you will enjoy using these features more and more.

Part 1 introduced you to the fundamentals of MFC programming. It showed you the basic form of any MFC application and demonstrated how to customize controls and respond to their events. In Part 2 you learned about the wide variety of classes available in MFC. You use these different classes as application "building blocks," combining them in unique ways to meet the goals of your project.

In Part 3 we begin to bring these building blocks together to create actual applications. Visual C++ provides three different tools that make this process much easier: the AppWizard, the ClassWizard, and the resource editors.

You will use the AppWizard as you begin each new application. It creates an *application framework*. This framework acts as the starting point for your program. The framework that the AppWizard creates is extremely thorough and robust. The App-Wizard framework also gives your application an organized document-centric orientation. The AppWizard integrates document and view classes into the framework, making it extremely easy to think about applications that contain multiple documents and multiple views. You will use the AppWizard once at the beginning of every application development cycle.

The ClassWizard gives you an automated way to modify message maps and is specifically tuned to work within the framework that the AppWizard provides. You will use the ClassWizard to add event processing into your application, create new classes, manipulate virtual functions, and integrate new dialogs into your applications.

The resource editors, in conjunction with the ClassWizard, give you an easy way to add menus, dialogs, and other resources to your applications. You will design and lay out any dialog box, menu, accelerator table, string resource, or bitmap with the resource editors. You will then modify your code, either by hand or with the aid of the ClassWizard, to take advantage of these new resources.

Part 3 demonstrates these tools using five different sample applications. Each application demonstrates a different style. Part 4 then builds on this introduction by showing you how to add the advanced features that let you create truly professional applications.

Understanding the AppWizard and ClassWizard

All the concepts covered in Parts 1 and 2 have been building to the point where you can create your own full-scale Windows applications. You are now ready to begin the process. Visual C++ contains several tools that make this process easier, and in this chapter you will learn about the first one, the AppWizard.

The AppWizard is a "framework generator." It builds a framework that acts as the starting point for an application. The first time you look at one of these frameworks, however, it will seem outrageously complicated. The goal of this chapter and the other chapters in this section is to help you feel comfortable with this framework. Once you understand the intent of the framework, and once you know where to correctly insert your own code, you will be able to rapidly create your own applications from the framework that the AppWizard provides.

One thing you should be aware of before embarking on your study of the AppWizard is that its proper use demands a fairly complete knowledge of the MFC class hierarchy. That is why Part 2 spent so much time going over the different classes in MFC. You may want to work through all examples in Part 2 before starting on Part 3. Alternatively, Part 3 includes a tremendous number of pointers back into Part 2 so you can quickly learn about or review the concepts when you need them.

14.1 The Goal of the AppWizard

Say that you want to begin building a new Windows application. How would you begin? If you already had created several other Windows applications, chances are you would pick out one of these previous applications and build from it as a starting point. For example, you might start with Listing 2.1, strip out the **CStatic** control for the "Hello World" message, and begin adding in your own controls as required by your new design. If you want to build a new drawing program, you might start with one of the drawing programs in Chapter 11 and build from there.

In other words, whenever you start a new program, you generally begin by taking an old program that works and has most of the important features that your new program needs. You strip out the parts of the old program that you do not need in the new application and then start building from there.

The AppWizard is designed to make this process easier. You can think of it as an automatic framework generator. Instead of stripping down an old program to create a starting point for a new program, you use the AppWizard to create a fresh, new template. The AppWizard has a number of options that let you customize the template to perfectly match the needs of your new application. From this new, standardized, and consistent template, you begin building your new application.

Note that the AppWizard is nothing more than a framework generator. For any new application you will use the AppWizard exactly once, at the very beginning of the process. Once it generates the application's framework you will start adding code and developing your application from that starting point, but you will never again use the AppWizard for that application. The AppWizard's goal is simply to generate a clean, new starting point that is consistent and tuned to the needs of the application. It does not contain any facilities to change a framework after it has been generated. The App-Wizard simply saves you the step of stripping out code from an old program to create a starting point.

Whenever you create a new framework from the AppWizard, you have a number of options. For example, you must decide whether you want to create an SDI application (Single-Document Interface, like Notepad, where only one file can be open at a time) or an MDI application (Multiple-Document Interface, like Microsoft Word, where several windows can be open in the application at one time). Here are some of the other features that the AppWizard lets you add to a new application framework:

- Tool bars and status bars
- Printing
- Help menu and context-sensitive help
- OLE client or server capabilities
- ODBC database capabilities

In this chapter we will start with the very simplest framework that the AppWizard creates so you can completely understand what the AppWizard is doing. The AppWizard, even for the simplest framework, generates about 15 different files. It will take a little time and experience before you will feel completely comfortable with all these files. In this chapter we will discuss, in a general way, what all the different files do and what the AppWizard is trying to accomplish with each of them. Then, in the next chapter, we will create a simple application from this framework so you can see what is involved. From there we move into different variations of the framework and more advanced features. By taking the time to go through the different examples, you will bring yourself to the point where you completely understand what each part of the framework does. You will then be able to quickly create your own applications using the AppWizard as a comfortable starting point.

14.2 Creating a Simple Framework with the AppWizard

To create a new framework you should start Visual C++ and then refer to Appendix B.6.1 for specific instructions.

At this point you should build the project that the AppWizard has created for you. Simply choose the **Build** option as described in Appendix B.6.1. It will form an executable and you should run it. What you will find is that you have a remarkably complete starter application. The menu bar works and contains all the normal menu options you would expect to find. The **Open**, **New**, and **Exit** options will all do the expected things. The application has an About box. The AppWizard's files create a very good starting point for a new application.

14.3 The AppWizard's Document-Centric Approach

One of the interesting things about the AppWizard is that it takes a *document-centric approach* to application design. The MFC class hierarchy contains two classes that help support this approach: **CDocument** and **CView**. The AppWizard and MFC use this approach because most Windows applications work this way. Built into the framework generated by the AppWizard is the assumption that your application will want to load and work with multiple *documents*, and that each document will have one or more *views* open at a time. This approach makes it extremely easy to create both SDI and MDI applications. There is a very small number of simple applications that do not need the document concept. A simple digital clock is an example. All other applications can be thought of in terms of documents and views. In the case of a simple digital clock, you can leave the document class in place and simply ignore it.

Before looking at the files created by the AppWizard, it is useful to have a feeling for what this document-centric approach means. It is easiest to understand the document/view architecture if you think about a typical MDI word processor like Microsoft Word, as pictured in Figure 14.1. At any given time you can have one or more documents open. A document represents a single open file. The user generally has one view open on each document. The view shows the user a part of the document in an MDI window and lets the user edit the document. However, Microsoft Word allows the user to split a window into multiple frames so the user can have two or more views on the document if desired. When the user edits in one of the views, it changes the data in the document associated with the view. If a document has multiple views open and the user changes data in one of the views, the document and all other related views should reflect the change. When the user saves the document, it is that data held by the document that gets saved to disk.

Many applications allow the user to open just one type of document. Microsoft Word, for example, works only with Microsoft Word documents. It may open other types of documents, but it first filters them to turn them into Word documents. Other applications open several different types of documents and can display all of them simultaneously in its MDI framework. Visual C++ is an example of this type of application. The most common type of document Visual C++ works with is a text file that contains code. However, you can open a browser file (see Appendix B.4) as well

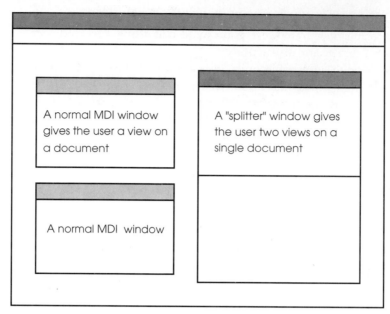

Figure 14.1
A typical MDI application can have several documents open at once. The user can have one or more views into each document

and it will display itself as a second type of document in the MDI framework. Microsoft Works is similar. It can open word processing documents, but it can also open spreadsheet and database documents. Each of these documents has a completely unique view in the MDI frame, but all the different views live there in harmony with one another. In addition, database documents can be viewed both in a spreadsheet-like list or in a customizable form that shows one complete record at a time.

Therefore, in the most general case an application may be able to open several different types of documents simultaneously. Each type of document can have a unique viewing window. Any document may have multiple views open at once. In fact, a document might have more than one way of viewing its data. Each document stores its data on disk. The views give the user a way to view and edit that data. Figure 14.2 shows that the application, documents, and views represent a tree. Because this arrangement is typical of most applications, the framework generated by the AppWizard supports this structure implicitly. The MFC class hierarchy contains classes that make this structure easy to create.

At a code level, the document and view classes separate functionality. The document class is responsible for data. It reads the data from a file on disk and holds it in memory. The view class is responsible for presentation. The view class takes data from the document class and presents it to the user in a view. The multiple views for a single document synchronize themselves through the data in the document. The separation between documents and views is explained in more detail in the following section. See also Tech Note Number 25.

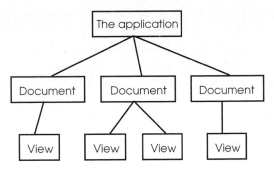

Figure 14.2
An MDI application can have several documents open at once. The documents could potentially be of different types. Each document can display itself to the user in one or more views

14.4 Understanding the AppWizard's Files

Before you can build a new application from any framework that the AppWizard creates, you must understand what all the different files do. You must also understand how they work together to create a complete application once they are compiled. *One of the best things that you can do at this point is print out all the different files and start marking them up with notes and pointers to other files.* This section takes you on a brief tour of all the different files, showing you what each file does. You should also look at the README file the AppWizard generated for information about the different files.

From your experience with the programs in Parts 1 and 2, you now have a great deal of experience with MFC code. What you will find as we walk though all these AppWizard files is that this experience is extremely useful. For example, every MFC program that you see in Parts 1 and 2 has a class that inherits behavior from **CWinApp**. You will find the same thing happening in the framework files. The framework files simply do it in a more thorough and complete fashion. The framework files also leverage off the strengths of resource files (see Chapter 6) as well as the document-centric classes described in the previous section of this chapter.

14.4.1 STDAFX Files

Using the sample framework you generated in Section 14.2, let's start the tour of the AppWizard files with the STDAFX files. When you look at your printouts of these files, you will find that both files are extremely short.

The STDAFX files handle pre-compiled header optimization. If you look inside STDAFX.H, it simply includes two AFX header files. The first, AFXWIN.H, is the same file that you have included in every sample program seen so far. The second, AFXEXT.H, contains extensions that are useful to the AppWizard. STDAFX.CPP contains nothing but an include statement for STDAFX.H. In the project file generated by the AppWizard, Visual C++ is instructed to compile STDAFX.CPP and then save its symbol table into a pre-compiled header file. By separately compiling just the

AFX header files into a pre-compiled header, the system ensures that the pre-compiled portion of the header is the same for all source files used in the framework.

You will notice that all the other CPP files generated by the AppWizard include STDAFX.H first. This file brings in the pre-compiled header file containing all the standard MFC symbols. Any other includes come below that. Because each CPP file is already aware of all MFC symbols after it includes STDAFX.H, the additional header files can use all those symbols rather than including them themselves. This structure speeds up the build process tremendously when you compile the project.

14.4.2 SAMP Files

The SAMP.H and SAMP.CPP files house the **CWinApp** object. Every sample program created in Parts 1 and 2 contains a single instance of **CWinApp**, and the applications generated by the AppWizard are just the same. The AppWizard simply isolates the **CWinApp** class in the files SAMP.H and SAMP.CPP.

The SAMP.CPP file contains the implementation of the new application class. The important function is the **InitInstance** function. In Parts 1 and 2, **InitInstance** has consistently been four lines long. In the AppWizard framework it expands somewhat. In particular, the framework adds code that reads profile strings (see Chapter 6), checks for command line parameters, and creates a *document template.* See Chapter 10 for more details on these features. You will often modify the framework's standard **InitInstance** function, including in it things like database or device initialization that must occur when the application starts.

An important line in the **InitInstance** function is the call to **AddDocTemplate,** duplicated below:

```
CSingleDocTemplate* pDocTemplate;
pDocTemplate = new CSingleDocTemplate(
    IDR_MAINFRAME,
    RUNTIME_CLASS(CSampDoc),
    RUNTIME_CLASS(CMainFrame),          // main SDI frame window
    RUNTIME_CLASS(CSampView));
AddDocTemplate(pDocTemplate);
```

This code links the application to its frame window, its document, and the document's view. In an application that supports multiple document types, there will be one of these lines for each type of document. See Section 16 for more information on multiple-document applications.

The bottom part of the SAMP.CPP file contains a derived dialog class to handle the application's About box. Generally, derived dialog classes go in their own separate files, but the About dialog is always placed at the bottom of SAMP.CPP by the framework. Chapter 15 gives a complete description of how to create and use your own dialog classes.

14.4.3 The MAINFRM Files

The MAINFRM files handle the main frame window for the application. In all the programs shown in Parts 1 and 2, a new class has been derived from **CFrameWnd** to act as the application's main window on the screen. MAINFRM.H and MAIN-

FRM.CPP hold the frame window's class declaration and implementation. Generally, you will not manipulate these files.

14.4.4 SAMPDOC Files

The SAMPDOC files hold the document class for the application. The SAMPDOC.H file derives a new document class from **CDocument**, and SAMP-DOC.CPP begins the implementation.

Note that SAMPDOC.H contains four sections: Attributes, Operations, Overrides and Implementation. You can also see this arrangement in SAMPVW.H and MAINFRM.H. Each of these sections has an intended purpose. In the *Attributes* section you place new data members, along with access functions (generally beginning with **Get** and **Set**) that let you manipulate the member variables. For example, if your document needs an array data member to hold the document's data, you would declare the instance of the array here, probably as a protected value, and if necessary you would also create **GetArray** and **SetArray** functions to get and set the contents of the array. These two functions could be either protected or public, depending on how your application uses the array. In the *Operations* section go member functions that will be called by other classes to operate on the document class. These would be either protected or public depending on their use. Normally you develop the interface for the document class in this section, and the view class calls these functions to manipulate the document. In the *Overrides* section go functions that override virtual functions in the **CDocument** class. This section is manipulated automatically by the ClassWizard, and you will have no occasion to manipulate it yourself. In the *Implementation* section go functions that are used internally by the document class or derived classes. Generally they will be protected. If you created a special function, used internally by the document class to clear some data structures or manipulate a database, these functions would go here. See the article entitled "MFC: Using the MFC Source Files" in the MFC encyclopedia in books on-line for further details.

Note that the document class's implementation in SAMPDOC.CPP contains **Serialize**, **AssertValid,** and **Dump** functions as discussed in Chapters 12 and 13. These are standard functions that every object derived from **CObject** needs to fit properly into the MFC hierarchy. Because **CDocument** is derived from **CObject**, the framework stubs out these functions for you and you simply fill in the blanks. See the example in the next chapter for a further discussion.

The document class should *completely* encapsulate the data known to the document. When the user opens a new document, the class should load the document from a file and then provide member functions that let the view display the document to the user. The document class should also provide member functions that let the view class add and change data in the document. The document should do nothing but hold the data for multiple views, as shown in Figure 14.3..

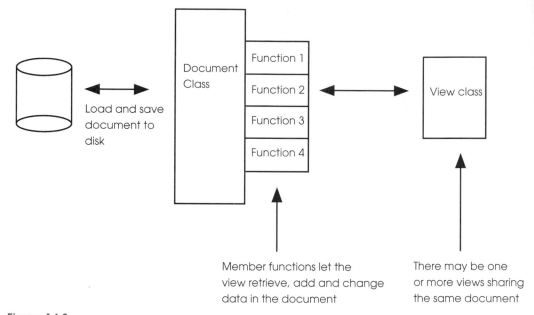

Figure 14.3
The relationship between a document and its view(s)

14.4.5 SAMPVIEW Files

The SAMPVIEW files hold the view of the document. The view normally has two jobs: It displays the data in the document to the user and it obtains new or modified data from the user and stores it back in the document (it is also possible for the document class to gather data from the user, as will be seen in Chapter 18). SAMP-VIEW.H contains the declarations for a new class derived from **CView**. SAMPVIEW.CPP implements the new class. This class will normally be heavily modified, and you will see examples of this in the following chapters.

One part of SAMPVIEW.CPP to pay particular attention to is the **OnDraw** function. It replaces the **OnPaint** function discussed extensively in Chapter 11, and is explained in detail in the next chapter.

You should note that all four CPP files described above have a message map. How do you decide which messages to put where? Your decision will come mostly from experience, and you will gain this experience from the examples shown in the other chapters in Part 3. In general, application-wide messages go in the application class (the SAMP files). The About box is a good example: Regardless of how many documents and views are active, the About box appears as a single dialog for the application. Other messages will go either in the document or view classes, and you base those decisions on coding convenience. Some events are much more easily handled in the document, while others are handled more easily in the view.

14.4.6 RESOURCE Files

RESOURCE.H is a resource header file like those that you saw in Chapter 6. It contains new constants you declare in the process of creating menus, dialogs, and so on. For example, if you create an edit control in a dialog and assign it a special constant value, the constant will appear in RESOURCE.H

SAMP.RC is the resource for the application framework. It initially contains sections for the application's icon, the menu bar, its accelerator table, the application's string table, the toolbar and the About dialog. It also contains version information. You should not manipulate this file yourself—you should always edit it using the resource editors available in Visual C++. See Chapter 6 for details.

One good way to get a feel for the contents of the SAMP.RC file is to examine its sections using the resource editors built into Visual C++. Open the resource view as described in Appendix B.6.2. Now double-click on any of the individual resources such as the dialog box or the menu. Visual C++ will display the resource in the appropriate editor. If you want to experiment, try customizing the About dialog or adding options to the menu bar. Change some of the version information.

Each change that you make gets written into SAMP.RC. If you look into the file with a text editor such as Notepad, you will be able to see the changes you make.

The first time you look at all these files it can be quite intimidating. The goal of the next four chapters is to show you several different example applications so you feel comfortable with this group of files. By the end of this section you will have touched all the different files and you will understand what to put where when you create your own applications.

14.5 Understanding the ClassWizard

The AppWizard is a tool that you use once for each application that you create. It is the very first step you take in creating a new application. Once you have created the framework you are done with the AppWizard tool. See Appendix B.7.

The ClassWizard, on the other hand, is used constantly. It allows you to do many things, but three of its different capabilities are most commonly used:

1. It gives you an easy way to modify message maps and to override virtual functions.
2. It creates new classes derived from many of the classes declared by MFC.
3. It lets you easily implement DDX (dialog data exchange) and DDV (dialog data verification) in dialog boxes.

The only way to learn how to use the ClassWizard is by example, and the following chapters contain plenty of opportunities to use it. Right now let's look at how you can use the ClassWizard to manipulate a message map so you can begin to get comfortable with this tool.

If you look at the message maps contained in the files the AppWizard generated, you will find they contain some rather odd-looking comments. The AFX_MSG tag inside a message map is a special string understood by the ClassWizard. The Class-

Wizard can look into the file, find these tags, and manipulate any message map that contains them. As the comments indicate, you should not modify the tags or the code within them because that will upset the ClassWizard's ability to orient itself in the code. There are some cases where it is valid to add entries into the ClassWizard's section, and we will see several examples of this in Part 4. In general, however, it is a good idea to steer clear of the sections tagged for the ClassWizard's use.

To demonstrate how the ClassWizard can modify a message map, let's make a very simple addition to the message map for the view class in the framework we just generated with the AppWizard. We will add an handler function for the WM_MOUSEMOVE message.

Open the file named SAMPVIEW.CPP. Look at the message map and you will find that it is empty. Do the same in SAMPVIEW.H, and you will again find that the message map is empty.

Now open the ClassWizard. Following the instructions in Appendix B.7.1 add a new message map entry for the WM_MOUSEMOVE event to SAMPVIEW.CPP. You will find that the message map gains a new entry for **OnMouseMove**. Edit the OnMouseMove function.

The new **OnMouseMove** function looks like this:

```
void CSampView::OnMouseMove(UINT nFlags, CPoint point)
{
    // TODO: Add your message handler code here and/or call default

    CView::OnMouseMove(nFlags, point);
}
```

It contains a comment that you can replace with your own code. It also contains a call down to the base implementation of **OnMouseMove**. You can keep this call or remove it, depending on how you plan to use the new function. Generally it is a good idea to keep it, but we will see examples in later chapters where it is useful to remove it or move it elsewhere.

Modify the **OnMouseMove** function so that it looks like this:

```
void CSampView::OnMouseMove(UINT nFlags, CPoint point)
{
    if (nFlags == MK_LBUTTON)
    {
        CClientDC dc(this);
        dc.SetPixel(point,RGB(0,0,255));
    }

    CView::OnMouseMove(nFlags, point);
}
```

This code should look familiar if you worked with any of the drawing programs in Chapters 11 and 12.

Now build the project and run it. You will find that you can draw points just like you could with the previous drawing applications. However, in this case you were able to create the drawing program by adding just five lines of code to an automatically generated framework, rather than typing an entire program as you did in Chapter 11.

As mentioned before, you will see a number of examples that demonstrate the uses of the ClassWizard in the following chapters. From the example here you can see that using it to add entries to any message map is extremely easy, and its other capabilities are just as easy to learn.

14.6 Conclusion

The next chapter will show you how to expand the drawing program started in the previous section, adding to it the ability to open and save documents. To do this will require you to extensively modify the document class, and from this experience you will learn a great deal about how documents and views work together in a framework to create an application.

Creating a Drawing Program

Several different chapters in Part 2 work with a simple drawing program that does nothing more than draw points. For example, in Chapter 11 this simple program introduced the concept of mouse motion events. In Chapter 12 it was modified to demonstrate how to create **CObject**-derived classes and **CObArray**s.

In this chapter we will use these same concepts to create a complete drawing application from an AppWizard framework. First we will create an SDI (Single Document Interface) version of the application, and then we will start over again and create an MDI (Multiple Document Interface) version. Then we will expand the program to include scrolling and splitter windows. We will add a new menu option and dialog to the application to demonstrate the use of the Visual C++ resource editors and the **CDialog** class first seen in Chapter 6. We will also add printing capabilities so you can see how to use the Print Preview and Print options that are implemented in the AppWizard framework.

Once you have finished working through the examples in this Chapter, you will have a much clearer view of how the different pieces in an AppWizard framework work together. Chapter 18 will then reinforce and continue the process, showing you additional features like the tool bar, status bar, and additional printing options.

15.1 The Goal of the Application

In this chapter you will create a drawing program using a framework generated by the AppWizard as the starting point. To simplify the program, it will draw nothing but points: When you move the mouse while holding down the left mouse button, the program will paint the pixels that the mouse moves over. It would be an easy extrapolation to create more sophisticated editors able to draw lines, rectangles, circles, polygons, and so on using the rubber-banding techniques seen in Chapter 11. Our goal here is not to create a complete drawing editor, but instead to expose you to the features available in the AppWizard's framework and show you how to use them without bogging you down with extraneous details.

By creating this application within an AppWizard framework, the application will have a number of standard features derived from the framework's inherent capabilities. The program will initially be an SDI application with the following features:

1. It will be able to draw points, just like the previous programs in Chapters 11 and 12.

2. It will properly refresh the window on exposure.

3. It will properly implement the Open, Close, Save, and Save-As menu options so you can open and save drawings.

4. It will put the proper file extension in File Open dialog, have a proper title bar, etc.

5. It will recognize that you have to save before closing.

6. It will have an appropriate About box and icon.

To create this application, you will take the following steps:

1. Create an SDI framework using the AppWizard.

2. Wire in **OnMouseMove** event in the view.

3. Create a complete document class for documents generated with this application. The document class needs to have a way to accept points from the view, store them in the document class, serialize the document, and retrieve points for the view.

4. Create the **OnDraw** function in the view to handle exposure.

5. Modify the IDM_MAINFRAME string resource. You can do this in AppWizard or after the fact. See the **CDocTemplate::GetDocString** page in the MFC documentation for documentation on this string resource.

6. Properly set the dirty bit with **SetModified** so the document knows when it has to save itself.

7. Customize the application's about box and icon.

The next section walks you through the process of creating this application in a detailed, step-by-step manner. The following section then explains what you have done at a high level so you can understand why you made each change to the framework. Subsequent sections show you how to change the application over to an MDI format and then extend its capabilities.

15.2 Creating a Drawing Program

Chapter 14 described the steps you need to take to create an SDI application framework with the AppWizard (see Appendix B.6.1 for details). You will start creating your drawing application by creating a new SDI framework for it in the same way. You will then add modifications piece by piece until you have fully integrated a complete drawing application into the framework.

15.2.1 Step 1—Create the Framework

Create a new SDI framework with the AppWizard, following the exact same steps that you saw in Chapter 14. See Appendix B.6.1 for details.

- Choose the **Single-Document** option.
- Choose **None** for database support.
- Choose **None** for OLE support.
- Disable all application features: Disable the dockable tool bar, Initial Status bar, printing, context-sensitive help, and 3-D controls (you can come back and enable these when you do this exercise a second time later in the chapter). Leave the MRU list set to 4. *Change the file extension to "drw" in the **File Extension** field as described in Appendix B.6.3.*
- Leave all file names as chosen by the AppWizard.

When you added the word "drw" to the **File Extension** field, you told the AppWizard to create a framework that will automatically append the DRW extension to files without extensions. The application will also be able to associate itself with files ending with the DRW extension.

Create the framework.

15.2.2 Step 2—Examine the Framework

Look around at all the files that the AppWizard created. There are many, as described in the previous chapter. The main categories are:

- A CPP and H file for the precompiled headers (stdafx)
- Four CPP files for the application, window, document, and view
- Four H files for the CPP files
- Resource files: an RC file and RESOURCE.H
- Project files

We will focus all our changes in this section on the document and view files. Note: The EXAMPLES directory on the diskette makes it easy to work through this example.

15.2.3 Step 3—Handle Mouse Movement Events

Add in an **OnMouseMove** event handler. This step is described in detail at the end of the previous chapter (see Section 14.6). You will use the ClassWizard tool to do this. Add the code in Listing 15.1 in place of the TODO comment in that function:

Listing 15.1
Mouse motion handler code. See Section 14.5 for further information

```
if (nFlags == MK_LBUTTON)
{
    CClientDC dc(this);
    dc.SetPixel(point,RGB(0,0,255));
```

```
          }
```

See Chapter 11 for more information on drawing and device contexts.

15.2.4 Step 4—Compile and Run

Compile the program and try it out. You should be able to draw by dragging the mouse. The program will not handle exposure right now because there is no data structure to remember the points. This is the purpose of the document class, and all the necessary modifications to it occur in Step 5.

15.2.5 Step 5—Adjust the Document Class

Modify the document class so it can remember points. We are going to add in a data structure based on **CObArray**, add code to serialize the data, and then add member functions to access the data in the document. The document will then be a completely self-contained class that can hold, load, and save the data of any drawing. See Chapter 12 for information on **CObArray**.

15.2.6 Step 5a

Create COBPOINT.H and COBPOINT.CPP. These two files create a point class derived from the **CObject** class. See Chapter 12 for information on deriving classes from **CObject** and an explanation of the process and advantages. See Chapter 13 for information on **AssertValid** and **Dump** functions. Listing 15.2 contains COB-POINT.H, while Listing 15.3 contains COBPOINT.CPP.

Listing 15.2
The COBPOINT.H file

```
// cobpoint.h
class CObPoint : public CObject
{
DECLARE_SERIAL( CObPoint )
protected:
    LONG x, y;
public:
    CObPoint();
    CObPoint(const CObPoint &p);
    CObPoint operator=(const CObPoint& p);
    CObPoint(int ix, int iy);
    CObPoint(CPoint &p);
    virtual void Serialize(CArchive &archive);
    CPoint GetPoint() const;
#ifdef _DEBUG
    virtual void Dump( CDumpContext& dumpSite ) const;
    virtual void AssertValid() const;
#endif
};
```

Choose the **New** option in the **File** menu, create a new text file, and copy the code in Listing 15.2 into the window. Save the file in the project's directory and give the file the name COBPOINT.H. Now create a second new file to hold the implementation, as shown in Listing 15.3.

Listing 15.3
The COBPOINT.CPP file

```
// cobpoint.cpp

#include "stdafx.h"
#include "cobpoint.h"

CObPoint::CObPoint()
{
    x=y=0;
}

CObPoint::CObPoint(const CObPoint &p)
{
    x=p.x;
    y=p.y;
}

CObPoint CObPoint::operator=(const CObPoint& p)
{
    x=p.x;
    y=p.y;
    return *this;
}

CObPoint::CObPoint(int ix, int iy)
{
    x=ix;
    y=iy;
}

CObPoint::CObPoint(CPoint &p)
{
    x=p.x;
    y=p.y;
}

void CObPoint::Serialize(CArchive &archive)
{
    CObject::Serialize(archive);
    if (archive.IsStoring())
        archive << x << y;
    else
        archive >> x >> y;
}

// The (int) casts in the function below are
// needed only in Windows 3.1. Remove in
```

```
// WIN32 environments
CPoint CObPoint::GetPoint() const
{
    return CPoint((int)x, (int)y);
}

#ifdef _DEBUG
    void CObPoint::Dump( CDumpContext& dumpSite ) const
    {
        CObject::Dump(dumpSite);

        dumpSite << "x: " << x << "y: " << y;
    }

    void CObPoint::AssertValid() const
    {
        // check base class first
        CObject::AssertValid();

        // check data members.
    }
#endif //_DEBUG

IMPLEMENT_SERIAL(CObPoint, CObject, 0)
```

Save the second file as COBPOINT.CPP. *Add COBPOINT.CPP to the project file* (see Appendix B.1.4). *Include COBPOINT.H in the Document file*: That is, somewhere below the include statement for the file STDAFX.H in the file DRAWDOC.H you should include the file COBPOINT.H, as shown here:

```
// drawdoc.cpp : implementation of the CDrawDoc class
//

#include "stdafx.h"
#include "draw.h"

#include "drawdoc.h"
#include "cobpoint.h"

#ifdef _DEBUG
#undef THIS_FILE
static char BASED_CODE THIS_FILE[] = __FILE__;
#endif
...
```

You might also consider deriving a class from **CObArray** in the same manner to override its **delete** and **RemoveAll** functions. Here we will do that work in the Document class, instead of creating a stand-alone class derived from **CObArray**, to save typing.

15.2.6.1 Step 5b In the document's header file (DRAWDOC.H), add the following declaration to the "attributes" section as a protected member:

```
CObArray array;
```

This array will be used to remember what the user has drawn. The top of DRAWDOC.H should look like this when you are done:

```
// drawdoc.h : interface of the CDrawDoc class
//
///////////////////////////////////////////////////////////////

class CDrawDoc : public CDocument
{
protected: // create from serialization only
    CDrawDoc();
    DECLARE_DYNCREATE(CDrawDoc)

// Attributes
protected:
    // holds the document's points in the drawing.
    CObArray array;

// Operations
public:
...
```

15.2.6.2 Step 5c In the Document's DRAWDOC.CPP file, add an overriding implementation of the virtual function named **DeleteContents**. To do this, use the **ClassWizard** as described in Appendix B.7.2. Modify the **DeleteContents** function so it looks like the version shown in Listing 15.4.

Listing 15.4
Modifications to the **DeleteContents** virtual function

```
void CDrawDoc::DeleteContents()
{
    int x;
    for (x=0; x<array.GetSize(); x++)
        delete(array.GetAt(x));
    array.RemoveAll();
    CDocument::DeleteContents();
}
```

This function gets called whenever the user selects the **New** option and also when the program exits. In this implementation it empties the array.

Note that, as described in Chapter 12, the elements of the **CObArray** must actually be deleted. As mentioned above, you could derive a new class from **CObArray** and handle the deletion there. Handling the deletion inside the document class simply saves some typing.

15.2.6.3 Step 5d Add the following line to the end of document's **Serialize** function in DRAWDOC.CPP:

```
    array.Serialize(ar);
```

Because the **CObArray** knows how to serialize itself, and because the **CObPoint** elements it contains also know how to serialize themselves, this single line is all that is needed to save or load the array to and from disk. See Chapter 12, as well as the MFC Encyclopedia's entry on Serialization in books on-line, for information on serialization. After you have added the line, the serialize function should look as shown in Listing 15.5.

Listing 15.5
The modified Serialize function in the Document class

```
void CDrawDoc::Serialize(CArchive& ar)
{
    if (ar.IsStoring())
    {
        // TODO: add storing code here
    }
    else
    {
        // TODO: add loading code here
    }
    array.Serialize(ar);
}
```

15.2.6.4 Step 5e Find the **AssertValid** and **Dump** functions in the DRAW-DOC.CPP file. Modify them so the document complies with the debugging and dumping features of MFC, as shown in Listing 15.6.

Listing 15.6
Completing the **AssertValid** and **Dump** functions in the document class

```
void CDrawDoc::AssertValid() const
{
    CDocument::AssertValid();
    ASSERT_VALID(&array);
}

void CDrawDoc::Dump(CDumpContext& dc) const
{
    CDocument::Dump(dc);
    dc << array;
}
```

15.2.6.5 Step 5f As the final modification to the document class, we need to create three access functions that allow the view to access the data held in the document. These functions will add points to the array, get points from the array, and indicate the number of points currently held in the array. Add the following prototypes for these functions to the Attributes section of the document's header file:

```
void CDrawDoc::AddPoint(CPoint p);
CPoint CDrawDoc::GetPoint(int x);
int CDrawDoc::GetNumPoints();
```

This book is continuously updated. See http://www.iftech.com/mfc

These functions should be declared as **public** functions so functions in the View class can call them. You will have to add these prototypes manually—the ClassWizard will not help with adding new attribute functions like these. When you are done modifying the attributes section of DRAWDOC.H, it should look like this:

```
class CDrawDoc : public CDocument
{
protected: // create from serialization only
    CDrawDoc();
    DECLARE_DYNCREATE(CDrawDoc)

// Attributes
protected:
    // holds the document's points in the drawing.
    CObArray array;
public:
    // functions allow access to the array
    void CDrawDoc::AddPoint(CPoint p);
    CPoint CDrawDoc::GetPoint(int x);
    int CDrawDoc::GetNumPoints();

// Operations
public:
...
```

Toward the bottom of the document's DRAWDOC.CPP file add a section called "Attributes" and add the implementations for these three functions as shown in Listing 15.7

Listing 15.7
Implementations for the three array encapsulation functions

```
/////////////////////////////////////////////////////
// Attributes

void CDrawDoc::AddPoint(CPoint p)
{
    array.Add(new CObPoint(p));
    SetModifiedFlag();
}

CPoint CDrawDoc::GetPoint(int x)
{
    return ((CObPoint *)(array.GetAt(x)))->GetPoint();
}

int CDrawDoc::GetNumPoints()
{
    return array.GetSize();
}
```

You have now finished your modification to the document class. It handles all data manipulations, including file saving and loading, for the application.

15.2.7 Step 6—Add Points to the Document

Open the ClassWizard. Select the **CDrawView** class and edit the code for the **OnMouseMove** function. Change the code by adding the two lines shown in Listing 15.8.

Listing 15.8

Modifications to the **OnMouseMove** function that allow it to save new points to the document class.

```
void CDrawView::OnMouseMove(UINT nFlags, CPoint point)
{
    if (nFlags == MK_LBUTTON)
    {
        CClientDC dc(this);
        dc.SetPixel(point,RGB(0,0,255));

        // Add each point to the array
        GetDocument()->AddPoint(point);
    }

    CView::OnMouseMove(nFlags, point);
}
```

The new line that calls **AddPoint** causes points to get added to the document class each time the user drags the mouse.

Note that this function, as well as the function in Step 7, both call the **GetDocument** function. Each view contains a pointer back to its document. The **GetDocument** function retrieves that pointer and lets the view talk to its document. In the case of this **OnMouseMove** function, the view needs to call the **AddPoint** member function in the document, so it retrieves its document pointer to do that.

15.2.8 Step 7—Handle Exposure Events

Open the ClassWizard. Select the **CDrawView** class and edit the code for the **OnDraw** function. Place the code shown in Listing 15.9 in place of the TODO comment that you find in the **OnDraw** function.

Listing 15.9

Exposure-handling code for the view's **OnDraw** function.

```
int x;
// Redraw all points in the array
for (x=0; x<pDoc->GetNumPoints(); x++)
    pDC->SetPixel(pDoc->GetPoint(x),
        RGB(0,0,255));
```

This code causes the view to properly refresh itself during exposure events by retrieving all the points held by the array and redrawing them. See Chapter 11 for details.

15.2.9 Step 8—Compile and Run

Recompile and run the project. You should be able to draw. You should be able to re-size or iconify the window and it should update properly on exposure. The **On-Draw** function accomplishes this. The file should also properly save itself when you use the **Save** option in the **File** menu, and then reload again with the **Open** option. This occurs because the document's **Serialize** function now works and it gets called automatically by the **Open** and **Save** menu options (see Section 15.3 for an explanation). If you try to quit without saving you will get a dialog asking you if you want to save. This occurs because of the call to **SetModifiedFlag** in the document's **AddPoint** function (see Step 5f).

15.2.10 Step 9—Change the Icon and About Box

Use the dialog editor and icon editor to modify the About Box and icon resources for the application to suit your tastes. To do this, open the resource file by double-clicking on it in the project window (see Section 14.4). Then double-click on the dialog and icon resources that you find there. Change both resources as appropriate. You may also wish to modify the version information in the version resource. Recompile and run. The application is now complete.

15.3 Understanding the Drawing Program

In the previous section you made a series of changes to a standard SDI framework produced by the AppWizard. These changes resulted in the creation of a complete drawing program. But how? There are two things that make it difficult to understand why the nine steps described in Section 15.2 resulted in a complete drawing editor:

1. You made so many small changes to so many different pieces that it is hard to get a global understanding of what you did.
2. So many things happen automatically in the framework and the base MFC classes that it is difficult to know why certain things work the way they do. For example, the **Open** option in the **File** menu of the drawing program works correctly, yet there does not seem to be any code that causes that to happen.

The purpose of this section is to help you understand why the code you entered in Section 15.2 actually works.

Let's start by summarizing the changes you made to the framework's code to produce the drawing program. Here is a list of the different modifications:

1. In the view, you used the ClassWizard to add an **OnMouseMove** function. Initially (Step 3) that function simply drew pixels into the view, but later (Step 6) it also added the pixels into the document.

2. In the view you also modified the existing **OnDraw** function (Step 7). By doing so you gave the program the ability to refresh its screen on exposure.

3. You implemented a complete **CObPoint** class derived from **CObject** (Step 5a). The reasons for, and advantages of, this step are described in Chapter 12. The **CObPoint** class is designed to hold one point of the drawing. You then added an instance of a **CObArray** to the document class (Step 5b) to hold the collection of all points drawn by the user.

4. You overrode the document's **DeleteContents** member function (Step 5c). By default this function does nothing. You overrode it to clear the member variable you added to the document class. The function gets called by the framework during destruction of the document. In an SDI application, it is also called each time the user opens or creates a new document, because an SDI application reuses the same document object throughout the run of the program. In an MDI application, a new document instance is created each time the user selects the **New** or **Open** option, so **DeleteContents** only gets called during destruction.

5. You modified the document's **Serialize** function (Step 5d) by adding one line to it. This line serializes the array to or from disk automatically. The document's **Serialize** function gets called automatically by the framework each time the user chooses the **Open, Save,** or **Save As** options.

6. You modified the **AssertValid** and **Dump** functions of the document class (Step 5e) so these functions work properly. See Chapter 13 for more information on these functions.

7. You added three functions to the document class (Step 5f) to complete its encapsulation: **AddPoint**, **GetPoint**, and **GetNumPoints**. The view class uses these three functions when it wants to manipulate data in the document class.

Note that these changes were made strictly to the document and view classes.

The goal of the document class is to completely encapsulate the data for one open document. It knows how to load the data from the disk and save it to the disk. It also has member functions that the view class uses to manipulate the data in the document. In this case the document has only three functions that the view uses: **AddPoint**, **GetPoint**, and **GetNumPoints**. In more complicated programs the interface will be more complicated, but here those three functions are enough to satisfy all the needs of the view.

The view class is responsible for letting the user view the contents of the document. In this case the document is a drawing. The view accepts drawing events from the user and adds new points to the document.

The relationship between the document and view classes is summarized in Figure 15.1. When you are designing your own applications, you want the document class to completely encapsulate the data, and you want the view to display information to the user. There should be a clear and obvious way for the view to interact with the document through member functions.

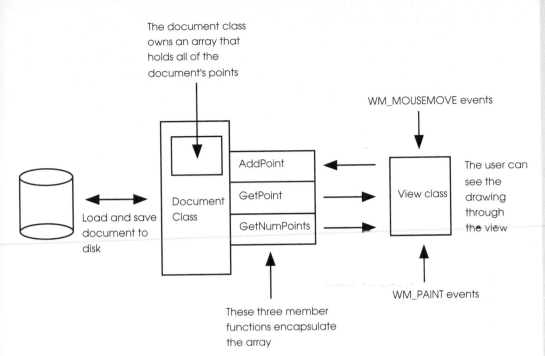

The document class owns an array that holds all of the document's points

WM_MOUSEMOVE events

AddPoint

GetPoint

GetNumPoints

Document Class

View class

The user can see the drawing through the view

Load and save document to disk

These three member functions encapsulate the array

WM_PAINT events

Figure 15.1
The relationship between the document and the view

With a clear understanding of what the document and view classes do in this application, it is easier to see how the total application handles events. Much of the event handling happens automatically in the framework. When an event occurs, code in the framework processes the event and then ends up calling certain functions in the document and view classes in response to those events. By understanding how events are processed in the framework, you get a much clearer understanding of why certain functions in the document and view classes should be modified.

Before proceeding, take a moment to look in the MFC documentation at the member functions for the **CDocument** and **CView** classes. When you look through the documentation for the document class you should recognize two functions that we have used in this chapter's example program: **SetModifiedFlag** and **DeleteContents**. In the view class you will also recognize two functions: **OnDraw** and **GetDocument**. Take a moment to read about some of the other functions in these two classes. You will find that many of them are called automatically by code or classes built into the framework. We will see examples of many of these functions in the chapters that follow.

Right now the application accepts only eight events that we care about in our implementation. Six of these come in the form of menu commands, while the other two are system events:

- The Open option in the File menu
- The New option in the File menu
- The Save option in the File menu

- The Save As option in the File menu
- The Exit option in the File menu
- The About option in the Help menu
- WM_PAINT messages in the view
- WM_MOUSEMOVE messages in the view

Let's look at each one of these individually to understand what happens when one of the events is recognized by the application. You may also want to peruse Tech Note 22 for more information on default menu behavior. Also be aware of the fact that you can look at the MFC source code and that this code is very educational. Using the debugger (see Appendix B.2) you can step right into the source and see what is happening.

15.3.1 The Open Menu Option

If you look in the message map generated by the AppWizard for the application class in DRAW.CPP, you will find an entry for the ID_FILE_OPEN command. The AppWizard built a default menu bar when it generated the framework, and the **Open** option in that menu bar generates this ID when the user selects it. As you can see in the application's message map, this message map entry calls **CWinApp::OnFile-Open**. If you walk through the source code for this function, you will see it displays the dialog to get a file name from the user and then calls the **OpenDocumentFile** function in the **CWinApp** class. The **OpenDocumentFile** function is more complicated, but essentially all that it does is attempt to create (in an MDI application) or reuse (in an SDI application) an instance of the document and view classes. Eventually the **OnOpenDocument** function in the **CDocument** class gets called. We have not overridden this function, so its default behavior executes. It first calls **DeleteContents**, which we have overridden to clear the document's array, and then calls **Serialize,** which we have modified to load the file.

There are many ways you can modify default behavior. You can, for example, override any of the functions in this chain of events. In most cases, however, the default behavior described above handles everything in an appropriate way. You simply modify **DeleteContents** and **Serialize** to take the appropriate actions and everything else happens automatically.

15.3.2 The New Menu Option

The **New** menu option, like the **Open** menu option, is handled in the message map of the application class. Eventually the framework calls the **OnNewDocument** function in the **CDocument** class. This function actually appears in the **CDrawDoc** class that the framework created, but we did not modify it. You can examine it with the ClassWizard. By default it calls **CDocument::OnNewDocument**, which eventually calls **DeleteContents**. The **DeleteContents** function that we created in Step 5c clears the array.

15.3.3 The Save Menu Option

Deep inside the core implementation for the **CDocument** class, the document's message map handles the ID_FILE_SAVE message. You can modify this behavior by creating your own message map entry for that ID in your derived **CDocument** class, but the default behavior is so rich that it is better to override some function in the standard chain of events to accomplish any goals that you have. First the **CDocument** message map calls **CDocument::OnFileSave**, which calls **CDocument::OnSave**, which calls **CDocument::OnSaveDocument**, which calls the overridden **Serialize** function of Step 5d. The **Serialize** function saves the document to disk. Both **OnSaveDocument** and **Serialize** can be easily overridden or modified.

15.3.4 The Save As Menu Option

The **Save As** option, like the **Save** option, is handled by a message map in the core of **CDocument**. The only difference between **Save** and **Save As** is that the **Save As** option additionally uses a dialog to get a new file name. It then calls **CDocument::OnSaveDocument** as described in the previous section.

15.3.5 The Exit Menu Option

The **Exit** option in the **File** menu is handled by the core behavior for the **CWinApp** class. Eventually the following overridable functions get called in the **CDocument** class:

- CanCloseFrame
- SaveModifed
- OnSaveDocument
- Serialize

The **SaveModified** function is the one that asks the user if the document should be saved before exiting. You can override it if you want a fancier query dialog. The call to **Serialize** is made only if the user wishes to save the document.

15.3.6 The About Menu Option

The **About** menu option is handled in the derived application class's message map in DRAW.CPP. It calls **OnAppAbout**, located at the bottom of DRAW.CPP as well. See Chapter 6 for a discussion of dialog classes and their implementation.

15.3.7 The WM_PAINT Message

We first discussed the WM_PAINT message in Chapter 11. This message is generated any time any part of a window gets exposed. In the framework generated by the AppWizard the **CView** class receives this message. Its implementation for the event's handler is extremely simple:

```
void CView::OnPaint()
{
    // standard paint routine
    CPaintDC dc(this);
    OnPrepareDC(&dc);
```

```
    OnDraw(&dc);
}
```

As you can see, the framework simply reroutes the drawing activity over to **On-Draw**. It does this so it can simplify printing, as discussed later in this chapter. Here we simply place the code for exposure handling into the **OnDraw** function rather than the **OnPaint** function.

15.3.8 The WM_MOUSEMOVE Message

The WM_MOUSEMOVE event calls the **OnMouseMove** function. **On-MouseMove** is called because we added an entry to the view's message map to handle that message using the ClassWizard. Our implementation appears in Listing 15.10 (from Step 6):

Listing 15.10
The **OnMouseMove** function from Section 15.2.6.

```
void CDrawView::OnMouseMove(UINT nFlags, CPoint point)
{
    if (nFlags == MK_LBUTTON)
    {
        CClientDC dc(this);
        dc.SetPixel(point,RGB(0,0,255));

        // Add each point to the array
        GetDocument()->AddPoint(point);
    }

    CView::OnMouseMove(nFlags, point);
}
```

This implementation simply paints one pixel at the appropriate position, and then adds the position into the document's data structure with the **AddPoint** function.

Unlike the previous functions, there is no magic framework processing going on in the background and no virtual functions to override. Most standard Windows messages you see under the **CView** class in the ClassWizard (with the exception of WM_PAINT) are handled directly like this.

15.4 Creating an MDI Application

In Section 15.2 the application we created can edit only one document at a time. In this section we will recreate the application so that it can edit multiple documents in an MDI framework. In the process you will learn about the **UpdateAllViews** function in the **CDocument** class and the **OnUpdate** virtual function in the **CView** class.

The process involved in creating an MDI application is nearly identical to that of creating an SDI application. The only modification occurs in Section 15.2. When you create the framework with the AppWizard, simply choose the **Multiple Docu-**

ment Interface option instead of the **Single Document Interface** option. You may also want to choose several of the other options like the tool bar to try out some of the AppWizard's capabilities.

To create an MDI version of the drawing program, complete all the steps exactly as you did for the SDI application in Section 15.2. Compile and run the new version and you should be able to open and edit multiple documents simultaneously.

It may surprise you to see that *exactly identical* code, applied to two different frameworks, can yield both SDI and MDI functionality. This is possible because both the implementations use the document and view classes, and the document and view classes created above were implemented in their intended manner. In the SDI version, there is only one document and one view. However, the **CDocument** and **CView** classes we created are general enough to handle multiple documents and multiple views. Because we complied with the requirements of the document and view classes during the initial implementation, we gained the power of MDI functionality "for free."

The differences between the MDI and SDI frameworks reside in the document templates used in the framework's application and frame classes, and in the resource file. For example, if you compare the resource file of the SDI and MDI applications, you will find the MDI version differs in that it has two menu bars, two accelerator tables, and two icons. The two menu bars (and their associated accelerator tables) handle the two possible states an MDI application can enter. When the application has no windows visible, the IDR_MAINFRAME menu bar appears. It contains a minimum of options, as appropriate for a no-windows state. When there are windows open, the second menu bar appears and displays to the user the standard menu options for the application. We will see in Chapter 16 that you can add multiple document types to a single MDI application and each document type can have its own menu bar to go with it. The framework handles all the details of displaying the appropriate menu bar.

There is one subtle way in which the MDI version that you just created is lacking. To see this, run the MDI drawing program again. Close any windows that are open (note how the menu bar changes) and create a new document by selecting the **New** option in the **File** menu. Draw something in this window. Now select the **New Window** option in the **Window** menu. You now have two views into the same document. Then select the **Tile** option in the **Window** menu so you can see both windows simultaneously. You can see that both views contain the same drawing. If you like, open several more new windows on the same document. They should all display the same drawing.

Now draw into one of the windows. You will find that the other windows do not update properly. What we would like is total synchronization in real time—as you draw into one view, the other views should get updated with the same information simultaneously. If you iconify one of the windows and then double-click on the icon, that view will suddenly synchronize itself because its **OnDraw** function redraws all the points in the document and the document knows about the entire drawing.

You can use two functions to fix this problem. The **CDocument** class contains a function called **UpdateAllViews**. This function calls the **OnUpdate** function in the **CView** class. The **UpdateAllViews** function is designed so that the document traverses its list of views and calls the **OnUpdate** function in each one. This allows all the views to know when any changes to the document occur.

If you look up the **UpdateAllViews** function in the **CDocument** class, you will find that it accepts three parameters:

1. The first parameter points to a view. If you set it to NULL when you call **UpdateAllViews**, the document calls the **OnUpdate** function in all of its views. If, on the other hand, you pass a pointer to a view in this parameter, the document will call all its views *except* the one specified.

2. The second parameter accepts a value of type LPARAM. You can pass any four-byte value you like through this parameter and it will be passed to the **OnUpdate** function of each view. You can design your code to use this value in any way you like.

3. The third parameter accepts a pointer to a **CObject**. The pointer will be passed to the **OnUpdate** function of each view. You can design your code to use this value in any way you like.

The latter two parameters are hints. You can use them in any way you please to pass information to the views. Generally you use this information to tell the views what to do or to help them optimize redrawing. We can modify our MDI program to take advantage of this update facility in several different ways.

The steps below present one way to use the **UpdateAllViews** function to synchronize the different views of a drawing document. Here are the modifications you will make to the MDI application:

1. Change the **OnMouseMove** function so it does not draw each pixel but instead simply calls **AddPoint** to add the points to the document.

2. Modify the **AddPoint** function so it calls **UpdateAllViews** to notify all views whenever any point is added to the document.

3. Override the **OnUpdate** function to the view class and cause it to draw the most recently added pixel in the document.

Note: The EXAMPLES directory on the diskette makes it easy to work through this example.

15.4.1 Step 1—Modify OnMouseMove

Modify the **OnMouseMove** function in the view and eliminate the **dc** variable and the call to **SetPixel**. We are going to move this functionality to the **OnUpdate** function. The revised **OnMouseMove** function is shown in Listing 15.11.

Listing 15.11
The revised **OnMouseMove** function calls **UpdateAllViews**

```
void CDrawView::OnMouseMove(UINT nFlags, CPoint point)
{
    if (nFlags == MK_LBUTTON)
    {
        // Add each point to the array
        GetDocument()->AddPoint(point);
    }

    CView::OnMouseMove(nFlags, point);
}
```

Use the ClassWizard to find this piece of code so you can modify it.

15.4.2 Step 2—Create OnUpdate

Create a new **OnUpdate** function in the **CDrawView** class (DRAW-VIEW.CPP) file using the ClassWizard. Edit the function so its code appears as shown in Listing 15.12.

Listing 15.12
The view's **OnUpdate** function

```
void CDrawView::OnUpdate(CView *pSender,
    LPARAM lHint, CObject *pHint)
{
    CDrawDoc* pDoc = GetDocument();
    int numPoints = pDoc->GetNumPoints();
    if (numPoints==0)
        return;
    CPoint point = pDoc->GetPoint(numPoints - 1);
    CClientDC dc(this);
    dc.SetPixel(point,RGB(0,0,255));
}
```

You can see from this implementation that, in the **OnUpdate** function, the view simply retrieves the last point in the data structure held by the document. It then paints this point on the screen.

15.4.3 Step 3—Add UpdateAllViews

Modify the **AddPoint** function in the document class (DRAWDOC.CPP) so it calls **UpdateAllViews**. When you are finished, **AddPoint** should look like Listing 15.13.

Listing 15.13
The modified **AddPoint** function in the document class.

```
void CDrawDoc::AddPoint(CPoint p)
{
    array.Add(new CObPoint(p));
```

```
    SetModifiedFlag();
    UpdateAllViews(NULL, 0, NULL);
}
```

In this implementation, the document simply updates all the views each time it gets a new point added to the data structure. The **OnUpdate** function in the view class draws the point that got added and all views are updated appropriately.

15.4.4 Step 4—Compile and Run

Compile and run the program, create a new document, and then select the **New Window** option in the **Window** menu. Tile the windows. When you draw on one window of the document, the second window will update itself as well. The two views are completely synchronized.

There are many other ways to implement this same behavior. For example:

1. The document could pass the point number as the second parameter in the call to **UpdateAllViews**. By doing this, you save each view from having to call **Get-NumPoints**.

2. The view could draw its own pixel and then call **UpdateAllViews** itself, passing **this** in the first parameter. The document would then update any other views if they existed.

3. The view could update itself as in the previous approach and then pass the point as the third parameter to **UpdateAllViews**. This would probably be the most efficient way to implement the updating in this particular application.

Also note that you can override the **OnInitialUpdate** function in the view class. This function is called immediately after the view is created, but before it appears on the screen, and is useful for initialization of data or visuals that you use inside the **On-Update** function.

15.5 Scrolling

The two simple drawing programs presented in the previous sections demonstrate the basic steps involved in creating any application with the AppWizard. However, the programs are fairly limited in several respects. One of the most important limitations is the fixed image size: At present, the user cannot draw a picture any larger than the maximum screen size. Fortunately, MFC and the AppWizard framework make it easy to add scrolling to your drawing program using a class called **CScrollView**. We saw how to handle scrolling by hand in Chapter 11, but it is much easier in MFC. The **CScrollView** class inherits behavior from **CView** and automatically adds horizontal and vertical scroll bars to the client area so the user has access to a client area that is potentially much larger than the screen itself.

It would be possible for you to duplicate the scrolling activity of the **CScroll-View** class fairly easily by adding your own scroll bars to the view and managing their horizontal and vertical scrolling events (see Chapter 4). The **CScrollView** class simply saves you the work. It also automatically handles sizing and mapping mode issues. Several useful member functions make the class extremely easy to adjust and manipulate. See the MFC documentation for details.

Using the **CScrollView** class is easy because you can specify its inclusion when you create an application framework with the AppWizard. Once you create a framework that includes the **CSrollView** class, there are only two things you have to add to the drawing program to make it handle scrolling properly:

1. You must set the size of the scrolled client area.
2. You must handle the translation of the coordinate system from the scrolling view to your data structure whenever the user adds points to the drawing.

The best way to understand these two issues is to create an application containing the **CScrollView** class and then watch how it works.

Create a new MDI framework with the AppWizard. Give the new project the name "draw."

As you go through the AppWizard option screens, select the following options:

- Choose the **Multiple-Document** option.
- Choose **None** for database support.
- Choose **None** for OLE support.
- Enable or disable any application features as you see fit. (However, leave printing turned off for the moment. See Section 15.8 for details on printing.) Add the file extension "drw" as described in Appendix B.6.3.
- Leave all file and class names as chosen by the AppWizard. However, change the **Base Class** of the **CDrawView** class to **CScrollView** as described in Appendix B.6.4.

The last step simply modifies the base class of the view. If you look in the file DRAWVIEW.H, you will find that **CDrawView** now inherits its behavior from **CScrollView** as shown below:

```
// drawview.h : interface of the CDrawView class
//
/////////////////////////////////////////////////////////////

class CDrawView : public CScrollView
{
    ...
```

Note: Use the files in the EXAMPLES directory on the diskette to work through the examples.

Now recreate the drawing application by following all the steps in Section 15.4 to create an MDI program that can update multiple views properly. At this point you should be getting good at modifying AppWizard code and it should only take about five minutes to recreate the application. Compile and run the application to confirm that it works exactly as the program did in Section 15.4. The **CScrollView** class is completely silent because we have not yet activated it.

To activate scrolling, you first have to tell the scrolling view class how big an area it needs to handle. You do this by calling the **SetScrollSizes** function in the **CScroll-**

View class. Additionally, the document class needs to hold the size of the document and then initialize the size of the views as they open. To do this, take the following steps.

15.5.1 Step1—Add a Document Size Variable and Access Functions

Add a size variable to the document class by adding a new protected attribute variable and access function to the DRAWDOC.H header file as shown in Listing 15.14

Listing 15.14
Changes to the DRAWDOC.H file

```
// Attributes
protected:
    CObArray array;
    CSize docSize;
public:
    void CDrawDoc::AddPoint(CPoint p);
    CPoint CDrawDoc::GetPoint(int x);
    int CDrawDoc::GetNumPoints();
    CSize GetDocSize();
    void SetDocSize(CSize s);
```

The access function **GetDocSize** simply retrieves the size of the document, while the **SetDocSize** function sets it. Add the two functions shown in Listing 15.15 below the **GetNumPoints** function in the attributes section of DRAWDOC.CPP.

Listing 15.15
Functions to allow manipulation of the document size

```
CSize CDrawDoc::GetDocSize()
{
    return docSize;
}

void CDrawDoc::SetDocSize(CSize s)
{
    docSize = s;
}
```

15.5.2 Step 2—Initialize the Document Size

The initial document size needs to be set to something. You might typically read this initial value in from an application profile file or document file, but for this example we will initialize it to a constant value of 2,000 x 2,000. The best place to do this is either in the document's constructor or in the **OnNewDocument** virtual function. The **OnNewDocument** function is preferred because, in the SDI case, only one instance of the document class gets created and it is reused each time the user requests a new document. The **OnNewDocument** function is also easier to use because you can get to it through the ClassWizard (you have to find the constructor by hand). Open the ClassWizard and add the **OnNewDocument** function to the **CDrawDoc** class (see Appendix B.7.2). Modify the function as shown in Listing 15.16.

Listing 15.16
The **OnNewDocument** function for the document class

```
BOOL CDrawDoc::OnNewDocument()
{
    if (!CDocument::OnNewDocument())
        return FALSE;

    docSize = CSize(2000,2000);

    return TRUE;
}
```

15.5.3 Step 3—Serialize the Document's Size

The document will need to save the document size with the document itself. Because we are using a constant document size of 2,000 x 2,000 right now, this step is not strictly required, but it will be useful when we create a variable-size document option later in the Chapter. To save the document size you need to modify the document's **Serialize** function so that it can load and save the **docSize** member. Modify the function as shown in Listing15.17.

Listing 15.17
The new **Serialize** function can save the document size

```
void CDrawDoc::Serialize(CArchive& ar)
{
    if (ar.IsStoring())
    {
        ar << docSize;
    }
    else
    {
        ar >> docSize;
    }
    array.Serialize(ar);
}
```

As you saw in Chapter 12, classes that serialize themselves can specify a version number in the file so the application can ignore old versions of the data files. To turn on this capability, change the DELCARE_DYNCREATE macro at the top of DRAWDOC.H to DECLARE_SERIAL and change the

IMPLEMENT_DYNCREATE macro at the top of DRAWDOC.CPP to IMPLEMENT_SERIAL. The IMPLEMENT_SERIAL macro should look like this when you are done:

```
IMPLEMENT_SERIAL(CDrawDoc, CDocument, 1)
```

The third parameter to the macro specifies the version number. See the MFC documentation and Chapter 12 for more information. Each time you change the **Serialize** function in the document you should increment the version number.

After you make this change and compile the code in Step 5, you might try an experiment: load a drawing created in one of the earlier sections in this chapter and see what happens.

15.5.4 Step 4—Set the Scrolling Size

The view contains the scroll bars. Therefore, the **CDrawView** class needs to set the size of the scrolling area. To do this, use the ClassWizard to find the **OnInitialUpdate** function in the **CDrawView** class and modify it so it contains the change shown in Listing 15.18.

Listing 15.18

The modified **OnInitialUpdate** function in the view class.

```
void CDrawView::OnInitialUpdate()
{
    SetScrollSizes(MM_TEXT, GetDocument()->GetDocSize());
    CScrollView::OnInitialUpdate();
}
```

The call to **SetScrollSizes** sets the mapping mode (see Chapter 11) and sets the maximum size of the virtual drawing area. Additionally you can set the amount the document scrolls when the user clicks on the arrows or the shaft of the scroll bar. See the documentation's description of **CScrollView::SetScrollSizes** for more information.

15.5.5 Step 5—Compile and Run

Compile and run the program. You will find the drawing window now has scroll bars. You can click in the scroll bars and they will respond appropriately. However, you will notice that something is not quite right. If you draw on the screen, and then scroll down and draw some more, and then scroll back to the top of the drawing, the two parts of the drawing are superimposed. In fact, you can scroll all the way to the bottom right hand corner of the drawing, draw the word "hi", and then scroll back to the top left corner. You will find that the word "hi" displays in the top left corner of the drawing.

15.5.6 Step 6—Synchronize Coordinate Systems

This problem results from the fact that mouse coordinates that come back in the **OnMouseMove** function are always in *device coordinates*. Therefore, every time you click on a point to draw it, the mouse coordinates received by the **OnMouseMove** function are always in pixel coordinates based on an origin of 0,0 for the window's upper left hand corner. However, the **CScrollView** class is correctly adjusting things to the *logical coordinate system* of the 2,000 x 2,000 pixel drawing space and adjusting the logical origin of the window to reflect that fact.

The solution to the problem lies in translating the coordinates coming from the **OnMouseMove** function so they match the logical coordinate system of the scrolling view. To do this, change the **OnMouseMove** function in the **CDrawView** class so it matches Listing 15.19.

Listing 15.19
A revised Version of the **OnMouseMove** function in the view class.

```
void CDrawView::OnMouseMove(UINT nFlags, CPoint point)
{
    if (nFlags == MK_LBUTTON)
    {
        // Convert device coordinates to logical coordinates
        // of the view.
        CClientDC dc(this);
        OnPrepareDC(&dc);
        dc.DPtoLP(&point);
        // Add each point to the array
        GetDocument()->AddPoint(point);
    }

    CScrollView::OnMouseMove(nFlags, point);
}
```

The first line of the modification creates a client DC (see Chapter 11). The call to **OnPrepareDC** changes the DC so it understands the logical coordinate system of the **CDrawView** class.

The **CDrawView** class is "preparing" the DC so it understands the view's logical coordinate system. A properly prepared DC is essential to translating the point to logical coordinates. The third line translates the point from device coordinates to logical coordinates using the DC's **DPtoLP** function. Because of the translation, the point that gets stored in the data structure is properly adjusted to fit inside the 2,000 x 2,000 coordinate framework. An extremely useful exercise is to walk through the code in Listing 15.19 with the debugger and watch the point change from device to logical coordinates.

You have to make one other change, this time to the **OnUpdate** function as shown in Listing 15.20.

Listing 15.20
Modifying the DC in **OnUpdate.**

```
void CDrawView::OnUpdate(CView* pSender, LPARAM lHint,
    CObject* pHint)
{
    CDrawDoc* pDoc = GetDocument();
    int numPoints = pDoc->GetNumPoints();
    if (numPoints==0)
        return;
    CPoint point = pDoc->GetPoint(numPoints - 1);
    CClientDC dc(this);
    // match the DC to the CScrollView
    OnPrepareDC(&dc);
    dc.SetPixel(point,RGB(0,0,255));
}
```

In this code the call to **OnPrepareDC** simply makes the DC aware of the coordinate system of the **CScrollView** class. The DC therefore starts using the correct origin, which changes as you scroll around. See Chapter 11's discussion of virtual drawing specifications for a description of the sorts of origin calculations that the **CScrollView** class has to do.

Note that the **OnDraw** function requires no changes. The DC used in this function is provided as a parameter from the **CScrollView** class, so it is already properly prepared.

15.5.7 Step 7—Compile and Run

Compile and run the program. You should now be able to draw into a 2,000 x 2,000 pixel drawing space. As you scroll around, points will remain in their proper places.

15.6 Splitter Windows

When you use scroll bars to scroll through large drawings, you have a problem: It becomes impossible to look at the entire drawing at one time at normal resolution. So, while scroll bars do add a useful capability, they also create a difficulty for the user. When the drawing is extremely large, the user may wish to look at one portion of the drawing while modifying another. One option for the user is to open two separate windows on the same document and scroll them separately. However, it is then the user's responsibility to tile the windows properly. The overall effect is bothersome.

In applications like Microsoft Word or Excel, this problem is solved by using *splitter windows*. For example, if you create a 100-page document in Word and you wish to look at page two while you modify part of page 95, you can split the document's window and scroll through the document in two separate panes. MFC and the

AppWizard let you do this same thing by adding splitter windows to the application framework that the AppWizard creates.

Adding splitter windows is easy. See Appendix B.6.5. If you do this and then use the code shown in Section 15.5, you will have an application with scrollable and splittable windows. If you want to try this out, take the following steps.

Note: The EXAMPLES directory on the diskette will help you to work through this example quickly.

15.6.1 Step 1—Create the Framework

Create a new scrolling MDI framework with the AppWizard as described in Appendix B.6.1. In the New Project dialog, give the new project the name "draw".

As you go through the AppWizard option screens, select the following options:

- Choose the **Multiple-Document** option.
- Choose **None** for database support.
- Choose **None** for OLE support.
- Enable or disable any application features as you see fit. (However, leave printing turned off for the moment. See Section 15.8 for details on printing.) Use the file extension "drw" in the **File Extension** field as described in Appendix B.6.3. *Select the **Use Splitter Windows** check box as described in Appendix B.6.5.*
- Leave all file and class names as chosen by the AppWizard. *Change the **Base Class** of the **CDrawView** class as described in Appendix B.6.4.*

If you look at the generated framework you will find that the set of files in the framework contains a pair of files named CHILDFRM.H and CHILDFRM.CPP. These two files create a class called **CChildFrame**. This class holds an instance of the **CSplitterWnd** class. The **CChildFrame** class is then used as the child window in the document template in DRAW.CPP. That is all that is necessary to bring in the capabilities of splitter windows to this application.

Recreate the application by following all the steps in the previous sections. These steps are consolidated below so you have them all in one place.

15.6.2 Step 2—Create a New CObPoint Class

Create COBPOINT.H and COBPOINT.CPP. These two files create a point class derived from the **CObject** class. See Chapter 12 for information on deriving classes from **CObject** and an explanation of the process and advantages. See Chapter 13 for information on **AssertValid** and **Dump** functions. Listing 15.21 contains COBPOINT.H. Listing 15.22 contains COBPOINT.CPP.

Listing 15.21
The COBPOINT.H file.

```
// cobpoint.h

class CObPoint : public CObject
```

```
{
DECLARE_SERIAL( CObPoint )
protected:
    LONG x, y;
public:
    CObPoint();
    CObPoint(const CObPoint &p);
    CObPoint operator=(const CObPoint& p);
    CObPoint(int ix, int iy);
    CObPoint(CPoint &p);
    virtual void Serialize(CArchive &archive);
    CPoint GetPoint() const;
#ifdef _DEBUG
    virtual void Dump( CDumpContext& dumpSite ) const;
    virtual void AssertValid() const;
#endif
};
```

Choose the **New** option in the **File** menu, create a new text file, and copy the code above into the window. Save the file in the project's directory with the file name COBPOINT.H. Do the same for COBPOINT.CPP.

Listing 15.22
The COBPOINT.CPP file.

```
// cobpoint.cpp

#include "stdafx.h"
#include "cobpoint.h"

CObPoint::CObPoint()
{
    x=y=0;
}

CObPoint::CObPoint(const CObPoint &p)
{
    x=p.x;
    y=p.y;
}

CObPoint CObPoint::operator=(const CObPoint& p)
{
    x=p.x;
    y=p.y;
    return *this;
}

CObPoint::CObPoint(int ix, int iy)
{
    x=ix;
    y=iy;
}
```

```
CObPoint::CObPoint(CPoint &p)
{
    x=p.x;
    y=p.y;
}

void CObPoint::Serialize(CArchive &archive)
{
    CObject::Serialize(archive);
    if (archive.IsStoring())
        archive << x << y;
    else
        archive >> x >> y;
}

// The (int) casts in the function below are
// needed only in Windows 3.1. Remove in
// WIN32 environments
CPoint CObPoint::GetPoint() const
{
    return CPoint((int)x, (int)y);
}

#ifdef _DEBUG
    void CObPoint::Dump( CDumpContext& dumpSite ) const
    {
        CObject::Dump(dumpSite);

        dumpSite << "x: " << x << "y: " << y;
    }

    void CObPoint::AssertValid() const
    {
        // check base class first
        CObject::AssertValid();

        // check data members.
    }
#endif //_DEBUG

IMPLEMENT_SERIAL(CObPoint, CObject, 0)
```

Add COBPOINT.CPP to the project file as described in Appendix B.1.4. Include COBPOINT.H in the Document file: That is, somewhere below the include statement for the file STDAFX.H in the file DRAWDOC.H you should include the file COB-POINT.H, as shown in Listing 15.23:

Listing 15.23
Including COBPOINT.H in the document file.

```
// drawdoc.cpp : implementation of the CDrawDoc class
//
```

```
#include "stdafx.h"
#include "draw.h"

#include "drawdoc.h"
#include "cobpoint.h"

#ifdef _DEBUG
#undef THIS_FILE
static char BASED_CODE THIS_FILE[] = __FILE__;
#endif
...
```

15.6.3 Step 3—Create an Array in the Document Class

In the document's header file (DRAWDOC.H), add the following line to the "attributes" section as a protected member:

```
CObArray array;
```

Create three access functions that allow the view to access the data held in the document. These functions will add points to the array, get points from the array, and indicate the number of point currently held in the array. Add prototypes for these functions to the Attributes section of the document's header file:

```
void CDrawDoc::AddPoint(CPoint p);
CPoint CDrawDoc::GetPoint(int x);
int CDrawDoc::GetNumPoints();
```

These functions should be declared as public so functions in the view class can call them. Put them in the Attributes section of the header file. Toward the bottom of the document's DRAWDOC.CPP file add a section called "Attributes" and add the three functions that appear in Listing15.24.

Listing 15.24
Adding attribute functions to the document class

```
/////////////////////////////////////////////////////
// Attributes

void CDrawDoc::AddPoint(CPoint p)
{
    array.Add(new CObPoint(p));
    SetModifiedFlag();
    UpdateAllViews(NULL, 0, NULL);
}

CPoint CDrawDoc::GetPoint(int x)
{
    return ((CObPoint *)(array.GetAt(x)))->GetPoint();
}

int CDrawDoc::GetNumPoints()
{
    return array.GetSize();
```

```
}
```

See Section 15.2, Steps 5b and 5f, for more information.

15.6.4 Step 4—Override DeleteContents

Using the ClassWizard, add an override for the **DeleteContents** function in the document class. See Section 15.2, Step 5c, for more information. The new function should appear as shown in Listing 15.25.

Listing 15.25
The modified **DeleteContents** file in the document class

```
void CDrawDoc::DeleteContents()
{
    int x;
    for (x=0; x<array.GetSize(); x++)
        delete(array.GetAt(x));
    array.RemoveAll();
    CDocument::DeleteContents();
}
```

15.6.5 Step 5—Add a Size Variable to the Document

Add a size variable to the document class by adding a new protected attribute variable and access function to the DRAWDOC.H header file as shown in Listing 15.26.

Listing 15.26
Adding the document size variable and functions to the document class

```
// Attributes
protected:
    CObArray array;
    CSize docSize;
public:
    void CDrawDoc::AddPoint(CPoint p);
    CPoint CDrawDoc::GetPoint(int x);
    int CDrawDoc::GetNumPoints();
    CSize GetDocSize();
    void SetDocSize(CSize s);
```

The access function **GetDocSize** needs to simply retrieve the size, while the **SetDocSize** function needs to set it. Add the two functions in Listing 15.27 below the **GetNumPoints** function in the attributes section of DRAWDOC.CPP.

Listing 15.27

The implementations for the document size functions

```
CSize CDrawDoc::GetDocSize()
{
    return docSize;
}

void CDrawDoc::SetDocSize(CSize s)
{
    docSize = s;
}
```

15.6.6 Step 6—Initialize the Document Size

Use the ClassWizard to find the **OnNewDocument** function in the document class list and double-click to edit it. Modify it as shown in Listing 15.28 to set the initial document size.

Listing 15.28
Initializing the document size

```
BOOL CDrawDoc::OnNewDocument()
{
    if (!CDocument::OnNewDocument())
        return FALSE;

    docSize = CSize(2000,2000);

    return TRUE;
}
```

See Section 15.5, Step 2, for more information.

15.6.7 Step 7—Serialize the Document

Modify the serialize function so it saves the document size and the array as shown in Listing 15.29.

Listing 15.29
Modifying the **Serialize** function

```
void CDrawDoc::Serialize(CArchive& ar)
{
    if (ar.IsStoring())
    {
        ar << docSize;
    }
    else
    {
        ar >> docSize;
    }
```

```
    array.Serialize(ar);
}
```

Classes that serialize themselves can specify a version number in the file so that the application can ignore old versions of the data files. To turn on this capability, change the DELCARE_DYNCREATE macro at the top of DRAWDOC.H to DECLARE_SERIAL, and change the IMPLEMENT_DYNCREATE macro at the top of DRAWDOC.CPP to IMPLEMENT_SERIAL. The IMPLEMENT_SERIAL macro should look like this when you are done:

```
IMPLEMENT_SERIAL(CDrawDoc, CDocument, 1)
```

See Section 15.2, Step 5d, and Section 15.5, Step 3, for more information.

15.6.8 Step 8 Modify the Document's AssertValid and Dump Functions

Find the **AssertValid** and **Dump** functions in the DRAWDOC.CPP file. Modify them so the document complies with the debugging and dumping features of MFC, as shown in Listing 15.30.

Listing 15.30
The documents **AssertValid** and **Dump** functions

```
void CDrawDoc::AssertValid() const
{
    CDocument::AssertValid();
    ASSERT_VALID(&array);
}

void CDrawDoc::Dump(CDumpContext& dc) const
{
    CDocument::Dump(dc);
    dc << "document size:\n" << docSize;
    dc << array;
}
```

See Section 15.2, Step 5e, for more information.

15.6.9 Step 9—Handle Mouse Movement Events

Open the ClassWizard and select the **CDrawView** class. Add an event handler for the WM_MOUSEMOVE event. Change the code by adding the lines shown in Listing 15.31.

Listing 15.31
Modifying the **OnMouseMove** function

```
void CDrawView::OnMouseMove(UINT nFlags, CPoint point)
{
```

```
        if (nFlags == MK_LBUTTON)
        {
            // Convert device coordinates to logical coordinates
            // of the view.
            CClientDC dc(this);
            OnPrepareDC(&dc);
            dc.DPtoLP(&point);
            // Add each point to the array
            GetDocument()->AddPoint(point);
        }

        CScrollView::OnMouseMove(nFlags, point);
    }
```

See Section 15.2, Step 6, and Section 15.5, Step 6, for more information.

15.6.10 Step 10—Set the Scrolling Size

Use the ClassWizard to find the **OnInitialUpdate** function in the **CDrawView** class and modify it so it looks like Listing 15.32.

Listing 15.32
Modifying the **OnInitialUpdate** function

```
    void CDrawView::OnInitialUpdate()
    {
        SetScrollSizes(MM_TEXT, GetDocument()->GetDocSize());
        CScrollView::OnInitialUpdate();
    }
```

See Section 15.5, Step 4, for more information.

15.6.11 Step 11—Update Views

Use the ClassWizard to override the **OnUpdate** function in the **CDrawView** class and modify it so it looks like Listing 15.33.

Listing 15.33
Modifying the **OnUpdate** function

```
    void CDrawView::OnUpdate(CView* pSender, LPARAM lHint,
        CObject* pHint)
    {
        CDrawDoc* pDoc = GetDocument();
        int numPoints = pDoc->GetNumPoints();
        if (numPoints==0)
            return;
        CPoint point = pDoc->GetPoint(numPoints - 1);
        CClientDC dc(this);
        // match the DC to the CScrollView
        OnPrepareDC(&dc);
```

```
        dc.SetPixel(point,RGB(0,0,255));
    }
```

See Section 15.4, Step 2, and Section 15.5, Step 6, for more information.

15.6.12 Step 12—Modify the OnDraw Function

Use the ClassWizard to find the **OnDraw** function in the **CDrawView** class and modify the function as shown in Listing 15.34.

Listing 15.34
Modifying the **OnDraw** function

```
void CDrawView::OnDraw(CDC* pDC)
{
    CDrawDoc* pDoc = GetDocument();
    ASSERT_VALID(pDoc);

    int x;
    // Redraw all points in the array
    for (x=0; x<pDoc->GetNumPoints(); x++)
        pDC->SetPixel(pDoc->GetPoint(x),
            RGB(0,0,255));
}
```

See Section 15.2, Step 7, for more information.

15.6.13 Step 13—Compile and Run

Compile and run the application. The application will correctly support splitter windows. Because the document and view were correctly created and their responsibilities appropriately subdivided in the previous sections, the framework handles splitter windows automatically and transparently. Figure 15.2 shows a typical run of the application with the splitter windows turned on.

15.7 Adding New Menu Options and Dialogs.

One of the most important features of an AppWizard framework is its ability to allow you to easily add new menus, menu options, and dialogs. The ease with which you can add and manipulate these features comes from the fact that much of the manipulation occurs in the resource file. You modify the menu and dialog resources using standard graphical editors. Then the ClassWizard makes it easy to add a new dialog class to handle the dialog.

To get a feeling for how you can easily add menu options and dialogs to the framework, this example will add a new **Options** menu to the drawing application created in Section 15.6. This menu will contain an item named **Drawing Size** that lets the user change the size of the drawing. The **Drawing Size** option will present a

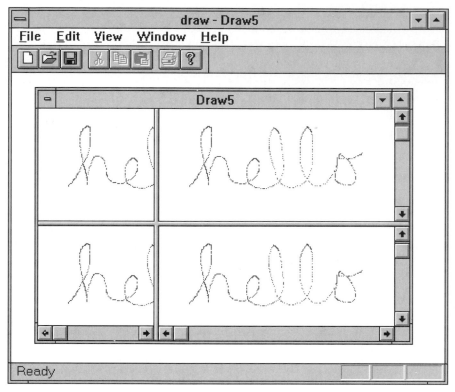

Figure 15.2
The draw application using splitter windows

dialog box that lets the user change the height and width of the scrollable drawing area. You will take the following steps to accomplish this:

1. Add the new **Options** menu and **Drawing Size** menu option to the menu bar.
2. Add an event handler function for the new menu option.
3. Create a new dialog resource that lets the user enter the document's width and height.
4. Create a new dialog class with the ClassWizard to manage the dialog.
5. Wire in the code so the document can activate the dialog and retrieve its data.

You will want to review Chapter 6 to get a good overview of how to create and use menus and new dialog classes.

Note: The EXAMPLES directory on the diskette contains listings that will help you do this example.

15.7.1 Step 1—Start the Application

Start with the completed program from the previous section. This application has scrollable and splittable windows in an MDI framework.

15.7.2 Step 2—Add a New Menu

Open the program's resources as described in Appendix B.6.2. Open the IDR_DRAWTYPE menu (note that the IDR_DRAWTYPE menu is visible when the MDI framework has open views, while the IDR_MAINFRAME menu is visible when there are no views open). Add a new menu named **Options** and add a new menu item named **Drawing Size**. When creating the name for the menu item, be sure to add an "&" symbol in front of the character you wish to use for the mnemonic (see Chapter 6). For example, if you wish to use the "O" in "Options" as the mnemonic, enter the name as "&Options". Move the new menu into a suitable position in the menu bar by dragging it.

If you now double-click on the **Drawing Size** item in the menu resource editor, you will find that the editor has automatically assigned this item the ID of ID_OPTIONS_DRAWINGSIZE. This is the ID that will identify the menu item when you create an event handler for it.

15.7.3 Step 3—Create a Menu Handler Function

Now wire in a handler for the **Drawing Size** menu option. Before doing this it is important to ask yourself a question: "There are several message maps in this application that *could* handle this menu option—which one should I use?" In this case, because it is the **docSize** member variable in the document class that will be affected by the dialog, you should choose the message map in the document class.

Use the ClassWizard to add a new menu handler function as described in Appendix B.7.3. Edit the new event handler and add the following line of code to the new function:

```
AfxMessageBox("Test", MB_OK);
```

15.7.4 Step 4—Compile and Run

Compile and run the program. You will find that when you choose the **Drawing Size** menu option, a message box that says "Test" will appear. Now you can implement the actual dialog box for this option.

15.7.5 Step 5—Create the Dialog Box

Create a new dialog resource as described in Appendix B.5.6. Then take the following steps.

15.7.5.1 Step 5a—Create Static Labels Add two new static items to the dialog as described in Appendix B.5.6. Double-click on each one so you can change the captions. One should display the word "Height" and the other should display the word "Width." You can change the IDs of both if you like, but this is not necessary because we will not be using the IDs.

See Chapter 6 for more information on adding controls to dialogs.

15.7.5.2 Step 5b—Add Edit Controls Add two new Edit controls in a similar manner. Arrange things as shown in Figure 15.3. Double-click on the first edit control and change its ID to IDC_HEIGHT. Change the second control's ID to IDC_WIDTH.

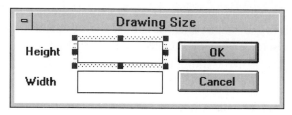

Figure 15.3
The Drawing Size dialog

15.7.5.3   Step 5c—Change the Dialog ID Double-click on the title bar of the new dialog. Change the ID of the dialog to IDD_DRAWINGSIZE and change the caption to "Drawing Size".

15.7.6   Step 6—Create a Dialog Class

Now that you have a new dialog, you need to create a new class to manage the dialog. This class, as described in Chapter 6, will handle the transfer of data to and from the dialog's edit fields and also control when the dialog appears on the screen.

To create the new dialog class see Appendix B.7.4. Name the new class **CSizeDlg** and make sure the **Class Type** is set to **CDialog**. Make sure the **Dialog** field is set to IDD_DRAWINGSIZE.

15.7.7   Step 7—Make the New Dialog Appear

To make the dialog appear in response to the **Drawing Size** menu option, you need to modify the **OnOptionsDrawingsize** function in the **CDrawDoc** class. *You also need to include the SIZEDLG.H file in the DRAWDOC.CPP file. Edit DRAW-DOC.CPP and include SIZEDLG.H as shown in Listing 15.35.*

Listing 15.35
Including the new dialog class

```
// drawdoc.cpp : implementation of the CDrawDoc class
//

#include "stdafx.h"
#include "draw.h"

#include "drawdoc.h"
#include "cobpoint.h"
#include "sizedlg.h"
```

Then find the **OnOptionsDrawingsize** function in the DRAWDOC.CPP file either manually or with the ClassWizard's **Edit Code** button. Change the **OnOp-**

tionsDrawingsize function so instead of displaying a message box it displays the new dialog. The new code is shown in Listing 15.36.

Listing 15.36
Modifying the menu handler for the dialog function

```
void CDrawDoc::OnOptionsDrawingsize()
{
    CSizeDlg dlg(AfxGetMainWnd());
    if (dlg.DoModal()==IDOK)
        AfxMessageBox("OK selected", MB_OK);
}
```

15.7.8 Step 8—Create Member Variables

Now that the dialog appears properly, we need to modify it so the program can assign initial values into the edit field and then retrieve any changes that the user makes. This is done by using the ClassWizard to add two DDX variables to the dialog, one for each edit control. Through a mechanism called Dialog Data Exchange (DDX), these two variables will directly mirror the values in the edit controls. See Chapter 22 for more information about DDX. We can also use another mechanism, called Dialog Data Verification (DDV), to make sure the values the user enters are appropriate.

To add the two variables, see Appendix B.7.5. Add a variable for both the IDC_HEIGHT and IDC_WIDTH controls. Name the new variables **m_height** and **m_width** respectively. Make them value variables, and for the variable type choose **UINT**. Type in whatever you want for the minimum and maximum values for each of these variables.

If you now look at the top of the SIZEDLG.H file, you will find the two variables **m_height** and **m_width** have been added, as shown in Listing 15.37.

Listing 15.37
The ClassWizard's modifications to the dialog

```
/////////////////////////////////////////////////////////////
// CSizeDlg dialog

class CSizeDlg : public CDialog
{
// Construction
public:
    CSizeDlg(CWnd* pParent = NULL);   // standard constructor

// Dialog Data
    //{{AFX_DATA(CSizeDlg)
    enum { IDD = IDD_DRAWINGSIZE };
    UINTm_height;
    UINTm_width;
```

```
//}}AFX_DATA
```

You will also see evidence of the two new variables in SIZEDLG.CPP. The constructor will initialize them to zero, and the **DoDataExchange** function will verify them, as shown in Listing 15.38.

Listing 15.38
The ClassWizard's modification's to the dialog's constructor and **DoDataExchange** functions

```
CSizeDlg::CSizeDlg(CWnd* pParent /*=NULL*/)
    : CDialog(CSizeDlg::IDD, pParent)
{
    //{{AFX_DATA_INIT(CSizeDlg)
    m_height = 0;
    m_width = 0;
    //}}AFX_DATA_INIT
}

void CSizeDlg::DoDataExchange(CDataExchange* pDX)
{
    CDialog::DoDataExchange(pDX);
    //{{AFX_DATA_MAP(CSizeDlg)
    DDX_Text(pDX, IDC_HEIGHT, m_height);
    DDV_MinMaxUInt(pDX, m_height, 1, 1000000);
    DDX_Text(pDX, IDC_WIDTH, m_width);
    DDV_MinMaxUInt(pDX, m_width, 1, 1000000);
    //}}AFX_DATA_MAP
}
```

See Chapter 22 for details on DDX and DDV.

15.7.9 Step 9—Get and Set the Variables

There are two ways to modify member variables in a dialog class. One is to access them directly. This technique is easier and therefore common and was demonstrated in Chapter 6. It has the disadvantage of breaking the encapsulation of the dialog class. The second way involves the use of functions to get and set the member variables. This technique is stylistically pure but takes a bit more work. We will use the second technique in this section. The first technique is shown in Chapter 18.

Modify the constructor of the **CSizeDlg** class so it accepts initial values for the two DDX member variables, and also create a **GetSize** function, as described in Chapter 6, that retrieves the values that the user sets when the dialog is on the screen. Manually modify the constructor in SIZEDLG.CPP so it looks like Listing 15.39.

Listing 15.39
Modifying the dialog's constructor

```
CSizeDlg::CSizeDlg(CSize size, CWnd* pParent /*=NULL*/)
    : CDialog(CSizeDlg::IDD, pParent)
{
    //{{AFX_DATA_INIT(CSizeDlg)
    m_height = size.cy;
    m_width = size.cx;
    //}}AFX_DATA_INIT
}
```

Also manually modify the prototype for this function in SIZEDLG.H to reflect the new parameter, as shown in Listing 15.40.

Listing 15.40
Modifying the constructor's prototype

```
class CSizeDlg : public CDialog
{
// Construction
public:
    CSizeDlg(CSize size, CWnd* pParent = NULL);
...
```

Now, in SIZEDLG.H, manually add a new function named **GetSize**. The purpose of this function is to extract the new width and height the user enters in the dialog. The function prototype should appear as shown in Listing 15.41.

Listing 15.41
Adding a prototype for the **GetSize** function to the dialog.

```
...
// Dialog Data
    //{{AFX_DATA(CSizeDlg)
    enum { IDD = IDD_DRAWINGSIZE };
    UINTm_height;
    UINTm_width;
    //}}AFX_DATA
    CSize GetSize();

// Overrides
...
```

In SIZEDLG.CPP, manually add the new **GetSize** function at the bottom of the file. Its implementation should appear as shown in Listing 15.42.

Listing 15.42
Implementing the dialog's **GetSize** function

```
CSize CSizeDlg::GetSize()
```

```
    {
        CSize size(m_width, m_height);
        return size;
    }
```

Change the **OnOptionsDrawingsize** function in DRAWDOC.CPP so the function properly calls the dialog's constructor with the current document size and then sets the document's size if the user clicks the OK button in the dialog, as shown in Listing 15.43.

Listing 15.43
Fully implementing the **OnOptionsDrawingSize** function.

```
void CDrawDoc::OnOptionsDrawingsize()
{
    CSizeDlg dlg(docSize, AfxGetMainWnd());
    if (dlg.DoModal()==IDOK)
    {
        if (AfxMessageBox("OK to delete drawing?",
            MB_OKCANCEL)==IDOK)
        {
            docSize = dlg.GetSize();
            DeleteContents();
            UpdateAllViews(NULL, 1, NULL);
        }
    }
}
```

Note that this function has to handle several problems. First, because the drawing size can potentially shrink when the user changes it, the document must be cleared if the user changes the size. Otherwise, the document could contain points that are outside the boundaries of the new drawing size. This is the same thing that the Paintbrush application does when the user changes the drawing size. Therefore, the function calls **AfxMessageBox** to ask the user if it is OK to delete the current drawing. If it is, the code changes the document's size, deletes the contents of the document, and then calls **UpdateAllViews**.

The call to **UpdateAllViews** is solving a second problem. Now that the document's size has changed and the document contains no data, the document class has to inform all the document's views. **UpdateAllViews** is the best way to do this. Note that the call to **UpdateAllViews** passes a special hint value of 1 to signify this special type of update. You must now modify the **OnUpdate** function in DRAWVIEW.CPP to recognize this hint, as shown in Listing 15.44.

Listing 15.44
Modifying the **OnUpdate** function

```
void CDrawView::OnUpdate(CView* pSender,
```

```
                LPARAM lHint, CObject* pHint)
    {
        CDrawDoc* pDoc = GetDocument();
        if (lHint==1)
        {
            SetScrollSizes(MM_TEXT, GetDocument()->GetDocSize());
            Invalidate();
            return;
        }
        int numPoints = pDoc->GetNumPoints();
        if (numPoints==0)
            return;
        CPoint point = pDoc->GetPoint(numPoints - 1);
        CClientDC dc(this);
        // match the DC to the CScrollView
        OnPrepareDC(&dc);
        dc.SetPixel(point,RGB(0,0,255));
    }
```

In this new version of **OnUpdate**, the hint value of 1 causes the view to reset its scroll sizes and then invalidate its contents to clear the view. The integer 1 is used here for clarity—in production code, you would declare a constant or use a different technique to signal change.

15.7.10 Step 10—Compile and Run

Compile and run the program. When you choose the **Drawing Size** item in the **Options** menu you should see the Drawing Size dialog with a default width and height of 2,000. When you change these sizes and click the **OK** button, you should see a dialog asking if it is OK to delete the drawing. If you click the **OK** button here, any views on the document will clear and the scroll bars will reflect the new drawing size.

15.7.11 Understanding the New Dialog

You made a number of changes to the drawing program to add a new dialog to it. Let's review the steps that you *must* take whenever you add any new dialog to an application, and then look at the specific additional changes made here to integrate the dialog into the application.

To add a new dialog to an application, you must do the following:

1. Create the dialog's template with the dialog resource editor. To do this, create a new dialog resource and then add all the appropriate controls to the dialog.
2. Create a dialog class for the dialog with the ClassWizard as described in Appendix B.7.4.
3. In the ClassWizard, create DDX variables for each control on the dialog that will contain data entered by the user. This section showed how to add DDX variables for Edit controls. See Chapter 22 for information on adding DDX variables for all other control types.
4. Create a menu option that will invoke the new dialog.

5. In the menu option's handler function, create an instance of the dialog class and call the dialog's **DoModal** function. You may wish to initialize dialog variables before calling **DoModal**. See Chapters 6 and 22 for details. *Be sure to include the dialog class's H file at the top of the file that contains the menu's handler.*

6. Extract the values from the DDX variables and apply them to the application in whatever way is appropriate.

In this application, we applied these general steps when creating the dialog. Additionally, we applied the results of the dialog to the application. In this case we did the following:

1. Set the document's size variable.
2. Cleared the document's data structure.
3. Notified all the views of the change.

There are numerous additional changes that you could make to further adapt this program to changing drawing sizes. For example, if the user is *increasing* the size of the drawing, there is no real need to clear the contents of the document. That is easily handled with an **if** statement. If the user is shrinking the drawing size, however, you may have noticed a problem. Say the user shrinks the document size to 20 x 20 for some reason. The size of the view does not change. What you would probably like to do is, in the **OnMouseMove** event handler, ignore points that fall outside the valid drawing size. You might also like to draw two lines, as Paintbrush does, to show the user the maximum document size.

15.8 Printing

In the previous sections of this chapter we have dealt with the internal structure and user interface for a simple drawing program. In this section we will examine the printing model that the AppWizard framework uses and demonstrate how to use this structure to add printing options to this program.

Printing functionality is built into the **CView** class and is activated when you request the **Printing and Print Preview** option in the AppWizard. When you select this option, the AppWizard will create three extra options in the **File** menu named **Print**, **Print Preview,** and **Print Setup**.

Selection of the printing option also causes small but fundamental changes in the AppWizard's framework. If you create a new framework, turn on printing, and then look at the view class generated by the AppWizard, you will find that the class contains several specific changes related to printing. In particular, you will find that the view's message map contains entries to handle the **Print** and **Print Preview** menu options (the application class handles **Print Setup**), and you will find stubs to manage the **OnPreparePrinting**, **OnBeginPrinting,** and **OnEndPrinting** functions.

Printing is not particularly easy, and there is no single or best way to do it. The code shown in this section is optimized for ease of understanding, but there are many other ways to accomplish the same thing. See the documentation, the MFC Encyclopedia, and sample programs like CHKBOOK in the Visual C++ Samples directory for additional information.

15.8.1 Understanding the Native Features

To understand how the framework implements printing, let's start by building a new framework and creating the same application demonstrated in Section 15.6. The only difference here will be that the framework includes printing capabilities. We can then examine what the framework handles automatically and why. This knowledge will allow us to customize the program to take full advantage of framework's printing facilities.

Note: See the EXAMPLES directory on the diskette.

15.8.1.1 Step 1— Reconstruct the Program Start by recreating the program

discussed in Section 15.6. This program is a drawing area application with scrollable, splittable windows of size 2,000 x 2,000. When you create the framework with the AppWizard, enable the printing capability by clicking on the **Printing and Print Preview** option in the AppWizard's setup screen.

15.8.1.2 Step 2—Test the Printing Features Compile and run the program. You

will find three new options in the **File** menu: **Print, Print Preview,** and **Print Setup**.

The **Print Setup** menu does exactly what you expect, leveraging off the standard Print dialog you saw in Chapter 7 to give the user the ability to change printers. This is an automatic capability that you will probably never change.

The **Print Preview** option gives you just the sort of preview capability you would expect in any advanced Windows application, as shown in Figure 15.4. You can view one or two pages, move forward and backward between the pages, zoom, and print. The **Print** button on the preview's button bar lets you print directly from the preview screen.

If you try drawing something in a drawing view and then switch to the print preview screen, you will see that your drawing appears there. You can choose the **Print** option in the **File** menu to actually print the drawing on your printer.

Given the fact that you have had to do absolutely nothing to get it, this is a startling amount of functionality. Again, it all works at no cost because the original program was designed to properly exploit the document/view paradigm.

15.8.2 Understanding Printing

The view class contains several functions that allow the framework to handle printing. These functions are listed below:

- OnBeginPrinting
- OnEndPrinting
- OnEndPrintPreview
- OnPrepareDC
- OnPreparePrinting
- OnPrint

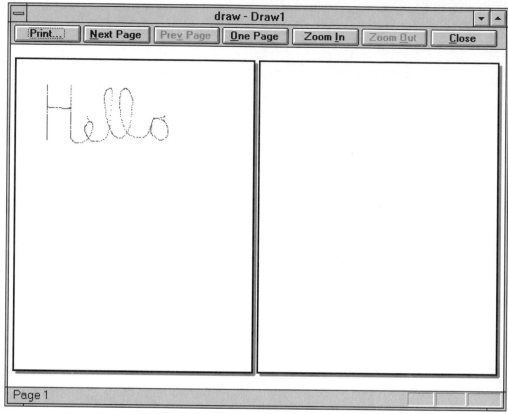

Figure 15.4
The print preview screen

Also important to the process is a class called the **CPrintInfo** class. To gain a full understanding of these functions and the **CPrintInfo** class, you should read the detailed description of each one in books on-line. You should also find and read the sections on printing in the MFC Encyclopedia.

For any printing operation, the framework goes through a very specific, choreographed set of function calls. If you understand the choreography, the whole printing system is much easier to understand. See Figure 15.5 for a summary of the flow.

Each of the functions shown in Figure 15.5 has a specific intended purpose that is described in the documentation. That purpose is facilitated by the parameters that each function receives. All of them receive a pointer to an instance of the **CPrintInfo** class. This class contains information about the current print job, as summarized below:

Data Members

m_pPD	Pointer to the Print dialog
m_bPreview	Flag that is TRUE if in preview mode
m_bContinuePrinting	Set this flag to FALSE in OnPrint to halt print loop

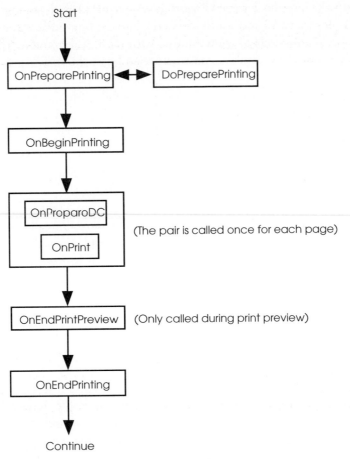

Figure 15.5
Printing function choreography

m_nCurPage	Page number currently being printed (starts at 1)
m_nNumPreviewPages	Either 1 or 2, depending on preview mode
m_lpUserData	User data
m_rectDraw	Usable page area
m_strPageDesc	Format string for page number

Attribute Functions

SetMinPage	Sets page number for the first page in the document
SetMaxPage	Sets page number for the last page in the document
GetMinPage	Page number for the first page in the document
GetMaxPage	Page number for the last page in the document
GetFromPage	Returns contents of From box in dialog
GetToPage	Returns contents of To box in dialog

Because the same instance of **CPrintClass** is passed to all the functions in Figure 15.5, the instance acts as a way for the framework to communicate with your code, as well as a way for your code to communicate with itself. For example, you can point the **m_lpUserData** data member to a structure and pass the structure from function to function.

The functions shown in Figure 15.5 have the following intended purposes:

- OnPreparePrinting—Override this function to do any general initialization. In particular, you should call **SetMaxPage** if possible here to initialize the maximum number of pages before the display of the Print dialog.

- DoPreparePrinting—This function displays the Print dialog. You generally will not change this function. In some cases, however, you will want to eliminate the printing dialog altogether. If you want to avoid displaying the dialog, then override **OnPreparePrinting** and remove the call to this function.

- OnBeginPrinting—Override this function to do any general initialization, such as creation of GDI objects needed during printing. Also override to check any information relating to the results in the Print dialog. At this point the printer DC is known and complete.

- OnPrepareDC—Each time a page is printed, this function will be called, immediately followed by **OnPrint**. Do any preparation to the DC here. Note that the **m_rectDraw** member in **pInfo** will be invalid the first time this function is called.

- OnPrint—This function does the actual printing. By default it simply calls **OnDraw**. That is why, without any modification, the drawing appeared in the print preview screen and on the printer when you added printing capabilities to the drawing program. If the application does not use **OnDraw** to update the display, this step will require modification. See Chapter 18 for an example.

- OnEndPrintPreview—If in Print Preview mode, this function will be called when the user closes the preview screen. You can use this opportunity to check the current page number and set the display to that page.

- OnEndPrinting—Clean up anything you created in **OnBeginPrinting**.

15.8.3 Improving Printing

Rerun the program that you created in Section 15.8.1, draw something recognizable, and print the page by selecting the **Print** option in the **File** menu. There are several important problems to notice in this printout. In this section we will look at those problems and then work toward some solutions.

If you printed the drawing on a typical 300 DPI laser printer, then what you will first notice is that the entire drawing fits on a single sheet of paper, but that it is fairly small compared to how it appears on your screen. If you printed it on a 100 or 150 DPI dot matrix printer, you probably noticed that the entire drawing did not fit on a single sheet of paper, but that only one sheet was printed. If you are fortunate to own a 2500 DPI printer, you will notice that the entire drawing fits in about a 0.80 inch square. Obviously there is a scaling problem as you move from printer to printer.

This scaling problem arises because the mapping mode (see Chapter 11) of the drawing is set to MM_TEXT in the call to **SetScrollSizes** in Section 15.6.10. The MM_TEXT mapping mode causes drawing coordinates to be interpreted in the *device coordinate system* of whatever device happens to be handling the output. On the screen, the device coordinates are the pixels that you see and their density is 75 to 100 per inch of screen space depending on monitor size, dot pitch, etc. As you print the same drawing on printers with different dot densities, the size of the drawing changes accordingly.

The solution to this problem is to change the drawing to a mapping mode that is device independent. Windows offers several different device-independent mapping modes as described in Chapter 11. We can try one of these out by modifying the call to **SetScrollSizes** in Section 15.6.10 to the following:

```
SetScrollSizes(MM_LOENGLISH, GetDocument()->GetDocSize());
```

You could just as easily use any of the other mapping modes. The **LOENGLISH** mode happens to use 1/100th of an inch as its unit of measure. Therefore, a 100 x 100 rectangle drawn on the screen will appear as a one-inch x one-inch square on any printer, regardless of the printer's dot density.

If you change the mapping mode and recompile the program, you will notice absolutely no change in the program's screen appearance. It will work exactly as it did before. However, you will notice a significant difference when you print the image to a printer. If you print it to a 300 DPI laser printer, you will find that the **SetPixel** call that draws the image on the printer creates individual dots that are very tiny—so tiny that they appear on the page as a light gray fog. These dots are 1/300th of an inch across and spaced much more widely on the page. However, the figure on the page will accurately mimic the size of the drawing on the screen. It will have the exact same size no matter what sort of printer you print it on.

To correct the dot-size problem, modify the program so it prints small rectangles instead of dots. The rectangles will have an identical size regardless of the printer chosen. For example, replace the two calls to **SetPixel** in the view class with the following:

If you see:

```
dc.SetPixel(point,RGB(0,0,255));
```

replace it with:

```
dc.Rectangle(point.x, point.y, point.x+5, point.y-5);
```

You may also want to use a brush (Chapter 11) to fill in the rectangle. Note that five is *subtracted* from the Y coordinate. The MM_LOENGLISH mapping mode uses a negative coordinate on the Y axis rather than a positive one, as described in Chapter 11.

15.8.4 Multi-Page Printing

Now that the drawing program uses the LOENGLISH mapping mode, you have created another problem. A 2,000 x 2,000 drawing measures 20 inches x 20 inches on any printer and this is much too big to fit on a single sheet of paper. To solve this problem, you need to override and modify the **OnBeginPrinting**, **OnPrint,** and **OnPrepareDC** functions in the view class to handle multi-page printing. Use the ClassWizard to override them and then modify them both as shown in Listing 15.45.

Listing 15.45
Modifications to the **OnPrint** and **OnPrepareDC** functions to allow multi-page printing

```
BOOL contPrint;

void CDrawView::OnBeginPrinting(CDC* pDC, CPrintInfo* pInfo)
{
    contPrint = TRUE;
}

void CDrawView::OnPrint(CDC* pDC, CPrintInfo* pInfo)
{
    // Page size
    CRect rectPage = pInfo->m_rectDraw;
    // Document size
    CSize sizeDrawing = GetDocument()->GetDocSize();

    // Figure out number of pages down and across
    int nPagesAcross = sizeDrawing.cx / rectPage.Width();
    if (sizeDrawing.cx % rectPage.Width() != 0)
        nPagesAcross++;
    int nPagesDown = sizeDrawing.cy / abs(rectPage.Height());
    if (sizeDrawing.cy % rectPage.Height() != 0)
        nPagesDown++;

    // Handle the end of the document
    // print mode
    pInfo->SetMaxPage(nPagesDown * nPagesAcross);
    // preview mode
    if (!pInfo->m_bPreview)
        if (pInfo->m_nCurPage >= UINT(nPagesDown * nPagesAcross))
            contPrint = FALSE;

    // Figure out appropriate origin
    int nAcross = (pInfo->m_nCurPage - 1) % nPagesAcross;
    int nDown = (pInfo->m_nCurPage - 1) / nPagesAcross;
    pDC->SetWindowOrg(CPoint(
        nAcross*rectPage.Width(),
        nDown*rectPage.Height()));

    // do the actual printing
    CScrollView::OnPrint(pDC, pInfo);
}

void CDrawView::OnPrepareDC(CDC* pDC, CPrintInfo* pInfo)
{
    CScrollView::OnPrepareDC(pDC, pInfo);
    // handle end of document in print mode
    if (pInfo)
```

```
        if (!pInfo->m_bPreview)
            pInfo->m_bContinuePrinting = contPrint;
}
```

If you use the ClassWizard to add the code as shown in Listing 15.45 to your program, what you will find is that the print preview screen works correctly, allowing you to use the **Next** and **Previous** buttons to move between pages. The **Print** option in the **File** menu also works, printing the entire drawing. If you were to remove the code that is shown in bold face in Listing 15.1, you would find that the print preview functionality still works correctly, but that the **Print** option in the **File** menu has a tendency to produce an infinite number of pages.

It is important to look at this code in some detail to fully understand what it is trying to accomplish. It also demonstrates several subtle features of the underlying framework that you need to be aware of so you can step around them.

The fundamental printing problem in this drawing application involves pagination. You need to figure out how to divide a large drawing across multiple pages. In order to perform the pagination, you need to know the size of a sheet of paper in logical coordinates. In the ideal case, this information would be available to you in an easy-to-use form when the framework calls the **OnPreparePrinting** function. With this information in hand, you could calculate the number of sheets of paper required to print the drawing and then call **pInfo->SetMaxPage** there.

In theory the information *is* available in the **m_rectDraw** member of the **pInfo** parameter. Unfortunately, this member does not get initialized until the point immediately following the first call to **OnPrepareDC** and just before the first call to **OnPrint**. To know the page size in **OnPreparePrinting**, therefore, you would have to call the **GetPrinterDeviceDefaults** in the **CWinApp** class, get the printer DC with the **GetPrinterDC** function of the Print dialog class, and then get the horizontal and vertical resolution of the printer from the DC using code like that shown below (see also Chapter 11):

```
pageWidth = dc->GetDeviceCaps(HORZRES);
pageHeight = dc->GetDeviceCaps(VERTRES);
```

Then you would need to convert this device information into the LOENGLISH logical coordinate system (or you could set the mapping mode of the DC before calling **GetDeviceCaps**). If you were to do all of that, you could call **SetMaxPage** properly in **OnPreparePrinting**. The print preview screen would then provide you with the extra bonus of a scroll bar that allows the user to scroll through all the available pages. This technique is used in the CHKBOOK Sample.

An alternative would be to set the maximum number of pages in the **OnBeginPrinting** function, because in that function the DC is available from the parameter list. You still need to set the DC's mapping mode and call **GetDeviceCaps**, but at least you are saved the trouble of extracting the DC from the dialog.

The code in Listing 15.45 has taken the option of postponing the number-of-pages determination until the **OnPrint** function. At this point in the code, the

m_rectDraw member of the **pInfo** parameter contains valid information about the page size. The code in Listing 15.45 uses that information, along with the document size, to calculate the number of pages needed across and down. It combines that knowledge with the current page number to modify the origin of the DC. The preferred place for this origin-modification activity is **OnPrepareDC**, but as stated before, the **m_rectDraw** member of the **pInfo** parameter does not contain valid information until the *second* call to **OnPrepareDC**. You may want to modify the structure of the code to see how to take advantage of that fact.

Note also that the **OnPrint** function is doing a certain amount of redundant calculation. You could calculate the number of pages across and down once, and then store them in static variables, member variables, or in user data structures that you associate with the user data member in the **pInfo** parameter.

By calling **SetMaxPage** in **OnPrint**, you satisfy the print preview screen's requirements and it will work properly. However, during an actual printing operation this action is insufficient. Instead, during an actual printing operation, you have to set the **m_bContinuePrinting** member to FALSE *in the **OnPrepareDC** function*. It will not work if you set it in the **OnPrint** function, at least in version 3.0 of MFC. The lines shown in bold face in Listing 15.45 handle this problem. Note that, in **OnPrepareDC**, you need to make sure **pInfo** is not NULL before checking its members. When **OnPrepareDC** is called during a screen update, **pInfo** will be NULL.

For more information on printing, See Chapter 18.

15.9 Conclusion

In this chapter you have learned how to take an AppWizard framework and turn it into a fairly complete drawing application with scrollable and splittable windows and a new dialog that lets the user set the drawing's size. The application can also print its documents.

There are numerous additions that you can make to this application. For example, you might give the user the ability to change colors and/or dot size and modify the **CObPoint** class appropriately to handle the new data. Add menu items and dialogs to accept necessary input for these options from the user. You might also want to look at Chapter 11 and then add code that lets the user create rubber-banded lines, circles, and rectangles in the drawing. The possibilities are almost endless. The nice thing, as you have seen in the sections above, is that the AppWizard framework, the ClassWizard, and the resource editors built into Visual C++ make it extremely easy to add features to the application.

One useful activity at this point would be to review all the functions available in the **CDocument**, **CView**, and **CScrollView** classes in the MFC documentation. By being aware of what functions are available, you can have a much better idea of the different possibilities when adding capabilities to your applications. You may also wish to work through the Scribble tutorial in the on-line documentation, because it contains many of the same capabilities described here. You will find that the tutorial is extremely easy to understand because of the experience you have gained in this chapter.

You should now understand all the basic concepts involved in working with an AppWizard framework. In the remaining chapters in Part 3, you will learn how to create other types of applications by modifying the behavior of AppWizard frameworks.

CREATING AN EDITOR
WITH CEDITVIEW

16

It is surprisingly easy to create an MDI text editor application with the AppWizard. In fact, you can do it without writing a single line of code. The thing that makes it so easy is a class in MFC called **CEditView**, which you first saw in Chapter 10. In this chapter you will learn how to use this class, both on its own to create a text editor application and together with other document templates to create applications that display multiple document types simultaneously.

16.1 Creating an MDI Text Editor

This section shows you the steps that you take to create an MDI text editor with the AppWizard.

16.1.1 Step 1—Create the Framework

Create a new MDI framework with the AppWizard. Give the new project the name "ed". See Appendix B.6.1 for more details.

As you go through the AppWizard option screens, select the following options:
- Choose the **Multiple-Document** option.
- Choose **None** for database support.
- Choose **None** for OLE support.
- Use the file extension "tex". See Appendix B.6.3 for details
- Leave all file and class names as chosen by the AppWizard. You should now be able to change the base class of the view to **CEditView**. See Appendix B.6.4 for details. (The **CScrollView** class is discussed in Chapter 15 and the **CFormView** class is discussed in Chapter 17.)

This last step simply modifies the base class of the view. If you look in the file ED-VIEW.H, you will find that **CEdView** now inherits its behavior from **CEditView** as shown below:

```
// edview.h : interface of the CEdView class
```

391

```
//
/////////////////////////////////////////////////////////////////

class CEdView : public CEditView
{
...
```

16.1.2 Step 2—Compile and Run

Compile the program and run it. You should find that you have a complete MDI editor. All the clipboard options should work properly. You should be able to create as many new windows as you like. **Open**, **Save,** and **Save As** should present the proper dialogs and work as expected.

16.2 Understanding the Editor

In Chapter 8 you learned about the multi-line text control. The **CEditView** control simply combines that control with code that gives the class the ability to automatically handle certain command IDs, such as ID_FILE_PRINT or ID_EDIT_CUT. These IDs are generated by the menu bar of the AppWizard framework. If you look in the MFC documentation for the **CEditView** class, you will find it automatically does just about everything you would expect from a simple text editor including file opening and closing, clipboard operations, and find operations.

The command IDs that the **CEditView** class automatically recognizes are listed below:

ID_EDIT_CUT	Normal clipboard cut operation
ID_EDIT_COPY	Normal clipboard copy operation
ID_EDIT_PASTE	Normal clipboard paste operation
ID_EDIT_UNDO	Normal undo operation
ID_EDIT_CLEAR	Normal clipboard delete operation
ID_EDIT_SELECT_ALL	Selects entire document
ID_EDIT_FIND	Finds occurrence of the specified string
ID_EDIT_REPLACE	Replaces string with specified string
ID_EDIT_REPEAT	Repeats last find/replace operation
ID_FILE_PRINT	Prints the current document

The standard framework generated by the AppWizard includes the first four options automatically as part of its standard menu structure for the **Edit** menu. The **CEditView** class automatically detects these commands as the user selects them in the menu because the AppWizard by default chooses ID names identical to what the **CEditView** class expects.

To activate the other options, you can simply add new options to the menu bar using the menu resource editor. As long as the IDs of your new menu options match what the **CEditView** class expects, the options will work automatically. Simply by adding menu options, you enable the capabilities.

To try out some of these options, open the resource view. Then open the menu labeled IDR_EDTYPE and add the menu items shown in Figure 16.1 to the application's menu. Double-click on each menu option after you add it to make sure its ID is correct.

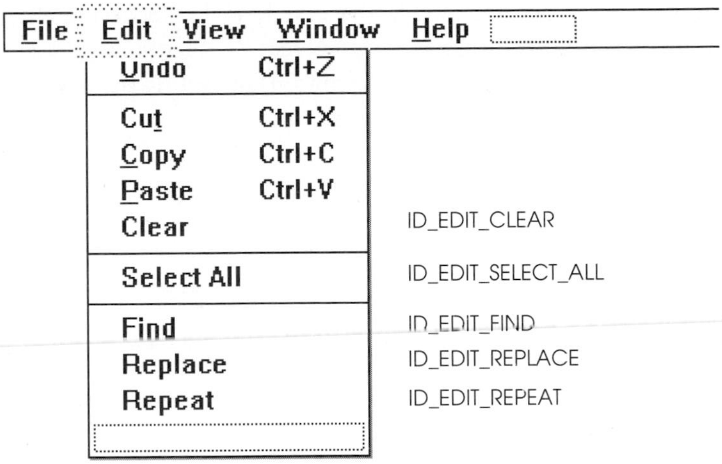

Figure 16.1
Adding new menu options to the editor application

After you have added the new menu options, close the menu resource editor window and rebuild the application. Visual C++ will recompile the resource file and then relink. Execute the application and open a text file. You will find that all the new options work as expected.

There is nothing forcing you to add the options to the **Edit** menu as shown in Figure 16.1. For example, you could create a **Search** menu and add the **Find**, **Replace,** and **Repeat** options to it. You will have to correct the IDs that the Menu editor automatically assigns to these options because it will automatically name them ID_SEARCH_FIND, ID_SEARCH_REPLACE, and ID_SEARCH_REPEAT. Simply rename the IDs as ID_EDIT_FIND, ID_EDIT_REPLACE, and ID_EDIT_REPEAT. Once you do that, the **CEditView** class will recognize them and these options will work as expected.

As you can see, the **CEditView** class is a tremendous convenience. It encapsulates all the behavior associated with a text editor in a single, easy-to-use class that fits the document/view paradigm, and it handles the details of that editor internally. However, you should be aware of one problem with the **CEditView** class while you are using it: The **CEditView** class violates the document data-handling guidelines that you learned about in Chapters 14 and 15.

The **CEditView** class is built from a normal **CEdit** control. As discussed in Chapter 8, this control stores all its data internally. If a **CEdit** control is displaying a 15,000 byte text file, the characters are stored inside the control itself. The same holds true for the **CEditView** class. One advantage of this structure is that it makes the class extremely easy to use. On the other hand, it makes it difficult or impossible to support the **UpdateAllViews** capability described for the drawing editor in Section 15.4. The document class in this editor application is not storing the data for the document. Instead, each individual view is.

A good question to ask, then, is, "Do we even need a document class in this editor application?" Technically, we do not. However, the document class automatically handles the **Open**, **Save,** and **Save As** menu options by calling the **Serialize** function. By leaving the document class in place you can take advantage of this automatic handling mechanism. A single line in the document's **Serialize** function serializes the ASCII text data held by the control. The document class's built-in functionality is easily tapped to implement these menu options. The document class really does nothing else. It does not hold any data. It is simply used as a convenience.

You should eliminate the **New Window** option from the **Window** menu in the editor application because it will never work properly unless you add code that keeps multiple views synchronized. While it is possible to implement multi-view functionality for a single document, you would have to write a good bit of code to make the synchronization work in an efficient way.

16.3 Combining Two Documents and Views in a Single Application

When you generate any MDI framework with the AppWizard, you have the option of allowing the application to handle several different document types simultaneously. That is, the MDI framework can allow the user to open several different types of documents in the same MDI application. It is very easy to demonstrate this capability by combining the editor application demonstrated above with the drawing application seen in the previous chapter. After combining them, we will have a single application capable of opening and editing both drawings and text files simultaneously.

The feature that makes this combination possible is the "document template" capability built into the MFC class hierarchy. Templates are created in the **InitInstance** function in the application class. For example, the **InitInstance** function in the editor application we created above looks like this:

```
CMultiDocTemplate* pDocTemplate;
pDocTemplate = new CMultiDocTemplate(
    IDR_EDTYPE,
    RUNTIME_CLASS(CEdDoc),
    RUNTIME_CLASS(CChildFrame), // custom MDI child frame
    RUNTIME_CLASS(CEdView));
AddDocTemplate(pDocTemplate);
```

This is the section of the program that bonds a document to a view and then links both of them to the application's frame window. The **AddDocTemplate** function adds a document template to the application. The constructor for the **CMultiDocTemplate** class creates the template to add. The template consists of four parts:

1. A constant that is used to extract standard resources from the resource file
2. The document class

3. The view's window frame
4. The view class.

The constant, in this case IDR_EDTYPE, is particularly interesting because it has several side effects. If you look at the resources in the resource file, you will find three different resources tagged with that same constant:

1. One of the application's two menu bars is named IDR_EDTYPE
2. One of the application's icons is named IDR_EDTYPE
3. One of the strings near the top of the string table is named IDR_EDTYPE (see the MFC documentation's description of **CDocTemplate::GetDocString** for more information on this string)

You can see that the IDR_EDTYPE ID references the three different things in the resource file that go with an individual view window: its icon, its menu, and its document string.

When you add a second document template to an application, the application becomes able to handle two different types of documents simultaneously in the same MDI framework. For example, say that you create an application that contains templates for both a text editor and drawing editor. When the user chooses the **New** option in the **File** menu, the application will display a dialog asking the user what type of document it should create. Once the user has several MDI windows open, when the user clicks on a text editor window the menu bar will change to a text editor menu, and when the user clicks on a drawing editor window the menu bar will change to a drawing editor menu. Minimizing either type of window will yield the correct icon.

The best way to get a feel for the possibilities is to create an application that includes multiple document types. To do this, take the following steps.

16.3.1 Step 1—Create a Drawing Program

Go back to Chapter 15 and create, from scratch, an MDI drawing editor application as you did in Section 15.4 (or, if you have a working drawing editor from that chapter available, you can use it). Compile the application and make sure it is working properly. Keep that project open and apply the following changes to it.

16.3.2 Step 2—Create a New Class

You now have an MDI application that can edit drawings. Our goal is to add to that application the ability to edit text files at the same time. First create a new document and view class for the text editor.

Open the ClassWizard. Create a new class of type **CDocument** (see Appendix B.7.6). Name the new class **CTextDoc**. Now add another new class of type **CEdit-View.** Name this new class **CTextView**.

16.3.2.1 Step 3—Modify the Document Class
In the new TEXTDOC.CPP file, find the **Serialize** function and add the following line to the end of it:

```
((CTextView*)m_viewList.GetHead())->SerializeRaw(ar);
```

This line will cause the edit windows to properly serialize themselves. This line was added automatically to the framework that the AppWizard generated in Section 16.1 because the AppWizard created the document and view classes. Here we have to add it manually because the ClassWizard does not have any idea that the document and view classes we just created have any relationship to one another. After modification the **Serialize** function in the **CTextDoc** class should look like this:

```
void CTextDoc::Serialize(CArchive& ar)
{
    // Serialize the text view
    ((CTextView*)m_viewList.GetHead())->SerializeRaw(ar);
}
```

In addition, you will have to add a #include statement at the top of TEXT-DOC.CPP so it includes TEXTVIEW.H, as shown here:

```
// textdoc.cpp : implementation file
//

#include "stdafx.h"
#include "draw.h"
#include "textdoc.h"
#include "textview.h"
...
```

16.3.3 Step 4—Add the Document Template

In the application file named DRAW.CPP, find the **InitInstance** function, and in it find the code that creates the document template. Duplicate that function call and modify it for the new edit classes. When you are done you should have a pair of templates that look like this:

```
CMultiDocTemplate* pDocTemplate;
pDocTemplate = new CMultiDocTemplate(
    IDR_DRAWTYPE,
    RUNTIME_CLASS(CDrawDoc),
    RUNTIME_CLASS(CChildFrame), // standard MDI child frame
    RUNTIME_CLASS(CDrawView));
AddDocTemplate(pDocTemplate);
pDocTemplate = new CMultiDocTemplate(
    IDR_EDTYPE,
    RUNTIME_CLASS(CEdDoc),
    RUNTIME_CLASS(CChildFrame), // custom MDI child frame
    RUNTIME_CLASS(CEdView));
AddDocTemplate(pDocTemplate);
```

Also add the following two include files at the top of DRAW.CPP:

```
#include "textdoc.h"
#include "textview.h"
```

These are the include files for the new editor document and view. If you have named them something different, adjust accordingly.

16.3.4 Step 5—Create New Resources

Open the resource file and use the resource editors to create a new menu bar, an icon, and a string resource for the text editor portion of this application. The easiest way to do this is to duplicate the existing resources for the drawing editor and modify them to handle the text editor.

Find the menu named IDR_DRAWTYPE. Select it by single-clicking on it. Copy it to the clipboard with Ctrl-C and then paste it. Visual C++ will create a new menu resource named IDR_DRAWTYPE1. Rename it to IDR_TEXTTYPE by using the Property dialog. Open the new IDR_TEXTTYPE menu and eliminate the **New Window** option from the **Window** menu. If you would like, add in the menu options for selecting, finding, and printing, as described previously in Section 16.2.

Now move to the icon section of the resource view. Copy the IDR_DRAWTYPE icon and paste it back. Visual C++ will create a new icon resource named IDR_DRAWTYPE1. Rename it IDR_TEXTTYPE. Customize the new icon in any way you like.

Now move to the string table section. Find the string named IDR_DRAWTYPE. Copy and paste it and rename the new string IDR_TEXTTYPE. Modify the new string so that it looks like this:

```
\nText\nText\nText Files (*.tex)\nTEX\nText.Document\nText Document
```

See the MFC documentation description of **CDocTemplate::GetDocString** for more information on this string.

16.3.5 Step 6—Compile and Run

Compile the new application by selecting the **Rebuild All** option in the **Project** menu. Execute it. When the application starts running you should see a dialog asking you what type of document you wish to initially create. Choose either type and draw or type in the new window. Create a second new window of the other type and draw or type into it as appropriate.

With this new application, you should be able to create and manipulate both text and drawing files. As you can see, the addition of the second document template, along with some additions to the resource file, lets the application know about two different document templates. The application can then handle both types equally well.

16.4 Fixing a Subtle Problem

There is one subtle problem with the code presented in Section 16.3. You may notice the problem if you try to open a file that has neither a TEX nor DRW extension. For example, if you try to open a CPP file with the program created in Section 16.3 you will get an error dialog. What you would like for the program to do is understand that anything other than a drawing file should be interpreted as a text file and opened in a text-editing window.

The error dialog appears because the application framework that the AppWizard generated has the following behavior: If the document you are trying to open has an extension that matches none of the document templates, the application uses the first registered document template to try to open the document. In the program in Section 16.3, this behavior causes the application to attempt to open unknown file types as drawing files. Text files, of course, fail when the **CDrawDoc** class tries to read in a text file as serialized drawing information, and it is that failure that produces the dialog.

To get around this particular problem, the solution is straightforward. You need to register the text file template first so it becomes the default template. Then any non-drawing program will be opened as a text file by default.

16.5 Handling Multiple Views on One Document

Imagine an application where you have a single document type, but where you would like to create multiple views on the document's data. For example, you might want to allow the user to view numeric data textually and also as a graph. To create this sort of functionality, you need to create two document templates as demonstrated in the previous exercise. Both templates will use the same document class but different view classes.

If you were to follow the steps described in the previous exercise to add the second document template, the second document template would need to have the same document class and the same window class as the initial template. Only the resource ID and the view class would be different. If you then ran the application, however, you would note a problem: the application would think that the two document templates were separate entities. It would not understand that you are trying to create two separate views on the same document.

The solution to this problem is straightforward. In the document string resource that you create for the second document template, leave the third sub-string blank. The third substring, as described in the documentation under the **GetDocString** function, identifies the name of the document type. By leaving this string out, the framework assumes that you do not want to create a separate document type. Both views are then available for the same document.

This now creates a second problem: There is no way to create an instance of the second view. To solve this problem you can create menu options that invoke instances of the two views. This process is demonstrated in Microsoft's Check Book sample program, which contains a very nice function named **CreateOrActivateFrame** that solves the problem completely (look in SAMPLES\MFC\CHKBOOK for the sample code). You will want to examine this function and use it if you want to create this sort of multi-view functionality.

While examining the Check Book sample code, look also at the document class for the application. It avoids serialization and instead writes directly to a binary file in the same way that Microsoft Money and Quicken do each time the user modifies a transaction. This technique is useful in a variety of applications, and the checkbook example handles it in a very nice way.

16.6 Conclusion

In this chapter you have seen how you can create simple text editor applications. You have also seen how you can add multiple document templates to a single application to create a single MDI program that can open multiple document types. You will find that this is an extremely useful capability when creating high-end applications having a variety of data to display.

Creating a Fahrenheit-to-Celsius Converter

In Chapter 5 you used a basic knowledge of controls, styles, and message maps to create your first real, albeit simple, application: a Fahrenheit to Celsius converter. Now that you know about the AppWizard, the ClassWizard, and the Resource editors, you can implement that same program again using these advanced tools. This will allow you to compare the tools with the "by hand" approach demonstrated in Chapter 5.

This application will also allow you to gain experience with the **CFormView** class in the AppWizard. The **CFormView** class is a specialized view class derived from **CView** that lets you place controls on the face of an SDI application or in the windows of an MDI application. We will use another form view in the next chapter to create an address list application.

One of the best examples of a form view type of interface in the standard Windows interface is the PIF editor, as seen in Figure 17.1. The PIF editor is nothing but a collection of standard Windows controls arranged to form the application's main user interface window. You may also use form views to emulate a paper form that you might be using around the office for order entries, payroll deductions, etc. The form view class makes it easy to create form-like interfaces that exist in the application as a main window rather than as a dialog.

17.1 Creating the Converter

The goal of this application, as it was in Chapter 5, is to allow users to convert Fahrenheit temperatures to Celsius. The application presents the user with a **CEdit** control in which to type a Fahrenheit temperature. The Celsius equivalent will appear in a **CStatic** control below it. In this section we will use the **SetDlgItemInt** and **Get-DlgItemInt** functions that you learned about in Part 1. In Section 17.3 we will revisit this application using DDX and DDV.

17.1.1 Step 1—Creating the Framework

Create a new SDI framework with the AppWizard. Give the new project the name "f2c."

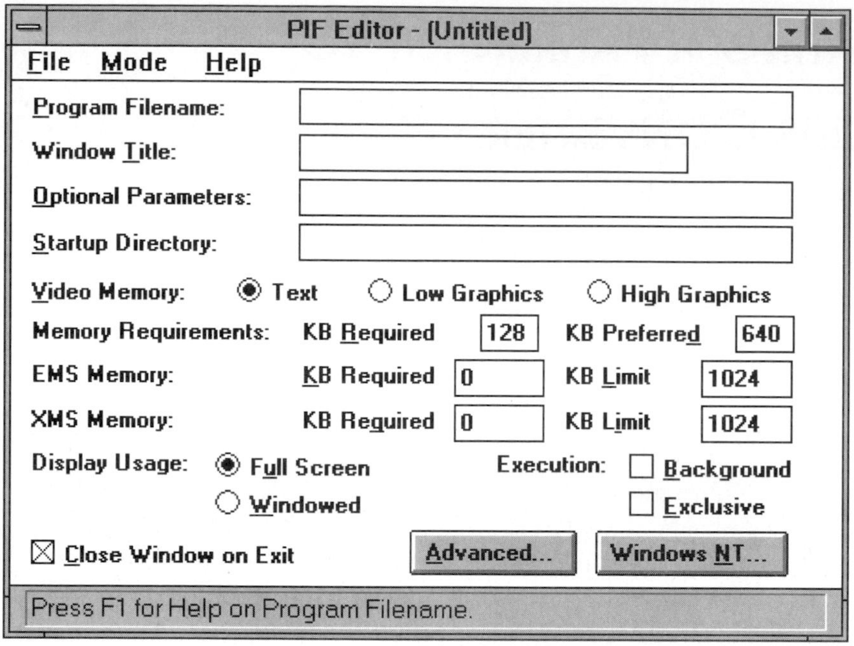

Figure 17.1
The PIF editor, an example of a form-type application interface

As you go through the AppWizard option screens, select the following options:
- Enable or disable any application features as you see fit. Use the file extension "f2c" as described in Appendix B.6.3.
- Chang the base class of the **CF2cView** class to **CFormView** as described in Appendix B.6.4.

The second change simply modifies the base class of the view. If you look in the file F2CVIEW.H, you will find that **CF2cView** now inherits its behavior from **CFormView** as shown below:

```
// f2cview.h : interface of the CF2cView class
//
/////////////////////////////////////////////////////////////

class CF2cView : public CFormView
{...
```

17.1.2 Step 2—Adding Controls to the Form

Open the resource file. Open the dialog named IDD_F2C_FORM. The IDD_F2C_FORM dialog is the form that will act as the main user interface for this application. Delete the TODO static control already in the form. Add in three new statics and a **CEdit** control, as shown in Figure 17.2. *Name the **CEdit** control IDC_FAHRENHEIT and the **CStatic** control containing the zero IDC_CELSIUS.* Double-click on the two controls to change their IDs.

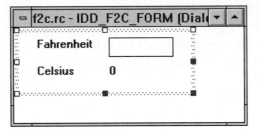

Figure 17.2
Creating the form with the dialog editor

17.1.3 Step 3—Handling Messages

You now need to wire in a message handler for the **CEdit** control so you can detect its changes and then reflect them as the Celsius temperature displayed in the IDC_CELSIUS control. Open the ClassWizard and look at the Message Map section for the **CF2cClass** as described in Appendix B.7.7. Double-click on the IDC_FAHRENHEIT control in the **Object IDs** list of the ClassWizard. Double-click on the EN_CHANGE message. Name the function whatever you like, although the default is a good name.

Edit the code for the new function. Add the code shown in Listing 17.1.

Listing 17.1
The **OnChangeFahrenheit** function

```
void CF2cView::OnChangeFahrenheit()
{
    // Get the fahrenheit temperature
    int temp = GetDlgItemInt(IDC_FAHRENHEIT);
    // Set the Cesius temperature
    SetDlgItemInt(IDC_CELSIUS, (temp - 32)*5/9);
}
```

17.1.4 Step 4—Compile and Run

Compile and run the program. You should see an application like the one shown in Figure 17.3. When you type a Fahrenheit temperature into the edit control, you should immediately see changes in the displayed Celsius temperature.

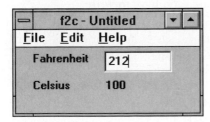

Figure 17.3
The new F2C application

17.2 Understanding the Program

In the previous section you created an application that uses a dialog box resource as the main window for an application. This style of window is called a "form." This style gives you a little more flexibility when designing your applications: For example, if you need to collect information from the user you can either present the user with a modal dialog box to collect information or you can present the user with an MDI child window that contains the same controls. When the request for information is presented as an MDI child window, users have the option to create multiple identical forms simultaneously if they so desire. You might try recreating the F2C application, this time with an MDI style, simply to demonstrate that the MDI implementation is no different from the SDI implementation. You can open several conversion windows simultaneously in the MDI shell.

One interesting thing that you should notice about this Fahrenheit-to-Celsius application is the fact that, for the first time in a very long time, you can see a reduction in your workload. The total amount of code that you had to write to create an application is actually *declining*. To understand this phenomenon, think about the following comparison. If you wanted to create an extremely simple text-based version of this f2c program in C, it might take you four or five lines of code as shown in Listing 17.2.

Listing 17.2
Text-based version

```
void main()
{
    int temp;
    printf("Enter fahrenheit temperature: ");
    scanf("%d", &temp);
    printf("The celsius temeperature is %d\n", (temp-32)*5/9);
}
```

If you were to do this program "properly" in C, creating new functions for input, processing, and output, it might take 10 or 15 lines of code. If you created a C++ class for I/O and another for temperature conversions, it might take 30 to 50 lines to implement the code properly in C++. If you look back at Chapter 5 and examine the straight MFC implementation in Listing 5.1, you will find that the pretty GUI version of the program is about 150 lines long. In other words, the more advanced the programming system and user interface requirements, the more code you have to write.

However, using the AppWizard and the ClassWizard, the tables have finally turned. Now to create a complete GUI Fahrenheit-to-Celsius application with every bell and whistle possible, you only had to write two or three lines of code. We have finally gotten back to the point we were at in the original C program, where the code you write deals mainly with the task at hand, rather than with the user interface. It's an interesting turn of events.

17.3 Using DDX

The previous section used techniques that you learned in Part 1 of this book to manipulate the controls. However, you can also use DDX and DDV to work with controls on a form view. This section will recreate the application from Section 17.1 using DDX and DDV. Be sure to look at Chapter 22 for more information on this topic.

17.3.1 Step 1—Create the Framework

Recreate the SDI framework from Section 17.1 using the AppWizard.

17.3.2 Step 2—Add Controls to the Form

Recreate the form for the application as you did in Section 17.1.2.

17.3.3 Step 3—Add a DDX Variable

You now need to set up a mechanism to get data from the Edit control. In Section 17.1 we used **GetDlgItemText**. However, if you had 30 controls in the form this technique would leave a lot to be desired. The easiest way to handle the controls, especially if there are a lot of them, is to use DDX, as discussed in Chapters 15, 18, and 22.

Open the ClassWizard. Add a member variable for the IDC_FAHRENHEIT control. Name the new variable **m_fahrenheit**, set its category to **Value,** and set its type to **int** as described in Appendix B.7.5. Give the new variable minimum and maximum values if you like—for the sake of this example choose 0 and 200.

Repeat these steps to add a variable for the IDC_CELSIUS control as well. Name the valiable **m_celsius**.Set its category to **Value** and set the type to **CString**.

17.3.4 Step 4—Respond to Input

When using DDX, you need a way to tell the DDX controls to transfer and verify their data. When we used DDX in Chapter 15, we used DDX inside a dialog box and the **CDialog** class handled the transfers automatically. When the user caused the dialog to appear, DDX moved data from the member variables to the controls, and when the user clicked the dialog's **OK** button, DDX moved data back from the controls to the member variables.

In the case here we need to wire the code so some specific event forces a DDX transfer. We could use the EN_CHANGE event as we did in Section 17.1. Or we could add a button to the form and use its BN_CLICKED event. Let's use the former right now, because it is easier.

Create a new function for the EN_CHANGED event in the IDC_FAHRENHEIT control owned by the view class. See Appendix B.7.7 for details. Inside that function place the code as shown in Listing 17.3.

Listing 17.3
The **OnChangeFahrenheit** function

```
void CF2cView::OnChangeFahrenheit()
{
```

```
    UpdateData(TRUE);
    m_celsius.Format("%d",(m_fahrenheit-32)*5/9);
    UpdateData(FALSE);
}
```

The **UpdateData** function, as discussed in Chapter 22, is extremely important to DDX. It moves data in and out of DDX controls. When the parameter passed to **UpdateData** is FALSE, data move from the variables into the controls. When it is TRUE, data move from the controls into the variables. At the same time, any DDV checking takes place.

The code above, therefore, causes the application to copy data from the controls into the DDX variables. It then performs a Fahrenheit to Celsius conversion and leaves the result in the variable for the static control. It then calls DDX again to move the changed data back to the controls. It may seem like overkill to use DDX to do this, but if you had 30 controls on the form and wanted to read or update them all, you can see that the single call to **UpdateData** that DDX provides would be extremely helpful. Read about this function both in Chapter 22 and in the MFC documentation.

17.3.5 Step 5—Compile and Run

Compile and run the program. You should see an application that behaves almost exactly like the one you created in Section 17.1. When you type a Fahrenheit temperature into the edit control, you should immediately see changes in the displayed Celsius temperature. However, if you type an invalid integer, or an integer value that is out of range, you should see an error dialog. DDV provides that dialog for you automatically.

You may want to change the constructor in the view class so that the **m_celsius** member variable starts with the value 0.

17.4 Using the Document Class

In the applications created in Sections 17.1 and 17.3, the document class is not doing anything. Because the document is available, however, you might want to make use of it. In this simple form-based application, you could allow the document to store the current Fahrenheit temperature so you can move it to and from a file. Although this seems like overkill here, it can be useful.

In a larger form-based application this practice actually has merit. For example, say that you create a form-based application to help loan officers in a bank write up mortgage estimates for customers. Perhaps the application displays a form that accepts the customer's name and address, the cost of the home, the amount of the down payment, and the current interest rate. The document could hold all this information and allow the loan officer to save the form to disk. Then, if the customer returns with questions, the officer could pull up the stored form quite easily.

To use the document class with the F2C application, let's consider what we are trying to accomplish. When the user types a Fahrenheit temperature into the edit control, we want that value stored in the document class so the user can save the "form." At a later time, the user should be able to go back and reload the "form," which in this case will contain the previously entered temperature. Once loaded, the value in the file should get moved to the edit control on the form so the user can see it.

As you can see, the view and the document need to talk to each other for this to work. As discussed in Chapters 14 and 15, the document should hold the data and handle the interface to the disk. The view should handle user I/O and presentation. Therefore, every time the user changes the number on the form, the new value should get transmitted to the document. Whenever the user loads a temperature file, the loaded value should get transmitted to the view so it can display the loaded temperature.

In the document, we need to create a variable that can hold the current Fahrenheit temperature seen in the view. We also need to create **Set** and **Get** functions so the view can set and get the value of that variable. Whenever the user changes the edit control, the view needs to set the variable. Whenever the user loads a file, the document needs to inform the view by using the **UpdateAllViews** function to call the view's **OnUpdate** function.

Take the following steps to demonstrate the process:

17.4.1 Step 1—Add a Variable to the Document

Start with the application you created in Section 17.3. Create a variable in the document class of type LONG and call it **fahrenheit**. Note that we use the type LONG here, rather than **int**, because the **CArchive** class's **>>** and **<<** operators do not know how to serialize **int**s—see the description of the **CArchive** class in the MFC documentation for more information.

Also create functions named **SetTemp** and **GetTemp** in the document class so the view has a way to get and set this variable. See Chapter 15 for numerous examples on how to add functions to a document class. You may wish to call the **SetModifiedFlag** function in the new **SetTemp** function. When you get done, the F2CDOC.H file should contain the code shown in Listing 17.4 in its Attributes section.

Listing 17.4
Attributes Section of F2CDOC.H FILE

```
class CF2cDoc : public CDocument

{
protected: // create from serialization only
    CF2cDoc();
    DECLARE_DYNCREATE(CF2cDoc)

// Attributes
protected:
    LONG fahrenheit;
public:
```

```
void SetTemp(LONG temp) { fahrenheit = temp; }
LONG GetTemp() { return fahrenheit; }
```

17.4.2 Step 2—Change the Constructor

Change the document's constructor so it initializes the **fahrenheit** variable:

```
CF2cDoc::CF2cDoc()
{
    fahrenheit = 0;
}
```

17.4.3 Step 3—Serialize the Document

Find the **Serialize** function in the document class and change it as shown below:

```
if (ar.IsStoring())
{
    ar << fahrenheit;
}
else
{
    ar >> fahrenheit;
}
```

Now when the user saves a file, the file will contain a single value. Note that the << and >> operators in the **CArchive** are not able to serialize variables of type **int**. That is why **fahrenheit** is declared as LONG.

17.4.4 Step—Set the Document's Variable

Now you need to modify the program so that the **fahrenheit** variable gets set properly when the user changes the control. Use the ClassWizard to find the **OnChangeFahrenheit** function in F2CVIEW.CPP and modify it as shown in Listing 17.5.

Listing 17.5
The **OnChangeFahrenheit** function

```
void CF2cView::OnChangeFahrenheit()
{
    UpdateData(TRUE);
    m_celsius.Format("%d",(m_fahrenheit-32)*5/9);
    UpdateData(FALSE);
    // Change the document and all other related views
    GetDocument()->SetTemp(m_fahrenheit);
    GetDocument()->UpdateAllViews(this, 0, NULL);
}
```

The call to **SetTemp** causes the temperature variable in the document class to get modified each time the user changes the temperature. The call to **UpdateAllViews** causes all views attached to the same document to get updated. This mechanism is completed in the next section.

17.4.5 Step 5—Handle File Opening and Newing

Finally, you need to modify the document and view classes so the application handles file opening and newing properly. When the user opens a document file, for example, that action will load a new temperature into the document's variable. All the document's views need to know about the change. The preferred mechanism for handling this sort of thing uses the **UpdateAllViews** function in combination with an **OnUpdate** function in the view class. Using the ClassWizard, modify the **OnNewDocument** and **OnOpenDocument** functions in the document class so they appear as in Listing 17.6.

Listing 17.6
The OnNewDocument and OnOpenDocument functions

```
BOOL CF2cDoc::OnNewDocument()
{
    if (!CDocument::OnNewDocument())
        return FALSE;

    fahrenheit = 0;
    UpdateAllViews(NULL, 0, NULL);

    return TRUE;
}

BOOL CF2cDoc::OnOpenDocument(LPCTSTR lpszPathName)
{
    if (!CDocument::OnOpenDocument(lpszPathName))
        return FALSE;

    UpdateAllViews(NULL, 0, NULL);

    return TRUE;
}
```

Then in the view class use the ClassWizard to add a new **OnUpdate** function, as shown in Listing 17.7.

Listing 17.7
The OnUpdate function

```
void CF2cView::OnUpdate(CView* pSender, LPARAM lHint,
    CObject* pHint)

{
    m_fahrenheit = GetDocument()->GetTemp();
    m_celsius.Format("%d",(m_fahrenheit-32)*5/9);
```

```
    UpdateData(FALSE);
}
```

17.4.6 Step 6—Compile and Run

Now compile and run the application. You will find you can save and load F2C files. When you save a file, the current value of the Fahrenheit temperature is saved. When you open the file again that value is restored.

Although this is an extremely simple use of the document class, it shows how easy it is to use it in your own form applications.

17.4.7 Step 7—Handle Incidentals

If the document contained any variables that needed destruction, you would handle this action in the document's **DeleteContents** function. It is important that you do it here, rather than in the document's destructor, because an SDI framework reuses a single instance of the document class.

You should also update the **AssertValid** and **Dump** functions in the document class, as discussed in Chapters 13 and 15.

17.5 Using Form Views

You will find that form views are extremely useful in a variety of database-type applications. For example, if you are creating a customer database, you can use a form view to create a "form" that the user fills in when adding a customer record. The same form can also act as a customer information browser. Even though the application could be implemented instead using dialog boxes to gather information from the user, the use of a form view allows the user to pull up several records in an MDI framework at the same time. Form views also automatically scroll if the window is not large enough, so you can create long or wide forms and let the user scroll to the different fields rather than having to use multiple dialogs. There is really no limit to form size when you use a form view, although extremely large forms become cumbersome from a user standpoint.

To gain an understanding of how forms "feel" to a user, you might want to create a new application following the instructions in Section 17.1. Create a sample entry form in the dialog editor in place of the Fahrenheit-to-Celsius converter form. For example, create a form that allows the user to enter a typical "patient information" form that you fill out at a doctor's office. Or create an employment application form. Place on the form all the fields that you find on the paper version of the form. Then try it out by compiling and running the application. If you create the application with an MDI framework, you will be able to open and fill in several forms at once. You will find that these electronic forms are just as easy to use as the paper equivalents.

17.6 Conclusion

In this chapter you have seen how easy it is to create form-based applications in MFC. In the next chapter, we will use a form view in a slightly different way to create a complete address list application. Chapter 18 combines many of the different techniques you have learned in this part of the book. See also Chapter 33, where form views are used for Database access.

CREATING AN ADDRESS LIST APPLICATION

In this chapter you will create an address list application, combining many of the techniques you have learned in the previous chapters. The purpose of this application is to help review the process of adding dialogs and new menu options to an AppWizard application. You will also have the opportunity to see how to modify the tool bar and status bar, use the clipboard, and accommodate printing of textual information.

Once you have completed this program you will have implemented a list-based application with a document class that can load and save an array of address structures. A custom dialog that you create with the ClassWizard allows you to add new elements to the list. You will also be able to delete and change elements.

18.1 Creating the Application

Imagine that you want to create an address-list application—the sort of application that holds the names and addresses of your friends and business associates. As the designer and implementer of this application, there are a number of different user interfaces from which to choose. For example, you could create a simple form, as demonstrated in Chapter 17, and let the user enter and view addresses using that form. This technique provides an interface that is extremely easy to implement with the AppWizard. The disadvantage of this approach is that the user can see only one address at a time in an SDI application. In an MDI application the user can open several different views into a single address list file, but the user is still fairly limited in the number of addresses that can be viewed simultaneously.

An alternative user interface for the application might present the user with a list of names and addresses. To add a name to the list, the user clicks on an **Add** menu option that presents an address entry dialog. The advantage of this approach is that it may make the interface "feel" better. The user can see a large number of names and addresses simultaneously and then scroll through them quickly and easily. A more complicated derivative of this same interface might paint the list into a rolodex-like graphical device on the screen. You could then leverage the rolodex metaphor to make the application easier for novice users to understand.

The address list application implemented in this chapter uses the second approach. It consists of a resizable **CListBox** control held in a resizable MDI window. The list displays names and addresses (here the program stores only the city and state but it is easy to handle other address or phone information). To add a new element to the list, a **Data** menu contains an **Add** option that presents a dialog with all the address fields. Other options allow the user to change an existing address record or delete a record. Figure 18.1 shows a rough view of how the application will look upon completion.

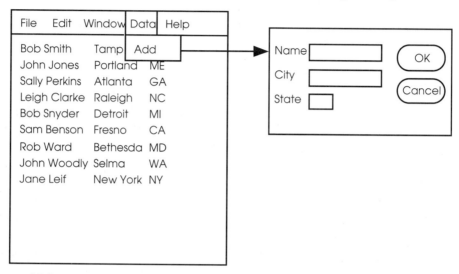

Figure 18.1
The address list application

Here's a road map that shows you where we are headed in the first stage of this program's development:

1. Create the framework with the AppWizard. Use a form for the main application window.
2. Put a list box in the main window and make it resize properly with the window.
3. Add a new menu named "Data" and a new menu option named "Add" so we can add data to the list.
4. Create a new data entry dialog containing fields for the address information.
5. Hook in the dialog so it appears when the Add menu option is selected.
6. Modify the document class so it can hold, load, and save address records.

From that starting point we will then add features to turn this program into a complete application. Many of the techniques described in this chapter are techniques discussed previously. Where appropriate we will provide pointers back to the earlier sections.

18.1.1 Step 1—Create the Framework

Create a new SDI framework with the AppWizard (see Chapter 14). Give the new project the name "Addr."

As you go through the AppWizard option screens, select the following options:

- Choose the **Single-Document** option.
- Enable or disable any application features as you see fit. Add the file extension "adr" as described in Appendix B.6.3.
- Change the Base Class of the **CAddrView** class to **CFormView** as described in Appendix B.6.4.

18.1.2 Step 2—Add a List

Add a list control onto the main form. The goal is to have the form display a single list box that resizes with the form. Open the IDR_ADDR_FORM dialog resource. Delete the TODO static object. Add a new list box to the dialog by dragging a list from the dialog palette (See Chapter 15 for a description of adding controls to a dialog). Place the upper left corner of the list in the upper left corner of the dialog and make the list control as small as possible. You need to do this because if the list is larger the application will automatically apply scroll bars to the *form view* as soon as it is resized smaller than the list. We want the list to automatically resize with the window, so we do no want those scroll bars to appear.

The ID chosen by the dialog editor (IDC_LIST1) is fine. *Double-click on the list and in the Styles section of the Property Sheet turn off sorting.* We need to do this so the document's data order prevails—we cannot have the document and view data in different orders.

18.1.3 Step 3—Compile and Run

Compile and run the program. You will find the application displays a very small list box. When you resize the application, it does not handle resizing at all.

18.1.4 Step 4—Add a Control Variable

Add the code so the list box resizes with the window. Use the ClassWizard and look at the member functions of the View class. First we need to add a member variable to let us access the list control in the view. Click on the **Member Variables** tab at the top of the ClassWizard. You will see a list of control IDs, and IDC_LIST1 will be the only value in the list. Select it and click the **Add Variable** button. Give the variable the name **m_list1**. In the **Category** field choose "Control" (see Chapter 22). In the **Variable Type** field choose **CListBox**. Click the **OK** button to create the variable. The purpose of this variable is to act as the instantiation of the list. We will use it to control the list. See Section 18.3 for an explanation of this step, as well as an explanation of DDX.

18.1.5 Step 5—Add Resizing Code

To add the code to resize the list properly, go to the ClassWizard again. Select the **Message Maps** tab and look at the view class. Under **Object Ids** choose the **CAddrView** class itself and double-click on the WM_SIZE message. Click the Edit Code button for the **OnSize** function. Add the code in Listing 18.1 to the **OnSize** function in place of the TODO comment.

Listing 18.1
The OnSize Function

```
void CAddrView::OnSize(UINT nType, int cx, int cy)
{
    CFormView::OnSize(nType, cx, cy);
    CRect r;

    // Ignore the first resize message
    if (GetDlgItem(IDC_LIST1)==NULL)
        return;
    UpdateData(FALSE);
    GetClientRect(&r);
    m_list1.MoveWindow(r);
}
```

There are two slight problems with the **OnSize** function that this piece of code is overcoming. First, the **OnSize** function gets called initially very early in the window's life, long before the list control exists. If the code tries to resize a non-existent list, it will crash. The **if** statement solves that problem. Second, when the **OnSize** function is next called, the window's list control exists but the **m_list1** variable is not yet connected to it. The call to **UpdateData** solves that problem. On this and all subsequent calls, the list resizes appropriately using the **MoveWindow** function.

18.1.6 Step 6—Compile and Run

Compile and run the code. You will find that the list box is now practically invisible because it is resizing properly with the window. To see it we will have to place some data in it. To do that we are going to add a menu option and a new dialog.

18.1.7 Step 7—Add a Menu

Modify the application's menu to contain a new "Data" menu with an "Add" option. Because this is an SDI application at the moment, you do this by opening the IDR_MAINFRAME menu and then adding the new menu and item in the menu resource editor. If this is an MDI application, there would be two menu resources: one for the application when it has no windows open named IDR_MAINFRAME, and the other for the application when it has a window open named IDR_ADDRTYPE. You would want to modify the latter in the MDI case. Open the menu resource. Follow the directions given in the example in Appendix B.5.5 to modify the menu to contain the new elements. The ID chosen by the ClassWizard for the new menu option is fine.

18.1.8 Step 8—Create a New Dialog

Create a new dialog resource as described in Appendix B.5.6. See also Chapter 6 for a discussion. Add three static controls and three edit controls to the dialog. When you get done it should look like the dialog shown in Figure 18.2. Change the IDs of the three edit areas to IDC_NAME, IDC_CITY, and IDC_STATE. The name IDD_DIALOG1 chosen for the dialog itself is fine.

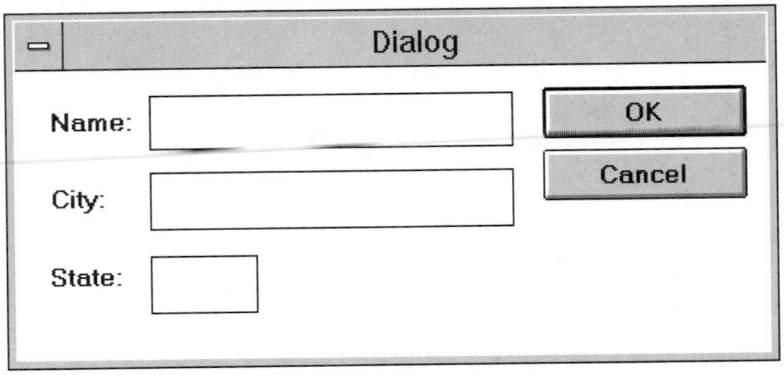

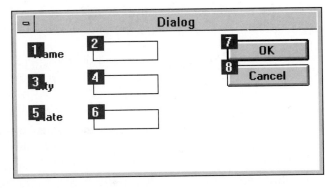

Figure 18.2
The Add Data dialog

You may want to adjust the tab order of the dialog once you finish it by selecting the **Tab Order** option or toolbar button. Set up the tab order as shown in Figure 18.3 by clicking on each control in the desired tab order.

Figure 18.3
An appropriate tab order

18.1.9 Step 9—Create a Dialog Class and Member Variables

Now we need to create a dialog class to go with the dialog. See Section 15.5 and Chapter 6 for a discussion of dialog classes. *With the new dialog visible as the topmost window in Visual C++*, open the ClassWizard. The ClassWizard will immediately make the assumption that you want to add a new dialog class for this dialog. In the

Class Name field, type **CAddDlg**. Everything else will be fine. The ClassWizard will create two new files for the new dialog class in the current directory. The files will be named ADDDLG.CPP and ADDDLG.H. The ClassWizard will add AD-DDLG.CPP to the project for you.

You should next add DDX variables to the dialog class for the three **CEdit** objects so you will be able to access their contents. See Appendix B.7.5. Click on IDC_NAME and name the variable **m_name**. Give it a **Value** category and a **CString** type. Do the same for IDC_CITY and IDC_STATE, calling their variables **m_city** and **m_state**.

18.1.10 Step 10—Activate the Dialog

Now we need to wire the dialog into the code and make it appear when we choose the **Add** menu option.

Consider for a moment where to handle the **Add** menu option. The ClassWizard will let you easily handle it in the message map for the application, for the frame window, or for the document. Clearly you do not want to handle it at the application level—if this were an MDI application you would want Add dialogs being associated with specific documents. Because the data that the Add dialog obtains is intended for the document, you should have the document handle it.

Add a **#include** statement at the top of the document's CPP file so that AD-DDLG.H is included in the document class. Then open the ClassWizard and select the document class. In the **Object IDs** list select the ID_DATA_ADD ID. Add in a COMMAND message map entry for it as described in Appendix B.7.3. The Class-Wizard will automatically choose the function name **OnDataAdd**, and this name is fine. Edit the code for the function and add the following two lines in place of the TODO statement:

```
CAddDlg addDlg;
addDlg.DoModal();
```

This code will cause the Add dialog to appear and then disappear when the user presses its **OK** or **Cancel** button.

18.1.11 Step 11—Compile and Run

Compile and run the program. You should see a new **Data** menu. When you select its **Add** option, you should see the dialog and you should be able to type in the dialog and press the **OK** button. If you add the following TRACE statements to the code following the **DoModal** call in Step 10, you can verify the dialog is working properly *when you run the program under the debugger* (see Chapter 13 for more information about TRACE statements):

```
TRACE("Name: %s\n", addDlg.m_name);
TRACE("City: %s\n", addDlg.m_city);
TRACE("State: %s\n", addDlg.m_state);
```

When you run the program you will notice that the status bar is not being updated properly. Under the debugger, you may also notice the status bar is generating error messages about this problem. See Section 18.4.5.4 for the solution to this problem.

18.1.12 Step 12—Modify the Document Class

Now we want to modify the document so it encapsulates the data for address documents. We also want to supply the document class with enough functions so the view class can access the data it needs. First, we are going to create a **CObject**-derived class that can hold one address record and then modify the document class as needed to accommodate an array of these address records. This is the same process we used in Chapter 15 to store points in the document.

18.1.12.1 Step 12a—Create a Data Class We need to modify the document class so it can accept and hold address records. First create the address record class. It is derived from **CObject** and has a header and CPP file. This technique was demonstrated in Chapter 12. Both the header file (ADDRREC.H) and the C++ implementation (ADDRREC.CPP) are shown in Listings 18.2 and 18.3.

Create two new files in Visual C++. Save the files under their appropriate names. *Add an include statement for ADDRREC.H into the document file. Add ADDRREC.CPP to the project.*

Listing 18.2
The header file for the address record class (ADDRREC.H)

```
// addrrec.h

class CAddrRec : public CObject
{
DECLARE_SERIAL( CAddrRec )
protected:
    CString name, city, state;
public:
    CAddrRec();
    CAddrRec(const CAddrRec &p);
    CAddrRec operator=(const CAddrRec& p);
    CAddrRec(CString nm, CString ct, CString st);
    virtual void Serialize(CArchive &archive);
    void GetAddr(CString &nm, CString &ct, CString &st) const;
};
```

Listing 18.3
The implementation file for the address record class (ADDRREC.CPP)

```
// addrrec.cpp

#include "stdafx.h"
#include "addrrec.h"
```

```
CAddrRec::CAddrRec()
{
    name = "";
    city = "";
    state = "";
}


CAddrRec::CAddrRec(const CAddrRec &p)
{
    name = p.name;
    city = p.city;
    state = p.state;
}


CAddrRec CAddrRec::operator=(const CAddrRec& p)
{
    name = p.name;
    city = p.city;
    state = p.state;
    return *this;
}


CAddrRec::CAddrRec(CString nm, CString ct, CString st)
{
    name = nm;
    city = ct;
    state = st;
}


void CAddrRec::Serialize(CArchive &archive)
{
    CObject::Serialize(archive);
    if (archive.IsStoring())
        archive << name << city << state;
    else
        archive >> name >> city >> state;
}


void CAddrRec::GetAddr(CString &nm, CString &ct, CString &st) const
{
    nm=name;
    ct=city;
    st=state;
}


IMPLEMENT_SERIAL(CAddrRec, CObject, 0)
```

Create two new files in Visual C++ to hold the above two listings. Save the files under their appropriate names. *Add an include statement for ADDRREC.H into the document file. Add ADDRREC.CPP to the project.*

18.1.12.2 Step 12b—Add an Array Let the document hold an array of address records. In the document header file, in the Attributes section of the document class, add the following line:

```
          CObArray array;
```

Make this a protected variable. If you choose to, you can instead derive a new class from **CObArray**.

18.1.12.3 Step 12c—Encapsulate the Array As first demonstrated in Chapter 15, add three member functions to the document class to allow access to the array. First add their prototypes as shown in Listing 18.4 as public member functions in the document header file:

Listing 18.4
Adding prototypes as public member functions

```
// Attributes
protected:
    CObArray array;
public:
    void CAddrDoc::AddAddr(CString name, CString city,
        CString state);
    int CAddrDoc::NumAddrs();
    void CAddrDoc::GetAddr(int x, CString &name, CString &city,
        CString &state);
```

Then add the function implementations in Listing 18.5 into the document's CPP file:

Listing 18.5
Function implementations

```
/////////////////////////////////////////////////////////////
// CAddrDoc Attributes

void CAddrDoc::AddAddr(CString name, CString city, CString state)
{
    array.Add(new CAddrRec(name, city, state));
    SetModifiedFlag();
}

int CAddrDoc::NumAddrs()
{
    return array.GetSize();
}

void CAddrDoc::GetAddr(int x, CString &name, CString &city,
    CString &state)
{
    ((CAddrRec *)array.GetAt(x))->GetAddr(name, city, state);
}
```

See Chapter 15 for details

18.1.12.4 Step 12d—Modify DeleteContents Add the **DeleteContents** function in Listing 18.6 to the document class using the ClassWizard. The function itself is identical to the function shown in Section 15.2, Step 5c.

Listing 18.6
The **DeleteContents** function

```
void CAddrDoc::DeleteContents()
{
    int x;
    for (x=0; x<array.GetSize(); x++)
        delete(array.GetAt(x));
    array.RemoveAll();
    CDocument::DeleteContents();
}
```

This function gets called whenever the user selects the **New** option and also when the program exits. It cleans up the array. See Chapter 15 for more information.

18.1.12.5 Step 12e—Serialize the Array Add the following line to the end of the **Serialize** function in Listing 18.7 so the document can serialize itself.

Listing 18.7
The **Serialize** function

```
void CAddrDoc::Serialize(CArchive& ar)
{
    if (ar.IsStoring())
    {
        // TODO: add storing code here
    }
    else
    {
        // TODO: add loading code here
    }
    array.Serialize(ar);
}
```

See Chapters 15 and 17 for more information.

18.1.12.6 Step 12f—Update AssertVAlid and Dump   Update the **AssertValid** and **Dump** functions as shown in Listing 18.8.

Listing 18.8
The **AssertValid** and **Dump** functions

```
void CAddrDoc::AssertValid() const
{
    CDocument::AssertValid();
```

```
    ASSERT_VALID(&array);
}

void CAddrDoc::Dump(CDumpContext& dc) const
{
    CDocument::Dump(dc);
    dc << array;
}
```

See Chapter 13 for more information.

18.1.12.7 Step 12g—Update OnDataAdd Update the **OnDataAdd** function, first seen in Step 10, as shown in Listing 18.9 so additions are placed into the array.

Listing 18.9
The **OnDataAdd** function

```
void CAddrDoc::OnDataAdd()
{
    CAddDlg addDlg;
    if (addDlg.DoModal()==IDOK)
    {
        AddAddr(addDlg.m_name, addDlg.m_city, addDlg.m_state);
        UpdateAllViews(NULL);
    }
}
```

Now the document class should be complete. It is totally self-contained and can write its data to disk.

18.1.13 Step 13—Handle OnUpdate

Note that in Step 12f the **OnDataAdd** function calls **UpdateAllViews** after data are added. This function calls the **OnUpdate** virtual function in each view to tell it to refresh its window (see Section 15.4 for details). Using the ClassWizard, override the **OnUpdate** function in the view's CPP file as in Listing 18.10. Add a prototype for it into the view's header file.

Listing 18.10
The **OnUpdate** function

```
void CAddrView::OnUpdate( CView* pSender, LPARAM lHint,
    CObject* pHint )
{
    m_list1.ResetContent();
    CAddrDoc *pDoc = GetDocument();
    int x;
    for (x=0; x<pDoc->NumAddrs(); x++)
    {
        CString name, city, state;
```

```
                pDoc->GetAddr(x,name, city, state);
                m_list1.AddString(name);
        }
    }
```

Currently this function displays only the name in the list. In a later exercise we will improve the program so it shows name, city, and state.

18.1.14 Step 14 Compile and Run

Recompile and run the program. You should be able to choose the **Add** menu option to add data to the application, and you should be able to see the data in the window's list. The **Open** and **Save** menu options should work properly.

18.1.15 Step 15—Create an MDI version

Rebuild the program from the beginning, this time using an MDI rather than an SDI format. You will find that the program now allows you to open multiple address lists simultaneously and also to open different views on those lists using the **New Window** option in the **Window** menu. Because the SDI version was built in a way that correctly uses the document/view paradigm, the MDI functionality works without any modification to the code.

18.2 Understanding the Address List Program

In this address list program, we have used the document and view structure to effectively handle the storage and viewing of address records. You made a series of changes to a standard SDI or MDI framework produced by the AppWizard. Let's start by summarizing the changes you made to the framework's code to produce the address list program:

1. You replaced the standard **CView** with a **CFormView**. Onto the form you placed a list box. This list box resizes with the form because of the addition of a handler for the **OnSize** event.
2. You added a new **Data** menu containing an **Add** option, and you created a dialog that appears in response to the **Add** option. You created a dialog class to manage the new dialog. This dialog class contains member variables used by DDX (See Section 18.3) that move data in and out of the dialog. When the user enters data on the dialog and presses the OK button, the **OnDataAdd** function adds the data to the array and then calls **UpdateAllViews** so the views reflect the addition.
3. You implemented a complete **CAddrRec** class derived from **CObject** (Step 12a). The reasons for, and advantages of, this step are described in Chapter 12. The **CAddrRec** class is designed to hold one address record. You then added an instance of a **CObArray** to the document class (Step 5b) to hold the collection of all addresses added by the user.

4. You added three functions to the document class (Step 12c) to complete its encapsulation: **AddAddr**, **GetAddr**, and **NumAddrs**. The **AddAddr** function actually adds a record to the document. The view class uses the other two functions when it wants to retrieve data from the document class to update a view.

5. You overrode the document's **DeleteContents** member function (Step 12d). By default this function does nothing. You override it to clear the member variables you add to the document class—here it clears the array. The function gets called by the framework during destruction of the document. In an SDI application, it is called each time the user opens or creates a document because an SDI application reuses the same document object throughout the run of the program. In an MDI application, a new document instance is created each time the user selects the **New** or **Open** options.

6. You modified the document's **Serialize** function (Step 12e) by adding one line to it. This line serializes the array of address records to or from disk automatically. The document's **Serialize** function gets called automatically by the framework each time the user chooses the **Save** or **Save As** options.

7. You modified the **AssertValid** and **Dump** functions of the document (Step 12f) so these functions work properly for your document class. See Chapter 13 for more information on these functions.

8. In Steps 12g and 13, you caused the dialog to appear, accept data, and update the list control when the user clicks the OK button.

Note that these changes were made to the document and view classes, a new dialog class, and to a new class derived from **CObject**.

The goal of the document class is to completely encapsulate the data for one open document. It knows how to load the data from the disk and save it to the disk. It also has member functions that the view uses to display the data in the document. When the user selects the **Add** option, it handles that.

The view class is responsible for letting the user view the contents of the document. In this case the document is a list of address information.

The relationship between the document and view classes is summarized in Figure 18.4. When you are designing your own applications, you want the document class to completely encapsulate the data, and you want the view to display information to the user. There should be a clear and obvious way for the view to interact with the document through member functions.

18.3 Understanding DDX and DDV

MFC contains two features, called Dialog Data Exchange (DDX) and Dialog Data Validation (DDV), that help you work with controls held by a dialog box or a form. DDX handles data movement, while DDV makes it easier to validate the data held in different dialog fields.

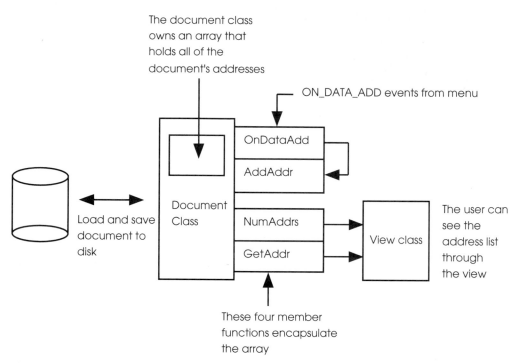

The document class
owns an array that
holds all of the
document's addresses

ON_DATA_ADD events from menu

OnDataAdd

AddAddr

Document
Class

Load and save
document to
disk

NumAddrs

GetAddr

View class

The user can
see the
address list
through
the view

These four member
functions encapsulate
the array

Figure 18.4
The relationship between the document and the view in the address list program

We have used the DDX feature of MFC in two different ways in this address list application. First we used it to obtain a variable, **m_list1**, that allows access to the list control in the main application window. This **m_list1** variable is called a *control member variable*. It acts as a synonym for the list itself, allowing us to call functions such as **MoveWindow** directly on the control. The program also uses DDX to obtain data from the dialog box once the user presses the **OK** button. With DDX, the string values in the three edit fields are automatically moved from the three **CEdit** controls and placed in the **CString** variables named **m_name**, **m_city**, and **m_state**. These variables are called *value member variables* of the dialog.

DDX is nothing magic. It is simply a convenience, implemented by the Class-Wizard and a set of functions that actually handle the data transfer. See Chapter 22 for information on the transfer functions. If you look at the dialog class, where we used the ClassWizard to add three member variables, you will see code like that shown in Listing 18.11.

Listing 18.11
DDX changes

```
CAddDlg::CAddDlg(CWnd* pParent /*=NULL*/)
    : CDialog(CAddDlg::IDD, pParent)
```

This book is continuously updated. See http://www.iftech.com/mfc

```
{
    //{{AFX_DATA_INIT(CAddDlg)
    m_city = _T("");
    m_name = _T("");
    m_state = _T("");
    //}}AFX_DATA_INIT
}

void CAddDlg::DoDataExchange(CDataExchange* pDX)
{
    CDialog::DoDataExchange(pDX);
    //{{AFX_DATA_MAP(CAddDlg)
    DDX_Text(pDX, IDC_CITY, m_city);
    DDX_Text(pDX, IDC_NAME, m_name);
    DDX_Text(pDX, IDC_STATE, m_state);
    //}}AFX_DATA_MAP
}
```

You can see in Listing 18.11 that the ClassWizard wrote code to initialize the three member variables in the dialog's constructor and then used the **DDX_Text** functions to implement the transfer.

When you create *value* member variables, you have the option of setting up automatic validation using DDV. For example, if you create a string member variable to allow data transfer from a **CEdit** control, you have the option to limit the length of the string entered by the user. You can also retrieve data from an edit control as an integer and validate the number within a range.

If MFC did not have DDX and DDV, you would have to implement the features yourself. For example, you would use functions like **GetDlgItemText** and **GetDlgItemInt** to do the same thing as a *value* member variable, using the control's ID to tell the functions which control to act on. You would use the **GetDlgItem** function to get the pointer to the control, and then use that pointer to accomplish the same thing that a *control* member variable does.

In your own applications, you will use DDX just as it is demonstrated here. If you have controls in a dialog or a form that you want to control directly, create a control member variable as described in Step 4 of Section 18.1. If you want to extract the data from a field on a dialog or a form, create a value member variable as described in Step 9. See Chapter 22 for a complete description of how to use DDX with every type of field.

18.4 Improving the Application

The purpose of this section is to walk through several different modifications to the address list program so you can see examples of some more advanced techniques. Although each change by itself is small, the net effect will be to create a much more complete application. Here is a list of the changes:

1. Add tabs to the list to display all fields of the addresses properly.
2. Add a **Delete** option to the data menu.

3. Add menu enabling and disabling for the delete option.
4. Add a **Change** option to the data menu and implement its dialog.
5. Modify the tool bar
6. Modify the status bar
7. Add clipboard support.

Before you make these changes, you should start by recreating an MDI version of this application that has the tool bar and status bar features enabled. This will give you a chance to try out modifications to the tool bar and status bar. Also add in Printing and Print Preview capabilities so we can add printing in Section 18.5. Figure 18.5 shows the feature summary for the new application. Follow all of the steps in Section 18.1 to create the MDI version of the application.

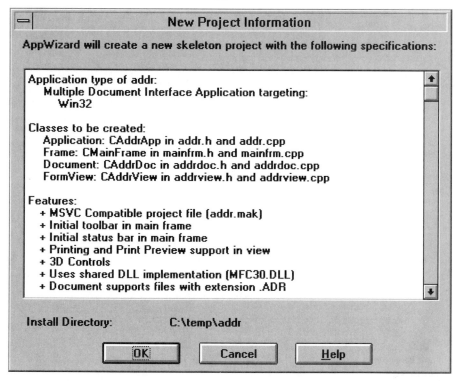

New Project Information

AppWizard will create a new skeleton project with the following specifications:

Application type of addr:
    Multiple Document Interface Application targeting:
        Win32

Classes to be created:
    Application: CAddrApp in addr.h and addr.cpp
    Frame: CMainFrame in mainfrm.h and mainfrm.cpp
    Document: CAddrDoc in addrdoc.h and addrdoc.cpp
    FormView: CAddrView in addrview.h and addrview.cpp

Features:
    + MSVC Compatible project file (addr.mak)
    + Initial toolbar in main frame
    + Initial status bar in main frame
    + Printing and Print Preview support in view
    + 3D Controls
    + Uses shared DLL implementation (MFC30.DLL)
    + Document supports files with extension .ADR

Install Directory: C:\temp\addr

[OK]   [Cancel]   [Help]

Figure 18.5
The feature list for the application framework used in this section

18.4.1 Add Tabs to the List

The application created in Section 18.1 displays only one of the three fields collected in the dialog. To display all three fields you need to convert the list to a tabbed list and then draw all three pieces of information into the list. Take the following steps.

18.4.1.1 Step 1—Modify the List Box Properties Open the resource file and then open the IDD_ADDR_FORM dialog. Double-click on the list control to view its property sheet. In the **Styles** section click on the **UseTabstops** check box to enable the tab stops in the list. See Chapter 9 for more information on tab stops

18.4.1.2 Step 2—Add an Include File At the top of the view class's ADDR-VIEW.CPP file, add in the STRSTREA.H header file as shown in Listing 18.12.

Listing 18.12
Adding the STRSTREA.H header file

```
// addrview.cpp : implementation of the CAddrView class
//

#include "stdafx.h"
#include "addr.h"
#include <strstrea.h>

#include "addrdoc.h"
#include "addrview.h"
```

18.4.1.3 Step 3— Add an OnInitialUpdate Function Using the ClassWizard, override the view's **OnInitialUpdate** function. The modified function should appear as in Listing 18.13.

Listing 18.13
The **OnInitialUpdate** function

```
void CAddrView::OnInitialUpdate()
{
    // Set two tab stops at 50 and 100 dialog units
    int ta[2] = {50, 100};
    m_list1.SetTabStops(2, ta);

    CFormView::OnInitialUpdate();
}
```

The goal of this code is to set the tab positions in the list. See Chapter 9 for details on tabbing.

18.4.1.4 Step 4—Modify OnUpdate In the view class, modify the **OnUpdate** function as shown in Listing 18.14.

Listing 18.14
The **OnUpdate** function

```
void CAddrView::OnUpdate(CView* pSender, LPARAM lHint,
    CObject* pHint)
{
    m_list1.ResetContent();
    CAddrDoc *pDoc = GetDocument();
```

```
int x;
char s[100];
ostrstream ostr(s,100);
for (x=0; x<pDoc->NumAddrs(); x++)
{
    CString name, city, state;
    pDoc->GetAddr(x, name, city, state);
        ostr.seekp(ios::beg);
    ostr << name << '\t';
    ostr << city << '\t';
    ostr << state << ends;
    m_list1.AddString(s);
}
}
```

The new code creates a string that contains the name, city, and state separated by tabs. When inserted into the list with the **AddString** function, the list displays the different parts of the string at the proper tab stops.

18.4.1.5 Step 5—Compile and Run Compile and run the program. You should find that all three parts of every address record are displayed properly.

18.4.2 Add a Delete Option

To delete an item, the user selects the item in the list and then chooses the **Delete** menu option in the **Data** menu. Adding such an option to this application is conceptually straightforward. You need to add a new **Delete** menu item, extract from the list the index of the currently selected item, and then delete that item from the list and the document.

The best place to handle the **Delete** menu option is in the document, but this presents a problem: The document class does not have any way to know which item has been selected in the list. There are two ways to solve this problem. In the first technique, the document can query the view that has focus (remember that an MDI framework allows multiple views on a single document to be open at the same time) and ask it for its currently selected item. In the second technique, the view with focus updates a variable in the document that keeps track of the current selection. In this second approach, the document class needs a variable to remember which item is selected. The view class also needs a mechanism that keeps this variable updated properly as the user selects items in the list.

We will implement the second technique here. To use this technique, the document class needs to have a variable that holds the currently selected item. The view class needs to update this variable each time the selection changes. In addition, because multiple views can be open, there is a need to update the variable when focus changes from one open view to another. Furthermore, when the selection is canceled, the variable should be set to some value indicative of that state (like LB_ERR). By handling these different events, the selection variable is guaranteed to contain the correct value at all times. The document class can then delete an item simply by referencing this variable.

18.4.2.1 Add in Current Selection Variable In the Attributes section of the document class's header file (ADDRDOC.H), add a variable to hold the current selection, along with two manipulation functions, as shown in Listing 18.15.

Listing 18.15
Modification of ADDRDOC.H file

```
// Attributes
protected:
    CObArray array;
    int currentSelection;
public:
    void SetSelection(int sel) { currentSelection = sel; }
    UINT GetSelection() { return currentSelection; }
    void CAddrDoc::AddAddr(CString name, CString city,
        CString state);
    int CAddrDoc::NumAddrs();
    void CAddrDoc::GetAddr(int x, CString &name, CString &city,
        CString &state);
```

Additionally, you should initialize the value of the **currentSelection** *variable to LB_ERR in the document's constructor. Add the same line to* **DeleteContents** *for completeness.*

18.4.2.2 Update the Current Selection from the View The view knows which item in the list the user has selected. It knows this because the list sends an LBN_SELCHANGE event to it each time the user changes the selection. It also sends an LBN_SELCANCEL message if the user clears the current selection. It sends an LBN_SETFOCUS event when the user gives the list focus. By handing these events in the view and calling the document's **SetSelection** function in response, the document will always know the current selection

Open the ClassWizard. In the **Message Maps** section choose the **CAddrView** class. Select the IDC_LIST1 control in the **Object IDs** list. Add message handler functions for LBN_SELCHANGE, LBN_SELCANCEL and LBN_SETFOCUS. Edit the code for all three new functions and change them as shown in Listing 18.16.

Listing 18.16
The **OnSelchangeList1**, **OnSetfocusList1**, and **OnSelcancelList1** functions

```
void CAddrView::OnSelchangeList1()
{
    GetDocument()->SetSelection(m_list1.GetCurSel());
}

void CAddrView::OnSetfocusList1()
```

```
{
    GetDocument()->SetSelection(m_list1.GetCurSel());
}

void CAddrView::OnSelcancelList1()
{
    GetDocument()->SetSelection(LB_ERR);
}
```

At this point you have wired in the document's selection variable so it is always valid.

18.4.2.3   Add the Delete Item to the Menu Open the resource file and double-click on the Menu folder. Open the IDR_ADDRTYPE menu resource by double-clicking on it. Add a new **Delete** option to the **Data** menu. The ID ID_DATA_DELETE chosen by the resource editor is fine.

18.4.2.4   Add an OnDataDelete Function Open the ClassWizard, choose the Message Maps section, and select the document class. Add in a COMMAND event handler for the ID_DATA_DELETE menu ID. Since the document knows exactly which item to delete, this function shown in Listing 18.17 is easy to implement.

Listing 18.17
The **OnDataDelete** function

```
void CAddrDoc::OnDataDelete()
{
    if (currentSelection != LB_ERR)
    {
        delete array.GetAt(currentSelection);
        array.RemoveAt(currentSelection);
        UpdateAllViews(NULL, 0, NULL);
        SetModifiedFlag();
        currentSelection = LB_ERR;
    }
}
```

The code first checks to make sure there is a valid item to delete. If so, it deletes the item from the array, tells all the views to update themselves, and then sets the document's modified flag.

18.4.2.5   Compile and Run Compile and run the program. You will find that it correctly deletes the selected item. If multiple views on the same document are open, all update correctly.

18.4.3 Enabling and Disabling Menu Options

You may have noticed in the previous section that, if the list is empty, the **Delete** menu item does not disable itself as you would expect. You would like the **Delete** item to disable itself whenever the list is empty or there is no selection. To add this functionality, you can make use of the UPDATE_COMMAND_UI message in MFC. This message gives you an extremely efficient way to enable and disable menu items. Take the following steps to correctly handle the **Delete** item's state.

18.4.3.1 Step 1—Add an UPDATE_COMMAND_UI Message Handler Open the ClassWizard, select the **Message Maps** section and the document class. In the **Object IDs** list, choose ID_DATA_DELETE. Then choose the UPDATE_COMMAND_UI message and create a new function for it. The framework will create a function named **OnUpdateDataDelete.**

The framework will call the **OnUpdateDataDelete** function just before it displays the menu that contains the **Delete** item. Therefore, inside this function you should tell the framework whether to enable or disable the **Delete** menu item based on the internal state of the application. In our case, we want to disable the menu option if **currentSelection** is LB_ERR and enable it otherwise.

To set the enable state, use the code in Listing 18.18 for the **OnUpdateData-Delete** function.

Listing 18.18
The **OnUpdateDataDelete** Function

```
void CAddrDoc::OnUpdateDataDelete(CCmdUI* pCmdUI)
{
    pCmdUI->Enable(currentSelection != LB_ERR);
}
```

If the Boolean expression resolves to TRUE, the menu option will be enabled. Otherwise it will be disabled.

18.4.3.2 Step 2—Compile and Run Compile and run the application. You will find that the **Delete** menu item correctly enables and disables itself in all situations.

18.4.3.3 Step 3—Understanding Menu Option Updating You can see from the previous steps that it is extremely easy to add the code to enable and disable menu items in an MFC program created using the AppWizard. You must do three things:

1. Create a function that handles the UPDATE_COMMAND_UI message for each menu option.
2. In each function, determine whether the option should be enabled or disabled.
3. Call **pCmdUI->Enable** to set the enable state of each menu option based on that determination.

If a menu option has an associated toolbar button (see below), then the toolbar button is also enabled or disabled at the same time.

MFC implements the UPDATE_COMMAND_UI capability in one of two different ways. If your program does not contain a tool bar, then UPDATE_COMMAND_UI is implemented using the same **OnInitMenu** approach that was discussed in Chapter 8. When the **OnInitMenu** function is called, MFC handles it by sending a message to trigger the UPDATE_COMMAND_UI handler for each relevant menu option. When you think about it, this is a tremendous simplifying step. Instead of a single, large handler for **OnInitMenu** as seen in Chapter 8, MFC chops it up and calls an individual enabling function for every single menu option in the program. That subdivides the task nicely and makes things much easier to understand. It is also efficient because these functions are called only if the user pulls down a menu.

If the tool bar is visible, a different and less-efficient mechanism is used. The tool bar buttons, unlike menu options, are always visible. Therefore, their enable state has to be updated constantly. This need is met by calling all the UPDATE_COMMAND_UI handlers in the application's **OnIdle** function (see Chapter 10). Because they are called continuously, you want to be careful to keep the amount of processing that you do in UPDATE_COMMAND_UI handlers to a minimum.

18.4.4 Adding a Change Option

This application would be more useful if the user had the ability to change items in the list. This option is now fairly easy to add because the **currentSelection** variable we added previously makes changing items straightforward. Take the following steps:

18.4.4.1 Step 1—Add the Change Menu Option Open the resource file and double-click on the Menu folder. Open the IDR_ADDRTYPE menu resource by double clicking on it. Add a new **Change** option to the **Data** menu. The ID ID_DATA_CHANGE chosen by the resource editor is fine.

18.4.4.2 Step 2—Add a Menu Handler Open the ClassWizard, choose the **Message Maps** section, and select the document class. Add in a COMMAND event handler for the ID_DATA_CHANGE menu ID. Because the document knows exactly which item to change through the **currentSelection** variable, the function shown in Listing 18.19 is easy to implement.

Listing 18.19
The OnDataChange function

```
void CAddrDoc::OnDataChange()
{
    CAddDlg addDlg;
    CAddrRec *temp;
    // init the dialog with selected data
    temp = (CAddrRec *) array.GetAt(currentSelection);
    temp->GetAddr(addDlg.m_name, addDlg.m_city, addDlg.m_state);
    // show the dialog
    if (addDlg.DoModal()==IDOK)
    {
        // Store changes back in array
        temp = new CAddrRec(addDlg.m_name,
         addDlg.m_city, addDlg.m_state);
        delete array.GetAt(currentSelection);
```

```
            array.SetAt(currentSelection, temp);
            UpdateAllViews(NULL);
    }
}
```

The code here retrieves the selected record from the array, uses it to initialize the fields of the dialog, presents the dialog to the user, and saves any changes the user makes back into the array.

18.4.4.3 Step 3—Add an UPDATE_COMMAND_UI Message Handler Open the ClassWizard and select the **Message Maps** section and the document class. In the **Object IDs** list, choose ID_DATA_CHANGE. Then choose the UPDATE_COMMAND_UI message and create a new function for it. The framework will create a function named **OnUpdateDataChange**.

Change the function as shown in Listing 18.20.

Listing 18.20
The **OnUpdateDataChange** function

```
void CAddrDoc::OnUpdateDataChange(CCmdUI* pCmdUI)
{
    pCmdUI->Enable(currentSelection != LB_ERR);
}
```

If the Boolean expression resolves to TRUE, the menu option will be enabled. Otherwise it will be disabled.

18.4.4.4 Step 4—Compile and Run When you run the program, you will find that the **Change** option lets you modify any record in the list.

18.4.5 Modify the Tool Bar

Because the user will select the options in the **Data** menu frequently, it would be useful to create buttons in the tool bar for them. To do this, you need to understand how to create new tool bar buttons and how the buttons on the toolbar are associated with the different items in the menu.

Adding buttons to the tool bar is easy. The button faces are stored in a bitmap that is already a part of the application framework. Open the resource file and then open the IDR_MAINFRAME toolbar. You will see a long narrow bitmap like the one shown in Figure 18.6. These are the tool bar buttons. Each button is 15 pixels high and 16 pixels wide. If you click on any of the buttons they will appear in the editable area and you can modify them.

In this case you would like to add three new buttons to the toolbar, one each for the **Add**, **Delete** and **Change** options. Take the following steps.

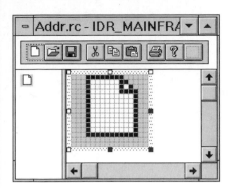

Figure 18.6
The tool bar

18.4.5.1   Step 1—Add Bitmaps The first thing that you need to do is add three new button faces to the bitmap. Figure 18.7 shows the new button faces. If you are more artistic you can create buttons that are far more glamorous.

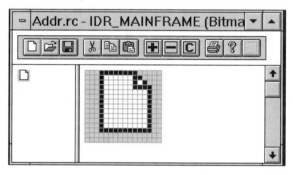

Figure 18.7
Adding new button faces to the end of the bitmap

18.4.5.2   Step 2—Modify the Buttons IDs To wire the new buttons in, you have to modify each of the new buttons' IDs. Double click on the button face in the toolbar image. A property dialog will appear. In the ID field, type or select the ID of the menu option that you want the button to activate.

To add the three buttons shown in Figure 18.7 to the tool bar, click on each new button and give it the appropriate ID. Give them the IDs of ID_DATA_ADD, ID_D ATA_DELETE and ID_DATA_CHANGE respectively.

18.4.5.3   Step 3—Compile and Run Compile and run the application. Your new tool bar should appear as shown in Figure 18.8. When you click on the new buttons, they should respond as expected. They should also enable and disable themselves properly.

436   This book is continuously updated. See http://www.iftech.com/mfc

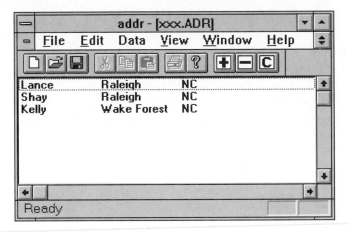

Figure 18.8
Adding new buttons to the tool bar

18.4.5.4 Step 5—Add in Labels and Status Bar Messages When you run the program and let the cursor rest on existing tool bar buttons for several seconds, you will notice that a helpful label appears to identify the button. You will also notice that these labels do not appear for the new buttons. In addition, the status bar does not update properly for the **Add**, **Delete,** and **Change** menu options. Both problems can be repaired by adding prompt strings to the menu items.

Open the resource file and double-click on the IDR_ADDR_TYPE menu. Double click on the **Add** menu option to view its property sheet, as shown in Figure 18.9.

Figure 18.9
The property sheet for the Add menu option

You can change the prompt string, as shown in Figure 18.9, and change both the status line and tool bar behavior of the menu option. The status bar entry appears in the prompt first, followed by "\n", followed by the tool bar label.

18.4.5.5 Step 5—Compile and Run When you rerun the application, you will find that the status bar updates properly and the tool bar buttons are properly labeled.

18.4.6 Adding Fields to the Status Bar

If you look at the status bar for the current application, you will see it currently is divided into four *panes*. In Figure 18.8 you can see three of those panes. As you have seen, the first pane displays information about the currently selected menu option. The next three panes display the status of the caps lock, num lock, and scroll lock keys, respectively. The leftmost pane is stretchy but has a minimum size. In Figure 18.8, the width of the window has been reduced to the point where the leftmost pane is at its limit. In this case, the framework will clip right-hand panes that do not fit.

It is easy for you to customize the status bar in three different ways:

1. You can easily display new status messages in the leftmost pane.
2. You can add new panes to the status bar and display any information that you choose.
3. You can customize the appearance of panes with the **SetPaneInfo** function.

In this section we will examine the steps you can take to add a new pane to the status bar and use it to display information about the currently selected item in the address list.

The framework generated by the AppWizard uses another array of integers in the MAINFRAME.CPP file to control the panes in the status bar. It is called the **indicators** array, and the stock version is shown in Listing 18.21.

Listing 18.21
The indicators array

```
static UINT BASED_CODE indicators[] =
{
    ID_SEPARATOR,            // status line indicator
    ID_INDICATOR_CAPS,
    ID_INDICATOR_NUM,
    ID_INDICATOR_SCRL,
};
```

The leftmost pane, known as *pane 0,* is unique. It is always present and it stretches to include all available space on the status bar minus the space required by any other panes. However, pane 0 has a minimum width and it will always consume at least that much space regardless of window size. That is why Figure 18.8 shows only three of the four available panes—the fourth was clipped off because of lack of space.

The array next indicates that the status bar should contain three additional panes for the caps, num and scroll lock keys. These are automatic panes in the sense that if you include them, they will work completely automatically with no further coding effort on your part.

To add a new pane, take the following steps.

18.4.6.1 Step 1—Add an ID to the Indicator Array Adding a new pane to the status bar is as simple as adding a new ID to the **indicators** array. As you can see in the array shown above, MFC supports three standard panes and their management is automatic. The easiest way to add a new standard indicator is to add its ID to the **indicators** array. Look in the string table in resource file and you will find six standard indicators. The string resource will give you an ID name, a constant value, and a string value. The string value will determine the width of the new pane.

Look in the application's string table resource. You will see there is already a value there for ID_INDICATOR_OVR. Modify the **indicators** array so that it contains the entries shown in Listing 18.22.

Listing 18.22
Modification of the indicators array

```
static UINT BASED_CODE indicators[] =
{
    ID_SEPARATOR,              // status line indicator
    ID_INDICATOR_CAPS,
    ID_INDICATOR_NUM,
    ID_INDICATOR_SCRL,
    ID_INDICATOR_OVR
};
```

The new pane can be identified as pane 4 or by the ID_INDICATOR_OVR ID.

18.4.6.2 Step 2—Compile and Run Compile and run the program. You will now see five menu panes. To make the new pane do anything, we need to wire in code to enable it.

18.4.6.3 Step 3—Update the New Pane To update the new pane, we need to enable it. Once enabled, it will display its string table string, in this case "OVR". You enable and disable the pane using the standard ON_COMMAND_UPDATE_UI mechanism that you used with menu options. When the status bar is visible, the UI message gets sent continuously so you can enable and disable the pane whenever you like. Unlike menu options, however, you will have to wire this handler in by hand because the ClassWizard will not handle it automatically.

To do this, open the MAINFRM.CPP and MAINFRM.H files and modify the message map as shown in the following listings (refer to Chapter 4 for an explanation of the message map modifications we are making). In MAINFRM.H add the changes shown in Listing 18.23.

Listing 18.23
Modifications to the message map in MAINFRM.H

```
    // Generated message map functions
protected:
    //{{AFX_MSG(CMainFrame)
    afx_msg int OnCreate(LPCREATESTRUCT lpCreateStruct);
    afx_msg void OnUpdateInsert(CCmdUI* pCmdUI);
```

```
    //}}AFX_MSG
    DECLARE_MESSAGE_MAP()
};
```

In MAINFRM.CPP add the changes shown in Listing 18.24.

Listing 18.24
Modifications to the message map in MAINFRM.CPP

```
/////////////////////////////////////////////////////////////////
// CMainFrame

IMPLEMENT_DYNAMIC(CMainFrame, CMDIFrameWnd)

BEGIN_MESSAGE_MAP(CMainFrame, CMDIFrameWnd)
    //{{AFX_MSG_MAP(CMainFrame)
    ON_WM_CREATE()
    ON_UPDATE_COMMAND_UI(ID_INDICATOR_OVR, OnUpdateInsert)
    //}}AFX_MSG_MAP
END_MESSAGE_MAP()
```

Finally, add the function in Listing 18.25 to the bottom of MAINFRM.CPP.

Listing 18.25
The **OnUpdateInsert** function

```
void CMainFrame::OnUpdateInsert(CCmdUI* pCmdUI)
{
    pCmdUI->Enable(TRUE);
}
```

These are the same three steps that the ClassWizard takes whenever it wants to add a new function to the message map—we have simply done it manually here.

18.4.6.4   Step 4—Compile and Run Compile and run the program and you will find that the new pane now consistently displays the word "OVR." If you were writing a text editor and wanted to display the state of the insert key, you could quite easily maintain a Boolean variable that toggles with the changes in insertion state. You could then pass this Boolean to the **Enable** function to toggle on and off the display of the word "OVR."

If you add an entry to the Accelerator portion of resource file that has the ID of ID_INSERT_KEY (or name the ID whatever you like), Key VK_INSERT, and Type VIRTKEY, then in your MAINFRM.CPP file you can use the ClassWizard to add a command handler for ID_INSERT_KEY. This handler will get called every time the user hits the Insert key, and you can use that signal to toggle a Boolean variable that controls the status pane.

18.4.6.5 *Step 5—Modify the New Pane* To demonstrate the use of the new pane for an alternative purpose, we can modify it so that it displays the index of the currently selected address record. To do this, we can modify the **SetSelection** function in the document class so it calls a new function in MAINFRM.CPP to modify the ID_INDICATOR_OVR pane. This modification function needs to reside in MAIN-FRM.CPP because the variable pointing to the status bar is protected.

Recall that the **SetSelection** function, created in Section 18.4.2, is used by the view class to tell the document which record the user currently has selected. This is a perfect place to update the status bar. Modify the **SetSelection** function in the ADDRDOC.CPP file so it appears as in Listing 18.26.

Listing 18.26
The **SetSelection** function

```
void CAddrDoc::SetSelection(int sel)
{
    CString s;

    currentSelection = sel;
    if (sel != LB_ERR)
        s.Format("%d/%d",sel,array.GetSize());
    else
        s="";
    CAddrApp *app = (CAddrApp *) AfxGetApp();
    CMainFrame *mf = (CMainFrame *) app->m_pMainWnd;
    mf->SetRecStatus(s);
}
```

This function now formats a string with information about the current selection and the number of address records in the array and then calls the **SetRecStatus** function in MAINFRM.CPP. This is a new function added to handle status bar updates. The new function appears in Listing 18.27.

Listing 18.27
The **SetRecStatus** function

```
void CMainFrame::SetRecStatus(CString s)
{
    m_wndStatusBar.SetPaneText(
        m_wndStatusBar.CommandToIndex(ID_INDICATOR_OVR), s);
}
```

Add a prototype for MAINFRM.H as well. As you can see, the function calls the **SetPaneText** function in the status bar class to change the text displayed in the new status bar pane. See the documentation for details on this function. You may also want to look at the **SetPaneInfo** function and use it to experiment with different styles and sizes. Note also that if you replace the first parameter passed to **SetPaneText** with a zero, you can place any text you like into the leftmost pane to inform the user of progress within your program.

18.4.6.6 Step 6—Compile and Run Compile and run the program. You will find that now when you select an address record in the list the status bar displays the index of the selection. There are a variety of ways that you can use the status bar to display useful information like this for the user.

If you want to create your own status bar pane, rather than modifying the OVR pane as demonstrated here, create a new string resource and add the ID of that resource to the **indicators** array. Then create a Command UI handler for it in the manner shown for the OVR UI handler.

18.4.7 Adding Clipboard Support

Every program that we have created in this part of the book has contained an **Edit** menu, but only the text editor created in Chapter 16 has really used it. In this section we will look at how you can add **Cut**, **Copy,** and **Paste** support to an application by adding clipboard functionality to this address list program.

One of the nice things about the clipboard is the fact that it is extremely easy to use. There are two functions in the 32-bit API that manipulate the clipboard: **SetClipboardData** and **GetClipboardData**. These functions either add or retrieve a block of memory from the clipboard.

To make the clipboard even easier to use, we will create a simple class that can handle the movement of text to and from the clipboard. Then we will use that new class when we create the handlers for the **Cut**, **Copy**, and **Paste** options. Take the following steps.

18.4.7.1 Step 1—Creating a Clipboard Class The clipboard class contains the two functions that let you add text data to or retrieve text data from the clipboard. The header file for the new class is shown in Listing 18.28.

Listing 18.28
Header file for the clipboard class

```
// cbtext.h
// CBText class: moves text on and off the clipboard

class CBText
{
public:
    CString GetText();
    BOOL SetText(CString s);
};
```

Create a new text file in Visual C++ and add the above information to it. Then save the file under the name CBTEXT.H. The implementation of the class appears in Listing 18.29.

Listing 18.29
Clipboard class implementation

```cpp
// cbtext.cpp
// CBText class: moves text on and off the clipboard

#include "stdafx.h"
#include "cbtext.h"
#include <memory.h>

CString CBText::GetText()
{
    CString s;
    HGLOBAL temp;
    LPTSTR str;

    // Get the frame wnd for the app
    CWinApp *app = AfxGetApp();
    CFrameWnd *fw = (CFrameWnd *)app->m_pMainWnd;

    // Open the clipboard
    if (!::OpenClipboard(fw->m_hWnd))
        return s;

    // Get the data from the clipboard
    temp = GetClipboardData(CF_TEXT);
    if (temp == NULL)
    {
        CloseClipboard();
        return s;
    }
    // Extract the text
    str = (char *)GlobalLock(temp);
    LPTSTR t = s.GetBuffer(strlen(str) + 1);
    memcpy(t, str, strlen(str) + 1);
    s.ReleaseBuffer();
    GlobalUnlock((void *)temp);

    CloseClipboard();

    return s;
}

BOOL CBText::SetText(CString s)
{
    HGLOBAL temp;
    CWinApp *app = AfxGetApp();
    CFrameWnd *fw = (CFrameWnd *)app->m_pMainWnd;
    LPTSTR str;

    // Open and clear the clipboard
    if (!::OpenClipboard(fw->m_hWnd))
        return FALSE;
    ::EmptyClipboard();
```

```
    // Allocate a block and copy text in
    temp = GlobalAlloc(GHND, s.GetLength() + 1);
    if (temp == NULL)
    {
        CloseClipboard();
        return FALSE;
    }
    str = (char *)GlobalLock(temp);
    memcpy(str, LPCTSTR(s), s.GetLength() + 1);
    GlobalUnlock((void *)temp);

    // Send data to clipboard
    SetClipboardData(CF_TEXT, temp);
    CloseClipboard();

    return TRUE;
}
```

Create a new text file in Visual C++ and add this information to it. Then save the file under the name CBTEXT.CPP. *Add the CBTEXT.CPP file to the project. Include the CBTEXT.H file at the beginning of the document class as shown in Listing 18.30.*

Listing 18.30
Adding the CBTEXT.H file to the document class

```
// addrdoc.cpp : implementation of the CAddrDoc class
//

#include "stdafx.h"
#include "addr.h"

#include "addrdoc.h"
#include "adddlg.h"
#include "addrrec.h"
#include "mainfrm.h"
#include "cbtext.h"

#ifdef _DEBUG
...
```

You will find that the **CBText** class is a generally useful class whenever you have any text data to add to or retrieve from the clipboard. If you like, you can also register your own clipboard classes and use the same techniques shown here to move any sort of data on or off the clipboard.

18.4.7.2   Step 2—Handle the Copy Option The easiest clipboard option to handle is the **Copy** option, and we will use it here to demonstrate the process. Open the ClassWizard, make sure you are looking at the **Message Maps** section, and select

444

the **CAddrDoc** class. Choose ID_EDIT_COPY from the **Object IDs** list, and COM-MAND from the **Messages** list. Click on the **Add Function** button and add a function with the name **OnEditAdd**. Add the code in Listing 18.31 to that function:

Listing 18.31
The **OnEditCopy** function

```
void CAddrDoc::OnEditCopy()
{
    if (currentSelection == LB_ERR)
        return;CBText t;
    CString name, city, state;
    char s[1000];
    ostrstream ostr(s,1000);
    GetAddr(currentSelection, name, city, state);
    ostr << name << '\t';
    ostr << city << '\t';
    ostr << state << ends;
    t.SetText(s);
}
```

This code extracts the currently selected record from the array and formats it into a text string that it sends to the clipboard.

18.4.7.3 Step 3—Compile and Run Compile and run the program. Because it has a command message handler, the **Copy** menu option will now be enabled. If you select an address record and then select the **Copy** option in the **Edit** menu, the currently selected record will be copied to the clipboard as text. You can then try pasting it into any other application that accepts text, such as the notepad.

18.4.7.4 Step 4—Handle Incidentals You can now add more detail to the program. For example, you want to add a UI handler to the program so the **Copy** option is disabled unless one of the items in the address list is currently selected. You can then implement a **Cut** option that does exactly the same thing that the **Copy** option does, but additionally deletes the current record. To handle the **Paste** option, you can reverse what the **Copy** option does and add the new record to the list.

18.5 Printing

Section 15.8 explains how the printing process works in an AppWizard framework. It showed how to apply those principles to Chapter 15's drawing application. In that example, printing could leverage off of the **OnDraw** function that we had already created to handle screen refreshing.

In this chapter, we have created an address list application that uses a list control to handle viewing. We have totally ignored the **OnDraw** function because the form handles all the I/O details for us. Therefore, the printing process will be slightly different in this application. However, the general concerns and process discussed in

Section 15.8 are still applicable here. We will simply have to do more work in the **On-Print** function.

In this address list program, printing and viewing are totally separated. When it comes time to print the information, a completely separate piece of code needs to format the page in the **OnPrint** function. This code will get each record from the document class, format it onto a sheet of paper, and then eject the page. If multiple pages are needed, the code can handle it dynamically during the print process.

Let's start by printing a single page. Take the following steps.

18.5.1 Step 1—Create a Framework

Start with the framework that you created in Section 18.4. This framework should have its printing capabilities already activated because the first step in Section 18.4 asks you to enable printing when you create the framework. Compile and run the program and you will find that the menu options **Print**, **Print Preview,** and **Printer Setup** are all present in the **File** menu.

18.5.2 Step 2—Set the Font

To print the address information, it is necessary either to use the default system font available in the printer DC or specify a font. We will do the latter as a demonstration. The best place to put the font creation is in the **OnBeginPrinting** function of the view class. Alternatively, you could create a menu option that lets the user select the font from the standard font dialog. The code is in Listing 18.32.

Listing 18.32
The **OnBeginPrinting** function

```
CFont *font=NULL;

void CAddrView::OnBeginPrinting(CDC* pDC, CPrintInfo* pInfo)
{
    font = new CFont;
    font->CreateFont (16,0,0,0,700,0,0,0,
        ANSI_CHARSET,OUT_DEFAULT_PRECIS,
        CLIP_DEFAULT_PRECIS,
        DEFAULT_QUALITY,
        DEFAULT_PITCH|FF_DONTCARE,
        "Arial");
}
```

Use the ClassWizard to edit the code for this function. You can declare the **font** variable anywhere you like. Placing it as an attribute member of the view class is the easiest thing to do now, but in the long term you will probably want to make it a member of the document (so you can save it with the document) or of the application (so you save it as an application variable). See Chapter 11 for more information on fonts.

Now also modify the **OnEndPrinting** function so it cleans up the allocated font as in Listing 18.33.

Listing 18.33
The **OnEndPrinting** function

```
void CAddrView::OnEndPrinting(CDC* pDC, CPrintInfo* pInfo)
{
    delete font;
}
```

18.5.3 Step 3—Prepare the DC

The **OnPrepareDC** function prepares the DC before the call to **OnPrint** is made. This function needs to set the mapping mode and select the font into the DC. Use the ClassWizard to find the **OnPrepareDC** function and modify it as shown in Listing 18.34.

Listing 18.34
The **OnPrepareDC** function

```
void CAddrView::OnPrepareDC(CDC* pDC, CPrintInfo* pInfo)
{
    CFormView::OnPrepareDC(pDC, pInfo);
    if (pInfo)
    {
        pDC->SetMapMode(MM_LOENGLISH);
        pDC->SelectObject(font);
    }
}
```

The **if** statement checks to make sure the function is being called for a print operation. If it is, the code sets the mapping mode to LOENGLISH. This is done as a convenience here, because it is easier to think about tab distances and margins in inches rather than pixels. The code then selects the font into the DC. Note the efficiency of allocating the font only once in **OnBeginPrinting** and then reusing it over and over again in **OnPrepareDC**.

18.5.4 Step 4—Print One Page

To print the list, the code needs to extract all the items from the list, format each one into a single line, and then print those lines with the proper inter-line spacing. The code in Listing 18.35 does this.

Listing 18.35
The **OnPrint** function

```
void CAddrView::OnPrint(CDC* pDC, CPrintInfo* pInfo)
{
    CAddrDoc *pDoc = GetDocument();
    int x;
    int tab=200;
    char s[100];
    ostrstream ostr(s,100);

    // Figure height of one line
    CSize size = pDC->GetTabbedTextExtent("Fg", 2, 1, &tab);
    // Set the left margin
    pInfo->m_rectDraw.left += 100;

    for (x=0; x<pDoc->NumAddrs(); x++)
    {
        // form the string to print
        CString name, city, state;
        pDoc->GetAddr(x, name, city, state);
            ostr.seekp(ios::beg);
        ostr << name << '\t';
        ostr << city << '\t';
        ostr << state << ends;
        // print the string
        pDC->TabbedTextOut(pInfo->m_rectDraw.left, -x*(size.cy + 5),
            s, strlen(s), 1, &tab, 100);
    }
}
```

Be sure to include STRSTREA.H at the top of the view class.

This code first uses **GetTabbedTextExtent** to figure out how high a line of text is in the chosen font. It will use this height plus 5/100ths of an inch for the inter-line spacing. It also gives the page a one-inch left-hand margin by modifying the **m_rectDraw** member. Then it is a simple matter of painting all the lines onto the page using the **TabbedTextOut** function. If the document is longer than one page, the excess will simply get clipped and ignored.

18.5.5 Step 5—Compile and Run

Compile and run the program. Enter some address information into the list. If you select the **Print Preview** menu option, it will work correctly. If you select the **Print** option, you will find that the output appears on the printer in a 16-point Arial font. Feel free to adjust the font size to something larger or smaller and see what happens.

18.5.6 Step 6—Add in Pagination

To add in pagination, follow the same sort of plan seen in Section 15.8. First, we need a Boolean that can control the **m_bContinuePrinting** flag. It is initialized in **OnBeginPrinting**. Declare the **continuePrinting** variable anywhere appropriate to your code structure. See Listing 18.36.

Listing 18.36
The continuePrinting variable

```
CFont *font=NULL;
BOOL continuePrinting = TRUE;

void CAddrView::OnBeginPrinting(CDC* pDC, CPrintInfo* pInfo)
{
    font = new CFont;
    font->CreateFont (16,0,0,0,700,0,0,0,
        ANSI_CHARSET,OUT_DEFAULT_PRECIS,
        CLIP_DEFAULT_PRECIS,
        DEFAULT_QUALITY,
        DEFAULT_PITCH|FF_DONTCARE,
        "Arial");
    continuePrinting = TRUE;
}
```

Next, modify the **OnPrepareDC** function, as shown in Listing 18.37 and discussed in Section 15.8, so it can halt printing during an actual **Print** operation.

Listing 18.37
The **OnPrepareDC** function

```
void CAddrView::OnPrepareDC(CDC* pDC, CPrintInfo* pInfo)
{
    CFormView::OnPrepareDC(pDC, pInfo);
    if (pInfo)
    {
        pDC->SetMapMode(MM_LOENGLISH);
        pDC->SelectObject(font);
        if (!pInfo->m_bPreview)
            pInfo->m_bContinuePrinting = continuePrinting;
    }
}
```

Finally, modify the **OnPrint** function as shown in Listing 18.38 so it calculates the number of lines per page and space lines appropriately on each page.

Listing 18.38
The **OnPrint** function

```
void CAddrView::OnPrint(CDC* pDC, CPrintInfo* pInfo)
{
    CAddrDoc *pDoc = GetDocument();
    int tab=200;
    char s[100];
    ostrstream ostr(s,100);
```

```
    // Figure heigh of one line
    CSize size = pDC->GetTabbedTextExtent("Fg", 2, 1, &tab);
    // Set the left margin
    pInfo->m_rectDraw.left += 100;
    // calc max number of pages and lines per page
    int linesPerPage =
        abs(pInfo->m_rectDraw.Height()) / size.cy - 1;
    int maxPage = pDoc->NumAddrs() / linesPerPage;
    if (pDoc->NumAddrs() % linesPerPage)
        maxPage++;
    pInfo->SetMaxPage(maxPage);

    int i, x;
    for (i=0; i < linesPerPage; i++)
    {
        x = (pInfo->m_nCurPage - 1) * linesPerPage + i;
        if (x >= pDoc->NumAddrs())
        {
            continuePrinting = FALSE;
            break;
        }
        // form the string to print
        CString name, city, state;
        pDoc->GetAddr(x, name, city, state);
            ostr.seekp(ios::beg);
        ostr << name << '\t';
        ostr << city << '\t';
        ostr << state << ends;
        // print the string
        pDC->TabbedTextOut(pInfo->m_rectDraw.left, -i*(size.cy + 5),
            s, strlen(s), 1, &tab, 100);
    }
}
```

This code uses the line height to calculate the number of lines per page and from that is able to calculate the number of pages necessary to print the document. This step allows the **Print Preview** screen to manage the **Next** and **Previous** buttons correctly. The code also sets **continuePrinting** correctly so the **OnPrepareDC** can stop print operations appropriately.

As mentioned in Chapter 15, there are many ways to handle printing. See the MFC Encyclopedia in Books, On-Line as well as the Check Book sample for more information.

18.6 Conclusion

In this chapter we have combined a number of different techniques discussed in previous chapters to create a complete application that successfully uses the document and view classes in a standard AppWizard framework. We have also had a chance to discuss some of the more subtle design issues that arise in creating a complete application.

There are a number of ways in which you can extend this application to further experiment with the application framework. For example, you might try adding a second view type to the application so the user can view lists *or* forms in the MDI framework. This can be accomplished by creating a new view class and adding a new document template for it as discussed in Chapter 16.

You might also work with the updating mechanism currently used in this application. As implemented now, each addition to the list causes the list control to be completely reloaded. This is obviously wasteful when there is a large number of records in the list. There are a variety of ways you can use **UpdateAllViews** to improve the updating mechanism so each insertion and deletion takes minimal CPU effort.

You might also try adding more fields to the dialog and the display so you can make the application more useful. For example, you could add full address and/or phone number information. You might also extend the document class to give the application the ability to re-sort the list in different ways, check for duplicates, and so on.

You might also want to check on the database handling classes in MFC, as described in Chapter 33. You may find it useful to convert this application to a database approach so you can experiment with the ODBC classes.

CONTEXT-SENSITIVE HELP

One of the greatest achievements of the Windows line of operating systems is the consistent and uniform help facility that it offers. This facility can handle everything from simple two-page help files to help files that contain many thousands of fully indexed pages.

Help files are created by the Help Compiler, a specialized tool that is able to read help source files and produce normal Windows help files. Like any compiler, you could spend quite a bit of time understanding its every nuance. If you wish to do this, see the "Help Compiler User's Guide" in the on-line documentation. In this chapter, the goal is to cover the essentials so you can create simple help files without a great deal of effort. You are aided in this endeavor by features that you can automatically add to an application using the AppWizard.

19.1 Understanding the AppWizard's Help Framework

The AppWizard has the ability when it is creating a new application to add help source files, a help project file, and context sensitive help features to its standard framework. The best way to begin understanding these features is to activate them and try them out. To do this, create a new application framework by taking the following steps.

19.1.1 Step 1—Create the Framework

Create a new MDI framework with the AppWizard (see Appendix B.6.1 for an introduction). Give the new project the name "Samp." Select the location for the new application directory and rename the directory if necessary. Click the **Create** button.

As you go through the AppWizard option screens, select the following options:
- Enable all application features, including the tool bar, status bar, printing, and *Context-Sensitive Help*.
- Leave all file and class names as chosen by the AppWizard.

If you examine the files that the AppWizard creates, you will find some new titles. First, there is a completely new HLP directory that contains two RTF files and a lot of bitmaps. In the project's main directory, you will also find a help project file named SAMP.HPJ, along with a batch file named MAKEHELP.BAT. The batch file compiles the help project and help source files in the HLP directory to create a standard HLP file. MAKEHELP.BAT is automatically executed by the project file when you build the project, or you can run it manually from a command line.

19.1.2 Step 2—Compile and Run

Compile the application by selecting the **Build** option in the **Build** menu. The project should automatically run MAKEHELP.BAT.

When you run the application, you will find that the **Help** menu now contains a new option: It opens a help window that contains information about this application. You will notice a number of "blanks" in this help file that you eventually will want to change to customize the help file for your application. You will also notice that every menu option in the program already has an entry in the help file. In addition, the help buttons on the various dialogs that appear in the framework work correctly.

The tool bar now has a new button for help. This button lets you select menu options and get help on them directly. You can click the button (or press the Shift-F1 key) and then select any menu option to get help on it.

The F1 and Shift-F1 keys provide *context-sensitive help*. This is the most advanced feature of the help system that the AppWizard built for you. If you press F1, the help system will give you information about the current document. As you add new menu options, dialogs, document templates, and so on, you can add additional context-sensitive help pages for each one. If a dialog box is open, F1 will give you help on that dialog, equivalent to pressing the dialog's **Help** button.

19.2 Understanding and Modifying the Help Files

Help files are simply text files written in a specific format and then compiled through the help compiler. The source code for a typical help file for an application consists of a "project" file that identifies the components and their names and one or more "code" files that contain the actual help information. In the framework created in the previous section, the project file is called SAMP.HPJ, and the code files are in the HLP directory under the names AFXCORE.RTF and AFXPRINT.RTF. The AFXPRINT.RTF file handles all the printing options and dialogs in the **File** menu, while the AFXCORE.RTF file handles everything else. The pair of files helps to demonstrate how easy it is to subdivide a large help file into separate RTF (Rich Text Format) files.

An HLP file generated by the help compiler contains a number of components. In particular it contains help topic pages from RTF files, as well as bitmaps. The project file tells the help compiler about the relationships between these components. Listing 19.1 shows the project file that the AppWizard created.

Listing 19.1
The help project file

```
[OPTIONS]
CONTENTS=main_index
TITLE=SAMP Application Help
COMPRESS=true
WARNING=2
BMROOT= ..,.
ROOT= ..,.

[FILES]
afxcore.rtf
afxprint.rtf

[ALIAS]
HIDR_MAINFRAME = main_index
HIDR_SAMPTYPE = HIDR_DOC1TYPE
HIDD_ABOUTBOX = HID_APP_ABOUT

HID_HT_SIZE = HID_SC_SIZE
HID_HT_HSCROLL = scrollbars
HID_HT_VSCROLL = scrollbars
HID_HT_MINBUTTON = HID_SC_MINIMIZE
HID_HT_MAXBUTTON = HID_SC_MAXIMIZE
AFX_HIDP_INVALID_FILENAME       = AFX_HIDP_default
AFX_HIDP_FAILED_TO_OPEN_DOC     = AFX_HIDP_default
AFX_HIDP_FAILED_TO_SAVE_DOC     = AFX_HIDP_default
AFX_HIDP_ASK_TO_SAVE            = AFX_HIDP_default
AFX_HIDP_FAILED_TO_CREATE_DOC   = AFX_HIDP_default
AFX_HIDP_FILE_TOO_LARGE         = AFX_HIDP_default
AFX_HIDP_FAILED_TO_START_PRINT  = AFX_HIDP_default
AFX_HIDP_FAILED_TO_LAUNCH_HELP  = AFX_HIDP_default
AFX_HIDP_INTERNAL_FAILURE       = AFX_HIDP_default
AFX_HIDP_COMMAND_FAILURE        = AFX_HIDP_default
AFX_HIDP_PARSE_INT              = AFX_HIDP_default
AFX_HIDP_PARSE_REAL             = AFX_HIDP_default
AFX_HIDP_PARSE_INT_RANGE        = AFX_HIDP_default
AFX_HIDP_PARSE_REAL_RANGE       = AFX_HIDP_default
AFX_HIDP_PARSE_STRING_SIZE      = AFX_HIDP_default
AFX_HIDP_FAILED_INVALID_FORMAT  = AFX_HIDP_default
AFX_HIDP_FAILED_INVALID_PATH    = AFX_HIDP_default
AFX_HIDP_FAILED_DISK_FULL       = AFX_HIDP_default
AFX_HIDP_FAILED_ACCESS_READ     = AFX_HIDP_default
AFX_HIDP_FAILED_ACCESS_WRITE    = AFX_HIDP_default
AFX_HIDP_FAILED_IO_ERROR_READ   = AFX_HIDP_default
```

```
AFX_HIDP_FAILED_IO_ERROR_WRITE        = AFX_HIDP_default
AFX_HIDP_STATIC_OBJECT                = AFX_HIDP_default
AFX_HIDP_FAILED_TO_CONNECT            = AFX_HIDP_default
AFX_HIDP_SERVER_BUSY                  = AFX_HIDP_default
AFX_HIDP_BAD_VERB                     = AFX_HIDP_default
AFX_HIDP_FAILED_MEMORY_ALLOC          = AFX_HIDP_default
AFX_HIDP_FAILED_TO_NOTIFY             = AFX_HIDP_default
AFX_HIDP_FAILED_TO_LAUNCH             = AFX_HIDP_default
AFX_HIDP_ASK_TO_UPDATE                = AFX_HIDP_default
AFX_HIDP_FAILED_TO_UPDATE             = AFX_HIDP_default
AFX_HIDP_FAILED_TO_REGISTER           = AFX_HIDP_default
AFX_HIDP_FAILED_TO_AUTO_REGISTER      = AFX_HIDP_default

[MAP]
#include <C:\local\MSDEV\MFC\include\afxhelp.hm>
#include <samp.hm>
```

You can see in Listing 19.1 that the project file contains several standard sections: [OPTIONS], [FILES], [BITMAPS], [ALIAS], and [MAP] are the sections seen in this file. These sections are explained in more detail below. However, just a quick scan reveals that the [FILES] section contains a list of all the help source files and the [BITMAPS] section lists all the bitmaps in the HLP directory.

A help source file uses the RTF text description language for its "programming language." Because the help compiler reads RTF, it is possible to create and edit help code files using any RTF-compatible editor (Microsoft Word, Word Perfect, etc.). Once you know a few things about formatting with the RTF syntax, it is easy to create massive help files very quickly.

To change or add new help information to the RTF files that the AppWizard provides, you need to edit the RTF files in the HLP directory for your project. The main file is named AFXCORE.RTF. Use any editor that understands RTF files to open this file. When you load a help file as shown in Figure 19.1, you will notice several conventions. The editor shown in Figure 19.1 happens to be Microsoft Word version 6.0, and it has been adjusted so that it shows footnotes, hidden text, and formatting characters like tab keys and paragraph symbols. You may find that the file looks slightly different depending on the editor that you use to open it.

Here are some of the conventions you will find as you browse through a help RTF file:

1. Any text you need to modify has "<<...>>" around it. You can modify any text you find, but these particular pieces *must* be changed to customize the files for your application.
2. Each *topic*, or page, in the help file is specified by a specific page break in the RTF file.

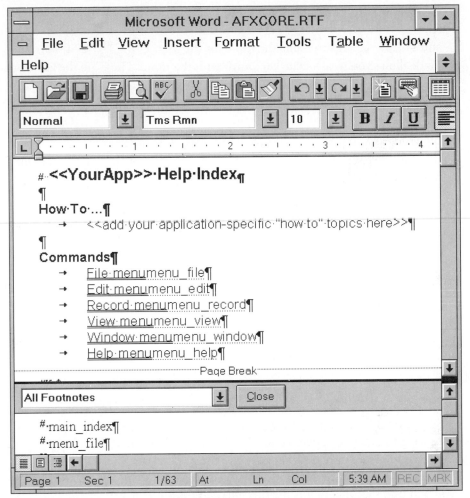

Figure 19.1
Loading a help file into Microsoft Word. By putting Word into Page Layout mode for the file, you can actually see and edit the footnotes at the bottom of each page

3. Hypertext links have double underlining for the tag, followed by hidden text that points to a new help topic page. The hidden text is called a *context string* and references another help topic. To create hidden text, type in the string, drag over it to select it, and then choose the *hidden* style in whatever editor you are using.

4. The "footnote" specifier from RTF has been borrowed to specify topic titles and key words. Using "#" as a footnote mark creates a context string for a help topic. This string is used in links (and in the mapping table in the help project file—see below) to allow the system to jump to a specific topic. In general, every topic should have a context string. In Figure 19.1 the context string for

the displayed topic is set to "menu_index". Using "$" as a footnote mark allows you to give the topic a title. The title is used in the help system's Search and History dialogs to name the topic for the user. Using "K" as a footnote mark allows you to associate key words with the topic. These are the key words displayed in the help system's Search dialog. A topic can have more than one key word—they are separated by semicolons. Different topics can also share the same key words.

5. Big groupings of items can be placed in tables.
6. All standard fonts, formatting, and so on that the editor supports are handled normally when the help source file is compiled and eventually displayed in the help window.

To try your hand at modifying a help file, open AFXCORE.RTF yourself and try the following steps.

19.2.1 Step 1—Change Several <<...>> Items

Open the AFXCORE.RTF file with an editor capable of handling RTF files. Put the editor into Page View mode if possible and turn on viewing for hidden text. Page through the file to get the lay of the land and then return to the first page.

At the top of the file, find the string "<<YourApp>>" and replace it with your application's name. Then, below that find the string "<<add your application-specific 'how to' topics here>>" and replace it with some descriptive text.

19.2.2 Step 2—Save, Compile, and Run

Save the RTF file to disk (being sure that when you save it it remains in RTF format rather than being converted to the editor's native format). Rerun the MAKE-HELP batch file as described earlier in the chapter. Then run the sample application and select the option in the **Help** menu. When you see the opening page of the help file you will find that it contains the title and description that you added.

19.2.3 Step 3—Add New Key Words

Adding key words to a help topic allows the user to look up the topic with the **Search** button. Many of the topics already have key words, and in those examples you can see that you can have multiple key words associated with any topic, with the different words or phrases separated by semicolons.

To add key words to the first help topic in AFXCORE.RTF, position the cursor so it is just to the right of the "#" symbol on the first line of the help topic. Use your editor's "Insert Footnote" feature to add a footnote. Set the reference character to "K". In the text of the footnote, add your key words or phrases, separated by semicolons.

Reposition the cursor next to the "K" on the first line of the file and then insert a second footnote. Set the reference character on this one to "$". The "$" reference specifies the title of the topic, and it is the string that appears in the bottom part of the **Search** dialog when you select a key word. Type a title into the footnote text.

Make sure that, in the actual footnote, there is only one blank separating the "K" and the "$" from their associated strings.

19.2.4 Step 4—Save, Compile, and Run

Save the RTF file to disk (being sure that when you save it it remains in RTF format rather than being converted to the editor's native format). Rerun the MAKE-HELP batch file as described earlier in the chapter. Then run the sample application and select the option in the **Help** menu. You will find the key words and when you select one of them it makes the proper topic page appear.

19.2.5 Step 5—Add a New Hypertext Link

In the first page of the file, create a new hypertext link. To do this, you have to add a piece of text for the reference that the user sees, along with a context string that tells the system what topic to jump to when the user clicks on the text. Recall that the context string for a help topic is specified by the topic's "#" footnote. As you can see throughout the RTF file, the text that the user sees for the hypertext link is formatted with double underlining, while the context string is formatted as hidden text. Create a new hypertext link somewhere on the first page.

19.2.6 Step 6—Save, Compile, and Run

Save the RTF file to disk (being sure that when you save it it remains in RTF format rather than being converted to the editor's native format). Rerun the MAKE-HELP batch file as described earlier in the chapter. Then run the sample application and select the option in the **Help** menu. Once you see the opening page of the help file, find your new hypertext link and click on it to try it out.

19.2.7 Step 7—Add Topics

The RTF file contains one page for each help topic and the AppWizard created a stock set of topics for the application framework it generated. You will frequently want to add your own new material to this starter set.

Adding a new topic to a help file is easy. First, at the bottom of the RTF file, add a page break. Then create the new topic by adding a title and some body text. Use the pages already in the RTF file as examples when you create your new page.

Now add a context string, a title, and key words to the topic. Click at the beginning of the title line for the topic page. Add a footnote with the reference character "#" associated with it. This is the context string for the page. In the footnote text, add the string "new_topic". Then add key words and a title as described in Section 19.2.3.

To get to the new page, you will have to add a hypertext link to it elsewhere in the help file. Do that using the instructions in Section 19.2.5.

19.2.8 Step 8—Save, Compile, and Run

Save the RTF file to disk (being sure that when you save it it remains in RTF format rather than being converted to the editor's native format). Rerun the MAKE-

HELP batch file as described earlier in the chapter. Then run the sample application and select the option in the **Help** menu. Once you see the opening page of the help file, find your new hypertext link and click on it to try out the new topic page.

19.2.9 Step 9—Add a New Bitmap

It is easy to add a new bitmap to your new page. Use the Paintbrush application or some other bitmap editor to create a new bitmap. Save the new bitmap to the HLP directory of your project under the name NEW.BMP. Edit the SAMP.HPJ file and add the bitmap name to the list of bitmaps.

If you add a string like the one below anywhere on any topic page, the bitmap will appear at that point:

```
{bmc hlp\new.bmp}
```

That string can exist by itself on a line of its own or embedded within text.

19.2.10 Step 10—Save, Compile, and Run

Save the RTF file to disk (being sure that when you save it it remains in RTF format rather than being converted to the editor's native format). Rerun the MAKE-HELP batch file as described earlier in the chapter. Then run the sample application and select the option in the **Help** menu. Once you see the opening page of the help file, find your new bitmap.

19.3 Context-Sensitive Help

The help system uses an ID-driven mechanism to allow context-sensitive help for menu options and dialog boxes. Tech Note 28 describes the mechanism in detail. You can activate context-sensitive help for new menu options and dialogs very easily using a tool called MAKEHM, which is already called by MAKEHELP.BAT.

The help project file contains a section called the [MAP] section. This section maps integer values to help context strings. To get a better idea of how the map section works, try the following example.

19.3.1 Step 1—Add a Menu Option

Start with the example application that you generated in Section 19.2. Open the resource file, open the IDR_SAMPTYPE menu, and add a new menu option to the bottom of the **Edit** menu. Call the new menu option **Test**. The ID_EDIT_TEST ID that the resource editor chooses for the new option is fine. Close the menu editor window.

19.3.2 Step 2—Add a Menu Handler

Open the ClassWizard. Select the **CSampApp** class and the **Message Maps** section. Add a COMMAND function for ID_EDIT_TEST. Edit the function so it appears as in Listing 19.2.

Listing 19.2
The OnEditTest function

```
void CSampApp::OnEditTest()
{
    WinHelp(2500);
}
```

This code tells the application to open the help system and to pass it the value 2,500 as a help context when it opens it. This value is a completely arbitrary choice.

19.3.3 Step 3—Add a Topic

Add a new topic to the AFXCORE.RTF file, as discussed in Section 19.2.7. Give it the context string HID_TEST by adding a footnote with the reference character "#" and the text HID_TEST.

19.3.4 Step 4—Modify the MAP Section

To the bottom of the MAP section in the help project file SAMP.HPJ, add the following line:

```
HID_TEST 2500
```

This line tells the help system to associate the value 2500 with the HID_TEST help context.

19.3.5 Step 5—Compile and Run

Save the RTF file to disk (being sure that when you save it it remains in RTF format rather than being converted to the editor's native format). Rerun the MAKE-HELP batch file as described earlier in the chapter. Choose the **Build** option in the **Build** menu to build the application. Run the application and select its new **Test** option in the **Edit** menu. The help window should open and the topic shown should be the one with the HID_TEST context ID.

The previous steps demonstrate that it is possible, from within an application, to activate the help system and cause it to produce a specific help page when it appears. This technique is the basis of the context-sensitive help system created by the App-Wizard. When you press the F1 key in a dialog, or when you click on a menu option with the cursor in the arrow-question state (activated by Shift-F1), the framework responds to the keystroke or mouse click by calling **WinHelp** and passing it an integer. The integer is the sum of the ID for the menu item or the dialog and a constant (the constants are defined in on-line documents in Tech Note 28). For example, if the user has pressed F1 while inside a dialog, the integer passed to **WinHelp** by the framework is the sum of the dialog's ID and the constant 0x200000.

The help system can respond to that ID if it has an association, in the help project file's MAP section, between the integer and a help context. You can type the line in by hand as demonstrated in Section 19.3.4, but this practice is discouraged.

Instead you should allow a tool called MAKEHM, which is called automatically by MAKEHELP.BAT, to modify the SAMP.HM file in the project's HLP directory. SAMP.HM is a help mapping file, and you can see it being included into the MAP section of the help project file at the bottom of Listing 19.1.

The MAKEHM tool simply looks at the IDs in the RESOURCE.H file (the file that contains the integer IDs for all the resource constants you define) and uses them to create help mappings between help IDs and help context strings. This is best seen through an example, so take the following steps.

19.3.6 Step 6—Prepare Yourself

Search the on-line documentation for pages containing MAKEHM in the title. These pages will explain that the tool can create help mapping files from resource header files.

19.3.7 Step 7—Look at MAKEHELP.BAT

If you look in MAKEHELP.BAT in your project's directory, you will find that this batch file automatically calls MAKEHM on all different standard IDs and creates the file HLP/SAMP.HM each time you run MAKEHELP.BAT.

19.3.8 Step 8—Look at SAMP.HM

Run MAKEHELP.BAT. Open the file SAMP.HM. You will find the following mapping entries as shown in Listing 19.3.

Listing 19.3
SAMP.HM file

```
// MAKEHELP.BAT generated Help Map file.  Used by SAMP.HPJ.

// Commands (ID_* and IDM_*)
HID_EDIT_TEST                           0x18003

// Prompts (IDP_*)

// Resources (IDR_*)
HIDR_MAINFRAME                          0x20080
HIDR_SAMPTYPE                           0x20081

// Dialogs (IDD_*)
HIDD_ABOUTBOX                           0x20064
```

Note that the MAKEHELP.BAT batch file system automatically has translated ID_EDIT_TEST into the context string HID_EDIT_TEST and given it a constant. This constant is the value that the application framework is going to emit to the help system when the user requests context-sensitive help on the **Test** option in the **Edit** menu.

19.3.9 Step 9—Look at SAMP.HM

In the AFXCORE.RTF file, create a new help topic and give it the context string HID_EDIT_TEST. See Section 19.2.7.

19.3.10 Step 10—Compile and Run

Save the RTF file to disk (being sure that when you save it it remains in RTF format rather than being converted to the editor's native format). Rerun the MAKE-HELP batch file as described earlier in the chapter. Run the application, press Shift-F1, and select the new **Test** option in the **Edit** menu. The help window should open and the topic shown should be the one with the HID_EDIT_TEST context ID.

As you can see, the AppWizard framework has done everything possible to make the creation of context-sensitive help pages straightforward. All that you have to do, essentially, is add topics with the proper help IDs for menu items and dialogs to the RTF file and recompile the help file.

19.4 Aliases

A big part of the help project file is the [ALIAS] section. This section allows you to point multiple help contexts to the same topic page in a help file. You might do this, for example, because you have multiple dialogs that do approximately the same thing, but each one is different enough to have its own ID. In this case you can create a single help topic and map all of the IDs to that topic.

AFX also predefines a number of help IDs and, in the ALIAS section, maps them to a default page. Many of these IDs are associated with dialogs that the application framework presents automatically. For example, the "Save Changes" dialog appears when you try to close a file that has not yet been changed. The framework generates this dialog automatically. The help ID associated with that dialog is AFX_HIDP_ASK_TO_SAVE, and this ID is currently aliased to the help ID AFX_HIPD_Default. You can write separate help pages for these different dialogs in one of two ways.

One way is to create a new help topic (see Section 19.2.9) and set its context string to one of the help IDs in the ALIAS section. For example, you could create a new help topic in the RTF file with the context string AFX_HIDP_ASK_TO_SAVE. Then, if you remove that entry from the ALIAS section and recompile, your new help topic will appear if the user presses the F1 key while the "Save Changes" dialog is on the screen.

Another way to handle the new topic is to create a new topic page and give it a new, unique help context. Then, in the ALIAS section, replace the AFX_HIPD_Default alias for AFX_HIDP_ASK_TO_SAVE with your new help context.

19.5 Conclusion

As mentioned at the beginning of the chapter, the help system and the help compiler are a world unto themselves. If you want to exploit the system completely you need to become intimately familiar with the compiler and its capabilities. Tech Note 28 and the Help Compiler User's Manual are good places to start the process.

In this chapter, you have seen that creating a straightforward help system with hypertext links, text, and bitmaps is easy. You can modify the help topics that the AppWizard created for you and add your own new pages. Using these techniques, you can obtain basic help functionality for any AppWizard application very quickly.

COMMON CONTROLS

In Windows 3.1 and earlier versions of Windows NT, Windows supports six different controls. These controls are available in the dialog editor, and can also be created in code using MFC classes for each of the controls. With Windows 95 came a whole new set of controls that add better appearance and functionality to dialogs that use them. The new common controls are supported in the following environments:

- Windows 95
- Windows NT, version 3.51 or later
- Win32s, version 1.3 or later

The different controls available are listed below:

- CListCtrl - List control (also called list view control)
- CTreeCtrl - Tree control (also called tree view control)
- CSpinButtonCtrl - Spin button control (also called up-down control)
- CImageList - Image list
- CRichEditCtrl - Rich edit control
- CSliderCtrl - Slider control (also called a trackbar)
- CProgressCtrl - Progress control
- CAnimateCtrl - Animation control
- CHeaderCtrl - Header control
- CHotKeyCtrl - Hot key control

These controls already exist within MFC and are rarely used outside of MFC:

- CStatusBarCtrl - Status window (CStatusBar)
- CTabCtrl - Tab control (Property Sheets)
- CToolBarCtrl - Toolbar control
- CToolTipCtrl - Tool tip control

Most of these controls are demonstrated in a huge and extensive MFC example program called CMNCTRLS, available from the developer' network CD.

20.1 A Simple Example Using the Spin Button, List, and Tree Controls

Most of these controls are remarkably easy to use once you see a bit of example code. You could spend a week studying each control in detail, but for normal use there is not a lot of complexity. In this example we will create a simple application that demonstrates how to use the spin control, the new list control and the tree control. Create a new SDI application framework with a form view. On the form, replace the existing static control with a Tree control, List control (not the list box), Spin control, and an Edit box. Change the properties for the following controls:

- Change the list control View style to Report
- Enable the tree control styles Has buttons, Has lines, and Lines at root
- Enable the spin control styles Auto buddy and Set buddy integer

In order for the Auto buddy style of the spin control to know which control is its "buddy" you must change the Tab Order so the edit box and the spin control are in sequential order with the edit box first.

20.2 CSpinButtonCtrl

If you compile and run the application now you will notice that the spin button control is fully functional. Its buddy edit box contains the value zero and when you press the down arrow the value increases and when you press the up arrow the value decreases. This somewhat odd behavior occurs because the default range for the spin button has the maximum set to zero and the minimum set to 100. Since the maximum value is less than the minimum value the function of the arrow buttons is reversed. We will use the control's **SetRange** method to change these values to achieve the desired functionality.

Use the ClassWizard to add Control member variables for each control in the view class. Also add the **OnInitialUpdate** handler to the class and add a call to the spin button's **SetRange**:

```
void CMyView::OnInitialUpdate()
{
    CFormView::OnInitialUpdate();

    m_ctlSpinButtonCtrl.SetRange( -10, 10 );
}
```

Now the spin button control will allow you to change the edit control's value from -10 to 10. You can use other methods of the spin button control to change other properties such as the base (decimal or hex) and the adjustment rate (acceleration).

20.3 CListCtrl

The new list control is more complex than the standard list box. Because the list control has four different ways to display itself, it has much more functionality. For this example we will demonstrate the Report view mode of the list control. In this mode, the list control looks a lot like a standard list box, except it more easily supports multiple columns which can be sorted and resized.

First we will fill the list control with three rows and three columns. Each row is made up of an item and two subitems. The subitems are only visible in Report mode.

The other three modes only show the item label for each element in the list. To add a column to the list use the **InsertColumn** method. Call it once for each column you want in the list. Inserting items and subitems is a two part process. First call **InsertItem** to insert an item in the list. Once there is an item in the list you use **SetItemText** to set the text for each subitem.

```
void CMyView::OnInitialUpdate()
{
    CFormView::OnInitialUpdate();

    m_ctlSpinButtonCtrl.SetRange( -10, 10 );

    m_ctlList.InsertColumn( 0, "Item" );
    m_ctlList.InsertColumn( 1, "Subitem 1" );
    m_ctlList.InsertColumn( 2, "Subitem 2" );

    int nItem;

    nItem = m_ctlList.InsertItem( 0, "Item A" );
    m_ctlList.SetItemText( nItem, 1, "Subitem A1" );
    m_ctlList.SetItemText( nItem, 2, "Subitem A2" );

    nItem = m_ctlList.InsertItem( 0, "Item B" );
    m_ctlList.SetItemText( nItem, 1, "Subitem B1" );
    m_ctlList.SetItemText( nItem, 2, "Subitem B2" );

    nItem = m_ctlList.InsertItem( 0, "Item C" );
    m_ctlList.SetItemText( nItem, 1, "Subitem C1" );
    m_ctlList.SetItemText( nItem, 2, "Subitem C2" );
}
```

Now you can run the application and see that the list has three rows and three columns. The columns can be resized by dragging the column dividers in the list header. Double-clicking the divider resizes the column so it exactly fits the column's contents.

A common thing to do with the list control is to allow the user to sort each column when the column header is clicked. To add this functionality to our example we have to do three things. First we have to know when a list column header is clicked. We can do this by adding a handler for the **LVN_COLUMNCLICK** message. When a column is clicked, we can sort the list on the selected column.

```
void CMyView::OnColumnclickList1(NMHDR* pNMHDR, LRESULT* pResult)
{
    NM_LISTVIEW* pNMListView = (NM_LISTVIEW*)pNMHDR;

    int nColumn = pNMListView->iSubItem;
    ASSERT( (nColumn >= 0) && (nColumn <= 2) );
    m_ctlList.SortItems(CompareFunc, nColumn);

    *pResult = 0;
}
```

This code tells the list control to call the **CompareFunc** function for each item in the list and to sort the items based on the result of the function. The arguments to the function are the item data for each item in the list and the second argument to **SortItems**. We can use this sort data to tell the sort function which column to base the sorting on. The only thing missing is the item data for each item in the list. Currently our items don't have any associated item data. Change **OnInitialUpdate** to call **SetItemData** for each item:

```
void CMyView::OnInitialUpdate()
{
    ...
    nItem = m_ctlList.InsertItem( 0, "Item A" );
    m_ctlList.SetItemText( nItem, 1, "Subitem A1" );
    m_ctlList.SetItemText( nItem, 2, "Subitem A2" );
    m_ctlList.SetItemData( nItem, 0 );

    ...
    m_ctlList.SetItemText( nItem, 2, "Subitem B2" );
    m_ctlList.SetItemData( nItem, 1 );

    ...
    m_ctlList.SetItemText( nItem, 2, "Subitem C2" );
    m_ctlList.SetItemData( nItem, 2 );
}
```

Add the sort function as a member of the view class:

```
static int CALLBACK CompareFunc(LPARAM, LPARAM, LPARAM);

int CALLBACK CMyView::CompareFunc(LPARAM lParam1, LPARAM lParam2,
    LPARAM lParamSort)
{
    switch(lParamSort)
    {
    case 0: // First column, sort A, B, C
        return lParam1 - lParam2;
        break;
    case 1: // Second column, sort C, B, A
        return lParam2 - lParam1;
        break;
    case 2: // Third column, no change
        return 0;
        break;

    default: // Invalid column
        ASSERT(FALSE);
        return 0;
    }
}
```

Notice that this function is defined as a static member function. This is because this function will be called as a callback from system, which expects the function to behave like a normal C callback function. For this compare function we have hard wired the function to sort the first column in the order of the item data elements (A, B, C), the second column sorts in reverse order (C, B, A) and the third column will not change the sorting of the list. If you wanted to make the sorting more intelligent you could make the item data a pointer to a structure that describes each item. Then you could sort based on the column text or a currency.

20.4 CTreeCtrl

The list control organized items and subitems in a linear form. The tree control organizes items and subitems in a hierarchical tree structure. Each item becomes a parent with subitems as its children. The most common example of a tree structure is the file system. Each directory is a parent which can contain other directories and files as children. If a parent has children, it can be expanded to show its children or collapsed to hide its children. As with the list control, you insert items into a tree control using its **InsertItem** method. There are many overloaded versions of this method. The most simple version of the method has arguments for the item label text and its position in the tree. **InsertItem** returns a handle to the new item. You can use this handle in other **InsertItem** calls to add children to a parent.

```
void CMyView::OnInitialUpdate()
{
    CFormView::OnInitialUpdate();
    ...

    HTREEITEM hRoot;
    HTREEITEM hChild;

    hRoot = m_ctlTree.InsertItem( "Root1" );
    m_ctlTree.InsertItem( "Child1 of Root1", hRoot );
    hChild = m_ctlTree.InsertItem( "Child2 of Root1", hRoot );
    m_ctlTree.InsertItem( "Child1 of Child2 of Root1", hChild );
    m_ctlTree.InsertItem( "Child3 of Root1", hRoot );

    hRoot = m_ctlTree.InsertItem( "Root2" );
    m_ctlTree.InsertItem( "Child1 of Root2", hRoot );
    hChild = m_ctlTree.InsertItem( "Child2 of Root2", hRoot );
    m_ctlTree.InsertItem( "Child1 of Child2 of Root2", hChild );
    m_ctlTree.InsertItem( "Child3 of Root2", hRoot );

    hRoot = m_ctlTree.InsertItem( "Root3" );
    m_ctlTree.InsertItem( "Child1 of Root3", hRoot );
    hChild = m_ctlTree.InsertItem( "Child2 of Root3", hRoot );
    m_ctlTree.InsertItem( "Child1 of Child2 of Root3", hChild );
    m_ctlTree.InsertItem( "Child3 of Root3", hRoot );
}
```

In this example, all the items in the tree are kept in the order they are added. The tree controls can also be sorted alphabetically or by a custom algorithm. If we wanted to sort the items in the list we could add the **TVI_SORT** flag as another argument to the InsertItem calls:

```
hChild = m_ctlTree.InsertItem("Child2 of Root3", hRoot, TVI_SORT);
```

20.5 Property Sheets

Property sheets help you create a single dialog containing numerous controls that share a common theme. For example, in a complicated application there can be hundreds of user-selectable options that control the behavior of the application. To display all these options without property sheets, applications were forced to create large complicated dialogs overpopulated with controls or a dialog-hierarchy that required multiple dialogs showing different options. Property sheets give applications a way to create a single dialog that contains multiple "pages" of options having the same theme. By selecting the tab at the top of each page you are able to view the different options.

MFC contains two classes that help you create property sheets and property pages. The **CPropertySheet** class, which is derived directly from **CWnd**, encapsulates the behavior of the property sheet itself and acts like a new version of the **CDialog** class. For example, it contains **DoModal** and **EndDialog** functions just like the dialog class does. The **CPropertyPage** class derives its behavior from **CDialog** and is used to create the pages in a property sheet. You derive a new class from **CPropertyPage** class for each page in a property sheet. This process mimics the creation of a new dialog class for each dialog in your application.

You create the property pages in exactly the same way you create a normal dialog. You use the dialog editor to create the controls and then use the ClassWizard to create a new class derived from **CPropertyPage** to handle the dialog resource. DDX and DDV let you access the controls on the property page just like you do with a dialog.

To create a property sheet, you either use the **CPropertySheet** class directly or use the ClassWizard to create a new class derived from **CPropertySheet**. You tell the instance of **CPropertySheet** about all its pages using its **AddPage** function.

The example in the next section shows how to create a new property sheet and its property pages and will help you to see how the whole system works.

20.6 A Property Sheet Example

It is remarkably easy to create a property sheet using principles you have already learned in this book. In this example we will create a simple modal property sheet dialog that contains two pages. Each page in a property sheet is a separate **CPropertyPage** object. The pages are actually based on dialog templates, which is the reason **CPropertyPage** is derived from the **CDialog** class. All you have to do is create a separate dialog template resource for each page.

Create two new dialog templates and change their Captions to the text you want to appear in the tab for this page. Also, set the Style to Child, set the Border to Thin, and enable the Disabled, Visible and Titlebar styles. If you don't set these options you will get an assertion failure when the page is created. Then some controls to the property page.

When creating a set of property pages, you will want to try to make the size and layout of each page consistent. When the property sheet is created, the size of the first property page in the sheet is used to determine how large the property sheet should be, so if your dialog template resources have different sizes, make sure the largest one is the first page.

When you create dialogs in MFC, you create a new dialog class that is derived from **CDialog**. The same concept applies to the **CPropertyPage** class. This allows each page to have its own member variables that can store the information from its controls. You will use DDX and DDV with property pages in the same way that you use them with normal dialogs. Use the ClassWizard to derive two new classes from **CPropertyPage**, one for each dialog template, named **CPage1** and **CPage2**.

20.7 The CPropertySheet Class

The **CPropertySheet** class is used to manage a group of property pages. Creating and displaying a modal property sheet dialog is simple using this class. To create and display a property sheet is done the following way:

```
void CMyApp::OnSomeCommand()
{
    // Create the property sheet
    CPropertySheet propSheet( "Information" );

    // Create and initialize page one
    CPage1 page1;
    page1.m_name = "Name";
    page1.m_phone = "Phone";
    page1.m_address = "Address";

    // Create and initialize page two
    CPage2 page2;
    page2.m_city = "City";
    page2.m_state = "State";

    // Add the pages to the sheet
    propSheet.AddPage( &page1 );
    propSheet.AddPage( &page2 );

    if( propSheet.DoModal() == IDOK )
    {
        TRACE( "Name: %s\nPhone: %s\nAddress: %s\n",
            (LPCSTR)page1.m_name,
            (LPCSTR)page1.m_phone,
            (LPCSTR)page1.m_address );
        TRACE( "City: %s\nState: %s\n",
            (LPCSTR)page2.m_city,
            (LPCSTR)page2.m_state );
    }
}
```

The code first creates a property sheet object, passing the constructor the title of the property sheet. Then it creates and initializes an object for each property page. DDX takes care of initializing the controls on the page with the values of the member variables. Each page is added to the property sheet with **AddPage**. As with normal dialogs, **DoModal** is used to display the property sheet dialog and will not return until the user selects either the OK or Cancel buttons.

Now that we have created a simple property sheet, we will explore how to better use these two classes. The property sheet above was created in two steps. First, the property sheet object was created and then its pages were created and added. Another, more object-oriented approach to creating a property sheet is to create a new class derived from **CPropertySheet**. The new class would contain a member variable for each property page and the constructor for the class would call **AddPage** for each page. You can use the ClassWizard to derive a class from **CPropertySheet** and then modify the new class as necessary.

```
class CMyPropertySheet : public CPropertySheet
{
public:
    CPage1 m_page1;
    CPage2 m_page2;

    CMyPropertySheet();
};

CMyPropertySheet::CMyPropertySheet() :
    CPropertySheet( "Information" )
{
    AddPage( &m_page1 );
    AddPage( &m_page2 );
}
```

The main reason to derive a class from **CPropertySheet** is to enhance it. With your own class you can add buttons or modify the default buttons. Or you can create a modeless property sheet dialog. If you wish to create a modeless property sheet dialog, you can use the class's **Create** member function. In this case, you must create your own **CPropertySheet**-derived class because the default buttons, OK, Cancel, and Apply are not created for modeless property sheets. You must also provide a way in the new class to close and destroy the modeless property sheet dialog, which is the purpose of **EndDialog**. This function is used to destroy the property sheet dialog when OK, Cancel or Close is selected.

There are also several page management functions in the **CPropertySheet** class. **RemovePage** performs the opposite of **AddPage** and removes the specified page from the property sheet. Only the property page's window is destroyed. The actual **CPropertyPage**-derived object is not destroyed until its property sheet is. **GetPage** will return a pointer to the page specified by an index between 0 and the value of **GetPageCount**. These can be used to iterate through the property sheet's pages.

As with normal dialogs, you override the virtual functions **OnCancel** and **OnOK** to handle the Cancel and OK buttons. The **OnCancel** function is called when the Cancel button is selected (it will be labeled Close instead of Cancel if it has been renamed with **CancelToClose**). The **OnOK** function is called for two different actions. It's called when the user chooses either the OK or Apply button. The difference is that the Apply button does not call **EndDialog** to dismiss the property sheet. If you need to handle the Apply button in a separate function, you can manually provide a message map entry for **ID_APPLY_NOW** in the page's parent **CPropertySheet**-derived class.

Two other virtual functions can be overriden to allow more control over the **CPropertyPage** class. **OnSetActive** is called when the page is chosen by the user and becomes the active page. The default action is to create the window for the page, if not previously created, and to make the page the active page. You can override this function to perform tasks that need to be done when a page is activated, such as custom initialization. Note that the controls for a property page are not created until the page itself is created, so make sure you call the base class **OnSetActive** to create the page before referencing any of the page's controls. **OnKillActive** is the opposite of **OnSetActive** and is called when the page is no longer to be the active page. The property page's **OnOK** function is only called if this function returns successfully. The default action is to call the DDX function **UpdateData** to copy settings from the controls in the property page to the member variables of the property page. If the data was not updated successfully because of a DDV error, the page retains focus. You can override this function to perform special data validation tasks that should be done before the active page loses focus. Note that the data is transferred from the controls to the member variables in **OnKillActive**, not in **OnOK**. Note that all these functions are page-dependent. That is, each property page class has its own **OnOK**, **OnCancel**, **OnSetActive**, and **OnKillActive**.

Some other useful functions are **CancelToClose** and **SetModified**. You can use the **CancelToClose** function to notify the user that he has made an unrecoverable change to the data in a page. This function will change the text of the Cancel button to read Close. This alerts the user that they have made a permanent change that cannot be cancelled. Note that the **CancelToClose** member function does nothing in a modeless property sheet because a modeless property sheet does not have a Cancel button by default.

The **SetModified** function is used to enable or disable the Apply button. Each page has a flag that marks the page as being "dirty." When the data for a page has been changed you can call **SetModified** with TRUE to enable the button. The Apply button will become disabled again only when none of the property pages is "dirty." Note that each page has its own "dirty" flag independent of the other pages.

20.8 OCX Controls

As we have discussed in this chapter and Part 2, Windows and MFC have a number of native controls. It is also possible to place custom controls, also known as

OCX controls, into your dialogs and form views. See Appendix B.8.4 and Section 34.8 for details on using and creating OCX controls.

20.9 Conclusion

You can see from the control examples that the simple use of common controls is extremely straightforward. You can learn about more complicated aspects of each control either through the documentation or the CMNCTRLS example mentioned above.

Property sheets are very useful, but you should be careful about exploiting them. Used to excess, or used in inconsistent ways, they can become quite confusing to the user. For another approach of arranging options in a dialog, take a look at Chapter 28 on expanding dialogs.

CREATING EXPLORERS

Windows 95 has established in the minds of most users the concept of an "explorer". An explorer typically consists of a split window with a tree control on the left side and a list control on the right. Figure 21.1 demonstrates a typical explorer-style application, this one called View IT! For Web Logs from Interface Technologies (you can download this application by visiting http://www.iftech.com/products/viewit/viewit.htm).

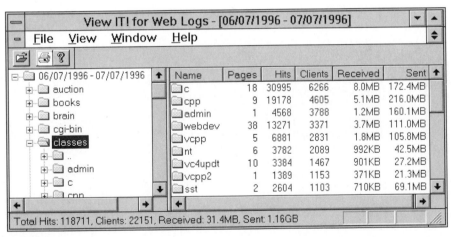

Figure 21.1
View IT! For Web Logs

In this chapter we will explore the steps necessary to create an explorer-style interface and see just how simple the basic application framework is.

21.1 Creating the basic framework

To create a basic explorer-style interface, take the following steps.

21.1.1 Step 1 - Create the Application Framework

Use the AppWizard to create a new application framework as described in Appendix B.6.1. Name the framework "Exp." Give it an MDI style and turn on the split window feature as described in Appendix B.6.5. Change the base class of the view to a tree view as described in Appendix B.6.4. Change the name of the view class to **CExpTreeView** and change the file names as appropriate. Create the framework.

21.1.2 Step 2 - Add a List View Class

Use the ClassWizard to add a new class to the application as described in Appendix B.7.6. The class name should be **CExpListView** and the base class should be **CListView**.

21.1.3 Step 3 - Change the Child Frame

Use the ClassWizard to override the **OnCreateClient** virtual function in the **CChildFrame** class of the framework (see Appendix B.7.2). Add the following code:

```
BOOL CChildFrame::OnCreateClient( LPCREATESTRUCT /*lpcs*/,
    CCreateContext* pContext)
{
    if (!m_wndSplitter.CreateStatic(this, 1, 2))
    {
        TRACE0("Failed to Create Static Splitter\n");
        return FALSE;
    }

    if (!m_wndSplitter.CreateView(0, 0,
        RUNTIME_CLASS(CExpTreeView), CSize(215, 0), pContext))
    {
        TRACE0("Failed to create first pane\n");
        return FALSE;
    }

    if (!m_wndSplitter.CreateView(0, 1,
        RUNTIME_CLASS(CExpListView), CSize(0, 0), pContext))
    {
        TRACE0("Failed to create second pane\n");
        return FALSE;
    }

    // activate the input view
    SetActiveView((CView*)m_wndSplitter.GetPane(0,0));

    return TRUE;
}
```

Also, add the following include files to the **CChildFrame** class:

```
#include "ExpDoc.h"
```

```
#include "ExpTreeView.h"
#include "ExpListView.h"
```

21.1.4 Step 4 - Compile and Run

If you run the program at this point, you will find that you have an MDI application that displays a split MDI child window.

21.1.5 Step 5 - Change the PreCreateWindow Functions

In the **CExpTreeView** class change the **PreCreateWindow** function to look like this:

```
BOOL CExpTreeView::PreCreateWindow(CREATESTRUCT& cs)
{
    cs.style |= TVS_HASLINES | TVS_LINESATROOT |
        TVS_HASBUTTONS;
    return CTreeView::PreCreateWindow(cs);
}
```

In the **CExpListView** class override the **PreCreateWindow** function with the ClassWizard (see Appendix B.7.2) and modify it to look like this:

```
BOOL CExpListView::PreCreateWindow(CREATESTRUCT& cs)
{
    cs.style |= LVS_REPORT;

    return CListView::PreCreateWindow(cs);
}
```

These changes tell the Tree and List views to change their embedded controls to the proper style. See Chapter 20 for details on these controls.

21.1.6 Step 6 - Initialize the Tree Control

To demonstrate the "look" of the application we will load some data into the tree and list views. Modify the **OnInitialUpdate** function in **CExpTreeView** so that it contains the following code:

```
void CExpTreeView::OnInitialUpdate()
{
    CTreeView::OnInitialUpdate();

    HTREEITEM hTreeRoot;
    HTREEITEM hTreeChild;
    CTreeCtrl& m_ctlTreeCtrl=GetTreeCtrl();

    hTreeRoot = m_ctlTreeCtrl.InsertItem( "Root1" );
    m_ctlTreeCtrl.InsertItem( "Child1 of Root1", hTreeRoot );
    hTreeChild=m_ctlTreeCtrl.InsertItem("Child2 of Root1",hTreeChild);
    m_ctlTreeCtrl.InsertItem("Child1 of Child2 of Root1",hTreeChild );
    m_ctlTreeCtrl.InsertItem( "Child3 of Root1", hTreeRoot );
```

```
    hTreeRoot = m_ctlTreeCtrl.InsertItem( "Root2" );
    m_ctlTreeCtrl.InsertItem( "Child1 of Root2", hTreeRoot );
    hTreeChild=m_ctlTreeCtrl.InsertItem("Child2 of Root2",hTreeRoot);
    m_ctlTreeCtrl.InsertItem( "Child1 of Child2 of Root2",hTreeChild );
    m_ctlTreeCtrl.InsertItem( "Child3 of Root2", hTreeRoot );

    hTreeRoot=m_ctlTreeCtrl.InsertItem( "Root3" );
    m_ctlTreeCtrl.InsertItem( "Child1 of Root3", hTreeRoot );
    hTreeChild=m_ctlTreeCtrl.InsertItem("Child2 of Root3",hTreeRoot );
    m_ctlTreeCtrl.InsertItem("Child1 of Child2 of Root3",hTreeChild );
    m_ctlTreeCtrl.InsertItem("Child3 of Root3",hTreeRoot );
}
```

This places several entries in the tree control, as described in Chapter 20.

21.1.7 Step 7 - Compile and Run

If you now execute the application you will find that the tree control on the left side of the window contains the tree structure that you created in Section 21.1.6. Obviously you could fill the tree control with any information that you like.

21.1.8 Step 8 - Adding List Updating

We would now like to modify the application so that when the user clicks on an entry in the tree control something gets loaded into the list control. First use the ClassWizard to add a =TVN_SELCHANGED event handler in the **CExpTreeView** class. Add the following code to the resulting function:

```
void CExpTreeView::OnSelchanged(NMHDR* pNMHDR, LRESULT* pResult)
{
    NM_TREEVIEW* pNMTreeView = (NM_TREEVIEW*)pNMHDR;

    CExpDoc* pDoc = GetDocument();
    ASSERT_VALID(pDoc);
    pDoc->UpdateAllViews(this, 0, NULL);

    *pResult = 0;
}
```

This modification uses the **UpdateAllViews** facility seen in Chapter 15 to send a signal to the list view. Therefore, you need to use the ClassWizard to add an **OnInitialUpdate** function to the **CExpListView** class (see Appendix B.7.2). Modify its code as shown here:

```
void CMyListView::OnInitialUpdate()
{
    //  CListView::OnInitialUpdate();

    CListCtrl& m_ctlListCtrl = GetListCtrl();
    m_ctlListCtrl.InsertColumn( 0, "Item" );
    m_ctlListCtrl.InsertColumn( 1, "Subitem 1" );
    m_ctlListCtrl.InsertColumn( 2, "Subitem 2" );
}
```

This code is similar to code seen in Chapter 20. It creates column headings. Finally, use the ClassWizard to add an **OnUpdate** function to the **CExpListView** class and modify it as shown here:

```
void CExpListView::OnUpdate(CView* pSender, LPARAM lHint,
    CObject* pHint)
{
    CListCtrl& m_ctlListCtrl = GetListCtrl();

    int nItem;

    nItem = m_ctlListCtrl.InsertItem( 0, "Item A" );
    m_ctlListCtrl.SetItemText( nItem, 1, "Subitem A1" );
    m_ctlListCtrl.SetItemText( nItem, 2, "Subitem A2" );

    nItem = m_ctlListCtrl.InsertItem( 0, "Item B" );
    m_ctlListCtrl.SetItemText( nItem, 1, "Subitem B1" );
    m_ctlListCtrl.SetItemText( nItem, 2, "Subitem B2" );

    nItem = m_ctlListCtrl.InsertItem( 0, "Item C" );
    m_ctlListCtrl.SetItemText( nItem, 1, "Subitem C1" );
    m_ctlListCtrl.SetItemText( nItem, 2, "Subitem C2" );
}
```

This code adds data to the list each time the user selects an item in the tree. Obviously you would engineer this section to add useful data into the list depending on what is clicked in the tree.

21.1.9 Step 9 - Compile and Run

Run the program and select any item in the tree. You will find that the list updates by growing slightly. Figure 21.2 shows a typical run of the application.

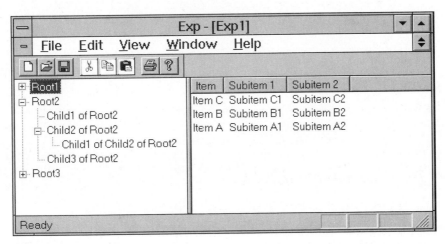

Figure 21.2
A typical run of the application

21.2 Conclusion

As you can see, the creation of this explorer-style framework is extremely simple and leverages a number of the different concepts that we have learned throughout the rest of Part 3. It is extremely easy to modify this framework to create explorer-style applications of any type.

Part 4

Using the tools described in Part 3, you can create any sort of application you can imagine. However, there are a wide variety of additional features, both inside and outside of MFC, that are frequently useful when creating advanced applications. Here are some examples:

- In Part 3 we saw several examples that demonstrate how to create standard dialogs that move data in and out of edit boxes using DDX. However, what if you want an intricate dialog containing lists, check boxes, and combo boxes?
- All of the examples in Part 3 open properly, but none of them announce their coming with a splash screen. What if you want to add splash screens to your own applications to make them more exciting?
- Many Windows applications can "float" above other windows so they are always on top. How can you make your own applications float?
- It is common to find list boxes that contain icons along with text. The normal File Open dialog uses this technique in its directory list. How can you add icons to your own lists?

None of these features are essential. However, they help to mark the difference between ordinary and extraordinary applications. Part 4 describes all these techniques, along with many others.

Dialog Data
Exchange and Validation

Dialog Data Exchange (DDX) and Dialog Data Validation (DDV) are two very simple yet very powerful concepts. Their availability in MFC makes the insertion and extraction of data from the fields of a dialog box, or any other **CWnd** derived class such as views, much easier. You first saw DDX and DDV in Part 3 of this book. In this chapter you will learn about DDX and DDV in detail. The chapter first explains the general principles and functions that drive DDX and DDV, and then works through a detailed example that shows how to set up and use most of the DDX and DDV routines. In the end we will design our own custom routines that deal with dates.

Every dialog has some assortment of controls in it. A simple message box has a static text control that displays information to the user along with one or more buttons. Most other dialogs are far more complicated, containing editable text areas, scrolling lists, combo boxes, and so on. The purpose of each control is to let the user manipulate data that the application uses. Once the data has been entered into the dialog, the application needs to check the data to make sure it meets certain criteria. For example, it might be the case that a number entered into an edit box should be positive, or within a range of values. Another field might need to accept no more than 20 characters. Together DDX and DDV help to simplify the process of gathering the data. DDX makes it easy to extract the data from the different entry fields in the dialog. Each control in a dialog has a corresponding member variable in the dialog's class, and this variable holds the field's data once the dialog is closed. DDX handles the transfer of data between the control and its member variable. DDV follows DDX, and handles the validation of the data in the member variable.

If a dialog contains an edit box, and if you want to restrict the input to a maximum string length of 5 characters in that edit box, then, as demonstrated in Part 3, it is very easy to set up and use DDX and DDV. The code below shows what is required to load the edit box with an initial value, display the dialog, and then extract the new value entered by the user, assuming that the variable **m_szText** has already been established as the DDX variable with the ClassWizard and DDV is set up to limit the field's length to 5 characters:

```
CMyDialog dlg;
dlg.m_szText = "Hello World";
dlg.DoModal();
TRACE( "String input was %s\n", dlg.m_szText );
```

As you can see in this code, DDX and DDV are completely invisible. When the dialog is created, the initial text in the edit box control associated with the **m_szText** member variable will be "Hello World". When the user closes the dialog with the OK button, the string printed by the **TRACE** statement will contain the value the user entered in the edit box. With DDV in place, the string will have a maximum length of five characters—if the user enters more than five characters they are notified of the problem and given a chance to fix the error. The advantage of DDX and DDV is that you, as the programmer, don't have to do any work. The framework takes care of everything associated with DDX and DDV automatically.

22.1 Understanding DDX

In the previous example, the initial text in the edit box control was "Hello World". How did the string get into the edit box? The answer lies behind the scenes, in the code that makes up the application framework and the classes it uses. The string "Hello World" was copied from the **m_szText** member variable to the edit box control in the call to **DoModal** through an overridden virtual function. In every class that handles DDX and DDV, this virtual function, called **DoDataExchange**, handles the data transfer. A standard **DoDataExchange** function looks like this:

```
void CMyDialog::DoDataExchange(CDataExchange* pDX)
{
    CDialog::DoDataExchange(pDX);

    //{{AFX_DATA_MAP(CMyDialog)
    ClassWizard edits this area...
    //}}AFX_DATA_MAP
}
```

The ClassWizard fills the middle of the function with code to exchange and validate the data in the dialog's member variables. As a programmer using a dialog class, you never call the **DoDataExchange** function directly. Instead, it is called automatically by **CWnd::UpdateData**. By default, **UpdateData** is called by **CDialog::OnInitDialog** and **CDialog::OnOK**. When **UpdateData** is called by **OnInitDialog**, it initializes each control with the data in its associated member variable. When **UpdateData** is called by **OnOK**, it reverses the process and initializes the member variables with the data in its associated control. In this way, **m_szText** is used to initialize the edit box on creation, and contains the user's input string on closure. A Boolean parameter passed to **UpdateData** tells it whether to load or save data.

22.2 Exchange Routines

The ClassWizard helps manage the association between the controls and the member variables. The table below shows some of the different DDX methods that ClassWizard uses. A DDX method is simply a function that manages data transfer between a control and its associated member variable. The table shows the control class the method is used with, the routines normally used with that control, and the value that is transferred by the routine. There are two sets of DDX methods. The first set, with the DDX_ prefix, is used for normal dialog exchange. The second set, with the DDX_Field prefix, is used for transferring the field data members of the CRecordset and CDaoRecordset classes. This chapter only discusses the first set, although the recordset methods work the same way.

Table 22.1
DDX methods available for the different controls

Control	Routine(s)	What is Transferred
CEdit	DDX_Text DDX_FieldText	Values such as BOOL, BYTE, short, int, UINT, long, DWORD, CString, float, double, COleCurrency, COleDateTime
CListBox	DDX_LBIndex DDX_FieldLBIndex	Index of the selected item
	DDX_LBString DDX_FieldLBString	String value of the selected item
	DDX_LBStringExact DDX_FieldLBStringExact	Exact string value of the selected item
CComboBox	DDX_CBIndex DDX_FieldCBIndex	Index of the selected item
	DDX_CBString DDX_FieldCBString	String value of the selected item
	DDX_CBStringExact DDX_FieldCBStringExact	Exact string value of the selected item
CButton	DDX_Check DDX_FieldCheck	Check box state
	DDX_Radio DDX_FieldRadio	Selected radio button index
CScrollBar	DDX_Scroll DDX_FieldScroll	Scroll bar position
CWnd	DDX_Control	Associates a CWnd object with a control

There are multiple overloaded versions of the **DDX_Text** routine, one for each data type that can be transferred. Each overloaded version handles a different variable type. **DDX_Text** handles the conversion between the string in the edit box and the appropriate member variable type. You could also use the **DDX_Text** routines with a **CStatic** control to display a variable's value. All of the data types are not available for every DDX routine. For example, the **DDX_FieldText** routine is only overloaded to transfer a **COleCurrency** between a **CDaoRecordset** and not a **CRecordset**.

DDX_LBIndex and **DDX_CBIndex** use the index of the selected item as the data, while **DDX_LBString** and **DDX_CBString** transfer the string value of the selected item between the member variable and control. **DDX_LBStringExact** and **DDX_CBStringExact** are the same as the DDX_String routines, except they use the exact string for item selection as opposed to the string prefix. For example, using a DDX_String routine with the string *help* will match both *helps* and *helping* whereas with DDX_StringExact it only matches *help*.

The **DDX_Check** routine exchanges the value of check buttons (on/off), and **DDX_Radio** exchanges the index of the currently selected button in a group. The **DDX_Scroll** routine exchanges data with the current scroll bar position. The last exchange routine is **DDX_Control**. It associates a dialog control with a **CWnd** object. See Chapter 23 for a description on how DDX_Control performs this association.

22.3 Transfer Direction

How does the DDX routine know which way to transfer the data? It needs to know whether to get the values from the dialog or set the values into the dialog. This is accomplished with the BOOL parameter to **UpdateData** called **bSaveAndValidate**. If **UpdateData(FALSE)** is called, the controls are initialized with the member variables' data. This is the case for **OnInitDialog**. If **UpdateData(TRUE)** is called, the member variables are initialized with the control contents. This is the case for **OnOK**. Notice that the **bSaveAndValidate** parameter is not passed to each individual DDX routine. The DDX and DDV routines communicate through a **CDataExchange** object, the **pDX** parameter to the routines. Using this **CDataExchange** object, each routine can determine what **bSaveAndValidate** is. Then based on its value, it might do something as simple as the following:

```
if (pDX->m_bSaveAndValidate)
{
    member variable = dialog control value
}
else
{
    set control value to member variable
}
```

The **CDataExchange** object also contains the handle of the control the DDX and DDV routines affect, along with some member functions that can be used when creating custom routines.

22.4 Understanding DDV

Dialog Data Validation is very similar to Dialog Data Exchange. The DDV routines check the data in a dialog's member variables to make sure the data meets certain criteria. Shown below are some validation routines. The MinMax routines constrain a value between a minimum and maximum value. Each data type has a different routine because function overloading in this case is not desirable.

```
DDV_MinMaxByte
DDV_MinMaxInt
DDV_MinMaxLong
DDV_MinMaxUInt
DDV_MinMaxDWord
DDV_MinMaxFloat
DDV_MinMaxDouble
```

Another validation routine used with strings allows you to restrict the length of the string.

```
DDV_MaxChars
```

Each of these validation routines perform something similar to the following:

```
if (pDX->m_bSaveAndValidate && member variable out of range)
{
    notify the user with a message box
    reset the focus to the offending control
    AfxThrowUserException()
}
```

DDV routines are only activated when you are getting data from controls, when **m_bSaveAndValidate** is TRUE. If the data is out of range, first a message box is displayed that describes the problem to the user. After the dialog is dismissed, the focus is automatically set to the control in question so the user can easily change it. This is the reason that the DDV routine is called immediately after the DDX routine for each control. The **CDataExchange** object keeps track of the last control that was used for an exchange. It assumes that the last control DDX used is the control with the invalid data. Last, DDV throws a user exception with **AfxThrowUserException**. By handling this exception, **UpdateData** can determine if any DDV routines failed during the call to **DoDataExchange**. No other exchange or validation routines are called after an exception is thrown from a DDV routine. This is the reason that member variables are guaranteed to be valid only after **DoModal** returns from **OnOK**. If **DoModal** returns from **OnCancel** the member variables could contain invalid data because only half of the DDX routines may have been called.

22.5 An Example

It is easier to understand the mechanisms of DDX and DDV for each of the different field types if you are looking at an actual example. In this section we will create a dialog to demonstrate some of the DDX and DDV routines, using the framework techniques discussed in Part 3.

Create a project and add the following controls to a dialog so it looks like the figure below. The dialog contains eight edit boxes, five radio buttons, five check boxes, three list boxes, three combo boxes, and a scroll bar. The scroll bar in this example will not be functional because we have not provided a handler for it.

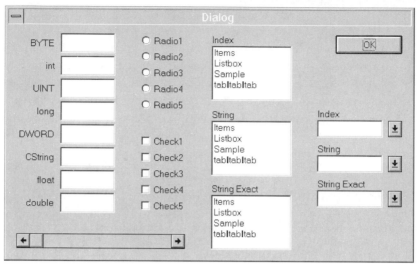

Figure 22.1
Demonstration dialog that contains every control type

To demonstrate the difference between the String and StringExact functions, it is necessary to turn off the Sort flag for all the list boxes and combo boxes. Also make sure the tab order is set correctly. The tab order is vital to the creation of a radio button group. The necessary tab order is shown below.

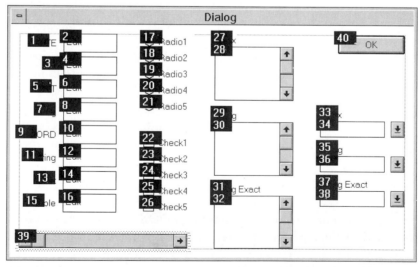

Figure 22.2
The required tab order

This book is continuously updated. See http://www.iftech.com/mfc

Notice that all the buttons in the radio button group have sequential numbers. Select the first radio button in the group (control 17), and set its Group and Tabstyle style flags. Make sure the Group flag is cleared for the other radio buttons (controls 18–21). Then set the Group flag for the control after the last radio button control (control 22). All the radio buttons between the first radio button and the next control in the tab order with the Group flag set will be a single group.

Now that we have created our dialog, we need to associate each control with a member variable. These are the variables that will be used for the data exchange and validation. Use the ClassWizard to create a dialog class (e.g. **CMyDialog**) and establish DDX and DDV connections with each of the modifiable controls in the dialog box. Add a Value member variable for each edit box control as shown below:

Table 22.2

Variable Name	Type	Variable Name	Type
m_edit1	BYTE	m_edit5	DWORD
m_edit2	int	m_edit6	CString
m_edit3	UINT	m_edit7	float
m_edit4	long	m_edit8	double

Notice that with each integral type (**BYTE**, **int**, and so on) we can specify range validation. We can specify a maximum and minimum value for each variable. Note also that each integral type inherently has its own boundaries. For example, a **BYTE** must be between 0 and 255, a **UINT** cannot be negative, and so on. With edit boxes that use a string type, the variable has length validation. Assign some boundaries to the edit variables so you can test them.

The next control is the radio button group. The only object ID in the ClassWizard list is for the first radio button in the group. This occurs because the variable we assign will be an integer value (0-based) that contains the index of the selected radio button. For example, if the first button in our group is selected, the value will be 0. If the last button is selected the value will be 4. Because only one button can be selected at a time, all we need is one variable per group. Add a value member variable named **m_nRadio** for this control.

Next, select one of the check boxes in the Control IDs list. Because this is a simple check box, there are only two values it can have: TRUE or FALSE. For this reason, the variable that is associated with each check box is of type **BOOL**. If the check box was tri-state, the variable would be of type int. Create a member variable for each check box control named **m_bCheck1**, **m_bCheck2**, to **m_bCheck5**.

Next, add a **CString** value member variable named **m_combo1**, **m_combo2**, and **m_combo3** for the combo boxes. The only value we can assign to a combo box with the ClassWizard is of type **CString**. By default this will use the **DDX_CBString** routine. We will change this later to include the other two combo box exchange routines. Notice that with the combo box **CString** type we can have length validation.

After the variable is added we can then set the "Maximum Characters" allowed in the string.

Now add a value member variables for each list box. The first list box, **m_list1** will have the type **int**. The other two, **m_list2** and **m_list3** will have the type **CString**. Because the user cannot change the strings in a list box, we don't have the option of string length validation as we did with the combo boxes. Next, add an **int** value member variable with the name **m_nScrollPos** for the scroll bar. If you now take a look at the **DoDataExchange** function for the dialog, you will notice that the ClassWizard has made quite a few changes.

The ClassWizard allowed us to add only one type of exchange for the list boxes and combo boxes. We must manually change two of the routines so we can demonstrate their use. Take a look at the member variable definitions in the dialog class definition. There are three variables for combo boxes. Change the first member variable to be of the type **int**.

```
int        m_combo1;
CString    m_combo2;
CString    m_combo3;
```

Next we must change the exchange routines used for these controls. Look at the dialog's **DoDataExchange** function. The exchange routine for the first list and combo box controls should be of the type **DDX_LBIndex** and **DDX_CBIndex**. The exchange routine for the second list and combo box controls should be **DDX_LBString** and **DDX_CBString**. The exchange routine for the third list and combo box controls should be **DDX_LBStringExact** and **DDX_CBStringExact**.

```
DDX_CBIndex(pDX, IDC_COMBO1, m_combo1);
DDX_CBString(pDX, IDC_COMBO2, m_combo2);
DDX_CBStringExact(pDX, IDC_COMBO3, m_combo3);

DDX_LBIndex(pDX, IDC_LIST1, m_list1);
DDX_LBString(pDX, IDC_LIST2, m_list2);
DDX_LBStringExact(pDX, IDC_LIST3, m_list3);
```

In the class constructor, where the variables are initialized, make sure each variable has an initial value that is valid. If the initial values for the dialog cannot be validated with the appropriate DDV function (if one is assigned), MFC will output warning messages notifying you. Initial values that you could use for this example are shown below.

```
m_edit1 = 1;
m_edit2 = 1;
m_edit3 = 1;
m_edit4 = 1;
m_edit5 = 1;
m_edit6 = _T("");
m_edit7 = 1.0f;
m_edit8 = 1.0;
m_nRadio = -1;
```

```
m_bCheck1 = FALSE;
m_bCheck2 = FALSE;
m_bCheck3 = FALSE;
m_bCheck4 = FALSE;
m_bCheck5 = FALSE;
m_combo1 = 2;
m_combo2 = _T("help");
m_combo3 = _T("help");
m_list1 = 2;
m_list2 = _T("help");
m_list3 = _T("help");
m_nScrollPos = 0;
```

Initially there are no radio buttons or check buttons selected. The code above selects the third (0-based) element in the list and combo boxes. The other strings ("help") for the list and combo boxes will be explained shortly.

The last thing we must do before we run the application is initialize the list and combo boxes with some strings. The place to do this is in the dialog's **OnInitDialog** message handler.

```
BOOL CMyDialog::OnInitDialog()
{
    int i;

    /* Initialize the list boxes. */
    int nListID[] = {IDC_LIST1, IDC_LIST2, IDC_LIST3};
    for( i=0; i < 3; i++ )
    {
        CListBox *pListBox =
            (CListBox *)GetDlgItem( nListID[i] );
        ASSERT( pListBox != NULL );

        pListBox->AddString( "helping" );
        pListBox->AddString( "help" );
        pListBox->AddString( "helpful" );
        pListBox->AddString( "helper" );
    }

    /* Initialize the combo boxes. */
    int nComboID[] = {IDC_COMBO1, IDC_COMBO2, IDC_COMBO3};
    for( i=0; i < 3; i++ )
    {
        CComboBox *pComboBox =
            (CComboBox *)GetDlgItem( nComboID[i] );
        ASSERT( pComboBox != NULL );

        pComboBox->AddString( "helping" );
        pComboBox->AddString( "help" );
        pComboBox->AddString( "helpful" );
        pComboBox->AddString( "helper" );
    }

    CDialog::OnInitDialog();
```

```
        return TRUE;
    }
```

Make sure **CDialog::OnInitDialog** is called last. If it is called before the list and combo boxes are initialized, MFC will warn you that no items can be selected because the lists are empty. If you wanted to use control member variables instead of using **GetDlgItem**, you would need to call **OnInitDialog** first, then call **UpdateData(FALSE)** after filling the controls. **OnInitDialog** would perform the control associations and then the **UpdateData** would select the items in the controls.

Now if you compile and run the application, all the exchanges and validations should work. It might be helpful to print out some of the member variables after **DoModal** returns using **TRACE** statements. This allows you to monitor the results of each exchange.

```
void CMyApp::OnDialog()
{
    CMyDialog dlg;

    // Set initial values here...

    dlg.DoModal();

    // Use new values here...

    TRACE( "m_nRadio = %d\n", dlg.m_nRadio );

    TRACE( "m_nScrollPos = %d\n", dlg.m_nScrollPos );

    TRACE( "m_bCheck1=%d, 2=%d, 3=%d, 4=%d, 5=%d\n",
        dlg.m_bCheck1, dlg.m_bCheck2, dlg.m_bCheck3,
        dlg.m_bCheck4,dlg.m_bCheck5 );

    TRACE( "m_combo1=%d, m_combo2=%s, m_combo3=%s\n",
        dlg.m_combo1, (LPCTSTR)dlg.m_combo2,
        (LPCTSTR)dlg.m_combo3 );

    TRACE( "m_list1=%d, m_list2=%s, m_list3=%s\n",
        dlg.m_list1, (LPCTSTR)dlg.m_list2,
        (LPCTSTR)dlg.m_list3 );

    TRACE("m_edit1=%d, m_edit=%d, m_edit3=%d, m_edit4=%d\n",
        dlg.m_edit1, dlg.m_edit2, dlg.m_edit3, dlg.m_edit4 );
    TRACE( "m_edit5 = %ld, m_edit6 = '%s', m_edit7 = %f\n",
        dlg.m_edit5,(LPCTSTR)dlg.m_edit6,dlg.m_edit7  );
    TRACE( "m_edit8 = %lf\n\n", dlg.m_edit8 );
}
```

If you want to modify the initial contents of the dialog, it would be done before **DoModal** is called. The values in the member variables at the time **DoModal** is called are the values used for the exchange. In the list and combo boxes, the order in which we added the strings allows us to show the difference between the DDX_String and DDX_StringExact routines. When the string is *help* and the function is DDX_String, the first item in the list that begins with *help* will be selected. Therefore, in the second combo and list box, the first item *helping* is selected. When the string is *help* and the function is DDX_StringExact, the first item in the list that matches the entire string (case insensitive) is selected. Therefore, in the third combo and list box, the first item *helping* is skipped and the second item *help* is selected. The **DDX_Index** routines for the combo and list boxes always selects based on an index value.

22.6 Custom Routines

What if you have a custom or not supported data type? If the routines provided by the framework don't suit your needs, you may want to create another set of exchange and validation routines. In this section we will demonstrate how to create simple DDX and DDV routines that will work with dates. We will use the standard time structure **struct tm** as the data type. The exchange routine is shown below.

```
void DDX_Time(CDataExchange* pDX, int nIDC, struct tm& tm)
{
    char sz[32];
    HWND hWndCtrl = pDX->PrepareEditCtrl(nIDC);

    if (pDX->m_bSaveAndValidate)
    {
        ::GetWindowText(hWndCtrl, sz, sizeof(sz));
        sscanf(sz, "%d-%d-%d",
            &(tm.tm_mon),
            &(tm.tm_mday),
            &(tm.tm_year));
        // Adjust values
        tm.tm_mon -= 1;
        tm.tm_year -= 1900;
    }
    else
    {
        sprintf(sz, "%d-%d-%d",
            tm.tm_mon + 1,
            tm.tm_mday,
            tm.tm_year + 1900);
        ::SetWindowText(hWndCtrl, sz);
    }
}
```

The exchange routine begins by calling the **CDataExchange** member function **PrepareEditCtrl**. Another member function **PrepareCtrl** would have been used if the control specified by **nIDC** was not an edit control. The purpose of these functions is to get the HWND of the specified control. This value is stored in the **CDataExchange** object so that it can be used by the DDV routine. The only difference between the **PrepareEditCtrl** and **PrepareCtrl** routine is the way the focus change is handled when validation fails. When a control prepared with **PrepareEditCtrl** fails validation, not only does it receive the focus, but all the text in the control is selected. The next step in the code depends on whether we are exchanging data to the control or from the control. If we are getting data from the control we must retrieve the text from the edit control and convert the string into values we can store in the tm structure. If we are setting the text in the control we create a string from the values in the tm structure and set the edit control text. The validation function makes sure the values in the **tm** structure have the valid ranges of a **CTime** object.

Day: 1 thru 31
Month: 0 thru 11, where January is 0
Year: 1970 to 2038, with a base of 1900

You may want to add far more stringent checks, but these comparisons are used here to demonstrate the process.

```
void DDV_Time(CDataExchange* pDX, struct tm& tm)
{
    if (pDX->m_bSaveAndValidate &&
        !(tm.tm_year >= 70 && tm.tm_year <= 138) ||
        !(tm.tm_mon >= 0 && tm.tm_mon <= 11) ||
        !(tm.tm_mday >= 1 && tm.tm_mday <= 31) )
    {
        CString str;
        str.Format("The date %d-%d-%d is invalid.",
                tm.tm_mon + 1,
                tm.tm_mday,
                tm.tm_year + 1900);
        AfxMessageBox(str, MB_ICONEXCLAMATION);
        pDX->Fail();
    }
}
```

This check only occurs if we are getting values from the edit control. If any of the values are invalid the user is notified and we call another **CDataExchange** member function named **Fail**. The **Fail** routine takes care of the focus change and throws an exception. If you want to extend the DDX and DDV capabilities of the Microsoft Developer Studio take a look at Technical Note 26 on DDX and DDV Routines for a description of how to add ClassWizard support for your new routines.

22.7 Conclusion

Using dialog data exchange and validation can accelerate your application development process. Just by overriding **DoDataExchange** you can save quite a bit of programming effort when requesting input of any type from the user. This is just another example of the way MFC helps simplify tasks for the programmer.

Understanding MFC

Do you know the answers to the following questions:

1. Have you ever gotten an assertion because you called a **CWnd** member function and **m_hWnd** was NULL? Do you know why?
2. Do you know why you can't use device contexts in a view's constructor?
3. Do you know why you can't add strings to a list box control in a dialog box until the dialog's **WM_INITDIALOG** message?
4. Do you know what window handles are and how messages work?
5. Have you been programming Windows using the C API and are trying to figure out how the MFC framework integrates with it?

In this chapter we will answer these questions and explore briefly how MFC works with the underlying C level API for Windows. This chapter is by no means a complete explanation—that would require another book. Instead, the purpose here is to give you some insight into how MFC does its job. Having this knowledge gives you better insight into how your application works. This is useful both when trying to debug and when it is necessary to go outside of the MFC boundaries.

23.1 What Are Window Handles?

Frames, views, dialogs, edit controls, buttons, list boxes, and so on are all windows. Every window in Windows has a unique handle associated with it. This handle, of type **HWND**, must be used whenever the window is referenced. Every operation on a window, such as setting the window text or sending the window a message, requires a handle to that window.

In an MFC application you rarely need to deal with window handles. You can create **CFrameWnd** and **CDialog** objects and never see an **HWND**. Does this mean that window handles are not used in MFC? No. MFC is simply hiding them from us and managing all of the details transparently. Almost everything MFC does to a window is eventually translated into the same C API call that would be made in a normal

495

C application. For example, if you take a look at AFXWIN1.INL and AFXWIN2.INL you will see how that translation occurs.

To get an idea of the type of activity that occurs behind the scenes in MFC, let's look at an example. To get the state of a button with the C API, you would normally send the button a **BBM_GETSTATE** message by making the following call:

```
LRESULT lState = SendMessage(hButton, BM_GETSTATE, 0, 0);
```

With MFC you instead call the **CButton** member function **GetState**:

```
UINT nState = ctlButton.GetState();
```

Here's how **CButton::GetState** is defined:

```
_AFXWIN_INLINE UINT CButton::GetState() const
{
    ASSERT(::IsWindow(m_hWnd));
    return (UINT)::SendMessage(m_hWnd, BM_GETSTATE, 0, 0);
}
```

Look familiar? MFC uses the **CWnd** member variable **m_hWnd** as the window handle to make the same API call. The **CWnd::Create** and **CWnd::CreateEx** member functions create a window with the API **CreateWindowEx** function. The returned **HWND** is stored in the **CWnd** member variable **m_hWnd** so MFC knows the window the **CWnd** object refers to. For instance, the **CEdit** object is a C++ class wrapping the windows EDIT control, so when you create a **CEdit** object something similar to the following occurs:

```
BOOL CEdit::Create( ... )
{
    m_hWnd = ::CreateWindowEx( ..., "EDIT", ... );
}
```

Keep in mind that every control you create in MFC is an instance of some class, like **CButton** or **CEdit**. Each instance of the class keeps track of its own **HWND** using the **m_hWnd** member variable. What this allows you to do, if you so choose, is to manipulate every MFC control by sending messages to it in the standard C style. Each member function is doing exactly that. The member functions simply give you a cleaner, easier way to send messages to a control via its window handle. You can use the **CWnd**'s **GetSafeHwnd** function to access the **m_hWnd** of a **CWnd** object.

Take a look at the first line in the **CButton::GetState** function above. It makes sure that **m_hWnd** is a valid window (i.e. it has been created and it is not NULL) using **IsWindow**. This is the answer to the first question. When you get this assertion, you are trying to send messages to a window that has not been created or one that has been destroyed. To understand how you can still have an object, such as a **CView** or **CDialog**, but why you can't use certain member functions, you must understand the creation and destruction of windows and objects.

23.2 The Life of Windows and Objects

To help illustrate the difference between object creation and window creation we will use an example. Say you have a frame window, **CMyFrame**, that is derived from **CFrameWnd**, and that this frame window has a single **CStatic** member variable named **m_static**. The following three lines of code create the frame window and its static control.

```
CMyFrame frame;
frame.Create( NULL, "My Frame", WS_OVERLAPPEDWINDOW,
    CRect(0,0,100,100) );
frame.m_static.Create( "Some Text Here",
    WS_CHILD|WS_VISIBLE|SS_CENTER,
    CRect(10,10,50,50), this );
```

The first line instantiates a **CMyFrame** object. This creates the frame object, calling its constructor, and it creates all of the frame objects' member variables, in this case **m_static**, and their constructors are called. At this point in time, we have two **CWnd** objects, **frame** and **m_static**. However, the window handles (**m_hWnd**) for both of these objects are NULL. What if you wanted to set the static's text in the frame's constructor:

```
CMyFrame::CMyFrame()
{
    m_static.SetWindowText( "Some Other Text" );
}
```

This won't work, you will get an assertion in **SetWindowText**. Why? Because we have an object (**m_static**) that does not have a window yet. The window for the object is not created until you call the object's **Create** function.

The second line calls the frame object's **Create** function. This is where the frame window is created. Now the frame's **m_hWnd** is valid. The static window still does not exist. The third line calls the static's **Create** function. Now the frame's static window has been created, the static's **m_hWnd** is valid, and we can call **SetWindowText** for the static control. You can move the static's **Create** call to the frame's constructor, this would be a more object-oriented approach. Just make sure you don't call any window oriented member functions on an object until the object has been **Create**'d.

What if you need to create or manage windows or window objects when the **CWnd** object is created? If you can't use the constructor, how do you do this? For example, say you have a view that you draw in and you need to initialize a variable to the height of the current font. You cannot do this in the view's constructor:

```
CMyView::CMyView()
{
    CClientDC dc(this);
    CSize size = dc.GetTextExtent("XXX", 3);
}
```

The reason is that the view window has not been created yet, and a device context is related to a particular window. We have to wait until the view's window is created. If we had called the view's **Create** function, we could do this after **Create** was called. For views however, the **Create** for the view is done by the framework when the frame is created. The solution to this is that when a window is created, but before it becomes visible, it receives a **WM_CREATE** message. In this message handler the window has been created and **m_hWnd** is valid. So, we can move the above code into the view's **WM_CREATE** message handler:

```
int CMyView::OnCreate(LPCREATESTRUCT lpCreateStruct)
{
    if(CView::OnCreate(lpCreateStruct) == -1)
        return -1;

    CClientDC dc(this);
    CSize size = dc.GetTextExtent("XXX", 3);

    return 0;
}
```

You can use the return value of **OnCreate** to keep the window from being created, in which case the **Create** function will return NULL.

The opposite of the **WM_CREATE** message is the **WM_DESTROY** message. This message is sent to the window after the window is removed from the screen, but before any of its children are destroyed. Therefore, any cleanup code you have that requires the use of windows can be done in **OnDestroy**.

In short, the constructor and destructor for a **CWnd** object should initialize and destroy any member variables that do not deal with windows, tasks such as initializing pointers to NULL. Tasks that involve windows, such as initializing controls, should be done in **OnCreate** and **OnDestroy**.

23.3 Initializing Dialogs

Dialogs are a bit different. As an example, say you have a dialog with a list box control in it and you want to initialize the list before the dialog is displayed. The following will not work:

```
CMyDialog dlg;
dlg.m_list.AddString("1");
dlg.m_list.AddString("2");
dlg.DoModal();
```

Again, this is because when the **CMyDialog** object is created, it does not have a window, or any children windows. You may also be tempted to do the following:

```
int CMyDialog::OnCreate(LPCREATESTRUCT lpCreateStruct)
{
    if (CDialog::OnCreate(lpCreateStruct) == -1)
        return -1;
```

```
    m_list.AddString("1");
    m_list.AddString("2");

    return 0;
}
```

This will not work either. The reason is because for dialogs, the dialog controls are not created by the time **OnCreate** is called. For dialogs, its controls do not exist until it receives the **WM_INITDIALOG** message. The solution to this problem is to initialize the list in **OnInitDialog**:

```
BOOL CMyDialog::OnInitDialog()
{
    CDialog::OnInitDialog();

    m_list.AddString("1");
    m_list.AddString("2");

    return TRUE;
}
```

Notice that **AddString** is called after the base class **OnInitDialog**. This is because **m_list** is a Control member variable of the type **CListBox**. This variable is not associated with the dialog's list box window until **CDialog::OnInitDialog** is called. If you are using DDX to select items in the list box you will have to add a call to **UpdateData** after calling **AddString**:

```
BOOL CMyDialog::OnInitDialog()
{
    CDialog::OnInitDialog();

    m_list.AddString("1");
    m_list.AddString("2");

    UpdateData(FALSE);

    return TRUE;
}
```

When **CDialog::OnInitDialog** calls **UpdateData**, the list box does not contain any items so there is nothing that can be selected. When we call **UpdateData** the list contains items that can be selected. You could also call **AddString** before **OnInitDialog** if you did not use Control member variables (i.e. by using **GetDlgItem** as shown in Chapter 22). In this case we would not need to call **UpdateData**.

For dialogs, you can still perform any dialog cleanup in **OnDestroy**.

23.4 From HWND to CWnd

The **CWnd** functions **Create** and **CreateEx** create a Windows window and associate the window with the **CWnd** object. But what if the window has already been created and we want to associate the window with a **CWnd** object? How do you convert an **HWND** into a **CWnd** object? This is the case for dialogs. Because dialogs are created from resource files, the controls (windows) on the dialog are not **CWnd** objects but Windows windows. Most of the time you want to manipulate the controls in a dialog using the functions offered by **CWnd**. There are two **CWnd** functions that solve this problem: **Attach** and **Detach**. (For dialogs you can also use the DDX routine **DDX_Control** to perform this association. This routine also subclasses the control and is discussed below). These two functions create and destroy a permanent association between an **HWND** and a new **CWnd** object. After a window has been attached to a **CWnd** object, the window can be referenced through the standard **CWnd** member functions. For example, if we had the handle to a button on a dialog and wanted to change the button text to "Hello" and disable it, we could do the following using the C API:

```
EnableWindow( hButtonWnd, FALSE );
SetWindowText( hButtonWnd, "Hello" );
```

(The easiest way to obtain the window handle for a control is to use the C API **GetDlgItem** function. This function accepts the handle for a dialog, along with a control ID, and returns the HWND for the control.) To use the **CWnd** member functions to perform the same task, you could use **Attach** to associate a permanent **CWnd** object with the control:

```
CButton button;
button.Attach( hButtonWnd );
button.EnableWindow( FALSE );
button.SetWindowText( "Hello" );
button.Detach();
```

Make sure to call **Detach** before the **CWnd** object is destroyed. Otherwise the associated window (the dialog button in this case) will be destroyed when the **CWnd** object is destroyed. You could also use one of the following methods to associate a temporary **CWnd** object with the button control:

```
CWnd* pWnd = CWnd::FromHandle(hButtonWnd);
pWnd->EnableWindow( FALSE );
pWnd->SetWindowText( "Hello" );
```

- or -

```
CWnd* pWnd = GetDlgItem( IDC_BUTTON );
pWnd->EnableWindow( FALSE );
pWnd->SetWindowText( "Hello" );
```

None of these methods allow the **CWnd** object to handle any of the window's messages. For this you need to subclass the window. This process is described below.

23.5 Permanent and Temporary Associations

The purpose of the **FromHandle** member function in classes such as **CWnd** and **CGdiObject** is to return a valid MFC object from any given Windows handle. If the specified handle already has an associated object, **FromHandle** will return that object. Otherwise it will create a temporary object and associate it with the handle. In the example above, if **hButtonWnd** was the handle of an existing **CButton** object, **FromHandle** would return a pointer to that object.

The difference between a permanent and temporary association is that when a temporary object is created, the object is stored in a temporary map. This map allows MFC to keep track of temporary objects so they can be cleaned up after they are used. Cleanup of this temporary map occurs in **DeleteTempMap** when the application becomes idle. Managing associations in this fashion allows you to create these associations during function calls without taking up a lot of resources. Because temporary associations are temporary, any objects obtained from **FromHandle** (or **GetDlgItem**) should not be cached or used between function calls.

23.6 Handles to Other Objects

Window handles aren't the only handles used in Windows. There are also handles to device contexts, menus, and the GDI objects: pens, brushes, fonts, bitmaps, palettes, and regions. The MFC classes for these objects, such as **CDC**, **CMenu**, **CPen**, and so on, work with handles in much the same way that the window class does.

If you look at the MFC hierarchy chart, you will find that all GDI objects share the same superclass: **CGdiObject**. The **CGdiObject** class has the member functions **GetSafeHandle**, **Attach**, and **Detach** that work in the same manner as the equivalent **CWnd** functions. Whenever you use one of these objects, the framework handles all the details for you so you can completely ignore the **HANDLE** types in your own code.

23.7 How Messages Work

When an event occurs in Windows, such as a window being created or the mouse moves, the system notifies the appropriate window through messages. For example, as the cursor moves across the screen, the window the cursor is in receives **WM_MOUSEMOVE** messages. When a window needs to paint itself it receives a **WM_PAINT** message. This leads to two questions: How does a window process events, and where do **CWnd** objects fit into the picture?

Every window in Windows has a function called a window procedure associated with it. When a message needs to be sent to a window, Windows finds what window procedure is associated with that window and calls it. This window procedure usually has a form similar to the following:

```
LRESULT WindowProc( hWnd, message, wParam, lParam )
{
    switch (message)
    {
    case WM_MOUSEMOVE:
        Do Something
        break;
    case WM_PAINT:
        Paint Something
        break;
    default:
        return DefWindowProc(...);
    }
}
```

The switch statement allows the window to perform different actions based on the message. For example, when the mouse moves the application might draw a line. If the window does not want to process a message, it can send the message along to a default window procedure that will perform the default action for it. Only windows can handle messages.

If only windows can handle message, where do **CWnd** objects fit in? Your **CWnd** objects use message maps to handle messages, not window procedures. Does that mean MFC doesn't use window procedures? Again, no. MFC simply hides them from us. In fact, the message map is the window procedure. Entries in the message map are used to route messages to pre-defined message handling functions. The message map, at the simplest level, simply automates the act of creating the switch statement.

When **WM_MOUSEMOVE** messages are being sent to your frame window, how do they get to your **CMyFrame** message handlers? Here are the steps MFC must take to get a message to a **CWnd** object's message handler:

1. Determine what **CWnd** object the message is destined for.
2. Determine what member function is associated with the message.
3. Call the member function.

To make message maps possible, two things happen to every **CWnd** object you create in your application. First, the **CWnd** object is associated with the window created through **Attach**. We already know **Attach** saves the window's **HWND** in **m_hWnd**, but it also performs another important operation: Attach adds the **CWnd** object to a permanent table that maps window handles (**HWND**) to **CWnd** objects. Second, the window procedure for the **CWnd**'s window is set to the function **Afx-WndProc**. All windows in an MFC application have the same window procedure.

When a message is sent to any window that was created by MFC, it is sent to the window's window procedure, **AfxWndProc**. **AfxWndProc** can then use the **HWND** of the destination window to look up its associated **CWnd** object. This is done by **CWnd::FromHandlePermanent**. This function uses the permanent window map to match an **HWND** with a **CWnd** object. Once it has the **CWnd** object, it can look up the message in the object's message map to find the member function to call. If there is no entry for the message in the message map, the message is sent to a default message handler.

23.8 Subclassing

The act of replacing one window procedure with another is called subclassing. This is not subclassing in the C++ sense, but subclassing in the Windows sense. For example, when MFC replaces the window procedure for every window created by a **CWnd** object with **AfxWndProc**, MFC is actually subclassing each window. This process lets **AfxWndProc** get the messages destined for the window before its original window procedure does.

You, as an MFC programmer, can subclass windows as well. You would do this because subclassing can save a great deal of time and effort when you are trying to add functionality to an existing MFC class. Take the edit control for example. If you need an edit control that accepts only numbers, it is much more productive to use the capabilities of the standard edit control than it is to design your own from scratch. To create the new behavior, all we need to do is monitor the keys pressed and make sure all of them are numbers. The rest of the functionality, like painting and control manipulation, can be left to the standard control. This technique is demonstrated in the next chapter.

Earlier we mentioned that **Attach** doesn't allow the **CWnd** object to process the messages destined for the attached window. The reason now should be obvious. **Attach** does not change a window's window procedure. The window procedure for the attached window is not **AfxWndProc**. Because of this, messages have no way of being mapped to **CWnd** member functions. To route the messages for the attached window through the **CWnd**'s message map, we must subclass the attached window. There are two functions that do just that. The **CWnd::SubclassWindow** function takes an **HWND** as a parameter and does two things to the window:

1. Performs an Attach to associate the CWnd with the window.
2. Replaces the window's window procedure with AfxWndProc.

The companion function **CWnd::SubclassDlgItem** does the same thing, except it takes a dialog control ID as a parameter. Therefore, if we created a new class **CMyEdit**, and if we wanted to route messages from an edit control through the **CMyEdit** message map, we could do the following:

```
CMyEdit edit;
edit.SubclassWindow( hEditWnd );
```

Then any messages in the **CMyEdit** message map would be rerouted until the **CMyEdit** object was destroyed or until **UnsubclassWindow** is called.

What you may be noticing is that this is exactly what is happening when you create a Control member variable for a dialog control in the ClassWizard. A Control variable is a variable that lets you access all the member functions and handle the messages for a specific type of control in a dialog box. When you create a Control member variable, the dialog data exchange function **DDX_Control** is added to the **DoDataExchange** function of the dialog. The first time **DoDataExchange** is called, the framework goes to all the trouble of getting the handle of the control, attaching it to the **CWnd** object, and then subclassing it. Then, using the Control variable, you can call all the standard member functions appropriate for the control. You can also handle any of the messages for the control. The ClassWizard is not doing anything mysterious—it is simply taking a standard technique and making it easier to use. You could just as well do it by hand, but it would take a lot more code.

23.9 Conclusion

You may have already realized that the MFC framework classes do not replace the original C API. They simply form a C++ interface to it. The tremendous advantage of this approach is that you can seamlessly call any of the C API functions from within an MFC application. MFC doesn't try to redefine any of the Windows paradigms familiar to C programmers. Instead, it makes those paradigms transparent, and easier to use, with member functions and message maps. The advantage of this approach, especially if you are used to programming to the Windows API in C, is that you don't have to learn any new concepts. The way MFC interacts with the Windows API is in most cases straightforward. However, if you ever have a problem or question about how MFC works, the source code is the best place to look for the reason behind the problem.

ENHANCING THE EDIT CONTROL

In the previous chapter we discussed how subclassing can be used to change the behavior of a window. In this chapter we will use subclassing to demonstrate how to change the **CEdit** control. The **CEdit** control is used in a variety of ways: It is useful as an edit field for simple text input in a dialog box and also as the basis of a complete text editor. Subclassing **CEdit** allows you to gain much greater control over the data accepted by an instance of the **CEdit** class. Using subclassing you can, for example, limit the characters accepted by an edit control to digits.

Edit controls are most commonly used as simple data entry devices in dialog boxes. Frequently the type of data entered in a dialog requires some sort of validity checking. For example, you may want to request a number from the user. In that case, you want to make sure that the user can enter only digits into the field. You may want to request a name from the user and guarantee that the user enters no digits in the field. One approach to validating the data in an input field is to wait until the user has performed an action such as when they tab to another control. Or you could wait until they pressed the OK button on a dialog using DDX and DDV. On this action you could retrieve the string from the edit control and then check it for validity. If there is a problem with the input, you can then display an error message.

Another approach is to monitor the input from the user and validate the string in real-time, as they type. This technique gives the user instant feedback. In this example we will implement the latter approach and create an edit control that accepts only numbers. If the user tries to type something that isn't a number, the new control will beep and ignore the input.

24.1 An Example

We want to create a new class that has all the functionality of a **CEdit** control, but we also want the new control to monitor its input and reject input that is not a digit. To do this, we need to derive a class from **CEdit** and handle some of the **CEdit**

505

messages in that new class. You can use the ClassWizard to create a new class that is derived from **CEdit**.

The **CEdit** control receives a **WM_CHAR** message when it needs to handle a keyboard event. This is the message that we need to monitor to intercept characters. You can use the ClassWizard to add **WM_CHAR** to the edit control's message map. Then our new class can capture characters before they reach the edit control. The checks that we need to make in **OnChar** are shown below:

```
void CMyEdit::OnChar(UINT nChar, UINT nRepCnt, UINT nFlags)
{
    // Always allow control characters
    if( (nChar < 0x20) || ((nChar >= '0') && (nChar <= '9')) )
    {
        CEdit::OnChar( nChar, nRepCnt, nFlags );
    }
    else
    {
        ::MessageBeep( 0xFFFFFFFF );
    }
}
```

This code checks to make sure **nChar** is a number or a control character such as the delete key. If it is, then we call the **CEdit**'s **OnChar** function so it can handle the character in the standard way and display it in the edit box. If the character is invalid we beep and ignore the input. This way the user knows invalid input as they fill in the edit box.

Now that we have an enhanced edit class, we need a way to test it. Create a dialog that contains an edit control. We have to subclass this edit control so it is wired to an object of our new edit control. This is how we get the messages from the dialog edit control through our new edit control's message map.

There are two ways to perform this subclassing. We could do it by hand and add an explicit call to the **SubclassDlgItem** function in the dialog's **OnInitDialog** function. However, a simpler way to perform this subclassing is through member variables using DDX. Use the ClassWizard to add a Control member variable of your class type (not **CEdit**) for the edit control in the dialog. If the ClassWizard doesn't let you select your edit control class when creating the member variable, you may have to do it manually.

Now you will find that you can type numbers into the edit control, but when you type letters the control rejects them and beeps.

24.2 Understanding the Process

Let's examine the process. When the dialog is created, the dialog's **DoDataExchange** is called. The **DDX_Control** function associates the dialog's edit control (i.e. **IDC_EDIT1**) with the dialog's member variable (i.e. **m_edit**) using the **SubclassWindow** function. Now all messages for the dialog's edit control will be re-routed through the **m_edit** object. Note that if the enhanced edit control was created with its **Create** function, the **DDX_Control** function would not have been necessary.

24.3 Conclusion

You can use the same technique demonstrated here to create any sort of modified edit control. For example, you might create an edit control that handles **WM_KEYUP** and **WM_KEYDOWN** messages or that handles **WM_VSCROLL** messages. Other controls can also be customized. You can create a **CStatic**, for example, and handle its **WM_PAINT** message to draw pictures. Subclassing is relatively simple to implement when you use DDX. You can also use this same technique to subclass controls in a **CFormView**.

Self-Managing Controls

In an object oriented world, each object should be self contained. Objects should be able to handle all their functionality themselves. For example your **CDocument** class knows how to serialize itself and your **CView** class knows how to display itself. Neither class tells the other how to manage itself. With Windows controls though, things are different. When you click a button, the button's parent handles the button's **BN_CLICKED** notification. When you select an item in a list view control, its parent handles the **NM_CLICK** notification. Sometimes this is the desired functionality. For example, in a dialog you want the dialog to handle the OK button notification so it can close itself. But what if you want to do something special when the user clicks an item in a special type of list view control? If you handle this special case in the list view's parent, what happens when you want to use this list in ten different places. With the current model you would have to copy the implementation ten times. In this chapter we will examine the MFC solution to this type of problem. The first solution relates to self-drawing controls. Next is a general solution for making controls manage themselves using a process called message reflection.

The list box and combo box controls are useful when you need to present the user with a list of choices. One limitation of these controls is that they can only display a list of strings. There are many cases, however, where you would like to have more control over the appearance of the items in the list. In such cases, a graphical list or combo box is often appropriate. For example, you might want to create a list that displays a set of icons. Or you may need to create a list having items containing bitmaps that represent disk drives or font types. You might want to display a combo box of colors. To create these different custom lists, you need the ability to draw the items in the list yourself.

The example in this chapter shows you how to enhance the standard combo box to display items containing a bitmap. You can also create custom list boxes, menus, buttons, and most other controls in a similar manner.

25.1 Owner-Drawing vs. Self-Drawing

If you have done any Windows programming previous to your exposure to MFC, you have probably heard of or used owner-drawn controls. With this type of control, the parent, or "owner," of a control draws whatever is necessary in the client area of the control. An owner-drawn button, for example, signals its parent whenever it needs repainting. The parent then draws whatever it likes on the face of the button.

This method of customizing controls makes poor use of the OOD philosophy. If you want to have the same custom control in several dialog boxes, using owner-drawn controls forces you to duplicate the code among all the potential parents. Each dialog needs to update all its custom controls itself. Another problem is more sublime: If a dialog has 20 owner-drawn lists, the dialog must take care of drawing each of those lists individually. Code management in these cases becomes a lot of work.

A self-drawing control is the object-oriented approach to owner-drawn controls. With self-drawing controls, the control itself, rather than its parent, is responsible for any customized drawing operations.

25.2 Owner-Drawn Messages

There are four messages associated with owner-drawn controls. The core message is the **WM_DRAWITEM** message. It is sent when a visual aspect of the control has changed. This may be due to refreshing or because an item's focus or selected state has changed. Three other messages are used with particular controls such as lists and combo boxes. The **WM_MEASUREITEM** message is sent when Windows needs to know the dimensions of an item. The **WM_COMPAREITEM** message is used during sorting to compare two items. For example, a sorted list box will call out to its parent with **WM_COMPAREITEM** messages so it can determine the correct ordering. The **WM_DELETEITEM** message is used to delete an item from a control and should take care of freeing any resources associated with items.

25.3 The Self-Drawing Framework

All that is necessary to make a control self-drawing is to override one of the virtual functions that handle these messages. The table below shows the relationship between the messages and the virtual **CWnd** member functions.

As you can see, not all the messages are used for every control. The list and combo box use all four but the status bar and button only uses the **WM_DRAWITEM** message. For the list and combo box, all the messages must be handled except the **WM_DELETEITEM** message. Handling this message is only necessary when the list or combo box has special cleanup actions to perform when deleting an item.

Table 25.1
Owner-drawing messages

Windows Message	CWnd Function	Classes
WM_DRAWITEM	DrawItem	CStatusBar, CListView, CBitmapButton, CButton, CListBox, CComboBox, CStatusBarCtrl, CListCtrl, CHeaderCtrl, CTabCtrl, CCheckListBox, CMenu
WM_MEASUREITEM	MeasureItem	CListBox, CComboBox, CMenu, CCheckListBox
WM_COMPAREITEM	CompareItem	CListBox, CComboBox
WM_DELETEITEM	DeleteItem	CListBox, CComboBox

25.4 Behind the Scenes

MFC takes the owner-drawn capability and reworks it to create self-drawing controls. It is interesting to understand how the translation takes place. You can skip over this section if the details don't interest you.

In Windows, when an owner-drawn control needs to be updated, the system sends messages to its parent. Then the parent proceeds to update the specified control. In MFC, the process is the same except the parent has the control update itself. This is done using the **CWnd::OnChildNotify** function. This function allows the control to determine if it wants to process the message itself. For example, if an owner-drawn **CListBox** in a **CDialog** needs to be drawn, the system sends the dialog a **WM_DRAWITEM** message. The **CWnd::OnDrawItem** function in the dialog (the parent) handles the message. **OnDrawItem** then sends the message to the **CListBox::OnChildNotify** function. In any self-drawing control, **OnChildNotify** determines if it wants to process the message and calls the appropriate function—in this case **CListBox::DrawItem** is called. After the item is drawn, **OnChildNotify** tells the dialog that the message has been processed. In other words, the owner-drawn message issued by the system gets sent to the dialog, which immediately routes it to the list so the list can handle it itself. Notice that the self-drawing control doesn't require any changes to its message map. All the messages are handled by the control's parent, which communicates with the control through virtual functions.

Although self-drawn controls are better than owner-drawn controls because they offer better encapsulation, you can still create owner-drawn controls in MFC. For example, to have a **CDialog** object handle the messages for its owner-drawn controls, just add **ON_WM_DRAWITEM** to the dialog's message map and implement its **OnDrawItem** function.

25.5 A General Solution

Overriding the previous four virtual functions is a special case solution for the self-drawing control problem. MFC also provides a way to handle the more general cases for having controls manage themselves. For example, if you want a specialized

CListCtrl that handles item selection different, you can have the list control object handle the **NM_CLICK** that the list control's parent would normally take care of. This process is called message reflection. Messages are reflected from the parent back to the control. The message the control receives is the original message the parent received (e.g. **WM_COMMAND**) plus the constant **WM_REFLECT**. So, in the case of the special **CListCtrl**, the list would receive the message **WM_NOTIFY + WM_REFLECT**. The message map entry necessary to handle this message is **ON_NOTIFY_REFLECT**. The ClassWizard will put an equal symbol (=) next to any reflected message a control can handle. Any message a control sends to its parent such as **WM_COMMAND**, **WM_NOTIFY**, the **WM_CTLCOLOR** family, **WM_HSCROLL**, **WM_VSCROLL** and **WM_PARENTNOTIFY** are reflected to controls.

For an example, if we wanted to make a **CMyButton** class that would handle its own **BN_CLICKED** notification, all we have to do is use the ClassWizard to create a new **CButton** derived class and add a message handler for the **=BN_CLICKED** notification. The message map entry for the button would look like this:

```
BEGIN_MESSAGE_MAP(CMyButton, CButton)
    //{{AFX_MSG_MAP(CMyButton)
    ON_CONTROL_REFLECT(BN_CLICKED, OnClicked)
    //}}AFX_MSG_MAP
END_MESSAGE_MAP()

void CMyButton::OnClicked()
{
    ::AfxMessageBox("Hello");
}
```

Now when you click a **CMyButton** button, the dialog receives a **WM_COMMAND** message with a **BN_CLICKED** notification and reflects that back to the button so it can display a message box.

You can also use message reflection for self-drawing controls that do not support the virtual function solution. All you need to do is add a message map entry such as **ON_WM_DRAWITEM_REFLECT** to the control. Some of the reflection message map entries and their function prototypes are shown below:

Table 25.2
Reflection message map entries

ON_CONTROL_REFLECT(wNotifyCode, memberFxn)   afx_msg void memberFxn ( );
ON_NOTIFY_REFLECT(wNotifyCode, memberFxn)   afx_msg void memberFxn (NMHDR * pNotifyStruct, LRESULT* result);
ON_UPDATE_COMMAND_UI_REFLECT()   afx_msg void memberFxn (CCmdUI* pCmdUI);
ON_WM_CTLCOLOR_REFLECT()   afx_msg HBRUSH CtlColor (CDC* pDC, UINT nCtlColor);

```
ON_WM_DRAWITEM_REFLECT( )
    afx_msg void DrawItem ( LPDRAWITEMSTRUCT );
ON_WM_MEASUREITEM_REFLECT( )
    afx_msg void MeasureItem ( LPMEASUREITEMSTRUCT);
ON_WM_DELETEITEM_REFLECT( )
    afx_msg void DeleteItem ( LPDELETEITEMSTRUCT );
ON_WM_COMPAREITEM_REFLECT( )
    afx_msg int CompareItem ( LPCOMPAREITEMSTRUCT );
ON_WM_CHARTOITEM_REFLECT( )
    afx_msg int CharToItem ( UINT nKey, UINT nIndex );
ON_WM_VKEYTOITEM_REFLECT( )
    afx_msg int VKeyToItem ( UINT nKey, UINT nIndex );
ON_WM_HSCROLL_REFLECT( )
    afx_msg void HScroll ( UINT nSBCode, UINT nPos );
ON_WM_VSCROLL_REFLECT( )
    afx_msg void VScroll ( UINT nSBCode, UINT nPos );
ON_WM_PARENTNOTIFY_REFLECT( )
    afx_msg void ParentNotify ( UINT message, LPARAM lParam );
ON_NOTIFY_REFLECT_EX( wNotifyCode, memberFxn )
    afx_msg BOOL memberFxn ( );
ON_COMMAND_REFLECT_EX( wNotifyCode, memberFxn )
    afx_msg BOOL memberFxn ( NMHDR * pNotifyStruct, LRESULT* result );
```

25.6 A Self-Drawing Combo Box

In this example we will create a self-drawing combo box that displays a list of bitmaps instead of strings.

Create an application framework using the AppWizard. Create a dialog and add a combo-box control to the dialog. To make the combo-box a self-drawing control change the following combo-box styles: Change the Type to Drop List and Owner draw to Variable. The Owner draw style cannot be Fixed because of some limitations of MFC. Also, pay attention to the Has Strings checkbox. When checked, it indicates that the combo box should hold strings for each item in the list, even though it may not display them (if it is owner-drawn, it will not display the strings). If this option is not checked you cannot use the string functions such as AddString to manage strings. Here, because the list displays only bitmaps, there is no need for it to manage any strings. You may also have to resize the combo box drop down size in order to see the bitmaps when you expand the combo box drop down list.

Create three bitmaps, **IDB_BITMAP1**, **IDB_BITMAP2**, and **IDB_BITMAP3**. These will be the items we put in the list so you can draw anything you like on them.

Now we need a new class that is derived from **CComboBox** that can handle the messages required to perform the drawing operations needed to display the bitmaps in the control. Use the ClassWizard to create a **CMyComboBox** that is derived from **CComboBox**. Then use the ClassWizard to override **DrawItem**, **MeasureItem**, and

CompareItem. We could also override the **DeleteItem** function, but it is only necessary when the items in the control have special memory requirements and need extra cleanup code. If you do not override these three functions in your new class, you will get an assertion when the base class functions are called.

The **CompareItem** function is shown below. This function is only used if we create a combo box that is sorted. Since we are drawing arbitrary bitmaps, the order is not important, and we return 0 so all the items are considered equal.

```
int CMyComboBox::CompareItem(LPCOMPAREITEMSTRUCT
    lpCompareItemStruct)
{
    return 0;
}
```

Next is the **MeasureItem** function. Its purpose is to return the height of a specified item.

```
void CMyComboBox::MeasureItem(LPMEASUREITEMSTRUCT
    lpMeasureItemStruct)
{
    static int cyItem = (-1);

    // Have we already set the height?
    if( cyItem < 0 )
    {
        // Load one of the bitmaps to retrieve
        // its height.
        BITMAP bm;
        CBitmap cBitmap;
        VERIFY(cBitmap.LoadBitmap(IDB_BITMAP1));
        VERIFY(cBitmap.GetObject(sizeof(BITMAP), &bm));
        VERIFY(cBitmap.DeleteObject());

        cyItem = bm.bmHeight;
    }

    ASSERT( cyItem > 0 );
    VERIFY( SetItemHeight( 0, cyItem + 8 ) != CB_ERR );
    VERIFY( SetItemHeight( -1, cyItem + 8 ) != CB_ERR );

    lpMeasureItemStruct->itemHeight = cyItem;
}
```

The **MeasureItem** function takes as a parameter a pointer to a **MEASUREITEMSTRUCT** structure. Among other things, this structure contains the ID of the requested item and a variable in which to return the height of the item. All items in our combo box are of fixed size, but because of MFC restrictions we must use **CBS_OWNERDRAWVARIABLE** for our derived class (see MFC Technical Note 14). Because our items are all the same height, it is sufficient to determine the height of a single item and to always return the same value. This step is performed by loading one of the bitmaps for the list and finding its height. After the initial call, this same

514

height value will always be returned. The calls to the **SetItemHeight** function determine how high the combo box edit area is. A pad of eight pixels is added to the height to space out the items. This helps solve the deficiency of not being able to use a Fixed style which would let us use the No Integral Height style instead of using **SetItemHeight**.

The rest of the functionality is in the **DrawItem** function. This is the function that will determine what item the control needs to draw, where it needs to draw it, and what state to give it on the screen.

```
void CMyComboBox::DrawItem(LPDRAWITEMSTRUCT
    lpDrawItemStruct)
{
    if( lpDrawItemStruct->itemID < 0 )
        return;

    // Create a temporary CDC object.
    CDC* pDC = CDC::FromHandle( lpDrawItemStruct->hDC );

    if( lpDrawItemStruct->itemAction &
        (ODA_DRAWENTIRE | ODA_SELECT) )
    {
        CBitmap cBitmap;
        COLORREF crOldText;
        COLORREF crOldBack;

        // If the item is selected then highlight it.
        if( lpDrawItemStruct->itemState & ODS_SELECTED )
        {
            crOldText = pDC->SetTextColor(
                ::GetSysColor(COLOR_HIGHLIGHTTEXT) );
            crOldBack = pDC->SetBkColor(
                ::GetSysColor(COLOR_HIGHLIGHT));
        }

        // Erase the entire area.
        pDC->ExtTextOut( lpDrawItemStruct->rcItem.left,
            lpDrawItemStruct->rcItem.top,
            ETO_OPAQUE, &(lpDrawItemStruct->rcItem),
            "", 0, NULL );

        // Load the appropriate bitmap
        switch( lpDrawItemStruct->itemID )
        {
        case 0: VERIFY(cBitmap.LoadBitmap(IDB_BITMAP1));
            break;
        case 1: VERIFY(cBitmap.LoadBitmap(IDB_BITMAP2));
            break;
        case 2: VERIFY(cBitmap.LoadBitmap(IDB_BITMAP3));
            break;
        default:VERIFY(cBitmap.LoadBitmap(IDB_BITMAP1));
            break;
        }

        // Get the dimensions of the bitmap to draw.
```

```
        BITMAP bm;
        VERIFY(cBitmap.GetObject(sizeof(BITMAP), &bm) );

        // Draw the bitmap using TransBitBlt.
        TransBitBlt( pDC,
            lpDrawItemStruct->rcItem.left,
            lpDrawItemStruct->rcItem.top,
            cBitmap, RGB(255,255,255) );

        // Delete the bitmap.
        VERIFY( cBitmap.DeleteObject() );

        // Draw the focus state.
        if( lpDrawItemStruct->itemState & ODA_FOCUS )
        {
            pDC->DrawFocusRect(
                &(lpDrawItemStruct->rcItem) );
        }

        // Return the DC to its original state.
        if( lpDrawItemStruct->itemState & ODS_SELECTED )
        {
            pDC->SetTextColor( crOldText );
            pDC->SetBkColor( crOldBack );
        }
    }

    if( lpDrawItemStruct->itemAction & ODA_FOCUS )
    {
        pDC->DrawFocusRect(&(lpDrawItemStruct->rcItem));
    }
}
```

The only argument to this function is a pointer to a **DRAWITEMSTRUCT**. This structure contains a variety of information about the object to be drawn. Inside the function, the code needs to know the ID of the item to draw, the coordinates at which to draw the item, the device context, and whether the item is selected or has the current focus. The code extracts all this information from the **DRAWITEM-STRUCT** structure.

We start the process by getting a device context. We must use the device context that is in the **lpDrawItemStruct**. Use the **FromHandle** function to create a temporary **CDC** object from the raw **DC**. Remember that this object is temporary, so we must create the object each time **DrawItem** is called. Next we check the **itemAction** value to determine if the entire item is being redrawn (**ODA_DRAWENTIRE**) or if the item is being selected (**ODA_SELECT**). The **itemAction** member tells us what drawing action is required. Both branches perform the same action because the only difference is the item's background color. The **itemState** member tells us what visual state the item should be in. If the item is selected we change the text and background colors to the default highlight colors. The entire area is then erased with the background color by **ExtTextOut**. We could have used **FillRect**, but **ExtTextOut** is usually faster and easier to use. Then based on the requested **itemID** we load the bitmap that needs to be drawn. The bitmap is drawn transparently using the **TransBlt** function described below. Then we check to see if we need to draw a focus rectangle around the item (**ODA_FOCUS**). **DrawFocusRect** will draw a dotted rectangle around the item using an XOR function. Before returning, we must make sure the device context is restored to its original state, so we restore the foreground and background colors if they were changed.

25.7 Drawing Transparent Bitmaps

Drawing the item bitmaps could be easy, but there is a catch. The bitmaps drawn are usually odd-shaped. If they were just drawn on the screen using **BitBlt**, the bitmap would overwrite the current background in the combo box and the result would look incorrect. The proper way to perform this action, therefore, is to draw the bitmap "transparently" onto the existing image, leaving the background intact. In this case, we want to draw only the black parts of the image. We want the white part of the bitmap to become the same as the background. There are a few different ways to implement transparent blitting. Here I will briefly describe the theory and then describe the technique seen in **TransBitBlt**.

There are three images involved with the transparent **BitBlt**: the source image (the face), the destination (screen), and the mask. The key to the process is the mask. We want to create a mask so we can "paint through" the mask and only affect the parts of the destination that the mask defines. The mask is a simple monochrome (black and white) bitmap. Only the parts of the mask that are black affect the destination (screen). Once all three bitmaps exist, three steps are necessary to paint the source onto the destination. Here are the steps involved when using individual **BitBlt** calls.

```
BitBlt( Destination, ..., Source,  ..., SRCINVERT );
BitBlt( Destination, ..., Mask,    ..., SRCAND );
BitBlt( Destination, ..., Source,  ..., SRCINVERT );
```

The three steps in the process are as follows:

1. The first step XORs the source bitmap onto the destination. This has the effect of copying the bitmap onto the destination without destroying the destination pixels. We use the fact that a second XOR will restore the destination to its original state.
2. The second step performs the masking. When the mask is ANDed to the destination, all the pixels that are white (the parts we want to be transparent) leave the destination pixels unchanged, while the pixels that are black (the parts of the image we want to paint) set the destination to black.
3. The third step XORs the source to the destination again. The parts that were not blacked out by the mask are restored to their original state (two XORs restore the original). Where the mask produced black, the pixels are copied directly from the source to the destination because value XOR black = value.

The **TransBitBlt** function performs the same operations as above, but it does them in a single step. Because we will be painting our bitmap image over a background color and not another bitmap (or complex image) we can use this second process to accomplish the three steps more quickly. In **TransBitBlt** we will use a custom ternary raster operation (ROP). The most common ROPs are ones like **SRCCOPY**, **SRC-PAINT**, **SRCAND**, and **SRCINVERT**. There are 15 pre-defined ROPs in WINDOWS.H, but there are 256 in all. (Search for "ternary raster operations" in books on-line for a complete list.) The 226th ROP performs the same operations as the three steps above, except it uses a source, destination, and pattern (brush):

ROP_DSPDxax = 0x00E20746

The constant for this Boolean function is written in reverse Polish notation (D=Destination, P=Pattern, S=Source, x=XOR, and a=AND). It translates to the following:

1. XOR the pattern with the destination (**SRCINVERT**).
2. AND the result with the source (**SRCAND**).
3. XOR the previous result with the destination (**SRCINVERT**).

Here is the complete **TransBitBlt** function:

```
BOOL TransBitBlt( CDC* pdcScreen, UINT x, UINT y,
    CBitmap& cImageBitmap, COLORREF crTransparent )
{
    ASSERT( pdcScreen != NULL );

    // Get the dimensions of the bitmap image.
    BITMAP bm;
    VERIFY(cImageBitmap.GetObject(sizeof(BITMAP), &bm));

    // Create a DC for the image bitmap.
    CDC dcImage;
    VERIFY( dcImage.CreateCompatibleDC( pdcScreen ) );
    CBitmap* pOldImageBitmap =
        dcImage.SelectObject( &cImageBitmap );

    // Create a DC and monochrome bitmap for the mask.
    CDC dcMask;
    CBitmap cMaskBitmap;
    VERIFY( dcMask.CreateCompatibleDC( pdcScreen ) );
    VERIFY( cMaskBitmap.CreateBitmap( bm.bmWidth,
        bm.bmHeight, 1, 1, NULL ) );
    CBitmap* pOldMaskBitmap =
        dcMask.SelectObject( &cMaskBitmap );

    // Create a memory DC and bitmap to work on.
    CDC dcMem;
    CBitmap cMemBitmap;
    VERIFY( dcMem.CreateCompatibleDC( pdcScreen ) );
    VERIFY( cMemBitmap.CreateCompatibleBitmap( pdcScreen,
```

```
            bm.bmWidth, bm.bmHeight ) );
    CBitmap* pOldMemBitmap =
        dcMem.SelectObject( &cMemBitmap );

    // Create a monochrome mask of the image.
    COLORREF crBack = dcImage.SetBkColor( crTransparent );
    dcMask.BitBlt( 0, 0, bm.bmWidth, bm.bmHeight,
        &dcImage, 0, 0, SRCCOPY );
    dcImage.SetBkColor( crBack );

    // Create and select a brush of the background color.
    CBrush cBrush;
    cBrush.CreateSolidBrush( pdcScreen->GetBkColor() );
    CBrush *cOldBrush = dcMem.SelectObject( &cBrush );

    // Copy the unmodified image in the temporary bitmap.
    dcMem.BitBlt( 0, 0, bm.bmWidth, bm.bmHeight,
        &dcImage, 0, 0, SRCCOPY );

    // Force conversion of the monochrome to stay B&W.
    COLORREF crText = dcMem.SetTextColor( 0L );
    crBack = dcMem.SetBkColor( RGB(255,255,255) );

    // Perform the masking copy.
    dcMem.BitBlt( 0, 0, bm.bmWidth, bm.bmHeight,
        &dcMask, 0, 0,
        0x00E20746 /* ROP_DSPDxax */ );

    // Copy the final image to the screen.
    pdcScreen->BitBlt( x, y, bm.bmWidth, bm.bmHeight,
        &dcMem, 0, 0, SRCCOPY );

    // Restore the original device context.
    dcMem.SetTextColor( crText );
    dcMem.SetBkColor( crBack );
    dcMem.SelectObject( cOldBrush );

    // Select the bitmaps out of the DCs.
    dcImage.SelectObject( pOldImageBitmap );
    dcMask.SelectObject( pOldMaskBitmap );
    dcMem.SelectObject( pOldMemBitmap );

    // Delete all the objects we CREATEd.
    VERIFY( dcImage.DeleteDC() );
    VERIFY( dcMask.DeleteDC() );
    VERIFY( dcMem.DeleteDC() );

    VERIFY( cBrush.DeleteObject() );
    VERIFY( cMemBitmap.DeleteObject() );
    VERIFY( cMaskBitmap.DeleteObject() );

    return( TRUE );
}
```

The **TransBitBlt** function takes as arguments the screen device context, the destination coordinates, the bitmap image to draw, and the color in the image to make transparent. We want the white parts of the bitmap to be transparent (only draw the black portions) so **crTransparent** will be **RGB(255, 255, 255)**.

The code first retrieves the dimensions of the bitmap. Then it creates three device contexts. The first is associated with the image bitmap. The second DC contains a monochrome bitmap (1 plane, 1 bit-per-pixel) that will be used as the mask. All drawing operations will be performed on the third DC so there is no flicker on the screen.

Next we create the monochrome mask of the image bitmap.

```
dcImage.SetBkColor( crTransparent );
dcMask.BitBlt( 0, 0, bm.bmWidth, bm.bmHeight,
    &dcImage, 0, 0, SRCCOPY );
```

Because **dcImage** is a color (multi-plane) bitmap, while **dcMask** is monochrome, the **BitBlt** converts the color bitmap in **dcImage** to a monochrome bitmap before copying it to the bitmap in **dcMask**. The **SetBkColor** function tells **BitBlt** which color in **dcImage** (the source DC) should be converted to white pixels. All other pixels will be converted to black. The result is a black and white image of the source. Then we create a brush that has the color of the background and copy the bitmap image to the temporary image. Before we use **BitBlt** with the custom ROP, we make sure the foreground and background colors in **dcMem** (the destination DC) are black and white. This step is important because **dcMask** is monochrome and **dcMem** is color. In this case **BitBlt** will try to perform another conversion between monochrome and color. **BitBlt** will convert the black pixels of the monochrome bitmap to the destination's foreground color and the white pixels to its background color. We want the conversion to stay black and white so we explicitly set the background and foreground colors of the destination to black and white. The next call to **BitBlt** performs the three necessary steps:

1. The current background pattern is XORd with the bitmap image in **dcMem**.
2. That result is ANDed with the monochrome mask of the bitmap image in **dcMask**.
3. The final result is XORd with the bitmap image in **dcMem** again, leaving the bitmap image with a background of the pattern color.

Now the image in **dcMem** contains our face with the same background as the screen so we can copy the final image to the screen without overwriting anything. The remaining code handles cleanup.

25.8 Subclassing the Combo Box

Now that we have the **CMyComboBox** class, we need to associate it with the combo box we created in the dialog. When we subclassed the **CEdit** control to handle numbers in Chapter 24 we used **DDX_Control** to simplify the process. In this example we will use **SubclassDlgItem** instead. **SubclassDlgItem** is a convenience function for **SubclassWindow** that takes a dialog control ID instead of a window handle.

The place to call **SubclassDlgItem** is in the dialog's **OnInitDialog** function. Use the ClassWizard to add a handler for the **WM_INITDIALOG** message. Then manually add a **CMyComboBox** member variable to the dialog class as shown in below.

```
// Member variables
public:
    CMyComboBox     m_combo;
```

Remember also to include the **CMyComboBox** header file where necessary. Here's the **OnInitDialog** function:

```
BOOL CMyDialog::OnInitDialog()
{
    CDialog::OnInitDialog();

    m_combo.SubclassDlgItem( IDC_COMBO1, this );

    /* Add the items to the combo box. */
    m_combo.AddString( NULL );
    m_combo.AddString( NULL );
    m_combo.AddString( NULL );

    return TRUE;
}
```

OnInitDialog does two things. First, it subclasses the combo box we added to the dialog. **SubclassDlgItem** takes the ID of the control in the dialog template (**IDC_COMBO1**) and the parent dialog. Second, **OnInitDialog** adds some items to our list. Because we have three bitmaps, we need three list items. You could also use the item data of the combo box (**SetItemData**) to associate list items with bitmaps.

25.9 Conclusion

Self-drawn controls give you the freedom to create controls with almost any sort of appearance. Simply by implementing three functions we have created a completely customized combo box. To create self-drawn lists and menus, follow the same process as the one shown here. Note also that the **CBitmapButton** class in MFC is a self-drawn button that handles bitmaps automatically.

ANOTHER LOOK—
A SELF-DRAWING LIST BOX

It is sometimes useful to request from the system a list of the available fonts. For example, you might want to know which fonts are available to use when drawing to the display or which fonts are supported by the current printer. Such a list can be created through a process called font enumeration. Enumeration is a general capability that allows you to access a particular list of objects.

In this chapter you will learn how to enumerate fonts. The enumeration is displayed using a customized list box that benefits from several of the techniques used in the previous chapter.

26.1 Introduction to Font Enumeration

Many different items in a Windows system can be enumerated. For example, you can enumerate lists of objects such as child windows, tasks, fonts, clipboard formats, metafile records, pens, and brushes. To use enumeration, you set up a procedure that Windows can call each time it recalls an item in the list being enumerated. With fonts, for example, you can set up an enumeration procedure and Windows will call that procedure each time it finds a font that matches a certain specification.

The function that performs font enumeration is **EnumFontFamilies** and is shown below.

```
int EnumFontFamilies( HDC hDC, LPCTSTR lpszFamily,
                      FONTENUMPROC lpEnumFontFamProc,
                      LPARAM lParam );
```

The first argument is a device context. This argument specifies the device with which we want the fonts to be compatible. For example, there might be many fonts that can be displayed on the screen, but only a select few that can be used on a printer. This is the case when you are using a text-only printer. The second argument is the font family name. Font families are general font names, like "Courier" or "Times." The family allows us to narrow the search. If this argument is NULL, then one font in each font family is enumerated. If this argument is a family name (e.g. "Courier"), then each available style or size of the font family is enumerated. Styles are specific characteristics such as "Courier Bold" or "Courier Italic." The third argument is the enumeration procedure. This is the function that will be called for each font matching our family specification. This procedure has the prototype shown below and is explained later. The fourth argument **lParam** is a call data parameter that allows us to pass something to the callback function. For example, you might pass a pointer to an integer and use the integer to keep track of the number of items.

Each enumeration procedure accepts different parameters depending on the object being enumerated. When enumerating child windows, the enumeration procedure receives the handle of the child window found. When enumerating pens, the enumeration procedure receives the style or color of the enumerated pen. In our case, the enumeration procedure will receive information describing each font.

```
int CALLBACK EnumFontFamProc( LPENUMLOGFONT lplf,
                              LPNEWTEXTMETRIC lpntm,
                              int nFontType,
                              LPARAM lParam );
```

The first two arguments are pointers to structures that describe the current font. We can determine attributes such as its weight (bold, italic), height, width, and underlining. The **nFontType** parameter lets us determine if the font is a TrueType font, a device font, a raster font, or a vector font. The **lParam** argument is the call data parameter passed from the calling function. The procedure returns an integer that determines if the enumeration process should continue. Enumeration will stop when there are no more fonts to enumerate or when the procedure returns 0. This allows us to search for a particular item and then stop.

26.2 Enumerating Font Families

To begin, we will create a function that will fill a list box with the name of each font family. It needs to enumerate one font from each family and add that font to the list, saving the font type along with the name.

```
void UpdateFamilyList( CListBox& ctlFontList )
{
    // Create an array of CStrings that we can store the
    // font family names in.
    CStringArray* fontNameArray = new CStringArray;

    // Get a device context for the default printer.
    CPrintDialog cPrintDlg( FALSE );
    VERIFY( cPrintDlg.GetDefaults() == TRUE );
    HDC hdcPrint = cPrintDlg.GetPrinterDC();
    ASSERT( hdcPrint != NULL );

    // Enumerate ALL the font families.
    EnumFontFamilies( hdcPrint, NULL,
        (FONTENUMPROC)EnumAllFontFamiliesCB,
        (LPARAM)fontNameArray );

    VERIFY( ::DeleteDC(hdcPrint) == TRUE );
```

```
    // Fill the list box with the fonts.
    ctlFontList.ResetContent();
    for( int i=0; i < fontNameArray->GetSize(); i++ )
    {
        // The item text looks like the following:
        //      FONTNAME:[T|P|R|V]
        // where the character specifies the font type.
        // Remove the ':' before we display the font.

        CString curFontName = fontNameArray->GetAt( i );
        int i = curFontName.FindOneOf( ":" );
        ASSERT( i >= 0 );
        char cch = curFontName[ i + 1 ];
        char* s = curFontName.GetBuffer( 256 );
        ASSERT( s != NULL );
        s[i] = '\0';
        curFontName.ReleaseBuffer( -1 );

        // The last character in the item text tells us if
        // the font it a TRUETYPE or PRINTER font.
        UINT nType = 0;
        switch( cch )
        {
        case 'T': nType = IDB_TRUETYPE; break;
        case 'P': nType = IDB_PRINTER;  break;
        }

        UINT nItemPos = ctlFontList.AddString( curFontName );
        ASSERT( nItemPos != LB_ERR );
        ASSERT( nItemPos != LB_ERRSPACE );
        VERIFY( ctlFontList.SetItemData( nItemPos,
            MAKELONG(nType, 0) ) != LB_ERR );
    }

    // Set the current selection.
    ctlFontList.SetCurSel( 0 );

    delete fontNameArray;
}
```

The enumeration callback will create a list of font family names and their types. We will use an array of **CString**s to hold the list. This array will be passed to the enumeration callback function as the **lParam** parameter. Next, because we want to enumerate the fonts available for the default printer, the function needs a device context for the default printer. The **CPrintDialog** and its member functions make this simple. If you want to instead enumerate the screen fonts, change the device context accordingly. Now for the enumeration. Notice that the second parameter to **Enum-FontFamilies** is NULL. This is done so that when the enumeration is complete the array will contain the font family names. When the enumeration is complete we have to clean up the printer device context and fill the list box with the returned items.

Our enumeration procedure uses the last character in each name to represent the font type (TrueType, printer, and so on). For each font in the array, we have to parse it to determine its type, then add the name to the list box. We will store the type of each font family in the item data value associated with each entry in the list box. Using **MAKELONG** you can store two separate numbers in the item data—one in the **HI-WORD** and one in the **LOWORD**. In this case we need only one value. Remember when adding strings to a self-drawing list box to make sure the Has Strings style is checked or the list will not allocate space for the item data. Last of all, we set the current selection to the first item in the list and delete the array of font names.

The enumeration function called for each font simply needs to add each family name to the array passed through **lParam**.

```
int CALLBACK EnumAllFontFamiliesCB( LPENUMLOGFONT lplf,
    LPNEWTEXTMETRIC lpntm, int nFontType, LPARAM lParam )
{
    ASSERT( lplf != NULL );
    ASSERT( lpntm != NULL );
    ASSERT( lParam != NULL );

    ASSERT( lplf->elfLogFont.lfFaceName != NULL );
    CString curFontName( lplf->elfLogFont.lfFaceName );

    if( nFontType & TRUETYPE_FONTTYPE )
        curFontName += ":T"; // TrueType font
    else if( (nFontType & DEVICE_FONTTYPE) &&
            (nFontType & RASTER_FONTTYPE) )
        curFontName += ":P"; // Raster printer font
    else if( nFontType & RASTER_FONTTYPE )
        curFontName += ":R"; // Raster font
    else // Vector font type
        curFontName += ":V";

    // The parameter passed in was an array of CStrings.
    // Add the font name found to this array.
    CStringArray* fontNameArray = (CStringArray *)lParam;
    fontNameArray->Add( curFontName );

    TRACE( "Enumerated Font Family (%s).\n",
        (LPCSTR)curFontName );

    // Return 1 so we will get called again
    return( 1 );
}
```

EnumAllFontFamiliesCB starts by getting the name of the font family. The **ENUMLOGFONT** structure contains this name. Next, the function determines the type of the font. It appends a character to the end of the font name depending on the type. The font can be either a TrueType, raster, or vector font. If the font is both Raster and device, it is available to the printer, either in hardware or by downloading. There is no special flag for the vector type. You can assume that if it is not TrueType or Raster, then it is a vector font. After the font name is added to the array of font names, the function returns the value 1 so enumeration will continue.

26.3 Enumerating Font Styles

When a font family is selected in the first list box we want to display the available styles in the second list box we created. This process is very similar to enumerating the families.

```
void UpdateStyleList( CListBox& ctlFontList,
    CListBox& ctlStyleList )
{
    // Create an array of CStrings that we can store the
    // font style names in.
    CStringArray* styleNameArray = new CStringArray;

    // Get a device context for the default printer.
    CPrintDialog cPrintDlg( FALSE );
    VERIFY( cPrintDlg.GetDefaults() == TRUE );
    HDC hdcPrint = cPrintDlg.GetPrinterDC();
    ASSERT( hdcPrint != NULL );

    // Get the currently selected font family.
    int nCurSel = ctlFontList.GetCurSel();
    ASSERT( nCurSel != LB_ERR );
    char szFontFamily[ 256 ];
    VERIFY( ctlFontList.GetText( nCurSel,
        szFontFamily ) != LB_ERR );

    // Enumerate the font styles for the current family.
    EnumFontFamilies( hdcPrint, szFontFamily,
        (FONTENUMPROC)EnumFontStylesCB,
        (LPARAM)styleNameArray );

    VERIFY( ::DeleteDC(hdcPrint) == TRUE );

    // Fill the combo box with the font styles.
    ctlStyleList.ResetContent();
    for( int i=0; i < styleNameArray->GetSize(); i++ )
    {
        CString curStyleName = styleNameArray->GetAt( i );
        UINT nItemPos = ctlStyleList.AddString( curStyleName );
        ASSERT( nItemPos != LB_ERR );
        ASSERT( nItemPos != LB_ERRSPACE );
    }

    ctlStyleList.SetCurSel( 0 );

    delete styleNameArray;
}
```

Notice the similarity between this and **UpdateFamilyList**. The main difference is the second argument to **EnumFontFamilies**. Now it is the name of the currently selected font family. This will enumerate the styles available for each font. This can also enumerate the sizes available for certain fonts, but we are only using the styles in this example. After the enumeration is complete, each style in the array is added to the style list box.

The styles callback function shown below determines which styles are available for the family being enumerated and adds each style to an array.

```
int CALLBACK EnumFontStylesCB( LPENUMLOGFONT lplf,
    LPNEWTEXTMETRIC lpntm, int nFontType, LPARAM lParam )
{

    // The parameter passed in was an array of CStrings.
    // Add the style found to this array.
    CStringArray *szFamilyArray = (CStringArray *)lParam;

    // If the font is not TrueType assume there are only 4
    // style possibilities.
    if( !(nFontType & TRUETYPE_FONTTYPE) )
    {
        szFamilyArray->Add( "Regular" );
        szFamilyArray->Add( "Italic" );
        szFamilyArray->Add( "Bold" );
        szFamilyArray->Add( "Bold Italic" );

        // We don't need to enumerate any more.
        return( 0 );
    }

    // If the font is TrueType, the styles are defined
    // in the elfStyle string.
    ASSERT( lplf->elfStyle != NULL );
    CString curStyleName( lplf->elfStyle );
    szFamilyArray->Add( curStyleName );

    // Return 1 so we will get called again for the next style.
    return( 1 );
}
```

If the font family is not TrueType, we assume there are four style possibilities: normal, bold, italic, and bold italic. This is the first check performed by the callback. We add these four styles to the array and then stop the enumeration with a return value of 0. If the family is TrueType, the procedure will be called once for each available style. As each style is enumerated, it is added to the array and a return value of 1 lets the enumeration continue.

26.4 An Example

As an example, we will create a dialog with two list boxes. One list box will be a self-drawing control and will contain a list of the available printer fonts. This list box will contain both the name of the font family and a bitmap that denotes its type. The other list box will contain the styles available for the currently selected font family.

Create a new application framework. Then create a new dialog resource. On the dialog, place two list boxes next to each other. Change the IDs of each to **IDC_FONTLIST** and **IDC_STYLELIST** respectively. We want the font list box to be self-drawn, so change the styles of **IDC_FONTLIST** so the Owner Draw style is

Variable and the Has Strings flag is set. The Variable value in the Owner Draw box indicates that each item in the list can have a variable size. With MFC, all owner-drawn lists and combo boxes must have this option set. The Has Strings checkbox, when checked, indicates that the list box will hold the strings for each item in the list. For this example, be sure that Has Strings is set.

Also create two bitmaps named **IDB_TRUETYPE** and **IDB_PRINTER** that are 16x16 in size. These two bitmaps will represent True Type and Printer fonts.

Similar to the process described in the previous chapter, we need to create our own list box class to handle the messages required to display our custom list items. Use the ClassWizard to derive a new class **CFontListBox** that is derived from **CListBox**. Then override its **DrawItem**, **MeasureItem**, and **CompareItem** functions.

For this example we will ignore sorting so the **CompareItem** function does not do anything. Return 0 so all the items are considered equal.

```
int CFontListBox::CompareItem(LPCOMPAREITEMSTRUCT
    lpCompareItemStruct)
{
    return 0;
}
```

Each item in the list will have a string and a bitmap. The height of the each item needs to be the tallest of the two, either the height of the bitmap or the height of the current font. Because our items are all the same height, it is sufficient to determine the height of a single item and to always return the same value.

```
void CFontListBox::MeasureItem(LPMEASUREITEMSTRUCT
    lpMeasureItemStruct)
{
    static int cyItem = (-1);

    // Have we already set the height?
    if( cyItem < 0 )
    {
        // Load one of the bitmaps to retrieve its height.
        BITMAP bm;
        CBitmap cBitmap;
        VERIFY( cBitmap.LoadBitmap( IDB_TRUETYPE ) );
        VERIFY( cBitmap.GetObject( sizeof(BITMAP), &bm ) );
        VERIFY( cBitmap.DeleteObject() );

        // Get the height of the current font.
        TEXTMETRIC tm;
        CDC* pDC = GetDC();
        ASSERT( pDC != NULL );
        pDC->GetTextMetrics( &tm );
        VERIFY( ReleaseDC( pDC ) );

        // The height of each item is the greatest of the two
        cyItem = max( bm.bmHeight, tm.tmHeight );
    }
```

```
        ASSERT( cyItem > 0 );
        lpMeasureItemStruct->itemHeight = cyItem;
    }
```

The rest of the functionality is handled in **DrawItem**.

```
    void CFontListBox::DrawItem(LPDRAWITEMSTRUCT lpDrawItemStruct)
    {
        if( lpDrawItemStruct->itemID < 0 )
            return;

        // Get the font type stored in the item data.
        DWORD wItemData = GetItemData( lpDrawItemStruct->itemID );
        ASSERT( wItemData != LB_ERR );

        // Get the name of the font.
        char szItem[ 256 ];
        VERIFY(GetText(lpDrawItemStruct->itemID, szItem) != CB_ERR);
        ASSERT( strlen(szItem) > 0 );

        // Get a device context to draw with.  We MUST use
        // this device context, and when we are finished with
        // it we have to make sure we didn't change any of its
        // values.
        CDC *pDC = CDC::FromHandle( lpDrawItemStruct->hDC );
        ASSERT( pDC != NULL );

        if( lpDrawItemStruct->itemAction &
            (ODA_DRAWENTIRE | ODA_SELECT) )
        {
            COLORREF crText;
            COLORREF crBack;

            // If the item is selected then highlight it.
            if( lpDrawItemStruct->itemState & ODS_SELECTED )
            {
                crText = pDC->SetTextColor(
                    ::GetSysColor(COLOR_HIGHLIGHTTEXT) );
                crBack = pDC->SetBkColor(
                    ::GetSysColor(COLOR_HIGHLIGHT) );
            }

            // The LOWORD of the item data tells us if the
            // font it a TRUETYPE or PRINTER font.
            CBitmap cBitmap;

            switch( (UINT)LOWORD(wItemData) )
            {
            case IDB_TRUETYPE:
                VERIFY(cBitmap.LoadBitmap(IDB_TRUETYPE)); break;
            case IDB_PRINTER:
                VERIFY(cBitmap.LoadBitmap(IDB_PRINTER));  break;
            default :
                VERIFY(cBitmap.LoadBitmap(IDB_TRUETYPE)); break;
            }
```

```
        // Get the dimension of the bitmap to draw.
        BITMAP bm;
        VERIFY( cBitmap.GetObject( sizeof(BITMAP), &bm ) );

        // Draw the font label text.
        VERIFY( pDC->ExtTextOut(
                lpDrawItemStruct->rcItem.left + bm.bmWidth + 4,
                lpDrawItemStruct->rcItem.top,
                ETO_OPAQUE | ETO_CLIPPED,
                &lpDrawItemStruct->rcItem,
                szItem, strlen(szItem),
                (LPINT)NULL ) == TRUE );

        // Draw the type bitmap on the left of the text.
        if( LOWORD(wItemData) != 0 )
        {
            TransBitBlt( pDC,
                lpDrawItemStruct->rcItem.left,
                lpDrawItemStruct->rcItem.top,
                cBitmap, RGB(255,255,255) );
        }

        VERIFY( cBitmap.DeleteObject() );

        // Return device context to its original state.
        if( lpDrawItemStruct->itemState & ODS_SELECTED )
        {
            pDC->SetTextColor( crText );
            pDC->SetBkColor( crBack );
        }
    }

    // Draw the focus rectangle if needed.
    if( (lpDrawItemStruct->itemAction & ODA_FOCUS) ||
        (lpDrawItemStruct->itemState & ODS_FOCUS) )
    {
        pDC->DrawFocusRect( &lpDrawItemStruct->rcItem );
    }
}
```

This **DrawItem** performs the same actions as the **DrawItem** function described in the previous chapter. The main difference is dealing with the bitmaps. First the name of the font retrieved with **GetText** is drawn with **ExtTextOut**. This clears the area, selecting it if necessary, and draws the text. The appropriate bitmap to draw next to the font is stored in the lower word of the item data associated with each item. This value was retrieved with **GetItemData**. If the font is a TrueType or Printer font, the bitmap is drawn with the same **TransBitBlt** as in Chapter 25 (you must copy this function into this project). The text is offset to the right to add some spacing between the text and bitmap.

We need to make the font list box in the dialog a **CFontListBox** object so use the ClassWizard to add a control member variable of the type **CFontListBox** for **IDC_FONTLIST** and a control member variable of the type **CListBox** for

IDC_STYLELIST. Also, add a message handler for the **IDC_FONTLIST**'s **LBN_SELCHANGE** message. The **OnInitDialog** and **OnSelchangeFontlist** functions are shown below.

```
BOOL CMyDialog::OnInitDialog()
{
    CDialog::OnInitDialog();

    UpdateFamilyList( m_ctlFontList );
    UpdateStyleList(m_ctlFontList, m_ctlStyleList);

    return TRUE;
}
```

The **OnSelchangeFontlist** function will update the style combo box each time a new family is selected.

```
void CMyDialog::OnSelchangeFontlist()
{
    UpdateStyleList(m_ctlFontList, m_ctlStyleList );
}
```

To see how the font enumeration changes, use the Control Panel and change the default printer. With each printer, the available printer fonts that are shown in the family list will change. For example, the "Generic/Text Only" printer displays perhaps five fonts, and only one is a printer font. A PostScript printer has many fonts, most of which are TrueType fonts.

26.5 Conclusion

Enumeration can be very involved, especially with fonts. One aspect of font enumeration not demonstrated here is font size enumeration. Determining what sizes are available for each font is similar to enumerating the font styles. With TrueType and vector fonts, there are an infinite number of font sizes, so the enumeration procedure is not used to enumerate the sizes. With raster fonts, the enumeration procedure is called once for each font size. With a few modifications to the **EnumFontStylesCB** function, you can add size enumeration easily.

CREATING A SPLASH SCREEN

Most applications display what is called a splash screen as they first start. Some applications display a splash screen that contains an enlarged application icon and a copyright message. Others display a bitmap containing a graphic and the name of the application. The purpose of a splash screen is to give the user some visual feedback while the program is loading. It is also a good place to display a copyright or registration information.

In this chapter we will create a class that implements splash screens. The approach used here is one solution for implementing splash screens. Another solution is to use the Component Gallery to insert another implementation of splash screens into an application. The class presented here has the same functionality, it just does it a different way.

When you think about how a splash screen works, you might think they are something special. They don't look like ordinary windows because they don't have any borders or decorations, and they don't stay around too long. In fact, a splash screen can be nothing more than a modeless dialog. The dialog is tuned so that it has no borders and a standard timer limits its lifespan. The application displays the dialog when it first becomes visible and it disappears either when the user presses a key or mouse button or when some amount of time has elapsed.

27.1 An Example

In this example we will create a simple application that displays a splash screen when it begins. After the application's main frame is created, the splash screen is displayed. It will remain on the screen until either the user presses a key or mouse button or two and a half seconds passes.

To start, create an SDI or MDI application framework. Then create a dialog template to use as the splash screen. We don't want the splash screen to have a title bar or system menu, so uncheck the Titlebar style. Delete the OK and Cancel buttons from the template and add whatever controls you want. After the dialog template is

533

finished, use the ClassWizard to create a new class, **CSplashWnd**, that is based on this template. Add a handler for the dialog's **WM_CREATE**, **WM_INITDIALOG**, and **WM_TIMER** messages. Also override the dialog's **PreTranslateMessage** function. Then add the following member variable and function to the class definition.

```
public:
    BOOL ShowSplashScreen( DWORD dwDisplayTime = 2500 );

protected:
    // Number of ticks the dialog is to be displayed
    DWORD m_dwDisplayTime;
```

Normally, when you want to display a dialog, you use the **CDialog::DoModal** member function. We want the splash dialog to be modeless, so we don't want to call **DoModal** because it does not return until the dialog is closed. We want to continue processing application events while the splash screen is displayed, so we must take another approach. We will create a function named **ShowSplashScreen** that will display the dialog and immediately return.

```
BOOL CSplashWnd::ShowSplashScreen( DWORD dwDisplayTime )
{
    m_dwDisplayTime = dwDisplayTime;

    // Update the main window.
    CWnd* pMainWnd = AfxGetMainWnd();
    ASSERT( pMainWnd != NULL );

    if (pMainWnd->IsIconic())
        return FALSE;

    if (!Create(CSplashWnd::IDD, pMainWnd))
        return FALSE;

    ShowWindow( SW_SHOW );
    UpdateWindow();
    pMainWnd->UpdateWindow();

    return TRUE ;
}
```

If the user started the application in an iconified state, we don't want to display the splash screen because it may get in the user's way. So, first we use **IsIconic** to see if the main window is iconified. If not, we call **Create**. This is how you make the dialog modeless. The dialog will now exist until we explicitly destroy it. After the dialog is created, we display it using **ShowWindow**, then **UpdateWindow** is used to make sure the main window and splash screen are displayed correctly.

When the splash screen is created, we use **SetTimer** to notify us when the specified time period has elapsed. When it's time for the splash screen to disappear we will get a **WM_TIMER** message notifying us.

```
int CSplashWnd::OnCreate(LPCREATESTRUCT lpCreateStruct)
{
    if (CDialog::OnCreate(lpCreateStruct) == -1)
        return -1;

    SetTimer( 1, m_dwDisplayTime, NULL );

    return 0;
}
```

When we receive the **WM_TIMER** message it is time for us to close the splash screen.

```
void CSplashWnd::OnTimer(UINT nIDEvent)
{
    // Check only if the splash dialog exists.
    if (m_hWnd != NULL)
    {
        DestroyWindow();

        // Update the main window.
        CWnd* pMainWnd = AfxGetMainWnd();
        ASSERT( pMainWnd != NULL );
        pMainWnd->UpdateWindow();
    }

    CDialog::OnTimer(nIDEvent);
}
```

The function starts by making sure the dialog still exists. It may be the case that the dialog was dismissed in response to a mouse or key message. When a window is destroyed by **DestroyWindow**, the actual **CWnd** object is not destroyed, but the Windows window is and its handle (**m_hWnd**) is set to NULL. If there is no dialog, there is no need to continue. Otherwise, we use **DestroyWindow** to close the splash screen. When the dialog is removed, there will be a blank area in the application window so we use **UpdateWindow** again to fix it.

When the user clicks the mouse or presses a key we want the splash screen to go away. This means the splash screen needs to know when the user causes any mouse or keyboard messages. A good place to filter these messages as they occur is in the **Pre-TranslateMessage** function. It will dismiss the splash screen when any user input occurs. To get this to work we will need to hook this function into the calling application.

```
BOOL CSplashWnd::PreTranslateMessage(MSG* pMsg)
{
    if (m_hWnd == NULL)
        return FALSE;

    // If the user causes any input destroy the dialog
    if( pMsg->message == WM_KEYDOWN ||
        pMsg->message == WM_SYSKEYDOWN ||
        pMsg->message == WM_LBUTTONDOWN ||
        pMsg->message == WM_RBUTTONDOWN ||
```

```
                  pMsg->message == WM_MBUTTONDOWN ||
                  pMsg->message == WM_NCLBUTTONDOWN ||
                  pMsg->message == WM_NCRBUTTONDOWN ||
                  pMsg->message == WM_NCMBUTTONDOWN )
     {

          DestroyWindow();

          // Update the main window.
          CWnd *pMainWnd = AfxGetMainWnd();
          ASSERT( pMainWnd != NULL );
          pMainWnd->UpdateWindow();

          return TRUE;
     }

     return CDialog::PreTranslateMessage(pMsg);
}
```

Again, this function first makes sure the dialog is still visible by checking **m_hWnd**. It may be the case that the dialog timed-out before the user pressed anything. Then it checks to see if the current message is a keyboard or mouse event, ignoring mouse movements. If so, the dialog is destroyed and the main window is updated the same way as before.

Last, we need to modify the **OnInitDialog** function to perform a trivial but essential task, call **CenterWindow**. This function centers a window within its parent. It ensures that the splash screen dialog is centered in the application's frame window.

```
BOOL CSplashWnd::OnInitDialog()
{
     CDialog::OnInitDialog();

     // Center the dialog in it's parent.
     CenterWindow();

     return TRUE;
}
```

To add this splash screen to an application first add a member variable of the type **CSplashWnd** to the application's **CWinApp** class:

```
     CSplashWnd m_splash;
```

Remember to include the splash screen include file where necessary. Next, we have to display the splash screen when the application starts, following the appearance of the main frame. To do this we use **ShowSplashScreen**. Add this line to the end of the application's **InitInstance** function. You must call **ShowSplashScreen** after the application's main frame window is created.

```
     m_splash.ShowSplashScreen();
```

The last thing we have to do is add the call to the splash screen's **PreTranslate-Message**. Use the ClassWizard to override the application's **CWinApp** derived class **PreTranslateMessage** function and have it call the splash screen.

```
BOOL CMyApp::PreTranslateMessage(MSG* pMsg)
{
    // Let the splash screen check for input.
    if (m_splash.PreTranslateMessage(pMsg))
        return TRUE;

    return CWinApp::PreTranslateMessage(pMsg);
}
```

Now, if you run the application, the splash screen dialog should pop up after the main window is created and disappear when you hit a key, press a mouse button, or wait for two and a half seconds.

27.2 Conclusion

The splash screen in this example is fairly simple and boring. Splash screens can be much more elaborate and can include detailed images and even animation. See Chapter 29 for a discussion of how to stretch a bitmap across your splash screen. The splash screen generated by the Component Gallery is not based on a dialog. It just creates a window and paints a bitmap into it.

EXPANDING DIALOGS

There are many cases where you need to present users with a complex dialog, but you do not want to intimidate them by initially displaying all of the complexity. It may be, for example, that some of the controls are not used very often, or that portions of the dialog contain more advanced options that are not relevant to novices. As a designer, you don't want to overwhelm beginning users with too much information and complexity, but you also don't want to keep advanced users from being able to customize your application.

A good compromise in situations like these is an expanding dialog. Expanding dialogs allow you to cater to both needs. An example of an expanding dialog is the dialog shown in Figure 28.1. This is the Color dialog from the Control Panel that allows you to customize the Windows color scheme. Most of the time users only need to pick a color scheme they like from the Color Schemes combo. For this purpose the dialog on the left is adequate. But in order to facilitate more advanced users, there is the Color Palette button. If you select this button, the dialog expands so that more controls are visible. This second pane gives advanced users more control, allowing them to change the color of individual screen elements.

In this chapter we will create an expanding dialog class that you can derive from and reuse in your applications. This will explain how expanding dialogs work and also give you an example of how to create reusable classes.

28.1 The CExpandingDialog Class

The class we are going to create will be named **CExpandingDialog** and it will be derived from **CDialog**. Its goal will be to allow you to create expanding dialogs as easily as you can create normal dialogs. The only thing you will have to do differently is add two special dialog controls to your dialog template. The expanding dialog class will automatically handle the expansion of the dialog.

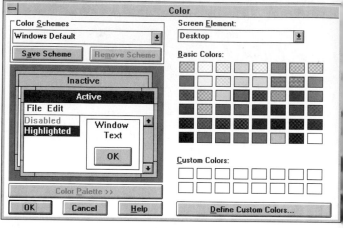

Figure 28.1
A typical expanding dialog

In order to for the expanding dialog class to be able to automatically handle the expansion of the dialog, the derived dialog's template must have two special controls. The first will be the button that will cause the expansion. This button must have an ID of **IDC_EXPAND**. The second control will be used to mark the division between the controls that are visible in the expanded portion of the dialog versus the non-expanded portion. This control can be of any type, but it must have an ID of **IDC_EXPAND_MARKER**.

To start, use the ClassWizard to create a **CExpandingDialog** class that is derived from **CDialog** and add a handler for the dialog's **WM_INITDIALOG** message. The class the created by the ClassWizard is supposed to be used in connection with a dialog template. Our case is special. We want our expanding dialog class to be a base class for other dialogs, it cannot be used directly with a dialog template. To make the class a base dialog class you must change the default constructor and remove the dialog template **IDD** enumeration from the **AFX_DATA** portion of the class definition. This is because the class is a base class, it does not have an associated dialog template, derived classes are intended to provide the template to use. The new class definition for the expanding dialog class is shown below. It includes the changes above as well as a few member variables and functions.

```
class CExpandingDialog : public CDialog
{
// Construction
public:
    CExpandingDialog(UINT nIDTemplate, CWnd* pParentWnd = NULL);

// Dialog Data
    //{{AFX_DATA(CExpandingDialog)
    CButton m_ctlExpandBtn;
    CWnd m_ctlExpandMarker;
```

```
        //}}AFX_DATA

// Overrides
public:
    // ClassWizard generated virtual function overrides
    //{{AFX_VIRTUAL(CExpandingDialog)
    protected:
    virtual void DoDataExchange(CDataExchange* pDX);
    //}}AFX_VIRTUAL

    CString m_strShrinkCaption;
    CString m_strExpandCaption;
    virtual void EnableExtraControls( BOOL bEnabled );

// Implementation
protected:
    void ShrinkDialog( void );

    int m_nNormalHeight;
    int m_nExpandedHeight;
    BOOL m_bExpanded;

    // Generated message map functions
    //{{AFX_MSG(CExpandingDialog)
    virtual BOOL OnInitDialog();
    afx_msg void OnExpand();
    //}}AFX_MSG
    DECLARE_MESSAGE_MAP()
};
```

Manually add an entry for the **IDC_EXPAND** button command to the dialog's message map:

```
BEGIN_MESSAGE_MAP(CExpandingDialog, CDialog)
    //{{AFX_MSG_MAP(CExpandingDialog)
    ON_BN_CLICKED(IDC_EXPAND, OnExpand)
    //}}AFX_MSG_MAP
END_MESSAGE_MAP()
```

The class constructor initializes the member variables to a default state. Derived classes can change the caption strings in their constructors to customize the dialog.

```
CExpandingDialog::CExpandingDialog(UINT nIDTemplate,
    CWnd* pParentWnd) : CDialog(nIDTemplate, pParentWnd)
{
    m_nNormalHeight = 0;
    m_nExpandedHeight = 0;
    m_bExpanded = TRUE; // Dialogs are created at normal size

    m_strShrinkCaption = _T("Details <<");
    m_strExpandCaption = _T("Details >>");

    //{{AFX_DATA_INIT(CExpandingDialog)
    //}}AFX_DATA_INIT
}
```

Manually edit **DoDataExchange** to use the **DDX_Control** routine to associate the control member variables with the two special controls on the dialog.

```
void CExpandingDialog::DoDataExchange(CDataExchange* pDX)
{
    CDialog::DoDataExchange(pDX);

    //{{AFX_DATA_MAP(CExpandingDialog)
    DDX_Control(pDX, IDC_EXPAND, m_ctlExpandBtn);
    DDX_Control(pDX, IDC_EXPAND_MARKER, m_ctlExpandMarker);
    //}}AFX_DATA_MAP
}
```

When the dialog is initially displayed we want it to be in its non-expanded form. First we check to make sure the expanding marker control exists, then we call **Shrink-Dialog** so the dialog is displayed in it's non-expanded state.

```
BOOL CExpandingDialog::OnInitDialog()
{
    // The expand marker control must exist
    if( GetDlgItem(IDC_EXPAND_MARKER) == NULL )
    {
        TRACE0( "Expanding control marker does not exist\n" );
        EndDialog( -1 );
        return TRUE;
    }

    CDialog::OnInitDialog();

    // The initial dialog is not expanded
    ShrinkDialog();

    return TRUE;
}
```

The expanding button's **OnExpand** message handler uses the **MoveWindow** function to toggle the dialog's height between normal and expanded.

```
void CExpandingDialog::OnExpand()
{
    CRect rcDlg;

    GetWindowRect( rcDlg );

    if( m_bExpanded )
    {
        rcDlg.SetRect( rcDlg.left, rcDlg.top,
                rcDlg.left + rcDlg.Width(),
                rcDlg.top + m_nNormalHeight );
    }
    else
    {
        rcDlg.SetRect( rcDlg.left, rcDlg.top,
                rcDlg.left + rcDlg.Width(),
```

```
                        rcDlg.top + m_nExpandedHeight );
    }

    // Keeps the window from flashing by hiding it
    SetWindowPos(NULL, -1, -1, -1, -1,
        SWP_HIDEWINDOW | SWP_NOMOVE | SWP_NOSIZE |
        SWP_NOZORDER | SWP_NOACTIVATE);

    // Resize the dialog
    MoveWindow( rcDlg, TRUE );

    // Keep the dialog centered
    if( CheckAutoCenter() )
    {
        CenterWindow();
    }

    // Toggle the expanded flag
    m_bExpanded = !m_bExpanded;

    // Change the button text
    m_ctlExpandBtn.SetWindowText(
        (m_bExpanded) ? m_strShrinkCaption :
        m_strExpandCaption );

    // Enable/Disable the extra controls
    EnableExtraControls( m_bExpanded );

    // Keeps the window from flashing
    SetWindowPos(NULL, -1, -1, -1, -1,
        SWP_SHOWWINDOW | SWP_NOMOVE | SWP_NOSIZE |
        SWP_NOZORDER | SWP_NOACTIVATE);
}
```

The function uses the **m_bExpanded** flag to determine what mode the dialog should be in. Then it can use **MoveWindow** to modify the height of the dialog to be **m_nNormalHeight** or **m_nExpandedHeight**. It also changes the button caption to let the user know the dialog can change between normal and expanded views. After the dialog is resized we have to enable or disable the controls in the expanded portion of the dialog.

EnableExtraControls allows us to enable and disable the extra controls on the dialog depending on what mode the dialog is in.

```
void CExpandingDialog::EnableExtraControls( BOOL bEnabled )
{
    HWND hWndChild = ::GetDlgItem( m_hWnd, IDC_EXPAND_MARKER );

    // Enable the extra controls when the dialog is expanded
    // and disable them when it is in normal mode.  This
    // keeps the user from being able to tab to the controls.
    // The default is to enable all the controls including and
    // after the IDC_EXPAND_MARKER control.

    while( hWndChild != NULL )
```

```
    {
        ::EnableWindow( hWndChild, bEnabled );
        hWndChild = ::GetNextWindow( hWndChild, GW_HWNDNEXT );
    }
}
```

This is where the expanding marker control is used. All the controls after the marker, including the marker itself, are enable or disabled automatically depending on the dialog's mode. We have to disable the controls that will not be visible when the dialog is shown in the normal (not expanded) state. This keeps the controls from gaining focus. If you did not disable these controls, the user could tab to them or use any mnemonics they might have. This would become very confusing for the user. If the derived class cannot use the automatic enabling and disabling of controls, it can override **EnableExtraControls** to do any special processing.

The **ShrinkDialog** function initializes the dialog to it's non-expanded mode.

```
void CExpandingDialog::ShrinkDialog( void )
{
    CRect rcDlg, rcMarker;

    // Calculate the expanded (max) height of the dialog
    GetWindowRect( rcDlg );
    m_nExpandedHeight = rcDlg.Height();

    // The top of this control is considered the bottom
    // of the normal height dialog.
    m_ctlExpandMarker.GetWindowRect( rcMarker );

    // Calculate the normal height of the dialog
    const int nPadding = ::GetSystemMetrics( SM_CYFRAME ) * 3;
    m_nNormalHeight = (rcMarker.top - rcDlg.top) /*+ nPadding*/;

    // Shrink the height dimension of the dialog
    rcDlg.SetRect( rcDlg.left, rcDlg.top,
            rcDlg.left + rcDlg.Width(),
            rcDlg.top + m_nNormalHeight );

    // Resize the dialog to the new (normal) size
    MoveWindow( rcDlg, TRUE );

    // The dialog is normal size
    m_bExpanded = FALSE;

    // Change the button text
    m_ctlExpandBtn.SetWindowText(
        (m_bExpanded) ? m_strShrinkCaption :
            m_strExpandCaption );

    // Enable/Disable the extra controls
    EnableExtraControls( m_bExpanded );
}
```

The expanded height of the dialog is the original height of the dialog when it is created. We can use **GetWindowRect** to get this value. The normal (non-expanded) height of the dialog is the distance between the top of the dialog and the top of the expanding control marker. To determine this height, we find the top of the marker and add some padding to it. This value is stored in **m_nNormalHeight**. These variables are used each time the user selects the expand button to toggle between normal and expanded views. Because we want the dialog to be shown initially in its normal state, the last thing we do is shrink the dialog to its normal height. The key part of this function is the **MoveWindow** call. This is the function that we will use to expand and shrink the dialog. It changes the position and dimensions of a window. Because we only modified the dialog's height in **SetRect**, that is the only dimension that will change. The **m_bExpanded** flag is used to keep track of what state the dialog is in.

28.2 An Example

Create a new dialog resource. Add a button below the Cancel button and make this button's ID be **IDC_EXPAND**. Add a control (the Picture control makes a good divider) and place it as a divider between the upper and lower portions of the dialog. Give this control an ID of **IDC_EXPAND_MARKER**. (You can make this control not visible if you like.) Now add some other controls to the dialog. Controls above the divider will always be visible. Controls below the divider will only be visible when the dialog is expanded. After you add all the controls to the dialog check the tab order. All controls below the divider must be after the divider itself. An example is shown in Figures 28.2 and 28.3.

When the dialog is complete, use the ClassWizard to create a new dialog class that is based on this template. If the ClassWizard will not let you specify **CExpandingDialog** as the base class, you will have to edit the new class generated by the ClassWizard and manually change all references of **CDialog** to **CExpandingDialog** using Replace All . Also, remember to include the expanding dialog class header file where necessary.

Now wire this dialog into an application and play with the expand button.

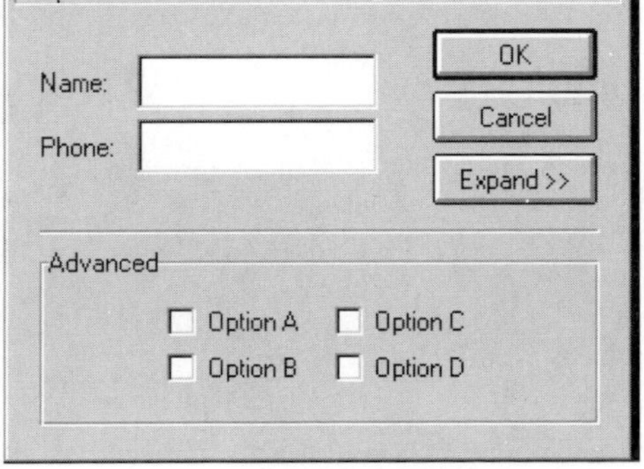

Figure 28.2
Sample dialog

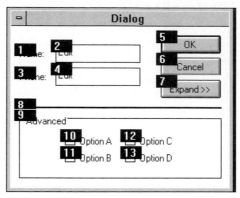

Figure 28.3
Tab order for sample dialog

28.3 Conclusion

If you wanted to make the dialog expand horizontally you could make the class a bit smarter so you could have either a horizontal or vertical divider. The only change necessary would be to change the dialog's width instead of its height.

Although expanding dialogs are useful, they may not be the only solution to the problem of complex dialogs. In some cases it might be more appropriate to use another auxiliary dialog (nested dialogs), or perhaps a property sheet containing the advanced options.

DRAWING AND CONTROLS

29

In this chapter we will explore two types of unusual drawing areas. The first is a static text control. You usually use static text controls as labels for other controls such as lists or edit fields. In this chapter we will explain how to convert a static text control into a miniature drawing area. The second unusual area is the background of a dialog. We will explain how to use the background of a dialog to display a bitmap.

29.1 Drawing in CStatic Controls

You usually don't think of a static text control as a place to draw. The technique used in this chapter allows you to think of the face of a static text area as a normal drawing area where you can use any of the **CDC** drawing functions. This approach has several advantages:

1. It allows the control to draw itself. This is not the same type of self-drawing described in Chapter 25, but it keeps the drawing's functionality self-contained. This lessens the work required when drawing.
2. It allows the programmer to position and size a control in the dialog editor. The alternative to drawing on a **CStatic** control is to try to draw on the dialog's background in a small, specified sub-area of the dialog. The problem with this approach is that you have to position and clip the sub-area yourself. Using a **CStatic** control you can visually position the drawing area in a dialog with respect to other dialog controls using the dialog editor. The **CStatic** control will handle positioning and clipping of the drawing itself.

In this section we will convert a static text control into a drawing area that plots points as the mouse moves when the left mouse button is pressed. The drawing area can be used for any kind of drawing, however, including static drawing commands, animated bitmaps, and other techniques.

Create an application framework and then create a new dialog template. Add a static text control to the dialog and change its ID to something other than

IDC_STATIC. If you use **IDC_STATIC** as the ID (the default), the control will not appear in the ClassWizard object list because this ID is filtered out.

In a manner similar to the process described in previous chapters for self-drawing controls, we need to create our own class to handle the messages required to draw into the static control. Use the ClassWizard to derive a new class, **CMyStatic**, from **CStatic**. The most important message to handle in the **CMyStatic** class is the **WM_PAINT** message. This message will allow the class to draw itself when necessary, in effect making the control self-drawing. The other messages we will handle are the mouse messages **WM_MOUSEMOVE**, **WM_LBUTTONDOWN**, **WM_LBUTTONUP**, and **WM_NCHITTEST**. These messages will allow us to turn the static control into a miniature drawing area. Use the ClassWizard to add handlers for these messages.

First, add the following member variable to the **CMyStatic** class definition and modify the class constructor to initialize the member variable:

```
protected:
   BOOL m_bButtonDown;


CMyStatic::CMyStatic()
{
    m_bButtonDown = FALSE;
}
```

The **OnPaint** message for the new class is shown below. This function is called each time the control needs to be repainted or refreshed. The function is simple for this example because we are not storing the points that are being drawn. If you were storing the data or wanted to draw a picture, it would be done in the **OnPaint** function.

```
void CMyStatic::OnPaint()
{
    CPaintDC dc(this); // device context for painting

    CRect r;
    GetClientRect(&r);

    // Draw a border around the control
    dc.Rectangle(r);

    // If you were storing the data being drawn
    // this is where you would place the code to
    // draw on refreshes.

    TRACE( "OnPaint\n" );

    // Do not call CStatic::OnPaint() for painting
}
```

The **CStatic** control class does not usually handle any input messages. However, we want our **CMyStatic** class to handle button presses and mouse movement so we can draw. Because the **CStatic** class will not automatically handle the **WM_LBUTTONDOWN** message and other messages like it, we have to do a little extra work.

The key to making the **CMyStatic** class understand messages lies in the **WM_NCHITTEST** message. This message is sent to a control when the mouse moves or when a mouse button is pressed or released inside the control. The value returned from the message lets Windows know what the cursor shape should be and when to change it. The default **CStatic::OnNcHitTest** function returns the value **HTTRANSPARENT**. This value tells Windows that the mouse is in a window that is covered by another window. When a control returns **HTTRANSPARENT**, Windows does not send the control any mouse events. Therefore, to allow the **CMyStatic** class to receive mouse events, its **OnNcHitTest** function needs to return **HTCLIENT** instead. This value tells Windows that the cursor is in the client area of a window and that the control should receive mouse events.

```
UINT CMyStatic::OnNcHitTest(CPoint point)
{
    // Do not call CStatic::OnNcHitTest
    return( HTCLIENT );
}
```

The handling of the button events for this example is simple. We want to draw in the client area of the static text control when the user moves the mouse when the left button is pressed. To begin drawing we need to know when the mouse button is pressed. The **OnLButtonDown** and **OnLButtonUp** functions use a Boolean flag that tells us when to draw points on mouse movement. Note, to make this process more accurate, you would need to use the **SetCapture** function.

```
void CMyStatic::OnLButtonDown(UINT nFlags, CPoint point)
{
    TRACE( "OnLButtonDown\n" );

    m_bButtonDown = TRUE;

    CStatic::OnLButtonDown(nFlags, point);
}

void CMyStatic::OnLButtonUp(UINT nFlags, CPoint point)
{
    TRACE( "OnLButtonUp\n" );

    m_bButtonDown = FALSE;

    CStatic::OnLButtonUp(nFlags, point);
}
```

When the mouse is moved in the static text control's client area, **OnMouse-Move** is called. If the left button is pressed while the mouse is moving, **OnMouseMove** will set a pixel at each mouse point using **SetPixel**. You could, if you like, improve the process by modifying the code to store each point drawn and draw lines between adjacent points.

```
void CMyStatic::OnMouseMove(UINT nFlags, CPoint point)
{
    if( m_bButtonDown )
    {
        TRACE( "OnMouseMove with button down\n" );

        CClientDC dc( this );
        dc.SetPixel( point, RGB(0,0,0) );
    }

    CStatic::OnMouseMove(nFlags, point);
}
```

Now that we have a **CMyStatic** class, we need to associate it with the static text control we created in the dialog. Use the ClassWizard to create a control member variable of the type **CMyStatic** for the static text control.

Before continuing, test the **CMyStatic** class. Run the application and move the mouse over the static text control and move the mouse while holding the left mouse button down. You should see a black pixel drawn at each point where the mouse moves. Remember, the lines will be jumpy unless you move the mouse slowly. (You may wish to remove the **TRACE** statements from the code once it is working.)

29.2 Drawing in Dialogs

The background of most windows is one solid color. The background of views may be white, and the background of most dialogs is gray. But what if you want to customize the background of a dialog or make the background of each view in your application different? By having a window manage the **WM_ERASEBKGND** message, we can customize what is drawn as the background. Instead of having Windows erase the background with some boring color we can draw any sort of pattern or bitmap in the background.

First, create a new bitmap resource with an ID of **IDB_BACKGROUND**. The width and height of the bitmap can be anything you like because we will use **Stretch-Blt** to draw the bitmap. This function will stretch the bitmap to fit a given rectangle. To lessen the distortions caused by **StretchBlt** though, the bitmap dimensions should be close to the dimensions of the window it will be drawn in.

The **WM_ERASEBKGND** message is sent to a window when some portion of the window's background needs erasing. It is usually sent before the **WM_PAINT** message is sent to the window. The default response to this message is to erase the background with the window's class background brush. By overriding this function we can draw whatever we want in the window's background.

Try to use the ClassWizard to add a handler for the **WM_ERASEBKGND** message. If you search through the list of available messages to add, you will not see the **WM_ERASEBKGND** message. This is because the ClassWizard filters that message, along with several others because they are not used in dialogs often. To show all the available messages in the list, switch to the Class Info tab. Notice the Message Filter combo box. Each item in the list causes different messages to be filtered from the message list. For example, the Not a Window item filters out all messages and no items will appear in the Messages list. The ClassWizard filters the messages in this fashion to simplify the process of adding messages to a class. A dialog initially has the Dialog message filter and the **WM_ERASEBKGND** message isn't shown. Change the filter to Window and all messages will be available. Change back to the Message Maps tab and add a function for the **WM_ERASEBKGND** message.

```
BOOL CMyDialog::OnEraseBkgnd(CDC* pDC)
{
    // Load bitmap to display
    CBitmap bmpBackground;
    VERIFY( bmpBackground.LoadBitmap( IDB_BACKGROUND ) );

    // Get the dimensions of the bitmap.
    BITMAP bm;
    bmpBackground.GetObject( sizeof(BITMAP), &bm );

    // How big is the destination window?
    RECT clientRect;
    GetClientRect( &clientRect );

    // Get the position to draw the upper
    // left corner of the bitmap.
    CPoint point( clientRect.left, clientRect.top );

    // Get the width and height the bitmap
    // needs to be drawn.
    CSize size( clientRect.right, clientRect.bottom );

    // Create a memory DC compatible with the window's DC.
    CDC memDC;
    VERIFY( memDC.CreateCompatibleDC( pDC ) );

    // Select the background bitmap into the memory DC.
    CBitmap* pOldBmp = memDC.SelectObject( &bmpBackground );
    ASSERT( pOldBmp != NULL );

    // StretchBlt the bitmap onto the window's background.
    pDC->StretchBlt( point.x, point.y, size.cx, size.cy,
        &memDC, 0, 0, bm.bmWidth-1, bm.bmHeight-1,
        SRCCOPY );

    // Select out the bitmap.
    VERIFY( memDC.SelectObject( pOldBmp ) );

    // Delete the bitmap that was loaded.
    bmpBackground.DeleteObject();

    return TRUE;
}
```

First, the function loads the bitmap from the resource file and determines its dimensions. Then it determines the dimensions of the destination window and where the bitmap should be drawn. A memory device context compatible with the window device context is created and the bitmap is selected into it. **StretchBlt** copies the bitmap from the memory DC to the background of the window. The bitmap will be stretched or compressed as necessary to fit the dimensions of the destination. This way we completely fill the window's background with the bitmap. If you only want to draw at a particular position without distortion, you can use the normal **BitBlt** function instead of **StretchBlt**. After the bitmap is copied, the DC is returned to normal and the bitmap is deleted.

29.3 Dialog Controls and the Background

If you rebuild the application and display the dialog, you will find it displays your bitmap on the background of the dialog. For this example everything looks fine. But if you add some controls to the dialog, such as other static text controls, you will notice something peculiar. You will notice that the rectangular regions around the static text controls are gray and they overwrite the bitmap. This is because the default background of the dialog is gray. The static control usually erases its client area with its parent's background color. To keep the controls from overwriting the bitmap, we need to handle the **WM_CTLCOLOR** message. The **OnCtlColor** function is called when a child control is about to be drawn. It gives you a chance to prepare the device context that will be used to draw the control. Here we will change the background mode of the device context to **TRANSPARENT** so the background bitmap will not be erased before the static text control is drawn. Then we return a handle to a **HOLLOW** brush that will be used for painting the control's background.

```
HBRUSH CMyDialog::OnCtlColor(CDC* pDC, CWnd* pWnd,
    UINT nCtlColor)
{
    // Don't erase bitmap when drawing controls.
    pDC->SetBkMode( TRANSPARENT );

    return( (HBRUSH)::GetStockObject( HOLLOW_BRUSH ) );
}
```

Compile and run the application. You will find that the dialog appears and that the bitmapped background has been stretched over it. The controls are then painted on top of the background.

29.4 Conclusion

The examples discussed in this chapter are greatly simplified for illustrative purposes. In the drawing area, for example, we didn't store the points drawn so they could be redrawn in the **OnPaint** function. You could add a variety of functionality to the **CMyStatic** class by using other drawing techniques.

You could also enhance the dialog's handling of the **OnCtlColor** and **OnErase-Bkgnd** functions to be more efficient. For example, if you load the hollow brush in **OnInitDialog**, **GetStockObject** wouldn't need to be called each time **OnCtlColor** was called. It would also be more efficient to load and select the bitmap being drawn into a class member variable in the **OnInitDialog** function. This would keep the code from having to load the bitmap every time the background needs erasing. Two points to remember when using this approach:

1. The window's **OnDestroy** member function needs to deselect and delete the bitmap.
2. The **CBitmap** pointer returned by **SelectObject** is temporary, so to keep track of **pOldBmp** between the **OnInitDialog** call and the **OnDestroy** call you would need to save the Windows handle of the bitmap that is returned by the **GetSafeHandle** function.

The same bitmap techniques shown in this chapter can also be used to customize the background of views in an SDI or MDI shell. For example, you could also modify the background of a view with a product logo or bitmap. Try out several variations and see if any of them appeal to you.

DIALOG BARS

One of the classes in the MFC visual object hierarchy is the **CControlBar** class. This is the base class for the **CToolBar**, **CStatusBar**, and **CDialogBar** classes. These classes demonstrate how MFC can tremendously simplify the creation of desirable application features. For example, the **CToolBar** class gives your application the ability to create a row of buttons across the top of your frame window. These buttons allow access to common menu items. You saw how easy it was to add tool bar buttons in Chapter 18. Also in Chapter 18 you saw how the **CStatusBar** class allows you to create a set of status panes across the bottom of your frame window to notify the user about the state of the application. Both these classes perform a substantial amount of their work "behind the scenes" and, therefore, make your job as a programmer much easier. You don't have to think about what happens when the frame window resizes or when a menu item is selected or disabled. The classes handle these details automatically.

The **CDialogBar** class is a member of this family. It is an extremely flexible and powerful class that gives you the freedom to place almost any control that you choose into a toolbar-like window. In this chapter we will explore the **CDialogBar** class and give you an example of how to use it.

The most common example of a dialog bar is the standard set of buttons that appear in the tool bar at the top of every MFC print preview window.

Figure 30.1
The print preview dialog box

The **CDialogBar** class is unique in the fact that it behaves much like a modeless dialog. It can contain any type of control: buttons, edit boxes, lists, and so on. It also supports tabbing between controls in the dialog bar. Dialog bars are extremely useful when you need a toolbar–like window in your application that requires more flexibility than a simple line of buttons.

Creating the dialog bar is as simple as creating a normal dialog. First you create a dialog template resource, then you create a **CDialogBar** object using that template. The controls on the dialog bar behave as normal, sending notification messages to the dialog bar's parent window. Additionally the **CDialogBar** class has the ability to align itself with its parent window and even "float" like a normal **CToolBar** object so that it works like a palette.

30.1 An Example

In this example we will create a **CDialogBar** containing several different controls. The bar will initially align itself to the top of the main frame window of an application.

Create a new application framework and create a dialog template to use for the dialog bar. Give the dialog an ID of **IDD_DIALOGBAR** and change the dialog style to Child, the Border to None, and make sure all the options are unchecked. Delete the two default buttons and add some controls to the dialog. For this example you can add an edit box, a combo box, and a push button. We will use the default control IDs, **IDC_EDIT1**, **IDC_COMBO1**, and **IDC_BUTTON1**. The size of the dialog bar will be the size of the dialog template, so resize the dialog template so it is shaped like a regular tool bar.

Now we need to modify the **CMainFrame** class so it contains our dialog bar. The main frame is probably already creating a toolbar and status bar so we can add the dialog bar where these are created. Add a **CDialogBar** member variable named **m_dlgBar** to the **CMainFrame** class definition. Also, so we can later add a message handler for the button on the dialog bar, modify the **AFX_MSG** section of the class by adding the **OnButton1** function. Sections of the resulting class are shown here:

```
class CMainFrame : public CFrameWnd
{
    protected:
        CDialogBar m_dlgBar;
    ...

    //{{AFX_MSG(CMainFrame)
    afx_msg void OnButton1();
    afx_msg int OnCreate(LPCREATESTRUCT lpCreateStruct);
    //}}AFX_MSG

    ...
};
```

To create the dialog bar, call the **m_dlgBar** object's **Create** function in the frame window's **OnCreate** after calling the base class **OnCreate**.

```
if (!m_dlgBar.Create(this,IDD_DIALOGBAR,CBRS_TOP,
    IDD_DIALOGBAR))
{
    TRACE( "Failed to create dialog bar!\n" );
    return -1;
```

This book is continuously updated. See http://www.iftech.com/mfc

}

This creates a dialog bar using the dialog resource template **IDD_DIALOGBAR**. The **CBRS_TOP** flag makes the dialog bar span the top of the frame window. Try changing this to **CBRS_BOTTOM**, **CBRS_LEFT**, and **CBRS_RIGHT** to see how the dialog bar changes. The height of the dialog bar is determined by the height of the dialog resource template, and the width becomes the width of the frame window it is attached to.

For the button we created on the dialog bar to actually do something, it must have a message handler. Because the parent of the dialog bar will be the main frame window, **CMainFrame** is the class that will receive the control messages from the dialog bar. We already added the function prototype to the **CMainFrame** class. All that's left is to add the function **OnButton1** to the class's message map by adding the **ON_COMMAND** for the **IDC_BUTTON1** command ID.

```
BEGIN_MESSAGE_MAP(CMainFrame, CFrameWnd)
    //{{AFX_MSG_MAP(CMainFrame)
    ON_WM_CREATE()
    ON_COMMAND(IDC_BUTTON1, OnButton1)
    //}}AFX_MSG_MAP
END_MESSAGE_MAP()
```

An example **OnButton1** function is shown here.

```
void CMainFrame::OnButton1()
{
    TRACE( "Button Pressed\n" );
    Beep(500, 500);
}
```

What we have done here is add the button's message handler into the message map manually. Once we have added the control into the map manually, its ID will appear in the ClassWizard and you will be able to later manipulate it from there as you would with any control in a dialog.

If you make several minor modifications to the application, you can give the dialog bar tool tips and display helpful information in the status bar as well. First, add the **CBRS_FLYBY** and **CBRS_TOOLTIPS** flags to the **Create** call.

```
if( !m_dlgBar.Create(this, IDD_DIALOGBAR,
    CBRS_TOP | CBRS_FLYBY | CBRS_TOOLTIPS,
    IDD_DIALOGBAR) )
{
    TRACE( "Failed to create the dialog bar!\n" );
    return -1;
}
```

Then you must add a string to the String Table resource. The ID of this new string must be the same as the control command ID of the control with which the message is to be associated, just like for tool bars. The message contains two sections separated by a newline (\n). The first part of the string is the message that will be displayed in the status bar if the **CBRS_FLYBY** flag is used. The second part of the string is the message that will appear in the tool tip for the control when **CBRS_TOOLTIPS** is specified. By adding a string resource for **IDC_BUTTON1**, **IDC_EDIT1**, and **IDC_COMBO1** you can have tool tips for each control.

The dialog bar can also be turned into a floating dialog bar just as tool bars can. Add the two lines shown below after the dialog bar has been created in the **OnCreate** function in. The **EnableDocking** call tells the dialog bar that it can align itself to any side of its parent (as long as its parent accepts docking on that side by calling **Enable-Docking** also).

```
m_dlgBar.EnableDocking(CBRS_ALIGN_ANY);
DockControlBar(&m_dlgBar);
```

The final **DockControlBar** call docks the dialog bar to the frame window. The opposite of this is the **FloatControlBar** call that undocks the dialog bar and makes it a floating window. You usually call these functions when the application is starting.

Compile and run the application. You will find that your new dialog bar initially appears at the top of the window. However, you can drag it to other positions, or drag it out so it converts automatically to a floating palette. The tool tips and status bar will respond appropriately. Something you may notice is that the tool tips and fly-by messages don't always appear when the cursor is over a control in the dialog bar. For example, notice how the tool tip disappears after you click the button once. No tool tips or fly-by messages will appear for that dialog bar until another window in the application takes away the focus from the dialog bar. This is so that when you start typing in an edit control in a dialog bar, the fly-by message will not get in the way.

30.2 Data Exchange

As you get more involved with dialog bars, you will eventually want to exchange data with the dialog bar's controls. Ideally you would like to use DDX as you do with normal dialogs. For example, when the ClassWizard creates a new **CDialog**-derived class, it automatically adds the **DoDataExchange** function. Then you can use Class-Wizard to add member variables to the dialog class.

The **CDialogBar** class is different because you cannot use ClassWizard to create a **CDialogBar**-derived class. There are two solutions to this problem:

1. The simpler solution is to use functions such as **GetDlgItemText** to access the data inside dialog bar controls. The dialog bar's parent can use these functions to exchange and validate the data in each control. This technique can become difficult if the dialog bar is complicated, but is extremely straightforward for simple dialog bars.

2. The other solution is to use the dialog data exchange functions described in Chapter 22. This technique allows you to use the existing DDX and DDV functions. This approach is more difficult because you must create your own

class derived from **CDialogBar** and override its **DoDataExchange** function (inherited from **CWnd**). This must be done manually, either by creating a new class from scratch or by starting from a **CDialog**-derived class created by Class-Wizard and modifying that class to be derived from **CDialogBar**. Then the dialog bar's parent can call the dialog bar's **UpdateData** function to validate the data in the dialog bar.

30.3 Conclusion

You can literally do anything you want with dialog bars. You simply use the same principles demonstrated in Part 1 to extract the data from the bar. You will find a number of important ways to use these extremely flexible controls in your own applications.

Dialog and View Idle Command Updating

In Part 3 of this book you learned how to use **UPDATE_COMMAND_UI** to have your applications' menus and toolbar buttons enable and disable themselves automatically. Using this method of command update handling is very simple and very useful. The **UPDATE_COMMAND_UI** mechanism however only works for menus, and controls that are children of toolbars, status bars, and dialog bars. In this chapter we will create a dialog and view class that will also be able to enable and disable children controls using the **UPDATE_COMMAND_UI** mechanism. Note: The information in this chapter depends on some undocumented features of the framework. Future versions of MFC may require changes for this functionality.

31.1 How Idle Updates Work

When an applications' message queue becomes empty, the application goes into an idle state. When the application enters this idle state, a **WM_IDLEUPDATECMDUI** message is sent to the applications' main window, all the main windows' descendants, and to all frame windows and their descendants. The handler for this message, usually **OnIdleUpdateCmdUI,** does different things for different windows. For example, the **CFrameWnd** updates elements such as the menu bar, title, and window layout.

The interesting class is **CControlBar.** This is where you usually see the affects of idle updates because its affects are visible, i.e. when buttons on a **CToolBar** are enabled and disabled. Its **OnIdleUpdateCmdUI** eventually calls its virtual function **OnUpdateCmdUI.** Derived classes handle this call differently as well, but the power of this function is that it calls **CWnd::UpdateDialogControls.** This function iterates through all the controls in the window and either calls the controls' **OnCmdMsg** (for message reflection), the controls' parents' **OnCmdMsg** or **CCmdUI::DoUpdate** on the control. **DoUpdate** is the major player in the idle update process. (This is also the function called in **CFrameWnd OnInitMenuPopup** to enable/disable menu commands). This function calls the target window's **OnCmdMsg** with the message **CN_UPDATE_COMMAND_UI** which will call the familiar **ON_UPDATE_COMMAND_UI** handlers that actually **Enable, SetText,** etc. the toolbar or menu commands.

All we need to do to make views and dialogs have the same idle update mechanism is to have them handle the **WM_IDLEUPDATECMDUI** message and then use the **UpdateDialogControls** function to enable and disable their children controls.

31.2 Idle Updating in Views

Making a view class, such as **CFormView**, have idle command update capability is simple because a view can handle the **WM_IDLEUPDATECMDUI** message and then call **UpdateDialogControls**.

In the view header file add **OnIdleUpdateCmdUI** to the message map declarations.

```
//{{AFX_MSG(CMyView)
afx_msg void OnIdleUpdateCmdUI();
//}}AFX_MSG
```

In the view source file add **WM_IDLEUPDATECMDUI** to the message map and have the message handler call **UpdateDialogControls**. You must include AFX-PRIV.H to define the **WM_IDLEUPDATECMDUI** message. We also call **UpdateDialogControls** in **OnInitialUpdate** so the controls are updated before the view becomes visible.

```
#include "afxpriv.h"

BEGIN_MESSAGE_MAP(CMyView, CFormView)
    //{{AFX_MSG_MAP(CMyView)
    ON_MESSAGE_VOID(WM_IDLEUPDATECMDUI, OnIdleUpdateCmdUI)
    //}}AFX_MSG_MAP
END_MESSAGE_MAP()

void CMyView::OnInitialUpdate()
{
    CFormView::OnInitialUpdate();

    // Update before becoming visible
    UpdateDialogControls( this, TRUE );
}

void CMyView::OnIdleUpdateCmdUI()
{
    // Don't bother if the user can't see us
    if( !IsWindowVisible() )
        return;

    UpdateDialogControls( this, TRUE );
}
```

The first argument to **UpdateDialogControls** is the parent window of the controls to update. The second argument determines if controls that do not have any command handlers are disabled. Because this argument is TRUE, any controls in the view that do not have an **ON_COMMAND** or **ON_BN_CLICKED** handler will be disabled.

31.3 An Example

Say you have a form view that contains a list box and a button. If you wanted to enable and disable the button depending on whether an item in the list is selected. There are two solutions to this problem. You could handle some control notifications such as **LBN_SELCHANGE** and enable the button when an item is selected and disable the button when no items are selected. Another solution would be to use idle command updating. For this approach all we need to do is add a command update handler for the button to the view.

In the view header add the handler function to the message map declarations.

```
//{{AFX_MSG(CMyView)
afx_msg void OnIdleUpdateCmdUI();
afx_msg void OnUpdateSomeCommand(CCmdUI* pCmdUI);
//}}AFX_MSG
```

In the view source add an **ON_UPDATE_COMMAND_UI** for the button to the message map.

```
BEGIN_MESSAGE_MAP(CMyView, CFormView)
    //{{AFX_MSG_MAP(CMyView)
    ON_MESSAGE_VOID(WM_IDLEUPDATECMDUI, OnIdleUpdateCmdUI)
    ON_UPDATE_COMMAND_UI(IDC_COMMAND, OnUpdateSomeCommand)
    //}}AFX_MSG_MAP
END_MESSAGE_MAP()
```

In the update handler we can just check to see if any items in the list are selected using **GetCurSel**.

```
void CMyView::OnUpdateSomeCommand(CCmdUI* pCmdUI)
{
    pCmdUI->Enable(
        ((CListBox*)GetDlgItem(IDC_LIST))->GetCurSel() != LB_ERR);
}
```

31.4 Idle Updating in Dialogs

Adding idle command updating to modal dialogs is not as simple as with views. Modal dialogs don't use the same message processing loop as the main application. The message loop for modal dialogs doesn't handle the idle state the same as the application message loop. This means there are no **WM_IDLEUPDATECMDUI** messages being sent around. Therefore we have to do some extra work to get idle command updating to work in dialogs.

The key to this process is the **WM_KICKIDLE** message. When there are no messages in the application message queue, the modal dialog message loop enters an idle state by sending a **WM_ENTERIDLE** message to its parent. Next, it sends itself a **WM_KICKIDLE** message with a **wParam** of **MSGF_DIALOGBOX** and **lParam** containing the idle count. Because the **WM_KICKIDLE** message is sent while the application is idle, we can use it to tell us when to perform idle update processing. When the application enters the idle state, the idle count is zero. Here, our **OnKick-Idle** function can do the same thing the main message loop does, it can send itself a **WM_IDLEUPDATECMDUI** message then send all its descendants an **WM_IDLEUPDATECMDUI** message.

In the dialog header file add an **OnUpdateCmdUI** virtual function. Also add **OnKickIdle** and **OnIdleUpdateCmdUI** to the message map declarations.

```
virtual void OnUpdateCmdUI(CDialog* pTarget,
    BOOL bDisableIfNoHndler);

//{{AFX_MSG(CMyDialog)
virtual BOOL OnInitDialog();
afx_msg LRESULT OnKickIdle(WPARAM, LPARAM);
afx_msg LRESULT OnIdleUpdateCmdUI(WPARAM, LPARAM);
//}}AFX_MSG
```

In the dialog source file add **WM_KICKIDLE** and **WM_IDLEUPDATECMDUI** to the message map. You must include AFXPRIV.H to define **WM_IDLEUPDATECMDUI**. In **OnInitDialog** we call **OnIdleUpdate-CmdUI** to update the controls before the dialog becomes visible.

```
#include "afxpriv.h"

BEGIN_MESSAGE_MAP(CMyDialog, CDialog)
    //{{AFX_MSG_MAP(CMyDialog)
    ON_MESSAGE(WM_KICKIDLE, OnKickIdle)
    ON_MESSAGE(WM_IDLEUPDATECMDUI, OnIdleUpdateCmdUI)
    //}}AFX_MSG_MAP
END_MESSAGE_MAP()

BOOL CMyDialog::OnInitDialog()
{
    BOOL bInit = CDialog::OnInitDialog();

    // Update controls before becoming visible
    OnIdleUpdateCmdUI(TRUE, 0L);

    return bInit;
}

LRESULT CMyDialog::OnKickIdle(WPARAM nFilterCode,
    LPARAM lIdleCount)
{
    // Only update commands on enter idle
    if( (nFilterCode == MSGF_DIALOGBOX) &&
        (lIdleCount == 0) )
    {
        if (m_hWnd != NULL && IsWindowVisible())
        {
```

```
        AfxCallWndProc(this, m_hWnd,
            WM_IDLEUPDATECMDUI,
            (WPARAM)TRUE, 0);

        SendMessageToDescendants(
            WM_IDLEUPDATECMDUI,
            (WPARAM)TRUE, 0, TRUE, TRUE);
        }
    }

    return Default();
}

LRESULT CMyDialog::OnIdleUpdateCmdUI(WPARAM wParam,
    LPARAM)
{
    OnUpdateCmdUI(this, (BOOL)wParam);
    return 0L;
}

void CMyDialog::OnUpdateCmdUI(CDialog* pTarget,
    BOOL bDisableIfNoHndler)
{
    UpdateDialogControls(pTarget, bDisableIfNoHndler);
}
```

Now we have a dialog that can have idle update handlers for its controls. Notice here that we delegated the call to **UpdateDialogControls** to **OnUpdateCmdUI** instead of **OnIdleUpdateCmdUI**. This was done in order to keep the process flexible. This way you can have a derived class that can override **OnUpdateCmdUI** to do any special processing it may need. You could also enhance this model by adding a virtual function such as **OnDialogIdle** that you could call each time **OnKickIdle** is called. This would give you the opportunity to have idle processing in the dialog. If you do this however, you should not call the application's **OnIdle** because the framework performs tasks in **OnIdle**, such as cleaning up temporary handles, that may adversely affect the dialog.

31.5 An Example

Say you have a dialog with an edit control and you want to enable the OK button only when the user has typed something in the control. One solution would be to use a control notification such as **EN_CHANGE** to enable and disable the OK button manually. Another solution is to use idle command updating to enable the button automatically.

In the dialog header add **OnUpdateOK** to the message map declaration.

```
//{{AFX_MSG(CMyDialog)
virtual BOOL OnInitDialog();
afx_msg LRESULT OnKickIdle(WPARAM, LPARAM);
afx_msg LRESULT OnIdleUpdateCmdUI(WPARAM, LPARAM);
afx_msg void OnUpdateOK(CCmdUI* pCmdUI);
```

```
//}}AFX_MSG
```

In the dialog source add an **ON_UPDATE_COMMAND_UI** for the OK button. Then in its command update handler we can use **GetWindowText** to determine if the user has typed anything.

```
BEGIN_MESSAGE_MAP(CMyDialog, CDialog)
    //{{AFX_MSG_MAP(CMyDialog)
    ON_MESSAGE(WM_KICKIDLE, OnKickIdle)
    ON_MESSAGE(WM_IDLEUPDATECMDUI, OnIdleUpdateCmdUI)
    ON_UPDATE_COMMAND_UI(IDOK, OnUpdateOK)
    //}}AFX_MSG_MAP
END_MESSAGE_MAP()

void CMyDialog::OnUpdateOK(CCmdUI* pCmdUI)
{
    CString strInput;
    GetDlgItem(IDC_EDIT)->GetWindowText(strInput);
    pCmdUI->Enable(strInput.GetLength()>0);
}
```

31.6 Conclusion

Notice how idle command updating can simplify the task of enabling controls. If you had a dialog or view with a lot of controls, handling the necessary control notifications for each control would be complicated and error prone.

To make this process reusable, a good object-oriented approach would be to derive a class such as **CMyDialog** from **CDialog**, then have all other dialogs in your application be derived from **CMyDialog**. An example of creating a base dialog class in this way is shown in Chapter 28. The same process could be done for a **CIdleUpdateFormView** class. This allows you to hide the implementation details and complexity in a base class.

ODDS AND ENDS

This chapter covers several topics that don't fit into any other section of the book. The topics covered include dragging files to your application, creating modeless dialogs and handling mini-frame windows. Small out-of-the-way topics such as these are not discussed often, but are extremely useful in special situations.

32.1 Accepting Files from the File Manager

If your application deals with files, it may be useful for the user to be able to select files in the File Manager and drag them to your application. Your application can process the files as if the user had opened them individually. The File Manager is called a drag-and-drop source. This means that files selected in the File Manager can be dragged to another application called the target. It is very simple for an application to become a drag-and-drop target. There is only one function that must be called for your main window and all its child windows to accept files dropped from the File Manager. This is the **CWnd::DragAcceptFiles** function. Calling this function from the main window in your **CWinApp**-derived class will turn any example into a target. Just add the following line to then end of its **InitInstance** function:

```
m_pMainWnd->DragAcceptFiles();
```

The default argument for **DragAcceptFiles** is TRUE. To stop accepting dragged files, call this function with an argument of FALSE. Remember **m_pMainWnd** is NULL until a document is created.

Now, if you select files from the File Manager and then drag them to the example window, you will notice that the cursor does not change into a circle with a slash through it as it normally does. This notifies the user that the application is a drag-and-drop target. When the mouse button is released, a **WM_DROPFILES** message is sent to the application.

The default processing done by the **CFrameWnd** class is to get the name of each dropped file and try to open it with **OpenDocumentFile**. In many cases, therefore, you may not need to add any code to your application for it to handle drag-and-drop properly. In special cases where you want to handle the message yourself, you have to add a message handler for **WM_DROPFILES** to the **CFrameWnd**-derived class in your application.

```
void CMainFrame::OnDropFiles(HDROP hDropInfo)
{
    // How many files were dropped?
    UINT nFiles = ::DragQueryFile( hDropInfo, 0xFFFFFFFF,
        NULL, 0 );

    // Where were they dropped?
    POINT point;
    ::DragQueryPoint( hDropInfo, &point );

    for( UINT i = 0; i < nFiles; i++ )
    {
        char szFileName[_MAX_PATH];

        ::DragQueryFile( hDropInfo, i, szFileName, _MAX_PATH );

        TRACE( "Filename (%s) dropped at %d,%d\n",
                    szFileName,
                    point.x, point.y );
    }

    ::DragFinish( hDropInfo );
}
```

This function simply determines how many files were dropped and then it prints the name of each file to the debug window. If the position of the drop determines what action takes place, you can use the **DragQueryPoint** function to decide where the files were dropped. Remember not to call the base class **OnDropFiles** or you will invoke the framework's default behavior, which opens the files.

32.2 Making an Application the Topmost Window

Some applications such as WinHelp, the Windows clock, and other small status windows such as the RAS monitor, have an option that allows them to remain on "top" of other windows, even though another application is active. Sometimes this can be useful. For example, it is nice to be able to keep the clock in the corner of the screen and for it always to be visible. Making an application the topmost window is a simple task. To make any application the topmost window, just add the following function to then end of its InitInstance function:

```
m_pMainWnd->SetWindowPos( &CWnd::wndTopMost, 0,0,0,0,
    SWP_NOMOVE | SWP_NOSIZE );
```

After you add this line, the application's window will always be the topmost window. Only other topmost windows are allowed to overlap yours. With

SetWindowPos you can make the window topmost, bottommost, and anywhere in between. It will also change the size and location of the window, but we use the **SWP** flags that keep the original dimensions.

Usually an application provides a check box in its options dialog or an Always on top menu option, which allows the user to make the application topmost or normal.

32.3 Starting an Application Minimized

To make your application initially appear minimized (as an icon) when it starts, all you need to do is change the value of the **CWinApp** member variable **m_nCmdShow**. For an MDI application you add the following line to the **InitInstance** function of your **CWinApp**-derived class. This value must be set before ShowWindow is called.

```
m_nCmdShow = SW_SHOWMINIMIZED;
pMainFrame->ShowWindow(m_nCmdShow);
pMainFrame->UpdateWindow();
```

For an SDI application you add the same line before you call **ProcessShellCommand**.

```
m_nCmdShow = SW_SHOWMINIMIZED;
ProcessShellCommand();
```

The variable **m_nCmdShow** is initialized by Windows when your application starts. This value is used by **ShowWindow** to determine how a window is displayed. You can also use the value **SW_SHOWMAXIMIZED** to initially maximize the window.

32.4 Modeless Dialog Boxes

A modeless dialog box is the same as a modal dialog box except that the user can interact with other application windows while the dialog box is active. For example, when you create a modal dialog box using **CDialog** and call **DoModal**, the user cannot interact with any other window in the application. This behavior occurs because the dialog box processes all command events and does not let them get to the application. Also, because **DoModal** does not return until the user closes the dialog box, the application cannot continue until the dialog is closed. Modeless dialog boxes, on the other hand, can be active along with the application's other windows. Both the application's window and the modeless dialog can process events simultaneously.

To create a modeless dialog, you must first create a new class that is derived from **CDialog**. For this example, use the ClassWizard to create a new class named **CFindNameDialog**. Add a Cancel and a Next button to the dialog. Then, override the **CDialog** functions **Create** and **PostNcDestroy** and then create handlers for the two buttons called **OnClose** and **OnNext**.

In the class definition for the new class change the class constructor so it accepts no arguments and change **Create** so it only takes the argument **pParentWnd**.

```
CFindNameDialog();
virtual BOOL Create(CWnd* pParentWnd);
```

Then change the constructor, **Create**, **PostNcDestroy**, **OnClose**, and **OnNext**.

```
CFindNameDialog::CFindNameDialog() : CDialog()
{
    //{{AFX_DATA_INIT(CFindNameDialog)
    //}}AFX_DATA_INIT
}

BOOL CFindNameDialog::Create(CWnd* pParentWnd)
{
    return CDialog::Create(IDD, pParentWnd);
}

void CFindNameDialog::PostNcDestroy()
{
    CDialog::PostNcDestroy();
    delete this;
}

void CFindNameDialog::OnClose()
{
    DestroyWindow();
}

void CFindNameDialog::OnNext()
{
    if( !UpdateData(FALSE) )
    {
        TRACE0( "UpdateData failed in OnNext()\n" );
        return;
    }
}
```

The constructor, **Create**, and **PostNcDestroy** all work together to create and destroy the dialog box. The constructor is changed so it calls the protected constructor that does not take any arguments. This creates the object itself: **Create** is the function that actually creates the dialog box window. Now the window is like any other window and can process messages independently of the other application windows. Note, however, that the dialog window is still a child of the application so it will iconify along with the application.

The **PostNcDestroy** function is special in this case. It is used to destroy the **this** pointer. The dialog's life cycle usually lasts longer than a function call. For this reason, the dialog is allocated on the heap with **new**. When the dialog box is destroyed, its resources need to be freed with delete. Because **PostNcDestroy** is called after the dialog window has been destroyed, it is the appropriate place to delete **this**.

The **OnClose** and **OnNext** functions perform the same actions as they would for modal dialogs. The **OnClose** function closes the dialog using **DestroyWindow**. The **OnNext** function calls **UpdateData** to perform any data exchanges that are necessary. Notice that we can still use DDX and DDV with modeless dialogs. Because we might want to be able to search for multiple names without closing the dialog, **OnNext** does not close the dialog. Make sure your modeless dialog does not call the base class **CDialog::OnOK** or **CDialog::OnCancel** functions. These functions will call **EndDialog**, which should only be used with modal dialogs.

When you want to create an instance of the modeless dialog, you would do something similar to this.

```
void CMainFrame::OnFindName()
{
    CFindNameDialog* pFindName = new CFindNameDialog;
    pFindName->Create( this );
}
```

This constructs a **CFindNameDialog** object on the heap and calls its **Create** function. Make sure the dialog is created on heap with **new** or it will be destroyed when it goes out of scope. Also be careful of dereferencing the pointer after creation because the dialog may have been closed, which will delete the pointer and make it invalid.

Modeless dialogs have some unique problems that you must be careful to avoid. With modeless dialogs, you can create multiple instances of the dialog. If you only want a single dialog at a time you must keep track of the dialog's condition and modify the dialog's menu option to disable it when the dialog is visible. Also you must be able to communicate with the dialog. This can be done through messages and the **Send-Message** function or by careful access to a pointer to the dialog. The dialog can get access to the application through functions such as **AfxGetMainWnd**.

32.5 Mini-Frame Windows

When the tool bars in an MFC application are floating, they have a thin border (or frame) around them called a mini-frame. This thin border is handled by the **CMiniFrameWnd** class. This class behaves the same as the **CFrameWnd** class except it draws a half-height frame around its window. It also does not have minimize/maximize buttons or menus, and you only have to single-click on the system menu to dismiss it. In this section we will describe how to convert the modeless dialog described above in into a mini-framed window.

Use the ClassWizard to derive a new class **CMiniFindNameDialog** from **CMiniFrameWnd**. Add to it the following member variable and make the constructor and destructor public:

```
public:
    CMiniFindNameDialog();
    virtual ~CMiniFindNameDialog();
```

```
public:
    CFindNameDialog* m_pFindNameDialog;
```

Remember to include the **CFindNameDialog** include file at the top of the **CMiniFindNameDialog** include file. Initialize the pointer to NULL in the constructor:

```
CMiniFindNameDialog::CMiniFindNameDialog()
{
    m_pFindNameDialog = NULL;
}
```

Now use the ClassWizard to add handlers for the **WM_ACTIVATE**, **WM_CREATE**, and **WM_SETFOCUS** messages.

When the mini-frame window is created we need to create the modeless dialog it manages. This dialog must be modeless because otherwise we would have to call **CDialog::DoModal** and that would be unacceptable.

```
int CMiniFindNameDialog::OnCreate(LPCREATESTRUCT lpCreateStruct)
{
    if (CMiniFrameWnd::OnCreate(lpCreateStruct) == -1)
        return -1;

    // Create the modeless find dialog
    m_pFindNameDialog = new CFindNameDialog;
    if (m_pFindNameDialog->Create(this) == -1)
    {
        delete m_pFindNameDialog;
        m_pFindNameDialog = NULL;
        return -1;
    }

    CRect clientRect, frameRect;
    m_pFindNameDialog->GetWindowRect( clientRect );
    frameRect = clientRect;

    // CMiniFrameWnd::CalcWindowRect adds the extra width
    // and height needed for the mini-frame
    CalcWindowRect( frameRect );
    SetWindowPos( NULL, frameRect.left, frameRect.top,
            frameRect.Width(), frameRect.Height(),
            SWP_NOZORDER | SWP_NOACTIVATE);
    m_pFindNameDialog->SetWindowPos( NULL, 0, 0,
            clientRect.Width(), clientRect.Height(),
            SWP_NOZORDER | SWP_NOACTIVATE);

    return 0;
}
```

First we call the base class **OnCreate**. Then we create the modeless find dialog the same way we did before. If the modeless dialog cannot be created, we clean up the resources and return. Otherwise we need to size the mini-frame window so it fits around its child dialog. This is done using **SetWindowPos**. Using **GetWindowRect** we get the dimensions of the modeless dialog. Then **CalcWindowRect** is called to increase those dimensions by the amount necessary for the frame border. The resulting rectangle is used to resize the mini-frame window.

When you select the caption of the mini-frame window it becomes the active window. In this example we want the dialog to become the active window because it is managing the controls. The mini-frame window needs to handle the **WM_ACTIVATE** and **WM_SETFOCUS** messages because we need to forward these messages to the child dialog. This allows the dialog to reset the focus to the child that previously had the focus, such as a button or edit control.

```
void CMiniFindNameDialog::OnActivate(UINT nState,
    CWnd* pWndOther, BOOL bMinimized)
{
    CMiniFrameWnd::OnActivate(nState, pWndOther, bMinimized);

    // Forward message to the dialog
    ASSERT_VALID( m_pFindNameDialog );
    const MSG* pMsg = GetCurrentMessage();
    ASSERT( pMsg->message == WM_ACTIVATE );
    m_pFindNameDialog->SendMessage( pMsg->message, pMsg->wParam,
        pMsg->lParam );
}

void CMiniFindNameDialog::OnSetFocus(CWnd* pOldWnd)
{
    CMiniFrameWnd::OnSetFocus(pOldWnd);
    ASSERT_VALID( m_pFindNameDialog );
    m_pFindNameDialog->SetFocus();
}
```

OnActivate uses **GetCurrentMessage** to get a pointer to the message currently being processed. This message can then be forwarded to the dialog. **OnSetFocus** sets the focus to the dialog using **SetFocus**.

This completes the **CMiniFindNameDialog** class. Before we can use the class however, we must modify the original **CFindNameDialog** dialog template. Because the dialog will be a child of another window it must have the **WS_CHILD** style, so set it's style to Child. It cannot have a border because the **CMiniFindNameDialog** class is providing one, so set the Border to None. Also make sure the Visible style is set or it will not appear in the window.

Next we have to change the way the **CFindNameDialog** class is destroyed. The **CFindNameDialog OnClose** function calls **DestroyWindow**. This will destroy the dialog itself. In this case we don't want to close the dialog. Instead we want to close the mini-frame window of which the dialog is a child. If you were just to close the dialog, you would be left with a hollow mini-frame window. The new **OnClose** is shown here.

```
void CFindNameDialog::OnClose()
{
    TRACE( "CFindNameDialog::OnClose\n" );
```

```
                GetParent()->SendMessage( WM_CLOSE, 0, 0);
        }
```

Using **GetParent**, the dialog can get a pointer to the mini-frame window. It then sends the mini-frame a **WM_CLOSE** message causing it to destroy both the mini-frame window and the child dialog.

Creating the mini-frame window is the same as creating a modeless dialog. First you create the mini-frame object on the heap and then call its **Create** function.

```
void CMainFrame::OnFindName()
{
    CMiniFindNameDialog* pMiniFindName = new CMiniFindNameDialog;

    if (!pMiniFindName->Create( NULL, "Find Name",
            WS_POPUP | WS_CAPTION | WS_SYSMENU,
            CRect(0,0,0,0),
            AfxGetMainWnd() ))
    {
        delete pMiniFindName;
        pMiniFindName = NULL;
        return;
    }

    pMiniFindName->CenterWindow();
    pMiniFindName->ShowWindow( SW_SHOW );
}
```

The arguments to the **Create** function are: an optional class name for the window, the window caption, the window style attributes, the dimensions of the window, and the parent window. We specify the typical style attributes, and the window dimensions can be empty because the **CMiniFindNameDialog** window will resize itself. The window is displayed using **CenterWindow** to position the window and then having **ShowWindow** show the window. We could have used the **WS_VISIBLE** style attribute instead of **ShowWindow**, but this will cause the window to flash between being created and being centered with **CenterWindow**.

This same process of creating a mini-frame with a dialog as its child can also be used to create modeless property sheets or any other type of window that needs a mini-frame.

32.6 Context Popup Menus

In certain types of programs, drawing editors for example, popup menus (also called shortcut or context menus) can eliminate a great deal of back-and-forth motion required to select common options from the menu bar. Instead of having to move the cursor from its current position in the drawing all the way up to the menu bar, the user simply clicks the right mouse button and a menu appears immediately.

You can use the Component Gallery to insert a context menu in your application. The implementation shown here is to give you an explanation of how they work. You should use the Component Gallery to insert context menus into your application because it will also add the code necessary to display the context menu using the keyboard.

To demonstrate a popup menu, create a menu with an ID of **IDR_POPUP**. Then add a message handler for the view's **WM_CONTEXTMENU** message.

```
void CMyView::OnContextMenu(CWnd* /*pWnd*/, CPoint point)
{
    // Make sure window is active
    GetParentFrame()->ActivateFrame();

    // Load menu from resource file
    CMenu menu;
    if (menu.LoadMenu(IDR_POPUP))
    {
        // Display menu
        CMenu* pPopup = menu.GetSubMenu(0);
        ASSERT(pPopup != NULL);
        pPopup->TrackPopupMenu(
            TPM_LEFTALIGN | TPM_RIGHTBUTTON,
            point.x, point.y, AfxGetMainWnd());
    }
}
```

When you run the application, click the right mouse button in the client area of the view. The popup menu will appear, and you use it like any other menu. Any menu handlers and update command handlers for identical menu options in the menu bar will be called.

The code then uses the **GetSubMenu** function to get the zeroth element of the menu resource. This step must be taken because we need a popup frame for the popup menu itself. Because the **IDR_POPUP** resource is intended for use in a normal menu bar, we need the dummy popup to act as a replacement for the menu bar in the popup menu.

Finally, the code calls **TrackPopupMenu** so the menu appears and the user's mouse actions are tracked appropriately. The **TPM_LEFTALIGN** constant indicates that the menu should be left aligned in relation to the point where the mouse button was clicked. Other options are right and center alignment. The **TPM_RIGHTBUTTON** constant indicates that the right mouse button's clicks should traverse the menu in the same way left mouse button clicks do. This is simply a convenience for the user—because the user has a finger on the right button to activate the menu, then it should be possible to use that same finger to traverse the menu as well.

A popup menu can, if you choose, completely echo the main menu bar. Generally, however, the popup contains only those items needed within a document. This minimization of popup options makes it easier and quicker for the user to traverse the popup menu structure. The popup menu items should not contain mnemonics—since you have to use the mouse to activate the popup anyway, keyboard traversal is not needed. You can leave out the accelerator labels if you like to minimize the size of the popup menu or leave them in to remind the user of the available accelerator keystrokes.

32.7 Modifying the System Menu

The system menu that appears when you click the box on the left side of the title bar is a normal menu. It sends messages just like any other. You can obtain a pointer to it so that you can modify it using the **CWnd::GetSystemMenu** function.

```
CMenu* pMenu;
pMenu = m_pMainWnd->GetSystemMenu(FALSE);
pMenu->AppendMenu(MF_SEPARATOR);
pMenu->AppendMenu(MF_STRING, 1000, "Always On Top");
```

This code gets the system menu and then appends two menu items to it: a separator and an Always on Top option. The new menu option generates the arbitrary command ID of 1,000 in this case, and you would probably use a named constant instead. Handle the option by manually modifying one of the message maps to recognize it.

See the MFC help file for more information on **GetSystemMenu** and the functions, such as **AppendMenu**, in the **CMenu** class.

32.8 Conclusion

Using the concepts in this chapter you can create a variety of interesting application effects. For example, you might create an application that is displayed as an icon that is always on the top of the screen and that processes files from the Windows File Manager. You should understand more clearly the difference between modal and modeless dialogs and how they can be used. This chapter also gives you a better understanding on what window classes are and how they can be used.

Part 5

Several of classes in MFC provide access to advanced features that are not necessarily needed in every application. However, by understanding these features you can take advantage of them when necessary. For example, if you are a corporate programmer needing to hook to SQL databases on client/server networks, the first chapter in this section will show you how to use the ODBC classes in MFC to provide an easy interface to a variety of database servers.

Although you may not have an immediate need for the features discussed in this section, you will want to browse through it occasionally to keep in mind the variety of solutions that MFC has to offer.

ADVANCED MFC CLASSES

DATABASE ACCESS

Most enterprises today store their data in database servers that are available to employees anywhere on the enterprise's client/server network. Users run client applications to view or modify the data. Because this type of data access is so prevalent, MFC contains classes that allow your code to interact with database servers using a facility called ODBC (Open Database Connectivity). The database-access class called **CRecordSet** makes this possible. Using the **CRecordSet** class, you can easily access database servers and manipulate their data from your MFC applications.

This chapter starts with the assumption that you know nothing about databases, SQL (Structured Query Language), or ODBC, and will teach you the basic concepts behind the system as well as specific ways of accessing databases through MFC. If you are already familiar with SQL and ODBC, you may want to skim the first portion of the chapter to map your vocabulary to the vocabulary used here and then proceed to the MFC specifics.

33.1 Understanding Relational Databases

If you have experience working or programming in a corporate environment, you are already familiar with the concept of databases and database servers. If, on the other hand, you have been programming in college, at home, or on a small peer-to-peer network, these concepts may be foreign to you. It is important that you understand what client/server databases are and why they have become so prevalent in the corporate world for you to completely understand the MFC database classes.

Almost any MFC application you create with Visual C++ uses data stored on a hard disk. This configuration is so prevalent, in fact, that the AppWizard makes the assumption that any application it creates will have a document class associated with it. One of the document class's primary jobs is to load and store the disk-based information that the application uses. In Part 3 of this book, for example, every application we created had the ability to load documents, display their data, and then save changes that the user made. The drawing program in Chapter 15 stores drawing information in its documents. The text editor in Chapter 16 stores text information in its documents. The address list program in Chapter 18 stores address information in its documents. While it is possible to imagine and create applications that do not store data, they are few and far between. A simple digital clock is an example of such a program.

Many applications can get by without sharing the information they store on disk. For example, if you create a text file with a text editor, it is likely that you will be the only one who ever sees it. If someone else needs one of your text files, you simply make a copy of it. As you can see, the concept of multiple users somehow "sharing" the text file, simultaneously viewing and editing it, is completely unknown. In Chapter 18 you created an address list application that had these same constraints. It lets you load an address list file into memory, modify it, and save it. This is an acceptable programming style when address lists are small and they have only one user. However, there are many cases where data is frequently shared among users, and this simple file model breaks down in that sort of environment.

Think about how any large company uses address lists. For example, if the company maintains a list of employees, this data is used all over the company. In the personnel department this data is used to send out mailings to employees. Many people in the personnel department need to look at this list, and there are also people in the department adding employees to the list and deleting employees from the list every day. People in the security department use the list, as do people at the switchboard looking up office phone numbers. A company statistician might want to access the list. There may be hundreds or thousands of different people in the company who want to look at the list of employees, add to it, modify entries, and so on.

You can see that the simple document-based approach used in Chapter 18 simply will not work in this sort of environment. Here are three of the problems with the document-based approach:

1. The address list may be huge, so loading the entire thing into memory is unacceptable.
2. Many people need to access the list at once, but giving everyone a private copy is wasteful.
3. All changes need to be reflected company-wide. If everyone keeps a separate copy of the list and modifies it on their own, then there is no easy way to synchronize all the changes.

To solve these problems, the company will generally create a *database server* on the company's network to hold the list. This server contains a single copy of the list and makes it available to everyone on the network. Hundreds of people can look at the same list simultaneously and all modifications are immediately available company-wide.

Most large corporate databases use the *relational* database model. In this model, data are subdivided into separate lists, or *tables*, that are related to one another through unique IDs called *keys*. This model helps to reduce duplicate data and, therefore, saves space, time and frustration. For example, the company might store name and address information for its employees in one table, as shown in Figure 33.1.

EmpID	LastName	FirstName	Address	ZipCode
1	Brain	Marshall	853-I Durham Rd.	27587
2	Lovette	Lance	496-J Raleigh Rd.	27611
3	Campbell	Kelly	901-K Halifax Rd.	27597
			Ano so on...	

Figure 33.1
The employee table

Each line in the table is called a *row* or a *record*. It contains the information about the employee, as well as a unique ID for each employee record. This ID is known as the *primary key*, and must be unique. The primary key can consist of one column in the table, as shown in Figure 33.1, or it might consist of two or more columns that, taken together, are unique. In Figure 33.1, the **EmpId** field is unique to each employee and would be the primary key for that table. The database will enforce uniqueness on values in the primary key column. Not all tables need to have primary keys, but most do.

The power of a relational database comes when you add other tables that relate to existing tables. For example, in Figure 33.1 you might have noticed that there is no city or state information stored in the employee table. That's because the storage of city and state information would be redundant. Instead, it is easier to store it in another table, as shown in Figure 33.2.

ZipCode	City	State
27587	Durham	NC
27611	Raleigh	NC
27597	Halifax	NC
	And so on ...	

Figure 33.2
The zip code table

In the zip code table shown in Figure 33.2, the **ZipCode** field would act as the primary key. In the **Employee** table, the zip code field is now referred to as a *foreign key*. It references into the primary key of the zip code table. The power of this storage technology comes from the fact that there might be 200 employees who have the

27611 zip code, but the words "Raleigh, NC" only exist in the database once. That saves a lot of space, and also eliminates a lot of typing errors.

When you want to display employee information on the screen in a client's application, you need to somehow merge information from the employee table and the zip code table. This operation is called a *join*. A join relates the data in tables that have at least one field in common—the foreign key in one table is related to the primary key in another. The joined view of the data contains fields from both tables. By joining the employee table in Figure 33.1 to the zip code table in Figure 33.2, you can create a result that contains city and state information for each employee in the employee table.

A database server can hold many different tables. Normally the tables do not exist as individual entities, however. They are collected together into *databases* or *data sources* of two or more tables. A large database storing complex data for a corporate process might have hundreds of tables to store all the different types of data relevant to the process. The organization of the tables and their columns is called the *schema* of the database and is determined by the database designer.

The collection of tables in one database is seen as one entity by the database server, and the server can therefore provide some interesting services for the entity. For example, the database server can maintain *referential integrity* in any database. That is, the database server will ensure that any entry in a foreign key column actually has a partner in the primary key of the corresponding table. The server can also provide multi-table entry protection using *transactions*. For example, a single complex operation in a large database might need to update five tables simultaneously. However, if the operation were to start, update two of the five tables, and then fail to complete because of a power failure, the entire database would be corrupted. You can therefore bracket the five table operations in a single transaction. You signal to the database the start of the transaction, perform the five operations, and then signal the end. If the power fails before the server receives the end signal, the server will *roll back* (or restore) the database to the state before the beginning of the transaction when it reboots.

You can see from this discussion that a database server offers a large enterprise a number of significant data-handling advantages. That is why these servers have become so prevalent and why MFC contains classes to access them.

33.2 Understanding SQL

Most companies now use relational database servers to store all their data. These servers hold such things as employee lists, customer lists, payroll information, inventory information, billing information, factory statistics, and so on. To access this data, a language called *Structured Query Language*, or SQL, has evolved as a standard. Although all database server manufacturers extend SQL in various ways, the core of the SQL language is compatible across all SQL servers. This core language allows you to retrieve information from any server, add data to specific tables, and update fields in tables. The language is simple and very powerful.

The most common reason to access an SQL server is to perform a *query*. Using SQL commands, you can ask questions of a database. SQL servers have an interesting property that makes them popular in client/server environments: the database server actually performs all the work of processing the queries. For example, you can issue an SQL statement that asks the server to retrieve only those rows in a table that match certain criteria and then sort the selected rows on a certain field. In a large database it might take a tremendous amount of work to perform the selection and ordering, but all that work takes place on the server rather than on your local machine. The advantage of this configuration is that as the company grows and stores and retrieves more and more data from its databases, only the database servers must be upgraded to handle the additional load.

The **CRecordSet** class in MFC exists primarily to handle queries. It can also be used to add and delete records, but its primary emphasis is queries. To feel completely comfortable with the **CRecordSet** class in MFC, you need to understand SQL query syntax. That does not mean that you have to understand the entire SQL language— you simply need to understand a subset that the **CRecordSet** class uses.

The most commonly used command in SQL is SELECT. This command allows you to retrieve data from a table and also performs joins between multiple tables. The following sections contain examples of the SELECT command so you can understand its different features.

33.2.1 Basic SELECT Statements

To retrieve all the information from the EMPLOYEE table shown in Figure 33.1, you can use the following SELECT command:

```
SELECT EmpID, LastName, FirstName, Address, ZipCode FROM EMPLOYEE
```

As you can see, the SELECT statement names the columns it wishes to select and the table that it wishes to select them from. The general form of the statement is:

```
SELECT <columns> FROM <table>
```

When you issue this command to an SQL server, the server retrieves the requested information into a record set and makes that record set available to the client application over the network. The client application can retrieve the records of the record set one at a time by sending requests to the server.

Using the SELECT statement, you can create a record set containing one, some, or all of the columns from any table in the database. The SQL server will check to make sure that the table you selected contains all the requested fields. If one of the field names is incorrect, it will return an error.

33.2.2 WHERE Clauses

To select data more specifically from a table, you can add a WHERE clause to a SELECT statement. For example, if you want to retrieve the names of all employees in the 27611 zip code, you can use the following SELECT statement:

```
SELECT LastName, FirstName FROM Employee WHERE (ZipCode=27611)
```

The SQL server will respond to this request by building a record set that contains only the **LastName** and **FirstName** columns. In those columns will be the names of only those employees whose **ZipCode** fields equal 27611. In the WHERE clause, you can add AND and OR statements to further qualify the selection. For example:

```
SELECT LastName, FirstName FROM EMPLOYEE WHERE (ZipCode=27611) AND
    (LastName='Smith')
```

This query would return all the Smiths living in the 27611 area code.

33.2.3 ORDER BY Clauses

The ORDER BY clause can be added to a SELECT statement to force the SQL server to sort information in a record set. For example, you might use the following statement:

```
SELECT LastName, FirstName FROM Employee ORDER BY LastName
```

This statement causes the server to sort the record set on the **LastName** column. To sort by last name and first name you can simply extend the ORDER BY clause like this:

```
SELECT LastName, FirstName FROM Employee ORDER BY LastName, FirstName
```

By adding the ASC and DESC key words, you can set the sorting order to ascending or descending on a field-by-field basis. For example:

```
SELECT LastName, FirstName FROM Employee
    ORDER BY LastName ASC, FirstName DESC
```

You can also combine ORDER BY and WHERE clauses to select and order information very specifically, like this:

```
SELECT LastName, FirstName FROM Employee WHERE (ZipCode=27611) AND
    (LastName='Smith') ORDER BY FirstName
```

This statement causes the SQL server to select all the Smiths in the 27611 zip code and then sort all the information in the record set by first name.

33.2.4 Joining Tables

You join two tables by adjusting the WHERE clause. For example, to display all of the information in the **Employee** table, join it to the **ZipCode** table in Figure 33.2 and display the city and state as well, you would use the following SELECT statement:

```
SELECT Employee.LastName, Employee.FirstName,
    Employee.Address, ZIPCODE.City, ZIPCODE.State,
    Employee.ZipCode
FROM Employee, ZIPCODE
WHERE Employee.ZipCode=ZIPCODE.ZipCode
```

The WHERE clause instructs the SQL server to join the two tables on the **Zip-Code** fields and to create a record set containing fields from both tables. The FROM statement tells the server which tables to use. Notice that each field is scoped by its table name, e.g., EMPLOYEE.LastName. This is necessary because it is possible for two tables to have column names that match. The use of the table name lets you distinguish between columns in the different tables. It is possible to join any number of fields from any number of tables.

33.2.5 Other SQL Key Words

SQL contains several other key words that are frequently useful when performing common database operations:

DELETE
INSERT
UPDATE
CALL

The CALL command in particular is important in corporate environments. It is possible, in many SQL servers, to create *stored procedures* that execute on the database server. A stored procedure is pre-written SQL code, and it is common to use a collection of stored procedures to encapsulate and protect a database. Rather than allowing direct access to tables, many companies will allow access only through stored procedures to enforce business rules in the database. The CALL command lets you call a stored procedure in the database.

33.3 Understanding ODBC

As you can see in the previous section, SQL is extremely simple, but it is also extremely powerful. It is a useful, general tool for accessing data from database servers. Unfortunately, SQL is not universal. In fact, there is a wide variety of other database formats that are quite common, including:

- DBase databases and other XBase derivatives
- Excel and Lotus 123 databases
- Access databases
- BTrieve databases

This proliferation of database access methods presents a problem: How can you allow programmatic access to this wide variety of database systems without requiring programmers to understand a wide variety of access languages, libraries, and so on? That is where ODBC comes in.

ODBC is a layer that lets any Windows application access any database using a single, SQL-like query language. Database manufacturers create ODBC drivers that let ODBC access the database. Under this system, any program that knows how to talk to ODBC can talk to any database provided that the system contains the appropriate ODBC driver for the database. ODBC drivers are available from Microsoft, many database vendors, and third-party companies.

The MFC **CRecordSet** class uses the ODBC facility to access databases. Therefore, to access a database you must be able to access it through ODBC. To set up connections to databases, you use the ODBC Administrator, located in the Control Panel. The ODBC Administrator is able to show you all the drivers known to ODBC, as well as the different databases available through the different drivers. It can also create new databases.

This is a nearly ideal solution because it standardizes all database interaction. One problem that arises, however, is that not all databases can support all the features in the SQL language. For example, while all true SQL servers support the concept of transactions that can be rolled back, many lower-level database systems like DBase and Excel do not. Therefore, ODBC contains the ability to handle transactions, but simply disables that feature when it is talking to a low-functionality driver.

Another minor problem arises in the area of data types (e.g., integers, strings). SQL supports certain data types, but these types differ from standard C++ types and can also differ between ODBC drivers. Therefore, ODBC does its best to map the different data types in the different database drivers to SQL types. You then map the standard SQL types to C++ data types. The article "SQL: SQL and C++ Data Types" in the MFC documentation explains the mapping.

ODBC is encapsulated in its own API called the ODBC API (your machine may have a file called ODBCAPI.HLP or ODBC20.HLP available to describe the API's functions). This API offers direct access to database servers through the ODBC calls. The MFC classes that access databases use this API to do their manipulations. There are some cases where special programming problems can be solved by accessing the ODBC API directly.

33.4 Microsoft Query

[This example demonstrates how to use Microsoft Query (which comes with Microsoft Office) to access an SQL server. You could also use tools that come with the SQL server to build and query the tables. See the web site for another example that uses Microsoft Access to build and query a sample database.]

To work with the examples in this chapter, you need to be able to create a database and the tables within it. The ODBC administrator allows you to create the database itself. To create tables in the database, you can either send direct SQL table-creation statements through ODBC, use a database administration tool provided with your database, or use a tool called Microsoft Query. The Microsoft Query tool is widely available—for example, it comes with Microsoft Office and many other products. The tool interacts with the ODBC facility to talk to any database that is a registered ODBC data source. It is able to create tables as well as the columns in those tables; add, update, and delete rows from tables; and perform queries by allowing you to visually or manually create SQL SELECT statements. If your machine has no ODBC drivers, or if you need Microsoft Query, contact Microsoft. The tutorial for the Enroll example in books on-line contains ordering information for ODBC drivers.

What we need to do here is use the ODBC administrator and Microsoft Query to create a simple two-table database that we will use in the following sections. The goal of this sample database is to provide a very simple test case you can use to understand the **CRecordSet** class and many of its features. The two tables will contain employee and zip code information as described earlier in this chapter. To create the database, take the following steps. Or, take similar steps with Microsoft Access, Transact-SQL, or other database interaction tool.

33.4.1 Create the Database

In this example, we will use the Microsoft SQL server. However, any database for which you have ODBC drivers will do. In this particular case, assuming that you have installed the SQL server on an NT machine, you need to start by opening the ODBC Administrator in the Control Panel. You will see a screen like the one shown in Figure 33.3.

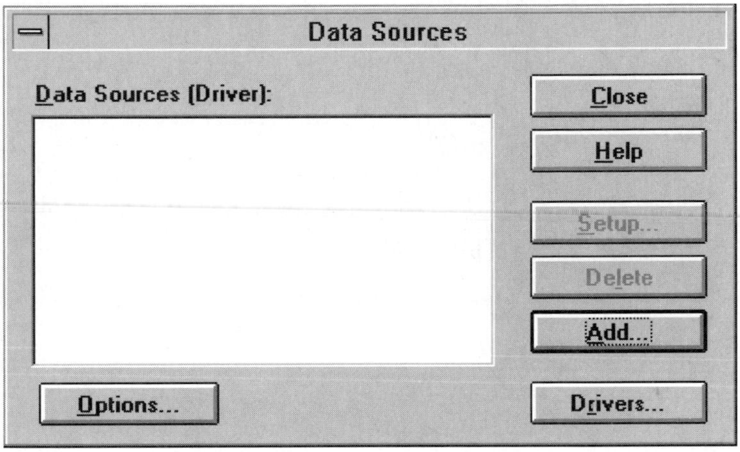

Figure 33.3
The ODBC administrator

The view shown in Figure 33.3 indicates that the system currently knows about no data sources (databases) at all. To add a new data source, click the **Add** button. You will see a dialog like the one shown in Figure 33.4.

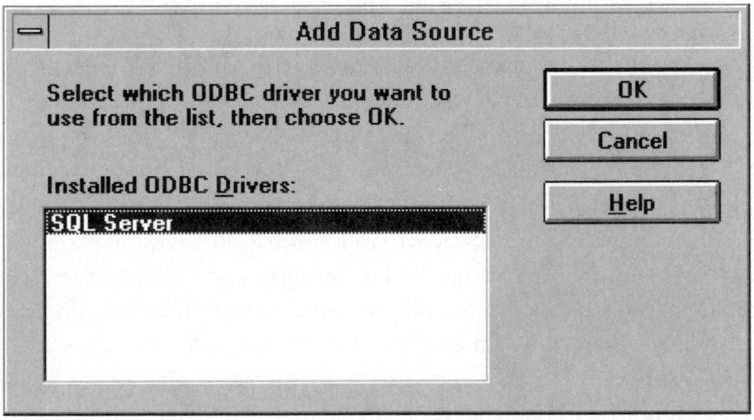

Figure 33.4
Selecting an ODBC driver

The dialog in Figure 33.4 shows you all the ODBC drivers known to your system. In this case, only SQL drivers exist on this system. Choose the driver you wish to use and then click on the **OK** button. You will see a dialog like the one shown in Figure 33.5. In this dialog, you name your new data source. The dialog will change slightly depending on the type of driver you are using.

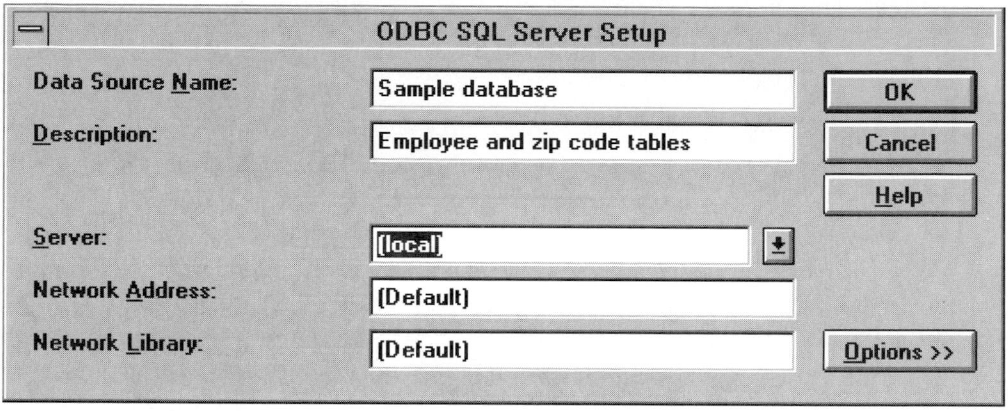

Figure 33.5
Creating a new data source

You can call the new data source anything you like. For this example, name it "Sample database" as shown. When you click the **Close** button you will return to the ODBC Administrator, and the new data source will be visible in the list. Close the Administrator and the Control Panel.

33.4.2 Create the Employee and ZipCode Tables

At this point we have created a database, but it has no tables. You need to add tables. The amount of difficulty you will experience in adding tables relates to the type of database engine that holds the tables. For example, if you are working with the Microsoft SQL server, you will probably want to use the administration tools that come with the server to create a new device and database, as well as a user account for yourself, and then set permissions. If you are using something like the Access database engine, things will be much easier.

We will add the EMPLOYEE table first. Start Microsoft Query. Choose the **Table Definition** option in the **File** menu. You will see the Select Data Source dialog. At this point you can choose the data source you just created or create a new one by clicking the **Other** button and following the same sort of procedure described above. Choose your data source and then click the **Use** button. You will see a dialog like the one shown in Figure 33.6.

Click the **New** button in the Select Table dialog to create a new table. Add columns to the table to duplicate the columns shown in Figure 33.1. When you are done you should see a dialog like the one shown in Figure 33.7. Click the **Create** button when you are done adding columns to the table.

Repeat the same steps to create a new ZIPCODE table. When you are done it should resemble Figure 33.8.

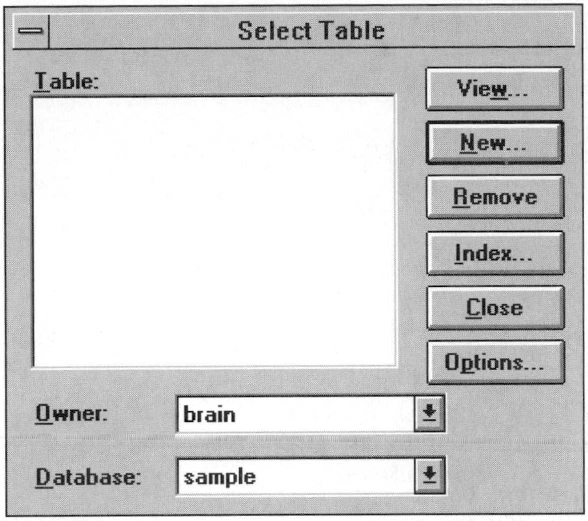

Figure 33.6
The Select Table dialog

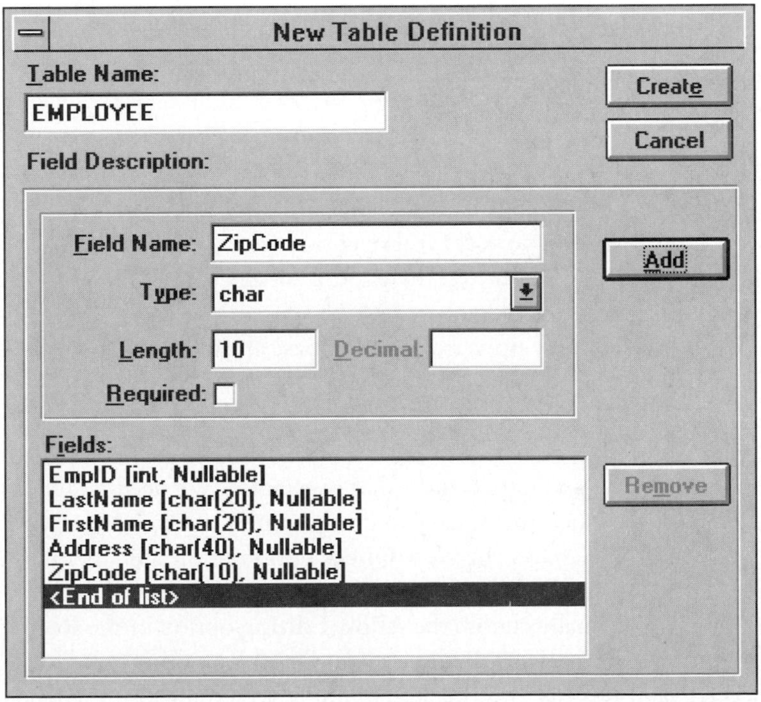

Figure 33.7
The New Table dialog for the EMPLOYEE table

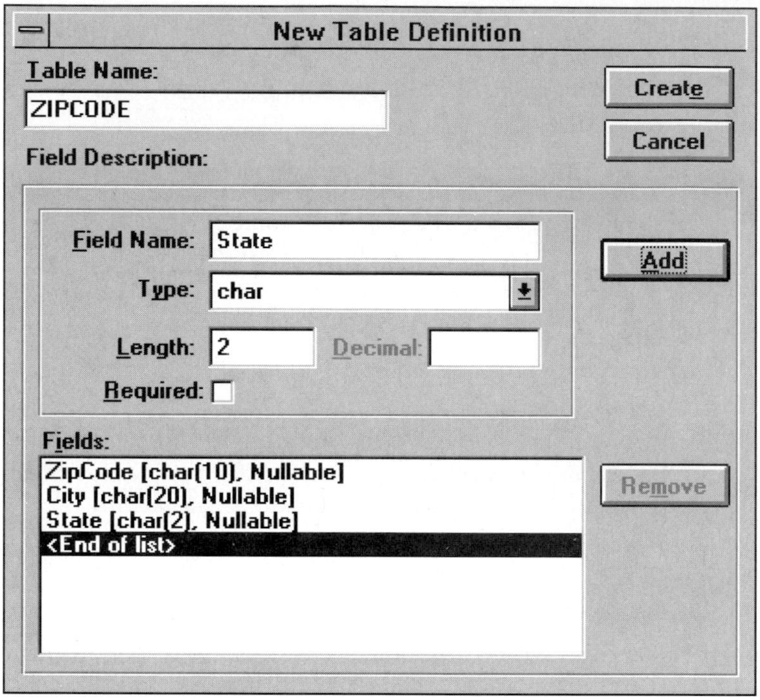

Figure 33.8
The New Table dialog for the ZIPCODE table

When you are through creating your tables, click the **Close** button.

Note that you can use your database's specific tools to create these same tables, and you will probably have more control over how you create and adjust things like primary keys, indexes, and so on. On many SQL servers you will have to use specific tools to grant users access to the database. We have used Microsoft Query here simply because it is generic and fairly universal. If a database already exists, then the only step to take is step 1, which creates the data source.

33.4.3 Add Data to the Tables

Now you have a Data Source and it has two tables. We need to add data to the tables. To do this, use Microsoft Query to create a "new query." A query in this case is a view on the database. Select the **New Query** option in the **File** menu. Select your data source. Then add the **Employee** table to the query. Click the "*" field at the top of the list of fields and finally choose the **Allow Editing** option in the **Records** menu. Add the data shown in Figure 33.1 to the table. Or add anything you like. The point is to get several valid records into the table. Simply type right into the fields you see. As you enter each value press the tab key to move to the next column. When you press the tab key on the last column, the record will be added to the database.

Now close that query. There is no need to save it. Create a second new query so you can add data to the **ZipCode** table and add several records there. Make sure there is one record in the **ZipCode** table for each unique zip code in the EMPLOYEE table.

33.4.4 Experiment with Queries

Now that the tables contain data, you can use the Microsoft Query application to play with SQL. The **View** menu contains an **SQL** option you can use to modify the current query. You can modify this statement in any way you like to experiment with WHERE clauses, ORDER BY clauses, join statements and so on. The application will immediately show you show you the results graphically, and you can learn quite a bit about SQL by experimenting with statements this way. You can also use the different menu options to modify the SQL statement graphically and then view the text you've created. The **Execute SQL** option in the **File** menu is also useful. See the MS Query documentation for further information Experiment freely until you feel comfortable with SQL.

33.5 The CRecordSet Class

The **CRecordSet** class supports the concept of a record set. The idea behind the **CRecordSet** class is extremely simple: An instance of the **CRecordSet** class holds one SELECT statement and can send it to the database server. The instance then lets you retrieve the records in the resulting record set from the database server one at a time. You might display those records immediately as you retrieve them, and if that is your goal the **CRecordView** class (see Section 33.7) makes your life extremely simple. Or you might spin through all the records in the record set so you can display them in a list box, show them in some sort of viewer, or print them.

One way to gain an understanding of the **CRecordSet** class is to read through all its member functions. The list below briefly describes each one. You will want to read the detailed description of each function in the MFC documentation at some point so you have a complete understanding of these different functions. Another way to feel comfortable with this class is to work through some examples, as described in the following sections.

Data Members

m_hstmt	Used by ODBC API to access database
m_nFields	Number of fields in record set
m_nParams	Number of parameters supported by the record set
m_strFilter	String used in SQL WHERE clause for this record set
m_strSort	String used in SQL ORDER BY clause by this record set

Opening and Closing

CRecordset	Constructor
Open	Performs the record set's query, the record set can then retrieve the records one by one using the Move functions
Requery	Reruns the SELECT statement to update record set
Close	Closes the record set and disconnects from the database

Getting Data

Move	Moves the record set's pointer up or down by amount specified and gets that record from the database
MoveFirst	Moves the record set's pointer to first record and gets that record from the database
MoveLast	Moves the record set's pointer to the last record and gets that record from the database
MoveNext	Moves the record set's pointer to the next record and gets that record from the database
MovePrev	Moves the record set's pointer to the previous record and gets that record from the database

Information Functions

CanAppend	Returns TRUE if you can use AddNew
CanRestart	Returns TRUE if you can use Requery
CanScroll	Returns TRUE if you can use MoveNext and MovePrev
CanTransact	Returns TRUE if you can use transactions in CDatabase object
CanUpdate	Returns TRUE if you can update records
GetRecordCount	Returns the number of records resulting from latest query
GetStatus	Returns the record set status
GetTableName	Returns the name of the record set's table
GetSQL	Returns this record set's SQL SELECT string
IsOpen	Returns TRUE if the record set is open
IsBOF	Returns TRUE if record set pointer is before the first record
IsEOF	Returns TRUE if record set pointer is past the last record
IsDeleted	Returns TRUE if current record has been deleted
IsFieldDirty	Returns TRUE if field has changed
IsFieldNull	Returns TRUE if field is NULL
IsFieldNullable	Returns TRUE if NULL is a valid field value

Modifying Records

AddNew	Initiates an Add operation. Call Update at completion
Delete	Deletes the current record
Edit	Initiates an Edit operation. Call Update at completion
Update	Saves the data of an AddNew or Edit operation
Cancel	Cancels asynchronous operations

Setting Characteristics

SetFieldDirty	Sets field's dirty bit
SetFieldNull	Sets field to NULL
SetLockingMode	Sets the locking mode

Overridables

DoFieldExchange	Override to exchange data between database and field variables
GetDefaultConnect	Override to change the connect string

This book is continuously updated. See http://www.iftech.com/mfc

GetDefaultSQL	Override to modify the SQL string
OnSetOptions	Override to set options for the ODBC statement
OnWaitForDataSource	Override to yield CPU to other applications

33.6 Simple CRecordSet Operations

The easiest way to begin your understanding of the **CRecordSet** class is to create an instance of it that can access the **Employee** table we created in Section 33.4. In this section we will do this using the simplest and most primitive code possible so that you can see exactly what is happening. Take the following steps.

33.6.1 Create the Application Framework

Create a new SDI framework with the AppWizard. Give the new project the name "db." As you go through the six AppWizard option screens, select the following options:

- Choose the **Single-Document** option.
- *In the database support screen, choose **Only Include Header Files.***
- Choose **None** for OLE support.
- Enable or disable any application features as you see fit.

Make sure you choose the header files specified in Step 2. We are not going to use this Application Framework as anything but a foundation to support and activate an instance of the **CRecordSet** class.

33.6.2 Create a CRecordSet Class

Open the ClassWizard and prepare to add a new class. In the dialog that appears, set the class type to **CRecordSet**. Name the class **CEmpSet**. Create the new class. You will see a dialog asking you to pick the data source (database). Choose the employee database you created in Section 33.4. You will then be asked to choose a table in that data source. Choose the **Employee** table.

If you look at the files the ClassWizard created, you will find they appear as shown in Listings 33.1 and 33.2

Listing 33.1
The EMPSET.H file

```
// empset.h : header file
//

/////////////////////////////////////////////////////////////
// CEmpSet recordset

class CEmpSet : public CRecordset
{
public:
    CEmpSet(CDatabase* pDatabase = NULL);
    DECLARE_DYNAMIC(CEmpSet)
```

```
// Field/Param Data
    //{{AFX_FIELD(CEmpSet, CRecordset)
    longm_EmpID;
    CStringm_LastName;
    CStringm_FirstName;
    CStringm_Address;
    CStringm_ZipCode;
    //}}AFX_FIELD


// Overrides
    // ClassWizard generated virtual function overrides
    //{{AFX_VIRTUAL(CEmpSet)
    public:
    virtual CString GetDefaultConnect();    // Default connection string
    virtual CString GetDefaultSQL();     // Default SQL for Recordset
    virtual void DoFieldExchange(CFieldExchange* pFX);  // RFX support
    //}}AFX_VIRTUAL

// Implementation
#ifdef _DEBUG
    virtual void AssertValid() const;
    virtual void Dump(CDumpContext& dc) const;
#endif
};
```

Listing 33.2
The EMPSET.CPP file

```
// empset.cpp : implementation file
//

#include "stdafx.h"
#include "db.h"
#include "empset.h"

#ifdef _DEBUG
#undef THIS_FILE
static char BASED_CODE THIS_FILE[] = __FILE__;
#endif

/////////////////////////////////////////////////////////////////
// CEmpSet

IMPLEMENT_DYNAMIC(CEmpSet, CRecordset)

CEmpSet::CEmpSet(CDatabase* pdb)
    : CRecordset(pdb)
{
    //{{AFX_FIELD_INIT(CEmpSet)
    m_EmpID = 0;
    m_LastName = _T("");
    m_FirstName = _T("");
```

```
    m_Address = _T("");
    m_ZipCode = _T("");
    m_nFields = 5;
    //}}AFX_FIELD_INIT
}


CString CEmpSet::GetDefaultConnect()
{
    return _T("ODBC;DSN=Sample database;");
}


CString CEmpSet::GetDefaultSQL()
{
    return _T("brain.EMPLOYEE");
}

void CEmpSet::DoFieldExchange(CFieldExchange* pFX)
{
    //{{AFX_FIELD_MAP(CEmpSet)
    pFX->SetFieldType(CFieldExchange::outputColumn);
    RFX_Long(pFX, "EmpID", m_EmpID);
    RFX_Text(pFX, "LastName", m_LastName);
    RFX_Text(pFX, "FirstName", m_FirstName);
    RFX_Text(pFX, "Address", m_Address);
    RFX_Text(pFX, "ZipCode", m_ZipCode);
    //}}AFX_FIELD_MAP
}

/////////////////////////////////////////////////////////////////
// CEmpSet diagnostics

#ifdef _DEBUG
void CEmpSet::AssertValid() const
{
    CRecordset::AssertValid();
}

void CEmpSet::Dump(CDumpContext& dc) const
{
    CRecordset::Dump(dc);
}
#endif //_DEBUG
```

You can see that the ClassWizard did not have to do a lot of work to create the new class. What it did do is use the ODBC API to query the **Employee** table and find its fields. It created a member variable in the class for each field in the table and then created RFX function calls in the **DoFieldExchange** function to hold data from each field. The class uses these member variables and RFX functions to hold one record's data when it transfers a record from the database to the class. It also uses these fields to hold user changes before transferring those changes to the database.

The RFX functions are similar to DDX functions. A DDX function, as described in Chapter 22, transfers data back and forth between member variables in a dialog or form view class and the controls in the dialog template. An RFX function transfers data between a member variable in a record set class and the database.

The ClassWizard automatically assumes you want to retrieve all columns from a table and sets up its member variables and RFX functions accordingly. If you do not want to retrieve all the columns from a table, simply remove the variable names using the ClassWizard.

33.6.3 Create Viewing Code

To view the data in the record set, we will use here an extremely primitive method that has the advantage of being extremely clear. The code we are about to create will recognize when the user clicks in the view. In response to that click, the code will present a succession of message boxes that display the record set's SQL statement followed by information from the database.

Open the ClassWizard, select the **Message Maps** tab, and then select the view class. What we want to do is detect when the user clicks anywhere in the view and use that as a signal to display the data in the record set. Select the **CDbView** class and then select its WM_LBUTTONUP message. Add a function for that message and edit the function. Add the following code to the new function:

```
void CEmpView::OnLButtonUp(UINT nFlags, CPoint point)
{
    int x;
    CEmpSet set;
    set.Open();

    AfxMessageBox(set.GetSQL());
    while (!set.IsEOF())
    {
        AfxMessageBox(set.m_LastName + set.m_FirstName);
        set.MoveNext();
    }

    CView::OnLButtonUp(nFlags, point);
}
```

Be sure you include EMPSET.H at the top of the CBBVIEW.CPP file.

33.6.4 Compile and Run

Compile and run the program. Provided the employee database exists and the **Employee** table contains data as shown in Section 33.4, you can click anywhere in the view to trigger the code you just entered. This code will first create an instance of the record set and **Open** it. That is, the record set class will attach to the database server and send the class's SELECT statement to it. The database will respond to the SELECT statement and form a result set. In addition, the **CEmpSet** class will retrieve the first record in the record set and store it in its member variables.

The code then uses a message box and the **GetSQL** function to display the SQL statement held by the record set class. A typical SQL statement would be:

```
SELECT EmpID,LastName,FirstName,ZipCode FROM EMPLOYEE FOR UPDATE OF
```

The "FOR UPDATE OF" clause specifies that updates will be allowed on the records in the record set.

The code then begins looping. Each time through the loop the code gets the last name field and displays it in a message box. Then it moves to the next record and displays it, repeating until it has shown all the records in the table.

33.6.5 Trap Exceptions

The code you've just tested is a bit too loose. If any problem occurs in accessing the database, the program will fail catastrophically. You can make the code much more stable by trapping database exceptions. See Chapter 13 for information on exception handling. Replace the code from Section 33.6.3 with the following:

```
void CEmpView::OnLButtonUp(UINT nFlags, CPoint point)
{
    try
    {
        int x;
        CEmpSet set;
        set.Open();

        AfxMessageBox(set.GetSQL());
        while (!set.IsEOF())
        {
            AfxMessageBox(set.m_LastName + set.m_FirstName);
            set.MoveNext();
        }
    }
    catch(CDBException *theException)
    {
        AfxMessageBox(theException->m_strError);
    }

    CView::OnLButtonUp(nFlags, point);
}
```

If you compile and run this code, it will work exactly as it did before. If you want to force a database exception to occur, replace the **for** statement with the following:

```
for (x=0; x<set.GetRecordCount() + 1; x++)
```

The loop will try to access one too many records and this will lead to an exception. If you look up the **CDBException** exception in the MFC documentation, you will find that it contains the extremely handy **m_strError** member. This member contains an English error string produced by the database server at the time of the error.

33.6.6 Add an ORDER BY Clause

You can sort the data in the record set by adding an ORDER BY clause, as discussed in Section 33.2.3. The **m_strSort** member variable in the **CRecordSet** class facilitates this process. You simply specify the field names you want to use for sorting.

To demonstrate the ORDER BY clause, modify the code as shown below:

```
void CDbView::OnLButtonUp(UINT nFlags, CPoint point)
{
    try
    {
        int x;
        CEmpSet set;
        set.m_strSort = "LastName ASC, FirstName ASC";
        set.Open();

        AfxMessageBox(set.GetSQL());
        while (!set.IsEOF())
        {
            AfxMessageBox(set.m_LastName + set.m_FirstName);
            set.MoveNext();
        }
    }
    catch(CDBException *theException)
    {
        AfxMessageBox(theException->m_strError);
    }

    CView::OnLButtonUp(nFlags, point);
}
```

The single line that sets the **m_strSort** variable is all that's needed. You must set this variable after instantiating the class but before opening the record set. Do not include the words "ORDER BY" in the string because the class will apply them itself.

33.6.7 Compile and Run

Compile and run the program. You will find the data returned in the record set is appropriately sorted.

33.6.8 Add a WHERE Clause

You can filter the data in the record set by adding a WHERE clause, as discussed in Section 33.2.2. The **m_strFilter** member variable in the **CRecordSet** class facilitates this process. You simply specify the field names that you want to use for filtering.

To demonstrate the WHERE clause, modify the code as shown below:

```
void CDbView::OnLButtonUp(UINT nFlags, CPoint point)
{
    try
    {
        int x;
        CEmpSet set;
```

```
        set.m_strFilter = "(ZipCode = '27612')";
        set.m_strSort = "LastName ASC, FirstName ASC";
        set.Open();

        AfxMessageBox(set.GetSQL());
        while (!set.IsEOF())
        {
            AfxMessageBox(set.m_LastName + set.m_FirstName);
            set.MoveNext();
        }
    }
    catch(CDBException *theException)
    {
        AfxMessageBox(theException->m_strError);
    }

    CView::OnLButtonUp(nFlags, point);
}
```

The single line that sets the **m_strFilter** variable is all that's needed. You must set this variable after instantiating the class but before opening the record set. Do not include the word "WHERE" in the string because the class will apply the word itself.

You can make the string as long and complicated as you want, using ANDs and ORs to extend it.

33.6.9 Compile and Run

When you compile and run the code, you will find only those rows with a 27612 zip code appear in the output, and they will be sorted by last name and first name.

33.6.10 Parameterize the WHERE Clause

In many cases you will not know at compile time the values you want to use for the filter and sort strings. The **CRecordSet** class, therefore, allows you to *parameterize* these strings. To parameterize a record set, you have to modify both the H and CPP files generated by the ClassWizard.

In this example, we will parameterize the zip code field in the filter string. You can parameterize as many values as you like in both the filter and sort strings. Making the modifications to the code requires four steps.

33.6.10.1 Add a Parameter Member Start by adding a parameter member to the record set class. In EMPSET.H, add this variable to the bottom of the Field/Param Data section:

```
// Field/Param Data
    //{{AFX_FIELD(CEmpSet, CRecordset)
    long        m_EmpID;
    CString     m_LastName;
    CString     m_FirstName;
    CString     m_Address;
    CString     m_ZipCode;
    //}}AFX_FIELD
    CString m_ZipCodeParam;
```

This string variable will hold the value of the parameter and send it to the database server.

33.6.10.2   Set up and Initialize the Parameter Member The new member must be initialized. You must also set the **m_nParams** parameter in the **CRecordSet** class to let it know you are using parameter values. Add the following two lines of code to the constructor in EMPSET.CPP:

```
CEmpSet::CEmpSet(CDatabase* pdb)
    : CRecordset(pdb)
{
    //{{AFX_FIELD_INIT(CEmpSet)
    m_EmpID = 0;
    m_LastName = _T("");
    m_FirstName = _T("");
    m_Address = _T("");
    m_ZipCode = _T("");
    m_nFields = 5;
    //}}AFX_FIELD_INIT
    m_nParams = 1;
    m_ZipCodeParam = "";
}
```

33.6.10.3   Modify DoFieldExchange You must then modify the **DoFieldExchange** function so that: 1) it knows to pass parameters, and 2) it knows how to pass the parameters. Modify the function by adding two lines as shown below:

```
void CEmpSet::DoFieldExchange(CFieldExchange* pFX)
{
    //{{AFX_FIELD_MAP(CEmpSet)
    pFX->SetFieldType(CFieldExchange::outputColumn);
    RFX_Long(pFX, "EmpID", m_EmpID);
    RFX_Text(pFX, "LastName", m_LastName);
    RFX_Text(pFX, "FirstName", m_FirstName);
    RFX_Text(pFX, "Address", m_Address);
    RFX_Text(pFX, "ZipCode", m_ZipCode);
    //}}AFX_FIELD_MAP
    pFX->SetFieldType(CFieldExchange::param);
    RFX_Text(pFX, "ZipCodeParam", m_ZipCodeParam);
}
```

The second parameter passed to **RFX_Text** is immaterial and can contain any string you like.

If you were passing multiple parameters, you would simply add more RFX statements following the **RFX_Text** statement (you need to call **SetFieldType** just once). MFC has ten different **RFX_** functions to handle all SQL data types—see the MFC documentation for more information.

33.6.10.4   Apply the Parameters To apply the parameters, you simply set the parameter member variables before calling **Open** or **Requery**. In DBVIEW.CPP, make the changes shown below:

```
void CDbView::OnLButtonUp(UINT nFlags, CPoint point)
{
    try
    {
        int x;
        CEmpSet set;
        set.m_strFilter = "(ZipCode = ?)";
        set.m_strSort = "LastName ASC, FirstName ASC";

        set.m_ZipCodeParam = "27587";
        set.Open();

        AfxMessageBox(set.GetSQL());
        while (!set.IsEOF())
        {
            AfxMessageBox(set.m_LastName + set.m_FirstName);
            set.MoveNext();
        }

        set.m_ZipCodeParam = "27612";
        set.Requery();

        AfxMessageBox("Requerying");
        for (x=0; x<set.GetRecordCount(); x++)
        {
            AfxMessageBox(set.m_LastName + set.m_FirstName);
            set.MoveNext();
        }
    }
    catch(CDBException *theException)
    {
        AfxMessageBox(theException->m_strError);
    }

    CView::OnLButtonUp(nFlags, point);
}
```

Note the use of the question mark in setting **m_strFilter**. This question mark indicates where to substitute the parameter. The code then sets the parameter member variable in the record set and calls **Open**. The **CRecordSet** class automatically passes the parameter to the database server at the same time it sends the SQL statement. You can later respecify the parameter and call **Requery** to query the database with the new parameter value. This is significantly more efficient than calling **Open** again.

You can fill the **m_ZipCodeParam** member with any string. Typically, you would fill it with a string supplied by the use in a dialog box or chosen by the user from a list.

Note that if you want to use multiple parameters, you follow the same steps: 1) add a member variable, 2) initialize the member variable and set the number of parameters, 3) add an **RFX_** function to transfer the parameter to the database, and 4) use a question mark in the filter string, set the parameter member, and query the database. When you use multiple question marks in a filter string, the question marks are filled from the parameter member variables in the order specified. That is, the first

601

question mark is filled with the first **RFX_** function's value, the second with the second, and so on.

33.6.11 Compile and Run

When you compile and run the program, you will find that the SQL query string sent to the database server contains the question mark. Behind the scenes the **CRecordSet** sends the query string first, and then passes the parameter(s). The database fills the question marks with the parameters in the order received.

You will find the code displays all rows that contain the 27587 zip code, followed by all records containing the 27612 zip code.

33.7 Using the CRecordView Class

As you can see from the examples in the previous section, the **CRecordset** class is designed to make the retrieval of data from a database server simple. The class issues a SELECT statement to the database and then makes it easy to retrieve all the records that result from the query. You can easily imagine creating applications that contain a number of record sets for a complicated database.

In the previous examples, we displayed all the data from the record set in a message box. This made the code simple, compact, and easy to understand. It would have been nearly as easy to walk through all the records resulting from a query and add them to a list. In many cases, however, what you would like to do is take the values from the record set and display them in a form, with each field in its own edit field so the user can view and modify the individual fields easily. Because this display technique is so common and so desirable, MFC contains a class called **CRecordView**. The AppWizard and ClassWizard can work with record views and record sets to quickly generate forms for the application.

The easiest way to understand a record view is to create one.

33.7.1 Create an Application Framework

Create a new SDI framework with the AppWizard. Give the new project the name "db." Select the location for the new application directory and rename the directory if necessary.

As you go through the AppWizard option screens, select the following options:
- Choose the **Single-Document** option.
- *In the database support screen, choose **A Database View, Without File Support.*** You will then need to click the **Data Source** button and choose a data source and a table. Use the sample data source we created earlier in this chapter, and choose the EMPLOYEE table.
- Choose **None** for OLE support.
- Enable or disable any application features as you see fit.

Make sure you choose the correct database option and data source as specified in Step 2. When you get done you should see a New Project Information dialog. This dialog summarizes the choices you made in the customization screens. See Appendix B.6 for details.

33.7.2 Compile and Run

Compile and run the new application. You will find, first of all, that the **File** menu contains nothing but an **Exit** option. This is because we specified *A Database View, Without File Support* when creating the application. This selection implies that you want to create an application that automatically opens the specified data source and uses it for all the application's data needs. Therefore, the **Open**, **New**, **Save**, and **Save As** options in the **File** menu are unnecessary.

There is also a complete new menu called **Record** that gives you the ability to move to the first, last, next, and previous records in the record set. These options don't really seem to do anything right now. However, if you try them out you will notice you can choose the **Next** option a limited number of times and that limit happens to correspond to the number of records you have in your sample **Employee** table. Try out the options in the **Record** menu.

You will also notice that the body of your SDI window is occupied with the standard TODO label. Our main goal with this application will be to fill the window with appropriate controls.

Take some time to look around at the files the AppWizard created. The DBSET files look exactly as they did in the previous section. This class simply provides an interface to the **Employee** table in the database. The DBVIEW files look remarkably like the files for a normal form view. For example, there is a dialog in the resource file for the form view, and this dialog's ID appears in DBVIEW.H and is referenced in DBVIEW.CPP. The only real differences between the view class here and a normal form view are:

1. DBVIEW.CPP knows about the record set class via an assignment that occurs in **OnInitialUpdate**.
2. DBVIEW.CPP does not contain a **Serialize** function. This difference occurs because we did not request file support when we created the application. If we had, the **File** menu would contain appropriate options and the **Serialize** function would be included here.

All other files look about the same as they normally do.

33.7.3 Modify the Dialog Template

To use a **CRecordView**-derived class, you create a set of edit controls to display the data in the different fields, and then you attach those fields through DDX to the different fields in the record set. The ClassWizard makes this easy.

Start by opening the resource file for the application and looking at the IDD_DB_FORM dialog. Remove the TODO static control already in the dialog and add to the dialog five static labels and five edit controls as shown in Figure 33.9. Double-click on each edit control and rename it with a meaningful ID. For example, rename the employee ID edit control with IDC_EMPID. Rename the edit control for the last name with IDC_LASTNAME. Do this for all five controls. Save and close the modified dialog.

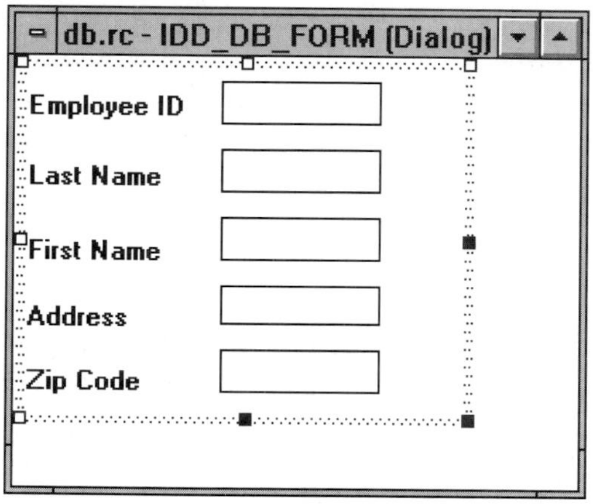

Figure 33.9
The form for the application

33.7.4 Connect the Controls

Open the ClassWizard and make sure the **Member Variables** tab is selected. Select the **CDbView** class. If you click on the IDC_ADDRESS control and click the **Add Variable** button, you will see the Add Member Variable dialog. Click on the arrow next to the **Member Variable Name** combo box and you will see a list that contains all the member variables *in the record set class*. This is unusual, but extremely useful. What we will do is wire the edit control for the address *directly to the RFX member variable in the record set class*. Select the proper variable from the record set class and press **OK**. Do this for all five controls in the view. Then adjust the DDX limits as appropriate.

The mechanism that allows the ClassWizard to hook the controls in the view class to variables in the record set class can be found in the **Class Info** section of the ClassWizard. If you look in that section you will find you have the ability to set a *foreign class* and a *foreign variable* in that class. The foreign class capability is designed specifically to allow you to form links between dialog or form classes and **CRecordset** classes.

33.7.5 Compile and Run

Compile and run the application. You will find the program comes up and displays the first record of the record set in the form. You can move forward and backward between the records in the record set using the menu options in the **Record** menu. You can also modify the fields in a record. When you move to another record, the database will be updated with the new information.

This is a remarkable amount of functionality, especially when you consider that you have written zero lines of code. All of this is accomplished by leveraging off the standard capabilities built into the **CRecordset** and **CRecordView** classes. Any record set that you can create (see Section 33.7) can be viewed in a record view.

33.7.6 Noticing a Problem

Try the following experiment. Open two copies of the application. Modify one of the records in the first copy. Save the changes by moving to the next record and moving back. You will find that the record has changed correctly.

Now scroll through all the records in the second copy of the application. You will find that the changes do not appear in that copy. If you start a third copy, it will contain the changes but the second one will never pick up the changes.

This problem occurs because the record set class, by default, is in *snapshot* mode. That is, the record set class sends a SELECT statement to the database, and the database responds to the statement and forms a result set. Then that result set is fed one record at a time to the record set as it requests them. However, the result set is separate from the actual data in the tables. It is possible to update the snapshot by calling the **Requery** function, but the code as it stands now does not contain that call.

The **CRecordset** class has another capability, called a *dynaset* that solves some of these problems. In a dynaset, the database correctly updates records each time it sends them to the record set. You determine whether the record set uses snapshots or dynasets in the call to the record set's **Open** function.

33.8 Adding and Deleting Records

As you saw in the previous section, the record set class automatically updates records in the database when you change field values and move to a different record. The **CRecordset** class also contains functions that allow you to add and delete records. You can experiment with these functions by taking the following steps.

33.8.1 Add Menu Options

Start with the application that you created in Section 33.7. Open the resource file and add four options to the bottom of the **Record** menu: **Requery**, **Add**, **Update**, and **Delete**. Save and close the file.

33.8.2 Create the Code for Requery

Using the ClassWizard, create a COMMAND handler for the **Requery** menu option in the **CDbView** class (if the menu IDs do not appear in the object ID list for the **CDbView** class, try opening the menu resource and, with it open as the topmost window in Visual C++, open the ClassWizard). Use the following code in the function:

```
void CDbView::OnRecordRequery()
{
    m_pSet->Requery();
```

```
        UpdateData(FALSE);
    }
```

When you compile and run the program you will find that you can requery the database whenever you like to reform the record set's snapshot. You can add to this function exception handling code if you like.

33.8.3 Create the Code for Delete

You can also delete records from the database. Using the ClassWizard, create a COMMAND handler for the **Delete** menu option in the **CDbView** class (if the menu IDs do not appear in the object ID list for the **CDbView** class, try opening the menu resource and, with it open as the topmost window in Visual C++, open the ClassWizard). Use the following code in the function:

```
void CDbView::OnRecordDelete()
{
    m_pSet->Delete();
    m_pSet->MoveNext();
    // Check for empty file
    if (m_pSet->IsBOF())
    {
        m_pSet->SetFieldNull(NULL);
        m_pSet->Requery();
    }
    // Check for end of file
    else if (m_pSet->IsEOF())
        m_pSet->MoveLast();
    UpdateData(FALSE);
}
```

This function deletes the current record. Then it moves to the next one in the record set. At that point the code checks for two conditions: 1) an empty file, and 2) end of file. In either case it responds appropriately.

33.8.4 Create the Code for Adding Records

Because there are so many different ways that a programmer might want to implement adding records to a database, it is suggested that you read through a variety of documentation entries (see Section 33.10 for a list) and also examine the Enroll tutorial provided by Microsoft in books on-line for some ideas. The basic principle, however, is that you need to call **AddNew** in the **CRecordset** class to start the add process and then call **Update** in the **CRecordset** class to actually add the record. We have previously created two menu options to handle these two activities. Other approaches might include calling **Update** when the user moves off the record (this is the approach described in the Enroll tutorial) or creating a separate Add dialog.

For the example here, the following minimalist code implements the **Update** and **Add** menu options. Wire in these two functions with the ClassWizard.

```
void CDbView::OnRecordUpdate()
{
    UpdateData();
    m_pSet->Update();
    m_pSet->Requery(); // not necessary in all databases
    UpdateData(FALSE);
}

void CDbView::OnRecordAdd()
{
    m_pSet->AddNew();
    UpdateData(FALSE);
}
```

To use this code, you should choose the **Add** menu option, enter your new values, and then choose the **Update** menu option. You will want to add exception-handling code to see specific error messages generated by the database.

33.9 Conclusion

SQL is its own science, and the **CRecordSet** and **CDatabase** classes are quite intricate as well. Therefore, the goal of this chapter has not been to cover these topics exhaustively, but instead to help you get started in creating your own understanding of these topics and their use in MFC applications.

The following pages in the advanced section of the MFC documentation may also prove useful in further understanding databases and the database classes in MFC: SQL, ODBC, Recordset, Database, Record, Record Field Exchange, Record View, Data Source and Data Object. Use the **Search** button to find these pages. See also the documentation on the **CRecordSet**, **CDatabase** and **CRecordView** classes, as well as the ODBCAPI.HLP documentation. Alternative examples for the **CRecordSet** and **CRecordView** classes are available in the Enroll example in the Visual C++ tutorials, available in books on-line. The MFC Encyclopedia in books on-line contains related articles as well. You may also want to pick up a book on SQL databases to increase your understanding of the SQL language.

OLE

OLE is one of the most interesting and intricate subsystems inside Windows. OLE is so intricate, in fact, that Microsoft plans to let it completely overwhelm and dominate Windows, eventually becoming the core technology inside forthcoming object-oriented operating systems. At present OLE has developed to the point of being a complete inter-application communication mechanism, and you can use this mechanism in your own applications to provide a wide variety of extremely interesting features and capabilities.

Because of the complexity of OLE, it would be impossible in any one chapter, or in fact in any book, to completely explain everything OLE can do. However, the MFC classes and different tools provided by Visual C++ go a long way toward making OLE usable, provided you understand the basic concepts that drive the whole system. Therefore, the goal of this chapter is to explain in a general way what OLE is and what it can do for you as a programmer. This chapter will also show you how to use the AppWizard and the new ControlWizard to create OLE servers, OLE containers, and OLE controls. Once you have a good grounding in these basic concepts, you can use the prodigious documentation provided by Microsoft to expand your knowledge in almost any way you desire.

34.1 Understanding OLE

To get started, here is a simple definition of OLE: *Object Linking and Embedding, also know as OLE, is a facility that allows separate Windows applications to communicate with one another. It is a standard protocol that lets one application request the services of another and also allows for specific forms of communication to occur between any two applications.*

OLE, at a conceptual level, is truly that simple. You can describe it in just a sentence or two. One program, through OLE, can communicate with another program. This simple definition is extremely important, because if you can keep this basic concept in mind at all times it is easy to keep the system in perspective. This simple definition also immediately generates two important questions: "Why do programs need to communicate with each other?" and "What are the implications of the communication system once it exists?" By answering these two questions you can gain a clear understanding of why OLE exists and what it can accomplish.

The first question is best answered by example. Let's say you wanted to design and create your own simple GUI environment. For the moment imagine that Windows, the Macintosh, X, and other windowing environments do not exist, and you want to create the first windowed operating system that the world has ever seen. You would probably want to start with something simple. The initial system might allow a programmer to create a window, draw shapes or text into that window, and send output to a printer. With such a system, it is fairly easy to create such things as word processors and drawing programs. Therefore, your first product release might consist of the GUI operating system, a word processor, and some sort of drawing program. This is, by the way, exactly the sort of configuration the world saw when the Macintosh made its appearance in 1984.

Once you release this new windowed operating system and its two applications and people start using it, one thing that your users will immediately demand is a way to put pictures into their word processor documents in a seamless way. For example, a user might want to create a figure for a technical paper and incorporate it into the paper itself. There are several ways you might create this capability, one of those being a temporary storage space in memory that applications use to pass data to one another: a clipboard. A clipboard is nothing more than an area of memory managed by the operating system to facilitate a form of inter-application communication. The concept of the clipboard gets a little murky, however, when applications want to share data that is fundamentally unexpected. For example, a "word processor" is meant to process words, not pictures. So when a word processor receives pictures on the clipboard it doesn't know what to do with them and therefore has a problem.

Clearly the easiest way to solve this problem is to brute-force a solution. You might define one or more specific formats for clipboard data, and then decree that each program must be able to accept those formats and render them. For example, you might allow programs to copy either text or bitmaps (and nothing else) to the clipboard. Then you can give each application the code it needs to handle and display and print both text and bitmap insertions. This simplification makes it easy to insert drawings into word processor documents.

This approach works well initially, but it eventually runs into problems for two reasons. First, as the number of applications proliferate, the two formats allowed probably are insufficient. For example, spreadsheet data works well neither as text nor as a bitmap. It may be too grainy, for instance, when rendered as a bitmap. When rendered as text it loses its fundamental spreadsheetness—all the nice boxes that divide the cells and line things up disappear. Second, the document that holds the pasted spreadsheet data cannot use that data in any way. All it has is a bitmap and there is no way to use it for anything other than rendering an image. Or all it has is some text and none of the formulas get transmitted.

One alternative is to allow the number of clipboard formats that each application supports to proliferate with the applications. For example, you could add spreadsheet-format data to your list of clipboard formats that all applications must support. Unfortunately, this approach will quickly become cumbersome because the number of applications in a GUI environment grows very quickly. There is no way that all the applications can keep up with the growing number of other applications and the clipboard formats they demand.

As the developer of this GUI environment, you might therefore scratch your head and begin to look for a better solution to the problem. A second, much more general approach is to allow applications to communicate at a deeper level and to interact with each other in more meaningful ways. For example, say that each application on a system is responsible for rendering its own data regardless of which application is actually holding the data. If the user has pasted spreadsheet data into a word processing document, and the word processing document needs to print the spreadsheet data, the word processor would somehow send a message to the spreadsheet application to request assistance. The spreadsheet application would start up, properly format and print the spreadsheet data for the word processor, and then terminate. This sort of system could be complicated, but it would allow applications to proliferate without putting an undue strain on developers. As long as each application is coded so it can communicate with the others about the clipboard data it is holding, the problem of proliferating clipboard data formats is solved.

This is exactly the sort of problem faced by GUI designers in their operating systems. And this is exactly the sort of evolutionary process clipboard data handling has gone through. The ultimate solution to the clipboard data problem is to let each application be in charge of changing and rendering its data no matter where that data actually lives. You can see from this example that any two applications need to be able to communicate and cooperate with one another at a fairly intimate level for this sort of clipboard formatting to occur properly.

Why limit inter-application communication strictly to clipboard data, however? If this communication capability is generalized just a bit, you suddenly end up with something much more powerful. What you end up with is a general system of communication that allows cooperation between applications for a variety of different tasks. In such a general communication environment, applications can request all sorts of services from one another. For example, a word processor can ask a spreadsheet to allow the user to edit a spreadsheet object. A spreadsheet can automatically update spreadsheet objects in other applications whenever it needs to. A spreadsheet can receive a data feed from another application connected to a modem that is querying a remote database. Once a general inter-application communication system exists, there is almost no end to the ways creative programmers can use the system.

The implications of this simple capability are tremendous. By giving applications a way to communicate, OLE ends up implementing the foundation of an object oriented-operating system. Each application acts as a stand-alone object, and all applications can communicate with one another. OLE's facilities are general enough to allow this sort of interaction. One of the things you will discover later in this chapter is that OLE will form the base of Microsoft's upcoming object-oriented operating system, currently known as "Cairo."

The ability to allow different applications to generally communicate with one another may not initially seem to be very important. For example, any Windows programmer using the Win32 API can already easily create two applications and let them communicate through shared memory, named pipes, mailslots, and any variety of other standardized inter-process communication mechanisms. Windows has also supported fairly general communications mechanisms such as DDE for some time. C++ and Smalltalk programmers constantly create objects and send messages between them. All these types of communication are limiting, however, because they expect that the application writer will specify the communication protocol and know how to use it. The beauty of a *general* system like OLE is that *any* two applications, regardless of the manufacturer, can communicate about a wide variety of topics. In the absence of a general scheme, developers come up with all sorts of proprietary schemes, and this diversity discourages interoperability. With one standardized scheme like OLE in place, any application can communicate with any other.

To implement a completely general communication system, OLE offers capabilities not normally found in other object-oriented systems. When you create an object oriented program in C++, for example, you have an important advantage that is not available to OLE: You know what each of the classes in your program does and therefore you can call specific functions in your different classes. This makes communication easy, because you inherently know which functions each class supports. But what if two applications, developed totally independently of one another, need to communicate? OLE is unique in this regard. In an OLE system, the different applications generally know *nothing* about one another. In fact, they cannot even be sure that other applications exist on the system. Yet they can communicate through OLE.

For OLE to allow independent applications to communicate, OLE applications must do something that is unusual in object-oriented programming: They must ask one another what can be done. OLE defines a set of pre-defined *interfaces* that any application may or may not choose to implement. These interfaces are simply standardized collections of functions that applications can call to communicate with one another. For example, if an application supports *visual editing* (see the next section for an example of this capability), it must implement the interfaces (the specific collections of functions) that other applications will use to access the visual editing features. Interfaces act as the communication channels between different applications, and each interface handles a specific type of communication. OLE originally defined 43 standard interfaces, each made up of a set of specific functions. These standard interfaces together handle most normal forms of communication between applications. Programmers can also define new interfaces of their own to handle special situations, so the number of interfaces grows constantly. Any application can choose to implement any number of known interfaces, depending on what the application does and how it wants to be able to interact with other applications.

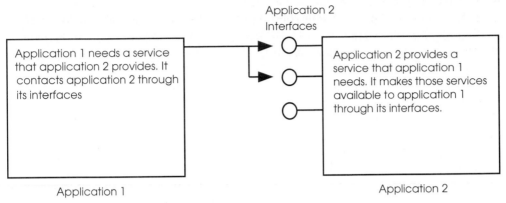

Application 2
Interfaces

Application 1 needs a service that application 2 provides. It contacts application 2 through its interfaces

Application 2 provides a service that application 1 needs. It makes those services available to application 1 through its interfaces.

Application 1

Application 2

Figure 34.1
Communication between two applications

Because the collections of functions in an interface are predeclared and publicly documented, any application can make use of an interface with the knowledge that it will work in a specific way. This expectation allows applications to communicate safely with one another.

Applications may also support, through a set of standard interfaces, a feature called *automation*. Using automation, an application can export an arbitrary set of operations that allow external manipulation of the application. These operations can be invoked by other applications, generally through some form of programming language or macro facility. A programmer can write code that calls the automated operations directly. The automation facility makes it possible for programmers to treat applications as reusable objects that become integral parts of other applications.

You can see from this discussion that OLE allows two forms of inter-application communication: 1) Independent applications can communicate with one another through standardized OLE interfaces, and 2) programmers can access the capabilities of certain applications through automation, if those applications support the automation interfaces. It is important to understand and accept OLE at this high level of generality. As you can see from the description given above, OLE is simply a communication mechanism used between separate applications.

Interfaces are, by design, standardized. The functions in any given interface have predefined and publicly declared names and parameter lists. Therefore, the code inside of a given interface will generally be similar across applications. The goal of the MFC classes that support OLE is to encapsulate this commonality in classes so you do not have to write the code yourself. These classes make standard OLE interactions extremely easy to implement because the bulk of the code is already written.

34.2 An Example

Because it is a general communication system, and because it has also been tuned to handle certain specific communication tasks, OLE expresses itself in a number of different ways in a Windows system. One way to understand OLE is to look at one of its most obvious capabilities and see how that capability is implemented.

Let's take the very common operation of pasting information from one application to another using the clipboard. For example, you might wish to paste something into a document that you have created using Microsoft Word version 6.0. This is a "traditional" use of OLE. Word 6.0 allows you to paste at least three different types of objects into a document:

1. Raw text—When Word sees raw text on the clipboard, it simply pastes it into the document at the current insertion point. It will apply some default formatting to the text.
2. Formatted text from Word and other word-processing applications—When Word sees specifically formatted text on the clipboard, it performs any translations required and then pastes the formatted text into the document.
3. OLE objects—When Word sees an OLE object on the clipboard, it pastes the object into the document. It also keeps track of the originating application, so that it can later request the services of that application to deal with the foreign data.

It is the third type of paste operation that is of interest, not because of the paste itself, but because of what can happen later. If the object is pasted properly, and if the object originated in an OLE application, then the user can double-click on the object to edit it within Word itself.

You can, and should, try this out yourself if you have OLE-aware versions of Word (versions 6.0 and above are OLE aware) and Excel (versions 5.0 and above are OLE aware) on your system. Open Word and type several lines of text into a new document. Then take the following steps:

1. Open Excel and enter four or five numbers in a column.
2. Select the numbers by dragging over them and copy them from Excel onto the clipboard.
3. In Word, choose the **Paste Special** option in the **Edit** menu and indicate that you want to paste the object in a native Excel format, as shown in Figure 34.2. Click the OK button on the dialog.
4. Once the paste operation is complete, double-click on the spreadsheet object in the Word document. What you will see is interesting: the Microsoft Excel application will take over Word's tool bar and menu, and you will also see scroll bars and a frame surround the spreadsheet data in the Word document, as shown in Figure 34.3. This capability is called *visual editing*. Excel has, in a way, momentarily taken over Word. You can use Excel from within Word to edit the

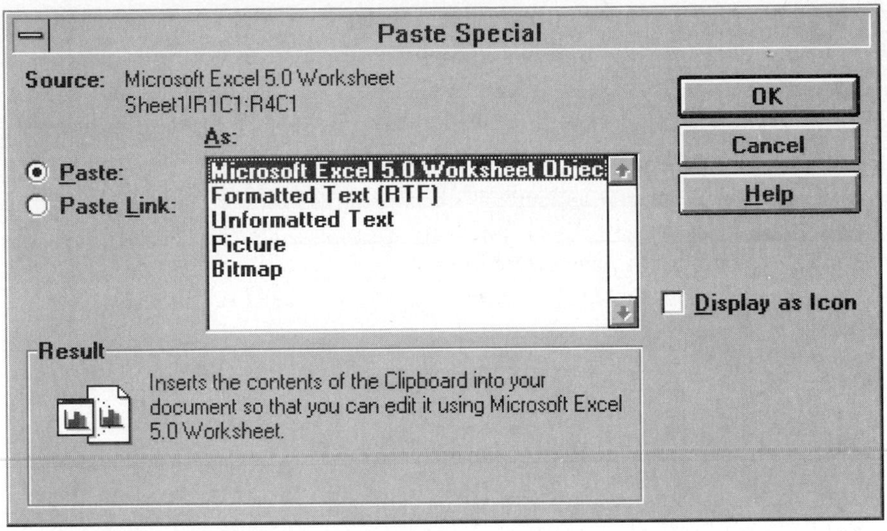

Figure 34.2
The Paste Special dialog

spreadsheet object directly. Single-click anywhere else in the document and Excel will disappear.

When you double-click on the spreadsheet object to indicate you want to edit it, OLE goes into action. The Word application and the Excel application begin to communicate with one another using a standard OLE conversation. Here is what happens in this particular conversation:

1. Word can be thought of as a *container* for the OLE object it holds. The user double-click on the object that Word holds. Word doesn't really care where the object originated, but it does know that the object came from an OLE-aware application. Word, therefore, requests that OLE start the application that created the object on which you double-clicked.

2. The OLE-aware application that created the object starts. In this case that application is Excel. Excel doesn't really care who started it. It simply knows, by the way that it was started, that a user wants to edit one of its objects currently residing in another application. It therefore needs to determine what level of editing the container is willing to support.

3. To figure out what the container can do, Excel queries Word through a standard OLE interface and asks, "Do you know how to do visual editing?" If the container answers negatively, Excel will pull in the data, open itself on the screen as a stand-alone application, change its **File** menu to include an **Update** option, and let the user edit the data. When the user chooses the **Update** option, Excel will write the data back to the document and quit.

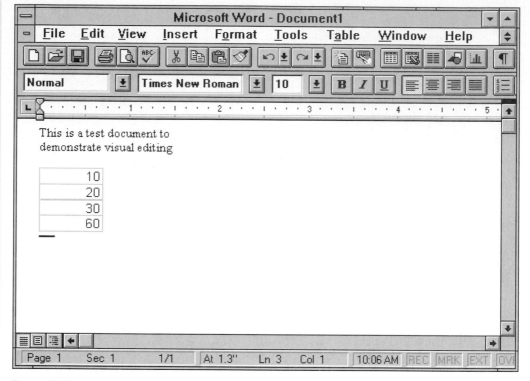

Figure 34.3
Visual editing in OLE. A Word document contains a piece of an Excel spreadsheet

4. If the container allows visual editing, Excel and the container enter into an OLE conversation to negotiate how the visual editing will take place. Word and Excel communicate with one another: They talk back and forth through standard interfaces to give Excel the space it needs to display its scroll bars, tool bar, status line, menus, and so on. Once the user is done editing the object, Excel saves the modified data in the document and terminates.

The entire conversation between Excel and Word occurs through standard interfaces pre-defined by OLE to perform this common conversation. Coded into each application is the appropriate response to each question that applications can ask of a given interface. The questions are asked, or services requested, by calling functions known to exist in the defined interfaces.

Your job as a programmer when you create an OLE application is to decide which capabilities your application needs to support and to then implement those interfaces so they correctly interact with other applications. You can do this directly yourself on an interface-by-interface basis using C or C++. However, because much of the behavior of any interface is fairly standard, the MFC class hierarchy contains classes that implement a great deal of the standard boilerplate code needed by OLE. These classes can make your programming task much easier.

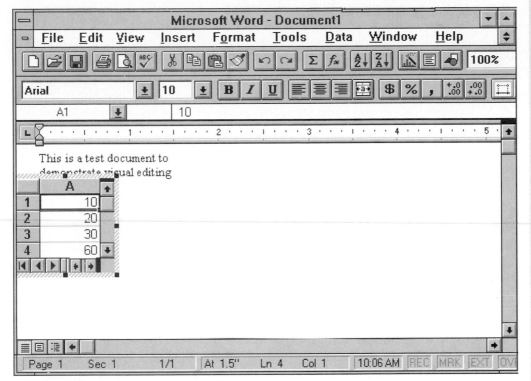

Figure 34.4
Visual editing in OLE. The user has double-clicked on the spreadsheet portion of the Word document and is now editing it with Excel. Note how Excel has taken over the menu, the tool bars, and the area immediately surrounding the spreadsheet object

Either way you do it, through MFC or standard C++, your application ends up possessing the OLE interfaces that other applications need to communicate with it. Once these interfaces are in place, your application becomes a full participant in the universe of OLE applications.

34.3 OLE as a Vision of the Future

OLE sets the stage for a new way of designing and implementing software. Once an operating system has an easy and efficient way for applications to communicate with one another, it opens up the possibility of creating applications with replaceable parts. It also opens the possibility of creating applications that are really little more than combinations of other applications. For example, a word processor might use a spelling checker, a drawing program, a table editor, and an e-mail routing system that are all stand-alone applications attached to the word processor through OLE. All these OLE parts are replaceable, independent sub-assemblies completely separate from the word processor. This vision of the future is called *Component Software*.

Under this component model, each application is a stand-alone software object that contains a set of capabilities. The application makes those capabilities available to other applications through its OLE interfaces. Other applications that need certain specific capabilities then tend to obtain them from the pool of applications on the current system, rather than implementing them internally. This tendency creates an environment in which individual components tend to be fairly small and single-minded. Programmers and users can then combine different sets of components to create specific applications.

The move toward component software has a number of important advantages:

1. Given a single, standard communication mechanism, any application can communicate with any other. This saves the cost of developing and supporting a number of proprietary communication systems and protocols.

2. Application designers and implementers can focus on the "meat" of their applications rather than having to waste time on peripheral issues like spelling checkers, address lists, and so on. Instead of implementing these extraneous pieces, the application developer simply connects to existing components that perform these tasks through OLE.

3. Users are no longer bound to specific vendors. They can mix and match components based on merit. Because all components communicate through the same standardized mechanism, they are interchangeable.

4. Small and innovative software companies can enter the software marketplace with sanely-sized products. Vendors can implement individual components that do just one thing. They are no longer required to invent huge, monolithic applications. At the same time, a developer can combine many existing pieces from other vendors to create large applications in much less time.

In the future, OLE will have two important effects. First, the mechanism will be extended to allow object connections over networks, so that distributed computing can be integrated into the workplace in a standard and simple way. Second, the entire Windows operating system will rapidly migrate toward OLE, so eventually all of the features of the operating system itself will be made available through their own stand-alone software objects. Instead of a programmer accessing the file system through an API, the programmer will access it in a standard way through an OLE interface. The operating system will itself become a set of components that the user extends by purchasing other components from a variety of software vendors.

34.4 Standard OLE Features

Although OLE is a general intercommunication system, it is used in several specific and stylized ways to accomplish common intercommunication tasks. It is these common tasks that the MFC classes support. Here is a list of the application features you commonly see in OLE applications.

1. Embedding—An application can embed an OLE object into one of its documents. The object comes in via the clipboard or through an Insert Object menu option. Under embedding, the application holds a complete copy of the object

in its document. The user can double-click on the object to edit it in its proper server.

2. Visual Editing—If an application supports visual editing, and if an embedded OLE object inside that application comes from an application that also supports visual editing, the user can edit the object in-place, as described in the example in the previous section.

3. Linking—An application can form a link to data held in a file on disk, as long as the file is owned by an OLE application. Under linking, the application simply stores a pointer to the data in the second file, and many documents can point to the same data. If the linked file changes, all documents linked to the file see the changes.

4. Drag-and-Drop—Rather than forcing the user to cut or copy information to the clipboard and then paste it in the destination document, OLE applications can speed up the process by allowing the user to drag information from one application and drop it in another. This action is equivalent to embedding.

5. Automation—An application can, if it chooses, allow other applications to activate and use it through automation. For example, a Visual Basic programmer can use automation to start up Word, open a document, change the document, and then print it. All of this happens invisibly, so the programmer can use Word in an application as a report generator and document-printing engine.

Behind the scenes, there is one other technology new to OLE that makes a number of these other features possible. It is called *structured storage*. If you think about how OLE might efficiently implement several of its features, it becomes easy to understand where structured storage comes from and why it is important.

Imagine that a word-processing document contains an embedded spreadsheet object. The user of the document double-clicks on the spreadsheet object to edit it. It is important to keep in mind two things: 1) the embedded object can, potentially, be quite large, and 2) when the user changes the object, the spreadsheet is going to want to save the modifications and the embedded object may therefore change in size. So how does the spreadsheet get the data, and how does it return the changes?

One way to implement OLE would be for the word processor to transmit the data to the spreadsheet and then accept the changes and write them back. To do that, however, the word processor would have to read the object off disk and into memory. Then it would have to transmit a copy of the data to the spreadsheet object. If the embedded object is large, the two copies of the data take up too much memory space, and the creation and transmission of the copy takes too much time.

Another way to implement OLE is to make it possible for the spreadsheet to manipulate the object directly inside the word-processing document's file. The word processor would tell the spreadsheet where the data is. The spreadsheet would load it and manipulate it independently of the word processor. However, this is rather risky in a conventional file because the spreadsheet may need to grow the object larger and there would be no room in the file to allow that.

One solution to this problem would be to store all embedded OLE objects in separate files outside the word processor file. Then the spreadsheet could manipulate a file that contains just the embedded object. This approach would solve a lot of problems, but has the disadvantage that a single document now consists of multiple physical files.

Structured storage, at least at a high level, can be thought of as a system that allows you to place multiple files inside a single file. The structured storage model lets you create what appears to be a hierarchical file structure inside a single file. Structured storage manages this entire abstraction for you and makes it possible for you to nearly forget that it is happening, especially when using the MFC classes.

Another feature that makes OLE possible is an external table that holds all the known OLE servers on each Windows machine. This table is used, for example, to populate the list you see when you select the **Insert New Object** menu option in any application that can embed OLE objects. This table gets updated each time you install a new server on your system or move a server's directory to another location on your hard disk. On any Windows machine, this table is known as the *registry*.

Any Windows NT programmer is familiar with the registry as a place to store system values for different applications as well as a variety of user information. This data is accessed with the REGEDT32 application. One of the subsections in the registry is called HKEY_CLASSES_ROOT. This subsection contains information about the OLE servers on the system. This particular subsection of the registry is also accessible through an application called REGEDIT.

If you run REGEDIT *with the /v option* from a command line on your machine, you will find that it displays two different kinds of information, as shown in Figures 34.5 and 34.6. In Figure 34.5, for example, you can see that Microsoft Equation 2 has been identified by name. The top part of the OLE registry is nothing but a list of the different servers identified by name. Underneath the name is additional information about the particular server, including the *class ID* of the server and the path to the server's executable. The system uses this part of the registry whenever it needs to create a list of all available servers for the user.

When the user picks an object server, for example, from a dialog that appears in response to an **Insert New Object** menu option, the dialog returns the *class ID* of the server. The word *class* in the name again demonstrates the object-oriented nature of OLE. Each object server known to the system is said to produce objects of a specific class. This is identical to the terminology used to talk about instantiation in any object-oriented language. The ID portion of the name signifies that different available severs have unique identifiers that OLE uses when specifying servers.

The identifiers used for OLE servers are called *UUIDs*, or Universally Unique Identifiers. UUIDs will be familiar to you if you have ever worked with Remote Procedure Calls (RPCs) in the Win32 API. A UUID is a 128-bit value represented as a hex number containing 32 digits. For example, the universally unique identifier for Microsoft Equation version 2.0 is:

00021700-0000-0000-C000-000000000046

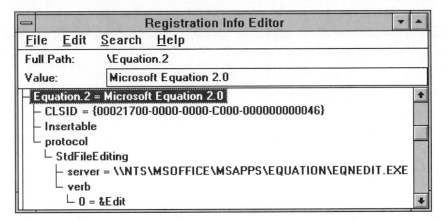

Figure 34.5
The first registry entry for Microsoft Equation 2

Every single Windows machine on the entire planet, now and until the end of time, will use that specific string to represent Microsoft Equation 2.

Each OLE server on the planet needs to have its own unique ID. When creating a server, you (or the AppWizard) can generate a UUID using a utility named UUID-GEN. This utility uses your machine's name, the time, and the date as input to a random number generator. The generator creates a value that has an extremely high probability of being completely and universally unique. After all, what is the probability of someone else on the planet generating a UUID at exactly the same millisecond on the same day using the same machine name you used? Pretty slim.

Given a class ID, also known as a CLSID, you can uniquely identify an OLE server. Therefore, if you pass a class ID to the OLE DLL and ask it to create an object of that type, the DLL can do so provided that your machine has a copy of that server available. OLE.DLL looks into the lower part of the registry to look up the name and the executable path of the server associated with the ID. Figure 34.6 shows that, in the lower part of the registry, all of the servers on the machine are listed a second time, but here they are sorted by UUIDs.

When you embed an OLE object in a document, the data for the object is stored along with the class ID of the application that generated the object. The application managing the document simply hands the class ID to the OLE server whenever it wants to request services on an OLE object.

34.5 An Introduction to OLE Containers

An OLE container is an application that can hold embedded or linked objects created by OLE servers. The AppWizard makes it extremely easy to create OLE containers that support linking, embedding, and visual editing of embedded objects. In this section you will learn how to create the AppWizard container framework and modify it to properly support multiple embedded objects. The following steps guide you through the process and explain it.

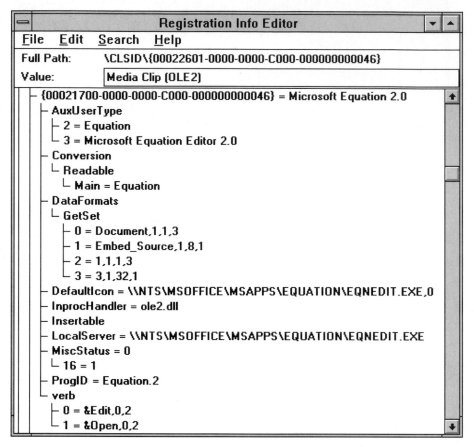

Figure 34.6
The second registry entry for Microsoft Equation 2

34.5.1 Create the Framework

Create a new SDI framework with the AppWizard. Give the new project the name "Samp."

As you go through the AppWizard option screens, select the following options:

- *Choose* **Container** *for OLE support. Select* **No Automation** *under automation support. See Appendix B.6.6 for details.*
- Enable or disable any application features as you see fit. *Be sure to enable printing.*

34.5.2 Compile and Run

Compile the application and run it. You will find that it looks like any other AppWizard application. The only real difference you will be able to see is in the **Edit** menu, which contains several new options that allow you to paste or directly insert OLE objects into the application.

This book is continuously updated. See http://www.iftech.com/mfc

Choose the **Insert New Object** option in the **Edit** menu. From the list, choose a server that you know to be OLE capable and able to handle visual editing. You will find that the server will create a new object in the upper left corner of the client area, and will allow you to visually edit that object. If you save the document and reopen it, you will find that it opens correctly.

There are a few problems, however. You cannot move the embedded object, so when you insert another it overlays the original. You cannot change the size of the object properly either. You cannot reselect the object to edit it a second time, and the only way to deselect it is to press escape. You can print the object, but its size will be minuscule on the sheet of paper. The application is obviously suffering from the same print scaling problem that was discussed in Chapter 15. The goal in the remainder of this section is to solve several of these problems.

34.5.3 Understanding the Differences

If you look at the source code that the AppWizard generated for this OLE container, you will find that the basic structure of the framework is very familiar. However, look though the code and note the following differences:

- SAMP.CPP—The application file looks almost exactly like it normally would, but at the beginning of the **InitInstance** function you should note the call to **AfxOleInit**, which starts the OLE DLL and initializes it.
- MAINFRM.CPP—No changes.
- SAMPDOC.CPP—This file is nearly identical to a normal document file, but instead of inheriting its behavior from **CDocument** it uses **COleDocument**. That simple change, however, makes monumental changes in the capabilities of the class. See the MFC documentation for a list of functions and a description. The fundamental difference in **COleDocument** is the fact that it can automatically maintain a list of OLE objects, which it can serialize to structured storage and also make available to its views. Also note the additional entries in the message map that call down to specific functions in **COleDocument**.
- SAMPVIEW.CPP—This file contains modifications that allow it to handle events on OLE objects, OLE insertions, and other OLE-related tasks. For example, the **OnDraw** function contains code that redraws OLE objects held by the document. A completely new section handles OLE client support.
- CNTRITEM.CPP—This file contains a class derived from the MFC **COleClientItem** class. If you look this class up in the MFC documentation, you will find that it is a large and extremely flexible class that encapsulates the code that handles the *client site* interfaces for OLE. Each OLE object in a document can be thought of as residing in a client site. The client site interfaces are the interfaces that an OLE server uses to talk with the client site for its object. For example, when an OLE server wants to know whether to use in-place activation when it opens, it can ask this question of the client site. Every OLE object embedded in the document is an instance of this class. Look

through the functions for the **COleClientItem** class in the MFC documentation to get an idea of what you can do with/to the OLE objects that a document contains. Look through the comments in CNTRITEM.CPP to get an idea of some of the behaviors you can modify or enable.

As you can see, much of the code used to implement this OLE container is the same as the code in any other AppWizard framework. The document class has been extended so that it can hold a list of OLE objects, but the management of those objects is largely hidden. The view class has been extended so it can display the OLE objects for the user, but the details are largely hidden here as well.

34.5.4 Thinking about PowerPoint

If you have ever used the slide editor in Microsoft PowerPoint, you may have noticed that a PowerPoint slide is nothing but a collection of pieces. There are text pieces, drawing pieces, chart pieces, and so on. Now that you know a little about OLE, you can begin to see that PowerPoint is little more than an OLE container combined with a drawing editor. Using the OLE container framework we have just built, you can create an application that contains a surprising percentage of PowerPoint's capabilities.

To create this application, there are three things we have to do:

1. Modify the framework so it can correctly place and size OLE objects in the view.
2. Adjust things so printing works correctly.
3. Add in drawing capabilities.

We will tackle these tasks in the order presented.

34.5.5 Adjusting Object Handling

There are three simple adjustments that need to be made to the existing framework in order for the OLE objects held in the container to seem like they are behaving properly:

1. The user should be able to move an object to a new position.
2. The user should be able to resize the objects.
3. The user should be able to double-click on an object to edit it, or click elsewhere on the screen to stop editing it.

To accomplish the first two tasks, you need to modify the class inside CNTRITEM.CPP. Each OLE item held in the document is an instance of this class. Therefore, when the document serializes the OLE objects it contains, it is serializing instances of this class. Also, when the view class draws the OLE objects, it is drawing instances of this class. Therefore, we need to modify this class so it can remember where each OLE object belongs and how big each OLE object is.

We need to add a member variable to the class that will hold the rectangle describing the size and position of the each object on the screen. This rectangle needs to be adjusted whenever the user moves or resizes the object. It also needs to be saved when the object is serialized, or made available to the view when the view wants to draw the object.

Open the CNTRITEM.H file and add a new member to the attribute section:

```
CRect m_SizeAndPositionRect;
```

If you do not like long variable names, consider calling it **r**. However, it will help make things clearer if you give this member an extremely descriptive name. Now in CNTRITEM.CPP find the constructor and modify it to initialize the new member:

```
CSampCntrItem::CSampCntrItem(CSampDoc* pContainer)
    : COleClientItem(pContainer)
{
    m_SizeAndPositionRect = CRect(10, 10, 200, 200);
}
```

The size and position chosen here are arbitrary.

Next, find the function named **OnChangeItemPosition**. This function is called any time the OLE object's position changes. We need to update **m_SizeAndPositionRect** whenever that happens, so modify the function as shown below:

```
BOOL CSampCntrItem::OnChangeItemPosition(const CRect& rectPos)
{
    ASSERT_VALID(this);

    if (!COleClientItem::OnChangeItemPosition(rectPos))
        return FALSE;

    m_SizeAndPositionRect = rectPos;
    GetDocument()->UpdateAllViews(NULL, 0, NULL);
    GetDocument()->SetModifiedFlag();

    return TRUE;
}
```

This code should make sense: When the position changes, you need to store the change, update any other views displaying the same information, and mark the document as dirty so the changes get written to a file.

Also modify the corresponding function, **OnGetItemPosition**, in the same file so it retrieves the rectangle properly:

```
void CSampCntrItem::OnGetItemPosition(CRect& rPosition)
{
    ASSERT_VALID(this);

    rPosition = m_SizeAndPositionRect;
}
```

Modify the **Serialize** function so that it saves the rectangle properly when the object is written to a file:

```
void CSampCntrItem::Serialize(CArchive& ar)
{
    ASSERT_VALID(this);

    COleClientItem::Serialize(ar);

    if (ar.IsStoring())
```

625

```
        ar << m_SizeAndPositionRect;
    else
        ar >> m_SizeAndPositionRect;
}
```

Finally, in the view class in SAMPVIEW.CPP, you need to adjust the **OnDraw** function so that it loops through all the OLE items held by the document and takes advantage of the size and position information held in each one, as shown below:

```
void CSampView::OnDraw(CDC* pDC)
{
    CSampDoc* pDoc = GetDocument();
    ASSERT_VALID(pDoc);

    POSITION pos = pDoc->GetStartPosition();
    while (pos != NULL)
    {
        CSampCntrItem *item =
            (CSampCntrItem*)pDoc->GetNextClientItem(pos);
        item->Draw(pDC, item->m_SizeAndPositionRect);
    }
}
```

You can see that this code asks the document for each of its objects, and then draws them at the proper position using the **Draw** function inside of **COleClientItem**.

If you compile and run now, and if you insert an OLE object, you will find that you can resize and move the object to a new position and the document will remember it.

Note that you can run this code under the debugger, but you need to be careful about how you exit the debugger. If, for example, you have a 16-bit OLE server open in your container and you select the **Stop Debugging** option, the server is going to have a very difficult time understanding what has happened. It is likely that it will corrupt your 16-bit subsystem, and you will need to reboot to fix it. Exit cleanly if at all possible using the container's **Exit** option.

Now we need to add two more bits of code so you can double-click on the object to select it again, and single-click elsewhere to deselect it. Use the ClassWizard to add a function for the WM_LBUTTONDBLCLK message to the view class. Inside that function, the code needs to scan through the list of all objects in the document and open one if the point clicked is inside the object's rectangle. Use the following code:

```
void CSampView::OnLButtonDblClk(UINT nFlags, CPoint point)
{
    CSampDoc* pDoc = GetDocument();
    m_pSelection = NULL;

    // determine selected item
    POSITION pos = pDoc->GetStartPosition();
    while (pos != NULL)
    {
        CSampCntrItem *item =
            (CSampCntrItem*)pDoc->GetNextClientItem(pos);
        if (item->m_SizeAndPositionRect.PtInRect(point))
        {
            m_pSelection = item;
```

```
            break;
        }
    }

    // activate the object
    if (m_pSelection != NULL)
    {
        if (GetKeyState(VK_CONTROL) < 0)
            m_pSelection->DoVerb(OLEIVERB_OPEN, this);
        else
            m_pSelection->DoVerb(OLEIVERB_PRIMARY, this);
    }

    CView::OnLButtonDblClk(nFlags, point);
}
```

The view class maintains a member named **m_pSelection** that keeps track of the currently selected item. Here the **OnLButtonDblClk** function scans through the list of OLE objects in the document until it determines that the point clicked is inside one of them. It then calls the OPEN or PRIMARY verb on that object to open it inside its proper OLE server.

Use the ClassWizard a second time to add a function for the WM_LBUTTONDOWN message to the view class. Inside that function, the code needs to determine if an OLE object is currently active and deactivate it if it is. Use the following code:

```
void CSampView::OnLButtonDown(UINT nFlags, CPoint point)
{
    COleClientItem* pActiveItem
        = GetDocument()->GetInPlaceActiveItem(this);
    if (pActiveItem != NULL)
        pActiveItem->Close();
    m_pSelection = NULL;

    CView::OnLButtonDown(nFlags, point);
}
```

The document class knows which object is active, and you deactivate it by closing it.

If you compile and run now, you will find that if you insert objects from OLE servers you can move and resize them. You can double-click on them to edit each one. Using the different OLE servers available on most machines, you can create fairly respectable screens. With a remarkably small amount of code we have been able to tap very nicely into the **COleDocument** and **COleClientItem** classes in a productive way.

What you cannot do with this particular implementation is handle OLE1 objects very well. You cannot, for example, move and resize them. The tutorial named "Contain" in books on-line goes into this topic in some detail and shows you how to handle it. It also discusses cursor tracking.

34.5.6 Handling Printing

When you try to print one of your views, you are going to find that there is a sizing problem caused by the mapping mode, as originally discussed in Chapter 15. By adding just a few lines of code you can solve this problem.

Use the ClassWizard to add an override for the **OnPrepareDC** function to the view class. Set the mapping mode in this function, as shown below:

```
void CSampView::OnPrepareDC(CDC* pDC, CPrintInfo* pInfo)
{
    pDC->SetMapMode(MM_HIMETRIC);

    CView::OnPrepareDC(pDC, pInfo);
}
```

If you compile and run now, you will find that you can insert an OLE object and edit it, but as soon as you click elsewhere in the view the object will completely disappear. If you run the application under the debugger and look at what **m_SizeAndPositionRect** is being set to when it is set in **OnChangeItemPosition**, you will see that the object's rectangle is being saved in device coordinates rather than logical coordinates. To fix this problem, change the **OnChangeItemPosition** function in CNTRITEM.CPP as shown below:

```
BOOL CSampCntrItem::OnChangeItemPosition(const CRect& rectPos)
{
    ASSERT_VALID(this);

    if (!COleClientItem::OnChangeItemPosition(rectPos))
        return FALSE;
    m_SizeAndPositionRect = rectPos;
    CClientDC dc(NULL);
    dc.SetMapMode(MM_HIMETRIC);
    dc.DPtoLP(&m_SizeAndPositionRect);
    GetDocument()->UpdateAllViews(NULL, 0, NULL);
    GetDocument()->SetModifiedFlag();

    return TRUE;
}
```

This code creates a client DC so it can translate the rectangle's device coordinates to HIMETRIC logical coordinates.

Compile and run the application. You will now be able to print a document, and all OLE objects will be properly sized both in print preview and on the sheet of paper.

34.5.7 Handling Drawing

Chapter 15 discussed how to create simple drawing applications and also showed how to create scrolled views that handle printing. If you look at the instructions for the first drawing program in Chapter 15 and make the changes specified there to this OLE framework, you will find you can draw around your OLE objects. The document will properly serialize the data and reload it. Everything will work as expected. If you like, create the drawing application with scrolling and printing seen in Section 15.8 and add to it the OLE container capabilities described here. It will work properly.

34.6 An Introduction to OLE Servers

An OLE server is an application that produces OLE objects that a user can insert in OLE containers. The AppWizard makes it extremely easy to create OLE servers that work with containers that support visual editing. In this section you will learn how to create an AppWizard server framework and modify it to implement a typical server. The following steps guide you through the process and explain what is going on.

34.6.1 Create the Framework

Create a new SDI framework with the AppWizard. Give the new project the name "Mand."

As you go through the AppWizard option screens, select the following options:
- *Choose **Full-Server** for OLE support. Select **No Automation** under automation support. See Appendix B.6.6 for details.*
- Enable or disable any application features as you see fit.

34.6.2 Compile and Run

Compile the application and run it. You will find that it looks like any of the AppWizard applications we created in Part 3. All the menu options are the same, the tool bar is the same, and so on. Exit the application.

The real difference comes when you try to *insert* objects created by this new server into OLE containers. You will find that the "Mand Document" server shows up in the OLE server list when you choose the **Insert New Object** menu option in an OLE container. For example, if you run Microsoft Excel and choose the **Object** option in the **Insert** menu, you will find "Mand Document" in that list. If you insert an object from this server, it will take over the Excel menu and tool bar and create a new object on the spreadsheet. The object will be white, and you will not be able to do anything with it.

34.6.3 Understanding the Differences

If you look at the source code that the AppWizard generated for this OLE server, you will find that the basic structure of the framework is very familiar. However, look through the code and note the following differences:
- MAND.CPP—The application file looks almost exactly like it normally would. You will note that the code declares a static global named **clsid** that acts as the class ID for the application (see Section 34.4). At the beginning of the **InitInstance** function you should note the call to **AfxOleInit**, which starts the OLE DLL and initializes it. Several things also happen at the bottom of the **InitInstance** function. The most important of these is the call to **UpdateRegistry**, which registers the application's name and class ID with the registry.

- MAINFRM.CPP—No changes.
- SAMPDOC.CPP—This file is nearly identical to a normal document file, but instead of inheriting its behavior from **CDocument** it uses **COleServerDoc**. See the MFC documentation for a list of functions and a description. **COleServerDoc** interacts with **COleServerItem** to support the activities of an OLE server.
- SAMPVIEW.CPP—Besides the addition of the **OnCancelEditSrvr** function, the view class is identical to any of the view classes seen in Chapter 15.
- IPFRAME.CPP—This file contains a class derived from **COleIFrameWnd**, which handles the frame window for an object embedded in a container and being edited in-place. See the MFC documentation for detailed information on the **COleIFrameWnd** class.
- SRVRITEM.CPP—This file contains a class derived from **COleServerItem**. This class encapsulates the interfaces that OLE containers will use to talk to the server for an embedded object. See the MFC documentation for detailed information on the **COleServerItem** class.

Because the document and view classes are nearly identical to the document and view classes seen in Chapter 15, you could easily create a simple drawing server using the code that you find in that chapter. However, there are a few details that change. In the following sections, we will develop an application that implements a simple mandelbrot set server to demonstrate the steps that you must take when creating any server.

34.6.4 Add a Menu Option

Open the resource file for the application and look at the menu resources. There are three:

1. IDR_SRVR_EMBEDDED—This is the menu that will appear when the server is invoked in a container that does *not* support visual editing. Note that the **File** menu contains the **Update** option that all fully open servers require.
2. IDR_SERVER_INPLACE—This is the menu that will appear when the server is invoked in a container that *does* support visual editing. Note that the menu bar does not contain a **File** menu and that there are two odd vertical separators on the menu bar. This peculiar structure is necessary so the server can integrate this menu bar into the menu bar of the container during in-place activation.
3. IDR_MAINFRAME—This is the menu that appears when the server is executed as a normal application.

We want to add a menu option named **Change** that will pop up a dialog to set the width, height, and number of iterations for the mandelbrot set created by this mandelbrot server. Open all three of the menu resources. In all three, delete the existing values from the **Edit** menus and add a new menu option named **Change** to the **Edit** menus.

34.6.5 Modify the Document Class

Now open the document files, MANDDOC.CPP and MANDDOC.H. The **Edit** menu now contains a menu option named **Change** that will pop up a dialog to set the width, height, and number of iterations for the mandelbrot server. The program will use the information from this dialog to recalculate the mandelbrot set's picture and place it in an array held by the document. This array will act as a cache for the pixel values, and will allow the view to draw the mandelbrot set quickly. The sections below add the appropriate variables and code to the document file so it can calculate the mandlebrot set and fill the cache array. The dialog and dialog class are also created.

34.6.5.1   Add Variables Add the following variables to the public attribute section of the document header file:

```
CSize size;
WORD numberOfIterations;
CUIntArray cachedPictColors;
COLORREF colors[64];
```

34.6.5.2   Add Function Prototypes Add the following two functions to the private operation section of the document header file:

```
void CreatePict();
int CalcColor(double real, double imag);
```

34.6.5.3   Initialize the Variables Add the following lines of code to the constructor in MANDDOC.CPP so the new member variables are properly initialized:

```
size.cx=size.cy=30;
numberOfIterations=10;
int x;
BYTE r=0, g=0, b=0;

for (x=0; x<64; x++)
{
    colors[x]=RGB(r, g, b);
    if (!(r+=64))
        if (!(b+=64))
            b+=64;
}
```

34.6.5.4   Add Helper Functions Add the following two helper functions to the bottom of MANSEDOC.CPP:

```
void CMandDoc::CreatePict()
{
    double xstep, ystep;
    double x, y;
    int i, j;
    int index;

    ystep=2.0/size.cy;
    xstep=2.0/size.cx;

    cachedPictColors.SetSize(size.cx*size.cy);
```

```
        index=0;
        for (j=0, y=-1; j<size.cy; j++, y+=ystep)
        {
            for (i=0, x=-1; i<size.cx; i++, x+=xstep)
            {
                cachedPictColors.SetAt(index, CalcColor(x, y));
                index++;
            }
        }
    }


int CMandDoc::CalcColor(double real, double imag)
{
    double r, i;
    double spread;
    double tr, ti;
    WORD iteration;

    r=i=0.0;

    for (iteration=0; iteration<numberOfIterations-1; iteration++)
    {
        tr=r + real;
        ti=i + imag;
        r=tr*tr - ti*ti;
        i=2*tr*ti;
        spread=r*r + i*i;
        if (spread > 4.0)
            break;
    }

    if (iteration > 63) TRACE("Color Array Overflow!!!\n");

    return(iteration);
}
```

These two functions together calculate the values for the pixels that make up the mandelbrot set when it is displayed. It stores the values in the cache array.

34.6.5.5   Create a Dialog Open the resource file. Create a new dialog resource. Create three edit areas (see Chapters 15 or 18. for details). Label the three edit areas with statics named "Width", "Height", and "Iterations". When you are finished, the new dialog should look like the one shown in Figure 34.7.

Open the ClassWizard while the dialog is visible. Create a new dialog class for the dialog called **CDlg**. Switch to the member variable section of the ClassWizard and add member variables for the width, height, and iterations with the names **m_cx**, **m_cy** and **m_iter**. All three should be *value* members of type **UINT**. When you click OK in the ClassWizard it will create the **CDlg** class. *Include DLG.H at the top of the document file MANDDOC.CPP.*

34.6.5.6   Wire in Menu Handlers Open the ClassWizard. In the Message Maps section, select the document class. Create a new COMMAND handler for the

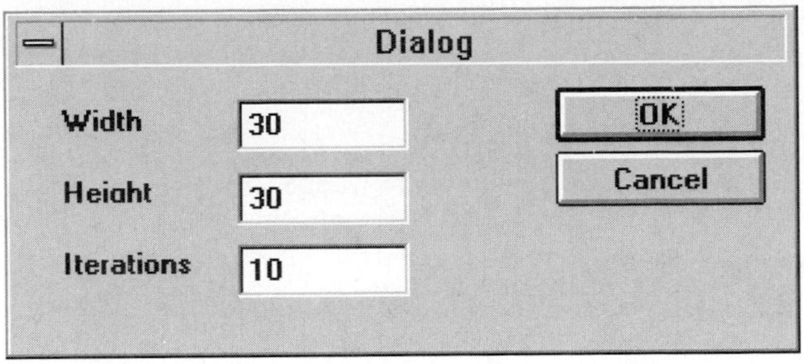

Figure 34.7
The Parameters dialog

ID_EDIT_CHANGE menu option. Edit the code for the **OnEditChange** function and change it to the following:

```
void CMandDoc::OnEditChange()
{
    CDlg dlg;
    int ret;

    dlg.m_cx=size.cx;
    dlg.m_cy=size.cy;
    dlg.m_iter=numberOfIterations;
    ret=dlg.DoModal();
    if (ret == IDOK)
    {
        size.cx=dlg.m_cx;
        size.cy=dlg.m_cy;
        numberOfIterations=dlg.m_iter;
        // build cache of picture colors
        BeginWaitCursor();
        CreatePict();
        EndWaitCursor();

        UpdateAllItems(NULL);
        UpdateAllViews(NULL);
    }
}
```

This code fills the cache array with values by calling the helper functions that do the actual math.

34.6.6 Modify OnDraw

Now that the document has a way to calculate the mandelbrot set and store it, the view can display it. Modify the **OnDraw** function in MANDVIEW.CPP so it contains the following code:

```
void CMandView::OnDraw(CDC* pDC)
{
    CMandDoc* pDoc = GetDocument();
    ASSERT_VALID(pDoc);

    int x, y, i;
    RECT r;
```

```
    CBrush brush;
    CRect cr;
    GetClientRect(&cr);

    pDC->SetMapMode(MM_ANISOTROPIC);
    pDC->SetWindowExt(pDoc->size.cx, pDoc->size.cy);
    pDC->SetViewportExt(cr.Width(), cr.Height());

    if (pDoc->cachedPictColors.GetSize() != 0)
    {
        i=0;
        for (y=0; y < pDoc->size.cy; y++)
            for (x=0; x < pDoc->size.cx; x++)
            {
                brush.CreateSolidBrush(
                    pDoc->colors[pDoc->cachedPictColors.GetAt(i++)]);
                r.left=x;
                r.right=x + 1;
                r.top=y;
                r.bottom=y + 1;
                pDC->FillRect(&r, &brush);
                brush.DeleteObject();
            }
    }
}
```

34.6.7 Compile and Run

All of the prior work creates a normal document/view style program that implements a mandelbrot set viewer. If you compile this code and *run it as a normal application*, you will find that, when you choose the **Change** option in the **Edit** menu and enter values such as a width of 32, a height of 32, and iterations of 16 and press the OK button, the program produces a mandelbrot set of the size indicated. It then stretches that small number of pixels across the face of the application's client area. You can increase the number of pixels, but as you would expect the calculation time will grow.

Now we will make final adjustments so that the application can update itself properly when used as an OLE server.

34.6.8 Make Server Modifications

To make the program work properly as an OLE server, open the file named SRVRITEM.CPP. Find the **OnGetExtent** function and find the following line:

```
    rSize = CSize(3000, 3000);   // 3000 x 3000 HIMETRIC units
```
Replace it with:

```
    rSize = GetDocument()->size;
    CClientDC dc(NULL);
    dc.LPtoHIMETRIC(&rSize);
```
Or replace it with:

```
    rSize = m_sizeExtent;
```

When a container asks the server how big its object is, the framework calls **OnGetExtent**. The first piece of replacement code asks the document for its current size and returns that value after translating it to HIMETRIC units. The second piece of replacement code uses the current size that the user has selected for the item in the container. The **m_sizeExtent** variable is a member of the **COleServerItem** class and is set by the container.

34.6.9 Make Server Modifications

In SRVRITEM.CPP, find the **OnDraw** function. Replace it with the following:

```
BOOL CMandSrvrItem::OnDraw(CDC* pDC, CSize& rSize)
{
    CMandDoc* pDoc = GetDocument();
    ASSERT_VALID(pDoc);

    int x, y, i;
    RECT r;
    CBrush brush;

    pDC->SetMapMode(MM_ANISOTROPIC);
    pDC->SetWindowExt(pDoc->size.cx, pDoc->size.cy);
    pDC->SetViewportExt(rSize.cx, rSize.cy);

    if (pDoc->cachedPictColors.GetSize() != 0)
    {
        i=0;
        for (y=0; y < pDoc->size.cy; y++)
            for (x=0; x < pDoc->size.cx; x++)
            {
                brush.CreateSolidBrush(
                    pDoc->colors[pDoc->
                    cachedPictColors.GetAt(i++)]);
                r.left=x;
                r.right=x + 1;
                r.top=y;
                r.bottom=y + 1;
                pDC->FillRect(&r, &brush);
                brush.DeleteObject();
            }
    }

    return TRUE;
}
```

For more information on the anisotropic drawing mode, see Chapter 11. This **OnDraw** function handles drawing into an OLE container's window. The code uses an anisotropic mapping mode so it can stretch the pixels in the cached array into the available space in the container. It then draws the cached array into the container. You can see that it looks remarkably similar to the **OnDraw** function in the view class. The only real difference is the use of **rSize** instead of **GetClientRect**. When you create your own servers, simply remember that you have to handle **OnDraw** in two places and make the appropriate adjustments.

34.6.10 Compile and Run

Compile the application, and then insert it into an OLE container that supports in-place activation. For example, in Excel you can chose the **Object** item from the **Insert** menu and choose "Mand Document" from the list. Note that the server properly takes over the menu bar and tool bar of the container. Select the **Change** option in the **Edit** menu, and then click OK. The new mandlebrot set will be drawn into the container. You can then stretch and move the embedded item.

Try out both pieces of replacement code for the **OnGetExtent** function in the previous section and choose the one that feels better to you.

34.7 An Introduction to OLE Automation

One of the key features of the OLE specification is the automation interface. Automation allows a programmer to call an OLE-aware application that supports automation and to use its services by calling functions on the application. For example, a Visual Basic programmer can easily activate Microsoft Word, which is OLE compliant and automation-aware, from a VB program. The VB program can open a Word document, insert text into that document, and print it. In this case, Word is being used as a print engine for customized reports. Or the programmer might activate Excel, which is also OLE compliant and automation-aware, insert several values in a spreadsheet, and then perform a complex mathematical operation on the values. The programmer can then retrieve the result. In this case, Excel is being used as a math engine.

It is extremely easy to add automation to your own OLE servers. You simply click a check box when you create the application in the AppWizard to make it OLE automation aware. You can then add two things to the application that other programmers will access: *properties* and *method*. A property is a variable that the programmer can set or read. A method is a function that can have parameters just like a C++ function. If you like, you can supply **get** and **set** methods for each property and eliminate open properties to completely encapsulate an automation server.

The following sections show you how easy it is to create and use an automation server. Once you have seen how to add and call one automation function, it will be trivial to add any number of automation functions to the OLE applications that you create.

34.7.1 Create the Server

We are going to start by repeating the steps seen in the previous section to create an OLE server. This time, however, *we will turn on the automation capability*. To do this uae the AppWizard. Give the new project the name "Auto."

As you go through the six AppWizard option screens, select the following options:

- *Choose **Full-Server** for OLE support. Be sure to enable automation support. See Appendix B.6.6 for details.*
- Enable or disable any application features as you see fit.

636

This book is continuously updated. See http://www.iftech.com/mfc

34.7.2 Compile and Run

Compile the application and run it. This step is important because it will register the server in the registry. You will find that the application looks just like the server did in Section 34.6.2. If you embed it in an application that is OLE aware, it will create a blank white rectangle.

34.7.3 Add an Automation Class

Open the ClassWizard. Go to the OLE Automation section. You need to create a new class that will contain the automation functions for the application, so add a new class as described in Appendix B.7.6. Set up the new class with the name "Beeper" and the class type of **CCmdTarget**.

34.7.4 Add a Method

Add a new method to the new Beeper class by clicking the **Add Method** button in the automation section of the ClassWizard. Call the function **BeepSamp** and give it a void return value.

Modify the **BeepSamp** function by adding a single line of code:

```
void Beeper::BeepSamp()
{
    Beep(1000, 1000);
}
```

34.7.5 Compile and Run

Compile the application and run it as a normal application. *This step will update the registry, and is a very important step.* Close the application.

34.7.6 Examine the Registry

Now go to a command line and execute REGEDIT /V. You will find that there are four sections of the registry that deal with the Auto application we just executed, as shown in Figures 34.8 and 34.9. All four parts are related. Simply find all four parts so that you understand that the application you have created has a corresponding section in the registry. Auto.Document and Auot.Beeper are joined, and both of them have unique class IDs.

34.7.7 Activate the Automation Server

This section shows you three different ways to activate the automation server that you just created.

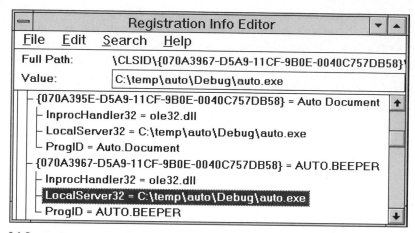

Figure 34.8
The first and second entries in the registry for this application. Having found these, you can use the class IDs in the Find option to find the other two parts.

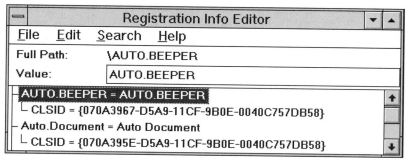

Figure 34.9
The third and fourth entries for this application in the registry

34.7.7.1 Activate from Visual Basic If you have Visual Basic and are familiar with the fundamentals, you can easily activate the automation server with a tiny Visual Basic program. Note also that Visual C++ ships with an application called DISPTEST (in the BIN directory) that is a stripped down version of VB that you can also use for automation testing.

Create a new application in VB. Create a new form. Create a new button on the form. Edit the code for the button so it looks like this:

```
Sub Command1_Click ()
    Dim O As Object
    Set O = CreateObject("Auto.Beeper")
    O.BeepSamp
End Sub
```

Run the VB program. Click the button. It will beep.

This code causes Visual Basic to open a connection to "Beeper," the name for the automation portion of this application. If you don't like the name "Beeper," then create a new application and change it when you create the automation class). The **O** variable then acts as a proxy for the open automation server, and you call functions in the server through the proxy.

34.7.7.2 Activation from Excel To connect to the automation server through Excel, do the following. Select the **Macro** and then **Module** options in the **Insert** menu. In the Macro Module, type the following code:

```
Function sample ()
    Dim O As Object
    Set O = CreateObject("Auto.Beeper")
    O.BeepSamp
End Function
```

This step creates an Excel macro named "sample". Then, in any sheet, you can call the macro with a formula like this:

```
=sample()
```

Every time the sheet recalculates, you will hear a beep.

34.7.7.3 Activate from other Visual C++ Programs Create a new Visual C++ application. Use the following code anywhere in your program:

```
COleDispatchDriver beepDisp;
beepDisp.CreateDispatch("Auto.Beeper");
beepDisp.InvokeHelper(1,NULL,VT_EMPTY,NULL,NULL);
beepDisp.ReleaseDisp();
```

The "1" in the call to **InvokeHelper** is the dispatch ID of the Beep function. Each function is numbered sequentially see the ODL file. Optionally, you can call **GetIdsOfName** before **InvokeHelper** to translate a function name to the dispatch ID at runtime. This technique is preferred.

34.7.8 Add a Second Function

Add a new method to the Beeper class by clicking the **Add Method** button in the automation section of the ClassWizard. Call the function **xxx** and give it a void return value. Additionally, click in the **Parameters** section of the Add Method dialog and add a parameter called **x** of type **short**.

Click the **Edit Code** button in the automation section of the ClassWizard. Modify the **xxx** function by adding a single line:

```
void Beeper::xxx(short x)
{
    Beep(500,x);
}
```

34.7.9 Activate from Visual Basic

Modify your VB code or Excel macro so that it looks like this:

```
Function sample()
    Dim O As Object
    Set O = CreateObject("Auto.Beeper")
    O.BeepSamp
```

```
        O.xxx (100)
    End Function
```

Now the program will beep twice, the second time for 100 milliseconds because of the parameter passed.

Experiment with other parameters, return values, and so on. Add properties and try setting them. It should be easy to see that the automation interface provides an extremely flexible and easy-to-use inter-application communication mechanism that you will be able to exploit in a variety of ways.

34.8 An Introduction to OLE Controls

Using the new ControlWizard built into Visual C++, you can create OLE controls, also known as OCXs. OLE controls replace what were formerly known as VBXs used in Visual Basic. Because they are based on OLE and have a well-designed interface, OCXs are much more flexible and portable than VBXs. In addition, the Control-Wizard makes their creation extremely easy.

You can understand the concepts driving OLE controls most easily if you try to think about normal Windows controls such the button control or the list box control in an extremely abstract way. These abstractions can then be mapped onto the OCX framework and you can work on examples that demonstrate each feature.

Imagine that you are a programmer and you want to create a dialog that contains a push button control. Imagine further that there is no such thing as a Windows button control or the **CButton** class. Instead, think about the abstract concept of a button control. There are two things that you need from this control:

1. The control has certain attributes—things like background and foreground color, a text string displayed on the button, alignment of the text string, and so on—and you need to be able to change those attributes. In a normal Windows button you set attributes like these using a variety of techniques: styles, **SetDlg-ItemText, SetFont**, and so on. In an abstract control it would be nice to have some straightforward, simple way to set attributes.

2. The control will receive user events and you need a way to be notified of those events so you can respond to them in your code. When the user clicks on the button, for example, you need a way for the button to notify your code of that event so you can respond to it in appropriate way. In a normal Windows buttons this step is handled using command IDs and message maps, as described in Chapter 4.

Now imagine that you would like to put a list box in the same dialog. An abstract list box will, like the abstract button, need to have attributes and a way to change them. It will also handle user events and want to communicate them back to the program. For example, when the user double-clicks on an element in the list, the list will want to have a way to communicate that event to the program so the program can respond to it. In addition, the list will need to have certain functions so the programmer using the control can manipulate the list. For example, the abstract list control needs a way for the programmer to add strings to the list. This task is most easily accomplished using a function call similar to the **AddString** function in the **CListBox** class.

OCX controls work in this sort of abstract way. As the implementer of an OCX control you can specify attributes that will determine the appearance or behavior of the control. In OCX controls they are called *properties*. Every OCX is expected to support a known set of properties called the *stock properties*, and then you add your own properties beyond that. The stock properties are listed below:

Background color
Border style
Enabled
Foreground color
Font
Text string

You can add other properties as you see fit. For example, if you are implementing a push button control, you might add a "fill color" property that determines what color the button uses to highlight itself when clicked.

Incidentally, the container that holds a control has a say in how the controls it contains should look. The container can specify *ambient properties*, and every control in the container should take on these ambient properties initially and use them unless they are specifically overridden by the programmer using the control. The ambient properties of any container are listed below:

Background color
Foreground color
Font
Text alignment
User mode (indicates whether control is in design or use mode)

OCXs also support function calls. They are called *methods*. There are a set of methods that every OCX supports, called *stock methods*. These stock methods fall into two categories: property methods and control methods. The stock methods are listed below. The first two are control methods and the rest manipulate the stock properties:

DoClick Lets the programmer simulate a click
Refresh Redraws the control

GetBackColor, SetBackColor
GetBorderStyle, SetBorderStyle
GetEnabled, SetEnabled
GetForeColor, SetForeColor
GetFont, SetFont
GetText, SetText
GetHwnd

You can add other *custom methods*. For example, if you are creating a list control you might add an **AddString** method to add strings to the list. When you add a property of your own to a control, you will add two methods to manipulate the new property.

Finally, as the implementer of a control you can create *events* for it to send to the application using the control. There is a set of *stock events* that a control should always send to its container, as listed below:

Click
Double Click
Error
Key Down
Key Press
Key Up
Mouse Down
Mouse Move
Mouse Up

You can add other events as you see fit. When you send an event to the OCX's container, it is referred to as *firing* the event. If you are creating a list control, you might add one event that gets fired when the user single-clicks on an item in the list, and another that gets fired when the user double-clicks on an item. The stock events are in place to handle all of the obvious, low-level events that any application might want to receive from a control.

34.8.1 Implementing OCXs

The OCX ControlWizard is a separate component of Visual C++ that makes the creation of OCXs easier. You have to load this component after you install Visual C++, and you access it from the **Tools** menu in Visual C++. In addition to the ControlWizard, three other new options in the **Tools** menu let you register and unregister the controls that you create and also run a test container that lets you test your controls.

The joy of working with the Visual C++ ControlWizard is that it makes the process of creating an OCX extremely easy. The ControlWizard creates a framework that contains all the code necessary to implement the stock properties, stock methods, and stock events. The ControlWizard also uses MFC classes that tend to follow patterns you are already familiar with. For example, to draw the face of your control, you override the **OnDraw** function and place into it drawing commands just like those seen in Chapter 11 and throughout the rest of the book. The ClassWizard makes it extremely easy for you to add new events, properties, and methods.

The dread of working with the ControlWizard, and more specifically the framework that it creates, comes from its flexibility. The flexibility expresses itself as complexity. For example, the **COleControl** class, a class central to the activities of the ControlWizard, has 117 member functions. Many other control classes further enhance the flexibility, and therefore the complexity. The key thing to keep in mind when approaching the Control-creation features of Visual C++ is that they all stem from the basic (and simple) ideas discussed in the previous section. Also keep in mind that you can approach the topic incrementally. Start your learning process here. Then work through the examples and documentation in the CDK books on-line and experiment on your own until you feel comfortable in this space.

The best way to get started down the OCX path is to use the ControlWizard to create the base control, see what it does, and then add properties, methods, and events to the control to see how they work. In the following sections we take this approach, starting with the base files and modifying them to create a simple "adjuster" control.

The adjuster control handles two user messages: a left mouse click and a right mouse click. A left mouse click increments the adjuster, which shows the adjustment visually with a painted bar on the face of the control. A right mouse click decrements the adjuster. The control fires an event whenever it is adjusted by the user. Additionally, the control has two properties that the programmer can set: the *range*, which determines the maximum value of the adjuster, and the *value*, which the programmer can set or get to change or read the current value of the control. The control also supports a *zero* method that zeros the adjuster. Take the following steps to create this control.

34.8.2 Create the Base OCX

Whenever you start the process of creating a new OCX, you will use the Control-Wizard to create the base framework. The process is identical to using the AppWizard to create a base application framework. See Appendix B.8.1 for details. Name the control "Adj" when you create it.

Look at the code files that the ControlWizard created. Of them, the only one we will modify in the section is ADJCTL.CPP. This file contains a class derived from **COleControl**, which embodies almost all of the modifiable behavior for an OLE control. It has quite a few different areas that the ClassWizard can modify. Look up this class in the on-line documentation and briefly review some of its capabilities.

34.8.3 Experiment with the Control

Compile the code for the new control. To test the control, you must register it. See Appendix B.8.2.

To actually execute the control to test it, you can use the test container for OCX controls that comes with Visual C++ (see Appendix B.8.3) or you can insert the control into a normal dialog or form view as described in Appendix B.8.4. The test container is much easier for debugging. Select the **Test Container** option as described in Appendix B.8.3. Choose the **Insert OLE Control** option in the **Edit** menu. Select "Adj Control" from the list to insert the new control. If you do not find an entry for the "Adj Control" in the dialog, you either forgot to register the control or you failed to select the **Available in Insert Dialog** option as described in Appendix B.8.1. Try again.

The control should appear in the test container. It will look like a rectangle filled with an ellipse. You can resize and move the control. Otherwise it is benign.

Now experiment with some of the features of the test container (make sure that you click on the control to select it before trying these options). In the edit menu you can insert and delete controls. You can set ambient properties on the container (although the control will currently ignore them). You can invoke methods on the control. Currently the only method available is **About**, which displays an About box for the control. You can invoke different OLE verbs on the control. The most interesting verb right now is **Properties**, but there are several other ways to invoke that option. The Properties dialog will eventually give programmers an easy way to adjust the properties of the control when they develop applications with it.

In the **View** menu you can open up windows to view events and notifications, although the control generates neither right now. You can also view the control's properties in two different ways. Either you can enter the name of a property directly or you can display the property dialog for those controls that support it.

Read through the documentation that comes with the test container for further information.

34.8.4 Activate the Stock Properties

When the ControlWizard created the base files, it wired into them the stock properties for the control. You can activate those properties using the ClassWizard. Open the ClassWizard and select the **OLE Automation** tab. Make sure the class name is **CAdjCtrl**. Click the **Add Property** button and select the **ForeColor** property from the **External Name** combo box list as described in Appendix B.8.5. Do the same thing for **BackColor**. Close the ClassWizard.

This action alone will not accomplish anything because the code currently does not ever use the foreground or background color properties. Find the **OnDraw** function in the ADJCTL.CPP file. You can see that it simply paints the background of the control in white and then draws an ellipse. Replace the old implementation with the following:

```
void CAdjCtrl::OnDraw(
          CDC* pdc, const CRect& rcBounds, const CRect& rcInvalid)
{
    CBrush brush(TranslateColor(GetBackColor()));
    pdc->FillRect(rcBounds, brush);
    CPen pen(PS_SOLID, 2, TranslateColor(GetForeColor()));
    CPen *oldPen;
    oldPen = pdc->SelectObject(&pen);
    pdc->Ellipse(rcBounds);
    pdc->SelectObject(oldPen);
}
```

This code simply applies the background color to the brush used to paint the background and the foreground color to the pen used to draw the ellipse. See Chapter 11 for additional information on pens and brushes.

Compile the code. Open the Test Container. Select the **Set Ambient Properties** option in the **Edit** menu and set the **BackColor** ambient property to something other than white. You change the color by clicking the **Choose** button that you will find toward the bottom of the dialog. Now create an Adj control. You will find it initially has the appropriate background color. This color was picked up from the container. Now choose the **Properties** button in the **View** menu. Select **ForeColor** from the **Properties** combo box. A small button displaying "..." will appear next to the **Value** field. Click it and chose the foreground color. You will find that the control responds appropriately. If you change the background color of the control, you will find it overrides the ambient color.

Open the Notifications window by selecting the **Notification Log** option in the **View** menu of the test container. Change the foreground property again and you will see that a new *notification* is issued when the property changes. You can change the behavior of the notification using the radio box at the bottom of the dialog. If you want to gain more control over how your code handles property changes, then you can create the property differently in the ClassWizard. Open the ClassWizard and delete the **ForeColor** property. Add the property again, but this time try the **Member Variable** or **Get/Set Function** options. The latter adds two functions to the ADJCTL.CPP file that you can fill with appropriate code to handle property changes. We will see more on notifications below.

34.8.5 Activate the Stock Methods

The two stock methods named **DoClick** and **Refresh** also already exist in the code generated by the ControlWizard. To activate them, open the ClassWizard. Select the **OLE Automation** tab and click the **Add Method** function. Pull down the **External Name** combo box and select **DoClick**. The dialog will specify the setup for the **DoClick** stock method. Press **OK** and do the same thing for **Refresh**. No further changes are required.

Compile the code and reinsert the control into the Test Container. You will find that the **Invoke Methods** option in the **Edit** menu can now invoke **Refresh** and **DoClick** methods, although, right now, these methods do not appear to do anything.

34.8.6 Add Custom Properties

This control needs two custom properties: **range** and **value**. They are integers. The **range** property holds the maximum value for the adjuster, while the **value** property holds the current value of the adjuster.

Open the ClassWizard and select the **OLE Automation** tab. Add a property named **value**, as described in Appendix B.8.6. The ClassWizard gives the property two names. The external name is used by a programmer to adjust the property. When the value is modified, the notification function gets called so you can respond to the change in your code. The variable name is used inside the control's code to access the property in C++. Use the external property name of **value** and the ClassWizard will choose the variable name **m_value** for the variable name. Use the type **short**.

Create the **value** and **range** properties. Compile the code and insert the control into the test container. You will find you can use the **Properties** option in the **View** menu to modify the two properties.

Find the constructor in the ADJCTL.CPP file and add code to initialize the two member variables as shown here:

```
m_range = 10;
m_value = 0;
```

Add the same two lines to the **OnResetState** function further down in the file.

Edit the two notification functions in ADJCTL.CPP so the members stay within range:

```
void CAdjCtrl::OnRangeChanged()
{
    if (m_range < 0)
        m_range = 10;

    SetModifiedFlag();
    Refresh();
}

void CAdjCtrl::OnValueChanged()
{
    if (m_value < 0)
        m_value = 0;
    if (m_value > m_range)
        m_value = m_range;

    SetModifiedFlag();
    Refresh();
}
```

34.8.7 Add Message Handlers

The **value** property will be incremented every time the user clicks the left mouse button, and decremented whenever the user clicks the right mouse button. Mouse clicks in a control are detected using the same message map technology used throughout this book. Open the ClassWizard. Choose the **Message Maps** tab and make sure the class is set to **CAdjCtrl**. Add functions for WM_LBUTTONUP and WM_RBUTTONUP. Edit the two new functions so they look like this:

```
void CAdjCtrl::OnLButtonUp(UINT nFlags, CPoint point)
{
    if (m_value < m_range)
        m_value++;

    COleControl::OnLButtonUp(nFlags, point);
    Refresh();
}

void CAdjCtrl::OnRButtonUp(UINT nFlags, CPoint point)
{
    if (m_value > 0)
        m_value--;

    COleControl::OnRButtonUp(nFlags, point);
    Refresh();
}
```

Now find the **OnDraw** function in ADJCTL.CPP and change it to the following:

```
void CAdjCtrl::OnDraw(
            CDC* pdc, const CRect& rcBounds, const CRect& rcInvalid)
{
    CBrush brush1(TranslateColor(GetBackColor()));
    pdc->FillRect(rcBounds, &brush1);
    CRect r = rcBounds;
    r.right = r.left + r.Width() * m_value / m_range;
    CBrush brush2(TranslateColor(GetForeColor()));
    pdc->FillRect(r, &brush2);
}
```

You can see that this code simply draws a rectangle on the control. The rectangle stretches from the left side toward the right. The length of the rectangle is proportional to **m_value/m_range**.

34.8.8 Test the Program

Compile the control and insert it into the test container. When you click with the left mouse button, the adjuster will increment and display the new value. When you click the right button, it decrements. You can also adjust the **m_value** and **m_range** properties using the **Properties** option in the **View** menu.

34.8.9 Add the Zero Method

The specification for this control calls for a **Zero** method to reset the adjuster to zero. Add the method as described in Appendix B.8.7. Give the method a void return type and no parameters. Edit the method's code by clicking the **Edit Code** button and add the following:

```
void CAdjCtrl::Zero()
{
    m_value = 0;
    Refresh();
}
```

Use the **Invoke Method** option in the **Edit** menu of the test container to invoke the **Zero** method.

34.8.10 Add the Event

This control needs to fire an event whenever the user clicks in it. We will call this event **Adjusted**. To add the event, open the ClassWizard and see Appendix B.8.8. The external name of the event should be **Adjusted**, giving it an internal name of **Fire-Adjusted**. Give it a parameter named **value** of type **short**.

Now we need to call **FireAdjusted** at appropriate points in the program. We will call it in only two places, but different designers might call it in other places as well (for example, when the **value** property is set). Modify the functions for the two mouse messages, as shown below:

```
void CAdjCtrl::OnLButtonUp(UINT nFlags, CPoint point)
{
```

```
        if (m_value < m_range)
            m_value++;

        COleControl::OnLButtonUp(nFlags, point);
        Refresh();
        FireAdjusted(m_value);
    }

    void CAdjCtrl::OnRButtonUp(UINT nFlags, CPoint point)
    {
        if (m_value > 0)
            m_value--;

        COleControl::OnRButtonUp(nFlags, point);
        Refresh();
        FireAdjusted(m_value);
    }
```

Compile the code and insert the control into the test container. Select the **Event Log** option in the **View** menu. Click on the control. You will see that an event gets fired on every mouse click.

34.8.11 Adding Stock Property Pages

If you select the **Properties** option in the **View** menu and click on the **Invoke Properties Verb** option, you will see an empty dialog that is designed to make it easier to set the properties in an OCX. It is easy to fill in this empty dialog.

The pages for the stock properties are already implemented and you can add them in with very minor effort. If you look toward the top of ADJCTL.CPP, you will find a property page section. Modify it so it looks like this:

```
/////////////////////////////////////////////////////////////////
// Property pages

// Add more property pages as needed.
// Remember to increase the count!!!!!!!
BEGIN_PROPPAGEIDS(CAdjCtrl, 4)
    PROPPAGEID(CAdjPropPage::guid)
    PROPPAGEID(CLSID_CColorPropPage)
    PROPPAGEID(CLSID_CFontPropPage)
    PROPPAGEID(CLSID_CPicturePropPage)
END_PROPPAGEIDS(CAdjCtrl)
```

This code specifies that the three stock property pages should be included. *Note that the BEGIN_PROPPAGEIDS macro accepts the number of pages, and this value must be updated properly.*

Compile the code and insert the control into the test container. Invoke the property verb. You will see a property sheet containing four property pages. The General page is currently empty. The Colors page lets you change the foreground and background colors. The Font and Picture pages are currently disabled because we have not added those stock properties into the application yet. For this control, the latter two pages would probably not be included because the control does not use fonts or pictures.

34.8.12 Modifying the General Page

The ControlWizard created the general property page for you when it created the control's framework. It is currently blank. You normally add to it controls that allow you to change your control's custom properties. In our case, we want to add controls so that the dialog allows modification of the **range** and **value** properties.

To add the controls to the general page, open the resource file. Open the dialog named IDD_PROPPAGE_ADJ. Add two statics and two edit boxes so the dialog appears as shown in Figure 34.10. Rename the two edit controls IDC_RANGE and IDC_VALUE.

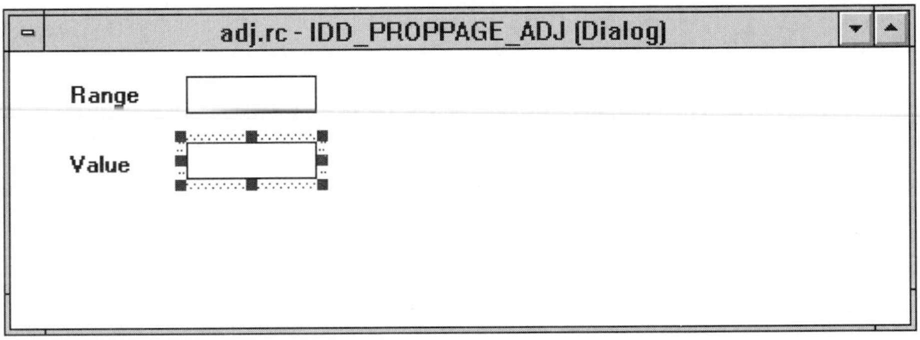

Figure 34.10
Creating the General property sheet

Now, with the dialog template open as the topmost window in Visual C++, open the ClassWizard. Choose the **Member Variables** tab. Double-click on IDC_RANGE. Your goal is to create a variable that can transfer a value to the **range** property in the control. Name the variable **m_range,** give it a **value** category and a **UINT** type. The **Optional OLE Property Name** field lets you type in a property name for the control. Use **range**. See Appendix B.8.9 for details. Do this for the IDC_VALUE control as well.

When you compile the control's code and insert it in the test container, you can invoke the properties verb and see your general properties page. It will work exactly as you expect it to. If it doesn't, you have probably misspelled the OLE Property Name. Note that case matters.

34.8.13 Overview of OCX Coding

In the preceding sections, we added stock properties, custom properties, stock methods, custom methods, and events to the base control. We also added message handlers and modified the appearance of the control. In all, we wrote a grand total of about 25 lines of code. The ClassWizard did absolutely everything else, in conjunction with the MFC classes that make up the control.

You should be able to appreciate how incredibly easy the ClassWizard makes this process. To add your own methods, properties, and events, simply follow the previous examples and use the tools that the ClassWizard provides.

34.9 Conclusion

You have seen almost the entire range of OLE functionality at a high level. You have created containers that can hold OLE servers, servers that fit into OLE containers, automation servers that fit with OLE automation clients, and OLE controls. You should be able to use this starting point to bootstrap yourself into the OLE space. Read through the descriptions of the different classes in the on-line documentation, the MFC encyclopedia, and technical notes. See the section inthe documentation on OLE. There is also a book and a variety of other OLE information, including the spec and programmer's reference, on Microsoft's Developer's Network CD.

MFC THREADS

The Win32 API provides Windows programmers with a number of advanced capabilities. These capabilities are discussed in detail in the book *Win32 System Services, The Heart of Windows 95 & Windows NT* by Marshall Brain, ISBN 0-13-324732-5, and also in the on-line documentation. Many of these advanced capabilities have yet to be incorporated into MFC. However, the threading and synchronization capabilities of Win32 have been encapsulated and are available in MFC classes. The MFC class called **CWinThread** is the subject of this chapter.

The **CWinThread** class gives you the ability to significantly improve the responsiveness and general "feel" of your applications. The purpose of this chapter is to introduce you to the class and show you several different ways to use it in your own applications. This introduction will help you become familiar with the class itself and its many possibilities.

35.1 Understanding the Possibilities

Threads give you a way to perform seamless background processing in your applications. If you have never thought about this sort of capability before, it may not be obvious how important background processing can be. Here are several examples that will help you to appreciate the value of multi-threading:

- If you create an MDI application, it is often useful to assign a separate thread to each window. For example, in an MDI communications program that lets you connect to multiple hosts via multiple modems simultaneously, it simplifies things considerably if each window has its own thread that communicates with each host.
- In a program that takes a long time to refresh its display because of the complexity of the graphics involved (for example, a visualization program may have to draw 10,000 polygons to refresh the display in a complicated drawing), it is useful to create a separate thread to handle the redrawing. The user

interface, with its own thread, remains active for the user while the redrawing takes place in the background.

- In a complicated simulation program, for example a program that simulates the activity of organisms in an environment, the design of the program is often conceptually simpler if each entity has its own thread. The entities are then fully independent of one another and can respond to their own simulation events individually.

- If you have part of a program that needs to respond to certain high-priority events very quickly, the problem is easily solved using thread priorities. The high-priority portion of the code is placed in its own thread and that thread is given a higher priority than other threads running on the machine. The high-priority thread then waits for the necessary events. When it senses one, it will awaken and receive almost all of the CPU cycles available until it completes its task. It can then go back to sleep waiting for the next event to arrive.

- If you are using an NT machine with multiple processors and you want to take full advantage of all he CPU power available, you need to break applications into multiple threads. NT's unit of division across CPUs is the thread, so if you have an application that contains only one thread it will, by default, use only one CPU out of those available. If the program breaks up its work into multiple threads, NT can run each thread on a different CPU.

- Any task that needs to happen "in the background" while the user continues to work with the application is easily handled with threads. For example, you might place lengthy recalculations, page formatting operations, file reading and writing, and so on. in separate threads that let the activities proceed in the background without disturbing the user.

As you read through this chapter, keep these examples in mind. They will help you to understand how you might apply the different techniques that are presented here.

35.2 Understanding Threads

The basic idea behind a thread is simple. A *thread* is a separate stream of execution. That may not mean a thing to you, however, if you are coming from a DOS background. Let's start by looking at what multi-processing and multi-threading actually mean from an operating system standpoint so you can clearly understand how threads fit into the big picture.

The MS-DOS operating system is a *single-process* operating system. It can run one program at a time. You load a program, work with it, quit it, and then run another. TSRs can, in certain situations, give an impression of multi-processing, but the problems that TSRs normally cause show that they are at best an illusion that MS-DOS was never intended to support.

Microsoft Windows 3.1, as well as Apple's Macintosh operating system up to System 7, are *cooperative multi-tasking* operating environments. Both can run multiple programs (processes) at the same time. For example, you can run a word processor in one window, a spreadsheet in another window, and download a file from a BBS in a third window. The word *cooperative* is used because it is up to each program to properly relinquish control at appropriate times so that all the processes appear to be working simultaneously. Cooperative multi-tasking works to some degree. However, a lengthy disk access or other undividable task performed by one program will tend to monopolize the entire system for a moment and the cooperation breaks down. This makes cooperative multi-tasking systems seem jerky and unstable in many cases. If one program locks up, the whole system often dies with it. As soon as one program locks, it cannot relinquish control to the others and everything stops.

UNIX is a *preemptive multi-tasking* operating system. The operating system, rather than individual applications, is in charge of giving CPU time to all the running processes and it does so as it best sees fit. UNIX gives a process a *time slice* of CPU time—perhaps 20 milliseconds or so—and when that amount of time expires the operating *preempts* the process and gives the next slice of CPU time to another process. A UNIX machine can therefore have literally hundreds of processes running at one time and still feel very smooth to the user. If one process locks it has no effect on the others because the operating system is still in control of slicing the CPU time.

Windows 95 and Windows NT are a *preemptive multi-tasking, multi-threaded* operating systems. Because they use preemptive multi-tasking, they share with UNIX the same smoothness of operation and process independence. Each process, or application, gets time slices from the operating system. Multi-threading goes one step further. An individual application by default contains one thread, but it can break itself into several (or many) independent threads of execution so that, for example, one thread of an application can send a file to the printer while another is responding to user input. The operating system gives each thread slices of CPU time. This simple change in a program's design can significantly reduce any waiting that the user normally has to do during lengthy recalculations, screen painting, file reading and writing, and so on.

Multi-threading also lets you take advantage of multiple CPUs available in many high-end NT machines. Say, for example, that you purchase an advanced RISC machine capable of using up to 10 CPU chips, but initially you purchase only one CPU for it. As part of your learning cycle you write a simple Mandelbrot set program, and you find that for a window of a certain size it takes 15 seconds to redraw the image of the Mandelbrot set.

Now you add nine more CPU chips to the machine. When you rerun the Mandelbrot program, you will find that it still takes almost 15 seconds to execute. NT has the ability to run different threads on different CPUs, but it cannot do anything with a single-threaded program but devote one CPU to it. There is no way for NT to divide a single thread across CPUs. Because NT is itself multi-threaded, the Mandelbrot program will speed up slightly because it is not competing with NT's system threads for CPU time. However, any one program cannot harness more than one tenth of the CPU power in a 10-CPU machine unless it is multi-threaded.

If you multi-thread your Mandelbrot program, NT can run the separate threads on separate CPUs, and this allows the program to take full advantage of all the available CPU power. For example, if the Mandelbrot program breaks itself into 10 threads, then one thread will run on each CPU and the program will run roughly ten times faster. There is no reason to use more than ten threads on a 10-CPU machine, because each thread incurs a very slight amount of overhead and it is therefore wasteful to have more than 10. However, you could break the program into 100 threads if you like, or use one thread for each scan-line of the drawing, if that makes things conceptually easier for you in a certain application. There are many cases where breaking an application into multiple threads actually makes the whole program much easier to understand, and threads turn out to be remarkably easy to create.

When any process starts in Windows, it by default contains one thread of execution. For example, when you type "notepad" on the command line or double click on notepad's icon in the Program Manager, Windows creates a process, and that process has one thread that "runs" notepad's code. The process is essentially a container for the global variables, environment strings, the heap owned by the application, and the thread. The thread is what actually executes the code.

All threads in one process *share* the variable space of their parent process. Each thread also has its own stack. When you create a new thread within a process, it has access to all the global variables and the heap of the parent process. See Figures 35.1 and 35.2. All the problems that arise from the careless use of globals in a normal program are therefore compounded in a multi-threaded program, because now several different threads can modify the same global variables independently of one another. To solve the problems that tend to arise in such situations, there are *synchronization mechanisms* built into the Win32 API and MFC.

If you read through Chapter 10, or if you are a long-time user of MFC, you may be familiar with the **OnIdle** capability built into the **CWinApp** class. It is important to understand the difference between a thread and **OnIdle**. A thread is a completely separate stream of execution, and the operating system gives the thread time slices. Once you start a thread it will perform its tasks in a completely independent manner. A background thread has no effect on the other threads. The **OnIdle** capability, on the other hand, is intimately tied to the application's user interface and central event loop. When there are no events in the event loop, then **OnIdle** gets called. However, the event loop will not process the next event until **OnIdle** returns. Therefore, the processing that occurs in **OnIdle** must be subdivided into tasks with a maximum duration of perhaps one-tenth of a second. Otherwise, the user interface stalls. The fact that there is only one **OnIdle** function, intimately tied to the application's event loop, and that **OnIdle** tasks have to be finely subdivided, makes the management of the **OnIdle** function very complicated. All of these problems disappear with threads.

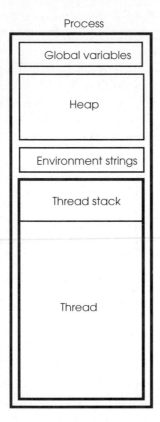

Process

Global variables

Heap

Environment strings

Thread stack

Thread

Figure 35.1
A process just after creation, with one thread. The process holds the global variables, heap, and environment strings, while the thread owns its stack (and therefore any local variables).

35.3 MFC Worker Threads

MFC divides threads into two types: *worker* threads and *user-interface* threads. Worker threads are simple background threads. They are extremely easy to understand and use, and are therefore much more common. Probably the easiest way to get started with threading is to start with small worker thread examples.

Let's do that by creating a simple AppWizard application that creates a worker thread that beeps in the background. This is the simplest threading example you can possibly create because the thread is *completely* independent of the application that spawned it.

To create this threading example, start by creating an AppWizard framework. Call the application "Thd." Specify an SDI interface and trim the features to a minimum because we will not use them. Open the ClassWizard and override the **OnInitalUpdate** function in the view class. Add the following code:

```
UINT ThreadFunction( LPVOID pParam )
{
    while (1)
    {
        Beep(100, 100);
        Sleep(1000);
    }
    return 0;
```

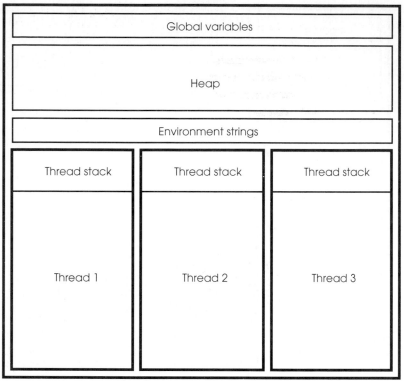

Process

Figure 35.2
A process holding three threads. The threads share the globals, heap and environment strings, while each thread has its own stack (and therefore its own local variables).

```
}

void CThdView::OnInitialUpdate()
{
    AfxBeginThread(ThreadFunction, NULL);

    CView::OnInitialUpdate();
}
```

The **OnInitialUpdate** function creates the thread by calling **AfxBeginThread**, which accepts the name of the *thread function* and a parameter to pass to the thread function. The thread function here is named **ThreadFunction**, but can be named anything you like. The thread function must, however, accept an LPVOID parameter and return a UINT. Also, the thread function cannot be the member of a class. It must be independent of the class, as shown in this example, because the **CWinThread** class uses Win32's **CreateThread** function, which only accepts normal functions.

Run the program. You will find that the application beeps once each second until you terminate the application.

When the system executes the program, the view's **OnInitialUpdate** function gets called as the view is created. The call to **AfxBeginThread** creates an instance of the **CWinThread** class, which calls the function in the Win32 API that actually creates the thread. The thread function executes in the new thread, so the function executes in a manner that is entirely independent of the application. If the thread function returns (or if it calls **AfxEndThread**), the thread dies. Otherwise, the thread function runs until the process that owns the thread—in this case the application— terminates.

One thing you should note in the thread function is the fact that it calls **Sleep**. The **Sleep** function suspends the thread for the length of time specified. While it is sleeping, the thread consumes no CPU resources. This is an extremely efficient way to perform this background task—the thread only executes one line of code (the **Beep** function) every second. Because the thread runs in a manner that is totally independent of the application, the thread function and its call to **Sleep** have absolutely no effect on the user interface for the application.

Run the application again under the debugger. You can set breakpoints in the thread function, or in the main application thread, and the system will honor them. You can also select the **Break** option in the **Debug** menu to stop a threaded application. All the threads will stop. When the program is stopped like this, you can use the **Threads** option in the **Debug** menu to view a list of running threads. You can selectively suspend and resume each thread. Try creating two separate thread functions that beep at different frequencies to experiment with the debugger features.

35.4 Thread Termination

When you run it under the debugger, one thing that you will notice about this simple beeping program is that it has a memory leak. To understand and fix this memory leak, you need to have a good working knowledge of the **CWinThread** class in MFC. Take a moment now to review the data members and member functions for **CWinThread** in the MFC documentation. You will also find there several general information pages that you should scan.

The **CWinThread** class creates a thread (using Win32's **CreateThread** function) and holds onto its handle with a member variable named **m_hThread**. The **CWinThread** class also contains several member functions that let you control the thread or get information about it. For example, you can get or set the thread's priority, and you can suspend and resume the thread. The **CWinThread** class additionally contains several data members and member functions that are useful when creating user-interface threads. These features are discussed later in this chapter.

When the beeping code in the previous section called the **AfxBeginThread** function, the function created an instance of the **CWinThread** class for you and returned a pointer to it. To eliminate the memory leak, you need to hold onto the pointer that **AfxWinThread** returns and delete that pointer before program termination. Before deleting the pointer, however, you should terminate the thread. This termination must be done by the thread itself.

A thread terminates itself in one of two ways. When the thread function returns, that terminates the thread. The thread can also call **AfxEndThread** to terminate itself. The **AfxEndThread** function is useful when the thread function has called another function and that function wants to terminate the thread. The value returned by **return,** or the parameter passed to **AfxEndThread**, acts as the exit code for the thread.

We can use all this information to correctly handle termination of the beeping thread in the previous section. First we need to give the thread a way to know that it is time to die. In this example we will use the simplest mechanism possible: a global variable. There is a variety of more exotic methods you can use if you so desire. See *Win32 System Services: The Heart of Windows NT* for details. You may also want to look at the MTRECALC example in the MFC samples directory for another view.

When the view is about to die, it can change the global variable so that the thread dies also. The **CWinThread** class is smart enough to delete itself once it senses the death of its associated thread so that should solve the problem. The following code attempts to use this technique. To make use of it, open the ClassWizard and add an override function for the WM_DESTROY message to the view class:

```
/////////////////////////////////////////////////////////////////
// CThdView message handlers

// Set to true to kill the thread
BOOL bKill = FALSE;

// The thread function
UINT ThreadFunction( LPVOID pParam )
{
    while (!bKill)
    {
        Beep(100, 100);
        Sleep(1000);
    }
    return 0;
}


CWinThread *pThread;

// Override for OnInitialUpdate VF. Create with ClassWizard.
void CThdView::OnInitialUpdate()
{
    pThread = AfxBeginThread(ThreadFunction, NULL);

    CView::OnInitialUpdate();
}

// Handler for WM_DESTROY message. Create with ClassWizard.
void CThdView::OnDestroy()
{
    bKill = TRUE;

    CView::OnDestroy();
}
```

In this code, you can see that the thread function uses the **bKill** Boolean to control the while loop. When it is time for the thread to die, the **OnDestroy** function sets **bKill** to TRUE. This should cause the thread's loop to terminate, which should cause the thread to return and therefore die, which should cause the instance of **CWinThread** pointed to by **pThread** to delete itself, which should end the memory leak. However, if you run this code under the debugger, you will find that, in most cases, the memory leak persists.

This problem is caused by the **Sleep** function in the thread. Although the **OnDestroy** function has set **bKill** to TRUE, the thread is probably sleeping. Therefore, the view proceeds to destroy itself before the thread wakes up and realizes it needs to die. The following code, although a bit more complicated, truly solves the problem:

```
/////////////////////////////////////////////////////////////////
// CThdView message handlers

// Set to true to kill the thread
BOOL bKill = FALSE;

// The thread function
UINT ThreadFunction( LPVOID pParam )
{
    while (!bKill)
    {
        Beep(100, 100);
        Sleep(1000);
    }
    return 0;
}


CWinThread *pThread;

// Override for OnInitialUpdate VF. Create with ClassWizard.
void CThdView::OnInitialUpdate()
{
    pThread = AfxBeginThread(ThreadFunction, NULL);
    pThread->m_bAutoDelete = FALSE;

    CView::OnInitialUpdate();
}

// Handler for WM_DESTROY message. Create with ClassWizard.
void CThdView::OnDestroy()
{
    bKill = TRUE;
    WaitForSingleObject(pThread->m_hThread, INFINITE);
    delete pThread;

    CView::OnDestroy();
}
```

This code creates the thread with **AfxBeginThread**, and then sets its **m_bAutoDelete** member to FALSE. This change eliminates the auto-deletion capability from the **CWinThread** instance, thereby causing the **CWinThread** object to remain in memory after the thread dies. Because we know that the **CWinThread** object always exists, we can safely use the **WaitForSingleObject** function in the Win32 API to wait for the thread to terminate. The **WaitForSingleObject** function blocks until the thread dies or the time-out expires. Because the time-out is infinite in this case, the function waits for the thread to terminate and then returns. Once the thread dies, we can delete the instance of **CWinThread** and allow the view to close. The memory leak is eliminated.

35.5 Passing Parameters to Threads

Any thread function can accept one four-byte parameter, which you can use in any way you like. You can pass in an integer, a Boolean, a pointer to a structure or class, and so on. One common way to use the parameter is to pass in a pointer that refers back to the parent of the thread.

To demonstrate the use of the thread function parameter, use the AppWizard to create a new *MDI* application. Use the ClassWizard to override the **OnInitialUpdate** function and add a WM_DESTROY handler function in the view. Add the following two lines to the view's header file in the attributes section:

```
BOOL bKill;
CWinThread *pThread;
```

Then add the following code to the view class:

```
//////////////////////////////////////////////////////////////
// CDotsView message handlers

// Thread function
UINT DotThread(LPVOID pParam)
{
    CDotsView *view = (CDotsView *) pParam;
    CRect r;
    srand(GetTickCount());

    while (!view->bKill)
    {
        CClientDC dc(view);
        view->GetClientRect(&r);

        int i = rand() % r.Width();
        int j = rand() % r.Height();

        dc.SetPixel(i, j, RGB(0,0,0));
    }
    return 0;
}

// Override for OnInitialUpdate VF. Create with ClassWizard.
void CDotsView::OnInitialUpdate()
{
    bKill = FALSE;
    pThread = AfxBeginThread(DotThread, this);
    pThread->m_bAutoDelete = FALSE;
```

```
        CView::OnInitialUpdate();
}

// Message handler for WM_DESTROY. Create with ClassWizard.
void CDotsView::OnDestroy()
{
    bKill = TRUE;
    WaitForSingleObject(pThread->m_hThread, INFINITE);
    delete pThread;

    CView::OnDestroy();
}
```

This code creates a thread function that draws random dots into the view. It can do this because the thread function receives a pointer to the view in its parameter. It then uses this pointer to access the view's member variables and to create a DC for the view. If you run this program, you will find that you can create multiple windows in the MDI shell, and they will update themselves properly. In addition, because the code correctly deletes threads as discussed in the previous section, you can close MDI windows and they will clean themselves up properly.

35.6 Suspending and Resuming Threads

The **CWinThread** class includes functions that let your application suspend and resume the threads that it creates. To demonstrate these functions, start with the application that you created in the previous section. We will add two menu options to it that will suspend and resume the thread's drawing activities.

Open the resource file and open the IDR_DOTSTYPE menu. Add a new menu named **Thread** and add to it two options named **Suspend** and **Resume**. With the menu open as the topmost window in Visual C++, open the ClassWizard and create handler functions for both menu options in the view class. Use the following code in the handlers:

```
// Handler for suspend option in thread menu
void CDotsView::OnThreadSuspend()
{
    pThread->SuspendThread();
}

// Handler for resume option in thread menu
void CDotsView::OnThreadResume()
{
    pThread->ResumeThread();
}
```

Compile and run the application. When you select the **Suspend** menu option, the thread will suspend. Click the **Resume** option to resume drawing. Open several windows using the **New** option in the **File** menu, and you will find that you can selectively suspend individual threads. Also note that if you suspend one thread twice, you have to resume it twice—the thread maintains a suspend count rather than a binary flag.

35.7 Thread Priorities

The Win32 API uses a round-robin priority queue structure to schedule CPU time among available threads. To understand thread priorities and how to set them, you need to be familiar with the priority and scheduling mechanisms used by Windows. This section contains a brief overview.

All the threads in a process have a priority relative to their parent process. The priority of the threads determines the amount of CPU time they receive relative to one another and relative to other threads in other processes of the same process priority. You set a thread's priority using the **SetThreadPriority** function and retrieve it using the **GetThreadPriority** function.

Every process starts with a base priority determined by its *priority class*. NT defines four different classes:

Class	Base priority
IDLE_PRIORITY_CLASS	4
NORMAL_PRIORITY_CLASS	9 foreground, 7 background
HIGH_PRIORITY_CLASS	13
REALTIME_PRIORITY_CLASS	24

A regular process, such as one launched from the Program Manager or the command line, is "normal." Operating system threads are given a high or real-time priority class.

The threads within a process can then adjust their priority relative to the base priority of the process. When you call **SetThreadPriority**, it accepts one of the following values:

THREAD_PRIORITY_LOWEST	-2
THREAD_PRIORITY_BELOW_NORMAL	-1
THREAD_PRIORITY_NORMAL	+0
THREAD_PRIORITY_ABOVE_NORMAL	+1
THREAD_PRIORITY_HIGHEST	+2

For example, if a foreground process has a normal priority class and one of its threads sets its priority to THREAD_PRIORITY_LOWEST, then the thread's priority value is 7 (9 - 2 = 7).

Two additional thread priorities set a thread's priority value to an absolute number:

THREAD_PRIORITY_TIME_CRITICAL	15 or 31 absolute
THREAD_PRIORITY_IDLE	1 or 16 absolute

Setting a thread's priority to THREAD_PRIORITY_IDLE makes the thread's priority value 16 if its process's class is REALTIME_PRIORITY_CLASS and makes it 1 otherwise. Setting a thread's priority to THREAD_PRIORITY_TIME_CRITICAL makes the thread's priority value 31 if its process's class is REALTIME_PRIORITY_CLASS and makes it 15 otherwise. (Find the **SetPriority-Class** description in the Win32 API documentation for a complete chart.)

Based on the different base priorities of processes and the possible thread priorities, there are a total of 22 different priority values possible, ranging between 1 and

31. The thread scheduler uses the priority value of all the threads currently in existence to determine which thread gets the next slice of CPU time.

Think about a typical Windows system in the middle of operation on a typical day. It has all sorts of threads running. Under Windows NT, if you open the Performance Monitor and look at the Threads counter under the Objects object, it will tell you exactly how many threads currently exist on your machine. On my machine at this particular moment there are 155. By killing off all the extraneous windows, I can get it down to 138. All the others are threads associated with different background services, operating system tasks, and so on.

At any given moment, a thread can be in any of several states. Some threads are *suspended*. For example, you might have clicked on the **Suspend** option for one of the windows in the previous section, so the thread for that window is suspended. These threads consume no CPU time and will not be scheduled for CPU time until they resume. Some threads are *sleeping* because they called the **Sleep** function. These threads also consume no CPU time, but will be scheduled for CPU time once the sleep time expires. Some of the threads are *waiting* for something. For example, one thread might need user input from the keyboard, while another is waiting for a network packet, and another is waiting for a sector from the hard disk. They will be scheduled once the resource or event they await arrives.

The rest of the threads are *ready*. They have something to do, and the only thing preventing them from doing it is the fact that there is only one CPU and perhaps five threads needing to share it. On a multi-CPU machine, there might be two CPUs and five threads waiting for one of them. Threads in that case are dispatched to both CPUs by the scheduler.

Windows NT, like most preemptive operating systems, picks a ready thread and lets it use the CPU for a specified amount of time, a *time slice*, of perhaps 20 milliseconds. The thread will normally end up requesting something that is not available, like a keystroke or a disk sector, before its time slice completes, so the operating system will stop it and let it wait for what it needs. Otherwise the time slice will elapse and the scheduler will preempt the thread. It then picks another ready thread and gives it the next time slice, and so on.

Windows picks the thread that will receive the next time slice using a set of ready queues arranged by priority. Figure 35.3 shows a typical arrangement. Each queue works in a round-robin fashion, so a thread that is ready gets put on the end of one of the priority queues. The queue chosen is determined by the priority number of the thread. The operating system services all the threads in a given queue in order. If a thread uses up its time slice and is still ready, it gets put onto the end of its ready queue again. All the ready threads in the highest priority queue get serviced until that queue is empty. The system then moves down to the next lower queue and begins servicing its threads, and so on.

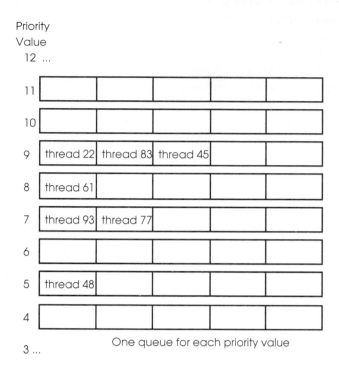

Figure 35.3

The priority queue structure used by the scheduler, here with seven different threads ready and waiting for CPU time. The three threads with priority value 9 will be serviced until they are all waiting for something and there are no ready threads at priority 9. Then the thread at priority 8 will be serviced, and so on.

Given this description of Windows' priority structure, it is easy to see how one can easily wreak havoc with it. For example, say that you take a thread that is CPU-bound—that is, one that never sleeps, requests keyboard input or disk sectors, and so on—and you then set the thread's priority just one level up by changing it to THREAD_PRIORITY_ABOVE_NORMAL after you create the thread. This simple act will essentially lock up all the other normal processes currently running. The scheduler services it continually, at the expense of *all* threads below it. The operating system threads that are in higher process classes still run, so the whole machine does not lock up, but all of the normal processes would appear to die. There are some safeguards, including variable thread priorities for threads with priorities below 16, but in general high priority threads that are CPU-bound cause problems.

There is an important lesson here. If you have a thread you know will always be ready—that is, a thread that is compute bound—you should probably lower its priority so that it does not stall all the threads below it in the scheduler. Alternatively, you can cause it to sleep occasionally or frequently to give the threads below it some time slices. An idle thread with priority value 1 *never* gets a time slice unless *all* threads above it are waiting for something. Therefore, it may be a reasonable practice to set your compute-bound threads to the absolute priority THREAD_PRIORITY_IDLE so that they don't cut off any other processes. If every application did that, things would work well.

Similarly, you should never give a thread a high priority unless you *know* that it will frequently wait, and that it will not use much CPU time when it becomes ready. For example, you might place a call to **WaitCommEvent** in a high-priority thread so that it is waiting for a certain communications event such as the arrival of a character. The thread can then quickly process that character and wait again. Design the application so a normal priority thread actually does something with the character retrieved, or set the priority of the high-priority thread back to normal during processing so you do not starve everything else.

You can use the following code to demonstrate thread priorities and experiment with different possibilities. It is a modification of the code from the previous section. This version creates two separate threads, one that draws red dots (a low-priority thread), and another that draws blue dots (a normal priority thread). You can suspend and resume the blue dot thread from the menu. Add the following three lines to the view's header file in the attributes section:

```
BOOL bKill;
CWinThread *pThread1;
CWinThread *pThread2;
```

Then modify the code in the **CDotsView** class so it looks like this:

```
//////////////////////////////////////////////////////////////
// CDotsView message handlers

// Thread function for blue dots
UINT DotThread1(LPVOID pParam)
{
    CDotsView *view = (CDotsView *) pParam;
    CRect r;
    srand(GetTickCount());

    while (!view->bKill)
    {
        CClientDC dc(view);
        view->GetClientRect(&r);

        int i = rand() % r.Width();
        int j = rand() % r.Height();

        dc.SetPixel(i, j, RGB(0,0,255));
    }
    return 0;
}

// Thread function for red dots
UINT DotThread2(LPVOID pParam)
{
    CDotsView *view = (CDotsView *) pParam;
    CRect r;
```

```
        srand(GetTickCount());

        while (!view->bKill)
        {
            CClientDC dc(view);
            view->GetClientRect(&r);

            int i = rand() % r.Width();
            int j = rand() % r.Height();

            dc.SetPixel(i, j, RGB(255,0,0));
        }
        return 0;
    }

    // Override for OnInitialUpdate VF. Create with ClassWizard.
    void CDotsView::OnInitialUpdate()
    {
        bKill = FALSE;
        pThread1 = AfxBeginThread(DotThread1, this);
        pThread1->m_bAutoDelete = FALSE;
        pThread2 = AfxBeginThread(DotThread2, this);
        pThread2->m_bAutoDelete = FALSE;
        pThread2->SetThreadPriority(THREAD_PRIORITY_LOWEST);

        CView::OnInitialUpdate();
    }

    // Message handler for WM_DESTROY. Create with ClassWizard.
    void CDotsView::OnDestroy()
    {
        bKill = TRUE;
        WaitForSingleObject(pThread1->m_hThread, INFINITE);
        delete pThread1;
        WaitForSingleObject(pThread2->m_hThread, INFINITE);
        delete pThread2;

        CView::OnDestroy();
    }

    // Handler for suspend option in thread menu
    void CDotsView::OnThreadSuspend()
    {
        pThread1->SuspendThread();
    }

    // Handler for resume option in thread menu
    void CDotsView::OnThreadResume()
    {
        pThread1->ResumeThread();
    }
```

The **OnInitialUpdate** function creates the two threads, and it adjusts the red thread's priority to the THREAD_PRIORITY_LOWEST. The **OnDestroy** function terminates both threads. The **OnThreadSuspend** and **OnThreadResume** functions handle the corresponding menu options and suspend and resume the blue thread.

When you run the application, you will find that the window fills quickly with blue dots. You will also find an occasional red dot, as the scheduler's variable priorities kick in to prevent total starvation of the red thread. Note, however, that the red thread's execution is *extremely* rare. If you suspend the blue thread, the red thread will pick up to full speed because it is not competing with anything (provided no other process on the system has a compute-bound thread at higher priority).

Now try a second experiment. Open a second child window in the MDI frame. In one of the windows suspend the blue thread. Now tile the windows. You can see exactly how often the red thread gets executed in relation to the blue thread. Try running two separate instances of the same application and run the same experiment. Use this framework to conduct a variety of priority experiments of your own until you feel comfortable with the different thread priorities and how they work.

35.8 Subclassing CWinThread

One problem frequently faced by application designers is the "long redraw" problem. For example, if you have a complex drawing or painting program that requires several minutes to update the screen, it can be annoying for the user when the hourglass cursor prevents the use of the rest of the application. In this section we examine how to solve this problem by subclassing the **CWinThread** class.

To simulate a long calculation, we will again use the Mandelbrot set. Even on extremely fast machines, the redraw time for a large Mandelbrot set can be quite annoying. To experience the annoyance for yourself, create a new MDI application with the AppWizard. Call it "Mandel". Open the resource file and in the IDR_MANDTYPE menu add an option called **Draw** to the **Window** menu. In the view class, use the ClassWizard to add a menu handler for this new menu option and put into it the following code:

```
// Command handler for Draw menu option
void CMandelView::OnWindowDraw()
{
    GetDocument()->UpdateAllViews(0, NULL, 0);
}
```

Add a variable of the following type to the attributes section of the view's header file:

```
DWORD colors[64];
```

Change the view class's constructor so that it initializes the member variable:

```
CMandelView::CMandelView(): m_thread(0)
{
    WORD x;
    BYTE red=0, green=0, blue=0;

    for (x=0; x<64; x++)
    {
        colors[x] = RGB(red, green, blue);
        if (!(red += 64))
            if (!(green += 64))
                blue += 64;
```

```
    }
    colors[63] = RGB(255,255,255);
}
```

Use the ClassWizard to override the **OnInitialUpdate** function in the view class and delete its code so it looks like this:

```
void CMandelView::OnInitialUpdate()
{
}
```

You are doing this so **OnUpdate** does not get called when the application first starts. This means that the only time **OnUpdate** will be called is when you select the **Draw** menu option.

Then use the ClassWizard again and add code to the view's **OnUpdate** function as shown below:

```
const int NUM_ITERATIONS=64;

const double left = -1.0;
const double right = 1.0;
const double top = -1.0;
const double bottom = 1.0;

typedef struct
{
    double real;
    double imag;
} complex;

void CMandelView::OnUpdate(CView* pSender,
    LPARAM lHint, CObject* pHint)
{
    CRect r;
    double xstep, ystep;
    double x, y;
    int i,j;
    WORD iter;
    complex k;
    complex z;
    double real, imag, spread;

    CClientDC dc(this);
    GetClientRect(&r);

    ystep = (double) (bottom - top) / r.Height();
    xstep = (double) (right - left) / r.Width();

    for (y=top, j=0; y <= bottom; y += ystep, j++)
    {
        for (x=left, i=0; x<=right; x += xstep, i++)
        {
            k.real = x;
            k.imag = y;
            z.real=z.imag=0.0;

            for (iter=0; iter<NUM_ITERATIONS-1;
                iter++)
```

```
            {
                real = z.real + k.real;
                imag = z.imag + k.imag;
                z.real = real * real -
                    imag * imag;
                z.imag = 2 * real * imag;
                spread = z.real * z.real +
                    z.imag * z.imag;
                if (spread > 4.0)
                    break;
            }
            dc.SetPixel(i, j, colors[iter]);
        }
    }
}
```

Compile the code and *run it under the debugger.* By running under the debugger you will have an easy way to terminate the application should you find it too annoying. Resize the MDI child window so it is fairly small, and choose the new **Draw** menu option in the **Window** menu. The Mandelbrot set will redraw. Note that, while it is redrawing, the rest of the application's user interface is locked. You cannot click in the menus, move the child windows, etc. If you use the **New Window** option in the **Window** menu to create several MDI windows for the same document, you will find that the problem is multiplied as all windows slowly update one by one.

The problems seen here can be solved with threads. However, we may not want to use the simple approach taken in the previous examples. There are two conflicting problems that can arise from the simple approach:

1. In the previous examples, the structure of the code guaranteed that the thread would start at the same time the view did and that it would only need to start once. Therefore, the **OnDestroy** function could simply delete **pThread**. In this Mandelbrot code, the **OnWindowDraw** function will need to start the thread many times. Therefore, the deletion of the **CWinThread** object becomes more complicated. It would be nice to have the thread object auto-delete and eliminate this problem, but you need it for menu item enabling and disabling.

2. Once the application starts drawing the set, it would be nice to have the **Draw** menu option disable itself and then re-enable itself once the thread completes. This means that the thread object needs to remain in existence following the completion of the thread so you can examine the thread exit code with the Win32 API's **GetExitCodeThread** function. This function returns STILL_ACTIVE while the thread is active, and the thread's return value once it terminates. If the instance of **CWinThread** automatically deletes itself, then there is no way to determine completion of the thread.

The easiest way to solve both these problems is to derive a class from **CWinThread** and then create an instance of this derived class in the view's constructor. This way you are able to start the thread multiple times, using the **CreateThread** function in **CWinThread**, without having to worry about deletion. Also, you can structure the implementation of the derived class so that some of the messiness seen in prior examples gets encapsulated in the derived class.

The ClassWizard gives you an easy way to derive a new class from **CWinThread**. Add a new class using the ClassWizard. Give the class the name **CMandelThread**. Select **CWinThread** for the class type. Take a look at the overridable functions for this class in the MFC documentation—several of them are interesting.

There are a number of changes we need to make to the **CMandelThread** class to adapt it to the task at hand. First we need to create a thread function and copy into it the Mandelbrot drawing code. We can also copy the color array, the color array initialization, and other constants and structures having to do with the Mandelbrot calculation. The drawing code needs to know about the view so we can pass that in through the constructor. The class can also handle starting, termination, and detection in member functions. When you get done, the header and code files for the **CMandelThread** class should look like those shown in Listings 35.1 and 35.2.

Listing 35.1
The mandel.h file

```
// mandelth.h : header file
//


/////////////////////////////////////////////////////////////////
// CMandelThread thread


class CMandelThread : public CWinThread
{
    DECLARE_DYNCREATE(CMandelThread)
protected:
    CMandelThread(); // protected constructor used by dyncreate
public:
    CMandelThread(CView *view); //public constructor

// Attributes
public:
    CView *pView;
    BOOL bKill;
    DWORD colors[64];

// Operations
public:

// Overrides
    // ClassWizard generated virtual function overrides
    //{{AFX_VIRTUAL(CMandelThread)
    public:
    virtual BOOL InitInstance();
    virtual int ExitInstance();
    //}}AFX_VIRTUAL
    void Kill();
```

```
        BOOL Start();
        BOOL Running();

// Implementation
public:
    virtual ~CMandelThread();

        // Generated message map functions
        //{{AFX_MSG(CMandelThread)
            // NOTE - the ClassWizard will add and
            // remove member functions here.
        //}}AFX_MSG

        DECLARE_MESSAGE_MAP()
};

//////////////////////////////////////////////////////////////////
```

Listing 35.2
The mandelth.cpp file

```
// mandelth.cpp : implementation file
//

#include "stdafx.h"
#include "mandel.h"
#include "mandedoc.h"
#include "mandelth.h"

#ifdef _DEBUG
#undef THIS_FILE
static char BASED_CODE THIS_FILE[] = __FILE__;
#endif

//////////////////////////////////////////////////////////////////
// Thread function

const int NUM_ITERATIONS=64;

const double left = -1.0;
const double right = 1.0;
const double top = -1.0;
const double bottom = 1.0;

typedef struct
{
    double real;
    double imag;
} complex;

UINT HandleDrawing(LPVOID pParam)
{
    CMandelThread *thread = (CMandelThread *) pParam;
```

```
CRect r;
double xstep, ystep;
double x, y;
int i,j;
WORD iter;
complex k;
complex z;
double real, imag, spread;

CClientDC dc(thread->pView);
thread->pView->GetClientRect(&r);

ystep = (double) (bottom - top) / r.Height();
xstep = (double) (right - left) / r.Width();

for (y=top, j=0; y <= bottom; y += ystep, j++)
{
    for (x=left, i=0; x<=right; x += xstep, i++)
    {
        if (thread->bKill)
            return 0;
        k.real = x;
        k.imag = y;
        z.real=z.imag=0.0;

        for (iter=0; iter<NUM_ITERATIONS-1;
            iter++)
        {
            real = z.real + k.real;
            imag = z.imag + k.imag;
            z.real = real * real -
                imag * imag;
            z.imag = 2 * real * imag;
            spread = z.real * z.real +
                z.imag * z.imag;
            if (spread > 4.0)
                break;
        }
        dc.SetPixel(i, j, thread->colors[iter]);
    }
}
return 0;
}


/////////////////////////////////////////////////////////////////
// CMandelThread

IMPLEMENT_DYNCREATE(CMandelThread, CWinThread)

CMandelThread::CMandelThread()
{
}

CMandelThread::CMandelThread(CView *view)
{
```

```
        pView = view;
        m_bAutoDelete = FALSE;
        m_pThreadParams = this;
        m_pfnThreadProc = HandleDrawing;

        WORD x;
        BYTE red=0, green=0, blue=0;
        for (x=0; x<64; x++)
        {
            colors[x] = RGB(red, green, blue);
            if (!(red += 64))
                if (!(green += 64))
                    blue += 64;
        }
        colors[63] = RGB(255,255,255);
}

CMandelThread::~CMandelThread()
{
}

BOOL CMandelThread::InitInstance()
{
    return TRUE;
}

int CMandelThread::ExitInstance()
{
    return CWinThread::ExitInstance();
}

// Kills a running thread
void CMandelThread::Kill()
{
    bKill = TRUE;
    WaitForSingleObject(m_hThread, INFINITE);
};

// Starts the thread running
BOOL CMandelThread::Start()
{
    bKill = FALSE;
    return CreateThread();
};

// Returns TRUE if the thread is running
BOOL CMandelThread::Running()
{
    DWORD bStatus;
    ::GetExitCodeThread(m_hThread, &bStatus);
    if (bStatus == STILL_ACTIVE)
        return TRUE;
    else
        return FALSE;
}
```

```
BEGIN_MESSAGE_MAP(CMandelThread, CWinThread)
    //{{AFX_MSG_MAP(CMandelThread)
        // NOTE - the ClassWizard will add and
        // remove mapping macros here.
    //}}AFX_MSG_MAP
END_MESSAGE_MAP()


/////////////////////////////////////////////////////////////////
// CMandelThread message handlers
```

The most interesting thing happening in this code is inside the constructor. There are two undocumented member variables in the **CWinThread** class named **m_pfnThreadProc** and **m_pThreadParams**. They hold the address of the thread function and the thread function's parameter, respectively. When you call **CreateThread** in the **CWinThread** class, it looks at these two members so it can start the thread function. Having set them, **CreateThread** will work properly. The top part of the class contains the thread function along with several declarations and constants that it needs.

In the view class, the constructor and destructor work together to allocate and destroy the thread:

```
/////////////////////////////////////////////////////////////////
// CMandelView construction/destruction

CMandelView::CMandelView()
{
    pThread = new CMandelThread(this);
}

CMandelView::~CMandelView()
{
    delete pThread;
}
```

You can then use the ClassWizard to create message handlers for **OnInitialUpdate**, **OnUpdate**, and **OnDestroy**, as well as for the **Draw** menu option's COMMAND and UPDATE_COMMAND_UI messages:

```
/////////////////////////////////////////////////////////////////
// CMandelView message handlers

void CMandelView::OnUpdate(CView* pSender,
    LPARAM lHint, CObject* pHint)
{
    pThread->Start();
}

void CMandelView::OnWindowDraw()
{
    GetDocument()->UpdateAllViews(0, NULL, 0);
}

void CMandelView::OnUpdateWindowDraw(CCmdUI* pCmdUI)
{
```

```
        pCmdUI->Enable(!pThread->Running());
}

void CMandelView::OnInitialUpdate()
{
}

void CMandelView::OnDestroy()
{
    pThread->Kill();
    CView::OnDestroy();
}
```

As you can see, the encapsulation of the thread into a thread class significantly simplifies the implementation of the view class that uses it.

35.9 User Interface Threads

In all the previous examples we have concentrated on worker threads. There is another form or thread in MFC called a *user-interface thread*. While a worker thread performs its tasks in the background and has no real connection to the user interface unless you create one with the thread function's parameter, a user interface thread is intended to operate as a part of the user interface. It has its own window and can process events separately from the main window.

To create a user interface thread, you use the ClassWizard to derive a new class from **CWinThread**. Inside that class you create your user interface. Then at some point in the program you create the user-interface thread by calling **AfxBeginThread**.

To try this out, create an application with the ClassWizard. Then derive a new class from **CWinThread**. Call the new class **CUIThread**. In the CPP file for that class place the code shown in Listing 35.3.

Listing 35.3
The implementation for the CUIThread class

```
// uithread.cpp : implementation file
//

#include "stdafx.h"
#include "uit.h"
#include "uithread.h"

#ifdef _DEBUG
#undef THIS_FILE
static char BASED_CODE THIS_FILE[] = __FILE__;
#endif

/////////////////////////////////////////////////////////////////
// CUIThread

IMPLEMENT_DYNCREATE(CUIThread, CWinThread)

CUIThread::CUIThread()
```

```
    {
    }

CUIThread::~CUIThread()
    {
    }

class CWindow : public CFrameWnd
    {
        CStatic *cs;
public:
        CWindow();
        ~CWindow();
    };

CWindow::~CWindow()
    {
        delete cs;
    }

CWindow::CWindow()
    {
        Create(NULL, "Extra Window", WS_OVERLAPPEDWINDOW,
            CRect(0,0,200,200));
        cs = new CStatic();
        cs->Create("Hello World",
            WS_CHILD | WS_VISIBLE | SS_CENTER,
            CRect(50, 80, 150, 150), this);
    }

BOOL CUIThread::InitInstance()
    {
        // create a new frame window
        m_pMainWnd = new CWindow();
        m_pMainWnd->ShowWindow(SW_SHOWNORMAL);
        m_pMainWnd->UpdateWindow();
        return TRUE;
    }

int CUIThread::ExitInstance()
    {
        return CWinThread::ExitInstance();
    }

BEGIN_MESSAGE_MAP(CUIThread, CWinThread)
    //{{AFX_MSG_MAP(CUIThread)
        // NOTE - the ClassWizard will add and
        // remove mapping macros here.
    //}}AFX_MSG_MAP
END_MESSAGE_MAP()
```

If you look through Listing 35.3, you will find that it looks remarkably like the program in Chapter 1. This code creates a new window that displays the words "Hello World." When you create an instance of the thread, it will create a new window separate from the main window. That window can contain anything you like, as discussed throughout the rest of this book.

To create this extra window from anywhere else in the program, you can call the following line:

```
AfxBeginThread(RUNTIME_CLASS(CUIThread));
```

That will create an instance of the new thread and, therefore, the new window. See the MFC documentation for further information on user-interface threads.

35.10 Conclusion

The code in Listing 35.3 has a nice circularity to it. We started in Chapter 1 with the simplest possible MFC program. From there we have worked through a tremendous quantity and variety of information to get to a point where you can now create applications inside applications using **CWinThread** class.

It is our hope that this information is useful to you, and that you are able to take it and build exciting applications of your own. If you manage to put a really neat app together, send us some e-mail as described in Appendix C and let us know. We would like to hear from you.

Understanding C++:
An Accelerated Introduction

A.1 Tutorial One—Introduction

For many people the transition from C to C++ is not easy. In fact, this transition is often accompanied by quite a bit of anxiety because C++ is surrounded by a certain aura that makes it inaccessible. For example, you can pick up a book on C++, randomly turn to a page, and encounter paragraphs like this:

> "From a design perspective, private derivation is equivalent to containment except for the (occasionally important) issue of overriding. An important use of this is the technique of deriving a class publicly from an abstract base class defining an interface and privately from a concrete class providing an implementation. Because the inheritance implied in private derivation is an implementation detail that is not reflected in the type of the derived class, it is sometimes called 'implementation inheritance' and contrasted to public declaration, where the interface of the base class is inherited and the implicit conversion to the base type is allowed. The latter is sometimes referred to as sub-typing or 'interface inheritance'."
>
> *(From "The C++ Programming Language, second edition", by Bjarne Stroustrup, page 413)*

It is difficult to get started in an environment that is this obtuse.

The goal of these tutorials is to help you to gain an understanding of the fundamental concepts driving C++ in a quick and painless way. They let you begin thinking in an "object-oriented way." Once you understand the fundamentals, the rest of the language is relatively straightforward because you will have a framework on which to attach other details as you need them. Once you understand its underlying themes and vocabulary, C++ turns out to be a remarkable language with quite a bit of expressive power. Used correctly, it can dramatically improve your productivity as a programmer.

These tutorials answer three common questions:
- Why does C++ exist, and what are its advantages over C?
- What tools are available in C++ to express object-oriented ideas?
- How do you design and implement code using object-oriented principles?

Once you understand the basic tools available in C++ and know how and why to use them, you have become a C++ programmer. These tutorials will start you down that road and make other C++ material much easier to understand.

These tutorials assume you already know C. If that isn't the case, spend a week or two acclimating yourself to the C language and then come back to these tutorials. C++ is a superset of C, so almost everything that you know about C will map straight into this new language.

The tutorials start with a brief explanation of why C++ exists, and what it is trying to accomplish. C++ is a response to a number of problems that arise in large programming projects, and the language makes a lot more sense if you view it in that light. The next section describes enhancements in C++ that overcome and correct deficiencies in the C language. The remainder of the tutorials introduce the concepts of object-oriented programming, and the ways in which C++ handles those ideas:

- Tutorial One—Introduction
- Tutorial Two—C++ Enhancements to C
- Tutorial Three—Vocabulary
- Tutorial Four—Classes
- Tutorial Five—Inheritance
- Tutorial Six—Operator Overloading
- Tutorial Seven—Working with Pointers
- Tutorial Eight—Virtual Functions

Tutorials Six and Seven get a little deep into pointer details—if you feel uncomfortable with pointers right now skip them and move to Tutorial Eight.

The market is flooded with C++ books. If you want another source of C++ information go to a bookstore and find one that you feel comfortable with. It won't hurt to have several perspectives on this language.

A.1.1 Why does C++ Exist?

People who are new to C++, or who are trying to learn about it from books, often have two major questions: 1) "Everything I read always has this crazy vocabulary— 'encapsulation,' 'inheritance,' 'virtual functions,' 'classes,' 'overloading,' 'friends'— Where is all of this stuff coming from?" and 2) "This language—and object-oriented programming in general—obviously involve a major mental shift, so how do I learn to think in a C++ way?" Both these questions can be answered, and the design of C++ as a whole is much easier to swallow, if you know what the designers of C++ were trying to accomplish when they created the language. If you understand why the designers made the choices they did, and why they designed certain features into the language, then it is much easier to understand the language itself.

Language design is an evolutionary process. A new language is often created by looking at the lessons learned from past languages, or by trying to add newly conceived features to a language. Languages also evolve to solve specific problems. For example, Ada was designed primarily to solve a vexing problem faced by the Pentagon. Programmers writing code for different military systems were using hundreds of different languages and it was impossible to later maintain or upgrade the systems because of this. Ada tries to solve some of these problems by combining the good features of many different languages into a single language.

Another good example of the evolutionary process in computer languages occurred with the development of structured languages. These languages arose in response to a major problem unforeseen by earlier language designers: the overuse of the goto statement in large programs. In a small program, goto statements are not a problem. But in a large program, especially when used by someone who *likes* goto statements, they are terrible. They make the code completely incomprehensible to anyone who is trying to read it for the first time. Languages evolved to solve this problem, eliminating the goto statement entirely and making it easier to break large programs down into manageable functions and modules.

C++ is an "object-oriented" language. Object-oriented programming is a reaction to programming problems that were first seen in large programs being developed in the 70s. All object-oriented languages try to accomplish three things as a way of thwarting the problems inherent in large projects:

1. Object-oriented languages all implement "data abstraction" in a clean way using a concept called "classes." We will look at data abstraction in much more detail later because it is a central concept in C++. Briefly, data abstraction is a way of combining data with the functions used to manipulate the data so that implementation details are hidden from the programmer. Data abstraction makes programs much easier to maintain and upgrade.

2. All object-oriented languages try to make parts of programs easily reusable and extensible. This is where the word "object" comes from. Programs are broken down into reusable objects. These objects can then be grouped together in different ways to form new programs. Existing objects can also be extended. By giving programmers a very clean way to reuse code, and by virtually forcing programmers to write code this way, it is much easier to write new programs by assembling existing pieces.

3. Object-oriented languages try to make existing code easily modifiable without actually changing the code. This is a unique and very powerful concept, because it does not at first seem possible to change something without changing it. Using two new concepts however—*inheritance* and *polymorphism*—it is possible to do just that. The existing object stays the same and any changes are layered on top of it. The programmer's ability to maintain and adjust code in a bug-free way is drastically improved using this approach.

Because C++ is an object-oriented language, it possesses the three object-oriented benefits discussed above. C++ adds two other enhancements of its own to clean up problems in the original C language or to make programming in C++ easier than it is in C:

1. C++ adds a concept called "operator overloading." This feature lets you specify new ways of using standard operators like "+" and ">>" in your own programs.

For example, if you want to add a new type such as a complex number type to a C program, the implementation will not be clean. To add two complex numbers, you will have to create a function named "add" and then say "c3=add(c1,c2);", where c1, c2, and c3 are values of the new complex number type. In C++, you can *overload* the "+" and "=" operators instead, so that you can say, "c3 = c1 + c2". In this way, new types are added to the language in a completely seamless manner. The overloading concept extends to all functions created in C++.

2. C++ also cleans up the implementation of several portions of the C language, most importantly I/O and memory allocation. The new implementations have been created with an eye toward operator overloading, so it is easy to add new types and provide seamless I/O operations and memory allocation for them.

Let's look at some examples of problems that you have probably run across in your C programming exploits and then look at how they are solved in C++.

The first example can be seen in every library that is built in C. The problem is demonstrated in the code below, which sets a string to a value and then concatenates another string onto it:

```
char s[100];

strcpy(s, "hello ");
strcat(s, "world");
```

This code is not very pretty, but the format is typical of every library you create in C. The string type is built out of the array-of-characters type native to C. Because the new type is not part of the original language, the programmer is forced to use function calls to do anything with it. What you would like to do instead is be able to create a new type and have it seamlessly blend in with the rest of the language. Something like this:

```
string s;

s = "hello ";
s += "world";
```

If this were possible, the language would be infinitely extensible. C++ supports this sort of extension through *operator overloading* and *classes*. Notice also that by using the **string** type, the implementation is completely hidden. That is, you do not know that—or if—**string** has been created using an array of characters, a linked list, etc., and it appears to have no maximum length. Therefore it is easy to change the implementation of the type in the future without adversely affecting existing code.

Another example using a library can be seen in the implementation of a simple stack library. The function prototypes for a typical stack library (normally found in the header file) are shown below:

```
void stack_init(stack s, int max_size);
int stack_push(stack s, int value);
int stack_pop(stack s, int *value);
void stack_clear(stack s);
void stack_destroy(stack s);
```

The user of this library can push, pop and clear the stack, but before these operations are valid the stack must be initialized with **stack_init**. When finished with the stack, the stack must be destroyed with **stack_destroy**. But what if you forget the initialization or destruction steps? In the former case, the code will not work and it can be very difficult to track down the problem unless all the routines in the library detect initialization failure and report it. In the latter case, the failure to destroy the stack properly can cause memory leaks that are again very difficult to track down. C++ solves this problem using *constructors* and *destructors*, which automatically handle initialization and destruction of objects such as stacks.

Continuing with the stack example, notice that the stack as defined can push and pop integers. What if you want to create another stack that can handle reals and another for characters? You will have to create three separate libraries, or alternatively use a union and let the union handle all different types possible. In C++, a concept called *templates* lets you create just one stack library and redefine the types stored on the stack when it is declared.

Another problem you might have had as a C programmer involves changing libraries. Say, for example, you are using the **printf** function defined in the stdio library but you want to modify it so it can handle a new type you have recently created. For example, you might want to modift **printf** so it can print complex numbers. You are out of luck unless you happen to have the source code for **printf**. And even if you have the source, modification won't do a lot of good because that source is not portable, nor do you have the right to copy it. There really is no way to extend a C library easily once it has been compiled. To solve your output problem, you will have to create a new function to print your new type. If you have more than one new type, you probably will have to create several different output functions and they will all be different. C++ handles all of these problems with its new technique for standard output. A combination of operator overloading and classes allow new types to integrate themselves into the standard C++ I/O scheme.

While thinking about the **printf** function, think about its design and ask yourself this: Is that a good way to design code? Inside **printf** there is a **switch** statement or an if-else-if chain that is parsing the format string. A %d is used for decimal numbers, a %c is used for characters, a %s is used for strings, and so on. There are at least three problems with this implementation:

1. The programmer has to maintain that **switch** statement and modify it for each new type that is to be handled. Modification means that new bugs might be introduced.
2. There is no guarantee that the user will match up the data parameters with the format string, so the whole system can fail catastrophically.
3. It is inextensible—unless you have the source you cannot extend the **printf** statement.

C++ solves these problems completely by forcing the programmer to structure the code in a new way. The switch statement is hidden and handled automatically by the compiler through *function overloading*. It is impossible to mismatch the parameters, first because they are not implemented as parameters in C++, and second because the type of the variable automatically controls the switching mechanism that is implemented by the compiler.

C++ solves many other problems as well. For example, it solves the "common code replicated in many places" problem by letting you factor out common code in a third dimension. It solves the "I want to change the parameter type passed into a function without changing the function" problem by letting you overload the same function name with multiple parameter lists. It solves the "I want to make a tiny change to the way this works, but I don't have the source for it" problem, and at the same time it also solves the "I want to redo this function completely but not change the rest of the library" problem using inheritance. It makes the creation of libraries much cleaner. It drastically improves the maintainability of code. And so on.

You have to change your way of thinking slightly in order to take advantage of much of this power, and it turns out that you generally have to consider the design of your code up front a little more. If you don't, you lose many of the benefits. As you can see however, you gain a great deal in return for your investment. As in everything else, there is a tradeoff, but overall the benefits outweigh the disadvantages.

A.1.2 Cleaning up C

The changes that make C++ different from C come in two categories: 1) changes that fix problems in C or enhance it, and 2) changes that add object-oriented extensions to C. The second category of changes is far more significant because they are the ones that involve a mental shift. The first category of changes enables many of those in the second category, however, so we will start with them first.

A.2 Tutorial Two—C++ Enhancements to C

Everything you ever wrote in C works in C++. However, in many cases C++ offers a better way to handle a given task. In other cases C++ offers a second way to do something, and the option gives you more flexibility. In this section we will examine C++ extensions to C. Many of these extensions were not added for their own sake, but instead "enable" object-oriented features that we will see in later tutorials.

This tutorial contains a lot of detail. Don't panic—just scan it for now if you like, and then come back and study the necessary sections as they are needed later on. These concepts have been collected here for easy reference because they are used at many different places.

A.2.1 Comments

C++ supports the old-style multi-line C comment, as well as a new single line form denoted by the "//" symbol. For example:

```
// get_it function reads in input values
void get_it()
{
    // do something.
}
```

Everything from the "//" to the end of the line is ignored. You can use both commenting styles interchangeably in a C++ program.

A.2.2 Type Casting

In C, you cast a type by placing a type name in parentheses and placing it in front of the variable name, as shown below:

```
int i;
float f;

f = (float) i;
```

In C++ a second format is also supported. It makes the cast look like a function call, as shown here:

```
int i;
float f;

f = float(i);
```

We will see later, when we begin discussing classes, that there is a reason for this new format.

A.2.3 Input and output

A.2.3.1 Terminal I/O One of the most obvious differences between C and C++ is the replacement of the stdio library in C with the iostream library in C++. The iostream library takes advantage of a number of the features of the C++ object-oriented extensions (we will see detailed examples later), and therefore makes the addition of new user-defined type I/O much easier. The iostream library also replaces all the capabilities found in the stdio library, so it is important to know how to use the basic features of the new library as you translate code to C++.

Use of the iostream library for basic input and output is straightforward. Two simple examples are shown below:

```
cout << "hello\n";
```

or equivalently:

```
cout << "hello" << endl;
```

Both forms produce the same output, and cause the word "hello" followed by a new line to appear on standard out. The word **cout** indicates stdout as the destination for the output, and the **<<** operator (the *insertion operator*) is used to gather the items. Two other standard output destinations are predefined: **cerr** for unbuffered error information and **clog** for buffered error information.

Any of the standard types can be written using the technique shown above: integers, floats, characters, and pointers to characters. Multiple items can either be strung together on a single line or stacked on multiple lines. For example:

```
int i = 2;
float f = 3.14
char c = 'A';
char *s = "hello";

cout << s << c << f << i << endl;
```

produces the output:

```
helloA3.142
```

and it is the same as:

```
cout << s << c;
cout << f;
cout << i << endl;
```

The **cout** mechanism automatically understands addresses and formats them for hex output. For example, if **i** is an integer, the statement:

```
cout << &i <<endl;
```

prints the address of **i** in hex format. If **p** is a pointer to **i**, printing **p** also prints the address of **i** in hex format. There are cases, however, where this formatting rule does not hold. Printing **s**, where **s** is a pointer to a character, produces the string pointed to by **s** rather than the address held by **s**. To remedy this situation, cast **s** to a void pointer as shown below if you want to see its address:

```
cout << (void *) s;
```

Now the address held by **s** will be shown in hex format. If you wish to display an address as a decimal number rather than in hex format, cast it to a **long** integer:

```
cout << long(&i);
```

This line prints the address of **i** in decimal format. In the same way, an **int** cast is used to print out the integer value of a character:

```
cout << int('A');// produces 65 as output
```

You may notice that the << operator—known in C as the shift left operator—has been stolen to handle output in C++. If you wish to use it for shifting left within an output line, then parentheses should be used:

```
cout << (2 << 4);// produces 32 as output
```

To format output, you can use several techniques. Information can be spaced by adding in spaces or tabs as literal strings, as shown below:

```
int i = 2;
float f = 3.14
char c = 'A';
char *s = "hello";

cout << s << " " << c << "\t" << f
    << "\t"<< i << endl;
```

There are several other manipulators that can be inserted into an output stream (on many systems you will have to include "iomanip.h" to use these):

- dec   Use decimal base
- oct   Use octal base
- hex   Use hex base
- endl   End of line
- ends   End of string ('\0')
- flush   Flush output buffer
- setw(w)   Set output width to w (0 is default)
- setfill(c)   Set fill character to c (blank is default)
- setprecision(p) Set float precision to p

The statement:

```
cout << "[" << setw (6) << setfill('*') << 192;
cout << "]" << endl;
cout << hex << "[" << setw (6);
cout << setfill('*') << 192 << "]" << endl;
cout << setprecision(4) << 3.14159 << endl;
```

produces:

```
[***192]
[****c0]
3.142
```

You can see from the above examples that certain variable and function names should not be used to avoid losing the manipulators built into the iostream library.

Input is handled in a similar manner, using the **cin** input stream and the ">>" *extraction* operator. For example, the statement:

```
int i,j,k;

cin >> i >> j >> k;
```

will read three integer values from stdin into **i, j**, and **k**. White space is automatically used as a separator and ignored. When reading into a string variable, the input is read word by word, where words are separated by white space. White space characters are ignored when reading into a character. This behavior can be overridden by explicitly reading strings and lines (see below). All of the standard types handled by **cout** are handled by **cin**. The **cin** stream can also be used in a while loop that terminates when EOF is detected, as shown below:

```
while (cin >> i)
    cout << i;
```

The **cin** stream automatically breaks string input into words and terminates on EOF.

A.2.4 File Input and Output

Input and output to text files are handled by including the file "fstream.h" and by then declaring variables of type **ifstream**, and **ofstream** respectively. For example, the following program reads from a file named "xxx" and writes to a file named "yyy":

```
#include <iostream.h>
#include <fstream.h>

void main()
{
    char c;
    ifstream infile("xxx");
    ofstream outfile("yyy");

    if (outfile && infile) // They will be 0 on err.
        while (infile >> c)
            outfile << c;
}
```

The **infile** and **outfile** variables are passed the file name on initialization and are used just as **cin** and **cout** are used. This code does not work as expected, however, because blanks, tabs, and '\n' characters at the end of each line are ignored as white space when using << on a character. Instead, the "get" function can be used, as shown below:

```
while (infile.get(c))
    outfile << c;
```

or:

```
while (infile.get(c))
    outfile.put(c);
```

It is also possible to read complete lines by calling the "getline" function in the same manner as used for the "get" function. To open a file for appending, use the following:

```
ofstream("xxx", iosapp);
```

This line, along with the ".get" function notation, will make more sense once you know more about C++. The fact that **ofsteam** sometimes takes one parameter and other times takes two is built into C++ (see Section 2.6).

Note that no "close" function is needed for file input and output. A file automatically closes itself when the file variable goes out of scope. If you do need to explicitly close a file, you can say:

```
outfile.close();
```

A.2.5 String I/O

Input can be read from strings in memory, and output can be sent to strings in memory, duplicating the action of **sscanf** and **sprintf**. To do this, you must include the file "strstrea.h" and then declare input and output strings. An output string is shown below:

```
char s[100];
ostrstream outstring(s,100);

outstring << 3.14 << " is pi" << ends;
cout << s;
```

The string **s** is filled with the text "3.14 is pi". If **s** is overfilled, **outstring** will automatically stop placing values into it.

If a string **s** exists and you wish to read from it, you can use an input string stream as shown below:

```
char *s = "3.14  12  cat";
istrstream instring(s, strlen(s));
float f;
int i;
char t[100];

instring >> f >> i >> t;
```

The iostream library has many other capabilities not discussed here. For more information see the C++ documentation supplied with the compiler—it contains a complete reference on the I/O library.

A.2.6 Variable Declarations

Variables are declared in C++ as they are in C. Variables can be declared anywhere in the code in C++, returning things almost to the point of FORTRAN in terms of flexibility. The variable comes into existence when it is declared and ceases to exist when the ending brace of the current block of code is reached. For example, in the following code:

```
{
    int i;
    ... code ...
    int j;
    ... code ...
    int k=func(i,j);
    ... code ...
}
```

All three variables come into existence at the point of declaration and disappear at the closing brace.

A.2.7 Constants

In C you create a constant by using the macro preprocessor. An example is shown below:

```
#define MAX 100
```

When the program is compiled, the preprocessor finds each occurrence of the work MAX and replaces it with the string 100.

In C++, the word "const" is used instead, and it is applied to normal variable declarations as shown below:

```
const int MAX=100;
```

The **int MAX=100;** portion is formatted exactly the same way as a normal declaration. The word **const** in front of it simply defines that the variable MAX cannot be subsequently changed.

The use of uppercase characters for constant variable names is a C tradition which you may choose to uphold or ignore.

The **const** modifier can also be used in parameter lists to specify the valid usage of a parameter. The three functions below demonstrate different uses of const.

```
void func1(const int i)
{
    i=5;    // cannot modify a constant
}

void func2(char * const s)
{
    s="hello";  // cannot modify the pointer
}

void func3(const char * s)
{
    s="hello";  // this is OK
    *s='A';     // cannot modify what is pointed to
}
```

The usage shown in **func2** should almost always be used when a **char*** parameter is passed.

A.2.8   Function Overloading

One of the most powerful new features in C++ is called "function overloading." An overloaded function has several different parameter lists. The language distinguishes which function to call based on pattern-matching the parameter list types. Here is an extremely simple demonstration of the process:

```
#include <iostream.h>

void func(int i)
{
    cout << "function 1 called" << endl;
    cout << "parameter = " << i << endl;
}

void func(char c)
{
    cout << "function 2 called" << endl;
    cout << "parameter = " << c << endl;
}

void func(char *s)
{
    cout << "function 3 called" << endl;
    cout << "parameter = " << s << endl;
}

void func(char *s, int i)
{
    cout << "function 2 called" << endl;
    cout << "parameter = " << s;
    cout << ", parameter = " << i << endl;
}

main()
{
    func(10);
    func('B');
    func("hello");
    func("string", 4);
    return 0;
}
```

When this code is executed, each version of the function **func** is called based on parameter-list matching. You will use this capability a great deal in C++ once you get used to the idea. For example, if you create a function that initializes a module, you can have it call different code depending on whether it is passed a string, an integer, a float, and so on.

A.2.9   Default Arguments

C++ also allows you to give default values to parameters—if the parameter is not passed, the default value is used. This capability is demonstrated in the following code:

```
#include <iostream.h>
```

```
void sample(char *s, int i=5)
{
    cout << "parameter 1 = " << s << endl;
    cout << "parameter 2 = " << i << endl;
}

main()
{
    sample("test1");
    sample("test1",10);
    return 0;
}
```

The first function call will output the default value 5 for the parameter **i**, while the second call will output the value 10.

When creating default parameters, you need to avoid ambiguity between the default parameter lists and other overloaded parameter lists. For example, given the above function definition for **sample**, it is not possible to create an overloaded version that accepts a single **char*** parameter—the compiler would be unable to pick which function to call in the case where it is passed a string.

A.2.10 Memory Allocation

C++ replaces the C memory allocation function **malloc** and the deallocation function **free** with **new** and **delete**, respectively, and in the process makes them much easier to use. **New** and **delete** allow user-created types to be allocated as easily as existing types.

The following code shows the simplest use of new and delete. A pointer to an integer points to a block of memory created by **new**:

```
int *p;
p = new int;
*p = 12;
cout << *p
delete p;
```

It is also possible to allocate blocks consisting of arrays of varying length using a similar technique. Note the use of **delete []** for deleting the array:

```
int *p;
p = new int[100];
p[10] = 12;
cout << p[10];
delete [] p;
```

The value 100 can be a variable if desired.

When working with user-defined types, **new** works just the same way. For example:

```
typedef node
{
    int data;
    node *next;
} node;

main()
{
```

```
        node *p;
        p=new node;
        p->date = 10;
        delete p;
}
```

We will see in later tutorials that the **delete** operator is very sophisticated when working with user-defined classes.

A.2.11 Reference Declarations

In C, pointers are frequently used to pass parameters to functions. For example, the following **swap** function swaps the two values passed:

```
void swap(int *i, int *j)
{
    int t = *i;
    *i = *j;
    *j = t;
}

main()
{
    int a=10, b=5;

    swap(&a, &b);
    cout << a << b <<endl;
}
```

C++ provides a *referencing* operator to clean up the syntax a bit. The following code works in C++:

```
void swap(int& i, int& j)
{
    int t = i;
    i = j;
    j = t;
}

main()
{
    int a=10, b=5;

    swap(a, b);
    cout << a << b <<endl;
}
```

The parameters **i** and **j** declared as type **int&** act as references to the integers passed (read **int&** as "a reference to an integer"). When a variable is assigned to the reference variable, the reference picks up its address and mimics the actual location of the assigned variable. For example:

```
int a;
int &b=a;

a=0;
b=5;
cout << a << endl;
```

This code produces 5 as its output because **b** references **a**. It is the same as using pointers and address operators in C but the syntax has been greatly simplified. Note that **b** must be initialized at creation as shown.

A.3 Tutorial Three—Vocabulary

The last tutorial focused on elements of the C++ language that extend C or correct problems inherent in it. These modifications are fairly easy to understand. The other part of C++ is the object-oriented extensions. These additions to the language are not so easy to understand. Whereas the **cout** capability is simply another way to handling printing—which you already understand—many of the object-oriented extensions will be unfamiliar. The purpose of this chapter is to give you your first exposure to some of the general ideas. Then we will look at the C++ syntax that supports these concepts and come back and look at the concepts again.

A.3.1 C++ Vocabulary

Look at the world around you. You can understand a good bit about the structure, vocabulary, and organization of C++ by looking at the structure and organization of the real world as well as the vocabulary that we use to talk about it. Many of the design elements of C++—and object-oriented languages in general—try to emulate the way we interact with the real world.

For example, whenever you look around yourself you see a large number of objects. We organize all the objects around us in our minds by arranging them in hierarchical categories or "classes." For example, you have in your hands a book. A book is a general class of object. You might say, "This object I am holding is classified as a book."

A hierarchy of object classes surrounds the class "book," and it extends in two directions. Books are a member of the more general class "publications." Specific types of books also exists: computer books, fiction books, biographical books, and so on. The hierarchy extends both toward the general and the more specific. At this point you are holding a single, particular book. In OOP lingo, you are holding an "instance" of the class "book."

Books have certain attributes that are shared by all books: They have a cover, several chapters, no advertising, and so on. They also have attributes shared by publications in general: a title, a date of publication, a publisher, and so on. They have attributes that are shared by all physical objects: a location, size, shape, and weight. This idea of shared attributes is very important in C++. C++ models the concept of shared attributes using *inheritance*.

There are certain things you do with and to different objects, and those actions change from object to object. For example, you can read a book, and you can flip its pages. You can look at the title, find a specific chapter, look something up in the index, count the number of pages, and so on. These actions are largely unique to publications: You never find yourself flipping the pages of a hammer, for example. However, there are actions that are generic to all physical objects, such as picking them up. C++ takes this fact about the world into account as well, again using inheritance.

The hierarchical nature of object categories, as well as our hierarchical organization of object attributes and actions, are all embedded into the syntax and vocabulary of C++. For example, when designing a program you will break it down into objects, each of which has a "class." You will "inherit" features of a "base class" when you create a "derived class." That is, you will create general object classes and then make more specific classes from them, deriving the particular from the general. You will "encapsulate" the data found in an object with "member functions", and as you extend a class you will "overload" and "override" the functions of the base class. Confused? Let's look at a quick example to see what all these words actually mean.

The classic example of object-oriented programming is a graphics program that allows you to draw objects—lines, rectangles, circles, and such—on the screen. What do all these objects share in common? All objects have a location on the screen. They might also have a color. These attributes are possessed by every shape shown on the screen. Therefore, as a program designer you would create a "base class"—another way to think about it is "a generic object class"—that holds attributes found in all objects appearing on the screen. The base class might be called "shape" to identify it in a generic sort of way. You would then "derive" different objects—circles, squares, lines—from this base class, adding in new attributes that are specific to these objects. A specific circle drawn on the screen using the circle class would then be an "instance" of the circle class, which inherited some of its behavior from the more generic shape class.

It is possible to create this sort of hierarchy with normal structures in C, but it is not nearly as easy to do as it is in C++. C++ contains syntax to handle inheritance. For example, in C you could create a base structure that holds the object's location on the screen and color. Then specific object structures could include this base structure and add to it. C++ makes this process easier, and then goes one step further. In C++, functions can be bonded into a structure as well and this is called a "class." So the base class might have "member functions", as they are called in C++, that allow an object to be moved and recolored. The "derived classes" can use these member functions as they are, or add in new member functions to increase functionality, or override existing member functions to change behavior.

The most important feature differentiating C++ from C is this idea of a "class," both at a syntactic and a conceptual level. Classes let you use all the normal object-oriented programming features—encapsulation, inheritance, and polymorphism—in your C++ programs. They also are the framework on which other features, such as "operator overloading" (the ability to redefine operators such as "+" and ">" for newly created data types), are built. That all may sound like gibberish now, but as you become familiar with the concepts and vocabulary you will begin to see the power of these new techniques.

A.3.2 The Evolution of Classes

Given the amount of conceptual power embodied in the class concept, it is interesting to note that the syntax remains fairly straightforward. A class is simply an extension of a C structure. Basically a class allows you to create a structure and then permanently bind all related functions to that structure. This process is known as *encapsulation*. It is a very simple concept, but it is the heart of object-oriented programming: *data + functions = object*. Classes can also be built on top of other classes using *inheritance*. Under inheritance, a new class extends its base class. Finally, new classes can modify the behavior of their base classes, a capability known as *polymorphism*.

This is a new way of thinking about your code—it is three-dimensional thinking. You can consider a straight-line piece of code (one that has no functions) as one-dimensional code. It starts at the beginning and ends at the end and that's it. Then you add functions to it to remove some of the redundancies and give names to some of the big pieces. That's two-dimensional code. Now we are going to add a third dimension to that, grouping functions and data together into classes so that the code is further organized. The class hierarchy created by inheritance adds the third dimension. And just as flying is much harder to master than driving because flying adds a third dimension to the mix, object-oriented programming can take some time to master.

One of the best ways to understand classes and their importance to you as a programmer is to understand how and why they evolved. The roots of the class concept lie in a topic known as "data abstraction."

Let's imagine that you are watching a typical room full of college freshmen write a program. Imagine a group of such students who are in their first-semester Pascal course. Once they know how to create **if** statements and loops and arrays they are pretty much ready to write code, but they don't yet know how to organize their thinking. If you ask them to create a simple program they create a blob of code that does the job somehow. It won't be pretty, but it will work.

Imagine that you have asked these students to create a program that can play the "cannon" game. If you have been around computers for 15 years or so then you are familiar with this game because it was very common on early personal computers: The player sees a cannon and a target sitting on terrain that changes from game to game. The goal is to set the angle of the cannon and the amount of powder so that the cannon ball hits the target, missing any hills or other obstacles in the terrain.

Assume that the terrain data exists in a text file consisting of pairs of coordinates. The coordinates are endpoints of the line segments that define the terrain. The students figure out that they need to read this file in so they can draw it, and they also need it in memory so they can check for intersections of the cannon ball's path with the terrain to determine where the cannon ball "lands." So what do they do? They declare a global array to hold the coordinates, read the file into the array, and then use the array whenever it is needed anywhere in the program.

The problem with this approach is that the array has now embedded itself in their code. If a change is ever required—say from an array to a linked list—the pro-

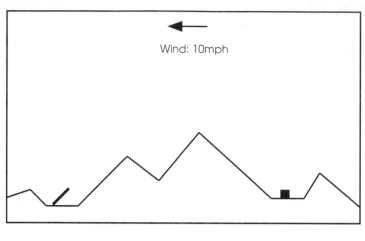

Wind: 10mph

gram will probably be thrown out and rewritten because it contains so many specific references to the array that change is impossible. From a production-programming standpoint this is not good because data structures frequently change in a large program.

A better way to design the program is to use an "abstract data type." In this approach, the programmer first tries to decide how the data will be used. In our terrain example, the programmer might think, "Well, I need to be able to load in the terrain data from wherever it comes from, and to draw the terrain on the screen, and to see if the cannon ball's path intersects with the terrain." Notice that this is done abstractly—there is no mention of an array or a linked list anywhere. Then the programmer creates functions to implement those capabilities. The functions might be named **load_terrain**, **draw_terrain**, and **check_terrain_intersection**. These functions are used throughout the program.

The functions act as a barrier. They hide the actual data structure from the program. If the data structure later has to change, say from an array to a linked list, the majority of the program remains unaffected—only the three functions have to change. The programmer has succeeded in creating an "abstract data type."

Many languages formalize this concept. In Pascal you can use a "unit," in C you can use a "library." Both allow you to create and separately compile a file containing the data structure and the functions that access it. You can specify that the data structure be "hidden," which means that the array can only be accessed by the functions in that unit. In addition, the unit can be compiled so the code inside is hidden as well: Other programmers can call the functions because of a publicly available interface, but they cannot see or modify the actual code.

Pascal units and C libraries represent a step in an evolutionary chain. They start to attack the problem of data abstraction but they do not go far enough. They work, but there are problems:

1.   Most importantly, there is no easy way to modify or extend the behavior of the unit after it is compiled.

2. These abstract types don't mesh with the original language very well. Syntactically they are a mess, and they don't use any of the operators like the "normal" types do. For example, if you create a new type for which an addition operation is natural, there is no way for you to use the plus sign to signify the operation—you have to create a function called **add** instead.

3. If you hide an array in a unit, you can have only one array. You cannot create multiple instances of the data type unless you modify the code and break the data-hiding principle in the process.

C++ classes eliminate these deficiencies.

A.3.3 C++ and Data Abstraction

In response to these problems, object-oriented languages such as C++ offer easy, extensible ways to implement data abstraction. All you have to do is modify your thinking patterns so you think about problems in an "abstract" way. This mental shift is fairly easy once you have seen some examples.

First of all you want to try to think in terms of "data types." Whenever you create a data type you need to think of all the things you will want to do with that data type and then bind the functions you create to the type. For example, say that you are creating a program that requires a rectangle data type containing two coordinate pairs. You should think, "What will I need to do with this type?" You might come up with the following actions: set it to a value, check for equality with another rectangle, check for intersection with another rectangle, and check to see if a point is inside the rectangle. If you need a terrain data type, you go through the same process and come up with functions to load the terrain data, draw the data, and so on. You then bind these functions to the data. Doing this for each data type you need in a program is the essence of object-oriented program.

The other essential technique used when thinking in an object-oriented way involves training your mind to think in a "generic-to-specific" hierarchy. For example, when thinking about a terrain object, you might notice some similarities between it and a list. After all, somewhere in there is a list of coordinates that is loaded from the file. A list is a generic object that can be used in many places. So you would try to create a generic list class and then build the terrain object on top of it. We will examine this process in detail as we go through more examples in the following tutorials.

A.4 Tutorial Four—Simple Classes

We can use a specific example to firm up some of the ideas from the last section. In this tutorial we will look at a simple address list program implemented in C and see how it can be moved to C++ by adding a class.

A.4.1 An Address List Program

Let's say you want to create an address list program that manages a list of names and addresses. The first thing you want to do to create this program is describe the program in English. It turns out that a good English description also helps to find objects in a program, and this is useful when designing C++ code. The description helps you to see the objects you need to create, as well as the functions that will go with each object. Here is a typical description:

> I want to create an address list program. The program will hold a list of names and addresses. The user will be able to add entries to the list, print the list to the screen, and find entries in the list.

You can see that this is a very high-level description. It doesn't talk about the user interface, loading and saving information on disk, error checking, the record format, or the data structure used. All of that would come later. The point of this description is to see what it *does* talk about. In particular, it talks about an object—a **list**—and a set of actions that go with the object—adding, printing, and finding. Now let's take the description further:

> The list can be loaded from disk and saved to disk. When the program begins, it will load the list and then display a menu that lets the user select from the following options: add, delete, find, and quit. When the user selects quit, the list will be saved and the program will terminate.

From this description, you can see that there are two more actions for the list object—load and save. You can also see two new objects developing—the **menu** object and the **program** object. Two actions are listed for the menu: display and selection. The program object currently has three actions: initialization, menu display, and termination.

The point to gain from this example is that an application breaks down into objects fairly naturally. As you describe the program, you begin to see objects in the description. They are generally the nouns in the description. You also can see the functions for the object—they are the verbs. One technique for finding objects in a program is to describe it, make a list of nouns from that description, and then throw out obvious things like "the user." What's left is a set of objects that the program will have to deal with. Then make a list of verbs and use them to form functions for each object.

A.4.2 An Old-Style Program

Let's start creating this address list program by implementing it in C. Then we will move it to C++ by adding a class. The following listing shows a very simple implementation of the address list using normal functions. The program can add elements to the list, print the list to the screen, or find an item in the list. The list is held in a global array.

```
#include <iostream.h>
#include <string.h>

typedef struct
{
    char name[20];
    char city [20];
    char state[20];
```

```
} addrStruct;

const int MAX=10;
addrStruct list[MAX];
int numInList;

void addName()
{
    if (numInList<MAX)
    {
        cout << "Enter Name: ";
        cin >> list[numInList].name;
        cout << "Enter City: ";
        cin >> list[numInList].city;
        cout << "enter State: ";
        cin >> list[numInList].state;
        numInList++;
    }
    else
    {
        cout << "List full\n";
    }
}

void printOneName(int i)
{
    cout << endl;
    cout << list[i].name << endl;
    cout << list[i].city << endl;
    cout << list[i].state << endl;
}

void printNames()
{
    int i;

    for (i=0; i<numInList; i++)
        printOneName(i);
    cout << endl;
}

void findName()
{
    char s[20];
    int i;
    int found=0;

    if (numInList==0)
    {
        cout << "List empty\n";
    }
    else
    {
        cout << "Enter name to find: ";
        cin >> s;
        for (i=0; i<numInList; i++)
```

```
        {
            if (strcmp(s,list[i].name)==0)
            {
                printOneName(i);
                found=1;
            }
        }
        if (!found)
            cout << "No match\n";
    }
}

void paintMenu()
{
    cout << "Address list Main Menu\n";
    cout << "  1 - add to list\n";
    cout << "  2 - print list\n";
    cout << "  3 - find name\n";
    cout << "  4 - quit\n";
    cout << "Enter choice: ";
}

void main()
{
    char choice[10];
    int done=0;
    numInList=0;
    while (!done)
    {
        paintMenu();
        cin >> choice;
        switch(choice[0])
        {
            case '1':
                addName();
                break;
            case '2':
                printNames();
                break;
            case '3':
                findName();
                break;
            case '4':
                done=1;
                break;
            default:
                cout << "invalid choice.\n";
        }
    }
}
```

This program has a fairly typical structure and organization. Functions are used to break up the code. One function handles each of the menu options, one paints the menu, and the function **printOneName** holds a piece of redundant code used in two places in the program. This program demonstrates the two main uses for functions— decomposition/naming and redundancy removal.

There is one fundamental problem with this program: The code is strongly bonded to the global array variable. As shown in the figure below, the array is global and it is referenced directly throughout the program:

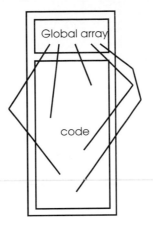

There is no easy way to change the array to another data structure without re-writing most of the code. This code has nothing to do with the list implemented by the array—it simply is in the wrong place.

The idea behind data abstraction is to protect variables such as the global array from direct manipulation by the program. By isolating the variables implementing the list from the rest of the program with function calls, we can accomplish three things:

1. It is much easier to replace the list with different data structures later on, because only the list functions need changing.
2. The program is better organized—the list concept is separated from the rest of the code as much as possible.
3. The list functionality can be used elsewhere in other programs now that it stands on its own.

In C you would make the program look like this:

```
#include <iostream.h>
#include <string.h>

typedef struct
{
    char name[20];
    char city [20];
    char state[20];
} addrStruct;


//-------- data and functions for the list -------
const int MAX=10;
addrStruct list[MAX];
int numInList;
```

```
void listInit()
{
    numInList=0;
}

void listTerminate()
{
}

int listFull()
{
    if (numInList>=MAX) return 1; else return 0;
}

int listEmpty()
{
    if (numInList==0) return 1; else return 0;
}

int listSize()
{
    return numInList;
}

int listAdd(addrStruct addr)
{
    if (!listFull())
    {
        list[numInList++]=addr;
        return 0;  // returns 0 if OK
    }
    return 1;
}

int listGet(addrStruct& addr, int i)
{
    if (i<listSize())
    {
        addr=list[i];
        return 0;  // returns 0 if OK
    }
    return 1;
}
//------------------------------------------------


void addName()
{
    addrStruct a;

    if (!listFull())
    {
        cout << "Enter Name: ";
        cin >> a.name;
        cout << "Enter City: ";
```

```
            cin >> a.city;
            cout << "enter State: ";
            cin >> a.state;
            listAdd(a);
        }
    else
        cout << "List full\n";
}

void printOneName(addrStruct a)
{
    cout << endl;
    cout << a.name << endl;
    cout << a.city << endl;
    cout << a.state << endl;
}

void printNames()
{
    int i;
    addrStruct a;

    for (i=0; i<listSize(); i++)
    {
        listGet(a,i);
        printOneName(a);
    }
    cout << endl;
}

void findName()
{
    char s[20];
    int i;
    int found=0;
    addrStruct a;

    if (listSize==0)
        cout << "List empty\n";
    else
    {
        cout << "Enter name to find: ";
        cin >> s;
        for (i=0; i<listSize(); i++)
        {
            listGet(a, i);
            if (strcmp(s,a.name)==0)
            {
                printOneName(a);
                found=1;
            }
        }
        if (!found)
            cout << "No match\n";
    }
}
```

```
void paintMenu()
{
    cout << "Address list Main Menu\n";
    cout << "  1 - add to list\n";
    cout << "  2 - print list\n";
    cout << "  3 - find name\n";
    cout << "  4 - quit\n";
    cout << "Enter choice: ";
}

void main()
{
    char choice[10];
    int done=0;
    listInit();
    while (!done)
    {
        paintMenu();
        cin >> choice;
        switch(choice[0])
        {
            case '1':
                addName();
                break;
            case '2':
                printNames();
                break;
            case '3':
                findName();
                break;
            case '4':
                done=1;
                break;
            default: cout << "invalid choice.\n";
        }
    }
    listTerminate();
}
```

At the top of the program are seven functions as well as the variables used to implement the list. The goal of the functions is to completely protect, or *encapsulate*, the variables. Using the **list...** functions it is possible to do anything that this program needs to do to the list without using any of the actual variables that implement the list. The functions act as a wall between the variables and the program. With this program structure, any change to the implementation of the list (for example, changing the array to a linked list) has no effect on the program itself—only the seven functions must be modified. The structure of this program is shown in the following diagram:

Many of these functions may seem trivial. For example, the **listTerminate** function contains no actual code at all. But it is there because of future possibilities—if the implementation changes to a linked list, there will need to be a function that deletes all the elements in the list to avoid memory leaks. The **listSize** function contains just one line here, but if the list were implemented using a binary tree the function would

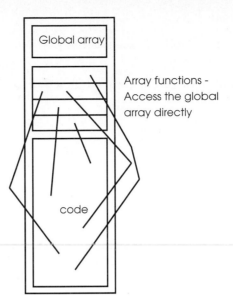

have to recursively traverse the tree to count all the elements and it would be much larger. What we have done is think of all the functions that might actually be needed for a generic list no matter how it is implemented.

While the implementation above is successful in isolating the list from the rest of the program, it has several problems. For example, anyone could come along and modify the program, calling the variables directly and defeating the wall of functions. In other words, there is no enforcement of the wall. Also, it is not easy to use two of these lists in one program. All the functions are tightly bound to a single array. You could get around this problem by passing the array in as a parameter, but that gets messy. C++ solves both problems with classes.

A.4.3 Creating a Class

The following code takes the data and the seven list functions from the previous listing and implements them as a C++ class. It then uses that class in the program:

```
#include <iostream.h>
#include <string.h>

typedef struct
{
    char name[20];
    char city [20];
    char state[20];
} addrStruct;

const int MAX = 10;

class List
{
    addrStruct list[MAX];
```

```
        int numInList;
public:
    List(): numInList(0) // constructor
    {
    }
    ~List() // destructor
    {
    }
    int Full()
    {
        if (numInList>=MAX) return 1; else return 0;
    }
    int Empty()
    {
        if (numInList==0) return 1; else return 0;
    }
    int Size()
    {
        return numInList;
    }
    int Add(addrStruct addr)
    {
        if (!Full())
        {
            list[numInList++]=addr;
            return 0;  // returns 0 if OK
        }
        return 1;
    }
    int Get(addrStruct& addr, int i)
    {
        if (i<Size())
        {
            addr=list[i];
            return 0;  // returns 0 if OK
        }
        return 1;
    }
};
//-----------------------------------------------

List list;

void addName()
{
    addrStruct a;

    if (!list.Full())
    {
        cout << "Enter Name: ";
        cin >> a.name;
        cout << "Enter City: ";
        cin >> a.city;
        cout << "enter State: ";
        cin >> a.state;
        list.Add(a);
```

This book is continuously updated. See http://www.iftech.com/mfc

```
    }
    else
        cout << "List full\n";
}

void printOneName(addrStruct a)
{
    cout << endl;
    cout << a.name << endl;
    cout << a.city << endl;
    cout << a.state << endl;
}

void printNames()
{
    int i;
    addrStruct a;

    for (i=0; i<list.Size(); i++)
    {
        list.Get(a,i);
        printOneName(a);
    }
    cout << endl;
}

void findName()
{
    char s[20];
    int i;
    int found=0;
    addrStruct a;

    if (list.Size()==0)
        cout << "List empty\n";
    else
    {
        cout << "Enter name to find: ";
        cin >> s;
        for (i=0; i<list.Size(); i++)
        {
            list.Get(a, i);
            if (strcmp(s,a.name)==0)
            {
                printOneName(a);
                found=1;
            }
        }
        if (!found)
            cout << "No match\n";
    }
}

void paintMenu()
{
    cout << "Address list Main Menu\n";
```

```
        cout << "  1 - add to list\n";
        cout << "  2 - print list\n";
        cout << "  3 - find name\n";
        cout << "  4 - quit\n";
        cout << "Enter choice: ";
    }

    int main()
    {
        char choice[10];
        int done=0;

        while (!done)
        {
            paintMenu();
            cin >> choice;
            switch(choice[0])
            {
                case '1':
                    addName();
                    break;
                case '2':
                    printNames();
                    break;
                case '3':
                    findName();
                    break;
                case '4':
                    done=1;
                    break;
                default:
                    cout << "invalid choice.\n";
            }
        }
        return 0;
        // list destroys itself when it goes out of scope.
    }
```

The list class is near the top of the program and starts with the words **class List**. This is just a type declaration—the actual *instance* of the list appears at the line:

```
    List list;
```

This line declares a variable named **list** of the type **class List.**

Notice that the **List** class starts off looking very much like a structure. It declares two variables in the same way a structure would. These are called *data members*. It then contains the word "public": This word indicates that the following functions will be known to any code using this class. The opposite word is "private" and is used when functions or variables are to remain hidden from the rest of the program. The variables and functions defined in a class are by default private unless you specifically make them public as shown here (the two data members are private by default and the seven functions are public).

Following the data members come the *member functions*. These are the functions that can be applied to instances of this class. The first two functions—**List** and **~List**—are unique and are called the *constructor* and the *destructor*, respectively. The constructor is *automatically* called when any instance of this class comes into existence. In this case, the instance comes into existence at the start of program execution because it is declared as a global variable, but constructors of local variables are called when the local variable comes into existence and constructors of pointers are activated when **new** is called on the pointer. The constructor has the same name as the class itself:

```
List(): numInList(0) // constructor
{
}
```

The initialization of the **numInList** data member is unique here. Another way to do it would be to say:

```
List() // constructor
{
    numInList = 0;
}
```

However, the first form is more efficient at runtime because of the way C++ internally initializes classes. The syntax, when used as shown in this constructor, initializes the data member **numInList** to 0 and should be used whenever initializing data members in a constructor.

The destructor **~List** is called *automatically* when the instance goes out of scope or is deleted. The remaining functions look just like C functions. They are unique only in that they are tightly bound to the class variables and can reference the class variables at any time.

The variable **list** is an instance of this class. If **list** were a plain structure it would be declared in about the same way, and it acts the same here. The variable **list** is as big as the size of its data members. The functions do not actually take up any space in each instance of the class. The syntax of the language simply allows them to be declared, and used, with instances of the class.

The instance **list** is used throughout the program. Each time something needs to be done to **list** you find the instance name **list** followed by a dot and then a function name. This again follows the syntax of a structure. The dot says, "call the member function of the class **List** on the specific instance **list**."

This may not all make immediate sense and that's OK. The important thing to gather from this example is that all we have done is take some data—in this case, an array and an integer—and the functions needed to manipulate the variables, and we have bound them together into a *class*. Now the variables cannot be directly accessed by the rest of the code. Because they are private within the class, they can be accessed only by the class's member functions and not by any other part of the program. The list object—data and functions glued together into an object—can only be accessed via the member functions.

A.4.4 A Simpler Example

The last example was fairly large. Let's look at a **Stack** class to review some of the concepts learned in a smaller setting.

```
#include <iostream.h>
```

```
        class Stack
        {
            int stk[100];
            int top;
        public:
            Stack(): top(0) {}
            ~Stack() {}
            void Clear() {top=0;}
            void Push(int i) {if (top<100) stk[top++]=i;}
            int Pop()
            {
                if (top>0) return stk[--top];
                else return 0;
            }
            int Size() {return top;}
        };

        int main()
        {
            Stack stack1, stack2;

            stack1.Push(10);
            stack1.Push(20);
            stack1.Push(30);
            cout << stack1.Pop() << endl;
            stack2=stack1;
            cout << stack2.Pop() << endl;
            cout << stack2.Pop() << endl;
            cout << stack1.Size() << endl;
            cout << stack2.Size() << endl;
            return 0;
        }
```

This program consists of two parts: the **Stack** class and the **main** function. The class defines the **Stack** type and two instances of this type are declared inside of **main**. Each of the instances will have its own copy of the **stk** and **top** data members, and a **sizeof** operation on each would indicate that just enough space (202 or 404 bytes, depending on the environment) is allocated for each. A class uses just as much space as a structure with the same data members would—there is no memory overhead for the member functions.

   The class contains a constructor, a destructor, and four other functions, each of which is public. Because the functions are public they can be called by any instance of the class. The constructor is called when stack variables are instantiated, and the destructor is called when they go out of scope. Inside the **main** function, different calls to the other four functions are made by using the instantiation name followed by a dot followed by a function name. For example:

```
        stack1.Push(10);
```

This line indicates that the value 10 should be pushed onto **stack1**. The instance **stack1** holds two pieces of data (**stk** and **top**) which contain values. This line says, "Call the function **Push** on the structure help in **stack1**—apply the statements in **Push** and the value 10 to the actual array and integer held within **stack1**. There are two completely separate stacks in this program: **stack1** and **stack2**. A statement like `stack2.Push(5)` means that 5 should be pushed onto the structur **stack2**.

The assignment statement midway down the **main** function is interesting. It does the same thing that an assignment between two structures would—the values of the data members on the right side are copied to the data members on the left:

```
stack2 = stack1;
```

After the assignment statement the two stacks contain the same values. This normally works fine, but if any of the data members are pointers you have to be careful. We will see a good example of this problem in Tutorial Seven.

A.4.5 A Rectangle Class

How do you decide what should be turned into an object and what shouldn't? Essentially what you do is take each little group of related data elements that you can find in a program, attach some functions to it, and make a class. In the stack example above, the array **stk** and the integer **top** are the data elements needed by the stack. Several useful functions relate to that little data grouping (**Push**, **Pop**, **Clear**, and **Size**). Together the data and functions make a class.

Say you have to remember the coordinates for a rectangle in one of your programs. Your variables are labeled **x1**, **y1**, **x2**, and **y2**—**x1** and **y1** represent the upper left corner and **x2** and **y2** represent the lower right corner. Together they represent a rectangle. What are some useful functions that go with these values? You need to be able to initialize them (a perfect job for the constructor), and maybe it would be handy to find the area and perimeter of the rectangle. The class might look like this:

```
class Rect
{
    int x1, y1, x2, y2;
public:
    Rect(int left=0,int top=0,
        int right=0,int bottom=0):
        x1(left),  y1(top),  x2(right),  y2(bottom)
    {
    }
    ~Rect() {}
    int Height() { return (y2-y1); }
    int Width() { return (x2-x1); }
    int Area() { return Width()*Height(); }
    int Perimeter() { return 2*Width()+2*Height();}
};
```

If you simply look at a program you are building and try to find each natural grouping of data along with some functions that are useful for manipulating that data, you will go a long way toward objectifying your programs.

A.4.6 Class Specifics

Let's review a few of the specifics learned in this tutorial. First, each class has a constructor and a destructor. The constructor is called when an instance of the class comes into existence and the destructor is called when the instance is destroyed. The following program can help you learn about constructors and destructors:

```
#include <iostream.h>

class Sample
{
    int num;
public:
    Sample(int i): num(i)
    {
        cout << "constructor " << num
            << " called" << endl;
    }
    ~Sample()
    {
    cout << "destructor " << num
        << " called" << endl;}
};

int main()
{
    Sample *sp;
    Sample s(1);

    cout << "line 1" << endl;
    {
        Sample temp(2);
        cout << "line 2" << endl;
    }
    cout << "line 3" << endl;
    sp = new Sample(3);
    cout << "line 4" << endl;
    delete sp;
    cout << "line 5" << endl;
    return 0;
}
```

Try running this code on paper and predict what it will do. Then run the program with a single-stepping debugger and see what happens.

Data members and member functions can be public or private, depending on their role in the program. It is good to strive toward the goal of no public data members. A public member can be used anywhere in the program, while a private member can only be used by a function that is a member of the class. Let's modify the **Rect** class slightly to see what this means:

```
class Rect
{
    int x1, y1, x2, y2;
public:
    Rect(int left=0,int top=0,
        int right=0,int bottom=0):
        x1(left),  y1(top),  x2(right),  y2(bottom)
    {
    }
    ~Rect() {}
private:
    int Height() { return (y2-y1); }
    int Width() { return (x2-x1); }
```

```
public:
    int Area() { return Width()*Height(); }
    int Perimeter() { return 2*Width()+2*Height();}
};
```

Now the **Width** and **Height** functions are private. They can be called as shown here because **Area** and **Perimeter** are member functions. But if you try the following:

```
Rect r;
...
cout  << r.Height();
```

You will get a compiler error because **Height** is private.

Assignment between two instances of a class simply copies the data members from one instance to the other. For example:

```
Rect r1,r2;
...
r1=r2;
```

is the same as saying:

```
r1.x1 = r2.x1;
r1.y1 = r2.y1;
r1.x2 = r2.x2;
r1.y2 = r2.y2;
```

Finally, there are two accepted ways to specify member functions. The examples seen previously represent one method, called **inline** functions. The code below shows the second method, here applied to the **Rect** class:

```
class Rect
{
    int x1, y1, x2, y2;
public:
    // the constructor uses default param. See tutor 2
    Rect(int left=0,int top=0,
        int right=0,int bottom=0);
    ~Rect();
    int Height();
    int Width();
    int Area();
    int Perimeter();
};

Rect::Rect(int left, int top, int right, int bottom):
    x1(left),  y1(top),  x2(right),  y2(bottom)
// default values are understood from the prototype
{
}

Rect::~Rect()
{
}

int Rect::Height()
{
    return (x2-x1);
}

int Rect::Width()
```

```
{
    return (y2-y1);
}

int Rect::Area()
{
    return Width()*Height();
}

int Rect::Perimeter()
{
    return 2*Width()+2*Height();
}
```

This form is generally much easier to read when the functions in the class are long. The **Rect::** portion specifies the class to which the function belongs. The class definition itself contains what are essentially prototypes for the class functions.

There are many other things you can do with a class, but to create simple data-abstracting collections of functions and data the material presented here is all you need. Now we can start creating hierarchies from these classes.

A.5 Tutorial Five—Inheritance

Let's say you have a list class and now you want to modify it. In the old world of programming you would take the source and start changing things. In the object-oriented world of programming you do things differently. What you do instead is leave the existing class alone and then layer your changes on top of it using a process called *inheritance*. Layering through inheritance lies at the very heart of object-oriented programming. It is a totally different way of doing things, but it has several important advantages:

1. Let's say you bought the list class from someone else, so you don't have the source code. By leaving the existing class alone and layering your changes on top of it you don't *need* to have the source.
2. The existing class is completely debugged and tested. If you modify its source, it has to go through the testing process again to be re-certified. Changes you make might also have side effects that aren't detected immediately. By layering the changes on top of the existing class, the existing class never changes and therefore remains bug-free. Only the new pieces must be tested.
3. The layering process forces you to think in a generic-to-specific way. You create a generic class like a list, and then layer specificity on top of it. A nice bonus to this way of thinking is that the generic classes are useful in many different programs. A list, for example, is useful in a lot of places. Each new program layers its own specifics onto the generic list, but the generic list stays the same everywhere.
4. If the "base class" is improved, all classes built on top of it take advantage of those improvements without modification. For example, say the list class is

714

changed so it sorts 10 times faster than it used to. Now every class built on top of the list class sorts 10 times faster as well, without modifying anything.

It is these benefits that get people excited about object-oriented programming.

A.5.1 Inheritance Example

Let's look at a specific example to get a feel for how inheritance works. Say you have purchased a simple list manager. It has the ability to insert at a specified location, to get items from the list, and to return the size of the list. The code for this list class is shown below, along with a small piece of test code:

```
#include <iostream.h>

class List
{
    int array[100];
    int count;
public:
    List(): count(0) {}
    ~List() {}
    void Insert( int n, int location )
    {
        int i;
        for (i=count; i>=location; i--)
            array[i+1] = array[i];
        array[location]=n;
        count++;
    }
    int  Get( int location ) {return array[location];}
    int Size() { return count; }
};

void main()
{
    List list;
    int i, value;

    for (i=0; i<10; i++)
        list.Insert(i,i);
    list.Insert(100,5);
    list.Insert(200,7);
    list.Insert(300,0);
    for (i=0; i<list.Size(); i++)
        cout << list.Get(i) << endl;
}
```

The class contains no error checking to keep it small—obviously you would want to add some if this were a commercial product.

Now let's say you want to modify this class to add two features. First, you want to have a sorted insertion function so that the class maintains a sorted list. Second, you want to keep track of the total sum of all items in the list. Rather than cycling through all elements in the list each time the **sum** function is called, you want to keep a running total as each item is inserted.

Obviously, one way to do this is to simply modify the **List** class shown above. In C++ you use inheritance to make the changes instead. We will create a **SortedList** class by inheriting the **List** class and modifying it. Let's start by adding the sorted insertion feature:

```
class SortedList: public List
{
public:
    SortedList():List() {}

    SortedInsert(int n)
    {
        int i,j;

        i=0;
        do
        {
            j = Get(i);
            if (j < n ) i++;
        } while (j < n && i<Size());
        Insert(n, i);
    }
};
```

The **List** class is totally unchanged—we have simply created the **SortedList** class on top of it. The **SortedList** class *inherits* its behavior from the **List** class—it is *derived* from the **List** class. The **List** class is the *base class* for **SortedList**.

The **List** class is inherited on the fist line:

```
class SortedList: public List
```

The colon indicates that we are inheriting something. The word **public** indicates that we want the public functions and variables in **List** to remain public in the **SortedList** class. We could have also used **private** or **protected**. In either of these cases any **public** variables and functions in the inherited class would be converted in the derived class. The use of **public** here is standard.

The following diagram shows what is happening:

The **SortedList** class simply extends the **List** class. Anyone using the **SortedList** class has access to the functions available in **List** as well as the new functions available in **SortedList**.

The constructor for **SortedList** is also new—we have used a colon here to call the constructor for the inherited class:

```
SortedList():List() {}
```

This line says that the constructor named **List** from the base class should be called and the **SortedList** constructor needs to do nothing of its own.

In the remainder of the **SortedList** class we simply add the new **SortedInsert** function into the class. This new function makes use of the old **Insert**, **Get**, and **Size** functions from the **List** class as needed, but it does not access any of the **List** class data members directly because it can't—they are private to the **List** class, so they cannot be seen in the inheriting class.

Say you wanted to have a variable or a function that seems private to outside users of a class but seems public to classes that inherit the class. For example, say that the

SortedList class

List class

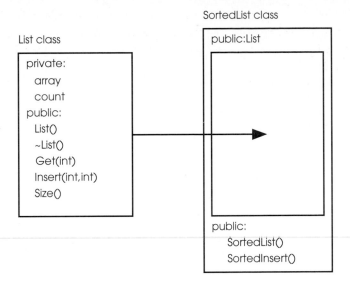

```
private:
    array
    count
public:
    List()
    ~List()
    Get(int)
    Insert(int,int)
    Size()
```

```
public:List
```

```
public:
    SortedList()
    SortedInsert()
```

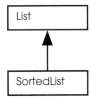

List

SortedList

SortedList class needed direct access to the **array** variable in **List** to improve its performance, but we still want to keep normal instances of **List** and **SortedList** from accessing the array directly. The word **protected:** can be used in the same manner as **public:** or **private:** to indicate this behavior. By declaring **array** as a protected member in **List**, it would be accessible by the derived-class **SortedList** but not by normal instances of **List** or **SortedList**.

Now let's add the totaling capability to the **SortedList** class. To do this we will need to add a new variable, and we will also need to modify the **Insert** function so that each insertion adds to the total. The code is shown below:

```
class SortedList: public List
{
private:
    int total;
public:
    SortedList():List(), total(0) {}
    void Insert( int n, int location )
    {
        total = total + n;
        List::Insert(n, location);
    }
    int GetTotal() { return total; }
    SortedInsert(int n)
```

```
    {
        int i,j;
        i=0;
        do
        {
            j = Get(i);
            if (j < n ) i++;
        } while (j < n && i<Size());
        Insert(n, i);
    }
};
```

In this version of the **SortedList** class we have added a new data member named **total**, a new member function **GetTotal** to retrieve the current total, and a new function **Insert** that *overrides* the existing **Insert** function. We have also modified the **SortedList** constructor so it initializes **total**. Now whenever the **SortedList** class is used and the **Insert** function is called, the *new* version of the **Insert** function will be accessed instead of the old version in **List**. The same goes for the **SortedInsert** function as well—when it calls **Insert** it is calling the *new* version.

The code for the new **Insert** function is straightforward:

```
void Insert( int n, int location )
{
    total = total + n;
    List::Insert(n, location);
}
```

This function first adds the new value to the total. It then calls the *old* **Insert** function inherited from the base class so the value is inserted in the list properly. The **List::** specifies from which class in the hierarchy the **Insert** function should be chosen. This is only a two-level hierarchy so it is a simple decision here, but in a hierarchy that has several layers of inheritance you can use this technique to choose a specific function from many. It is this layering, and the ability to work and think in a multi-level inheritance hierarchy as shown here, that gives C++ its 3-dimensional feel.

A.5.2 A More Advanced Example

Let's take what we have learned about inheritance and use it to create a realistic example class. What we would like to do is create a new number class called a "multi-precision integer," or mint. This integer type will work like a normal integer, but it will have up to 100 digits (for now—later we will see how to extend it to have as many digits as memory will hold using linked lists). A mint allows you to do things like find the actual value for 60! or find the 300th value in a Fibonacci series.

What is a good way to create the new class in an object-oriented programming environment? One way to think about it is to think in a generic-to-specific way. For example, what is a multi-precision integer? It is simply a list of digits. Therefore, you can start by creating a generic list class that has all the insertion features needed to implement a mint and then layer the mint functionality on top of it.

How do we decide which features are needed in the list? A good way to do this is to think about what you will have to do with the digits in typical mint operations, and then use those thoughts to create the list class. Alternatively, you would have a list class lying around and you would simply build on top of it. Let's take the first approach because we don't have a good list class lying around.

How do you initialize a mint? The mint will start off containing no digits. We will then add one digit at a time to create the new mint. For the value 4,269 the mint would look like this:

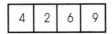

Each square in this diagram represents one element in the list, and each element in the list contains an integer value between 0 and 9. At the list level we need to be able to add digits to the beginning or the end of the list, depending on where the initial value came from.

Now let's look at a simple addition, as shown in the figure below:

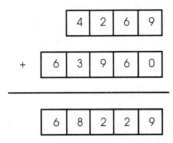

To implement addition we will want to start with the last digits of the two mints being summed, add them together, and insert the resulting digit in the new mint being formed as the sum. Then we will go to the previous two digits and do the same thing, and so on. We will therefore need an efficient way to move through the lists from end to beginning (for example, **GetLast** and **GetPrevious** functions), and we will also need a way to be able to tell when we have hit the beginning of the list (perhaps a return value from **GetPrevious** can indicate that the action is not possible or a **Size** function can indicate how far to go).

From this discussion and our previous work with lists we can surmise that the list will probably need to have the following capabilities:

constructor and destructor
AddToFront
AddToEnd
GetFirst
GetLast
GetPrevious
GetNext
Size
Clear

The code below implements the list:

```
class List
```

```
{
    int array[100];
    int count;
    int pointer;
public:
    List(): count(0), pointer(0) {}
    ~List() {}
    void AddToFront(int n)
    {
        int i;
        for(i=count; i>=1; i--)
            array[i]=array[i-1];
        array[0]=n;
        count++;
    }
    void AddToEnd(int n)
    {
        array[count++]=n;
    }
    // &n is a reference - see tutor 2
    int GetFirst(int &n)
    {
        if (count==0)
            return 1;
        else
        {
            n=array[0];
            pointer=0;
            return 0;
        }
    }
    int GetLast(int &n)
    {
        if (count==0)
            return 1;
        else
        {
            n=array[count-1];
            pointer=count-1;
            return 0;
        }
    }
    int GetPrevious(int &n)
    {
        if (pointer-1<0)
            return 1;
        else
        {
            pointer--;
            n=array[pointer];
            return 0;
        }
    }
    int GetNext(int &n)
    {
        if (pointer+1>count-1)
```

```
            return 1;
        else
        {
            pointer++;
            n=array[pointer];
            return 0;
        }
    }
    int Size() { return count; }
    void Clear() { count = 0; }
};
```

This code should all be fairly straightforward to you at this point. **List** is simply a generic list of integers. A data member named **pointer** points to one of the elements in the list and is moved by the four **Get...** functions. Each of these functions returns 0 on success and 1 on failure (for example, if **pointer** is not on element 0 of the list then there is a previous element to get and **GetPrevious** function will return a 0). The two **Add...** functions add at the beginning and end of the list respectively—they currently contain no error checking. The **AddToFront** function contains an inherent inefficiency because it must move the entire contents of the array down one element for each insertion.

The **Mint** class inherits **List** and uses it to build the actual mint type. It implements two constructors (a *default constructor* that accepts no parameters and a second constructor that accepts a string and uses it to fill the list), as well as functions that add two mints and print a mint. The code is shown below:

```
class Mint: public List
{
public:
    Mint():List() {}
    Mint(char *s):List()
    {
        char *p;
        for (p=s; *p; p++)
            AddToEnd(*p-'0');
    }
    void Add(Mint &a, Mint &b)
    {
        int carry, temp;
        int erra, errb, na, nb;

        carry=0;
        Clear();
        erra=a.GetLast(na);
        errb=b.GetLast(nb);
        while (!erra || !errb)
        {
            if (erra)
                temp=nb+carry;
            else if (errb)
                temp=na+carry;
            else
                temp=na+nb+carry;
            AddToFront(temp%10);
```

```
                carry=temp/10;
                erra=a.GetPrevious(na);
                errb=b.GetPrevious(nb);
            }
            if (carry>0)
                AddToFront(carry);
        }
        void Print()
        {
            int n, err;

            err=GetFirst(n);
            while( !err )
            {
                cout << n;
                err=GetNext(n);
            }
             cout << endl;
        }
    };
```

The following **main** function tests the mint class by adding two numbers and printing the sum:

```
    void main()
    {
        Mint a("1234567");
        Mint b("1234");
        Mint c;

        c.Add(a,b);
        c.Print();
    }
```

The constructors and the **Print** function are simple and straightforward. The **Add** function may remind you of your grade school days, because it is doing addition the old-fashioned way. It starts with the last digits of the two numbers being summed, adds those digits, saves the result in the current mint, and remembers the carry value. It then moves forward through the list. Because it is likely that the two mints will not have an equal number of digits, the code must continually check to make sure it has not run out of digits in one or the other mint. It does this using **erra** and **errb**. As soon as both mints have run out it checks **carry** and saves one last digit if necessary.

Running the test code you will see that the **Mint** class works as advertised and can add two numbers of up to 100 digits each. After you use the **Mint** class for awhile, however, you begin to see a problem with the **Add** function—there is no way to say something like "m = m + 1", or in the format necessary here "m.Add(m, one);" where **one** has been initialized to "1". The reason for this lies in the fact that **Add** must clear out the destination of the result before it can place a value into it, and this forces the loss of needed data in the case shown here.

The solution to this problem lies in the creation of a temporary holding value for the result during the actual addition. Then at the end of the function, the final result is copied into the current instance. The **this** pointer is used to solve the problem, as shown below:

```
void Add(Mint &a, Mint &b)
{
    int carry, temp;
    int erra, errb, na, nb;
    Mint x;


    carry=0;
    erra=a.GetLast(na);
    errb=b.GetLast(nb);
    while (!erra || !errb)
    {
        if (erra)
            temp=nb+carry;
        else if (errb)
            temp=na+carry;
        else
            temp=na+nb+carry;
        x.AddToFront(temp%10);
        carry=temp/10;
        erra=a.GetPrevious(na);
        errb=b.GetPrevious(nb);
    }
    if (carry>0)
    x.AddToFront(carry);
    *this = x;
}
```

In this version of **Add** a temporary value named **x** has been created. The results of the addition are placed into **x** digit by digit. The last line of the function copies **x** into the current instance. The **this** pointer is available in every instance of a class in C++—it points to the current instance. That is, **this** is a pointer that points to the data members (the structure) that make up the current instance. In this case we use **this** because it saves code. The alternative would be to replace the last line with:

```
array = x.array;
count = x.count;
pointer = x.pointer;
```

The value ***this** is the structure pointed to by **this**, and it is more expedient to copy the whole structure at once.

As a final example of the **Mint** class, let's use it to implement a Fibonacci number finder. The Fibonacci series is as follows:

1, 1, 2, 3, 5, 8, 13, 21, 34, etc.

Each number in the series is the sum of the prior two numbers. To implement this feature we will need a way to check for equality in mints so we can make a loop. The following member function can be added to the **Mint** class to check for equality between two mints:

```
int Equal(Mint &a)
{
    if (a.Size()!=Size())
        return 0;
    else
    {
        int i, na, nb;
        a.GetFirst(na);
```

```
            GetFirst(nb);
            for (i=0; i<a.Size(); i++)
                if (na!=nb)
                    return 0;
                else
                {
                    a.GetNext(na);
                    GetNext(nb);
                }
            return 1;
        }
    }
```

Given the existence of this function, then the following code will find the 100th number in the Fibonacci series:

```
void main()
{
    Mint max("100");
    Mint counter("1"), one("1");
    Mint t1("0"), t2("1");
    Mint d;

    do
    {
        d.Add(t1,t2);
        t1=t2;
        t2=d;
        counter.Add(counter,one);
    } while (!counter.Equal(max));
    d.Print();

}
```

The code uses two values **t1** and **t2** to remember the previous two values. They are added together and then shifted down by one. The counter is then incremented and the loop continues until the counter has reached the desired value. Using this code, the 100th number was found to be 354,224,848,179,261,915,075.

A.5.3 Conclusion

In this tutorial you have seen how inheritance is used to create class hierarchies and how the existence of inheritance tends to favor the development of code using a generic-to-specific style. The **Mint** class is a perfect example of this phenomena—a generic list was used to build the **Mint** class because a mint is nothing more than a list of digits.

Although we have accomplished our goal, the **Mint** class is not very well-integrated into the language. We would like to use the "+" operator for addition and the "==" operator to check for equality. We will see how to do this in the next section.

A.6 Tutorial Six—Operator Overloading

In the last tutorial we implemented a version of the **Mint** class, ending up with code that calculates members of the Fibonacci series. The code used to perform the calculation looked like this:

This book is continuously updated. See http://www.iftech.com/mfc

```
void main()
{
    Mint max("100");
    Mint counter("1"), one("1");
    Mint t1("0"), t2("1");
    Mint d;

    do
    {
        d.Add(t1,t2);
        t1=t2;
        t2=d;
        counter.Add(counter,one);
    } while (!counter.Equal(max));
    d.Print();

}
```

What we would like instead is to be able to write code that looks "normal," like this:

```
void main()
{
    Mint max("100");
    Mint counter("1");
    Mint t1("0"), t2("1");
    Mint d;

    do
    {
        d = t1 + t2;
        t1=t2;
        t2=d;
        counter = counter + "1";
    } while (! (counter==max));
    cout << d << endl;

}
```

C++ allows this sort of seamless melding of new types using a process called *operator overloading*. The normal operators like "+", "==", and "<<" are overloaded so that they can handle the new types.

Some operator overloading involves the use of *friend* functions. A friend function is just like a normal C function, but it is permitted to access private members of the class within which it is declared. The fact that it is a normal C function means that it does not have access to a **this** pointer and it can be called without having to name a class that it operates on. For example, a normal member function such as **Insert** in the **List** class requires an instantiation of the list to be called:

```
List lst;
...
lst.Insert(5);
```

A friend function does not necessarily require a class instantiation because it does not have a **this** pointer.

Almost every operator in C++ can be overloaded:

+	-	*	/	%	^	&	|
~	!	,	=	<	>	<=	>=
++	—	<<	>>	==	!=	&&	||
+=	-=	/=	%=	^=	&=	|=	*=
<<=	>>=	[ ]	( )	->	->*	new	delete

Many of these are never seen, much less overloaded, but by overloading all the common operators like "+" and "==" you can make a class much easier to use.

The code below shows the **Mint** class redone so the "+", "==", and "<<" operators are overloaded, along with a piece of test code that uses all three:

```
class Mint: public List
{
public:
    Mint():List() {}
    Mint(char *s):List()
    {
        char *p;
        for (p=s; *p; p++)
            AddToEnd(*p-'0');
    }

    friend Mint operator+ (Mint &a, Mint &b)
    {
        int carry, temp;
        int erra, errb, na, nb;
        Mint x;

        carry=0;
        erra=a.GetLast(na);
        errb=b.GetLast(nb);
        while (!erra || !errb)
        {
            if (erra)
                temp=nb+carry;
            else if (errb)
                temp=na+carry;
            else
                temp=na+nb+carry;
            x.AddToFront(temp%10);
            carry=temp/10;
            erra=a.GetPrevious(na);
            errb=b.GetPrevious(nb);
        }
        if (carry>0)
            x.AddToFront(carry);
        return x;
    }

    int operator==(Mint &a)
    {
        if (a.Size()!=Size())
            return 0;
        else
```

```
        {
            int i, na, nb;
            a.GetFirst(na);
            GetFirst(nb);
            for (i=0; i<a.Size(); i++)
                if (na!=nb)
                    return 0;
                else
                {
                    a.GetNext(na);
                    GetNext(nb);
                }
            return 1;
        }
    }

    friend ostream& operator<< (ostream& s, Mint &m)
    {
        int n, err;

        err=m.GetFirst(n);
        while( !err )
        {
            s << n;
            err=m.GetNext(n);
        }
        return s;
    }
};

void main()
{
    // add two numbers
    Mint a("1234567");
    Mint b("1234");
    Mint c;

    c = a + b;
    cout << "it's fine " << c << "...really" << endl;
    cout << a + "3333" << endl;

    // find the 100th fibbinocci number
    Mint counter;
    Mint t1, t2;
    Mint d;

    t1 = "0";
    t2 = "1";
    counter = "1";
    do
    {
        d = t1 + t2;
        t1 = t2;
        t2 = d;
        counter = counter + "1";
    } while (! (counter == "100") );
```

```
        cout << d << endl;
    }
```

Let's start by looking at the "==" function:

```
    int operator== (Mint &a)
```

Because this function is a member of the **Mint** class, this header says that the operator should return an integer, use what's on the left side of the == as **this**, and use what is on the right hand side of the == as **a**. In the code for the == operator function, when we use a function like **GetFirst** directly we are referring to the value on the left side of the ==. A function call of the form **a.GetFirst** refers to the right side of the ==:

```
    Mint b, m;
    ...
    if (b == m)
```

The rest of the code is identical to the **Equal** function we saw in Tutorial Five. The returned integer value is used as the result of the comparison. With this function in place, our "==" operator is called whenever the compiler finds an "==" operator between two values of type **Mint**.

The over loaded "+" operator is a friend function:

```
    friend Mint operator+ (Mint &a, Mint &b)
```

It is declared as a friend because we do not want it to automatically use the left side of a plus statement as **this** because that would clear it (as discussed in Tutorial Five). Because it is a friend it acts as a normal C function without a **this** pointer. It adds the two mints passed and returns the resulting mint.

In the **main** function there are several statements of the following form:

```
    c = "3333"
```

and

c = c + "1";

How does the compiler know what to do? How does it know to convert "1" to a mint? Because we have a mint constructor that accepts a **char*** type, the constructor is automatically invoked in an attempt to make the + operator's types match up. If we created another constructor that accepted a **long** parameter, then we would also be able to write code like this:

```
    c = c + 1;
```

The conversion of the integer value would be automatic as well. The following statement will *not* work:

```
    c = "2222" + "3333";
```

The compiler does not have anything to tell it that the "+" should be adding mints, so it cannot make the conversion—one side of the "+" must be a mint to cue the compiler.

The << operator is also overloaded. The function must be a friend because the left parameter is not of the class type. It must accept a reference to an **ostream** parameter and then to a parameter of the class type. It must also return a reference to **ostream**. Having done this however, the code is simple. With this function in place any C++ output operation using a mint will work.

The >> operator is overloaded in a similar way:

```
    friend istream& operator>> (istream& s, Mint& m)
    {
```

```
            buf[100];

            s >> buf;
            m = buf; // calls the constructor
            return s;
    }
```

Other operators such as ++, +=, !=, etc. are easily overloaded using the examples above. For some of the more esoteric operators, see a book such as Lippman's.

A.7 Tutorial Seven—Working with Pointers

When a class contains data members that are pointers, there are several concerns that must be addressed to make the class "work". For example, when an instantiation of the class is destroyed, the destructor should make sure that all allocated blocks of memory within the class are deleted. Another example involves the assignment operator: the standard "copy all data members" behavior for the "=" operator that we have seen until now has worked fine, but it does not work with pointers.

To get a feel for the differences let's implement a stack class both with an array and with pointers. Here is the array version, along with a main function containing test code (this is identical to the code we saw in Tutorial Four):

```
    #include <iostream.h>

    class Stack
    {
        int stk[100];
        int top;
    public:
        Stack(): top(0) {}
        ~Stack() {}
        void Clear() {top=0;}
        void Push(int i) {if (top<100) stk[top++]=i;}
        int Pop()
        {
            if (top>0) return stk[--top];
            else return 0;
        }
        int Size() {return top;}
    };

    void main()
    {
        Stack stack1, stack2;

        stack1.Push(10);
        stack1.Push(20);
        stack1.Push(30);
        cout << stack1.Pop() << endl;
        stack2=stack1;
        cout << stack1.Size() << endl;
        cout << stack2.Size() << endl;
        cout << stack2.Pop() << endl;
        cout << stack2.Pop() << endl;
    }
```

The code below implements the same stack using pointers, but it has several problems that will be discussed in a moment:

```
typedef struct node
{
    int data;
    node *next;
} node;

class Stack
{
    node *top;
public:
    Stack(): top(0) {}
    ~Stack() { Clear(); }
    void Clear()
    {
        node *p=top;
        while (p)
        {
            top = top->next;
            delete p;
            p = top;
        }
    }
    void Push(int i)
    {
        node *p = new node;
        p->data = i;
        p->next = top;
        top = p;
    }
    int Pop()
    {
        if (top != 0)
        {
            int d = top->data;
            node *p=top;
            top = top->next;
            delete p;
            return d;
        }
        else return 0;
    }
    int Size()
    {
        int c=0;
        node *p=top;
        while (p)
        {
            c++;
            p = p->next;
        }
        return c;
    }
};
```

This is a fairly complete class. It properly cleans up after itself in its destructor and works the same way as the previous stack class. However, this class does not work as expected after an assignment statement such as:

```
stack1 = stack2;
```

The following diagram demonstrates what is happening. When the assignment operation executes, it simply copies the data members from **stack2** to **stack1**, leaving one copy of the data on the heap with two pointers accessing it:

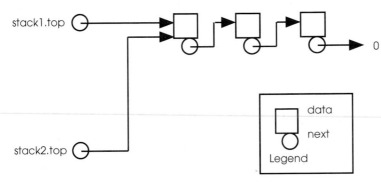

After the assignment, the pointers **stack1.top** and **stack2.top** both point to the same chain of memory blocks. If one of the stacks is then cleared, or if one executes a **Pop**, the other pointer will be pointing to memory that is no longer valid. On many machines, the code will compile fine and everything will look OK for awhile during execution. But as the system runs, the rot sets in and things gets flakier and flakier for no apparent reason until the program finally crashes.

What is needed is a way to redo the assignment operation to create a copy of the memory blocks. But where is the assignment operator coming from and how can it be modified?

A.7.1 Default Functions

Whenever you create any class, four *default* functions are created automatically unless you override them by creating your own. They are:
- The default constructor
- The default copy constructor
- The default assignment operator
- The default destructor

The default constructor is invoked whenever you declare an instance of a class and pass it no parameters. For example, if you create a class **Sample** and you create no constructors for it, then the following statement invokes the default constructor on **s**:

```
Sample s;
```

The following initialized declaration of **s2** invokes the copy constructor:

```
Sample s1;

Sample s2 = s1;
```

The default destructor is called whenever a variable goes out of scope, and the default assignment operator is called whenever a normal assignment occurs. You can override any of the defaults by creating functions of your own. For example, if you create *any* constructor then the default constructor is not created.

The code below can be used to gain an understanding of what the default constructor and destructor do:

```
#include <iostream.h>

class Class0
{
    int data0;
public:
    Class0 () { cout << "class0 constructor" << endl; }
    ~Class0 () { cout << "class0 destructor" << endl; }
};

class Class1
{
    int data1;
public:
    Class1 () { cout << "class1 constructor" << endl; }
    ~Class1 () { cout << "class1 destructor" << endl; }
};

class Class2: public Class1
{
    int data2;
  Class0 c0;
};

void main()
{
    Class2 c;
}
```

The class **Class2** has neither constructor nor destructor, but when you run this code the following output is produced:

```
class1 constructor
class0 constructor
class0 destructor
class1 destructor
```

What has happened is that the compiler created a default constructor and destructor for **Class2**. The behavior of the default constructor is to call the base class default constructor as well as the default constructor for all data members that are classes. The default constructor calls the destructors for the base class and class data members.

Let's say you create a new constructor for **Class2** that accepts an integer. The compiler will still call the necessary default constructors for the base class and class data members. The following code demonstrates the process:

```
class Class2: public Class1
{
    int data2;
```

This book is continuously updated. See http://www.iftech.com/mfc

```
        Class0 c0;
public:
    Class2(int i)
    {
        cout << "class2 constructor" << endl;
    }
};

void main()
{
    Class2 c(1);
}
```

This also works, producing the following output:

```
class1 constructor
class0 constructor
class2 constructor
class0 destructor
class1 destructor
```

But now you cannot declare an uninitialized variable of type **Class2** because there is no default constructor. The following code demonstrates:

```
Class2 c(1);// OK
Class2 e;// not OK--no default constructor
```

It is also impossible to declare arrays of a class unless there is no default constructor defined. Therefore, you should recreate the default constructor yourself by creating a constructor with an empty parameter list whenever you create other constructors.

The assignment operator and copy constructor are created automatically as well. Both simply copy the data members from the right side of the equal sign to the left. In the case of our stack class we want to eliminate these default functions and use our own so that assignment works correctly. Below are the two new functions for the stack class, along with a function **Copy** that is shared by both:

```
void Copy(const Stack& s)
{
    node *q=0;
    node *p=s.top;

    while (p)
    {
        if (top==0)
        {
            top = new node;
            q=top;
        }
        else
        {
            q->next = new node;
            q = q->next;
        }

        q->data = p->data;
        p = p->next;
    }
    q->next=0;
```

```
    }
    Stack& operator= (const Stack& s) //assignment
    {
        if (this == &s)
            return *this;
        Clear();
        Copy(s);
        return *this;
    }
    Stack(const Stack& s): top(0) // copy constructor
    {
        Copy(s);
    }
```

The function for the assignment operator starts by checking for the case of equivalent assignment, as in:

```
    s = s;
```

If it finds this situation it does nothing. It then clears the recipient and copies the linked list on the heap so that the left side of the assignment has its own copy of the stack. The copy constructor is just like any other constructor and is used to handle the following cases:

```
    Stack s1;
    s1.Push(10);
    s1.Push(20);
    Stack s2(s1);// copy constructor invoked
    Stack s3 = s1;// copy constructor invoked
```

With the assignment operator and copy constructor in place, the **Stack** class is complete—it can handle any condition that may arise.

A.7.2 Conclusion

This may all seem like a lot of work to go through, but generally it is only necessary when working with pointers. What is happening is that you are actually having to secure your pointer-based structures against any contingency so the data is *always* valid. In many C programs the programmer will make an assumption such as, "I can point several pointers at the same blocks on the heap and it will be OK because in this part of the code nothing modifies the blocks." However, if another programmer comes along and violates that assumption accidentally, the program can break in mysterious and hard-to-track ways. That can never happen with a secure C++ class because all the contingencies are covered.

You can see that the implementation shown above is inefficient, however. What if, in certain places, you *want* to have only one copy of the blocks on the heap. For example, what if the data on the heap occupies many megabytes, and you can't afford to make a copy? What you can do in that case is use a technique such as a reference count—each instance increments a static global variable that keeps count of the number of instances using the single copy of the data on the heap. Then in each destructor you can decrement the counter. Only when a destructor, after decrementing the counter, detects that no other instance is using the data in the heap does it actually delete all the heap blocks containing the data.

A.8 Tutorial Eight—Virtual Functions

In these tutorials we have seen many examples of inheritance because inheritance is very important to object-oriented programming. We have seen that inheritance allows data members and member functions to be added in the derived class. We have also seen several examples where we used inheritance to *change* the behavior of a function. For example, in Tutorial Three we saw an example where the **Insert** function of a base **List** class was overridden to implement a totaling feature. A similar hierarchy is shown below, using a base class called **List** and a derived class called **TotalingList**:

```
#include <iostream.h>

class List
{
    int array[100];
    int count;
public:
    List(): count(0) {}
    void Insert(int n) { array[count++]=n; }
    int Get(int i) { return array[i]; }
    int Size() { return count; }
};

void ManipList(List list)
{
    // do things to the list
    list.Insert(100);
    list.Insert(200);
    // do things to the list
}

class TotalingList: public List
{
    int total;
public:
    TotalingList(): List(), total(0) {}
    void Insert(int n)
    {
        total += n;
        List::Insert(n);
    }
    int GetTotal() { return total; }
};

void main()
{
    TotalingList list;
    int x;

    list.Insert(10);
    list.Insert(5);
    cout << list.GetTotal() << endl;
    ManipList(list);
    cout << list.GetTotal() << endl;
    for (x=0; x<list.Size(); x++)
        cout << list.Get(x) << ' ';
```

```
        cout << endl;
    }
```

In this code, the class **List** implements the simplest possible list with the three member functions **Insert**, **Get**, and **Size**, as well as the constructor. The function **ManipList** is an example of some arbitrary function that uses the **List** class, and it calls the insert function twice simply as an example.

The **TotalingList** class inherits the **List** class and adds in a data member named **total**. This member holds the current total of all the numbers held in the list. The **Insert** function is overridden so that **total** is updated at each insertion.

The **main** function declares an instance of the **TotalingList** class. It inserts 10 and 5, and prints out the total. It then calls **ManipList**. It might surprise you that this actually compiles—if you look at the prototype for **ManipList** you can see that it expects a parameter of type **List**, not **TotalingList**. But C++ understands certain things about inherited classes, one of them being that a parameter of a base class type should accept any class derived from that base class as well. Therefore, because **TotalingList** is derived from the **List** class, **ManipList** will accept it. This is one of the features of C++ that makes inheritance so powerful—you can create derived classes and pass them to existing functions that know only about the base class.

When the code shown above runs, however, it does not produce the correct result. It produces the output:

15

15

10 5

This output indicates that not only did the totaling not work, but the 100 and 200 were never inserted in the list during the call to **ManipList**. Part of this problem is occurring because of an outright error in the code—the parameter accepted by **ManipList** must be a pointer or a reference or no values are returned. Modifying the prototype for **ManipList** to the following partially fixes the problem:

```
    void ManipList(List& list)
```

Now the output looks like this:

15

15

10 5 100 200

It is educational to single-step through the **ManipList** and watch what happens. When the calls to the **Insert** functions occur, they route themselves to **List::Insert** rather than **TotalingList::Insert**.

This problem can also be solved, however. It is possible in C++ to create a function with the prefix **virtual**, and this causes C++ to call the version of the function *in the derived class*. That is, when a function is declared as virtual, the compiler can call versions of the function that did not even exist when the code calling the function was written. To see this, add the word **virtual** in front of the **Insert** functions in both the **List** and **TotalingList** classes, as shown below:

```
    class List
    {
```

```
        int array[100];
        int count;
public:
        List(): count(0) {}
        virtual void Insert(int n) { array[count++]=n; }
        int Get(int i) { return array[i]; }
        int Size() { return count; }
};

void ManipList(List& list)
{
        // do things to the list
        list.Insert(100);
        list.Insert(200);
        // do things to the list
}

class TotalingList: public List
{
        int total;
public:
        TotalingList(): List(), total(0) {}
        virtual void Insert(int n)
        {
                total += n;
                List::Insert(n);
        }
        int GetTotal() { return total; }
};
```

Actually it is only necessary to place it in front of the function name in the base class, but it's a good habit to perpetuate it in all derived classes as well to give some indication of what is happening.

Now when you execute the program, you will get the correct output:

15

315

10 5 100 200

What is happening? The word **virtual** in front of a function tells C++ that *you plan to create new versions of this function in derived classes*. That is, it lets you state future intentions for a class. When the virtual function is called, C++ looks at the class that called the function and picks the version of the function *for that class*, even if the derived class did not exist at the time that the function call was written.

What all this means is that in many cases you have to think into the future when you are writing code. You have to think, "will I or anyone else ever need or want to change the behavior of this function?" If the answer is "yes," the function should be declared as a virtual function.

You have to pay attention to several things for virtual functions to work correctly. For example, you have to actually predict the need for the function and remember to make it virtual in the base class. Another point can be seen in the program above— try removing the **&** from the parameter in the **ManipList** function and then single-step through the code. Even though the **Insert** function is tagged as virtual, the

List::Insert function is called instead of the **TotalingList::Insert** function. The behavior changes because the parameter type **List** is acting like a type cast when the **&** is not there. Any class passed in is cast back to the base **List** class. With the **&** in place, this casting does not happen.

You see virtual functions everywhere in C++ class hierarchies. A typical hierarchy *expects* you to be changing behavior in the future to customize the library to your application. Virtual functions are also frequently used when the creator of the class *cannot* know what you will do with the class. For example, say that you are using a user interface class that implements buttons on the screen. When you create an instance of the button it paints itself onto the screen and behaves as a button should by highlighting itself when the button is clicked by the user. However, the person who wrote the class has no idea what people using the class plan to have the button do when it is clicked. In such cases, the author will create a virtual function named something like **handleEvent** that is called whenever the button is clicked. Then you override that virtual function with a function of your own that handles the button event properly.

A.8.1 Conclusion

We have covered quite a bit of ground in these tutorials, but you are probably left with the impression that we have only scratched the surface. And that is true to a certain degree—C++ is a very deep language, with many subtleties and quirks that are only mastered with experience. C is like that, only on a much smaller scale.

The only way to fully understand this language is to write, and read, a lot of C++ code. You can learn a great deal by using and studying class libraries that other people have developed.

The many advantages of this language become apparent once it is fully understood. So start coding. . .

USING THE VISUAL C++ COMPILER AND TOOLS

This book is designed to be "version free." The goal is to create a book that can be updated on the web each time Visual C++ changes versions so that we can save you the cost of buying a new book every six months. To accomplish this goal, we have isolated all version-specific features in this appendix. When a new version appears on the market, we will update this appendix on the web immediately, and you can access our updates, changes and supplements free of charge. See http://www.iftech.com/mfc for details.

The purpose of this appendix is to give you a tour of the Visual C++ compiler and the different tools that you can use with it to make programming easier. These tools include the debugger, the browser, the AppWizard and the ClassWizard. By understanding these tools completely you can make the most of this rich and powerful programming environment. This appendix was produced using VC++ version 4.1.

To simplify this discussion as much as possible, we will start with *console programs*. A console program works strictly in text mode. Once you have mastered these simple programs, we will then move on to try a small MFC application, followed by larger applications using the AppWizard and ClassWizard.

For information on the different resource editors, see Chapter 6. For information on the AppWizard and ClassWizard, see Chapters 14 through 18, as well as Part 5. See also the Visual C++ User's Guide in the on-line documentation for specific reference information about Visual C++ tools and features.

B.1 Compiling and Executing a Console Program with Visual C++

Given its power and flexibility, Visual C++ is remarkably easy to use. This section shows you how to enter, compile, and execute a simple program using Visual C++ so you can quickly become familiar with the basic features. You will take the following steps:

1. Prepare the environment
2. Enter the code

3. Create a project file
4. Build the project
5. Execute the program

For this simple example, you should use the program shown in Listing B.1.

Listing B.1
A simple console program

```cpp
// simple.cpp

#include <iostream.h>

void loop()
{
    int x=0;
    while (x<5)
    {
        cout << x << endl;
        x++;
    }
}

void main()
{
    cout << "Starting the loop\n";
    loop();
    cout << "ending\n";
    cout << "Press return to continue: ";
    char s[100];
    cin.getline(s, 100);
}
```

B.1.1 Preparing the Environment

Open Visual C++ by double-clicking on its icon. If you are opening from a new installation, Visual C++ will open in an empty state. However, if Visual C++ has been used previously it is possible that it will automatically open project and/or code files because it remembers the open windows from its last session. For this exercise you will want to close these files. In the **Windows** menu you will find a **Close All** option. If it is enabled select it. Also, use the **Close Workspace** option in the **File** menu to close any open project. Now Visual C++ is in an empty state and you can begin a new project.

B.1.2 Creating a Project

Every application you create in Visual C++ must have a *project workspace*. If you are familiar with the concept of a makefile, you can think of project file as a makefile that you manipulate graphically using tools in Visual C++. The project file stores several important pieces of information about your program:

1. It remembers all of different source files that make up the application. In this simple application there is only one small source file, but most real applications contain several source code files. The project file will also keep track of which files have already been compiled so it compiles only those that have changed.

2. It remembers the type of application that you want to build: console, windows, etc. It is also possible to build such things as libraries and DLL files by changing the type of the project.

3. It remembers options specific to your project. These include compiler, linker, and resource options, as well as other specifics about the project.

To create a new project for Listing B.1, choose the **New** option in the **File** menu again. It will present you with the New dialog we have already seen in Figure B.1. This time select the **Project Workspace** option and click the **OK** button.

You will see a **New Project Workspace** dialog like the one shown in Figure B.2.

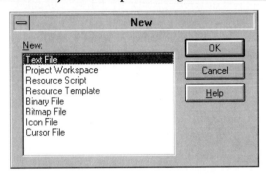

Figure B.1
Opening a new window

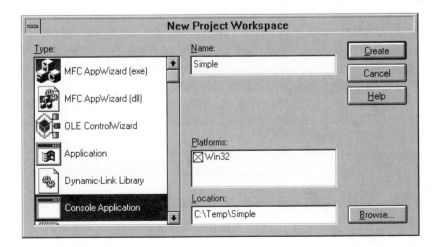

Figure B.2
The new project workspace dialog

Enter the name "Simple" in the **Project Name** field of the New Project dialog. Select the project type from the Project Type combo box. You will want your project to be a **Console Application** as shown in Figure B.2. Choose the directory in which you want your new project directory to be created. Click the **Create** button. Visual C++ will create a new Project Workspace as well as a new directory for it.

B.1.3 Entering the Code

Choose the **New** option in the **File** menu to open a new editing window. You will see a dialog like the one shown in Figure B.1 that lets you choose the type of file you wish to create. In this case we want to create a **Text** window so we can enter the code in Listing B.1. Click the **OK** button on the New dialog and you will see a new text window.

This new window will act a great deal like any standard text editor you have used in Windows. The only real difference is that the editor will color certain words to help you see them better. Type in the code shown in Listing B.1. Save the code to a file named SIMPLE.CPP using the **Save** option in the **File** menu.

You may notice certain behaviors in the editor that you do not like. In many cases you can change those behaviors by selecting the **Options** option in the **Tools** menu. You will see a dialog like the one shown in Figure B.3. You can change the editor's colors, its font, its treatment of tabs and so on in this dialog.

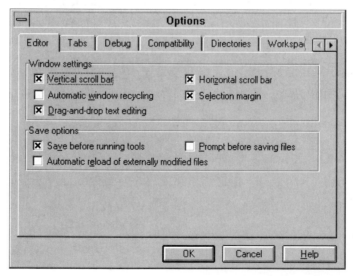

Figure B.3
The Options dialog

B.1.4 Adding the Code to the Project

Choose the **Files In Project** option in the **Insert** menu. See Figure B.4. Select SIMPLE.CPP from the list and click the **OK** button.

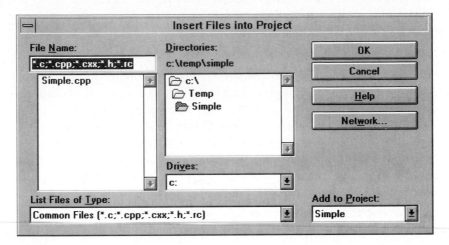

Figure B.4

The Insert Files into Project dialog

B.1.5 Examining the Windows

You will now have two windows open in Visual C++. The first is the source file itself. The second is the Project Workspace window. See Figure B.5. The workspace window contains three tabs: one for the FileView, one for the ClassView and one for the InfoView (see section B.6.2 also). If you look at the FileViewit contains one file: SIMPLE.CPP.

Figure B.5
The project workspace window for this project

The steps you have taken in this section have let you:

1. Create and name the project
2. Choose the type of project.
3. Choose the directory for the project files.
4. Add a source file to the project.

You are now ready to build the application.

B.1.6 Building the Application

To build the application, choose the **Build** option in the **Build** menu. This option will compile the source file and link it to form an executable.

As it compiles and links, Visual C++ will place progress messages in an Output pane at the bottom of the Visual C++ window. (If for some reason this pane is not visible, choose the **Output** option in the **View** menu. This pane is dockable, so you can move it or place it in a free-floating window.) This pane also shows you any compiler errors that the system detects. You can double-click on an error message and the system will jump to the offending line in your program and show you an error message on the status line. You can also get more information about the error message itself by single-clicking on the error message in the output pane and pressing the F1 key.

B.1.7 Executing the Application

To execute the application, choose the **Execute** option in the **Project** menu. You will see a text window and it will display the output of the application. Press the Enter key to terminate the application.

B.2 Debugging

The Visual C++ debugger is extremely powerful, but also extremely easy to use. You can use it to find problems in your own code. When working with MFC code, you can also use the debugger to step into the actual MFC source code to learn about what it is doing. As discussed in Chapter 13, looking at the MFC source can also help you to resolve assertions that you have violated.

In order to use the debugger, you must create a *debug version* (as opposed to a *release version*) of your application when you build it. This is the default, but you can make sure you are building a debug version by choosing the **Set Default Configuration** option in the **Build** menu. A debug version of the program contains a wide variety of information required by the debugger and makes the size of your executable larger than the release version. See Chapter 13 for more information about the specific features of the debugging version of an MFC application.

There are many different things that you can do with the debugger:

1. You can run a program under the debugger using the **Go** option.

2. You can stop execution of a program running under the debugger using the **Stop Debugging** option, or restart it from the beginning with the **Restart** option. You can also interrupt it midstream in a resumable way using the **Break** option.

3. You can single step through the program one line at a time. If the current line of code calls a function, you can either **Step Into** the function or **Step Over** it. In the first case you are taken to the first line of the function. In the second case, the function executes completely and returns. If you are inside a function,

you can **Step Out** of it. In this case the function will complete, return to its caller and stop there.

4. You can place the cursor on any executable line in the program and step to that line by selecting the **Step To Cursor** option.

5. You can examine specific exceptions or Threads. See Chapters 13 and 35 for details.

6. You can set breakpoints in your code and manipulate them with the **Break-points** option.

7. You can examine a variable in the **Quick Watch** window. This window lets you see the current value of any variable, modify the variable's value, or add the variable to the *watch window* so that its value is visible at each step of the program's execution.

8. At the bottom of the **View** menu you can monitor the state of the program with the following windows: **Watch**, **Locals**, **Registers**, **Memory**, **Call Stack**, and **Disassembly**. The first five windows are dockable. The **Watch**, **Locals**, and **Call Stack** windows deal with information at the source code level and are generally more useful to the C++ programmer. The call stack window is particularly useful in the case of crashes: It shows the set of function calls currently pending on the call stack. For example, if the **main** function called a function named **A**, and function **A** called a function named **B** and you are currently on a line within function **B**, then the call stack will show **main, A**, and **B**. You can double-click on any line in the call stack to see the function in your source code.

Many of the options just described are echoed in the standard and debug tool bars, as shown in Figure B.6. The debug tool bar should become visible once you begin debugging by selecting the **Go** option in the **Debug** menu of the **Build** menu, but if you cannot find it choose the **Toolbars** option in the **View** menu and click on **Debug**.

One of the best ways to become familiar with the debugger is to use it to walk through some simple code. To try out the debugger with SIMPLE.CPP, take the following steps.

B.2.1 Run the Program

If you select the **Go** option in the **Debug** menu of the **Build** menu (or press the equivalent tool bar button), the program will execute under the debugger. It will appear to run in exactly the same way as it did when you used the **Execute** option in the **Project** menu. However, if the program enters an infinite loop you have the option to use the **Break** option in the **Debug** menu to halt execution and examine the problem.

You can also set breakpoints. Then when you select the **Go** option, the program will run until it hits a breakpoint. To set a breakpoint you can click on a line of code

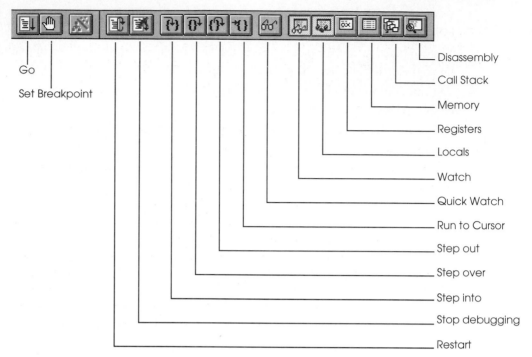

Figure B.6
The debugging tool bar options

and click the tool bar button that sets breakpoints. A small dot to the left of the line marks it as a breakpoint. Set a breakpoint, and then select **Go**. Execution will halt at the breakpoint. You can then select **Go** to continue execution, or perform any other debugger operation.

B.2.2 Single-Step

Choose the **Stop Debugging** option if it is available to stop execution of the current program. Then resize the Visual C++ window so it takes up about half the screen. Set a breakpoint somewhere in the code. Choose the **Go** option. The debugger will begin execution of the program, display the output window, and stop on the breakpoint. Reposition the output window so both it and Visual C++ are visible simultaneously. Choose **Step Over** or press its accelerator key repeatedly to step through the entire program to completion. Note that when you step over the call to the **loop** function the entire function executes and returns all in one step.

Now step through the application again, but when you get to the **loop** function choose the **Step Into** option instead. Now you can single-step through the function itself.

Note that if you choose **Step Into** on a line that produces output, you will single step into the source code for its implementation. This is sometimes useful.

746

At any time while you are single-stepping, you can choose the **Go** option to complete execution of the program or to run to a breakpoint. You can also click on a line and choose **Run to Cursor** to run to a specific line without setting a breakpoint. If you are inside the **loop** function you can also choose the **Step Out** function to complete the **loop** function and return to its caller. Try out all these options.

B.2.3 Getting Information

Single step into the **loop** function and select the **Call Stack** option in the **View** menu. You will see a window that shows you the call stack. In this program, the **main** function has called the **loop** function. This is fairly obvious here, but in a large program this little window can be a lifesaver. The Call Stack window is dockable, so you can leave it floating or dock it anywhere along the edge of the Visual C++ window.

Now highlight the variable **x** and choose the **Quick Watch** option. You can see its current value (or you can see its value simply by letting the cursor rest on it). You can change its value if you like or add the variable to the **Watch** window. If you add it to the **Watch** window, choose the **Watch** option in the **View** menu to make the **Watch** window visible. The **Watch** window is dockable, so you can watch variables there as you single-step. The **Quick Watch** window, on the other hand, is a dialog. With the **Watch** window visible, single-step through the program and watch **x** increment.

Now choose the **Variables** option. This window shows you all of the local variables for the current function. This window is also dockable.

B.3 Compiling MFC Programs

The code from Chapters 1 and 2 appears again in Listing B.2. This section shows you how to create a project file and compile the code. You will find that many of the steps echo the steps for the console program: You have to create a project, type in the code, add the code file to the project, and build the project.

Listing B.2
hello.cpp - A simple "Hello world" program in MFC.

```
//hello.cpp

#include <afxwin.h>

// Declare the application class
class CHelloApp : public CWinApp
{
public:
    virtual BOOL InitInstance();
};

// Create an instance of the application class
CHelloApp HelloApp;
```

```
// Declare the main window class
class CHelloWindow : public CFrameWnd
{
    CStatic* cs;
public:
    CHelloWindow();
};

// The InitInstance function is called each
// time the application first executes.
BOOL CHelloApp::InitInstance()
{
    m_pMainWnd = new CHelloWindow();
    m_pMainWnd->ShowWindow(m_nCmdShow);
    m_pMainWnd->UpdateWindow();
    return TRUE;
}

// The constructor for the window class
CHelloWindow::CHelloWindow()
{
    // Create the window itself
    Create(NULL,
        "Hello World!",
        WS_OVERLAPPEDWINDOW,
        CRect(0,0,200,200));
    // Create a static label
    cs = new CStatic();
    cs->Create("hello world",
        WS_CHILD|WS_VISIBLE|SS_CENTER,
        CRect(50,80,150,150),
        this);
}
```

To create a new project for HELLO.CPP, choose the **New** option in the **File** menu. You will see a dialog like the one shown in Figure B.1. You want to create a new project workspace, so select **Project Workspace** from the list and click the **OK** button. You will see a new project dialog like the one shown in Figure B.2. This dialog lets you specify the name of the project, the directory in which to store the project file, and the type of project you want to create.

Type the word "hello" into the **Project Name** field in the upper left corner of the dialog. *For the **Project Type** field choose the **Application** option because for this example you will be creating a simple MFC application. DO NOT CHOOSE THE "MFC APPWIZARD" PROJECT TYPE - CHOOSE "APPLICATION".* Choose an appropriate directory. Create the project.

Now you need to type in the code from Listing B.2. In the **File** menu select the **New** option. You will see a selection dialog like the one that you see in Figure B.1. Choose the **Text** option and click the **OK** button. This will create a new editor window. Type the code into the editor window (or copy and paste the file from the diskette—it would be beneficial to actually type it because it will force you to look at every word in the program and start to get used to each one). Once you are finished entering the file, save it into the new project directory, giving it the name HELLO.CPP.

Add the HELLO.CPP file to the project by choosing the **Files Into Project** option in the **Insert** menu and selecting HELLO.CPP.

*Choose the **Settings** option in the **Build** menu. In the **General** tab, change the **Microsoft Foundations Classes** combo box to **Use MFC in a Shared DLL**. If you fail to do this the project will not link.*

Having created the project file, added the code file to it, and having set up the project properly for MFC code, you are ready to compile the program. In the **Build** menu you will find three different compile options:

1. Compile HELLO.CPP
2. Build HELLO.EXE
3. Rebuild All

The first option simply compiles the source file listed and forms the object file for it. This option does not perform a link, so it is useful only for quickly compiling a file to check for errors. The second option compiles all the source files in the project that have been modified since the last build and then links them to form an executable. The third option recompiles all the source files in the project and relinks them. It is a "compile and link from scratch" option that is useful after you change certain compiler options or move to a different platform.

In this case, choose the **Build HELLO.EXE** option in the **Project** menu to compile and link the code. You will see, in the bottom area of the Visual C++ window, messages that indicate progress as the code compiles.

If you see compiler errors, simply double click on the error message in this output area. The editor will take you to that error. Compare your code against Listing B.2 and fix the problem. If you see a mass of linker errors, it probably means that you specified the project type incorrectly in the workspace dialog. Delete your new directory and recreate it again following the instructions given above.

To execute the program, choose the **Execute HELLO.EXE** option in the **Build** menu. A window appears with the words "Hello World." The window itself has the usual decorations: a title bar, re-size areas, minimize and maximize buttons, and so on. Inside the window is a static label displaying the words "Hello World." Note that the program is complete. You can move the window, re-size it, minimize it, and cover and uncover it with other windows. With a very small amount of code you have created a complete Windows application. This is one of the many advantages of using MFC.

To terminate the program, click on its system menu and select the **Close** option.

Here is a recap of the steps you took in this chapter. You may want to repeat them just so they become more familiar to you:

1. You created a new project named "hello"
2. You created a new code file named "hello.cpp" from Listing B.2,
3. You added the code file to the project,

4. You adjusted the settings in the project file to identify the code as MFC code,
5. You compiled and ran the program.

For further instructions on compiling code, please turn to Appendix B.

When you begin working with and creating your own MFC code, there are two mistakes commonly made. These two errors are notoriously hard to track down, but the Visual C++ debugger can help you. The two errors are described in the following sections.

B.3.1 Addressing Errors

Addressing errors are generally caused when a pointer writes to memory that it should not be writing to. This occurs when the pointer has not been initialized or when it has been loaded with a corrupt address. It is easy to simulate an addressing error in Listing B.2 and then see how the debugger helps you to find the problem.

To simulate an addressing error, find the following line in the constructor for the **CHelloWindow** class:

```
cs = new CStatic();
```

Comment the line out, rebuild the project, and then execute it by selecting the **Execute** option in the **Project** menu. You will see a dialog notifying you of a problem, but the dialog gives you no clue as to the problem's cause.

Now try to execute the program again under the debugger. Choose the **Go** option. The program will eventually halt with an application error on a specific line inside one of MFC's source files. To find out where you were in your application's code at the time of the error, choose the **Call Stack** option in the **Debug** menu. Figure B.7 is representative of what you will see.

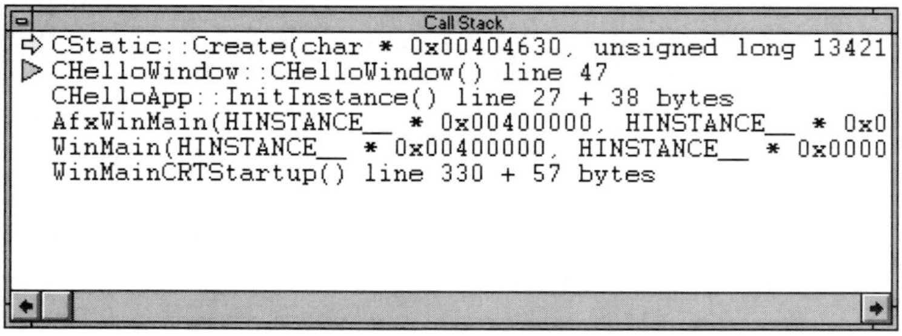

```
                          Call Stack
⇨ CStatic::Create(char * 0x00404630, unsigned long 13421
▷ CHelloWindow::CHelloWindow() line 47
  CHelloApp::InitInstance() line 27 + 38 bytes
  AfxWinMain(HINSTANCE__ * 0x00400000, HINSTANCE__ * 0x0
  WinMain(HINSTANCE__ * 0x00400000, HINSTANCE__ * 0x0000
  WinMainCRTStartup() line 330 + 57 bytes
```

Figure B.7
The Call Stack

The highlighted line in Figure B.7 shows the constructor for the **CHelloWindow** class. You can see that the constructor was called by the **InitInstance** function. You can also see that the constructor called the **Create** function for the **CStatic** class.

By double-clicking on the line for the constructor in the call stack dialog, Visual C++ will take you to the specific line in your source code that called **CStatic::Create**.

You therefore know that something is wrong with this line, either with the parameters passed to the **CStatic::Create** function or with **cs**. You can check **cs** by highlighting it and then choosing the **Quick Watch** option in the **Debug** menu. Figure B.8 shows the dialog you will see.

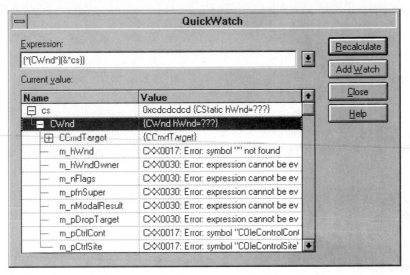

Figure B.8
The Quick Watch dialog

The error messages seen in Figure B.9 indicate that there is a problem with this variable. You should therefore check back through the code to see where the variable gets initialized (the Browse tool, described in Section B.4, can help you find all uses of **cs**). In this code the **cs** variable is used before initialization, and that is the source of the problem.

B.3.2 Omissions

Let's say you accidentally were to leave out the **InitInstance** function in Listing B.2. This function is essential to an application's successful execution. Try removing it now (both the function and its definition in the **CHelloApp** class), and then rebuild and execute the application. Absolutely nothing will happen, and Visual C++ gives you no clue as to why.

Now rerun the application under the debugger by choosing the **Go** option. Again nothing will happen. However, the debugger will give you a clue in the form of a trace statement that is part of MFC's source code. You will see the message shown in Figure B.9 in the Output window. This message indicates that **m_pMainWnd** was never initialized.

If you look up **m_pMainWnd** in the MFC help file, the help information will point you to the **InitInstance** function, and its explanation should jog your memory or at least cause you to look up references to it in the example code in this book.

Figure B.9
The Output window when the **InitInstance** fuction is missing

If you return the program to its original state (Listing B.2) and rerun it under the debugger, the program will run fine but complain of memory leaks when it exits. Note that you do note see this message when you executed the program—you must use the **Go** option. See Chapter 2 for an explanation. For more information on the debugging features built into MFC, see Chapter 13.

B.4 The Browser

The browser acts like an animated cross-reference listing for your application. Visual C++ forms a special file for the browser after each build (a .BSC file), and this file contains the information presented by the browser. The browse file takes a noticeable amount of time to create, especially with MFC applications, and you therefore have the ability to enable and disable the file's creation. By default the file is rebuilt every time you compile an application. However, if you select the **Settings** option in the **Build** menu and then select the **Browser** section of the dialog, the **Build Browse Info File** check box turns the browser file creation on and off. You must also select the **Browse Info** check box in the **C/C++** tab of the same dialog.

Using the browser you can immediately find any of the following pieces of information:

1. You can find where any variable, type, function, class, or macro in your application is declared, and every place where it is used (*definitions and references*).
2. You can list all the functions, classes, variables, macros, etc., that you have declared (the *file outline*).
3. You can find all the functions that a given function calls (a *call graph*).
4. You can find all the functions that call a given function (a *caller graph*).
5. You can find what classes a specific class derives its behavior from (a *base class graph*)
6. You can find out which classes are derived from a specified class (a *derived class graph*).

In a large program, especially one written by another programmer, and most especially when you are looking at the program for the first time, these different views can be a tremendous time-saver. You can quickly answer questions that you have about the different classes, functions and variables in a program. The browser is also extremely useful to anyone as they begin learning MFC, because it helps you to find out information about the MFC class hierarchy very quickly.

You can learn a great deal about the browser by trying a few exercises using Listing B.2 as a sample program for experimentation. The following sections contain several different demonstrations. Try these and then make up some exercises of your own. You will quickly become adept with this tool because it is so easy to use. For additional information, look up information on the browser in books on-line.

To open the browser for the following examples, choose the **Browse** option in the **Tools** menu. The general way to use the browser is to highlight a name in your program and the choose the **Browse** option. You will see a dialog like the one shown in Figure B.10. This dialog lets you select the browser mode that you are interested in using. Once you select the mode you will see the browser itself, and it will display the requested information in a modeless dialog.

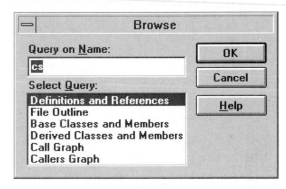

Figure B.10
The Browse dialog lets you choose the browser's mode

B.4.1 Finding Declarations and References

Listing B.2 contains a variable named **cs**. Let's say you want to find the declaration for **cs** along with all references to it. If you highlight **cs** anywhere in the program and select the **Browse** option in the **Tools** menu, you can select the **Definitions and References** option for the Browse dialog. You will see a display similar to the one shown in Figure B.11. The list on the right shows the location of the variable's definition, as well as all of the references to it. If you double-click on the line numbers shown in the right hand list, Visual C++ will take you to that specific line in the edit window so you can see the variable in context.

In a large program, it is possible for a name to be used in several different classes or files. When this happens, it is not possible for the browser to tell which reference you are interested in viewing. It will, therefore, present a list showing you the different possibilities on the left-hand side of the dialog. In Figure B.11, this left-hand list contains only one item because there is only one use of the name **cs**.

For definitions and references to variables, types, classes, etc., the browser offers a second way to quickly move through a file using the **Browse** tool bar. If this tool bar

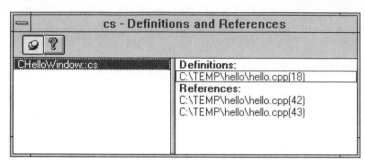

Figure B.11
Finding the definitions and references of **cs**

is not visible, select the **Toolbars** option in the **Tools** menu and click on **Browse**. This is a dockable tool bar. Let the cursor rest on each button in the tool bar to identify its function—they are all self-explanatory. Many of them echo the five browse options that you find at the bottom of the **Search** menu.

For example, find a reference to the variable **cs** in the editor window and highlight the variable **cs**. Now choose the **Go To Definition** option in the **Browse** tool bar or the **Search** menu. You will be taken to the line that defines the variable **cs**. Now select the **Go To Reference** option in the **Browse** tool bar and you will be taken to the line containing the first reference to the variable in the file. Use the **Next** and **Previous** options in the **Browse** tool bar to move to other references. This technique is limited to a single file, while the browse window shown in Figure B.11 spans files, so each technique is appropriate in different circumstances.

Try out the same techniques on the class name **CHelloWindow**. That is, highlight the name **CHelloWindow** in the edit window and select the **Browse** option.

Note that the Browser is case sensitive.

B.4.2 Finding all Names in a File

You can find all of the functions, classes, variables types and macros declared in a file using the browser's File Outline feature. Figure B.12 shows a typical view for Listing B.2.

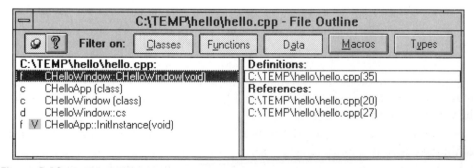

Figure B.12
The File Outline display for Listing B.2

Along the top of Figure B.12 you can see that you can select the specific types of information shown in the window. The left-hand list shows all the filtered names. Then you can click on the declarations or references in the right-hand list.

B.4.3 Finding All the Functions Called by a Function

You can easily find all the functions called by a given function by creating a *call graph* for the function in question. Figure B.13 shows the call graph for the **InitInstance** function in Listing B.2. If you look in Listing B.2 you will find that the **InitInstance** function calls four functions and all four are represented in the call graph. Clicking on any function in the graph displays the function's definitions and references in the list on the right.

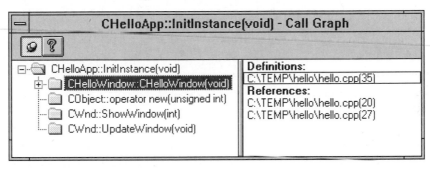

Figure B.13
The call graph for the **InitInstance** function

B.4.4 Finding All Functions that Call a Function

A *caller graph* lets you see all the functions that call a specific function. This can help you to track down side effects. For example, if you modify a function and the program suddenly breaks in a mysterious way, you can use the caller graph to quickly find every call to the function and then pinpoint the problem.

The caller graph is no different from the definitions and references list created for a variable in Section B.4.1. In the list on the right it shows the definition of and references to the function. Try this with the **InitInstance** function and see Section B.4.1 for more information.

B.4.5 Finding the Base-Class Graph

The *Base-Class Graph* shows what classes act as base classes for a specified class. This graph can be very useful in large programs or when you are learning about MFC or another programmer's class hierarchy. Figure B.14 shows the base class graph for the **CHelloWindow** class.

As you can see in Figure B.14, the graph shows each of the classes that **CHelloWindow** is derived from. In the upper right-hand list it shows the class's member functions and variables. In the lower right-hand list it shows the lines where the class is defined and used.

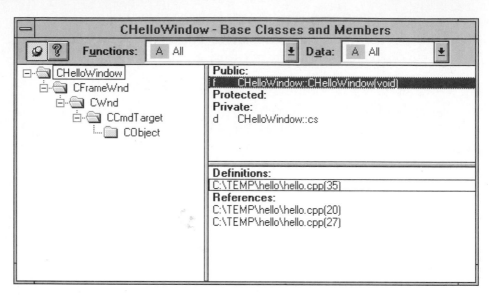

Figure B.14
The base class graph for **CHelloWindow**

B.4.6 The Derived-Class Graph

A *derived-class graph* shows all the classes derived from a given class. You can use this graph to track use of a given class and also to point out parts of your program that may be affected by a change you make to a given class. Figure B.15 shows the derived class graph for the class **CFrameWnd**. Because **CHelloWindow** is derived from **CFrameWnd**, it appears in the graph. If other classes were derived from **CHelloWindow**, they would appear in the graph as well.

Like the base-class graph shown in Section B.4.5, the derived-class graph shows you the selected class's member functions and variables in the upper right-hand list. It also shows you the lines where the class is defined and used in the lower right hand list.

B.5 Resources and resource files

As described in Chapter 6, resource files hold program elements such as menus, dialogs, strings and so on. These elements are created with graphical resource editors. This section describes normal techniques for working with the different resources described throughout the rest of the book.

B.5.1 Resources in General

Whenever you work with resources in an application, you start by creating a *resource script*. If you are using the AppWizard then the resource script is created automatically. If you are working on small programs of the style described in Chapter 6 then you create the resource script separately and add it into the project. Once you have created the script you can add individual resources to it. You do this by choosing the **Resource** option in the **Insert** menu.

This book is continuously updated. See http://www.iftech.com/mfc

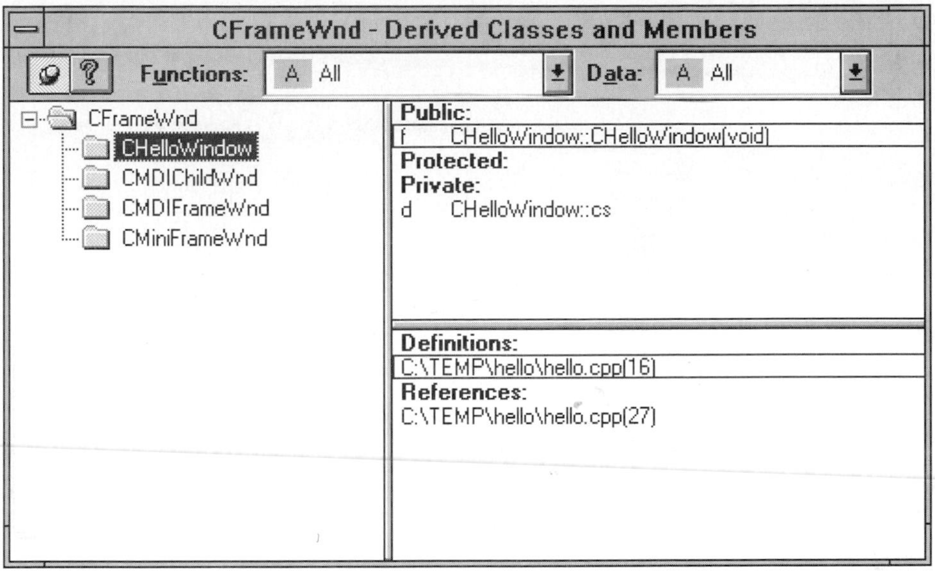

Figure B.15
The derived class graph shows for **CFrameWnd**

B.5.2 Creating a Resource Script

To create a new resource script, choose the **New** option in the **File** menu. You will see a dialog like the one shown earlier in Figure B.1. Select the **Resource Script** option to create a new, empty script. You can then choose the **Save** option in the **File** menu to save the script file to disk. You can name it anything you like, and it will be assigned the .RC file extension. Once you have saved the file, you can add it to the project. Choose the **Files into Project** option in the **Insert** menu and add the new script file to the project.

B.5.3 Icon Resources

To create a new icon resource, choose the **Resource** option in the **Insert** menu. You will see a dialog like the one shown in Figure B.16 that lets you choose the resource type. Choose Icon. You will see the new icon in an icon editor, as shown in Figure B.17. The palettes to the right as seen in Figure B.17 should be visible. If they are not visible choose the **Toolbars** option in the **View** menu and enable them. Draw into the icon as you would with any bitmap editor.

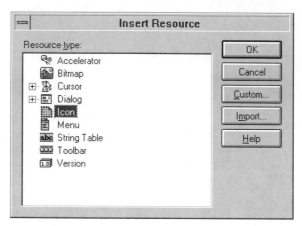

Figure B.16
Choosing the type of resource to create

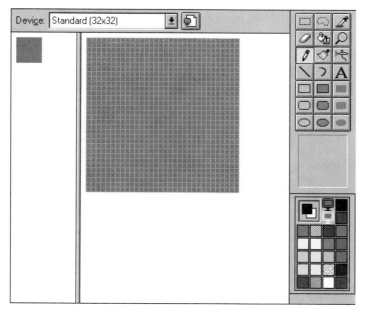

Figure B.17
Creating a new icon

In Figure B.17 you can see a **Device** combo box at the top of the figure. This combo box allows you to create several different sizes of icon for the same icon ID. That way the icon can fit into several different working situations. You should always be in the habit of creating all available sizes for every icon that you create.

To change the icon's ID, choose the **Properties** option in the **Edit** menu.

B.5.4 Resource Palettes

The palettes to the right in Figure B.17 should be visible. If they are not choose the **Toolbars** option in the **View** menu and enable them. Several of the resource editors have palettes like this, including the bitmap and the dialog editors.

B.5.5 Menu Resources

To create a new menu resource, choose the **Resource** option in the **Insert** menu and select the Menu resource from the list. You can click on the empty, dotted rectangle that you see and type the new menu string into it. You can do this either on the menu bar or in a menu itself to create new individual menu options. When you begin typing, a properties window will appear. When you have finished typing the string, press the return key and the properties dialog will close automatically.

If you create a menu option, close its property dialog, and then double click on the menu option again you will see that Visual C++ has created an appropriate ID for the menu option automatically, as shown in Figure B.18. Generally you will leave these automatically generated IDs alone because they are appropriate, but you can customize them if you wish.

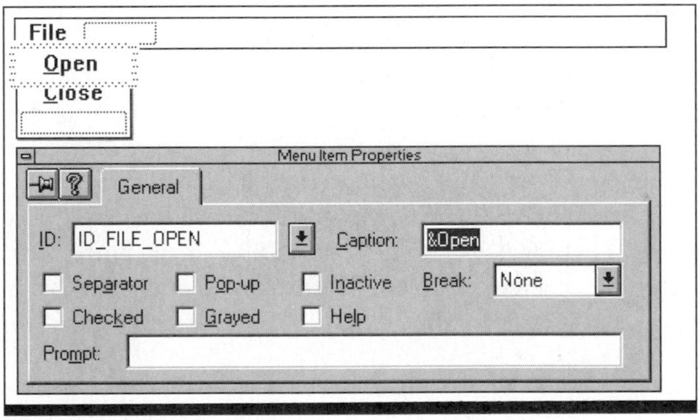

Figure B.18
A menu bar under construction, and the properties dialog for the Open option. Note the automatically created ID for this option.

B.5.6 Dialog Resources

To create a new dialog resource, choose the **Resource** option in the **Insert** menu and select the Dialog resource from the list. You will see an arrangement like the one shown in Figure B.19. Here you see a new dialog with an OK and Cancel button, as well as the Controls palette. If the palette is not visible choose the **Toolbars** option in the **View** menu and enable it.

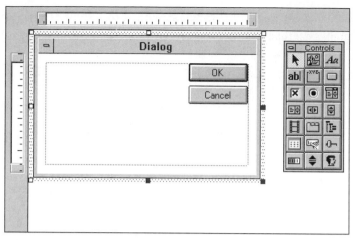

Figure B.19
A new dialog and the controls palette

If you let the cursor rest on each of the buttons in the Controls palette, the buttons will display a small tag that tells you what control the button represents. For example, the button at the end of the first row creates static controls, while the button at the left of the second row creates edit controls. Click on the type of control that you wish to create in the Controls palette and drag out an area in the dialog. A new control of the selected type will be created in the rectangle you specified. You can then double-click on the new control to view its properties. The property dialog can also be displayed by choosing the **Properties** option in the **Edit** menu.

Note that, when you have a dialog resource open in the dialog editor, a **Layout** menu will appear. There will also be a Layout toolbar at the bottom of the window. This menu helps you arrange controls. The **Tab Order** option in this menu lets you set the tab order of the controls in the dialog.

B.5.7 String Tables

To create a new string table resource, choose the **Resource** option in the **Insert** menu and select the String Table resource from the list. You will see an arrangement like the one shown in Figure B.20. You can double click on the empty dotted rectangle to pull up the property dialog. Then type the new string and change the ID of the string resource. You can reference the string from within your code using the ID as described in Chapter 6.

ID	Value	Caption
IDS_STRING1	1	Hello World
IDS_STRING2	2	There is a %1 error in the valve

String Properties

General

ID: IDS_STRING2

Caption: There is a %1 error in the valve

Figure B.20

B.6 AppWizard Files

As described in Part 3 of the book, you can use the AppWizard to create new projects. You will only use the AppWizard once at the beginning of any new project to create the project's *framework*. You will then use the ClassWizard to manipulate the framework.

B.6.1 Creating AppWizard Projects

As described in Part 3 of the book, you can use the AppWizard to create new projects. You will only use the AppWizard once at the beginning of any new project to create the project's *framework*. You will then use the ClassWizard to manipulate the framework.

To start the AppWizard, choose the **New** option in the **File** menu. You will see a New dialog like the one shown in Figure B.21. Select **Project Workspace** from the list and click OK. You will then see a dialog like the one shown in Figure B.22. Select the **MFC AppWizard (exe)** option and name the project.

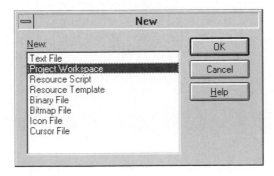

New

New:
Text File
Project Workspace
Resource Script
Resource Template
Binary File
Bitmap File
Icon File
Cursor File

OK
Cancel
Help

Figure B.21

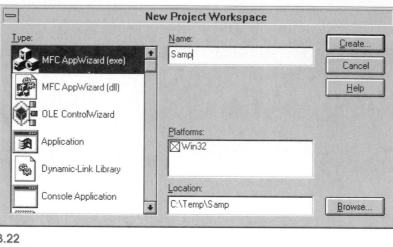

Figure B.22

The AppWizard presents six different options screens to you so that you can tune each framework to your specific needs. These screens are shown in Figures B.23 through B.28. The captions on each figure explain the general purpose of each screen. The help button on the screens will provide detailed information and is extremely educational when you first start using the AppWizard.

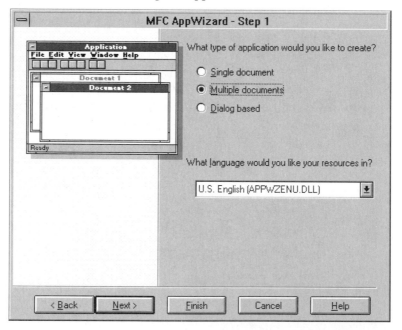

Figure B.23

The first screen lets you select between SDI, MDI and Dialog applications. Dialog applications are stripped down mini-applications that have a very simple form view type of interface.

This book is continuously updated. See http://www.iftech.com/mfc

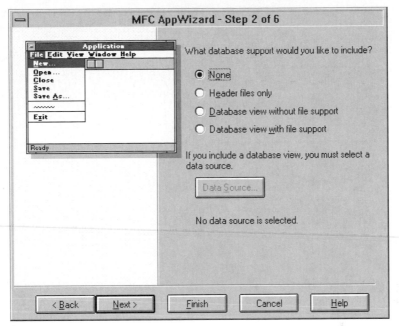

Figure B.24
The second screen lets you select your level of database support. Chapter 33 discusses database applications.

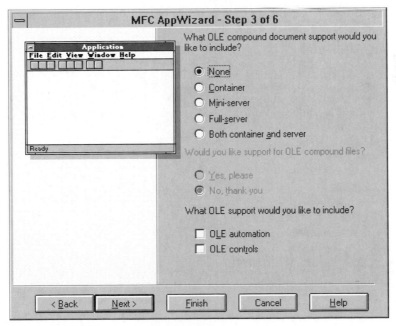

Figure B.25
The third screen selects OLE options. See Section B.6.6.

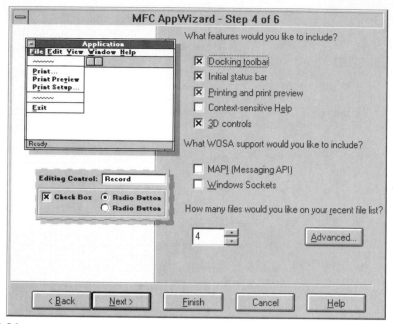

Figure B.26
The fourth screen selects application options. Such as toolbars and printing. The **Advanced** button brings up a subsidiary dialog discussed in sections B.6.3 and B.6.5.

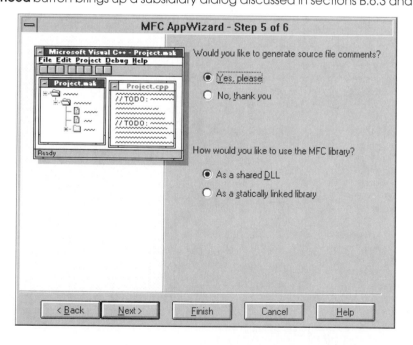

Figure B.27
The fifth screen lets you change the level of comments and linking. Generally you leave this screen as-is.

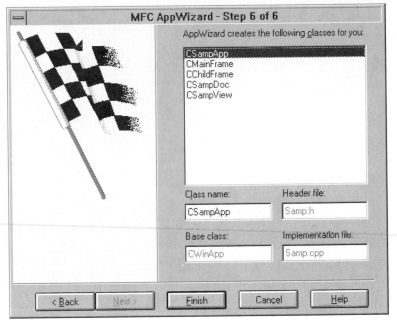

Figure B.28
This screen lets you choose the file names for the classes, and also lets you change the base class of the view as described in section B.6.4.

To create the simplest possible framework, choose the SDI option in the first screen, clear the different options that are selected in screen 4, and then click the **Finish** button. You can then click the OK button on the confirmation screen and the AppWizard will create the files for your framework.

The AppWizard will proceed to create 20 different files. Seventeen of those files will be in the directory named SAMP, while two others will be found in a new subdirectory of SAMP named RES. Take a moment to look at the new directories and also open up and look inside several of the files. The AppWizard creates the following directory tree:

```
samp
    mainfrm.cpp
    mainfrm.h
    readme.txt
    resource.h
    samp.clw
    samp.cpp
    samp.h
    samp.mak
    samp.ncb
    samp.rc
    samp.reg
    sampdoc.cpp
    sampdoc.h
    sampview.cpp
```

```
sampview.h
stdafx.cpp
stdafx.h
res
    samp.ico
    samp.rc2
    toolbar.bmp
```

You are free, and expected, to modify all these files as you create your application, with the exception of a few ancillary files like SAMP.NCB, SAMP.REG and SAMP.CLW (This file holds the ClassWizard database. If you accidentally erase it, the ClassWizard can regenerate it automatically.) Chapter 14 explains what all these different files do.

At this point you should build the project that the AppWizard has created for you. Simply choose the **Build** option in the **Build** menu. Visual C++ will form an executable and you should run it. What you will find is that you have a remarkably complete starter application. The menu bar works and contains all the normal menu options you would expect to find. The Open, New, and Exit options will all do the expected things. The application has an About box. The AppWizard's files create a very good starting point for a new application.

B.6.2 Project views

Once the AppWizard creates your project framework, you will see a project workspace window like the one shown in Figure B.29. This window gives you four different views:

- The ClassView - Shows you all of the different classes in your application, as well as members, variables, etc.
- The ResourceView - Shows you all of the resources (menus, dialogs, icons, etc.) in your application.
- The FileView - Shows you all of the different files that hold the code for your application.
- The InfoView - Shows you all of the on-line books that are available.

Simply click on the different tabs to change your view.

B.6.3 Adding File Extensions

To add a file extension, click the **Advanced** button in the fourth AppWizard customization screen (Figure B.26). You will see a dialog like the one shown in Figure B.30. Add the file extension in the **File Extension** field.

B.6.4 Changing the Base Class

In the AppWizard's sixth customization screen (Figure B.28) you can change the base class of the view class. Choose the view class in the list. Then change the base class as shown in Figure B.31.

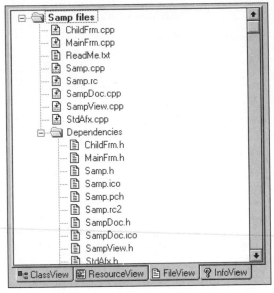

Figure B.29
The Project Workspace window. If your tabs do not have the names shown in the figure, drag the window wider.

B.6.5 Adding Splitter Windows

To add a splitter window, click the advanced button in the fourth AppWizard customization screen (Figure B.26). You will see a dialog like the one shown in Figure B.30. Click the **Window Styles** tab to reveal a dialog like the one shown in Figure B.32. Click the **Use Split Window** check box.

B.6.6 OLE Applications

The third AppWizard customization screen (Figure B.25) lets you customize the OLE features of your application. This screen is exercised in Chapter 34, which demonstrates how to create a Container, a Full Server, and an Automation-aware application. Note that this screen has radio buttons for Containers and Full Servers, and a check box for automation. Also note the check box for OLE controls, which you will want to use if you want to use OLE controls in the application. Select these different options as appropriate to the applications that you create.

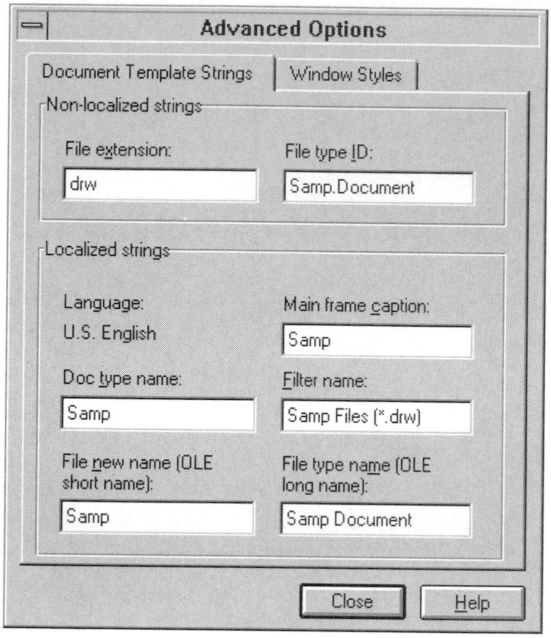

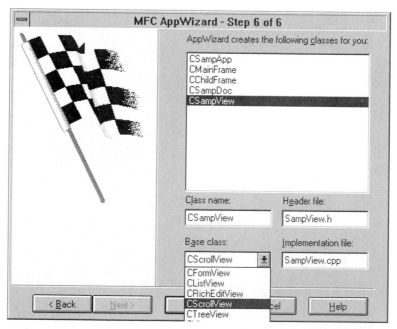

Figure B.30

Adding a file extension

Figure B.31

Changing the base class of the view class

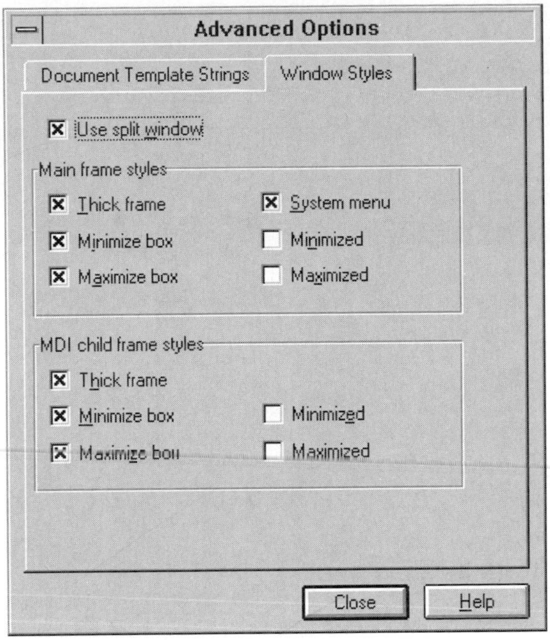

Figure B.32
Selecting the splitter window option

B.7 Using the ClassWizard

The ClassWizard manipulates frameworks generated by the AppWizard. You open the ClassWizard by selecting the **ClassWizard** option in the **View** menu. See Part 3 of the book for details on the ClassWizard. The following sections demonstrate many of the different features of the ClassWizard.

B.7.1 Creating New Message Map Entries for Events

The ClassWizard allows you to add message map entries for any system event. The different system events are documented in the **CWnd** class. Every member function in this class that begins with **On...** is associated with a WM_ message. See Chapter 4 for details.

The ClassWizard makes it easy to add message map entries for system events. For example, if you want to add a message map entry for the WM_MOUSEMOVE event (see the **OnMouseMove** function documentation for details), open the Class-Wizard and set it up as shown in Figure B.33. Select the **Message Maps** tab and then select the class whose message map you want to add the function to. In Figure B.33 the view class has been chosen. Make sure the view class name is selected in the **Object IDs** list. Then find WM_MOUSEMOVE in the **Messages** list. Click the **Add Function** button to add the function. You can then press the **Edit Code** button to be taken immediately to the new function in the view class.

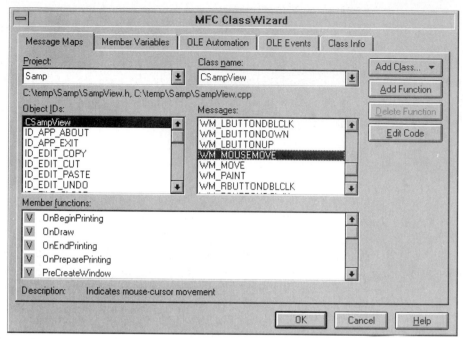

Figure B.33
Adding a system event handler with the ClassWizard

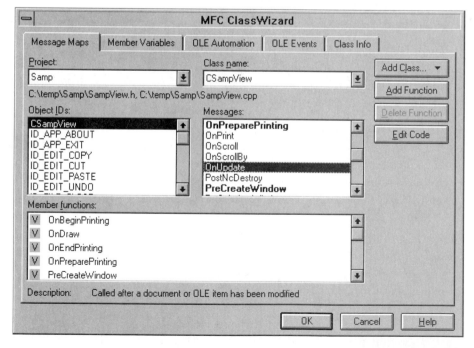

Figure B.34
Overriding a virtual function with the ClassWizard

B.7.2 Overriding Virtual Functions

Most MFC classes (for example CDocument, CView and so on) contain virtual functions that are described in the MFC documentation. The ClassWizard gives you an easy way to override these functions. Figure B.34 shows an example. Here the programmer wishes to override the **OnUpdate** function in the view class. Choose the **Message Maps** tab, choose the correct class, and then find the virtual function that you wish to override. Click the **Add Function** button and the click the **Edit Code** button.

B.7.3 Creating Menu Handlers

Each menu option in the menu bar has an ID. For example, ID_EDIT_COPY is the ID for the **Copy** option in the **Edit** menu. When you create a new menu option, the menu editor will automatically name the ID for the option, and you can change the name if you like.

To add a handler function to handle the given menu option, use the ClassWizard as shown in Figure B.35. Select the class whose message map you want to handle the menu option, and then select the menu ID in the **Object IDs** list. Choose the **Command** value in the **Messages** list. Click the **Add Function** button. You will see a dialog asking you to confirm the function name. Then click the **Edit Code** button to edit the code.

B.7.4 Creating New Dialog Classes

When you create a dialog resource, you must also create a dialog class to go with it. The class acts as a liaison between the application and the dialog resource and is especially important for holding DDX variables. To create a new dialog class, create the dialog resource. Rename the ID for the dialog resource from the default name of IDD_DIALOG1 to something appropriate (e.g. - IDD_ADDRESSDIALOG). Now, *with the dialog editor for the new dialog visible as the top-most window*, open the ClassWizard. You will see a dialog like the one shown in Figure B.36. The ClassWizard will recognize, since it is a new dialog, that you would probably like to create a dialog class to go with it. Click OK, and you will see the standard **Add Class** dialog as shown in Figure B.37, but it will have been preset for use with your dialog. Simply type in the new class name in the name field and you are set.

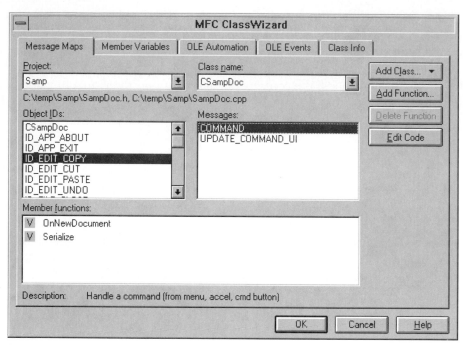

Figure B.35
Adding a menu handler function with the ClassWizard

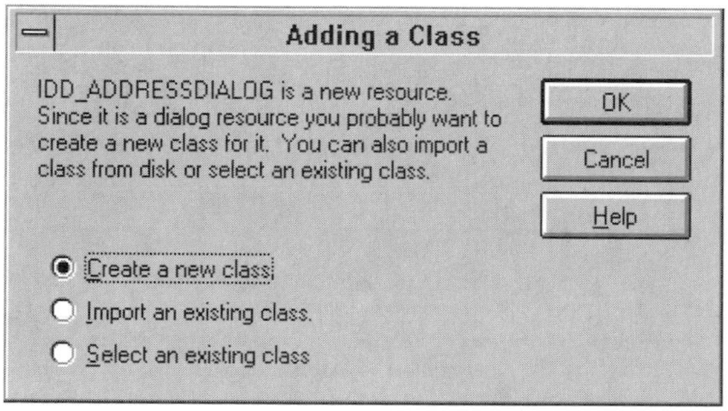

Figure B.36
Creating a new dialog class with the ClassWizard

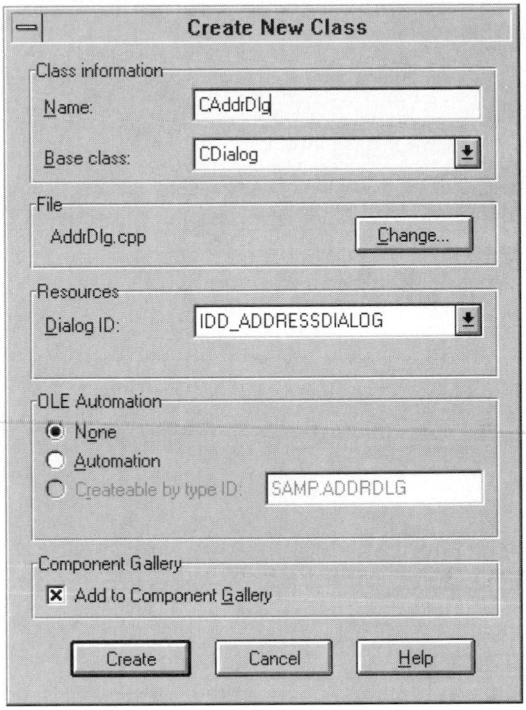

Figure B.37
Adding the new dialog class

B.7.5 Adding DDX Value Variables

The ClassWizard makes it extremely easy to add DDX value variables to a dialog class. See Chapters 15, 18 and 22 for an introduction to DDX variables. A value variable gives you an easy way to get and set the value of edit (and other) controls in a dialog.

As an example, imagine that you have an edit control on a dialog. You have given the control an ID of IDC_NAME. To create a DDX variable for the control, open the ClassWizard. Select the **Member Variables** tab. Select the appropriate dialog class. Select the IDC_NAME control. You will see a display like that shown in Figure B.38. Click the **Add Variable** button and you will see a dialog like the one shown in Figure B.39. Give the variable a name and select the appropriate type. Leave the category set to Value.

B.7.6 Adding New Classes

The ClassWizard gives you an easy way to add any class that inherits from an existing MFC class to your application. Simply click the **Add Class** button. Name the class and select the appropriate base class and the ClassWizard will do the rest. *Be aware that you must include the header file for the new class in any files that use the class.*

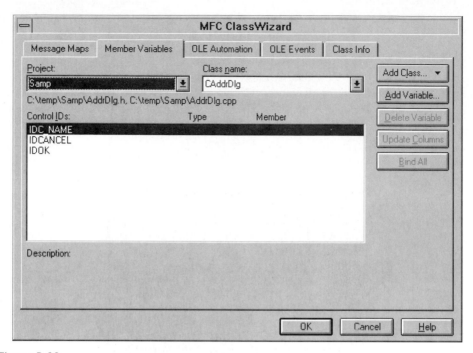

Figure B.38
Selecting the control

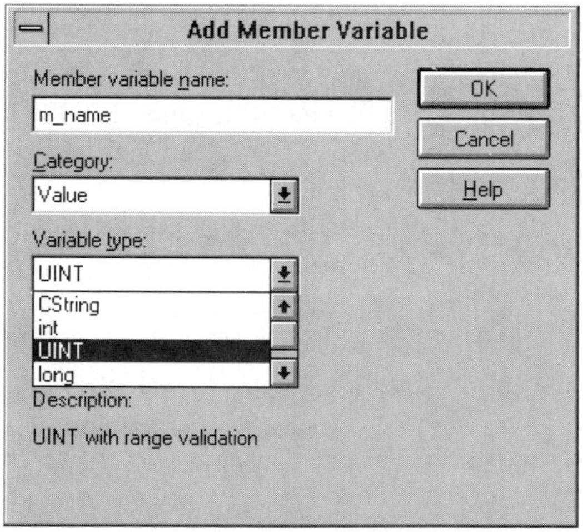

Figure B.39
Adding the DDX variable

B.7.7 Adding DDX Control Variables and Handlers

A DDX control variable lets you get a pointer to a control so that you can call member functions on the control. See Chapters 18 and 22 for details. Typically you will want to do this for a List control in a dialog or form view.

To add a DDX control variable, open the ClassWizard. Select the Member Variables tab for the appropriate dialog class. Choose the control ID from the list and click the **Add Variable** button. You will see a dialog like the one shown in Figure B.40. Name the variable and choose the Control category. The variable type indicates the class from which you can call member variables.

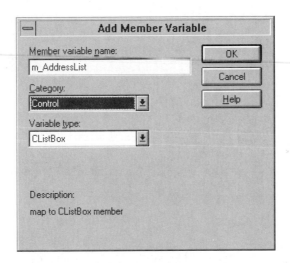

Figure B.40
Adding a control variable

B.8 OLE Controls

The OCX ControlWizard creates OCX control classes, which are then manipulated with the ClassWizard. See Section 34.8 for details on OCX controls.

B.8.1 Creating a New OCX Control with the ControlWizard

Whenever you start the process of creating a new OCX control, you will use the ControlWizard to create the base framework. The process is identical to using the AppWizard to create a base application framework. In the **File** menu choose the **New** option and in the dialog choose **Project Workspace**. You will see a dialog like the one shown in Figure B.41. Name the new control as shown and choose a directory for it.

The ControlWizard will appear. It has two customization screens. The first one you will generally leave alone, and is shown in Figure B.42. On the second screen, shown in Figure B.43, you will generally want to check the **Available in "Insert Object" dialog** check box or you will be unable to test the control.

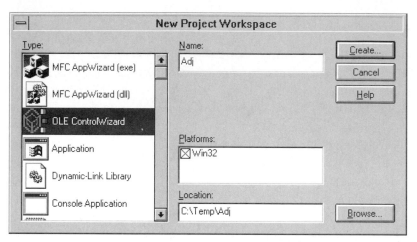

Figure B.41
Creating a new OCX control with the ControlWizard

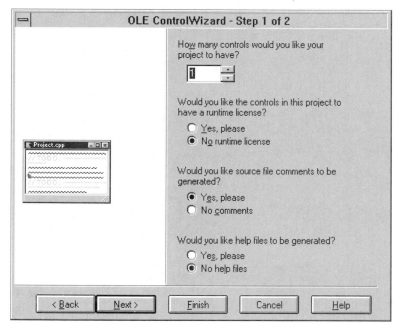

Figure B.42
The first ControlWizard screen

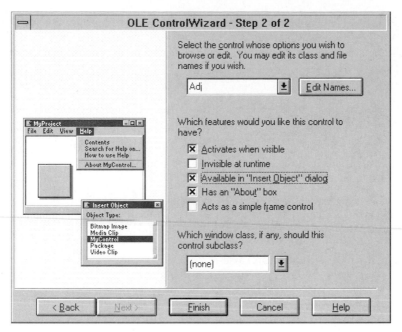

Figure B.43
The second ControlWizard screen

Press the **Finish** button and let the ControlWizard generate its files. Look at the code files that the ControlWizard created. Of them, the only one you will generally modify is ADJCTL.CPP (or whatever). This file contains a class derived from **COle-Control**, which embodies almost all of the modifiable behavior for an OLE control. It contains quite a few different areas that the ClassWizard can manipulate.

Compile the code for the new control by choosing the **Build** option in the **Build** menu. To test the control, you must do two things. First, you have to register the control in the registry using the **Register Control** option in the **Tools** menu. You need to do this only once for each control that you create. To actually execute the control to test it, you can use the test container for OCX controls that comes with Visual C++. Select the **Test Container** option in the **Tools** menu. Choose the **Insert OLE Control** option in the **Edit** menu. Select "Adj Control" (or whatever) from the list to insert the new control. If you do not find an entry for the "Adj Control" in the dialog, you either forgot to register the control or you failed to select the **Available in Insert Dialog** option as shown in Figure B.43.

B.8.2 Registering a new OCX Control

You have to register the control in the registry using the **Register Control** option in the **Tools** menu before you can use it. If this option is not available in the menu, it means that portions of the OCX functionality were not installed with Visual C++. Reinstall these parts.

B.8.3 Using the OCX Test Container

Select the **Test Container** option in the **Tools** menu. Choose the **Insert OLE Control** option in the **Edit** menu. Select "Adj Control" (or whatever) from the list to insert the new control. If this option is not available in the menu, it means that portions of the OCX functionality were not installed with Visual C++. Reinstall these parts.

B.8.4 Testing OLE Controls in Dialogs

It is extremely easy to use standard OCX controls shipped by Microsoft or new OCX controls that you create in dialog boxes or in form views. Take the following steps:

- Create a new dialog resource in an application that will use the OCX control.
- Choose the **ComponentÖ** option from the **Insert** menu. You will see a dialog like the one shown in Figure B.44. Select the Adj control and click **Insert**.
- You will see a Confirm Classes dialog. Click OK.
- Click Close
- Visual C++ will add a new control to the bottom of the dialog Controls palette.
- Add the OCX control to the dialog as you would any other control
- Double-click on the control to change its properties

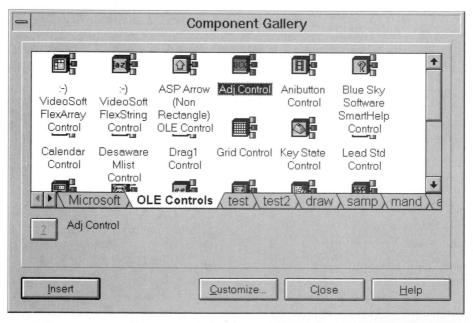

Figure B.44

Adding an OCX control

This book is continuously updated. See http://www.iftech.com/mfc

B.8.5 Activating Stock Properties

When the ControlWizard creates the base files, it wires into them the stock properties for the control. You can activate these properties using the ClassWizard. Open the ClassWizard and select the **OLE Automation** tab. Make sure the class name is **CAdjCtrl** (or whatever). Click the **Add Property** button and select the property from the **External Name** combo box list as shown in Figure B.45.

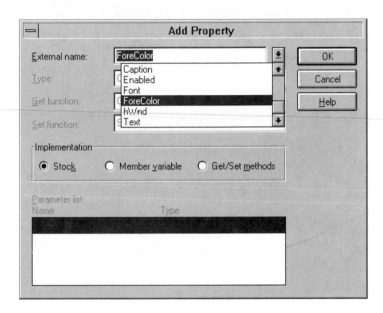

Figure B.45

Adding a stock property

B.8.6 Adding Custom Properties

Open the ClassWizard and select the **OLE Automation tab**. Click the **Add Property** button. Add a property, as shown in Figure B.46. The ClassWizard gives the property two names. The external name is used by a programmer to adjust the property. The variable name is used inside the control's code to access the property in C++.

B.8.7 Adding Methods

The two stock methods named **DoClick** and **Refresh** already exist in the code generated by the ControlWizard. To activate them, open the ClassWizard. Select the **OLE Automation** tab and click the **Add Method** button. Pull down the **External Name** combo box and select **DoClick**. The dialog will specify the setup for the **DoClick** stock method. Press OK and do the same thing for **Refresh**. No further changes are required.

To add a custom method, do the same thing but type a new name in the **External Name** field as shown in Figure B.47. You can give the method a return type and parameters just as you would any function.

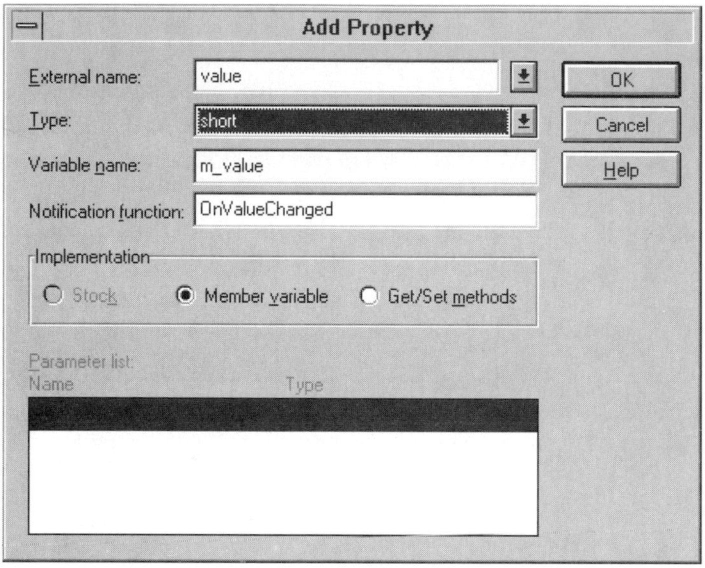

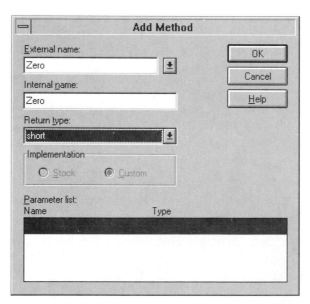

Figure B.46
Adding a custom property

Figure B.47
Adding a custom method

B.8.8 Adding Events

To add an event, open the ClassWizard. Choose the **OLE Events** tab and click the **Add Event** button. Add a new event as shown in Figure B.48. That is, give the event a name and click on the first location in the parameter list to add parameters.

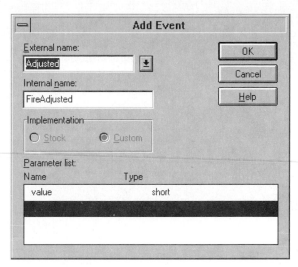

Figure B.48
Adding an event

B.8.9 Adding Member Variables for Property Sheets

Create the controls in your property sheet. With the dialog template for the property sheet open as the topmost window in Visual C++, open the ClassWizard. Choose the **Member Variables** tab, as shown in Figure B.49. Now double-click on a control ID. Figure B.50 shows the setup for the IDC_RANGE variable discussed in Section 38.8.12. The **Optional OLE Property Name** field lets you type in a property name for the control.

B.9 Conclusion

The Visual C++ environment provides you with a huge variety of tools. Those tools further include resource editors, which are described in detail in Chapter 6, along with the different wizards described in Parts 3 and 5.

For further information on all these tools, see the "Visual C++ User's Guide" in books on-line.

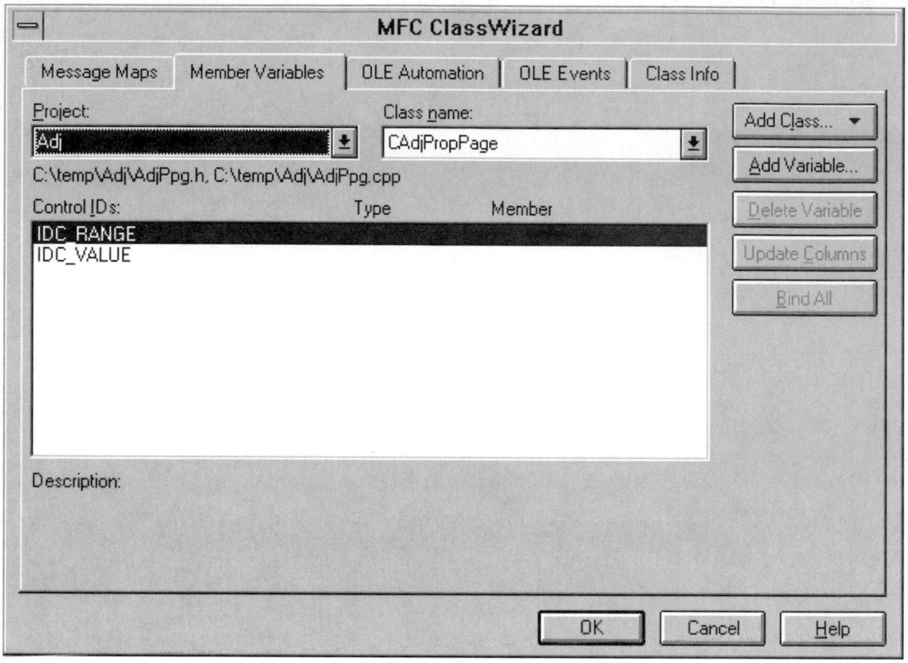

Figure B.49

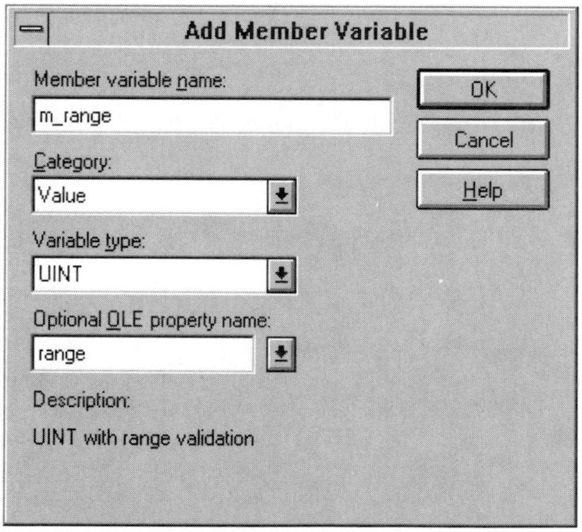

Figure B.50

Contacting the Authors

If you have any questions, comments, or suggestions for improving this book, we would like to hear from you. Your comments will help us improve later editions, and we will post your corrections so other readers can take advantage of them.

To send suggestions, comments, questions or corrections via electronic mail, address e-mail to:

mfc@iftech.com

To view available update and correction pages, as well as supplements, visit the web site for this book at:

http://www.iftech.com/mfc

This book is designed to be "version free." The goal is to create a book that can be updated on the web each time Visual C++ changes versions so that we can save you the cost of buying a new book every six months. To accomplish this goal, we have isolated all version-specific features in Appendix B. When a new version appears on the market, we will update this appendix on the web immediately, and you can access our updates, changes and supplements free of charge. See http://www.iftech.com/mfc for details.

C.1 About Interface Technologies

Interface Technologies, Inc., has distinguished itself as a premier supplier of software development and programmer training services in a variety of computing environments. These services are supplied with the specific goal of helping the client increase programmer productivity by improving software design, documentation, and development processes.

Technical classes offered by Interface Technologies give programmers the skills they need to rapidly master new, advanced programming environments. These skills are necessary in any company that wants to create leading-edge applications. Our classes feature extensive hands-on exercises, expert instruction, and an intensive pace that builds confidence and self-assurance. Programmers leave the class ready to begin creating their own applications immediately. All ITI classes are delivered at the client's site, an approach that saves both time and money for the client and ensures that programmers are available to handle any emergencies that may arise during the course of training.

As authors of Prentice Hall's five-book series on Windows NT, Digital Press's "Motif Programming: The Essentials and More," and numerous other books and articles, ITI's areas of specialty include object-oriented design and C++ programming, Windows 95 and Windows NT application development, and GUI design and implementation using MFC and Motif. ITI also offers consulting services such as project management and auditing, human factors and design analysis, software testing and verification, and network design and administration. Our clients include a number of large firms in the financial district of New York City, several large telecommunications companies, and numerous smaller firms, all dedicated to the creation of modern, reliable systems using either in-house programming staff or outside resources.

If you would like more information on ITI's services or classes, please call 1-800-224-4965 today. Or visit our web site at http://www.iftech.com.

Using OpenGL with MFC

D

By Alan Oursland, Interface Technologies, Inc.

With the release of Windows NT 3.5, OpenGL became a part of the Windows operating system. Now with Windows 95 support for OpenGL and low price graphics accelerators becoming readily available even on low end machines, the prospects of using OpenGL on any Windows machine is becoming more attractive every day. If you are interested in creating quality 2-D or 3-D graphics in Windows, or if you already know another variant of GL, this tutorial will show you how to use OpenGL and some of its basic commands.

GL is a programming interface designed by Silicon Graphics. OpenGL is a generic version of the interface made available to a wide variety of outside vendors in the interest of standardization of the language. OpenGL allows you to create high quality 3-D images without dealing with the heavy math usually associated with computer graphics. OpenGL handles graphics primitives, 2-D and 3-D transformations, lighting, shading, Z-buffering, hidden surface removal, and a host of other features. I'll use some of these topics in the sample programs following; others I'll leave to you to explore yourself.

D.1 Writing an OpenGL Program

The first program demonstrated here will show you the minimum requirements for setting up a Windows program to display OpenGL graphics. As GDI needs a Device Context (DC) to draw images, OpenGL requires a Rendering Context (RC). Unlike GDI, in which each GDI command requires that a DC is passed into it, OpenGL uses the concept of a current RC. Once a rendering context has been made current in a thread, all OpenGL calls in that thread will use the same current rendering context. While multiple rendering contexts may be used to draw in a single window, only one rendering context may be current at any time in a single thread.

To start, create a new SDI application framework. First we must include all necessary OpenGL libraries in this project. In the project build settings, add the following libraries to the linker Object/Library Modules setting:

```
opengl32.lib glu32.lib glaux.lib
```

Now add the OpenGL include files to the end of STDAFX.H:

```
#include <gl\gl.h>
#include <gl\glu.h>
```

OpenGL requires that the window performing the GL operations have styles
WS_CLIPCHILDREN and WS_CLIPSIBLINGS. These options must be set in the
view's PreCreateWindow:

```
BOOL COpenGLView::PreCreateWindow(CREATESTRUCT& cs)
{
    cs.style |= (WS_CLIPCHILDREN | WS_CLIPSIBLINGS);

    return CView::PreCreateWindow(cs);
}
```

There are three steps to creating and making current a rendering context:

1. Set the window's pixel format.
2. Create the rendering context.
3. Make the rendering context current.

The first step to creating a rendering context is to define the window's pixel format. The pixel format describes how the graphics that the window displays are
represented in memory. Parameters controlled by the pixel format include color
depth, buffering method, and supported drawing interfaces. We will look at some of
these below. Use the ClassWizard to add a handler for the view's WM_CREATE and
WM_DESTROY messages and add the following member variables and functions to
the class definitions:

```
protected:
    int m_GLPixelIndex;
    HGLRC m_hGLContext;

    BOOL SetWindowPixelFormat(HDC hDC);
    BOOL CreateViewGLContext(HDC hDC);
```

Initialize the member variables in the constructor:

```
COpenGLView::COpenGLView()
{
    m_hGLContext = NULL;
    m_GLPixelIndex = 0;
}
```

When the view is created we want to set its pixel format. Add a call to our SetWindowPixelFormat after calling the base class OnCreate:

```
int COpenGLView::OnCreate(LPCREATESTRUCT lpCreateStruct)
```

```
    {
        if (CView::OnCreate(lpCreateStruct) == -1)
            return -1;

        HDC hDC = ::GetDC(GetSafeHwnd());
        if (SetWindowPixelFormat(hDC) == FALSE)
            return 0;

        return 0;
    }

    BOOL COpenGLView::SetWindowPixelFormat(HDC hDC)
    {
        PIXELFORMATDESCRIPTOR pixelDesc;
        memset(&pixelDesc, 0, sizeof(pixelDesc));

        pixelDesc.nSize = sizeof(PIXELFORMATDESCRIPTOR);
        pixelDesc.nVersion = 1;

        pixelDesc.dwFlags = PFD_DRAW_TO_WINDOW | PFD_DRAW_TO_BITMAP |
            PFD_SUPPORT_OPENGL | PFD_SUPPORT_GDI | PFD_STEREO_DONTCARE;

        pixelDesc.iPixelType = PFD_TYPE_RGBA;
        pixelDesc.cColorBits = 32;
        pixelDesc.cRedBits = 8;
        pixelDesc.cRedShift = 16;
        pixelDesc.cGreenBits = 8;
        pixelDesc.cGreenShift = 8;
        pixelDesc.cBlueBits = 8;
        pixelDesc.cBlueShift = 0;
        pixelDesc.cAlphaBits = 0;
        pixelDesc.cAlphaShift = 0;
        pixelDesc.cAccumBits = 64;
        pixelDesc.cAccumRedBits = 16;
        pixelDesc.cAccumGreenBits = 16;
        pixelDesc.cAccumBlueBits = 16;
        pixelDesc.cAccumAlphaBits = 0;
        pixelDesc.cDepthBits = 32;
        pixelDesc.cStencilBits = 8;
        pixelDesc.cAuxBuffers = 0;
        pixelDesc.iLayerType = PFD_MAIN_PLANE;
        pixelDesc.bReserved = 0;
        pixelDesc.dwLayerMask = 0;
        pixelDesc.dwVisibleMask = 0;
        pixelDesc.dwDamageMask = 0;

        m_GLPixelIndex = ChoosePixelFormat( hDC, &pixelDesc);
        if (m_GLPixelIndex == 0) // Let's choose a default index.
        {
            m_GLPixelIndex = 1;
            if (DescribePixelFormat(hDC,  m_GLPixelIndex,
                sizeof(PIXELFORMATDESCRIPTOR), &pixelDesc) == 0)
            {
                return FALSE;
            }
        }
```

```
    if (SetPixelFormat(hDC, m_GLPixelIndex, &pixelDesc) == FALSE)
    {
        return FALSE;
    }

    return TRUE;
}
```

If you run the program now it will look like a generic MFC shell. Try playing with the pixel format descriptor. You may want to try passing other indices into DescribePixelFormat to see what pixel formats are available. I'll spend some time now explaining what the code does and precautions you should take in the future.

A PIXELFORMATDESCRIPTOR contains all of the information defining a pixel format. I'll explain some of the important points here, but for a complete description look in the online help.

- dwFlags - Defines the devices and interfaces with which the pixel format is compatible. Not all of these flags are implemented in the generic release of OpenGL. Refer to the documentation for more information. dwFlags can accept the following flags:

Table D.1
Values for dwFlags

PFD_DRAW_TO_WINDOW	Enables drawing to a window or device surface.
PFD_DRAW_TO_BITMAP	Enables drawing to a bitmap in memory.
PFD_SUPPORT_GDI	Enables GDI calls. Note: This option is not valid if PFD_DOUBLEBUFFER is specified.
PFD_SUPPORT_OPENGL	Enables OpenGL calls.
PFD_GENERIC_FORMAT	Specifies if this pixel format is supported by the Windows GDI library or by a vendor hardware device driver.
PFD_NEED_PALETTE	Tells if the buffer requires a palette. This tutorial assumes color will be done with 24 or 32 bits and will not cover palettes.
PFD_NEED_SYSTEM_PALETTE	This flag indicates if the buffer requires the reserved system palette as part of its palette. As stated above, this tutorial will cover palettes.
PFD_DOUBLEBUFFER	Indicates that double-buffering is used. Note that GDI cannot be used with windows that are double buffered.
PFD_STEREO	Indicates that left and right buffers are maintained for stereo images.

- iPixelType - Defines the method used to display colors. PFD_TYPE_RGBA means each set of bits represents a Red, Green, and Blue value, while PFD_TYPE_COLORINDEX means that each set of bits is an index into a color lookup table. All of the examples in this program will use PFD_TYPE_RGBA.

- cColorBits - Defines the number of bits used to define a color. For RGBA it is the number of bits used to represent the red, green, and blue components of the color (but not the alpha). For indexed colors, it is the number of colors in the table.
- cRedBits, cGreenBits, cBlueBits, cAlphaBits - The number of bits used to represent the respective components.
- cRedShift, cGreenShift, cBlueShift, cAlphaShift - The number of bits each component is offset from the beginning of the color.

In SetWindowPixelFormat we initialize our structure, then call ChoosePixel-Format to find the system pixel format that is closest to the one we want. ChoosePixelFormat takes a DC and a PIXELFORMATDESCRIPTOR, and returns an index used to reference that pixel format or 0 if the function fails. If the function fails, we just set the index to 1 and get the pixel format description using DescribePix-elFormat. There are a limited number of pixel formats, and the system defines what their properties are. If you ask for pixel format properties that are not supported, ChoosePixelFormat will return an integer to the format that is closest to the one you requested. Once we have a valid pixel format index and the corresponding description we can call SetPixelFormat. A window's pixel format may be set only once.

After the pixel format is set we have to create the rendering context and make it current. This is done by calling our CreateViewGLContext function in OnCreate:

```
int COpenGLView::OnCreate(LPCREATESTRUCT lpCreateStruct)
{
    if (CView::OnCreate(lpCreateStruct) == -1)
        return -1;

    HDC hDC = ::GetDC(GetSafeHwnd());
    if (SetWindowPixelFormat(hDC) == FALSE)
        return 0;

    if (CreateViewGLContext(hDC) == FALSE)
        return 0;

    return 0;
}

BOOL COpenGLView::CreateViewGLContext(HDC hDC)
{
    m_hGLContext = wglCreateContext(hDC);
    if (m_hGLContext == NULL)
    {
        return FALSE;
    }

    if (wglMakeCurrent(hDC, m_hGLContext) == FALSE)
    {
        return FALSE;
    }
```

```
        return TRUE;
    }
```

When the view is destroyed we need to clean up:

```
void COpenGLView::OnDestroy()
{
    if(wglGetCurrentContext()!=NULL)
    {
        // make the rendering context not current
        wglMakeCurrent(NULL, NULL) ;
    }

    if (m_hGLContext != NULL)
    {
        wglDeleteContext(m_hGLContext);
        m_hGLContext = NULL;
    }

    CView::OnDestroy();
}
```

Now if you run the program it will still look like a generic MFC program, but it is now enabled for OpenGL drawing. You may have noticed that we created one rendering context at the beginning of the program and used it the entire time. This goes against most GDI programs where DCs are created only when drawing is required and freed immediately afterwards. This is a valid option with RCs as well, however creating an RC can be quite processor intensive. Because we are trying to achieve high performance graphics, the code only creates the RC once and uses it the entire time.

CreateViewGLContext creates and makes current a rendering context. wglCreateContext returns a handle to an RC. The pixel format for the device associated with the DC you pass into this function must be set before you call CreateViewGLContext. wglMakeCurrent sets the RC as the current context. The DC passed into this function does not need to be the same DC you used to create the context, but it must have the same device and pixel format. If another rendering context is current when you call wglMakeCurrent, the function simply flushes the old RC and replaces it with the new one. To make no rendering context current you may call:

```
wglMakeCurrent(NULL, NULL);
```

Because OnDestroy releases the window's RC, we need to delete the rendering context there. But before we delete the RC, we need to make sure it is not current. We use wglGetCurrentContext to see if there is a current rendering context. If there is, we remove it by calling wglMakeCurrent. Next we call wglDeleteContext to delete out the RC. It is now safe to allow the view class to release the DC. Note that since the RC was current to our thread we could have just called wglDeleteContext without first making it not current. Don't get into the habit of doing this. If you ever start using multi-threaded applications that convenience is going to bite you.

D.2 Simple 2-D Graphics

The sample program presented in this section will show you how to create the viewport, set up matrix modes, and draw some simple 2-D images. Use the ClassWizard to add handlers for the view's WM_SIZE and WM_PAINT messages.

```
void COpenGLView::OnPaint()
{
    CPaintDC dc(this); // device context for painting

    glLoadIdentity();
    glClear(GL_COLOR_BUFFER_BIT);

    glBegin(GL_POLYGON);
    glColor3f(1.0f, 0.0f, 0.0f);
    glVertex2f(100.0f, 50.0f);
    glColor3f(0.0f, 1.0f, 0.0f);
    glVertex2f(450.0f, 400.0f);
    glColor3f(0.0f, 0.0f, 1.0f);
    glVertex2f(450.0f, 50.0f);
    glEnd();

    glFlush();
}

void COpenGLView::OnSize(UINT nType, int cx, int cy)
{
    CView::OnSize(nType, cx, cy);

    GLsizei width = cx;
    GLsizei height = cy;
    GLdouble aspect = (cy == 0) ? (GLdouble)width :
        (GLdouble)width/(GLdouble)height;

    glViewport(0, 0, width, height);
    glMatrixMode(GL_PROJECTION);
    glLoadIdentity();
    gluOrtho2D(0.0, 500.0*aspect, 0.0, 500.0);
    glMatrixMode(GL_MODELVIEW);
    glLoadIdentity();
}
```

If you run the program now you should see a black window with a large multi-colored triangle in it. Try resizing the window and watch the triangle resize along with it. OnPaint is where we draw the triangle. First we clear the current matrix using glLoadIdentity. This isn't really necessary since we are doing any transformations, but it is there just in case you decide to add one. Next we clear the color buffer with glClear (which in this case happens to be the screen, but could be a print buffer or bitmap depending on the type of device context you used to create rendering context). glBegin changes the state of the rendering context. From an object oriented perspective, it creates an internal object of type GL_POLYGON, which is defined by all commands issued until glEnd is called. Our triangle is defined with three vertices.

glColor3f sets the current color. The first call sets the color to Red by specifying the Red component to 1 and the Green and Blue components to 0. We then define a vertex at point (100,50) in our world coordinates by calling glVertex2f. We now have a red vertex at point (100,50). We repeat this process, setting the color to Green and Blue respectively, for the next two vertices. The call to glEnd ends the definition of this polygon. At this point there should still be nothing on the screen. OpenGL will save the list of commands in a buffer until you call glFlush. glFlush causes these commands to be executed. OpenGL automatically interpolates the colors between each of the points to give you the multi-hued triangle you see on the screen. Play with some of the different shapes you can create with glBegin. In the next section, we will move our drawing routines into the document class. I will also show you how to use the basic transforms and the importance of pushing and popping matrices onto and off of the matrix stack.

OnSize defines the viewport and the viewing coordinates. We change the viewport in OnSize so it changes when you resize the window. The viewport is the area of the window that the OpenGL commands can draw into. It is set by calling glViewport. This sets the lower left hand corner of the viewport to the lower left hand corner of the window and sets the height and width to that of the window. The parameters passed into the function are in screen coordinates. If you changed the glViewport command to the following:

```
glViewport(width/4, height/4, width/2, height/2);
```

Then made the window taller than it is wide, because the viewport is smaller than the screen, part of the triangle will be clipped. The next OpenGL call is glMatrixMode. OpenGL maintains three internal matrices to control various transformations, Projection, ModelView, and Texture. The Projection matrix handles transformations from the eye coordinates to clip coordinates. The ModelView matrix converts object coordinates to eye coordinates. The Texture matrix converts textures from the coordinates they are defined in to the coordinates need to map them onto a surface. glMatrixMode sets which of these matrices will be affected by matrix operations. Don't worry if you don't understand these right now, I'll explain them as needed. glLoadIdentity initializes the projection matrix. gluOrtho2D sets the project matrix to display a two dimension orthogonal image. The numbers passed into this function define the space within which you may draw. This space is known as the world coordinates. We now initialize the ModelView matrix and leave OpenGL in this matrix mode. Matrix operations (which include transformations) carried out while in the ModelView mode will affect the location and shape of any object drawn. For example if we called:

```
glRotated(30, 0, 0, 1);
```

Just before our glBegin call in OnPaint, our triangle would be rotated 30 degrees around the lower left corner of the screen. We will look at this more a little later. (For those of you who have used IRIS GL, we have just set up the equivalent of calling mmode(MSINGLE). There is an entire section in the online documentation detailing the differences between IRIS GL and OpenGL for those who are interested.)

Let me take a moment at this point to discuss the naming conventions OpenGL uses. All OpenGL commands use the prefix "gl". There are also a number of "glu" commands which are considered "GL Utilities". These "glu" commands are simply combinations of "gl" commands that perform commonly useful tasks—like setting up 2-D orthographic matrices. Most "gl" commands have a number of variants that each take different data types. The glVertex2f command, for instance, defines a vertex using two floats. There are other variants ranging from four doubles to an array of two shorts. Read the list of glVertex calls in the online documentation and you will feel like you are counting off an eternal list. glVertex2d, glVertex2f, glVertex3i, glVertex3s, glVertex2sv, glVertex3dv...

D.3 Transformations and the Matrix Stack

In this section we will add a "robot arm" that you can control with your mouse. This "arm" will actually be two rectangles where one rectangle rotates about a point on the other rectangle. To begin, add the following member variables and functions to the application's document class:

```
protected:
    enum GLDisplayListNames { ArmPart=1 };
    double m_transX; // x offset of arm from the WCS origin
    double m_transY; // y offset of arm from the WCS origin
    double m_angle1; // angle of 1st arm part with respect to WC axis
    double m_angle2; // angle of 2nd arm part with respect to 1st part

    void COpenGLDoc::RenderScene(void)
```

Initialize the member variables in the document's constructor:

```
COpenGLDoc::COpenGLDoc()
{
    m_transY=100;
    m_transX=100;
    m_angle2=15;
    m_angle1=15;
}
```

Here we will change the painting model so the document actually renders the scene. With this model, the document defines the scene and the view defines how the scene is displayed. For example, if you had two views and you wanted each to be different, you could set view specific transformations in OnPaint before calling RenderScene. Then both views would be rendered with the same scene but they would be displayed differently.

```
void COpenGLView::OnPaint()
{
```

```
    CPaintDC dc(this); // device context for painting

    // Set view specific transformations here

    COpenGLDoc* pDoc = GetDocument();
    pDoc->RenderScene();
}
```

We will be using what is known as a display list to draw the parts of our arm. A display list is simply a list of OpenGL commands that have been stored and named for future processing. Display lists are often preprocessed, giving them a speed advantage over the same commands called without using a display list. Once a display list is created, its commands may be executed by calling glCallList with the integer name of the list. We will create the display list each time a document is created. You would also do this if you wanted to read the scene data from a file.

```
BOOL COpenGLDoc::OnNewDocument()
{
    if (!CDocument::OnNewDocument())
        return FALSE;

    glNewList(ArmPart);
        glBegin(GL_POLYGON);
            glVertex2f(-10.0f,  10.0f);
            glVertex2f(-10.0f, -10.0f);
            glVertex2f(100.0f, -10.0f);
            glVertex2f(100.0f,  10.0f);
        glEnd();
    glEndList();

    return TRUE;
}
```

Rendering the scene just consists of executing the display list:

```
void COpenGLDoc::RenderScene(void)
{
    glClear(GL_COLOR_BUFFER_BIT);

    glColor3f(1.0f, 0.0f, 0.0f);
    glCallList(ArmPart);

    glFlush();
}
```

If you were to run the program now, all you would see is a small red rectangle in the lower left hand corner of the screen. Now add the following lines:

```
void COpenGLDoc::RenderScene(void)
{
    glClear(GL_COLOR_BUFFER_BIT);

    glRotated( m_angle1, 0, 0, 1);
```

```
    glTranslated( m_transX, m_transY, 0);
    glColor3f(1.0f, 0.0f, 0.0f);
    glCallList(ArmPart);

    glFlush();
}
```

These two commands affect the ModelView matrix, causing our rectangle to rotate the number of degrees stored in m_angle1 and translate by the distance defined by (m_transX, m_transY). Run the program now to see the results. Notice that every time the program gets a WM_PAINT event the rectangle moves a little bit more. The effect occurs because we keep changing the ModelView matrix each time we call gl-Rotate and glTranslate. Note that resizing the window resets the rectangle to its original position because OnSize clears the matrix to an identity matrix. To keep from having this effect, after rotating and translating the matrix, we need to leave the matrix in the same state in which we found it. To do this we will use the matrix stack.

```
void COpenGLDoc::RenderScene(void)
{
    glClear(GL_COLOR_BUFFER_BIT);

    glPushMatrix();
        glRotated( m_angle1, 0, 0, 1);
        glTranslated( m_transX, m_transY, 0);
        glColor3f(1.0f, 0.0f, 0.0f);
        glCallList(ArmPart);
    glPopMatrix();

    glFlush();
}
```

glPushMatrix takes a copy of the current matrix and places it on a stack. When we call glPopMatrix, the last matrix pushed is restored as the current matrix. Our gl-PushMatrix call preserves the initial identity matrix, and glPopMatrix restores it after we dirtied up the matrix. We can use this technique to position objects with respect to other objects. Once again, edit RenderScene to match the code below.

```
void COpenGLDoc::RenderScene(void)
{
    glClear(GL_COLOR_BUFFER_BIT);

    glPushMatrix();
        glRotated( m_angle1, 0, 0, 1);
        glTranslated( m_transX, m_transY, 0);
        glPushMatrix();
            glRotated( m_angle2, 0, 0, 1);
            glTranslated( 90, 0, 0);
            glColor3f(0.0f, 1.0f, 0.0f);
            glCallList(ArmPart);
        glPopMatrix();
        glColor3f(1.0f, 0.0f, 0.0f);
        glCallList(ArmPart);
```

```
        glPopMatrix();

        glFlush();
    }
```

When you run this you will see a red rectangle overlapping a green rectangle. The translate commands actually move the object's vertex in the world coordinates. When the object is rotated, it still rotates around its own vertex, thus allowing the green rectangle to rotate around the end of the red one.

D.4 Mouse Action

Now we will add mouse handling so we can translate and rotate the arm using the mouse. Add the following member variables to the view class definition, and add message handlers for the WM_LBUTTONDOWN, WM_RBUTTONDOWN, and WM_MOUSEMOVE messages.

```
protected:
    CPoint m_ptLDown;
    CPoint m_ptRDown;
```

All we need to do in OnLButtonDown and OnRButtonDown is save the point where the mouse was clicked:

```
void COpenGLView::OnLButtonDown(UINT nFlags, CPoint point)
{
    m_ptLDown = point;
    CView::OnLButtonDown(nFlags, point);
}

void COpenGLView::OnRButtonDown(UINT nFlags, CPoint point)
{
    m_ptRDown = point;
    CView::OnRButtonDown(nFlags, point);
}
```

OnMouseMove changes the scene as the mouse moves when a button is pressed:

```
void COpenGLView::OnMouseMove(UINT nFlags, CPoint point)
{
    if (nFlags & MK_RBUTTON)
    {
        CSize rotate = m_ptRDown - point;
        m_ptRDown = point;

        COpenGLDoc* pDoc = GetDocument();
        pDoc->m_angle1 += rotate.cx/3;
        pDoc->m_angle2 += rotate.cy/3;

        InvalidateRect(NULL);
    }

    if (nFlags & MK_LBUTTON)
```

```
{
    CSize translate = m_ptLDown - point;
    m_ptLDown = point;

    COpenGLDoc* pDoc = GetDocument();
    pDoc->m_transX -= translate.cx/3;
    pDoc->m_transY += translate.cy/3;

    InvalidateRect(NULL);
}

CView::OnMouseMove(nFlags, point);
}
```

Now if you run the program you can drag with the left mouse button to move (translate) the arm, and drag with the right button to rotate the parts of the arm. On-MouseMove uses the current mouse point to change the values of the document then invalidates the window so the scene will be repainted. The only problem now is an annoying flicker from the full screen refreshes. We can fix this problem using double buffering.

D.5 Double Buffering

Double buffering is a very simple concept used in most high performance graphics programs. Instead of drawing to one buffer that maps directly to the screen, two buffers are used. One buffer is always displayed (known as the front buffer), while the other buffer is hidden (known as the back buffer). We do all of our drawing to the back buffer and, when we are done, swap it with the front buffer. Because all of the updates happen at once we don't get any flicker. The only drawback to double buffering is that it is incompatible with GDI. GDI was not designed with double buffering in mind. Because of this, GDI commands will not work in an OpenGL window with double buffering enabled.

The first step to eliminating the flicker is to change all of the InvalidateRect calls to:

```
InvalidateRect(NULL, FALSE);
```

This keeps the background from being erased before painting the window. This will solve most of our flicker problem (the rest of the flicker was mainly to make a point). To enable double buffering for the pixel format, change the pixelDesc.dwFlags definition in our SetWindowPixelFormat to the following:

```
pixelDesc.dwFlags = PFD_DRAW_TO_WINDOW | PFD_SUPPORT_OPENGL |
                    PFD_DOUBLEBUFFER | PFD_STEREO_DONTCARE;
```

There are no checks when we set the pixel format to make sure that the one returned from ChoosePixelFormat has double buffering.

To use the double buffering we need to tell OpenGL to draw only onto the back buffer. Up until now we have been drawing on the front buffer. Add the following line to the end of the view's OnSize:

```
glDrawBuffer(GL_BACK);
```

Now each time we draw the scene we need to swap the buffer, so add this to the end of OnPaint:

```
SwapBuffers(dc.m_ps.hdc);
```

Now if you run the program you should see absolutely no flicker. However, the program will run noticeably slower. If you still see any flicker then ChoosePixelFormat is not returning a pixel format with double buffering. Remember that ChoosePixel-Format returns an identifier for the pixel format that it believes is closest to the one you want. Try forcing different indices when you call SetPixelFormat until you find a format that supports double buffering.

In the final sample program, we will construct a three dimensional cube. There may be some 3-D graphics concepts in this section that those uninitiated to graphics will not understand. Explaining these concepts is beyond the scope of this tutorial. For those people, I recommend reading one of the books listed at the end of this tutorial.

D.6 A Three Dimensional Cube

First we need to change our viewing coordinate system. gluOrtho2D, the function we have been calling to set up our projection matrix, actually creates a 3 dimensional view with the near clipping plane at z=-1 and the far clipping plane at 1. You've actually been doing 3-D programming all along. All of the "2-D" commands we have been calling have actually been 3-D calls where the z coordinate was zero. To view our cube, we would like to use perspective projection. To set up a perspective projection we need to change OnSize to the following:

```
void COpenGLView::OnSize(UINT nType, int cx, int cy)
{
    CView::OnSize(nType, cx, cy);

    GLsizei width = cx;
    GLsizei height = cy;
    GLdouble aspect = (cy == 0) ? (GLdouble)width :
        (GLdouble)width/(GLdouble)height;

    glViewport(0, 0, width, height);
    glMatrixMode(GL_PROJECTION);
    glLoadIdentity();
    gluPerspective(45, aspect, 1, 10.0);
    glMatrixMode(GL_MODELVIEW);
    glLoadIdentity();
    glDrawBuffer(GL_BACK);
}
```

Orthogonal projection maps everything in three dimensional space onto a two dimensional surface at right angles. The result is everything looks the same size regardless of its distance from the eye point. Perspective project simulates light passing through a point (as if you were using a pinhole camera). The result is a more natural picture where distant object appear smaller. The gluPerspective call above sets the eye point at the origin, gives us a 45 angle field of view, a front clipping plane at 1, and a back clipping plane at 10. Now lets draw our cube. Edit RenderScene to look like this:

```
void COpenGLDoc::RenderScene(void)
{
    glClear(GL_COLOR_BUFFER_BIT);

    glPushMatrix();
        glTranslated(0.0, 0.0, -8.0);
        glRotated(m_xRotate, 1.0, 0.0, 0.0);
        glRotated(m_yRotate, 0.0, 1.0, 0.0);

        glBegin(GL_POLYGON);
            glNormal3d(  1.0,  0.0,  0.0);
            glVertex3d(  1.0,  1.0,  1.0);
            glVertex3d(  1.0, -1.0,  1.0);
            glVertex3d(  1.0, -1.0, -1.0);
            glVertex3d(  1.0,  1.0, -1.0);
        glEnd();

        glBegin(GL_POLYGON);
            glNormal3d( -1.0,  0.0,  0.0);
            glVertex3d( -1.0, -1.0,  1.0);
            glVertex3d( -1.0,  1.0,  1.0);
            glVertex3d( -1.0,  1.0, -1.0);
            glVertex3d( -1.0, -1.0, -1.0);
        glEnd();

        glBegin(GL_POLYGON);
            glNormal3d(  0.0,  1.0,  0.0);
            glVertex3d(  1.0,  1.0,  1.0);
            glVertex3d( -1.0,  1.0,  1.0);
            glVertex3d( -1.0,  1.0, -1.0);
            glVertex3d(  1.0,  1.0, -1.0);
        glEnd();

        glBegin(GL_POLYGON);
            glNormal3d(  0.0, -1.0,  0.0);
            glVertex3d( -1.0, -1.0,  1.0);
            glVertex3d(  1.0, -1.0,  1.0);
            glVertex3d(  1.0, -1.0, -1.0);
            glVertex3d( -1.0, -1.0, -1.0);
        glEnd();

        glBegin(GL_POLYGON);
            glNormal3d(  0.0,  0.0,  1.0);
            glVertex3d(  1.0,  1.0,  1.0);
            glVertex3d( -1.0,  1.0,  1.0);
            glVertex3d( -1.0, -1.0,  1.0);
```

```
        glVertex3d(  1.0,  -1.0,   1.0);
    glEnd();

    glBegin(GL_POLYGON);
        glNormal3d(  0.0,   0.0,  -1.0);
        glVertex3d( -1.0,   1.0,  -1.0);
        glVertex3d(  1.0,   1.0,  -1.0);
        glVertex3d(  1.0,  -1.0,  -1.0);
        glVertex3d( -1.0,  -1.0,  -1.0);
    glEnd();
  glPopMatrix();
}
```

Add member variables to the document class for m_xRotate and m_yRotate (look at the function definitions to determine the correct type). Add member variables and event handlers to the view class to modify the document variables when you drag with the left mouse button just like we did in the last example (hint: Handle the WM_LBUTTONDOWN, WM_LBUTTONUP, and WM_MOUSEMOVE events. Look at the sample source code if you need help). Compile and run the program. You should see a white cube that you can rotate. You will not be able to see any discernible feature yet since the cube has no surface definition and there is no light source. We will add these features next. Add the following lines to the beginning of RenderScene:

```
GLfloat RedSurface[]   = { 1.0f, 0.0f, 0.0f, 1.0f};
GLfloat GreenSurface[] = { 0.0f, 1.0f, 0.0f, 1.0f};
GLfloat BlueSurface[]  = { 0.0f, 0.0f, 1.0f, 1.0f};
```

These defines surface property values. Once again, the numbers represent the red, green, blue and alpha components of the surfaces. The surface properties are set with the command glMaterial. Add glMaterial calls to the following locations:

```
glMaterialfv(GL_FRONT_AND_BACK, GL_AMBIENT, RedSurface);
glBegin(GL_POLYGON);
...
glEnd();

glBegin(GL_POLYGON);
...
glEnd();

glMaterialfv(GL_FRONT_AND_BACK, GL_AMBIENT, GreenSurface);
glBegin(GL_POLYGON);
...
glEnd();

glBegin(GL_POLYGON);
...
glEnd();

glMaterialfv(GL_FRONT_AND_BACK, GL_AMBIENT, BlueSurface);
glBegin(GL_POLYGON);
```

```
...
glEnd();

glBegin(GL_POLYGON);
...
glEnd();
```

These new calls make two of the cube faces red, two faces green, and two faces blue. The commands set the ambient color for front and back of each face. However, the cube will still appear featureless until the lighting model is enabled. To do this add the following command to the end of OnSize:

```
glEnable(GL_LIGHTING);
```

Now if you run the program you should see one of the blue faces of the cube. Rotate the cube with your mouse. You will notice the cube looks very strange. Faces seem to appear and disappear at random. This is because we are simply drawing the faces of the cube with no regard as to which is in front. When we draw a face that is in back, it draws over any faces in front of it that have been drawn. The solution to this problem is z-buffering.

D.7 Z-Buffering

The z-buffer holds a value for every pixel on the screen. This value represents how close that pixel is to the eye point. Whenever OpenGL attempts to draw to a pixel, it checks the z-buffer to see if the new color is closer to the eye point than the old color. If it is, the pixel is set to the new color. If not, then the pixel retains the old color. As you can guess, z-buffering can take up a large amount of memory and CPU time. The cDepthBits parameter in the PIXELFORMATDESCRIPTOR we used in Set-WindowPixelFormat defines the number of bits in each z-buffer value. Enable z-buffering by adding the following command at the end of OnSize:

```
glEnable(GL_DEPTH_TEST);
```

We also need to clear the z-buffer when we begin a new drawing. Change the glClear command in RenderScene to the following:

```
glClear(GL_COLOR_BUFFER_BIT | GL_DEPTH_BUFFER_BIT);
```

Now if you run the program you should have a colorful cube that rotates in space and draws correctly, but it is very faint. Let's add a light to the scene so that we can see the cube better. Add the following declaration to the beginning of RenderScene:

```
GLfloat LightAmbient[]  = { 0.1f, 0.1f, 0.1f, 0.1f };
GLfloat LightDiffuse[]  = { 0.7f, 0.7f, 0.7f, 0.7f };
GLfloat LightSpecular[] = { 0.0f, 0.0f, 0.0f, 0.1f };
GLfloat LightPosition[] = { 5.0f, 5.0f, 5.0f, 0.0f };
```

These will serve as the property values for our light. Now add the following commands just after glClear in RenderScene:

```
glLightfv(GL_LIGHT0, GL_AMBIENT, LightAmbient);
glLightfv(GL_LIGHT0, GL_DIFFUSE, LightDiffuse);
glLightfv(GL_LIGHT0, GL_SPECULAR, LightSpecular);
glLightfv(GL_LIGHT0, GL_POSITION, LightPosition);
glEnable(GL_LIGHT0);
```

glLight defines properties for light sources. OpenGL's light sources are all created within the implementation of OpenGL. Each light source has an identifier GL_LIGHTi where i is zero to GL_MAX_LIGHTS. The above commands set the ambient, diffuse, and specular properties , as well as the position, of light zero. glEnable turns on the light.

The program is currently wasting time by drawing the interior faces of the cube with our colored surfaces. To fix this, change the GL_FRONT_AND_BACK parameter in all of the glMaterialfv calls to GL_FRONT. We also want to set the diffuse reflectivity of the cube faces now that we have a light source. To do this, change the GL_AMBIENT parameter in the glMaterialfv calls to GL_AMBIENT_AND_DIFFUSE. Now if you run the program you should have a program that displays a lighted, multi-colored cube in three dimensions that uses z-buffering and double buffering.

D.8 Conclusion

You should now know how to set up an OpenGL program using MFC, and should also understand some of the basic graphics commands. If you wish to explore OpenGL further you should look through the sample programs or read through the documentation in Books Online. You may also find the following OpenGL books useful. These books are also referred to as the "Red Book" and the "Blue Book" (as per their respective colors).

1. OpenGL Programming Guide, The Official Guide to Learning OpenGL, Release 1 . OpenGL Architecture Review Board, 1992, Addison Wesley, ISBN 0-201-63274-8.
2. OpenGL Reference Manual, The Official Reference Document for OpenGL, Release 1 . OpenGL Architecture Review Board, 1992, Addison Wesley, ISBN 0-201-63276-4.

If you would like to learn more about graphics in general, the following books would be helpful.

1. Foley, J. D. and Dam, A. V. and Feiner, S. K. and Hughes., J. F. Computer Graphics, Principles and Practice. Addison-Wesley Publishing Company: Reading, Massachusetts, 1990
2. Hill, F. S. Computer Graphics. MacMillian Publishing Company: New York, 1990.

It really is necessary to understand the basics of the material in either of these books if you want to do any serious 3-D graphics.

This is a "single-word 30% index, by section." Every word in the text of the book that appears in 30% or less of the book's sections is displayed, along with the sections in which it appears. The 30% barrier eliminates common words.

This index is supplemented by a comprehensive electronic index on the CD.

_BLACK _BLACK A
_BLACK 11.5.4
_COPYPEN 11.3, 11.5.4
_DEBUG 13.1
_dos_gettime 12.1.3
_MASKNOTPEN 11.5.4
_MASKPEN 11.5.4
_MASKPENNOT 11.5.4
_MAX_PATH 12.1.1
_MERGENOTPEN 11.5.4
_MERGEPEN 11.5.4
_MERGEPENNOT 11.5.4
_NOP 11.5.4
_NOT 11.5.4
_NOTCOPYPEN 11.5.4
_NOTMASKPEN 11.5.4
_NOTMERGEPEN 11.5.4
_NOTXORPEN 11.5.4
_WHITE 11.5.4
_XORPEN 11.5.4
AB 13.5
abbreviated 12.1.3
abbreviation 11.6.2
abilities 3.3, 12.3
Abort 7.1
Aborts 13.7
AboutDialog 8.5
absence 34.1
absolute 12.1.1, 35.7
Absolutely B.3.2, D.5, 0.4, 15.8.1, 15.8.3, 34.8.13, 35.3
abstract A.1, A.3.2, A.3.3, 34.8
abstraction A.1.1, A.3.2, A.3.3, A.4.2, 1.3, 12.1.1, 34.4
abstractions 11.3, 34.8
abstractly A.3.2
abstracts 11.1
accelerate 0.1, 0.2, 6.1, 22.7, Prf
accelerated 0.3
accelerates 2.1
acceleration 20.2
accelerator B.2.2, 0.1, 0.4, 3.2, 6, 6.1, 6.3, 6.5.3, 8.4, 10.4.10, 14.4.6, 15.4, 18.4.6, 32.6
accelerators D.0, 0.4, 6.5.3, 8.4
accept A.6, A.8, D.1, 0.4, 4.3, 4.4, 5.1, 5.3, 5.4, 6.7.3, 7.1, 7.6, 8.1, 8.6.1, 9.3, 11.4.1, 11.4.4, 11.6.1, 12.2, 13.3, 15.1, 15.9, 18.1.12, 18.2, 22.0, 32.1, 34.1, 34.4, 35.3, 35.5
acceptable 33.1
acceptance 5.3, 7.0
accepted A.4.6, A.6, A.8, 7.4, 11.5.2, 11.5.3, 12.1.3, 24.0
accepting 5.1, 8.4, 32.1
accepts A.2.9, A.5.2, A.6, A.7.1, 2.3.2, 3.1, 4.2, 4.3, 4.5, 5.2, 7.2, 7.3, 8.4, 10.2, 11.4.2,

11.4.3, 11.4.4, 11.4.5, 11.4.6, 11.4.8, 11.6.1, 12.1.1, 12.1.2, 12.2, 13.5, 13.6, 13.6.1, 15.3, 15.4, 15.7.9, 17.4, 18.4.7, 23.4, 23.8, 24.0, 26.1, 30.1, 32.4, 34.8.11, 35.3, 35.7
access A.3.2, A.5.1, A.6, B, B.8.6, C.0, 0.4, 6.1, 6.5.3, 6.6.8, 7.2, 8.3, 10.1, 11.3, 12.1.1, 12.1.2, 12.3, 12.4, 12.5, 13.1, 14.4.4, 15.2.5, 15.2.6, 15.5, 15.5.1, 15.6.3, 15.6.5, 15.7.9, 17.6, 18.1.4, 18.1.9, 18.1.12, 18.3, 20.5, 23.1, 23.8, 26.0, 30.0, 30.2, 32.4, 33.0, 33.1, 33.2, 33.2.5, 33.3, 33.4, 33.4.2, 33.5, 33.6, 33.6.5, 34.1, 34.3, 34.7, 34.8.1, 34.8.6, 35.2, 35.5, Prf
accessed A.3.2, A.4.3, A.5.1, 34.4
accesses 11.3
accessible A.5.1, 12.1.1, 34.4
accessing A.5.1, A.7, 2.1, 33.0, 33.3, 33.6.5, 34.3
accessory 5.2
accidentally A.7.2, B.3.2, B.6.1, 9.3
acclimating A.1
accommodate 6.7, 9.1, 12.2, 18.0, 18.1.12
accompanied A.1
accompanies 6.1
accomplish A.1, A.1.1, A.4.2, B, 2.2, 5.1, 11.4.6, 14.1, 15.3.3, 15.7, 15.8, 15.8.4, 17.4, 18.3, 25.7, 34.1, 34.4, 34.5.5, 34.8.4, Prf
accomplished A.5.3, 0.0, 18.6, 22.3, 33.7.5, 34.8
accomplishes 8.4, 15.2.9
accordingly 1.1, 4.4, 4.6, 5.2, 15.8.3, 16.3.4, 26.2, 33.6.2
account A.3.1, 5.4, 33.4.2
accumulating 9.4
accurate 11.4.6, 29.1, Prf
accurately 15.8.3
achieve D.1, 11.5.2, 20.2
achievements 19.0
Acknowledgments Prf
acquiring 11.6.3
across A.1.1, 1.1, 11.2, 11.4.1, 11.4.8, 11.5.3, 11.5.4, 12.1.1, 15.8.3, 15.8.4, 23.7, 27.2, 30.0, 33.2, 34.1, 34.6.7, 35.1, 35.2
act A.2.11, A.3.2, A.4.2, B.1.3, B.4.5, 0.2, 1.4, 7.2, 7.6, 9.3, 11.5.1, 11.5.2, 14.4.3, 17.1.2, 17.5, 18.1.4, 18.3, 23.7, 23.8, 32.6, 33.1, 34.1, 34.6.5, 35.7
acting A.8
action A.2.5, A.5.2, 0.4, 1.3, 4.6, 4.7, 5.2, 7.1, 7.2, 7.4, 9.3, 11.5.2, 11.5.4, 12.1.1, 12.2, 13.2, 15.8.4, 17.4.5, 17.4.7, 20.7, 23.7, 24.0, 25.6, 25.7, 32.1, 34.2,

34.4, 34.8.4
actions A.3.1, A.3.3, A.4.1, 1.3, 4.6, 7.2, 7.3, 9.3, 10.6, 12.1.4, 15.3.1, 20.7, 23.7, 25.3, 26.4, 32.4, 32.6
activate B.8.5, B.8.7, 6.5.3, 10.5, 15.5, 15.7, 16.2, 18.4.5, 19.1, 19.3, 19.3.5, 32.6, 33.6.1, 34.4, 34.7, 34.7.7, 34.8.4, 34.8.5
activated A.4.3, 0.4, 8.2, 11.5.2, 11.6.1, 15.5, 15.8, 18.1.5, 19.3.5, 20.7, 22.4
Activates 10.4.10
activation 34.5.3, 34.6.4, 34.6.10
active 4.5, 4.6, 10.1, 13.1, 13.2, 13.4, 14.4.5, 20.7, 32.2, 32.4, 32.5, 34.5.5, 35.1, 35.8
activities 1.3, 10.3, 33.8.4, 34.6.3, 34.8.1, 35.1, 35.6
activity 2.3, 10.3, 11.5.4, 15.3.7, 15.5, 15.8.4, 15.9, 23.1, 35.1
acts A.4.3, A.6, B.4, B.7.4, 2.2, 2.3, 2.5, 7.6, 11.1, 13.6, 14.0, 15.8.2, 18.3, 20.5, 34.1, 34.6.3, 34.7.7, 35.4
actual A.2.11, A.3.2, A.4.2, A.4.3, A.4.4, A.5.2, B.2, 2.2, 3.3, 7.0, 8.1, 8.5, 8.6, 8.6.10, 11.3, 11.5.4, 11.6.3, 15.7.4, 15.8.2, 15.8.4, 18.5.6, 19.2, 19.2.3, 20.7, 22.5, 27.1, 33.7.6, 34.6.5
Ada A.1.1
adapt 11.7, 15.7.11, 35.8
adapter 11.6.2
AddAddr 18.2
ADDDLG 18.1.9, 18.1.10
AddDocTemplate 10, 10.4.10, 14.4.2, 16.3
added A.1.1, A.2, A.5.1, A.5.2, A.8, B.3, 2.3, 4.4, 4.5, 6.3.3, 7.2, 9.1, 10.4.10, 11.5.3, 11.5.5, 12.3, 13.1, 15.2.1, 15.2.6, 15.2.7, 15.3, 15.3.8, 15.4, 15.4.3, 15.7.8, 15.8.2, 16.2, 16.3.3, 18.1.13, 18.2, 18.4.4, 18.4.6, 19.2.2, 20.4, 20.7, 22.5, 23.8, 25.6, 25.8, 26.2, 26.3, 30.1, 33.2.3, 33.4.3, 34.8.11, 34.8.13
AddHead 12.4
adding A.2.3, A.3.1, A.4, A.4.1, A.4.2, A.5.1, A.5.2, A.6, B.6.6, B.7.1, B.7.4, B.7.6, B.7.7, B.8.4, B.8.5, B.8.7, B.8.8, D.7, 2.1, 6.3, 6.5, 6.5.2, 10.5, 11.5.3, 11.5.5, 12.2, 12.4, 14.1, 14.4.6, 14.5, 14.6, 15.2.6, 15.2.7, 15.3, 15.5, 15.5.1, 15.6, 15.6.3, 15.6.5, 15.6.9, 15.7.5, 15.7.9, 15.7.11, 15.9, 16.2, 17.5, 18.0, 18.1.2, 18.1.7, 18.1.12, 18.2, 18.4.1, 18.4.2, 18.4.5, 18.4.6, 18.4.7, 18.6, 19.2.3, 19.2.7, 19.3.3,

20.3, 26.2, 29.2, 30.1,
31.4, 33.1, 33.2.3, 33.4.2,
33.6.6, 33.6.8, 33.6.10,
33.8.4, 34.5.6, 34.7.4,
34.7.8, Prf
addition A.2.3, A.3.2, A.5.2, A.5.3, 2.1,
5.2, 9.1, 9.4, 10.1, 10.5,
11.5.2, 11.5.5, 12.1.2,
12.1.3, 12.1.4, 12.4, 14.3,
14.5, 16.3.6, 18.2, 18.4.2,
18.4.5, 18.6, 19.1.2,
33.6.4, 34.6.3, 34.8,
34.8.1, 35.5
additional B.4, 0.2, 3.0, 4.6, 4.7,
11.5.5, 12.1.2, 13.5, 13.6,
13.6.2, 14.4.1, 15.0,
15.7.11, 15.8, 18.4.6,
19.1.2, 33.4, 34.4, 34.5.3,
34.8.4, 35.7
Additionally 12.1.3, 12.3, 12.4, 15.3.4,
15.5, 15.5.4, 15.7.11,
18.4.2, 18.4.7, 30.0,
34.7.8, 34.8.1, 35.4
additions A.3, 15.9, 16.3.6, 18.1.12
AddNew 33.5, 33.8.4
AddPage 20.5, 20.7
AddPoint 15.2.6, 15.2.7, 15.2.9, 15.3,
15.3.8, 15.4, 15.4.3,
15.6.3
Addr 18.1.1, 18.4.2, 18.4.4, 18.4.5,
18.4.6
ADDRDOC 18.4.2, 18.4.6
address A.2.3, A.2.11, A.4, A.4.1,
A.4.2, B.3.1, C.0, 0.4, 3.3,
6, 7.0, 8.6.2, 9.2, 12.3,
13.7, 17.0, 17.4, 17.6,
18.0, 18.1, 18.1.12,
18.1.15, 18.2, 18.3, 18.4,
18.4.1, 18.4.6, 18.4.7,
18.5, 18.5.2, 18.5.5, 18.6,
33.1, 33.2.1, 33.2.4,
33.7.4, 34.3, 35.8, Prf
addressed A.7
addresses A.2.3, A.4.1, C.0, 18.1, 18.2,
18.4
Addressing B.3.1
ADDRREC 18.1.12
ADDRVIEW 18.4.1
adds A.1.1, A.3.2, A.5.1, A.5.2, A.6,
A.8, 9.1, 9.4, 10.4.10,
10.5, 11.5.3, 12.2, 12.4,
12.5, 13.4, 14.4.2, 15.3,
15.3.8, 15.5, 16.3, 18.2,
21.1.8, 23.7, 25.8, 26.3,
30.2, 34.8.4
AddString 5.2, 9.1, 9.4, 18.4.1, 23.3,
25.6, 34.8
AddTail 12.4
AddToEnd A.5.2
AddToFront A.5.2
AddToRecentFileList 10.4.10, 10.5
adept B.4
adequate 28.0
Adj B.8.1, B.8.3, B.8.4, 34.8.2, 34.8.3,
34.8.4
adjacent 29.1
ADJCTL B.8.1, 34.8.2, 34.8.4, 34.8.6,
34.8.7, 34.8.11
adjust A.1.1, B.8.6, 11.4.6, 11.5.5,
11.6.1, 15.5, 16.3.4,

18.1.8, 18.5.5, 33.4.2,
33.7.4, 34.5.4, 34.5.5,
34.8.3, 34.8.6, 34.8.8,
35.7
adjusted B.3, 15.5.6, 19.2, 34.5.5,
34.8.1, 34.8.10
adjuster 34.8.1, 34.8.6, 34.8.8, 34.8.9
adjusting 13.5, 15.5.6, 33.2.4
adjustment 20.2, 34.8.1
adjustments 34.5.5, 34.6.7, 34.6.9
adjusts 4.4, 4.6, 35.7
administration C.1, 33.4, 33.4.2
Administrator 33.3, 33.4, 33.4.1
adr 18.1.1
Advanced B.6.1, B.6.3, B.6.5, C.1, 0.0,
0.1, 1.2, 5.3, 11.0, 11.5.2,
11.6.2, 12.3, 14.1, 15.8.1,
17.0, 17.2, 18.4, 19.1.2,
28.0, 28.3, 33.9, 35.0,
35.2, Prf
advantage A.1.1, A.2.3, A.5, C.0, D.3,
0.1, 1.0, 1.1, 2.1, 5.2, 6.7,
10.3, 11.5.1, 12.2, 12.3,
13.1, 13.2, 13.5, 15.4,
15.8.1, 15.8.4, 16.2, 18.1,
22.0, 23.9, 33.2, 33.6.3,
34.1, 34.5.5, 35.1, 35.2
advantages A.1, A.5, A.8.1, B.3, 0.4,
1.1, 6.1, 8.5, 12.1.2, 12.2,
15.2.6, 15.3, 15.6.2, 18.2,
29.1, 33.1, 34.3
adversely A.1.1, 31.4
advertised A.5.2
advertising A.3.1
aesthetics 11.5.1
affect D.2, D.3, 22.3, 25.7, 31.4
affected B.4.6, D.2, 1.3, 11.6.1, 15.7.3
affecting A.1.1
affects 31.1
afford A.7.2, 11.6.2
afterward 12.1.3
afterwards D.1
Afx 13.6.2, 13.7, 14.4.1, 19.4
AFX_DATA 28.1
AFX_HIDP_ASK_TO_SAVE 19.4
AFX_HIPD_Default 19.4
AFX_IDI_STD_FRAME 6.3.7
afx_msg 4.3, 4.4, 14.5, 30.1
AfxAbort 13.7
AfxBeginThread 35.3, 35.4, 35.9
afxCheckMemory 13.5
AfxCheckMemroy 13.7
AFXCORE 19.2, 19.2.1, 19.2.3,
19.3.3, 19.3.9
AFXDLGS 7.2
AfxDoForAllClasses 13.7
AfxDoForAllObject 13.7
afxDump 13.4
AfxEnableMemoryTracking 13.7
AfxEndThread 35.3, 35.4
AFXEXT 14.4.1
AfxFormatString 6.7, 6.7.3
AfxFrameOrView 13.4
AfxGetApp 10.1, 11.5.3
AfxGetAppName 10.1
AfxGetInstanceHandle 10.1
AfxGetMainWnd 32.4
AfxGetResourceHandle 10.1
AfxIsMemoryBlock 13.7
AfxIsValidAddress 13.7

AfxIsValidString 13.7
afxMemDF 13.5
AfxMessageBox 6.7.3, 7.1, 15.7.3,
15.7.9
AfxOleInit 34.5.3, 34.6.3
AFXPRINT 19.2
AFXPRIV 31.2, 31.4
AfxRegisterWndClass 11.5.3
AfxSetAllocHook 13.7
AfxStringFormat 6.7.3
AfxThrowArchiveException 13.6.2
AfxThrowDBException 13.6.2
AfxThrowFileException 13.6.2
AfxThrowMemoryException 13.6.2
AfxThrowNotSupportedException
13.6.2
AfxThrowOleDispatchException
13.6.2
AfxThrowOleException 13.6.2
AfxThrowResourceException 13.6.2
AfxThrowUserException 13.6.2, 22.4
AfxTraceEnabled 13.7
afxTraceFlags 13.3, 13.7
afxwin 2.3, 14.4.1, 23.1
AfxWinThread 35.4
AfxWndProc 23.7, 23.8
against A.7.2, B.3, D.1, 13.1
aggressive 7.2
aided 19.0
albeit 17.0
alerts 20.7
algorithm 12.5, 20.4
ALIAS 19.2, 19.4
aliased 19.4
align 4.6, 11.4.6, 30.0, 30.1
aligned 9.2, 11.4.8, 32.6
alignment 4.6, 6.6.5, 32.6, 34.8
aligns 3.3
alleviates 11.3
allocate A.2.10, 8.6.2, 9.3, 12.3, 13.6,
26.2, 35.8
allocated A.2.10, A.4.4, A.7, 2.3.2,
2.3.3, 2.4, 12.2, 12.4,
13.5, 18.5.2, 32.4
allocates 2.3.2, 2.3.3, 3.1, 12.1.2, 12.2,
12.3, 13.2, 13.5
allocating 12.2, 18.5.3
allocation A.1.1, A.2.10, 13.5, 13.6,
13.6.1
allocations 13.5, 13.6, 13.7
allocator 13.5, 13.6.2
allocMemDF 13.5
almost A.1, A.2.6, A.2.7, A.6, B.8.1,
0.2, 1.3, 2.1, 2.3.1, 4.4,
5.1, 6.2, 8.6.4, 9.5, 11.2,
11.4.8, 11.5.5, 11.6.2,
15.9, 17.3.5, 23.1, 25.9,
30.0, 33.1, 34.0, 34.1,
34.5.3, 34.6.3, 34.8.2,
34.9, 35.1, 35.2
alone A.5, B.5.5, B.8.1, 4.6, 15.2.6,
34.1, 34.2, 34.3, 34.8.4
along A.2.4, A.4.2, A.4.5, A.5.1, A.7,
A.7.1, A.7.2, B.2.3, B.4.1,
B.4.2, B.9, D.2, D.6, 0.2,
1.2, 2.3.2, 3.0, 5.3, 6.6,
6.6.8, 7.3, 7.5, 7.6,
10.4.10, 12, 14.4.4,
15.8.4, 16.3.6, 18.4.2,
19.1.1, 19.2.5, 22.0, 22.3,

23.4, 23.7, 26.2, 29.2,
32.4, 34.4, 35.8, Prf
alpha D.1, D.6
alphabetically 20.4
Alt 1.2, 5.4, 6.5.3
alternate 9.2, 11.3, 11.4.2, 11.4.5
alternately 10.2, 11.5.2
alternates 10.2
alternative A.5.2, 5.2, 5.3, 11.2, 15.8.4,
18.1, 18.4.6, 29.1, 33.9,
34.1
alternatively A.1.1, A.5.2, 13.5, 14.0,
18.5.2, 19.2.8, 19.2.10,
35.7
Although A.5.3, 1.3, 2.5, 3.4, 6.4, 8.3,
9.5, 10.5, 11.0, 11.4.1,
12.3, 13.5, 17.1.3, 17.4,
17.4.6, 17.5, 18.4, 22.2,
25.4, 28.3, 33.2, 34.4,
34.8.3, 34.8.5, 35.4
altogether 5.2, 15.8.2
always A.1.1, A.2.7, A.7.2, B.5.3, D.5,
0.4, 2.3.3, 2.5, 3.1, 3.2,
3.3, 3.5, 4.4, 6.2, 6.5.3,
7.0, 8.6.10, 9.5, 11.2,
11.4.1, 11.4.6, 11.5.4,
11.6.1, 12.1.2, 13.2,
14.4.2, 14.4.6, 15.5.6,
18.4.2, 18.4.3, 18.4.6,
22.5, 25.6, 26.4, 28.2,
30.1, 32.2, 32.7, 32.8,
34.8, 35.4, 35.7
am A.3.1, 12.1.3
ambient D.6, D.7, 34.8, 34.8.3, 34.8.4
ambiguity A.2.9
among 2.3.2, 3.3, 12.1.1, 25.1, 25.6,
33.1, 35.7
amount A.3.2, B.3, B.4, D.7, 1.1, 1.3,
3.3, 4.2, 5.4, 6, 6.7, 7.2,
8.4, 8.5, 8.6.7, 10.4.10,
11.6.2, 12.2, 12.4, 13.6,
15.5.4, 15.8.1, 15.8.4,
17.2, 17.4, 18.4.3, 27.0,
30.0, 32.5, 33.2, 33.4.2,
33.5, 33.7.5, 34.5.5, 35.2,
35.7, Prf
ampersand 5.4, 6.5.2
ampersands 6.5.2
analysis C.1
anchors 11.5.4
ancillary B.6.1
anddrop 32.1
ANDed 25.7
ANDs 33.6.8
angle A.3.2, D.6, 11.4.4, 11.4.6
angles D.6, 11.4.4
animate 0.4
animated B.4, 0.4, 11.6.2, 29.1
animation 8.6.10, 10.2, 10.3, 11.3,
11.4.7, 11.6.2, 20.0, 27.2
anisotropic 11.6.1, 34.6.9
Ann Prf
annoyance 35.8
annoying D.4, 2.6, 11.5.3, 35.8
anomaly 4.2

ANSI 7.3, 8.1
ANSI_CHARSET 11.4.6
answer A.1, A.8, B.4, 13.2, 22.1, 23.0,
23.1

answered A.1.1, 1.2, 34.1
answering 1.4, 34.1, Prf
answers 0.4, 23.0, 34.2, Prf
anxiety A.1
anymore 11.2
anyone A.1.1, A.4.2, A.5.1, A.8, B.4
anything A.1.1, A.4.2, A.5, A.6, B.5.2,
C.0, 0.2, 1.3, 3.3, 4.2, 6.4,
8.4, 11.2, 11.4.1, 11.5.4,
11.6.3, 13.2, 15.8.2, 16.4,
17.4, 18.4.6, 23.8, 25.6,
25.7, 26.4, 27.1, 29.2,
30.3, 31.5, 33.4.1, 33.4.3,
33.6.1, 33.7.2, 34.1,
34.6.2, 34.8.4, 34.8.5,
35.2, 35.3, 35.7, 35.9
anyway 3.2, 32.6
anywhere A.2.6, A.3.2, A.4.6, B.2.3,
B.4.1, 3.3, 11.4.7, 12.1.1,
13.6, 18.5.2, 18.5.6,
19.2.9, 32.2, 33.0, 33.6.3,
33.6.4, 34.2, 34.7.7, 35.9
API 0.2, 1.0, 1.1, 1.3, 2.1, 2.3, 3.1, 3.3,
4.3, 5.2, 7.2, 7.3, 7.4, 7.5,
7.6, 8.2, 11.0, 11.1, 11.3,
11.4.1, 11.5.3, 11.7,
12.1.4, 18.4.7, 23.0, 23.1,
23.4, 23.9, 33.3, 33.5,
33.6.2, 34.1, 34.3, 34.4,
35.0, 35.2, 35.3, 35.4,
35.7, 35.8
APIs 12.1.1
App 13.3, 35.10
apparent A.7, A.8.1, 2.3
appeal 29.4
appealing 11.5.4
appearance 1.1, 1.3, 3.0, 3.1, 3.2, 4.0,
4.2, 4.5, 5.2, 7.2, 9.1, 9.6,
11.5.3, 15.8.3, 18.4.6,
20.0, 25.0, 25.9, 27.1,
34.1, 34.8, 34.8.13, Prf
appeared 15.8.2
append 15.2.1
appending A.2.4
AppendMenu 32.7
appends 26.2, 32.7
Apple 35.2
applicable 8.1, 18.5
applied A.2.7, A.4.3, A.4.6, 11.4.6,
11.5.5, 15.4, 15.7.11
applies 1.2, 2.5, 4.3, 4.6, 11.3, 11.5.5,
20.6, 34.8.4
apply A.4.4, 3.2, 3.5, 4.0, 4.6, 4.8, 5.3,
7.3, 8.3, 10.4.10, 15.7.11,
16.3.1, 18.1.2, 18.5, 20.7,
33.6.6, 33.6.8, 33.6.10,
34.2, 35.1
appreciate 5.1, 34.8.13, 35.1
approach A.1.1, A.3.2, A.5.2, C.1, 0.2,
3.3, 5.1, 5.2, 6.7, 11.4.6,
11.5.1, 11.5.5, 14.3,
15.4.4, 17.0, 18.1, 18.4.2,
18.4.3, 18.6, 20.7, 20.8,
23.2, 23.9, 24.0, 25.1,
27.0, 27.1, 29.1, 29.4,
30.2, 31.3, 31.6, 33.1,
33.8.4, 34.1, 34.4, 34.8.1,
35.8
approaches 8.1, 33.8.4
approaching 34.8.1

approximately 4.7, 19.4
AppWizard B, B.3, **B.5.1**, B.6, B.6.1,
B.6.2, B.6.3, B.6.4, B.6.5,
B.6.6, B.7, B.8.1, 0.1, 0.3,
0.4, 2.3, 2.5, 5.1, 5.4, 6.1,
6.3.7, 6.4, 7.0, 7.7, 8.0,
8.3, 8.6.10, 8.7, 10, 10.4,
10.4.9, 10.4.10, 11.5.3,
11.5.5, 11.6.3, 11.7, **14.0,
14.1, 14.2, 14.3, 14.4,
14.4.1, 14.4.2, 14.5,** 15.0,
15.1, 15.2, 15.2.1, 15.2.2,
15.3, 15.3.1, 15.3.7, 15.4,
15.5, 15.6, 15.6.1, 15.7,
15.8, 15.8.1, 15.9, 16.0,
16.1, 16.1.1, 16.2, 16.3,
16.3.3, 16.4, 17.0, 17.1.1,
17.2, 17.3.1, 18.0, 18.1,
18.1.1, 18.2, 18.4.3,
18.4.6, 18.5, 18.6, 19.0,
19.1, 19.1.1, 19.1.2, 19.2,
19.2.7, 19.3.5, 19.3.10,
19.5, 21.1.1, 25.6, 33.1,
33.6.1, 33.7, 33.7.1,
33.7.2, 34.0, 34.4, 34.5,
34.5.1, 34.5.2, 34.5.3,
34.6, 34.6.1, 34.6.2,
34.6.3, 34.7, 34.7.1,
34.8.2, 35.3, 35.5, 35.8,
Prf
aquarium 11.6.2
ar 15.2.6, 16.3.3, 34.5.5
arbitrarily 12.3
arbitrary A.8, 4.2, 6.3.4, 6.5.3, 11.4.7,
11.6.1, 19.3.2, 25.6, 32.7,
34.1, 34.5.5
arc 11.4.4
Architecture 2.1, 14.3
Archive 12, 12.1.1, 12.3, 13.6
arcs 11.1, 11.4
area A.4.5, A.4.6, B.3, B.5.6, D.2, 0.4,
1.2, 1.3, 3.1, 3.3, 5.1, 5.3,
7.4, 8.1, 9.1, 9.2, 9.5,
11.2, 11.3, 11.4.6, 11.4.7,
11.4.8, 11.5.3, 11.5.5,
11.6.1, 11.6.2, 11.6.3,
12.3, 15.5, 15.5.4, 15.7,
15.8.1, 15.8.2, 18.4.5,
25.1, 25.6, 26.4, 27.1,
29.0, 29.1, 29.3, 29.4,
32.6, 33.2.2, 33.3, 34.1,
34.2, 34.5.2, 34.6.7, Prf
areas B.3, B.8.1, C.1, 1.2, 1.3, 3.4, 5.1,
5.3, 5.4, 6.4, 11.5.3,
11.5.5, 18.1.8, 22.0, 29.0,
34.6.5, 34.8.2, Prf
aren A.5, 23.6
argument 13.3, 20.3, 20.4, 25.6, 26.1,
26.3, 31.2, 32.1, 32.4
arguments 20.3, 20.4, 25.7, 26.1, 32.4,
32.5
arial 3.5, 11.4.6, 11.6.3, 18.5.5
arise A.1, A.7.1, C.1, 3.3, 11.5.4, 18.6,
35.2, 35.8
arises 0.0, 15.8.3, 33.3
arm D.3, D.4
arose A.1.1
around A.3.1, A.3.2, A.4.2, A.5.2, D.2,
D.3, 0.1, 1.2, 2.3, 4.7,
11.4.3, 13.2, 15.2.2,

15.5.6, 15.5.7, 15.8.4,
16.4, 17.0, 19.2, 25.6,
27.0, 29.3, 31.4, 32.5,
33.7.2, 34.5.7
arrange B.5.6, 6.6.5, 15.7.5
arranged 1.1, 1.3, 2.2, 3.0, 5.1, 11.1,
17.0, 35.7
arrangement B.5.6, B.5.7, 3.3, 4.4,
11.6.1, 14.3, 14.4.4,
17.1.2, 35.7
arranging A.3.1, 20.8
array A.1.1, A.2.10, A.3.2, A.4.2, A.4.3,
A.4.4, A.4.5, A.5.1, A.5.2,
A.7, D.2, 8.2, 9.2, 9.3,
11.4.5, 11.4.8, 11.5.3,
11.5.5, 12, 12.1.2, 12.2,
12.3, 13.2, 13.3, 13.4,
13.5, 14.4.4, 15.2.6,
15.2.8, 15.3, 15.3.1,
15.3.2, 15.6.3, 15.6.7,
18.0, 18.1.12, 18.2,
18.4.2, 18.4.4, 18.4.6,
18.4.7, 26.2, 26.3, 34.6.5,
34.6.9, 35.8
array_u 13.5
arrays A.2.10, A.3.2, A.7.1, 0.4, 11.4.5,
12, 12.1.2, 12.1.3, 12.2,
12.3
arrival 35.7
arrive 35.1
arrives 4.7, 10.3, 11.4.6, 35.7
arrow 9.3, 9.5, 10.2, 11.5.3, 19.1.2,
19.3.5, 20.2, 33.7.4
arrows 4.6, 15.5.4
article 14.4.4, 33.3
articles C.1, 33.9
artistic 18.4.5
ASC 33.2.3
ascending 33.2.3
ASCII 6.5.3, 16.2
ask A.1.1, A.3.2, C.0, D.1, 7.2, 13.4,
15.7.3, 15.7.9, 16.2,
18.4.2, 33.2, 34.1, 34.2,
34.4, 34.5.3
asked A.3.2, 33.6.2, 34.2
asking B.7.3, 7.6, 8.5, 10.4.9, 15.2.9,
15.7.10, 16.3, 16.3.6,
33.6.2, Prf
asks 15.3.5, 18.5.1, 33.2, 34.2, 34.5.5,
34.6.8
aspect 11.6.2, 25.2, 26.5
aspects 0.2, 2.1, 5.2, 20.8
assemblies 34.3
assembling A.1.1
ASSERT 0.4, 12.2, 13.2
ASSERT_VALID 13.2
ASSERTed 13.2
assertion 13.2, 20.6, 23.0, 23.1, 23.2,
25.6
assertions B.2, 13.2
asserts 12.4
AssertValid 13.2, 14.4.4, 15.2.6, 15.3,
15.6.2, 15.6.8, 17.4.7,
18.1.12, 18.2
assign 14.4.6, 15.7.8, 22.5, 35.1
assigned A.2.11, B.5.2, 6.1, 6.4, 12.1.2,
15.7.2, 22.5
assigning 13.5
assignment A.4.4, A.4.6, A.7, A.7.1,
12.1.4, 12.3, 12.4, 33.7.2

assigns 16.2
assistance 34.1
assisted Prf
associate 6.5.3, 10.5, 12.5, 15.2.1,
15.8.4, 19.2, 19.3.4, 22.5,
23.4, 23.5, 23.8, 25.8,
28.1, 29.1
associated B.7.1, D.0, D.1, 6.1, 10.5,
11.3, 11.6.2, 12.1.1, 12.5,
13.5, 13.6, 14.3, 15.4,
16.2, 18.1.10, 18.4.3,
18.4.5, 19.2.3, 19.2.7,
19.4, 20.3, 22.0, 22.1,
22.2, 22.5, 23.1, 23.3,
23.4, 23.5, 23.7, 25.2,
25.7, 26.2, 26.4, 28.1,
30.1, 33.1, 34.4, 35.4,
35.7
associates 12.5, 18.1, 22.2, 24.2
association 12.5, 19.3.5, 22.2, 23.4,
23.5
associations 12.5, 22.5, 23.5
assortment 11.1, 22.0
assume A.1, A.3.2, 6.4, 26.2, 26.3
assumed 11.5.5, 13.2
assumes D.1, 5.2, 13.2, 16.5, 22.4,
33.6.2
assuming 22.0, 33.4.1
assumption A.7.2, 13.2, 14.3, 18.1.9,
33.0, 33.1
assumptions 13.2
assurance C.1
Asterisk 10.2
asynchronous 33.5
ATA_DELETE 18.4.5
attach A.1, A.4.5, 0.3, 11.6.3, 23.4,
23.6, 23.7, 23.8, 33.6.4,
33.7.3
attached 4.6, 11.1, 11.3, 11.4.3, 11.4.6,
11.6.1, 11.6.2, 17.4.4,
23.4, 23.8, 30.1, 34.3
attaches 12.3
attaching 11.4.3, 11.6.2, 23.8
attachment 11.6.3
attack A.3.2
attempt A.6, 0.2, 7.2, 12.1.1, 12.2,
13.6, 15.3.1, 16.4
attempting 13.6
attempts D.7, 12.1.1, 13.6, 35.4
attention A.8, 0.3, 7.6, 9.4, 12.3, 13.3,
14.4.5, 25.6, Prf
attractive D.0
attractively 4.4
attribute 2.3.2, 3.2, 3.3, 3.4, 5.4, 6.2,
12.1.1, 15.2.6, 15.5.1,
15.6.3, 15.6.5, 15.8.2,
18.5.2, 32.5, 34.5.5,
34.6.5
attributes A.3.1, 2.3.2, 2.3.3, 3.2, 3.3,
4.0, 4.2, 5.2, 5.3, 9.1,
11.3, 11.4.6, 14.4.4,
15.2.6, 15.5.1, 15.6.3,
15.6.5, 17.4.1, 18.1.12,
18.4.2, 26.1, 32.5, 34.8,
35.5, 35.7
Audience Prf
auditing C.1
augmented 9.3
Auot 34.7.6
aura A.1

author A.8
authors C.1, Prf
Auto 20.1, 34.7.1, 34.7.6, 34.7.7, 35.4,
35.8
automated C.0, 6.1, 34.1
automates 6.5, 6.5.1, 23.7
automatic A.6, 2.3, 5.1, 6.3.7, 10.5,
12.3, 14.1, 15.8.1, 16.2,
18.3, 18.4.6, 28.1
Automation B.6.6, B.8.5, B.8.6, B.8.7,
0.4, 13.6, 34.1, 34.4,
34.5.1, 34.6.1, 34.7,
34.7.1, 34.7.3, 34.7.4,
34.7.7, 34.7.8, 34.7.9,
34.8.4, 34.8.5, 34.8.6,
34.9
auxiliary 28.3
availability 22.0
avoid A.2.3, A.2.9, A.4.2, 3.1, 10.5,
11.6.2, 12.4, 15.8.2, 32.4
avoids 16.5
await 35.7
awaken 35.1
aware B.6.6, B.7.6, 8.0, 14.0, 14.4.1,
15.3, 15.5.6, 15.8.4, 15.9,
16.2, 34.2, 34.7, 34.7.2
away 11.5.4, 11.5.5, 11.6.2, 27.1, 30.1
awhile A.5.2, A.7
axes 11.6.1
axis 11.6.1, 15.8.3
babbling Prf
back A.1, A.2, A.3, A.8, B.3.1, D.5,
D.6, 1.3, 5.3, 6, 6.4, 6.5.1,
6.6.8, 7.2, 7.6, 8.6.1,
8.6.2, 8.6.3, 11.4.5,
11.5.3, 11.5.4, 11.5.5,
11.6.1, 12.3, 13.4, 14.0,
14.4.5, 15.2.1, 15.2.7,
15.5.5, 15.5.6, 16.3.1,
16.3.5, 17.2, 17.3.4, 17.4,
18.1, 18.4.4, 25.5, 29.2,
32.6, 33.1, 33.3, 33.6.2,
33.7.6, 34.2, 34.4, 34.8,
35.1, 35.5, 35.7
BackColor 34.8.4
background D.5, 0.4, 3.4, 7.4, 10.3,
10.5, 11.3, 11.4.8, 11.5.3,
11.5.4, 11.6.2, 15.3.8,
25.6, 25.7, 29.0, 29.1,
29.2, 29.3, 29.4, 34.8,
34.8.4, 34.8.11, 35.1,
35.2, 35.3, 35.7, 35.9
backgrounds 0.1, 3.2, Prf
backing 11.5.3
backward 8.7, 15.8.1, 33.7.5
balance 5.4
ball A.3.2
band 11.5.4
banded 0.4, 11.5.4, 11.6.2, 15.9
banding 11.5.4, 11.5.5, 11.6.2, 15.1
bank 17.4
barrier A.3.2
Baseline 11.4.6
basic A.1, A.2.3, B.1, D.0, D.2, D.8,
0.1, 0.4, 1.2, 1.3, 2.1, 3.0,
5.0, 5.1, 9.1, 11.4.1,
11.5.4, 12.2, 13.2, 13.3,
15.5, 15.9, 17.0, 19.1,
19.5, 21, 21.1, 33.0,
33.8.4, 34.0, 34.1, 34.4,

34.5.3, 34.6.3, 34.7,
34.7.7, 34.8, 34.8.1, 35.2
Basically A.3.2
Basics 1.5, 10.7, 11.0, Prf
basis 4.6, 4.7, 5.4, 11.4.6, 19.3.5, 24.0,
33.2.3, 34.2
BAT 19.1.1, 19.1.2, 19.3, 19.3.5,
19.3.7, 19.3.8
batch 19.1.1, 19.2.2, 19.2.4, 19.2.6,
19.2.8, 19.2.10, 19.3.5,
19.3.7, 19.3.8, 19.3.10
BBM_GETSTATE 23.1
BBS 35.2
Beam 10.2
bear 5.1
bearings 0.0, Prf
beauty 34.1
became D.0
become A.1, A.3.1, A.8.1, B.1, B.2,
B.3, B.4, 0.0, 0.1, 0.2, 2.1,
3.3, 6.7, 10, 17.5, 19.5,
20.7, 20.8, 25.7, 28.1,
30.2, 32.1, 32.5, 33.1,
34.1, 34.3, 35.0
becomes 1.3, 4.1, 6.4, 11.2, 11.4.1,
15.6, 16.3, 16.4, 20.4,
20.7, 23.2, 23.5, 25.1,
27.0, 30.1, 31.1, 31.2,
31.4, 32.5, 34.2, 34.4,
35.7, 35.8
becoming D.0, 34.0
Beep 4.3, 4.5, 4.6, 9.3, 24.0, 24.1,
34.7.7, 34.7.9, 35.3
beepDisp 34.7.7
Beeper 34.7.3, 34.7.4, 34.7.6, 34.7.7,
34.7.8
beeping 4.5, 35.4
beeps 4.3, 4.5, 24.1, 35.3
BeepSamp 34.7.4
begin A.1, A.2.2, A.3.1, A.4.1, A.5.2,
B.1.1, B.2, B.2.2, B.3, B.4,
B.5.5, C.1, D.3, D.7, 0.0,
0.1, 0.2, 1.1, 1.4, 2.3, 5.1,
6.4, 11.5.4, 11.6.2, 14.0,
14.1, 14.5, 19.1, 26.2,
29.1, 33.6, 34.1, 34.2,
34.5.4, Prf
BEGIN_MESSAGE_MAP 4.3, 4.7
BEGIN_PROPPAGEIDS 34.8.11
beginning A.3.2, A.5.2, B.2, B.6, B.6.1,
D.1, D.6, D.7, 0.1, 0.4,
3.3, 4.4, 8.2, 12.1.2,
12.1.3, 12.4, 14.1, 14.4.4,
18.1.15, 18.4.7, 19.2.7,
19.5, 28.0, 33.1, 34.5.3,
34.6.3
BeginPaint 11.4.1
begins A.4.1, B.7.1, 2.3, 8.6.2, 10.3,
11.5.4, 14.4.4, 22.5, 22.6,
27.1, 33.6.4, 35.7
BeginWaitCursor 10.2
behave 2.1, 7.3, 8.6, 13.2, 20.3, 30.0
behaves A.8, 17.3.5, 30.0, 32.5
behaving 34.5.5
behaviors B.1.3, 8.2, 9.1, 10.4.10,
34.5.3
behind A.4.2, 0.4, 1.0, 4.1, 5.1, 8.3,
9.1, 12.4, 13.2, 22.1, 23.1,
23.9, 30.0, 33.0, 33.5,
33.6.11, 34.4, 35.2, Prf

believes D.5
bell 17.2
belongs A.4.6, 2.3.3, 12.4, 34.5.5
beneficial B.3, 8.5
benefits A.1.1, A.5, 12.3, 26.0
benign 34.8.3
beside 11.5.5
besides 10.5, 34.6.3
best A.3.2, B.2, 0.3, 1.4, 2.1, 2.3, 3.3,
5.1, 5.4, 11.4.6, 12.2,
12.4, 13.2, 14.4, 15.5,
15.5.2, 15.7.9, 15.8, 16.3,
17.0, 18.4.2, 18.5.2, 19.1,
19.3.5, 23.9, 33.3, 34.1,
34.8.1, 35.2
bets 11.4.6
better A.2, A.3.2, A.4.2, B.1.3, D.7,
5.1, 10.3, 10.5, 15.3.3,
15.9, 18.1, 19.3, 20.0,
20.7, 23.0, 25.4, 32.8,
34.1, 34.6.10
beyond D.5, 8.1, 34.8
bFindDialogOnly 7.6
bFlag 2.3
big A.3.2, A.4.3, 1.1, 3.3, 11.3, 11.4.6,
11.6.1, 11.6.2, 13.5, 15.5,
15.8.4, 19.2, 19.4, 34.5.5,
34.6.8, 35.2
bigger 11.4.6, 12.2
billing 33.2
billion 13.6
bin 13.3, 34.7.7
binary A.4.2, 0.4, 6.1, 12, 12.1.1, 12.3,
12.4, 16.5, 35.6
bind A.3.2, A.3.3
biographical A.3.1
bItalic 11.4.6
BitBlt 11.4.7, 11.6.2, 25.7, 29.2
bitblts 11.6.2
bite D.1
bitmap B.5.3, B.5.4, D.1, D.2, 0.4, 6.1,
6.3, 11.3, 11.4.3, 11.6.2,
18.4.5, 19.2.9, 19.2.10,
25.0, 25.6, 25.7, 26.4,
27.0, 27.2, 29.0, 29.2,
29.3, 29.4, 34.1
bitmapped 0.1, 29.3
bitmaps 0.4, 6, 11.1, 11.6.2, 19.1.1,
19.2, 19.2.9, 19.5, 23.6,
25.0, 25.6, 25.7, 25.8,
25.9, 26.4, 29.1, 34.1, Prf
bits D.1, D.7, 11.4.7, 11.6.2, 11.7,
12.1.1, 34.5.5
bizarre 4.7
Bjarne A.1
bKill 35.4
black D.2, 3.1, 3.4, 11.3, 11.4.2,
11.4.7, 11.5.2, 11.5.4,
25.7, 29.1
blacked 25.7
blank A.2.3, 6.4, 6.5.3, 6.7.2, 8.6.1,
11.4.1, 16.5, 19.2.3, 27.1,
34.7.2, 34.8.12
blanks A.2.4, 14.4.4, 19.1.2
blend A.1.1
blended 3.3
blitting 25.7
blob A.3.2
block A.2.6, A.2.10, 8.2, 8.6.2, 8.6.7,
11.4.6, 11.6.2, 12.1.1,

12.1.2, 12.2, 13.2, 13.5,
13.6, 13.6.1, 13.7, 18.4.7
blocks A.2.10, A.7, A.7.2, 1.2, 8.2,
12.1.1, 12.4, 13.5, 13.6.1,
35.4
blown 0.1
Blue D.1, D.2, D.6, D.8, 7.4, 11.4.2,
11.4.6, 11.5.2, 35.7
BlueSurface D.6
bmc 19.2.9
BMP 19.2.9
BN_CLICKED 17.3.4, 25.0, 25.5
boards C.0
body C.0, 19.2.7, 33.7.2
bogging 15.1
boilerplate 2.1, 34.2
bold 3.5, 11.4.6, 15.8.4, 26.1, 26.3
boldface 4.3
bonded A.3.1, A.4.2
bonds 10, 10.4.10, 16.3
bonus A.5, 15.8.4
book A.1, A.3.1, A.6, B, B.3.2, B.5,
B.6, B.6.1, B.7, C.0, C.1,
D.8, 0.0, 0.1, 0.2, 0.3, 0.4,
1.1, 1.3, 1.4, 1.5, 2.3,
2.3.2, 3.0, 5.2, 6.2, 10,
10.4, 10.4.10, 10.5, 11.7,
12.6, 13.3, 16.5, 17.3,
17.6, 18.4.7, 18.5.6, 20.6,
22.0, 23.0, 31.0, 32.0,
33.1, 33.9, 34.0, 34.8.1,
34.8.7, 34.9, 35.0, 35.9,
Prf
books A.1, A.1.1, A.3.1, B.4, B.6.2,
B.9, C.1, D.5, D.8, 0.1,
0.2, 1.1, 12.2, 13.6.2,
14.4.4, 15.2.6, 15.8.2,
18.5.6, 19.0, 19.3.5,
19.3.6, 25.7, 33.4, 33.8.4,
33.9, 34.5.5, 34.8.1
bookstore A.1
BOOL 2.3, 7.2, 7.3, 7.4, 7.5, 7.6,
11.4.4, 11.4.6, 21.1.5,
22.2, 22.3, 22.5
Boolean 2.3, 7.2, 7.3, 8.6.1, 10.3,
11.5.2, 11.5.4, 13.2, 13.5,
18.4.3, 18.4.4, 18.4.6,
18.5.6, 22.1, 25.7, 29.1,
35.4, 35.5
bootstrap 34.9
bOpenFileDialog 7.2
border 3.1, 3.2, 3.3, 3.4, 5.2, 11.4.3,
11.4.7, 11.5.2, 20.6, 30.1,
32.5, 34.8
borders 9.1, 27.0
boring 27.2, 29.2
borrowed 19.2
borrows 11.5.4
bothersome 6, 12.2, 15.6
bottom B.1.6, B.2, B.3, B.4.1, B.5.6,
B.8.4, 4.6, 5.3, 5.4, 8.6.1,
8.6.10, 9.1, 9.3, 11.1,
11.4.1, 11.4.3, 11.4.6,
12.1.4, 12.2, 13.2, 13.4,
14.4.2, 15.2.6, 15.3.6,
15.5.5, 15.6.3, 15.7.9,
19.2, 19.2.3, 19.2.4,
19.2.7, 19.3.1, 19.3.4,
19.3.5, 30.0, 33.6.10,
33.8.1, 34.6.3, 34.6.5,

34.8.4
bottommost 32.2
BottomRight 12.1.4
bought A.5
bounces 13.6.1
bound A.4.2, A.4.3, 34.3, 35.7
boundaries 11.4.6, 12.2, 15.7.9, 22.5, 23.0
boundary 12.2, 13.5
bounding 3.3, 5.3, 11.4.6
bounds 11.4.4, 12.2
bPrintSetupOnly 7.5
brace A.2.6
braces 13.5
bracket 33.1
Brain 10.5, 13.5, 35.0, Prf
branches 25.6
breadth 11.1
break A.1.1, A.3.1, A.3.2, A.4.2, A.7.2, B.2, B.2.1, 11.2, 11.4.6, 19.2, 19.2.7, 35.1, 35.2, 35.3
breaking 15.7.9, 35.2
breakpoint B.2.1, B.2.2
breakpoints B.2, B.2.1, 35.3
breaks A.2.3, A.4.1, B.4.4, 2.3.1, 8.2, 33.1, 35.1, 35.2
brief A.1, 0.1, 14.4, 35.7
Briefly A.1.1, 2.2, 3.2, 7.6, 11.4.6, 12.1.4, 13.3, 13.7, 23.0, 25.7, 33.5, 34.8.2
bring 5.1, 10.4.10, 14.1, 15.6.1
brings B.6.1, 9.4, 12.3, 14.4.1
broadly 12.3
broken A.1.1, 2.1, 11.1, 11.6.3, Prf
Browse B.3.1, B.4, B.4.1, 2.3.1, 8.2, 19.2, Prf
browser B, B.4, B.4.1, B.4.2, 0.4, 1.5, 10.4.10, 14.3, 17.5
browsing 4.4, 8.2, 11.4.8
Brush 11.3, 11.4.3, 11.4.6, 11.4.7, 11.4.8, 11.5.2, 15.8.3, 25.7, 29.2, 29.3, 29.4, 34.8.4
brushes 11.1, 11.4.6, 23.6, 26.1, 34.8.4
brute 34.1
BS 4.2
BS_PUSHBUTTON 4.2
bSaveAndValidate 22.3
BSC B.4
BTrieve 33.3
bubbling 12.2
buddy 20.1, 20.2
buffer A.2.3, D.1, D.2, D.5, D.7, 8.6.1, 12.1.2
buffered A.2.3, D.1
buffering D.0, D.1, D.4, D.5, D.6, D.7
buffers D.1, D.5
bug A.1.1, A.5, 8.7, 13.0
bugs A.1.1, 8.7, 12.2
build A.3.3, A.5.2, A.5.3, B.1, B.1.2, B.1.5, B.1.6, B.2, B.2.1, B.3, B.4, B.6.1, B.8.1, D.1, 3.0, 3.2, 5.5, 6.1, 6.3.7, 6.4, 6.5, 6.5.1, 6.6.7, 8.3, 13.1, 13.2, 13.3, 14.1, 14.2, 14.4, 14.4.1, 14.5, 19.1.2, 19.3.5, 33.4, 34.8.3, 35.10, Prf

building A.4.5, B.2, 11.5.5, 13.3, 14.0, 14.1, 15.8.1, 33.2.2
builds C.1, 14.0
built A.1.1, A.2.3, A.2.4, A.3.1, A.3.2, A.5, B.3.2, 0.4, 5.1, 8.3, 8.6.7, 9.0, 10.4, 10.5, 11.4.8, 12.3, 12.6, 13.0, 13.1, 13.5, 13.6.2, 14.3, 14.4.6, 15.3, 15.3.1, 15.8, 15.9, 16.2, 16.3, 18.1.15, 19.1.2, 33.7.5, 34.5.4, 34.8, 35.2, Prf
builtin 11.7
bulk 1.1, 34.1
bulletin C.0
bUnderline 11.4.6
business 18.1, 33.2.5
busy 10.2
buttons A.8, B.3, B.5.6, B.6.6, 1.1, 1.2, 1.3, 2.1, 4.6, 4.7, 5.1, 5.2, 6.5, 6.6.4, 7.1, 7.3, 7.6, 8.5, 8.6.7, 11.4.3, 11.5.1, 11.5.2, 15.8.4, 18.4.3, 18.4.5, 18.5.6, 19.1.2, 20.1, 20.2, 20.7, 22.0, 22.2, 22.5, 23.1, 25.0, 27.1, 30.0, 30.1, 31.0, 31.1, 32.4, 32.5, 34.8, Prf
buying B, Prf
bypass 7.5
byte 12.1.1, 12.3, 16.2, 22.2, 22.5, 35.5
bytes A.4.4, 12.1.1, 13.5, 13.6
C_FORM 17.1.2
cache 34.6.5
cached 23.5, 34.6.9
cachedPictColors 34.6.5
caches 11.3
CAD 11.1
CAddDlg 18.1.9
CAddrDoc 18.4.7
CAddrRec 18.2
CAddrView 18.1.1, 18.1.5, 18.4.2
CAdjCtrl B.8.5, 34.8.4, 34.8.7
Cairo 34.1
CalcColor 34.6.5
calculate 5.1, 5.4, 11.4.6, 15.8.4, 18.5.6, 34.6.5, 34.6.6
calculates A.6, 5.3, 5.4, 11.4.4, 11.4.6, 12.1.3, 18.5.6
calculation A.6, 10.2, 15.8.4, 34.6.7, 35.8
calculations 15.5.6
calculator 5.0, 5.1, 5.2, 5.4, 6
CalcWindowRect 32.5
callback 20.3, 26.1, 26.2, 26.3
caller B.2, B.2.2, B.4, B.4.4, 11.6.3
cAlphaBits D.1
cAlphaShift D.1
came A.5.2, 5.2, 20.0, 34.2
camera D.6
CanAppend 33.5
Cancel B.5.6, 6.6.4, 7.1, 7.2, 7.6, 8.5, 8.6.1, 8.6.7, 12.1.1, 18.1.10, 20.7, 27.1, 28.2, 32.4, 33.5
canceled 18.4.2
cancelled 20.7
cancels 7.6, 33.5
CancelToClose 20.7

CanCloseFrame 15.3.5
CAnimateCtrl 20.0
canned 6.6.8, 7.0, 7.1, 7.2, 8.0, 8.3, 8.5, Prf
cannon A.3.2
cannot A.1.1, A.2.7, A.3.2, A.4.3, A.5.1, A.6, A.7.1, A.8, B.2, D.1, 4.2, 4.3, 5.2, 6.4, 6.5.2, 7.1, 8.6.2, 9.5, 11.5.1, 11.5.4, 11.6.2, 12.1.2, 13.6, 15.5, 18.1.2, 20.7, 22.5, 23.2, 25.6, 28.1, 30.2, 32.4, 32.5, 34.1, 34.5.2, 34.5.5, 35.2, 35.3, 35.8
CanRestart 33.5
CanScroll 33.5
CanTransact 33.5
CanUndo 8.2
CanUpdate 33.5
capabilities A.2.3, A.2.5, A.3.2, A.5.2, 2.1, 3.3, 3.6, 7.6, 8.0, 8.7, 9.5, 10, 10.4.9, 10.7, 11.0, 11.1, 11.3, 11.4.1, 11.4.6, 11.6, 12.1.2, 12.2, 12.3, 13.0, 13.5, 14.1, 14.5, 15.0, 15.1, 15.4, 15.6.1, 15.8.1, 15.8.2, 15.9, 16.2, 18.4, 18.5.1, 19.5, 22.6, 23.8, 33.7.5, 34.0, 34.1, 34.2, 34.3, 34.5.3, 34.5.4, 34.5.7, 34.8.2, 35.0, Prf
capability A.2.8, A.2.9, A.3, A.3.2, A.5.1, 4.5, 4.8, 10.5, 11.5.5, 11.6.1, 12, 12.1.2, 13.5, 15.5.3, 15.6, 15.6.7, 15.8.1, 16.2, 16.3, 16.6, 18.4.3, 25.4, 26.0, 31.2, 33.7.4, 33.7.6, 34.1, 34.2, 34.7.1, 35.1, 35.2, 35.4
capable 4.4, 9.3, 9.5, 16.3, 19.2.1, 34.5.2, 35.2, Prf
capitalization 6.4
CApp 5.2, 13.2
caps 18.4.6
caption 1.2, 6.4, 6.5.2, 6.5.3, 6.7.2, 10.4.6, 10.5, 13.4, 15.7.5, 28.1, 32.5
captions B.6.1, 6.5.2, 15.7.5, 20.6
capture 24.1
captured 13.6.1
capturing 11.5.4
CArchive 12, 12.1.2, 12.1.3, 12.3, 16.3.3, 17.4.1, 17.4.3, 34.5.5
CArchiveException 12, 13.6
card Prf
care 15.3, 20.7, 22.0, 22.6, 25.1, 25.2, 25.5, 34.2
career 5.2
careful A.4.4, 18.4.3, 20.8, 32.4, 34.5.5
carefully 13.5
careless 35.2
CArray 12.2, 12.3
carriage 11.4.6
carried D.2
carry A.5.2
Cartesian 11.6.1
cast A.2.2, A.2.3, A.8, 11.5.3
casting A.8

catastrophically A.1.1, 33.6.5
catch 10.6, 12, 13.1, 13.6, 13.6.1, 25.7
catches 13.6
catching 13.2, 13.6, 13.6.1
categories A.1.2, A.3.1, 2.1, 6.1, 9.0,
    12.1.1, 15.2.2, 34.8
category A.1.2, B.7.5, B.7.7, 5.1, 6.1,
    12.3, 17.3.3, 18.1.4,
    18.1.9, 34.8.12
cater 28.0
caught 13.6, 13.6.1
cause A.1.1, A.2.3, B.3.1, B.3.2, 4.5,
    6.6.2, 11.4.1, 11.6.2,
    13.5, 15.4, 16.3.3,
    18.1.10, 19.3.5, 28.1,
    32.5, 35.2, 35.4, 35.7
caused B.3.1, 13.2, 17.3.4, 18.2, 29.2,
    34.5.6, 35.4
causes A.8, D.2, 2.3, 3.3, 4.6, 7.4, 7.5,
    8.1, 8.2, 8.6.10, 9.2, 10.5,
    11.4.6, 11.5.2, 11.5.4,
    11.6.1, 13.1, 13.3, 13.5,
    13.6.1, 15.2.7, 15.2.8,
    15.3, 15.7.9, 15.8, 15.8.3,
    16.4, 17.3.4, 17.4.4, 18.6,
    27.1, 29.2, 33.2.3, 34.7.7
causing D.3, 2.3, 13.1, 32.5, 35.4
caution 7.1
CBBVIEW 33.6.3
CBitmap 11.4.3, 29.4
CBitmapButton 25.3, 25.9
cBlueBits D.1
cBlueShift D.1
CBRS_BOTTOM 30.1
CBRS_FLYBY 30.1
CBRS_LEFT 30.1
CBRS_RIGHT 30.1
CBRS_TOOLTIPS 30.1
CBRS_TOP 30.1
CBrush 11.4.3
CBS_DROPDOWN 9.5
CBS_DROPDOWNLIST 9.5
CBS_OWNERDRAWVARIABLE
    25.6
CBS_SIMPLE 9.5
CBTEXT 18.4.7
CButton 3.0, 4.0, 4.2, 4.3, 4.4, 5.1, 5.2,
    22.2, 23.1, 23.5, 25.3,
    25.5, 34.8
CButtonWindow 4.3, 4.4
CByteArray 12.2
CC_FULLOPEN 7.4
CC_PREVENTFULLOPEN 7.4
CC_RGBINIT 7.4
CC_SHOWHELP 7.4
CCheckListBox 25.3
CChildFrame 15.6.1, 21.1.3
cClass 17.1.3
CClientDC 11.4.1, 11.4.6, 15.2.3,
    34.6.8
CCmdTarget 10.2, 34.7.3
CCmdUI 6.5.1, 8.6.10, 31.1
cColorBits D.1
CColorDialog 7.4
CComboBox 3.0, 22.2, 25.3, 25.6
CControlBar 30.0, 31.1
CD 0.0, 0.1, 0.2, 0.3, 20.0, 34.9, Prf
CD_TEXT 8.6.10
CDaoRecordset 22.2
CDatabase 33.5, 33.9

CDataExchange 22.3, 22.4, 22.6
CDBException 13.6, 33.6.5
CDbView 33.6.3, 33.7.4, 33.8.2,
    33.8.3
CDC 7.3, 11.3, 11.4.1, 11.4.3, 11.4.4,
    11.4.6, 11.4.7, 11.4.8,
    11.5.4, 11.6.1, 11.6.2,
    11.6.3, 23.6, 25.6, 29.1
cDepthBits D.7
CDialog 2.1, 6, 6.6, 6.6.8, 15.0, 15.7.6,
    17.3.4, 20.5, 20.6, 22.1,
    22.5, 23.1, 23.3, 25.4,
    27.1, 28.1, 28.2, 30.2,
    31.6, 32.4, 32.5
CDialogBar 30.0, 30.1, 30.2
CDialogderived 6.6
CDK 34.8.1
CDlg 34.6.5
CDOC 17.4.1
CDocTemplate 10.4.6, 15.1, 16.3,
    16.3.5
CDocument B.7.2, 12.3, 14.3, 14.4.4,
    15.3, 15.3.1, 15.3.2,
    15.3.3, 15.3.4, 15.3.5,
    15.4, 15.5.3, 15.6.7, 15.9,
    16.3.2, 25.0, 34.5.3,
    34.6.3
CDotsView 35.7
CDrawDoc 15.2.6, 15.3.2, 15.5.2,
    15.5.3, 15.6.3, 15.6.4,
    15.6.7, 15.7.7, 16.4
CDrawView 15.2.7, 15.2.8, 15.4.1,
    15.4.2, 15.5, 15.5.4,
    15.5.6, 15.6.1, 15.6.9,
    15.6.10, 15.6.11, 15.6.12
CDumpContext 12
CDWordArray 12, 12.2
ceases A.2.6
CEdit 0.4, 3.0, 5.2, 5.3, 5.4, 6.6.5,
    6.6.7, 6.6.8, 8.0, 8.1, 8.2,
    8.3, 8.4, 8.6.6, 9.0, 9.1,
    10.4, 16.2, 17.1, 17.1.2,
    17.1.3, 18.1.9, 18.3, 22.2,
    23.1, 24.0, 24.1, 25.8
CEditView 8.0, 8.3, 8.7, 10.4, 10.4.10,
    16.0, 16.1.1, 16.2, 16.3.2
CEditWindow 8.6.1, 8.6.2
CEdView 16.1.1
cells 34.1
Celsius 1.3, 5.0, 5.1, 5.2, 17.0, 17.1,
    17.1.3, 17.1.4, 17.2,
    17.3.4, 17.3.5, 17.5
CEmpSet 33.6.2, 33.6.4
center 3.2, 3.3, 8.1, 32.6
centered 2.3.3, 3.3, 11.4.6, 27.1, 32.5
centering 11.6.1
centers 27.1
CenterWindow 27.1, 32.5
central A.1.1, 1.5, 8.6.10, 10, 10.7,
    34.8.1, 35.2
centric 14.3, 14.4
century 12.1.3
cerr A.2.3
certain A.1, A.1.1, A.2.3, A.3.1, A.7.2,
    A.8, A.8.1, B.1.3, B.3, 3.1,
    3.5, 10.3, 10.4, 11.3,
    11.4.7, 12.1.1, 13.4, 13.6,
    15.3, 15.8.4, 16.2, 22.0,
    22.4, 23.1, 26.1, 26.3,
    32.6, 33.2, 33.3, 34.1,

    34.2, 34.3, 34.8, 35.1,
    35.2, 35.7
certified A.5
CException 12, 13.6.2
CExpandingDialog 28.1, 28.2
CExpListView 21.1.2, 21.1.5, 21.1.8
CExpTreeView 21.1.1, 21.1.5, 21.1.6,
    21.1.8
CF 13.4, 17.1.1, 17.1.3
CF_ANSIONLY 7.3
CF_APPLY 7.3
CF_BOTH 7.3
CF_EFFECTS 7.3
CF_FIXEDPITCHONLY 7.3
CF_FORCEFONTEXIST 7.3
CF_INITTOLOGFONTSTRUCT
    7.3
CF_LIMITSIZE 7.3
CF_NOFACESEL 7.3
CF_NOOEMFONTS 7.3
CF_NOSIMULATIONS 7.3
CF_NOSIZESEL 7.3
CF_NOSTYLESEL 7.3
CF_NOVECTORFONTS 7.3
CF_PRINTERFONTS 7.3
CF_SCALABLEONLY 7.3
CF_SCREENFONTS 7.3
CF_SHOWHELP 7.3
CF_TTONLY 7.3
CF_USESTYLE 7.3
CF_WYSIWYG 7.3
CFile 8.6.2, 12, 12.1.1, 12.3, 13.6,
    13.6.2
CFileDialog 7.2, 12.1.1
CFileException 12, 12.1.1, 12.5, 13.6
CFileStatus 12.1.1
CFindDialog 7.6
CFindNameDialog 32.4, 32.5
CFindReplaceDialog 7.6
CFont 3.5, 11.4.6
CFontDialog 7.3
CFontListBox 26.4
CFormView 16.1.1, 17.0, 17.1.1,
    18.1.1, 18.2, 24.3, 31.2
CFrameWnd B.4.6, 2.1, 2.3, 2.3.2,
    2.3.3, 2.5, 3.3, 4.4, 5.2,
    6.5, 11.4.1, 11.5.3, 13.4,
    14.4.3, 23.1, 23.2, 31.1,
    32.1, 32.5
CGdiObject 23.5, 23.6
cGreenBits D.1
cGreenShift D.1
ch 13.5
chain A.1.1, A.3.2, A.7, 3.3, 7.2,
    15.3.1, 15.3.3
chance 8.6.11, 18.4, 18.6, 22.0, 29.3
chances 14.1
Chang 17.1.1
changing A.1.1, A.4.2, A.5, A.8, B.1.2,
    B.6.6, D.3, 3.1, 5.2, 10.2,
    10.5, 11.4.7, 11.4.8,
    11.5.4, 11.6.1, 13.4, 13.6,
    15.7.11, 16.3.5, 18.4.4,
    30.1, 34.1, 35.7
channels 34.1
char A.1.1, A.2.3, A.2.7, A.2.9, A.6,
    2.3, 11.4.6, 12.1.1, 12.3
character A.2.3, A.2.4, 2.3, 5.3, 5.4,
    6.5.2, 6.5.3, 7.2, 8.1, 8.2,
    8.6.7, 11.4.6, 12.1.1,

12.1.2, 12.1.3, 12.4, 15.7.2, 19.2.3, 19.2.7, 19.3.3, 24.1, 26.2, 35.7, Prf

characteristics 11.4.2, 11.6.2, 12.3, 26.1, 33.5

characters A.1.1, A.2.3, A.2.4, A.2.7, 3.2, 5.3, 6.5.2, 6.5.3, 7.1, 7.2, 8.1, 8.2, 9.2, 9.5, 11.3, 11.4.6, 11.4.8, 12.1.1, 12.1.2, 13.5, 16.2, 19.2, 22.0, 22.5, 24.0, 24.1

charge B, 34.1, 35.2, Prf

chart 11.5, 11.6.1, 23.6, 34.5.4, 35.7

Charts 4.7, 11.5, 11.6.1, 12.3

CHeaderCtrl 20.0, 25.3

check A.3.2, A.3.3, A.5.2, A.5.3, B.3, B.3.1, B.4, B.6.5, B.6.6, B.8.1, 1.2, 2.3.2, 3.1, 6.4, 6.5.1, 6.6.4, 6.6.5, 7.2, 7.3, 7.5, 7.6, 8.5, 8.6.5, 11.5.4, 13.2, 13.3, 13.5, 13.6, 15.6, 15.6.1, 15.8.2, 16.5, 18.4.1, 18.5.6, 18.6, 22.0, 22.2, 22.4, 22.5, 22.6, 24.0, 25.6, 26.3, 28.1, 28.2, 31.3, 32.2, 33.2.1, 34.7

check_terrain_intersection A.3.2

checkAlwaysMemDF 13.5

checkbook 16.5

checkbox 25.6, 26.4

Checked 6.4, 6.5.1, 7.6, 13.2, 25.6, 26.2, 26.4

checker 34.3

checkers 34.3

checking A.4.1, A.5.1, A.5.2, A.7.1, 10.3, 11.5.2, 13.2, 15.8.4, 17.3.4, 24.0, 27.1

CheckMenuItem 6.5.1

CheckPoint 13.5

checks A.5.2, D.5, D.7, 7.5, 7.6, 8.6.1, 8.6.10, 10.4.10, 11.5.3, 12.1.2, 12.2, 13.3, 13.5, 13.7, 14.4.2, 18.4.2, 18.5.3, 22.6, 24.1, 27.1, 33.8.3

CHelloApp B.3.2, 2.1, 2.3, 2.3.1, 2.3.2

CHelloWindow B.3.1, B.4.1, B.4.5, B.4.6, 2.1, 2.3, 2.3.2, 2.3.3, 2.4

child 1.2, 1.3, 2.3.3, 3.1, 3.2, 3.5, 4.3, 4.4, 15.6.1, 17.2, 20.4, 20.6, 21.1.4, 26.1, 29.3, 30.1, 32.1, 32.4, 32.5, 35.7, 35.8

CHILDFRM 15.6.1

children 11.5.3, 20.4, 23.2, 23.3, 31.0, 31.1

chips 35.2

CHKBOOK 15.8, 15.8.4, 16.5

choice 1.2, 10.3, 11.4.6, 19.3.2

choices A.1.1, 1.1, 9.2, 25.0

ChooseColor 7.4

CHOOSEFONT 7.3

ChoosePixelFormat D.1, D.5

chooses 10.4.10, 15.3, 16.2, 16.3, 18.2, 18.4.2, 19.3.1, 20.7, 34.2, 34.4

choosing B.2, B.3, B.3.1, B.3.2, B.5.1, B.5.3, B.5.6, B.8.1, 6.5.3, 6.6.5, 9.1, 34.8.3

chops 18.4.3

chord 11.4.4

choreographed 15.8.2

choreography 15.8.2

chose 7.2, 34.6.10, 34.8.4

chosen A.5.1, B.7.1, 6.1, 6.4, 6.5, 7.2, 7.3, 7.4, 8.3, 8.5, 10.5, 11.0, 11.4.6, 11.5.2, 11.6.1, 11.6.3, 12.6, 15.2.1, 15.5, 15.6.1, 15.8.3, 16.1.1, 18.1.2, 18.1.7, 18.1.8, 18.4.2, 18.4.4, 18.5.4, 19.1.1, 20.7, 33.6.10, 34.5.5, 35.7

CHotKeyCtrl 20.0

CIdleUpdateFormView 31.6

CImageList 20.0

cin A.2.3, A.2.4

circle A.3.1, 5.3, 11.3, 32.1

circles A.3.1, 0.4, 11.0, 11.4, 11.4.4, 11.5.4, 15.1, 15.9

circularity 35.10

circumstances B.4.1

City C.1, 11.5.5, 18.1, 18.1.13, 18.4.1, 33.1, 33.2.4

civilian 12.1.3

clarify 2.3

clarity 15.7.9

classic A.3.1

classified A.3.1

classing 9.6

ClassView B.1.5, B.6.2

ClassWizard B, **B.6, B.6.1, B.7, B.7.1, B.7.2, B.7.3, B.7.4, B.7.5, B.7.6, B.7.7, B.8, B.8.1,** B.8.5, B.8.6, B.8.7, B.8.8, B.8.9, D.1, D.2, 0.1, 0.3, 0.4, 1.2, 5.1, 6.1, 6.5, 6.6, 6.6.8, 14.4.4, 14.5, **15.2.3, 15.2.6, 15.2.7, 15.2.8, 15.3, 15.3.2, 15.3.8, 15.4.1, 15.4.2, 15.5.2, 15.5.4, 15.6.4, 15.6.6, 15.6.9, 15.6.10, 15.6.11, 15.6.12, 15.7, 15.7.3, 15.7.7, 15.7.8, 15.7.11, 15.8.4, 15.9,** 16.3.2, 16.3.3, 17.0, 17.1.3, 17.2, 17.3.3, 17.3.4, 17.4.4, 17.4.5, **18.0, 18.1.4, 18.1.5, 18.1.7, 18.1.9, 18.1.10, 18.1.12, 18.1.13, 18.3, 18.4.2, 18.4.3, 18.4.4, 18.4.6, 18.4.7, 18.5.2, 18.5.3,** 19.3.2, 20.2, 20.5, 20.6, 20.7, 21.1.2, 21.1.3, 21.1.5, 21.1.8, 22.0, 22.1, 22.2, 22.5, 22.6, 23.8, 24.1, 25.5, 25.6, 25.8, 26.4, 27.1, 28.1, 28.2, 29.1, 29.2, 30.1, 30.2, 32.4, 32.5, 33.6.2, 33.6.3, 33.6.10, 33.7, 33.7.3, 33.7.4, 33.8.2, 33.8.3, 33.8.4, 34.5.5, 34.5.6,

34.6.5, 34.7.3, 34.7.4, 34.7.8, 34.8.1, 34.8.2, 34.8.4, 34.8.5, 34.8.6, 34.8.7, 34.8.10, 34.8.12, 34.8.13, 35.3, 35.4, 35.5, 35.6, 35.8, 35.9, Prf

clause 33.2.2, 33.2.3, 33.2.4, 33.5, 33.6.4, 33.6.6, 33.6.8

clauses 33.2.3, 33.4.4

clean A.1.1, A.2.11, 10.6, 11.4.3, 12.4, 14.1, 15.8.2, 26.2, 32.5, 35.5

cleaned 23.5

cleaner A.1.1, 12.1.2, 23.1

cleaning 31.4

cleanly 34.5.5

cleans A.1.1, A.7, 11.5.4, 18.1.12, 18.5.2

cleanup 23.2, 23.3, 23.5, 25.3, 25.6, 25.7

clear A.1.1, A.4.5, A.5.2, A.6, B.6.1, D.2, D.7, 8.1, 8.2, 8.5, 11.5.2, 11.6.2, 14.4.4, 14.5, 15.3, 15.3.1, 15.7.9, 15.7.10, 15.7.11, 18.2, 33.6.3, 34.1, Prf

cleared A.7, 11.6.2, 15.7.9, 15.7.11, 22.5

clearer 15.0, 15.3, 34.5.5

clearing 8.6.1

Clearly 18.1.10, 32.8, 34.1, 35.2

clears A.7.1, D.3, 8.2, 8.6.1, 10.4.10, 11.4.1, 11.5.3, 15.3.2, 18.2, 18.4.2, 26.4

clicked A.8, D.4, 1.3, 4.2, 4.3, 7.6, 11.5.2, 17.3.4, 20.3, 21.1.8, 32.6, 34.2, 34.5.5, 34.8, 35.7

clicking B.1.1, B.1.6, B.3.1, B.4.3, 1.2, 1.3, 4.2, 5.2, 6.3.5, 6.6.4, 7.1, 9.3, 11.5.2, 15.2.10, 15.8.1, 16.2, 16.3.5, 18.1.8, 18.4.2, 18.4.4, 19.2.4, 20.3, 33.4.2, 34.7.4, 34.7.8, 34.8.4, 34.8.9

clicks 0.4, 1.1, 1.3, 3.2, 4.1, 4.2, 4.3, 4.4, 4.6, 6.5, 7.2, 7.6, 9.3, 11.5.1, 11.5.2, 11.5.3, 11.5.4, 11.5.5, 12.1.1, 13.6, 15.5.4, 15.7.9, 16.3, 18.1, 18.2, 19.2.5, 21.1.8, 25.0, 27.1, 32.6, 33.6.3, 34.4, 34.8, 34.8.7, 34.8.10

client C.1, 0.3, 1.2, 3.1, 3.3, 4.4, 4.6, 9.1, 11.2, 11.3, 11.4.1, 11.4.6, 11.5.3, 11.5.5, 11.6.2, 11.6.3, 12.3, 14.1, 15.5, 15.5.6, 25.1, 29.1, 29.3, 32.6, 33.0, 33.1, 33.2, 33.2.1, 34.5.2, 34.5.3, 34.5.6, 34.6.7, Prf

clients C.1, 34.9, Prf

clip D.2, 18.4.6, 29.1

CLIP_CHARACTER_PRECIS 11.4.6

CLIP_DEFAULT_PRECIS 11.4.6

clipboard 0.4, 8.1, 8.2, 8.3, 8.6.6, 8.6.10, 16.1.2, 16.2, 16.3.5, 18.0, 18.4, 18.4.7,

26.1, 34.1, 34.2, 34.4
clipped D.2, 3.2, 3.3, 11.2, 11.5.5, 18.4.6, 18.5.4
clipping D.6, 11.1, 11.3, 11.4.6, 29.1
CList 3.0, 12.4
CListBox 5.2, 9.1, 9.2, 9.5, 18.1, 18.1.4, 22.2, 23.3, 25.3, 25.4, 26.4, 34.8
CListCtrl 20.0, 25.3, 25.5
CListView 21.1.2, 25.3
Clock 1.2, 4.5, 4.8, 11.4.6, 12.1.3, 14.3, 32.2, 33.1
Clockwise 3.1
clog A.2.3
close A.2.4, B.1.1, B.3, B.5.5, B.8.4, D.7, 6.3.5, 6.4, 6.5, 6.6.7, 6.7.2, 8.6.11, 10.5, 11.4.5, 11.5.3, 12.2, 12.3, 15.1, 15.4, 16.2, 19.1.1, 19.3.1, 19.4, 20.7, 25.0, 27.1, 29.2, 32.4, 32.5, 33.4.1, 33.4.2, 33.4.3, 33.5, 33.7.3, 33.8.1, 34.7.5, 34.8.4, 35.4, 35.5
closed 11.4.5, 22.0, 27.1, 32.4
closer D.7
closes A.2.4, 2.3.2, 8.6.11, 11.2, 11.4.5, 12.1.1, 15.8.2, 22.0, 32.4, 33.5
closest D.1, D.5, 11.4.2
closing A.2.6, 12.1.1, 15.1, 16.2, 32.4, 33.5, 34.5.5
closings 10.6
closure 22.1
clrInit 7.4
CLSID 34.4, 34.6.3
clue B.3.1, B.3.2
clustered 11.5.3
clutter 1.2
CLW B.6.1
CMainFrame 30.1
CMandelThread 35.8
CMap 12.5
CMapPtrToPtr 12, 12.5
CMapPtrToWord 12, 12.5
CMapStringToOb 12, 12.5
CMapStringToPtr 12, 12.5
CMapStringToString 12, 12.5
CMapWordToOb 12, 12.5
CMapWordToPtr 12, 12.5
CMDIChildWnd 16.3
CMDIFrameWnd 2.5
CMemFile 12, 12.1.1
CMemoryException 12, 13.6
CMemoryState 12, 13.5
CMenu 23.6, 25.3, 32.7
CMetaFileDC 11.4.1
CMiniFindNameDialog 32.5
CMiniFrameWnd 2.5, 32.5
CMNCTRLS 20.0, 20.8
CMultiDocTemplate 16.3
CMyButton 25.5
CMyComboBox 25.6, 25.8
CMyDialog 22.5, 23.3, 31.6
CMyEdit 23.8
CMyFrame 23.2, 23.7
CMyStatic 29.1, 29.4
CN_UPDATE_COMMAND_UI 31.1
CNotSupportedException 12, 13.6

cnt 13.3
CNTRITEM 34.5.3, 34.5.5, 34.5.6
coarse 5.3
CObArray 11.5.3, 12, 12.3, 13.4, 15.2.5, 15.2.6, 15.3, 15.6.3, 18.1.12, 18.2
CObArrays 15.0
CObject 2.1, 3.3, 12, 12.2, 12.3, 12.4, 12.5, 13.0, 13.2, 13.4, 13.5, 13.7, 14.4.4, 15.0, 15.2.6, 15.3, 15.4, 15.6.2, 18.1.12, 18.2
CObjects 12.5
CObList 12, 12.4
CObPoint 12.3, 13.2, 15.2.6, 15.3, 15.6.2, 15.9
coded 34.1, 34.2
codes 1.1, 12.5, 13.6, 13.6.2
coding A.8.1, 12.4, 14.4.5, 18.4.6
COleClientItem 34.5.3, 34.5.5
COleControl B.8.1, 34.8.1, 34.8.2
COleCurrency 22.2
COleDateTime 22.2
COleDispatchDriver 34.7.7
COleDispatchException 13.6
COleDocument 34.5.3, 34.5.5
COleException 12, 13.6
COleIFrameWnd 34.6.3
COleServerDoc 34.6.3
COleServerItem 34.6.3, 34.6.8
collapsed 20.4
collate 7.5, 12.1.2
collect 3.4, 17.2
collected A.2, 18.4.1, 33.1
collection 0.2, 1.1, 3.0, 5.1, 6.3, 10.4.10, 12.6, 13.4, 15.3, 17.0, 18.2, 33.1, 33.2.5, 34.5.4, Prf
collections A.4.6, 2.1, 11.1, 12.2, 12.4, 13.4, 34.1
collects 2.1
college A.3.2, 33.1
colon A.5.1
color A.3.1, B.1.3, D.1, D.2, D.6, D.7, 0.4, 3.2, 3.4, 7.0, 7.4, 10.5, 11.3, 11.4.2, 11.4.3, 11.4.6, 11.4.7, 11.4.8, 11.5.3, 11.5.4, 11.6.2, 25.6, 25.7, 26.1, 28.0, 29.2, 29.3, 34.8, 34.8.4, 35.8
COLOR_ACTIVEBORDER 11.5.3
COLOR_ACTIVECAPTION 11.5.3
COLOR_APPWORKSPACE 11.5.3
COLOR_BACKGROUND 11.5.3
COLOR_BTNFACE 11.5.3
COLOR_BTNSHADOW 11.5.3
COLOR_BTNTEXT 11.5.3
COLOR_CAPTIONTEXT 11.5.3
COLOR_GRAYTEXT 11.5.3
COLOR_HIGHLIGHT 11.5.3
COLOR_HIGHLIGHTTEXT 11.5.3
COLOR_INACTIVEBORDER 11.5.3
COLOR_INACTIVECAPTION 11.5.3
COLOR_MENU 11.5.3
COLOR_MENUTEXT 11.5.3
COLOR_SCROLLBAR 11.5.3
COLOR_WINDOW 11.5.3

COLOR_WINDOWFRAME 11.5.3
COLOR_WINDOWTEXT 11.5.3
colored D.7
colorful D.7
COLORREF 7.3, 7.4, 34.6.5
colors B.1.3, D.1, D.2, D.8, 7.4, 9.0, 10.5, 11.1, 11.4.2, 11.4.6, 11.5.3, 11.5.4, 11.6.2, 15.9, 25.0, 25.6, 25.7, 34.6.5, 34.8.11
column 0.4, 9.2, 20.3, 21.1.8, 33.1, 33.2.3, 33.2.4, 33.4.3, 34.2
columns 9.2, 9.5, 20.3, 33.1, 33.2.1, 33.2.2, 33.2.4, 33.4, 33.4.2, 33.6.2
com B, C.0, C.1, 21, Prf
combination A.1.1, 0.1, 6.5.3, 6.6, 9.5, 10.4, 11.5.4, 16.3, 17.4.5
combinations D.2, 6.5.3, 34.3
combine 5.5, 33.2.3, 34.3
combined 5.5, 7.1, 9.5, 11.5.1, 12.5, 18.6, 19.1.2, 34.5.4
combines 0.1, 0.4, 6.6.8, 8.4, 9.0, 9.5, 15.8.4, 16.2, 17.6
combining A.1.1, 3.0, 13.8, 16.3, 18.0
combo B.1.2, B.3, B.5.3, B.8.5, B.8.7, 0.4, 1.2, 2.1, 9.0, 9.2, 9.4, 9.5, 13.1, 13.2, 13.3, 22.0, 22.5, 25.0, 25.2, 25.3, 25.6, 25.7, 25.8, 25.9, 26.4, 28.0, 29.2, 30.1, 33.7.4, 34.8.4, 34.8.5
come A.1, A.1.2, A.2, A.2.6, A.3, A.3.3, A.4.1, A.4.2, A.4.3, 0.3, 2.3, 2.6, 3.2, 3.3, 6.7.3, 7.2, 8.2, 8.3, 10.2, 12.2, 13.3, 14.4.1, 14.4.5, 15.2.1, 15.3, 15.5.6, 33.4, 33.4.2, 34.1, Prf
comes A.1.1, A.2.6, A.3.2, A.4.3, A.4.6, A.7.2, B.8.1, 0.1, 2.1, 3.5, 4.6, 8.3, 13.3, 15.7, 18.5, 33.1, 33.3, 33.4, 33.7.5, 34.4, 34.6.2, 34.8.1, 34.8.3
comfortable A.1, 0.1, 1.0, 6.3.7, 6.6.5, 6.8, 14.0, 14.1, 14.4.6, 14.5, 33.2, 33.4.4, 33.5, 34.8.1, 35.7, Prf
comfortably 5.1
coming A.1.1, A.7, 4.4, 9.4, 13.3, 15.5.6, 35.2
Command B.7.3, D.1, D.2, D.6, D.7, 0.0, 1.3, 4.3, 4.4, 6.5.3, 8.3, 10.1, 13.1, 14.4.2, 15.3.1, 16.2, 18.1.10, 18.4.2, 18.4.4, 18.4.6, 18.4.7, 19.1.2, 19.3.2, 30.1, 31.0, 31.2, 31.3, 31.4, 31.5, 31.6, 32.4, 32.6, 32.7, 33.2, 33.2.1, 33.2.5, 33.8.2, 33.8.3, 34.4, 34.6.5, 34.7.6, 34.8, 35.2, 35.7, 35.8
commands D.0, D.2, D.3, D.5, D.6, D.7, D.8, 1.3, 11.1, 11.6.2, 13.3, 15.3, 16.2, 29.1, 31.1, 33.2, 34.8.1
comment A.2.1, B.3.1, 13.6.1, 14.5,

15.2.3, 15.2.8, 18.1.5
commenting A.2.1
comments B.6.1, C.0, 13.2, 14.5,
    19.1.1, 34.5.3, Prf
commercial A.5.1
common A.1, A.1.1, A.3.1, A.3.2, A.6,
    0.1, 0.4, 2.1, 2.3, 3.3, 5.1,
    6.1, 7.0, 8.1, 9.1, 9.4, 10,
    11.1, 11.2, 11.5.2, 11.5.4,
    12, 12.1.2, 12.1.3, 12.1.4,
    12.2, 14.3, 15.7.9, 20.0,
    20.3, 20.4, 20.5, 20.8,
    25.7, 30.0, 32.6, 33.1,
    33.2, 33.2.5, 33.3, 33.7,
    34.2, 34.4, 35.3, 35.5, Prf
commonality 34.1
commonly B.3, D.2, 2.1, 6.1, 6.4, 11.2,
    12, 14.5, 24.0, 33.2, 34.4
communicate 2.3.2, 7.6, 15.8.2, 22.3,
    32.4, 34.1, 34.2, 34.3,
    34.8
communicates 25.4, 35.1
communicating 6
communication 34.0, 34.1, 34.2, 34.3,
    34.7.9
communications 9.4, 34.1, 35.1, 35.7
compact 33.7
companies C.1, 33.2, 33.2.5, 33.3, 34.3
companion 6.7, 23.8
company C.1, 6, 6.7, 33.1, 33.2
Compare B.3, 0.4, 3.3, 12.1.2, 12.1.3,
    13.5, 15.4, 17.0, 20.3,
    25.2
compared 1.3, 7.4, 11.6.1, 15.8.3
CompareFunc 20.3
CompareItem 25.3, 25.6, 26.4
CompareNoCase 12.1.2
comparing 11.4.6
comparison A.6, 11.4.7, 17.2
comparisons 22.6
compatible D.1, 11.6.2, 12.3, 19.2,
    26.1, 29.2, 33.2, Prf
competing 12.1.1, 35.2, 35.7
compilation 13.1
compiled A.1.1, A.2.7, A.3.2, B.1.2,
    B.3, 1.5, 2.3, 6.1, 6.4,
    14.4, 14.4.1, 19.2
compiler A.1.1, A.2.5, A.2.9, A.4.6,
    A.6, A.7.1, A.8, B, B.1.2,
    B.1.6, B.3, 0.1, 0.3, 0.4,
    1.0, 1.5, 6.1, 6.4, 12.3,
    13.2, 19.0, 19.2, 19.5, Prf
compilers Prf
compiles A.8, B.1.2, B.1.6, B.3, 2.1,
    13.1, 19.1.1
compiling B.3, 3.3, 6.1, 12.3, 14.4.1,
    17.5, 19.1.2
complain B.3.2
complaints 2.4
completeness 11.1, 18.4.2
completes 1.0, 32.5, 35.1, 35.7, 35.8
Completing 15.2.6
completion B.2.2, 11.5.4, 18.1, 33.5,
    35.8
complex A.1.1, 2.1, 6, 20.3, 25.7, 28.0,
    28.3, 33.1, 34.7, 35.8
complexity 0.0, 20.1, 28.0, 31.6, 34.0,
    34.8.1, 35.1
compliant 34.7
complicated 2.1, 2.3, 5.5, 7.6, 8.6.10,

9.1, 11.5.3, 14.0, 15.3,
    15.3.1, 18.1, 20.5, 20.8,
    22.0, 30.2, 31.6, 33.6.8,
    33.7, 34.1, 35.1, 35.2,
    35.4, 35.8
complied 15.4
complies 15.2.6, 15.6.8
comply 2.3
Component B.8.4, D.1, D.2, 27.0,
    27.2, 32.6, 34.3, 34.8.1
components D.1, D.2, D.6, 10.4.6,
    19.2, 34.3
compounded 35.2
compressed 29.2
compromise 28.0
Compuserve C.0, 0.2
compute 35.7
computer A.1.1, A.3.1, D.0, 11.2,
    11.4.7, 11.6.2
computers A.3.2
computing C.1, 34.3
concatenate 12.1.2
concatenated 12.1.2
concatenates A.1.1
conceived A.1.1
concentrate 2.1, 6.1
concentrated 35.9
concept A.1.1, A.3.1, A.3.2, A.4.2,
    B.1.2, D.1, D.5, 1.3, 6,
    11.2, 13.4, 13.6, 14.3,
    15.0, 20.6, 21, 33.1, 33.3,
    33.5, 34.1, 34.8
concepts A.1, A.1.1, A.2, A.3, A.3.1,
    A.4.4, D.5, 0.0, 0.4, 1.0,
    1.3, 1.5, 2.3, 3.0, 4.0, 4.8,
    6.8, 8.3, 8.4, 11.0, 11.2,
    11.5.4, 11.7, 12, 12.1,
    14.0, 15.0, 15.9, 21.2,
    22.0, 23.9, 32.8, 33.0,
    33.1, 34.0, 34.8, Prf
conceptual A.3.1, A.3.2, 2.0, 34.1
conceptually 18.4.2, 35.1, 35.2
concerned 10.3, 11.6.1, 11.6.3
concerns A.7, 18.5
concise 13.5
concludes 0.1
concrete A.1
condition A.7.1, 32.4
conditional 13.1
conditions 2.3.2, 8.6.10, 33.8.3
conduct 35.7
confidence C.1
confidently 0.0, Prf
Configuration B.2, 10.5, 11.5, 11.6.1,
    33.1, 33.2, 34.1
confirm B.7.3, B.8.4, 15.5
confirmation B.6.1, 7.2
Confirms 13.7
conflicting 35.8
Confused A.3.1
confusing 20.8, 28.1
conjunction 4.5, 5.1, 34.8.13
connect 11.5.3, 11.5.4, 33.5, 34.7.7,
    35.1
connected C.0, 18.1.5, 34.1
connection 28.1, 34.7.7, 35.9
connections 7.2, 22.5, 33.3, 34.3
connectivity 0.1, 33.0
connects 34.3
conquer Prf

consider A.1.1, A.3.2, 5.2, 11.5.5,
    15.2.6, 17.4, 18.1.10,
    33.7.5, 34.5.5
considerably 35.1
considered D.2, 13.2, 25.6, 26.4
consist 33.1, 34.1
consistent 0.1, 11.4.8, 14.1, 19.0, 20.6
consistently 14.4.2, 18.4.6
consisting A.2.10, A.3.2, 6.6.2, 11.6.3,
    12.4
consists A.4.4, 1.1, 2.3, 6.5.3, 8.4, 11.2,
    11.6.2, 16.3, 18.1, 19.2,
    21, 34.4
console B, B.1, B.1.2, B.3
consolidate 5.0
consolidated 15.6.1
const A.2.7, 7.3, 7.4, 7.5, 7.6, 11.4.6,
    12.1.2
constant A.2.7, 2.3.2, 3.3, 4.2, 4.6, 6.1,
    6.3.4, 6.3.5, 6.3.7, 6.4,
    6.5.3, 11.4.6, 12.1.3,
    12.2, 12.4, 14.4.6, 15.5.2,
    15.5.3, 15.7.9, 16.3,
    18.4.6, 19.3.5, 19.3.8,
    25.5, 25.7, 32.6, 32.7, Prf
constantly 6.3.7, 14.5, 18.4.3, 34.1, Prf
constants 3.2, 3.5, 4.2, 4.6, 5.2, 6.4,
    7.1, 7.2, 11.4.6, 12.1.3,
    14.4.6, 19.3.5, 35.8
constrain 8.1, 11.5.5, 22.4
constrained 5.1
constraint 6.5.2
constraints 4.3, 33.1
construct D.5, 6.6.8
constructed 11.5.3
construction B.5.5, 4.7, 12.1.1
constructors A.1.1, A.4.3, A.4.6, A.5.2,
    A.7.1, 12.1.2, 12.1.3,
    12.3, 23.2, 28.1
constructs 32.4
consulting C.1
consume 11.6.2, 12.1.1, 18.4.6, 35.7
consumes 3.3, 35.3
consumption 3.3
contact 33.4
Contacting Prf
Container B.6.6, B.8.1, B.8.3, 10.1,
    13.2, 34.2, 34.5, 34.5.1,
    34.5.3, 34.5.4, 34.5.5,
    34.5.7, 34.6.2, 34.6.3,
    34.6.4, 34.6.8, 34.6.9,
    34.6.10, 34.8, 34.8.1,
    34.8.3, 34.8.4, 34.8.5,
    34.8.6, 34.8.8, 34.8.9,
    34.8.10, 34.8.11, 34.8.12,
    35.2
Containers B.6.6, 0.4, 34.0, 34.5, 34.6,
    34.6.2, 34.6.3, 34.9
containing A.3.2, A.3.3, A.5.2, A.7,
    A.7.2, B.4.1, 0.2, 1.2, 1.4,
    2.3.2, 4.3, 6.5, 6.6.7, 6.7,
    8.2, 8.5, 9.5, 11.3, 11.5.2,
    11.6.3, 12.1.1, 12.1.2,
    12.4, 14.4.1, 15.5, 17.1.2,
    18.1, 18.2, 19.3.6, 20.5,
    22.0, 25.0, 27.0, 28.3,
    30.1, 31.4, 33.2.1, 33.2.4,
    33.6.11, 34.4, 34.8.11
containment A.1
contention 12.1.1

contents A.5.2, 4.4, 5.3, 5.4, 8.1, 8.2, 8.4, 9.1, 9.3, 9.4, 11.4.3, 11.5.3, 12.1.2, 12.2, 12.4, 13.4, 14.4.4, 14.4.6, 15.3, 15.7.9, 15.7.11, 15.8.2, 18.1.9, 18.2, 20.3, 22.3, 22.5

context B.4.1, D.1, D.2, 0.4, 4.5, 6.2, 7.3, 7.5, 10.1, 10.4.10, 11.3, 14.1, 15.2.1, 19.1, 19.1.1, 19.1.2, 19.2, 19.2.5, 19.2.7, 19.3, 19.3.2, 19.3.3, 19.3.4, 19.3.5, 19.3.8, 19.3.9, 19.3.10, 19.4, 23.2, 25.6, 25.7, 26.1, 26.2, 29.2, 29.3, 32.6

contexts D.1, 15.2.3, 19.4, 23.0, 23.6, 25.7

contiguous 8.2, 11.4.7

contingencies A.7.2

contingency A.7.2

continually A.5.2, 35.7

continue B.2.1, 3.3, 7.1, 8.1, 12.3, 13.6, 15.0, 26.1, 26.2, 26.3, 27.1, 32.4

continuePrinting 18.5.6

continues A.5.2, 0.1, 10.3, 13.6, 35.1

Continuing A.1.1, 29.1

continuous 11.2

continuously 18.4.3, 18.4.6

contrast 5.1, 8.3

contrasted A.1

controllable 4.0

controlled D.1, 6.6.8, 9.5

controlling 11.3

ControlWizard B.8, B.8.1, B.8.5, B.8.7, 34.0, 34.8, 34.8.1, 34.8.2, 34.8.4, 34.8.5, 34.8.12

convenience D.1, 3.3, 9.5, 14.4.5, 16.2, 18.3, 18.5.3, 25.8, 32.6

convenient 4.3, 12.1.1, 12.1.3

conventional 34.4

conventions D.2, 19.2

conversation 34.2

conversion A.1, A.6, 1.3, 5.1, 12.1.3, 17.2, 17.3.4, 22.2, 25.7

conversions 17.2

convert A.6, 5.3, 8.1, 9.3, 11.5.3, 12.1.3, 15.8.4, 17.1, 18.4.1, 18.6, 22.6, 23.4, 25.7, 29.0, 29.1, 32.5

converted A.5.1, 1.3, 5.3, 19.2.2, 19.2.4, 19.2.6, 19.2.8, 19.2.10, 19.3.5, 19.3.10, 25.7

converter 1.3, 5.0, 5.1, 5.2, 17.0, 17.5

converting 8.1, 12.3

converts D.2, 5.3, 12.1.2, 12.1.4, 25.7, 30.1

convincing 11.6.2

cooperate 34.1

cooperation 34.1, 35.2

cooperative 35.2

coordinate A.3.3, D.6, 11.1, 11.2, 11.5.5, 11.6.1, 11.6.3, 13.2, 15.5, 15.5.6, 15.8.3, 15.8.4

coordinates A.3.2, A.3.3, A.4.5, D.2,

D.3, 3.3, 5.3, 11.2, 11.3, 11.4.1, 11.5.2, 11.5.5, 11.6.1, 12.1.4, 13.2, 15.5.6, 15.8.3, 15.8.4, 25.6, 25.7, 34.5.6

copied A.4.4, A.5.2, 7.5, 18.4.7, 22.1, 25.7, 29.2

copies A.4.6, A.5.2, A.7, A.7.1, 7.5, 8.1, 8.2, 8.6.10, 11.6.2, 12.2, 12.4, 29.2, 33.7.6, 34.4

copy A.1.1, A.4.4, A.5.2, A.7, A.7.1, A.7.2, B.3, B.7.3, D.3, 6.6, 7.3, 8.1, 8.2, 8.3, 8.5, 8.6.10, 10.1, 11.3, 11.4.7, 11.6.2, 12.1.1, 12.1.2, 12.3, 13.3, 15.2.6, 15.6.2, 16.2, 16.3.5, 17.3.4, 18.4.7, 20.7, 25.0, 25.7, 26.4, 33.1, 33.7.6, 34.1, 34.2, 34.4, 35.8

copying 12.2, 25.7

CopyRect 12.1.4

copyright 27.0

core 0.1, 15.3.3, 15.3.4, 15.3.5, 25.2, 33.2, 34.0

corner A.4.5, B.3, D.2, 2.3.2, 3.1, 3.3, 5.3, 11.2, 11.4.1, 11.4.6, 11.6.1, 15.5.5, 15.5.6, 18.1.2, 32.2, 34.5.2

corners 11.4.3

corporate 0.3, 33.1, 33.2.5

correct A.1, A.3, A.8, B.7.2, D.6, 2.1, 6.4, 11.4.6, 11.5.3, 12.4, 12.5, 15.5.6, 15.8.3, 16.2, 16.3, 18.4.2, 25.2, 33.7.1

correction C.0, Prf

corrections C.0, 2.4

correctly A.1, A.7.1, A.8, D.7, 1.1, 2.3.2, 2.4, 4.4, 6.3.6, 6.5.3, 7.3, 8.4, 9.1, 9.3, 11.5.3, 13.6.1, 14.0, 15.3, 15.5.6, 15.6.13, 15.8.4, 18.1.15, 18.4.2, 18.4.3, 18.5.5, 18.5.6, 19.1.2, 22.5, 27.1, 33.7.6, 34.2, 34.5.2, 34.5.4, 35.4, 35.5, Prf

correspond 33.7.2

corresponding D.1, 4.4, 8.1, 11.4.4, 11.4.8, 22.0, 33.1, 34.5.5, 34.7.6, 35.7

corresponds 4.4, 6.5.3

corrupt B.3.1, 13.5, 34.5.5

corrupted 13.5, 33.1

corruption 13.7

cost B, 15.8.1, 17.4, 34.3, Prf

couldn Prf

count A.3.1, A.4.2, A.7.2, 9.3, 12.4, 31.4, 35.6

counter A.5.2, A.7.2, 13.5, 35.7

counting D.2, 12.1.2

couple 2.3.2

Courier 3.5, 11.4.6, 26.1

course A.3.2, C.1, 16.4

cout A.2.3, A.2.4, A.3

cover A.3.1, B.3, D.1, 0.2, 11.4.7, 11.7, 19.0, 33.9, Prf

coverage 12.1.2

covered A.7.2, A.8.1, 2.3.2, 11.0, 11.2, 14.0, 29.1, 32.0

covering 0.2, 2.1, 11.4.1, Prf

covers 1.0, 11.7, 32.0

CPage 20.6

CPaintDC 11.4.1, 11.4.6

CPen 11.4.2, 23.6

CPoint D.4, 11.4.3, 11.4.4, 11.4.5, 12, 12.1.4, 14.5, 15.2.6, 15.2.7, 15.4.1, 15.6.3

CPrintClass 15.8.2

CPrintDialog 7.5, 26.2

CPrintInfo 15.8.2

CProgressCtrl 20.0

CPromptDialog 6.6.8

CPropertyPage 20.5, 20.6, 20.7

CPropertySheet 20.5, 20.7

CPtrArray 12, 12.2

CPtrList 12, 12.4

CPU D.7, 4.7, 18.6, 33.5, 35.1, 35.2, 35.3, 35.7

CPUbound 35.7

CPUs 35.1, 35.2, 35.7

crash 18.1.5

crashes A.7, B.2

crazy A.1.1

crColor 11.4.2, 11.4.3

creat Prf

CreateCompatibleBitmap 11.6.2

CreateCompatibleDC 11.6.2

CreateDispatch 34.7.7

CreateEx 23.1, 23.4

CreateFont 11.4.6

CreateOrActivateFrame 16.5

CreatePict 34.6.5

CREATESTRUCT 21.1.5

CreateThread 35.3, 35.4, 35.8

CreateViewGLContext D.1

CreateWindowEx 23.1

creation A.1.1, A.2.11, A.5.2, B.4, C.1, 1.1, 1.2, 1.3, 2.3, 2.3.3, 2.6, 3.1, 3.2, 3.3, 3.4, 4.1, 4.2, 4.3, 4.6, 5.1, 5.2, 5.3, 6.1, 6.2, 6.6, 6.6.8, 6.7, 7.0, 7.1, 7.3, 7.6, 8.7, 9.0, 9.1, 9.2, 9.3, 9.5, 11.4.5, 11.6.1, 11.6.3, 12.1.1, 12.3, 13.5, 15.3, 15.8.2, 18.5.2, 19.3.10, 20.5, 21.2, 22.1, 22.5, 23.1, 23.2, 30.0, 32.4, 34.4, 34.8, 34.8.1, 35.2, Prf

creative 34.1

creator A.8

CRecordset 0.4, 22.2, 33.0, 33.2, 33.3, 33.4, 33.5, 33.6, 33.6.1, 33.6.2, 33.6.6, 33.6.8, 33.6.10, 33.6.11, 33.7, 33.7.4, 33.7.5, 33.7.6, 33.8, 33.8.4, 33.9

CRecordView 33.5, 33.7, 33.7.3, 33.7.5, 33.9

CRect 3.3, 11.4.3, 11.4.4, 11.4.6, 11.5.2, 12, 12.1.4, 34.5.5

cRedBits D.1

cRedShift D.1

CResourceException 12, 13.6

CRichEditCtrl 20.0

criteria 22.0, 22.4, 33.2

critical 2.1

cross B.4, 10.2, 11.4.5, 11.5.3

crossing 11.4.5

crTransparent 25.7
CRuntimeClass 12
cs B.3.1, B.4.1, 3.4, 21.1.5
CS_BYTEALIGNCLIENT 11.5.3
CS_BYTEALIGNWINDOW 11.5.3
CS_CLASSDC 11.5.3
CS_DBLCLKS 4.3, 11.5.3
CS_GLOBALCLASS 11.5.3
CS_HREDRAW 11.5.3
CS_NOCLOSE 11.5.3
CS_OWNDC 11.5.3
CS_PARENTDC 11.5.3
CS_SAVEBITS 11.5.3
CS_VREDRAW 11.5.3
CSampApp 19.3.2
CSampCntrItem 34.5.5
CSampDoc 34.5.5
CSampView 14.5
CScrollBar 3.0, 4.0, 4.6, 22.2
CScrollView 11.5.5, 15.5, 15.5.4,
        15.5.6, 15.9, 16.1.1
CSize 11.4.6, 12, 12.1.4, 15.7.9,
        34.6.5, 34.6.8
CSizeDlg 15.7.6, 15.7.9
CSliderCtrl 20.0
CSpinButtonCtrl 20.0
CSplashWnd 27.1
CSplitterWnd 15.6.1
CSrollView 15.5
CStatic B.3.1, 0.4, 2.3.3, 2.4, 2.6, 3.0,
        3.1, 3.2, 3.3, 3.4, 3.5, 3.6,
        4.0, 4.2, 5.1, 5.2, 6.2,
        6.3.7, 6.6.4, 6.7.3, 8.1,
        9.0, 10.2, 11.4.6, 11.4.8,
        14.1, 17.1, 17.1.2, 22.2,
        23.2, 24.3, 29.1
CStatusBar 20.0, 25.3, 30.0
CStatusBarCtrl 20.0, 25.3
CStdioFile 12, 12.1.1
CSting 12.1.2
cStrikeOut 11.4.6
CString 5.2, 7.3, 7.5, 7.6, 8.6.2, 8.6.7,
        12, 12.1.2, 12.3, 12.4,
        12.5, 17.3.3, 18.1.9, 18.3,
        22.2, 22.5
CStringArray 12, 12.2
CStringList 12, 12.4
CStrings 7.2, 12.1.2, 12.2, 12.4, 26.2
CTabCtrl 20.0, 25.3
CTestWindow 3.3, 3.4, 3.5
CTextDoc 16.3.2, 16.3.3
CTextView 16.3.2, 16.3.3
CTime 12, 12.1.1, 12.1.3, 22.6
CTimeSpan 12, 12.1.3
CTLCOLOR 3.2
CToolBar 30.0, 31.1
CToolBarCtrl 20.0
CToolTipCtrl 20.0
CTreeCtrl 20.0
Ctrl 6.5.3, 9.3, 16.3.5
cube D.5, D.6, D.7
cue A.6
CUIntArray 12, 12.2, 13.2, 13.3, 13.4,
        13.5, 34.6.5
CUIThread 35.9
cumbersome 17.5, 34.1
currency 20.3
currentSelection 18.4.2, 18.4.3, 18.4.4
cursor B.2, B.2.2, B.2.3, B.4.1, B.5.6,
        0.4, 6.1, 6.3, 8.1, 8.6.7,

10.2, 11.5.2, 11.5.3,
        11.5.4, 18.4.5, 19.2.3,
        19.3.5, 23.7, 29.1, 30.1,
        32.1, 32.6, 34.5.5, 35.8
cursors 10.2, 11.5.3
curve 11.4.4
CUserException 12, 13.6
custom B.8.7, 0.4, 1.4, 5.1, 6.6, 6.7,
        7.0, 7.2, 7.4, 7.6, 8.2, 8.3,
        8.5, 10.2, 18.0, 20.4, 20.7,
        22.0, 22.3, 22.6, 25.0,
        25.1, 25.7, 26.4, 34.8,
        34.8.6, 34.8.12, 34.8.13
customer 17.4, 17.5, 33.2
customers 17.4
customizable 14.3
customization B.6.3, B.6.4, B.6.5,
        B.6.6, B.8.1, 1.0, 1.2, 1.5,
        7.4
customize A.8, B.5.5, B.6.6, 0.4, 2.1,
        3.5, 4.0, 5.3, 7.1, 7.3, 7.6,
        8.1, 9.4, 9.6, 10, 13.7,
        14.1, 15.1, 15.8.1, 16.3.5,
        18.4.6, 19.1.2, 19.2, 28.0,
        28.1, 29.2, 29.4, Prf
customized 3.0, 6, 24.3, 25.1, 25.9,
        26.0, 34.7, Prf
customizes 1.1
customizing 2.6, 7.5, 14.4.6, 25.1
Cut 8.1, 8.2, 8.3, 8.5, 8.6.10, 16.2,
        18.4.7, 34.4, 35.7
Cuts 8.2
CView B.7.2, 10.4, 14.3, 14.4.5, 15.3,
        15.3.7, 15.3.8, 15.4, 15.5,
        15.8, 15.9, 17.0, 17.1.1,
        17.4.4, 18.2, 23.1, 25.0
CWinApp 2.1, 2.3, 2.3.1, 2.3.2, 2.5,
        4.1, 5.2, 10, 10.1, 10.2,
        10.3, 10.4, 10.4.10, 10.5,
        10.6, 10.7, 11.4.1, 13.3,
        13.6, 13.6.1, 14.4, 14.4.2,
        15.3.1, 15.3.5, 15.8.4,
        27.1, 32.1, 32.3, 35.2
CWindow 5.2, 6.5, 6.5.1, 9.2, 9.3,
        11.5.3, 12.3, 13.2, 13.3,
        13.4
CWindowDC 11.4.1
CWinThread 35.0, 35.3, 35.4, 35.6,
        35.8, 35.9, 35.10
CWnd B.7.1, 2.1, 2.3.2, 3.2, 3.3, 3.5,
        3.6, 4.3, 4.4, 4.5, 4.6, 4.7,
        5.2, 5.4, 7.1, 8.1, 8.6.10,
        8.6.11, 11.2, 11.5.2,
        11.5.3, 11.5.4, 11.6.1,
        13.3, 13.4, 15.7.9, 20.5,
        22.0, 22.1, 22.2, 23.0,
        23.1, 23.2, 23.4, 23.5,
        23.6, 23.7, 23.8, 25.3,
        25.4, 27.1, 30.2, 31.1,
        32.1, 32.7
CWordArray 12, 12.2
cx 12.1.4
cy 12.1.4
cycle 0.1, 1.1, 1.3, 2.1, 5.5, 8.5, 12,
        32.4, 35.2, Prf
cycles 35.1
cycling A.5.1
d A.1.1, D.0, D.1, D.2, D.5, D.6, 10.5,
        12.1.3, 13.3, 15.2.1, 15.3,
        15.3.3, 15.6.7, 18.2, 23.2,

25.7
D_DEBUG 13.1
dataabstracting A.4.6
database B.6.1, 0.1, 0.3, 0.4, 2.1, 6, 8.1,
        10.2, 11.5.5, 12, 13.3,
        13.6, 14.1, 14.3, 14.4.2,
        14.4.4, 15.2.1, 15.5,
        15.6.1, 16.1.1, 17.5, 17.6,
        18.6, 19.1.1, **33.0, 33.1,**
        33.2, 33.2.1, 33.2.5, 33.3,
        33.4, 33.4.1, 33.4.2,
        33.4.3, 33.5, 33.6.1,
        33.6.2, 33.6.3, 33.6.4,
        33.6.5, 33.6.10, 33.6.11,
        33.7, 33.7.1, 33.7.2,
        33.7.5, 33.7.6, 33.8,
        33.8.2, 33.8.3, 33.8.4,
        33.9, 34.1, Prf
databases 0.4, 33.0, 33.1, 33.2, 33.3,
        33.4.1, 33.9, Prf
date A.3.1, 12.1.3, 34.4
dates 22.0, 22.6
daunting 0.1, 11.0
Dave Prf
Davis Prf
day D.0, 9.0, 12.1.3, 22.6, 33.1, 34.4,
        35.7
days A.5.2, 12.1.3
DB 13.3, 33.6.1, 33.7.1
DBase 33.3
DBException 12
dblClicked 11.5.2
DBSET 33.7.2
DBVIEW 33.6.10, 33.7.2
DC D.1, D.5, 7.5, 10.6, 11.3, 11.4.1,
        11.4.2, 11.4.3, 11.4.6,
        11.5.3, 11.6.2, 11.6.3,
        15.2.3, 15.4.1, 15.5.6,
        15.8.2, 15.8.3, 15.8.4,
        18.5.2, 18.5.3, 25.6, 25.7,
        29.2, 34.5.6, 34.6.8, 35.5
dcImage 25.7
dcMask 25.7
dcMem 25.7
dControls 10.5
DCs D.1, 7.3, 11.3, 11.4.1, 11.4.6
DDE 34.1
DDV 0.4, 6.6, 6.6.8, 14.5, 15.7.8,
        17.1, 17.3, 17.3.4, 17.3.5,
        18.3, 20.5, 20.6, 20.7,
        22.0, 22.1, 22.3, 22.4,
        22.5, 22.6, 24.0, 30.2,
        32.4
DDV_MinMaxByte 22.4
DDV_MinMaxDouble 22.4
DDV_MinMaxDWord 22.4
DDV_MinMaxFloat 22.4
DDV_MinMaxInt 22.4
DDV_MinMaxLong 22.4
DDV_MinMaxUInt 22.4
DDX B.7.4, B.7.5, B.7.6, B.7.7, 0.4,
        6.6, 6.6.8, 14.5, 15.7.8,
        15.7.9, 15.7.11, 17.1,
        17.3, 17.3.3, 17.3.4,
        18.1.4, 18.1.9, 18.2, 18.3,
        20.5, 20.6, 20.7, 22.0,
        22.1, 22.2, 22.3, 22.4,
        22.5, 22.6, 23.3, 23.4,
        24.0, 24.1, 24.3, 30.2,
        32.4, 33.6.2, 33.7.3,

33.7.4
DDX_CBIndex 22.2, 22.5
DDX_CBString 22.2, 22.5
DDX_CBStringExact 22.2, 22.5
DDX_Check 22.2
DDX_Control 22.2, 23.4, 23.8, 24.2,
    25.8, 28.1
DDX_Field 22.2
DDX_FieldCBIndex 22.2
DDX_FieldCBString 22.2
DDX_FieldCBStringExact 22.2
DDX_FieldCheck 22.2
DDX_FieldLBIndex 22.2
DDX_FieldLBString 22.2
DDX_FieldLBStringExact 22.2
DDX_FieldRadio 22.2
DDX_FieldScroll 22.2
DDX_FieldText 22.2
DDX_Index 22.5
DDX_LBIndex 22.2, 22.5
DDX_LBString 22.2, 22.5
DDX_LBStringExact 22.2, 22.5
DDX_Radio 22.2
DDX_Scroll 22.2
DDX_String 22.2, 22.5
DDX_StringExact 22.2, 22.5
DDX_Text 18.3, 22.2
deactivate 34.5.5
deal A.1.1, A.2.8, A.4.1, A.8.1, B.1.3,
    B.2, B.4, 0.3, 1.2, 9.0, 9.1,
    9.5, 10.1, 11.3, 11.4.3,
    11.4.6, 11.4.7, 11.4.8,
    12.3, 14.4, 14.6, 19.0,
    22.0, 23.1, 23.2, 23.8,
    32.6, 34.2, 34.7.6
dealing D.0, 11.3, 26.4
deallocation A.2.10, 13.5
deals 2.1, 12, 17.2, 32.1
dealt 2.1, 15.8
death 35.4
debug B.2, B.2.1, B.3.1, 0.1, 0.3, 12.2,
    13.0, 13.1, 13.2, 13.3,
    13.5, 23.0, 32.1, 35.3
DEBUG_NEW 13.5
debugged A.5, 0.1, 13.2
debugger A.4.6, B, B.2, B.2.1, B.2.2,
    B.3, B.3.1, B.3.2, 0.4, 1.5,
    2.4, 13.1, 13.2, 13.3, 13.4,
    13.5, 15.3, 15.5.6,
    18.1.11, 34.5.5, 34.5.6,
    35.3, 35.4, 35.8
debugging B.2, B.2.2, B.3.2, 0.1, 0.4,
    12, 12.2, 12.3, 12.6, 13.1,
    13.2, 13.3, 13.4, 13.5,
    13.7, 15.2.6, 15.6.8,
    34.5.5, 34.8.3, Prf
dec A.2.3
decide A.3.2, A.4.5, A.5.2, D.2, 1.1,
    5.1, 7.6, 8.6.3, 11.4.6,
    11.5.2, 12.3, 14.1, 14.4.5,
    32.1, 34.2
decided 2.2
decides 4.6, 8.6.7, 10.4.10
deciding 10.3
decimal A.1.1, A.2.3, 12.1.3, 20.2
decision A.5.1, 8.6.1, 8.6.4, 14.4.5
decisions 14.4.5
declaration A.1, A.2.6, A.2.7, A.4.3,
    A.7.1, B.4.1, D.7, 3.1, 3.3,
    4.3, 7.6, 14.4.3, 15.2.6,

31.5
declarations A.2.7, B.4.2, 14.4.5, 31.2,
    31.3, 31.4, 35.8
declare A.2.5, A.3.2, A.7.1, 2.3.2, 4.7,
    11.4.1, 11.5.3, 14.4.4,
    14.4.6, 15.7.9, 18.5.2,
    18.5.6
DECLARE_DYNAMIC 12.3
DECLARE_DYNCREATE 12.3
DECLARE_MESSAGE_MAP 4.3, 4.7
DECLARE_SERIAL 12.3, 15.5.3,
    15.6.7
declared A.1.1, A.2.6, A.2.11, A.4.3,
    A.4.4, A.6, A.8, B.4,
    B.4.2, 2.3, 2.3.1, 2.5, 3.3,
    3.4, 3.5, 4.4, 7.2, 11.4.1,
    11.5.3, 12.1.2, 12.3, 12.5,
    14.5, 15.2.6, 15.6.3,
    17.4.3, 34.1
declares A.4.3, A.8, 2.3, 2.3.3, 5.2,
    12.1.1, 12.3, 13.2, 13.6,
    34.6.3
declaring A.2.4, A.5.1, 12.1.1, 13.4
declining 17.2
decoding 13.6.1
decomposition A.4.2
decorations B.3, 5.2, 27.0
decreased 3.3
decreases 3.3, 20.2
decree 34.1
decrement A.7.2
decremented 34.8.7
decrementing A.7.2
decrements 34.8.1, 34.8.8
dedicated C.1
deductions 17.0
deep A.1, A.8.1, 13.6.1, 15.3.3
deeper 34.1
deeply Prf
DEFAULT_PITCH 11.4.6
DEFAULT_QUALITY 11.4.6
defaults A.7.1, 3.4, 11.3, 11.4.2
defeating A.4.2
deficiencies A.1, A.3.2
deficiency 25.6
define A.2.7, A.3.2, D.1, D.2, 1.3, 2.2,
    6.5.3, 11.6.1, 13.5,
    19.3.5, 31.2, 31.4, 34.1
defined A.1.1, A.2.3, A.2.10, A.4.3,
    A.7.1, B.4.5, B.4.6, D.2,
    D.3, 2.3.2, 3.2, 3.3, 4.2,
    4.3, 4.6, 5.2, 6.1, 7.1, 7.2,
    10.2, 10.3, 11.5.3, 12.2,
    19.3.5, 20.3, 23.7, 25.7,
    34.1, 34.2
defines A.2.7, A.4.4, B.4.1, D.1, D.2,
    D.3, D.6, D.7, 2.3.2, 3.3,
    5.2, 6.5.3, 25.7, 34.1, 35.7
defining A.1, D.1
definitely 5.1
definition A.2.9, A.4.6, B.3.2, B.4.1,
    B.4.4, D.2, D.4, D.5, D.6,
    3.3, 4.4, 6.1, 6.5.1, 22.5,
    27.1, 28.1, 29.1, 30.1,
    32.4, 33.4.2, 34.1
definitions B.4, B.4.1, B.4.3, B.4.4,
    D.1, D.6, 1.2, 22.5
deflated 4.4
degree A.8.1, 11.4.6, 35.2
degrees D.2, D.3, 11.4.4

delayFreeMemDF 13.5
DELCARE_DYNCREATE 15.5.3,
    15.6.7
delegated 31.4
delete A.2.10, A.4.1, A.6, A.7.2, B.3,
    D.1, 0.4, 2.3.2, 2.4, 6.6.7,
    8.3, 8.6.10, 12.1.1, 12.3,
    13.5, 15.2.6, 15.7.9,
    15.7.10, 16.2, 17.1.2,
    18.0, 18.1, 18.1.2, 18.4,
    18.4.2, 18.4.3, 18.4.5,
    24.1, 25.2, 26.2, 27.1,
    29.4, 30.1, 32.4, 33.2,
    33.2.5, 33.4, 33.5, 33.8,
    33.8.1, 33.8.3, 34.6.4,
    34.8.3, 34.8.4, 35.4, 35.8
DeleteContents 15.2.6, 15.3, 15.3.1,
    15.3.2, 15.6.4, 17.4.7,
    18.1.12, 18.2, 18.4.2
deleted A.4.3, A.7, 3.4, 12.1.1, 15.2.6,
    29.2, 33.5
DeleteItem 25.3, 25.6
deletes A.4.2, 8.1, 8.2, 8.4, 9.4, 12.1.1,
    12.2, 12.3, 12.4, 12.5,
    15.7.9, 18.4.2, 18.4.7,
    33.5, 33.8.3, 35.5, 35.8
DeleteString 9.4
DeleteTempMap 23.5
deleting A.2.10, 12.3, 25.3, 33.1, 35.4
deletion 12.2, 15.2.6, 18.6, 35.4, 35.8
delivered C.1
demand 4.7, 34.1
demands 14.0
demonstrations B.4, 11.4.6
denoted A.2.1
denotes 26.4
densities 15.8.3
density 3.5, 15.8.3
dental 11.5
department 33.1
depend 1.3
dependent 11.2, 11.3, 11.6.1, 12.1.2,
    13.5
depending A.2.8, A.4.4, A.4.6, A.5.2,
    D.2, 9.4, 11.3, 12.3,
    14.4.4, 14.5, 15.8.2,
    15.8.3, 19.2, 21.1.8, 26.1,
    26.2, 28.1, 31.3, 33.4.1,
    34.1
depends 10.3, 11.6.1, 22.6, 31.0
depth D.1, 10.4, 13.4, Prf
dereferencing 32.4
derivation A.1, 2.1, 2.3.2, 13.2
derivations 2.3.2
derivative 18.1
derivatives 33.3
derive A.3.1, 2.1, 2.3, 2.3.1, 4.7, 7.4,
    7.5, 12.3, 12.4, 12.5, 13.2,
    15.2.6, 16.3, 18.1.12,
    20.5, 20.6, 20.7, 24.1,
    26.4, 28.0, 29.1, 31.6,
    32.5, 35.8, 35.9
derives B.4, 2.3.3, 11.4.1, 13.4, 14.4.4,
    20.5
deriving A.1, A.3.1, 15.2.6, 15.6.2
DESC 33.2.3
descendants 31.1, 31.4
descending 33.2.3
DescribePixelFormat D.1
describes A.1, B.5, D.1, 3.1, 6.1, 8.4,

8.5, 13.7, 19.3, 20.3, 22.4,
　　33.5
describing 6.6.8, 11.4.4, 11.5.5, 26.1,
　　34.5.5
description A.4.1, D.1, 2.3.2, 4.3, 5.3,
　　5.4, 6.2, 7.2, 7.3, 7.5, 8.4,
　　9.2, 10.5, 11.5.3, 13.6,
　　14.4.2, 15.5.4, 15.5.6,
　　15.8.2, 16.3, 16.3.5,
　　17.4.1, 18.1.2, 18.3, 19.2,
　　19.2.2, 22.2, 22.6, 33.5,
　　34.1, 34.5.3, 34.6.3, 35.7
descriptions 0.2, 3.0, 7.2, 7.6, 9.5, 13.7,
　　34.9, Prf
descriptive 19.2.1, 34.5.5
descriptor D.1
deselect 29.4, 34.5.2, 34.5.5
design A.1, A.1.1, A.3.1, A.3.2, C.1,
　　0.1, 1.1, 2.2, 5.1, 5.5, 8.3,
　　11.3, 11.5.5, 14.1, 14.3,
　　15.4, 18.6, 22.0, 23.8,
　　34.1, 34.8, 35.1, 35.2,
　　35.7
designated 7.6
designed A.1.1, B, D.0, D.5, 0.0, 0.1,
　　5.1, 6.6.8, 10.2, 13.2,
　　14.1, 15.3, 15.4, 15.8.1,
　　18.2, 33.7, 33.7.4, 34.8,
　　34.8.11, Prf
designer A.3.1, 6.5.3, 18.1, 28.0, 33.1,
　　Prf
designers A.1.1, 34.1, 34.3, 34.8.10,
　　35.8
designing A.3.1, A.4.1, 11.5.5, 15.3,
　　17.2, 18.2, 34.3
desirable 22.4, 30.0, 33.7
desire 10.3, 12.5, 17.2, 34.0, 35.4
desired A.2.10, A.5.2, 1.2, 3.3, 8.3, 9.2,
　　11.3, 11.4.6, 14.3, 17.3.3,
　　18.1.8, 20.2, 25.0
desktop 1.2, 3.2, 6.3.7, 11.5.4
Despite 3.3, Prf
destination A.2.3, A.5.2, 23.7, 25.7,
　　29.2, 34.4
destinations A.2.3
destined 23.7, 23.8
destroy A.1.1, 20.7, 23.2, 23.4, 27.1,
　　32.4, 32.5, 35.4, 35.8
destroyed A.1.1, A.4.6, A.7, 7.6, 13.6,
　　20.7, 23.1, 23.2, 23.4,
　　23.8, 27.1, 32.4, 32.5
destroying 25.7
destroys 6.6.8, 11.5.4, 12.3
DestroyWindow 5.2, 6.5, 27.1, 32.4,
　　32.5
destruction A.1.1, 6.6.8, 12.4, 15.3,
　　17.4.7, 18.2, 23.1
destructor A.4.3, A.4.4, A.4.6, A.5.2,
　　A.7, A.7.1, A.7.2, 2.3.2,
　　2.4, 2.5, 3.4, 11.4.1, 12.3,
　　12.4, 13.3, 17.4.7, 23.2,
　　32.5, 35.8
destructors A.1.1, A.4.6, A.7.1
Detach 23.4, 23.6
detail A.1, A.1.1, A.2, A.3.3, B.9, 1.3,
　　1.4, 1.5, 2.1, 2.3, 2.3.1,
　　2.3.2, 2.3.3, 3.1, 5.3, 8.3,
　　10.4.10, 11.0, 14.3,
　　14.4.5, 15.2.3, 15.8.4,
　　18.4.7, 19.2, 19.3, 20.1,

22.0, 34.5.5, 35.0
detailed A.2.3, B.6.1, 1.0, 11.5.5, 15.1,
　　15.8.2, 22.0, 27.2, 33.5,
　　34.6.3
detailing D.2
details A.1, A.1.1, B, B.2, B.7, B.7.1,
　　B.7.7, B.8, C.0, 1.1, 1.3,
　　1.4, 2.3.1, 2.3.2, 3.1, 3.3,
　　3.5, 4.3, 4.7, 5.1, 5.3,
　　6.3.7, 6.5.4, 6.7.3, 7.1,
　　7.2, 8.6.6, 8.6.7, 8.7, 10.6,
　　11.3, 11.4.4, 11.5, 11.6.1,
　　11.6.3, 12.6, 13.1, 14.4.2,
　　14.4.4, 14.4.6, 15.1, 15.2,
　　15.2.1, 15.2.8, 15.4, 15.5,
　　15.6.1, 15.7.8, 15.7.11,
　　16.1.1, 16.2, 18.1.13,
　　18.4.1, 18.4.6, 18.5,
　　21.1.5, 23.1, 23.6, 25.4,
　　30.0, 31.6, 34.5.1, 34.5.3,
　　34.6.1, 34.6.3, 34.6.5,
　　34.7.1, 34.8.2, 34.8.12,
　　35.4, Prf
detect A.1.1, 0.4, 6.4, 10.4, 11.5.2,
　　13.0, 13.5, 13.6, 13.6.1,
　　17.1.3, 33.6.3
detected A.2.3, A.5, 7.6, 11.5.4, 13.3,
　　13.5, 34.8.7
Detecting 11.5.2, 12.5, 13.5
detection 35.8
detects A.7.2, B.1.6, 10.4.10, 13.3,
　　13.5, 16.2
determination 15.8.4, 18.4.3
determine A.3.2, D.6, 4.3, 4.6, 7.2, 7.3,
　　8.6.7, 8.6.10, 10.4.10,
　　11.4.2, 11.4.5, 11.4.6,
　　11.4.8, 11.5.2, 13.6,
　　18.4.3, 18.4.6, 20.6, 22.3,
　　22.4, 23.7, 25.2, 25.4,
　　25.6, 26.1, 26.2, 26.4,
　　28.1, 31.5, 32.3, 33.7.6,
　　34.2, 34.5.5, 34.8, 35.7,
　　35.8
determined 3.2, 3.3, 5.2, 6.5.3, 11.4.6,
　　30.1, 33.1, 35.7
determines 1.3, 2.3.3, 3.4, 5.2, 7.3, 8.2,
　　11.4.6, 25.4, 26.1, 26.2,
　　26.3, 29.2, 31.2, 32.1,
　　34.5.5, 34.8, 34.8.1, 35.7
Determining 26.5
develop 0.0, 6, 8.3, 8.5, 14.4.4, 34.6.3,
　　34.8.3, Prf
developed A.1.1, A.8.1, 6.2, 34.0, 34.1
Developer 0.2, 1.1, 20.0, 22.6, 34.1,
　　34.3, 34.9
developers 34.1
developing A.4.1, 1.1, 11.6.2, 13.0,
　　13.3, 14.1, 34.3
development A.1.1, A.5.3, C.1, 0.1,
　　0.3, 0.4, 1.0, 1.1, 1.2, 2.1,
　　5.5, 6.1, 12, 13.0, 18.1,
　　22.7, Prf
Device B.5.3, D.1, D.2, 7.3, 7.5, 11.0,
　　11.1, 11.2, 11.3, 11.4.6,
　　11.6.1, 11.6.3, 14.4.2,
　　15.2.3, 15.5.6, 15.8.3,
　　15.8.4, 18.1, 23.0, 23.2,
　　23.6, 25.6, 25.7, 26.1,
　　26.2, 29.2, 29.3, 33.4.2,
　　34.5.6

devices D.1, 11.1, 11.2, 24.0
devote 35.2
devoted 1.3
diagnostic 12.3
Diagonal 10.2, 11.4.1, 11.4.2, 11.6.3
diagram A.4.2, A.5.1, A.5.2, A.7, 2.1,
　　3.3
dialogs B.5, B.6.2, 0.1, 0.3, 0.4, 2.1,
　　3.0, 5.1, 6, **6.1, 6.6, 6.6.8,
　　6.7**, 7.0, 7.6, 7.7, 8.0, 8.3,
　　8.5, 10.5, 14.4.6, 15.7,
　　15.7.5, 15.9, 16.1.2, 17.5,
　　18.0, 18.1.10, 19.1.2,
　　19.2, 19.3, 19.3.10, 19.4,
　　20.0, 20.5, 20.6, 20.7,
　　20.8, 22.0, 23.1, 23.3,
　　23.4, 28.0, 28.1, 28.3,
　　29.2, 30.2, 31.1, 31.4,
　　31.6, 32.0, 32.4, 32.8, Prf
did A.1.1, A.8, B.2.1, D.6, 4.6,
　　10.4.10, 11.5.2, 13.2,
　　13.6, 14.5, 15.3, 15.3.2,
　　15.4, 15.5, 15.7.11,
　　15.8.3, 16.3.1, 17.3.2,
　　17.3.4, 18.3, 22.1, 22.5,
　　23.3, 28.1, 32.5, 33.6.2,
　　33.6.5, 33.7.2, 34.7.2,
　　34.8.13, 35.7, 35.8
didn 4.7, 11.4.1, 29.4
die 13.2, 35.4, 35.7
dies 35.2, 35.3, 35.4
differ 1.3, 4.3, 33.3
difference B.1.3, 0.4, 3.4, 8.6.4, 11.6.1,
　　12.1.3, 13.5, 15.3.4,
　　15.8.1, 15.8.3, 20.7, 22.5,
　　22.6, 23.2, 23.5, 25.6,
　　26.3, 26.4, 32.8, 33.7.2,
　　34.5.2, 34.5.3, 34.6.2,
　　34.6.9, 35.2, Prf
differences A.2.3, A.7, D.2, 1.3, 12.1.3,
　　13.5, 15.4, 33.7.2, 34.5.3,
　　34.6.3
differentiating A.3.1
differently A.5, D.3, 1.3, 13.2, 28.1,
　　31.1, 34.8.4
differs 9.2, 15.4
difficult A.1, A.1.1, 0.1, 3.3, 10.1, 12.2,
　　15.3, 16.2, 30.2, 34.5.5
difficulty 15.6, 33.4.2
diffuse D.7
digit A.5.2, 24.1
Digital C.1, 4.5, 4.8, 11.4.6, 11.6.2,
　　14.3, 33.1
digits A.5.2, A.5.3, 5.3, 24.0, 34.4
dimension A.1.1, A.3.2, D.2, 28.1
dimensional A.3.2, A.5.1, D.5, D.6
dimensions D.7, 11.4.1, 11.4.6, 25.2,
　　25.7, 28.1, 29.2, 32.2,
　　32.5
Dir 9.4
direct A.4.2, A.5.1, 8.2, 10.5, 33.2.5,
　　33.3, 33.4
directed C.0
direction 0.0, 7.6, 9.1, 11.2, 12.3
directions A.3.1, 10.4.6, 10.4.7, 10.4.8,
　　11.4.7, 18.1.7, Prf
directly A.4.2, A.4.3, A.5.1, A.6, D.5,
　　1.3, 2.1, 4.4, 4.5, 5.1,
　　6.6.8, 6.7, 6.7.3, 7.5,
　　10.4.10, 11.4.7, 11.5.4,

11.6.1, 11.6.2, 12.1.2,
13.3, 13.5, 15.3.8, 15.7.8,
15.7.9, 15.8.1, 16.5, 18.3,
19.1.2, 20.5, 22.1, 25.7,
28.1, 33.3, 33.7.4, 34.1,
34.2, 34.4, 34.5.2, 34.8.3
directories B.6.1, 7.2, 20.4
directory B.1.2, B.1.5, B.3, B.6.1,
B.8.1, 0.2, 1.5, 3.1, 3.3,
5.2, 6.4, 6.6, 7.2, 9.4,
10.4.10, 10.5, 12.1.1,
13.3, 15.2.2, 15.2.6, 15.4,
15.5, 15.6, 15.6.2, 15.7,
15.8, 15.8.1, 18.1.9,
19.1.1, 19.1.2, 19.2,
19.2.9, 19.3.5, 19.3.7,
20.4, 33.7.1, 34.4, 34.7.7,
35.4, Prf
dirtied D.3
dirty 15.1, 20.7, 33.5, 34.5.5
disable B.4, 0.4, 5.2, 6.5.1, 8.6.10,
15.2.1, 15.5, 15.6.1,
17.1.1, 18.1.1, 18.4.3,
18.4.5, 18.4.6, 20.7, 23.4,
28.1, 31.0, 31.1, 31.3,
31.5, 32.4, 33.6.1, 33.7.1,
34.5.1, 34.6.1, 34.7.1,
35.8
disabled 7.6, 18.4.3, 18.4.4, 18.4.7,
20.6, 20.7, 28.1, 30.0,
31.1, 31.2, 34.8.11
disables 5.2, 7.5, 8.6.10, 11.5.3, 13.7,
18.4.3, 33.3
disabling 3.2, 8.6.10, 18.4, 28.1, 35.8
disadvantage 3.3, 6.7, 11.5.1, 12.2,
15.7.9, 18.1, 34.4
disadvantages A.1.1
disappear A.2.6, D.6, 6.4, 9.1, 18.1.10,
27.1, 34.1, 34.2, 34.5.6,
35.2
disappearance 11.2
disappears 11.4.1, 27.0, 30.1
Disassembly B.2
discard 8.6.1
discern 0.1
discernible D.6
disconnects 33.5
discouraged 19.3.5
discourages 34.1
discover 5.2, 13.5, 34.1
discovers 13.5
discretion 8.2
discussion A.5.2, B, 0.4, 1.1, 1.2, 2.3,
5.3, 10.2, 10.4, 11.2,
12.1.1, 14.4.4, 15.3.6,
15.5.6, 18.1.8, 18.1.9,
27.2, 33.1, 34.1
discussions 0.2
disk A.4.1, B.5.2, 3.3, 8.6.3, 11.5.3,
12.1.1, 12.3, 13.3, 13.6,
14.3, 15.2.6, 15.3, 15.3.3,
17.4, 18.1.12, 18.2,
19.2.2, 19.2.4, 19.2.6,
19.2.8, 19.2.10, 19.3.5,
19.3.10, 25.0, 33.1, 34.4,
35.2, 35.7, Prf
diskette B.3, 13.3, 15.2.2, 15.4, 15.5,
15.6, 15.7, 15.8.1, Prf
disks 12.1.1
dislike 2.3

dismiss 20.7, 27.1, 32.5
dismissed 7.2, 22.4, 27.1
Dispatch 13.3, 34.7.7
dispatched 10.6, 35.7
dispatches 10
dispose 12.3
DISPTEST 34.7.7
distance D.3, D.6, 28.1
distances 11.4.6, 18.5.3
distant D.6, 6.1
distinction 6.5.3
distinguish 1.1, 12.2, 33.2.4
distinguished C.1, 11.2
distinguishes A.2.8, 4.6, 6.5
distortion 29.2
distortions 29.2
distributed 34.3
district C.1
disturbing 11.4.3, 35.1
diversity 34.1
divide 13.6.1, 15.8.4, 34.1, 35.2
divided 10.5, 18.4.6
divider 20.3, 28.2, 28.3
dividers 20.3
divides 35.3
division 28.1, 35.1
dlg 8.5, 34.6.5
DLL B.1.2, B.3, 13.1, 19.1.1, 34.4,
34.5.3, 34.6.3
dock B.2.3
dockable B.1.6, B.2, B.2.3, B.4.1,
15.2.1
DockControlBar 30.1
docking 30.1
docks 30.1
DoClick B.8.7, 34.8, 34.8.5
docSize 15.5.3, 15.7.3
doctor 17.5
document D.2, D.3, D.4, D.6, 0.4, 1.2,
2.1, 7.5, 8.2, 10, 10.4,
10.4.6, 10.4.10, 10.5,
11.6.3, **14.1, 14.3, 14.4,
14.4.2, 14.4.4, 14.4.5,
14.6**, 15.0, 15.1, 15.2.1,
15.2.2, 15.2.4, 15.2.5,
15.2.6, 15.2.7, 15.2.9,
15.3, 15.3.1, 15.3.3,
15.3.5, 15.3.8, 15.4,
15.4.2, 15.4.3, 15.4.4,
15.5, 15.5.1, 15.5.2,
15.5.3, 15.5.4, 15.6,
15.6.1, 15.6.2, 15.6.3,
15.6.4, 15.6.5, 15.6.6,
15.6.7, 15.6.8, 15.6.13,
15.7, 15.7.3, 15.7.9,
15.7.10, 15.7.11, 15.8.1,
15.8.2, 15.8.4, 16.0,
16.1.1, 16.2, 16.3, 16.3.2,
16.3.3, 16.3.4, 16.3.5,
16.3.6, 16.4, 16.5, 16.6,
17.4, 17.4.1, 17.4.3,
17.4.4, 17.4.5, 17.4.6,
17.4.7, 18.0, 18.1, 18.1.1,
18.1.2, 18.1.10, 18.1.12,
18.1.15, 18.2, 18.4.2,
18.4.3, 18.4.4, 18.4.6,
18.4.7, 18.5, 18.5.2,
18.5.4, 18.5.6, 18.6,
19.1.1, 19.1.2, 32.1, 32.6,
33.1, 33.6.1, 33.7.1, 34.1,

34.2, 34.4, 34.5.2, 34.5.3,
34.5.5, 34.5.6, 34.5.7,
34.6.2, 34.6.3, 34.6.5,
34.6.6, 34.6.7, 34.6.8,
34.6.10, 34.7, 34.7.6,
35.8, Prf
documentcentric 14.3
documented B.7.1, 0.2, 34.1
documents 1.2, 3.3, 14.3, 14.4.5, 14.6,
15.1, 15.4, 15.6.8, 15.9,
16.3, 18.1.10, 18.1.12,
33.1, 34.1, 34.4
docview 10.4.1, 10.4.2, 10.4.3, 10.5
DoDataExchange 22.1, 22.4, 22.5,
22.7, 23.8, 24.2, 28.1,
30.2
doesn A.4.1, 5.3, 11.5.3, 23.7, 23.8,
23.9, 24.1, 25.4, 31.4,
34.1, 34.2, 34.8.12
DoFieldExchange 33.5, 33.6.2, 33.6.10
Doing A.3.3, A.5, A.5.2, B.2, D.1, D.2,
D.6, 2.3.3, 3.5, 4.7, 5.1,
8.2, 12.2, 14.1, 15.3,
15.4.4, 15.7.3, 15.8.4,
17.4, 23.1, 23.8, 35.7,
35.8
DoMessageBox 10.4.10
dominate 34.0
DoModal 6.6.8, 7.2, 7.3, 7.4, 7.5, 7.6,
15.7.11, 18.1.11, 20.5,
20.7, 22.1, 22.4, 22.5,
27.1, 32.4, 32.5
don A.1.1, A.2, A.3.2, A.5, A.5.2, D.1,
D.2, D.5, 1.4, 2.1, 2.3,
2.6, 20.3, 20.6, 22.0, 22.5,
22.6, 23.2, 23.9, 25.4,
27.0, 27.1, 28.0, 29.1,
30.0, 30.1, 31.4, 32.0,
32.5, 33.7.2, 34.7.7, 35.7
DoPreparePrinting 15.8.2
DOS 1.3, 35.2
dot A.4.3, A.4.4, B.2.1, 11.2, 11.6.1,
15.8.3, 15.9, 35.7
dots 11.2, 15.8.3, 35.5, 35.7
dotted B.5.5, B.5.7, 25.6
double B.1.1, B.1.6, B.2, B.3, B.3.1,
B.4.1, B.5.5, B.5.7, B.8.4,
B.8.9, D.1, D.4, D.5, D.7,
6.1, 6.3.5, 6.4, 6.5.2,
6.5.3, 6.6.4, 6.6.5, 6.7.2,
9.3, 10.4.7, 11.5.2,
11.5.3, 11.5.4, 13.2,
14.4.6, 15.2.10, 15.4,
15.6.6, 15.7.2, 15.7.5,
16.2, 16.3.5, 17.1.2,
17.1.3, 18.1.2, 18.1.5,
18.4.1, 18.4.2, 18.4.4,
18.4.5, 19.2, 19.2.4,
19.2.5, 20.3, 22.2, 22.5,
33.7.3, 34.2, 34.4, 34.5.5,
34.6.5, 34.8, 34.8.12,
35.2
doubleclick B.5.6, 17.1.3
doubles D.2
doubly 12.4
DoUpdate 31.1
DoWaitCursor 10.2
down A.1, A.1.1, A.3.1, A.4.1, A.4.4,
A.5.2, B.3, B.4.4, B.6.1,
B.8.7, 0.4, 1.2, 1.3, 2.1,

3.3, 7.6, 8.2, 8.6.11, 9.5,
10.3, 11.5.1, 11.5.2,
11.5.3, 11.5.4, 11.5.5,
11.6.1, 12.2, 13.2, 14.1,
14.5, 15.1, 15.5.5, 15.8.4,
17.4, 18.4.3, 20.0, 20.2,
25.6, 29.1, 33.1, 33.5,
34.5.3, 34.7.7, 34.8,
34.8.1, 34.8.5, 34.8.6,
35.2, 35.7, Prf
download 21, 35.2
downloading 26.2
downward 11.2, 11.6.1
dozen 13.6
dpi 11.1, 11.2, 11.6.1, 15.8.3
DPtoLP 11.6.1, 15.5.6
DRAFT_QUALITY 11.4.6
drag B.5.6, B.6.4, D.4, D.6, 4.6, 6.4,
6.6.4, 6.6.5, 11.5.4, 19.2,
30.1, 32.1, 34.4
DragAcceptFiles 32.1
dragged 0.4, 4.6, 32.1
dragging 4.2, 10.2, 15.2.4, 15.7.2,
18.1.2, 20.3, 32.0, 34.2
DragQueryPoint 32.1
drags 4.6, 11.5.4, 15.2.7
dramatic 11.5.3
dramatically A.1
drastically A.1.1
draw A.3.1, A.3.2, A.3.3, B.5.3, D.1,
D.2, D.3, D.5, D.6, D.7,
0.4, 5.1, 11.0, 11.2, 11.3,
11.4, 11.4.1, 11.4.2,
11.4.3, 11.4.4, 11.4.6,
11.5, 11.5.3, 11.5.4,
11.5.5, 11.6.1, 11.6.2,
11.6.3, 12.3, 14.5, 15.0,
15.1, 15.2.4, 15.2.9,
15.2.10, 15.3.1, 15.3.6,
15.4, 15.4.4, 15.5, 15.5.5,
15.5.6, 15.5.7, 15.6.1,
15.6.13, 15.7.11, 15.8.3,
16.3.4, 16.3.5, 16.3.6,
18.4.1, 23.2, 23.7, 24.3,
25.0, 25.6, 25.7, 26.4,
29.1, 29.2, 29.3, 34.1,
34.5.5, 34.5.7, 34.6.5,
34.8.1, 34.8.4, 35.1, 35.8
draw_terrain A.3.2
drawback D.5
DRAWDOC 15.2.6, 15.4.3, 15.5.1,
15.5.3, 15.6.2, 15.6.3,
15.6.5, 15.6.7, 15.6.8,
15.7.7, 15.7.9
DrawFocusRect 11.4.3, 25.6
DrawIcon 11.4.8, 11.5.2
drawings 0.4, 4.5, 5.1, 11.4.6, 11.5,
15.1, 15.6, 16.3, 16.3.2,
34.1
DrawItem 25.3, 25.4, 25.6, 26.4
DRAWITEMSTRUCT 25.6
drawn A.3.1, D.2, D.6, 0.1, 0.3, 0.4,
11.0, 11.1, 11.2, 11.3,
11.4.1, 11.4.2, 11.4.3,
11.4.4, 11.4.6, 11.4.8,
11.5.1, 11.5.2, 11.5.3,
11.5.4, 11.5.5, 11.6.2,
15.2.6, 15.3, 15.8.3, 25.1,
25.2, 25.4, 25.6, 25.7,
25.9, 26.4, 29.1, 29.2,

29.3, 29.4, 34.6.10
draws D.6, D.7, 11.2, 11.4.1, 11.4.3,
11.4.5, 11.4.6, 11.4.7,
11.5.3, 11.5.4, 11.5.5,
11.6.2, 15.4.3, 15.8.3,
25.1, 26.4, 32.5, 34.5.5,
34.6.9, 34.8.4, 34.8.7,
35.5, 35.7
DrawText 11.4.6
DRAWVIEW 15.4.2, 15.5, 15.7.9
dread 34.8.1
drew 11.4.2, 11.4.6, 15.3
drive 1.5, 13.6, 22.0, 34.0
driven 0.0, 0.3, 1.0, 1.3, 19.3, Prf
driver D.1, 7.5, 11.3, 33.3, 33.4.1
drivers 33.3, 33.4, 33.4.1
drives 7.2, 25.0
driving A.1, A.3.2, 34.8
drop 0.4, 25.6, 32.1, 34.4
dropped 9.5, 32.1
drops 9.5
drw 15.2.1, 15.5, 15.6.1, 16.4
DT_BOTTOM 11.4.6
DT_CALCRECT 11.4.6
DT_CENTER 11.4.6
DT_EXPANDTABS 11.4.6
DT_EXTERNALLEADING 11.4.6
DT_LEFT 11.4.6
DT_NOCLIP 11.4.6
DT_NOPREFIX 11.4.6
DT_RIGHT 11.4.6
DT_SINGLELINE 11.4.6
DT_TABSTOP 11.4.6
DT_TOP 11.4.6
DT_VCENTER 11.4.6
DT_WORDBREAK 11.4.6
due 25.2
dummy 8.6.1, 32.6
dump 1.4, 3.3, 3.4, 3.5, 4.2, 4.6, 5.2,
5.4, 6.2, 7.1, 8.1, 9.1, 9.2,
9.3, 12.1.1, 13.3, 13.4,
13.5, 14.4.4, 15.2.6, 15.3,
15.6.2, 15.6.8, 17.4.7,
18.1.12, 18.2
DumpAllObjectsSince 13.5
dumped 13.3, 13.4
Dumping 10.1, 12.3, 13.3, 13.4, 13.5,
15.2.6, 15.6.8
dumps 7.2, 12.3, 13.4, 13.5
DumpStatistics 13.5
duplicate 4.7, 12.1.1, 12.1.3, 12.5,
15.5, 16.3.4, 16.3.5, 25.1,
33.1, 33.4.2
duplicated 6.6.8, 9.3, 14.4.2
duplicates 12.1.1, 18.6
duplicating A.2.5
duration 10.3, 35.2
dv D.2
dwFlags D.1, D.5, 7.2, 7.3, 7.4, 7.6
DWORD 11.4.3, 12, 12.3, 22.2, 22.5
dwStyle 3.1, 3.2
dynamic 12.3
dynamically 6.5.1, 11.5.4, 12.1.2, 12.3,
18.5
dynaset 33.7.6
dynasets 33.7.6
DYNCREATE 10.4, 12.3
earlier A.1.1, B.5.2, 1.1, 8.7, 11.6.1,
15.5.3, 18.1, 19.2.2,
19.2.4, 19.2.6, 19.2.8,

19.2.10, 19.3.5, 19.3.10,
20.0, 23.8, 33.4, 33.7.1
early A.3.2, 8.5, 13.2, 18.1.5
ease 7.0, 15.7, 15.8
eats 4.7
EC 13.4
eccentrics 4.7
echo B.3, B.4.1, 32.6
echoed B.2
ed 3.2, 11.4.6, 13.5, 16.1.1, 16.2, 16.3
edge B.2.3, C.1, 11.2
edges 11.4.3
Editable 1.2, 1.3, 2.1, 3.4, 5.4, 18.4.5,
22.0
edited 34.6.3
editing B.1.3, 0.1, 5.1, 6, 6.3.4, 11.0,
16.3, 16.4, 33.1, 33.4.3,
34.1, 34.2, 34.4, 34.5,
34.5.2, 34.5.5, 34.6,
34.6.4
edition A.1
editions C.0
edits 14.3
educational A.8, B.6.1, 15.3
EDVIEW 16.1.1
effect A.4.2, D.3, 3.3, 5.2, 6.3.7, 6.5.1,
7.2, 11.5.2, 13.2, 15.6,
18.4, 25.7, 29.1, 35.2,
35.3
effective 0.1, 3.0
effectively 0.3, 18.2
effects A.5, B.4.4, 7.3, 13.2, 16.3, 32.8,
34.3
efficiency 1.1, 18.5.3
efficient A.4.3, A.5.2, 0.1, 9.0, 11.4.6,
12.1.2, 12.2, 12.3, 15.4.4,
16.2, 18.4.3, 29.4,
33.6.10, 34.3, 35.3
efficiently 34.4
effort 1.2, 6.7, 18.4.6, 18.6, 19.0, 22.7,
23.8, 34.8.11
Eight A.1, 5.4, 6, 11.4.4, 11.6.2, 15.3,
22.5, 25.6
eject 18.5
elaborate 27.2
elapse 35.7
elapsed 12.1.3, 27.0, 27.1
elapses 4.5
electronic C.0, 17.5
element A.5.2, 11.2, 12.2, 12.3, 12.4,
18.1, 20.3, 22.5, 32.6,
34.8
elementary 11.5.2, 12.5
elements A.3, A.3.1, A.4.2, A.4.5,
A.5.1, A.5.2, B.5, 0.4, 1.2,
1.3, 3.1, 5.1, 6.1, 6.6.5,
6.7, 11.2, 11.5.1, 11.5.2,
12.2, 12.3, 12.4, 13.2,
13.3, 13.4, 13.5, 15.2.6,
18.0, 18.1.7, 20.3, 28.0,
31.1
Eleven 4.2
eliminate A.3.2, A.7.1, 6.4, 11.4.1,
11.5.3, 15.4.1, 15.8.2,
16.2, 16.3.5, 32.6, 34.7,
35.4, 35.8
eliminated 35.4
Eliminates 7.5, 33.1, 35.4
eliminating A.1.1, D.5
ellipse 11.0, 11.4.3, 11.4.4, 34.8.3,

34.8.4
ellipses 11.1, 11.4.3, 11.4.4, 11.4.7, 11.5.4, 13.6.1
else A.1.1, A.5, A.8, 4.2, 11.5.3, 15.3.1, 16.2, 18.1.9, 19.2, 33.1, 34.1, 34.2, 34.4, 34.8.13, 35.7, 35.9
elsewhere A.4.2, 3.3, 11.5.4, 14.5, 19.2.7, 34.5.5, 34.5.6
email C.0, Prf
embarking 14.0
embed 11.5.5, 34.4, 34.7.2
embedded A.3.1, A.3.2, 6.7, 8.2, 9.2, 10.4.10, 11.4.6, 19.2.9, 21.1.5, 34.4, 34.5, 34.5.2, 34.5.3, 34.6.3, 34.6.10
Embedding 34.1, 34.4, 34.5
embodied A.3.2
embodies B.8.1, 10, 34.8.2
emergencies C.1
emit 19.3.8
emphasis 33.2
EmpId 33.1, 33.2.1, 33.6.4
employ 11.5.2
employee 33.1, 33.2, 33.2.1, 33.2.2, 33.2.3, 33.2.4, 33.4, 33.4.2, 33.4.3, 33.6, 33.6.2, 33.6.4, 33.7.1, 33.7.2, 33.7.3
employees 33.0, 33.1, 33.2.2
employment 17.5
EMPSET 33.6.2, 33.6.3, 33.6.10
Empties 12.4, 15.2.6
empty A.7.1, B.1.1, B.5.2, B.5.5, B.5.7, 3.4, 10.3, 11.4.1, 11.5.2, 12.1.2, 12.4, 14.5, 18.4.3, 22.5, 31.1, 32.5, 33.8.3, 34.8.11, 35.7
EmptyUndoBuffer 8.2
emulate A.3.1, 9.0, 17.0
EN 5.3
EN_CHANGE 5.3, 5.4, 17.1.3, 17.3.4, 31.5
EN_CHANGED 17.3.4
enable A.2, B.4, B.5.3, B.5.4, B.5.6, D.5, D.7, 0.4, 6.5.1, 10.5, 12.3, 13.3, 15.2.1, 15.5, 15.6.1, 15.8.1, 16.2, 17.1.1, 18.1.1, 18.4.1, 18.4.3, 18.4.5, 18.4.6, 18.5.1, 19.1.1, 20.1, 20.6, 20.7, 28.1, 31.0, 31.1, 31.3, 31.5, 33.6.1, 33.7.1, 34.5.1, 34.5.3, 34.6.1, 34.7.1, 35.8
enabled B.1.1, D.1, D.5, D.6, 6.4, 6.5, 8.6.7, 8.6.10, 18.4, 18.4.3, 18.4.4, 18.4.6, 18.4.7, 31.1, 34.8
EnableDocking 30.1
EnableExtraControls 28.1
EnableMenuItem 6.5.1, 8.6.10
enables A.1.2, D.1, 7.5, 7.6, 8.6.10, 13.5, 13.7, 18.4.3
EnableShellOpen 10.5
EnableWindow 7.6
enabling 6.5.1, 8.6.10, 13.4, 18.4, 18.4.3, 28.1, 31.6, 35.8
encapsulate A.3.1, A.4.2, 11.5.5, 12, 14.4.4, 15.3, 18.2, 33.2.5,

34.1, 34.7
encapsulated 12.1.1, 33.3, 35.0, 35.8
encapsulates 1.0, 2.1, 7.2, 7.3, 7.4, 7.5, 7.6, 11.0, 11.4.1, 12.1, 12.1.1, 12.1.2, 12.1.3, 16.2, 18.1.12, 20.5, 34.5.3, 34.6.3
encapsulating 0.1
encapsulation A.1.1, A.3.1, A.3.2, 1.1, 15.2.6, 15.3, 15.7.9, 18.2, 25.4, 35.8
encapsulations 12.1.4
encodes 2.3
encounter A.1
Encyclopedia 0.2, 14.4.4, 15.2.6, 15.8, 15.8.2, 18.5.6, 33.9, 34.9
end A.2.1, A.2.3, A.2.4, A.3.2, A.5.2, B.5.6, D.0, D.1, D.3, D.5, D.6, D.7, 1.5, 3.3, 5.3, 6.4, 7.2, 8.0, 8.6.7, 9.4, 12.1.1, 12.1.2, 12.2, 12.4, 13.6, 14.4.6, 15.2.3, 15.2.6, 16.3.3, 16.6, 18.1.12, 18.4.5, 22.0, 26.2, 27.1, 32.1, 32.2, 33.1, 33.8.3, 34.1, 34.4, 35.2, 35.4, 35.7, Prf
END_MESSAGE_MAP 4.3
EndDialog 6.6.8, 20.5, 20.7, 32.4
endeavor 19.0
ended 6
ending A.2.6, A.6, 8.1, 8.2, 11.3, 11.4.1, 11.4.4, 11.5.4, 15.2.1
endl A.2.3
endless 15.9
EndPage 11.6.3
EndPaint 11.4.1
endpoints A.3.2
ends A.2.3, A.3.2, D.2, 4.3, 11.6.3, 15.3, 34.1, 34.2
EndWaitCursor 10.2
enforce 33.1, 33.2.5
enforcement A.4.2
engine 7.6, 8.6.7, 8.6.8, 33.4.2, 34.4, 34.7
engineer 21.1.8
engines 5.1
English A.4.1, 5.4, 6.1, 6.7, 11.6.1, 12.5, 33.6.5, Prf
enhance A.1.2, 0.4, 8.3, 20.7, 25.0, 29.4, 31.4, 34.8.1
enhanced 24.1, 24.2
enhancements A.1, A.1.1
enjoy 13.8
enjoyable 12
enlarged 27.0
enough A.3.2, A.4.4, 2.3.2, 3.4, 5.1, 5.3, 8.6.2, 9.1, 11.4.6, 11.5, 11.5.3, 11.5.4, 11.6.2, 13.5, 15.3, 15.4, 17.5, 18.1.12, 19.4, 34.1, 35.4
Enroll 33.4, 33.8.4, 33.9
ensure 7.0, 33.1
ensures C.1, 5.3, 14.4.1, 27.1
enter B.1, B.1.2, B.1.3, B.1.7, 1.0, 1.3, 1.4, 5.3, 6, 6.5.3, 6.6.4, 7.2, 8.1, 8.6.3, 11.5, 15.4, 15.7, 15.7.2, 17.5, 18.1,

18.5.5, 24.0, 33.4.3, 33.8.4, 34.2, 34.3, 34.6.7, 34.8.3, Prf
entered 2.3, 6.6.7, 6.6.8, 7.2, 8.1, 8.6.7, 15.3, 15.7.11, 17.4, 18.3, 22.0, 24.0, 33.6.4
entering B.3, 3.3, 12.4, Prf
enterprise 33.0, 33.1
enterprises 33.0
enters B.2.1, 6.6, 8.1, 8.6.1, 11.4.6, 12.1.1, 15.7.8, 15.7.9, 18.2, 22.0, 24.0, 31.1, 31.4
entire A.5.2, B.2.2, D.1, D.2, 0.1, 1.2, 2.6, 7.3, 8.2, 9.1, 10.4, 11.4.6, 11.4.7, 11.5.3, 11.5.4, 11.5.5, 11.6.2, 12.6, 13.5, 14.5, 15.4, 15.6, 15.8.3, 15.8.4, 16.2, 22.5, 25.6, 33.1, 33.2, 34.2, 34.3, 34.4, 34.9, 35.2
entirely A.1.1, 11.4.1, 35.3
entities 16.5, 33.1, 35.1
entitled 14.4.4
entity 33.1, 35.1
entries A.4.1, B.7.1, 4.4, 10.5, 14.5, 15.8, 17.0, 18.4.6, 19.3.8, 21.1.6, 23.7, 25.5, 33.1, 33.8.4, 34.5.3, 34.7.6, 34.7.7
entry B.7.1, B.8.1, 4.4, 4.7, 5.3, 6.5, 6.5.3, 7.6, 11.4.1, 11.4.6, 11.5.3, 12.1.1, 12.2, 14.5, 15.2.6, 15.3.1, 15.3.3, 15.3.8, 17.5, 18.1, 18.1.10, 18.4.5, 18.4.6, 19.1.2, 19.4, 20.7, 21.1.8, 22.0, 23.7, 24.0, 25.5, 26.2, 33.1, 34.4, 34.8.3, Prf
EnumAllFontFamiliesCB 26.2
enumerate 0.4, 26.0, 26.1, 26.2, 26.3, 26.5
enumerated 26.1, 26.3
enumerating 26.1, 26.3, 26.5
enumeration 26.0, 26.1, 26.2, 26.3, 26.4, 26.5, 28.1
enumerations 13.5
EnumFontFamilies 26.1, 26.2, 26.3
EnumFontFamProc 26.1
EnumFontStylesCB 26.5
ENUMLOGFONT 26.2
environment A.1, A.4.4, A.5.2, B, B.1, B.9, 0.0, 0.1, 1.0, 1.1, 1.2, 1.4, 13.2, 33.1, 34.1, 34.3, 35.1, 35.2
environments C.1, 0.0, 0.2, 20.0, 33.2, 33.2.5, 34.1, 35.2
EOF A.2.3
equal A.5.2, A.6, A.7.1, 7.6, 11.4.5, 25.5, 25.6, 26.4, 33.2.2
equality A.3.3, A.5.2, A.5.3, 12.1.4
equally 16.3.6
EqualRect 12.1.4
Equation 34.4
equipped 6.4
equivalent A.1, A.7.1, B.2.1, D.2, 2.1, 4.3, 8.3, 12.2, 17.1, 19.1.2, 23.6, 34.4

equivalently A.2.3
equivalents 12.1.2, 17.5
erase B.6.1, 11.5.4, 11.6.2, 29.2
erased D.5, 11.5.4, 11.6.2, 25.6, 29.3
erases 29.3
erasing 11.4.8, 11.5.4, 29.2, 29.4
erra A.5.2
errb A.5.2
erroneous 13.2
error A.2.3, A.4.1, A.4.6, A.5.1, A.5.2,
    A.8, B.1.6, B.3, B.3.1, 3.1,
    6.7, 6.7.2, 6.7.3, 8.6.2,
    11.6.3, 12.1.1, 12.2, 12.4,
    12.5, 13.2, 13.3, 13.5,
    13.6, 13.6.1, 13.6.2, 13.7,
    16.4, 17.3.5, 18.1.11,
    20.7, 22.0, 24.0, 31.6,
    33.2.1, 33.6.5, 33.8.4,
    34.8
errors B.1.6, B.3, B.3.1, 7.1, 7.2, 12.4,
    13.0, 13.1, 13.3, 13.6,
    13.6.1, 33.1
ErrorTranslate 12.5
ES_AUTOHSCROLL 8.1, 8.2
ES_CENTER 8.1
ES_LEFT 8.1
ES_LOWERCASE 8.1
ES_MULTILINE 8.2
ES_NOHIDESEL 8.1
ES_OEMCONVERT 8.1
ES_PASSWORD 8.1
ES_READONLY 8.1
ES_RIGIIT 8.1
ES_UPPERCASE 8.1
escape 34.5.2
esoteric A.6, 4.5, 7.2, 10.1
especially A.1.1, B.4, B.7.4, 9.2, 10.5,
    11.3, 11.6.1, 17.3.3, 23.9,
    26.5, 33.7.5, 34.4
essence A.3.3
essential A.3.3, B.3.2, 15.5.6, 27.1
Essentially A.4.5, A.4.6, 8.2, 15.3.1,
    19.3.10, 35.2, 35.7
Essentials C.1, 19.0
establish 11.5.4, 22.5
established 6.6.8, 11.6.3, 21, 22.0
estimates 17.4
etc A.1.1, A.5.2, A.6, B.1.2, B.4, B.4.1,
    B.6.2, 0.4, 1.3, 4.1, 5.2,
    6.1, 7.3, 11.3, 11.6.2,
    12.3, 12.4, 13.6, 15.1,
    15.8.3, 17.0, 19.2, 31.1,
    35.8, Prf
eternal D.2
ETO_CLIPPED 11.4.6
ETO_OPAQUE 11.4.6
ette 6.3.4
evaluates 13.2
even A.1.1, A.8, D.0, 5.1, 6.5, 6.5.1,
    7.6, 8.1, 9.1, 11.4.7,
    11.5.4, 11.6.1, 11.6.2,
    13.5, 14.1, 16.2, 17.5,
    18.4.7, 25.6, 27.2, 30.0,
    32.2, 34.1, 35.8
event A.8, B.7.1, B.8.8, D.3, D.6, 0.3,
    1.0, 1.1, 1.3, 1.5, 2.2, 2.3,
    2.3.1, 3.0, 4.0, 4.1, 4.4,
    4.5, 4.6, 4.7, 9.3, 10, 10.3,
    11.2, 11.3, 11.4.1, 11.4.6,
    11.5.1, 11.5.2, 11.5.3,

11.5.4, 12.3, 14.5, 15.1,
    15.2.3, 15.3, 15.3.7,
    15.3.8, 15.6.9, 15.7,
    15.7.2, 15.7.3, 15.7.11,
    17.3.4, 18.2, 18.4.2,
    18.4.4, 21.1.8, 23.7, 24.1,
    27.1, 34.8, 34.8.1,
    34.8.10, 35.1, 35.2, 35.7,
    Prf
events B.7.1, B.8.8, D.6, 0.4, 1.0, 1.3,
    2.3, 2.3.2, 3.0, 3.2, 4.0,
    4.1, 4.2, 4.4, 7.1, 7.6, 9.1,
    9.3, 10, 10.3, 11.2, 11.4.1,
    11.4.6, 11.5.1, 11.5.3,
    11.5.4, 12.3, 14.4.5, 15.0,
    15.2.8, 15.3, 15.3.1,
    15.3.3, 15.5, 17.2, 18.4.2,
    23.7, 27.1, 29.1, 32.4,
    34.5.3, 34.8, 34.8.1,
    34.8.3, 34.8.13, 35.1,
    35.2, 35.9, Prf
eventual 8.5
eventually B.3.1, 4.7, 15.3.1, 15.3.2,
    15.3.5, 19.1.2, 19.2, 23.1,
    30.2, 31.1, 34.0, 34.1,
    34.3, 34.8.3
everyone 8.3, 33.1
everything A.1, A.1.1, A.2, A.2.1, A.7,
    D.6, 1.3, 8.6.5, 8.7, 10,
    11.0, 11.2, 11.4.1, 12.1.1,
    13.3, 13.5, 15.3.1, 16.2,
    18.1.9, 19.0, 19.2,
    19.3.10, 22.0, 23.1, 29.3,
    34.0, 34.5.7, 34.8.13,
    35.2, 35.7
everywhere A.5, A.8, 9.0
evolutionary A.1.1, A.3.2, 34.1
evolve A.1.1
evolved A.1.1, A.3.2, 33.2
exact 1.3, 11.4.6, 13.2, 13.6, 15.2.1,
    15.8.3, 22.2, Prf
exactly A.2.7, B.2.1, 0.3, 4.2, 6.3.3,
    6.5.4, 8.6.4, 9.1, 11.1,
    11.5.4, 12.1.2, 12.2, 13.5,
    14.1, 15.4, 15.5, 15.8.1,
    15.8.3, 17.3.5, 18.4.2,
    18.4.4, 18.4.7, 20.3, 20.5,
    23.1, 23.8, 33.6, 33.6.5,
    33.7.2, 34.1, 34.4, 34.5.3,
    34.6.3, 34.8.12, 35.7
examine A.2, A.3.3, B.2, B.2.1, 1.4,
    1.5, 2.0, 3.0, 4.0, 4.2, 4.6,
    7.0, 7.2, 11.4, 11.4.7,
    11.5.5, 12.3, 12.4, 13.1,
    13.6, 14.4.6, 15.3.2, 15.8,
    15.8.1, 16.5, 17.2, 18.4.6,
    19.1.1, 24.2, 25.0, 33.8.4,
    35.8
examining 11.5.2, 11.5.4, 12.3, 16.5
examples A.1.1, A.2.3, A.3.3, A.4.6,
    A.6, A.8, B.4, D.1, 0.1,
    2.1, 2.3, 3.1, 3.5, 4.8, 5.1,
    5.2, 6.6.8, 7.6, 11.3,
    11.5.1, 11.5.3, 11.5.4,
    11.5.5, 11.6.1, 11.6.3,
    13.6, 13.6.2, 14.0, 14.1,
    14.4.5, 14.5, 15.0, 15.2.2,
    15.3, 15.4, 15.5, 15.6,
    15.7, 15.8.1, 17.0, 17.4.1,
    18.4, 19.2.3, 19.2.7, 20.8,

29.4, 33.2, 33.4, 33.5,
    33.7, 33.9, 34.8, 34.8.1,
    34.8.13, 35.1, 35.3, 35.8,
    35.9, Prf
Excel 15.6, 33.3, 34.2, 34.6.2, 34.6.10,
    34.7, 34.7.7, 34.7.9
except A.1, 3.3, 4.6, 12.1.1, 12.4, 15.4,
    20.3, 22.2, 23.8, 25.3,
    25.4, 25.7, 32.4, 32.5
exception B.6.1, 0.4, 9.0, 12, 12.1.1,
    12.3, 12.5, 13.0, 13.6,
    13.6.1, 13.6.2, 15.3.8,
    22.4, 22.6, 33.6.5, 33.8.2
exceptional 13.0, 13.6
exceptionhandling 33.8.4
exceptions B.2, 10.6, 12, 12.1.1, 12.5,
    13.6, 13.6.1, 13.6.2,
    33.6.5
excess 18.5.4, 20.8
Exchange 6.6.8, 14.5, 15.7.8, 18.3,
    22.0, 22.1, 22.2, 22.4,
    22.5, 22.6, 22.7, 23.8,
    30.2, 33.5, 33.9
exchanges 22.2, 22.5, 32.4
exchanging 22.6
excited A.5
exciting 35.10
exclamation 7.1, 10.2
excluded 13.2
excluding 11.4.6
exclusive 12.1.1
EXE B.3, B.6.1, 10.1, 13.3
executable B.1.6, B.2, B.3, B.6.1, 3.3,
    6.1, 6.3.6, 13.1, 13.3,
    14.2, 34.4
executables 3.3
execute A.8, B.1, B.1.7, B.2.1, B.3,
    B.3.1, B.3.2, B.8.1, 1.3,
    1.4, 2.3, 3.3, 4.4, 5.3, 6.4,
    6.6.7, 6.7.3, 11.5.2,
    11.6.3, 12.1.1, 13.1, 13.2,
    13.3, 16.2, 16.3.6, 21.1.7,
    33.2.5, 33.4.4, 34.7.5,
    34.7.6, 34.8.3, 35.2
executed A.2.8, B.3.2, D.2, D.3, 1.5,
    2.3, 34.6.4, 34.7.6, 35.7
executes A.7, B.2, B.2.2, 1.2, 4.1, 13.6,
    15.3.1, 35.2, 35.3
executing 2.3, 6.7, 10.2
execution A.4.3, A.7, B.2, B.2.1, B.2.2,
    B.3.2, 1.3, 1.4, 2.3, 2.3.2,
    5.2, 5.4, 9.3, 11.5.3, 13.2,
    13.5, 13.6, 35.2, 35.7
exercise B.1.1, 8.0, 15.2.1, 15.5.6, 16.5,
    18.1.13
exercised B.6.6, 3.3, 8.1
exercises B.4, C.1, 8.7
EXEs 3.3
exhaustively 12.6, 33.9
exist A.1, A.2.6, A.8, B.8.7, 0.4, 2.3.1,
    3.5, 6.7, 7.2, 7.3, 12.5,
    13.0, 13.2, 13.6, 17.0,
    19.2.9, 20.0, 23.2, 23.3,
    25.7, 27.1, 33.1, 33.4.1,
    34.1, 34.2, 34.8.5, 35.7
existed 15.4.4
existence A.2.6, A.4.3, A.4.6, A.5.2,
    A.5.3, 35.7, 35.8
existent 11.4.1, 12.5, 18.1.5
Existing A.1.1, A.2.10, A.3.1, A.5,

A.5.1, A.8, B.7.6, 0.4, 2.1,
 2.3.1, 6.4, 7.2, 8.3, 8.7,
 10.4.10, 11.4.6, 11.5.2,
 11.5.4, 12.1.2, 12.2, 12.4,
 13.3, 15.3, 16.3.5, 18.1,
 18.4.5, 20.1, 23.5, 23.8,
 25.7, 30.2, 33.1, 34.3,
 34.5.5, 34.6.4, Prf
exists A.1, A.2.5, A.3.1, A.3.2, 4.7, 6.5,
 6.5.3, 6.6.8, 8.3, 18.1.5,
 27.1, 28.1, 33.2, 33.4.2,
 33.6.4, 34.1, 35.4
Exit B.6.1, 1.3, 6.4, 6.5.3, 6.6.2, 8.3,
 8.5, 8.6.5, 8.6.10, 8.6.11,
 10.4.7, 10.4.10, 12.1.1,
 14.2, 15.3, 15.3.5, 33.7.2,
 34.5.5, 34.6.2, 35.4, 35.8
exiting 1.3, 6.5.3, 15.3.5
ExitInstance 10.6
exits B.3.2, 7.2, 8.6.5, 10.4.9, 10.4.10,
 15.2.6, 18.1.12
exotic 35.4
Exp 21.1.1
expand 1.2, 14.6, 15.0, 25.6, 28.1,
 28.2, 28.3, 34.0
expanded 1.2, 11.4.6, 20.4, 28.1, 28.2
expanding 0.1, 0.3, 0.4, 20.8, 28.0,
 28.1, 28.2, 28.3, Prf
expands 14.4.2, 28.0
expansion 28.1
expect B.6.1, 4.2, 6.5.3, 11.5.4, 14.2,
 15.8.1, 16.2, 18.4.3, 34.1,
 34.6.7, 34.8.12
expectation 34.1
expected A.2.4, A.7, B.6.1, 1.3, 3.3,
 4.1, 4.6, 6.4, 7.1, 9.3,
 12.1.2, 14.2, 16.1.2, 16.2,
 18.4.5, 34.5.7, 34.8
expecting 12.1.4
expects A.8, 16.2, 20.3
expedient A.5.2
expense 35.7
experience A.8.1, 0.3, 3.5, 5.2, 13.8,
 14.1, 14.4, 14.4.5, 14.6,
 15.9, 17.0, 33.1, 33.4.2,
 35.8, Prf
experienced 0.0
experiment 2.3.2, 5.3, 8.1, 10.5,
 11.5.3, 11.6.3, 12.2,
 14.4.6, 15.5.3, 18.4.6,
 18.6, 33.4.4, 33.7.6, 33.8,
 34.7.9, 34.8.1, 34.8.3,
 35.3, 35.7
experimentation B.4, 8.2
experimented 6.2
experimenting 11.4.6, 33.4.4
experiments 35.7
expert C.1
expires 35.2, 35.4, 35.7
explain B.6.1, D.1, D.2, 19.3.6, 28.0,
 29.0, 34.0, 34.5, 34.6
explained 6.4, 14.3, 14.4.5, 19.2, 22.5,
 26.1, Prf
explaining D.1, D.5
explains B.6.1, 11.6.1, 15.1, 18.5, 22.0,
 33.3
explanation A.1, B.3.2, 1.0, 2.3.3,
 15.2.6, 15.2.9, 15.6.2,
 18.1.4, 18.4.6, 23.0, 32.6
explanations 0.2

explanatory B.4.1, 1.3, 3.1, 7.5
explicit 2.3.3, 24.1
explicitly A.2.3, A.2.4, 25.7, 27.1
exploit 1.0, 4.7, 15.8.1, 19.5, 34.7.9
exploiting 20.8
exploits A.1.1
explore D.0, D.8, 13.3, 20.7, 21, 23.0,
 29.0, 30.0
explorer 21, 21.1, 21.2
Explorers 21
explores Prf
export 34.1
expose 15.1
exposed 11.2, 11.4.1, 11.5.3, 15.3.7
exposure A.3, 2.3, 11.2, 11.3, 11.4.1,
 11.4.6, 11.5.1, 11.5.2,
 11.5.3, 12.3, 15.1, 15.2.4,
 15.2.8, 15.2.9, 15.3,
 15.3.7, 25.1
express A.1
expressed 11.2
expresses 34.2, 34.8.1
expression 13.2, 18.4.3, 18.4.4
expressive A.1
extend A.1.1, A.3, A.3.1, A.3.2, A.5.2,
 11.5.5, 11.6.1, 12.3, 15.1,
 18.6, 22.6, 33.2, 33.2.3,
 33.6.8
extended A.1.1, 2.1, 9.3, 9.4, 34.3,
 34.5.3
extending 10.4.9
extends A.1.1, A.3.1, A.3.2, A.5.1,
 11.2, 11.5.5, 11.6.1,
 12.1.1, 34.3
extensible A.1.1, A.3.3
extension A.1.1, A.3.2, B.5.2, B.6.3,
 B.6.6, 6.1, 6.6.8, 7.2,
 8.6.2, 10.5, 15.1, 15.2.1,
 15.5, 15.6.1, 16.1.1, 16.4,
 17.1.1, 18.1.1
extensions A.1.2, A.2, A.2.3, A.3, 8.7,
 10.4.10, 14.4.1, 15.2.1
extensive C.1, 2.1, 12.1.2, 20.0
extensively 6.2, 6.8, 7.7, 11.4.7, 13.2,
 14.4.5, 14.6
extent 9.1, 11.6.1
extents 13.2
External B.8.5, B.8.6, B.8.7, 34.1, 34.4,
 34.8.4, 34.8.5, 34.8.6,
 34.8.10
ExtFloodFill 11.4.7
Extra 3.2, 5.2, 6.7, 11.4.8, 12.1.2, 12.2,
 15.8, 15.8.4, 25.6, 28.1,
 29.1, 31.4, 35.9
extract 5.3, 6.6, 6.6.8, 6.7, 7.0, 7.2, 9.1,
 10.6, 12.1.3, 15.7.9,
 15.7.11, 16.3, 18.3,
 18.4.2, 18.5.4, 22.0, 30.3
extracting 7.6, 15.8.4
extraction A.2.3, 22.0
extracts 5.4, 6.6.8, 12.3, 18.4.7, 25.6
extraneous 15.1, 34.3, 35.7
extrapolation 11.5.5, 15.1
extreme Prf
ExtTextOut 11.4.6, 25.6, 26.4
eye A.1.1, D.2, D.6, D.7
eyes 11.6.2
f A.2.3, B.1.6, D.2, D.6, D.7, 6.3.7,
 6.4, 6.5.3, 6.6.5, 6.6.8,
 15.2.9, 15.3, 15.6.3,

15.8.4, 17.1.1, 17.1.4,
 17.2, 17.4, 17.4.1, 17.4.4,
 17.4.6, 18.1.13, 18.2,
 19.1.2, 19.3.5, 19.4
face D.6, 0.1, 0.4, 4.5, 11.3, 11.4.6,
 15.8.4, 17.0, 18.4.5, 25.1,
 25.7, 29.1, 34.6.7, 34.8.1,
 Prf
faced A.1.1, 34.1, 35.8
faces D.6, D.7, 18.4.5
facilitate 6.6.8, 10.4, 28.0, 34.1
facilitated 10.5, 15.8.2
facilitates 33.6.6, 33.6.8
facilities 0.4, 12.6, 13.1, 13.7, 14.1,
 15.8.1, 34.1
facility 0.2, 6.7.3, 10.3, 10.4.10, 13.3,
 15.4, 19.0, 21.1.8, 33.0,
 33.3, 33.4, 34.1
fact A.1, A.2.4, A.3.1, A.5.2, A.6, 2.1,
 6.4, 6.6.8, 6.7.3, 9.5, 11.3,
 11.5.5, 12.1.1, 12.2, 13.2,
 13.3, 14.3, 15.1, 15.3,
 15.5.5, 15.5.6, 15.7,
 15.8.1, 15.8.4, 16.0, 17.2,
 18.4.7, 23.7, 25.7, 27.0,
 30.0, 33.1, 33.3, 34.0,
 34.1, 34.5.3, 35.2, 35.3,
 35.7
factor A.1.1
factors C.1, 11.6.1
factory 33.2
facts 6.1
Fahrenheit 1.3, 5.0, 5.1, 5.2, 17.0,
 17.1, 17.1.4, 17.2, 17.3.4,
 17.3.5, 17.4, 17.4.1,
 17.4.3, 17.4.4, 17.4.6,
 17.5
fail A.1.1, B.3, 13.2, 13.6, 16.4, 22.6,
 33.1, 33.6.5
failed B.8.1, 13.2, 13.6, 22.4, 34.8.3
fails D.1, 13.6, 22.6, 33.1
failure A.1.1, A.5.2, 13.2, 16.4, 20.6,
 33.1
faint D.7
fair 1.3, 8.6.7
fairly A.3, A.3.2, A.3.3, A.4.1, A.4.2,
 A.4.4, A.5.2, A.7, B.2.3,
 2.1, 3.5, 6.6.8, 7.4, 8.2,
 8.7, 9.1, 10.3, 10.4.10,
 11.0, 11.6.2, 14.0, 15.5,
 15.8.3, 15.9, 18.1, 18.4.4,
 27.2, 33.4.2, 34.1, 34.2,
 34.3, 34.5.5, 35.8
fall 5.3, 6.4, 12.3, 15.7.11, 34.8
FALSE D.5, 2.3.1, 3.1, 7.2, 8.6.1,
 8.6.10, 10.3, 11.5.4,
 12.1.1, 13.2, 15.8.2,
 15.8.4, 17.3.4, 22.3, 22.5,
 32.1, 33.8.2, 35.4
familiar A.3.1, A.3.2, B.1, B.1.2, B.2,
 B.3, 0.3, 1.1, 1.3, 3.3, 4.2,
 5.1, 5.2, 12.1.1, 14.5,
 19.5, 23.1, 23.9, 31.1,
 33.0, 33.1, 34.4, 34.5.3,
 34.6.3, 34.7.7, 34.8.1,
 35.0, 35.2, 35.7, Prf
familiarity 2.3.2, 11.4.6
families 26.1, 26.3
family 25.5, 26.1, 26.2, 26.3, 26.4,
 30.0

fancier 15.3.5
far A.1.2, A.3.2, A.5.2, D.6, 2.3.2, 2.4, 3.3, 4.4, 4.5, 10.3, 11.3, 11.4.6, 11.4.8, 11.6.1, 11.6.3, 12.3, 13.1, 14.4.1, 18.4.5, 22.0, 22.6, 33.1
fashion 14.4, 23.5, 29.2, 35.7
fashioned A.5.2
fast 12.1.1, 12.4, 35.8
faster A.5, 12.1.1, 12.1.2, 25.6, 35.2
FAT 12.1.1
fatal 13.7
favor A.5.3
feature A.1.1, A.3.1, A.5.1, A.5.2, A.8, B.4.2, C.1, D.6, 3.3, 5.2, 5.4, 6.5.1, 7.3, 9.5, 11.5.2, 12.3, 13.5, 13.6, 16.3, 18.3, 18.4, 19.1.2, 19.2.3, 21.1.1, 33.3, 34.1, 34.4, 34.8, Prf
featured 1.2, Prf
featureless D.6
fed 33.7.6
feed 34.1
feedback 1.3, 4.2, 11.5.2, 11.5.4, 24.0, 27.0
feel A.1, A.5.1, A.7, D.2, 0.1, 1.0, 1.3, 5.3, 6.6.5, 8.5, 14.0, 14.1, 14.4.6, 16.3, 17.5, 18.1, 18.5.5, 33.2, 33.4.4, 33.5, 34.8.1, 35.0, 35.2, 35.7, Prf
feeling 2.3, 14.3, 15.7
feels 34.6.10
fenetre 12.5
few A.4.6, B.4, B.6.1, B.8.1, 1.2, 2.5, 4.1, 11.0, 11.2, 11.6, 19.2, 22.5, 25.7, 26.1, 26.5, 28.1, 33.1, 34.5.2, 34.5.6, 34.6.3, 34.8.2
FF_DECORATIVE 11.4.6
FF_DONTCARE 11.4.6
FF_MODERN 11.4.6
FF_ROMAN 11.4.6
FF_SCRIPT 11.4.6
FF_SWISS 11.4.6
fgets 12.1.1
Fibonacci A.5.2, A.6
fiction A.3.1
field B.1.2, B.3, B.6.3, B.7.4, B.8.7, B.8.9, D.6, 6.1, 6.3.5, 6.3.7, 6.4, 7.5, 8.1, 12.5, 15.2.1, 15.6.1, 15.7.6, 15.7.8, 18.1.4, 18.1.9, 18.3, 18.4.5, 22.0, 22.2, 22.5, 24.0, 33.1, 33.2, 33.2.1, 33.2.3, 33.2.4, 33.4.3, 33.5, 33.6.2, 33.6.4, 33.6.6, 33.6.8, 33.6.10, 33.7, 33.8, 33.9, 34.8.4, 34.8.12
fields 1.3, 6.4, 6.6.8, 15.7.6, 17.5, 18.1, 18.3, 18.4, 18.4.1, 18.4.4, 18.6, 22.0, 29.0, 33.1, 33.2, 33.2.1, 33.2.2, 33.2.4, 33.4.3, 33.5, 33.6.2, 33.7, 33.7.3, 33.7.5
fifth B.6.1, 4.2, 7.2, 7.6, 11.2, 12.1.2
filenames 7.2

FILETIME 12.1.3
FileView B.1.5, B.6.2
FileViewit B.1.5
fill A.2.3, A.5.2, 1.1, 1.2, 5.1, 9.1, 11.3, 11.4.3, 11.4.5, 11.4.7, 11.5, 12.1.3, 12.6, 13.6, 14.4.4, 15.8.3, 17.5, 20.3, 21.1.7, 24.1, 26.2, 29.2, 33.6.10, 33.7.2, 34.6.5, 34.8, 34.8.4, 34.8.11
filled A.2.5, 1.2, 3.2, 3.4, 7.2, 11.4.3, 11.4.4, 11.4.5, 11.4.7, 11.4.8, 11.6.2, 33.6.10, 34.8.3
filling 9.5, 11.3, 11.4.5, 11.4.7, 12.4, 22.5
FillRect 11.4.3, 25.6
fills 5.1, 8.4, 9.1, 9.3, 11.4.3, 11.4.5, 11.4.6, 11.4.7, 11.5.4, 12.1.3, 12.2, 17.5, 22.1, 33.6.11, 34.6.5, 35.7
filter 7.2, 27.1, 29.2, 33.6.8, 33.6.10
filtered B.4.2, 29.1, 29.2
filtering 7.2, 12.1.1, 33.6.8
Filters 7.2, 14.3, 29.2
final A.5.2, D.5, 5.4, 8.5, 11.5.3, 11.5.4, 11.6.2, 13.1, 13.2, 15.2.6, 25.7, 30.1, 34.6.7
Finally A.3.2, A.4.6, A.7, 0.1, 1.0, 1.4, 2.1, 4.3, 8.6.7, 11.4.1, 11.4.3, 11.5.4, 12, 12.1.3, 17.2, 17.4.5, 18.5.6, 21.1.8, 32.6, 33.4.3, 34.5.5, 34.8
financial C.1
finder A.5.2
FindHelper 7.6
FindIndex 12.4
finding A.4.1, B.4.1, 3.3, 16.3.5, 25.6
findMessage 7.6, 8.6.7
FindNext 7.6
FindOneOf 12.1.2
FINDREPLACE 7.6
findReplaceDialog 8.6.7
finds A.2.7, A.6, A.7.1, 1.1, 9.4, 11.4.6, 11.4.7, 12.1.2, 13.5, 16.2, 23.7, 26.1
FindString 9.4
FindText 7.6
fine A.4.4, A.7, B.3.2, 6.6.4, 6.6.5, 10.2, 11.6.1, 18.1.2, 18.1.7, 18.1.8, 18.1.9, 18.1.10, 18.4.2, 18.4.4, 19.3.1, 29.3
finely 35.2
finger 32.6
Finish B.6.1, B.8.1, 18.1.8, 19.1.1, Prf
finished A.1.1, B.3, B.5.5, 1.1, 6.3.4, 11.3, 11.6.2, 15.0, 15.2.6, 15.4.3, 27.1, 34.6.5
finishes 8.6.1, 12.3, 12.4
fire 34.8.10
FireAdjusted 34.8.10
fired 34.8, 34.8.10
fires 34.8.1
firing 34.8
firm A.4
firms C.1
FirstName 33.2.1, 33.2.2, 33.2.3, 33.2.4, 33.6.4

fish 11.6.2
fist A.5.1
fit B.5.3, 3.3, 5.1, 8.1, 8.3, 9.1, 10.4.10, 11.4.6, 11.5.1, 11.5.5, 14.4.4, 15.5, 15.5.6, 15.6.1, 15.8.3, 15.8.4, 17.1.1, 18.1.1, 18.4.6, 23.7, 29.2, 32.0, 33.6.1, 33.7.1, 34.5.1, 34.6.1, 34.7.1, 34.8, 34.9, 35.2
fits 2.5, 11.4.6, 15.8.3, 16.2, 20.3, 32.5
Five A.1, A.6, B.2, B.4.1, C.1, 3.1, 3.5, 4.2, 5.1, 6.1, 7.2, 10.2, 11.4.6, 11.6.1, 12.1.2, 12.2, 14.5, 15.5, 15.8.3, 17.2, 18.4.6, 22.0, 22.5, 26.4, 33.1, 33.7.3, 33.7.4, 34.2, 35.7, Prf
fix A.1.2, B.3, D.4, D.7, 2.4, 6.4, 9.1, 13.2, 15.4, 22.0, 27.1, 34.5.5, 34.5.6, 35.4
fixed 7.3, 8.2, 9.1, 11.6.1, 11.6.2, 12.1.1, 12.2, 15.5, 25.6
FIXED_PITCH 11.4.6
fixes A.8, 8.7
flag D.1, 8.2, 8.6.1, 8.6.3, 11.5.2, 15.8.2, 18.4.2, 18.5.6, 20.4, 20.7, 22.5, 26.2, 26.4, 28.1, 29.1, 30.1, 35.6
flags D.1, 7.2, 7.3, 7.4, 7.5, 7.6, 11.5.3, 22.5, 30.1, 32.2
flakier A.7
flash 32.5
flavors 2.1, 12.2
fledged 6.3.7
flexibility A.2, A.2.6, B.1, 0.1, 11.4.6, 17.2, 30.0, 34.8.1, Prf
flexible 12.2, 30.0, 30.3, 31.4, 34.5.3, 34.7.9, 34.8
flicker D.4, D.5, 11.5.3, 11.6.2, 25.7
flight 11.6.2
flip A.3.1, 8.1
flipping A.3.1
float A.2.3, A.2.8, 0.4, 1.2, 7.6, 11.5.1, 22.2, 22.5, 30.0
FloatControlBar 30.1
floating B.1.6, B.2.3, 0.4, 5.3, 11.5.4, 30.1, 32.5, Prf
floats A.2.3, D.2
flood 11.4.7
flooded A.1
FLOODFILLSURFACE 11.4.7
flooding 11.4.7
flow 7.2, 15.8.2
flush A.2.3, 12.1.1
flushes D.1, 12.1.1
fly 7.3, 9.4, 30.1
flying A.3.2
FmtLines 8.2
focus 5.3, 8.1, 8.6.1, 11.4.3, 15.2.2, 18.4.2, 20.7, 22.4, 22.6, 25.2, 25.6, 28.1, 30.1, 32.5, 34.3
focused A.3, 9.4
focuses Prf
fog 15.8.3
folder 18.4.2, 18.4.4
follow 0.3, 2.3, 3.3, 6.5, 7.2, 9.1,

11.4.1, 12.3, 15.3, 16.5,
  18.1.7, 18.4, 18.5.6, 25.9,
  33.6.10, 34.8.1, 34.8.13,
  Prf
followed A.2.3, A.4.3, A.4.4, B, 4.3,
  6.3.6, 6.4, 11.4.5, 15.8.2,
  18.4.5, 19.2, 33.6.3,
  33.6.11
follows A.4.3, A.5.2, 1.3, 6.6.8, 7.4,
  11.4.6, 11.5.4, 13.6, 22.0,
  25.7
font B.1.3, 0.4, 3.5, 7.0, 7.3, 8.2, 8.7,
  9.2, 11.3, 11.4.2, 11.4.6,
  11.6.1, 11.6.3, 18.5.2,
  18.5.3, 18.5.4, 18.5.5,
  23.2, 25.0, 26.0, 26.1,
  26.2, 26.3, 26.4, 26.5,
  34.8, 34.8.11
fonts 0.4, 3.5, 3.6, 7.3, 9.0, 11.1,
  11.4.6, 18.5.2, 19.2, 23.6,
  26.0, 26.1, 26.2, 26.3,
  26.4, 26.5, 34.8.11
footnote 19.2, 19.2.3, 19.2.5, 19.2.7,
  19.3.3
footnotes 19.2
force B.3, 33.2.3, 33.6.5, 34.1
forced A.1.1, 5.3, 9.5, 20.5
forces A.5, A.5.2, 3.3, 10.5, 12.5,
  17.3.4, 25.1
forcing A.1.1, D.5, 16.2, 34.4
ForeColor 34.8.4
foreground 7.4, 25.6, 25.7, 34.8,
  34.8.4, 34.8.11, 35.7
foreign 1.3, 33.1, 33.7.4, 34.2
foremost 12.2
forest 0.2
forget A.1.1, 34.4
forgot B.8.1, 34.8.3
form A.1.1, A.2.1, A.4.1, A.4.3, A.4.6,
  A.6, B.1.6, B.3, B.3.2,
  B.6.1, B.7.7, B.8.4, 0.1,
  0.4, 1.1, 1.2, 2.1, 3.4, 4.4,
  9.2, 11.4.3, 11.4.4,
  11.5.2, 11.6.2, 12.1.3,
  12.2, 12.5, 14.2, 14.3,
  15.3, 15.8.4, 17.0, 17.1.2,
  17.2, 17.3, 17.3.2, 17.3.3,
  17.3.4, 17.4, 17.4.6, 17.5,
  17.6, 18.1, 18.1.2, 18.2,
  18.3, 18.5, 20.1, 20.4,
  23.7, 23.9, 28.1, 31.3,
  33.2.1, 33.6.2, 33.6.4,
  33.7, 33.7.2, 33.7.3,
  33.7.4, 33.7.5, 34.1, 34.4,
  34.7.7, 34.8.3, 35.9
formal 5.1
formalize A.3.2
format A.1.1, A.2.2, A.2.3, A.4.1,
  A.5.2, D.1, D.5, 5.2,
  6.5.3, 8.6.10, 9.0, 12.1.3,
  15.1, 15.8.2, 18.1.15,
  18.5, 18.5.4, 19.2, 19.2.2,
  19.2.4, 19.2.6, 19.2.8,
  19.2.10, 19.3.5, 19.3.10,
  34.1, 34.2
FormatGmt 12.1.3
formats A.2.3, D.1, 3.1, 9.2, 11.4.6, 12,
  12.1.3, 18.4.6, 18.4.7,
  26.1, 33.3, 34.1
formatted A.2.7, 7.0, 11.4.6, 19.2.5,

34.2
formatting A.2.3, 8.2, 11.4.6, 12.1.3,
  19.2, 34.1, 34.2, 35.1
formbased Prf
formed A.5.2, 4.6
former A.1.1, 11.6.3, 17.3.4
formerly 34.8
forms A.2.3, B.3, B.4, 0.2, 3.1, 5.4,
  12.1.3, 13.2, 17.2, 17.5,
  18.6, 33.7, 33.7.6, 34.1
formula 34.7.7
formulas 34.1
forth 6.5.1, 13.4, 32.6, 33.6.2, 34.2
forthcoming 34.0
fortitude Prf
FORTRAN A.2.6
fortunate 15.8.3
Fortunately 1.3, 2.1, 6.7, 15.5
forum 0.2
forward A.5.2, 15.8.1, 32.5, 33.7.5
forwarded 32.5
found A.1.1, A.2.3, A.3.1, A.5.2, B.6.1,
  D.3, 0.4, 1.1, 2.1, 3.2, 3.3,
  3.5, 4.2, 5.2, 7.5, 8.6.7,
  9.5, 11.5.3, 12.1.2,
  12.1.3, 12.4, 13.6, 26.1,
  33.7.4, 34.1, 34.7.6, Prf
Foundation 0.0, 1.0, 1.5, 2.1, 11.7,
  33.6.1, 34.1
Foundations B.3
Four A.1, A.4.4, A.5.2, A.7, A.7.1,
  B.4.3, B.6.2, D.2, 0.1, 0.2,
  2.3.2, 3.0, 3.1, 3.2, 4.2,
  4.6, 5.0, 5.2, 5.4, 6.5.3,
  7.3, 7.6, 10.4.10, 10.5,
  11.4.1, 11.4.5, 11.4.6,
  11.6.2, 12.1.3, 12.1.4,
  13.2, 13.5, 14.4.2, 14.4.4,
  14.4.5, 14.4.6, 15.2.2,
  16.2, 16.3, 17.2, 18.4.6,
  20.3, 25.2, 25.3, 25.5,
  26.3, 33.6.10, 33.8.1,
  34.2, 34.7.6, 34.8.11,
  35.5, 35.7, Prf
fourbyte 15.4
fourth B.6.1, B.6.3, B.6.5, 2.3.2, 2.3.3,
  7.2, 7.3, 7.6, 12.1.2,
  12.1.3, 13.5, 18.4.6, 26.1,
  34.7.7
fputs 12.1.1
FR_DOWN 7.6
FR_FINDNEXT 7.6
FR_HIDEMATCHCASE 7.6
FR_HIDEUPDOWN 7.6
FR_HIDEWHOLEWORD 7.6
FR_MATCHCASE 7.6
FR_NOMATCHCASE 7.6
FR_NOUPDOWN 7.6
FR_NOWHOLEWORD 7.6
FR_REPLACE 7.6
FR_REPLACEALL 7.6
FR_SHOWHELP 7.6
FR_WHOLEWORD 7.6
fragment 6.5.1, 8.2, 11.6.2
frame 0.4, 1.2, 2.3.2, 3.1, 3.3, 3.4, 4.4,
  5.2, 11.3, 11.4.7, 11.6.2,
  14.3, 14.4.2, 14.4.3, 15.4,
  16.3, 18.1.10, 23.2, 23.7,
  27.1, 30.0, 30.1, 31.1,
  32.0, 32.5, 32.6, 34.2,

34.6.3, 35.7
framed 2.1, 3.2, 32.5
FrameRect 11.4.3
frames 3.2, 3.4, 11.6.2, 14.3, 23.1
framework A.1, A.3.1, B.6, B.6.1,
  B.6.2, B.8.1, D.1, 0.1, 0.4,
  2.0, 2.1, 2.3, 5.1, 6.1, 7.7,
  10, 10.2, 10.3, 10.4,
  11.6.3, 11.7, **14.0, 14.1,
  14.2, 14.3, 14.4, 14.4.1,
  14.4.2, 14.4.4, 14.4.6,
  14.5, 14.6, 15.0, 15.1,**
  15.2, 15.2.1, 15.3, 15.3.1,
  15.3.2, 15.3.7, 15.3.8,
  15.4, 15.5, 15.5.6, 15.6,
  15.6.1, 15.6.13, 15.7,
  15.7.1, 15.7.2, 15.8,
  15.8.1, 15.8.2, 15.8.4,
  15.9, 16.1.1, 16.2, 16.3,
  16.3.3, 16.4, 16.5, 17.1.1,
  17.3.1, 17.4.7, 17.5, 18.1,
  18.1.1, 18.2, 18.4, 18.4.2,
  18.4.3, 18.4.4, 18.4.5,
  18.4.6, 18.5, 18.5.1, 18.6,
  19.1, 19.1.1, 19.1.2, 19.2,
  19.2.7, 19.3.5, 19.3.8,
  19.3.10, 19.4, 20.1, 21,
  21.1.1, 21.1.3, 21.2, 22.0,
  22.1, 22.5, 22.6, 23.0,
  23.2, 23.6, 23.8, 23.9,
  25.6, 26.4, 27.1, 29.1,
  30.1, 31.0, 31.4, 32.1,
  33.6.1, 33.7.1, 34.5,
  34.5.1, 34.5.3, 34.5.4,
  34.5.5, 34.5.7, 34.6,
  34.6.1, 34.6.3, 34.6.8,
  34.8, 34.8.1, 34.8.2,
  34.8.12, 35.3, 35.7, Prf
frameworks B.7, 7.0, 14.0, 15.4, 15.9,
  Prf
free A.1.1, A.2.10, A.5, B, B.1.6, B.6.1,
  2.4, 12.3, 12.4, 13.0, 13.5,
  13.7, 15.4, 18.5.5, Prf
freed D.1, 13.5, 32.4
freedom 25.9, 30.0
FreeExtra 12.2
freeing 25.2
freely 33.4.4
French 6.1, 6.7, 12.5
frequencies 35.3
frequently A.2.11, A.3.2, A.8, 6.5.3,
  9.0, 10.1, 10.3, 12, 12.1,
  12.1.4, 12.2, 13.1, 18.4.5,
  19.2.7, 24.0, 33.1, 33.2.5,
  35.7, 35.8
fresh 8.6.1, 14.1
freshmen A.3.2
friend A.6
friendly 7.0
friends A.1.1, 18.1
FromHandle 23.5, 25.6
FromHandlePermanent 23.7
front A.1.1, A.2.2, A.2.7, A.8, D.5,
  D.6, 6.5.2, 12.4, 13.3,
  15.7.2
frustrating 6.7
frustration 33.1
fstream A.2.4
FTP C.0
fuction B.3.2

full A.3.2, B.6.6, D.4, 0.1, 1.2, 2.6, 5.1,
    6.3.7, 7.2, 11.6.2, 12.2,
    12.3, 14.0, 15.8.1, 15.8.2,
    18.6, 34.2, 34.6.1, 34.7.1,
    35.1, 35.2, 35.7, Prf
fully A.8.1, 1.0, 2.3.2, 10.5, 13.2, 15.2,
    15.8.4, 19.0, 20.2, 34.6.4,
    35.1
func A.2.7, A.2.8
functional 2.3.2, 10.5, 20.2, 22.5
functionality A.3.1, A.4.2, A.5.2, B.8.2,
    B.8.3, 3.0, 8.3, 8.4, 10.3,
    10.4, 11.4.1, 11.5.2,
    11.5.5, 12, 12.1.1, 12.1.2,
    12.2, 14.3, 15.4, 15.4.1,
    15.8, 15.8.1, 15.8.4, 16.2,
    16.5, 18.1.15, 18.4.3,
    18.4.7, 19.5, 20.0, 20.2,
    20.3, 23.8, 24.1, 25.0,
    25.6, 26.4, 27.0, 29.1,
    29.4, 31.0, 33.3, 33.7.5,
    34.9
functionscalls 11.6.1
fundamental A.1, A.4.2, 1.0, 1.5, 4.7,
    15.8, 15.8.4, 34.1, 34.5.3
fundamentally 34.1
fundamentals A.1, 0.3, 34.7.7, Prf
further A.3.1, A.3.2, A.4.1, B.3, B.8.7,
    B.9, C.0, D.8, 6.5.4, 9.6,
    10.2, 10.4.10, 12.1.2,
    12.1.4, 12.2, 12.4, 12.5,
    13.2, 14.4.4, 15.2.3,
    15.7.11, 18.4.6, 18.6,
    33.2.2, 33.4.4, 33.9, 34.8,
    34.8.1, 34.8.3, 34.8.5,
    34.8.6, 35.2, 35.9
Furthermore 18.4.2
future A.1.1, A.4.2, A.8, D.1, D.3, 0.4,
    5.4, 31.0, 34.3, Prf
FW 3.5
FW_BOLD 3.5
FW_NORMAL 3.5
g B.7.4, 4.2, 4.3, 5.3, 18.2, 22.5, 25.5,
    26.1, 33.2.4, 33.3
gain A.1, A.1.1, A.4.1, A.7.1, 0.2, 1.4,
    1.5, 2.0, 2.3, 2.3.2, 3.0,
    3.3, 4.0, 4.2, 5.2, 11.4.6,
    12.3, 12.4, 13.8, 14.4.5,
    15.8.2, 17.0, 17.5, 24.0,
    33.5, 34.1, 34.8.4
gained 4.0, 5.5, 11.7, 15.4, 15.9
gaining 5.2, 28.1
gains 14.5
Gallery 27.0, 27.2, 32.6
game A.3.2, 11.5
Games 11.6.2
gap 12.2
gather A.2.3, A.4.3, 2.2, 5.1, 11.7,
    14.4.5, 17.5
gathered 7.5
gathering 22.0
gave 6.3.5, 15.3
GDI D.1, D.5, 11.0, 11.1, 11.2, 11.3,
    11.5, 11.6, 11.7, 15.8.2,
    23.6
general A.1.1, A.3, A.3.1, B.3, B.4,
    B.6.1, 1.3, 2.1, 6, 7.2,
    10.2, 10.3, 11.1, 11.2,
    11.4.1, 11.4.6, 11.4.8, 12,
    13.2, 14.1, 14.3, 14.4.5,

14.5, 15.4, 15.7.11,
    15.8.2, 18.5, 19.2, 22.0,
    25.0, 25.5, 26.0, 26.1,
    33.2.1, 33.3, 34.0, 34.1,
    34.2, 34.4, 34.8.11,
    34.8.12, 35.0, 35.4, 35.7
generality 34.1
generalized 34.1
generally A.1.1, A.4.1, A.4.6, A.7.2,
    B.2, B.3.1, B.5.5, B.6.1,
    B.8.1, 3.3, 6.1, 9.5,
    10.4.10, 11.2, 11.3,
    11.6.1, 11.6.2, 12.1.2,
    13.5, 14.1, 14.3, 14.4.2,
    14.4.3, 14.4.4, 14.5, 15.4,
    15.8.2, 18.4.7, 32.6, 33.1,
    34.1
generate B.8.1, 0.3, 2.3, 4.6, 6.4, 8.5,
    9.3, 11.4.6, 11.5.2,
    11.6.3, 13.2, 13.6.1,
    13.6.2, 14.1, 16.3, 33.7,
    34.4
generated B.5.5, B.7, B.8.7, 0.4, 2.2,
    2.5, 4.4, 5.3, 6.5.3, 8.5,
    8.6.10, 9.3, 10, 11.4.1,
    11.4.6, 11.5.3, 11.5.5,
    11.6.1, 11.7, 13.6, 14.1,
    14.3, 14.4, 14.4.1, 14.4.2,
    14.5, 15.1, 15.3.1, 15.3.7,
    15.6.1, 15.8, 16.2, 16.3.3,
    16.4, 18.4.6, 19.2, 19.2.7,
    19.3.1, 27.2, 28.2,
    33.6.10, 33.8.4, 34.4,
    34.5.3, 34.6.3, 34.8.5
generates 0.3, 0.4, 4.4, 5.1, 9.1, 11.4.1,
    13.3, 14.1, 15.3.1, 19.4,
    32.7, 34.1, 34.8.3
generating 0.1, 13.2, 18.1.11, 34.4
generator 0.1, 14.0, 14.1, 34.4
generic A.3.1, A.3.3, A.4.2, A.5, A.5.2,
    A.5.3, D.0, D.1, 13.6.1,
    26.4, 33.4.2
geographical 11.5.5
German 6.1, 6.7
GetAddr 18.2
GetArray 14.4.4
GetAt 11.5.3, 12.1.2, 12.2, 12.3, 12.4
GetBackColor 34.8
GetBkColor 11.4.8
GetBorderStyle 34.8
GetBuffer 12.1.2
GetBufferSetLength 12.1.2
GetCaretIndex 9.4
GetClientRect 3.3, 4.4, 9.1, 11.6.1,
    34.6.9
GetClipboardData 18.4.7
GetColor 7.3, 7.4
GetCopies 7.5
GetCount 9.3, 12.4, 12.5
GetCurrentMessage 32.5
GetCurrentTime 12.1.3
GetCurSel 9.3, 9.5, 31.3
GetDays 12.1.3
GetDefaultConnect 33.5
GetDefaults 7.5
GetDefaultSQL 33.5
GetDeviceCaps 11.3, 11.6.3, 15.8.4
GetDeviceName 7.5
GetDevMode 7.5
GetDlgItem 8.1, 18.3, 22.5, 23.3, 23.4,

23.5
GetDlgItemInt 5.3, 17.1, 18.3
GetDlgItemText 5.3, 12.1.2, 17.3.3,
    18.3, 30.2
GetDocSize 15.5.1, 15.6.5, 15.8.3
GetDocString 10.4.6, 15.1, 16.3,
    16.3.5, 16.5
GetDocument 15.2.7, 15.3, 15.8.3,
    34.6.8
GetDriverName 7.5
GetEnabled 34.8
GetEnglish 12.5
GetExceptionCode 13.6.1
GetExitCodeThread 35.8
GetFaceName 7.3
GetFileExt 7.2
GetFileName 7.2
GetFileTitle 7.2
GetFindString 7.6
GetFirst A.5.2, A.6
GetFirstVisibleLine 8.2
GetFont 34.8
GetForeColor 34.8
GetFromPage 7.5, 15.8.2
GetGmTime 12.1.3
GetHandle 8.2
GetHead 12.4, 16.3.3
GetHeadPosition 12.4
GetHours 12.1.3
GetHwnd 34.8
GetIdsOfName 34.7.7
GetInputString 6.6.8
GetItemData 26.4
GetLast A.5.2
GetLength 12.1.1, 12.1.2
getline A.2.4, 8.2
GetLineCount 8.2
GetLocalTm 12.1.3
GetMaxPage 15.8.2
GetMinPage 15.8.2
GetMinutes 12.1.3
GetModify 8.1, 8.2, 8.6.1
GetNext A.5.2, 12.4
GetNextAssoc 12.5
GetNotifier 7.6
GetNumPoints 15.2.6, 15.3, 15.4.4,
    15.5.1, 15.6.3, 15.6.5
GetOpenFileName 7.2
GetPage 20.7
GetPageCount 20.7
GetParent 32.5
GetPathName 7.2
GetPoint 12.3, 15.2.6, 15.3, 15.6.3
GetPortName 7.5
GetPosition 12.1.1
GetPrev 12.4
GetPrevious A.5.2, 12.4
GetPrinterDC 7.5, 15.8.4
GetPrinterDeviceDefaults 10.6, 15.8.4
GetProfileInt 10.5
GetProfileString 10.5
GetReadOnlyPref 7.2
GetRecordCount 33.5, 33.6.5
GetRect 8.2
GetReplaceString 7.6
GetSafeHandle 23.6, 29.4
GetSafeHwnd 23.1
GetSaveFileName 7.2
GetScrollPos 4.6
GetSeconds 12.1.3

GetSel 8.1, 8.2
GetSelCount 9.3
GetSelItems 9.3
GetSize 7.3, 12.2, 12.3, 15.7.9
GetSQL 33.5, 33.6.4
GetStartPosition 12.5
GetState 23.1
GetStatus 12.1.1, 33.5
GetStockObject 29.4
GetStyleName 7.3
GetSubMenu 32.6
GetSystemMenu 32.7
GetTabbedTextExtent 18.5.4
GetTableName 33.5
GetTail 12.4
GetTailPosition 12.4
GetTemp 17.4.1
GetText 9.3, 26.4, 34.8
GetTextExtent 11.4.6
GetThreadPriority 35.7
GetTime 12.1.3
getting 3.0, 10.1, 11.0, 11.4.1, 11.5.4,
    15.5, 22.4, 22.6, 23.8,
    25.6, 26.2, 33.5, Prf
GetToPage 7.5, 15.8.2
GetTotal A.5.1
GetTotalHours 12.1.3
GetTotalMinutes 12.1.3
GetTotalSeconds 12.1.3
GetUpperBound 12.2
GetWeight 7.3
GetWindowRect 28.1, 32.5
GetWindowText 31.5
GetWindowTextLength 8.2
gibberish A.3.1
gigabyte 11.5.5
gigantic Prf
GIS 11.5.5
giving A.1.1, B.3, D.3, 8.1, 12.3, 33.1,
    34.1, 34.8.10, 35.2
GL D.0, D.1, D.2
GL_AMBIENT D.7
GL_AMBIENT_AND_DIFFUSE D.7
GL_BACK D.5
GL_COLOR_BUFFER_BIT D.7
GL_DEPTH_BUFFER_BIT D.7
GL_DEPTH_TEST D.7
GL_FRONT D.7
GL_FRONT_AND_BACK D.7
GL_LIGHT D.7
GL_LIGHTi D.7
GL_LIGHTING D.6
GL_MAX_LIGHTS D.7
GL_POLYGON D.2
glamorous 18.4.5
glaux D.1
glBegin D.2
glCallList D.3
glClear D.2, D.7
glColor D.2
glDrawBuffer D.5
glEnable D.6, D.7
glEnd D.2
GLfloat D.6, D.7
glFlush D.2
glLight D.7
glLightfv D.7
glLoadIdentity D.2
glMaterial D.6
glMaterialfv D.7

glMatrixMode D.2
global A.3.2, A.4.2, A.4.3, A.7.2, 2.3,
    2.5, 7.6, 8.6.7, 11.4.1,
    13.4, 13.5, 13.6.1, 15.3,
    34.6.3, 35.2, 35.4
globally 2.3.1, 10.5, 11.5.3, 12.5
globals 35.2
glPopMatrix D.3
glPushMatrix D.3
glRotate D.3
glRotated D.2
glTranslate D.3
glu D.1, D.2
glued A.4.3
gluOrtho D.2, D.6
gluPerspective D.6
glVertex D.2
glViewport D.2
GMT 12.1.3
goal A.1, A.3.2, A.4.2, A.4.6, A.5.3, B,
    C.1, 0.2, 0.4, 1.1, 1.4, 2.5,
    6.1, 11.0, 13.0, 14.0, 14.1,
    14.4.6, 15.1, 15.3, 16.3.2,
    17.1, 18.1.2, 18.2, 18.4.1,
    19.0, 28.1, 33.4, 33.5,
    33.7.2, 33.9, 34.0, 34.1,
    34.5.2, 34.8.12, Prf
goals 0.3, 5.1, 11.3, 12, 15.3.3, Prf
goes A.2.4, A.3.1, A.4.3, A.5.1, A.7.1,
    D.1, 1.2, 4.1, 4.5, 6.4,
    11.4.6, 11.4.7, 12.3, 12.4,
    15.8.2, 23.8, 31.1, 32.4,
    34.2, 34.5.5, 35.2
going A.3.2, D.1, 0.4, 2.3.2, 5.1, 8.3,
    11.5.5, 14.0, 15.2.5,
    15.3.8, 15.4.1, 18.1.6,
    18.1.12, 19.3.8, 28.1,
    33.6.1, 34.4, 34.5.5,
    34.5.6, 34.6, 34.7.1
gone 34.1
good A.1.1, A.3.1, A.3.2, A.4.1, A.4.4,
    A.4.6, A.5.2, A.8, B.6.1,
    0.3, 1.1, 1.2, 2.3, 3.0, 3.5,
    10.4, 11.2, 11.4.6, 12.1.1,
    12.3, 12.6, 13.3, 14.2,
    14.4.5, 14.4.6, 14.5, 15.5,
    15.7, 16.2, 17.1.3, 19.5,
    27.0, 27.1, 28.0, 28.2,
    31.6, 34.0, 35.4, Prf
got 15.4.3
goto A.1.1
gotten 17.2, 23.0
gradations 5.3
grade A.5.2, Prf
grainy 34.1
grand 34.8.13
grant 33.4.2
graph B.4, B.4.3, B.4.4, B.4.5, B.4.6,
    11.5.4, 16.5
graphic 27.0
graphical B.5, 0.1, 0.4, 6.1, 9.0, 11.0,
    15.7, 18.1, 25.0
graphically B.2, 33.4.4
graphics A.3.1, D.0, D.1, D.5, D.8,
    0.4, 5.1, 11.0, 11.2, 35.1
graphs 11.5, 11.6.1
gray 3.4, 15.8.3, 29.2, 29.3
Grayed 6.4
great A.1.1, A.2.8, A.8.1, B.1.3, B.4,
    0.3, 1.2, 9.1, 9.5, 10.1,

    11.3, 11.4.6, 11.4.7,
    11.4.8, 12.3, 14.4, 14.6,
    19.0, 23.8, 32.6, 34.2
greater 2.1, 24.0
greatest 19.0
greatly A.2.11, 0.1, 1.1, 11.6.3, 29.4
Green D.1, D.2, D.3, D.6, 7.4
GreenSurface D.6
ground A.8.1, 11.7, Prf
grounded Prf
grounding 34.0
group A.3.2, A.4.5, 1.3, 3.1, 3.4,
    14.4.6, 20.7, 22.2, 22.5
grouped A.1.1
grouping A.3.2, A.4.5
groupings 19.2
groups 11.1, 11.4.5, 11.4.7
grow 4.6, 12.2, 34.4, 34.6.7
growing 21.1.9, 34.1
grown Prf
grows 2.1, 12.1.2, 12.2, 33.2, 34.1
growth 12.2
guarantee A.1.1, 9.4, 11.3, 13.2, 24.0
guaranteed 11.5.3, 18.4.2, 22.4, 35.0
guess D.7
GUI C.1, 0.1, 1.3, 17.2, 34.1, Prf
Guide B, B.9, 0.3, 19.0, 34.5, 34.6
guidelines 16.2
guides 11.4.6
GUIs 1.3, 5.1
habit A.8, B.5.3, D.1, 12.1.2, Prf
had A.1.1, D.3, 2.3.1, 3.3, 6, 14.1,
    15.8.1, 17.2, 17.3.3,
    17.3.4, 18.4.4, 18.5, 18.6,
    23.2, 23.4, 31.6, 32.1,
    32.5, 33.1, 33.7.2
hair 10.2
hairs 11.5.3
half B.2.2, 3.5, 6.6, 11.4.1, 12.6, 22.4,
    27.1, 32.5
Hall C.1
halt B.2.1, B.3.1, 13.1, 15.8.2, 18.5.6
halted 13.2
halts 13.2
hammer A.3.1
hampered 0.0
hand A.6, B.2.3, B.4.1, B.4.2, B.4.5,
    B.4.6, D.2, 2.1, 5.1, 6,
    6.1, 6.6, 8.1, 10.2, 11.5.5,
    13.2, 14.5, 15.4, 15.5,
    15.5.2, 15.5.5, 15.5.6,
    15.8.4, 16.2, 17.0, 17.2,
    18.4.6, 18.5.4, 19.2,
    19.3.5, 23.8, 24.1, 32.4,
    33.1, 35.2, 35.8
handing 8.6.1, 18.4.2
HandleButton 4.3, 5.2, 5.4, 7.1, 7.3,
    7.6, 11.6.3, 12.1.1,
    12.1.3, 12.4, 12.5, 13.6
HandleChange 5.3, 5.4
handled A.1.1, A.2.3, A.2.4, 1.3, 4.6,
    6.2, 11.2, 11.5.3, 11.5.4,
    13.6, 13.6.1, 14.4.5,
    15.3.2, 15.3.4, 15.3.5,
    15.3.6, 15.3.8, 15.7.11,
    17.3.4, 19.2, 22.6, 25.3,
    25.4, 26.4, 32.5, 34.8,
    35.1
handleEvent A.8
HandlePrint 11.6.3

HandleQuit 6.5
handler B.7.1, B.7.3, B.7.4, D.1, 1.3,
2.3.2, 4.3, 4.4, 4.6, 4.7,
5.2, 7.1, 7.6, 8.6.1, 9.3,
10.2, 11.5.2, 13.6, 13.6.1,
14.5, 15.2.3, 15.3.7,
15.6.9, 15.7, 15.7.2,
15.7.3, 15.7.7, 15.7.11,
17.1.3, 17.3.4, 18.2,
18.4.2, 18.4.3, 18.4.4,
18.4.6, 18.4.7, 20.2, 20.3,
21.1.8, 22.5, 23.2, 23.7,
25.5, 25.8, 26.4, 27.1,
28.1, 29.2, 30.1, 31.1,
31.2, 31.3, 31.5, 32.1,
32.6, 33.8.2, 33.8.3,
34.6.5, 35.5, 35.6, 35.8
handlers D.2, D.4, D.6, 6.5, 18.4.3,
18.4.7, 23.7, 29.1, 31.1,
31.2, 31.4, 32.4, 32.5,
32.6, 34.8.13, 35.6, 35.8
handles A.1, A.1.1, A.4.2, A.8, D.0,
D.2, 0.4, 1.3, 1.4, 2.1, 2.2,
2.3.1, 4.3, 4.5, 4.6, 4.7,
6.7.3, 7.1, 7.2, 7.6, 8.2,
8.6.6, 8.6.11, 10.2,
10.4.10, 11.3, 11.4.1,
11.4.6, 11.5.4, 11.5.5,
12.4, 13.2, 13.6, 13.6.1,
15.2.6, 15.3, 15.3.1,
15.3.3, 15.4, 15.5,
15.6.13, 15.8, 15.8.1,
16.2, 16.5, 17.4.5, 18.2,
18.3, 18.4.3, 18.5, 19.2,
22.0, 22.1, 22.2, 23.0,
23.1, 23.2, 23.6, 23.7,
24.3, 25.0, 25.4, 25.5,
25.7, 25.9, 31.4, 34.1,
34.5.3, 34.6.3, 34.6.9,
34.8.1, 34.8.4
HandleSelchange 9.3
handling A.3, D.4, 0.4, 1.1, 1.5, 2.3,
3.0, 4.0, 4.1, 4.4, 4.6, 4.7,
4.8, 6.5.1, 7.6, 8.6.7, 9.1,
10.2, 10.5, 12, 12.1.1,
13.0, 13.6, 15.2.6, 15.2.8,
15.3, 15.3.7, 15.8.3, 16.2,
17.4.5, 18.4.2, 18.6,
19.2.1, 22.4, 23.7, 25.3,
29.1, 29.4, 31.0, 31.6,
32.0, 33.1, 33.6.5, 33.8.2,
34.1
hands A.3.1, C.1, 8.6.2, 34.4
handy A.4.5, 33.6.5
happen A.1.1, A.7.2, A.8, B.3.2, D.5,
11.4.5, 11.4.6, 12.4, 13.1,
15.3, 23.7, 34.2, 34.6.3,
35.1
happened A.7.1, 4.5, 34.5.5
happening A.5.1, A.7, A.7.2, A.8, 0.4,
7.6, 13.2, 14.4, 15.3, 23.8,
33.6, 34.4, 35.8
happens A.4.6, A.8, B.4.1, D.2, 4.1,
10.4.10, 11.5.2, 11.5.4,
15.3, 15.3.1, 15.5.3,
15.8.3, 18.5.5, 19.2, 25.0,
30.0, 33.7.2, 34.2, 34.4,
34.5.5
hard A.7.2, B.3, 2.1, 15.3, 20.3, 33.1,
34.4, 35.7

harder A.3.2
hardware D.1, 26.2
harmony 7.6, 14.3
harness 35.2
hash 0.4
hashing 12.5
hatched 11.4.3
haven 4.2
having A.6, A.7.2, B.3, D.3, 2.3.3, 6,
10.4.10, 11.4.7, 11.5.3,
13.6, 15.4.4, 16.6, 17.5,
20.5, 23.0, 25.0, 25.5,
29.2, 29.4, 32.5, 32.6,
34.3, 34.7.6, 35.8
havoc 35.7
hbrBackground 11.5.3
HBRUSH 11.5.3
hButtonWnd 23.5
hChild 20.4
HCURSOR 11.5.3
hdc D.5, 7.5
hdcPrinter 7.3
he 20.7, 35.1, Prf
head 12.4, 34.1
headed 10.2, 18.1
header A.1.1, A.6, B.7.6, 2.3, 3.3, 6.1,
12.3, 13.1, 14.4.1, 14.4.6,
15.2.6, 15.5.1, 15.6.3,
15.6.5, 18.1.12, 18.1.13,
18.4.1, 18.4.2, 18.4.7,
19.3.6, 20.0, 20.3, 25.8,
28.2, 31.2, 31.3, 31.4,
31.5, 33.6.1, 34.6.5, 35.5,
35.7, 35.8
headers 15.2.2
headings 21.1.8
healthy 13.2
heap A.7, A.7.1, A.7.2, 8.2, 12.1.2,
12.2, 13.2, 13.5, 13.6,
13.7, 32.4, 32.5, 35.2
hear C.0, 34.7.7, 35.10, Prf
heard 25.1
heart A.3.2, A.5, 10.5, 35.0, 35.4
heavily 14.4.5
heavy D.0
hEditWnd 23.8
Height A.4.6, D.2, 3.3, 5.3, 6.1, 11.2,
11.4.3, 11.4.6, 11.5,
11.5.5, 11.6.2, 12.1.4,
15.7, 15.7.5, 15.7.9,
15.7.10, 18.5.4, 18.5.6,
23.2, 25.6, 26.1, 26.4,
28.1, 28.3, 29.2, 30.1,
32.5, 34.6.4, 34.6.5,
34.6.7
heights 11.4.6
held A.2.3, A.4.2, A.4.4, A.8, 1.2,
2.3.2, 4.4, 5.1, 10.4.10,
12.1.3, 12.3, 12.4, 13.5,
14.3, 15.2.6, 15.2.8,
15.4.2, 15.6.3, 16.2, 18.1,
18.3, 33.6.4, 34.4, 34.5.3,
34.5.5, 34.6.5
hello A.1.1, A.2.3, B.3, 0.4, 1.4, 2.2,
2.3, 2.5, 3.3, 6.7.2, 6.7.3,
11.6.3, 12.1.2, 14.1, 22.0,
22.1, 23.4, 35.9
help A.1, A.4.4, A.4.6, B.1.3, B.2, B.3,
B.3.1, B.3.2, B.4.4, B.6.1,
C.0, D.1, D.6, 0.0, 0.1,

0.2, 0.4, 2.3.1, 2.3.2, 3.1,
3.2, 3.3, 3.5, 4.2, 4.3, 4.4,
4.6, 4.7, 5.2, 5.3, 6, 7.1,
7.2, 7.3, 7.4, 7.5, 7.6, 8.3,
8.4, 10.1, 10.4.10, 10.7,
11.4.3, 11.4.6, 11.5.3,
11.6.1, 11.6.3, 12, 12.6,
13.0, 13.1, 13.3, 13.6,
13.6.2, 14.0, 14.1, 14.3,
15.2.1, 15.2.6, 15.3, 15.4,
15.6, 15.7, 16.3, 16.3.5,
16.5, 17.3.4, 17.4, 18.0,
18.3, 18.4.6, **19.0, 19.1,
19.1.1, 19.1.2, 19.2,
19.2.2, 19.2.3, 19.2.4,
19.2.5, 19.2.6, 19.2.7,
19.2.8, 19.2.10, 19.3,
19.3.2, 19.3.4, 19.3.5,
19.3.6, 19.3.8, 19.3.9,
19.3.10, 19.4, 19.5,** 20.5,
22.0, 22.2, 22.5, 23.2,
32.7, 33.4.4, 33.6.5,
33.6.10, 33.8.4, 33.9,
34.5.3, 34.5.5, 34.6.3,
34.8.3, 35.0, 35.1, 35.4,
35.7, Prf
helper 7.2, 7.6, 8.5, 8.6.7, 12.2, 34.6.5
helpful 9.4, 17.3.4, 18.4.5, 22.5, 30.1,
Prf
helping C.1, 0.1, 22.2, 22.5
helps A.4.1, B.3.1, B.4, B.5.6, 0.1,
11.4.4, 11.6.2, 19.2, 22.2,
22.7, 25.6, 33.1
hex A.2.3, 12.1.1, 13.4, 20.2, 34.4
hi 15.5.5
hIcon 11.5.3
HID_EDIT_TEST 19.3.8, 19.3.9,
19.3.10
HID_TEST 19.3.3, 19.3.4, 19.3.5
hidden A.1.1, A.3.2, A.4.3, D.0, D.5,
0.0, 2.3, 4.1, 9.5, 10.1,
12.1.1, 19.2, 19.2.1,
19.2.5, 34.5.3
hide A.3.2, 2.1, 20.4, 31.6
Hides 7.2, 7.6, 9.5, 23.7
hiding A.3.2, 23.1
hierarchical A.3.1, 6.5.4, 20.4, 34.4
hierarchically 6.5.4
hierarchies A.4.6, A.5.3, A.8
hierarchy A.3.1, A.3.2, A.3.3, A.5.1,
A.8, B.4, B.4.5, 0.1, 0.2,
0.3, 1.0, 1.5, 2.1, 3.3, 4.7,
6, 10, 10.5, 11.4.1, 12.3,
12.6, 13.0, 13.6, 14.0,
14.3, 14.4.4, 16.3, 20.5,
23.6, 30.0, 34.2, Prf
high A.4.1, D.0, D.1, D.5, 11.5.5,
11.6.1, 11.6.2, 15.1, 16.6,
18.4.5, 18.5.4, 25.6, 34.1,
34.4, 34.9, 35.1, 35.2,
35.7
HIGH_PRIORITY_CLASS 35.7
higher 1.3, 35.1, 35.7
highest 35.7
highlight B.2.3, B.4, B.4.1, 4.1, 9.3,
11.5.2, 25.6, 34.8
highlighted B.3.1, 11.5.2
highlighting A.8, B.3.1, 1.3, 11.5.2
highlights 1.3, 4.2, 9.3
hills A.3.2

HIMETRIC 34.5.6, 34.6.8
hint D.6, 15.7.9
hints 0.2, 15.4
History 19.2
hit A.5.2, 1.2, 6.5.3, 27.1
hits A.3.2, B.2.1, 11.4.7, 18.4.6
HIWORD 26.2
HKEY_CLASSES_ROOT 34.4
HLP 19.1.1, 19.2, 19.2.9, 19.3.5,
        19.3.7, 33.3, 33.9
HM 19.1.1, 19.3.5, 19.3.7, 19.3.8
hold A.2.3, A.3.2, A.4.1, A.5.2, B.5,
        B.6.2, 1.2, 2.2, 3.4, 3.5,
        6.5.3, 8.2, 8.6.2, 10,
        11.4.6, 11.5.3, 11.6.2,
        12.3, 13.5, 13.6, 14.4.3,
        14.4.4, 14.4.5, 15.2.5,
        15.2.6, 15.3, 15.5, 16.2,
        17.4, 18.1, 18.1.12, 18.2,
        18.4.2, 25.6, 26.2, 26.4,
        33.1, 33.2, 33.6.2,
        33.6.10, 34.5, 34.5.3,
        34.5.5, 34.9, 35.4, 35.8
holding A.3.1, A.5.2, B.7.4, 0.2, 8.2,
        9.3, 13.5, 15.1, 29.1, 34.1,
        35.2
holds A.3.1, A.4.2, A.4.4, A.8, B.6.1,
        D.7, 1.2, 2.2, 3.5, 8.6.7,
        11.5.2, 12.3, 14.3, 15.6.1,
        16.2, 18.1, 18.4.2, 22.0,
        33.4.2, 33.5, 34.1, 34.2,
        34.4, 34.8, 34.8.6, 35.2,
        35.4
HOLLOW 29.3, 29.4, 32.5
home 17.4, 33.1
hone Prf
honor 35.3
Hook 18.1, 27.1, 33.7.4
hooked 11.4.2
hooks 2.2
hope 8.7, 35.10
horizontal 4.6, 6.4, 9.1, 9.2, 10.2, 11.3,
        11.5.3, 11.5.5, 15.5,
        15.8.4, 28.3
horizontally 8.1, 8.2, 11.4.6, 28.3
HORZRES 11.3, 15.8.4
host D.0, 35.1
hosts 35.1
hot 6.5.3, 20.0
hour 3.5, 8.7, 12.1.3
Hourglass 10.2, 35.8
hours 12.1.3, Prf
house C.1, 14.4.2
HPFS 12.1.1
HPJ 19.1.1, 19.2, 19.2.9, 19.3.4
hRoot 20.4
HS_BDIAGONAL 11.4.3
HS_CROSS 11.4.3
HS_DIAGCROSS 11.4.3
HS_FDIAGONAL 11.4.3
HS_HORIZONTAL 11.4.3
HS_VERTICAL 11.4.3
HTCLIENT 29.1
htm 21
http B, C.0, 21, Prf
HTTRANSPARENT 29.1
hued D.2
huge B.9, 0.1, 2.3.2, 11.1, 11.4.6, 20.0,
        33.1, 34.3
human C.1, 6.1, 6.7, 12.4

humor Prf
hundreds A.1.1, 0.0, 0.1, 1.1, 2.2, 5.1,
        6, 6.7, 11.6.2, 12.1.4,
        20.5, 33.1, 35.2
Hungarian 2.3
hurdle 0.1
hurt A.1
HWND 22.6, 23.1, 23.4, 23.7, 23.8
Hypertext 19.2, 19.2.5, 19.2.6, 19.2.7,
        19.2.8, 19.2.10, 19.5
icon B.1.1, B.5.3, 0.4, 1.2, 3.1, 3.2, 5.2,
        6.1, 6.2, 6.3, 6.3.1, 6.3.4,
        6.3.5, 6.3.7, 6.4, 7.1, 10.2,
        10.3, 10.4.8, 10.4.10,
        11.4.1, 11.4.8, 11.5.2,
        11.5.3, 11.5.4, 14.4.6,
        15.1, 15.2.10, 15.4, 16.3,
        16.3.5, 27.0, 32.3, 32.8,
        35.2
iconic 2.3.2
iconified 1.2, 27.1
iconifies 8.4
iconify 1.2, 15.2.9, 15.4, 32.4
icons B.6.2, 0.4, 1.3, 3.0, 6, 6.1, 6.2,
        6.3.7, 10.2, 11.5.2, 15.4,
        16.3, 25.0
iCurSel 7.2
ID_APP_EXIT 10.4.7, 10.4.10
ID_APPLY_NOW 20.7
ID_D 18.4.5
ID_DATA_ADD 18.1.10, 18.4.5
ID_DATA_CHANGE 18.4.4, 18.4.5
ID_DATA_DELETE 18.4.2, 18.4.3
ID_EDIT_CHANGE 34.6.5
ID_EDIT_CLEAR 16.2
ID_EDIT_COPY B.7.3, 16.2, 18.4.7
ID_EDIT_CUT 10.4, 16.2
ID_EDIT_FIND 16.2
ID_EDIT_PASTE 16.2
ID_EDIT_REPEAT 16.2
ID_EDIT_REPLACE 16.2
ID_EDIT_SELECT_ALL 16.2
ID_EDIT_TEST 19.3.1, 19.3.2,
        19.3.8
ID_EDIT_UNDO 16.2
ID_FILE_MRU_FILE 10.5
ID_FILE_NEW 10.4.7
ID_FILE_OPEN 6.4, 10.4.7, 15.3.1
ID_FILE_PRINT 16.2
ID_FILE_SAVE 15.3.3
ID_INDICATOR_OVR 18.4.6
ID_INSERT_KEY 18.4.6
ID_INSERT_TOGGLE 6.5.3
ID_OPTIONS_DRAWINGSIZE
        15.7.2
ID_SEARCH_FIND 16.2
ID_SEARCH_REPEAT 16.2
ID_SEARCH_REPLACE 16.2
IDABORT 7.1
IDB_BACKGROUND 29.2
IDB_BITMAP 25.6
IDB_PRINTER 26.4
IDB_TRUETYPE 26.4
IDC_ 4.2
IDC_ADDRESS 33.7.4
IDC_ARROW 10.2
IDC_BUTTON 4.2, 30.1
IDC_CELSIUS 17.1.2, 17.1.3, 17.3.3
IDC_CITY 18.1.8, 18.1.9
IDC_COMBO 25.8, 30.1

IDC_CROSS 10.2, 11.5.3
IDC_EDIT 6.6.5, 24.2, 30.1
IDC_EMPID 33.7.3
IDC_EXPAND 28.1, 28.2
IDC_EXPAND_MARKER 28.1, 28.2
IDC_FAHRENHEIT 17.1.2, 17.1.3,
        17.3.3, 17.3.4
IDC_FONTLIST 26.4
IDC_HEIGHT 15.7.5, 15.7.8
IDC_IBEAM 10.2
IDC_ICON 10.2
IDC_LASTNAME 33.7.3
IDC_LIST 18.1.2, 18.1.4, 18.4.2
IDC_NAME B.7.5, 18.1.8, 18.1.9
IDC_RANGE B.8.9, 34.8.12
IDC_SIZE 10.2
IDC_SIZENESW 10.2
IDC_SIZENS 10.2
IDC_SIZENWSE 10.2
IDC_SIZEWE 10.2
IDC_STATE 18.1.8, 18.1.9
IDC_STATIC 6.6.4, 29.1
IDC_STRING 12.1.2
IDC_STYLELIST 26.4
IDC_UPARROW 10.2
IDC_VALUE 34.8.12
IDC_WAIT 10.2
IDC_WIDTH 15.7.5, 15.7.8
IDCANCEL 7.1, 7.2
IDD 28.1
IDD_ADDR_FORM 18.4.1
IDD_ADDRESSDIALOG B.7.4
IDD_DB_FORM 33.7.3
IDD_DIALOG B.7.4, 18.1.8
IDD_DIALOGBAR 30.1
IDD_DRAWINGSIZE 15.7.5, 15.7.6
IDD_F 17.1.2
IDD_PROPPAGE_ADJ 34.8.12
idea A.2.8, A.3.1, A.4.2, A.8, 6.2, 6.8,
        9.1, 11.1, 11.6.3, 13.2,
        13.3, 14.5, 15.9, 16.3.3,
        19.3, 23.1, 33.5, 34.5.3,
        35.2
ideal 15.8.4, 33.3
Ideally 30.2
ideas A.1, A.3, A.4, 1.5, 11.5.5, 33.8.4,
        34.8.1
identical A.6, A.7, B.8.1, 3.3, 4.2, 5.2,
        6.5, 6.5.1, 11.3, 11.4.6,
        12.1.1, 12.1.2, 12.4, 15.4,
        15.8.3, 16.2, 17.2,
        18.1.12, 32.6, 34.4,
        34.5.3, 34.6.3, 34.8.2
identically 13.2
identification 6.1
identified 4.3, 5.4, 6.1, 13.6, 18.4.6,
        34.4
identifier D.5, D.7, 6.1, 6.3.7, 34.4
identifiers 34.4
identifies 4.1, 5.1, 6.1, 12.1.1, 13.4,
        13.6, 16.5, 19.2
identify A.3.1, B.3, B.4.1, 3.1, 3.3, 4.2,
        15.7.2, 18.4.5, 34.4
identities 6.1
identity D.3
IDI_APPLICATION 10.2
IDI_ASTERISK 10.2
IDI_EXCLAMATION 10.2
IDI_HAND 10.2
IDI_ICON 6.1, 6.3.4, 6.3.5

IDI_QUESTION 10.2
IDIGNORE 7.1
idle 0.4, 10.3, 23.5, 31.1, 31.2, 31.3,
    31.4, 31.5, 31.6, 35.7
IDLE_PRIORITY_CLASS 35.7
IDM_ 6.4
IDM_FILE_CLOSE 6.4, 6.5.1
IDM_FILE_EXIT 6.6.2
IDM_FILE_OPEN 6.4, 6.5.3
IDM_FILE_PROMPT 6.6.2
IDM_FILE_QUIT 6.4, 6.5
IDM_MAINFRAME 15.1
IDNO 7.1
IDOK 6.6.8, 7.1, 7.2
IDR_ADDR_FORM 18.1.2
IDR_ADDR_TYPE 18.4.5
IDR_ADDRTYPE 18.1.7, 18.4.2,
    18.4.4
IDR_DOTSTYPE 35.6
IDR_DRAWTYPE 15.7.2, 16.3.5
IDR_EDTYPE 16.2, 16.3
IDR_MAINFRAME 15.4, 15.7.2,
    18.1.7, 18.4.5, 34.6.4
IDR_MANDTYPE 35.8
IDR_MENU 6.4, 6.6.2
IDR_POPUP 32.6
IDR_SAMPTYPE 19.3.1
IDR_SERVER_INPLACE 34.6.4
IDR_SRVR_EMBEDDED 34.6.4
IDR_STANDARD 10.4.6, 10.4.7,
    10.4.8, 10.4.10
IDR_TEXTTYPE 16.3.5
IDRETRY 7.1
IDs B.5.5, B.7.1, B.7.3, 4.2, 6.4, 6.6.6,
    6.7, 10.4, 10.4.7, 15.7.5,
    16.2, 17.1.2, 17.1.3,
    18.1.4, 18.1.5, 18.1.8,
    18.1.10, 18.4.2, 18.4.3,
    18.4.4, 18.4.5, 18.4.7,
    19.3.5, 19.3.7, 19.3.10,
    19.4, 22.5, 26.4, 30.1,
    33.1, 33.8.2, 33.8.3,
    34.7.6, 34.8
IDS_ERROR 6.7.2
IDS_HELLOWORLD 6.7.2
IDYES 7.1
ifdef 13.2
ifdefed 13.1
ifstream A.2.4
iftech B, C.0, C.1, 21, Prf
ignore A.2.7, C.0, 2.6, 5.3, 7.1, 7.2,
    11.0, 14.3, 15.5.3, 15.6.7,
    15.7.11, 23.6, 24.0, 24.1,
    26.4, 34.8.3
ignored A.2.1, A.2.3, A.2.4, 3.2, 3.4,
    3.6, 5.3, 10.5, 18.5, 18.5.4
ignores 4.2
ignoring 27.1
illusion 35.2
illustrate 23.2
illustrates 6.1
illustrative 29.4
imag 34.6.5
image D.2, 11.4.3, 11.6.1, 12.3, 13.5,
    15.5, 15.8.3, 18.4.5, 20.0,
    25.7, 34.1, 35.2
images D.0, D.1, D.2, 7.0, 13.5, 25.7,
    27.2
imagine A.3.2, B.7.5, 2.2, 3.0, 4.7, 5.1,
    6, 6.7, 11.4.1, 11.5.4,

13.2, 16.5, 18.1, 33.1,
    33.7, 34.1, 34.4, 34.8
immaterial 33.6.10
immediate A.4.3, 4.7, 12.1.2, 13.2
immediately A.5, B, B.4, B.7.1, C.1,
    D.1, 1.0, 2.3.1, 4.6, 5.4,
    6.5.3, 8.3, 8.5, 10.3,
    11.4.6, 11.5.3, 11.5.4,
    13.2, 13.6, 15.4.4, 15.8.2,
    15.8.4, 17.1.4, 17.3.5,
    18.1.9, 22.4, 25.4, 27.1,
    32.6, 33.1, 33.4.4, 33.5,
    34.1, 34.2, Prf
impact 10.3, 13.1
impatient 5.1
implement A.1, A.1.1, A.3.2, A.3.3,
    A.4.2, A.5.2, A.7, A.8, 0.1,
    1.1, 2.1, 2.2, 2.3, 3.5, 5.1,
    5.2, 5.3, 6.1, 7.2, 7.7, 8.3,
    8.5, 8.6, 9.4, 10.2, 10.3,
    10.4.10, 11.5.4, 11.5.5,
    12.3, 12.5, 13.5, 14.5,
    15.1, 15.4.4, 15.7.4, 16.2,
    17.0, 17.2, 18.1, 18.3,
    18.4, 18.4.2, 18.4.4,
    18.4.7, 24.0, 24.3, 25.4,
    25.7, 33.8.4, 34.1, 34.2,
    34.3, 34.4, 34.5.3, 34.6,
    34.8.1
IMPLEMENT_DYNAMIC 12.3
IMPLEMENT_DYNCREATE 12.3,
    15.5.3, 15.6.7
IMPLEMENT_SERIAL 12.3, 13.2,
    15.2.6, 15.5.3, 15.6.2,
    15.6.7
implementation A.1, A.1.1, A.4.2,
    A.7.2, B.2.2, C.1, D.7,
    1.3, 5.2, 5.4, 9.1, 10.3,
    10.4.10, 11.4.6, 11.5.4,
    11.5.5, 12.2, 12.3, 14.4.2,
    14.4.3, 14.4.4, 14.5,
    15.2.6, 15.3, 15.3.3,
    15.3.6, 15.3.7, 15.3.8,
    15.4, 15.4.2, 15.4.3,
    15.7.9, 17.2, 18.1.12,
    18.4.7, 25.0, 27.0, 31.6,
    32.6, 34.5.5, 34.8.4, 35.8,
    35.9
implementations A.1.1, 6.6.8, 15.2.6,
    15.4, 15.6.5
implemented A.1.1, A.4, A.4.2, A.6,
    D.1, 1.2, 2.3, 5.4, 11.6.2,
    12.4, 15.0, 15.3, 15.4,
    17.5, 18.0, 18.1, 18.2,
    18.3, 18.4.3, 18.6, 34.2,
    34.8.11
implementer 18.1, 34.8
implementers 34.3
implementing A.4.2, 2.5, 7.0, 15.7.9,
    25.9, 27.0, 34.1, 34.3,
    34.8
implements A.4.3, A.5.2, A.7, A.8, 1.3,
    2.1, 3.0, 5.3, 5.4, 7.2, 9.1,
    10.4, 10.4.10, 11.5.4,
    11.5.5, 14.4.5, 15.8.1,
    18.4.3, 27.0, 33.8.4,
    34.6.3, 34.6.7
implications 10.4, 34.1
implicit A.1
implicitly 14.3

implied A.1
implies 13.6.1, 33.7.2
imply 4.6
importance A.3.2, D.2
important A.1, A.2.3, A.3.1, A.4.3, A.5,
    A.8, B.1.2, B.7.4, D.1,
    0.0, 2.3, 3.1, 4.5, 4.7, 5.1,
    6.1, 6.2, 6.4, 6.5, 6.7, 9.6,
    10, 10.5, 11.0, 11.6,
    11.6.3, 12.1.2, 12.2, 12.3,
    14.1, 14.4.2, 15.5, 15.7,
    15.7.3, 15.8.2, 15.8.3,
    15.8.4, 17.3.4, 17.4.7,
    23.7, 25.6, 25.7, 29.1,
    30.3, 33.1, 33.2.5, 34.1,
    34.3, 34.4, 34.6.3, 34.7.2,
    34.7.5, 35.1, 35.2, 35.7,
    Prf
importantly A.1.1, A.3.2
imposed 2.1
impossible A.1.1, A.3.2, A.7.1, 11.7,
    13.5, 15.6, 16.2, 34.0
impractical 11.5.5
impression A.8.1, 0.3, 1.2, 35.2
improve A.1, A.5.1, C.0, 0.4, 18.1.13,
    18.6, 29.1, 35.0, Prf
improved A.1.1, A.5
improvements A.5, 11.5.3
improves A.1.1, 5.4, 11.5.3
improving C.0, C.1, Prf
inaccessible A.1
inactive 6.4, 11.5.2
inappropriate 5.3
Inc C.1
inch 11.2, 11.6.1, 11.6.2, 15.8.3,
    18.5.4
inches 11.2, 11.3, 11.6.1, 15.8.4,
    18.5.3
Incidentally 34.8
inclined 8.7
inclusion 3.3, 15.5
incoming 13.2
incompatible D.5
incomprehensible A.1.1
inconsistent 20.8
incorporate 34.1
incorporated 35.0
incorrect 25.7, 33.2.1
incorrectly B.3
increase A.3.1, C.1, 1.1, 1.5, 32.5, 33.9,
    34.6.7
increased 0.1, 13.5
increases 3.3, 6.1, 11.4.6, 12.2, 20.2
increasing 11.1, 15.7.11
incredibly 13.6.2, 34.8.13
increment B.2.3, 4.5, 11.6.2, 13.2,
    15.5.3, 34.8.8
incrementally 34.8.1
incremented A.5.2, 34.8.7
incrementing 10.3
increments A.7.2, 10.3, 13.5, 34.8.1
incurs 35.2
independence 35.2
independent 4.6, 11.1, 11.2, 11.3,
    11.6.1, 13.2, 15.8.3, 20.7,
    34.1, 34.3, 35.1, 35.2,
    35.3
independently 3.3, 32.4, 34.1, 34.4,
    35.2
index A.3.1, D.1, 8.1, 8.2, 9.3, 9.4,

12.2, 12.4, 18.4.2, 18.4.6,
    19.1.2, 19.2.2, 19.2.4,
    19.2.6, 19.2.8, 19.2.10,
    20.7, 22.2, 22.5, Prf
indexed D.1, 12.1.2, 19.0
indexes 8.2, 9.3, 12.2, 33.4.2
indexing 8.6.7, Prf
indicate A.4.4, A.5.1, A.5.2, B.3, B.3.1,
    1.2, 2.3, 2.3.1, 3.2, 4.1,
    6.4, 9.3, 11.4.2, 11.4.6,
    11.6.1, 12.3, 13.1, 14.5,
    15.2.6, 15.6.3, 34.2
indicated 4.1, 4.3, 7.6, 12.2, 34.6.7
indicates A.2.3, A.4.3, A.4.4, A.5.1,
    A.8, B.3.2, B.7.7, D.1,
    2.3.2, 2.3.3, 3.1, 4.1, 4.2,
    4.3, 4.4, 5.4, 6.5.3, 8.2,
    10.3, 11.4.6, 11.5.2, 12.2,
    18.4.6, 25.6, 26.4, 32.6,
    33.4.1, 33.6.10, 34.8
indicating 4.2, 12.1.1, 13.5, 13.6
indication A.8
indicative 18.4.2
indicator 12.1.1, 18.4.6
indicators 18.4.6
indices D.1, D.5
individual B.5.1, B.5.5, 1.2, 11.2,
    11.4.7, 11.6.3, 13.5,
    14.4.6, 15.8.3, 16.2, 16.3,
    18.4.3, 22.3, 25.7, 28.0,
    33.1, 33.7, 34.3, 35.2,
    35.6
individually 3.3, 11.4.7, 12.3, 12.4,
    15.3, 25.1, 32.1, 35.1
inefficiency A.5.2, 13.5
inefficient A.7.2
inequality 12.1.4
inextensible A.1.1
infile A.2.4
infinite B.2.1, 8.1, 15.8.4, 26.5, 35.4,
    Prf
infinitely A.1.1, 11.5.5
InflateRect 3.3, 12.1.4
Info B.4, C.0, 29.2, 33.7.4
inform 4.6, 11.6.3, 15.7.9, 17.4, 18.4.6
informational 3.1
informing 7.2
informs 8.6.7
InfoView B.1.5, B.6.2
ing 3.2
inherent A.1.1, A.3, A.5.2, 13.0, 13.2,
    15.1
inherently 22.5, 34.1
inherit A.3.1, A.5.1, 5.4, 11.4.1,
    12.1.1, 12.1.2, 12.3,
    13.6.2
inheritance A.1, A.1.1, A.3.1, A.3.2,
    A.5, A.5.1, A.5.2, A.5.3,
    A.8, 1.1, 3.3
inherited A.1, A.3.1, A.5.1, A.8, 2.3.1,
    3.2, 3.3, 3.6, 4.4, 5.2, 5.4,
    8.1, 12.1.1, 13.6.2, 30.2
inheriting A.5.1, 34.5.3, 34.6.3
inherits A.5.1, A.5.2, A.8, B.7.6, 2.1,
    2.3.2, 3.2, 3.3, 3.5, 6.6.8,
    12.1.1, 14.4, 15.5, 16.1.1,
    17.1.1
INI 0.4, 10.1, 10.5
InitApplication 2.3.1, 10.6
initial A.5.2, D.3, 0.1, 2.3.2, 5.2, 5.5,

6.6.7, 6.6.8, 7.2, 7.3, 7.4,
    7.6, 10.4.10, 11.5.4, 12.2,
    13.2, 15.2.1, 15.4, 15.5.2,
    15.6.6, 15.7.8, 15.7.9,
    16.5, 22.0, 22.1, 22.5,
    25.6, 34.1
initialization A.1.1, A.2.4, A.4.1, A.4.3,
    B.3.1, 1.4, 2.3.1, 3.1,
    10.6, 14.4.2, 15.4.4,
    15.8.2, 20.7, 35.8
initialize A.4.5, A.5.2, D.1, D.2, 2.3.1,
    2.3.3, 6.6.8, 12.1.3, 15.5,
    15.5.2, 15.7.11, 15.8.2,
    18.3, 18.4.2, 18.4.4, 22.1,
    22.5, 23.2, 23.3, 29.1,
    32.5, 33.6.10, 34.5.5,
    34.8.6
initialized A.1.1, A.2.11, A.5.2, A.7.1,
    B.3.1, B.3.2, 2.3.1, 2.3.2,
    9.1, 11.5.3, 11.6.2,
    11.6.3, 12.3, 15.8.4,
    18.5.6, 22.3, 22.5, 32.3,
    33.6.10, 34.6.5
initializes A.2.8, A.4.3, A.5.1, D.2, 2.2,
    6.6.8, 9.2, 12.1.3, 20.7,
    22.1, 28.1, 34.5.3, 34.6.3
initializing A.4.3, 15.6.6, 20.7, 23.2
initially 0.1, 1.4, 2.1, 3.3, 5.3, 6.4,
    6.5.1, 7.2, 7.4, 7.5, 7.6,
    8.6.3, 10.1, 10.4, 14.4.6,
    15.1, 15.3, 16.3.6, 18.1.5,
    22.5, 28.0, 28.1, 29.2,
    30.1, 32.3, 34.1, 34.8,
    34.8.4, 35.2
Initiates 33.5
initiating 7.6
InitInstance B.3.1, B.3.2, B.4.3, B.4.4,
    2.3, 2.3.1, 2.3.2, 2.5, 5.2,
    10.5, 10.6, 13.2, 14.4.2,
    16.3, 16.3.4, 27.1, 32.1,
    32.2, 32.3, 34.5.3, 34.6.3
INL 23.1
inline A.4.6
inner 13.6.1
innovative 34.3
inplace 34.5.3
input A.2.3, A.2.4, A.2.5, 0.1, 1.2, 2.2,
    5.1, 5.3, 5.4, 6.6.8, 8.4,
    13.2, 15.9, 17.2, 22.0,
    22.1, 22.7, 24.0, 24.1,
    27.1, 29.1, 34.4, 35.2,
    35.7
inputString 6.6.8
insensitive 12.1.2, 22.5, Prf
insert A.5.1, A.5.2, A.6, A.8, B.1.4, B.3,
    B.5.1, B.5.2, B.5.3, B.5.5,
    B.5.6, B.5.7, B.8.1, B.8.3,
    B.8.4, 6.5.3, 9.1, 14.0,
    18.4.6, 19.2.3, 20.3, 20.4,
    27.0, 32.6, 33.2.5, 34.1,
    34.4, 34.5.2, 34.5.5,
    34.5.6, 34.6, 34.6.2,
    34.6.10, 34.7, 34.7.7,
    34.8.3, 34.8.6, 34.8.8,
    34.8.10, 34.8.11, 34.8.12
InsertAfter 12.4
InsertAt 12.2
InsertBefore 12.4
InsertColumn 20.3
inserted A.2.3, A.5.1, A.8, 9.2, 18.4.1

Inserting 20.3
insertion A.2.3, A.5.1, A.5.2, A.8, 5.3,
    9.2, 10.2, 12.2, 12.4,
    18.4.6, 18.6, 22.0, 34.2
insertions 12.4, 34.1, 34.5.3
InsertItem 20.3, 20.4
inserts A.8, 8.1, 9.4, 12.2, 12.4
InsertString 9.1, 9.4
Inside A.1.1, A.3.2, A.3.3, A.4.4, B.2,
    B.2.2, B.3, B.3.1, B.6.1,
    B.8.6, 0.1, 0.4, 1.2, 1.3,
    1.4, 2.3, 2.3.2, 2.3.3, 4.4,
    4.5, 4.6, 6.4, 7.7, 8.1,
    10.2, 11.4.1, 11.5.2,
    11.5.3, 11.5.4, 11.6.2,
    11.6.3, 12.1.4, 12.4, 13.2,
    13.3, 13.6, 13.6.1, 14.4.1,
    14.5, 15.2.6, 15.3.3,
    15.4.4, 15.5.6, 16.2,
    17.3.4, 18.4.3, 19.3.5,
    25.6, 29.1, 30.2, 34.0,
    34.1, 34.4, 34.5.5, 34.8.6,
    35.8, 35.9, 35.10
insight 23.0
inspect 7.2
inspects 7.3
install 0.1, 34.4, 34.8.1
installation B.1.1, 1.4
installations 1.4
installed B.8.2, B.8.3, 1.4, 33.4.1
installing 4.1
instance A.3.1, A.4.3, A.4.4, A.4.6,
    A.5.2, A.7.1, A.7.2, A.8,
    D.2, 1.2, 2.3, 2.3.1, 2.3.2,
    2.3.3, 2.5, 3.1, 3.5, 6.6.8,
    10, 10.1, 10.4, 10.4.10,
    10.6, 11.4.1, 11.4.2,
    11.4.6, 11.5.3, 11.6.3,
    12.1.1, 12.1.2, 12.1.3,
    12.1.4, 12.3, 13.2, 13.5,
    13.6, 14.4.2, 14.4.4, 15.3,
    15.3.1, 15.5.2, 15.6.1,
    15.7.11, 15.8.2, 16.5,
    17.4.7, 18.2, 20.5, 23.1,
    24.0, 32.4, 33.5, 33.6,
    33.6.1, 33.6.4, 34.1,
    34.5.3, 34.5.5, 35.3, 35.4,
    35.8, 35.9
instances A.3.2, A.4.3, A.4.4, A.4.6,
    A.5.1, A.7.2, 2.1, 2.3.1,
    8.6.7, 10.4.10, 12.1.1,
    12.1.2, 12.1.3, 12.3, 13.5,
    16.5, 32.4, 34.5.5, 35.7
instant 7.0, 24.0
instantaneous 6.6.8
instantiated A.4.4
instantiates 2.3.2, 23.2
instantiating 33.6.6, 33.6.8
instantiation A.4.4, A.6, A.7, 18.1.4,
    34.4
instructed 14.4.1
instruction C.1
instructions B.3, C.0, 2.3, 3.3, 8.5,
    10.4, 13.4, 14.2, 14.5,
    17.5, 19.2.7, 34.5.7
Instructs 7.6, 33.2.4
insufficient 15.8.4, 34.1
int A.2.3, A.2.7, A.2.11, A.6, 2.3, 7.3,
    7.5, 11.4.3, 11.4.6,
    12.1.4, 12.3, 15.2.6,

15.6.3, 17.3.3, 17.4.1,
17.4.3, 22.2, 22.5, 26.1,
34.6.5
intact 25.7
integer A.2.3, A.2.8, A.2.10, A.2.11,
A.4.3, A.4.4, A.4.5, A.5.2,
A.6, A.7.1, D.1, D.3, 3.1,
4.2, 5.2, 5.3, 5.4, 6.1,
6.5.3, 7.1, 7.2, 7.4, 8.1,
9.3, 10.3, 10.5, 11.4.4,
11.4.5, 11.6.1, 12.1.3,
13.2, 13.3, 13.5, 15.7.9,
17.3.5, 18.3, 19.3, 19.3.5,
20.1, 22.5, 26.1, 35.5
integers A.1.1, A.2.3, A.2.11, A.5.2,
5.3, 9.2, 9.3, 11.4.5, 12.2,
18.4.6, 33.3, 34.8.6
integral 22.5, 25.6, 34.1
integrate A.1.1, 0.4, 1.0, 6, 6.1, 10.5,
12.3, 15.7.11, 34.6.4
integrated A.5.3, 15.2, 34.3
integrates 3.0, 23.0
integrating 11.4.1
integration 12.3
integrity 33.1
intelligent 20.3
intended 1.0, 5.4, 14.4.4, 15.4, 15.8.2,
18.1.10, 28.1, 32.6, 35.2,
35.9
intensities 11.4.2
intensive C.1, D.1, 11.6.2
intent 14.0
intentions Λ.8
inter 18.5.4, 34.0, 34.1, 34.7.9
interact A.3.1, 3.5, 9.3, 11.5, 15.3,
18.2, 32.4, 33.0, 34.1,
34.2
interaction 5.1, 7.2, 11.0, 11.5.1, 33.3,
33.4, 34.1
interactions 11.5.3, 34.1
interactive 5.1
interacts 1.3, 23.9, 33.4, 34.6.3
intercept 4.1, 5.4, 24.1
intercepted 5.3
intercepts 4.3
interchangeable 5.3, 34.3
interchangeably A.2.1
intercommunication 34.4
interest D.0, 4.1, 5.0, 5.4, 6, 17.4, 25.4,
34.2
interested B.4, B.4.1, D.0, D.2
interesting A.3.2, A.4.4, 2.3, 4.1, 4.2,
4.4, 5.2, 6.3.7, 6.7, 8.1,
8.3, 11.4.8, 12.3, 13.6.2,
14.3, 16.3, 17.2, 19.1.2,
25.4, 31.1, 32.8, 33.1,
33.2, 34.0, 34.2, 34.8.3,
35.8
interface A.1, A.3.2, A.4.1, A.8, B.6.1,
C.0, C.1, D.0, 0.1, 0.4,
1.0, 1.1, 1.2, 1.3, 2.2,
2.3.2, 3.0, 3.1, 4.0, 5.1,
5.2, 5.3, 5.4, 5.5, 6.1, 7.0,
9.0, 9.1, 10.3, 11.0, 11.1,
11.5.4, 12.1.3, 14.1,
14.4.4, 15.0, 15.3, 15.4,
15.8, 17.0, 17.1.2, 17.2,
17.4, 18.1, 21, 21.1, 23.9,
33.7.2, 34.1, 34.2, 34.3,
34.7, 34.7.9, 34.8, 35.1,

35.2, 35.3, 35.4, 35.8,
35.9
interfaces D.1, 0.0, 3.0, 17.0, 18.1,
34.1, 34.2, 34.3, 34.5.3,
34.6.3
interfacing 1.3
interfering 10.3
interior D.7, 2.3.2, 11.3, 11.4.3, 11.5.2
internal D.2, 8.6.1, 9.4, 12.1.2, 13.2,
13.3, 15.8, 18.4.3,
34.8.10
internally A.4.3, 10.4.10, 13.1, 14.4.4,
16.2, 34.3
internationally 6.7
Internet C.0
interoperability 34.1
interpolates D.2
interpret 9.2
interpreted 9.2, 15.8.3, 16.4
interprets 5.3, 5.4, 9.2
interrelationships 1.1
interrupt B.2
intersection A.3.3, 4.6, 12.1.4
intersections A.3.2
IntersectRect 12.1.4
intersects A.3.2
intervals 4.5, 10.2, 10.3
inthe 34.9
intimate 34.1
intimately 19.5, 35.2
intimidate 28.0
intimidating 0.1, 14.4.6
intricate 9.1, 12.1.3, 33.9, 34.0, Prf
introduce A.1, 0.0, 0.3, 6, 11.0, 13.5,
35.0
introduced A.1.1, 1.1, 15.0
introduces 0.1, 1.0, 1.5
Introduction A.1, B.7.5, 0.1, 0.3, 1.0,
11.7, 12.6, 19.1.1, 35.0,
Prf
introductory Prf
ints 17.4.1
intuitive 1.3
inty 11.4.6
invalid 5.3, 6.7, 7.2, 12.1.3, 13.2, 13.5,
15.8.2, 17.3.5, 22.4, 22.6,
24.1, 32.4
Invalidate 11.5.2, 15.7.9
InvalidateRect D.5
invalidates D.4, 11.5.2, 11.5.5
invent 34.3
inventory 33.2
inverse 11.5.4
invert 11.5.2, 11.5.4
InvertRect 11.4.3, 11.5.2
inverts 11.4.3, 11.5.4
invest 0.1
investment A.1.1, Prf
invisible 2.3, 3.2, 3.4, 4.1, 18.1.6, 22.0
invisibly 34.4
invocation 10.1, 12.1.1, 12.3
invoke 2.1, 6.1, 15.7.11, 16.5, 32.1,
34.8.3, 34.8.5, 34.8.9,
34.8.11, 34.8.12
invoked A.6, A.7.1, 2.3.1, 6.1, 7.2,
10.4, 12.3, 13.7, 34.1,
34.6.4
InvokeHelper 34.7.7
invokes A.7.1, 6.1, 7.1, 10.4.10
Invoking 7.3

involve A.1.1, A.1.2, 6.7, 9.3, 23.2
involved 1.3, 2.3.2, 4.0, 11.5.5, 14.1,
15.4, 15.5, 15.9, 25.7,
26.5, 30.2, 35.1
involves A.1.1, A.3.3, A.6, A.7, 13.6.1,
15.7.9, 15.8.4
iomanip A.2.3, 5.3
iostream A.2.3, A.2.5, 3.3
IPFRAME 34.6.3
iPixelType D.1
IPO 5.1
IRIS D.2
irrelevant 5.3
ISBN 10.5, 35.0
IsBOF 33.5
IsBold 7.3
IsDeleted 33.5
IsDialogMessage 5.4
IsEmpty 12.1.2, 12.4, 12.5
IsEOF 33.5
IsFieldDirty 33.5
IsFieldNull 33.5
IsFieldNullable 33.5
IsIconic 27.1
IsItalic 7.3
IsKindOf 12.3, 13.6.1
isn A.1, D.2, 24.0, 29.2
isolated B, Prf
isolates 14.4.2
isolating A.4.2
IsOpen 33.5
isotropic 11.6.1
IsRectEmpty 12.1.4
IsRectNull 12.1.4
IsStoring 12.3
IsStrikeOut 7.3
issue A.1, 33.2, 33.2.1
issued D.2, 25.4, 34.8.4
issues 0.2, 1.3, 15.5, 18.6, 33.7, 34.3
IsTerminating 7.6
istream A.6
IsUnderline 7.3
IsWindow 23.1
Italic 26.1, 26.3
item A.4.2, A.5.1, B.4.1, 2.3.3, 3.2, 3.3,
6.3.5, 6.4, 6.5, 6.5.1,
6.5.2, 8.5, 9.1, 9.3, 9.4,
9.5, 10.4, 10.5, 15.7,
15.7.2, 15.7.10, 18.1.7,
18.4.2, 18.4.3, 18.4.4,
18.4.6, 19.3.5, 20.3, 20.4,
21.1.8, 21.1.9, 22.2, 22.5,
25.0, 25.2, 25.3, 25.4,
25.5, 25.6, 25.7, 25.8,
26.1, 26.2, 26.4, 29.2,
30.0, 31.3, 34.5.5, 34.6.8,
34.6.10, 34.8, 35.8
itemAction 25.6
itemID 25.6
items A.2.3, A.5.1, 5.1, 5.4, 6.4, 6.5.4,
8.3, 8.5, 9.0, 9.1, 9.2, 9.3,
9.4, 9.5, 15.7.5, 15.9,
16.2, 18.4.2, 18.4.3,
18.4.4, 18.4.5, 18.4.7,
18.5.4, 19.2, 19.3.10,
20.3, 20.4, 22.5, 23.3,
25.0, 25.2, 25.6, 25.8,
26.1, 26.2, 26.4, 29.2,
30.0, 31.3, 32.6, 32.7,
34.5.5

itemState 25.6
iterate 11.5.2, 20.7
iterates 11.4.6, 13.7, 31.1
iterating 12.5
iterations 34.6.4, 34.6.5, 34.6.7
ITI C.1
January 12.1.3, 22.6
jerky 35.2
job A.3.2, A.4.5, 1.1, 3.3, 10.4, 15.8.2,
     23.0, 30.0, 34.2
jobs 14.4.5, 33.1
jog B.3.2
join 33.1, 33.2.4, 33.4.4
joined 33.1, 34.7.6
joining 33.1
joins 33.2
joy 34.8.1
jump B.1.6, 19.2, 19.2.5
jumping 8.6.7
jumpy 29.1
justification 3.3
justified 3.2
justify 8.1
k A.2.3, 12.1.1, 19.2, 19.2.3
Kasparian Prf
keep A.5.1, B.1.2, D.3, 1.2, 3.3, 10.3,
     11.5.4, 11.6.2, 12.4, 13.1,
     14.5, 16.3.1, 18.4.3, 23.1,
     23.2, 23.5, 26.1, 28.0,
     28.1, 29.3, 29.4, 31.4,
     32.2, 32.4, 34.1, 34.4,
     34.8.1, 35.1
keeps A.7.2, D.5, 8.2, 8.6.1, 11.3,
     11.5.5, 16.2, 18.4.2, 22.4,
     23.1, 28.1, 29.1, 33.1,
     34.2, 34.5.5
kept 20.4
key B.1.6, B.1.7, B.2.2, B.5.5, 0.2, 5.4,
     6.3.7, 6.5.3, 6.6.5, 6.6.8,
     10.1, 10.4.10, 11.5.5,
     18.4.6, 19.1.2, 19.2,
     19.2.3, 19.2.4, 19.2.7,
     19.2.8, 19.2.10, 19.3.5,
     19.4, 20.0, 24.1, 25.7,
     27.0, 27.1, 28.1, 29.1,
     31.4, 33.1, 33.2.3, 33.2.5,
     33.4.3, 34.7, 34.8, 34.8.1
keyboard 1.2, 1.3, 5.4, 6.5.3, 24.1,
     27.1, 32.6, 35.7
keys 0.4, 6.5.3, 9.3, 11.5.2, 18.4.6,
     19.1.2, 19.2, 23.8, 33.1,
     33.4.2
keystroke 5.4, 6.5.3, 19.3.5, 35.7
keystrokes 1.3, 3.2, 5.4, 32.6
keyword 13.6, 13.6.2
kick 35.7
killing 35.7
kind 0.3, 5.1, 11.5.3, 29.1
kinds 12.4, 34.4, Prf
know A.1, A.1.1, A.2.3, A.2.4, A.3.2,
     A.6, A.8, B.3.1, D.0, D.8,
     0.0, 0.1, 0.2, 0.3, 1.3, 2.3,
     3.3, 3.5, 5.1, 6.5.3, 8.3,
     11.0, 11.2, 11.3, 11.4.1,
     11.5.3, 11.6.1, 12.2, 13.2,
     13.3, 14.0, 15.2.6, 15.3,
     15.4, 15.8.4, 16.3.6, 17.0,
     17.4.1, 17.4.5, 18.4.2,
     19.2, 20.1, 20.3, 22.3,
     23.0, 23.7, 25.2, 25.6,

26.0, 27.1, 28.1, 29.1,
     33.0, 33.6.10, 34.1, 34.2,
     34.5.2, 34.5.3, 34.5.4,
     35.4, 35.7, 35.8, 35.10
knowing 6.3.7, 13.2
knowledge 0.3, 1.5, 3.0, 5.0, 5.1, 5.5,
     8.3, 10, 11.7, 14.0, 15.8.1,
     15.8.4, 17.0, 23.0, 34.0,
     34.1, 35.4, Prf
known A.2.3, A.3.2, A.4.3, D.2, D.3,
     D.5, 10.4.10, 12.4,
     14.4.4, 15.8.2, 18.4.6,
     33.1, 33.3, 33.4.1, 34.1,
     34.2, 34.4, 34.8
knows 6.1, 12.1.2, 15.1, 15.2.6, 15.3,
     15.4, 18.2, 18.4.2, 18.4.4,
     23.1, 24.1, 25.0, 33.3,
     33.4.1, 33.6.10, 33.7.2,
     34.2, 34.5.5
l 2.3, 13.4
label B.3, 1.4, 2.2, 2.3.2, 2.3.3, 2.4, 3.1,
     3.2, 3.3, 3.4, 3.5, 5.0, 5.1,
     5.3, 5.4, 6.2, 6.7, 6.7.3,
     9.2, 9.3, 9.5, 10.2, 11.4.6,
     11.4.8, 18.4.5, 20.3, 20.4,
     33.7.2, 34.6.5
labeled A.4.5, 1.3, 4.1, 5.1, 5.4, 7.1,
     16.2, 18.4.5, 20.7
labels 1.2, 3.1, 3.3, 3.6, 4.6, 4.7, 5.2,
     5.4, 6.1, 18.4.5, 29.0,
     32.6, 33.7.3
labor 1.3
laced 13.3
lack 0.2, 4.3, 8.2, 13.6, 18.4.6
lacking 15.4
lacks 11.5.3
land 2.3, 19.2.1
lands A.3.2
Language A.1, A.1.1, A.2.8, A.3, A.3.2,
     A.4.3, A.5.3, A.8.1, D.0,
     1.0, 6.1, 6.7, 12.1.2, 12.5,
     13.3, 19.2, 33.0, 33.2,
     33.3, 33.9, 34.1, 34.4
languages A.1.1, A.3.1, A.3.2, A.3.3,
     0.2, 6.1, 6.7, 33.3
large A.1, A.1.1, A.3.1, A.3.2, A.4.4,
     B.2.3, B.4, B.4.1, B.4.5,
     C.1, D.2, D.7, 1.1, 1.2,
     1.3, 2.1, 3.4, 5.1, 5.3, 6.7,
     9.1, 9.2, 10.4, 11.2,
     11.4.6, 11.5.5, 11.7,
     12.1.2, 13.6.1, 15.6,
     15.8.4, 17.5, 18.1, 18.4.3,
     18.6, 19.2, 20.5, 20.6,
     33.1, 33.2, 34.3, 34.4,
     34.5.3, 35.8
largely A.3.1, 34.5.3
larger A.4.2, B, B.2, 0.4, 5.5, 8.2,
     11.4.1, 11.4.6, 11.5.5,
     15.5, 17.4, 18.1.2, 18.5.5,
     34.4, Prf
largest 11.4.6, 11.6.2, 13.5, 20.6
laser 11.1, 11.2, 11.6.1, 15.8.3
last A.3, A.4, A.4.4, A.5.2, A.6, B.1.1,
     B.3, C.0, D.3, D.6, 4.0,
     5.0, 5.2, 7.2, 8.1, 8.2,
     8.6.8, 11.4.2, 11.4.5,
     11.4.6, 11.5, 11.5.4,
     12.1.1, 12.2, 12.4, 15.4.2,
     15.5, 15.8.2, 16.1.1, 16.2,

22.2, 22.4, 22.5, 26.2,
     27.1, 28.1, 33.2.3, 33.4.3,
     33.5, 33.6.4, 33.6.9,
     33.7.2, 33.7.3
LastName 33.2.1, 33.2.2, 33.2.3,
     33.2.4, 33.6.4
lasts 32.4
later A.1.1, A.2, A.2.2, A.2.3, A.2.10,
     A.3.2, A.4.1, A.4.2, A.5.2,
     C.0, D.2, 2.3.1, 2.3.2, 4.2,
     7.0, 10.3, 11.4.1, 11.4.8,
     11.7, 12.3, 14.5, 15.2.1,
     15.3, 15.3.7, 15.5.3, 17.4,
     18.1.13, 20.0, 22.5, 26.1,
     30.1, 33.6.10, 34.1, 34.2,
     35.4
latest 33.5
latter A.1, A.1.1, 0.2, 6.6.8, 8.2, 11.5.2,
     11.6.3, 15.4, 18.1.7,
     18.5.2, 24.0, 34.8.4,
     34.8.11
launch 10.5
launched 35.7
lay 2.3, 6, 19.2.1
layer A.5, A.5.2, 33.3
layered A.1.1
Layering A.5, A.5.1
layers A.5, A.5.1
Layout B.5.6, 5.1, 19.2, 20.6, 31.1, Prf
lays 11.5.1
LB_ERR 18.4.2, 18.4.3
LBN_SELCANCEL 18.4.2
LBN_SELCHANGE 18.4.2, 26.4,
     31.3
LBN_SETFOCUS 18.4.2
LBS 9.1
LBS_EXTENDEDSEL 9.3
LBS_MULTICOLUMN 9.2
LBS_NOINTEGRALHEIGHT 9.1
LBS_NOTIFY 9.3
LBS_SORT 9.1, 9.4
LBS_STANDARD 9.1
LBS_USETABSTOPS 9.2
lCount 10.3
lead 12.2, 33.6.5
leading C.1
leads 23.7
leak 11.4.7, 11.6.2, 13.5, 35.4
leaks A.1.1, A.4.2, B.3.2, 0.4, 11.6.2,
     13.3, 13.5
learn A.1.1, A.4.6, A.8.1, B.2, B.4, 0.0,
     0.1, 0.3, 1.5, 2.3, 2.3.2,
     3.2, 3.5, 4.6, 6.1, 6.5, 7.7,
     11.0, 11.4, 11.4.8, 13.3,
     14.0, 14.5, 14.6, 15.4,
     15.9, 16.0, 20.8, 22.0,
     23.9, 26.0, 33.4.4, 34.5,
     34.6, Prf
learned A.1.1, A.4.4, A.4.6, A.5.2, 1.0,
     3.0, 5.0, 8.4, 10.7, 11.5,
     15.9, 16.2, 17.1, 17.3,
     17.6, 18.0, 20.6, 21.2,
     31.0
learning B.4, B.4.5, 1.1, 3.0, 11.0,
     12.1.1, 34.8.1, 35.2, Prf
least A.1.1, B.3.2, 3.2, 5.2, 10.3,
     10.4.10, 10.5, 13.2,
     15.8.4, 18.4.6, 33.1, 34.2,
     34.4
leave A.5, B.2.3, B.3.2, B.5.5, B.6.1,

B.7.5, B.8.1, C.1, D.0, D.2, D.3, 6.4, 12.6, 14.3, 15.2.1, 15.5, 15.6.1, 16.1.1, 16.5, 17.3.3, 19.1.1, 25.7, 32.6
leaves 11.5.4, 13.2, 17.3.4
leaving A.5, A.7, 5.2, 16.2, 16.5, 25.7
left A.2.3, A.4.1, A.4.4, A.4.5, A.6, A.7.1, A.8.1, B.2.1, B.3, B.4.1, B.4.2, B.5.6, D.1, D.2, D.4, D.6, 1.2, 2.3.2, 3.1, 3.2, 3.3, 3.6, 4.5, 4.6, 5.3, 8.1, 11.2, 11.4.3, 11.4.6, 11.5.2, 11.5.3, 11.6.1, 12.1.2, 12.1.4, 15.1, 15.5.5, 15.5.6, 18.1.2, 18.5.4, 21, 21.1.7, 23.8, 28.0, 29.1, 30.1, 32.5, 32.6, 32.7, 34.5.2, 34.8.1, 34.8.7, 34.8.8
leftmost 12.1.2, 18.4.6
Leigh Prf
len 8.2, 12.1.2
length A.1.1, A.2.10, 5.3, 8.1, 8.6.1, 11.4.6, 12.1.1, 12.1.2, 18.3, 22.0, 22.4, 22.5, 34.8.7, 35.3
lengthy 35.1, 35.2
less A.6, 4.2, 10.3, 11.1, 18.4.3, 20.2, 34.3
lessen 29.2
lessens 29.1
lesson 35.7
lessons A.1.1
letters 2.3, 24.1
letting A.1.1, B.2.3, 2.1, 11.5.5, 15.3, 18.2
level A.3.1, A.4.1, A.5.1, A.5.2, B.2, B.6.1, 1.1, 1.3, 2.2, 3.1, 6.2, 6.4, 14.3, 15.1, 18.1.10, 23.0, 23.7, 33.3, 34.1, 34.2, 34.4, 34.8, 34.9, 35.7
levels 0.2, 0.3
leverage 10.4.10, 14.4, 18.1, 18.5
leverages 6.3.7, 21.2
leveraging 15.8.1, 33.7.5
LHS 12.4
liaison B.7.4
lib D.1
libraries A.1.1, A.3.2, A.8.1, B.1.2, D.1, 0.2, 2.3, 12.1.3, 13.2, 33.3, Prf
library A.1.1, A.2.3, A.2.5, A.3.2, A.8, D.1, 1.1, 2.1, 3.3, 5.2, 5.3, 11.0, 11.1, 11.2, 11.3, 11.5, 11.6, 11.7, 12.1.1, 12.1.2, 12.1.3, 13.1, 13.3
lie A.3.2
lies A.5, A.5.2, 1.2, 15.5.6, 22.1, 29.1
life 0.1, 8.5, 12, 12.3, 13.2, 18.1.5, 32.4, 33.5
lifesaver B.2.3
lifespan 27.0
light A.1, D.6, D.7, 15.8.3
LightAmbient D.7
LightDiffuse D.7
lighted D.7
lighting D.0, D.6
LightPosition D.7

LightSpecular D.7
likelihood 13.2
likely A.5.2, 33.1, 34.5.5
likes A.1.1, 8.3, 25.1
limit 6.7, 10.3, 12.2, 12.4, 17.5, 18.3, 18.4.6, 22.0, 24.0, 33.7.2, 34.1
limitation 25.0
limitations 10.3, 15.5, 25.6
limited B.4.1, D.1, 8.1, 11.3, 15.5, 18.1, 33.7.2
limiting 34.1
limits 8.1, 27.0, 33.7.4
LimitText 5.3, 8.1, 8.2
  Prf
linear 20.4
LineArray 11.5.5
LineFromChar 8.2
LineIndex 8.2
LineLength 8.1, 8.2
LineScroll 8.2
LineTo 11.4.1
lingo A.3.1
link B.1.6, B.3, 6.1, 6.3.6, 12.3, 19.2.5, 19.2.6, 19.2.7, 19.2.8, 19.2.10, 34.4
linked A.1.1, A.3.2, A.4.2, A.5.2, A.7.1, 6.1, 6.4, 12, 12.4, 34.4, 34.5
linker B.1.2, B.3, D.1, 13.1
linking B.1.2, 6.1, 34.1, 34.4, 34.5
links B.1.6, B.3, 13.1, 14.4.2, 16.3, 19.2, 19.5, 33.7.4
Lippman A.6
listSize A.4.2
listTerminate A.4.2
literal A.2.3, 6.7
literally 3.3, 6.6.8, 30.3, 35.2
little A.1, A.1.1, A.4.5, B.2.3, D.2, D.3, 1.2, 2.1, 3.4, 12.4, 14.1, 17.2, 29.1, 34.1, 34.3, 34.5.4
live 1.2, 14.3
lived 11.4.1
lives 34.1
living 33.2.2
ll D.0, D.1, D.2, 2.3.1, 3.1, 4.0, 5.3, 11.4.1
load A.3.2, A.3.3, A.4.1, 0.0, 0.3, 0.4, 6.2, 6.4, 6.5.3, 6.6.7, 6.7, 10.2, 10.4.10, 11.4.8, 11.5.3, 12.3, 12.5, 14.3, 14.4.4, 15.2.5, 15.2.6, 15.3, 15.3.1, 15.5.3, 17.4.5, 17.4.6, 18.0, 18.1, 18.2, 19.2, 21.1.6, 22.0, 22.1, 25.6, 29.4, 33.1, 33.2, 34.4, 34.8.1, 35.2
load_terrain A.3.2
LoadAccelTable 6.5.3
LoadCursor 10.2, 11.5.3
loaded A.3.3, A.4.1, A.6, B.3.1, 2.3, 8.6.1, 10.2, 11.4.3, 11.5.2, 11.5.3, 17.4, 21.1.8
LoadIcon 6.3.7, 10.2
loading A.4.1, 6.5.3, 6.7, 8.4, 12.3, 13.6, 15.2.6, 19.2, 25.6, 27.0, 33.1
loads 6.1, 6.4, 8.5, 10.5, 12.3, 12.5,

17.4, 29.2
LoadStandardCursor 10.2, 11.5.3
LoadStandardIcon 10.2
LoadStdProfileSettings 10.5
loan 17.4
local A.4.3, B.2.3, 3.3, 11.4.1, 12.1.3, 33.2, 35.2
LocalLock 8.2
locally 12.5
Locals B.2
LocalUnlock 8.2
located 15.3.6, 33.3
location A.2.11, A.3.1, A.5.1, B.4.1, B.8.8, D.2, 3.3, 5.3, 8.2, 8.6.10, 9.1, 9.3, 9.4, 11.4.6, 11.4.7, 12.1.1, 12.2, 19.1.1, 32.2, 33.7.1, 34.4
locations D.6
lock 12.1.1, 18.4.6, 35.7
locked 8.2, 12.1.1, 35.8
locking 8.2, 12.1.1, 33.5
LockRange 12.1.1
locks 35.2
LOENGLISH 15.8.3, 15.8.4, 18.5.3
log 8.6.11, 34.8.4, 34.8.10
LOGFONT 7.3
logic 11.4.6
logical 11.6.1, 11.6.3, 15.5.6, 15.8.4, 34.5.6
logistical Prf
logo 29.4
logs 8.6.11, 21
long A.2.3, A.4.5, A.4.6, A.6, 1.2, 2.3, 6.7, 8.2, 10.2, 10.3, 11.2, 11.4.7, 12.1.1, 13.5, 14.4.2, 16.2, 17.2, 17.4.1, 17.4.3, 17.5, 18.1.5, 18.4.5, 18.5.2, 22.2, 22.5, 27.0, 30.1, 33.6.8, 34.0, 34.1, 34.4, 34.5.5, 35.1, 35.2, 35.8, Prf
longer A.7, 3.3, 8.6.1, 12.1.1, 12.1.2, 18.5.4, 20.7, 32.4, 34.3
lookup D.1, 12.5
loop A.2.3, A.5.2, B.2.1, B.2.2, B.2.3, 1.3, 2.3, 2.3.1, 4.1, 10, 10.6, 11.4.6, 11.6.2, 12.1.1, 12.3, 12.4, 13.2, 15.8.2, 31.4, 33.6.4, 33.6.5, 35.2, 35.4
looping 33.6.4
loops A.3.2, 34.5.5
loose 11.3, 33.6.5, Prf
lose A.1.1, 11.5.1
loses 20.7, 34.1
losing A.2.3
loss A.5.2
lost 13.2
lot A.1, A.1.1, A.2, A.5, A.7.2, A.8.1, 0.0, 1.4, 11.3, 11.7, 17.3.3, 19.1.1, 20.1, 20.3, 23.5, 23.8, 25.1, 31.6, 33.1, 33.6.2, 34.4
Lotus 33.3
low D.0, 1.3, 2.2, 33.3, 34.8, 35.7
lower A.4.5, B.4.5, B.4.6, D.2, 5.3, 8.1, 11.6.1, 26.4, 28.2, 33.3, 34.4, 35.7
lowercase 12.1.2

lowest 1.3
LOWORD 26.2
LPARAM 7.6, 15.4, 26.1, 26.2, 31.4
lpCount 11.4.6
LPCRECT 12.1.4
LPCSTR 7.2
LPDEVMODE 7.5
lpDrawItemStruct 25.6
lpDxWidth 11.4.6
lpDxWidths 11.4.6
LPENUMLOGFONT 26.1
lpFacename 11.4.6
LPINT 11.4.6
lplf 26.1
lplfInitial 7.3
LPNEWTEXTMETRIC 26.1
lpntm 26.1
lpRect 11.4.4, 11.4.6, 12.1.4
lpString 11.4.6
lpszDefExt 7.2
lpszFileName 7.2
lpszFilter 7.2
lpszFindWhat 7.6
lpszPathName 7.2
lpszReplaceWith 7.6
lpText 3.1
LPtoDP 11.6.1
LPtoHIMETRIC 34.6.8
LPVOID 35.3
lst A.6
luck A.1.1
LVN_COLUMNCLICK 20.3
lying A.5.2
m A.5.2, A.6, 2.3, 12.1.3
m_angle D.3
m_atime 12.1.1
m_attribute 12.1.1
m_bAutoDelete 35.4
m_bAutoMenuEnable 6.5, 8.6.10
m_bCheck 22.5
m_bContinuePrinting 15.8.2, 15.8.4, 18.5.6
m_bExpanded 28.1
m_bHelpMode 10.1
m_bPreview 15.8.2
m_bSaveAndValidate 22.4
m_cause 12.1.1, 12.5, 13.6
m_celsius 17.3.3, 17.3.5
m_city 18.1.9, 18.3
m_combo 22.5
m_ctime 12.1.1
m_ctlTree 20.4
m_cx 34.6.5
m_cy 34.6.5
m_dlgBar 30.1
m_edit 22.5, 24.2
m_fahrenheit 17.3.3
m_hAccelTable 13.4
m_height 15.7.8
m_hInstance 10.1
m_hPrevInstance 10.1
m_hstmt 33.5
m_hThread 35.4
m_hWnd 13.4, 23.0, 23.1, 23.2, 23.7, 27.1
m_iter 34.6.5
m_lf 7.3
m_list 18.1.4, 18.1.5, 18.3, 22.5, 23.3
m_lpCmdLine 10.1
m_lpCommandLine 2.3.1

m_lpUserData 15.8.2
m_mtime 12.1.1
m_name 18.1.9, 18.3
m_nCmdShow 2.3.1, 2.3.2, 10.1, 32.3
m_nCurPage 15.8.2
m_nExpandedHeight 28.1
m_nFields 33.5
m_nIDHelp 13.4
m_nIDLastMessage 13.4
m_nIDTracking 13.4
m_nNormalHeight 28.1
m_nNumPreviewPages 15.8.2
m_nParams 33.5, 33.6.10
m_nRadio 22.5
m_nScrollPos 22.5
m_nWindow 13.4
m_pActiveWnd 10.1
m_pfnThreadProc 35.8
m_pMainWnd B.3.2, 2.3, 2.3.2, 32.1
m_pPD 15.8.2
m_ps D.5
m_pSelection 34.5.5
m_pSet 33.8.2
m_pszAppName 2.3.1, 10.1
m_pszExeName 10.1
m_pszHelpFilePath 10.1
m_pszProfileName 10.1
m_pszRegistryKey 10.1
m_pThreadParams 35.8
m_ptRDown D.4
m_range 34.8.7, 34.8.8, 34.8.12
m_rectDraw 15.8.2, 15.8.4, 18.5.4
m_size 12.1.1
m_SizeAndPositionRect 34.5.5, 34.5.6
m_sizeExtent 34.6.8
m_state 18.1.9, 18.3
m_static 23.2
m_strError 33.6.5
m_strFilter 33.5, 33.6.8, 33.6.10
m_strPageDesc 15.8.2
m_strSort 33.5, 33.6.6
m_szFullName 12.1.1
m_szText 22.0, 22.1
m_transX D.3
m_transY D.3
m_value 34.8.6, 34.8.7, 34.8.8
m_viewList 16.3.3
m_width 15.7.8
m_xRotate D.6
m_yRotate D.6
m_ZipCodeParam 33.6.10
Mac 1.1, 1.3
machine D.0, 1.4, 3.5, 10.5, 11.6.1, 12.4, 33.2, 33.3, 33.4, 33.4.1, 34.4, 35.1, 35.2, 35.7
machines A.7, D.0, 3.4, 13.6, 34.5.5, 35.2, 35.8
Macintosh 0.0, 34.1, 35.2
macro A.2.7, B.4, 4.3, 4.4, 12.3, 13.2, 13.3, 13.5, 15.5.3, 15.6.7, 34.1, 34.7.7, 34.7.9, 34.8.11
macros B.4, B.4.2, 4.3, 4.7, 10.4, 12, 12.3, 13.2, 13.5, 13.6.1
made A.1.1, A.4.4, B.3, D.0, D.1, D.2, 3.3, 4.3, 8.5, 8.6.1, 8.6.2, 9.1, 13.2, 13.5, 15.1, 15.3, 15.3.5, 15.7.11, 18.2, 18.5.3, 20.3, 20.7, 22.5,

23.1, 33.1, 33.7, 34.1, 34.3, 34.5.5
magic 15.3.8, 18.3
mail C.0, 9.4, 34.3, 35.10
mailbox 9.4
mailings 33.1
mailslots 34.1
main A.4.2, A.4.4, A.5.2, A.6, A.7, A.8, B.2, B.2.3, 1.2, 1.3, 1.4, 2.2, 2.3, 2.3.1, 2.3.2, 2.5, 3.1, 4.1, 4.5, 5.1, 5.2, 5.3, 6, 6.4, 7.2, 10, 10.1, 13.3, 14.4.3, 15.2.2, 17.0, 17.1.2, 17.2, 18.1, 18.1.2, 18.3, 19.1.1, 19.2, 20.7, 26.3, 26.4, 27.1, 30.1, 31.1, 31.4, 32.1, 32.6, 33.7.2, 35.3, 35.9
MAINFRAME 18.4.6
MAINFRM 14.4.3, 14.4.4, 18.4.6, 34.5.3, 34.6.3
mainly D.5, 17.2
MainMenu 6.4
maintain A.1.1, 6.1, 10.5, 18.4.6, 33.1, 34.5.3
maintainability A.1.1
maintained D.1
maintaining 6.7, 12.1.2
maintains A.5.1, D.2, 8.2, 12.4, 33.1, 34.5.5, 35.6
major A.1.1, 11.0, 31.1
majority A.3.2, 2.1, 4.7, 12.3
MAK 16.2
makefile B.1.2, 19.1.1
MAKEHELP 19.1.1, 19.1.2, 19.2.2, 19.2.4, 19.2.6, 19.2.8, 19.2.10, 19.3, 19.3.5, 19.3.7, 19.3.8, 19.3.10
MAKEHM 19.3, 19.3.5, 19.3.6, 19.3.7
MAKELONG 26.2
MakeLower 12.1.2
MakeReverse 12.1.2
MakeUpper 12.1.2
making A.1.1, D.1, 0.1, 2.1, 6.4, 6.7, 8.6, 10.4, 10.5, 13.2, 13.3, 18.4.6, 23.1, 23.8, 25.0, 27.1, 29.1, 31.2, 32.2, 33.6.10, 34.0, Prf
malloc A.2.10, 13.6.2
manage 3.3, 11.5.3, 15.7, 15.7.6, 15.8, 18.2, 18.5.6, 20.7, 22.2, 23.2, 25.0, 25.5, 25.6, 29.2, 35.10
manageable A.1.1
managed 34.1
management C.1, 2.1, 8.6.10, 11.5.3, 18.4.6, 20.7, 25.1, 34.5.3, 35.2
manager A.5.1, 0.1, 0.4, 2.3.2, 5.1, 8.2, 8.6.7, 10.5, 32.1, 32.8, 35.2, 35.7
manages A.4.1, 1.3, 11.2, 11.5.3, 22.2, 32.5, 34.4
managing 15.5, 23.1, 23.5, 32.5, 34.4
Mand 34.6.1, 34.6.2, 34.6.3, 34.6.10
Mandatory 3.2
MANDDOC 34.6.5
Mandel 35.8
mandelbrot 34.6.3, 34.6.4, 34.6.5,

34.6.6, 34.6.7, 35.2, 35.8
mandlebrot 34.6.5, 34.6.10
MANDVIEW 34.6.6
ManipList A.8
manipulate A.1.1, A.4.3, B.1.2, B.2,
    B.6, B.6.1, B.8.1, 1.3, 3.1,
    3.3, 5.1, 6.1, 9.4, 11.4.7,
    12.1.2, 12.1.4, 14.4.3,
    14.4.4, 14.4.6, 14.5, 15.3,
    15.5, 15.7, 16.3.6, 17.3,
    18.4.7, 22.0, 23.1, 23.4,
    30.1, 33.0, 34.4, 34.8
manipulated B.8, 1.3, 2.2, 11.5.5,
    12.1.2, 14.4.4
manipulates B.7, 1.1, 1.3, 4.2, 4.6, 5.1,
    11.4.7
manipulating A.4.5
manipulation A.4.2, 4.6, 10.4.10, 11.0,
    15.5.1, 15.7, 18.4.2, 23.8,
    34.1
manipulations 11.5.5, 15.2.6, 33.3
manipulator 5.1
manipulators A.2.3
manner A.1.1, A.2.3, A.2.4, A.5.1,
    6.5.1, 11.6.1, 12.1.1,
    12.4, 15.1, 15.2.6, 15.4,
    15.7.5, 18.4.6, 23.6, 25.0,
    29.1, 35.2, 35.3
MANSEDOC 34.6.5
Manual 19.5
manually 6.4, 15.2.6, 15.7.7, 15.7.9,
    16.3.3, 18.4.6, 20.7, 22.5,
    24.1, 25.8, 28.1, 28.2,
    30.1, 30.2, 31.5, 32.7,
    33.4
manuals 0.1, 0.2
manufacturer 34.1
manufacturers 33.2, 33.3
manuscript Prf
map A.1, B.7.1, B.7.3, D.2, 0.3, 0.4,
    4.1, 4.2, 4.3, 4.4, 4.5, 4.6,
    4.7, 5.2, 5.3, 5.4, 6.5,
    6.5.1, 6.5.4, 6.6.8, 7.1,
    7.6, 8.5, 8.6.7, 9.3, 10.4,
    10.4.10, 11.2, 11.4.1,
    11.4.6, 11.5.1, 11.5.2,
    11.5.3, 11.5.5, 11.6.1,
    12.1.1, 12.5, 14.4.5, 14.5,
    15.3.1, 15.3.2, 15.3.3,
    15.3.4, 15.3.6, 15.3.8,
    15.7.3, 15.8, 17.1.3, 18.1,
    18.1.10, 18.4.6, 19.1.1,
    19.2, 19.3, 19.3.4, 19.3.5,
    19.4, 20.7, 23.5, 23.7,
    23.8, 24.1, 25.4, 25.5,
    30.1, 31.2, 31.3, 31.4,
    31.5, 33.0, 33.3, 34.5.3,
    34.8.7, Prf
mapped 11.5.5, 23.8, 34.8
mapping 11.0, 11.1, 11.2, 11.3, 11.4.2,
    11.6.1, 11.6.3, 12.5, 15.5,
    15.5.4, 15.8.3, 15.8.4,
    18.5.3, 19.2, 19.3.5,
    19.3.6, 19.3.8, 33.3,
    34.5.6, 34.6.9
mappings 11.2, 12, 12.5, 19.3.5
Maps B.7.1, B.7.2, D.5, D.6, 1.0, 1.5,
    4.0, 4.7, 6.1, 6.4, 6.5,
    6.5.3, 11.3, 11.5, 12, 12.5,
    13.3, 14.5, 15.7.3, 17.0,

17.3.4, 18.1.5, 18.4.2,
    18.4.3, 18.4.4, 18.4.7,
    19.3, 19.3.2, 19.4, 23.7,
    23.9, 29.2, 32.7, 33.6.3,
    34.6.5, 34.8, 34.8.7, Prf
margin 3.3, 18.5.4
margins 18.5.3
mark 6.4, 6.5.2, 6.5.4, 7.1, 7.2, 10.2,
    19.1.2, 19.2, 28.1,
    33.6.10, 33.6.11, 34.5.5
marker 28.1
market A.1, B, Prf
marketplace 34.3
marking 14.4
marks B.2.1, 6.5.1, 6.5.2, 13.6, 20.7,
    33.6.10, 33.6.11
Marshall 10.5, 35.0
mask 3.2, 25.7
masking 25.7
mass B.3
massive 6.7, 19.2
master A.3.2, C.1, 0.0, 2.3.2, 4.6, 11.0
mastered A.8.1, B, Prf
match A.1.1, A.6, D.3, 7.6, 9.5, 11.4.2,
    11.4.6, 11.6.2, 14.1,
    15.5.6, 16.2, 22.2, 23.7,
    33.2, 33.2.4, 34.3, Prf
MatchCase 7.6
matches 8.4, 15.5.6, 16.4, 22.2, 22.5,
    26.1, Prf
matching A.2.8, 26.1, Prf
MatchWholeWord 7.6
material A.1, A.4.6, 0.0, 0.2, 0.3,
    19.2.7, Prf
math D.0, 11.4.4, 34.6.5, 34.7
mathematical 34.7
matrices D.2
matrix D.2, D.3, D.6, 11.2, 11.6.1,
    15.8.3
matter A.4.2, 3.3, 3.5, 8.6, 11.5.3,
    11.6.1, 15.8.3, 18.5.4,
    34.1, Prf
matters 2.6, 34.8.12
MAX A.2.7
MAX_RANGE 4.6
maximization 5.2
maximize B.3, 1.2, 5.2, 32.3, 32.5
maximized 0.4, 2.3
maximizes 11.2
maximum A.1.1, 5.3, 8.1, 8.2, 9.1,
    11.3, 11.6.1, 12.1.2, 15.5,
    15.5.4, 15.7.8, 15.7.11,
    15.8.2, 15.8.4, 17.3.3,
    20.2, 22.0, 22.4, 22.5,
    34.8.1, 34.8.6, 35.2
maybe A.4.5
maze 11.5
MB_ABORTRETRYIGNORE 7.1
MB_APPLMODAL 7.1
MB_DEFBUTTON 7.1
MB_ICONEXCLAMATION 7.1
MB_ICONINFORMATION 7.1
MB_ICONQUESTION 7.1
MB_ICONSTOP 7.1
MB_OK 6.7, 7.1, 15.7.3
MB_OKCANCEL 7.1
MB_RETRYCANCEL 7.1
MB_SYSTEMMODAL 7.1
MB_YESNO 7.1
MB_YESNOCANCEL 7.1

MCImail C.0
MDI B.6.1, 0.4, 1.2, 2.1, 2.3.2,
    10.4.10, 14.1, 14.3, 15.0,
    15.1, 15.3, 15.3.1, 15.4,
    15.5, 15.6.1, 15.7.1,
    15.7.2, 16.0, 16.1, 16.1.1,
    16.1.2, 16.3, 16.3.1,
    16.3.2, 16.6, 17.0, 17.2,
    17.5, 18.1, 18.1.7,
    18.1.10, 18.1.15, 18.2,
    18.4, 18.4.2, 18.6, 19.1.1,
    21.1.1, 21.1.4, 27.1, 29.4,
    32.3, 35.1, 35.5, 35.7,
    35.8, Prf
me D.2, 0.4, 7.1, 7.6
mean A.3.1, 0.4, 23.1, 23.7, 33.2, 35.2
meaningful 33.7.3, 34.1
meanings 3.5
means A.1.1, A.3.2, A.4.4, A.4.6, A.6,
    A.8, B.3, B.8.2, B.8.3,
    D.1, 2.3, 11.4.2, 11.6.1,
    12.1.4, 13.6, 14.3, 23.0,
    27.1, 31.4, 32.1, 35.8
meant 34.1
measure 11.2, 15.8.3
measured 11.2, 11.6.1
MeasureItem 25.3, 25.6, 26.4
MEASUREITEMSTRUCT 25.6
measures 11.2, 15.8.4
meat 34.3
mechanism A.1.1, A.2.3, 4.1, 6.5,
    6.6.8, 7.6, 10.2, 12, 13.0,
    13.2, 13.6, 13.6.2, 15.7.8,
    16.2, 17.3.3, 17.4.4,
    17.4.5, 18.4.2, 18.4.3,
    18.4.6, 18.6, 19.3, 31.0,
    31.1, 33.7.4, 34.0, 34.1,
    34.3, 34.7.9, 35.4
mechanisms 0.4, 12.1.1, 22.5, 34.1,
    35.2, 35.7
Meehan Prf
meets 22.0, 22.4
megabyte 11.6.2
megabytes A.7.2, 0.0, 0.2, 5.2
melding A.6
memberFxn 25.5
members A.4.3, A.4.4, A.4.6, A.5.1,
    A.5.2, A.6, A.7, A.7.1,
    A.8, B.6.2, 2.1, 2.3.1, 3.0,
    7.1, 9.1, 11.5.2, 11.5.3,
    11.5.4, 12.1.1, 12.1.2,
    12.3, 13.2, 13.4, 14.4.4,
    15.8.2, 15.8.4, 22.2, 33.5,
    34.6.5, 34.8.6, 35.4, 35.8
memory A.1.1, A.2.5, A.2.10, A.3.2,
    A.4.2, A.4.4, A.5.2, A.7,
    B.2, B.3.1, B.3.2, D.1,
    D.7, 0.4, 2.1, 2.3, 2.3.2,
    2.3.3, 2.4, 3.1, 4.7, 5.2,
    8.2, 8.6.2, 8.6.7, 11.3,
    11.6.2, 12, 12.1.1, 12.1.2,
    12.2, 12.3, 12.4, 13.0,
    13.3, 13.5, 13.6, 13.6.1,
    13.6.2, 13.7, 14.3, 18.4.7,
    25.6, 29.2, 33.1, 34.1,
    34.4, 35.4
memstate 13.5
mental A.1.1, A.1.2, A.3.3, 0.0
mention A.3.2
mentioned 8.7, 11.6.1, 13.2, 14.5,

15.2.6, 18.5.6, 19.5, 20.8, 23.8
menu_index 19.2
menus B.5, B.6.2, 0.1, 0.4, 1.1, 1.3, 3.0, 5.1, 6, 6.1, 6.4, 6.5, 6.7, 8.4, 8.6.10, 14.4.6, 15.7, 23.6, 25.0, 25.9, 31.0, 32.5, 32.6, 34.2, 34.6.4, 35.8, Prf
merge 33.1
merit 17.4, 34.3
mesage 4.7
mesh A.3.2
mess A.3.2
MessageBeep 3.3, 4.3
MessageBox 6.7, 6.7.3, 7.1
messages B.1.6, B.3, B.3.1, B.7.1, B.7.3, D.1, D.2, D.4, 1.3, 2.2, 2.3.2, 3.1, 3.2, 4.0, 4.1, 4.2, 4.3, 4.4, 4.5, 4.7, 5.2, 5.4, 6.7, 7.0, 7.1, 7.6, 9.1, 9.3, 9.5, 10.3, 10.6, 11.4.1, 13.3, 14.4.5, 15.3, 15.3.8, 18.1.11, 18.4.6, 18.4.7, 22.5, 23.0, 23.1, 23.4, 23.7, 23.8, 24.1, 24.2, 24.3, 25.2, 25.3, 25.4, 25.5, 25.6, 26.4, 27.1, 29.1, 29.2, 30.0, 30.1, 31.4, 32.4, 32.5, 32.7, 33.8.4, 34.1, 34.8.1, 34.8.10, 35.8
messiness 35.8
messy A.4.2
met 18.4.3
metafile 26.1
Metafiles 11.1
metaphor 18.1
method A.4.6, B.8.7, D.1, 1.1, 5.1, 8.6.7, 20.2, 20.3, 20.4, 22.2, 25.1, 31.0, 33.6.3, 34.7, 34.7.4, 34.7.8, 34.8, 34.8.1, 34.8.3, 34.8.5, 34.8.9
methods B.8.7, 20.2, 22.2, 23.4, 33.3, 34.7, 34.8, 34.8.1, 34.8.3, 34.8.5, 34.8.13, 35.4
Metric 11.6.1
MF_BYCOMMAND 6.5.1
MF_DISABLE 6.5.1
Microsoft B.3, B.8.4, 0.0, 0.2, 1.0, 1.1, 1.5, 2.1, 2.3, 3.3, 4.7, 5.1, 14.1, 14.3, 15.6, 16.5, 19.2, 22.6, 33.3, 33.4, 33.4.1, 33.4.2, 33.4.3, 33.4.4, 33.8.4, 34.0, 34.1, 34.2, 34.4, 34.5.4, 34.6.2, 34.7, 34.9, 35.2, Prf
mid 12.1.2
middle 11.5.2, 12.1.2, 12.2, 12.4, 22.1, 35.7
midstream B.2
midway A.4.4
migrate 34.3
migrating Prf
migration 0.2
Mike Prf
military A.1.1, 12.1.3
millimeter 11.6.1
millimeters 11.3

millisecond 34.4
milliseconds 4.5, 34.7.9, 35.2, 35.7
mimic 15.8.3
mimics A.2.11, 12.1.1, 20.5
MIN_RANGE 4.6
mind A.3.3, D.5, 1.1, 10.3, 11.6.2, 12.4, 13.1, 23.1, 34.1, 34.4, 34.8.1, 35.1
minded 34.3
minds A.3.1, 21
mini B.6.1, 0.4, 32.0, 32.5
miniature 29.0, 29.1
miniframe 32.5
minimal 6.7, 11.4.6, 18.6
minimalist 33.8.4
minimization 11.5.3, 32.6
minimize B.3, 1.2, 7.6, 11.4.1, 32.5, 32.6
minimized 0.4, 1.2, 2.3, 2.3.2, 6.3.7, 11.5.4, 32.3
minimizes 3.3
Minimizing 16.3
minimum D.1, 15.4, 15.7.8, 17.3.3, 18.4.3, 18.4.6, 20.2, 22.4, 22.5, 35.3
MinMax 22.4
minor 1.3, 30.1, 33.3, 34.8.11
mint A.5.2, A.5.3, A.6
mints A.5.2, A.6
minus 7.2, 9.3, 18.4.6
minuscule 34.5.2
minute 2.3.2, 6.4, 12.1.3
minutes 2.3.2, 12.1.3, 15.5, 35.8
mirror 15.7.8
misbehave 8.6.10
Miscellaneous 11.1
misleading 3.4
mismatch A.1.1
missing A.3.2, B.3.2, 13.6, 20.3, Prf
misspelled 34.8.12
mistakes B.3
mix A.3.2, 34.3
MK_LBUTTON 15.2.3
MM_ANISOTROPIC 11.6.1
MM_HIENGLISH 11.6.1
MM_HIMETRIC 11.6.1
MM_ISOTROPIC 11.6.1
MM_LOENGLISH 11.6.1, 15.8.3
MM_LOMETRIC 11.6.1
MM_TEXT 11.6.1, 15.8.3
MM_TWIPS 11.6.1
mmode D.2
mnemonic 1.2, 5.4, 6.5.2, 6.5.3, 15.7.2
mnemonics 8.4, 28.1, 32.6
modal 0.4, 1.2, 2.1, 6.6.8, 7.1, 7.6, 8.3, 17.2, 20.6, 20.7, 31.4, 32.4, 32.8
mode B, B.4, D.2, 7.2, 8.0, 8.1, 8.2, 8.3, 8.6.1, 9.2, 9.3, 9.4, 9.5, 10.1, 11.2, 11.3, 11.4.2, 11.4.3, 11.4.5, 11.4.6, 11.4.7, 11.5.4, 11.6.1, 11.6.3, 12.2, 13.1, 13.5, 15.5, 15.5.4, 15.8.2, 15.8.3, 15.8.4, 18.5.3, 19.2, 19.2.1, 20.3, 28.1, 29.3, 33.5, 33.7.6, 34.5.6, 34.6.9, 34.8
model D.3, D.6, 6.6.8, 11.4.6, 15.8, 25.0, 31.4, 33.1, 34.3,

34.4, Prf
modeless B.4, 0.4, 1.2, 2.1, 7.6, 8.3, 8.5, 8.6.7, 20.7, 27.0, 27.1, 30.0, 32.0, 32.4, 32.5, 32.8
modelessly 8.5
models A.3.1
modelss 0.4
ModelView D.2, D.3
modem 34.1
modems 35.1
modern C.1, 0.0, 1.1, 7.0, 11.5.4
modes D.2, 0.4, 3.4, 8.0, 9.5, 11.4.6, 11.5.4, 11.6.1, 15.8.3, 20.3
modifiable A.1.1, B.8.1, 22.5, 34.8.2
modification A.1.1, A.5, 5.4, 8.2, 15.2.6, 15.4, 15.5.6, 15.8.2, 15.8.4, 16.3.3, 18.1.15, 18.4.6, 21.1.8, 34.8.12, 35.7
modifications A.3, 4.3, 6.5, 6.5.4, 8.6.1, 8.6.10, 15.2, 15.2.4, 15.2.7, 15.3, 15.4, 15.7.8, 15.8.4, 18.4, 18.4.6, 26.5, 30.1, 33.1, 33.6.10, 34.4, 34.5.3
modified A.4.2, A.5.1, A.7, B.3, 2.1, 3.0, 3.5, 6.1, 6.4, 6.5.1, 6.5.3, 8.1, 8.2, 11.4.6, 11.5.3, 11.5.4, 13.2, 14.4.5, 15.0, 15.2.6, 15.3, 15.3.1, 15.3.3, 15.4.3, 15.5.4, 15.6.4, 16.3.5, 17.4.4, 18.2, 18.4.2, 24.3, 28.1, 33.7.3, 34.2, 34.8.6, 34.8.13
modifier A.2.7
modifiers 1.3, 6.5.3
modifies A.7.2, 3.3, 5.3, 11.5.3, 11.6.1, 12.1.4, 12.4, 15.5, 16.1.1, 16.5, 17.1.1, 33.1
modift A.1.1
module A.2.8, 6.7.2, 34.7.7
modules A.1.1, D.1
mold 5.1
moment A.7, B.6.1, D.2, 2.3, 2.3.1, 6.4, 11.3, 13.2, 15.3, 15.5, 15.6.1, 18.1.7, 18.1.10, 34.1, 35.2, 35.4, 35.7
momentarily 34.2
Monday 12.1.3
money C.1, 16.5
monitor B.2, 11.1, 11.2, 11.4.2, 11.4.6, 15.8.3, 22.5, 23.8, 24.0, 24.1, 32.2, 35.7
monochrome 25.7
monolithic 34.3
monopolize 35.2
month 12.1.3, 22.6
months B, Prf
monumental 34.5.3
Morey Prf
mortgage 17.4
mostly 14.4.5
Motif C.1
motion 11.5, 11.5.3, 11.5.4, 15.0, 15.2.3, 32.6
mouse D.3, D.4, D.6, 0.4, 1.2, 1.3, 3.2, 4.6, 5.1, 5.4, 11.0, 11.4.1,

11.5, 11.5.2, 11.5.3,
11.5.4, 15.0, 15.1, 15.2.3,
15.2.4, 15.2.7, 15.5.6,
19.3.5, 23.7, 27.0, 27.1,
29.1, 32.1, 32.6, 34.8,
34.8.1, 34.8.7, 34.8.8,
34.8.10
move A.1, A.4.2, A.5.2, B, B.1.6, B.3,
B.4.1, D.2, D.3, D.4, 0.0,
0.4, 1.0, 1.1, 1.3, 4.6, 5.1,
6.1, 7.6, 8.2, 11.4.1,
11.4.8, 11.6.2, 13.2, 14.1,
14.5, 15.1, 15.4.1, 15.7.2,
15.8.1, 15.8.3, 15.8.4,
16.3.5, 17.3.4, 17.4, 18.2,
18.4.7, 23.2, 29.1, 32.6,
33.4.3, 33.5, 33.7.2,
33.7.5, 33.8, 34.3, 34.4,
34.5.2, 34.5.5, 34.6.10,
34.8, 34.8.3, 35.8, Prf
moved A.3.1, A.4, A.5.2, 2.3, 17.3.4,
17.4, 18.3, 29.1, Prf
MoveFirst 33.5
MoveLast 33.5
movement 4.6, 11.2, 11.5.4, 18.3,
18.4.7, 29.1
movements 27.1
MoveNext 33.5
MovePrev 33.5
moves A.5.2, D.3, 4.4, 4.5, 4.6, 11.4.1,
11.5.2, 11.5.3, 11.5.4,
11.5.5, 12.1.4, 12.4, 15.1,
17.3.4, 23.7, 29.1, 33.5,
33.6.4, 33.8.3, 33.8.4,
34.5.5, 35.7
MoveTo 11.4.1
MoveWindow 4.4, 18.1.5, 18.3, 28.1
moving 11.4.1, 11.5.3, 11.6.2, 29.1,
33.7.6
MRU 0.4, 10.4.10, 10.5, 15.2.1
MS 33.4.4, 35.2
MSDOS 35.2
MSGF_DIALOGBOX 31.4
MSINGLE D.2
MSLANG 0.2
MSMFC 0.2
MTRECALC 35.4
much A.1, A.1.1, A.2.3, A.2.10, A.3.2,
A.4.2, A.4.3, A.4.4, A.4.6,
A.6, A.8.1, B, 1.0, 1.3, 2.1,
3.3, 5.3, 6.1, 7.6, 8.0, 8.4,
8.7, 9.5, 10.3, 10.4, 10.7,
11.4.6, 11.5.5, 11.6.1,
12.1, 12.1.1, 12.1.2,
12.1.3, 12.3, 12.4, 13.5,
13.8, 14.0, 14.4.5, 15.0,
15.3, 15.5, 15.7, 15.8.2,
15.8.3, 15.8.4, 15.9, 18.4,
18.4.3, 18.4.6, 20.3, 22.0,
23.6, 23.8, 24.0, 27.2,
28.0, 30.0, 33.4.2, 33.6.5,
34.1, 34.2, 34.3, 34.4,
34.5.3, 34.8, 34.8.3, 35.2,
35.3, 35.7
multi A.2.1, A.5.1, A.5.2, D.1, D.2,
D.7, 0.4, 1.2, 3.3, 6.4, 8.0,
8.2, 8.3, 9.2, 11.4.6, 13.3,
15.8.4, 16.2, 16.5, 19.1.1,
25.7, 33.1, 35.1, 35.2,
35.7, Prf

multicolored D.2
multiline 8.2
multiple A.1.1, A.2.3, A.3.2, D.1, 0.4,
1.2, 2.3.1, 3.3, 3.6, 4.5,
7.2, 7.5, 8.6.7, 9.3, 9.5,
10.4.10, 11.3, 11.6.3,
13.6.1, 14.1, 14.3, 14.4.2,
14.4.4, 15.0, 15.4, 15.5,
15.6.1, 15.8.4, 16.0,
16.1.1, 16.2, 16.3, 16.5,
16.6, 17.2, 17.5, 18.1.15,
18.4.2, 18.5, 19.2.3, 19.4,
20.3, 20.5, 22.2, 32.4,
33.1, 33.2, 33.6.10, 34.4,
34.5, 35.1, 35.2, 35.5,
35.8, Prf
multiplied 35.8
multiprecision A.5.2
murky 34.1
my 0.4, 13.2, 35.7
mysterious A.7.2, B.4.4, 23.8
n A.2.3, A.2.4, 8.2, 10.4.6, 12.1.1,
12.1.2, 13.3, 18.4.5, 30.1
naming A.4.2, D.2, 6.4
narrow 18.4.5, 26.1
native A.1.1, 2.1, 3.2, 19.2.2, 19.2.4,
19.2.6, 19.2.8, 19.2.10,
19.3.5, 19.3.10, 34.2
natural A.3.2, A.4.5, D.6
naturally A.4.1
nature A.3.1, 1.0, 34.4
navigational 11.5.5
NC 33.1
NCB B.6.1
nChar 24.1
nCharSet 11.4.6
nClassStyle 11.5.3
nClipPrecision 11.4.6
nCode 7.2
nCount 11.4.6
near A.4.3, D.6, 10.5, 11.4.6, 16.3
nearly A.3.1, 4.2, 5.2, 6.6.8, 8.1, 8.3,
15.4, 33.3, 33.7, 34.4,
34.5.3, 34.6.3
neat 35.10
necessarily A.6, 11.4.6
necessary A.2, A.5.2, A.7.1, A.7.2, A.8,
C.1, D.1, D.2, 1.1, 1.3,
1.4, 2.1, 2.2, 11.4.6,
11.4.8, 12.1.2, 12.2, 12.3,
12.5, 14.4.4, 15.2.4,
15.6.1, 15.7.5, 15.9,
18.5.2, 18.5.6, 19.1.1,
20.7, 21, 22.5, 23.0, 24.2,
25.1, 25.3, 25.5, 25.6,
25.7, 25.8, 26.4, 27.1,
28.2, 28.3, 29.1, 29.2,
31.6, 32.4, 32.5, 32.6,
33.2.4, 33.7.1, 34.6.4,
34.8.1, 35.1
nEdit 10.4.6
negative 11.6.1, 13.2, 15.8.3, 22.5
negatively 34.2
negotiate 11.5, 34.2
neither A.7.1, 12.4, 16.4, 25.0, 34.1,
34.8.3
nEscapement 11.4.6
nest 13.6.1
nested 11.6.2, 28.3
nesting 13.6.1

net 18.4
network C.1, 0.2, 1.1, 7.2, 9.4, 11.5,
11.5.2, 11.5.4, 20.0, 33.0,
33.1, 33.2.1, 34.9, 35.7
networks 34.3
never A.3.1, A.5, A.6, A.7.2, A.8, B.3.2,
0.0, 0.3, 1.0, 1.3, 4.7, 6.1,
11.2, 11.4.1, 11.6.2, 13.2,
14.1, 15.8.1, 16.2, 22.1,
23.1, 33.7.6, 35.1, 35.2,
35.7, Prf
new_topic 19.2.7
newFile 8.6.1, 8.6.3
newing 17.4.5
newline 7.1, 30.1
newly A.1.1, A.3.1, 11.4.6
nFlags 11.4.6, 14.5, 15.2.3, 15.2.7,
15.4.1
nFontType 26.1
nFormat 11.4.6
nHeight 11.4.6
nice A.5, 11.4.6, 12.1.2, 15.9, 16.5,
18.4.7, 32.2, 34.1, 34.8,
35.8, 35.10
nicely 7.0, 8.6.10, 18.4.3, 34.5.5
nicest 8.6.6
nID 3.1
nIDBox 7.2
nIDC 22.6
nIndex 11.4.3
nine 15.3, 35.2
Ninety 12.3
NM_CLICK 25.0, 25.5
node 11.5.2
nodes 11.5, 11.5.2, 11.5.4
non 7.2, 7.3, 11.2, 11.4.1, 11.4.7, 12.2,
12.4, 12.5, 13.2, 13.4,
13.5, 18.1.5, 28.1
nondrawing 16.4
None 4.4, 6.4, 8.4, 13.6.1, 15.2.1,
15.5, 15.6.1, 16.1.1, 16.4,
19.1.1, 20.7, 23.4, 30.1,
32.5, 33.6.1, 33.7.1, 34.1
nOptions 11.4.6
nor A.1.1, A.7.1, 12.4, 16.4, 34.1
nOrientation 11.4.6
normal A.2.7, A.3.1, A.3.2, A.4.2,
A.5.1, A.5.2, A.6, A.7.1,
B.5, B.6.1, 1.3, 2.1, 2.3.2,
3.3, 3.5, 4.2, 4.3, 5.1, 5.2,
6.1, 6.2, 6.5.4, 7.6, 8.2,
8.3, 8.4, 8.6.1, 8.6.3, 9.2,
10.2, 10.6, 11.2, 11.4.1,
11.4.6, 11.5.1, 11.5.2,
11.5.3, 11.5.4, 11.6.1,
12.1.1, 12.1.2, 12.1.3,
12.2, 13.1, 13.5, 13.8,
14.2, 15.6, 16.2, 19.0,
20.1, 20.3, 20.5, 20.6,
20.7, 22.2, 23.1, 26.3,
28.1, 29.1, 29.2, 30.0,
30.2, 32.2, 32.6, 32.7,
33.7.2, 34.1, 34.5.3,
34.6.3, 34.6.4, 34.6.7,
34.7.5, 34.8, 34.8.3, 35.2,
35.3, 35.7, Prf
NORMAL_PRIORITY_CLASS 35.7
normally A.1.1, A.4.4, 1.1, 1.2, 1.3,
3.4, 7.6, 10.5, 11.3,
11.5.5, 13.6, 14.4.4,

14.4.5, 16.3, 19.2, 22.2, 23.1, 25.5, 27.1, 32.1, 33.1, 33.7.2, 34.1, 34.5.3, 34.6.3, 34.8.12, 35.2, 35.7
notation A.2.4, 2.3, 25.7
notational 2.3
Notepad 5.1, 8.3, 14.1, 14.4.6, 18.4.7, 35.2
Notes 0.2, 14.4, 34.9
nothing A.4.2, A.5.1, A.5.3, A.7.1, A.7.2, B.3.2, C.0, D.2, 2.3.1, 3.0, 3.3, 4.2, 5.1, 7.2, 9.5, 11.4.1, 11.5.2, 11.5.3, 11.5.4, 11.5.5, 14.1, 14.4.1, 14.4.4, 15.0, 15.1, 15.3, 15.8.1, 16.2, 17.0, 18.2, 18.3, 20.7, 23.3, 27.0, 33.0, 33.7.2, 34.1, 34.4, 34.5.4
Notice A.1.1, A.2.3, A.3.2, A.3.3, A.4.3, B.1.3, D.3, D.6, 0.0, 2.1, 2.3, 2.3.2, 4.2, 4.4, 5.2, 5.3, 5.4, 9.1, 11.4.1, 11.4.6, 11.5.3, 11.5.4, 14.4.1, 15.5.5, 15.8.3, 16.4, 17.2, 18.1.11, 18.4.5, 19.1.2, 19.2, 20.2, 20.3, 22.3, 22.5, 23.3, 25.4, 26.2, 26.3, 29.2, 29.3, 30.1, 31.4, 31.6, 32.1, 32.4, 33.2.4, 33.7.2, 35.4
noticeable B.4
noticeably D.5
noticed D.1, 4.4, 5.2, 11.5.4, 12.3, 15.7.11, 15.8.3, 18.4.3, 33.1, 34.5.4
noticing 23.8
Notification 5.3, 13.6, 25.0, 25.5, 30.0, 31.5, 34.8.4, 34.8.6
notifications 31.3, 31.6, 34.8.3, 34.8.4
Notified 15.7.11, 22.0, 22.6, 34.8
notifies 23.7, 32.1
notify 4.1, 15.4, 20.7, 27.1, 30.0, 34.8
notifying B.3.1, 22.5, 27.1
notoriously B.3
nouns A.4.1, 12.5
nOutPrecision 11.4.6
novice 18.1
novices 28.0
nowhere 12.3
nPenStyle 11.4.2
nPitchAndFamily 11.4.6
nQuality 11.4.6
NT C.1, D.0, 1.1, 5.1, 7.0, 10.5, 20.0, 33.4.1, 34.4, 35.0, 35.1, 35.2, 35.4, 35.7, Prf
nTEX 16.3.5
nText 16.3.5
NTFS 12.1.1
nuance 19.0
NULL D.1, D.5, 2.3, 2.3.2, 4.5, 7.2, 11.4.6, 11.5.3, 12.5, 15.4, 15.7.9, 15.8.4, 23.0, 23.1, 23.2, 26.1, 26.2, 27.1, 32.1, 32.5, 33.5, 34.6.8, 34.7.7
NULLs 12.1.4
num 18.4.6

NumAddrs 18.2
numbered 34.7.7
numberOfIterations 34.6.5
numbers A.1.1, A.5.2, A.8, B.4.1, D.2, D.6, 2.3, 5.3, 8.2, 12.5, 22.5, 23.8, 24.0, 24.1, 25.8, 26.2, 33.1, 34.2
numeric 5.1, 12.1.3, 12.5, 16.5
numerous C.1, 15.7.11, 15.9, 17.4.1, 20.5
numInList A.4.3
nWeight 11.4.6
nWidth 11.4.2, 11.4.6
O A.1.1, A.2.3, A.2.4, A.2.5, 6.5.3, 8.6.2, 12.1.1, 15.7.2, 17.2, 17.4, 18.5, 34.7.7
objectifying A.4.5
obscure 3.4, 5.3
obstacles A.3.2
obtain 11.3, 11.5, 11.6.3, 18.3, 19.5, 23.4, 32.7, 34.3
obtained 23.5
obtaining 11.4.6, 11.4.8
obtains 11.4.1, 11.4.6, 14.4.5, 18.1.10
obtuse A.1, 1.3
obvious A.2.3, A.4.1, B.2.3, 0.0, 6.4, 11.2, 12.1.3, 12.1.4, 13.2, 15.3, 18.2, 23.8, 34.2, 34.8, 35.1, Prf
obviously A.1.1, A.5.1, 0.2, 2.2, 2.3.2, 12.2, 15.8.3, 18.6, 21.1.7, 21.1.8, 34.5.2
occasion 14.4.4
occasional 35.7
occasionally A.1, 5.1, 35.7
occupied 33.7.2
occupies A.7.2
occur A.8, 11.5.2, 12.2, 13.2, 13.6, 13.6.1, 14.4.2, 15.2.4, 15.4, 27.1, 33.6.5, 34.1
occurred A.1.1, 6.7.2, 11.5.2, 13.5, 13.6.1
occurrence A.2.7, 16.2
occurring A.8, 13.5
occurs A.7.1, B.3.1, D.3, 4.1, 11.4.1, 11.5.3, 11.5.5, 13.6, 15.2.9, 15.3, 15.4, 15.7, 22.5, 22.6, 23.1, 23.5, 23.7, 27.1, 32.4, 33.6.5, 33.7.2, 33.7.6, 34.2, 35.2
oct A.2.3
octal A.2.3
OCX B.8, B.8.1, B.8.2, B.8.3, B.8.4, 0.4, 34.8, 34.8.1, 34.8.2, 34.8.3, 34.8.11
OCXs 34.8, 34.8.1
ODA_DRAWENTIRE 25.6
ODA_FOCUS 25.6
ODA_SELECT 25.6
ODBC 0.4, 14.1, 18.6, 33.0, 33.3, 33.4, 33.4.1, 33.5, 33.6.2, 33.9
ODBCAPI 33.3, 33.9
odd 2.3, 14.5, 20.2, 25.7, 34.6.4
ODL 34.7.7
OEM 7.3, 8.1
OEM_CHARSET 11.4.6
off A.4.3, A.5.2, B.4, D.2, 3.3, 4.5, 8.6.11, 11.2, 11.4.3, 11.4.6, 11.5.4, 11.5.5,

11.6.2, 12.2, 12.3, 13.5, 14.4, 15.5, 15.6.1, 15.8.1, 18.1.2, 18.4.6, 18.4.7, 18.5, 22.2, 22.5, 33.7.5, 33.8.4, 34.4, 35.7
offending B.1.6, 13.3
offer A.3.3, C.0, 25.4
offered C.1, 11.4.1, 23.4
offers A.2, B.4.1, C.1, 0.1, 11.1, 12.1.2, 12.1.3, 15.8.3, 19.0, 33.1, 33.3, 34.1
office 17.0, 17.5, 33.1, 33.4
officer 17.4
officers 17.4
offset D.1, 11.4.8, 11.5.5, 12.1.4, 26.4
OffsetRect 12.1.4
OFN_ALLOWMULTISELECT 7.2
OFN_CREATEPROMPT 7.2
OFN_EXTENSIONDIFFERENT 7.2
OFN_FILEMUSTEXIST 7.2
OFN_HIDEREADONLY 7.2
OFN_NOCHANGEDIR 7.2
OFN_NONETWORKBUTTON 7.2
OFN_NOREADONLYRETURN 7.2
OFN_NOTESTFILECREATE 7.2
OFN_NOVALIDATE 7.2
OFN_OVERWRITEPROMPT 7.2
OFN_PATHMUSTEXIST 7.2
OFN_READONLY 7.2
OFN_SHOWHELP 7.2
ofpages 15.8.4
ofsteam A.2.4
ofstream A.2.4
OK A.4.3, A.7, A.7.2, B.1.2, B.1.3, B.1.4, B.3, B.5.6, B.6.1, B.7.4, B.8.4, B.8.7, 6.6.4, 6.6.7, 6.6.8, 7.0, 7.1, 7.2, 8.6.2, 8.6.3, 11.6.3, 15.7.9, 15.7.10, 17.3.4, 18.1.4, 18.1.10, 18.1.11, 18.2, 18.3, 19.1.1, 20.7, 22.0, 24.0, 25.0, 27.1, 31.5, 33.4.1, 33.7.4, 34.2, 34.6.5, 34.6.7, 34.6.10, 34.8.5
old A.2.1, A.5, A.5.1, A.5.2, D.1, D.7, 2.1, 3.3, 11.5.4, 11.6.2, 12.3, 14.1, 15.5.3, 15.6.7, 34.8.4
older 11.3, 12.1.3
OLE B.6.1, B.6.6, B.8.1, B.8.3, B.8.5, B.8.6, B.8.7, B.8.8, B.8.9, 0.1, 0.4, 2.1, 10.1, 12, 13.3, 13.6, 14.1, 15.2.1, 15.5, 15.6.1, 16.1.1, 19.1.1, 33.6.1, 33.7.1, **34.0, 34.1, 34.2, 34.3, 34.4, 34.5, 34.5.1, 34.5.2, 34.5.3, 34.5.4, 34.5.5, 34.5.6, 34.5.7, 34.6, 34.6.1, 34.6.2, 34.6.3, 34.6.7, 34.6.8, 34.6.9, 34.6.10, 34.7, 34.7.1, 34.7.2, 34.7.3, 34.8, 34.8.2, 34.8.3, 34.8.4, 34.8.5, 34.8.6, 34.8.12, 34.9,** Prf
omit 9.3
omitted 6.2
ON_BN_CLICKED 4.3, 4.4, 31.2

ON_BN_DOUBLE 4.3
ON_BN_DOUBLECLICKED 4.3
ON_COMMAND 4.3, 4.4, 6.5, 30.1, 31.2
ON_COMMAND_REFLECT_EX 25.5
ON_COMMAND_UPDATE_UI 18.4.6
ON_CONTROL_REFLECT 25.5
ON_EN_CHANGE 5.3
ON_LBN_DBLCLK 9.3
ON_LBN_SELCHANGE 9.3
ON_NOTIFY_REFLECT 25.5
ON_NOTIFY_REFLECT_EX 25.5
ON_REGISTERED_MESSAGE 7.6
ON_UPDATE_COMMAND_UI 31.1, 31.5
ON_UPDATE_COMMAND_UI_RE FLECT 25.5
ON_WM_ 4.4
ON_WM_CHARTOITEM_REFLEC T 25.5
ON_WM_COMPAREITEM_REFLE CT 25.5
ON_WM_CTLCOLOR_REFLECT 25.5
ON_WM_DELETEITEM_REFLEC T 25.5
ON_WM_DRAWITEM 25.4
ON_WM_DRAWITEM_REFLECT 25.5
ON_WM_HSCROLL_REFLECT 25.5
ON_WM_MEASUREITEM_REFLE CT 25.5
ON_WM_MOUSEMOVE 11.5.3
ON_WM_MOVE 4.5
ON_WM_PAINT 4.5, 11.3, 11.4.1
ON_WM_PARENTNOTIFY_REFLE CT 25.5
ON_WM_SIZE 4.4, 11.4.6
ON_WM_TIMER 4.5
ON_WM_VKEYTOITEM_REFLEC T 25.5
ON_WM_VSCROLL_REFLECT 25.5
OnActivate 32.5
OnAppAbout 15.3.6
OnBeginPrinting 15.8, 15.8.2, 15.8.4, 18.5.2, 18.5.3, 18.5.6
OnButton 30.1
OnCancel 7.3, 7.4, 7.5, 20.7, 22.4, 32.4
OnCancelEditSrvr 34.6.3
OnChangeFahrenheit 17.4.4
OnChangeItemPosition 34.5.5, 34.5.6
OnChar 24.1
OnChildNotify 25.4
OnClose 8.6.11, 32.4, 32.5
OnCmdMsg 31.1
OnColorOK 7.4
OnContextHelp 10.4.10
OnCreate D.1, 23.2, 23.3, 30.1, 32.5
OnCreateClient 21.1.3
OnCtlColor 29.3, 29.4
OnDataAdd 18.1.10, 18.1.12, 18.1.13, 18.2
OnDataChange 18.4.4
OnDataDelete 18.4.2
OnDestroy D.1, 12.3, 23.2, 23.3, 29.4,

35.4, 35.7, 35.8
OnDialogIdle 31.4
OnDocumentOpen 10.4.10
OnDraw 14.4.5, 15.1, 15.2.8, 15.2.9, 15.3, 15.3.7, 15.4, 15.5.6, 15.6.12, 15.8.2, 18.5, 34.5.3, 34.5.5, 34.6.6, 34.6.9, 34.8.1, 34.8.4, 34.8.7
OnDrawItem 25.4
OnDropFiles 32.1
OnEditAdd 18.4.7
OnEditChange 34.6.5
OnEditCopy 18.4.7
OnEditTest 19.3.2
OnEndPrinting 15.8, 15.8.2, 18.5.2
OnEndPrintPreview 15.8.2
OnEraseBkgnd 29.4
ones A.1.2, 3.2, 3.3, 6.2, 25.7
OnExpand 28.1
OnFileNameOK 7.2
OnFileNew 10.4.10
OnFileOpen 10.4.10, 10.5, 15.3.1
OnFilePrintSetup 10.4.10
OnFileSave 15.3.3
OnGetExtent 34.6.8, 34.6.10
OnGetItemPosition 34.5.5
OnHelp 10.4.10
OnHelpIndex 10.4.10
OnHelpUsing 10.4.10
OnHScroll 4.6, 5.2
OnIdle 10.3, 18.4.3, 31.4, 35.2
OnIdleUpdateCmdUI 31.1, 31.2, 31.4
OnInitalUpdate 35.3
OnInitDialog 6.6.8, 22.1, 22.3, 22.5, 23.3, 24.1, 25.8, 26.4, 27.1, 29.4, 31.4
OnInitialUpdate 15.4.4, 15.5.4, 15.6.10, 20.2, 20.3, 21.1.6, 21.1.8, 31.2, 33.7.2, 35.3, 35.5, 35.7, 35.8
OnInitMenu 8.6.10, 18.4.3
OnInitMenuPopup 31.1
OnKickIdle 31.4
OnKillActive 20.7
OnLBSelChangedNotify 7.2
OnLBSelChangeNotify 7.2
OnLButtonDblClk 11.5.2, 34.5.5
OnLButtonDown D.4, 11.5.2, 11.5.4, 29.1
OnLButtonUp 11.5.2, 11.5.4, 11.5.5, 29.1
online D.1, D.2, D.8
OnMButtonDblClk 11.5.2
OnMButtonDown 11.5.2
OnMouseActivate 11.5.2
OnMouseMove B.7.1, D.4, 11.5.2, 11.5.3, 11.5.4, 11.6.1, 12.3, 14.5, 15.1, 15.2.3, 15.2.7, 15.3, 15.3.8, 15.4, 15.4.1, 15.5.6, 15.6.9, 15.7.11, 29.1
OnNcHitTest 29.1
OnNewDocument 15.3.2, 15.5.2, 15.6.6, 17.4.5
OnNext 32.4
OnOK 6.6.8, 7.3, 7.4, 7.5, 20.7, 22.1, 22.3, 22.4, 32.4
OnOpenDocument 15.3.1, 17.4.5

OnOptionsDrawingsize 15.7.7, 15.7.9
OnPaint D.2, D.3, D.5, 11.2, 11.4.1, 11.4.2, 11.4.3, 11.4.5, 11.4.6, 11.4.7, 11.5.1, 11.5.2, 11.5.3, 11.5.5, 11.6.1, 11.6.2, 12.3, 14.4.5, 15.3.7, 29.1, 29.4
OnPrepareDC 15.5.6, 15.8.2, 15.8.4, 18.5.3, 18.5.6, 34.5.6
OnPreparePrinting 15.8, 15.8.2, 15.8.4
OnPrint 15.8.2, 15.8.4, 18.5, 18.5.3, 18.5.4, 18.5.6
OnPrompt 6.6.8
OnQueryEndSession 8.6.11
OnRButtonDblClk 11.5.2
OnRButtonDown D.4, 11.5.2
OnRButtonUp 11.5.2
OnRecordRequery 33.8.2
OnResetState 34.8.6
OnSave 15.3.3
OnSaveDocument 15.3.3, 15.3.4, 15.3.5
OnSelcancelList 18.4.2
OnSelchangeFontlist 26.4
OnSelchangeList 18.4.2
OnSetActive 20.7
OnSetCursor 11.5.3
OnSetFocus 32.5
OnSetfocusList 18.4.2
OnSetOptions 33.5
OnShareViolation 7.2
OnSize D.2, D.3, D.5, D.6, D.7, 4.4, 9.1, 11.4.6, 18.1.5, 18.2
OnThreadResume 35.7
OnThreadSuspend 35.7
OnTimer 4.5, 10.2, 11.6.2
onto A.1.1, A.4.4, A.5, A.8, C.0, D.2, D.5, D.6, 0.4, 1.3, 2.3, 2.3.2, 8.6.10, 9.4, 11.0, 11.3, 11.4.1, 11.4.7, 11.5.4, 11.5.5, 11.6.2, 11.6.3, 18.1.2, 18.2, 18.5, 18.5.4, 25.7, 34.2, 34.8, 35.4, 35.7
OnUpdate B.7.2, 15.4, 15.4.1, 15.4.2, 15.4.3, 15.4.4, 15.5.6, 15.6.11, 15.7.9, 17.4, 17.4.5, 18.1.13, 18.4.1, 21.1.8, 35.8
OnUpdateCmdUI 31.1, 31.4
OnUpdateDataChange 18.4.4
OnUpdateDataDelete 18.4.3
OnUpdateOK 31.5
OnVScroll 4.6, 11.5.5
OnWaitForDataSource 33.5
OnWindowDraw 35.8
OOD 25.1
OOP A.3.1
OpenDocumentFile 10.4.10, 15.3.1, 32.1
opened 8.6.3, 8.6.4, 10.5, 16.4, 32.1
OpenFile 8.6.2
OPENFILENAME 7.2
OpenGL D.0, D.1, D.2, D.3, D.5, D.7, D.8
opening B.1.1, B.1.2, 0.0, 5.2, 7.2, 8.6.2, 12.1.1, 16.2, 16.3, 16.3.5, 17.4.5, 18.1.7, 19.2.2, 19.2.4, 19.2.6, 19.2.8, 19.2.10, 33.4.1,

33.5, 33.6.6, 33.6.8,
33.7.3, 33.8.2, 33.8.3
opens 8.6.2, 10.4.10, 11.4.1, 11.5.4,
12.1.1, 12.3, 14.4.4, 15.3,
17.4.5, 18.2, 19.1.2,
19.3.2, 32.1, 33.7.2, 34.3,
34.5.2, 34.5.3
operate 1.3, 5.1, 14.4.4, 35.9
operates A.6
operating D.0, 7.0, 10.3, 19.0, 34.0,
34.1, 34.3, 35.2, 35.7, Prf
operation A.3.2, A.4.4, A.6, A.7, B.2.1,
8.1, 8.2, 8.6.3, 10.7,
11.5.4, 11.6.3, 12.1.1,
12.1.2, 12.2, 13.5, 13.6,
15.8.2, 15.8.4, 16.2,
18.5.3, 18.5.6, 23.1, 23.7,
25.7, 33.1, 33.5, 34.2,
34.6.5, 34.7, 35.2, 35.7
operations A.1.1, A.5.2, D.1, D.2,
8.6.6, 10.3, 12.1.1,
12.1.2, 13.6, 14.4.4, 16.2,
18.5.6, 23.1, 25.6, 25.7,
33.1, 33.2.5, 33.5, 34.1,
35.1
Operator A.1, A.1.1, A.2.3, A.2.10,
A.2.11, A.3.1, A.5.3, A.6,
A.7, A.7.1, 5.3, 12.1.2,
12.2, 12.3, 12.5
operators A.1.1, A.2.11, A.3.1, A.3.2,
A.6, 3.3, 11.4.6, 12,
12.1.2, 12.1.3, 12.1.4,
12.3, 17.4.1, 17.4.3
opportunities 14.5
opportunity 13.6, 15.8.2, 18.0, 31.4
opposed B.2, 2.1, 11.4.1, 12.3, 13.1,
22.2
opposite A.4.3, 20.7, 23.2, 30.1
optimal 11.4.6
optimization 14.4.1
optimize 15.4
optimized 2.1, 15.8
Optional B.8.9, 3.2, 32.5, 34.8.12
optionally 13.6, 34.7.7
order A.1.1, B.2, B.5.6, 0.1, 3.4, 7.6,
8.5, 11.1, 11.3, 11.4.1,
11.4.5, 11.5.4, 12.4,
15.8.4, 17.0, 18.1.2,
18.1.8, 20.1, 20.3, 20.4,
22.5, 25.6, 28.0, 28.1,
28.2, 31.4, 33.2.3, 33.4.4,
33.5, 33.6.6, 33.6.10,
33.6.11, 34.5.4, 34.5.5,
35.7
ordering 25.2, 33.2, 33.4
orders 18.1.2
ordinal 12.3
ordinary 27.0
organisms 35.1
organization A.3.1, A.4.2, 1.2, 33.1, Prf
organize A.3.1, A.3.2, 12
organized A.3.2, A.4.2, 0.1, 3.3, 9.0,
20.4, Prf
organizes 0.1, 20.4
organizing 1.2
orient 14.5
orientation 4.6, 11.4.6
oriented A.1, A.1.1, A.1.2, A.2, A.2.3,
A.3, A.3.1, A.3.2, A.3.3,
A.5, A.5.2, A.8, C.1, D.2,

1.0, 20.7, 23.2, 25.0, 25.1,
31.6, 34.0, 34.1, 34.4
origin D.6, 0.0, 11.2, 11.4.8, 11.5.5,
11.6.1, 15.5.6, 15.8.4
original A.1.1, A.3.2, B.3.2, D.3, 1.1,
8.3, 8.6.3, 11.4.8, 11.5.4,
11.6.1, 11.6.2, 13.6,
15.8.1, 17.2, 23.8, 23.9,
25.5, 25.6, 25.7, 28.1,
32.2, 32.5, 34.5.2
originally 4.4, 34.1, 34.5.6
originated 34.2
originating 34.2
originY 11.5.5
oring 13.5
ORs 33.6.8
orthogonal D.2, D.6
orthographic D.2
ostream A.6
OUT_CHARACTER_PRECIS 11.4.6
OUT_DEFAULT_PRECIS 11.4.6
OUT_STRING_PRECIS 11.4.6
OUT_STROKE_PRECIS 11.4.6
outcome 11.6.3
outer 13.6.1
outfile A.2.4
outline B.4, B.4.2, 6.7
output A.1.1, A.2.3, A.2.4, A.2.5,
A.2.9, A.2.11, A.6, A.7.1,
A.8, B.1.6, B.1.7, B.2.2,
B.3, B.3.2, 2.2, 3.3, 5.1,
6.1, 6.2, 10.1, 11.2,
11.4.2, 11.4.6, 11.4.7,
11.5.1, 11.5.3, 11.6.1,
11.6.2, 11.6.3, 13.3, 13.4,
13.7, 15.8.3, 17.2, 18.5.5,
22.5, 33.6.9, 34.1
outrageously 14.0
outright A.8
outside A.5.1, C.1, D.0, 2.3.2, 6.1,
10.6, 11.5.2, 11.5.4,
11.5.5, 12.2, 15.7.9,
15.7.11, 20.0, 23.0, 34.4
outstring A.2.5
outweigh A.1.1
over A.1, A.6, B.2, B.2.2, D.3, D.6, 0.0,
0.4, 2.1, 9.1, 9.3, 9.4,
11.5.3, 11.5.4, 11.6.1,
11.6.2, 12.1.1, 12.1.2,
12.2, 12.3, 12.4, 14.0,
15.0, 15.1, 15.3.7, 18.5.3,
19.2, 20.7, 24.0, 25.0,
25.4, 25.7, 29.1, 29.3,
30.1, 33.1, 33.2.1, 33.4.2,
34.2, 34.3, 34.6.2,
34.6.10, 34.8.4, Prf
overall A.1.1, 13.5, 15.6
overburdening 10.3
overcome A.1
overcoming 18.1.5
overfilled A.2.5
overflowing 11.4.6
overhead A.4.4, 4.7, 35.2
overidden 10.3
overkill 17.3.4, 17.4
overlaid 1.2, 3.4
overlap 32.2
overlappable 2.3.2
overlapping D.3
overlay 11.5.1

overlays 34.5.2
overload A.1.1, A.3.1
overloaded A.2.8, A.2.9, A.6, 11.4.6,
12.1.2, 12.3, 20.4, 22.2
Overloading A.1, A.1.1, A.2.8, A.3.1,
A.6, 22.4
overloads 12.1.3
overlooked 11.0
overpopulated 20.5
overridable 15.3.5, 35.8
Overridables 33.5
overridden A.2.3, A.8, 2.3, 2.3.1, 2.3.2,
4.7, 6.6.8, 6.7.3, 10.3,
15.3.1, 15.3.3, 22.1, 34.8
override A.3.1, A.7.1, A.8, B.7.2, 2.5,
7.2, 7.3, 7.5, 10.3, 11.5.3,
12.2, 12.3, 13.2, 14.4.4,
14.5, 15.2.6, 15.3.1,
15.3.3, 15.3.5, 15.3.8,
15.4, 15.4.4, 15.6.4,
15.6.11, 15.8.2, 15.8.4,
18.1.13, 18.2, 20.7,
21.1.3, 21.1.5, 25.3, 25.6,
26.4, 27.1, 28.1, 30.2,
31.4, 32.4, 33.5, 34.5.6,
34.8.1, 35.3, 35.4, 35.5
overriden 20.7
overrides A.5.1, 2.3.1, 4.7, 5.2, 5.4,
11.5.3, 12.1.2, 12.3,
14.4.4, 34.8.4
overriding A.1, B.7.1, 10.2, 15.2.6,
22.7, 25.5, 29.2
overrode 15.3, 18.2
overuse A.1.1
overview 0.1, 2.1, 3.5, 4.4, 15.7, 35.7
overwhelm 28.0, 34.0
overwrite 7.2, 25.7, 29.3
overwrites 13.5
overwriting 7.2, 25.7, 29.3
OVR 18.4.6
owner 0.4, 25.1, 25.2, 25.3, 25.4, 25.6,
26.4
ownerdrawn 25.1, 26.4
owning 4.4
owns 35.2, 35.3
p A.2.3, 2.3, 12.1.3, 15.2.6, 15.6.3,
25.7
pace C.1
package 0.3
packet 35.7
pad 25.6
padding 28.1
page A.1, 0.4, 3.2, 3.3, 6.6.8, 7.5, 9.2,
11.6.1, 11.6.3, 15.1, 15.6,
15.8.2, 15.8.3, 15.8.4,
18.5, 18.5.4, 18.5.6, 19.0,
19.2, 19.2.1, 19.2.2,
19.2.4, 19.2.5, 19.2.6,
19.2.7, 19.2.8, 19.2.9,
19.2.10, 19.3.5, 19.4,
20.5, 20.6, 20.7, 34.8.11,
34.8.12, 35.1
pagedependent 20.7
pageHeight 15.8.4
pages A.3.1, C.0, 0.0, 0.1, 3.3, 7.5,
10.5, 11.4.6, 11.6.3,
15.8.1, 15.8.2, 15.8.4,
18.5, 18.5.6, 19.0, 19.1.2,
19.2, 19.2.7, 19.3.6,
19.3.10, 19.4, 19.5, 20.5,

20.6, 20.7, 33.9, 34.8.11, 35.4
pageWidth 15.8.4
pagination 15.8.4, 18.5.6
painfully 12.2
painless A.1, 1.4, 3.3, 6.7
paint 5.1, 7.2, 11.3, 11.4.1, 11.4.2, 11.4.3, 11.4.8, 11.5, 11.5.2, 11.5.3, 11.6.2, 15.1, 18.1, 23.7, 25.7, 34.8.4
Paintbrush 5.1, 8.6.10, 15.7.9, 15.7.11, 19.2.9
painted 2.3.2, 5.1, 29.3, 34.8.1
painting D.3, D.5, 6.3.4, 11.4.8, 11.5.2, 11.6.2, 18.5.4, 23.8, 25.7, 29.3, 35.2, 35.8
paints A.4.2, A.8, 1.3, 11.4.3, 11.4.6, 11.4.7, 11.5.2, 11.5.3, 11.5.4, 15.3.8, 15.4.2, 27.2, 34.8.4
pair 11.4.1, 11.4.4, 12.1.3, 15.6.1, 16.3.4, 19.2
pairs A.3.2, A.3.3, 12.5
pal 6.3.4
palette B.5.6, B.8.4, D.1, 6.3.4, 6.6.3, 6.6.4, 6.6.5, 7.4, 18.1.2, 28.0, 30.0, 30.1
palettes B.5.3, B.5.4, D.1, 0.4, 23.6, Prf
pane B.1.6, 7.5, 18.4.6, 28.0
Panel 3.4, 5.1, 10.5, 26.4, 28.0, 33.3, 33.4.1
panes 7.5, 15.6, 18.4.6, 30.0
panic A.2
paper A.4.6, 11.3, 11.5.5, 12.5, 15.8.3, 15.8.4, 17.0, 17.5, 18.5, 34.1, 34.5.2, 34.5.6
papier 12.5
paradigm 0.4, 10.4, 15.8.1, 16.2, 18.1.15
paradigms 23.9
paragraph 10.4.10, 19.2
paragraphs A.1
Param 33.6.10
parent 2.3.3, 3.1, 3.2, 4.1, 4.3, 4.4, 6.6.8, 7.2, 7.3, 7.4, 7.5, 7.6, 11.5.3, 13.4, 20.4, 20.7, 25.0, 25.1, 25.2, 25.4, 25.5, 25.8, 27.1, 29.3, 30.0, 30.1, 30.2, 31.2, 31.4, 32.5, 35.2, 35.5, 35.7
parentheses A.2.2, A.2.3, 4.3
parents 25.1, 31.1
parse 7.1, 7.2, 26.2
parses 1.3
parsing A.1.1, 1.3
partial 9.1
partially A.8, 3.3
participant 34.2
particular A.3.1, A.4.1, 0.3, 2.2, 2.3.1, 2.3.2, 3.3, 3.5, 7.3, 8.6.10, 9.5, 10, 10.1, 11.4.7, 11.5.2, 11.5.5, 11.6.1, 11.7, 12.1.2, 12.3, 13.1, 13.3, 13.5, 14.4.2, 14.4.5, 15.4.4, 15.8, 15.8.2, 16.4, 19.2, 23.2, 25.2, 26.0, 26.1, 29.2, 33.2.5, 33.4.1,

34.2, 34.4, 34.5.5, 35.7, Prf
particularly B.2, 0.2, 12.2, 15.8, 16.3
partner 5.2, 33.1
partners 7.6
parts A.1.1, A.4.4, B.4.6, B.8.2, B.8.3, B.9, D.3, D.4, 1.5, 2.3, 2.3.1, 7.0, 8.6.10, 11.2, 11.5.4, 12.3, 14.0, 14.1, 14.4, 14.4.2, 14.4.3, 15.5.5, 16.3, 18.4.1, 25.7, 34.1, 34.3, 34.7.6, Prf
party 33.3
Pascal A.3.2, 7.6
pass A.2.11, A.7.1, A.8, D.1, 7.3, 10.5, 11.3, 11.4.3, 11.4.4, 11.4.6, 12.1.2, 12.1.4, 12.5, 15.4, 15.4.4, 15.8.2, 18.4.6, 19.3.2, 26.1, 33.6.10, 34.1, 34.4, 35.3, 35.5, 35.8
passed A.1.1, A.2.4, A.2.7, A.2.8, A.2.9, A.2.11, A.6, A.8, B.3.1, D.1, D.2, 2.3.2, 3.2, 3.3, 3.4, 4.5, 4.6, 6.2, 6.6.8, 7.3, 8.2, 8.6.7, 9.2, 9.3, 10.5, 11.4.2, 11.4.4, 11.4.6, 11.5.3, 11.6.1, 15.4, 15.8.2, 17.3.4, 18.4.6, 19.3.5, 22.1, 22.3, 26.1, 26.2, 33.6.10, 34.7.9, 35.4
passes 5.4, 6.2, 6.6.8, 7.2, 9.3, 11.5.4, 15.7.9, 27.1, 33.6.10, 33.6.11
passing A.4.2, D.1, D.6, 3.3, 4.5, 6.6.8, 7.2, 9.2, 11.4.1, 15.4.4, 19.3.5, 20.7, 33.6.10
password 5.3, 8.1
past A.1.1, 0.0, 6.1, 11.4.6, 33.5
paste B.3, 8.1, 8.2, 8.3, 8.5, 8.6.10, 16.2, 16.3.5, 18.4.7, 34.2, 34.4, 34.5.2
pasted 34.1, 34.2
Pastes 8.2, 34.2
pasting 18.4.7, 34.2
PatBlt 11.6.2
path A.3.2, 7.2, 10.1, 10.5, 12.1.1, 34.4, 34.8.1
pathName 8.6.2
paths 12.1.2
patience Prf
patient 17.5
pattern A.2.8, 1.3, 6.5, 11.3, 11.4.3, 11.4.8, 25.7, 29.2
patterned 11.4.8
patterns A.3.3, 12.1.1, 34.8.1
pauses 13.2
pay A.8, 0.3, 12.3, 14.4.5, 25.6
paying 13.3
payment 17.4
payroll 17.0, 33.2
pBitmap 11.4.3
PC C.0
pCmdUI 18.4.3
pContainer 34.5.5
PCs 0.0
PD_ALLPAGES 7.5
PD_COLLATE 7.5
PD_DISABLEPRINTTOFILE 7.5

PD_NOPAGENUMS 7.5
PD_NOSELECTION 7.5
PD_NOWARNING 7.5
PD_PAGENUMS 7.5
PD_PRINTSETUP 7.5
PD_PRINTTOFILE 7.5
PD_RETURNDC 7.5
PD_RETURNDEFAULT 7.5
PD_RETURNIC 7.5
PD_SELECTION 7.5
PD_SHOWHELP 7.5
PD_USEDEVMODECOPIES 7.5
pDX 22.3
peculiar 29.3, 34.6.4
pedestrian 0.0
peer 33.1
pen 7.4, 11.3, 11.4.1, 11.4.2, 11.4.3, 11.4.6, 11.5.4, 26.1, 34.8.4
PEN_SOLID 11.4.2
penalty 2.1
pending B.2, 12.1.1
pens 11.1, 11.4.6, 23.6, 26.1, 34.8.4
Pentagon A.1.1
people A.1, A.1.1, A.5, A.8, A.8.1, D.5, 0.1, 0.3, 5.2, 11.0, 33.1, 34.1, Prf
per D.8, 6.7, 10.6, 11.2, 11.4.6, 11.6.2, 15.8.3, 18.5.6, 22.5, 25.7
perceived 11.5.4, 12.2
Percent 12.1.3, 12.3
percentage 34.5.4
perception 8.1
perfect A.4.5, A.5.3, 18.4.6, 19.2
perfectly 14.1
perform A.6, B.2.1, B.3, D.2, 0.4, 7.2, 7.6, 8.6.1, 9.4, 10.3, 10.6, 11.5.2, 12.2, 12.5, 13.2, 13.5, 13.7, 15.8.4, 20.7, 22.5, 23.3, 23.4, 23.7, 24.1, 25.3, 25.6, 25.7, 27.1, 30.0, 31.4, 32.4, 33.1, 33.2, 33.4, 34.2, 34.3, 34.7, 35.1, 35.2, 35.3
performance A.5.1, D.1, D.5, 2.1, 11.5.3, 12.2, 13.1, 35.7, Prf
performed 5.2, 10.3, 11.6.3, 24.0, 25.6, 25.7, 26.3, 35.2
performing D.1, 10.4, 33.2.5
performs 1.3, 3.1, 11.6.3, 12.1.2, 13.5, 17.3.4, 20.7, 22.2, 23.7, 23.8, 25.7, 26.1, 26.4, 31.4, 33.2, 33.5, 34.2, 35.9
perhaps A.5.2, 0.0, 1.3, 5.2, 11.5.5, 12.1.1, 12.5, 17.4, 26.4, 28.3, 35.2, 35.7
perimeter A.4.5, A.4.6
period 5.3, 7.2, 11.5.3, 27.1
periodically 0.4, 11.4.6
peripheral 10.4.10, 34.3
permanent 13.4, 20.7, 23.4, 23.5, 23.7
permanently A.3.2
permissions 33.4.2
permitted A.6
perpetuate A.8
persistence 11.5.3, 12.3
persists 35.4

person A.8, 8.3
personal A.3.2
personnel 33.1
perspective A.1, D.2, D.6, 2.6, 11.6.2, 34.1
perspectives A.1
peruse 15.3
PFD_DOUBLEBUFFER D.1
PFD_DRAW_TO_BITMAP D.1
PFD_DRAW_TO_WINDOW D.1
PFD_GENERIC_FORMAT D.1
PFD_NEED_PALETTE D.1
PFD_NEED_SYSTEM_PALETTE D.1
PFD_STEREO D.1
PFD_SUPPORT_GDI D.1
PFD_SUPPORT_OPENGL D.1
PFD_TYPE_COLORINDEX D.1
PFD_TYPE_RGBA D.1
phase 11.5.4, 12, 12.2, 13.2
phenomena A.5.3
phenomenon 17.2
philosophy 25.1
phone 9.2, 18.1, 18.6, 33.1, Prf
phrases 19.2.3
physical A.3.1, 11.5.5, 34.4
pi A.2.5
pick A.1, A.2.9, 0.0, 1.1, 14.1, 28.0, 33.6.2, 33.7.6, 33.9, 35.7
picked 34.8.4
picking A.3.1
picks A.2.11, A.8, 10.4.10, 34.4, 35.7
picture D.6, 6.6.2, 6.6.4, 11.0, 11.2, 11.5, 11.5.2, 12.3, 15.5, 23.7, 28.2, 29.1, 34.6.5, 34.8.11, 35.2
pictured 14.3
pictures 24.3, 34.1, 34.8.11
pie 11.4.4
piece A.3.2, A.4.2, A.5.1, 1.3, 2.0, 4.2, 5.2, 8.7, 11.4.6, 11.5.2, 11.5.5, 13.3, 13.5, 13.6, 15.2, 15.4.1, 18.1.5, 18.5, 19.2.5, 34.2, 34.6.8
pieces A.1.1, A.3.2, A.4.4, A.5, B.1.2, B.4, 2.1, 2.3, 2.5, 5.2, 7.2, 7.6, 8.3, 8.6, 9.2, 11.3, 11.5.3, 15.0, 15.3, 18.4.1, 19.2, 34.3, 34.5.4, 34.6.10
PIF 5.1, 17.0
pilot 11.6.2
pInfo 15.8.2, 15.8.4
pinhole D.6
pinpoint B.4.4
pipes 34.1
pitch 7.3, 15.8.3
pixel D.1, D.5, D.7, 11.2, 11.3, 11.4.2, 11.4.7, 11.5.3, 11.5.4, 11.6.1, 11.6.2, 15.3.8, 15.4, 15.4.4, 15.5.6, 15.5.7, 25.7, 29.1, 34.6.5
pixelDesc D.5
PIXELFORMATDESCRIPTOR D.1, D.7
pixels 2.3.2, 3.3, 9.2, 11.1, 11.2, 11.3, 11.4, 11.4.2, 11.4.3, 11.4.7, 11.4.8, 11.5.3, 11.5.4, 11.5.5, 11.6.1, 11.6.2, 15.1, 15.3, 15.8.3,

18.4.5, 18.5.3, 25.6, 25.7, 34.6.5, 34.6.7, 34.6.9
placed A.5.2, 2.3.2, 3.3, 4.4, 6.3.5, 9.3, 12.1.3, 13.2, 14.4.2, 18.1.12, 18.2, 18.3, 19.2, 35.1
placeholder 6.7.3
placeholders 13.3
Placement 2.3.3, 4.3, 5.1, 5.4
places A.1.1, A.2, A.3.3, A.4.2, A.5, A.7.2, D.3, 4.0, 4.5, 5.2, 7.6, 8.6.1, 9.1, 10.5, 12.1.2, 15.5.7, 19.5, 21.1.6, 25.0, 34.6.9, 34.8.10
placing A.2.2, A.2.5, 6.4, 6.5.2, 13.2, 18.5.2
plain A.4.3
plan A.8, 11.0, 11.6.1, 12.1.3, 14.5, 18.5.6
plane D.6, 25.7
planet 34.4
planning 11.5.5
plans 34.0
platform B.3, 1.1
platforms Prf
play A.3.2, D.2, 7.2, 28.2, 33.4.4
player A.3.2, 31.1
playing D.1
please B.3, C.1, 1.0, 1.3, 1.5, 2.3, 3.3, 4.7, 15.4
plenty 14.5
plots 29.1
plotter 11.2
plus A.3.2, A.6, 11.4.6, 18.5.4, 19.3.6, 25.5
PM 12.1.3
PointArray 11.5.3
pointed A.2.3, A.5.2, 8.2, 35.4
pointer A.1, A.2.3, A.2.10, A.4.3, A.5.2, A.6, A.7, A.7.2, A.8, B.3.1, B.7.7, 2.3, 3.1, 6.6.8, 8.1, 8.2, 8.6.7, 10.1, 11.4.3, 11.5.3, 12.1.1, 12.1.2, 12.1.3, 12.4, 13.7, 15.2.7, 15.4, 15.8.2, 18.3, 20.3, 20.7, 23.5, 25.6, 26.1, 29.4, 32.4, 32.5, 32.7, 33.5, 34.4, 35.4, 35.5
Pointers A.1, A.2.3, A.2.11, A.4.3, A.4.4, A.7, A.7.2, 5.2, 12.3, 12.4, 14.0, 14.4, 18.1, 23.2, 26.1
pointing A.7, 10.2, 18.4.6
points A.2.10, A.5.2, D.1, D.2, 3.5, 8.2, 8.6.1, 10.1, 11.2, 11.3, 11.4.4, 11.4.5, 11.5.3, 11.5.4, 12.3, 13.7, 14.5, 15.0, 15.1, 15.2.4, 15.2.5, 15.2.6, 15.2.7, 15.2.8, 15.3, 15.4, 15.5, 15.5.7, 15.6.3, 15.7.9, 15.7.11, 18.1.12, 19.2, 29.1, 29.4, 34.8.10, Prf
pOldBmp 29.4
Polish 25.7
polygon D.2, 11.0, 11.4.5, 11.6.2
polygons 11.3, 11.4, 11.4.5, 11.4.7, 11.6.2, 15.1, 35.1

Polyline 11.4.5, 11.5.3
polymorphism A.1.1, A.3.1, A.3.2
PolyPolygon 11.4.5
pool 13.7, 34.3
poor 25.1
pop A.1.1, A.4.5, A.7, 11.5.2, 27.1, 34.6.4, 34.6.5
popping D.2
popular 12.2, 33.2
populate 34.4
popup 0.4, 6.4, 6.5.4, 32.6, Prf
port 7.5, 9.4
portable A.1.1, 1.1, 34.8
portion A.2.7, A.4.6, 1.0, 2.1, 6.1, 7.5, 10.5, 11.2, 11.3, 11.5.5, 13.2, 14.4.1, 15.6, 16.3.5, 18.4.6, 28.1, 29.2, 33.0, 34.2, 34.4, 34.7.7, 35.1
portions A.1.1, B.8.2, B.8.3, 4.3, 8.4, 25.7, 28.0, 28.2
position D.3, D.7, 2.3.3, 3.1, 3.3, 4.6, 5.2, 6, 6.1, 8.2, 8.6.7, 9.1, 9.4, 10, 11.3, 11.4.1, 11.4.6, 11.5.2, 11.5.3, 11.5.4, 12.1.1, 12.3, 12.4, 15.3.8, 15.7.2, 19.2.3, 20.4, 22.2, 28.1, 29.1, 29.2, 32.1, 32.5, 32.6, 34.5.5
positioning 3.1, 3.2, 29.1
positions 6.4, 9.2, 18.4.1, 30.1
positive 11.2, 11.6.1, 13.2, 15.8.3, 22.0
possess 5.1
possessed A.3.1
possesses A.1.1, 10.4
possessing 34.2
possibilities A.4.2, B.4.1, 3.3, 12.1.1, 15.9, 16.3, 26.3, 35.0, 35.7
possibility 34.3
possibly 0.2, 35.3
post C.0
PostNcDestroy 32.4
postponing 15.8.4
PostScript 26.4
potential 7.2, 8.5, 12.3, 13.5, 25.1
potentially 2.6, 6.6.8, 13.6.1, 14.3, 15.5, 15.7.9, 34.4
powder A.3.2
power A.1, A.1.1, A.3.1, A.3.2, B.1, 1.1, 5.1, 15.4, 31.1, 33.1, 35.1, 35.2
powerful A.1.1, A.2.8, A.8, B, B.2, 0.1, 6, 6.6, 22.0, 30.0, 33.2, 33.3, 34.1
PowerPoint 34.5.4
pParent 15.7.9
pParentWnd 3.1, 7.2, 7.3, 7.4, 7.6, 32.4
practically 18.1.6
practice 17.4, 19.3.5, 35.7
pre 1.3, 4.5, 5.4, 6.6.7, 11.5.3, 12.2, 13.2, 14.4.1, 23.7, 25.7, 33.2.5, 34.1, 34.2
precautions D.1
preceding 34.8.13
preceeding 6.5.2, 6.7, 8.5
precision A.2.3, A.5.2, 11.4.6
precompiled 15.2.2
PreCreateWindow D.1, 11.5.3, 21.1.5

predeclared 34.1
predefined A.2.3, 11.5.3, 34.1
predefines 19.4
predict A.4.6, A.8
preempt 35.7
preemptive 35.2, 35.7
preempts 35.2
preface 6.4
prefer 6.1
preferences 2.3
preferred 1.1, 3.3, 15.5.2, 15.8.4, 17.4.5, 34.7.7
prefix A.8, C.0, D.2, 2.3, 22.2
prefixes 3.2, 13.3
prelude 11.0
premier C.1
Prentice C.1
Preparation 8.6.7, 15.8.2
Prepare B.1, 29.3, 33.6.2
PrepareCtrl 22.6
prepared 15.5.6, 22.6
PrepareEditCtrl 22.6
prepares 18.5.3
preparing 15.5.6
preprocessed D.3
preprocessor A.2.7
present B.1.2, B.4.1, 11.6.3, 15.4, 15.5, 15.7, 16.1.2, 17.2, 18.1, 18.4.6, 18.5.1, 25.0, 28.0, 33.6.3, 34.0
presentation 8.6.2, 10.4.10, 14.3, 17.4
presented A.4.6, B.4, D.2, 0.3, 5.1, 8.6.8, 11.4.6, 11.7, 15.5, 16.4, 17.2, 27.0, 34.5.4, 35.1
presents B.6.1, 1.2, 7.0, 8.5, 8.6.2, 8.6.3, 13.6, 14.3, 17.1, 18.1, 18.4.2, 18.4.4, 19.4, 33.3
preserve 12.1.4
preserves D.3
preset B.7.4
Press B.1.7, B.2.1, B.2.2, B.5.5, B.7.1, B.8.1, B.8.7, C.1, 5.3, 6.3.7, 6.4, 6.6.5, 6.6.7, 6.6.8, 7.6, 8.6.7, 18.1.11, 19.1.1, 19.1.2, 19.3.5, 19.3.10, 20.2, 27.1, 33.4.3, 33.7.4, 34.5.2, 34.6.7, 34.8, 34.8.5, Prf
pressed 1.3, 4.3, 7.2, 7.3, 7.6, 8.6.7, 19.3.5, 23.8, 24.0, 27.1, 29.1
presses 1.3, 4.1, 5.3, 6.6.8, 7.0, 7.2, 7.6, 8.6.2, 8.6.3, 11.5.2, 11.6.3, 18.1.10, 18.2, 18.3, 19.4, 27.0, 27.1, 29.1
pressing B.1.6, 7.1, 12.1.1, 19.1.2
PreTranslateMessage 5.4, 10.6, 27.1
pretty A.1.1, A.3.2, 17.2, 34.4
prevails 18.1.2
prevalent 33.0, 33.1
prevent 0.4, 7.4, 11.5.3, 11.5.4, 11.5.5, 12.1.1, 35.7
preventing 8.6.7, 35.7
prevents 12.1.1, 35.8
preview 10.5, 11.6.3, 15.0, 15.8, 15.8.1, 15.8.2, 15.8.4, 18.4, 18.5.1, 18.5.5,

18.5.6, 30.0, 34.5.6
previously A.4.6, B.1.1, 4.5, 8.6.1, 10.5, 12.1.3, 12.2, 13.2, 16.3.5, 17.4, 18.1, 18.4.4, 20.7, 32.5, 33.8.4
price D.0
primarily A.1.1, 33.2
primary 0.2, 1.1, 13.6, 33.1, 33.2, 33.4.2, 34.5.5
primes 11.5.4
primitive 33.6, 33.6.3
primitives D.0
principle A.3.2, 9.3, 33.8.4
principles A.1, 0.1, 11.5.4, 11.5.5, 18.5, 20.6, 22.0, 30.3, Prf
print A.1.1, A.2.3, A.4.1, A.4.2, A.5.2, D.2, 0.4, 7.5, 10.4.10, 10.5, 11.0, 11.3, 11.4.6, 11.6.1, 11.6.3, 12.1.3, 13.3, 13.4, 14.4, 15.0, 15.8, 15.8.1, 15.8.2, 15.8.3, 15.8.4, 15.9, 18.4, 18.5, 18.5.1, 18.5.2, 18.5.3, 18.5.4, 18.5.5, 18.5.6, 22.5, 30.0, 33.5, 34.1, 34.4, 34.5.2, 34.5.6, 34.7
PrintAll 7.5
PrintCollate 7.5
PRINTDLG 7.5
printed 15.8.2, 15.8.3, 22.0
printer 7.3, 7.5, 10.6, 11.1, 11.2, 11.3, 11.6.1, 11.6.3, 15.8.1, 15.8.2, 15.8.3, 15.8.4, 18.5.1, 18.5.2, 18.5.5, 26.0, 26.1, 26.2, 26.4, 34.1, 35.2
PrinterDlg 7.5
printers 7.5, 11.2, 11.3, 11.6.1, 11.6.3, 15.8.1, 15.8.3
printf A.1.1, 3.3, 12.1.3, 13.3
printing A.2.3, A.3, A.4.1, A.5.2, B.6.1, 0.4, 7.5, 8.7, 10.6, 11.0, 11.6.3, 14.1, 15.0, 15.2.1, 15.3.7, 15.5, 15.6.1, 15.8, 15.8.1, 15.8.2, 15.8.4, 16.3.5, 18.0, 18.4, 18.5, 18.5.1, 18.5.6, 19.1.1, 19.2, 34.4, 34.5.1, 34.5.4, 34.5.7, Prf
printOneName A.4.2
printout 15.8.3
printouts 14.4.1
PrintRange 7.5
prints A.2.3, A.8, 13.4, 15.8.3, 16.2, 32.1
PrintSelection 7.5
prior A.5.2, 0.3, 7.4, 10.3, 34.6.7, 35.8, Prf
priorities 0.4, 35.1, 35.7
priority 35.1, 35.4, 35.7
private A.1, A.4.3, A.4.6, A.5.1, A.6, 2.3.3, 11.5.5, 33.1, 34.6.5
privately A.1
pro Prf
probability 34.4
probably A.1.1, A.3.2, A.5.2, A.8.1, B.3, B.7.4, 0.0, 1.4, 5.1, 5.4, 8.7, 10.4, 11.6.2, 13.1, 13.5, 14.4.4, 15.4.4,

15.7.11, 15.8.1, 15.8.3, 18.5.2, 25.1, 30.1, 32.7, 33.4.2, 34.1, 34.8.11, 34.8.12, 35.3, 35.4, 35.7
probes Prf
problem A.1.1, A.3.2, A.4.2, A.4.4, A.5.2, A.8, B.2.1, B.3, B.3.1, B.4.4, D.4, D.5, D.6, 0.0, 2.4, 3.3, 4.7, 5.1, 5.2, 6.4, 6.7, 7.2, 7.4, 8.6.10, 9.1, 10.2, 11.4.1, 11.4.4, 11.4.6, 11.4.7, 11.5.3, 11.5.4, 11.6.1, 11.6.2, 12.1.1, 12.3, 13.2, 13.3, 13.6, 15.4, 15.5.6, 15.6, 15.7.9, 15.7.11, 15.8.3, 15.8.4, 16.2, 16.4, 16.5, 18.1.5, 18.1.11, 18.4.2, 22.0, 22.4, 23.3, 23.4, 23.9, 24.0, 25.0, 25.1, 25.5, 28.3, 29.1, 30.2, 31.3, 33.3, 33.6.5, 33.7.6, 34.1, 34.4, 34.5.2, 34.5.6, 35.1, 35.4, 35.8, Prf
problems A.1, A.1.1, A.1.2, A.3, A.3.2, A.3.3, A.4.2, A.7, B.2, 0.0, 6, 11.3, 11.4.1, 11.6.1, 12.2, 13.2, 13.5, 15.7.9, 15.8.3, 18.1.5, 18.4.5, 32.4, 33.1, 33.3, 33.7.6, 34.1, 34.4, 34.5.2, 35.2, 35.7, 35.8, Prf
procedure 0.4, 9.3, 11.5, 23.7, 23.8, 26.1, 26.2, 26.3, 26.5, 33.2.5, 33.4.2, 34.4
procedures 23.7, 33.2.5
proceed B.6.1, 0.3, 7.1, 8.6.1, 33.0, 35.1
proceeding 13.0, 15.3
proceeds 25.4, 35.4
processed 2.3, 5.4, 15.3, 25.4, 32.5
processes C.1, 4.5, 10.3, 12.1.1, 15.3, 32.4, 32.8, 35.2, 35.7
processing D.3, 0.4, 2.2, 10.3, 11.5.4, 14.3, 15.3.8, 17.2, 18.4.3, 27.1, 28.1, 31.4, 32.1, 33.2, 34.1, 34.2, 34.4, 35.1, 35.2, 35.7
ProcessMessageFilter 10.6
processor D.1, 13.2, 14.3, 34.1, 34.3, 34.4, 35.2
processors 34.1, 35.1
ProcessShellCommand 32.3
ProcessWndProcException 10.6
prodigious 34.0
produce A.2.3, A.8, 2.3.2, 6.3.6, 6.7, 11.4.6, 11.6.3, 12.1.3, 12.5, 13.5, 15.3, 15.8.4, 18.2, 19.0, 19.3.5, 34.4
produced A.7.1, B, 3.4, 3.5, 4.6, 7.0, 10.5, 11.4.5, 15.3, 18.2, 25.7, 33.6.5
produces A.2.3, A.2.11, A.8, B.2.2, 6.7, 9.3, 11.4.6, 11.6.1, 11.6.3, 12.1.1, 16.4, 34.6, 34.6.7
product A.5.1, 0.2, 8.5, 13.0, 13.1, 29.4, 34.1
production A.3.2, 11.5.5, 15.7.9, Prf

productive 0.1, 0.2, 23.8, 34.5.5
productivity A.1, C.1, 6.1
products 0.2, 1.1, 21, 33.4, 34.3, Prf
professional 0.0, 0.1, 0.3, 1.0, 1.1, 1.5, Prf
profile 14.4.2, 15.5.2
programmatic 33.3
programmatically 3.1
programmer A.1, A.1.1, A.3.2, A.7.2, B.2, B.4, B.4.5, B.7.2, B.8.6, C.1, 0.0, 0.1, 0.3, 1.1, 1.3, 2.3, 2.6, 8.1, 9.5, 10.3, 11.3, 12, 12.1.2, 22.0, 22.1, 22.7, 23.8, 29.1, 30.0, 33.8.4, 34.0, 34.1, 34.2, 34.3, 34.4, 34.7, 34.8, 34.8.1, 34.8.6, 34.9, Prf
Programmers A.1.1, A.3.2, C.1, 0.2, 13.2, 23.9, 33.3, 34.1, 34.3, 34.7, 34.8.3, 35.0, Prf
Programming A.1, A.1.1, A.3.1, A.3.2, A.5, A.5.2, A.8, B, C.1, D.0, D.6, 0.0, 0.2, 0.3, 1.0, 1.1, 1.3, 2.1, 6.1, 17.2, 19.2, 22.7, 23.0, 23.9, 25.1, 33.1, 33.3, 34.1, 34.2, Prf
programs A.1.1, A.3.1, A.4.2, A.4.5, A.5, A.7.2, B, B.4.5, B.5.1, D.0, D.1, D.5, D.8, 0.0, 0.1, 0.3, 1.5, 2.1, 3.3, 3.6, 4.1, 4.5, 5.1, 6.1, 6.6, 7.6, 11.4.1, 11.5.3, 11.5.4, 11.5.5, 11.7, 13.1, 13.8, 14.1, 14.4, 14.4.3, 14.5, 15.1, 15.3, 15.5, 15.8, 32.6, 34.1, 35.2, Prf
progress B.1.6, B.3, 10.2, 18.4.6, 20.0
progression 0.3
project B.1, B.1.1, B.1.2, B.1.4, B.1.5, B.1.7, B.2.1, B.3, B.3.1, B.5.1, B.5.2, B.6, B.6.1, B.6.2, B.6.4, B.8.1, C.1, D.1, D.2, D.6, 0.1, 1.5, 2.1, 3.3, 6.1, 6.3, 6.3.1, 6.3.3, 6.3.7, 6.4, 6.6, 6.6.1, 6.6.7, 6.7, 6.7.1, 6.7.3, 10.4.1, 10.4.3, 10.4.5, 13.1, 13.2, 13.3, 14.2, 14.4.1, 14.5, 15.2.2, 15.2.6, 15.2.9, 15.2.10, 15.5, 15.6.1, 15.6.2, 16.1.1, 16.2, 16.3.1, 16.3.6, 17.1.1, 18.1.1, 18.1.9, 18.1.12, 18.4.7, 19.1, 19.1.1, 19.1.2, 19.2, 19.2.9, 19.3, 19.3.4, 19.3.5, 19.3.7, 19.4, 22.5, 26.4, 33.6.1, 33.7.1, 34.5.1, 34.6.1, 34.7.1, 34.7.5, 34.8.3
Projection D.2, D.6
projects A.1, A.1.1, B.6, B.6.1, 11.7
proliferate 34.1
proliferating 34.1
proliferation 33.3
prompt 1.3, 6.4, 6.6.2, 6.6.7, 6.6.8, 18.4.5, 19.1.2

promptDialog 6.6.8
prompts 1.3, 7.2, 7.3
prone 31.6
PROOF_QUALITY 11.4.6
proper 6.4, 6.5.3, 11.3, 12.3, 12.4, 13.6, 14.0, 15.1, 15.5.7, 16.1.2, 18.4.1, 18.5.4, 19.2.4, 19.3.10, 21.1.5, 25.7, 33.7.4, 34.4, 34.5.5
Properties B.5.3, B.5.5, B.5.6, B.8.4, B.8.5, D.1, D.6, D.7, 2.3.2, 6.1, 6.3.5, 6.3.7, 6.4, 6.5.3, 6.5.4, 6.6.4, 6.6.5, 20.1, 20.2, 34.7, 34.7.9, 34.8, 34.8.1, 34.8.3, 34.8.4, 34.8.6, 34.8.8, 34.8.11, 34.8.12, 34.8.13
property B.5.5, B.5.6, B.5.7, B.8.5, B.8.6, B.8.7, B.8.9, D.6, D.7, 0.1, 0.3, 0.4, 6.1, 6.5.1, 6.5.2, 6.6.4, 6.7.2, 8.1, 18.1.2, 18.4.1, 18.4.5, 20.0, 20.5, 20.6, 20.7, 20.8, 28.3, 32.5, 33.2, 34.7, 34.8, 34.8.3, 34.8.4, 34.8.6, 34.8.7, 34.8.10, 34.8.11, 34.8.12, Prf
proportional 9.2, 34.8.7
proposed 5.1
proprietary 34.1, 34.3
prospects D.0
protect A.4.2, 33.2.5
protected A.5.1, 14.4.4, 15.2.6, 15.5.1, 15.6.3, 15.6.5, 18.1.12, 18.4.6, 32.4
protection 33.1
protocol 34.1
protocols 34.3
prototype A.8, 8.5, 15.7.9, 18.1.13, 18.4.6, 26.1, 30.1
prototypes A.1.1, A.4.6, 15.2.6, 15.6.3, 18.1.12, 25.5
prove 33.9
provide A.1.1, B.6.1, 0.2, 9.1, 10.3, 11.5.3, 12.1.1, 12.1.3, 12.1.4, 12.3, 14.4.4, 15.8.4, 18.1, 19.1.2, 20.7, 28.1, 33.1, 33.4, 34.0
provided 0.2, 6.3.6, 6.5.3, 10.2, 12.1.2, 12.1.3, 12.6, 13.3, 13.5, 13.6.2, 15.5.6, 22.5, 22.6, 33.3, 33.4, 33.6.4, 33.8.4, 34.0, 34.4, 35.7
provides A.2.11, B.9, 0.1, 0.2, 1.0, 1.1, 1.2, 6.4, 6.6.8, 9.4, 10.2, 10.5, 11.0, 11.5.3, 11.6.1, 11.7, 12, 12.1.1, 12.1.2, 12.1.3, 12.2, 12.3, 13.0, 14.0, 17.3.4, 17.3.5, 18.1, 19.2, 25.5, 32.2, 33.7.2, 34.7.9, 34.8.13, 35.0, Prf
providing A.1, 12, 32.5, Prf
proxy 34.7.7
PS_DASH 11.4.2
PS_DASHDOT 11.4.2
PS_DASHDOTDOT 11.4.2
PS_DOT 11.4.2
PS_INSIDEFRAME 11.4.2

PS_NULL 11.4.2
PS_SOLID 11.4.2
PSTR 8.2
ptEnd 11.4.4
pThread 35.4, 35.8
PtInRect 11.5.2, 12.1.4
ptStart 11.4.4
public A.1, A.4.3, A.4.4, A.4.6, A.5.1, 3.3, 4.3, 7.3, 14.4.4, 15.2.6, 15.6.3, 18.1.12, 32.5, 34.6.5
publication A.3.1
publications A.3.1
publicly A.1, A.3.2, 34.1
publisher A.3.1, Prf
pull B.5.7, B.8.7, 1.2, 1.3, 17.4, 17.5, 34.2, 34.8.5
pulls 18.4.3
pump 11.5.4, 13.3
purchase 0.1, 35.2
purchased A.5.1
purchasing 34.3
pure 15.7.9
purely 3.1
purist 4.7
purpose A.3, B, B.6.1, 0.0, 2.1, 2.3.1, 5.0, 5.4, 9.0, 9.4, 13.6, 14.4.4, 15.2.4, 15.3, 15.7.9, 15.8.2, 18.0, 18.1.4, 18.4, 18.4.6, 20.7, 22.0, 22.6, 23.0, 23.5, 25.6, 27.0, 28.0, 35.0
purposes 1.4, 3.1, 11.3, 15.8.2, 29.4
push A.1.1, A.4.4, A.4.5, 0.4, 1.2, 1.3, 2.1, 4.2, 6.5, 7.1, 7.6, 13.6, 30.1, 34.8
pushed A.4.4, D.3
pushing D.2
put 0.4, 4.1, 14.4.5, 14.4.6, 15.1, 15.6.3, 18.1, 18.5.2, 19.2.1, 25.5, 25.6, 34.1, 34.8, 35.7, 35.8, 35.10
puts 1.3, 3.1
putting 19.2, 34.1, Prf
Q 5.4, 6.5.3
qualified 13.6
qualify 13.6.1, 33.2.2
quality D.0, 11.4.6
quantity 35.10
queries 8.6.1, 11.6.3, 33.2, 33.4, 34.2
query 8.6.1, 12.3, 15.3.5, 18.4.2, 33.0, 33.2, 33.2.2, 33.3, 33.4, 33.4.2, 33.4.3, 33.4.4, 33.5, 33.6.2, 33.6.10, 33.6.11, 33.7
querying 8.6.1, 34.1
question B.4.3, C.0, 3.3, 3.5, 4.7, 7.1, 10.2, 15.7.3, 16.2, 19.1.2, 19.3.5, 22.4, 23.1, 23.9, 33.6.10, 33.6.11, 34.1, 34.2, 34.5.3
questions A.1, A.1.1, B.4, C.0, 0.4, 1.4, 3.3, 7.1, 13.2, 17.4, 23.0, 23.7, 33.2, 34.1, 34.2, Prf
queue 10.3, 31.1, 31.4, 35.7
queues 35.7
quick A.1, A.3.1, B.2, B.2.3, B.3.1, 1.4, 6.1, 19.2
Quicken 16.5
quicker 8.6.7, 12.1.2, 32.6

quickly B.1, B.3, B.4, B.4.1, B.4.4, 0.0,
        0.1, 0.2, 0.3, 0.4, 1.1, 2.3,
        6.1, 6.6, 8.5, 11.5.4,
        11.6.2, 12.1.1, 12.5, 13.1,
        14.0, 14.1, 15.6, 18.1,
        19.2, 19.5, 25.7, 33.7,
        34.1, 34.6.5, 35.1, 35.7,
        Prf
quirks A.8.1
quit A.4.1, 1.3, 4.1, 5.1, 5.2, 5.4, 6.4,
        6.5, 6.5.3, 15.2.9, 34.2,
        35.2, Prf
quite A.1, A.8.1, B.8.1, D.1, 0.2, 1.3,
        2.1, 2.4, 2.5, 3.2, 3.5, 4.4,
        4.7, 5.2, 6, 9.0, 9.5, 10.4,
        11.6.3, 12.2, 14.4.6,
        15.5.5, 17.4, 18.4.6, 19.0,
        20.8, 22.5, 22.7, 33.3,
        33.4.4, 33.9, 34.4, 34.8.2,
        35.8
quits 5.4, 11.4.6, 12.3
quitting 1.3, 4.1, 5.1, 5.4
quoted 6.3.7, 6.4
quotes 6.1, 6.3.5, 6.3.7, 6.4
r 3.3, 11.3, 11.4.6, 11.5.4, 13.4, 34.5.5
radically 1.3
radio B.6.6, 1.2, 7.5, 9.0, 9.5, 22.2,
        22.5, 34.8.4
radius 5.3
Raleigh 33.1
ran B.3, 6.1, 16.5
random D.6, 11.4.7, 34.4, 35.5
randomly A.1, 11.5.3
range 3.5, 4.6, 5.2, 5.3, 7.3, 7.5, 8.1,
        9.1, 11.4.2, 11.4.6,
        11.5.5, 12.1.1, 17.3.5,
        18.3, 20.2, 22.0, 22.4,
        22.5, 34.8.1, 34.8.6,
        34.8.12, 34.9
ranges 22.6
ranging D.2, 35.7
rapidly C.1, 0.0, 6, 12.1.1, 14.0, 34.3,
        Prf
rare 35.7
rarely 20.0, 23.1
RAS 32.2
raster 11.2, 25.7, 26.1, 26.2, 26.5
Rate 5.4, 11.6.2, 17.4, 20.2
rates 11.6.2
ratio 11.6.2
raw 25.6, 34.2
RC B.5.2, D.1, 6.1, 6.3.3, 6.4, 6.6.1,
        6.7.3, 8.4, 10.4.4, 10.4.5,
        14.4.6, 15.2.2, 15.2.10,
        16.2, 16.3, 16.3.5, 18.4.2,
        18.4.4, 18.4.5, 18.4.6,
        19.3.1, 33.8.1, 34.6.4,
        34.6.5, 35.8
RCs D.1
re A.5, B.3, 4.4, 4.5, 5.1, 5.2, 6.1, 6.6.5,
        6.7, 8.4, 9.1, 11.2, 11.4.1,
        11.4.6, 11.5.2, 11.5.3,
        11.5.4, 11.6.1, 11.6.2,
        15.2.9, 18.6, 24.2, 35.8
reach 24.1
reached A.2.6, A.5.2
reaches 8.6.7
reaction A.1.1
read A.1.1, A.2.3, A.2.4, A.2.5, A.2.11,
        A.3.1, A.3.2, A.4.6, A.8.1,

D.2, D.3, D.8, 1.0, 2.3,
        3.5, 5.2, 7.2, 7.6, 8.1, 8.7,
        10.4, 12.1.1, 12.1.3, 12.3,
        13.6, 15.3, 15.5.2, 15.8.2,
        16.4, 17.3.4, 19.0, 20.7,
        33.5, 33.8.4, 34.4, 34.7,
        34.8.1, 34.8.3, 34.9, 35.1,
        35.2
readable 12.3, 12.4
reader 0.1
readers C.0
ReadHuge 12.1.1
readily D.0
reading A.2.3, D.5, 0.2, 5.2, 5.3, 8.6.3,
        12.1.1, 12.3, 13.2, 35.1,
        35.2
readjust 5.2
README 14.4, Prf
reads A.2.4, 1.3, 8.6.2, 12.1.1, 12.3,
        14.3, 14.4.2, 19.2
ReadString 12.1.1
ready A.3.2, B.1.5, B.3, C.1, 0.1, 3.0,
        8.6.1, 8.6.5, 14.0, 35.7,
        Prf
real A.3.1, B.1.2, B.1.3, 5.3, 5.4, 6, 8.1,
        11.6.1, 15.4, 15.7.11,
        17.0, 24.0, 33.7.2, 34.5.2,
        34.6.2, 34.6.5, 34.6.9,
        35.7, 35.9
realistic A.5.2, 2.2
realized 23.9
realizes 35.4
reallocates 12.1.2, 12.2
reallocating 8.6.1, 13.5
really A.1.1, D.2, 0.4, 5.1, 11.6.2, 16.2,
        17.5, 18.4.7, 33.7.2, 34.2,
        34.3, 35.10, Prf
reals A.1.1
REALTIME_PRIORITY_CLASS 35.7
reappears 11.5.4
reason A.2.2, A.5.2, A.7, B.1.6, 7.0,
        11.0, 13.6, 15.7.11, 20.6,
        20.7, 22.4, 22.5, 23.2,
        23.3, 23.8, 23.9, 32.4,
        33.2, 35.2
reasonable 35.7
reasons 11.0, 12.3, 15.3, 18.2, 34.1
reboot 34.5.5
reboots 33.1
Rebuild B.3, B.3.1, B.3.2, 3.3, 13.2,
        16.2, 16.3.6, 18.1.15,
        29.3
rebuilt B.4
recalculate 34.6.5
recalculates 34.7.7
recalculating 11.4.6
recalculations 35.1, 35.2
recall 7.3, 12.1.2, 18.4.6, 19.2.5
recalls 26.1
recap B.3
receive 0.2, 1.3, 4.2, 4.5, 7.2, 7.6, 10.3,
        11.2, 11.5.4, 13.6, 15.8.2,
        22.6, 25.5, 26.1, 27.1,
        29.1, 30.1, 34.1, 34.8,
        35.1, 35.7
received 7.6, 11.6.1, 15.5.6, 25.5,
        33.6.11
receives 1.3, 4.4, 9.1, 11.2, 11.5.2,
        12.3, 13.2, 13.3, 15.3.7,
        15.8.2, 23.2, 23.3, 23.7,

24.1, 25.5, 26.1, 33.1,
        34.1, 35.5
recently A.1.1, 10.5, 15.4
recipient A.7.1
recognizable 15.8.3
recognize B.7.4, 6.5, 7.2, 9.4, 11.4.6,
        15.1, 15.3, 15.7.9, 16.2,
        32.7, 33.6.3
recognized 4.4, 6.3.7, 9.3, 15.3
recognizes 6.5, 10.4, 16.2
recognizing 4.4, 11.5.2
recolored A.3.1
recommend D.5
recommends 10.3
Recompile 2.3.2, 6.5.2, 10.5, 15.2.9,
        15.2.10, 15.8.3, 16.2,
        18.1.14, 19.3.10, 19.4
recompiles B.3
recompiling 6.1
reconstruction 11.5.4
record A.4.1, 9.2, 12.1.1, 13.2, 14.3,
        17.5, 18.1, 18.1.12, 18.2,
        18.4.1, 18.4.4, 18.4.6,
        18.4.7, 18.5, 33.1, 33.2.1,
        33.2.2, 33.2.3, 33.2.4,
        33.4.3, 33.5, 33.6.2,
        33.6.3, 33.6.4, 33.6.6,
        33.6.7, 33.6.8, 33.6.10,
        33.7, 33.7.2, 33.7.3,
        33.7.4, 33.7.5, 33.7.6,
        33.8, 33.8.1, 33.8.2,
        33.8.3, 33.8.4, 33.9
records 0.4, 12.1.1, 12.3, 12.5, 17.5,
        18.1, 18.1.12, 18.2,
        18.4.6, 18.6, 26.1, 33.2,
        33.2.1, 33.4.3, 33.5,
        33.6.4, 33.6.5, 33.6.11,
        33.7, 33.7.2, 33.7.5,
        33.7.6, 33.8, 33.8.3,
        33.8.4
recordset 22.2, 33.9
recreate A.7.1, B.3, 15.4, 15.5, 15.6.1,
        17.3, 17.3.1, 17.3.2
recreating 15.8.1, 17.2, 18.4
Rect A.4.6, 3.1, 3.2, 3.4, 12.1.4, 13.4
rectangle A.3.3, A.4.5, B.5.5, B.5.6,
        B.5.7, D.3, 3.1, 3.2, 3.3,
        3.4, 4.4, 4.6, 5.3, 6.6.4,
        6.6.5, 8.2, 11.0, 11.3,
        11.4.1, 11.4.3, 11.4.4,
        11.4.6, 11.4.8, 11.5.2,
        11.6.1, 11.6.2, 11.6.3, 12,
        12.1.4, 15.8.3, 25.6, 29.2,
        32.5, 34.5.5, 34.5.6,
        34.7.2, 34.8.3, 34.8.7
rectangles A.3.1, D.3, 0.4, 3.3, 3.4, 5.3,
        11.0, 11.1, 11.4, 11.4.3,
        11.4.4, 11.4.6, 11.4.7,
        11.5.2, 11.5.3, 11.5.4,
        11.6.2, 12.1.4, 15.1,
        15.8.3, 15.9
rectangular 3.1, 3.2, 3.4, 11.1, 11.4.7,
        29.3
rectDefault 2.3.2, 3.3
recursively A.4.2, 13.4
Red D.1, D.2, D.3, D.6, D.8, 7.4,
        11.5.2, 35.7
redefine A.1.1, A.3.1, 23.9
redo A.1.1, A.7
redone A.6

redraw 11.2, 11.4.6, 11.5.2, 11.5.3,
    11.6.2, 12.3, 35.2, 35.8
redrawing 11.5.4, 15.2.8, 15.4, 35.1,
    35.8
redrawn 11.5.2, 11.5.3, 11.5.4, 11.5.5,
    25.6, 29.4
redraws 11.4.1, 11.5.5, 15.4, 34.5.3,
    34.8
RedSurface D.6
reduce 10.4.10, 13.6, 33.1, 35.2
reduced 3.3, 18.4.6
reduces 1.1
reducing 0.1
reduction 17.2
redundancies A.3.2
redundancy A.4.2
redundant A.4.2, 3.2, 15.8.4, 33.1
Refer D.1, 2.3.2, 14.2, 18.4.6
reference A.2, A.2.5, A.2.11, A.4.3,
    A.6, A.7.2, A.8, B, B.4,
    B.4.1, B.5.7, D.1, 0.2, 1.1,
    8.2, 12.2, 12.4, 19.2.3,
    19.2.5, 19.2.7, 19.3.3,
    34.9
referenced A.4.2, 23.1, 23.4, 33.7.2
references A.2.11, A.3.2, B.3.2, B.4,
    B.4.1, B.4.2, B.4.3, B.4.4,
    16.3, 19.2, 28.2, 33.1
referencing A.2.11, 18.4.2, 20.7
referential 33.1
referred A.1, D.8, 1.1, 1.3, 33.1, 34.8
referring A.6, 2.3.2, 4.6
refers A.6, 23.1, 35.5
reflect 6.4, 12.1.1, 14.3, 15.5.6, 15.7.9,
    15.7.10, 17.1.3, 18.2
reflected A.1, 25.5, 33.1
reflection 25.0, 25.5, 31.1
reflectivity D.7
reflects 8.6.1, 25.5
reform 33.8.2
reformats 8.2
reformatting 8.2
Refresh B.8.7, 11.5.1, 12.3, 15.1,
    15.2.8, 15.3, 18.1.13,
    34.8, 34.8.5, 35.1
refreshed 11.2, 29.1
refreshes D.4, 11.4.1, 11.4.6
refreshing 18.5, 25.2
refreshRate 11.4.6
REG B.6.1
regard D.6, 11.3, 11.5.4, 34.1
regardless D.6, 0.0, 11.4.2, 11.6.1,
    13.6.1, 14.4.5, 15.8.3,
    18.4.6, 34.1
REGEDIT 34.4, 34.7.6
REGEDT 34.4
regenerate B.6.1
region 11.3
regions 11.1, 11.4.1, 23.6, 29.3
register B.8.1, B.8.2, 10.5, 11.5.3, 16.4,
    18.4.7, 34.7.2, 34.8.1,
    34.8.3
RegisterClass 11.5.3
registered 16.4, 33.4
registering 4.3
Registers B.2, 7.6, 8.5, 11.5.3, 34.6.3
RegisterShellFileTypes 10.5
registration 7.6, 27.0
registry B.8.1, B.8.2, 0.4, 10.1, 10.5,
    34.4, 34.6.3, 34.7.2,

34.7.5, 34.7.6, 34.7.7
regular 30.1, 35.7
reinforce 15.0
reinsert 34.8.5
Reinstall B.8.2, B.8.3
reject 3.2, 24.1
rejected 5.3
Rejects 7.2, 24.1
relate A.4.5, 8.3, 11.5, 33.1
related A.3.2, A.4.5, 3.1, 3.4, 10.5,
    11.0, 11.1, 13.2, 14.3,
    15.8, 23.2, 33.1, 33.9,
    34.5.3, 34.7.6
relates 25.0, 33.1, 33.4.2
relating 15.8.2
relation 32.6, 35.7
relational 0.4, 33.1, 33.2
relationship 11.5.5, 14.4.4, 15.3,
    16.3.3, 18.2, 25.3
relationships 19.2
relative 3.1, 11.2, 12, 35.7
relatively A.1, 3.3, 24.3
release B.2, D.0, D.1, 11.3, 11.5.2,
    11.5.4, 13.0, 13.1, 13.2,
    13.3, 13.5, 34.1
ReleaseBuffer 12.1.2
ReleaseCapture 11.5.4
released 11.4.1, 29.1, 32.1
ReleaseDisp 34.7.7
releases D.1, 11.5.2, 11.5.4, Prf
releasing 11.5.2
relevant 10.4.10, 18.4.3, 28.0, 33.1
reliable C.1
relink 16.2
relinks B.3
relinquish 35.2
reload 11.5.3, 12.3, 15.2.9, 17.4,
    34.5.7
reloaded 18.6
rely 12.4
remain A.4.3, A.5.1, 7.2, 7.6, 11.4.6,
    13.5, 15.5.7, 27.1, 32.2,
    35.4, 35.8
remainder A.1, A.5.1, 34.5.2
remaining A.4.3, 6.6.4, 13.6.1, 15.9,
    25.7
remains A.3.2, A.5, 8.2, 11.4.1, 11.5.4,
    19.2.2, 19.2.4, 19.2.6,
    19.2.8, 19.2.10, 19.3.5,
    19.3.10, 35.1
remarkable A.1, 33.7.5
remarkably B.1, B.6.1, 14.2, 20.1, 20.6,
    33.7.2, 34.5.5, 34.6.9,
    35.2, 35.9
remedy A.2.3, 6.4
remember A.4.5, A.5.2, A.8, D.5, 13.4,
    15.2.4, 15.2.5, 15.2.6,
    18.4.2, 25.6, 25.8, 26.2,
    27.1, 28.2, 29.1, 29.4,
    32.1, 32.5, 34.5.5, 34.6.9
remembers A.5.2, B.1.1, B.1.2, 8.6.1,
    11.3, 11.5.3
remind A.5.2, 32.6
remote 34.1, 34.4
removal A.4.2, D.0
remove A.3.2, D.1, 1.5, 3.3, 8.5,
    11.5.3, 12.1.1, 13.5, 14.5,
    15.8.2, 15.8.4, 19.4, 28.1,
    29.1, 33.6.2, 33.7.3
RemoveAll 12.2, 12.4, 12.5, 15.2.6

RemoveAt 12.2, 12.4
removed 11.4.3, 13.2, 23.2, 27.1
RemoveHead 12.4
RemoveKey 12.5
RemovePage 20.7
Removes 12.2, 12.5, 13.2, 20.7
RemoveTail 12.4
removing A.8, B.3.2, 1.2
Rename B.7.4, 6.4, 12.1.1, 13.6, 16.2,
    16.3.5, 19.1.1, 33.7.1,
    33.7.3, 34.8.12
renamed 20.7
Renames 12.1.1
renaming 13.6
render 34.1
rendered D.3, 11.2, 11.4.6, 34.1
Rendering D.1, D.2, 34.1
renders D.3
RenderScene D.3, D.6, D.7
reopen 34.5.2
reopens 12.1.1
repainted D.4, 4.5, 29.1
repainting 4.5, 25.1
repaints 11.5.3
repaired 18.4.5
repeat B.3, D.2, 13.3, 16.2, 17.3.3,
    33.4.2
repeated 11.4.8
repeatedly B.2.2, 12.4
repeating 33.6.4, 34.7.1
repeats 1.3, 4.7, 8.6.8, 16.2
replace A.4.2, A.5.2, 0.2, 0.4, 3.3, 6.1,
    7.6, 8.7, 9.2, 9.3, 11.4.3,
    11.4.4, 11.4.5, 11.4.6,
    11.4.7, 12.1.1, 12.4, 12.5,
    13.6, 14.5, 15.8.3, 16.2,
    18.4.6, 19.2.1, 19.4, 20.1,
    23.9, 28.2, 33.6.5, 34.6.8,
    34.6.9, 34.8, 34.8.4
replaceable 6.7, 34.3
ReplaceAll 7.6
ReplaceCurrent 7.6
replaced 4.5, 9.5, 11.5.4, 12.4, 13.5,
    18.2
replacement A.2.3, 3.3, 5.3, 7.3, 7.6,
    9.2, 9.3, 9.5, 12.1.1, 13.5,
    32.6, 34.6.8, 34.6.10
replaces A.2.3, A.2.7, A.2.10, D.1, 8.2,
    12.4, 14.4.5, 16.2, 23.8
ReplaceSel 8.1, 8.2
ReplaceText 7.6
replacing 2.3.2, 3.3, 8.6, 12.5, 13.5,
    23.8
replicated A.1.1
reply C.0
report A.1.1, 6.7, 20.1, 20.3, 34.4
reports 8.6.10, 13.3, 34.7
Reposition B.2.2, 6.1, 19.2.3
represent A.3.2, A.4.5, A.4.6, D.1, D.6,
    11.5.2, 12.5, 14.3, 25.0,
    26.2, 26.4, 34.4
representation 12.1.3
representations 12.1.3
representative B.3.1
represented B.4.3, D.1, 34.4
representing 9.2, 11.4.1, 11.5.5
represents A.5.2, B.5.6, D.1, D.7, 14.3
Requery 33.5, 33.6.10, 33.7.6, 33.8.1,
    33.8.2
request C.0, 2.3.3, 4.1, 7.0, 7.6, 11.3,

11.5.5, 13.6, 15.8, 17.2,
24.0, 26.0, 33.2.2, 33.7.2,
34.1, 34.2, 34.4
requested B.4, D.1, 7.2, 9.5, 10.4.10,
25.6, 33.2.1, 34.2
requesting 22.7, 35.7
requests 11.5.5, 15.5.2, 19.3.8, 33.2.1,
33.7.6, 34.2, 35.7
require A.6, 0.3, 8.6.6, 11.2, 11.4.4,
12.1.3, 14.6, 15.8.2, 23.0,
25.4, 31.0, 34.6.4
required A.3.2, B.2, B.8.7, D.1, 2.2,
2.3.2, 3.5, 6.5.4, 7.6, 8.3,
8.5, 8.6.7, 14.1, 15.5.3,
15.8.4, 18.4.6, 20.5, 22.0,
22.5, 25.6, 26.4, 29.1,
32.6, 34.2, 34.3, 34.8.5
requirement 2.3
requirements D.1, 4.4, 8.3, 12.1.2,
15.4, 15.8.4, 17.2, 25.6
requires A.3.3, A.6, D.1, 2.2, 3.6, 5.2,
5.3, 7.2, 11.6.2, 12.1.2,
15.5.6, 23.1, 23.2, 24.0,
30.0, 33.6.10, 35.8
requiring 13.2, 33.3
rerouted 23.8
reroutes 15.3.7
rerun B.3.2, 10.5, 12.3, 13.2, 15.8.3,
18.4.5, 19.2.2, 19.2.4,
19.2.6, 19.2.8, 19.2.10,
19.3.5, 19.3.10, 35.2
Reruns 33.5
RES B.6.1
reselect 34.5.2
resemble 33.4.2
reserved D.1, 4.2, 11.4.1
reset 15.7.9, 32.5, 34.8.9
ResetContent 9.4
resets D.3, 8.2, 8.6.1, 10.3
reside 15.4, 18.4.6
resides 13.7
residing 2.3.2, 34.2, 34.5.3
resizable 0.4, 2.3.2, 18.1
resize B.2.2, D.2, 1.2, 4.4, 4.6, 5.2,
18.1, 18.1.2, 18.1.3,
18.1.5, 25.6, 30.1, 32.5,
34.5.5, 34.8.3, 35.8
resized 2.3.2, 4.4, 11.6.2, 18.1.2, 20.3,
28.1
resizes 4.4, 18.1.2, 18.1.4, 18.1.5, 18.2,
20.3, 30.0, 34.5.5
resizing D.2, D.3, 4.4, 5.2, 10.2,
18.1.3, 18.1.6
resolution 11.3, 15.6, 15.8.4
resolutions 11.6.1
resolve B.2
resolves 18.4.3, 18.4.4
resource B, B.1.2, **B.5, B.5.1, B.5.2,
B.5.3, B.5.4, B.5.5, B.5.6,
B.5.7**, B.7.4, B.8.4, B.9,
0.1, 0.4, 1.2, 3.2, 3.6, 4.2,
5.1, 5.2, **6, 6.1, 6.2, 6.3,
6.3.2, 6.3.4, 6.3.5, 6.3.6,
6.3.7, 6.4, 6.5.1, 6.5.3,
6.5.4, 6.6, 6.6.1, 6.6.2,
6.6.3, 6.6.6, 6.6.8, 6.7,
6.7.2, 6.7.3, 6.8**, 7.2, 8.0,
8.4, 8.5, 10.1, 10.2,
10.4.4, 10.4.6, 10.4.7,
10.4.8, 10.4.10, 11.4.1,

11.4.3, 11.5.2, 11.5.3,
11.6.2, 12, 13.6, 14.4,
14.4.6, **15.0, 15.1, 15.2.2,
15.2.10, 15.4, 15.7,
15.7.2, 15.7.5, 15.7.11,**
15.9, 16.2, 16.3, 16.3.5,
16.3.6, 16.5, 17.0, 17.1.2,
17.2, 18.1.2, 18.1.7,
18.1.8, 18.4.1, 18.4.2,
18.4.4, 18.4.5, 18.4.6,
19.3.1, 19.3.5, 19.3.6,
20.5, 20.6, 23.4, 26.4,
28.2, 29.2, 30.0, 30.1,
32.6, 33.7.2, 33.7.3,
33.8.2, 33.8.3, 34.6.5,
34.8.12, 35.6, 35.7
resources B.5, B.5.1, B.6.2, C.1, 0.1,
0.4, 6, 6.1, 6.3.7, 6.6.8,
6.8, 10.2, 10.4, 10.4.10,
11.4.3, 11.5.3, 14.4.6,
15.2.10, 15.7, 15.7.2,
16.3, 16.3.5, 18.1.7, 20.6,
23.5, 25.2, 32.4, 32.5,
34.6.4, 35.3
ResourceView B.6.2
respecify 33.6.10
respect D.3, 29.1
respectable 34.5.5
respective D.1, D.8, 7.3
respectively A.2.4, A.2.10, A.4.3, A.5.2,
D.2, 1.2, 2.1, 5.2, 6.4,
10.4.7, 11.4.1, 11.6.1,
12.1.4, 15.7.8, 18.4.5,
18.4.6, 26.4, 35.8
respects 15.5
respond 0.1, 0.4, 1.3, 3.0, 4.2, 4.4, 6.5,
6.6.8, 7.1, 7.6, 9.1, 10.4,
11.4.1, 11.5.3, 13.2,
15.5.5, 18.4.5, 19.3.5,
30.1, 33.2.2, 33.6.4, 34.8,
34.8.6, 35.1, Prf
responded 4.4, 7.1
responding 4.0, 11.4.1, 35.2
responds 1.1, 1.3, 4.2, 5.4, 7.1, 7.6,
19.3.5, 33.7.6, 33.8.3,
34.8.4
response A.1, A.1.1, A.3.3, 2.3.2, 3.2,
4.1, 5.2, 6.5, 7.6, 9.1, 9.3,
11.3, 11.4.1, 11.5.2,
11.5.3, 11.5.4, 15.3,
15.7.7, 18.2, 18.4.2, 27.1,
29.2, 33.6.3, 34.2, 34.4
responses 8.5
responsibilities 15.6.13
responsibility 11.2, 15.6
responsible 4.5, 8.6.1, 8.6.2, 12.3, 14.3,
15.3, 18.2, 25.1, 34.1
responsiveness 35.0
rest A.1, A.1.1, A.4.2, A.4.3, A.6, B.2.3,
B.4.1, B.5, B.5.6, B.7.6,
D.5, 1.2, 1.4, 2.6, 4.1, 8.4,
11.2, 11.6.1, 11.6.2, 13.3,
18.4.5, 21.2, 23.8, 25.6,
26.4, 34.8, 34.8.1, 35.7,
35.8, 35.9
restart B.2
restarts 12.3
restore 11.4.1, 11.5.4, 25.6, 25.7, 33.1
restored D.3, 17.4.6, 25.6, 25.7
restores D.3, 11.4.1

restoring 11.5.4
restrict 22.0, 22.4
restricted 5.3, 12.2
restrictions 25.6
result A.5.2, A.6, A.8, D.6, 5.1, 5.4,
7.1, 7.2, 8.6.7, 11.4.1,
13.2, 17.3.4, 20.3, 25.7,
33.1, 33.6.4, 33.7, 33.7.6,
34.7
resulted 15.3
resulting A.5.2, A.6, 3.3, 21.1.8, 30.1,
32.5, 33.5, 33.7
results A.5.2, D.3, 5.2, 7.3, 15.5.6,
15.7.11, 15.8.2, 22.5,
33.4.4, Prf
resumable B.2
resume 35.3, 35.4, 35.6, 35.7
retains D.7, 9.1, 11.5.3, 20.7
Retrieval 5.3, 12.2, 33.7
retrieve A.5.1, 0.4, 5.3, 6.1, 6.6.8, 7.4,
8.1, 9.3, 9.4, 9.5, 10.5,
11.5.2, 11.5.3, 12.3, 12.5,
15.1, 15.6.5, 15.7, 15.7.8,
18.2, 18.3, 18.4.7, 22.6,
24.0, 33.2, 33.2.1, 33.2.2,
33.5, 33.6.2, 33.6.4, 33.7,
34.7, 35.7
retrieved 9.3, 26.4, 35.7
retrieves 4.4, 8.2, 8.6.1, 8.6.7, 9.3,
10.5, 15.2.7, 15.4.2,
15.5.1, 15.7.9, 18.4.4,
25.7, 33.2, 33.2.1, 34.5.5
retrieving 4.6, 6.6.8, 7.3, 8.6.7, 9.3,
15.2.8
Retry 7.1, 13.2
return A.1.1, A.5.1, A.5.2, A.6, B.2,
B.2.2, B.3.2, B.5.5, B.8.7,
D.1, 5.3, 6.4, 6.6.4, 7.2,
7.3, 8.6.1, 10.3, 10.4,
11.4.8, 11.6.1, 12.1.1,
12.1.3, 13.6, 19.2.1, 20.7,
23.2, 23.5, 25.6, 26.3,
26.4, 27.1, 29.1, 29.3,
32.4, 32.5, 33.2.1, 33.2.2,
33.4.1, 34.4, 34.7.4,
34.7.8, 34.7.9, 34.8.9,
35.3, 35.4, 35.8
returned A.6, A.8, D.5, 2.3.1, 5.2,
6.6.8, 9.3, 11.5.5, 12.1.1,
12.1.3, 13.6, 23.1, 25.6,
26.2, 29.1, 29.2, 29.4,
33.6.7, 35.4
returning A.2.6, D.5, 12.1.2, 12.4,
13.6, 25.6
returns A.5.2, A.6, B.2, B.2.2, D.1,
D.5, 2.3.1, 3.1, 3.3, 6.6.8,
6.7.3, 7.1, 7.2, 7.3, 7.4,
7.5, 7.6, 8.1, 8.2, 8.6.1,
8.6.2, 9.4, 10.1, 10.3,
10.6, 11.4.6, 11.6.1,
11.6.3, 12.1.1, 12.1.2,
12.1.3, 12.1.4, 12.2, 12.4,
12.5, 13.5, 15.8.2, 17.4,
20.4, 20.7, 22.4, 22.5,
23.4, 26.1, 26.2, 29.1,
33.5, 34.4, 34.6.8, 35.2,
35.3, 35.4, 35.8
retyping Prf
reusable A.1.1, 28.0, 31.6, 34.1
reuse A.1.1, 15.3.1, 28.0

reused 15.5.2
reuses 15.3, 17.4.7, 18.2
reusing 18.5.3
reveal B.6.5
reveals 19.2
reversal 8.6.3
reverse 10.6, 18.4.7, 20.3, 25.7
reversed 20.2
ReverseFind 12.1.2
Reverses 12.1.2, 12.3, 22.1
review A.4.4, A.4.6, 1.2, 6.3.7, 6.4,
     13.0, 14.0, 15.7, 15.7.11,
     15.9, 18.0, 34.8.2, 35.4
revised 15.4.1, 15.5.6
revisions 11.5.4
revisit 12.3, 17.1
rewarded 0.1
reworks 25.4
rewriting A.4.2, 0.4
rewritten A.3.2
RFX 33.6.2, 33.6.10, 33.7.4
RFX_Text 33.6.10
RGB 7.4, 11.4.2, 11.4.3, 11.4.7,
     11.4.8, 15.2.3, 15.8.3,
     25.7
RGBA D.1
RHS 12.4
rich B, 13.6.2, 15.3.3, 19.2, 20.0, Prf
right A.1, A.1.1, A.4.4, A.4.5, A.6,
     A.7.1, B.4.1, B.4.2, B.4.3,
     B.4.4, B.4.5, B.4.6, B.5.3,
     B.5.4, D.1, D.2, D.4, D.6,
     0.4, 1.2, 2.3, 3.2, 3.3, 4.1,
     4.6, 5.3, 6.4, 8.1, 8.7,
     10.4.7, 11.2, 11.4.1,
     11.4.3, 11.4.6, 11.5.2,
     11.5.3, 11.5.5, 11.6.1,
     12.1.2, 12.1.4, 13.2, 14.5,
     15.2.4, 15.3, 15.5.3,
     15.5.5, 17.3.4, 18.4.6,
     19.2.3, 21, 26.4, 32.6,
     33.4.3, 33.7.2, 34.8.1,
     34.8.3, 34.8.5, 34.8.7,
     34.8.8
rightmost 12.1.2
RISC 35.2
risky 34.4
road A.1, 0.3, 18.1
robin 35.7
robot D.3
robust 2.1, 12.2, 13.0, 13.8
robustness 0.1
role A.4.6
roll 33.1
rolled 33.3
rolodex 18.1
ROM 0.1, 0.2
Roman 3.5, 11.4.6
room A.3.2, 12.2, 34.4
root 10.5, 20.1, 20.4, Prf
roots A.3.2
ROP 25.7
ROP_DSPDxax 25.7
ROPs 25.7
rot A.7
rotate D.3, D.4, D.6
rotated D.2, D.3
rotates D.3, D.7
rotating D.3
Rotation 11.4.6

rough 1.1, 5.1, 18.1
roughly 35.2
round 11.4.3, 35.7
rounded 11.4.3
RoundRect 11.4.3
route A.8, 4.5, 11.5.1, 23.7, 23.8
routed 11.5.2, 13.3, 13.6.1, 24.2
routes 4.5, 4.7, 5.4, 25.4
routine 22.2, 22.3, 22.4, 22.5, 22.6,
     23.4, 28.1
routines A.1.1, D.2, 22.0, 22.2, 22.3,
     22.4, 22.5, 22.6
routing 4.3, 34.3
row B.5.6, 20.3, 30.0, 33.1
rows 20.3, 33.2, 33.4, 33.6.9, 33.6.11
RPCs 34.4
rSize 34.6.8, 34.6.9
RTF 19.1.1, 19.2, 19.2.1, 19.2.2,
     19.2.3, 19.2.4, 19.2.5,
     19.2.6, 19.2.7, 19.2.8,
     19.2.10, 19.3.3, 19.3.5,
     19.3.9, 19.3.10, 19.4
rubber 0.4, 11.5.4, 11.5.5, 11.6.2,
     15.1, 15.9
rudimentary 10.3
rule A.2.3
rules 5.5, 33.2.5
running A.4.6, A.5.1, A.5.2, B.2, 2.3,
     9.1, 10.5, 11.5.4, 13.3,
     16.3.6, 17.5, 35.1, 35.2,
     35.3, 35.7, 35.8
runs A.7, A.8, 4.5, 11.5.3, 12.2, 13.6,
     34.1, 35.2, 35.3
runtime A.4.3, 0.2, 12.3, 12.4, 13.0,
     13.1, 13.3, 34.7.7
RUNTIME_CLASS 35.9
safe D.1, 11.4.6
safeguards 35.7
safely 8.2, 34.1, 35.4
safety 11.5.2
said 34.4
sake A.2, 13.2, 17.3.3
SAMP B.6.1, 14.4.2, 14.4.5, 14.4.6,
     19.1.1, 19.2, 19.2.9,
     19.3.1, 19.3.4, 19.3.5,
     19.3.7, 19.3.8, 34.5.1,
     34.5.3
SAMPDOC 14.4.4, 34.5.3, 34.6.3
sample A.2.9, A.7.1, B.4, D.0, D.2,
     D.5, D.6, D.8, 0.0, 0.2,
     5.2, 6.5.1, 8.3, 8.5, 11.4.6,
     11.5.3, 12.1.3, 14.4.1,
     14.4.2, 15.8, 15.8.4, 16.5,
     17.5, 18.5.6, 19.2.2,
     19.2.4, 19.2.6, 19.2.8,
     19.2.10, 28.2, 33.4,
     33.4.1, 33.7.1, 33.7.2,
     34.7.7
samples 0.2, 5.2, 7.3, 15.8, 16.5, 35.4
SAMPVIEW 14.4.5, 14.5, 34.5.3,
     34.5.5, 34.6.3
SAMPVW 14.4.4
sanely 34.3
satisfy 12.1.2, 15.3, 15.8.4
SaveAllModified 10.4.10
SaveChanges 8.5, 8.6.1, 8.6.2, 8.6.5,
     8.6.11
saved A.4.1, B.5.2, 8.5, 8.6.1, 8.6.3,
     8.6.5, 12.1.2, 14.3,
     15.3.5, 15.8.4, 17.4.6,

     34.5.5, 34.5.6
SaveFile 8.6.3
SaveFileAs 8.6.3, 8.6.4
SaveModifed 15.3.5
SaveModified 15.3.5
saver B.4
saves A.5.2, C.1, 8.6.2, 10.4.10, 12.3,
     13.3, 14.1, 14.3, 15.2.6,
     15.3.3, 15.5, 15.6.7,
     17.4.3, 18.4.4, 23.7, 33.1,
     33.5, 34.2, 34.3, 34.5.5
saving A.4.1, 4.7, 6.4, 7.2, 10.4.10,
     13.3, 13.6, 15.2.6, 15.2.9,
     26.2
saw A.6, A.7, A.8, 4.0, 8.1, 8.5, 11.4.7,
     11.4.8, 12.1.2, 14.4.6,
     15.2.1, 15.5, 15.5.3,
     15.8.1, 16.0, 22.0, 30.0,
     33.8, 34.1
say A.1.1, A.2.4, A.3.1, A.3.2, A.3.3,
     A.4.1, A.4.3, A.4.5, A.5,
     A.5.1, A.5.2, A.7.1, A.8,
     B.3.2, B.4.1, 1.1, 3.3, 4.1,
     6.7, 11.4.1, 11.4.4,
     11.5.5, 11.6.1, 12.1.2,
     12.2, 12.3, 14.1, 15.7.11,
     16.3, 17.4, 23.2, 23.3,
     31.3, 31.5, 34.1, 34.8,
     35.2, 35.7
saying 4.7
says A.4.3, A.4.4, A.5.1, A.6, 1.3, 3.3,
     4.1, 6.6.4, 15.7.4
SB_BOTTOM 4.6
SB_LINEDOWN 4.6
SB_LINEUP 4.6
SB_PAGEDOWN 4.6
SB_PAGEUP 4.6
SB_THUMBPOSITION 4.6
SB_TOP 4.6
SBS_HORIZ 4.6
SBS_VERT 4.6
scalable 7.3, 11.4.6
scale A.8.1, 11.5.5, 14.0
scaled 11.4.6, 11.5.1, 11.6.1
scales 11.6.1
scaling 11.6.1, 15.8.3, 34.5.2
scan A.2, 0.4, 8.6.7, 19.2, 34.5.5, 35.2,
     35.4
scans 13.5, 34.5.5
scattered 12.1.1
scenario 1.3
scene D.3, D.4, D.5, D.7
scenes 0.4, 4.1, 5.1, 8.3, 22.1, 23.1,
     30.0, 33.6.11, 34.4
schedule 35.7
scheduled 35.7
scheduler 35.7
scheduling 35.7
schema 12.3, 33.1
scheme A.1.1, 1.2, 28.0, 34.1
Schemes 28.0, 34.1
school A.5.2
science 33.9
scope A.2.4, A.4.3, A.4.4, A.7.1, D.5,
     8.5, 32.4
scoped 33.2.4
scratch B.3, 11.5.5, 16.3.1, 23.8, 30.2,
     34.1
scratched A.8.1
scratches 11.7

screens B.6.1, B.8.1, 0.1, 0.3, 11.2,
15.5, 15.6.1, 16.1.1,
17.1.1, 18.1.1, 19.1.1,
27.0, 27.2, 33.6.1, 33.7.1,
34.5.1, 34.5.5, 34.6.1,
34.7.1, Prf
Scribble 15.9
script B.5.1, B.5.2, 6.1, 6.3, 6.3.2,
6.3.7, 6.4, 6.6.1, 6.7.2,
6.7.3, 8.4, 10.4.4, 10.4.5,
10.4.6, 10.4.7, 10.4.8
scripts 6.1, 6.3, 6.3.7
scroll 0.4, 1.1, 1.2, 1.3, 2.1, 4.6, 4.8,
5.0, 5.1, 5.2, 5.3, 8.1, 9.1,
9.2, 9.4, 9.5, 11.2, 11.5.5,
15.5, 15.5.4, 15.5.5,
15.5.6, 15.5.7, 15.6,
15.7.9, 15.7.10, 15.8.4,
17.5, 18.1, 18.1.2, 18.4.6,
22.2, 22.5, 33.7.6, 34.2
scrollable 5.1, 15.6, 15.7, 15.7.1,
15.8.1, 15.9
scrolled 15.5, 34.5.7
scrolling 0.4, 4.6, 9.1, 11.5.5, 15.0,
15.5, 15.5.4, 15.5.6,
15.6.1, 22.0, 34.5.7
scrolls 4.6, 8.1, 8.2, 8.4, 15.5.4
SDI B.6.1, D.1, 0.4, 14.1, 14.3, 15.0,
15.1, 15.2, 15.2.1, 15.3,
15.3.1, 15.4, 15.5.2, 17.0,
17.1.1, 17.2, 17.3.1,
17.4.7, 18.1, 18.1.1,
18.1.7, 18.1.15, 18.2,
20.1, 27.1, 29.4, 32.3,
33.6.1, 33.7.1, 33.7.2,
34.5.1, 34.6.1, 35.3
seamless A.1.1, A.6, 34.1, 35.1
seamlessly A.1.1, 23.9
Search B.4.1, 2.3.1, 3.3, 3.5, 4.4, 4.7,
5.1, 5.2, 7.6, 8.3, 8.4,
8.6.7, 8.6.8, 8.6.10, 10.2,
10.4.10, 13.3, 16.2, 19.2,
19.2.3, 19.2.4, 19.2.8,
19.2.10, 19.3.6, 25.7,
26.1, 29.2, 32.4, 33.9, Prf
SearchDown 7.6
searching 5.2, 6.7, 8.7, 9.4, 12.2, 12.3,
12.4
seconds 10.3, 12.1.3, 18.4.5, 27.1, 35.2
sections A.2, B.3, B.4, B.6.1, B.7, 0.2,
2.3, 3.1, 4.2, 6.1, 6.5, 6.7,
8.6, 10.4, 10.5, 11.3,
11.4.7, 11.5, 12.1, 13.1,
14.4.4, 14.4.6, 14.5, 15.1,
15.5, 15.5.3, 15.6.1,
15.6.13, 15.8, 15.8.2,
15.9, 17.4, 18.1, 19.2,
30.1, 33.2, 33.4, 33.5,
34.6.3, 34.6.5, 34.7,
34.7.6, 34.8.1, 34.8.13,
Prf
sector 35.7
sectors 35.7
secure A.7.2
security 33.1
seeing 8.7
seek 12.1.1
Seeking 12.1.1
seem A.1.1, A.4.2, A.7.2, D.6, 1.3, 2.3,
10.4, 14.0, 15.3, 17.3.4,

33.7.2, 34.1, 34.5.5, 35.2
seemed 8.7
seems A.5.1, 1.2, 4.7, 17.4, Prf
seen A.1.1, A.3.3, A.4.6, A.5.1, A.5.3,
A.6, A.7, A.8, B.1.2,
B.3.1, B.5.3, 1.3, 1.4,
2.3.3, 2.5, 3.3, 3.5, 4.2,
4.3, 4.5, 4.6, 5.2, 6, 6.6.8,
6.7, 7.2, 7.6, 8.1, 8.6.4,
8.6.11, 9.4, 11.2, 11.4.6,
11.6.2, 12.2, 12.3, 13.2,
13.8, 14.4.1, 14.4.5, 15.0,
15.1, 15.9, 16.3, 16.6,
17.0, 17.4, 17.6, 18.1.12,
18.4.3, 18.4.6, 18.5.6,
19.2, 19.3.5, 19.5, 21.1.8,
25.7, 33.1, 34.1, 34.5.7,
34.6.3, 34.7, 34.7.1,
34.8.1, 34.9, 35.8, Prf
sees A.3.2, 1.3, 8.5, 11.5.3, 11.6.2,
19.2.5, 33.1, 34.2, 35.2
segment 10.3
segments A.3.2, 11.4.5
selectable 20.5
selected B.4.6, B.5.6, B.6.1, B.7.1, 6.4,
6.5, 7.2, 7.3, 7.4, 7.5, 8.1,
8.2, 8.6.7, 8.6.10, 9.1, 9.3,
9.4, 11.4.6, 18.1, 18.4.2,
18.4.4, 18.4.6, 18.4.7,
19.1.1, 20.3, 20.7, 22.2,
22.5, 22.6, 23.3, 25.2,
25.6, 26.3, 26.4, 29.2,
30.0, 31.3, 32.1, 33.2,
33.2.1, 33.7.4, 34.5.5,
34.6.8
selecting B.1.3, B.2, B.3, B.3.1, B.6.6,
B.7, B.7.6, 0.2, 6.4, 9.4,
9.5, 11.4.6, 15.4, 15.8.3,
16.3.5, 16.3.6, 18.1.8,
19.1.2, 20.5, 26.4, 33.4.1,
34.6.5, 34.8.4
selection A.4.1, B.3, 1.3, 5.1, 7.2, 7.4,
7.5, 8.2, 9.1, 9.3, 9.4, 9.5,
15.8, 18.4.2, 18.4.3,
18.4.6, 22.2, 25.5, 26.2,
33.2, 33.2.2, 33.7.2
selections 7.3, 9.3, 9.5
selectively 35.3, 35.6
SelectObject 11.4.2, 11.6.2, 29.4
selects A.4.1, B.6.1, 1.3, 6.4, 6.5, 6.6.7,
6.6.8, 7.2, 8.6.7, 8.6.10,
9.1, 9.4, 15.2.6, 15.3,
15.3.1, 16.2, 18.1.12,
18.2, 18.4.2, 18.5.3, 20.7,
21.1.8, 22.5, 28.1
SelectString 9.4
self B.4.1, C.1, 0.1, 0.3, 3.1, 7.5,
15.2.5, 18.1.12, 25.0,
25.1, 25.3, 25.4, 25.5,
25.6, 25.9, 26.0, 26.2,
26.4, 29.1
selfdrawn 25.9
semester A.3.2
semicolons 4.3, 19.2, 19.2.3
send C.0, 4.1, 4.2, 4.3, 7.0, 21.1.8,
23.1, 23.7, 29.1, 31.4,
33.1, 33.4, 33.5, 33.6.4,
33.6.10, 34.1, 34.8, 35.2,
35.10
sending 1.3, 4.4, 18.4.3, 23.1, 30.0,

31.4, 33.2.1
SendMessage 32.4
sends 4.2, 4.3, 4.4, 4.5, 4.7, 6.5, 7.6,
18.4.2, 18.4.7, 25.4, 25.5,
31.4, 32.5, 32.7, 33.6.10,
33.6.11, 33.7.6
sense A.1, A.2.4, A.4.3, 0.4, 1.4, 2.3,
3.3, 13.6, 18.4.6, 23.8,
34.5.5
senses 35.1, 35.4
sensitive B.4.1, 0.4, 4.1, 4.4, 8.7,
10.4.10, 11.4.1, 13.6,
14.1, 15.2.1, 19.1, 19.1.1,
19.1.2, 19.3, 19.3.5,
19.3.8, 19.3.10
sensitivity 3.2
sent A.2.5, 4.4, 4.5, 5.2, 5.3, 18.4.6,
23.2, 23.7, 25.2, 25.4,
29.1, 29.2, 31.1, 31.4,
32.1, 33.6.11
sentence 34.1
separate A.1.1, A.4.4, 1.5, 3.3, 6.5.3,
7.2, 7.6, 10.3, 11.4.6,
12.3, 14.3, 14.4.2, 15.6,
16.5, 18.5, 19.2, 19.4,
20.6, 20.7, 26.2, 33.1,
33.7.6, 33.8.4, 34.1, 34.3,
34.4, 34.8.1, 35.1, 35.2,
35.3, 35.7, 35.9
separated A.2.3, A.4.2, 8.2, 18.4.1,
18.5, 19.2, 19.2.3, 30.1
separately A.3.2, B.5.1, 3.3, 12.4,
14.4.1, 15.6, 35.9
Separating 11.4.6, 19.2.3
separation 14.3
separator A.2.3, 6.4, 32.7
separators 3.1, 34.6.4
sequenced 10.2
sequential 12.4, 20.1, 22.5
sequentially 13.5, 34.7.7
SERIAL 12.3
serializable 12.3
serialization 12.3, 12.4, 13.6, 15.2.6,
16.5
Serialize 10.4.10, 12.3, 14.4.4, 15.1,
15.2.5, 15.2.6, 15.2.9,
15.3, 15.3.1, 15.3.3,
15.3.5, 15.5.3, 15.6.7,
16.2, 16.3.3, 17.4.1,
17.4.3, 18.1.12, 18.2,
25.0, 33.7.2, 34.5.3,
34.5.5, 34.5.7
serialized 12.3, 12.4, 16.4, 34.5.5
SerializeRaw 16.3.3
serializes 12.3, 15.3, 16.2, 18.2, 34.5.5
serializing 34.5.5
series A.5.2, A.6, C.1, 0.2, 15.3, 18.2
serve D.7, 3.1, 13.6
Server B.6.6, 0.3, 0.4, 10.1, 14.1, 33.0,
33.1, 33.2, 33.2.1, 33.2.2,
33.2.3, 33.2.4, 33.2.5,
33.4, 33.4.1, 33.4.2, 33.5,
33.6.4, 33.6.5, 33.6.10,
33.6.11, 33.7, 34.4,
34.5.2, 34.5.3, 34.5.5,
34.6, 34.6.1, 34.6.2,
34.6.3, 34.6.4, 34.6.5,
34.6.7, 34.6.8, 34.6.10,
34.7, 34.7.1, 34.7.2,
34.7.7, Prf

Servers B.6.6, 0.4, 33.0, 33.1, 33.2,
    33.2.5, 33.3, 33.4.2, 34.0,
    34.4, 34.5, 34.5.5, 34.6,
    34.6.4, 34.6.9, 34.7, 34.9,
    Prf
serves 11.3
serviced 35.7
services C.0, C.1, 10.5, 33.1, 34.1,
    34.2, 34.4, 34.7, 35.0,
    35.4, 35.7
servicing 35.7
session B.1.1, 0.1
SetArray 14.4.4
SetAt 12.1.2, 12.2, 12.4, 12.5
SetAtGrow 12.2
SetBackColor 34.8
SetBkColor 11.4.8, 25.7
SetBorderStyle 34.8
SetBrushOrigin 11.4.8
SetCapture 11.5.4, 29.1
SetCaretIndex 9.4
SetClipboardData 18.4.7
SetColumnWidth 9.2
SetCurSel 9.4
SetCursor 11.5.3
SetDepth 13.4
SetDialogBkColor 10.5
SetDlgItemInt 5.2, 5.3, 8.1, 17.1
SetDlgItemText 5.2, 5.3, 6.6.4, 8.1,
    34.8
SetDocSize 15.5.1, 15.6.5
SetEnabled 34.8
SetFieldDirty 33.5
SetFieldNull 33.5
SetFieldType 33.6.10
setfill A.2.3
SetFocus 5.3, 8.6.1, 32.5
SetFont 3.5, 5.2, 34.8
SetForeColor 34.8
SetHandle 8.2
SetHorizontalExtent 9.1
SetIcon 5.2, 6.3.7, 10.2
SetItemData 20.3, 25.8
SetItemHeight 25.6
SetItemRange 9.4
SetItemText 20.3
SetLength 12.1.1
SetLockingMode 33.5
SetMapMode 11.6.1
SetMaxPage 15.8.2, 15.8.4
SetMinPage 15.8.2
SetModified 15.1, 20.7
SetModifiedFlag 15.2.9, 15.3, 17.4.1
SetModify 8.2, 8.6.1
SetPaneInfo 18.4.6
SetPaneText 18.4.6
SetPasswordChar 8.1
SetPixel 11.4.7, 11.5.3, 15.2.3, 15.4.1,
    15.8.3, 29.1
SetPixelFormat D.1, D.5
SetPolyFillMode 11.4.5
setprecision A.2.3
SetPriorityClass 35.7
SetRange 4.6, 20.2
SetReadOnly 8.1, 8.2
SetRecStatus 18.4.6
SetRect 8.2, 12.1.4, 28.1
SetRectEmpty 12.1.4
SetRectNP 8.2
SetRegistryKey 10.1, 10.5

SetROP 11.5.4
sets A.1.1, A.7, B.2.1, D.1, D.2, D.6,
    3.5, 5.2, 5.3, 7.2, 7.5, 8.1,
    8.2, 8.6.1, 9.1, 10.2, 10.5,
    11.4.6, 11.4.7, 11.5.3,
    11.5.4, 11.5.5, 11.6.1,
    11.6.3, 12.1.1, 12.1.2,
    12.1.3, 12.1.4, 12.2, 12.3,
    13.2, 15.5.1, 15.5.4,
    15.7.9, 15.8.2, 18.4.2,
    18.5.3, 18.5.6, 22.2, 32.5,
    33.5, 33.6.2, 33.6.6,
    33.6.8, 33.6.10, 33.7,
    34.3, 35.4, 35.7
SetScrollSizes 15.5, 15.5.4, 15.8.3
SetSel 8.1, 8.2, 9.4
SetSelection 18.4.2, 18.4.6
SetSize 12.2, 13.2
SetStatus 12.1.1
SetTabStops 8.2, 9.2
SetTemp 17.4.1, 17.4.4
SetText 31.1, 34.8
SetTextAlign 11.4.6
SetTextCharacterExtra 11.4.8
SetThreadPriority 35.7
SetTimer 4.5, 27.1
setting A.4.4, B.2.2, D.1, D.2, 2.3.2,
    3.0, 4.6, 5.4, 11.5.3, 13.4,
    13.5, 18.3, 22.6, 23.1,
    33.5, 33,6,10, 34.7.9,
    35.7
Settings B.3, B.4, D.1, 1.2, 11.3,
    11.4.2, 20.7
SetTopIndex 9.4
setup B.8.7, B.8.9, 7.5, 10.4.10, 15.8,
    15.8.1, 18.5.1, 34.8.5
setw A.2.3
SetWindowLong 5.2
SetWindowPixelFormat D.1, D.5, D.7
SetWindowPos 32.2, 32.5
SetWindowText 23.2
Seven A.1, A.4.2, A.4.3, A.4.4, 0.2, 6.1,
    12.1.3, 35.7
Seventeen B.6.1
severe 11.5.3
severs 34.4
shading D.0
shaft 4.6, 15.5.4
shape A.3.1, D.2, 3.1, 4.4, 11.3, 11.4.8,
    11.5.3, 11.5.4, 11.6.1,
    29.1
shaped 25.7, 30.1
shapes D.2, 11.1, 11.3, 11.4, 11.4.3,
    11.5, 34.1
share A.3.1, 7.2, 7.6, 12.2, 19.2, 20.5,
    23.6, 34.1, 35.2, 35.7
shared A.3.1, A.7.1, B.3, 11.5.3, 12.3,
    19.1.1, 33.1, 34.1
sharing 12.1.1, 33.1
sheet B.8.9, 11.3, 15.8.3, 15.8.4,
    18.1.2, 18.4.1, 18.4.5,
    18.5, 20.5, 20.6, 20.7,
    28.3, 34.5.2, 34.5.6,
    34.7.7, 34.8.11, 34.8.12
sheets 0.1, 0.3, 0.4, 15.8.4, 20.0, 20.5,
    20.7, 20.8, 32.5, Prf
shell D.1, 10.4.10, 17.2, 29.4, 35.5
shift A.1.1, A.1.2, A.2.3, A.3.3, 6.5.3,
    9.3, 11.5.2, 19.1.2, 19.3.5
shifted A.5.2

ShiftF 19.3.10
shifting A.2.3
shipped B.8.4, 5.2, 8.3
ships 3.5, 11.4.6, 34.7.7
short 3.3, 9.2, 10.3, 11.4.1, 14.4.1,
    22.2, 23.2, 34.7.8, 34.8.6,
    34.8.10
shortcut 11.4.3, 32.6
shortly 4.3, 12.1.3, 22.5
shorts D.2
shot 11.6.2
shouldn A.4.5
show B.1.6, B.2, D.0, D.1, D.2, 0.3,
    0.4, 1.0, 1.1, 1.5, 6.1, 6.2,
    6.5.3, 6.8, 7.2, 8.5, 10.2,
    11.5.5, 13.0, 13.1, 14.4.6,
    14.6, 15.1, 15.7.11, 20.3,
    20.4, 22.5, 29.2, 32.5,
    33.3, 33.4.4, 33.5, 34.0,
    34.7, 35.0, 35.2, Prf
ShowDropDown 9.5
showed 15.7.11, 18.5, 34.5.7
showing B.4.1, 0.4, 1.3, 3.3, 6.4, 8.1,
    8.7, 9.2, 12.1.3, 14.4,
    15.0, 20.5
ShowSplashScreen 27.1
ShowWindow 2.3.2, 27.1, 32.3, 32.5
shrink 9.1, 12.2, 15.7.9, 28.1
ShrinkDialog 28.1
shrinking 15.7.11
shrinks 15.7.11
shut 8.6.11
shuts 8.6.11
side A.4.4, A.5, A.6, A.7.1, B.4.1,
    B.4.4, 6.3.7, 10.4.7, 13.2,
    16.3, 21, 21.1.7, 30.1,
    32.7, 34.8.7
sidebar 3.3
sides 3.3
sign A.3.2, A.7.1, 7.1, 10.2
signal 15.7.9, 18.4.6, 21.1.8, 33.1,
    33.6.3
signals 25.1
significant A.1.2, 0.1, 15.8.3, 33.1
significantly 1.0, 1.1, 2.1, 5.5, 10.4.10,
    12.1.2, 13.5, 33.6.10,
    35.0, 35.2, 35.8
signifies 34.4
signify A.3.2, 15.7.9
silent 15.5
Silicon D.0
similar A.2.3, A.2.10, A.6, A.8, B.4.1,
    1.3, 2.3.3, 3.3, 4.5, 8.3,
    9.3, 9.5, 11.4.6, 11.5.1,
    11.5.5, 11.6.3, 12.1.3,
    14.3, 15.7.5, 21.1.8, 22.4,
    23.1, 23.7, 25.0, 26.3,
    26.4, 26.5, 29.1, 32.4,
    33.4, 33.6.2, 34.1, 34.6.9,
    34.8
similarities A.3.3
similarity 11.4.6, 26.3
Similarly 11.4.8, 12.1.1, 35.7, Prf
simpler 24.1, 30.2, 35.1
simplest A.2.10, A.8, B.6.1, 2.5, 3.0,
    6.2, 7.1, 10.4, 10.5, 14.1,
    23.7, 33.6, 35.3, 35.4,
    35.10, Prf
simplicity 2.1, 2.3.1, 3.0, 11.5.1, 12.1.3
simplification 34.1

simplified A.2.11, 11.6.3, 29.4
simplifies 35.1, 35.8
simplify B, 12, 12.1.1, 15.1, 15.3.7, 22.0, 22.7, 25.8, 29.2, 30.0, 31.6
simplifying 18.4.3
simulate B.3.1, 11.5.3, 34.8, 35.8
simulated 7.3
simulates D.6, 35.1
simulation 35.1
simulator 11.6.2
simultaneously B.2.2, 1.2, 2.3.1, 3.3, 4.5, 7.6, 9.3, 11.4.5, 11.4.7, 14.3, 15.4, 16.0, 16.3, 17.2, 18.1, 18.1.15, 32.4, 33.1, 35.1, 35.2
sin 3.3
since B.3, B.7.4, D.1, D.2, D.6, 13.5, 18.4.2, 20.2, 25.6, 32.6
sincerely Prf 35.2
singleline 8.1
singlestep A.8
site C.1, 13.4, 33.4, 34.5.3
sites C.0
sits 1.1
sitting A.3.2, 11.4.1
situation A.2.3, A.7.1, 0.3, 11.3, 11.6.2, 12.4, 13.5, 13.6, 13.6.1
situations B.5.3, 7.0, 8.6.1, 9.4, 11.2, 11.4.6, 11.6, 11.6.2, 12.1.2, 13.0, 13.4, 13.6, 18.4.3, 28.0, 32.0, 34.1, 35.2
Six A.1, B, B.6.1, 2.1, 2.3, 2.5, 3.0, 3.1, 3.4, 7.2, 9.1, 10.5, 11.6.1, 11.6.2, 12.1.3, 12.2, 12.3, 15.3, 16.1.1, 18.1.1, 18.4.6, 19.1.1, 20.0, 33.6.1, 34.7.1, Prf
sixth B.6.4, 3.1, 13.5
sizable 5.1
sized 9.1, 11.4.1, 11.4.6, 34.3, 34.5.6
SIZEDLG 15.7.7, 15.7.8, 15.7.9
sizeof A.4.4
sizes B.5.3, 7.3, 8.4, 9.1, 11.2, 11.4.6, 11.6.1, 15.7.9, 15.7.10, 15.7.11, 18.4.6, 20.6, 26.3, 26.5
sizing 4.4, 4.5, 5.2, 7.3, 8.4, 11.2, 11.4.6, 11.5.3, 15.5, 34.5.6
sketch 1.1, 5.1
skill 11.0
skills C.1, Prf
skim 0.3, 33.0
skip A.1, 25.4
skipped 22.5
slash 32.1
sleep 35.1, 35.3, 35.4, 35.7
sleeping 35.3, 35.4, 35.7
sleeps 35.7
slice 35.2, 35.7
slices 35.2, 35.7
slicing 10.3, 35.2
slide 34.5.4
Slider 20.0
sliding 5.1
slight 18.1.5, 35.2

slightly A.1.1, A.4.6, 1.3, 2.3, 3.3, 5.3, 9.3, 11.5.3, 17.6, 18.5, 19.2, 21.1.9, 33.4.1, 35.2
slim 34.4
slow 11.4.7, 12.2, 12.4, 13.5
slower D.5
slowly 9.4, 13.1, 29.1, 35.8
small A.1.1, A.5.1, B, B.1.2, B.2.1, B.3, B.5.1, B.5.6, 1.1, 1.4, 2.1, 2.3, 3.1, 3.3, 4.6, 5.0, 5.3, 6, 6.6, 8.4, 8.5, 9.2, 9.5, 11.5.2, 11.5.5, 11.6.1, 11.6.2, 14.3, 15.3, 15.8, 15.8.3, 18.1.2, 18.1.3, 18.4, 29.1, 32.0, 32.2, 33.1, 34.3, 34.5.5, 34.6.7, 34.8.4, 35.3, 35.8
smaller A.4.4, A.8.1, C.1, D.2, D.6, 1.3, 2.1, 9.5, 11.4.6, 11.6.1, 13.1, 18.1.2, 18.5.5
Smalltalk 34.1
smart 5.3, 35.4
smarter 28.3
Smith 33.2.2, 33.2.3
Smiths 33.2.2, 33.2.3
smooth 11.2, 11.4.7, 35.2
smoother 10.3, 11.5.3
smoothly 11.6.2
smoothness 35.2
snapshot 13.5, 33.7.6, 33.8.2
snapshots 13.5, 33.7.6
socket 9.4
soft 8.2
software C.1, 0.1, 1.2, 2.1, 34.3
sold 6.7
solid 3.1, 3.4, 11.3, 11.4.2, 11.4.3, 11.5.4, 11.7, 29.2
solution A.5.2, D.6, 15.5.6, 15.8.3, 16.4, 16.5, 18.1.11, 23.2, 23.3, 25.0, 25.5, 27.0, 28.3, 30.2, 31.3, 31.5, 33.3, 34.1, 34.4
solutions 15.8.3, 30.2, 31.3
solve A.1.1, A.5.2, D.5, 0.0, 5.2, 6, 6.7, 11.4.4, 11.5.3, 11.6.1, 11.6.2, 13.3, 13.5, 15.8.4, 16.5, 18.4.2, 23.4, 25.6, 33.1, 34.1, 34.4, 34.5.2, 34.5.6, 35.2, 35.4, 35.8, Prf
solved A.1.1, A.8, 8.6.10, 15.6, 33.3, 34.1, 35.1, 35.8
solves A.1.1, A.4.2, 11.4.1, 16.5, 18.1.5, 33.7.6, 35.4
solving 15.7.9
somehow A.3.2, 33.1, 34.1
someone A.1.1, A.5, 33.1, 34.4
something A.1.1, A.2, A.3.1, A.4.3, A.5.1, A.5.2, A.8, B.3.1, B.7.4, 1.3, 2.3, 4.2, 6, 6.6.4, 7.3, 8.3, 8.6.10, 10.1, 11.3, 11.4.1, 11.4.6, 11.4.7, 11.5.2, 11.5.3, 11.5.4, 11.6.3, 12.3, 13.3, 13.6, 15.4, 15.5.2, 15.5.5, 15.8.1, 15.8.3, 16.3.4, 18.5.5, 21.1.8, 22.3, 23.1, 24.0, 25.0, 26.1, 27.0, 29.1, 29.3, 30.1, 31.5,

32.4, 33.4.2, 34.1, 34.2, 34.8.4, 35.7
sometimes A.1, A.2.4, B.2.2, 10.6, 12.1.1, 25.0, 26.0, 32.2, Prf
somewhat 1.3, 4.0, 13.1, 14.4.2, 20.2
somewhere A.3.3, B.2.2, 3.3, 13.2, 15.2.6, 15.6.2, 16.3.5, 19.2.5
soon A.5.2, 11.3, 11.4.6, 18.1.2, 34.5.6, 35.2
sophisticated A.2.10, 15.1
sort A.1.1, A.3.1, A.6, 0.0, 1.1, 1.3, 1.4, 5.1, 8.3, 10.4, 10.4.10, 10.5, 11.5.2, 11.5.5, 12.1.1, 13.6, 15.8.1, 15.8.3, 16.5, 17.4.5, 18.1, 18.4.7, 18.5.6, 18.6, 20.3, 20.4, 22.5, 24.0, 24.3, 25.9, 29.2, 33.1, 33.2, 33.2.3, 33.4.2, 33.5, 33.6.6, 33.6.10, 34.1, 34.8, 35.1
sorted A.5.1, 9.1, 9.4, 9.5, 12.4, 20.3, 20.4, 25.2, 25.6, 33.6.7, 33.6.9, 34.4
SortedInsert A.5.1
SortedList A.5.1
Sorting 9.1, 12.2, 18.1.2, 20.3, 25.2, 26.4, 33.2.3, 33.6.6
SortItems 20.3
sorts A.5, 6.7, 15.5.6, 20.3, 34.1, 35.7
sound A.3.1
sounds 11.5.3
source A.1, A.1.1, A.5, B.1.2, B.1.5, B.1.6, B.2, B.2.2, B.3, B.3.1, B.3.2, D.6, D.7, 0.2, 1.5, 3.3, 6.7, 10.2, 10.3, 10.4.10, 10.7, 12.1.1, 12.1.2, 13.2, 13.3, 14.4.1, 14.4.4, 15.3, 15.3.1, 19.0, 19.1, 19.1.1, 19.2, 23.9, 25.7, 31.2, 31.4, 31.5, 32.1, 33.4, 33.4.1, 33.4.2, 33.4.3, 33.6.2, 33.7.1, 33.7.2, 33.9, 34.5.3, 34.6.3, Prf
sources D.7, 0.4, 3.2, 33.1, 33.4.1
space A.2.3, A.2.4, A.4.3, A.4.4, D.2, D.6, D.7, 0.4, 3.3, 5.2, 9.0, 9.5, 11.5.5, 11.6.1, 12.1.1, 12.1.2, 12.2, 12.4, 13.6, 13.7, 15.5.6, 15.5.7, 15.8.3, 18.4.6, 18.5.6, 25.6, 26.2, 33.1, 34.1, 34.2, 34.4, 34.6.9, 34.8.1, 34.9, 35.2
spaced A.2.3, 15.8.3
spaces A.2.3
spacing 11.4.8, 18.5.4, 26.4
span 30.1
SpanExcluding 12.1.2
SpanIncluding 12.1.2
Spanish 6.1, 6.7
spans B.4.1
spawned 35.3
speaks 6.7
spec 34.9
special B.4, 4.3, 5.2, 6.1, 6.5.3, 7.3, 11.2, 11.4.3, 11.5.4, 11.6,

12.3, 13.6.2, 14.4.4,
14.4.6, 14.5, 15.7.9, 20.7,
25.0, 25.3, 25.5, 25.6,
26.2, 27.0, 28.1, 31.4,
32.0, 32.1, 32.4, 33.3,
34.1, 34.2
specialization 11.1
specialized 1.1, 1.3, 8.1, 11.1, 11.4.1,
17.0, 19.0, 25.5
specialty C.1
specifically A.4.3, 1.1, 3.2, 12.1.2,
33.2.2, 33.2.3, 33.7.4,
34.2, 34.8, 34.8.1
specification 1.1, 26.1, 34.7, 34.8.9
specifications 6.5.3, 15.5.6
specificity A.5
specifics A.4.6, A.5, B.1.2, 1.3, 13.3,
33.0
specified A.5.1, B.3, B.4, B.4.5, B.5.6,
D.1, 2.3.3, 3.2, 3.3, 3.4,
4.3, 4.7, 5.2, 6.7, 7.3, 8.1,
8.2, 9.1, 9.2, 9.4, 9.5,
10.4.10, 10.6, 11.4.5,
11.4.5, 11.4.6, 11.5.2,
12.1.3, 12.2, 13.6, 15.4,
16.2, 19.2, 19.2.5, 20.7,
22.6, 23.5, 25.4, 25.6,
27.1, 29.1, 30.1, 33.5,
33.6.1, 33.6.10, 33.7.1,
33.7.2, 34.5.7, 35.3, 35.7
specifier 19.2
specifies A.4.6, A.5.1, D.1, 2.3.2, 2.3.3,
3.1, 3.3, 3.5, 4.4, 5.3, 7.1,
7.2, 8.1, 9.1, 9.2, 9.3,
10.1, 10.4.10, 10.5, 11.3,
11.4.3, 11.4.4, 11.5.3,
15.5.3, 19.2.3, 26.1,
33.6.4, 34.8.11
specify A.1.1, A.2.7, A.3.2, A.4.6, B.3,
B.8.7, 3.3, 3.5, 4.1, 4.7,
6.6.8, 7.3, 7.4, 9.3, 11.4.5,
11.4.6, 12.1.2, 15.5,
15.5.3, 15.6.7, 18.5.2,
19.2, 22.5, 28.2, 32.5,
33.6.6, 33.6.8, 34.1, 34.8,
34.8.5, 35.3
specifying D.2, 5.3, 11.4.4, 34.4
spectacular 2.1
specular D.7
speed D.3, 0.4, 5.5, 11.5.5, 12.1.1,
13.2, 34.4, 35.2, 35.7, Prf
speeds 14.4.1
spell Prf
spelled Prf
spelling 34.3, Prf
spend A.1, D.1, 19.0, 20.1
spends 8.6.7
spent 8.7, 14.0
Spin 20.0, 20.1, 20.2, 33.5
spins 11.4.6
spirit 12
splash 0.1, 0.3, 0.4, 27.0, 27.1, 27.2,
Prf
Split B.6.5, 14.3, 15.6, 21, 21.1.1,
21.1.4
splittable 15.6, 15.7.1, 15.8.1, 15.9
splitter B.6.5, B.6.6, 0.4, 15.0, 15.6,
15.6.1, 15.6.13
spray 11.5.3
spread 11.2

spreadsheet 14.3, 34.1, 34.2, 34.4,
34.6.2, 34.7, 35.2
spreadsheetness 34.1
spreadsheets 5.1
sprintf A.2.5, 5.2
SQL 0.4, 33.0, 33.2, 33.2.1, 33.2.2,
33.2.3, 33.2.4, 33.2.5,
33.3, 33.4, 33.4.1, 33.4.2,
33.4.4, 33.5, 33.6.3,
33.6.4, 33.6.10, 33.6.11,
33.9
square A.5.2, 4.6, 15.8.3
squares A.3.1
SRCAND 25.7
SRCCOPY 25.7
SRCINVERT 25.7
SRCPAINT 25.7
SRVRITEM 34.6.3, 34.6.8, 34.6.9
SS 3.2
SS_BLACKFRAME 3.2, 3.4, 6.6.4
SS_BLACKRECT 3.2, 3.4
SS_CENTER 3.2, 3.3, 5.2
SS_GRAYFRAME 3.2, 3.4
SS_GRAYRECT 3.2, 3.4
SS_ICON 3.2, 3.6, 6.2, 6.3.7, 6.6.4
SS_LEFT 3.2, 3.3
SS_LEFTNOWORDWRAP 3.2, 3.3
SS_NOPREFIX 3.2
SS_RIGHT 3.2, 3.3
SS_SIMPLE 3.2
SS_USERITEM 3.2
SS_WHITEFRAME 3.2, 3.4
SS_WHITERECT 3.2, 3.4
sscanf A.2.5
stable 33.6.5
stack A.1.1, A.4.4, A.4.5, A.7, A.7.1,
B.2, B.2.3, B.3.1, D.2,
D.3, 13.1, 13.2, 35.2
stack_destroy A.1.1
stack_init A.1.1
stacked A.2.3
stacking 3.4
stacks A.1.1, A.4.4, A.7
staff C.1
stage 18.1, 34.3
stall 7.6, 10.3, 35.7
stalls 35.2
stand 4.6, 13.2, 15.2.6, 34.1, 34.2, 34.3
standalone 34.3
standard A.1.1, A.2.3, A.5.1, A.7,
B.1.3, B.2, B.7.4, B.8.4,
1.1, 1.2, 1.4, 2.1, 2.3, 3.1,
3.3, 4.7, 5.1, 6.5.3, 6.6.4,
7.2, 7.6, 8.3, 10.2, 10.4,
10.4.10, 11.4.2, 11.5.1,
11.5.3, 11.6.3, 12.1.1,
12.1.3, 12.3, 13.2, 13.4,
13.5, 14.4.1, 14.4.2,
14.4.4, 15.1, 15.3, 15.3.3,
15.3.8, 15.4, 15.7, 15.8.1,
16.2, 16.3, 17.0, 18.2,
18.4.6, 18.5.2, 18.6, 19.1,
19.1.1, 19.1.2, 19.2,
19.3.7, 20.3, 22.1, 22.6,
23.1, 23.4, 23.8, 24.1,
25.0, 27.0, 30.0, 33.2,
33.3, 33.7.2, 33.7.5, 34.1,
34.2, 34.3
standardization D.0
standardized 7.4, 14.1, 34.1, 34.3

standardizes 33.3
standpoint A.3.2, 1.3, 12.4, 17.5, 35.2
stands A.4.2, 33.7.6, Prf
startling 15.8.1
StartPage 11.6.3
starts A.3.2, A.4.3, A.5.2, A.7.1, 2.3,
3.5, 4.6, 8.6.7, 9.3, 10.3,
11.4.1, 11.4.3, 11.4.6,
11.5.4, 11.5.5, 11.6.1,
11.6.3, 12.1.1, 13.5,
14.4.2, 15.5.6, 15.8.2,
16.3.6, 17.3.5, 26.2, 27.1,
32.3, 33.0, 34.2, 34.5.3,
34.6.3, 35.2, 35.7, 35.8,
Prf
starvation 35.7
starve 35.7
state A.8, B.1.1, B.2, B.3.2, D.2, D.3,
0.4, 2.3.2, 6.5.1, 8.1,
11.4.7, 11.4.8, 11.5.4,
13.2, 13.4, 13.5, 15.4,
18.1, 18.1.13, 18.4.1,
18.4.2, 18.4.3, 18.4.6,
19.3.5, 22.2, 22.5, 23.1,
25.2, 25.6, 25.7, 27.1,
28.1, 30.0, 31.1, 31.4,
33.1, 33.2.4
stated D.1, 15.8.4
statement A.1.1, A.2.3, A.4.4, A.6, A.7,
A.7.1, B.3.2, 4.6, 7.1,
13.2, 13.3, 13.4, 13.5,
13.6.1, 14.4.1, 15.2.6,
15.6.2, 15.7.11, 18.1.5,
18.1.10, 18.1.12, 18.5.3,
22.0, 23.7, 33.2, 33.2.1,
33.2.2, 33.2.3, 33.2.4,
33.4.4, 33.5, 33.6.3,
33.6.4, 33.6.5, 33.6.10,
33.7, 33.7.6
states 15.4, 35.7
static A.7.2, B.3, B.5.6, 1.2, 1.4, 2.1,
2.2, 2.3, 2.3.2, 2.3.3, 3.0,
3.1, 3.2, 3.4, 3.5, 3.6, 4.6,
4.7, 5.0, 5.1, 5.2, 5.3, 5.4,
6.2, 6.6.4, 7.6, 9.2, 9.3,
9.5, 10.2, 11.5, 11.6.2,
12.1.3, 15.7.5, 15.8.4,
17.1.2, 17.3.4, 18.1.2,
18.1.8, 20.1, 20.3, 22.0,
23.2, 29.0, 29.1, 29.3,
33.7.3, 34.6.3
statics 17.1.2, 34.6.5, 34.8.12
statistician 33.1
statistics 13.5, 33.2
status B.1.6, 0.4, 6.4, 11.6.3, 12.1.1,
14.1, 15.0, 15.2.1, 18.0,
18.1.11, 18.4, 18.4.5,
18.4.6, 19.1.1, 20.0, 25.3,
30.0, 30.1, 31.0, 32.2,
33.5, 34.2, Prf
stay 4.4, 25.7, 27.0, 34.8.6
stays A.1.1, A.5
STDAFX D.1, 0.4, 14.4.1, 15.2.2,
15.2.6, 15.6.2
stdin A.2.3
stdio A.1.1, A.2.3
stdout A.2.3
steer 14.5
stem 34.8.1
stereo D.1

sticking 3.5
still A.5.1, A.7.1, D.1, D.2, D.3, D.5, D.6, 2.2, 4.6, 11.5.2, 11.5.5, 11.6.1, 13.3, 13.5, 15.8.4, 18.1, 18.5, 23.1, 23.2, 23.3, 25.4, 27.1, 32.4, 35.2, 35.7, Prf
STILL_ACTIVE 35.8
stipulation 13.2
stk A.4.4, A.4.5
stock B.8.5, B.8.7, 18.4.6, 19.2.7, 34.8, 34.8.1, 34.8.4, 34.8.5, 34.8.11, 34.8.13
stolen A.2.3
stop A.2.5, B.2, B.2.2, 7.1, 9.2, 10.2, 11.5.4, 13.2, 18.5.6, 26.1, 26.3, 32.1, 34.5.5, 35.3, 35.7
stopped 35.3, Prf
stops 4.7, 8.2, 9.2, 10.3, 18.4.1, 35.2
storage 18.2, 33.1, 34.1, 34.4, 34.5.3
store B.3, 6.7, 10.5, 11.4.6, 11.5.3, 12, 12.1.3, 12.3, 12.4, 15.1, 15.8.4, 17.4, 18.1.12, 20.6, 22.6, 26.2, 29.1, 29.4, 33.0, 33.1, 33.2, 33.6.4, 34.4, 34.5.5, 34.6.6
stored A.1.1, D.3, 8.2, 8.6.7, 10.5, 11.1, 11.4.6, 11.5.5, 12.1.1, 12.1.2, 12.3, 15.5.6, 16.2, 17.4, 18.4.5, 22.6, 23.1, 23.5, 26.4, 28.1, 33.1, 33.2.5, 34.4
stores B.1.2, 3.3, 10.5, 11.3, 11.4.6, 11.5.4, 13.5, 14.3, 14.4.5, 16.2, 18.1, 33.1, 33.2, 34.4, 34.6.5
storing 11.5.2, 13.6, 16.2, 29.1, 33.1
str 13.3
straight A.1, A.3.2, 1.0, 9.5, 17.2
straightforward A.1, A.2.3, A.3.2, A.5.1, A.5.2, 1.1, 1.4, 5.4, 6, 6.1, 8.7, 11.0, 11.5.5, 16.4, 16.5, 18.4.2, 18.4.4, 19.3.10, 19.5, 20.8, 23.9, 30.2, 34.8, Prf
strain 34.1
strange D.6
strategies 3.3
strcat A.1.1, 12.1.2
strcmp 12.1.2
strcoll 12.1.2
strcpy A.1.1, 12.1.2
stream A.2.3, A.2.5, 5.2, 12, 12.3, 35.2
strengths 14.4
stress 13.5
stretch 0.4, 11.5.4, 27.2, 29.2, 34.6.9, 34.6.10
StretchBlt 29.2
stretched 29.2, 29.3, Prf
stretches 11.5.4, 18.4.6, 34.6.7, 34.8.7
stretchy 18.4.6
strftime 3.3, 12.1.3
strictly B, 15.3, 15.5.3, 34.1
strikeout 7.3, 11.4.6
stringent 22.6
StringExact 22.5
stringHandle 8.2
stringPointer 8.2

strings A.1.1, A.2.3, A.2.5, B.5, 0.4, 5.2, 6.1, 6.7, 6.7.3, 7.6, 9.1, 9.4, 10.5, 12, 12.1, 12.1.2, 12.1.3, 12.5, 14.4.2, 16.3, 18.4.5, 19.2.3, 19.3, 19.3.5, 22.4, 22.5, 23.0, 25.0, 25.6, 26.2, 26.4, 28.1, 33.3, 33.6.10, 34.8, 35.2
strip 14.1
stripped B.6.1, 13.1, 34.7.7
stripping 14.1
strips 13.2
strive A.4.6
strlen 11.4.6, 12.1.2
stroke 11.5.4
stroked 11.2
strokes 11.2
strong 13.2
strongly A.4.2
Stroustrup A.1
strstr 12.1.2
strstrea A.2.5, 5.3, 18.4.1, 18.5.4
strstream 5.3
struct 12.1.4, 22.6
structur A.4.4
structure A.1.1, A.3.1, A.3.2, A.4.1, A.4.2, A.4.3, A.4.4, A.5.2, D.1, 1.2, 1.3, 1.4, 1.5, 2.0, 2.1, 2.5, 4.7, 5.0, 6.4, 7.2, 7.3, 7.5, 7.6, 8.2, 8.3, 8.5, 10.4.10, 10.6, 11.5.2, 11.5.3, 11.5.5, 12, 12.1.1, 12.1.2, 12.1.3, 14.3, 14.4.1, 15.2.4, 15.2.5, 15.3.8, 15.4.2, 15.4.3, 15.5, 15.5.6, 15.7.11, 15.8, 15.8.2, 15.8.4, 16.2, 18.2, 18.5.6, 20.3, 20.4, 21.1.7, 22.6, 25.6, 26.2, 32.6, 34.4, 34.5.3, 34.6.3, 34.6.4, 35.5, 35.7, 35.8
structured A.1.1, 0.3, 33.0, 33.2, 34.4, 34.5.3
structures A.3.1, A.3.2, A.4.2, A.4.4, A.7.2, 11.4.5, 11.7, 12, 12.1.1, 12.1.3, 12.1.4, 12.2, 14.4.4, 15.8.4, 18.0, 26.1, 35.8
struggle 11.5.3
strung A.2.3
stub 8.5
stubbed 8.5, 8.6
stubs 8.5, 8.6, 14.4.4, 15.8
students A.3.2
Studio 22.6
study A.2, 14.0
studying A.8.1, 20.1
stuff A.1.1
stunning Prf
style A.2.1, A.5.3, B.5.1, 1.3, 1.4, 2.3.2, 2.3.3, 3.1, 3.2, 3.3, 3.6, 4.0, 4.2, 4.3, 4.6, 5.2, 5.3, 6.2, 6.3.7, 7.1, 7.2, 7.3, 7.4, 7.5, 7.6, 8.1, 8.2, 9.1, 9.2, 9.3, 9.5, 11.3, 11.4.6, 11.5.3, 13.4, 17.2, 19.2, 20.1, 20.6, 21, 21.1, 21.1.1, 21.1.5, 21.2, 22.5, 23.1, 25.6, 26.1, 26.2,

26.3, 26.4, 27.1, 30.1, 32.5, 33.1, 34.6.7, 34.8
styles A.2.1, B.6.5, D.1, 0.4, 3.2, 3.4, 4.2, 4.3, 4.6, 5.3, 6.6.4, 6.6.5, 8.1, 9.1, 9.5, 17.0, 18.1.2, 18.4.1, 18.4.6, 20.1, 20.6, 25.6, 26.1, 26.3, 26.4, 26.5, 34.8
stylistically 15.7.9
stylized 34.4
sub A.1, 1.2, 1.3, 9.6, 16.5, 29.1, 34.3
subclass 23.4, 23.8, 24.1, 24.3
SubclassDlgItem 23.8, 24.1, 25.8
subclassed 25.8, Prf
subclasses 23.4, 25.8
subclassing 0.4, 23.8, 24.0, 24.1, 24.3, 35.8
SubclassWindow 23.8, 24.2, 25.8
subdirectory B.6.1
subdivide 19.2
subdivided 15.6.13, 33.1, 35.2
subdivides 18.4.3
subitem 20.3
subitems 20.3, 20.4
subject 2.3.2, 35.0, Prf
sublime 25.1
subsection 34.4
subsections 34.4
subsequent 11.3, 11.4.2, 11.4.6, 11.5.4, 15.1, 18.1.5
subsequently A.2.7
subset 33.2
subsidiary B.6.1
substantial 30.0
substitute 6.7, 6.7.3, 7.3, 11.4.5, 12.1.3, 12.5, 33.6.10
substitution 6.7.3
substring 8.6.7, 12.1.2, 16.5
subsystem 34.5.5
subsystems 34.0
subtle 15.4, 15.8.4, 16.4, 18.6
subtleties A.8.1
subtract 12.1.3
subtracted 11.5.5, 12.1.3, 15.8.3
subtraction 11.5.5, 12.1.3, 12.1.4
SubtractRect 12.1.4
succeeded A.3.2
success A.5.2
successful A.4.2, B.3.2, 3.1, 8.6.2, 11.5.4
successfully 1.5, 2.3.1, 18.6, 20.7
succession 33.6.3
suddenly B.4.4, 6.7, 15.4, 34.1
suffering 34.5.2
suffice C.0
sufficient 25.6, 26.4
suggested 33.8.4
suggestions C.0, Prf
suit 15.2.10, 22.6
suitable 1.4, 6.7, 15.7.2
suite 0.1
suited 5.1
sum A.5.1, A.5.2, 19.3.5
summarized 11.4.4, 15.3, 15.8.2, 18.2
summarizes 11.1, 13.5
summarizing 15.3, 18.2
summary 0.1, 15.8.2, 18.4
summed A.5.2
Sun 12.1.3
Sunday 12.1.3

superclass 23.6
superimposed 15.5.5
superset A.1
supplements B, C.0, 12.1.3, Prf
supplied A.2.5, C.1, 7.3, 12.5, 13.3, 33.6.10
supplier C.1
supplies 1.0, 10.4.10
supply 18.1.12, 34.7
support B.6.1, D.0, 0.4, 2.1, 6.7, 10.5, 11.3, 11.6.3, 12, 12.3, 13.4, 13.6, 14.3, 15.2.1, 15.5, 15.6.1, 15.6.13, 16.1.1, 16.2, 18.4, 18.4.7, 19.1.1, 22.6, 25.5, 33.3, 33.6.1, 33.7.1, 33.7.2, 34.1, 34.2, 34.4, 34.5, 34.5.1, 34.5.3, 34.6, 34.6.1, 34.6.3, 34.6.4, 34.7.1, 34.8, 34.8.3, 35.2, Prf
supported A.2.2, D.1, 6, 6.4, 6.6.5, 7.3, 10.4, 12.1.1, 13.6, 20.0, 22.6, 26.0, 33.5, 34.1
supporting 34.3
supports A.1.1, A.2.1, A.3, C.0, D.5, 0.2, 1.2, 2.1, 3.4, 4.6, 6.1, 6.6.4, 7.5, 9.3, 10, 11.4.5, 12, 12.1.4, 12.2, 12.4, 13.6, 14.3, 14.4.2, 18.4.6, 19.2, 20.0, 20.3, 30.0, 33.3, 33.5, 34.1, 34.4, 34.6.10, 34.7, 34.8, 34.8.1
supposed 28.1
surface A.8.1, D.0, D.1, D.2, D.6, 10.4.10, 11.4.1, 11.4.7, 11.5.4, 11.5.5, 11.6.1, 11.7
surfaces D.6, D.7
surgical 11.5
surmise A.5.2
surprise A.8, 15.4
surprising 5.1, 34.5.4
surprisingly 8.4, 16.0
surround 13.6, 34.2
surrounded A.1, 3.3
surrounding 3.3, 12.1.4, 34.2
surrounds A.3.1, 0.0
suspend 35.3, 35.4, 35.6, 35.7
suspended 35.7
suspends 35.3
sv D.2
SW_SHOWMAXIMIZED 32.3
SW_SHOWMINIMIZED 2.3.2, 32.3
swallow A.1.1
swap A.2.11, D.5, 11.6.2
SwapBuffers D.5
swaps A.2.11
switch A.1.1, 4.6, 7.1, 8.2, 11.6.1, 13.1, 15.8.1, 19.1.2, 23.7, 29.2, 34.6.5
switchboard 33.1
switching A.1.1, 5.2, 11.6.1
SWP 32.2
symbol A.2.1, 3.5, 11.4.6, 14.4.1, 15.7.2, 16.3.5, 19.2.3, 25.5
SYMBOL_CHARSET 11.4.6
symbols 14.4.1, 19.2

symmetrically 3.3
synchronization 15.4, 16.2, 35.0, 35.2
synchronize 14.3, 15.4, 33.1
synchronized 15.4.4, 16.2
synonym 4.3, 18.3
syntactic A.3.1
Syntactically A.3.2
syntax A.2.11, A.3, A.3.1, A.3.2, A.4.3, 19.2, 33.2
systems A.1.1, A.2.3, C.0, C.1, 1.3, 10.5, 11.1, 11.2, 11.5.5, 11.6.1, 12.1.1, 19.0, 33.3, 34.0, 34.1, 34.3, 35.2, 35.7
SYSTEMTIME 12.1.3
sz 2.3
szString 2.3
t A.1, A.1.1, A.2, A.3.2, A.4.1, A.4.5, A.5, A.5.1, A.5.2, A.7.2, D.1, D.2, D.5, 1.4, 2.1, 2.3, 2.6, 3.3, 4.2, 4.7, 5.3, 11.4.1, 11.5.3, 12.1.3, 13.4, 20.3, 20.6, 22.0, 22.5, 22.6, 23.0, 23.1, 23.2, 23.6, 23.7, 23.8, 23.9, 24.0, 24.1, 25.4, 27.0, 27.1, 28.0, 29.1, 29.2, 29.4, 30.0, 30.1, 31.4, 32.0, 32.5, 33.7.2, 34.1, 34.2, 34.7.7, 34.8.12, 35.7, Prf
TA_BASELINE 11.4.6
TA_BOTTOM 11.4.6
TA_CENTER 11.4.6
TA_LEFT 11.4.6
TA_NOUPDATECP 11.4.6
TA_RIGHT 11.4.6
TA_TOP 11.4.6
TA_UPDATECP 11.4.6
tab B.3, B.4, B.5.6, B.6.5, B.7.1, B.7.2, B.7.5, B.7.7, B.8.5, B.8.6, B.8.7, B.8.8, B.8.9, 0.4, 5.4, 8.2, 9.2, 17.3.4, 18.1.4, 18.1.5, 18.1.8, 18.1.9, 18.4.1, 18.5.3, 19.2, 20.0, 20.1, 20.5, 20.6, 22.5, 24.0, 28.1, 28.2, 29.2, 33.4.3, 33.6.3, 33.7.4, 34.8.4, 34.8.5, 34.8.6, 34.8.7, 34.8.12
tabbed 0.4, 9.2, 9.5, 18.4.1
TabbedTextOut 18.5.4
tabbing 18.4.1, 30.0
table B.5.7, D.1, 0.4, 2.3, 4.7, 6.1, 6.3, 6.5.3, 6.7, 6.7.2, 6.7.3, 8.4, 10.4.6, 10.4.10, 10.5, 11.5.4, 14.4.1, 14.4.6, 16.3, 16.3.5, 18.4.6, 19.2, 22.2, 22.5, 23.7, 25.3, 25.5, 30.1, 33.1, 33.2, 33.2.1, 33.2.2, 33.2.4, 33.4, 33.4.2, 33.4.3, 33.5, 33.6, 33.6.2, 33.6.4, 33.7.1, 33.7.2, 34.3, 34.4
tablecreation 33.4
tables 0.4, 4.7, 6, 6.1, 6.5.3, 6.7, 15.4, 17.2, 19.2, 33.1, 33.2, 33.2.4, 33.2.5, 33.4, 33.4.2, 33.4.3, 33.4.4, 33.7.6

tabs A.2.3, A.2.4, B.1.3, B.1.5, B.6.2, B.6.4, 6.6.5, 9.2, 9.5, 11.4.6, 18.4, 18.4.1
Tabstyle 22.5
tackle 34.5.4
tag B.5.6, 4.3, 4.4, 14.5, 19.2
tagged A.8, 14.5, 16.3
tags 14.5
tail 12.4
talk A.3.1, A.4.1, 1.2, 15.2.7, 17.4, 33.3, 33.4, 34.2, 34.4, 34.5.3, 34.6.3
talking 33.3
talks A.4.1, Prf
taller D.2
tallest 26.4
tap 34.5.5
tapped 16.2
target A.3.2, 12.1.2, 13.1, 13.2, 13.3, 31.1, 32.1
task A.2, 1.3, 2.2, 6, 9.4, 10.2, 10.3, 11.0, 12.1.2, 17.2, 18.4.3, 23.4, 27.1, 31.6, 32.2, 34.2, 34.8, 35.1, 35.2, 35.3, 35.8
tasking 35.2
tasks D.2, 7.0, 10.3, 10.4, 20.7, 22.7, 23.2, 26.1, 31.4, 34.1, 34.2, 34.3, 34.4, 34.5.3, 34.5.4, 34.5.5, 35.2, 35.7, 35.9
tastes 15.2.10
tCrtl 6.5.3
teach 0.3, 33.0, Prf
teaches 19.1.2
Tech 0.2, 14.3, 15.3, 19.3, 19.3.5, 19.5
Technical C.1, 0.2, 22.6, 25.6, 34.1, 34.9
technically 11.4.1, 12.3, 16.2
technique A.1, A.1.1, A.2.3, A.2.10, A.3.3, A.4.1, A.5.1, A.7.2, B.4.1, D.3, 3.1, 3.3, 5.1, 5.3, 5.4, 6.3.1, 6.7, 10.2, 11.4.1, 11.4.6, 11.5.3, 11.5.4, 11.6.2, 13.6.1, 15.7.9, 15.8.4, 16.5, 17.3.3, 18.1, 18.1.12, 18.4.2, 19.3.5, 23.8, 24.0, 24.3, 25.7, 29.1, 30.2, 33.7, 34.7.7, 35.4
techniques A.2.3, A.3.1, B.4.1, B.5, 0.0, 0.1, 0.2, 0.3, 1.1, 3.1, 5.1, 5.2, 5.3, 6.2, 8.4, 11.3, 11.4, 11.5, 13.0, 13.8, 15.1, 17.3, 17.6, 18.0, 18.1, 18.4, 18.4.7, 18.6, 19.5, 22.5, 26.0, 29.1, 29.4, 34.8, 35.1
Technologies C.0, C.1, 21
technology 11.5.4, 33.1, 34.0, 34.4, 34.8.7
telecommunications C.1
tell A.5.2, A.6, B.4.1, D.5, 1.3, 4.1, 11.3, 11.6.1, 13.2, 13.3, 13.4, 13.5, 15.4, 15.5, 17.3.4, 18.1.13, 18.3, 18.4.3, 18.4.6, 20.3, 20.5, 21.1.5, 31.4, 34.4, 35.7, Prf
telling 11.2, 13.5

tells A.8, B.5.6, D.1, 6.2, 10.4.10, 12.2,
12.3, 13.2, 18.4.2, 19.2,
19.2.5, 19.3.2, 19.3.4,
20.3, 22.1, 25.0, 25.4,
25.6, 25.7, 29.1, 30.1,
33.2.4
temperature 1.3, 5.1, 17.1, 17.1.3,
17.1.4, 17.2, 17.3.5, 17.4,
17.4.4, 17.4.5, 17.4.6
temperatures 5.2, 17.1
template B.8.9, 0.4, 3.1, 6.6, 10.4,
10.4.10, 10.5, 12.2, 12.3,
12.4, 12.5, 14.1, 14.4.2,
15.6.1, 15.7.11, 16.3,
16.3.4, 16.3.6, 16.4, 16.5,
18.6, 20.6, 25.8, 27.1,
28.1, 28.2, 29.1, 30.0,
30.1, 32.5, 33.6.2,
34.8.12
templates A.1.1, 6.6, 10.4, 10.4.10,
12.2, 15.4, 16.0, 16.3,
16.3.4, 16.3.6, 16.4, 16.5,
16.6, 19.1.2, 20.6
temporarily 9.5
temporary A.5.2, 12.1.1, 12.4, 23.4,
23.5, 25.6, 25.7, 29.4,
31.4, 34.1
tempted 23.3
ten 2.1, 2.3.2, 10.2, 11.2, 11.4.6,
11.5.3, 12.4, 25.0,
33.6.10, 35.2
tend 34.3, 34.8.1, 35.2
tendency 15.8.4, 34.3
tends A.5.3, 2.3, 11.3, 13.6
tens 0.0
tenth 35.2
term 18.5.2
terminate A.4.1, B.1.7, B.3, 2.3.1,
6.6.2, 7.6, 13.3, 34.1,
35.3, 35.4, 35.8
terminated 2.3, 11.4.6
terminates A.2.3, 4.1, 6.5, 8.5, 10.6,
11.6.3, 34.2, 35.3, 35.4,
35.7, 35.8
terminating 7.6
termination A.4.1, 11.5.3, 35.4, 35.8
terminology 34.4
terms A.2.6, A.3.3, 11.6.1, 14.3
ternary 25.7
terrain A.3.2, A.3.3
terrible A.1.1
test A.5.1, A.5.2, A.7, B.8.1, B.8.3,
6.6.5, 7.2, 13.2, 13.8,
15.7.3, 15.7.4, 19.3.1,
19.3.5, 19.3.8, 19.3.10,
22.5, 24.1, 29.1, 33.4,
34.8.1, 34.8.3, 34.8.4,
34.8.5, 34.8.6, 34.8.8,
34.8.9, 34.8.10, 34.8.11,
34.8.12
tested A.5, 0.1, 13.2, 33.6.5
testing A.5, C.1, 13.2, 13.3, 34.7.7
tests A.5.2, 13.1, 13.2, 13.4, 13.7
tex 10.4.6, 16.1.1, 16.3.5, 16.4
TEXTDOC 16.3.3, 16.3.4
textual 18.0
textually 16.5
Texture D.2
textures D.2
textview 16.3.4

th A.5.2, 11.6.1, 15.8.3, 25.7
thank Prf
Thd 35.3
theme 20.5
themes A.1
theory 15.8.4, 25.7, Prf
thousands 0.0, 0.1, 0.2, 2.1, 3.3,
11.6.2, 12.2, 19.0, 33.1
thread D.1, 0.4, 10.3, 35.1, 35.2, 35.3,
35.4, 35.5, 35.6, 35.7,
35.8, 35.9, Prf
THREAD_PRIORITY_ABOVE_NO
RMAL 35.7
THREAD_PRIORITY_BELOW_NO
RMAL 35.7
THREAD_PRIORITY_HIGHEST
35.7
THREAD_PRIORITY_IDLE 35.7
THREAD_PRIORITY_LOWEST
35.7
THREAD_PRIORITY_NORMAL
35.7
THREAD_PRIORITY_TIME_CRITI
CAL 35.7
threaded D.1, 35.2, 35.3, Prf
ThreadFunction 35.3
threading 35.0, 35.1, 35.2, 35.3
Threads B.2, 0.4, 10.3, 35.1, 35.2,
35.3, 35.4, 35.5, 35.6,
35.7, 35.8, 35.9, Prf
throw A.4.1, 12.1.1, 12.3, 13.6, 13.6.2
Throwing 13.6.2
thrown A.3.2, 13.6, 22.4
throws 12.1.1, 13.6, 22.4, 22.6
thru 22.6
ths 11.4.6, 11.6.1, 18.5.4
thumb 4.6
thus D.3, 7.6
thwarting A.1.1
tied 35.2
tightly A.4.2, A.4.3
Tile 15.4, 15.4.4, 15.6, 35.7
time_t 12.1.3
timed 27.1
timer 4.5, 4.8, 10.2, 11.4.6, 11.6.2,
27.0
timers 4.5
times A.2.4, A.5, 3.5, 6.3.7, 7.6, 9.5,
11.4.6, 11.5.3, 12.1.1,
12.1.3, 13.3, 18.4.2, 25.0,
26.1, 33.7.2, 34.1, 35.2,
35.8
Tina Prf
tiny A.1.1, 11.6.1, 15.8.3, 34.7.7
tip 20.0, 30.1
tips 30.1
title A.3.1, B.3, 1.2, 2.3.2, 6.3.5, 7.1,
7.2, 8.6.1, 8.6.2, 8.6.3,
10.4.10, 11.2, 15.1,
15.7.5, 19.2, 19.2.2,
19.2.3, 19.2.4, 19.2.7,
19.3.6, 20.7, 27.1, 31.1,
32.7
Titlebar 20.6, 27.1
titles 0.2, 6.7, 19.1.1, 19.2
tm 12.1.3, 22.6
today C.1, 11.2, 33.0
TODO 15.2.3, 15.2.8, 17.1.2, 18.1.2,
18.1.5, 18.1.10, 33.7.2,
33.7.3

together A.1.1, A.2.3, A.3.2, A.4.3,
A.4.5, A.5.2, 0.1, 1.1, 2.3,
3.2, 3.4, 5.2, 6.3, 6.3.6,
8.3, 9.5, 10.4.10, 13.5,
13.6.1, 14.4, 14.6, 15.0,
16.0, 22.0, 32.4, 33.1,
34.1, 34.6.5, 35.8, 35.10,
Prf
toggle 11.5.2, 18.4.6, 28.1
toggles 6.5.1, 11.5.2, 18.4.6
told 2.3.2, 4.2, 15.2.1
tongue 6.7
too 3.3, 5.3, 7.2, 11.4.6, 13.5, 15.8.4,
27.0, 28.0, 33.6.5, 34.1,
34.4, 35.8
took B.3, 8.7
tool B.2, B.2.1, B.3.1, B.4, B.4.1, 0.2,
0.4, 5.1, 6, 6.5, 11.5.3,
14.1, 14.5, 15.0, 15.2.1,
15.2.3, 15.4, 18.0, 18.4,
18.4.3, 18.4.5, 19.0,
19.1.1, 19.1.2, 19.3,
19.3.5, 19.3.6, 20.0, 30.0,
30.1, 32.5, 33.3, 33.4,
34.2, 34.6.2, 34.6.10, Prf
toolbar B.5.6, 6.1, 6.3, 6.6.5, 14.4.6,
18.1.8, 18.4.3, 18.4.5,
20.0, 30.0, 30.1, 31.0,
31.1, Prf
Toolbars B.2, B.4.1, B.5.3, B.5.4,
B.5.6, B.6.1, 31.0
tools A.1, B, B.1.2, B.1.3, B.4, B.4.1,
B.8.1, B.8.2, B.8.3, B.9,
0.0, 0.1, 0.2, 0.3, 1.3, 5.5,
6, 6.1, 6.3.4, 6.3.7, 6.6.5,
11.1, 12, 13.0, 14.0, 17.0,
33.4, 33.4.2, 34.0, 34.8.1,
34.8.13, Prf
tooth 11.5
top A.1.1, A.3.2, A.3.3, A.4.2, A.4.3,
A.4.4, A.4.5, A.5, A.5.1,
A.5.2, A.7, B.4.2, B.5.3,
B.7.4, 0.4, 1.1, 1.2, 3.1,
3.3, 4.2, 4.6, 5.2, 5.3, 6.4,
6.6.6, 8.2, 9.4, 10.5,
11.4.6, 11.5.1, 12.1.4,
12.3, 13.1, 13.2, 13.3,
15.2.6, 15.5.3, 15.5.5,
15.6.7, 15.7.8, 15.7.11,
16.3, 16.3.4, 18.1.4,
18.1.10, 18.4.1, 18.5.4,
19.2.1, 20.5, 28.1, 29.3,
30.0, 30.1, 32.2, 32.5,
32.7, 32.8, 33.4.3, 33.6.3,
34.4, 34.6.5, 34.8.11,
35.8
topeer 33.1
topic A.3.2, 9.1, 11.0, 12.2, 13.6.2,
17.3, 19.2, 19.2.3, 19.2.4,
19.2.5, 19.2.7, 19.2.8,
19.2.9, 19.2.10, 19.3.3,
19.3.5, 19.3.9, 19.3.10,
19.4, 34.5.5, 34.8.1
topics C.0, D.0, 11.0, 11.6, 19.2,
19.2.1, 19.2.3, 19.2.7,
19.3.10, 19.5, 32.0, 33.9,
34.1, Prf
TopLeft 12.1.4
topmost B.8.9, 1.2, 6.6.5, 18.1.9, 32.2,
33.8.2, 33.8.3, 34.8.12,

35.6
total A.5.1, A.8, 13.5, 15.3, 15.4, 17.2, 34.8.13, 35.7
totaling A.5.1, A.8
TotalingList A.8
totally A.5, A.5.1, 2.3, 11.2, 13.2, 18.1.12, 18.5, 34.1, 35.3
touch 6.1, 6.7, 11.4.7
touched 14.4.6
touching 6.1, 11.5.5
tour B, 14.4, 14.4.1
toward A.1.1, A.3.1, A.4.5, A.4.6, 1.2, 6.7, 15.2.6, 15.6.3, 15.8.3, 34.0, 34.3, 34.8.4, 34.8.7, 34.8.11
TPM_LEFTALIGN 32.6
TPM_RIGHTBUTTON 32.6
trace B.3.2, 0.4, 2.4, 13.3, 13.4, 13.7, 18.1.11, 22.0, 22.5, 29.1
tracer 13.3
tracing 10.7, 13.3
track A.1.1, A.5.1, A.7.2, B.1.2, B.3, B.4.4, B.4.6, 3.3, 8.2, 8.6.1, 11.3, 11.5, 11.5.3, 11.5.4, 11.5.5, 12.2, 13.2, 13.5, 18.4.2, 22.4, 23.1, 23.5, 26.1, 28.1, 29.4, 32.4, 34.2, 34.5.5
trackbar 20.0
tracked 34.5.5
tracking 13.7, 34.5.5
TrackPopupMenu 32.6
tracks 11.5.3
trade 12.2
tradeoff A.1.1
tradition A.2.7
traditional 34.2
training A.3.3, C.1
Transact 33.4
transaction 16.5, 33.1
transactions 33.1, 33.3, 33.5
TransBitBlt 25.6, 25.7, 26.4
transfer 11.6.2, 12.1.1, 15.7.6, 17.3.4, 18.3, 22.0, 22.1, 22.2, 22.3, 33.6.10, 34.8.12
transferable Prf
transferred 20.7, 22.2
transferring 22.2, 33.6.2
transfers 12.1.1, 17.3.4, 33.6.2
transformations D.0, D.2, D.3, 11.1
transforms D.2
transition A.1, 0.0
translatable 11.3
translate A.2.3, D.3, D.4, 6.7, 8.2, 11.5.5, 12.5, 34.5.6, 34.7.7
translated 10.6, 11.6.1, 19.3.8, 23.1
translates 11.5.5, 11.6.3, 12.5, 15.5.6, 25.7
translating D.3, 15.5.6, 34.6.8
translation 5.4, 11.2, 15.5, 15.5.6, 23.1, 25.4
translations 2.3, 11.6.1, 12.5, 34.2
transmission 34.4
transmit 34.4
transmitted 17.4, 34.1
transparent 23.9, 25.7, 29.3
transparently 8.3, 15.6.13, 23.1, 25.6, 25.7
trap 10.6, 13.6

trapping 12.1.1, 33.6.5
traversal 7.2, 32.6
traverse A.4.2, 7.2, 12.4, 32.6
traversed 7.2
traverses 11.5.5, 12.4, 15.4
treat 34.1
treated 6.5.4, 13.5
treatment B.1.3
tree A.4.2, B.6.1, 7.2, 14.3, 20.0, 20.1, 20.4, 21, 21.1.1, 21.1.5, 21.1.6, 21.1.7, 21.1.8, 21.1.9
tremendous B.4, 6, 7.2, 11.0, 14.0, 16.2, 18.4.3, 23.9, 33.2, 34.1, 35.10, Prf
tremendously 0.2, 2.1, 6.1, 14.4.1, 30.0
trend 5.2
tri 22.5
triangle D.2
tries A.1.1, A.3.2, 4.1, 4.2, 8.6.2, 11.5, 12.3, 16.4, 18.1.5, 24.0
trigger 8.6.7, 18.4.3, 33.6.4
triggering 11.5.5
triggers 11.5.3
trim 35.3
triplet 7.4, 11.4.8
trivial A.4.2, 2.1, 3.3, 10.2, 27.1, 34.7
trouble 12.3, 15.8.4, 23.8, Prf
true A.8.1, 2.3.1, 3.1, 3.5, 7.2, 7.3, 7.5, 7.6, 8.1, 8.6.1, 10.1, 10.3, 11.4.6, 11.5.4, 12.1.1, 12.1.2, 12.1.4, 12.4, 12.5, 13.5, 15.8.2, 16.2, 17.3.4, 18.4.3, 18.4.4, 20.7, 22.3, 22.4, 22.5, 26.4, 31.2, 32.1, 33.3, 33.5, 35.4
TrueType 11.4.6, 26.1, 26.2, 26.3, 26.4, 26.5
truly 34.1, 35.4
truncating 12.1.1
truncation 3.3
TSRs 35.2
tune B.6.1, 3.0, 8.1, 8.4, 13.5
tuned 1.1, 14.1, 27.0, 34.2
turn A.1, B.3, 0.3, 1.0, 2.4, 3.3, 11.4.3, 12.3, 13.1, 13.3, 13.5, 14.3, 15.5.3, 15.6.7, 15.8, 15.9, 17.2, 18.1, 18.1.2, 19.2.1, 21.1.1, 22.5, 29.1, 32.1, 34.7.1, 35.2
turned A.4.5, 13.2, 15.5, 15.6.1, 15.6.13, 17.2, 30.1
turning 11.5.3
turns A.1, A.1.1, A.4.1, B.4, D.7, 2.3.2, 3.3, 8.3, 11.0, 11.3, 11.5.2, 13.3
Tutorial A.1, A.2, A.3, A.4, A.4.4, A.4.6, A.5.3, A.6, A.7, A.8, D.0, D.1, D.5, 15.9, 33.4, 33.8.4, 34.5.5
tutorials A.1, A.2, A.2.10, A.3.3, A.8, A.8.1, 33.9
TVI_SORT 20.4
TVN_SELCHANGED 21.1.8
tweaked 8.5
tweaking 8.7
twice A.8, 12.4, 34.7.9, 35.6
twostep 2.3.3
typed 5.3, 6.1, 6.4, 6.5.3, 7.2, 9.5, 31.5
typedef 12.1.4

typeface 11.4.6
typical A.1.1, A.3.2, A.4.1, A.4.2, A.5.2, A.8, B.4.2, 0.1, 1.2, 1.3, 1.4, 2.1, 3.1, 6.1, 9.2, 10.1, 11.2, 11.4.4, 11.4.7, 11.5.3, 11.6.2, 12.1.1, 12.1.2, 12.1.3, 13.5, 14.3, 15.6.13, 15.8.3, 17.5, 19.2, 21, 21.1.9, 28.0, 32.5, 33.6.4, 34.6, 35.7
Typically B.7.7, 1.1, 1.2, 1.3, 2.3.2, 3.1, 3.4, 6.5.3, 9.1, 9.5, 11.5.5, 11.6.2, 12.1.1, 12.3, 15.5.2, 21, 33.6.10
typing A.1, B.5.5, 4.2, 4.4, 6.4, 14.5, 15.2.6, 19.1.2, 30.1, 33.1
U 12.1.3
uae 34.7.1
UI 18.4.6, 18.4.7
UINT 2.3, 7.2, 8.2, 11.4.6, 12, 12.2, 12.3, 13.4, 14.5, 15.2.7, 15.4.1, 15.7.8, 22.2, 22.5, 34.6.5, 34.8.12, 35.3
ultimate 11.6.1, 34.1
un 1.3, 11.5.2, 11.5.4
unable A.2.9, B.8.1
unacceptable 32.5, 33.1
unaffected A.3.2
unattractive 5.2
unbuffered A.2.3
unchanged A.5.1, 11.5.4, 25.7
uncheck 27.1
unchecked 6.5.1, 30.1
uncomfortable A.1
uncover B.3
undeleted 13.5
Under A.3.2, B.2, B.2.1, B.3.1, B.3.2, B.5.5, 0.4, 1.1, 1.2, 2.1, 2.2, 2.4, 4.4, 10.5, 13.3, 13.4, 13.5, 15.3.8, 16.5, 18.1.5, 18.1.11, 18.1.12, 18.4.7, 19.2, 19.2.9, 33.3, 34.3, 34.4, 34.5.1, 34.5.5, 34.5.6, 34.6.1, 35.3, 35.4, 35.7, 35.8
undergoes 13.5
underline 7.3
underlined 1.2
underlining 19.2, 19.2.5, 26.1
underlying A.1, 15.8.4, 23.0
underneath 3.4, 11.4.3, 11.5.4, 34.4
understood A.8.1, 4.4, 6.1, 11.6.1, 12.1.3, 14.5
undisturbed 11.5.4
undividable 35.2
Undo 8.1, 8.2, 8.3, 8.5, 8.6.10, 16.2
undocks 30.1
undocumented 31.0, 35.8
Undoes 8.1, 8.2
undue 34.1
unexpected 13.2, 34.1
unfamiliar A.3, 0.3, 2.6
unforeseen A.1.1
Unfortunately 0.3, 11.4.4, 15.8.4, 33.3, 34.1
unfreed 13.3
unhandled 10.6
uniform 19.0
unimportant 2.3.1
uninitialized A.7.1, 13.5

uninitiated D.5
union A.1.1, 11.4.6
UnionRectSets 12.1.4
unique A.1.1, A.3.1, A.4.3, 1.2, 2.2,
    2.3.2, 4.2, 4.7, 5.1, 5.2,
    5.4, 6.1, 6.6.4, 7.6, 11.4.1,
    12.1.2, 14.3, 18.4.6, 19.4,
    23.1, 30.0, 32.4, 33.1,
    33.4.3, 34.1, 34.4, 34.7.6,
    Prf
uniquely 34.4
uniqueness 33.1
unit A.3.2, 11.2, 11.6.1, 15.8.3, 35.1
units A.3.2, 9.2, 11.3, 11.6.1, 34.6.8
universal 33.3, 33.4.2
Universally 34.4
universe 34.2
UNIX 0.0, 1.3, 35.2
unknown 3.5, 16.4, 33.1
unless A.1.1, A.3.2, A.4.3, A.7.1, 0.3,
    3.2, 4.3, 6.4, 6.5, 11.2,
    13.2, 16.2, 18.4.7, 29.1,
    34.8, 35.2, 35.7, 35.9
Unlike D.1, 15.3.8, 18.4.3, 18.4.6
unlikely 2.3
Unlock 8.2, 12.1.1
unlocking 8.2
UnlockRange 12.1.1
unnecessary 33.7.2
unneeded 4.7
unprotected 12.2
unqualified 13.6
unrecoverable 20.7
unregister 34.8.1
unrelated 11.2
unsigned 12.2
unstable 35.2
UnsubclassWindow 23.8
Unsupported 12
until A.5.2, A.7, B.2.1, D.2, D.5, D.6,
    1.2, 6.6.5, 7.6, 8.4, 8.7,
    9.5, 10.3, 11.4.1, 11.4.2,
    11.4.6, 11.4.7, 13.4, 15.2,
    15.8.4, 20.7, 23.0, 23.2,
    23.3, 23.8, 24.0, 27.1,
    30.1, 32.1, 32.4, 33.4.4,
    33.6.4, 34.4, 34.5.5,
    34.8.1, 35.1, 35.2, 35.3,
    35.4, 35.7
unto 19.5
untold 0.0
unusual 3.3, 7.6, 12.4, 29.0, 33.7.4,
    34.1
upcoming 34.1
update B, C.0, 1.3, 4.2, 4.5, 9.4, 15.2.9,
    15.4, 15.4.4, 15.5, 15.7.9,
    15.8.2, 15.8.4, 17.3.4,
    17.4.7, 18.1.12, 18.2,
    18.4.2, 18.4.5, 18.4.6,
    25.1, 25.4, 31.0, 31.1,
    31.2, 31.3, 31.4, 31.5,
    32.6, 33.1, 33.2, 33.2.5,
    33.4, 33.5, 33.6.4, 33.7.6,
    33.8.1, 33.8.4, 34.1, 34.2,
    34.5.5, 34.6.4, 34.6.7,
    34.7.5, 35.5, 35.8, Prf
UPDATE_COMMAND_UI 18.4.3,
    18.4.4, 31.0, 35.8
UpdateAllViews 15.4, 15.4.1, 15.4.3,
    15.4.4, 15.7.9, 16.2, 17.4,

17.4.4, 17.4.5, 18.1.13,
    18.2, 18.6, 21.1.8
updated A.8, B, 7.0, 11.4.6, 15.4,
    15.4.3, 17.4.4, 18.1.11,
    18.4.2, 18.4.3, 20.7, 25.4,
    27.1, 31.2, 33.7.5, 34.4,
    34.8.11, Prf
UpdateData 17.3.4, 18.1.5, 20.7, 22.1,
    22.3, 22.4, 22.5, 23.3,
    30.2, 32.4, 33.8.2
UpdateDialogControls 31.1, 31.2, 31.4
UpdateFamilyList 26.3
UpdateRegistry 34.6.3
updates B, D.5, 5.2, 11.4.6, 12.1.2,
    15.4.3, 18.4.2, 18.4.5,
    18.4.6, 21.1.9, 31.1,
    33.6.4, 33.7.6, 33.8, Prf
UpdateWindow 2.3.2, 27.1
updating 1.3, 15.4.4, 18.6, 31.3, 31.4,
    31.5, 31.6
upgrade A.1.1
upgraded 33.2, Prf
uphold A.2.7
upon 9.3, 11.5.4, 12.5, 18.1
upper A.4.5, B.3, B.4.5, B.4.6, 2.3.2,
    3.1, 3.3, 5.3, 8.1, 11.2,
    11.4.3, 11.6.1, 15.5.6,
    18.1.2, 19.2.4, 28.2,
    34.5.2
uppercase A.2.7, 12.1.2
uppermost 11.4.6
upset 14.5
us A.3.1, C.0, D.6, 4.1, 13.6, 15.8.1,
    18.1.4, 18.3, 18.5, 22.5,
    23.1, 23.7, 25.6, 26.1,
    27.1, 28.1, 29.1, 31.4,
    35.10, Prf
Usable 15.8.2, 34.0
usage A.2.7
useful A.4.1, A.4.5, A.5, B.2, B.2.2,
    B.3, B.4, B.4.5, D.2, D.8,
    0.2, 1.0, 2.3.2, 3.0, 3.3,
    4.5, 5.1, 5.5, 8.1, 8.2, 9.2,
    9.5, 10, 10.1, 10.5, 10.6,
    11.3, 11.5.2, 11.5.4,
    11.6.1, 12, 12.1.1, 12.1.2,
    12.1.3, 12.1.4, 12.2, 12.5,
    13.2, 13.4, 13.5, 13.6.1,
    14.3, 14.4, 14.4.1, 14.5,
    15.4.4, 15.5, 15.5.3,
    15.5.6, 15.6, 15.9, 16.5,
    16.6, 17.4, 17.5, 18.4.4,
    18.4.5, 18.4.6, 18.4.7,
    18.6, 20.7, 20.8, 21.1.8,
    23.0, 24.0, 25.0, 26.0,
    28.3, 30.0, 31.0, 32.0,
    32.1, 32.2, 33.2.5, 33.3,
    33.4.4, 33.7.4, 33.9, 35.1,
    35.4, 35.10, Prf
usefulness 6.7
useless 12.1.2, 13.2
UseTabstops 18.4.1
usual B.3, 3.5, 11.5.1
usually D.0, 5.1, 6.5.3, 11.4.3, 13.2,
    23.7, 25.6, 25.7, 29.0,
    29.1, 29.2, 29.3, 30.1,
    31.1, 32.2, 32.4
UTC 12.1.3
Utilities D.2
utility 0.1, 11.4.8, 12, 12.1.2, 12.6,

34.4, Prf
utilization 12
UUID 34.4
UUIDGEN 34.4
UUIDs 34.4
v 34.4, 34.7.6
valiable 17.3.3
valid A.1.1, A.2.7, A.7, A.7.2, D.1, 3.2,
    7.1, 11.4.2, 12.1.1,
    12.1.3, 13.2, 13.3, 13.7,
    14.5, 15.7.11, 15.8.4,
    18.4.2, 22.4, 22.5, 22.6,
    23.1, 23.2, 23.5, 33.4.3,
    33.5
validate 7.4, 18.3, 22.1, 24.0, 30.2
validated 22.5
validating 24.0
Validation 6.6.8, 18.3, 20.7, 22.0, 22.4,
    22.5, 22.6, 22.7
validations 22.5
validity 13.2, 24.0
valuable 0.2
VARIABLE_PITCH 11.4.6
variant D.0
variants D.2
variations 14.1, 29.4
variety B.2, B.9, C.1, D.0, 0.1, 0.2, 0.3,
    3.0, 3.2, 4.5, 10.4.10,
    11.5, 11.5.5, 11.6.1, 13.4,
    16.5, 16.6, 17.5, 18.4.6,
    18.6, 24.0, 25.6, 29.4,
    32.8, 33.3, 33.8.4, 34.0,
    34.1, 34.3, 34.4, 34.7.9,
    34.8, 34.9, 35.4, 35.7,
    35.10, Prf
various D.2, 0.2, 6.3.4, 11.5.5, 12.1.3,
    13.6, 19.1.2, 33.2
vary 2.3
varying A.2.10, 0.3
vast 4.7, 12.3
VB 34.7, 34.7.7, 34.7.9
VBXs 34.8
VC B
VCPPBOOK 13.5
ve D.6, 1.4, 7.6, 11.2, 11.4.6, 11.6.1,
    11.6.3, 33.4.4, 33.6.5
vector 7.3, 26.1, 26.2, 26.5
vendor D.1
vendors D.0, 33.3, 34.3
verb 34.5.5, 34.8.3, 34.8.11, 34.8.12
verbs A.4.1, 34.8.3
verification C.1, 14.5, 15.7.8
verify 12.3, 13.2, 17.3.4, 18.1.11
verifying 13.2
version A.2.8, A.2.9, A.5.1, A.5.2, A.6,
    A.7, A.8, B, B.2, D.0, 0.2,
    0.3, 1.1, 2.1, 3.3, 5.2, 5.3,
    6.1, 6.3, 6.6.8, 6.7, 8.5,
    10.3, 11.4.3, 11.5.2,
    11.5.3, 12.2, 12.3, 13.1,
    13.2, 13.3, 13.5, 13.6.1,
    14.4.6, 15.0, 15.2.6,
    15.2.10, 15.4, 15.5.3,
    15.5.6, 15.6.7, 15.7.9,
    15.8.4, 17.2, 17.5,
    18.1.15, 18.4, 18.4.6,
    19.2, 20.0, 20.4, 20.5,
    22.2, 34.2, 34.4, 34.7.7,
    35.7, Prf
versions A.8, B, 1.1, 6.7, 7.0, 10.3,

11.3, 12.3, 13.2, 15.5.3,
15.6.7, 20.0, 20.4, 22.2,
31.0, 34.2, Prf
versus 28.1
vertex D.2, D.3
vertical 4.6, 9.1, 9.2, 10.2, 11.3, 11.5.3,
15.5, 15.8.4, 28.3, 34.6.4
vertically 11.4.6
vertices D.2
VERTRES 11.3, 15.8.4
vexing A.1.1
VGA 11.1, 11.2
via A.4.3, C.0, 1.3, 5.3, 23.1, 33.7.2,
34.4, 35.1, Prf
viewed 14.3, 18.1, 33.7.5
viewer 33.5, 34.6.7
viewing B.4.1, D.2, D.6, 14.3, 18.2,
18.5, 19.2.1, 33.1
viewit 21
viewport D.2
violate 13.2
violated B.2, 13.2
violates A.7.2, 13.2, 16.2
Violating 13.2
violations 7.2
VirtKey 6.5.3, 18.4.6
Virtual A.1, A.1.1, A.8, B.7.1, B.7.2,
2.3, 2.3.1, 4.7, 5.4, 6.5.3,
7.2, 7.3, 7.4, 7.5, 11.5.5,
12.2, 12.4, 13.2, 14.4.4,
14.5, 15.2.6, 15.3.8, 15.4,
15.5.2, 15.5.4, 15.5.6,
18.1.13, 20.7, 21.1.3,
22.1, 25.3, 25.4, 25.5,
31.1, 31.4
virtually A.1.1, 0.3, 13.5
vision 34.3
visit C.1, Prf
visiting 21
visualization 35.1
visualize 1.1
visually 3.1, 3.4, 4.6, 6, 6.1, 29.1, 33.4,
34.5.2, 34.8.1
visuals 15.4.4
vital 22.5
VK_INSERT 18.4.6
vocabulary A.1, A.1.1, A.3.1, 1.0, 1.2,
1.5, 11.2, 33.0
void A.2.3, A.2.11, A.8, 4.3, 7.2, 7.3,
7.4, 7.5, 8.6.2, 12, 12.4,
12.5, 14.5, 15.2.6, 15.2.7,
15.4.1, 15.6.3, 15.6.4,
16.3.3, 33.8.2, 34.5.5,
34.6.5, 34.7.4, 34.7.8,
34.8.9
Volume 12.1.1
VT_EMPTY 34.7.7
w A.2.3, 2.3, 12.1.3
wading 0.1
wait 8.7, 23.2, 24.0, 27.1, 35.4, 35.7
WaitCommEvent 35.7
WaitForSingleObject 35.4
waiting 11.4.1, 35.1, 35.2, 35.7
waits 1.3, 35.1, 35.4
wakes 35.4
walk B.2, 6.2, 6.3, 8.6, 11.5.5, 14.4,
15.3.1, 15.5.6, 18.4, 33.7
walking 2.3
walks 12.4, 15.1
wall A.4.2, 0.0

wanted A.5.1, D.3, 2.3.2, 6.6.4, 13.6.2,
17.2, 17.3.4, 18.4.6, 20.3,
20.4, 22.5, 23.2, 23.4,
23.8, 25.5, 28.3, 29.1,
31.3, 34.1
wants C.1, 8.6.1, 10.4.10, 15.3, 18.2,
18.4.6, 25.4, 34.1, 34.2,
34.4, 34.5.3, 34.5.5, 35.4
warn 22.5
warned 13.3
warning 7.5, 22.5
warnings 6.4
warns 13.6
wasn 3.3
waste 34.3
wasted 8.7, 12.2
wasteful 11.3, 18.6, 33.1, 35.2
wasting D.7
watch A.8, B.2, B.2.3, B.3.1, D.2, 0.4,
11.4.6, 11.5.4, 13.1, 15.5,
15.5.6
watching A.3.2
web B, C.1, 21, 33.4, Prf
wedge 11.4.4
week A.1, 12.1.3, 20.1
weeks 2.1
weight A.3.1, 26.1
went 4.5, 13.6
wglCreateContext D.1
wglDeleteContext D.1
wglGetCurrentContext D.1
wglMakeCurrent D.1
White A.2.3, A.2.4, D.6, 3.4, 11.3,
11.4.8, 11.5.2, 11.5.4,
11.6.2, 25.7, 29.2, 34.6.2,
34.7.2, 34.8.4
who A.1.1, A.3.2, A.8, D.2, 0.1, 0.3,
1.2, 4.7, 5.1, 8.3, 33.1,
34.2
whole A.1.1, A.5.2, 6.3, 7.6, 8.7,
15.8.2, 20.0, 20.5, 34.0,
35.2, 35.7
whose B.7.1, B.7.3, 12.1.1, 13.2,
33.2.2
Why A.1, A.1.1, A.3.2, B.3.2, 0.3, 0.4,
2.5, 4.3, 4.7, 7.6, 10,
10.4.10, 11.6.1, 12.1.2,
12.3, 13.2, 14.0, 15.1,
15.3, 15.8.1, 15.8.2,
17.4.3, 18.4.6, 23.0, 23.1,
23.2, 33.1, 34.1, 34.4
wide B.2, D.0, D.2, 0.2, 4.5, 10.2,
11.3, 11.4.2, 11.5, 11.5.5,
11.6.1, 14.4.5, 17.5,
18.4.5, 33.1, 33.3, 34.0,
34.1, Prf
widely 15.8.3, 33.4
wider B.6.4
width A.2.3, A.4.6, D.2, 5.3, 6.1, 9.1,
9.2, 11.2, 11.3, 11.4.2,
11.4.3, 11.4.6, 11.6.2,
12.1.4, 15.7, 15.7.5,
15.7.9, 15.7.10, 18.4.6,
26.1, 28.3, 29.2, 30.1,
34.6.4, 34.6.5, 34.6.7
widths 11.4.6
wild Prf
willing 34.2
Win 0.2, 1.1, 10.5, 11.1, 11.3, 13.6.1,
20.0, 34.1, 34.4, 35.0,

35.2, 35.3, 35.4, 35.7,
35.8, Prf
wind 0.2
WINDING 11.4.5
windowed 34.1
windowing 34.1
WindowProc 13.3
Windowsspecific 11.2
Wingdings 3.5, 11.4.6
WinHelp 10.4.10, 19.3.5, 32.2
WinMain 2.3, 13.2
WinMainCRTStartup 13.2
wire 4.2, 8.5, 9.5, 15.1, 15.7, 15.7.3,
17.1.3, 17.3.4, 18.1.10,
18.4.5, 18.4.6, 28.2,
33.7.4, 33.8.4
wired 4.5, 4.6, 18.4.2, 20.3, 24.1,
34.8.4
wires B.8.5, 4.6, 5.3, 11.5.3
wish A.2.3, A.2.5, B.1.3, B.5.5, B.5.6,
B.7.2, D.8, 0.4, 5.1, 5.2,
6.5.1, 6.7.3, 7.3, 7.6, 11.3,
11.5.2, 11.5.3, 13.0, 13.4,
15.2.10, 15.6, 15.7.2,
15.7.11, 15.9, 16.3.6,
17.4.1, 19.0, 20.7, 29.1,
33.4.1, 34.2
wishes B.7.2, 6.7, 15.3.5, 33.2.1
within A.2.3, A.4.3, A.4.4, A.6, A.7,
B.2, B.5.7, D.2, D.7, 1.2,
2.3.3, 3.3, 5.4, 5.3, 6.1,
6.5.4, 7.0, 7.1, 9.2, 9.4,
9.5, 10, 10.2, 10.4, 11.4.6,
11.5.2, 11.5.3, 11.6.3,
11.7, 12.1.1, 12.3, 14.5,
15.1, 18.3, 18.4.6, 19.2.9,
19.3.5, 20.0, 22.0, 23.9,
27.1, 32.6, 33.4, 34.2,
34.8.6, 35.2, 35.7
without A.1.1, A.4.2, A.5, A.6, B.2.2,
D.0, D.1, D.3, 0.4, 4.6,
4.7, 6.1, 7.2, 8.1, 8.2, 8.3,
10.3, 11.4.1, 11.4.2,
11.4.3, 11.4.6, 11.5.4,
11.5.5, 11.6.2, 15.1,
15.2.1, 15.2.9, 15.8.2,
16.0, 18.1.15, 19.0, 20.5,
23.5, 25.7, 29.2, 32.4,
33.1, 33.3, 33.7.1, 33.7.2,
34.1, 35.1, 35.8, Prf
wizards B.9
WM_ B.7.1
WM_ACTIVATE 32.5
WM_CHAR 24.1
WM_CLOSE 32.5
WM_COMMAND 13.3, 25.5
WM_COMPAREITEM 25.2, 25.3
WM_CONTEXTMENU 32.6
WM_CREATE D.1, 23.2, 27.1, 32.5
WM_CTLCOLOR 25.5, 29.3
WM_DELETEITEM 25.2, 25.3
WM_DESTROY D.1, 23.2, 35.4, 35.5
WM_DRAWITEM 25.2, 25.3, 25.4
WM_DROPFILES 32.1
WM_ENTERIDLE 31.4
WM_ERASEBKGND 29.2
WM_HSCROLL 25.5
WM_IDLEUPDATECMDUI 31.1,
31.2, 31.4
WM_INITDIALOG 23.0, 23.3, 25.8,

27.1, 28.1
WM_KEYDOWN 24.3
WM_KEYUP 24.3
WM_KICKIDLE 31.4
WM_LBUTTONDBLCLK 34.5.5
WM_LBUTTONDOWN D.4, D.6,
    29.1, 34.5.5
WM_LBUTTONUP D.6, 29.1,
    33.6.3, 34.8.7
WM_MEASUREITEM 25.2, 25.3
WM_MOUSEMOVE B.7.1, D.4,
    D.6, 14.5, 15.3, 15.3.8,
    15.6.9, 23.7, 29.1
WM_NCHITTEST 29.1
WM_NOTIFY 25.5
WM_PAINT D.2, D.3, 11.4.1, 15.3,
    15.3.7, 15.3.8, 23.7, 24.3,
    29.1, 29.2
WM_PARENTNOTIFY 25.5
WM_RBUTTONDOWN D.4
WM_RBUTTONUP 34.8.7
WM_REFLECT 25.5
WM_SETFOCUS 32.5
WM_SIZE D.2, 18.1.5
WM_TIMER 27.1
WM_VSCROLL 24.3, 25.5
WNDCLASS 11.5.3
wNotifyCode 25.5
won A.1, A.1.1, A.3.2, 23.2
wonder 2.3.2
worked A.7, 11.2, 14.5, 34.4, 35.10
worker 0.4, 35.3, 35.9
Working A.1, A.2.10, A.7.2, B.2, B.3,
    B.5, B.5.1, B.5.3, 8.1, 8.5,
    8.6, 9.3, 10, 11.3, 11.5.3,
    12.3, 13.1, 13.2, 15.0,
    15.9, 16.3.1, 18.1.11,
    29.1, 33.1, 33.4.2, 34.8.1,
    35.2, 35.4
workload 17.2
workplace 34.3
works A.1.1, A.2, A.2.10, A.2.11,
    A.4.4, A.5.1, A.5.2, A.7,
    A.7.1, B, B.6.1, 0.3, 1.3,
    2.1, 4.3, 4.7, 8.4, 8.6.4,
    9.3, 11.4.6, 13.3, 14.1,
    14.2, 14.3, 15.2.9, 15.3,
    15.5, 15.8.1, 15.8.4,
    18.1.15, 18.5, 19.3, 20.5,
    22.0, 23.0, 23.9, 27.0,
    30.0, 31.0, 34.1, 34.5.4,
    35.2, 35.7
Workspace B.1.1, B.1.2, B.1.5, B.3,
    B.6.1, B.6.2, B.6.4, B.8.1
workstation 11.1, 11.6.1
world A.1.1, A.3.1, A.5, B.3, D.2, D.3,
    0.4, 1.4, 2.2, 2.3, 2.3.2,
    2.5, 3.3, 6.7.2, 6.7.3,
    12.1.2, 14.1, 19.5, 22.0,
    22.1, 25.0, 33.1, 34.1,
    35.9, Prf
worry D.2, 1.4, 2.3, 2.6, 6.5.3, 35.8
worthless 0.3
worthwhile 2.2
wouldn 29.4
wParam 31.4
wrap 3.3, 6.5.1, 8.2, 11.4.6
wrapped 3.2, 3.3
wrapping 3.3, 8.2, 11.4.6, 13.6, 23.1
wreak 35.7

writable 12.3
write A.1.1, A.3.2, A.6, A.8.1, 0.0, 0.1,
    1.1, 1.4, 2.1, 2.2, 4.1, 4.2,
    5.1, 6, 6.6.8, 6.7, 10.4.10,
    11.5.3, 12.1.1, 12.3, 12.6,
    13.2, 13.6, 16.2, 17.2,
    17.4, 18.1.12, 19.4, 34.1,
    34.2, 34.4, 35.2
WriteHuge 12.1.1
WriteProfileInt 10.5
WriteProfileString 10.5
writer 34.1
writes A.2.4, B.3.1, 8.6.3, 12.1.1, 12.4,
    13.5, 16.5
WriteString 12.1.1
WriteToFile 12.4
writing A.1.1, A.8, B.3.1, 1.3, 2.1, 8.3,
    12.1.1, 12.3, 12.4, 16.0,
    18.4.6, 35.1, 35.2
written A.2.3, A.8, B.4, 0.1, 0.2, 1.1,
    2.1, 8.4, 12.1.1, 13.2,
    14.4.6, 19.2, 25.7, 33.2.5,
    33.7.5, 34.1, 34.5.5
wrong A.4.2, B.3.1, 13.6
wrote A.2, A.8, 18.3, 34.8.13
WS 3.2, 4.2, 9.1
WS_BORDER 3.2, 5.2
WS_CHILD 3.2, 4.2, 32.5
WS_CLIPCHILDREN D.1
WS_CLIPSIBLINGS D.1
WS_DISABLED 3.2
WS_MINIMIZE 5.2
WS_OVERLAPPED 5.2
WS_OVERLAPPEDWINDOW 5.2
WS_SYSMENU 5.2
WS_TABSTOP 5.4
WS_VISIBLE 3.2, 4.2, 32.5
www B, C.0, C.1, 21, Prf
x A.4.5, A.5.2, B.2.3, 0.2, 2.3.2, 6.3.7,
    11.1, 11.2, 11.4.1, 11.4.3,
    11.4.6, 11.4.8, 11.6.1,
    11.6.2, 12.1.1, 12.1.3,
    12.1.4, 13.2, 13.4, 15.2.6,
    15.5.2, 15.5.3, 15.5.6,
    15.5.7, 15.6.3, 15.7.11,
    15.8.1, 15.8.3, 15.8.4,
    19.3.5, 25.7, 26.4, 33.6.5,
    34.1, 34.6.8, 34.7.8
xA 13.4
XBase 33.3
xF 13.4
XOR 25.6, 25.7
XORd 25.7
XORs 25.7
year 12.1.3, 22.6
years A.3.2
yes A.8, 6.4, 7.1, 8.5, 8.6.1
yet A.3.2, D.6, 1.4, 2.3, 4.6, 5.1, 6.4,
    11.4.1, 11.5.5, 15.3, 15.5,
    18.1.5, 19.4, 22.0, 23.2,
    34.1, 34.8.11, 35.0
yield 13.2, 15.4, 16.3, 33.5
yields Prf
York C.1, 11.5.5
YourApp 19.2.1
yours 32.2
yourself A.1, A.1.1, A.3.1, A.7.1, D.0,
    2.1, 5.1, 7.6, 9.5, 11.5.3,
    13.6, 14.1, 14.4.4, 14.4.6,
    15.7.3, 18.3, 19.2, 25.0,

29.1, 32.1, 33.4.2, 34.1,
    34.2, 34.9, 35.8
Z D.0, D.6, D.7, 12.1.3
zbuffering D.7
zero D.6, D.7, 2.3, 5.3, 6.1, 9.3, 10.3,
    11.5.5, 12.1.1, 12.1.2,
    12.1.3, 12.1.4, 12.2, 12.3,
    13.4, 13.5, 13.6.1, 17.1.2,
    18.4.6, 20.2, 31.4, 33.7.5,
    34.8.1, 34.8.9
zeros 34.8.1
zeroth 32.6
Ziff Prf
zip 33.1, 33.2.2, 33.2.3, 33.4, 33.4.3,
    33.6.9, 33.6.10, 33.6.11
ZipCode 33.1, 33.2.1, 33.2.2, 33.2.3,
    33.2.4, 33.4.2, 33.4.3,
    33.6.4
zone 12.1.3
zoom 15.8.1